OXFORD PAPERBACK REFERENCE

THE CONCISE
OXFORD DICT

LIT

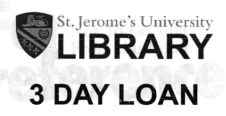

THE CONCISE
OXFORD DICTIONARY OF
FRENCH
LITERATURE

EDITED BY

Joyce M. H. Reid

Oxford   New York

OXFORD UNIVERSITY PRESS

Oxford University Press, Walton Street, Oxford OX2 6DP

Oxford New York Toronto
Delhi Bombay Calcutta Madras Karachi
Kuala Lumpur Singapore Hong Kong Tokyo
Nairobi Dar es Salaam Cape Town
Melbourne Auckland

and associated companies in
Beirut Berlin Ibadan Nicosia

Oxford is a trade mark of Oxford University Press

ISBN 0-19-866118-5
ISBN 0-19-281200-9 pbk

Printed in Great Britain by
Richard Clay (The Chaucer Press) Ltd.
Bungay, Suffolk

Abbreviations

anon.	anonymous, anonymously	m.	married
augm.	augmented	ms.	manuscript
b.	born	no., nos.	number(s)
bk., bks.	book(s)	p., pp.	page(s)
c.	century	perf.	performed
c.	*circa*, about	posth.	posthumous, posthumously
ch., chs.	chapter(s)	prod.	produced
d.	died	Prov.	Provençal
ed.	edited, edition, editor	pt., pts.	part(s)
Eng.	English	publ.	published
esp.	especially	r.	reigned
f.	founded	rev.	revised
fl.	*floruit*, flourished	ser..	series
Fr.	French	suppl.	supplement, supplemented
Ger.	German	trans.	translated, translation
inc.	included, including	*v.*	*vide*, see
L.	Latin	vol., vols.	volume(s)
l., ll.	line(s)		

An asterisk (*) preceding a word indicates a relevant article under that (or a closely similar, possibly plural) heading. In order to avoid an excess of asterisks, *this symbol has not been attached to the names of persons*, except in reference to a following work (e.g. *Corneille's *Andromède*, indicating that, though there is no article *Andromède*, this play is mentioned under *Corneille*). In the case of persons, it may in general be assumed that anyone referred to by surname only (preceded sometimes by a title or, for purposes of distinction, by initials) is the subject of a separate article under that surname, and that the presence of full Christian name and dates indicates the absence of a separate article.

Modernized spelling has been adopted for titles of works dating from 1500 onwards, except where there are strong reasons for retaining the original spelling (e.g. for the titles under *Dictionaries and Encyclopedias*).

Preface

THIS work is an abridged and revised version of *The Oxford Companion to French Literature*, first published in 1959. Abridgement has been effected by condensation and amalgamation rather than omission, in the belief that the briefest mention is more helpful than silence and that this approach would best preserve the unique scope and utility of the *Companion*, which ranges far beyond the strictly literary field. Many new articles have been added, and a great many existing articles revised or expanded, in an attempt to bring the whole work more nearly up to date (though, like the *Companion* before it, the *Dictionary* does not aspire or claim to be a complete guide to the contemporary scene); a few articles have also been added to fill gaps in the coverage of earlier periods. The articles omitted include most of those on French-Canadian literature, which is now covered by *The Oxford Companion to Canadian History and Literature*. Details of the abbreviations and conventions used will be found on p. vi.

I have had help and advice from many sources. My warmest thanks go to Mrs. J. E. Heseltine, joint editor of the *Companion*, who gave me kindly encouragement from the outset and provided an invaluable list of suggested additions and revisions; to Dr. K. O. Gore, for most generous help in the fields of contemporary literature and the modern theatre (he contributed 14 new articles, including that on Sartre, for which I am particularly grateful, and those on Adamov, Arrabal, Barrault, Barthes, H. Bazin, S. de Beauvoir, Beckett, and Céline); to Miss Ann Jefferson, who also compiled new articles on a number of 20th-c. authors (including exponents of the *nouveau roman* and the *nouvelle critique*, Merleau-Ponty, R. Roussel, F. Sagan, and Vian) and updated the article *Critics and Criticism*; and to my husband, Professor T. B. W. Reid, who revised many articles on medieval literature, the French language, and versification, contributed a number of new articles in these fields, and read the whole work in typescript and galley proof. The many others to whom I am indebted include Mr. J. P. Cooper and Professor Norman Hampson (for much-needed help in bringing the coverage of historians and the article *History* up to date), Professor C. A. Hackett, Dr. Robert Shackleton, Professor L. J. Austin, Mr. Giles Barber, Mrs. H. Temple Patterson, and, last but by no means least, the library staff of the Taylor Institution and the Maison Française in Oxford.

Oxford 1976   J. M. H. R.

A

Abailard, *v.* *Abélard*.

Abbaye, *v.* *Cluny*; *Saint-Denis*; *Saint-Germain-des-Prés*; *Saint-Victor*; *Trappe*.

Abbaye, L', a house at Créteil, near Paris, leased (1906) by a group of young writers and artists—Arcos, Duhamel, the painter Albert Gleizes, Barzun, Vildrac—who proposed to support themselves on the produce of the garden and by printing and selling books. It was a centre of artistic activity for 14 months. Lack of funds ended the venture, which is the subject of Duhamel's novel *Le Désert de Bièvres* (1937; *v.* *Chronique des Pasquier*).

The *Abbaye* was not a poetical 'school'; but because its press issued Romains's *La Vie unanime* and some poets of the community were later classed with him as *unanimistes*, it has been associated with **Unanimisme*.

Abbaye, Prison de l', f. 1522, a prison attached to **Saint-Germain-des-Prés*; used first for disorderly young nobles, later for military, then for political, offenders; demolished 1854. The September Massacres (1792; *v.* *Revolutions*, 1) began here.

Abbaye-aux-Bois, *v.* *Récamier*.

Abbaye de Thélème, *v.* *Gargantua*.

Abbé, in the Middle Ages, an abbot; later also any ecclesiastic, not necessarily in priest's orders and often leading a purely worldly life (e.g. Chaulieu).

Abbé Constantin, L', *v.* *Halévy, L.*

Abbé Tigrane, L', *v.* *Fabre, F.*

Abbesse de Jouarre, L', *v.* *Drames philosophiques*.

Abélard or **Abailard**, Pierre (1079–1142), philosopher and theologian. He studied under Roscellinus and later, in the Cathedral School of Paris (*v.* *Universities*, 1), under Guillaume de Champeaux, whose extreme Realism he brilliantly refuted before enthusiastic audiences in the Cathedral School and in that of **Sainte-Geneviève*. He also attained distinction as a theologian of independent and rational views, but his teaching career was cut short by his tragic love affair with his pupil Héloïse (1101–64), niece of Fulbert (a canon of Notre-Dame, in whose house he lodged), a woman of high character and great learning. They were secretly married after she had given birth to a child; but Fulbert, in revenge, caused Abélard to be castrated. He took refuge at **Saint-Denis* and later at other monasteries; some of his teachings were denounced by St. Bernard and condemned as heretical; eventually he was reconciled with the leaders of the Church and spent his last years at **Cluny*.

His many writings include works on dialectics (in which his final position lay between Nominalism and Realism), ethics, and theology, notably the *Sic et Non* (a collection of apparently contradictory excerpts from the Scriptures and the Fathers which had an important influence on scholastic method). He is now best known for his more personal writings, his hymns (e.g. *O quanta qualia*) and, above all, his correspondence with Héloïse—letters exchanged long after their parting, when she was abbess of the convent of the Paraclete which he had founded, in which he consoles and encourages her and advises her on the conduct of a nunnery.

Abencérage, *v.* *Aventures du dernier Abencérage, Les*.

Ablancourt, Nicolas Perrot d' (1606–64), translator and man of letters, noted for his style; a friend of Patru. His translations include works of Lucian (a free version described by Ménage as 'la belle infidèle'), Thucydides, Xenophon, Arrian, Caesar, Cicero, Tacitus.

About, EDMOND (1828–85), journalist (v. *XIXe Siècle, Le*) and novelist. He published *Causeries* (1865 and 1866), collected articles; *Le Roman d'un brave homme* (1880), a successful novel; and several shorter tales, wittily written and still amusing reading (e.g. *Le Roi des montagnes*, 1857; *L'Homme à l'oreille cassée*, 1862; *Le Nez d'un notaire*, 1862).

Abrantès, (1) JEAN-ANDOCHE JUNOT, DUC D' (1771–1813), 'Sergent la Tempête', a brave and dashing soldier (less effective as a commander), campaigned with Bonaparte in Italy and Egypt, becoming his *aide-de-camp*, distinguished himself at *Austerlitz, was military governor of Paris, then led the invasion of Portugal (1807), took Lisbon, and was made a duke and governor of Portugal. He fell from favour when, after being defeated by Wellington at Vimeiro (21 Aug. 1808), he signed the Convention of Cintra which led to the French evacuation of Portugal. He fought again in Spain, Germany, and Russia, and was made governor of the Illyrian provinces (1813); but his mind became unhinged and he committed suicide; (2) his wife LAURE PERMON, DUCHESSE D' (1785–1838), whose mother, a Corsican, was a close friend of the *Bonaparte family, became lady-in-waiting to Napoleon's mother and a brilliant hostess under the Empire. Her husband's death left her very badly off, so she took to writing for a living. Her *Mémoires historiques sur Napoléon, la Révolution, le Directoire ... et la Restauration* (1831–5), also (1836) of the first years of the July Monarchy, and her *Histoire des salons de Paris* (1836–8) give an excellent, racy, if not invariably reliable, picture of court, military, diplomatic, and literary society—formerly assembled in her own *salon*.

Académie, (1) a literary, scientific, or artistic society, v. the next 12 articles; *Literary Academies*; *Institut de France*; used alone, 'l'Académie' means the *Académie française*; (2) an administrative region, v. *Université de France*.

Académie de France à Rome, v. *École de Rome*.

Académie de Poésie et de Musique, v. *Baïf, J.-A. de*.

Académie des Beaux-Arts, v. *Académie royale de Peinture et de Sculpture*.

Académie des Inscriptions et Belles-Lettres, f. 1663 by Colbert for the encouragement of historical and archaeological learning (originally it provided mottoes for inscription on royal buildings); one of the five constituent bodies of the *Institut de France*. v. *Journal des savants, Le*.

Académie des Sciences, f. 1666 by Colbert for the study of mathematics, physics, and natural history (v. *Fontenelle*); one of the five constituent bodies of the *Institut de France*.

Académie des Sciences morales et politiques, f. 1795 by the *Convention for the study of philosophy, political economy, law, etc.; since 1832 one of the five constituent bodies of the *Institut de France*.

Académie du Palais, f. by Henri III for the discussion of philosophy and ethics; a successor of the *Académie* of J.-A. de Baïf and a short-lived precursor of the *Académie française*. Ronsard was a member.

Académie française. This had its origin in a group of men of letters (e.g. Conrart, Gombauld, Godeau, Chapelain) who used to meet *c.* 1630 in Paris, at Conrart's house, to discuss literary and other topics. Their meetings were, by agreement, secret, but in 1634 Richelieu heard of them and persuaded the group to become an official body of 40 (hence 'les Quarante'). The letters patent of the *Académie française*—the name adopted—were approved in 1635, but not officially registered till 1637. The members included some of the leading writers of the day, and critics and grammarians such as Chapelain and Vaugelas, but in general they were persons of literary taste rather than literary eminence. They continued to meet in private houses till 1672, when they were installed in the *Louvre. *v. Pellisson.*

The *Académie*'s purpose was to perfect the French language, and to this end members began to compile a Dictionary, in which the authority of Vaugelas had special weight. Progress was impeded by the invidious task (imposed by Richelieu) of passing judgement on *Le *Cid* (*v. Corneille*), then by the deaths of Richelieu and Vaugelas; and the first edition did not appear until 1694 (for details and later eds. *v. Dictionaries*, 1694). A *Grammar*, a *Rhetoric*, and a *Poetic* were also originally contemplated (*cf. Grammaire de l'Académie française*).

In the early 18th c. the main tendency of the *Académie* was to defend consecrated rules and models. Later, when the *philosophes* finally obtained a majority, it became a leading organ of opinion. It was suppressed in 1793, but re-established in substance in 1803, when Napoleon reorganized the *Institut national* (*v. Institut de France*), making the second *classe* one of French language and literature, with a self-elected membership of 40. In 1816 the name *Académie française* was officially restored, and it was made first of the *classes* of the *Institut de France*. In 1806 it had moved to its present quarters in the Palais Mazarin.

The *Académie* was at first hostile to the *Romantics, but eventually yielded to public opinion and admitted, for example, Lamartine (1829), Hugo (1841), and Vigny (1845). Though the institution has been the target of much wit, membership is an honour coveted by the great majority **of distinguished Frenchmen (women were ineligible until 1980; *v. Yourcenar*). Most**

great writers have been members (notable exceptions include Molière, Diderot, Balzac, Flaubert), also—for the distinction is not solely confined to men of letters—*savants*, clerics, soldiers, diplomats, etc. *v. Immortels, Les; Fauteuils acadèmiques.*

When a seat in the *Académie* falls vacant, the vacancy is declared. Candidates then write to each *académicien* and usually make a round of formal visits, though no *académicien* may pledge his support to a candidate. Election is by secret ballot. The public are admitted to the formal reception of the new member who, attired in the famous *habit vert* of the *Institut* (embroidered with palm-leaves, and complete with *bicorne* and sword), must pronounce a *discours de réception* (*v. Patru*) in the form of a eulogy of the *Académie* and of his predecessor. There follows a formal response on behalf of the *Académie*, in effect a laudatory biography of the new member.

For prizes in the gift of the *Académie, v. Prix littéraires.*

Académie Goncourt, a literary society f. by the will of E. de Goncourt, was recognized as a public body, and began to function, in 1903. It consists of 10 men, or women, of letters (excluding members of the *Académie française*). Their chief duty is to select annually (now in November), for the award of a money prize (the *Prix Goncourt*), the best imaginative prose work in French, preferably a novel, published in the preceding year. Prize-winners have included Proust (**A l'ombre des jeunes filles en fleurs*) and Malraux (*La *Condition humaine*).

Académie nationale de Musique, the official title of the *Théâtre de l'Opéra*, the home of grand opera in Paris. It began (1671) as the *Académie des Opéras*, under the direction of the poet Pierre Perrin (*c.* 1620–75). Perrin was ousted by Lulli, who obtained the king's *privilège* and established his *Académie royale de Musique* in a hall of the *Palais-Royal (1673, after Molière's death). After several changes of quarters and many more of title, it was installed in 1875 in its present home in the Place de l'Opéra. It is subsidized by the State.

Académie palatine (or du Palais), the 'Palace Academy' (*cf. École palatine*) for the promotion of learning formed on Charlemagne's initiative by the scholars and men of letters at his court (e.g. *Alcuin, Theodulfus, Paul the Deacon, Peter of Pisa, Angilbert). Members (inc. women, e.g. Charlemagne's daughters) discussed points of theology, grammar, and rhetoric, read poems, propounded riddles, etc. They assumed classical or Biblical names: Charlemagne was 'David', Alcuin 'Flaccus Albinus'. Their activities reflected and promoted the intellectual renaissance that marked Charlemagne's reign.

Académie royale de Peinture et de Sculpture, f. 1648 by Mazarin (Le Brun was its first rector). It was suppressed in 1793, then absorbed into the *Institut national* (*v. Institut de France*). In 1816, as the *Académie des Beaux-Arts*, it became one of the constituent bodies of the *Institut de France*. Associated with it is the *École nationale supérieure des Beaux-Arts* (f. 1648 as the *École académique*), an *école spéciale* for painters, sculptors, architects, etc. The *École des Beaux-Arts* awards the famous *Grand Prix de Rome*, tenable at the *École de Rome. v. Salon*, 2.

Acadie, roughly the present Canadian province of Nova Scotia, was discovered by the Cabots (1497), Italian navigators in the service of Henry VII of England. It was named 'Acadie' in 1524 by Verazzani, an Italian navigator in the service of François Iᵉʳ, who took possession of it (and of Newfoundland as 'Terre-Neuve') for France. There were French settlers (*habitants*) as early as 1598, but French occupation was continually disputed by the English. Louis XIV abandoned the French claim to both Acadie and Terre-Neuve at the Peace of Utrecht (1713). Many French settlers refused to acknowledge British sovereignty and were

deported (1755). Britain was finally confirmed in possession of the whole of French Canada by the Treaty of Paris (1763), which ended the Seven Years War. *Cf. Nouvelle France, La*.

Accusateur public, L', a counter-Revolutionary journal f. soon after the Terror (1794), and suppressed in 1797 (*v. Press*, 3).

Achard, MARCEL (1899–1974), playwright (a member of the *Académie*, 1959), author of comedies—a happy mixture of burlesque, pantomime, and unexpected pathos—e.g. *Voulez-vous jouer avec moâ?* (1924), *Marlborough s'en va-t-en guerre* (1924), *Jean de la lune* (1929), *Nous irons à Valparaiso* (1948), also of an adaptation of Jonson's *Silent Woman* (*La Femme silencieuse*, 1926). He collaborated in many films.

Ackermann, LOUISE CHOQUET, MME (1813–90), poetess, a contributor to *Le *Parnasse contemporain* (1876). Her work (collected in *Œuvres*, 1885; inc. *Ma vie*, an autobiography) is often coloured by her atheism and despairing view of human destiny.

Acomat, in Racine's *Bajazet*.

Acte additionnel aux constitutions de l'Empire (1 June 1815; *v. Champ de mai*), an act embodying the new liberal constitution (providing for liberty of the *Press—and v. Librairie—*, ministerial responsibility, and parliamentary government) inaugurated by Napoleon during the Hundred Days. It was drafted by B. Constant.

Acte gratuit, a gratuitous or inconsequent action performed on impulse, possibly to gratify a desire for sensation. The term occurs in the writings of Gide, part of whose doctrine of individualist morality is that our behaviour should be uninhibited, governed by our desires rather than by conventional (often hypocritical) standards. A typical *acte gratuit* occurs in his *Les Caves du Vatican*, where Lafcadio, alone in a railway compartment with the insignificant and irritating Amédée, obeys a sudden impulse to push him to his death through the door.

Actes des Apôtres, Les, (1) v. *Mystère*; (2) a famous Royalist journal, f. 1789 by Peltier. Its venomously witty satires of the Revolution and its 'Apostles' provoked such hostility that the king himself suppressed it (1791); v. *Rivarol*.

Action française, L', a political group, f. 1899, which stood for 'integral nationalism'. From 1908 it engaged in extreme monarchist, Roman Catholic, and anti-Semitic propaganda—though denounced from monarchist headquarters and excommunicated (1926–39) by Rome. Young members of the party (the *camelots du roi*) indulged in political hooliganism. Its organ, *L'Action française* (1899–1944), appeared daily from 1908, exercising considerable influence among die-hards and right-wing intellectuals. The editors and chief polemicists were Maurras and L. Daudet; contributors included Bainville, Massis, Bernanos (for a time), Rebatet and Brasillach (v. *Resistance*). The political comment was provocative and often scurrilous, the literary standard consistently high. From 1940 the paper supported Pétain. It was suppressed in 1944 (v. *Press*, 9).

Adam, Jeu, v. *Jeu de la Feuillée*.

Adam, Jeu d', v. *Religious Writings*, 1.

Adam, JULIETTE LAMBER, MME (1836–1936), a writer on foreign affairs, founder-editor of *La Nouvelle Revue* (1879–1940; a political and literary periodical); also a novelist (e.g. *Païenne*, 1883). After the *Franco-Prussian war she exercised political and literary influence through her *salon* (Gambetta and Loti were *habitués*). She left reminiscences of Paris in the 1870s.

Adam, PAUL (1862–1920), novelist, owed his reputation, at one time considerable, to

rather heavy novels of social history, e.g. *Robes rouges* (1891), *Le Vice filial* (1891), and *La Force du mal* (1896), depicting contemporary judicial, medical, and Bohemian circles; *Le Mystère des foules* (1895; on *Boulangisme*); *La Force* (1899), *L'Enfant d'Austerlitz* (1902), *La Ruse* (1903), and *Au soleil de juillet* (1903), four novels of family and military life in the years 1800–30, belonging to a group of some 16 in all entitled *Le Temps et la vie*; *En décor* (1891; provincial life); *La Ville inconnue* (1911; Paris). Two earlier novels, *Chair molle* (1885) and *Être, ou les Feux du Sabbat* (1888), were influenced by *Naturalism and *Symbolism respectively. His *Petit Glossaire pour servir à l'intelligence des auteurs décadents et symbolistes* (1888; under the pseud. 'Jacques Plowert') was apparently without satirical intention. v. *Thé chez Miranda, Le*.

Adam Billaut, v. *Billaut*.

Adam de la Halle or **Adam le Bossu** (*c.* 1240–*c.* 1288), a lyric poet of *Arras, later in the suite of Charles d'Anjou in Italy. He is famous for two dramatic works, the *Jeu de la Feuillée* and the *Jeu de Robin et Marion*. He also wrote songs on themes of courtly love (*amour courtois*), a satirical *congé*, etc.

Adamov, ARTHUR (1908–70), playwright of Armenian birth, settled in Paris in 1924 and became involved with *Surrealist circles. His first work for the theatre was an adaptation of Büchner's *La Mort de Danton*, produced at the Festival d'Avignon in 1948. There followed *L'Invasion* and *La Grande et la Petite Manœuvre* (1950), *La Parodie* (1952), *Le Professeur Taranne* (1953), and *Ping-Pong* (1955)— his best-known play, the story of two down-and-outs, which marks the turning-point towards an increasingly committed, Marxist theatre, e.g. *Paolo-Paoli* (1957), *La Politique des restes* (1962), *Le Printemps 71* (1963; a 'documentary' on the subject of the *Commune*), *Off Limits* (1969). His name is often associated with the Theatre of the Absurd (*v. Theatre of the 19th and 20th cs.*), although his increasing political commitment clearly marked him off from most other exponents of this form. *L'Aveu* (1946) was an autobiographical work.

Adenet le Roi, a 13th-c. **ménestrel* and poet of Brabant, long in the service of Count Guy of Flanders; author of the **chansons de geste* of **Berthe aux grands pieds*, the *Enfances *Ogier*, and *Beuve de Comarchis*, rehandlings of earlier *chansons*. He made certain innovations, substituting the **alexandrine* for the decasyllable and often linking the stanzas in pairs by similarity of rhymes, masculine in the first, feminine in the second. He also wrote the romance **Cléomadès*.

Adolescence Clémentine, *v. Marot.*

Adolphe (London 1816; written 1807), a remarkable early novel of psychological analysis by B. Constant. The story recalls his own liaison with Mme de Staël.

Adolphe, young and discontented, satisfies his *amour propre* by seducing the much older Ellénore. He has briefly fancied himself genuinely in love, but her devotion becomes irksome. Obliged to protest a love that is dead, tortured when with her and unhappy when away from her, but too compassionate and responsible, above all too weak, to abandon her, he subjects all his various feelings to minute analysis. Finally disillusioned and forced to abandon all hope of his love, Ellénore dies of grief, whereupon he realizes that the bondage of love may be preferable to loveless freedom.

Adrienne Lecouvreur (1849), a play about Adrienne **Lecouvreur* by Scribe and E.-W. Legouvé. *v. Bernhardt*; *Rachel.*

Affaire, L', *v. Dreyfus.*

Affaire Clemenceau, L', *v. Dumas fils.*

Agadir, a roadstead on the west coast of Morocco where in April 1911, after France had been subduing anarchy in the country,

Germany sent a gunboat ostensibly to protect German subjects. The ensuing crisis nearly ended in a European war.

Agathon, *v. Massis.*

Agésilas, *v. Corneille.*

Agincourt (Azincourt, a village near Arras). Here, in a famous battle (25 Oct. 1415), the English under Henry V defeated a much larger French army under the connétable d'Albret. *v. Armagnacs and Burgundians.*

Agnès, in Molière's *L'*École des femmes.*

Agnès de Saint-Paul, La Mère, *v. Arnauld, Arnauld d'Andilly* (3).

Agoult, MARIE DE FLAVIGNY, COMTESSE D' (1805–76), beauty and bluestocking, published novels (e.g. *Nélida*, 1845) as 'Daniel Stern' and wrote on history, politics, and philosophy for reviews. Liszt was her lover between 1830 and 1840, and their daughter Cosima married Wagner. She left *Souvenirs* (1877). *v. Salon*, 1.

Agrégation, agrégé. The *concours d'agrégation* is an annual competitive examination—open to men and women who have obtained their first university degree (the *licence*)—for appointment to a limited number of teaching posts in **lycées*. An *agrégé* is a successful candidate. The prestige of the *agrégation* has long been high, though it is no longer the sole method of recruiting *lycée* teachers.

Aguesseau, *v. Daguesseau.*

Aicard, JEAN (1848–1921), author of novels (e.g. *Le Roi de la Camargue*, 1890; *Maurin des Maures*, 1907) and poetry (e.g. *Les Poèmes de Provence*, 1874; *La Chanson de l'enfant*, 1875) depicting Provençal life and childhood.

Aigle de Meaux, L', i.e. Bossuet.

Aiglon, L' (1900), a verse drama by E. Rostand. The hero is Napoleon's son (*v.*

Napoleon II), tortured by dreams of glory which he has no means of realizing. *v. Bernhardt.*

Aignelet, in **Pathelin.*

Aimeri de Narbonne, a *chanson de geste (*Garin de Monglane cycle); one of the finest examples of the *genre*, written in the early 13th c. probably by Bertrand de Bar-sur-Aube, in nearly 5,000 rhyming deca-syllables. It recounts the taking of Nar-bonne by Aimeri (Garin's grandson) on Charlemagne's orders after Roncevaux; his courting of Ermenjart; further battles with the Saracens; and the marriage fes-tivities. It inspired Hugo's *Aymerillot* in the **Légende des siècles.*

Aimerides, Geste des, *v. Garin de Monglane.*

Aiol, a *chanson de geste of the 12th–13th cs., the first part in decasyllables, the second in *alexandrines. Aiol obtains the reinstatement of his father, banished through the intrigues of Macaire from the court of Louis, son of Charlemagne.

Aïssé, MADEMOISELLE (*c.* 1694–1733), a Circassian slave bought as a child by the French ambassador at Constantinople and educated in France. She entered Parisian society, where her beauty and charm were widely admired. Her *Lettres* throw light on social personages of the day. It was she who wrote: 'Il n'y a point de héros pour son valet de chambre.'

Akakia, *v. Diatribe du docteur Akakia.*

Alacoque, MARGUERITE-MARIE (1647–1690; canonized 1920), a nun of the Order of the Visitation (f. by St. François de Sales), chief founder of devotion to the Sacred Heart.

Alain, *v. Chartier, É.-A.*

Alain-Fournier, *pseudonym of* HENRI-ALBAN FOURNIER (1886–1914), author of an outstanding novel, *Le* *Grand Meaulnes (1913). A schoolmaster's son, he spent his youth at Épineuil (Cher), a small town which partly inspired the Sainte-Agathe of his novel. His later school and university years (at the **École normale supérieure*) were spent in Paris; he also took a clerical post for a time in England. Having failed the *agrégation, he took up journalism. He died in action in the 1914–18 war. *v. Rivière.*

'A la lanterne!' The 'lanterne de la Grève', a lamp bracket on the wall of a shop in the Place de *Grève in Paris, served for several summary executions after the fall of the *Bastille (1789), hence the cry 'A la lanterne!' *v. Ça ira; Desmoulins.*

A la recherche du temps perdu (1913–1927), by Proust, a novel in seven separately entitled but interrelated sections (*v.* 4, below). *v. Novel,* 3.

1. GENERAL. The novel is reminiscent in character, told in the first person by 'Marcel' (we never learn his surname; he resembles the author, though the work is not an autobiography). It evolves on several planes at once, and a point important for appreciation is Marcel's dual approach as narrator. He is the central character, whose life we follow from childhood, and who accepts experiences and contacts as they arrive, with no inkling of their future significance; but he is at the same time the middle-aged narrator, viewing and fully comprehending the same sensations, and their significance for himself and others, in retrospect ('sentant au fond de moi des terres reconquises sur l'oubli') and so, *recovering* time. Only with the last volume (*Le Temps retrouvé*, ii) does the reason for this dual standpoint in time become clear. Then, too, the long novel takes shape as the concrete framework for an inner plot—Marcel's awakening to his vocation as a creative writer.

2. THE INNER PLOT. As child, adolescent, and adult, Marcel observes the world of which he is the centre. He is at times vaguely, at certain almost transcendental moments urgently, aware of a reality, an essence, waiting to be captured. Such moments have usually

occurred when a trivial sensation or act (e.g. the taste of a 'madeleine' dipped in tea) has stimulated his 'involuntary' memory and illumined whole stretches of the past, registered hitherto only by his unconscious perceptions. More or less constantly, too, throughout life, and usually at moments of heightened aesthetic perception (e.g. when listening to music), he has played with the idea of writing. But he rebels unconsciously against the difficulties of creation, and a day comes in middle age when he decides that he will never write.

Just at this time (*Le Temps retrouvé*, ii), he returns to Paris after an absence of some years, and goes to an afternoon reception. As he waits in an ante-room to be announced, three trivial incidents stimulate three supreme flashes of 'involuntary' memory, and he re-experiences the sensations of moments of the past when he has been acutely aware of an intangible reality. Suddenly, as he reflects on this identity of past and present sensations, he penetrates to the essence. Reality, he sees, is the spiritual significance of all that we experience in life. Events, emotions, human contacts, and our reactions to them, are successive; but reality, which can be disengaged from them all, transcends time, and is universal.

He further realizes that this *essence* awaits the expression that only the writer can give it, and that writing is the vocation for which his whole life has been a preparation. He must now seek, in the depths of his consciousness, the 'vraie vérité' of his life and convert it by writing into its spiritual equivalent.

He is then announced, and finds a company known to him since, or through contacts of, childhood. All are witnesses, physically and socially, to time's disintegrating and transforming action (*v. Guermantes*). Here, he sees, in this visible link between past and present, is the concrete framework for his book. He will resurrect his life and those of the people whose story has at various points been interwoven with his own. The study of their relations to himself and to one another, and to the events and passions of

their lives, will be his means of reaching, and conveying, an understanding of the true significance of life itself and the emotions of which it is made up.

At what point in his life shall he begin? While in the ante-room, he had noticed G. Sand's *François le champi* on the bookshelves. It recalled an evening in childhood significant for the development of his personality. That evening, he decides, shall be the starting-point for his recovery of time, and of reality. The whole novel, which, after an introductory chapter, does, in fact, begin with this evening (*Du côté de chez Swann*, i. *Combray*), has led up to this moment; and with the choice the work ends.

3. THE FRAMEWORK. The child Marcel, a day-dreamer, sensitive and delicate (*cf.* Proust), with an adored and adoring mother and grandmother, leaves Paris regularly for family holidays at *Combray. We follow his developing interests and, as time passes and his social circle widens, study with him Parisian society of the late 19th and early 20th cs. He belongs to the wealthy, cultivated *bourgeoisie*, but also moves in the circles dominated by the *Guermantes aristocracy. Twice he spends the summer at *Balbec. His first love is *Gilberte Swann. Later, he is attracted by the duchesse de Guermantes, and he has an unhappy love affair with *Albertine Simonet. By way of many digressions (he pauses to emphasize the link between a past momentarily recaptured and the present from which he writes; he pursues subsidiary themes: 'involuntary' memory, love—particularly in the form of inversion—, jealousy, the arts, the social hierarchy) we end with him in middle age, at the reception described above.

For other leading characters (out of well over 200 in all) *v. Bergotte*; *Bloch*; *Charlus*; *Elstir*; *Françoise*; *Norpois*; *Odette*; *Saint-Loup*; *Swann*; *Verdurin*; *Villeparisis*; *Vinteuil*.

4. PUBLICATION. After completing the novel in its first form (1912), Proust contemplated publication in one volume entitled *A la recherche du temps perdu*. It was too long for this, and three volumes

were then envisaged. The first, *Du côté de chez Swann*, was published in 1913, and the remaining two were announced. The 1914–18 war—which provided Proust with a wealth of fresh material—interrupted publication, but this was resumed in 1917, by the publishing house of the *Nouvelle Revue française*. By then he had revised and enlarged his manuscript to such an extent (a practice he followed till his death in 1922) that further subdivision was continually necessary.

The work as published by the *N.R.F.* now became: *Du côté de chez Swann* (1917, 1 vol., reissued 1919, 2 vols.); *A l'ombre des jeunes filles en fleurs* (1918, 1 vol., later 2 and then 3 vols.); *Le Côté de Guermantes*, i (1920, 1 vol.) and *Le Côté de Guermantes*, ii with *Sodome et Gomorrhe*, i (1921, 1 vol.); *Sodome et Gomorrhe*, ii (1922, 3 vols.); *La Prisonnière* [originally *Sodome et Gomorrhe*, iii] (1923, 2 vols.); *Albertine disparue* (1925, 2 vols.); *Le Temps retrouvé*, i and ii (1927, 2 vols.). There is an excellent English translation, *Remembrance of Things Past* (1922–31), by C. K. Scott-Moncrieff and (last section only) S. Hudson.

Alba, *v. Chansons à personnages.*

Albatros, L', *v. Baudelaire.*

Albert-Birot, PIERRE (1876–1967), poet, dramatist, and essayist, an extreme individualist, was closely associated with *Cubism, *Futurism, and early *Surrealism, when his review *Sic* (f. 1916) was an outlet for *avant-garde* poets. Thereafter, he went his own way and made his name with the vast, unpunctuated, prose epic *Grabinoulor* (publ. at intervals from 1921; a rev. and augm. ed. appeared in 1964), whose hero has been called 'le Tarzan du fantastique'. His early verse is collected in *Poésie I, 1916–1924* (1967).

Albertine disparue (1925, 2 vols.), 6th section of Proust's *A la recherche du temps perdu*. His original choice of title appears to have been *La Fugitive*.

Marcel meets Albertine Simonet on his first holiday at *Balbec. On a second stay,

some years later, he is about to end an affair with her when a slight incident seems to confirm his suspicions of her Lesbianism and rekindles his love. He takes her to live with him in Paris and keeps her virtually a prisoner, alternately anxious and reluctant to marry her. She runs away and is killed when out riding. Marcel's love fades gradually and painfully into oblivion.

Earlier 'Albertine' sections are *A l'ombre des jeunes filles en fleurs*; *Sodome et Gomorrhe*, ii; *La Prisonnière*.

Albert Savarus, *v. Comédie humaine, La* (*Scènes de la vie privée*).

Albertus, ou l'Âme et le Péché (1832), a fantastic, but not too serious, poem by Gautier about a young poet of Leyden who offers his soul to the Devil for love.

Albigeois (Albigenses), members of a heretical sect, so named from Albi (though Toulouse was the main centre of the movement), who became conspicuous in the 12th c. for their piety and austere morality. Supported by the nobles and even the bishops of the region, they censured the corruptions of the papacy and were accused of Manichaean doctrines. Innocent III launched a crusade against them (1209–18), conducted, often with great cruelty, by Simon de Montfort (and the subject of a 13th-c. epic poem in Old Provençal). It led to the fall of Raymond VI, comte de Toulouse, their leader, who was supported by Peter of Aragon. Thus began the subjection of the princes of the Midi to the central government in Paris, and the decline of the literature they had fostered (*v. Troubadours*). Cf. *Vaudois*; *v. Oldenbourg.*

Album de vers anciens, *v. Valéry.*

Alcaforado or **Alcaforada**, MARIANNA, *v. Lettres portugaises.*

Alceste, in Molière's *Le *Misanthrope.*

Alceste, an opera (1) by Quinault (1674), with music by Lulli; (2) by Gluck, performed in Paris (1776) with a French adaptation of the original Italian libretto.

Alcionée, v. *Du Ryer*.

Alcuin (c. 730–804), a Northumbrian theologian, master of the cathedral school at York from 766. At the invitation of Charlemagne, whom he met at Parma in 781, he became head of the *École palatine* (for which he wrote manuals). He was soon the leading light of the *Académie palatine* and the emperor's 'premier ministre intellectuel' (Guizot). In 796 he became abbot of Tours, where he founded a school (soon the model for other cathedral or monastery schools), a library, and a scriptorium. Actively encouraged by Charlemagne, he did much to promote education in the seven liberal arts and his influence (exercised also through his theological writings) powerfully contributed to the intellectual renaissance of the Carolingian period. His letters shed light on contemporary society.

Aldomen, v. *Obermann*.

Alecis, v. *Alexis or Alecis*.

Alembert, JEAN LE ROND D' (1717–83), natural son of Mme de Tencin (who barbarously exposed him as an infant on the steps of Saint-Jean-le-Rond, whence his name), a *philosophe*, a mathematician who advanced the sciences of dynamics and astronomy (his *Traité de dynamique* was written when he was 26), and an ardent opponent of religion. He was Diderot's chief assistant on the *Encyclopédie* till 1758, when he withdrew, discouraged by the vexations entailed. He had contributed the remarkable *Discours préliminaire* (1751) and the article *Genève* (1757), which created a storm by its praise of the Genevan pastors (and v. *Lettre à d'Alembert sur les spectacles*). He published little else of importance, except scientific works (*Mélanges de littérature, d'histoire et de philosophie*, 1753; 2nd ed. 1758), but exercised influence as a member of the *Académie* (from 1754; from 1772 he was perpetual secretary), as a frequenter of *salons* (v. *Du Deffand*; *Lespinasse*), and through his European reputation. He enjoyed the patronage of the empress Catherine of Russia and Frederick the Great, and spent three months at the Prussian court in 1763. For *Le Rêve de d'Alembert*, v. *Diderot*.

Alexandre de Bernay (surnamed de **Paris**), v. *Alexandre le Grand* (1).

Alexandre le Grand. (1) A series of poems based on a 2nd-c. Alexandrian Greek original, later translated into Latin. Early in the 12th c. a popular epitome of the Latin was used for a version (in the Dauphiné dialect) by Albéric de Pisançon (or Besançon, or Briançon). Only a fragment remains of this first vernacular poem (in form recalling the *chansons de geste*, but in octosyllables) on a classical subject (v. *Romans d'antiquité*). A slightly later version in decasyllables was probably written in Poitou. At the end of the century the material was rehandled by other poets (inc. Alexandre de Bernay), still in rhymed *laisses*, but using the dodecasyllabic line later known as the *alexandrine*; it is this work that is generally called the *Roman d'Alexandre*. Oriental influence is marked in the descriptions of sumptuous palaces, strange scenery, rich apparel, and jewels, and in the hero's adventures. Liberality, a quality then much esteemed, is his chief characteristic. v. *Wauquelin*.

(2) A tragedy by Racine; produced 1665. Having reached the banks of the Hydaspes in his bid to conquer India, Alexandre (Alexander the Great) is confronted by the Indian kings Porus and Taxile, and a queen, Axiane, whom both kings love and who excites them against him. Porus is eager for battle; but Taxile, encouraged by his sister Cléophile, who is loved by Alexandre, betrays Porus and comes to terms. Porus is defeated. Alexandre proposes to reward Taxile with Axiane, but she repulses the traitor. Taxile in despair confronts Porus, who is still holding out with a few soldiers. Porus kills him and, satisfied with his revenge,

surrenders to Alexandre who, impressed by his courage, restores his kingdom and gives him Axiane.

Alexandrine, a dodecasyllabic line, the commonest metre in French verse. First found in the **Pèlerinage de Charlemagne* (probably mid-12th c.), it was used as the line appropriate to epic poetry in the **Roman d'Alexandre* (late 12th c.), whence its name. In the 13th c. it ousted the decasyllable as the metre of the **chansons de geste*. It fell into disuse in the 15th c., was revived (and extended to lyric poetry) by Ronsard and the poets of the **Pléiade* in the mid-16th c., and became the standard metre of tragedy and (from the 17th c.) of comedy and of serious poetry in general (*v. Tragiques, Les*). The strict rules applied to it in the 17th c., notably by Boileau, were relaxed in the 19th c. by the *Romantics and the *Symbolists. *v. Enjambement; Versification*.

Alexis or **Alecis**, GUILLAUME (*c.* 1425–1486), a monk whose poems *Les Faintises du monde* (proverbial philosophy) and *Le Blason des faulses amours* (on the dangers of illicit passion) had a great vogue; the latter poem was imitated by La Fontaine (*Janot et Catin*).

Alexis, PAUL (1847–1901), *Naturalist novelist and dramatist, a friend of Zola, contributed to Les *Soirées de Médan, published collected tales (e.g. *La Fin de Lucie Pellegrin*, 1880; *Le Besoin d'aimer*, 1885), and collaborated with Oscar Méténier (1859–1913) in writing plays (notably dramatizations of Les *Frères Zemganno, 1890, and *Charles Demailly*, 1893).

Alexis, Vie de Saint, one of the most remarkable early literary texts (in 125 stanzas of five assonanced decasyllables), written *c.* 1040 by an unknown author. Amplified versions were written in the 12th, 13th, and 14th cs. *v. Saints, Lives of*.

Alexis, son of a noble Roman, renounces the world on his wedding-night for a life of religion in complete poverty. After he has lived for 17 years at Edessa, in Syria, his saintliness is revealed by an image of the Virgin. He then returns, without making himself known, to his father's house, where he is given shelter and lives in saintly poverty for a further 17 years. Feeling near to death, he records the story of his life on a parchment, and from this his identity is later recognized. His character, and those of his wife and parents, are drawn with great literary skill.

Aliboron, Maître, a name of unknown derivation applied in the Middle Ages to a person of versatility and consequence, later to a foolish person and even to a donkey (La Fontaine, *Fables*, I, 13). A late 15th-c. poem, *Les Dits de Maistre Aliborum qui de tout se mesle*, describes this personage.

Aliénor d'Aquitaine, *v. Troubadours; Wace*.

Aliscans, *v. Guillaume, Chanson de*.

Alissa, in Gide's *La *Porte étroite*.

Allain, MARCEL, *v. Fantômas*.

Allainval, LÉONOR-J.-C. SOULAS D' (1700–53), author of *L'Embarras des richesses* (1725) and *L'*École des bourgeois* (1728), notable comedies of manners.

Allais, ALPHONSE (1854–1905), a humorist who wrote light verse (monologues; *cf. Cros*); tales and sketches, e.g. *Le Parapluie de l'Escouade* (1894), *On n'est pas des bœufs* (1896); and *L'Affaire Blaireau* (1899), a novel. He was associated with the *Chat-Noir* cabaret.

Allart de Méritens, HORTENSE, MME (1801–79), figured in the literary life of Paris as the mistress of Chateaubriand, Sainte-Beuve (their correspondence is of interest), and others. She wrote an autobiographical novel, *Les Enchantements de Prudence* (1873; as 'Mme de Saman').

Alliance, La Sainte (Holy Alliance) (1815), the alliance formed after the fall of Napoleon between the rulers of Russia, Austria, and Prussia, with the professed object of uniting their governments in a Christian fraternity. Its semi-religious character has been attributed to Tsar Alexander I (*cf. Krüdener*). Louis XVIII adhered to it *par politesse*, but it was ridiculed by Castlereagh and Metternich. It had dissolved by 1825.

Alliance française, L', a body f. 1883, with headquarters in Paris, 'for the propagation of the French language in the colonies and foreign countries', maintains or assists schools, libraries, and other organizations for the study of French in these fields. It draws its funds from an almost world-wide membership.

Almaviva, Comte, in Beaumarchais's *Le *Barbier de Séville*, Le *Mariage de Figaro*, and *La Mère coupable*.

A l'ombre des jeunes filles en fleurs, v. *A la recherche du temps perdu*.

Alternance des rimes, in French prosody, a rule requiring the alternation of *masculine and feminine rhymes. First consistently applied by Ronsard, it was generally accepted until the *Symbolists began to ignore it in the 19th c., since when it has been much less closely observed. v. *Rimes*.

Althusser, LOUIS, v. *Structuralism*.

Alzire, ou les Américains, a tragedy by Voltaire; produced 1736.

The scene is Lima. Alzire, daughter of a conquered Indian chief, and a Christian convert, reluctantly marries Gusman, a cruel Spanish conqueror and successor of his father, Alvarez, as governor of Peru; for she still loves Zamore, an Indian chief long presumed dead. Zamore, having survived Gusman's cruel tortures, now appears in Lima, reveals himself to Alvarez as the Indian who once saved his life, gains access to Alzire, and is amazed to learn of her marriage to the tyrant. Gusman discovers that Zamore is still alive

and, mad with jealousy, orders his execution. Zamore escapes, enters the council chamber in disguise, and mortally stabs Gusman. The council decide that Zamore and Alzire must die, unless Zamore becomes a Christian. Both proudly refuse the concession. Then Gusman, his eyes opened to his own barbarity by the approach of death, pardons Zamore and gives him Alzire. Zamore embraces a faith capable of inspiring such generosity.

Amadas et Idoine, a *roman d'aventure* composed in England in the first half of the 13th c.; the story of a squire of low degree, told with some power and originality.

Amadis de Gaule, a series of 15th-c. Spanish romances relating the chivalrous feats and marvellous adventures of the knight Amadis, son of King Perion of Gaul (? Wales), and, in a continuation, those of his son Esplandian. Nicolas Herberay des Essarts (d. *c.* 1552) published (1540–8) a French prose version of eight books and the translation was continued by others well into the 17th c. The element of gallantry and the love scenes were developed in the French version, which some deemed pernicious to youth. Even so, it was very popular and paved the way for the heroic romances of Mlle de Scudéry, Gomberville, etc. v. *Quinault*.

Amant rendu cordelier à l'observance d'amours, L', a poem of 1872 lines composed *c.* 1440, sometimes attributed to Martial d'Auvergne, treating of the code of gallantry.

Amants, v. *Donnay*.

Amants de Venise, Les, v. *Maurras*.

Amants magnifiques, Les, a 5-act prose *comédie-ballet* by Molière; produced 1670, as part of the *Divertissement royal*.

The very thin plot—two princes vie for the hand of a princess, but she prefers a humble warrior—is largely a pretext for the music and dances of the interludes. The theme, chosen by Louis XIV, recalled the duchesse de Montpensier's love for Lauzun.

Amaury, in Sainte-Beuve's *Volupté*.

Amboise, Conjuration d' (1560), an abortive conspiracy by the sieur de la Renaudie and *Huguenot supporters to overthrow the government of the *Guises (under François II) by a *coup de main* at Amboise. The young Agrippa d'Aubigné, passing the bodies of the conspirators hung from the balconies of Amboise, was required by his father to swear vengeance.

Ambroise, a Norman *jongleur* of the late 12th c. His *Estoire de la guerre sainte* (12,000 octosyllables), a history of the 3rd Crusade in which he took part, celebrates both the deeds of Richard Cœur de Lion and the trials of humbler pilgrims.

Âme et la danse, L', v. Valéry.

American Influence, v. *Foreign Influences*, 6.

Âmes du Purgatoire, Les, v. Mérimée.

Ami des hommes, L', i.e. the elder Mirabeau, so called from his book of that title.

Ami du peuple, L' (originally *Le Publiciste parisien*), a sensationalist daily, f. 1789 by Marat, widely read by the people and frequently suppressed. It ceased publication (as *Le Publiciste de la République française*) on 14 July 1793, the day after Marat's death. The title *Ami du peuple* was revived for later papers.

Ami du Roi, des Français, de l'ordre, et surtout de la vérité, L'. Two Royalist journals of this title, to some extent continuations of Fréron's *Année littéraire*, existed between 1790 and 1792. One was conducted by Galart de Montjoie (1746–1816). The other, conducted by the abbé Thomas Royou (1741–92), Fréron's brother-in-law and a virulent Royalist, became the official organ of the *émigrés* and clergy and was denounced (1792) by the *Assemblée législative*.

Amiel, Denys, *pseudonym of* GUILLAUME ROCHE (1884–1977), author of tragicomedies of everyday life, e.g. *La Souriante Mme Beudet* (1921; with Obey), depicting a latter-day *Madame Bovary; *Le Couple* (1923); *M. et Mme Un Tel* (1926); *Trois et une* (1932); *La Maison Monestier* (1939); *Le Mouton noir* (1945).

Amiel, HENRI-FRÉDÉRIC (1821–81), diarist and critic, a professor at the University of Geneva, his birthplace, became more widely known after the posthumous publication of parts of his diary (*Fragments d'un journal intime*, 1883–1887, re-ed. and augm. 1923 and 1927; *Philine*, further fragments, 1927). This remarkable piece of introspective literature, observing and analysing his creative impotence and inability to adopt a determined attitude to life ('Agir est mon supplice'), reveals rare intellectual and critical ability. His *Essais critiques* appeared in 1932 and *Lettres..., 1837–49* in 1935. The first English translation of his *Journal* (1885) was by Mrs. Humphry Ward.

Amiens, La Paix d', the Peace of Amiens between France and England (1802; v. *Coalitions* (2)), after which thousands of English tourists flocked to Paris. By this treaty the royal title of France, borne by English kings since Edward III, was relinquished.

Ami Fritz, L', v. Erckmann-Chatrian.

Amis de la constitution, Société des, v. *Jacobins*.

Amis des droits de l'homme et du citoyen, Société des, v. *Cordeliers*.

Amis et Amile, a 12th-c. romance in the form of a *chanson de geste*, of Oriental origin but associated with the *Charlemagne cycle. *Cf.* the 13th-c. English *Amis and Amiloun*.

It is the story of the deep devotion of two friends. Amile secretly replaces Amis in a trial by combat, for which deception he is punished with leprosy. To cure him,

Amis, at the bidding of Heaven, sacrifices his own children; but, on going to see their dead bodies, he finds them sleeping.

Amour, De l', v. *De l'amour.*

Amour courtois, a medieval conception of love, elaborated in the courts of S. France, whence—thanks partly to the influence of Eleanor of Aquitaine (v. *Troubadours*)—it spread to the nobility of the North, especially the court of Champagne. It is seen fully developed in the poems of Chrétien de Troyes, in extreme form in his **Chevalier à la charrette.* With the more subtle of the *troubadours* and **trouvères*, it is a disciplined and reasonable passion, directed to a worthy object—a beautiful and virtuous woman. Such a love is a service which ennobles, for the lover must win his lady by his prowess, courtesy, and patience; it is therefore an ordeal which he welcomes. The exaltation of woman is in strong contrast to the indignities she often suffers in the **chansons de geste.* Courtly love was governed by a code of conduct, set forth by Andreas Capellanus (André le Chapelain) in *De arte honeste amandi* (early 13th c.). The chief work inspired by the notion of courtly love was the first part of the **Roman de la Rose.*

Amour de Dieu, Traité de l', v. *François de Sales, St.*

Amoureuse, v. *Porto-Riche.*

Amour médecin, L', a 3-act prose **comédie-ballet* by Molière; produced 1665 at **Versailles.* It is said that Molière, secure in the royal favour, here caricatured the court doctors. v. *Lulli.*

Lucinde loves Clitandre, but her devoted father Sganarelle, a selfish *bourgeois*, is determined not to lose her, or her dowry. Her maid devises a stratagem. Lucinde, already in a melancholy, feigns illness. Four doctors are called, and disagree. Then Clitandre, disguised as a physician, is introduced. He proposes to cure her by an imaginary marriage, which he will perform. Sganarelle, duly

impressed, co-operates, only to find that he has signed a binding marriage agreement. v. *Josse.*

Amour peintre, L', v. *Sicilien, Le.*

Amours, Les, v. *Ronsard.*

Amours de Psyché et de Cupidon, Les, v. *La Fontaine.*

Amours du Chevalier de Faublas, Les (1789–90), a frivolous, licentious novel by Louvet de Couvray, typical of many of its time. The amorous adventures of the amiable Faublas, the victim of his own charms, are related with a certain lively force. The novel ends on a moral note: Faublas goes mad.

Amours jaunes, Les, v. *Corbière.*

Amour tyrannique, L', v. *Scudéry, G. de.*

Ampère, (1) ANDRÉ-MARIE (1775–1836), a pioneer in the study of electricity. His *Essai sur la philosophie des sciences* (1834–1844) and *Journal et correspondance* are both of interest to the lay reader; (2) his son JEAN-JACQUES (1800–64), historian and man of letters, the generous friend of many literary contemporaries. His works include an *Histoire littéraire de la France avant le XIIᵉ siècle* (1839–40).

Amphitryon, a 3-act comedy in **vers libres* by Molière, produced 1668; based on the *Amphitruo* of Plautus and imitating passages in **Rotrou's Les Sosies.*

Amphitryon, a Theban general, and his servant Sosie are returning to Thebes from a successful campaign. But Jupiter, enamoured of Amphitryon's wife Alcmène, has assumed Amphitryon's features and introduced himself to her on the previous night as her victorious husband. Mercury, in attendance on Jupiter, has similarly assumed the appearance of Sosie. The comedy arises from the presence at the palace of two indistinguishable Amphitryons and two indistinguishable Sosies. In the end

Jupiter explains the deception. The play contains the lines:

> Le véritable Amphitryon
> Est l'Amphitryon où l'on dîne,

the origin of the association of Amphitryon with gastronomy; and the now proverbial

> Le Seigneur Jupiter sait dorer la pilule.

Dryden drew on this play for his *Amphitryon*, and Giraudoux handles the same story in his *Amphitryon 38*.

Amphitryon 38, *v. Giraudoux.*

Amyot, JACQUES (1513–93), a humanist of humble birth, taught at the University of Bourges till 1543, then became known to François Ier, who gave him an abbacy. Under Charles IX, whose tutor he had been, he became grand almoner and bishop of Auxerre. He is famous as the translator into admirable French of Plutarch's *Lives* (*Les Vies des hommes illustres*, 1559) and *Moralia* (1572), works of Diodorus Siculus and Heliodorus, and Longus's *Daphnis and Chloe* (1559). Besides raising the quality of French prose, he popularized the wisdom of the ancients through his Plutarch. Montaigne quotes freely from it in his *Essais*; and North's translation of the *Lives*, on which Shakespeare drew, was from Amyot's version. *v. Renaissance.*

Anacharsis en Grèce, Voyage du jeune, *v. Barthélemy.*

Anarchisme, *v. Literary Isms.*

Anastasie, a nickname for the *censorship, apparently first applied during the Second Empire. 'Dame Censure', or 'Anastasie', was caricatured as an old hag with an owl on her shoulder and a large pair of scissors under one arm; or as a crow with a large beak formed by the blades of scissors.

'Anastasie' was often the name given to the ugly old maid in *vaudeville.

Ancelot, JACQUES-ARSÈNE (1794–1854) and his wife MARGUERITE-LOUISE-VIRGINIE CHARDON (1792–1875), a well-known couple in the literary life of mid-19th-c. Paris. He wrote numerous ephemeral comedies, *vaudevilles, and tragedies (his *Louis XI*, 1819, brought him short-lived fame and a pension), but is most often remembered as the husband of the pushing but kind-hearted Mme Ancelot. Her *salon (in its heyday during the July Monarchy) was one of the best known and most influential in Paris, often mentioned in letters and memoirs—e.g. by Mérimée and Stendhal. She also painted (pictures of her *salon* and its frequenters); and her *Salons de Paris, foyers éteints* (1858) and *Un Salon de Paris, 1824–1864* (1866) are still read.

Ancey, GEORGES (1860–1917), a dramatist associated with the *Théâtre Libre. His comedies include *M. Lamblin* (1888), *Les Inséparables* (1889), *L'École des veufs* (1889), *La Dupe* (1891), *Ces Messieurs* (1901).

Ancien régime, L', the term applied to the system of government, or the political structure, of pre-Revolutionary France.

Ancien Régime, L', *v. Tocqueville.*

Anciens et des modernes, Parallèles des, *v. Perrault.*

Anciens et des modernes, Querelle des, *v. Querelle.*

Anciens et les modernes, ou la Toilette de Mme de Pompadour, Les, a dialogue by Voltaire.

Ancre, MARÉCHAL D', *v. Concini.*

André Cornélis (1887), a novel of psychological analysis by Bourget. It turns on the hero's dilemma when he discovers that his father, believed to have died a natural death, was in fact murdered by the man who is now his stepfather and whom his mother, in all innocence, adores.

Andrieux, FRANÇOIS (1759–1833), judge, professor at the *Collège de France, and perpetual secretary of the *Académie, wrote several comedies, e.g. *Les Étourdis* (1787), *Le Vieux Fat* (1810). They were feeble, but won him official recognition.

Andromaque, a tragedy by Racine, produced 1667; based on the Greek legend of the fate of Andromache after the fall of Troy (except that with Racine she is merely the widow of Hector and mother of Astyanax, who has survived, and not also the mother of Molossus by Pyrrhus).

The scene is in Epirus. Pyrrhus, the king, is neglecting Hermione, his betrothed, for Andromaque, his captive. Hermione is jealous; Andromaque, faithful to the memory of Hector, hates her new suitor. Oreste, who has long loved Hermione, is sent to Epirus by the Greek States to demand the death of Astyanax. To bend Andromaque to his will Pyrrhus threatens to surrender him to the Greeks. Andromaque vacillates between hatred of Pyrrhus and fear for her son; Pyrrhus, between love for Andromaque and cruel anger against her; Hermione, between love for Pyrrhus and resentment at his neglect. Finally, to save her son, Andromaque agrees to marry Pyrrhus, but plans to kill herself thereafter. Hermione, infuriated by news of the intended marriage, agrees to fly with Oreste, but first demands the death of Pyrrhus, which Oreste reluctantly promises her. But when he comes to tell her that Pyrrhus is dead, she turns fiercely against him for having murdered the man she loves, and kills herself on Pyrrhus's body. Oreste goes mad.

Andromède, *v. Corneille*.

Aneau, BARTHÉLEMY, in Latin ANNULUS (*c.* 1500–65), a teacher of rhetoric in Lyons who was murdered as a suspected Protestant. His works include a *Mystère de la Nativité* (1539; perf. by his pupils); *Picta poesis* (1552), emblem verses; a translation of More's *Utopia*; and, almost certainly, *Le Quintil Horatien*, criticizing Du Bellay's *Défense et illustration de la langue française*.

Âne mort et la Femme guillotinée, L', v. Janin.

Angélique, in Molière's *George Dandin*.

Angélique, La Mère, *v.* Arnauld, *Arnauld d'Andilly* (2).

Angélique de Saint-Jean, La Mère, *v.* *Arnauld, Arnauld d'Andilly* (5).

Angellier, AUGUSTE (1848–1911), poet, worked as a journalist, then became professor of English at the University of Lille. His works include, notably, the sonnet-sequence *A l'amie perdue* (1896); also *Le Chemin des saisons* (1903; nature poems), *Dans la lumière antique* (1905–11; series of poems), and a study of Robert Burns (1892).

Angelo (1835), a prose drama by Hugo. Tisbe, a courtesan and mistress of Angelo, governor of Brescia, discovers that Rodolpho, whom she loves, has long been the lover of Angelo's wife Catarina, and also that, as a child, Catarina had saved her (Tisbe's) mother from the gallows. Now Angelo discovers that his wife has a lover, and plots to murder her with a poison to be procured by Tisbe. Tisbe substitutes a narcotic. Rodolpho sees Catarina's 'corpse', and stabs Tisbe. Catarina wakens, and the dying Tisbe plots escape for the lovers.

Angennes, JULIE D', *v. Rambouillet, Hôtel de; Guirlande de Julie*.

Ange Pitou, v. Dumas père.

Anglo-Norman or **Anglo-French,** that form of French which became current in Great Britain and Ireland as a result of the Norman Conquest and the intercommunication between France and these countries during the next 200 years; also applied to the literature written in this language, to the authors who produced it, and in a looser sense to such writers as Wace.

It was mainly the language of the superior classes, but there is evidence that it penetrated to the lower orders. Its basis was the French of Normandy, with an admixture of other elements. Typical Normanisms in English are *garden* and *war* (contrast Central French *jardin*, *guerre*) and dialectal variation is preserved in our *chattel* and *cattle*. Isolation from the Continent and contact with English greatly modified its grammar, spelling, and pronunciation; thus, it anticipated Continental French in discarding the distinctive nominative form in nouns, extended the infinitive ending *-er* of the first conjugation, and reduced many diphthongs to simple vowels. Heterogeneous in structure and largely individual in use, it degenerated rapidly and had ceased to be a literary and colloquial medium by the end of the 14th c. It continued in commercial and official use into the 15th c., and survived till *c.* 1700 in the form of Law French, remnants of which remain in such formulas as *Le roi le veult* and many legal terms of French origin.

Anglo-Norman was the vehicle of an extensive literature from *c.* 1120 (Philippe de Thaon) to *c.* 1400 (Gower), at its peak in the 12th c. It dealt largely with religious, moral, and historical themes (chronicles in the vernacular appear earlier in England than in France). Typical works are a *Voyage of St. *Brendan*, one of many lives of saints; the *Chasteau d'amour*, an allegorical poem in praise of the Virgin by Robert Grosseteste (1175–1253), bishop of Lincoln; translations of Biblical books. There were also *romans bretons* such as the *Tristan* of Thomas, and quasi-historical romances and *romans d'aventure* such as *Horn*, *Haveloc*, *Beuve de Haumtone*, *Gui de Warewic*, and *Ipomedon*. The important *Jeu d'Adam* (*v. Religious Writings*, 1) was written in Anglo-Norman in England; and the famous *Chanson de Roland* has survived in the manuscript (at Oxford) of an Anglo-Norman scribe.

Angoisses douloureuses qui procèdent d'amours, Les, *v. Crenne*.

Angot, Madame, the type of the lower-class woman grown suddenly rich who retains the coarse tastes and language of her former condition. The name comes from the popular *opéra-comique Madame Angot, ou la Poissarde parvenue* (1796), by Maillot or Desmaillot (i.e. Arthur-François Ève, 1747–1814), precursor of the even more famous operetta *La Fille de Madame Angot* (1872; with music by Alexandre-Charles Lecocq, 1832–1918) and the comedy *La Petite Fille de Madame Angot* (1934) by Clément Vautel (1876–1954).

Angoulême, *v. Marguerite d'Angoulême*; *Bourbon* (3).

Annales de la littérature et des arts, Les (1820–9), a literary review which published work by young *Romantics.

Annales: *Économies,* *Sociétés,* *Civilisations* (1946– ; six times a year), a continuation of the *Annales d'histoire économique et sociale* f. 1929 by M. Bloch and Febvre. *v. History*, 4.

Annales patriotiques et littéraires, Les (1789–97; also known as *La Tribune des hommes libres*, and later as *Les Annales politiques et littéraires*), a journal (f. and ed. by L.-S. Mercier) devoted to politics, commerce, and literature; widely read by *Jacobins in the provinces.

Annales philosophiques, Les (title borne 1800–1; f. 1796 as *Les Annales religieuses*), one of the early, and best remembered, literary and philosophical reviews (fortnightly). It existed, under various titles and with intervals of suppression, till 1859, then became a daily of more general interest.

Annales politiques, civiles et littéraires du dix-huitième siècle, Les (1777–92), often called *Les Annales politiques*, a periodical of political, economic, and literary interest, founded and edited in London by Linguet. It circulated in France, where Linguet's virulent articles created a stir. While he was in the *Bastille, it was conducted in Geneva (1780–3) by Mallet du Pan and noted for fair political comment. Linguet later resumed publication in London and (1790–2) in Paris.

Annales politiques et littéraires, Les, v.
Annales patriotiques et littéraires.

Annales romantiques, Les (1823–36), a
periodical publication issued in miscellany
form (12 vols., the first entitled *Tablettes
romantiques*) to avoid censorship (*v. Press*,
5); an organ of the *Romantic movement.

Anneau d'améthyste, L', v. Bergeret.

Anne d'Autriche (Anne of Austria)
(1602–66), wife of Louis XIII; mother of
Louis XIV and regent during his minority.
v. Mazarin.

Année littéraire, L' (1754–90; usually
publ. every 10 days), one of the first
reviews to devote considerable space to
literary criticism, conducted till 1775 by
Fréron, then by his son Stanislas (*v.
Orateur du peuple*), Royou (*v. Ami du Roi*),
Geoffroy, and others. It consistently
supported the monarchy and the Church.

Année philosophique, L', v. Renouvier.

Année terrible, L', v. Hugo.

Annonce faite à Marie, L' (1912; a later
version of *La Jeune Fille Violaine*), by
Claudel, a medieval mystery (4 acts and
prologue; *cf. Mystère; Miracle*).
  Anne Vercors departs on a pilgrimage,
leaving Jacques Hury, a labourer, to look
after his wife and two daughters—the
gentle, innocent Violaine, who is
betrothed to Jacques, and the violent,
jealous Mara, who is in love with him.
Mara sees Violaine, moved by pity, kiss the
leper Pierre de Craon in the mystical belief
that she may heal him. On her wedding eve
Violaine shows Jacques the marks of the
leprosy which has now attacked her. (The
leper, we learn later, was cured.) Jacques,
influenced by Mara's tales, refuses to
believe in Violaine's innocence and she
leaves home. He marries Mara. Years
later, on Christmas Eve, a distraught Mara
brings the corpse of her baby to the cave
where Violaine, now a blind pauper, has
taken refuge. At Violaine's request she
reads the Christmas Office while Violaine

holds the corpse. A miracle occurs, and
Violaine returns a living child to her sister.

Anonyme de Béthune, L', v. History, 1.

Anouilh, JEAN (1910–), a skilful and
successful playwright. His plays—many
fundamentally   pessimistic,   others
lighthearted and gay—have been collected
(1942–70) in several volumes with titles
indicative of their nature: (1) *Pièces noires*
(inc. *Le Voyageur sans bagage*, 1937; *La
Sauvage*, 1938; and three modernized
versions of Greek themes, played in
modern dress, but preserving some of the
conventions of classical tragedy, notably
Antigone, 1944, also *Eurydice* and *Médée*);
(2) *Pièces roses* (inc. *Le Bal des voleurs*, 1938;
Le Rendez-vous de Senlis, 1941); (3) *Pièces
brillantes* (inc. *L'Invitation au château*,
1947; *La Répétition*, 1950; *Colombe*,
1951); (4) *Pièces costumées* (inc. *L'Alouette*,
1953, about Joan of Arc; *Becket*, 1959); (5)
Pièces grinçantes (inc. *La Valse des
toréadors*, 1952; *Pauvre Bitos*, 1956;
L'Hurluberlu, 1959).

Anquetil-Duperron,   ABRAHAM-HYA-
CINTHE (1731–1805), Orientalist. At
23, he set out for India in search of the
sacred writings of the Parsees and, after
many adventures and hardships, returned
to Paris (1762) with a priceless collection
of 180 manuscripts. He spent the rest of
his life working on them. His translation
of the *Zend-Avesta* (1771, with a preface
on his Indian adventures) opened a new
era in Oriental studies.

Anseïs de Carthage, a *chanson de geste
(*Charlemagne cycle) of the late 12th or
early 13th c. Charlemagne has conquered
Spain and given it to the young knight
Anseïs. But Anseïs seduces the daughter
of one of his chief vassals, provoking her
father to lead the Moors from Africa into
Spain.

Anthinéa, v. Maurras.

Antier, BENJAMIN, *v. Macaire, R.*

Antin, LOUIS-ANTOINE, DUC D' (1665–

1736), legitimate son of Mme de Montespan, disgraced himself at the battle of Ramillies, but was restored to favour, succeeded Mansard as director of royal buildings, and was later a member of the council of regency. He left memoirs.

Antioche, Chanson d', a poem in monorhyme stanzas of *alexandrines written early in the 13th c. by Graindor de Douai. It recounts the incidents of the 1st Crusade (1096–9) prior to the capture of Jerusalem, including the disastrous end of the expedition of *Pierre l'Hermite and culminating in the siege and occupation of Antioch. Graindor completed the story in another poem, *La Conquête de Jérusalem*. The poems are of only moderate literary merit, and falsify some of the facts. With the poems on the house of Godefroi de Bouillon (*v. Chevalier au cygne*; *Baudouin de Sebourg*) they form the Crusade *cycle.

Antiquité dévoilée, L', *v. Boulanger, N.-A.*

Antiquités de Rome, Les, *v. Du Bellay.*

Anti-roman, a 17th-c. term, revived by Sartre and applied to N. *Sarraute's novel *Portrait d'un inconnu* (1948), which he compared with Nabokov, Evelyn Waugh, and Gide's *Les *Faux-Monnayeurs*. The *anti-roman* (proof 'that we are living in a period of reflection, and that the novel is in the process of reflecting upon itself') retains the shape and appearance of the novel, whilst in reality 'contesting the novel through itself, destroying it before our eyes while appearing to construct it, writing the novel of a novel which does not come into existence'. This questioning of the traditional form of the novel is related to the *nouveau roman. v. Novel*, 3.

Antoine, ANDRÉ-LÉONARD (1858–1943), theatre director. He was a keen amateur actor, and in 1887 threw up his job with the Paris Gas Co. and used his meagre savings to found the *Théâtre Libre*. He later directed the *Théâtre Antoine* and ended his active career in the theatre as director (1906–14) of the *Odéon*. He

published *Mes souvenirs sur le Théâtre Libre* (1921) and *Le Théâtre* (1932; a history of the French stage from 1859).

Antony (1831), a drama by Dumas *père*; a work which contained much then novel (e.g. the *Romantic hero—a deprived 'outsider'; the 'femme incomprise') and has a place in the evolution of the modern theatre.

Adèle, the misunderstood wife of an army officer, succumbs to the sadistic charms of Antony, a rich but nameless orphan. When he comes at night to urge her to flee with him, they are surprised by her husband—whereupon Antony stabs her, declaring: 'Elle me résistait, je l'ai assassinée!' He has saved her honour and ensured that no one else will enjoy what he has been denied.

Aphrodite, *v. Louÿs.*

Apollinaire, Guillaume, *pseudonym of* WILHELM APOLLINARIS DE KOSTROWITZKY (1880–1918), poet, b. in Rome (the illegitimate son of an aristocratic Polish mother and an Italian father) and educated at schools on the Riviera. After a visit to Belgium and travel as a tutor (1901–2) in Germany, he found work in a Paris bank and from 1903 was actively involved in literary and artistic life. He helped to found ephemeral reviews, frequented literary cafés, wrote for the *Mercure de France*, and became a leading figure in *Cubist and *Futurist circles, with many friends among painters (e.g. Picasso, Derain, Dufy, Modigliani) as well as poets. He joined the army (Dec. 1914) and fought bravely at the front, revelling in military life (some of his poems of this period glorify war as a marvellous adventure). He received a severe head-wound in 1916, never fully recovered, and died in the influenza epidemic of 1918. He was at once a notable love poet (tender and melancholy, broadly in the lyrical tradition of the great *Romantics and Nerval) and a man of fertile intellect and passionate curiosity whose works and ideas have strongly influenced modern poets, especially the *Surrealists. He called for 'un esprit nouveau' in poetry, meaning primarily (as emerges in his essay *L'Esprit nouveau et les poètes*, 1918) an element of surprise and a sense of wonder. He urged poets to explore new fields of poetic fancy, to look for the exciting resemblances between apparently disparate things, to endow 'mille phantasmes impondérables' with reality. He used little or no punctuation in his verse and experimented with pictorial typography (hence the title *Calligrammes*). His fame rests on the collections *Alcools* (1913; poems of 1898–1913, inc. the well-known *Chanson du mal-aimé*) and *Calligrammes* (1918; poems of 1913–16, inc. *Il pleut*, printed with the letters trickling like water down the page). Other works published in his lifetime include *L'Enchanteur pourrissant* (1909), a tale; *L'Hérésiarque et Cie* (1910), short stories; *Les Peintres cubistes* (1913), essays on Picasso, Braque, Fernand Léger, Marcel Duchamp, Marie Laurencin (one of the many women he loved), etc.; *Les Mamelles de Tirésias* (1918; prod. 1917, and *v. Poulenc*), which he called a 'drame surréaliste' (said to be the first use of the term *surréaliste*) because of its 'usage raisonnable des invraisemblances'; and *v. Enfer*. More appeared posthumously, e.g. the novel *Une Femme assise* (1920), poems and letters to women he loved (*Tendre comme le souvenir*, 1952; *Poèmes à Lou*, 1955; *Lettres à Lou*, 1969), and collected art criticism (*Chroniques d'art*, 1960). He had a taste for erotic themes and, underlying his 'esprit nouveau' and his modern images (of cars, aeroplanes, etc.), a deep attachment to Greco-Latin culture (seen in his many mythological allusions).

Apologie de Raimond Sebond, *v. Montaigne*.

Apologie pour Hérodote, *v. Estienne* (4).

Appel au soldat, L', *v. Barrès*.

Approximations, *v. Du Bos, C.*

Après-midi d'un faune, L', *v. Mallarmé*; *Debussy*.

Aquinas, *v. Thomas Aquinas, St.*

A quoi rêvent les jeunes filles (1833, in **Un Spectacle dans un fauteuil*), one of the most perfect of Musset's short comedies (verse), marked by the gay, tender lyricism that has sometimes prompted comparisons with Shakespeare.

Duke Laerte wishes to marry his twin daughters Ninon and Ninette to Silvio and Irus. Knowing that a husband who comes provided only with a father's blessing and a ring will never satisfy youth's romantic dreams, he contrives serenades, midnight assignations, even a duel.

Arago, FRANÇOIS (1786–1853), scientist, founded (1816) the journal *Annales de chimie et de physique*, became director of the *Observatoire*, and was famous for the lucidity of his public lectures on astronomy (1812–45). From 1830 to 1848 he was also active in politics, figured prominently in the 1848 **Revolution*, helped (with Lamartine) to form the provisional government, and was largely responsible for the abolition of slavery in the colonies. Besides scientific works, he left most interesting memoirs, *Histoire de ma jeunesse* (1854), describing his adventures on a scientific mission in Spain.

Aragon, LOUIS (1897–1982), poet, novelist, and journalist; editor of *Les *Lettres françaises*. He began as a **Dadaist*, then became a leading **Surrealist*. His works of this period include the poems of *Feu de joie* (1920) and *Le Mouvement perpétuel* (1926); *Le Paysan de Paris* (1926), a novel evoking the everyday marvels of the city; *Traité du style* (1928), essays on Surrealist theories. He became a Communist in 1927 and a visit to Russia in 1930 led him to break with Surrealism and his former literary life. Since then he has been a committed and politically active writer (*v. Littérature engagée*), also at times an outspoken critic of Soviet policy. He directed the Communist daily *Ce soir*, went to Madrid during the Spanish Civil War, supported the **Front populaire*, and, after the fall of France, emerged as a national bard and a leader of the intellectual **Resistance*, actively engaged in clandestine publishing. In *Le Crève-cœur* (1941), *Les Yeux d'Elsa* (1942), *Le Musée Grévin* (1943), *La Diane française* (1945), etc., his patriotism and yearning for liberty are often fused with his love for his companion Elsa (*v. Triolet, E.*) in poignant lyric poems, notable for his return to traditional forms (the *chanson, *sonnet, *alexandrine, etc.). His other poetical works include *Les Yeux et la mémoire* (1954); *Le Roman inachevé* (1956), an autobiography; *Elsa* (1959); *Les Poètes* (1960); *Le Fou d'Elsa* (1963); *Il ne m'est Paris que d'Elsa* (1964). His novels, which show his great skill as a narrator, all depict life from a Marxist standpoint (observing the slow decline of a corrupt *bourgeoisie*, the aspirations of the proletariat, etc.), e.g. *Les Cloches de Bâle* (1933); *Les Beaux Quartiers* (1936); *Les Voyageurs de l'impériale* (1942), which embodies the story of his own youth; *Aurélien* (1945); *Les Communistes* (1949–51, 6 vols.); *La Semaine sainte* (1958), centred on the painter Géricault and the France of 1815, and widely regarded as his best novel; *Blanche, ou l'Oubli* (1967). His critical works include *La Lumière de Stendhal* (1954) and *Je n'ai jamais appris à écrire, ou les Incipit* (1969).

Aramis, in Dumas *père*'s *Les *Trois Mousquetaires.*

Arbres de liberté, trees erected temporarily, or planted, during the Revolution as symbols of liberty and fraternity, and later—following a decree (1794) that one should be planted in every *commune* (*v. Département*)—to commemorate the constitution of 1793. The young trees (often poplars) were decked, borne in procession, and planted in the presence of local notabilities. The first are said to have been planted at Lille and Auxerre (1792), and one still survives at Bayeux. The practice, apparently adopted in reminiscence of May Day and May Tree rejoicings, was revived for a time during the 1848 Revolution.

Arc de Triomphe, L', a triumphal arch

on the Roman model, completed 1836, stands at the head of the Avenue des *Champs-Élysées in Paris (in the Place Charles-de-Gaulle, formerly Place de l'Étoile). After the 1914–18 war France's Unknown Soldier was buried beneath it, since when a torch (the *flamme du souvenir*) has burned continuously there.

Archives de philosophie (1923–38; 1950– , now quarterly), a learned philosophical journal.

Archives nationales, Les, a central depot for documents relating to French political and administrative history, the equivalent of the British Public Record Office. Centralization of archives was effected by a decree (1793) of the *Convention*. From 1808 they were housed in the Hôtel de Soubise in Paris, and, from 1927, also in the neighbouring Hôtel de Rohan.

Archives philosophiques, Les (1817–18), a literary and philosophical review; an organ of the *doctrinaires, ed. by Royer-Collard and Guizot.

Arcos, RENÉ (1881–1948), *unanimiste poet, a member of the *Abbaye group; author of poetry marked by social concern and faith in man's progress towards happiness, e.g. *L'Âme essentielle* (1902), *La Tragédie des espaces* (1908), *Ce qui naît* (1910), *L'Île perdue* (1913), *Le Sang des autres* (1918), and of the novels *Pays du soir* (1918) and *Autrui* (1926).

A rebours (1884), a novel by Huysmans. Des Esseintes (*v. Montesquiou-Fezensac*), the effete survivor of a worn-out family, tries to overcome his profound *ennui* by leading a life elaborately opposed to that of ordinary men. He experiments with exotic furnishings, perfumes, and pleasures; buys a tortoise and has its shell encrusted with jewels; reads Mallarmé (then barely known), and dreams of a perfect evocative prose. (Mallarmé reciprocated with *Prose (pour des Esseintes).*) He succeeds only in adding acute biliousness to his original neurasthenia. Cured of the former, he gives way to pessimism, but as the book ends is turning to religion as a last resource.

The work owed much to its appearance at the time when the *esprit décadent* was merging into *Symbolism, and is now also important as a compendium of *fin-de-siècle* tastes and interests (*cf.*, in English, the quarterly *Yellow Book* and Wilde's *Picture of Dorian Gray*).

Arène, PAUL (1843–96), novelist and poet of Provençal life, wrote *Jean des figues* (1868; a novel which includes a description of *décadent* circles—*v. Esprit décadent*), *La Gueuse parfumée, récits provençaux* (1876), *Au bon soleil* (1881), *Le Midi rouge* (1895), *Contes de Provence* (1920). He was also part-author of *Le Parnassiculet contemporain* (1867; *v. Pastiche*).

Argan, in Molière's *Le *Malade imaginaire*.

Argens, JEAN-BAPTISTE, MARQUIS D' (1704–71), *philosophe* and man of letters. His *Lettres juives* (1736), written in the assumed character of a Jew visiting France, were pungently critical of French customs and religious institutions.

Argenson, (1) RENÉ-LOUIS, MARQUIS D' (1694–1757), elder son of a famous *lieutenant général de *police* under Louis XIV, a man of original and enlightened views, a member of the *Club de l'Entresol* and an advocate of free trade, later minister of foreign affairs (1744–7). His *Considérations sur le gouvernement ancien et présent de la France* (1764; previously much read in ms.), on democracy under a monarchy, was approved by Voltaire and quoted by J.-J. Rousseau. He left a *Relation* of the battle of *Fontenoy (publ. by Voltaire in the *Commentaire historique*, 1776), at which both he and his brother were present; *Essais* in the style of Montaigne; and *Mémoires* revealing his sound views on political reform; (2) his brother MARC-PIERRE, COMTE D' (1696–1764), to whom the *Encyclopédie* was

dedicated, held a variety of offices (minister of war; *directeur de la *librairie*, 1737–40, etc.). When Desfontaines, defending a scandalous pamphlet, pleaded 'Il faut bien que je vive', it was he who retorted 'Je n'en vois pas la nécessité'.

Argent, L' (1891), one of Zola's *Rougon-Macquart* novels. Aristide Saccard, whose grandiose speculative mania had once before brought him to ruin (in *La *Curée*), founds a joint-stock company (involving disastrous competition with the Jewish banker Gundermann) for exploitation in the Near East. The inevitable crash entails the usual pitiful tragedies. The launching of the *Banque universelle*, the feverish atmosphere and manipulation of the Stock Exchange, with accompanying corruption and political intrigue, are described with impressionistic mastery of detail.

Argenton, Monsieur d', *v. Commines.*

Aricie, in Racine's *Phèdre.*

Arimène, *v. Nicolas de Montreux.*

Ariste, a character in Molière's *Les *Femmes savantes*; also in many other plays.

Aristocratisme, *v. Literary Isms.*

Aristote, Lai d', *v. Lai d'Aristote.*

Arland, MARCEL (1899–), novelist and critic (a member of the *Académie, 1968), editor of the *Nouvelle Revue française* from 1953 (at first with Paulhan). His works—sensitive, allusive, humanistic, and notable for the classical elegance of his style—include many volumes of short stories (e.g. *Les Vivants*, 1934; *La Grâce*, 1941; *Le Grand Pardon*, 1965; *Attendez l'aube*, 1970), novels (e.g. *L'Ordre*, 1929), and literary essays (e.g. *Essais critiques*, 1931; *La Prose française*, 1951; *Lettres de France*, 1951; *La Grâce d'écrire*, 1955; *Je vous écris*, 1960–3).

Arlequin (Harlequin) (from Ital. *Arlecchino*; possibly the same name as O. Fr. *Hellequin* and Ger. *Erlkönig*, a medieval demon), a stock character of the *commedia dell'arte* (*v. Italiens*). In the hands of Regnard, Dufresny, Lesage, Piron, Marivaux, etc., Arlequin became a protean character in comedy and **opéra-comique*, at once credulous and sly, blundering and witty; in Florian's *arlequinades* he became the simple, good-natured hero of the *comédie bourgeoise*. *v.* also *Cartouche*.

Arlequin poli par l'amour, *v. Marivaux*.

Arlésienne, L', *v. Daudet, A.*; *Bizet*.

Arlincourt, CHARLES-VICTOR PRÉVOST, VICOMTE D' (1789–1856), novelist; nicknamed 'le Vicomte inversif' because his style was full of inversions. His first novel, *Le Solitaire* (1821), was a best-seller, translated into six languages. The hero, a miraculously resurrected Charles the Bold, is a gloomy hermit who has gone to a mountain-top to expiate innumerable fearful crimes, but sallies forth to steal the hair-ribbons of the heroine, Élodie—a tender virgin who can accept the fact that he has killed her father and seduced her cousin, but cannot face love without a wedding-ring.

Armagnacs and Burgundians. After Charles VI became insane, hostilities broke out between Jean sans Peur, duke of Burgundy (son of the 4th son of Jean II), and supporters of the house of **Orléans*, led by Bernard VII, comte d'Armagnac. Their bitter feud (*c.* 1410–18) favoured the operations of the English under Henry V. After **Agincourt* (1415) the Burgundians allied themselves with the English and the Armagnacs appeared the national party; *v. Jeanne d'Arc*. The Treaty of Arras (1435) ended the dissension.

Armance, *v. Stendhal*.

Armande, in Molière's *Les *Femmes savantes*.

Armée, La Grande, now usually taken to mean the army with which Napoleon invaded Russia in 1812.

Napoleon raised four very different armies between 1803 and 1814. The first, a fine army wholly French in composition, known as *la Grande Armée* or *l'Armée d'Angleterre*, was raised to invade England and concentrated (1803–5) round Boulogne. It fought in Austria, Prussia, and Poland, and finally disintegrated in Spain. The second, raised 1809 from hastily levied French recruits and allied contingents, was of much poorer quality and victorious at great cost. The third, *l'Armée de Russie*, was international in composition and raised expressly for the Russian campaign in which it was defeated. The fourth, used in the campaign of 1813 and 1814, was largely French in composition.

Armée des émigrés (or des princes), L', the Royalist army formed late in 1791 by princes of the blood royal who had left France after the outbreak of the Revolution; first composed mainly of former army officers (inc. Chateaubriand), but later increasingly joined by civilian *émigrés*. The comte de Provence (later Louis XVIII) was commander-in-chief, but the army was organized at Worms under the prince de Condé (*v. Bourbon*). By 1792 it was attached to the **coalition forces in three corps under Prussian or Austrian command. The first (*l'Armée du centre*; *c.* 10,000 men) suffered a terrible defeat with the Prussians at **Valmy, and was soon disbanded. The third (4,000–5,000 men) was disbanded after the Austrian defeat at **Jemmapes. The second (*l'Armée de Condé*; *c.* 5,000 men) fought as an Austrian division in Alsace, Austria, Bavaria, on the Rhine, and in Italy, and was also in Russia. It was disbanded only in 1801, after the Treaty of Lunéville (*v. Coalitions* (2)).

Armide, an opera (1) by Lulli, with libretto by Quinault (1686), regarded as their masterpiece; (2) by Gluck (1777), also using Quinault's libretto. The subject is from Tasso's *Jerusalem Delivered*.

Arnaud, FRANÇOIS-THOMAS DE BACULARD D' (1718–1805), dramatist and novelist, wrote *Coligny* (1740), a tragedy; *Le Comte de Comminges* (1764), a horrific drama set in the burial crypt of a Trappist monastery (*cf. Tencin*); and romances. His poem *Les Lamentations de Jérémie* provoked Voltaire's epigram (later directed against Pompignan):

> Savez-vous pourquoi Jérémie
> A tant pleuré pendant sa vie?
> C'est qu'en prophète il prévoyait
> Que Baculard le traduirait.

Arnauld, Arnauld d'Andilly, a distinguished family of Auvergne, famous for its association with *Port-Royal. It included, notably, (1) ANTOINE ARNAULD (1612–94), 'le Grand Arnauld', *Jansenist theologian of *Port-Royal*, pupil of Du Vergier de Hauranne, and an ardent controversialist in defence of Jansenism against the *Jesuits. He was author of *La Fréquente Communion* (1643), denying that the profligate could atone for continued sin by frequent communion without repentance. His *Seconde Lettre à un duc et pair* in the Jansenist controversy was condemned by the *Sorbonne (1656; *v. Pascal*), and he went into hiding. He emerged (1669, during the period of ecclesiastical peace est. by Clement IX) and wrote, among many religious and controversial works, *La Perpétuité de la foi de l'Église catholique touchant l'Eucharistie* (1669–76; *v. Nicole*), against the Protestant doctrine of the Eucharist. In 1679 he had again to go into exile, where he died. Latterly, he wrote against Malebranche (*Traité des vraies et fausses idées*, 1683) and against William III (defending the rights of James II). For his educational works *v. Port-Royal*.

(2) JACQUELINE-MARIE-ANGÉLIQUE ARNAULD (1591–1661), 'la Mère Angélique (de Sainte-Madeleine)', sister of (1), (3), and (4). In 1602 (aged 11) she was installed as abbess of *Port-Royal*, which she reformed. Sainte-Beuve's *Port-Royal vividly describes 'la journée du guichet', the memorable day (25 Sept. 1609) when she insisted that her parents should observe the convent rules and speak to her only through a small grille. Her letters have been published.

(3) JEANNE-CATHERINE-AGNÈS ARNAULD (1594–1671), 'la Mère Agnès de Saint-Paul', sister of (1), (2), and (4); abbess of *Port-Royal* for six years from 1636. Her letters have been published.

(4) ROBERT ARNAULD D'ANDILLY (1589–1674), brother of (1), (2), and (3), was employed in the administrative service under Richelieu. In 1646 he retired and became a solitary of *Port-Royal*. He translated theological works and left memoirs. His son Simon, marquis de Pomponne, was minister of foreign affairs under Louis XIV and a close friend of Mme de Sévigné.

(5) ANGÉLIQUE ARNAULD D'ANDILLY (1624–84), 'la Mère Angélique de Saint-Jean', daughter of (4); abbess of *Port-Royal des Champs* (1678–84). She was among the recalcitrant nuns removed to other convents and deprived of the sacraments when the archbishop of Paris broke up the community of *Port-Royal de Paris* (1664; their removal is the subject of *Montherlant's drama *Port-Royal*). She describes her anguish at this time in her *Relation de captivité* (1760).

Arnault, ANTOINE-VINCENT (1766–1834), remembered for a short poem, *La Feuille*, sometimes included in anthologies and first published in his *Fables* (1812–16), a collection of mainly satirical verse.

Arnolphe, in Molière's *L'*École des femmes*.

Arnould, MADELEINE-SOPHIE (1744–1803), a famous opera singer (1757–78), notably in works by Rameau and Gluck; also renowned for her beauty and wit.

Aron, RAYMOND (1905–83), political journalist and sociologist; professor at the *Collège de France from 1970. He was editor in London of the *Resistance journal *La France Libre* (1940–4) and a columnist on *Le *Figaro* from 1947. From 1955 to 1968 he taught at the *Sorbonne, becoming a professor of sociology. At first closely associated with Sartre (*v. Temps modernes, Les*), he soon emerged as a stern critic of Communism. His many works include *Introduction à la philosophie de l'histoire* (1938), *Les Guerres en chaîne* (1951), *L'Opium des intellectuels* (1955), *La Tragédie algérienne* (1957), *Paix et guerre entre les nations* (1962), *La Révolution introuvable* (1968; on the rising of May 1968).

Arouet, FRANÇOIS-MARIE, *v. Voltaire*.

Arrabal, FERNANDO (1932–   ), a Spanish-born author, who writes in French. Among his numerous plays, the best known are *Pique-nique en campagne* (1952), *Le Cimetière de voitures* (1957), and three plays produced in Paris during the 1969–70 season: *Et ils passèrent des menottes aux fleurs*, *Le Jardin des délices*, and *Le Lai de Barabbas*. In Arrabal's theatre, one finds a mixture of elements reflecting a diversity of 20th-c. preoccupations and expressed in terms of poetry, personal fantasy, obscenity, violence, and protest at man's cruelty to man. He is often associated with the Theatre of the Absurd (*v. Theatre of the 19th and 20th cs.*).

Arras (Pas-de-Calais), once capital of the *province of Artois. In the 13th c., it was a rich town and a literary centre, the home of a *puy* and of poets including Bodel and Adam de la Halle. *v. Congé*.

Arrêts d'amour, Les, *v. Martial d'Auvergne*.

Arsenal, *v. Bibliothèque de l'Arsenal*.

Arsène Guillot, *v. Mérimée*.

Arsinoé, (1) in Molière's *Le *Misan-thrope*; (2) in Corneille's *Nicomède*.

Art, L', *v. Émaux et Camées*.

Art, Théâtre d', *v. Œuvre, Théâtre de l'*.

Artaban, the hero of *La Calprenède's *Cléopâtre*, proverbial for his pride: 'fier comme Artaban'.

Artaud, ANTONIN (1896–1948), actor and dramatist. He came to Paris in 1920, worked as an actor or assistant director in the theatre (with Dullin at the *Atelier* and with Pitoëff, Jouvet, etc.) and in the cinema (acting in Dreyer's *La Passion de Jeanne d'Arc* and Abel Gance's *Napoléon*), joined the *Surrealists, and published poetry (*L'Ombilic des limbes*, 1925; *Le Pèse-nerfs*, 1927). Disowned by the Surrealists in 1926, he was in 1927 a co-founder, with Roger Vitrac, of the short-lived *Théâtre Alfred-Jarry*. He then broke with the traditional Western conception of the drama to inaugurate the *théâtre de la cruauté*, exemplified in his only full-length play, *Les Cenci* (the monstrous story of the Cenci family, adapted from Stendhal and Shelley), which he staged in 1935. His dramatic theories (expounded in the essays and manifestos collected in *Le Théâtre et son double*, 1938) were strongly influenced by the Balinese dancers he saw in Paris in 1931, and by Mexican Indian culture and ritual (he visited Mexico in 1936 and experimented with the drug peyotl). He sought to restore myth and mystery to the theatre, to exploit man's deepest instincts through incantation, movement, and the spectacle of cruelty and destruction. Cruelty he regarded as a transforming force capable of exorcizing fear, the process of exorcism being a gruelling metaphysical experience shared by the actors and the audience. His other works include *Le Jet de sang* (1925, in *L'Ombilic des limbes*), *La Pierre philosophale* (1949, in *Les Cahiers de la Pléiade*), and other lost or unfinished plays; *Héliogabale, ou l'Anarchiste couronné* (1934) and *Van Gogh, le suicidé de la société* (1949), which have a marked autobiographical element. His mental balance was always precarious (he was confined in an asylum from 1937 to 1946), his works often fevered, anguished, and highly paradoxical. He had little success in his lifetime; but his dramatic theories have since aroused much interest both in France and in England (thanks to Peter Brook's production of the *Marat/Sade* in 1962). *v. Theatre of the 19th and 20th cs.*

Art d'être grand-père, L', *v. Hugo*.

Art de vérifier les dates des faits historiques, des chartes, des chroniques et anciens monuments depuis la naissance de Jésus-Christ, par le moyen d'une table chronologique..., avec un calendrier perpétuel, L' (1750, 1 vol.; rev. and augm. 1770, 1783–92), a vast work of erudition compiled by *Maurists. An *Art de vérifier les dates avant l'ère chrétienne* was added in 1820, an *Art de vérifier les dates depuis l'année 1770 jusqu'à nos jours (1827)* in 1821–44. v. Dictionaries, 1845–63.

Art poétique, (1) v. Verlaine; (2) v. Claudel.

Art poétique, L' (1674), a didactic poem by Boileau, an epitome of the *Classical doctrines of his *Satires; modelled on Horace's *Ars poetica*.

The first of its four cantos is on poetic composition, the need for good sense, fidelity to nature, nobility of style, observance of rules (*hiatus, *enjambement, etc.). The second is on specific types of poem, the idyll, the ode, etc., holding up the ancients as models for imitation. The third is on tragedy and comedy; and on the epic, which he deems an inappropriate medium for national and Christian themes (v. Desmarets de Saint-Sorlin). The fourth treats generally of the profession of letters and its dignity.

The famous couplet on the unities (v. Tragedy) is in the third canto:

Qu'en un Lieu, qu'en un Jour, un seul Fait accompli
Tienne jusqu'à la fin le Théâtre rempli...

Art pour l'art, L'. This expression occurs in an entry of 1804 in B. *Constant's *Journal intime* and later in *Cousin's *Cours de philosophie* (*Sorbonne lectures of 1818: 'Il faut de la religion pour la religion, de la morale pour la morale, comme de l'art pour l'art... le beau ne peut être la voie ni de l'utile, ni du bien, ni du saint; il ne conduit qu'à lui-même'). Though the actual words are not used in Gautier's prefaces to *Albertus (1832) and *Mademoiselle de Maupin (1835), these are manifestos of the theory that the achievement of formal beauty is the sole purpose of a work of art, that aesthetic value is what matters. The phrase became the rallying-cry of Gautier, Baudelaire, Banville, Flaubert, and others in their fight for liberty in art. It acquired the further meaning that beauty in a work of art is a matter of perfect expression and absolute unity of form and content. In poetry this led to 'l'horrible artistement exprimé' and 'la douleur rythmée et cadencée' of *Baudelaire's *Les Fleurs du mal*, and to the impassive, descriptive verse of the *Parnassiens; in the novel it led to *Realism, and sometimes, as with Flaubert, to a passionate devotion to style. v. English Literature, French Influence on, 5.

Artagnan, Mémoires de M. d', v. Courtilz de Sandras.

Artamène, v. Grand Cyrus, Le.

Arthénice, v. Rambouillet, Hôtel de.

Arthurian Romances, v. Romans bretons.

Artois, v. Provinces. The title comte d'Artois was borne by several princes of the blood, notably by Louis XVI's brother Charles-Philippe, later Charles X.

Arvers, FÉLIX (1806–50), poet and dramatist, remembered for his sonnet *Mon âme a son secret, ma vie a son mystère* (in *Mes heures perdues*, 1833), said to have been addressed to Nodier's daughter Marie.

Asmodée, in Lesage's Le *Diable boiteux

Asmodée, v. Mauriac.

Aspremont, a *chanson de geste (*Charlemagne cycle) of the late 12th or early 13th c. Charlemagne liberates Rome and Italy from the Saracens.

Assemblée constituante, L' (or *Assemblée nationale constituante*), the name taken (9 July 1789) by the representative body, consisting of the *Tiers État*, a majority of the clergy, and a minority of the *noblesse*, which developed out of the *Assemblée nationale*. It framed and voted the constitution of 1791 and was succeeded (Oct. 1791) by the *Assemblée législative*. *v. Revolutions*, 1; *Constitutions*.

Later *Assemblées constituantes*, charged with the framing of constitutions, were those elected under the Second and Fourth *Republics*.

Assemblée législative, L', (1) the second national assembly of the Revolution, succeeded the *Assemblée constituante* (Oct. 1791) and was replaced (Sept. 1792) by the *Convention* (*v. Corps législatif*; *Revolutions*, 1); (2) the assembly that succeeded (May 1849) the *Assemblée constituante* of 1848–9 and was dissolved by the *coup d'état* of 1851 (*v. Republics*, 2).

Assemblée nationale, L', the name taken (June 1789) by the *Tiers État*. It soon became the *Assemblée constituante*. *v. Revolutions*, 1.

For the *Assemblée nationale* of 1871–5 *v. Republics*, 3. From 1875 to 1940 the term *Assemblée nationale* denoted a joint session of the *Sénat* and the *Chambre des *Députés* to elect a President or revise the constitution (as in July 1940). Since 1946 the *Assemblée nationale* has been the lower house of the French parliament (replacing the *Chambre des Députés*), the upper house being first the *Conseil de la République*, then the *Sénat*. *v. Republics*, 3, 4, and 5; *Palais-Bourbon*.

Assemblée nationale, L' (later *Le Spectateur*), an opposition daily paper, f. after the 1848 *Revolution by former officials of Louis-Philippe's government; widely read, often suspended, and finally suppressed (1858).

Assignats. Interest-bearing bonds issued 1790 by the *Assemblée constituante* in an attempt to raise revenue. Their security was the *biens nationaux* to which holders were to have a preferential right of exchange. Later, they became paper currency pure and simple, bearing no interest, constantly over-issued and depreciating. Those in circulation were liquidated, at a bankruptcy value, in 1796.

Assommoir, L' (1877), one of Zola's *Rougon-Macquart* novels, a powerful, relentlessly drawn picture of working-class life, also a notable example of his effort to intensify his naturalistic atmosphere by describing life through the eyes of the characters, in their own vocabulary, with no artistic distinction between dialogue and narrative.

Gervaise, daughter of Antoine Macquart, is in Paris with her lover Auguste *Lantier and their children. He deserts her, and she marries Coupeau (*v. Nana*), a zinc-roofer. For a time they lead a contented, industrious life. She starts a laundry on borrowed money, and it flourishes. But then Coupeau has an accident and after a long convalescence becomes a lazy drunkard, squandering their money at the *assommoir* (drinking-shop). Gervaise, too, becomes indolent, and her inherited tendency to alcoholism soon shows itself. Lantier returns, and forms a *ménage à trois* with the couple until they are too poor to provide good living. The laundry fails, and they sink to besotted, bestial poverty, ending in squalid death. Memorable descriptions include that of a band of vicious young girls from the slums, patrolling the outer *boulevards* decked in their Sunday finery, arms linked and eyes roving.

Assonance, agreement in the last stressed vowel of two or more metrical lines, but not in the consonants following it (e.g. *tombe, onde*), is characteristic of the early *chansons de geste*. It was reintroduced by the *Symbolists, and has remained common in modern poetry. *Cf. Consonance*.

Assouci, CHARLES COUPPEAU D' (1605–75), musician and poet, author of burlesque poems and the *Aventures burlesques de d'Assouci* (a collection of four mainly autobiographical works in prose and verse).

Astrate, roi de Tyr, a tragedy by Quinault; produced 1664.

Élise has usurped the throne of Tyre, killing the true king and two of his sons (a third has escaped). Astrate, who loves the queen and is loved by her, discovers, as he receives the royal ring from her, that he is the son and brother of her victims.

Astrée, L' (1607–27), a prose romance by d'Urfé (in 4 pts.; the 4th publ. posth. by Baro, who in 1628 added a conclusion based on d'Urfé's notes). *v. Foreign Influences*, 1; *Pastoral*; *Novel*, 2.

The scene is by the river Lignon (a small tributary of the Loire in the Forez district of the Lyonnais) in the 5th c. The barbarians are invading Gaul, but this region, under Queen Amasis, is unaffected. The shepherd Céladon loves the shepherdess Astrée. She dismisses him on suspicion of infidelity. He throws himself into the river, is rescued by three 'nymphs' of the queen's court, and resists their coquetries. But he dares not return to Astrée (except disguised as a Druid's daughter) until she has revoked his dismissal, which (in Baro's conclusion) she finally does, after both have been exposed to great dangers and he has been wounded in an attack on the kingdom by the traitor Polémas. Skilfully interwoven into this main theme is the love story of Sylvandre (a more sane and robust lover than Céladon) and the virtuous Diane, the inconstancy of Hylas, and the adventures of a host of other couples.

This work, combining elements of history, chivalry, and pastoral life, interspersed with sonnets and madrigals, presents an ideal of polite and distinguished living, in which men and women of the world figure as shepherds and shepherdesses (the stories are said to have some factual basis). It is agreeably told, though mannered and diffuse. Ridiculed in C. *Sorel's Le Berger extravagant*, but nevertheless immensely popular, it provided plots for many dramas, and helped to improve the moral tone of society.

Astyanax, in Racine's *Andromaque*.

Atala, ou les Amours de deux sauvages dans le désert (1801), a tale by Chateaubriand; intended as part of *Les *Natchez*, but published separately and then included in *Le *Génie du christianisme* (1802).

The scene is Louisiana, in the 18th c. Chactas, an old Indian, tells his life-story to René (*v. René*). As a young man he was captured by a hostile tribe and saved by the maiden Atala, a Christian convert. The two fled and eventually reached the hermitage of the missionary Père Aubry. Atala would have married Chactas but for her mother's dying vow that she should take the veil. Too weak either to fulfil the vow or to resist her love, she took poison. (The account of her burial in the forest, near a mountain torrent, is one of the author's finest descriptive passages.) Returning in after years, Chactas learnt that Aubry had been murdered and was buried beside her.

Atalide, in Racine's *Bajazet*.

Atelier, Théâtre de l', a leading experimental theatre in Paris, f. 1922 and directed till 1940 by the actor and producer Charles Dullin (1885–1949), formerly of the *Vieux-Colombier*. He staged French classics and new plays, and foreign classics in translation (e.g. Aristophanes, Shakespeare, Pirandello). *v. Theatres and Theatre Companies*.

Ateliers nationaux. Under a scheme instituted in 1848 by the provisional government (*v. Revolutions*, 3) unemployed men, regardless of their former trades, were taken on and set to level the *Champ-de-Mars. Their numbers, and the purposeless employment, made it a ruinous proceeding, and in June 1848 the *ateliers* were abolished by decree. Serious riots ensued (*v. Republics*, 2).

Athalie, Racine's last play, deemed a model of *Classical tragedy; performed 1691 by the pupils of the *Institut de *Saint-

Cyr, but not publicly produced till 1716. It is based on the Biblical story of Athaliah and Joash, and includes songs for a chorus of Levite maidens.

The scene is the Temple of Jerusalem. Athalie, a devotee of Baal, is queen of Judah, and has attempted to exterminate all the children of the house of David. But the child Joas has been saved by his aunt Josabet, wife of the high priest Joad, and secretly brought up in the Temple as 'Éliacin'. The day has come on which Joad proposes to proclaim him king. Athalie, disturbed by an ominous dream in which her mother Jézabel warns her that the God of the Jews is about to take vengeance on her, enters the Temple (thereby profaning it) and recognizes in Joas an unknown boy in priest's robes who had threatened her life in the dream. Suspicious of his origin, she demands his surrender, under threat of destruction of the Temple. Joas is presented to the Levites in the Temple and acclaimed. Athalie is lured into the Temple and confronted with Joas, enthroned and surrounded by Levites. News is brought that he has been proclaimed to the people and received with rejoicing. Athalie, conceding victory to the God of the Jews, is hauled off to death.

Athénée (royal), L', *v. Lycée, Le*.

Athénée, Théâtre de l', *v. Jouvet*.

Athos, in Dumas *père*'s *Les *Trois Mousquetaires*.

Atlas linguistique de la France, *v. Gilliéron*.

Attaque au moulin, L', *v. Soirées de Médan, Les*.

Attila, a tragedy by Corneille, produced 1667; one of his least successful plays.

Attila, victorious king of the Huns, has two possible wives in view. He learns that he has rivals in the persons of two conquered kings in his suite. His scheme to play them off against each other with fatal consequences for both is interrupted by his own sudden death.

Atys, v. Quinault.

Aubanel, THÉODORE (1829–86), a poet of the **Félibrige*. His works include *La Mióugrano entreduberto* (i.e. *La Grenade entr'ouverte*, 1860), love poems; *Lou Pan dóu pecat*, a play produced 1891 in translation as *Le Pain du péché*.

Aube, v. Chansons à personnages.

Auber, DANIEL-FRANÇOIS-ESPRIT (1782–1871), a composer of light opera, long the musical partner of Scribe. He succeeded Cherubini (1842) as head of the Paris *Conservatoire de musique*.

Auberée, a typical **fabliau*. Auberée, a seamstress, engages to contrive a meeting between a young man and his love, who has been married off to a widower. She borrows the gallant's cloak, hides her needle and thimble in it, calls on the lady, and contrives to conceal it in her bed. The husband finds it, concludes that his wife has been unfaithful, and turns her out. Auberée appears and, professing to shelter her till he comes to his senses, takes the lady to her house, where the gallant joins her. To reassure the husband, Auberée causes him to find his wife praying in church, and explains the incriminating cloak by lamenting that she has mislaid in some house a cloak she was mending, and also her needle and thimble.

Auberge des Adrets, L', *v. Macaire, R*.

Auberge rouge, L', *v. Comédie humaine, La* (*Études philosophiques*).

Aubert de La Chesnaye des Bois, FRANÇOIS-ALEXANDRE, *v. Dictionaries*, 1767.

Aubignac, FRANÇOIS HÉDELIN, ABBÉ D' (*c.* 1604–*c.* 1673), author of a *Pratique du théâtre* (1657) in which, besides providing valuable information on the 17th-c. theatre, he vigorously defends the unities (*v. Tragedy*), as founded not on authority but on reason, and required by verisimilitude.

Aubigné, AGRIPPA D' (1552–1630), an ardent *Huguenot of heroic spirit (sworn to the cause by his father; v. *Amboise*); grandfather of Mme de Maintenon. A pupil of Bèze, he long served the future Henri IV as soldier, diplomat, and councillor, but was little at court after the king's conversion and lived latterly in Geneva. His works include, notably, Les *Tragiques* (1616), a work justly described as the epic of Calvinism; also *Printemps* (first publ. 1874), early love poems; an *Histoire universelle* (1616–20) of the period 1550–1601, which revolves around Henri IV and the Huguenot faction and is of historical value, though often laborious and obscure; the *Aventures du baron de *Fæneste* (1617–30); the *Confession de Sancy*, an imaginary confession of base motives by an apostate from Protestantism; *Sa vie à ses enfants*, an autobiography.

Au bon beurre, v. Dutourd.

Au bonheur des dames (1883), one of Zola's *Rougon-Macquart* novels. Octave Mouret (whose parents figure in La *Conquête de Plassans*), by exploiting his success with women and the Second Empire craze for luxury and building development, transforms a moderately prosperous Paris drapery into a huge, sensationally successful, department store, mercilessly ruining small competitors in the process. Human interest is supplied by staff intrigues and his relations with a saleswoman, whose charm and honesty defeat his hitherto all-conquering toughness. The book at times recalls Balzac (e.g. *César Birotteau*).

Aubusson (Creuse), the site of a famous carpet manufactory, established in the 15th c.

Aucassin et Nicolette, a *roman d'aventure* by an unknown author, probably of the early 13th c., who gave the name *chantefable* to his narrative in alternating passages of prose and heptasyllabic verse.

It is a story of young love in a world of mingled reality and fantasy, told with exquisite delicacy, and remarkable for the freshness and vividness of the scenes and characters it presents. Aucassin, son of the lord of Beaucaire in Provence, loves Nicolette, a captive bought from the Saracens by one of the lord's vassals, but his father forbids their union and causes Nicolette's master to imprison her. Aucassin is so lovesick that he will not even fight to defend his father's castle until promised a brief word with her and a single kiss. But the father breaks his promise and Aucassin is imprisoned. Nicolette escapes and sings outside his prison of her love for him, till warned by a friendly watchman that she is in danger. She flees to the forest and is presumed lost or killed. Aucassin's father releases him and tries to comfort him, but he leaves to search for Nicolette and eventually finds her. They take ship to the fabulous castle of Torelore, and spend three happy years there. Then Saracens attack the castle and carry everyone off. Nicolette is taken to Carthage, where the king recognizes her as his lost daughter. Aucassin is wrecked near Beaucaire and, his father being dead, becomes lord. Nicolette makes her way to Beaucaire disguised as a minstrel, and they are reunited.

Aude, in the *Chanson de Roland* and other *chansons de geste*, sister of *Olivier and *Roland's betrothed.

Aude, JOSEPH, CHEVALIER (1755–1841), author of ephemeral farces and *vaudevilles*; sometime secretary to Buffon. He exploited the character Cadet Roussel, for long a type of the well-meaning but pretentious nincompoop (*Cadet Roussel, ou le Café des aveugles*, 1793, etc.).

Audefroi le Bastart (13th c.), a poet of *Arras, author of *romances*, etc. v. *Lyric Poetry*, 1.

Au-dessus de la mêlée, v. Rolland.

Audiberti, JACQUES (1899–1965), a writer of amazing virtuosity whose work abounds in bold fantastic or grotesque images and metaphors. At times inspired, but often garrulous and undisciplined, he was most successful as a dramatist, though he also wrote poetry (e.g. *Race des hommes*, 1937; *Des tonnes de semence*, 1941; *La Nouvelle Origine*, 1942; *Toujours*, 1944; *Rempart*, 1953; *Ange aux entrailles*, 1964) and novels (e.g. *Abraxas*, 1938; *Cent Jours*, 1947). His plays (e.g. *Quoat-Quoat*, 1946; *Le Mal court*, 1947; *La Fête noire*, 1948; *Pucelle*, 1950; *L'Effet Glapion*, 1959) are a blend of fantasy, farce, and horrific melodrama, and often show man at the mercy of primitive forces of evil.

Audoux, MARGUERITE (1863–1937), a poor orphan who went to Paris (1881), became a dressmaker, and wrote when she had time. A chance meeting led to literary friendships and the publication of her autobiographical novel *Marie-Claire* (1910; with a preface by Mirbeau), continued in *L'Atelier de Marie-Claire* (1920).

Auerstadt (Saxony). Here the French under Davout defeated the Prussians (14 Oct. 1806; *cf. Jena*) in Napoleon's campaign against the 4th *Coalition.

Augé, CLAUDE, *v. Dictionaries*, 1866–76.

Augereau, PIERRE-FRANÇOIS-CHARLES, *v. Maréchal.*

Augier, ÉMILE (1820–89), dramatist, grandson of Pigault-Lebrun; a leader (with Ponsard) of the *école du bon sens*, in reaction against the exaggerations of *Romantic drama. His greatest successes, well-constructed, conventional dramas of *bourgeois* life, upholding the virtues of honesty, common sense, and conjugal love, included *Le *Gendre de M. Poirier* (1854; with Sandeau); *Les Lionnes pauvres* (1858); *Maître Guérin* (1865); *Les Effrontés* (1861), satirizing the Second Empire passion for money and speculation; *Le Fils de Giboyer* (1862), attacking contemporary efforts to mix religion and politics—its hard-hitting satire provoked great indignation. His first

plays, *L'Aventurière* (1848; a comedy set in 16th-c. Padua) and *Gabrielle* (1850), were in verse. *v. Theatre of the 19th and 20th cs.*

Augustinus, *v. Jansenism.*

Au jardin de l'infante, *v. Samain.*

Aulard, ALPHONSE (1849–1928), historian of the Revolution, noted for his studies of Danton (for him the hero of the Revolution; *cf. Mathiez*), the *Jacobins, the *Convention, etc., in such works as *Études et leçons sur la Révolution française* (1893–1921) and *Histoire politique de la Révolution française* (1901). *v. History*, 4.

Aulnoy, MARIE-CATHERINE LE JUMEL DE BARNEVILLE, COMTESSE D' (*c.* 1650–1705), author of fairy-tales (1698; *v. Children's Reading*), including the stories of *The Yellow Dwarf* and *The White Cat*, which remain popular; *Mémoires de la Cour d'Espagne* (1690); a lively *Relation d'un voyage d'Espagne* (1691), highly praised by Taine.

Aurélia, *v. Nerval.*

Aurore, L', (1) a daily paper (1897–1914; *v. Dreyfus*); (2) a daily paper f. 1944. *v. Press*, 9.

Austerlitz (Moravia). Here Napoleon won a striking victory (2 Dec. 1805) over the Austro-Russian armies led by their emperors. *v. Coalitions* (3).

Austrasia, *v. Merovingians.*

Autobiographies, *v. Memoirs.*

Auton, JEAN D', *v. Jean d'Auton.*

Autran, JOSEPH (1813–77), town librarian of Marseilles, wrote poetry influenced by Lamartine, e.g. *La Mer* (1835), *Ludibria ventis* (1838), *Laboureurs et soldats* (1854), and plays, e.g. the tragedy *La Fille d'Eschyle* (1848).

Autrichienne, L', i.e. Marie-Antoinette.

Autun, L'Évêque d', i.e. Talleyrand, early in his career. v. *Fédération, fédérés*.

Aux flancs du vase, v. *Samain*.

Avant-garde, Théâtre(s) d', v. *Theatres and Theatre Companies*.

Avare, L', a 5-act prose comedy by Molière, produced 1668; based on Plautus's *Aulularia*.

Harpagon, a rich miser, wants to marry his daughter Élise to the elderly Anselme, who would take her without a dowry. He himself, with an eye to obtaining a dowry, would marry Mariane, whom his son Cléante loves. Valère, who loves Élise, takes service with Harpagon as a steward, hoping to further his suit. Cléante, determined to win Mariane, removes a box containing part of his father's treasure, and Harpagon is distraught. Suspicion falls on Valère, who, supposing that he is being charged with designs on Élise, admits his guilt, blaming her 'beaux yeux' ('Les beaux yeux de ma cassette!', exclaims Harpagon). Finally the matter is cleared up. Harpagon surrenders Élise to Valère (who proves to be Anselme's lost son) and, in consideration of the return of his treasure, allows Cléante to marry Mariane—stipulating that he is to be put to no expense.

This grim comedy shows how avarice not only destroys all dignity and paternal affection in the miser himself, but also provokes revolt in his children; yet it was censured as immoral by J.-J. Rousseau.

A vau l'eau (1882), a tale by Huysmans. M. Folantin, an elderly, impecunious civil servant, lives alone, bullied by *concierges* and charwomen. His drab evening expeditions to cheap restaurants and the nauseating food he encounters are described in minute detail.

Avenir, L', v. *Lamennais*.

Avenir de la science, L' (1890), an essay by Renan, written in 1848, after his break with the Church, largely to take stock of his own views. He urges the need for

more, and more specialized, study of the philosophical sciences (esp. of comparative philology and comparative religion) as a means of arriving at ultimate truth. He also explores what will become the central theme of *Les Origines du christianisme*.

Avenir de l'intelligence, L', v. *Maurras*.

Avent (Advent). Bourdaloue (between 1670 and 1693) and Massillon (1699) delivered notable Advent sermons, later printed.

Aventures du baron de Fæneste, Les, v. *Fæneste*.

Aventures du dernier Abencérage, Les (1826), by Chateaubriand, a short tale of chivalry and fidelity in 16th-c. Spain, after the expulsion of the Moors. The noble, but infidel, Aben-Hamet, last of the tribe of the Abencérages, former rulers in Granada, loves and is loved by Bianca, daughter of the Spanish governor. Religion, and a history of blood and cruelty between their families, preclude their union and oblige them to live out their lives apart. He returns to the African desert, and (according to Chateaubriand) 'le tombeau du dernier Abencérage' can be seen in the cemetery by ruined Carthage. She grows old in Granada with her memories. Soon after 1814 Chateaubriand read this tale in Mme Récamier's *salon to a company including Mme de Staël, Wellington, and Bernadotte.

Aventures du roi Pausole, Les, v. *Louÿs*.

Aventurière, L', v. *Augier*.

Averroès et l'Averroïsme, v. *Renan*.

Aveugle, L', v. *Chénier, A*.

Aveugle et le Boiteux, L', a *moralité by La Vigne; performed 1496 (with his *mystère of St. Martin). Two drunken, rascally beggars, one blind, one lame, agree that their infirmities are very profitable. Disconcerted to hear of the miracles of healing wrought by the body of St. Martin, they resolve to flee, but meet the saint's procession and are healed. The blind man is delighted to see again; the lame man decides to feign his old infirmity.

Aveugles de Compiègne, Les Trois, a *fabliau. A merry clerk meets three blind men on the road, says to them 'Here's a bezant among you', but gives nothing. Each thinking that one of the others has the alms, they feast at an inn, observed by the clerk. Next morning, when their bill is presented, they find that none has the money to pay it. The clerk tells the landlord that he will pay it, or the parish priest for him. The two go to the church, where the clerk explains privately to the priest that the landlord is possessed and pays to have him exorcized. The priest tells the landlord that he will 'settle the affair' after Mass. The clerk makes off; the landlord, reassured, waits patiently. After Mass, he is forcibly exorcized, his loud demands for money being put down to his deluded state.

Aveugles, Lettre sur les, v. Lettre.

Avignon, originally capital of the marquisate of Provence, briefly a republic (from the late 12th c.), then captured by Louis VIII (1226) and ceded to the comte de Provence. Later the residence of seven successive popes (1309–78) and two anti-popes (1378–1408), it was sold to the papacy (1348) and remained a papal possession till 1791, when France annexed it. The town is famous for its connection with Petrarch, who migrated there in 1313 and there first saw Laura. *v. Vaucluse.*

Avril, v. Belleau.

Axël (1890), a drama of Wagnerian character (in highly poetical prose) by Villiers de l'Isle-Adam.

The period is *c.* 1828. Axël, the young lord of Auërsperg, fearful of arousing harmful passions, discourages interest in a treasure said to be hidden in the secret vaults of his castle, deep in a German forest. He kills Kaspar, a prying relative,

in a duel, but is then himself tempted by visions of the treasure. At night in the vault he surprises Sara, an escaped novice (her dramatic refusal to take her vows and her escape form part I of the drama). Having discovered the clue to the secret in *Rosicrucian writings, she has just worked the charm by which the walls and floor recede and gold and jewels cascade from every side. She tries to kill Axël. He disarms her and makes to retaliate, but is overcome by her rare beauty—and she by his. They talk of their sudden passion. She paints a future in which, thanks to the treasure, their every desire will be fulfilled; but Axël convinces her that life can offer no joys to equal this night of anticipation. The day dawns, and they drink poison from a jewelled cup found among the treasure.

Aymé, MARCEL (1902–67), author of novels, short stories, and plays marked by a racy, Rabelaisian humour, highly coloured farce, and a strain of wild fantasy, logically interwoven with vivid realism. During and after the 1939–45 war, his humour became more bitter, and he often pitilessly satirized contemporary evils (esp. political and judicial corruption and ineptitude). He made his name with the novel *La Jument verte* (1933), a robustly comic picture of late 19th-c. rural life in the Franche-Comté. His subsequent works include *Le Moulin de la Sourdine* (1936), *Travelingue* (1941), *Uranus* (1948), novels; *Le Passe-Muraille* (1943), *En arrière* (1950), short stories; *Lucienne et le Boucher* (1948; written 1932), *Clérambard* (1950), *La Tête des autres* (1952; attacking the magistracy), *Les Oiseaux de lune* (1955; introducing a character who can change people into birds), *Le Minotaure* (1964), plays; and his delightful *Contes du chat perché* (publ. from 1934), among the best children's stories of modern times.

Aymon, Les Quatre Fils, v. Renaud de Montauban; Bibliothèque bleue.

Azincourt, *v. Agincourt.*

Aziyadé, v. Loti.

B

Babeuf, FRANÇOIS-ÉMILE (1760–97), self-styled 'Caius-Gracchus, Tribun du peuple', a Revolutionary politician and journalist (editor 1794–6 of the *Journal de la liberté de la presse*, later *Le Tribun du peuple*) whose political views, based on bitter experience of poverty and oppression, were an interesting anticipation of modern Communism. By 1796 he was convinced that the Revolution had only led to the rise of a new dominating class. He engineered a conspiracy, which almost succeeded, to overthrow the **Directoire* and frame a constitution more akin to early Revolutionary ideals. It was betrayed and its leaders were arrested. He was sentenced to death (but committed suicide) after a trial at which he spoke movingly in defence of freedom of speech and action, equality, and the sovereign rights of the people. Thirty of his followers (*Babouvistes*) were executed and many more deported or imprisoned. In 1828 a fellow conspirator, Michel Buonarotti (1761–1837), published *La Conspiration pour l'égalité*, which reawakened interest in Babeuf and helped to stimulate the romantic socialism of the 1830s.

Babouc, ou le Monde comme il va (1749; a rev. ed. of *Le Monde comme il va: Vision de Babouc*, 1748), a philosophical tale by Voltaire.

Ituriel, one of the spirits that preside over the world's empires, angered at the follies and excesses of the Persians, sends the Scythian Babouc to report on Persepolis, in order to decide whether it shall be exterminated or corrected. Babouc is both disgusted and impressed: he finds cruelty, superstition, licentiousness, and venality; but also bravery, learning, fidelity, and generosity. Ituriel decides to 'laisser aller le monde comme il va, car, dit-il, si tout n'est pas bien, tout est passable'.

Babouvistes, *v. Babeuf*.

Bacbuc, in Rabelais's **Pantagruel*.

Baccalauréat (slang *bachot*), the State examination taken by pupils at the end of their secondary school education, a necessary first step to university studies and most forms of professional career.

Bachaumont, FRANÇOIS DE (1624–1702), author with **Chapelle* of the *Voyage en Provence et Languedoc* (1656).

Bachaumont, LOUIS PETIT DE (1690–1771), publicist. His *Mémoires secrets pour servir à l'histoire de la république des lettres en France depuis 1762* (1777; cont. by others till 1787), containing daily records of events and opinions, and general literary intelligence, are of some historical value.

Bachelard, GASTON (1884–1962), philosopher, began life as a country postman and ended it as a professor at the **Sorbonne*. He is best known for his exploration of the creative imagination, e.g. in *La Psychanalyse du feu* (1937), *L'Eau et les rêves* (1940), *L'Air et les songes* (1942), *La Terre et les rêveries du repos* (1945), *La Poétique de l'espace* (1958), *La Flamme d'une chandelle* (1961). His study of imagery as the poet's expression of the four elements, transposed through the unconscious, strongly influenced some exponents of the *nouvelle critique* (*v. Critics and Criticism*, 3).

Bachelier de Salamanque, Le, *v. Lesage*.

Bachot, *v. Baccalauréat*.

Backer, GEORGE DE, *v. Dictionaries*, 1718.

Baculard d'Arnaud, *v. Arnaud*.

Badebec, in Rabelais, wife of **Gargantua* and mother of **Pantagruel*.

Badinguet, *v. Napoléon III*.

Bague d'Annibal, La, *v. Barbey d'Aurevilly*.

Baïf, (1) LAZARE DE (1485–1547), French ambassador in Italy, translated Sophocles's *Electra* into clumsy *alexandrines (1537)—a step towards 16th-c. *tragedy; (2) his son JEAN-ANTOINE DE (1532–89), a poet of the *Pléiade* and founder (1570) of a short-lived *Académie de Poésie et de Musique*. His works include, notably, his *Mimes* (1581), a miscellany of moral and satirical pieces; also love poems, epitaphs, adaptations from classical dramatists (*Le Brave, ou Taillebras*, prod. 1567; *L'Eunuque*, publ. 1573; *Antigone*—from Plautus, Terence, and Sophocles respectively), and a translation of the Psalms. He used a wide variety of metres and verse-forms with ease and fluency, also experimented with quantitative verse and phonetic spelling; but he showed little taste or judgement, for his poetical talent was not equal to his great learning.

Baillet, ADRIEN (1649–1706), an erudite and assiduous compiler (e.g. *Jugements des savants sur les principaux ouvrages des auteurs*, 1685 and 1686, 9 vols.; *Des enfants devenus célèbres par leurs études et par leurs écrits*, 1688); also author of a *Vie de Descartes* (1691) still considered useful, and of devotional works. He was ascetic to a degree: slept little (usually in his clothes), ate once a day, and never had a fire when alone.

Bailli; Sénéchal. The kingdom of France was divided into *gouvernements*, each subdivided into *bailliages* (in N. France) and *sénéchaussées* (in S. France). The *bailli* or *sénéchal* was an official representing the king in these respective areas. His functions, first precisely defined by Philippe II in 1190, were originally at once judicial, administrative, financial, and military. His jurisdiction was subordinate to that of the *parlements. v. Prévôt; Police.*

Bailly, SYLVAIN (1736–93), a distinguished astronomer, prominent at the outbreak of the Revolution as president of the *Assemblée nationale*, then mayor of Paris (*v. Commune*, 1). He was a constitutional monarchist and later became highly unpopular. As he waited in the rain to be guillotined, someone remarked, 'Tu trembles, Bailly.' 'Oui, mon ami,' he replied, 'mais c'est de froid.'

Bainville, JACQUES (1879–1936), author of popular historical works, e.g. a history of France (1924), a study of Napoleon (1931). They were not always free from political bias, for he was a leading contributor to *L' *Action française*, and a founder and editor of the *Revue universelle*.

Baiser au lépreux, Le, *v. Mauriac.*

Bajazet, a tragedy by Racine, produced 1672; based on an actual event of 1638.

The scene is Constantinople. The sultan Amurat, away besieging Babylon, has left his brother Bajazet imprisoned in the seraglio. Acomat, the grand vizier, plots to overthrow Amurat, and to this end favours the sultana Roxane's love for Bajazet. She is to release Bajazet, marry him, and place him on the throne. Bajazet's supposed love for the princess Atalide serves as a pretext for their interviews. But Bajazet has deceived both Acomat and Roxane: he and Atalide really are in love, and he has feigned interest in Roxane only to gain his freedom. When Roxane demands immediate marriage, he temporizes. Her suspicion turns to rage when a letter found in Atalide's possession reveals his perfidy. Amurat sends an order for Bajazet's execution, and Roxane abandons him to the mutes, who strangle him. But Amurat, informed of her infidelity, has ordered Roxane's death also, and this follows. Atalide commits suicide.

Balafré, Le, *v. Guise; Ligue, La.*

Balbec, the seaside resort where Marcel, in Proust's *A la recherche du temps perdu*, stays on two occasions and meets Albertine (*v. Albertine disparue*). It figures notably in *A l'ombre des jeunes filles en fleurs* and *Sodome et Gomorrhe*, and was modelled on Cabourg (Normandy), where Proust used to stay.

Bal Bullier, v. Bals populaires.

Balcon, Le, v. Genet.

Bal de Sceaux, Le, v. Comédie humaine, La (Scènes de la vie privée).

Bal du comte d'Orgel, Le, v. Radiguet.

Ballade, a poem usually consisting either of three decasyllabic *dizains* with five-line *envoi* (rhyme-scheme: ababbccdcD, thrice, followed by ccdcD), or of three octosyllabic *huitains* with four-line *envoi* (ababbcbC, thrice, followed by bcbC). The last line of the first stanza is repeated as the last line of the other two and of the *envoi*, thus (as indicated by the capital letters) forming the refrain. There are occasional departures from the regular forms. Villon—the greatest writer of *ballades*, though there are good examples in Marot and later poets—sometimes used decasyllabic *huitains*.

The *double ballade* is composed of six *dizains* or *huitains* as above, usually without *envoi*.

Ballade des dames du temps jadis; **Ballade des pendus**; **Ballade et oroison pour Jehan Cotart**; **Ballade pour prier Nostre Dame,** v. Villon.

Ballanche, PIERRE-SIMON (1776–1847), Christian philosopher (cf. Bonald; Maistre, J. de), a friend of Joubert and Mme Récamier. His mystical conceptions of universal religion, of 'harmonies', and of poetry as the expression of the universal mind, had some influence on 19th-c. thought. His works, poetical but obscure, include Du sentiment considéré dans ses rapports avec la littérature et les arts (1801), in some degree a forerunner of Chateaubriand's Le *Génie du christianisme*; Antigone (1814); Essai sur les institutions sociales dans leurs rapports avec les idées nouvelles (1818); Essais de palingénésie sociale (1827–31; inc. La Vision d'Hébal and La Ville des expiations), a philosophical epic (prose, unfinished) inspired by the myth of Atlantis in Plato's Timaeus. v. Illuminisme.

Ballet, introduced from Italy in the time of Catherine de Médicis, was in vogue at court in the 17th c. Benserade added rhymed commentaries and epigrams to the pantomimic dances, and from this Molière evolved the *comédie-ballet*.

Ballette, v. Chansons à danser.

Balsamo, JOSEPH, v. Cagliostro.

Bals populaires, public dance-halls and places of amusement, sometimes out of doors, more often on the premises of cafés or drinking-shops, e.g. the Bal Bullier (Bullier was the proprietor) at the Closerie des Lilas, a café on the Boulevard Montparnasse. Forerunners of the night club, café-chantant, café-concert, dancing, etc., they were dotted all over Paris in the years between the Revolution and the end of the Second Empire and catered for every class of society (the different types are described in Taine's *Notes sur Paris*). There are many references to them in novels (e.g. in Balzac, Zola, *Murger's* Scènes de la vie de Bohème), light comedies, and *vaudevilles*. Most had disappeared by 1900.

Balzac, HONORÉ, self-styled DE (1799–1850), novelist, b. at Tours, where his father, who came of Midi peasant stock (the family name was originally Balssa), was concerned with army supplies. At the Collège des Oratoriens at Vendôme (1807–13; v. Louis Lambert) he seemed loutish and dull, but was secretly devouring the school library so fast that he had a breakdown. By 1814 the family was in Paris and he went to a private school, then into a lawyer's office, where he acquired the sound knowledge of law and lawyers that pervades his work. At the same time, he followed the popular *Sorbonne* lectures of Cousin, Guizot, and Villemain. In 1819 his parents allowed him to forsake law for literature, and gave him a meagre allowance. On this he scraped along in a garret and wrote poems, history, and a tragedy (Cromwell)—all equally bad. Between 1820, when his parents made him return home, and 1825 he published several bad, sensational novels under pseudonyms (notably 'Horace de Saint-Aubin'). Then, again on his own in Paris, he devoted himself to grandiose, often harebrained, commercial schemes, hoping to win freedom to write. Despite financial help from Mme de Berny (v. *Dilecta*, *La*), the first of many women friends, he was soon deeply in debt. His mania for speculation and equally strong collector's passion—the cause of his perpetual insolvency—date from these years. Undaunted, he returned to his pen and within five months wrote *Les *Chouans* (1829), his first success and the first novel published under his own name. His output now became prodigious—some 91 novels and tales between 1829 and 1848 over and above the increasing demands of regular journalism—and his life-history became that of his writing, his continual financial crises (with ingenious escapes from creditors), and his friendships with women. In 1832 he received from Poland a letter of admiration and criticism, signed 'L'Étrangère'. This began a long correspondence and a liaison with Mme Hanska (*Lettres à l'Étrangère*, 1899–1906, 2 vols.). They married in 1850, shortly before her death, and too late for her money to be of help to him.

Balzac's early idea of grouping his writings as sections of a composite whole, with a collective title indicative of purpose and scope, was realized in his 1842–8 collected edition (17 vols.), entitled *La Comédie humaine* (possibly in imitation of Dante) and divided into three main groups: *Études de mœurs*, *Études philosophiques*, *Études analytiques* (for the grouping and dates of individual works *v. Comédie humaine*). His system of classification, with the use of the word *étude*, implied a scientific basis for the work and shows him as the true child of an age in which Geoffroy Saint-Hilaire was breaking new ground in natural science. (His interest in Mesmer, Gall, Lavater, Swedenborg, etc., is also often evident, esp. in the *Études philosophiques*.)

La Comédie humaine—of which he said: 'Une génération est un drame à quatre ou cinq mille personnages saillants. Ce drame, c'est mon livre'—is a panorama of French society from the Consulate to the July Monarchy. Within the genealogical and geographical framework of the whole, the characters—over 2,000 in all, drawn from all strata of society—appear and reappear in the various volumes at different stages in their lives, playing now principal now minor parts. The underlying theme is that money can do everything. Restraints of religion, of monarchical and parental authority, have vanished, leaving self-interest as the supreme motive of human conduct.

Balzac's genius shows itself in his dynamic creative vigour; his super-abundant imagination, which has a fantastic, visionary strain all the more forcible for being allied to remarkable powers of realistic observation and delineation of character (he creates living persons, acting from plausible motives, and in his care for documentation is a precursor of *Realism); his masterly portrayal of passions which, if not always vicious in themselves, can wreck men's lives, e.g. avarice (*Eugénie Grandet*), jealousy (*La *Cousine Bette*); his grasp of such widely differing subjects as geology, architecture, mysticism, and commerce, e.g. his account of the launching of César Birotteau's hair-oil (*Histoire de la grandeur et de la décadence de César Birotteau*). His descriptive powers are at their most characteristic in long, cumulative portraits. He is not a great stylist: he hammers his way to comprehensive expression through the vast resources of his thought, achieving 'le style nécessaire, fatal, et mathématique de son idée' (Gautier). His greatness can be measured from the fact that his characters are discussed and used as types for comparison as if they had really lived: as Bourget remarked, 'Balzac semble avoir moins observé la société de son époque qu'il n'a contribué à en former une.'

His method of composition was laborious and costly. He worked from 10 to 14 hours daily; often he went to bed at 6 p.m. and rose to write from midnight to the following midday, fortifying himself with black coffee. He would send the printer a skeleton first draft, and then fill it out in a whole series of sets of proofs, each such a labyrinth of erasures and insertions that his bill for corrections exceeded his income from the book.

Besides the above works and letters, he wrote the *Contes drolatiques (1832-7) and historical and political articles for periodicals. Latterly, hoping to save his fortunes from wreck, he turned to the drama, with *Vautrin (1840), Les Ressources de Quinola (1842), La Marâtre (1848), and Le Faiseur (v. Mercadet). v. also Revue parisienne; Spoelberch de Lovenjoul; Surville.

Balzac, JEAN-LOUIS GUEZ DE (1594–1654), essayist and stylist, a gentleman of the Angoumois, is remembered as having perfected French prose (as Malherbe perfected French verse), making it orderly and lucid, constructing the eloquent period (based on assiduous study of Latin authors, esp. Cicero), and so preparing the way for Pascal and Bossuet. His works, much admired in their day, include Le Prince (1631), on the political situation of France under Louis XIII, with a flattering portrait of the king; Le Barbon (1648), a satire; Socrate chrétien (1652), dialogues and discourses on religious subjects; Entretiens (1657), mostly on literary subjects; Aristippe (1658), on wisdom in political administration. The first collection of his Lettres (elaborate dissertations) appeared in 1624. Though the matter of his works is less important than their form, he expresses sound, if rather pessimistic, views on ethics, politics, and literature, shows a love of rustic scenery, and can give an agreeable turn to his wisdom.

Banc d'œuvre, under the ancien régime, a special pew in church, a privilege accorded only to the nobility.

Bandello, MATTEO (1485–1561), an Italian Dominican who settled in France, became a bishop, but devoted himself mainly to writing his Novelle, tales much influenced by Boccaccio and later translated into French (v. Belleforest;

Foreign Influences, 1). One of his tales inspired Shakespeare's Romeo and Juliet, another Musset's *Barberine.

Ban et de l'arrière-ban, Appel du, under feudal custom, the summoning of the king's vassals and the population at large to his support in an emergency. Holders of fiefs were required to attend him on horseback, gratis, for three months.

Banquet, Le (1892, 8 nos.), a very promising but short-lived literary review, founded and written by former pupils of the Lycée Condorcet, including Proust and Blum.

Banquets. In 1847 the political opposition circumvented the law against public meetings by organizing banquets at which speakers, including Lamartine, agitated for liberal and electoral reform. The government's refusal to allow such a banquet to be held in Paris on 22 February 1848 provoked reactions which led to the 1848 *Revolution.

Banville, THÉODORE FAULLAIN DE (1823–91), poet, dramatist, and man of letters. His verse is notable for its delicately lyrical quality and mixture of sentiment and irony; he also had a great command of language and rhythm, and a remarkable facility for rhyming. His collections include Les Cariatides (1842); Les Stalactites (1846), Le Sang de la coupe (1857), and Les Exilés (1867), where perfection of form and choice of subject show him as a precursor of the *Parnassiens (he contributed to Le Parnasse contemporain in 1866); Odes funambulesques (1857), light verse; Roses de Noël (1878); Sonnailles et clochettes (1890); Dans la fournaise (1892). In Trente-six Ballades joyeuses à la manière de François Villon (1873) and Rondels à la manière de Charles d'Orléans (in Poésies, 1875) he employed forms long disused (*rondeau, *villanelle, *triolet). His comedies include *Gringoire (1866) and Riquet à la houppe (1885; a fairy play). He also wrote tales of Parisian life (e.g. Esquisses parisiennes,

1859; *Contes bourgeois*, 1891) and a *Petit Traité de poésie française* (1872), which remains useful and has one chapter of notable brevity: '*Licences poétiques*. Il n'y en a pas.'

Baour-Lormian, PIERRE (1770–1854), wrote verse, conventional tragedies (e.g. *Mahomet II*, 1810), translations of Tasso (*Jérusalem délivrée*, 1795) and *Ossian (1801), and—despite his Ossian—satires attacking the *Romantics.

Barante, GUILLAUME-PROSPER BRUGIÈRE, BARON DE (1782–1866), historian, literary critic, and diplomat; noted for his *Histoire des ducs de Bourgogne de la Maison de Valois* (1824–6), based on 15th-c. chronicles, an attempt to present history in the form of an objectively written narrative, with all the interest of an historical novel. In youth he was a devoted admirer of Mme de Staël.

Barbe-bleue, La, v. *Perrault*; *Retz or Rais*.

Barberine (1853, in *Comédies et Proverbes*), a prose comedy by Musset; an augmented version of his earlier *La Quenouille de Barberine* (1835, in the *Revue des Deux Mondes*; 1840, in *Comédies et Proverbes*), which he rewrote in 1850, as *Barberine*, with a view to its production at the *Comédie-Française. (It was rejected, but eventually produced there in 1882.) The subject—an absent husband uses a magic mirror to test his wife's fidelity—was taken from one of *Bandello's *Novelle*.

Barbey d'Aurevilly, JULES-AMÉDÉE (1808–89), novelist and critic (he began as a poet), studied law at Caen (where he met Beau Brummell, then British consul there), and from 1833 earned his living by journalism in Paris. His writings, and arrogant, flamboyantly *Romantic character, make him an interesting minor figure of 19th-c. French literature. Latterly, he had many disciples among younger writers (for whom he was 'le Connétable des Lettres'), and his reputation has grown since his death.

After the early *L'Amour impossible* (1841) and *La Bague d'Annibal* (1843), he wrote two novels of exceptional merit, *L'*Ensorcelée* (1854) and *Le *Chevalier des Touches* (1864); and others—*Une Vieille Maîtresse* (1851), *Un Prêtre marié* (1865), *Les *Diaboliques* (1874; tales), *Une Histoire sans nom* (1882), *Ce qui ne meurt pas* (1884), *Une Page d'histoire* (1886)—which are extravagant, at times ridiculous, in character. He excelled at conveying the atmosphere and traditions of the wild, lonely Cotentin country (v. *Chouannerie*)—the scene of his own childhood—in which most of them were set. He was literary or dramatic critic on several papers (Sainte-Beuve's successor on the *Constitutionnel*). His vigorous, paradoxical criticism (collected in *Le Théâtre contemporain*, 1887–9, 3 vols., 1892, 1896; *Les Œuvres et les hommes*, 1860–1909, 26 vols.) was often far-seeing in its appraisements, but impaired by his violent prejudices and militant Royalism and Catholicism (v. *Bloy*). His other works include *Du dandysme et de G. Brummell* (1845), one dandy on another; *Memoranda* (publ. at intervals during his lifetime), a form of journal. v. *Guérin, E. and M. de*.

Barbier, ANTOINE-ALEXANDRE, v. *Dictionaries*, 1806–9.

Barbier, AUGUSTE (1805–82), minor poet and satirist, made a sudden reputation with *La Curée* (1830, in the *Revue des Deux Mondes*), a verse satire on the place-hunters who tried to profit by the 1830 *Revolution. His other works include *Iambes* (1832; inc. *L'Idole*, a denunciation of Napoleon, *cf. Légende napoléonienne*; and *La Curée*), satires attacking contemporary evils; *Il Pianto* (1833), poems of Italy, lamenting her former glories; *Lazare* (1837), including melancholy impressions of the English industrial scene.

Barbier, EDMOND-JEAN-FRANÇOIS (1689–1771), an advocate whose *Journal historique et anecdotique* for the period 1718–63 contains valuable information.

Barbier de Séville, Le, a prose comedy by Beaumarchais; produced 1775. *v. Mariage de Figaro, Le. v. Lindor.*

Bartholo, a curmudgeonly old doctor, keeps his ward Rosine imprisoned and, against her will, intends to marry her. He is aided in his designs by her music-master, the villainous Bazile. The comte Almaviva, a young Spanish grandee, has seen Rosine and the two have fallen in love, though she does not know who he is. The play is concerned with the devices by which, abetted by the resourceful Figaro (once his servant, now a barber), Almaviva contrives to outwit Bartholo and marry Rosine.

Barbizon, a village near Fontainebleau, famous from the early 19th c. (esp. *c.* 1850) as an artists' colony. Painters of the Barbizon school included Corot, P.-É.-T. Rousseau, and Millet. Life there is depicted in the Goncourt brothers' *Manette Salomon.*

Barbusse, HENRI (1874–1935), novelist and journalist, made his name with *Le Feu: journal d'une escouade* (1916), a novel of the 1914–18 war, with realistic descriptions of life in the trenches, behind the lines, on leave, etc. His other works include *Pleureuses* (1895), poems; *Les Suppliants* (1903) and *L'Enfer* (1908), novels; *Clarté* (1919), another war novel; *La Lueur dans l'abîme* (1920) and *Paroles d'un combattant* (1920) political writings, pacifist and socialist in character.

Barclay, JOHN (1582–1621), a Scot, born in France, who wrote in Latin and is remembered for two works—*Argenis* (1621), an allegorical satire (enjoyed by Richelieu), in effect a history of the reigns of Henri III and Henri IV; and *Euphormionis Lusinini Satyricon* (in 2 pts.: 1602, London; 1603, Paris), also allegorical, directed against the *Jesuits. He lived for a time in England and was employed on editorial work by James VI and I.

Bargone, FRÉDÉRIC, *v. Farrère.*

Barlaam et Josaphat, a medieval religious romance, interesting as a christianized version of the story of Buddha. There are three 13th-c. French poems on the subject (one anonymous, one by an *Anglo-Norman poet named Chardri, one by Gui de Cambrai). *Cf.*, in English, *Barlaam and Josaphat.*

Josaphat, son of an Indian king and secluded from the world by his father, finally gains his liberty and is converted to Christianity by Barlaam, a holy man. He converts his father, abandons the kingdom when he succeeds to it, and dies a hermit.

Barnabooth, *v. Larbaud.*

Baro, BALTHAZAR (17th c.), d'Urfé's secretary, wrote the conclusion of *L'*Astrée* from d'Urfé's notes, also ephemeral plays and novels.

Baron, MICHEL BOYRON, *known as* (1653–1729), actor and dramatist, a disciple of Molière. His best comedies were *L'Homme à bonnes fortunes* (1686); and *L'Andrienne,* adapted from Terence.

Barras, PAUL-JEAN-FRANÇOIS-NICOLAS, VICOMTE DE (1755–1829), came of an old Provençal family and soldiered in India before taking to Revolutionary politics (allegedly to escape from his debts—he was always a man of pleasure). He voted for the death of Louis XVI (1792), was a member of the *Comité de salut public,* helped to overthrow Robespierre (1794), and then became a prominent *thermidorien* (*v. Revolutions,* 1), a member of the *Directoire,* and a protector of the young Bonaparte (who married his former mistress, the vicomtesse de Beauharnais). He retired to private life when Bonaparte became First Consul (1799).

Barrault, JEAN-LOUIS (1910–   ), actor-manager and director, began his theatrical career with Dullin at the *Atelier and worked for a time with Artaud. His success has lain in the cinema (*Drôle de drame*; *Les Enfants du Paradis*) as well as in the theatre, where one of his main contributions has been the introduction of Claudel to a wide public: *Le Soulier de satin* (1943), during his period at the *Comédie-Française; Partage de midi (1948), during his tenure (1946–56) of the Théâtre Marigny in Paris; Tête d'or (1959), while he was director of the *Odéon-Théâtre de France. His other creations include *Camus's L'État de siège (1948), *Ionesco's Rhinocéros (1960), *Beckett's Oh! les beaux jours (1963), *Genet's Les Paravents (1966), and his own adaptation of Rabelais (1968), produced in a wrestling hall in Montmartre after his dismissal from the Théâtre de France in the wake of the student rising of May 1968. His success is shared with his wife, the actress Madeleine Renaud, with whom he founded the Compagnie Renaud-Barrault.

Barrès, MAURICE (1862–1923), novelist, essayist, and politician, studied law at Nancy, then began his literary career in Paris c. 1884 by founding a short-lived review, Taches d'encre. After Huit Jours chez M. Renan (1888), imaginary conversations on an impertinently ironic note, he was soon in the first rank of authors with many disciples among other writers. A rather dilettante, sceptical aesthete, concerned to experience new sensations, he exalted his culte du moi in novels (partly essays), Sous l'œil des barbares (1888), Un Homme libre (1889), Le Jardin de Bérénice (1891); and in travel impressions, Du sang, de la volupté, et de la mort (1894; Spain), Amori et dolori sacrum: La Mort de Venise (1902), etc. But his patriotic conscience had been stirred by *Boulangisme, he had entered politics (*député for Nancy, 1889), and was soon drawn to a form of mysticonationalism. The individual, he now saw, was dependent on the group, and for true self-development must be conscious of being one of, and with, his race, allied by ties of blood to the soil of his ancestors. National education must encourage the young Frenchman to serve his country in his native province, where everything conspired to foster his capabilities, not to be a citizen of an abstract 'humanity' for whom France was an administrative fiction. These views inspired his trilogy Le Roman de l'énergie nationale: I. Les *Déracinés (1897), II. L'Appel au soldat

(1900; mainly about Boulangisme), III. Leurs figures (1902; v. Panama); Les Amitiés françaises (1902; essays); and Les Bastions de l'Est, two novels of Alsace-Lorraine: I. Au service de l'Allemagne (1905), II. Colette Baudoche (1909). These works, and his anti-*Dreyfus attitude, stamped him as a reactionary and lessened his influence.

During and after the 1914–18 war, as president of the *Ligue des patriotes, he wrote daily articles in L'Écho de Paris (collected in Chronique de la Grande Guerre, 1920–4, 14 vols.). His other works include La *Colline inspirée (1913) and Un Jardin sur l'Oronte (1922), novels; and Mes cahiers (1929–63), a voluminous journal intime.

Barricades, street blocks erected by the people of Paris in times of revolt or civil strife (v. Ligue, La and Fronde for the journées des barricades). Improvised from empty barrels (barriques—hence their name), uprooted paving-stones, vehicles, etc., they impeded the passage of troops through narrow streets and were a good cover for ill-armed insurgents. 'Aux barricades!' became a call to desperate measures against authority and the barricades a symbol of a revolutionary city populace in arms.

Barrière, THÉODORE (1823–77), dramatist, wrote both farce and drama. His characters were types of stupidity, egoism, or malice, as in Les Filles de marbre (1853; a study of courtesans); Les Faux Bonshommes (1856), written with Ernest Capendu (1826–68); Les Jocrisses de l'amour (1865), written with Lambert Thiboust (1826–67).

Barruel-Bauvert, ANTOINE-JOSEPH, ABBÉ (1756–1817), a champion of religious orthodoxy (Les Helviennes, 1781; against the *philosophes) and of the Royalist cause.

Barthélemy, JEAN-JACQUES, ABBÉ (1716–1795), a learned and amiable antiquarian. A period in Italy (1755–7) with his patron, the French ambassador, inspired his Voyage du jeune Anacharsis en Grèce (1788), a popular reconstruction of

Greek civilization in the 4th c. B.C. as seen by a young Scythian visitor, introducing Epaminondas, Xenophon, Alexander, etc. The fruit of 30 years' labour, it was highly successful, and he was admitted to the *Académie* (1789).

Barthes, ROLAND (1915–80), a leading critic whose influence dates mainly from 1953, when he helped to found the review *Théâtre populaire* and published *Le Degré zéro de l'écriture*. He is among the chief exponents of the *nouvelle critique* (v. *Critics and Criticism*, 3), deriving his inspiration as much from Freudian psycho-analysis as from Marxism, *Existentialism, and *Structuralism. His view that human communication must always imply a system of signs has led him in the direction of *Semiology, as can be seen in his successive volumes of criticism, e.g. *Michelet par lui-même* (1954), *Mythologies* (1957), *Sur Racine* (1963), *Essais critiques* (1964), *Critique et vérité* (1965), *Système de la mode* (1967), *L'Empire des signes* (1970), *Sade, Fourier, Loyola* (1971), *S/Z* (1971).

Bartholo, in Beaumarchais's *Le *Barbier de Séville* and *Le *Mariage de Figaro*.

Bartholomew, Massacre of St. (La Saint-Barthélemy), the massacre of *Huguenots in Paris and other large cities on St. Bartholomew's Eve, 23–4 August 1572, ordered by Charles IX at the instigation of his mother Catherine de Médicis and her advisers. Notable victims were Coligny and La Ramée. It is described in Mérimée's *Chronique du règne de Charles IX* and M.-J. Chénier's **Charles IX.* v. *Bussy d'Amboise*; *Coconas*; *Tavannes*.

Bartole (Bartolus) (1314–57), an Italian jurist and commentator on Justinian; often mentioned in early literature, e.g. by Rabelais.

'Baruch?, Avez-vous lu'. La Fontaine was so impressed by a chance reading of the prayer of the Jews in the book of Baruch that he put this question to all and sundry. It is used proverbially of a sudden, striking discovery.

Barzun, HENRI-MARTIN (1881–1966), poet, a member of the *Abbaye group and the founder of *Simultanéisme*. He published *La Terrestre Tragédie* (1907; collected verse) and *La Trilogie des forces* (1908–14; collections illustrating his *simultanéiste* theories).

Bashkirtseff, MARIE (1860–84), a Russian whose *Journal* (publ. posth. 1887; written in French) is one of the remarkable *journaux intimes* of the 19th c. She came, aged 12, to France with her mother, several other relations, and family retainers. The little party lived in Nice, Rome, and Paris (from 1877), in a succession of hotels and furnished houses, until Marie, always its centre, died of consumption. In her diary, kept from 1873 till 11 days before her death, she revealed herself 'tout entière', at first for her own benefit but soon intentionally as a means of leaving her imprint on posterity. She recorded her life of (at times precarious) luxury; her arrogance; her romantic fancies; her determination to improve her education; her ambition to be a great painter (she hastened her end by working feverishly at the well-known *Académie Julian*); her struggle against her illness and, in the final, moving pages, her realization that nothing could save her.

Basiliade du célèbre Pilpai, La, v. *Morelly*.

Basnage de Beauval, HENRI (1656–1710), *Huguenot scholar and compiler, settled in Holland after the revocation of the Edict of Nantes. His *Histoire des ouvrages des savants* (Rotterdam 1687–1709, 12 vols.)—a periodical collection in which his brother JACQUES (1653–1723; also a compiler) is said to have had a hand—continued *Bayle's *Nouvelles de la République des Lettres*. v. also *Dictionaries*, 1690.

Basoche, Basochiens (from L. *basilica*, 'tribunal'), the name given to associations of attorneys', registrars', and other law clerks, formed for mutual protection and amusement. In Paris the chief societies were the *Basoche du *Parlement* or *Royaume de la Basoche*, formed *c.* 1303, which had a king, chancellor, etc., and some jurisdiction over members; the *Basoche du *Châtelet*; and the *Empire de Galilée*, for clerks of the *Chambre des comptes*. They were obliged by statute to assemble at stated times for a *montre*, or general review. On these occasions they performed pantomimes, *tableaux vivants*, and, as time went on, dialogues, *farces*, and *moralités*, often written by members and usually satirizing the world of the judicature. On the *jours gras* of Carnival they pleaded burlesque law-suits (*causes grasses*; *v. Coquillart*). Their fondness for satire brought them into disrepute at court and with the authorities (except under Louis XII, who encouraged their audacities), and their performances were often censored and periodically prohibited. *Basochiens* and the closely related *Enfants sans souci* sometimes acted *farces* and *soties* in conjunction with a *mystère* from the *Confrérie de la Passion*, a mixture known as *pois pilés*. Later, the *Basochiens* produced many of Larivey's plays, and an occasional tragedy. Their dramatic activities (though not the *causes grasses*) ended *c.* 1590. The *Basoche du Parlement* survived as a corporation until the Revolution.

Provincial *Basoches* included those of Aix, Angers, Avignon, Bordeaux, Lyons, and Rouen; some were less given to play-acting and satire than those of Paris. *v. Marot*.

Basselin, OLIVIER (15th c.), a fuller of Vire in Normandy, reputed author of drinking-songs current in the *vau* ('valley') of the river Vire. This may be the origin of the term *vaudevire* (*v. Vaudeville*). Basselin is the subject of a 15th-c. dirge, which suggests that he was killed in the English wars.

Bassompierre, FRANÇOIS DE (1579–1646), soldier and diplomat, became *maréchal de France* after serving in many campaigns. Richelieu held him in the *Bastille* (1629–41), 'not for any wrong he had done, but for fear he might be led into mischief'. His memoirs give a lively account of himself and his contemporaries.

Bastard de Bouillon, Le, *v. Baudouin de Sebourg*.

Bastiat, CLAUDE-FRÉDÉRIC (1801–50), political economist, an early French advocate of Free Trade, wrote an account of the English movement (*Cobden et la ligue*, 1845). He met Cobden in England (1845). He was editor, with Blanqui and others, of the journal *Le Libre Échange* (1846–8). He died leaving his chief work, *Harmonies économiques*, unfinished.

Bastille, La, a fortress (erected 1370–82) at the Porte Saint-Antoine in the *Marais quarter of Paris. From the time of Richelieu it was the most redoubtable of the State prisons and had many famous inmates (e.g. Voltaire). To the people, its name spelt injustice and absolutism, and the first symbolic act of the *Revolution was *la Prise de la Bastille* on 14 July 1789. It proved little more than a venerable scarecrow, containing a few convicts and lunatics and a garrison of 125 men (95 of them *invalides*); the governor, the marquis de Launay, was murdered by the mob. The anniversary of its fall was at first marked by the *Fêtes de la *Fédération*; since 1880 it has been by law the chief national holiday.

Bataille, a medieval literary form, akin to the *débat* and *dispute* (*v. Dit*), depicting an armed combat between personifications, e.g. *Henri d'Andeli's *Bataille des Sept Arts*.

Bataille, GEORGES (1897–1962), novelist, essayist, and founder of *Documents*, *Critique*, and other reviews; a librarian at the *Bibliothèque nationale* (1922–42). He approached *Surrealism, but soon reacted against it, despite his concern with the erotic, oneiric, mystical, and metaphysical. He was much influenced by Nietzsche, Hegel, and Freud, and his preoccupation is with an 'apotheosis of the perishable'— expressed both in fictional works which herald the *anti-roman*, and in essays which mark him as a metaphysician of criticism and helped in the transition to the *nouvelle critique* (*v. Critics and Criticism*, 3). His works (often publ. under pseudonyms, e.g. 'Lord Auch', 'Pierre Angélique') include *Histoire de l'œil* (1928), *Madame Edwarda* (1941), *L'Expérience intérieure* (1943), *Le Coupable* (1944), *Sur Nietzsche* (1945), *Haine de la poésie* (1947; later entitled *L'Impossible*), *La Part maudite* (1949), *La Littérature et le mal* (1957; studies of Emily Brontë, Baudelaire, Sade, Proust, Genet, etc.), *L'Érotisme* (1957), *Le Bleu du ciel* (1957; a novel written in 1935), *Ma mère* (1966).

Bataille, HENRI (1872–1922), author of psychological dramas which combined audacity with false sentiment and had a wide appeal, e.g. *Maman Colibri* (1904; on a middle-aged woman's love for her son's friend), *La Marche nuptiale* (1905), *La Vierge folle* (1910), *L'Enfant de l'amour* (1911), *Le Phalène* (1913), *La Tendresse* (1921).

Bataille d'*Hernani*, **La**, *v. Hernani.*

Bateau ivre, Le, a poem by Rimbaud; written 1871. A boat's crew has been massacred: only the poet is left. Rudderless, the boat drifts through luminous seas, is tossed by hurricanes into birdless skies, becoming the symbol of his confused soul. The poem is full of continually shifting images which have the fleeting clarity of hallucinations.

Baty, GASTON (1885–1952), producer. After working in various theatres in Paris, he took over (1930) the *Théâtre Montparnasse*, where he staged new French plays, foreign classics, and dramatizations of novels (e.g. *Crime and Punishment*, *Manon Lescaut, *Madame Bovary), becoming noted for his novel *décors. v. Theatres and Theatre Companies.*

Baude, HENRI (*c.* 1430–*c.* 1496), poet and provincial official, an imitator of Villon. His works include a satirical *moralité (perf. by the *Basoche, 1486), containing reflections on the court which earned him

one of his many spells in prison; satirical poems, showing him cheerful in adversity, e.g. *Les Lamentations Bourrien* (against clerics), *Le Testament de la mule Barbeau* (against magistrates); and *Lettres à Mgr de Bourbon*, pleading for release from prison.

Baudelaire, CHARLES (1821–67), poet and critic. His poetic genius (little appreciated in his lifetime) and great influence on modern poetry are now universally recognized; his stature as a literary, art, and music critic is now also apparent. *v. Lyric Poetry,* 4; *Critics and Criticism,* 3.

He was born in Paris, in comfortable circumstances; his mother was 26, his father 60. In 1828 his widowed mother, whom he adored, married Colonel Aupick, and a new presence came (or intruded) into his life. The pair opposed his determination to be a poet and started him on a voyage to India (1841–2); but he left the ship at Mauritius, returned to Paris, and–being now of age and possessed of an inheritance—set up on his own. He wrote regularly for reviews, and discovered and translated Edgar Allan Poe, whose aesthetic theories appealed to him. He was also influenced by his reading of Swedenborg. His life was one of excess, and in time became desperate and sordid. One of his mistresses, the mulatto Jeanne Duval, is remembered as the 'Vénus noire' of his poems: he treated her with amazing kindness, long after she became a besotted wreck and their relationship agonizing. His pride and his faith in his genius—and also his finances—received a cruel blow when, on publication of his poems *Les Fleurs du mal* (1857), he was fined for offences against public morals (*cf.* Flaubert and *Madame Bovary). Six poems were banned, and the edition could not be sold without their deletion. (They were omitted from the 2nd and 3rd eds., 1861 and 1868, but printed illegally, as an appendix, in subsequent French eds. until the ban was lifted in 1949; they were also printed in *Les Épaves, v.* below.) By 1864 his resources were exhausted and he went to Brussels with hopes, which foundered pitifully, of making money by lecturing. He lived there squalidly until his constitution gave way and he was brought back to Paris (1866) with advanced syphilis and hemiplegic paralysis.

The poems of *Les Fleurs du mal* were written at various dates (the section *Tableaux parisiens*, for example, was not introduced till the 2nd ed.). Their theme is the antagonism between *spleen* and *idéal*, between evil and good, by which man is torn. In the first section (*Spleen et Idéal*) the poet discards the traditional criterion of idealized beauty: he will extract poetic magic from the hideous realities of life— 'l'horreur et l'extase de la vie'. In the next three sections (*Tableaux parisiens, Le Vin, Les Fleurs du mal*) he finds inspiration in the streets and the mysterious, hidden life of Paris, or in evil itself, lingering over it with an almost mystical acuity of sensation. He analyses himself morbidly and is haunted by a sense of damnation which exasperates him to revolt and blasphemy. But these cannot prevail against God, and he longs (*Révolte* and *La Mort*, the final sections) for death and the discovery of the Beyond: 'Nous voulons... Plonger au fond du gouffre, Enfer ou Ciel, qu'importe? Au fond de l'Inconnu pour trouver du *nouveau*!' (*cf.* Rimbaud, on whom his influence was strong). Famous poems in this collection include *L'Albatros*, *Correspondances, Harmonie du soir, L'Invitation au voyage, L'Héautontimorouménos* ('The Self-Tormentor'), *Un Voyage à Cythère, Le Voyage* (the final poem, ending with the lines quoted above), *Recueillement*. *v. Limbes, Les; Présidente, La; Parnassiens* (for *Nouvelles Fleurs du mal*).

Hugo said that Baudelaire introduced a *frisson nouveau* into poetry—an exacerbated sensibility that quickens only to a beauty containing the elements of corruption. His prosody was classical in its perfection, but he was a precursor of modern poetry by his perception of the symbolic *correspondances* of scents, colours, and sounds (*v. Symbolism*), by his exploration of the musical possibilities of language, and, above all, by his remarkable evocative power. *v. Art pour l'art, L'*.

His other works include *Les Épaves* (1866; publ. in Belgium), poems including the six banned from *Les Fleurs du mal* (*Les Bijoux, Le Léthé, A celle qui est trop gaie, Lesbos, Femmes damnées, Les Métamorphoses du vampire*); *Petits Poèmes en prose* (1869; later entitled *Le Spleen de Paris*; *v. Prose Poem*), influenced by A. *Bertrand's *Gaspard de la nuit*; *Les Paradis artificiels, opium et haschisch* (1860), essays including a study of, and translations from, De Quincey's *Opium Eater*; *Histoires extraordinaires* and *Nouvelles Histoires extraordinaires par Edgar Poë* (1856 and 1857), translations; criticism of the *Salons of 1845, 1846, and 1859, Richard Wagner et Tannhäuser* (1861), and *Eugène Delacroix* (1863)— all in *Curiosités esthétiques* and *L'Art romantique* (both 1868); *Fusées* and *Mon cœur mis à nu*, interesting, often poignant jottings (first publ. *in extenso* 1917).

Baudouin, JEAN (1590–1650), translator of Tacitus, Suetonius, Tasso, Bacon, etc.

Baudouin d'Avesnes, *v. History*, 1.

Baudouin de Condé, *v. Trois morts...*, *Dit des*.

Baudouin de Sebourg, an early 14th-c. romance in the form of the *chanson de geste* and, with its sequel *Le Bastard de Bouillon*, among the last examples of that form; attached to the Crusade *cycle. Many of the adventures of the hero (son of the king of Nimègue in Holland and educated by the lord of Sebourg), in Europe and the East, have the burlesque character of *fabliaux* and give a lively, realistic picture of contemporary manners.

Bayard, *v. Renaud de Montauban*.

Bayard, PIERRE DU TERRAIL, CHEVALIER DE (*c*. 1473–1524), 'le Chevalier sans peur et sans reproche', a famous captain whose brave exploits in the Italian wars (esp. his defence of the bridge of Garigliano against 200 Spaniards) were recorded in the *Très joyeuse... histoire du gentil seigneur de Bayart* by his 'loyal serviteur' (possibly Jacques de Mailles).

Bayle, PIERRE (1647–1706), lexico-grapher, philosopher, and critic; a man of erudition and intellectual probity. A Protestant who became a Catholic and then reverted to Protestantism, he ended as a Pyrrhonian in religion and a champion of toleration, holding that even reason leads to no certain conclusions and that morality is independent of religious faith. Forced to leave France, he taught philosophy at Sedan (1675) and as a professor at Rotterdam (1680), setting forth his views in his *Pensées sur la Comète* (1682; later augm.) and *Commentaire philosophique sur les paroles de Jésus-Christ*: '*Contrains-les d'entrer*' (1686; denying that these words justify persecution). He also founded and conducted (1684–7) the literary review *Nouvelles de la République des Lettres* (publ. in Holland). His anonymous *Avis important aux réfugiés sur leur prochain retour en France*, advocating passive obedience, was deemed a betrayal of their cause and cost him his professorship. Then came his chief work, the *Dictionnaire historique et critique* (Rotterdam 1697; augm. 1702, and suppl. 1704–6 by *Réponses aux questions d'un provincial*), the true precursor, in both ideas and form, of the **Encyclopédie*. It consists of articles on ancient and modern historical figures, indicating errors and omissions in earlier works (esp. that of Moreri; *v. Dictionaries*, 1674) and (in voluminous footnotes to a substantially orthodox text) freely investigating philosophical and theological subjects—for 'les erreurs pour être vieilles n'en sont pas meilleures'. By 1740 there were 11 editions, and an *Analyse* or abbreviation appeared in 1755. There were English editions from 1710. Bayle's correspondence has also been published.

Bazard, ARMAND, *v. Saint-Simonisme*.

Bazin, HERVÉ, *pseudonym of* JEAN-PIERRE HERVÉ-BAZIN (1911–   ), great-nephew of the following, was known first as a poet, with such volumes as *Parcelles* (1933), *Visages* (1934), and the prize-winning *Jour* (1947). He obtained notoriety with his novel *Vipère au poing* (1948), a transposi-tion of his own life, in which he launches an attack on his family, and in particular his mother. His subsequent novels con-tinue to reflect his critical attitude towards the *bourgeoisie* into which he was born: *La Tête contre les murs* (1949), *La Mort du petit cheval* (1950; a sequel to *Vipère au poing*), *Lève-toi et marche* (1952), *L'Huile sur le feu* (1954), *Qui j'ose aimer* (1956), *Au nom du fils* (1961). He is the author of two volumes of short stories, *Le Bureau des mariages* (1951) and *Chapeau bas* (1963), as well as of further collections of poetry, *A la suite d'Iris* (1948), *Humeurs* (1952), *Bestiaire* (1953).

Bazin, RENÉ (1853–1932), author of earthy novels of provincial life which had a great sentimental and patriotic appeal *c.* 1900, e.g. *La Terre qui meurt* (1899; Vendée), *Les Oberlé* (1901; an Alsatian family faces the choice between French and German nationality), *Donatienne* (1903; Brittany), *Le Blé qui lève* (1907; Burgundy and Picardy).

Béatrix, *v. Comédie humaine, La* (*Scènes de la vie privée*).

Beauclair, HENRI (1860–1919), journalist and poet, author with Vicaire of *Les *Déliquescences d'Adoré Floupette*. His *Les Horizontales* (1885) parodied Hugo's *Les *Orientales*.

Beauharnais, JOSÉPHINE TASCHER DE LA PAGERIE, VICOMTESSE DE (1763–1814), b. in Martinique. Her first husband was guillotined (1794). She then married (1796) Napoleon Bonaparte, becoming empress (1804); but she bore him no children, and he divorced her (1809). Her children by the vicomte de Beauharnais were EUGÈNE (1781–1824), whom Napoleon made viceroy of Italy, and HORTENSE (1783–1837), who married Louis Bonaparte (*v. Bonaparte Family*) and was the mother of Napoleon III (and *v. Morny*). *v. Malmaison*.

Beauharnais, MARIE-ANNE-FRANÇOISE ('FANNY') MOUCHARD, COMTESSE DE (1738–1813), wife of Claude de Beauharnais (a relative of the above), was the intimate friend of C.-J. Dorat and herself a minor authoress. Her house was a literary centre, frequented by Dorat, Restif de la Bretonne, L.-S. Mercier, etc.

Beaumanoir, PHILIPPE DE REMI, SIRE DE (*c.* 1250–96), an eminent jurist, author of the *Coutumes du Beauvaisis* (a treatise on French law), La *Manekine and *Jehan et Blonde (verse *romans d'aventure*), and La *Fole Largece (a *fabliau).

Beaumarchais, PIERRE-AUGUSTIN CARON DE (1732–99), dramatist, son of a Paris clock-maker named Caron. He received little education, being intended for his father's trade, but obtained (1755) a minor post in the royal household, married a rich widow, and took the name Beaumarchais from a property she owned. He lost his wife (and her fortune) soon afterwards, but his talent as a harpist earned him the post of music-master to Louis XV's daughters. Enriched by a service rendered to the financier Pâris-Duverney (*v. Pâris, Les frères*), he bought a brevet of nobility and a higher office, and plunged into a series of political and financial intrigues and adventures, involving more than one spell in prison. A sensational law-suit, relating to accounts between the deceased Pâris-Duverney and himself, provoked his four brilliant *Mémoires* (1773–4) about his dealings with the magistrate Goezman's wife with a view to an audience with her husband. A skilful blend of gaiety, irony, reason, and eloquence, they won public opinion to his side and carried him to the height of popularity (though he lost his case). His subsequent multifarious activities included: secret-service missions to England and elsewhere; organizing supplies and equipping ships for the insurgent American colonies; a successful defence of dramatists' financial rights against the chicanery of the actors' companies; the difficult—and unremunerative—task of issuing the famous Kehl edition of *Voltaire. During the Revolution, though an agent of the *Comité de salut public, he was in constant danger as a suspected *émigré*.

By way of diversion he wrote plays: *Eugénie* (1767; a girl is lured into a mock marriage by an English noble, who deserts her, but finally repents of his misdeeds); *Les Deux Amis, ou le Négociant de Lyon* (1770), an unsuccessful romantic drama; *Le *Barbier de Séville* (1775) and *Le *Mariage de Figaro* (1784), the two great comedies on which his fame rests; their very inferior sequel *L'Autre Tartufe, ou la Mère coupable* (1792), in which Figaro reappears, but prosy and morose (in the Tartufe of this play, by name Bégearss, he pilloried the advocate Bergasse, his bitter enemy); also the opera *Tavare* (1787), of little merit, though of temporary political importance.

As a man, he won renown but not respect, for, though amiable and generous, he was something of an adventurer. As a dramatist, he was important not only for his bold social satire and because he revived the comedy of intrigue that had suffered eclipse since Molière, but also as the first playwright to apply fully Diderot's theories of stagecraft and acting.

Beaumont, CHRISTOPHE DE (1703-81), archbishop of Paris, was active in repressing works critical of Catholicism (*v. Rousseau, J.-J.*).

Beaumont, MME DE, *v. Leprince de Beaumont.*

Beaumont de la Bonnière, GUSTAVE-AUGUSTE DE (1802–66), man of letters and politician (ambassador in London for some months in 1848), was sent (1831) with *Tocqueville to study the American penal system and collaborated in the ensuing report. His novel *Marie, ou l'Esclavage aux États-Unis* (1835) was based on his observation of slave life in America.

Beauvoir, **Roger de**, *pseudonym of* EUGÈNE-AUGUSTE-ROGER DE BULLY (1806–66), minor writer, a 'dandy' and one of the extreme *Romantics. His numerous works include *L'Écolier de Cluny, ou le Sophisme* (1832), a novel of medieval horrors said to have given Dumas *père* the plot of *La *Tour de Nesle*; and *Le Chevalier de Saint-Georges* (1840, 4 vols.).

Beauvoir, SIMONE DE (1908–   ), whose name is indissolubly linked with *Existentialism and with Sartre, with whom she has been associated since 1929, has herself produced a considerable body of work. Her writings include essays, e.g. *Pyrrhus et Cinéas* (1944) and *Pour une morale de l'ambiguité* (1947), both concerned with the ethical implications of Existentialism, *Privilèges* (1944), *L'Existentialisme et la sagesse des nations* (1948), *Le Deuxième Sexe* (1949, 2 vols.), *La Longue Marche* (1957), *Brigitte Bardot et le mythe de Lolita* (1960), *Djamila Boupacha* (1962; with Gisèle Halimi), *La Vieillesse* (1970); one play, *Les Bouches inutiles* (1945); a number of fictional works, largely centred on her own *milieu* and her preoccupations as a left-wing intellectual, e.g. *L'Invitée* (1943), *Le Sang des autres* (1945), *Tous les hommes sont mortels* (1946), *Les Mandarins* (1954; awarded the *Prix Goncourt*), *Les Belles Images* (1966), *La Femme rompue* (1967; short stories); and *Une Mort très douce* (1964), a remarkable account of her mother's terminal illness. Her most substantial publication in recent years has been four volumes of autobiography: *Mémoires d'une jeune fille rangée* (1958), *La Force de l'âge* (1960), *La Force des choses* (1963), *Tout compte fait* (1972).

Beaux-Arts, Académie des; **École des**, *v. Académie royale de Peinture et de Sculpture*.

Béchellerie, La, *v. France, A.*

Becket, Vie de Saint Thomas, *v. Thomas Becket*.

Beckett, SAMUEL BARCLAY (1906–   ), a figure of major contemporary importance in both the English and the French languages; winner of the *Prix Nobel* (1969). He studied modern languages at Trinity College in his native Dublin, then taught English at the *École normale supérieure* (1928–30; his close friendship

with James Joyce began at this time) and French at Trinity College (1930–2). Since 1932 he has lived mostly in France and many of his works were written first in French. In the 1930s, he published a study of Proust (1931), wrote poetry, and translated the work of French poets into English. 1938 saw the publication in English of his novel *Murphy* and this has been followed, in the post-war period, by a series of other prose works: *Malone meurt* (1951), *Molloy* (1951), *L'Innommable* (1953), *Nouvelles et textes pour rien* (1955), *From an abandoned work* (1957; collected as *D'un ouvrage abandonné* with *Assez* and *Bing* in *Têtes-mortes*, 1967), *Watt* (1958), *Le Dépeupleur* (1970), *Mercier et Camier* (1970). But his greatest impact has probably been made in the theatre, where *En attendant Godot* (Paris 1953; Eng. *Waiting for Godot*, London 1955) not only echoed the widespread feeling that man, in order to compensate for a life which seems to have no meaning in itself, turns with unfounded hope towards some transcendent justification for his existence, but also did so in a theatrical form which, by its break with traditional usage, marked Beckett as a master of the Theatre of the Absurd (*v. Theatre of the 19th and 20th cs.*). Subsequently, he seems to have worked out the implications of this situation in plays where language alone provides a defence (inadequate) against the emptiness and meaninglessness of human relations and of life itself: *Fin de partie* (1957; Eng. *End Game*, 1958), *Embers* (radio play, 1959; Fr. *Cendres*), *Krapp's Last Tape* (1958; Fr. *La Dernière Bande*, 1960), *Happy Days* (1961; Fr. *Oh! les beaux jours*, 1963), *All that fall* (1957, commissioned for radio by the B.B.C.; Fr. *Tous ceux qui tombent*, 1963), *Play* (1963; Fr. *Comédie*, 1964), *Come and go* (1965; Fr. *Va et vient*, 1966). With *Silence* and, particularly, *Breath* (1970), a piece lasting for about 30 seconds, during which the only sound, apart from a breath being drawn in and expelled, is a 'faint brief cry', Beckett seemed near to the Theatre of Nothingness. But 1973 saw the creation of *Not I*, an astonishing verbal flow in which, though discourse is fragmented, an attempt is made, through language, to impose an order on experience.

Beckford, WILLIAM, *v. Vathek.*

Becque, HENRI (1837–99), dramatist. His *Les *Corbeaux* (1882) and *La *Parisienne* (1885), in which plot was subordinated to the attempt to present a faithful picture of life (a new dramatic technique), helped to extend *Naturalism to the stage (*v. Théâtre Libre*). His other plays include *La Navette* (1879); *Les Honnêtes Femmes* (1880); and *Les Polichinelles* (1910), an unfinished study of the financial world.

Béda, NOËL (d. 1536), syndic of the *Sorbonne, head of the *Collège de Montaigu (from 1499), and one of the chief opponents of *Évangélisme. He questioned—not without reason—the orthodoxy of Marguerite de Navarre. François Ier banished him for his officiousness to the *Mont-Saint-Michel, where he died. Rabelais ridiculed his obesity by crediting him with a work *de optimitate triparum* (*v. Pantagruel*).

Bédier, JOSEPH (1864–1938), an eminent and influential medievalist, threw new light on the origins of the *fabliaux (*Les Fabliaux*, 1893) and the *chansons de geste (*Les Légendes épiques*, 1903–13, 4 vols.), published a Modern French reconstitution of the primitive *Tristan romance (*Le Roman de Tristan et Iseut*, 1900), and edited and translated the *Chanson de Roland (1921). *v.* also *Histories of French Literature.*

Béguin, ALBERT (1901–57), critic and journalist of Swiss birth, editor of *Esprit* (*v.* Mounier) from 1950. His works include *L'Âme romantique et le rêve* (1937) and studies of Nerval, Bloy, Balzac, Ramuz, Bernanos. *v. Critics and Criticism*, 3; *Resistance.*

Béjart, JOSEPH; MADELEINE; ARMANDE, *v. Molière.*

Bel-Ami (1885), a novel by Maupassant. Georges Duroy ('Bel-Ami') is an unscrupulous careerist with an unfailing attraction for women. His fortunes are at a low ebb when he accepts a chance offer of a newspaper post. He exploits his charm, becomes editor of an important paper, and marries the millionaire proprietor's daughter—but will clearly be no more faithful to her than to the other female rungs in his career. A brutally frank picture of a selfish, sensual man, also of journalistic life.

Belgiojoso, CRISTINA TRIVULZIO, PRINCESSE (1808–71), a mid-19th-c. Italian patriot, actively involved in the *Risorgimento*, and for a time a figure in Parisian intellectual circles. Her afternoon receptions were celebrated, and she inspired several passions.

Belin, the ram in the *Roman de Renart.

Bel Inconnu, Le, *v. Guinglain.*

Bélisaire, *v. Marmontel.*

Bélise, in Molière's *Les *Femmes savantes.*

Bella, *v. Giraudoux.*

Belleau, REMI (1528–77), a poet of the *Pléiade. His works include *Les Petites Inventions* (1556), short poems describing flowers, fruits, and insects; a *Bergerie* (1565 and 1572; prose and verse), containing pleasant descriptions of the seasons (inc. *Avril*, a famous *chanson); *Amours et nouveaux échanges des pierres précieuses* (1576), curious poems describing the origins and secret virtues of precious stones; also a verse translation (1566) of the pseudo-Anacreon (recently publ. by H. Estienne) and *La Reconnue*, an unfinished comedy based largely on Plautus's *Casina*. Ronsard called him 'le Peintre de la nature'. *v. Religious Writings*, 2.

Belle au bois dormant, La, *v. Perrault.*

Belle Dame sans merci, La, *v. Chartier, A.*

Belle et la Bête, La, the tale of Beauty and the Beast, originally in the *Contes marins* (1740–1, 4 vols.) of Mme de Villeneuve (d. 1755); abridged by Mme Leprince de Beaumont for her *Magasin des enfants* (1757).

Belleforest, FRANÇOIS DE (1530–83), a bad poet but a good literary hack, responsible, with Pierre Boaistuau or Boistuau (compiler and translator; d. 1566), for the *Histoires tragiques* (from 1559), mainly translations of *Bandello's *Novelle. v.* also *Pastoral.*

Belle Hélène, La, v. Offenbach.

Bellerophon, **H.M.S.,** *v. Napoleon;* O'*Meara.*

Bellerose, *stage-name of* PIERRE LE MESSIER (17th c.), an actor at the *Hôtel de Bourgogne* from *c.* 1622, noted as the first to introduce an element of grace and tenderness into French acting.

Belloy, PIERRE-LAURENT BUIRETTE, *known as* DORMONT DE (1727–75), dramatist, author of *Le Siège de Calais* (1764), a very successful patriotic tragedy. His other tragedies, mediocre and mainly historical, include *Gaston et Bayard, Gabrielle de Vergy, Pierre le Cruel.*

Belphégor, one of La Fontaine's *Contes et Nouvelles;* based on a story by Machiavelli.

Satan, aware that most souls in Hell attribute their damnation to their spouses, sends the devil Belphégor to investigate the earthly state of matrimony. When Belphégor, in human guise, takes a wife (to complete his inquiries), she proves such a shrew that he is thankful to escape back to Hell.

Belphégor is also the title of a work by Benda.

Benda, JULIEN (1867–1956), critic and essayist of Jewish parentage, studied classics, history, and philosophy at the *Sorbonne.* His works are the uncompromising expression of his conviction that human conduct should be dictated by reason, and of his contempt for any emotional or intuitional approach to life and literature (e.g. modern attempts to get behind words to the 'pure idea'). His views can be studied, evolving or fully mature, in the autobiographical *La Jeunesse d'un clerc* (1936) and *Un Régulier dans le siècle* (1938); *Dialogues à Byzance* (1900), on the *Dreyfus case; Le Bergsonisme, ou une Philosophie de la mobilité* (1912), an intellectual attack on Bergson; and two challenging works, *Belphégor* (1918) and *La Trahison des clercs* (1927). The first, an *Essai sur l'esthétique de la présente société française,* asserts that neither modern writers nor their readers understand the meaning of intellectual pleasure; for them, literature is solely a matter of emotion and sensation (a theme elaborated, with much hard hitting at Valéry, Gide, etc., in *La France byzantine,* 1945). The second maintains that not only have passions been mobilized as political forces during the last century (class hatred, anti-Semitism, etc.), but 'les clercs', the intelligentsia, formerly detached from politics, dedicated to intellectual pursuits (Goethe) and persuaded that conduct should be guided by abstract principles (Voltaire, Renan, Kant, etc.), have betrayed their own kind by descending into the arena.

Benedictines. For their special connection with literature *v. Maurists.*

Benoit, PIERRE (1886–1962), author of over 40 novels of adventure, notably *Kœnigsmark* (1918), *L'Atlantide* (1919).

Benoît de Sainte-Maure or **Sainte-More,** a 12th-c. poet, probably of Sainte-Maure (Touraine), author of the *Roman de Troie,* also, at the request of Henry II, of a history (43,000 octosyllables) of the dukes of Normandy down to 1135 (*cf. Wace*), based on the Latin chronicles.

Benserade, ISAAC DE (1612–91), poet, wrote several mediocre tragedies, then won fame, wealth, and election to the *Académie* as a composer (1651–81) of *ballets* or masques (many with music by Lulli) for performance at court. His translation (1676) of Ovid's *Metamorphoses* was less successful. In 1649, during the *Fronde*, the literary world was divided by such a fierce dispute about whether or not his sonnet on *Job* was superior to Voiture's sonnet on *Uranie* that Corneille had finally to intervene as peacemaker.

Béranger, PIERRE-JEAN, *self-styled* DE (1780–1857), writer of *chansons*, in his lifetime accounted the national poet of France. He owed his great popularity to a facility for turning simple, at times ribald, jests and pleasures into witty, gay, and lilting verses (though his later songs were often mordant political satires). Born in Paris, of humble parentage, he picked up an education (while living at an aunt's inn in Picardy) and became a printer's apprentice. In 1804 his verses were seen by Lucien Bonaparte, who procured him a small pension. Later, a minor clerical post at the University gave him the freedom to write the poems collected in *Chansons morales et autres* (1815). This included the famous *Le Roi d'Yvetot* (from the 14th to 16th cs. the lords of Yvetot, in Normandy, were exempt from duties of vassalage to the crown and were called *rois*), a song about the genial, easy-going ruler of a small contented country.

> [Il] n'agrandit point ses États,
> Fut un voisin commode,
> Et, modèle des potentats,
> Prit le plaisir pour code.

It was first sung at Le *Caveau c.* 1813, when France was growing weary of Napoleon's despotism and ambition. His *Chansons*, 2ᵉ *recueil* (1821), satirizing the abuses of the Restoration, cost him his post and a term in prison, where he began *Chansons nouvelles* (1825). Further imprisonment and a heavy fine (this time for expressing Bonapartist sympathies; *v.* *Légende napoléonienne*) rewarded *Chansons inédites* (1828). But persecution only increased his popularity, and his fine was paid by general subscription. After *Chansons nouvelles et dernières* (1833) he lived in retirement.

Berçuire, *v. Bersuire*.

Bérénice, a tragedy by Racine, produced 1670. The theme is from a passage in Suetonius telling how Titus, after promising to marry Berenice, queen of Judaea, on becoming emperor sent her away 'invitus invitam'. Racine's play was considered superior to Corneille's *Tite et Bérénice* on the same theme. There is said to be no truth in the story that the duchesse d'Orléans (*Henriette d'Angleterre) contrived for them to work simultaneously on the same subject, each unaware that the other was doing so.

Titus, having just succeeded Vespasian, is about to marry Bérénice. His friend Antiochus, king of Commagene, who has long secretly loved her, decides to quit Rome and takes leave of her. Titus learns that Roman opinion will not tolerate his marriage to a foreigner, and resolves to part from his beloved Bérénice. He asks Antiochus to tell her. She indignantly refuses to accept dismissal from anyone but Titus himself. From his lips, she accepts the verdict of Rome with dignified resignation, and bids him farewell. Antiochus hopes to follow her, but she puts him aside, resolved to love no one after Titus.

Bergerac, CYRANO DE, *v. Cyrano de Bergerac*.

Bergeret, Monsieur, the provincial professor in A. France's *L'Histoire contemporaine* (1896–1901), a keen satire of French life (politics, religion, monarchism, militarism, the *Dreyfus case; the various *coteries*, strata, and contending factions in a provincial town)—less a novel than a series of character-revealing discussions. There are four volumes: *L'Orme du mail* (1896; the *mail* is the avenue where the townspeople gossip on summer evenings); *Le Mannequin d'osier* (1897; Mme Bergeret's dressmaker's dummy—a symbol of the bullying M. Bergeret endures); *L'Anneau d'améthyste* (1899; two local clerics contend for a vacant see); *M. Bergeret à Paris* (1901; M. Bergeret quits the provinces for a chair at the *Sorbonne*).

Berger extravagant, Le, v. Sorel, C.

Bergotte, in Proust's *A la recherche du temps perdu*, a famous novelist, a hero to young Marcel.

Bergson, HENRI-LOUIS (1859–1941), philosopher, son of a Jewish musician and an Englishwoman, a teacher by profession, and from 1900 a professor at the *Collège de France*. His chief works were: *Essai sur les données immédiates de la conscience* (1888; Eng. trans. *Time and Free Will*); *Matière et mémoire* (1896); *L'Évolution créatrice* (1907); *Les Deux Sources de la morale et de la religion* (1932). He wrote many other monographs and lectures, some collected in *L'Énergie spirituelle* (1919); also *Le Rire, Essai sur la signification du comique* (1900). He was awarded the *Prix Nobel* (1927).

His philosophy profoundly influenced modern thought and literature (both creative and critical). Broadly speaking, he sought, as he said, 'to rebuild the bridge between metaphysics and science'—a breach created by Kant and widened by subsequent development of the sciences. Whereas Kant thought of science as mathematical physics, Bergson examined the non-mathematical sciences (biology, physiology, psychology) and sought in them a fresh approach to metaphysical problems. He observed that in describing change philosophers have taken time into account only as a conventional, spatial measure, ignoring real duration, *la durée réelle*, 'what each of us apprehends when he reflects on his own conscious life' (A. D. Lindsay); and he perceived that organic change can only be studied by methods that recognize this duration. He saw in psychical life, besides causal elements, an element of spontaneity or freedom, a subject treated in his *Essai sur les données immédiates de la conscience*. This freedom expresses itself in action in space, introducing something new and unpredictable amid the general laws of nature, deflecting the course of events. Mind thus acts on matter, and in a mysterious way, which is examined in *Matière et mémoire*.

The body, he contends, and particularly the brain, is solely an instrument of action. The brain, in perception, receives external impulses and places these in relation with motor mechanisms selected with more or less freedom. Above all, memories are not stored in the brain. The orthodox explanation of memory by 'physical traces' is plausible only because the word 'memory' is used in two quite different senses. There is habit-memory, as when we are said to remember how to play the piano; and there is pure memory or memory proper, the awareness of past experiences. Habit-memory depends on the brain. Pure memory does not: it is a psychical function. Past psychical states have the same sort of independent survival as the material world. In relation to pure memory, the brain is more the organ of forgetting than of remembering, for its function is to exclude from consciousness all but that small segment of our past which is relevant to the practical activity of the moment; and it is at this point of connection between memory and perception that spirit influences matter. (His presidential address to the London Society for Psychical Research—1913, in the Society's *Proceedings*—elucidates his doctrine.)

He was then led to consider various theories of evolution (*L'Évolution créatrice*). He finds it incredible that complex structures so similar (e.g. the eye) should have evolved in species that have developed along such divergent lines as the mollusc and the vertebrate if evolution were wholly due, as Darwin holds, to the preservation and accumulation of chance variations; and he finds in an original impulse of life, a common effort on the part of individual organisms (*l'élan vital*), that psychological factor in evolution which is the profound cause of the variations. But evolution cannot be explained by the efforts of isolated individuals; possibly development is effected by the effort of the species as a whole and the variations appear at the same time in all or most of its members, so that the whole is in some sense an individual (like a hive of bees). In this connection, he shows that instinctive and intelligent life are divergent directions, not different stages, of development. But intelligence, no less than instinct, has primarily a biological function: it presents to us a simplified and, above all, a specialized picture of the world, adapted to meet the needs of action, especially manipulative action. In so far as he is an intelligent animal, man is not *homo sapiens*, but *homo faber*. Ultimate reality (whose essential feature is *la durée réelle*) is not revealed to us by instinct or intelligence, but by a third function, intuition.

His conception of the world, set out in the same work, is of two opposing currents: inert matter pursuing its downward course; organic life striving upwards, overcoming the obstacles matter places in its way, displaying a single original impulse, but following divergent lines of development.

In *Le Rire*, he infers from an examination of comic situations and characters that at the root of the comic element is a certain rigidity or inadaptability to circumstances or conventions which causes a conscious being to behave like a mechanism, and that laughter is the means by which society tends to correct this defect.

He wrote in a brilliant, fluid, often poetical, style, using vivid metaphors and ingenious similes. These, it may be thought, sometimes gain assent to propositions which would hardly carry conviction if expressed in plain prose.

Berl, EMMANUEL (1892-1976), author of essays sternly critical of the *bourgeoisie* and the *bourgeois* mentality (*Mort de la pensée bourgeoise*, 1931, etc.), novels (notably *Sylvia*, 1952; romanticized autobiography), an *Histoire de l'Europe*, etc.

Berlioz, LOUIS-HECTOR (1803-69), composer, introduced the *Romantic spirit into French music, notably in his *Symphonie fantastique* (in five 'episodes in the life of an artist'), written after he saw and fell in love with the English actress Harriet Smithson (when she played

Ophelia in Paris in 1830), who became his wife. He was music critic on the *Journal des Débats* (1838-63) and published several collections of essays, also *Mémoires* (1870).

Bernadette, St. (1844-79; canonized 1933), Bernadette Soubirous, a peasant girl of Lourdes (Hautes-Pyrénées) to whom the Virgin is said to have appeared several times in 1858 while she was guarding sheep on the mountain-side. The happenings, and the tales of miraculous cures attendant on them, aroused both elation and scepticism, but after inquiry Rome pronounced the apparitions authentic. Bernadette became a nun; and Lourdes has become a great, and highly organized, place of pilgrimage. The story inspired *Zola's *Lourdes*.

Bernadotte, JEAN-BAPTISTE-JULES, *v. Maréchal*.

Bernanos, GEORGES (1888-1948), novelist and polemicist, of partly Spanish descent. He was active in the *Action française* group (as a *camelot du roi*, then as a journalist), served in the 1914-18 war, and after 1926 lived mainly by his pen. He subsequently broke with the *Action française* and went to Majorca. Despite his Catholic and Royalist sympathies, he denounced the atrocities committed by Franco's side in the Spanish Civil War. In 1938, shocked and disgusted by the Munich agreement with Hitler, he emigrated to S. America, where he remained till 1945.

The main theme of his novels, which all introduce the supernatural and are written with great force, is the struggle between the warring forces of good and evil in the souls of a saintly elect, especially humble village priests. They include, notably, *Sous le soleil de Satan* (1926), which made his name, *Le Journal d'un curé de campagne* (1936), and *Monsieur Ouine* (1946; written much earlier); also *La Joie* (1929), *Un Crime* (1935), *Nouvelle Histoire de Mouchette* (1937). As a polemicist, he fought hypocrisy of every kind. *La Grande Peur des bien-pensants* (1931), an appreciation of the anti-Semite Drumont, defined his own view of Royalism and Catholicism and reflected his disgust with the modern world. *Les Grands Cimetières sous la lune* (1937) was an indictment of Franco and the Church in Spain. Mention should also be made of his writings (e.g. *Lettre aux Anglais*, 1942) and broadcasts (from Brazil) during the 1939-45 war. His *Correspondance* (2 vols.) appeared in 1971.

Bernard, St. (1091-1153), founder of the Cistercian abbey of Clairvaux, one of the four 'Latin Fathers', and among the most influential ecclesiastics in Europe. He secured the recognition of Innocent II as pope (1130), relentlessly opposed Abélard, and preached the 2nd Crusade (1147-9). He left some remarkable letters and treatises, and was a founder of Latin hymnody. There are French translations, made *c.* 1200, of 84 of his Latin sermons.

Bernard, Charles de, *pseudonym of* CHARLES-BERNARD DU GRAIL DE LA VILLETTE (1805-50), journalist and novelist, a friend of Balzac, remembered for his novel *Gerfaut* (1838).

Bernard, CLAUDE (1813-78), experimental physiologist. His widely read *Introduction à l'étude de la médecine expérimentale* (1865) argued that the art of medicine was a matter of observation and experiment, and that natural phenomena were explicable in the light of environment and precedent causes. His theories, imperfectly comprehended, were applied by Zola to the art of the novel; *v. Naturalism*.

Bernard, JEAN-JACQUES, *v. Bernard, T.*

Bernard, JEAN-MARC (1881-1915), *fantaisiste* poet, founder (1909) of *Les Guêpes*, a satirical and critical review. He is remembered for the love and nature poems of *Sub tegmine fagi* (1913). His moving poem *De profundis*, written just before he was killed in action, is an anthology piece. His *Œuvres complètes* (1923, 2 vols.) include poetry, essays, and criticism.

Bernard, PIERRE-JOSEPH (1710-75), 'Gentil-Bernard' (a nickname he owed to Voltaire), wrote *vers de société* and an *Art d'aimer* after Ovid. He was a *protégé* of Mme de Pompadour.

Bernard, (1) TRISTAN (1866-1947), journalist and playwright, a noted *raconteur* and wit, author of successful comedies, farces, and *vaudevilles, gently poking fun at *bourgeois* life, e.g. *Le Fardeau de la liberté* (1897), *L'Anglais tel qu'on le parle* (1899), *Un Mari pacifique* (1901), *Triplepatte* (1905; with André Godfernaux, 1864-1906), *Le Petit Café* (1912), *Embrassez-moi* (1923); also of *Les Mémoires d'un jeune homme rangé* (1899), a novel; (2) his son JEAN-JACQUES (1888-1972), dramatist, author of *Le Feu qui reprend mal* (1921), *Martine* (1922), *L'Invitation au voyage* (1924), *L'Âme en peine* (1926), *Notre-Dame d'En-Haut* (1951), etc. He makes skilful use of modern theories of the unconscious; and he often uses meaningful silence, rather than words, to convey a character's feelings.

Bernard de Ventadour (*fl. c.* 1145-80), often deemed the greatest of the *troubadours*, was a singer at various courts, including that of Eleanor of Aquitaine. His poems, exclusively *chansons* and *tensons* (*v. Jeu parti*), combine technical mastery with passionate feeling; he is a notable exponent of the *trobar leu*, or 'simple' style of Provençal poetry. According to tradition, he was the son of a baker at the castle of Ventadour and ended his days at the abbey of Dalon.

Bernardin de Saint-Pierre, JACQUES-HENRI (1737-1814), naturalist and writer. Having lost a post as military engineer through his insubordinate temper, he led a vagrant life, travelling all over Europe to promote a scheme for the regeneration of society, often without resources. In 1768 he joined an expedition to Madagascar, but disembarked at the *Île de France, working there for a time as an engineer. His *Voyage à l'Île de France* (1773), published after his return, was only moderately successful, but his *Études de la*

Nature (1784; the famous *Paul et Virginie appeared first in the 1787 ed.), a pioneer work in the literature of the picturesque, brought him fame and profit. His other works include *La Chaumière indienne* (1791; a traveller seeking truth and wisdom finds them only in the hut of an Indian pariah); *Les Harmonies de la Nature* (1815), a poor echo of the *Études*. Briefly curator of the **Jardin des Plantes* (1792) and a member of the **Institut de France* from 1795, he was decorated and pensioned by Napoleon.

Adventurer, malcontent, and visionary, he found consolation for his hatred of society in a love of nature, which he depicted with careful accuracy but sought to explain in the light of sentiment rather than science. He was a friend of the mature J.-J. Rousseau (whose life he wrote, 1820), and developed his doctrines unintelligently and to extremes. Adducing the order and harmony of nature as an argument against atheism, he saw in it all sorts of providential arrangements, some quite absurd (the melon's ribs were designed for its division into portions). But some of his descriptions of natural scenes, written in a rich, supple style, have great charm, and his pictures of the sea and the tropics were something quite new. In his feeling for the melancholy aspects of nature he was a precursor of Chateaubriand.

Bernhardt, SARAH-HENRIETTE-ROSINE (1845–1923), a great actress, noted for her 'golden voice'. She made her *début* in 1862 and acted frequently (1862–80) at the **Comédie-Française* (though never permanently associated with it), and also much abroad. Latterly, she was her own manager in Paris, in the end at her own *Théâtre Sarah Bernhardt*. Her great parts included *Phèdre, *Doña Sol, **Adrienne Lecouvreur*, La Tosca and Fédora (*v. Sardou*), Marguerite (in *La *Dame aux camélias*), and—one of her greatest triumphs—Napoleon's son in *L'*Aiglon*. She also played Shakespeare's Cordelia in French (1872) and later Hamlet. Even after she lost a leg (1915) she still acted on occasion, appearing last in the name-part

of M. Rostand's *La Gloire* (1921)—specially written to allow her to remain seated. She published *Mémoires de ma vie* (1907).

Bernier, FRANÇOIS (*c.* 1625–88), physician, traveller, and a prominent *libertin, wrote *Voyages* (1699; on his travels in the East and India, where he was physician to Aurung-zeb) and philosophical works, e.g. *Abrégé de la philosophie de Gassendi* (1678; written for Mme de La Sablière), *Traité du libre et du volontaire* (1685).

Bernis, FRANÇOIS–JOACHIM, ABBÉ DE (1715–94), 'Babet la Bouquetière', so nicknamed by Voltaire because in his earlier years he frequented the duchesse du Maine's court at Sceaux and wrote light, flowery verses. He was admitted to the *Académie (1744). A *protégé* of Mme de Pompadour, he became minister of foreign affairs (1757) during the Seven Years War, proved unequal to the task, and was dismissed (1758)—though not disgraced, for he retired with a cardinal's hat and was soon archbishop of Albi, and later ambassador in Rome. His memoirs show Mme de Pompadour in her political role.

Bernstein, HENRY (1876–1953), author of closely constructed, 'powerful' dramas, e.g. *La Rafale* (1905), *Le Voleur* (1907), *Samson* (1907), *L'Assaut* (1912), *Le Secret* (1913), *Judith* (1922), *La Galerie des glaces* (1924), *Évangéline* (1952).

Berny, MME DE, *v. Dilecta, La.*

Béroalde de Verville, FRANÇOIS (1558–1612), a canon of Tours (from 1593), wrote a romance (*Les Aventures de Floride*, 1594–1601) and probably *Le Moyen de parvenir* (1610), the fantastic account of a symposium at which various grave personages, ancient and modern (e.g. Solon, Plutarch; Commines, Budé), exchange Rabelaisian anecdotes interspersed with satires on monks, women, tax-collectors, etc. The tales are well told, but much of the satire is now obscure.

Béroul, v. *Tristan* (*Tristram*).

Berquin, ARNAUD (1747–91), author of idylls, romances, and, in particular, many volumes of children's stories (*berquinades*), notably *L'Ami des enfants* (1782–3). Some were translated into English and proved very popular. v. *Children's Reading.*

Berquin, LOUIS DE (d. 1529), an early leader of *Évangélisme*, translated works of Luther into French and, though protected by Marguerite de Navarre, was executed as a heretic.

Berry, CHARLES, DUC DE, v. *Bourbon* (3).

Bersuire or **Berçuire,** PIERRE (d. 1362). His translation of Livy (1352–6) was a work of wide influence. He met Petrarch when the latter came to France (1361).

Bertaut, JEAN (1552–1611), poet, reader to Henri III, then official court poet under Henry III and Henri IV; bishop of Séez (now Sées) from 1606. He imitated Ronsard and Desportes with less talent, but with more propriety in his love poems. His verses are pointed and polished, sometimes tender and melancholy, but lack vigour. As court poet and bishop he celebrated great events and wrote canticles on religious subjects and paraphrases of the Psalms. He confined himself in the main to quatrains and sixains of *alexandrines. His love poems were published, anonymously, in 1602, his serious poems in 1601. He wrote a well-known quatrain:

> Félicité passée
> Qui ne peux revenir,
> Tourment de ma pensée,
> Que n'ai-je, en te perdant, perdu
> le souvenir!

Berthe aux grands pieds, a *chanson de geste* about Berthe (wife of Pépin le Bref and mother of Charlemagne) by Adenet le Roi; a rehandling of an earlier *chanson.* It tells how on her wedding-night another woman was substituted by traitors for the true Berthe. Thus ousted from the throne,

Berthe wandered in the forest, suffering great hardships until the imposture was discovered by her mother. The story is also the theme of one of the *Miracles de Notre-Dame.*

The adventures of the boy Charlemagne, driven by sons of the false Berthe to take refuge among the Saracens under the name 'Mainet', are related in the *chanson* entitled *Mainet,* of which fragments survive.

Berthelot, MARCELIN (1827–1907), famous for his work in organic chemistry, a *savant* of wide philosophical outlook who saw philosophical systems as the expression of the contemporary state of scientific knowledge. Soon after his *La Chimie organique fondée sur la synthèse* (1860; on the results of his researches and their philosophic bearing) he was offered a specially created chair of organic chemistry at the *Collège de France,* which he held till his death. From 1870 he was also active in politics (minister of national defence, and of education). His subsequent works included *Les Origines de l'alchimie* (1885), an historical study, with translations, of Greco-Egyptian texts on alchemy; *La Chimie au moyen âge* (1893); *Science et philosophie* (1886) and *Science et morale* (1897), collected essays and addresses, containing, among other items, a good picture of Paris during the *Franco-Prussian war, also a vision of the world c. 2000 (natural energy will be harnessed to provide heat and power; the earth will be a garden, for man will live on chemical pills, and stock and crops—even vineyards—will not be needed; and aerial navigation will have abolished trade barriers and wars—provided some spiritual alchemy has been found to transform human nature). v. also *Dictionaries,* 1885–1903.

He was a lifelong friend of Renan and influenced his thought. Their *Correspondance* (1898) extends from 1847 to 1892.

Berthier, LOUIS-ALEXANDRE, v. *Maréchal.*

Bertillon, ALPHONSE (1853–1914), for many years head of the *Service d'identité*

judiciaire at the Paris *Préfecture de *police*, did much to improve the science of detection. His system of identification based on the measurement and classification of certain bony structures, especially the head (anthropometry or *Bertillonnage*), was used in France and elsewhere until superseded by fingerprints.

Bertin, a family famous for its association with the **Journal des Débats*, purchased (1799) by Bertin *aîné*—LOUIS-FRANÇOIS BERTIN (1766–1841)—and his brother LOUIS-FRANÇOIS BERTIN DE VAUX (1771–1842). Bertin *aîné* was succeeded as editor by his sons ARMAND (1801–54) and FRANÇOIS-ÉDOUARD (1797–1871), a landscape artist. *v.* also *Journal universel*.

Bertin, ANTOINE (1752–90), poet, b. in the **Île Bourbon and a friend of Parny, wrote three books of graceful elegies on his life and loves (*Les Amours*, 1780).

Bertrand, HENRI-GRATIEN, COMTE DE (1773–1844), one of Napoleon's most faithful generals, served him from the Egyptian campaign onwards and followed him to Elba and St. Helena. On St. Helena he wrote, at Napoleon's dictation, a record of the *Campagne d'Égypte et de Syrie* (1847, 2 vols.) and also kept his own journal (1948) of life there.

Bertrand, LOUIS, *known as* ALOŸSIUS (1807–41), poet, lived mainly in Paris from 1829, moving in the **Romantic circles dominated by Nodier, Hugo, and Sainte-Beuve, always poor and, latterly, consumptive. His fame rests on one work, *Gaspard de la nuit* (1842; written *c.* 1830), a collection of 'fantaisies à la manière de Rembrandt et de Callot'. An early example of the **prose poem, written in ornate and rhythmical language with touches of delicate naturalistic description, it forms a series of scintillating, often grotesque, images. It reflected the Romantic revival of interest in the Middle Ages, but its author has also been seen as a precursor of **Symbolism and **Surrealism.

Baudelaire, in the preface to his *Petits Poèmes en prose*, recognized Bertrand's influence on him.

Bertrand, LOUIS (1866–1941), novelist of French colonial life (Africa), e.g. *Le Sang des races* (1899), *La Cina* (1901), *Pépète le bien-aimé* (1904).

Bertrand de Bar-sur-Aube, a late 12th-c. poet, author of the **chanson de geste* of **Girart de Viane* and probably of **Aimeri de Narbonne*. He is said to have been the first to suggest grouping the *chansons de geste* in three main **cycles or *gestes*.

Bertrand de Born (*c.* 1140–*c.* 1215), a famous **troubadour* of Guyenne. His poems inflamed Prince Henry against his father Henry II of England, earning him a place in Dante's *Inferno* among the 'sowers of schism'. After Prince Henry's death, he supported Henry II and Richard I against Philippe II.

Bertrand et Raton, the monkey and the cat in La Fontaine's fable *Le Singe et le Chat*. The cat draws the chestnuts from the fire and the monkey eats them. The names are sometimes used proverbially.

Bertrand et Raton (1833) was one of Scribe's most successful historical comedies. The scene is Copenhagen in 1772. Bertrand van Rantzau is a wily statesman. Raton is a rich merchant, popular, easily led, and eager to rise in the world. Alleging that Raton has been unjustly imprisoned, Bertrand engineers a popular rising which overturns Struensee, the powerful prime minister—whereupon Bertrand steps into his shoes.

Bérulle, PIERRE DE, *v. Oratoire*.

Berwick, JAMES FITZJAMES, DUKE OF (1670–1734), **maréchal de France*, natural son of the duke of York (James II) by Arabella Churchill, was born and educated in France and created duke of Berwick when he came to England after his father's accession. He served in, and successfully commanded, French armies all over Europe and was killed at the siege of

Philippsburg. His mainly military *Mémoires*, written in a simple, natural style, include a description of the battle of the Boyne (where he fought against William III) and other items of interest to English readers.

Besançon, ALBÉRIC DE, *v. Alexandre le Grand* (1).

Besant de Dieu, Le, a didactic religious poem in octosyllabic couplets by Guillaume le Clerc (12th–13th c.). He takes as theme the *besant* or talent entrusted to each by God, reviews the failings of the various social classes of the day, and urges amendment.

Bescherelle, LOUIS-NICOLAS, *v. Dictionaries*, 1843–6.

Besenval, PIERRE-VICTOR, BARON DE (1722–91), a Swiss officer who served with distinction in the French army and spent much of his life at court. His *Mémoires* shed light on court personages and on society at the close of the *ancien régime*.

Bessières, JEAN-BAPTISTE, *v. Maréchal*.

Bestiaire, in medieval literature, a collection of tales about animals (largely of Greek and Latin origin), from which moral conclusions are drawn; common in France from the 12th c., also popular in England. The earliest surviving example (early 12th c.) is the *Bestiaire* of Philippe de Thaon, mainly in hexasyllabic couplets. It gives fantastic descriptions of animals, adding moral interpretations. The *Bestiaire d'amour* (*c.* 1250) of Richard de Fournival is less pious in its interpretations.

Bête humaine, La (1890), one of Zola's *Rougon-Macquart* novels; a melodramatic round of passion, jealousy, and homicidal mania, involving a stationmaster, his wife, and her engine-driver (Jacques *Lantier), redeemed by forcible descriptive writing—notably about trains. The strongest personality in the book is 'La Lison', the engine.

Bêtes, Les, *v. Gascar*.

Béthune, L'Anonyme de, *v. History*, 1.

Bettine (1851, in the *Revue des Deux Mondes*; 1853, in *Comédies et Proverbes*), a one-act prose comedy by Musset; produced 1851. Bettine's lover elopes with a shady princess; she is heartbroken, but by the end of the play is half inclined to marry a faithful old admirer.

Beuve (or **Boeve**) **de Haumtone**. The oldest version of this popular tale is represented by a 13th-c. *Anglo-Norman *chanson de geste* (3,850 ll.); there are adaptations in Continental French, English (*Sir Beves of Hamtoun*), and many other languages.

Beuve's mother procures the murder of her husband, Gui, earl of Southampton, by Doon, emperor of Germany, whom she then marries; the 10-year-old Beuve kills the emperor, and is sold as a slave. After many adventures (e.g. the defeat and conversion of the pagan giant Escopart), in which his horse Arundel and sword Murgleie figure prominently, Beuve marries Josiane, daughter of the king of Egypt. Their son Miles marries the daughter of Edgar, king of England, and succeeds him on the throne.

Beyle, HENRI; **Beylisme**, *v. Stendhal*.

Bèze, THÉODORE DE, in Latin BEZA (1519–1605), Protestant and humanist, Calvin's successor as head of the Church of Geneva, wrote an *Histoire ecclésiastique des Églises Réformées au royaume de France* (1580); verse translations of the Psalms; *Abraham sacrifiant* (1550), a play which is a landmark between the medieval *mystère* and Renaissance drama (*v. Tragedy*); and *L'Épître de Benoît Passavant* (1553), a lively satire. He maintained relations with English churchmen and presented the *Codex Bezae* of the Gospels and Acts to Cambridge University.

Bible, a term sometimes used in the Middle Ages for didactic or satirical verse treatises (*v. Guiot de Provins*). The *Bible* of Hugues II de Berzé (c. 1220), a former crusader, is a more serious work than Guiot's and condemns the worldly life of the day.

Bible, French versions of the. The earliest known translations from the Scriptures are two *Anglo-Norman versions of the Psalter of the early 12th c. In the second half of the 12th c. there was a prose version of the four books of Kings, in pure and elegant French; also a metrical version of the Old and New Testaments (c. 1190) by Herman de Valenciennes (also author of several lives of saints). The first translation of the whole Bible, with glosses on some parts, was made in the reign of Louis IX (1226-70); it was very uneven in quality. Then came the *Bible historiale* (c. 1295; very popular in the 14th c.) of Guyart des Moulins, a free translation of Peter Comestor's *Historia scolastica* (an epitome of the Bible narrative with some glosses) with additional translations of various Scriptural passages. In the 14th c. Jean de Vignai prepared, by order of Jeanne de Bourgogne, consort of Philippe VI, versions of the Epistles and Gospels in the offices of the day. After the Middle Ages the first complete translation of the Bible was that of Lefèvre d'Étaples (completed 1528). It was followed by that of Olivetan (1535), the first Protestant version, published, as corrected by Calvin, at the expense of the *Vaudois. This was a model for the Catholic 'Louvain' Bible (1550), and for a new Protestant translation (1588; still authoritative) by members of the *Compagnie des pasteurs de Genève*, including Bèze. Various translations were made in the 17th and 18th cs., notably a version of the N.T. (Amsterdam 1667; known as the 'Nouveau Testament de Mons' because of its Mons imprint) by Le Maître de Saci, A. Arnauld, and other *Port-Royal solitaries. Le Maître de Saci later added a translation of the O.T. (1672-95). A version of the N.T. (Trévoux 1702) by Richard Simon (1638-1712; a Hebrew scholar expelled from the *Oratoire for unorthodox views) was condemned by *Bossuet, who himself

translated parts of the Bible. The text most widely used in French Protestant churches today is still the complete translation (1744) by the Swiss theologian Jean-Frédéric Osterwald (1663-1747). *v.* also *Religious Writings*.

Bible de l'humanité, La (1864), by Michelet, a study of the origins and evolution of religious belief; written with fervour and a strong sense of discovery of the past (the effect of recent revelations by Orientalists and archaeologists), and of the present within the past.

Bible Guiot, *v. Guiot de Provins*.

Bibliographie de la France, La, or *Journal de la Librairie et de l'Imprimerie*, an official weekly list (f. 1811 by decree) of all the newly printed books delivered, by State requirement (the *Dépôt légal*), to the *Bibliothèque nationale.

Bibliographies. General bibliographies include Lanson's *Manuel bibliographique de la littérature française moderne, 1500-1900* (1909-14, 5 vols.; rev. and augm. ed. 1921), continued by J. Giraud's *Manuel de bibliographie littéraire pour les XVIe, XVIIe, et XVIIIe siècles français, 1921-35* (1939), *1936-1945* (1956), *1946-1955* (1970); the *Bibliographie des auteurs modernes de langue française (1801-   ) (1928-   ; vol. 22, to MORGAN, 1976, 1973), ed. by H. Talvart and J. Place, then by G.-G. Place; H. P. Thieme's *Bibliographie de la littérature française de 1800 à 1930* (1933, 3 vols.), continued under the same title by S. Dreher and M. Rolli, *1930-1939* (1948), and by M. L. Drevet, *1940-1949* (1954-5); *A Critical Bibliography of French Literature* (Syracuse 1947-   ; 6 vols. by 1980, from the Middle Ages to the 20th c.), ed. by D. C. Cabeen and others; R. Bossuat's *Manuel bibliographique de la littérature française du moyen âge* (1951) and its supplements; the *Bibliographie der französischen Literaturwissenschaft* (Frankfurt a. M. 1960-   ; 21 vols. to date, covering publications from 1956), ed. by O. Klapp; the *Bibliographie de la littérature française* *moderne* (*XVIe-XXe siècles*) (1963-), continued from 1967 as the *Bibliographie de la littérature française du moyen âge à nos jours* (17 vols. in all to date, covering publications from 1962), ed. by R. Rancœur; A. Cioranescu's *Bibliographie de la littérature française du XVIIe siècle* (1965-7, 3 vols.) and ...*du XVIIIe siècle* (1969-70, 3 vols.); *The Year's Work in Modern Language Studies* (1931-).

Bibliothèque bleue, collections (bound in blue) of popular tales and romances of chivalry (e.g. *Les Quatre Fils Aymon*, a prose version of *Renaud de Montauban; *Robert le Diable*), first issued *c.* 1665 by Jean Oudot, a bookseller of Troyes; almost the sole reading-matter in country districts before 1789. *v. Children's Reading.*

Bibliothèque de l'Arsenal, on the site of the ancient Arsenal in Paris, ranks second (after the *Bibliothèque nationale*) among the great French libraries. Originally the private library of Antoine-René d'Argenson (son of the marquis d'Argenson), a great collector of books who occupied the Hôtel de l'Arsenal in an official capacity, it was bought (1786) by the comte d'Artois (later Charles X), confiscated by the State during the Revolution, but preserved intact and thrown open to the public (1797) as the *Bibliothèque de l'Arsenal*. Later, quantities of other confiscated books and manuscripts were added. In the reign of Charles X the library reverted temporarily to his possession, but readers were still admitted. It now contains over a million printed books, *c.* 120,000 prints, and a fine collection of illuminated manuscripts, being particularly rich in medieval and dramatic literature. Curators have included Nodier (it was the scene of his *salon; *v. Romanticism*) and Heredia.

Bibliothèque de la Sorbonne, the name from 1897 for a part of the *Bibliothèque de l'Université de Paris* (now the *Bibliothèque universitaire*) housed from 1823 in the *Sorbonne*.

Bibliothèque de l'Université de Paris, *v. Bibliothèque universitaire.*

Bibliothèque de Saint-Victor, *v. Saint-Victor, Abbaye de.*

Bibliothèque Mazarine, a famous Paris library (of special interest to students of the 17th c.), housed in the Palais Mazarin with the *Institut de France* and attached to that body in 1945. Its nucleus was the fine library of theological and historical works (*c.* 40,000 vols.) left by Mazarin to the *Collège des Quatre-Nations*. It was greatly enriched by books and manuscripts confiscated by the State during the Revolution.

Bibliothèque nationale, the greatest library in France. It had its origin in the libraries formed by such French kings as Charles V, Charles VIII, Louis XI, and François Ier. François Ier assembled the various royal collections at *Fontainebleau and appointed Budé the first royal librarian. Foreign manuscripts were now acquired, e.g. a large quantity of Greek manuscripts was bought (1541) in Venice and the Oriental scholar Guillaume Postel was sent to gather manuscripts in the East. Under Louis XIV, this *Bibliothèque du Roi*—by now in Paris—was almost doubled in size by the efforts of Colbert, who installed it on its present site in the city. From 1692, it was thrown open to the public twice a week. The collection was further enriched under both Louis XV and Louis XVI. With the Revolution it became State property, securing the largest share of confiscated books and manuscripts. After the Revolution, renamed the *Bibliothèque nationale* (and the *Bibliothèque impériale* under the First and Second Empires), it was opened daily (all day from 1859) to accredited readers.

It now has eight departments: manuscripts; printed books (*c.* 6,000,000 vols.; under the terms of the *Dépôt légal*— originating in a decree issued in 1537 by François Ier—one copy of every book publ. in France must be deposited, also of prints and of all photographs intended for sale); periodicals; maps; music; prints; medals, coins, and antiquities; new acquisitions. *v. Enfer; Bibliographie de la France, La; Delisle.*

Bibliothèque rose, *v. Children's Reading.*

Bibliothèque Sainte-Geneviève, originally the library of the abbey of *Sainte-Geneviève in Paris, was richly endowed and re-established *c.* 1624, and has been open to the public since 1759. It became State property in 1791 and was known for a time as the *Bibliothèque du Panthéon.* It was attached in 1930 to the *Bibliothèque de l'Université de Paris* (*v. Bibliothèque universitaire*).

Bibliothèque universitaire, until recently the *Bibliothèque de l'Université de Paris.* Under this general title are grouped the great specialist libraries of the 13 *Universities of Paris and the various institutions affiliated to them (e.g. the *Bibliothèque de la Sorbonne,* the *Bibliothèque Sainte-Geneviève*), also such bequests as the *Bibliothèque Victor Cousin.*

Bicêtre, now a hospital, originally the site of a palace built 1204 on the outskirts of Paris by a bishop of Winchester (whence *Bicêtre*), then of a hospital (built 1634) for disabled soldiers. After the soldiers moved to the *Invalides (1675), it became one of the most foul and notorious prisons of the pre-Revolutionary era, used to confine lunatics (inc. those conveniently classed as such), paupers, thieves, debauched youths, etc., also those on their way to penal servitude or execution (as in Hugo's Le *Dernier Jour d'un condamné*). It was a scene of the September Massacres (*v. Revolutions,* 1 (1792)).

Bien-avisé et Mal-avisé, *v. Moralité.*

Bien Bon, Le, *v. Coulanges* (1).

Biens nationaux, Crown, Church, and private (e.g. of *émigrés* or suspects) lands and property confiscated by the State during the Revolution. *Cf. Assignats.*

Bigorne, in the *Dit de *Chicheface.*

Bijoux indiscrets, Les, *v. Diderot.*

Billaut, ADAM (1602–62), 'Maître Adam',

carpenter-poet of Nevers. His three collections of verse (entitled, after his instruments, *Chevilles, Vilebrequin,* and *Rabot*) earned him a pension from Richelieu and the respect of Corneille and Voltaire.

Biographie universelle ancienne et moderne, or *Biographie Michaud,* first published 1811–28, 1834–54 (52 vols. and 29 suppl. vols.) and later revised and augmented, is still one of the best-known dictionaries of biography. It was launched by a Paris bookseller, Louis-Gabriel Michaud (1772–1858), brother of J. Michaud (who was also associated in the venture). The articles were written by distinguished scholars and critics.

Bip, *v. Marceau, M.*

Biribi, *v. Darien.*

Biron, ARMAND-LOUIS, DUC DE, *v. Lauzun, A.-L.*

Biron, CHARLES, DUC DE (1562–1602), a brave soldier, friend of Henri IV, who made him *maréchal de France, duc et pair,* and governor of Burgundy. Over-ambitious, he was executed for conspiring against France with Spain and Savoy.

Birotteau, César, in Balzac's *Histoire de la grandeur et de la décadence de César Birotteau.*

Bizet, GEORGES (1838–75), composer. His works include music for the *opéras-comiques La Jolie Fille de Perth (1867; based on Scott's novel) and *Carmen (1875), incidental music for A. *Daudet's L'Arlésienne (1872), etc.

Blanc, LOUIS (1811–82), left-wing politician and historian, at first a journalist, was a leader of the 1848 *Revolution (*v. also Republics,* 2), which his *Histoire de Dix Ans* (1841; an indictment of the July Monarchy) helped to bring about (*cf.* Lamartine's *Histoire des Girondins*). On the suppression of the *ateliers nationaux* (which were not organized as advocated in his pamphlet *L'Organisation du travail*, 1839), he fled to England. He returned to political life in France in 1871. His other works include an *Histoire de la Révolution française* (1847–62; written with a socialistic bias, but still a good guide), an *Histoire de la Révolution de 1848* (1870), *Dix Années de l'histoire d'Angleterre* (1879–81; articles on English political life first publ. in *Le *Temps*).

Blancandin et l'Orgueilleuse d'amour, a *roman d'aventure* of the second half of the 13th c. A knight offends a proud lady by daring to kiss her, but later wins her by his prowess in rescuing her from her enemies.

Blanc et le Noir, Le (1764), by Voltaire, a philosophical tale ridiculing Manichaeism.

Rustan, a young Indian whose wonderful adventures appear to have brought about his death, finds he has been attended during life by a good and an evil genius. He wonders how such contrary principles can co-exist in the universe, and what use they are, since their influence is overridden by destiny. Finally he wakes up—it was all a dream.

Blanche, JACQUES-ÉMILE (1861–1942), son of Antoine-Émile Blanche, the alienist who treated Nerval and Maupassant; painter (well known for his portraits of writers) and art critic (*Propos de peintre*, 1919–28, etc.). His memoirs (*Les Cahiers d'un artiste*, 1914–19; *Mes modèles*, 1928) depict artistic and literary circles.

Blanche et Guiscard, a tragedy by Saurin, on the theme of James Thomson's *Tancred and Sigismunda* (itself based on a story in *Gil Blas*); produced 1763.

The dying king of Sicily names Guiscard his heir provided that he marries Constance, the king's sister. But Guiscard loves Blanche, daughter of the chancellor Siffrédi, and she him. Siffrédi urges Guiscard to marry Constance for reasons of State and, without his consent, announces the intended marriage. Blanche, in despair, agrees to be married at once, as her father wishes, to Osmont, constable of Sicily. Too late she discovers Guiscard's

fidelity. He and Osmont fight a duel; Osmont is killed, but not before he has turned his sword against Blanche and slain her.

Blanchefleur, (1) in some *chansons de geste* of the *Charlemagne cycle (e.g. *Macaire*), the emperor's consort; (2) in the *Geste des Lorrains*, Pépin's wife, taken by him from *Garin le Loherain; (3) *v. Floire et Blancheflor*.

Blanchot, MAURICE (1907–), a writer who has some affinity with Kafka and Beckett, and whose work, which has a philosophical quality, stems from a personal vision of the 'absurdity' of the human condition (for which he seeks symbols in the unreal and the fantastic) and a preoccupation with the inefficacy of language. His writings include novels heralding the *anti-roman*, e.g. *Thomas l'Obscur* (1941; 2nd version 1950), *Aminadab* (1942), *L'Arrêt de mort* (1948), *Celui qui ne m'accompagnait pas* (1953), *Le Dernier Homme* (1957), *L'Attente, l'Oubli* (1961); and essays evolving a critical approach which influenced the *nouvelle critique* (*v. Critics and Criticism*, 3), e.g. *La Part du feu* (1949), *L'Espace littéraire* (1955), *Le Livre à venir* (1959), *L'Entretien infini* (1969), *L'Amitié* (1971).

Blanqui, LOUIS–AUGUSTE (1805–81), revolutionary agitator, often imprisoned. His *Blanquiste* party helped to bring down the Second Empire after *Sedan. He was imprisoned for life after the fall of the *Commune, but released in 1879.

Blason, *v. Rhétoriqueurs*.

Blémont, Émile, *pseudonym of* LÉON-ÉMILE PETITDIDIER (1839–1927), critic, dramatist, poet. His (usually one-act, verse) plays include *Les Ciseaux* (1896), *Mariage pour rire* (1898). *Théâtre moliéresque et cornélien* (1898) and *Théâtre légendaire* (1908) are works of criticism.

Bloch, in Proust's *A la recherche du temps perdu*; a brilliant, vulgar, pushing young Jewish intellectual, transformed by the passage of time into a much-sought-after writer.

Bloch, JEAN–RICHARD (1884-1947), man of letters, of Jewish birth, wrote three outstanding novels: *Lévy* (1912) and *...et Cie* (1913), studies of Jewish character and enterprise; *La Nuit kurde* (1925), an Oriental tale in which the beginnings of racialism are evoked with great imaginative force.

Bloch, MARC (1886–1944), medieval historian, professor at the University of Strasbourg and, latterly, at the *Sorbonne; leader, with Febvre, of an important school of historiography (*v. History*, 4). His works include *Rois et serfs, un chapitre d'histoire capétienne* (1920); *Les Rois thaumaturges. Essai sur le caractère surnaturel attribué à la puissance royale* (1924); *Les Caractères originaux de l'histoire rurale française* (1931); *La Société féodale* (1939-40, 2 vols.); a notable *Apologie pour l'histoire, ou Métier d'historien* (1949; unfinished); also *L'Étrange Défaite* (1946), recollections of the 'phoney war' (1939-40). He was a Jew and was shot by the Nazis for his activities in the *Resistance.

Bloch, OSCAR, *v. Dictionaries*, 1932.

Blocus continental, Le, the general economic blockade of the British Isles by the continental powers decreed (21 Nov. 1806) by Napoleon. His object, the destruction of British sea-power and sea-trade, was not fully achieved, and the resentment aroused by its adverse effects on those continental powers whose economic welfare was bound up with that of Britain was an ultimate factor in his downfall.

Blondel, MAURICE (1861–1949), Neo-Catholic, Modernist philosopher (*cf. Duchesne; Laberthonnière; Le Roy, É.; Loisy*; and *v. Teilhard de Chardin*), a disciple of Ollé-Laprune. His chief work was *L'Action: Essai d'une critique de la vie et d'une science de la pratique* (1893). Modernist doctrines—condemned by Rome in 1907 as anti-Thomist (*v. Thomas*

Aquinas) and a 'synthesis of all the heresies'—sought to bring traditional Catholicism into closer relation with modern philosophical and scientific ideas.

Blondel de Nesle, a late 12th-c. Picard poet, an early imitator in N. French of the *troubadours* (*v. Lyric Poetry*, 1). Nothing is known of his life. According to legend he was a follower of Richard Cœur de Lion and, when his master was imprisoned in Austria (1192), succeeded in discovering him by singing beneath the prison window a song they had composed together. He paused half-way through, and Richard took up the tune. *v. Sedaine.*

Bloy, LÉON (1846–1917), became an author and a Roman Catholic after an encounter with Barbey d'Aurevilly. His writings (essays and studies, religious, historical, and critical; novels and tales—each 'un aveu arraché par la torture') were violent and vituperative, but of an arresting visionary quality. They include *Le Désespéré* (1886) and *La Femme pauvre* (1897), autobiographical novels; *Le Mendiant ingrat* (1898–1920, 8 vols.), his journal; *Le Pèlerin de l'absolu* (1914).

Blum, LÉON (1872–1950), essayist, critic, journalist (*v. Press*, 9), and statesman (*v. Front populaire*), of Jewish birth. Before he devoted himself entirely to politics, this Socialist intellectual had made his mark as a writer. His early literary and dramatic criticism in the *Revue blanche* (much of it collected in *En lisant*, 1906–9; *Au théâtre*, 1906–10) is impressively mature and well written. Even more so are the *Nouvelles Conversations de Goethe avec Eckermann* (1901; first publ. in the *Revue blanche*), discussions (on literature, aesthetics, political concepts, etc.) revealing his intellectual, moral, and political ideals. His last purely literary work was the masterly *Stendhal et le Beylisme* (1914 and 1930). His other writings include *Du mariage* (1907); *Souvenirs sur l'Affaire* (1935), an informative survey of the social scene during the *Dreyfus crisis; and an inspiring portrait of Jaurès (1937), whose private secretary he had been.

Boaistuau or **Boistuau**, PIERRE, *v. Belleforest*.

Bocage, *stage-name of* PIERRE–MARTINIEN TOUSEZ (1797–1863), a leading actor of the *Romantic era, most successful in drama and melodrama (as the melancholy lover), e.g. in plays by Dumas *père* (**Antony*, *La *Tour de Nesle*, etc.) and G. Sand.

Bochetel, JEAN (16th c.), made a fine verse translation of Euripides' *Hecuba*, printed 1544 by Estienne.

Bodel, JEAN (late 12th–early 13th c.), poet of *Arras, became a leper and retired to a lazar-house *c*. 1202 (*v. Congé*). His *Chanson des Saxons* (or *des Saisnes*), a *chanson de geste about Charlemagne's victorious campaign against the Saxons under their king Guiteclin (Witikind) and the loves of Roland's brother Baudoin and Guiteclin's wife Sebille, contains the often-quoted lines:

> Ne sont que iij matières à nul homme
> atandant,
> De France et de Bretaigne et de
> Rome la grant.

His *Jeu de Saint Nicolas* (in octosyllabic couplets interspersed with other metres) is a dramatic *miracle, partly religious, partly comic. A crusading army is destroyed by the Saracens, but, in answer to the prayer of the sole survivor, the saint forces three thieves (represented as citizens of Arras) to return treasure stolen from the Saracen king, whereupon he and his people are converted to Christianity.

Bodin, JEAN (1530–96), political philosopher, a friend of Pibrac, was professor of Roman law at Toulouse, then became *procureur du roi*, taking an important part in the *États généraux of 1576. He visited England (1581) in connection with a projected marriage between the duc d'Alençon and Queen Elizabeth. His *Six Livres de la République* (1576; trans. into Latin by the author

(1586), English (1606), and other languages), an analysis of the State and the political and economic relations of its constituent parts, was the foundation of French political science. Writing with moderation and realism (though diffusely, with excursions into astrology, etc.), he rejects both *Hotman's doctrine of the sovereignty of the people and Machiavelli's absolute monarchy in favour of a strong hereditary monarchy, restrained by such checks as the control of taxation by the *États généraux*. He also wrote a *Methodus ad facilem historiarum cognitionem* (1566), advancing many novel ideas on the study of history; a *Démonomanie des sorciers* (1580), representing sorcery as a serious danger to society and intended as a judges' manual; *Universae naturae theatrum* (1596; trans. as *Théâtre de la Nature entière*, 1597), arriving at a knowledge of the Deity from a survey of natural science; *Heptaplomeres* (not publ. till the 19th c.), a discussion of seven creeds (all found worthy of respect) revealing some preference for 'natural religion' tinged with Judaism.

Boèce (Boethius), *v. Consolation de Philosophie*.

Boétie, *v. La Boétie*.

Bœuf sur le toit, Le, *v. Cocteau*.

Boïeldieu, FRANÇOIS–ADRIEN (1775–1834), composer of *opéras-comiques, e.g. *Le Calife de Bagdad* (1800); *La Dame blanche* (1823), which was inspired by Scott's *Guy Mannering* and started a vogue for tartans. He was director of the Royal Opera in St. Petersburg (1804–10) and later helped to make the *Opéra-Comique famous (*cf. Méhul*).

Boigne, LOUISE D'OSMOND, COMTESSE DE (1781–1866), remembered for her *salon, among the most brilliant of the July Monarchy, and her entertaining *Mémoires* (1907).

Boileau, ÉTIENNE (d. *c*. 1269), *prévôt de Paris, was responsible for the important

Livre des métiers, codifying the statutes and regulations of the trade guilds.

Boileau or **Boileau-Despréaux,** NICOLAS (1636–1711), 'le Législateur du Parnasse', son of a clerk to the Paris *parlement*, studied law at the University of Paris, became an advocate, then inherited money from his father (1657) and devoted himself entirely to literature. His first works were his *Satires*, nine of which had appeared by 1668. About 1669 he was presented to Louis XIV, to whom he read his first *Épître*. The king gave him a pension, later made him (with Racine) historiographer royal, and suggested his admission to the *Académie* (1684). The 1674 edition of his works contained, besides the above, four more *Épîtres*, the *Art poétique*, four cantos of the *Lutrin*, and a translation of Longinus. Publication of his *Dialogue des héros de romans* (written *c.* 1665) was delayed to avoid offending Mlle de Scudéry. The rest of the *Lutrin* and *Épîtres* VI–IX appeared in 1683. In later life his health was bad and his output declined, but he remained active, on the side of the *anciens*, in the *Querelle des anciens et des modernes*: in the *Art poétique* he had opposed Desmarets de Saint-Sorlin; later, in opposition to Perrault, he wrote the *Ode sur la prise de Namur* (1693; a feeble imitation of Pindar), the *Réflexions sur Longin* (1694), and some of his *Épîtres* and *Satires*—but yielded ground in his *Lettre à M. Perrault* (1700). He was the warm friend and champion of Racine, Molière, and La Fontaine, and was devoted to A. Arnauld (on whom he wrote a fine epitaph). His *Jansenist tendencies embroiled him with the *Jesuits (*v. Épîtres*; *Satires*).

He is less important as a poet (though a master of the verse-form, he lacked inspiration) than as a founder of French literary criticism. By his acute judgement, independence, sincerity, and brilliant power of expression, he made himself the arbiter of literary reputations, attacked affectation, insipidity, pedantry, and pomposity, and laid down the canons of good writing (derived from Malherbe), as practised by the *Classical school and

approved by the taste of his age. He was read and admired in England; *v. English Literature, French Influence on,* 3.

Boisrobert, FRANÇOIS LE MÉTEL, ABBÉ DE (1592–1662), dramatist, a member of the original *Académie française*, a familiar of Richelieu and one of his *cinq auteurs*; also something of a buffoon. His one good play, the comedy *La Belle Plaideuse* (1654), from which Molière borrowed a scene, depicts contemporary Parisian life (e.g. the Foire Saint-Germain) and manners.

Boissier, GASTON (1823–1908), ancient historian, author of *Cicéron et ses amis* (1865), *La Religion romaine d'Auguste aux Antonins* (1874), *Promenades* and *Nouvelles Promenades archéologiques* (1880 and 1886), *La Fin du paganisme en occident* (1891), etc.

Boiste, PIERRE–CLAUDE–VICTOIRE, *v. Dictionaries,* 1800.

Bollandistes, Belgian *Jesuit editors of the *Acta Sanctorum* (from 1643; work was interrupted in 1786 after the dispersal of the Order, but resumed in 1837), lives of saints arranged in date order of their feast-days; so called after Jean Bolland (1596–1665), first editor of the work.

Bonald, LOUIS, VICOMTE DE (1754–1840), political philosopher, emigrated in 1790 and was a conservative politician under the Restoration. An ardent defender of Altar and Crown against the Revolution (*cf. Maistre, J. de*), he held the Catholic faith and the divine right of kings to be truths as incontrovertible as the laws of nature. His chief works, written in a laborious, inelegant style, were the *Théorie du pouvoir politique et religieux dans la société civile* (1796), *Essai analytique sur les lois naturelles de l'ordre social* (1801), *La Législation primitive considérée... par les seules lumières de la raison* (1802).

Bonaparte, the French form of the Italian *Buonaparte*—Napoleon's original surname. From the time he took command in Italy (1796) until he became emperor

(1804) he signed himself 'Bonaparte'. In allusions to his career prior to 1804 he is more usually called 'Bonaparte' than 'Napoleon'.

Bonaparte, PRINCE LOUIS–NAPOLÉON, v. *Napoleon III.*

Bonaparte Family. Napoleon's father, CARLO MARIA BUONAPARTE (1746–85), b. at Ajaccio, came of a family of Italian descent established in Corsica from the 16th c. He married a Corsican of Genoese origin, MARIA LETIZIA RAMOLINO (1750–1836), a woman of great beauty and fine character. (Napoleon brought her to Paris in 1799, and she was known as 'Madame Mère'.) Eight of their children reached maturity: (1) JOSEPH (1768–1844). Napoleon created him king of Naples (1806), then king of Spain (1808–13); (2) NAPOLÉON (1769–1821), v. *Napoleon*; (3) ÉLISA (1773/4–1820), m. Prince Bacciochi. Napoleon created her grand duchess of Tuscany (1808); (4) LUCIEN (1775–1840). He presided effectively over the *Conseil des Cinq-Cents* (v. *Directoire*) at the time of the *coup d'état du 18 brumaire* (v. *Revolutions*, 1), held various offices under the Consulate and Empire, and patronized literature and the sciences. When he fell out with Napoleon and left for the U.S.A. he was captured by an English cruiser and held in England for three years. Later he lived in Italy. v. *Wyse*; (5) LOUIS (1778–1846), m. Hortense de *Beauharnais. Napoleon created him king of Holland (1806), but he abdicated (1810). Napoleon III was his third son; (6) PAULINE (1781–1825), a famous beauty, m. (1) General Leclerc (v. *Toussaint Louverture*), (2) Prince Camillo Borghese; (7) CAROLINE (1782–1839), m. Murat (v. *Maréchal*) and so became queen of Naples (1808); (8) JÉRÔME (1784–1860), king of Westphalia (1807–13), m. (1) Elizabeth Paterson of Baltimore, (2) Princess Catherine of Württemberg, by whom he had three children: Jérôme (1814–47); *Mathilde; and Napoléon-Joseph-Charles-Paul (1821–91), the Prince Napoléon ('Plon-plon') who was a patron of writers and artists under the Second Empire—and whose

grandson (b. 1914) is the present Bonapartist pretender to the throne.

Bonaparte-Wyse, v. *Wyse* (2).

Bonheur, v. *Verlaine.*

Bonjour Tristesse, v. *Sagan.*

Bonnard, Sylvestre, in A. France's *Le *Crime de Sylvestre Bonnard.*

Bonne Chanson, La, v. *Verlaine.*

Bonnefoy, YVES, v. *Lyric Poetry*, 4.

Bonnes, Les, v. *Genet.*

Bonnes lettres; Bonnes œuvres; Bonnes études, Société des, v. *Congrégation* (2).

Bonnet phrygien, v. *Bonnet rouge.*

Bonnet rouge, the red cap, the emblem of the Revolution. It seems to derive both from the *bonnet phrygien* (a name also used for it), the conical cap of liberty worn by the freed slaves of antiquity, and the *bonnet rouge* of the *galériens* (convicts). From 1789 onwards it appeared as a seal used on letters by officers who had fought with the insurgent American colonists, in engravings or on medals (showing Liberty with a *bonnet phrygien* on her head or her pike), on Voltaire's bust at the *Comédie-Française*, etc. Its colour, however, was often grey. But after mutinous troops at Nancy (1790) were sentenced to 30 years' convict labour at Brest (v. *Galères*) many outraged *Jacobins donned a *bonnet rouge*. And when the released mutineers arrived for a public welcome in Paris (April 1792) wearing the *bonnet rouge* of the *galériens*, the red cap finally ousted the grey as the symbol of liberty. Two months later, when the mob broke into the *Tuileries, the king consented to have a *bonnet rouge* placed on his head; and within days of his fall it was made the official emblem of the Revolution (14 Aug. 1792).

Bonneval, CLAUDE-ALEXANDRE, COMTE

DE (1675–1747), a gallant officer of unbalanced character who, after a dispute over his military accounts, went over to Prince Eugène and fought under him against the French and the Turks. The Regent rehabilitated him (1717), but his quick temper caused fresh difficulties. Finally, he joined the Turks, becoming a Moslem and a pasha. He repudiated the memoirs written in his name. Voltaire and Casanova mention him.

Bonstetten, CHARLES-VICTOR DE (1745–1832), a Swiss employed in the administrative service of his country, a man of learning and wide interests (philosopher, economist, antiquarian, traveller); a friend of the Neckers and Mme de Staël, also of Thomas Gray (whom he visited in 1769 and who wrote some extant letters to him). His works include *L'Homme du Midi et l'homme du Nord* (1824), showing the influence on him of Mme de Staël, and a pleasant *Voyage dans le Latium* (1804).

Bontemps, Roger, v. *Roger Bontemps*.

Booz endormi, v. *Légende des siècles, La*.

Borda, JEAN-CHARLES (1733–99), whose research did much to advance nautical science, was one of three experts asked to measure the arc of the meridian as a basis for the *metric system. The *Borda* was the training vessel for cadets at the State Naval College at Brest (1852–1913; life there is described in *Loti's Prime Jeunesse*).

Bordeaux, HENRI (1870–1963), wrote some 50 novels of provincial life, widely read in their day, often about homes (in his native Savoy) in which neither family ties nor religious beliefs suffice to preserve unity. Possibly his best were *La Peur de vivre* (1902), *Les Roquevillard* (1906), *La Robe de laine* (1910), *La Neige sur les pas* (1912).

Borderie, BERTRAND DE LA, v. *Héroët*.

Borel, PETRUS (1809–59), *Romantic poet and novelist, leader of the *bousingos*, self-styled 'le Lycanthrope' (apparently in reference to the saying 'Man is a wolf to man'). His works include *Rhapsodies* (1832), stark poems with a hard rhythm—obviously written by a malcontent; *Champavert, contes immoraux* (1833) and a novel, *Madame Putiphar* (1839), both full of melodramatic horrors, intended to scandalize; a translation (1836) of *Robinson Crusoe*.

Borel, PIERRE, v. *Dictionaries*, 1655.

Bornier, HENRI, VICOMTE DE (1825–1901), author of verse dramas, notably *La Fille de Roland* (1875; still played at the *Comédie-Française* on national occasions) and *Les Noces d'Attila* (1880).

Borodino (between Smolensk and *Moscow), the scene of *la bataille de la Moskova*, Napoleon's costly victory over the Russians under Kutusov (7 Sept. 1812).

Boron or **Borron**, ROBERT DE, v. *Perceval*.

Bosco, HENRI (1888–1976), a well-known regional novelist, author of *L'Ane culotte* (1937), *Le Mas Théotime* (1945), *Le Jardin d'Hyacinthe* (1946), *Barboche* (1957), etc., tales of country life in his native Provence, evoking its primitive mysteries and largely inspired by memories of his own childhood (described in *Souvenirs*, 1961–2, 2 vols.).

Bosse, ABRAHAM (1602–76), engraver, noted for his accurate portrayal of *bourgeois* life in his day.

Bossuet, JACQUES-BÉNIGNE (1627–1704), theologian, moralist, and orator, came of a family of magistrates, was educated by the *Jesuits at Dijon and at the *Collège de Navarre*, then entered the priesthood and preached for some years at Metz (a Protestant and Jewish centre). In 1659 he settled in Paris, won fame with his sermons, and was made bishop of Condom (1669) and tutor (1670) to the Dauphin ('le *Grand Dauphin')—a thankless task (the lad suffered from 'incuriosité') on which he spent the next 10 years. From 1681, when he was named bishop of Meaux, he concentrated on his ecclesiastical duties and polemical works.

His fame rests on his sermons and funeral orations, his educational works for the Dauphin, and his miscellaneous writings. He published only one sermon, *Sur l'unité de l'Église* (1682), a manifesto of the *Gallican position at the time of Louis XIV's conflict with Innocent XI. The rest survive only in drafts (often incomplete). His funeral orations (panegyric and sermon combined, drawing lessons from the life or character of the deceased) included those on Henrietta Maria (wife of Charles I of England; 1669), Henriette d'Angleterre (1670), Maria Theresa (wife of Louis XIV; 1683), Le Tellier (1686), 'le Grand Condé' (1687). They contain some of his most famous oratory, passages of greater pomp and solemnity than was usual in his sermons. His normal style of preaching was simple, touching, and persuasive; also courageous in its attack on royal failings.

For the Dauphin he wrote a *Discours sur l'histoire universelle* (1681), a chronological abstract of world history, with a commentary on the evolution of religion and the providential causes of the rise and fall of empires; the *Politique tirée de l'Écriture Sainte* (1709), on the divine right of kings and their duties to their subjects; the *Traité de la connaissance de Dieu et de soi-même* (1722) and the *Logique*, elementary philosophy. His miscellaneous (mainly polemical) works included (1) the *Histoire des variations des églises protestantes* (1688; 'le plus beau livre de la langue française'—Brunetière), exposing the Protestants' lack of community and continuity of doctrine, and the subordination of authority to individual judgement—and drawing replies to which he published rejoinders; (2) *Maximes et réflexions sur la Comédie* (1694; highly critical of the theatre) and the *Traité de la concupiscence* (1731; censuring intellectual curiosity), both revealing his *Jansenist sympathies (though he condemned the five propositions attributed to Jansenius); (3) the *Relation sur le Quiétisme* (1698),

against *Quietism—the fruit of an acute controversy with Fénelon; (4) the *Instructions sur la version du Nouveau Testament* and *Défense de la tradition et des saints Pères* (1702), opposing novelties of exegesis advanced by Richard Simon (*v. Bible, French versions*)—elsewhere he contested the doctrines of Malebranche and Spinoza; and (5), in a different category, his *Méditations sur l'Évangile* (1730–1) and *Élévations à Dieu sur les mystères*, works of religious edification.

La Bruyère hailed him as the last of the Fathers. His polemical work was a defence of traditional Catholic faith in its integrity, based on assiduous study of the Scriptures and the Fathers (esp. St. Augustine and Tertullian). He was practical and moderate in exposition, luminous in discussion, conciliatory in polemics; he approved the revocation of the Edict of Nantes, but opposed the use of force against the *Huguenots. His style is marked by a strong lyrical quality (e.g. the *Méditations* and *Élévations*) and the use of concrete and picturesque terms: Lanson calls him 'le grand poète lyrique du XVIIe siècle'.

Bottin, Le, short for the *Annuaire-Almanach du commerce et de l'industrie* (*Didot-Bottin*), the commercial directory (in several vols.—Paris, the *départements*, a foreign section) to be found in post offices and cafés. It is called after Sébastien Bottin, who took over (1819) and developed the *Almanach du commerce* (f. 1798), renaming it *L'Almanach Bottin*. After his death in 1853 this was merged with the *Annuaire général du commerce* (publ. by Firmin-Didot) and has since appeared under the present title.

Boubouroche, *v. Courteline.*

Bouchardon, EDME (1698–1762), sculptor. His work may be seen at *Versailles and in Paris (fountain in the Rue de Grenelle).

Bouchardy, JOSEPH (1810–70), wrote *mélodrames, e.g. *Gaspardo le pêcheur* (1837), *Le Sonneur de Saint-Paul* (1838),

Les Enfants trouvés (1843), and was for a time a *bousingo*.

Boucher, FRANÇOIS (1703–70), a painter of graceful pastoral and mythological pictures. He excelled at grouping and decorative treatment, but lacked Watteau's poetic spirit.

Bouchet, GUILLAUME (*c.* 1513–93), a bookseller of Poitiers, wrote three books of *Serées* (i.e. 'soirées'; 1584–98), in which citizens of Poitiers and their wives meet of an evening to discuss anything from marriage to fish, dogs, and wine, with anecdotes and maxims, local scandal, mockery of lawyers, etc.—doubtless a fair picture of provincial *bourgeois* society.

Bouchet, JEAN (1476–*c.* 1557), a successful attorney of Poitiers and a very long-winded *rhétoriqueur* poet, self-styled 'le Traverseur des voies périlleuses'; a friend of Rabelais, to whom he wrote in mediocre verse. His *Épîtres familières* (1547) are interesting for the personages mentioned.

Bouciquaut, JEAN LE MAINGRE, *known as* (1365–1421), *maréchal de France*, governor of Genoa 1401–9, was wounded and captured at Agincourt, and died in England. He was one of the originators of the *Cent Ballades*. The 15th-c. *Livre des faits du bon messire Jean le Maingre, dit Bouciquaut*, by an anonymous cleric, represents him as a fine type of a dying class, the feudal noble, and is very informative about the period of his governorship of Genoa. *v. History*, 1.

Boudin, EUGÈNE-LOUIS (1825–98), painter, often of Normandy coast scenes. *v. Impressionism*.

Bouffes-Parisiens, one of the homes of operetta and light comedy in Paris. Offenbach opened it in premises on the *Champs-Élysées* (1855) and later transferred it to its present site near the *Opéra-Comique*.

Boufflers, STANISLAS-JEAN, CHEVALIER DE

(1738–1815), cavalry officer and author of mediocre light verse, etc.; a member of the *Académie*.

His mother, the MARQUISE DE BOUFFLERS, a friend of Voltaire, is to be distinguished from both the DUCHESSE DE BOUFFLERS (*v. Luxembourg*), a patroness of J.-J. Rousseau, and the COMTESSE DE BOUFFLERS-ROUVERET, also a friend of Rousseau.

Bougainville, LOUIS-ANTOINE DE (1729–1814), naval officer, was sent (1766) to establish a colony in the Falkland Islands, visited many Pacific islands, and circumnavigated the globe, returning in 1769. He wrote a *Voyage autour du monde* (1771), and gave his name to the plant *Bougainvillea*. For the *Supplément au Voyage de Bougainville*, *v. Diderot*.

Bougeant, GUILLAUME-HYACINTHE, ABBÉ (1690–1743), *Jesuit author of plays, historical works, and an *Amusement philosophique sur le langage des bêtes* (1739; trans. into English and German). His Order disapproved of this book, which led to his imprisonment.

Bouhélier-Lepelletier, STÉPHANE-GEORGES DE, *v. Saint-Georges de Bouhélier*.

Bouhours, DOMINIQUE (1628–1702), 'le Père Bouhours', a *Jesuit man of letters, succeeded Vaugelas as chief grammarian of his period. His works include the *Entretiens d'Ariste et d'Eugène* (1671), assorted dialogues; *Doutes sur la langue française* (1674), etc., backing the *Académie*'s efforts to purify the language; a life of St. Francis Xavier (trans. 1686 by Dryden).

Bouilhet, LOUIS-HYACINTHE (1822–69), librarian at Rouen, a minor poet and dramatist, lifelong friend of Flaubert. He wrote *Madame de Montarcy* (1856) and *La Conjuration d'Amboise* (1866), historical dramas; and poetical works on historical and scientific subjects, e.g. *Melaenis* (1851; Rome under Commodus), *Festons et Astragales* (1859; the geological ages of the earth).

Bouillie de la comtesse Berthe, La, v. Dumas père.

Bouillon, GODEFROI DE, v. *Godefroi de Bouillon.*

Boulanger, GÉNÉRAL GEORGES (1837–91), became minister of war in 1886, and by energetic measures to reform the army, increase armaments, and strengthen the Franco-German frontier won popular prestige as a man of action, the 'général de la revanche', though many saw him as a warmonger and a tool for the anti-Republicans. His popularity so embarrassed the government that, to remove him from Paris, he was given an army command at Clermont-Ferrand (1887). A *Boulangiste* movement started there and soon became a national party, with 'Dissolution, Constituante [i.e. election of an *Assemblée constituante*], Revision' as slogan and a red carnation (his favourite flower) as emblem. In January 1889 he was elected *député* for the *département de la Seine* (i.e. Paris) by a huge majority, and by prompt use of force might have made himself master of France. But the popular hero temporized, giving the impression that, when it came to governing, he had no clear political policy. He also seems, at crucial moments, to have preferred the arms of his mistress, Mme de Bonnemains, to politics. On 1 April, fearing arrest, he disconcerted his followers by fleeing the country. He was tried and condemned *in absentia* for treason and for mishandling public funds, and finally discredited when found to have negotiated secretly (1888) with the monarchists. He committed suicide in Brussels on his mistress's grave. *Boulangisme* was seen in retrospect as having revived French morale. It is described in *Barrès's L'Appel au soldat* and P. *Adam's Le Mystère des foules*.

Boulanger, LOUIS (1806–67), a painter esteemed by the *Romantics, was a member of Hugo's *cénacle*. His pictures were often on subjects from Hugo's books.

Boulanger, NICOLAS-ANTOINE (1722–59), a *philosophe*. His *Antiquité dévoilée* (1766), a work of some influence in which d'Holbach was said to have had a hand, attributes the origin of religion to the fear inspired by such calamities as the Deluge.

Boulangisme, Boulangiste, v. *Boulanger, G.*

Boule or **Boulle,** ANDRÉ-CHARLES (1642–1732), wood-carver, introduced the metal or other inlay to ornament furniture, and gave his name (in Eng. usually Germanized as *Buhl*) to this style.

Boule-de-suif (in *Les *Soirées de Médan,* 1880), a masterly short story by Maupassant. 'Boule-de-suif', a prostitute, is one of a small party of refugees leaving Rouen during the *Franco-Prussian war. Her companions are fulsomely attentive to her so long as her food and ample personal charms (whence her nickname) serve to aid their escape. Once they are safe they revert to contemptuous hostility.

Boulevard du Crime, a section of the Boulevard du Temple in Paris (since demolished), so called in the early 19th c. because the theatres playing *mélodrame* were located there.

Bourbon, a royal family (*Capetian dynasty) descended from a younger son of Louis IX. It attained the throne (1589) in the person of Henri IV, from whom subsequent kings down to Louis-Philippe were directly descended. At the outbreak of the Revolution the chief members of the elder branch of this house were: (1) King Louis XVI and his three children by Marie-Antoinette: Marie-Thérèse-Charlotte de France (1778–1851), 'Madame Royale' (v. *Orpheline du Temple*); Louis-Joseph-François-Xavier (1781–9), succeeded as dauphin by Louis-Charles, duc de Normandie (1785–95; v. *Orphelin du Temple*); (2) the comte de Provence ('Monsieur'), the king's eldest brother, later Louis XVIII; (3) the comte d'Artois, the king's second brother, later Charles X, and his sons: the duc d'Angoulême, who married 'Madame

Royale' (v. (1)) in 1799 and became dauphin in 1824; and the duc de Berry (assassinated 1820; v. *Chambord, comte de*), whose widow was imprisoned for fomenting rebellion against Louis-Philippe in the Vendée (1832); (4) 'Mesdames', i.e. Adélaïde (1732–1800) and Victoire (1733–99), unmarried daughters of Louis XV who emigrated in 1791; (5) 'Madame Élisabeth' (1764–94), the king's sister, who was imprisoned with the royal family and executed.

Collateral branches were the houses of Bourbon-*Orléans and Condé (*cf. Condé, Le Grand; Conti*). The latter included Louis-Joseph de Bourbon, prince de Condé (1736–1818; v. *Armée des émigrés*), his son Louis-Henri-Joseph, duc de Bourbon (1756–1830), and his grandson, the duc d'*Enghien. v. also *Maine*; *Vendôme*.

The Bourbons also provided kings of Naples and of Spain (v. *Grand Dauphin*).

Bourdaloue, Louis (1632–1704), a famous *Jesuit preacher, an opponent of *Jansenism. His first sermons in Paris, delivered in 1669 (when Bossuet had almost ceased to preach), were much admired, and until his death he was deemed the greatest preacher of the day. In contrast to Bossuet, he appealed to reason rather than the emotions: his exposition was simple and popular, with no outstanding passages; his arguments were carefully marshalled; his subject rigorously analysed and subdivided. He usually chose moral and practical themes, exposing contemporary vices without fear or favour, and with a profound knowledge of the human soul. v. *Avent*; *Carême* (*Lent*).

Bourdet, ÉDOUARD (1887–1944), author of many successful comedies of manners, involving psychological analysis and social satire, e.g. *L'Homme enchaîné* (1924), *La Prisonnière* (1926), *Vient de paraître* (1927; satirizing the literary world), *Le Sexe faible* (1929), *Les Temps difficiles* (1934). As administrator (1936–40) of the *Comédie-Française*, he introduced reforms including the appointment of Copeau, Baty, Jouvet, and Dullin as producers.

Bourdigné, CHARLES, v. *Pierre Faifeu*.

Bourgeois de Molinchart, Les, v. *Champfleury*.

Bourgeois de Paris, Journal d'un, v. *History*, 1.

Bourgeois de Paris, Mémoires d'un, v. *Véron*.

Bourgeois Gentilhomme, Le, a 5-act prose *comédie-ballet by Molière; produced 1670. v. *Lulli*.

M. Jourdain, a vain, ignorant *bourgeois*, eager to appear a man of quality, takes up dancing, fencing, and philosophy (and finds he has been talking prose all his life without knowing it). A laughing-stock in his extravagant dress, fleeced by Dorante, a needy nobleman who flatters his conceit, he refuses his daughter to the worthy, but low-born, Cléonte. So Cléonte poses as the son of the Grand Turk who has come to Paris as her suitor, talks a ridiculous jargon which passes for Turkish, and creates Jourdain a 'Mamamouchi'. The foolish Jourdain, completely deceived, gladly gives his daughter to such an exalted suitor.

Bourges, ÉLÉMIR (1852–1925), author of long, grandiosely imaginative novels, influenced by his love of Wagner and the Elizabethan dramatists, e.g. *Le Crépuscule des dieux* (1884), *Les Oiseaux s'envolent et les feuilles tombent* (1893); also of *Sous la hache* (1885), a novel of the *Chouannerie, and *La Nef* (1904–22), a vast two-part prose poem.

Bourget, PAUL (1852–1935), novelist and critic, turned from medicine and philosophy to literature, tutoring by day and writing by night. After early poetical collections (*La Vie inquiète*, 1875; *Edel*, 1878, a long poem; *Les Aveux*, 1882), he won a reputation as a novelist with *Cruelle Énigme* (1885) and *André Cornélis* (1887)—novels of psychological analysis

(v. *Novel*, 3)—and confirmed it with such works as *Le *Disciple* (1889), *Cosmopolis* (1893), *L'*Étape* (1902). His theme was usually some dilemma of conscience and/ or sociological problem; and, like his friend Henry James, he described the life of the leisured classes. His later works were coloured by his moralistic attitude and deepening Catholic and Royalist sympathies (e.g. *Un Divorce*, 1904; *L'Émigré*, 1907; *Le Démon de midi*, 1914), though some of his shorter tales (*Le Justicier*, 1919; *L'Échéance*, 1921) were less burdened with ideology. He is now more highly esteemed as a critic than as a novelist, especially for his *Essais* and *Nouveaux Essais de psychologie contemporaine* (1883 and 1886), *Pages* and *Nouvelles Pages de critique et de doctrine* (1912 and 1922).

Bourgmestre de Stilmonde, Le, *v. Maeterlinck.*

Bourgogne, Hôtel de, *v. Hôtel de Bourgogne.*

Bourg régénéré, Le, *v. Romains.*

Boursault, EDME (1638–1701), dramatist, author of successful comedies of manners, notably *Le Mercure galant* (1683), in which a series of grotesque characters seek to exploit the publicity afforded by the *Mercure galant* (Donneau de Visé complained to the authorities and the play was renamed *La Comédie sans titre*). He quarrelled with Molière (v. *Impromptu de Versailles, L'*), Boileau, and Racine.

Bourse, La, the Stock Exchange. An Exchange was officially established in Paris in 1724 (being preceded by provincial Exchanges, e.g. at Lyons, Toulouse). Before then merchants and bankers had met in various quarters of Paris (e.g. the *Pont-au-Change, the Palais de Justice) to transact business, and speculative dealings had been rife since *Law's *système*. Since 1826 the Paris *Bourse* has functioned in the building specially erected for the purpose in the Rue Vivienne. It often figures in Zola's

novels of the Second Empire (v. *Rougon-Macquart, Les*; *Curée, La*), a period of feverish speculation.

Bousingo, bousingot, a name given after the 1830 *Revolution (esp. c. 1831–2 in *Le *Figaro*) to members of a band of turbulent young *Romantics. They are said to have acquired it, together with a reputation for Republicanism, after a night when they roamed the streets shouting 'Nous avons fait du bousingo' and ended in the lock-up. Their leaders included Petrus Borel, the *bousingo par excellence*, Gautier, and O'Neddy; their average age was 20 (*cf. Jeunes-France*). One of their eccentricities of costume was a wide-brimmed hat of the type worn by sailors. (This was often called a *bousingo*, a word which may come from Eng. *boozing*.) They are described in G. Sand's novel *Horace* (1842).

Bouteille à la mer, La (1854, in the *Revue des Deux Mondes*; 1864, in *Les Destinées*), a poem by Vigny. The captain of a sinking ship seals his last records in a bottle and tosses it to the waves, trusting that one day it will be salvaged. So should the 'jeune homme inconnu', to whom the poem is addressed, entrust his work to posterity.

Boutroux,   ÉMILE   (1845–1921), philosopher. He held that human evolution was ultimately governed by a creative principle which transcended determinist theories of cause and effect, or theories of the possible and non-possible, and permitted of spirituality and moral choice. His writings include *De la contingence des lois de la nature* (1874), his chief work; *Science et religion dans la philosophie contemporaine* (1908); *Questions de morale et d'éducation* (1895); various important studies of the history of philosophy; *De l'idée de loi naturelle dans la science et la philosophie contemporaines* (1895), *Sorbonne lectures of 1892–3.

Bouts rimés, a kind of competition, fashionable in the 17th c., in which contestants composed verses on a given set of rhymes.

Bouvard et Pécuchet (1881, posth.), an unfinished novel by Flaubert.

Two copying clerks meet by accident and find they are twin souls. One inherits money, the other realizes his savings, and they buy a farm. They embark on a series of experiments in agriculture, distilling, chemistry, etc., with a naïve enthusiasm for scientific progress which is doomed to continual disappointment. After science they try philosophy, religion, then an equally disastrous educational experiment with two orphans.

Flaubert worked on the book for over 10 years. The conclusion he had planned was that the pair should decide to end up, as they had begun, as copyists. They were to transcribe passages from books consulted for their many experiments—and unwittingly to compile an anthology of the amazing errors and ineptitudes of which even great minds are capable. This was to form a second volume, incorporating Flaubert's own collection of platitudes (*v. Dictionnaire des idées reçues*).

Bouvines (near Lille). Here Philippe II defeated (1214) the emperor Otho IV.

Bovary, *v. Madame Bovary*.

Boyer, ABEL (1667–1729), a *Huguenot who settled in England (1689) and produced an English–French/French–English dictionary (1702), histories in English of William III and Queen Anne, and English translations of the *Mémoires du comte de *Gramont* and Racine's *Iphigénie*. He attacked Swift, who vowed vengeance on the 'French dog' (*Journal to Stella*).

Boylesve, RENÉ (1867–1926), novelist of small-town provincial life (its cliques, prejudices, etc.), e.g. *Le Médecin des dames de Néans* (1896); *Mademoiselle Cloque* (1899; clerical strife); *La Becquée* (1901) and a sequel *L'Enfant à la balustrade* (1903); *La Jeune Fille bien élevée* (1909) and a sequel *Madeleine, jeune femme* (1912).

Bradamante (1582), the first French *tragicomedy, by Garnier; based partly on Ariosto's *Orlando Furioso*.

Bradamante, a warrior-maiden, and Roger, 'un simple chevalier', are in love; but her ambitious parents, Aymon and Béatrix, want her to marry Léon, heir to the emperor of Byzantium. Charlemagne decides that she shall marry whoever can defeat her in single combat. Meanwhile Léon has saved the life of an unknown knight (Roger in disguise) whom he begs, on hearing Charlemagne's verdict, to fight Bradamante on his behalf. Roger is torn between love and honour (*cf.* Corneille's *Le *Cid*). Honour prevails; he defeats Bradamante, and rides sadly away. But Charlemagne decides that, as she had originally been promised to Roger, Léon ought to fight and defeat Roger. It then emerges that Roger is the unknown knight, and Léon surrenders Bradamante to him. Finally, to overcome the obstinate objections of old Aymon (who provides the comic element), Roger is offered the crown of Bulgaria, and so raised to a position of sufficient dignity.

Braille, LOUIS (1809–52), inventor of 'Braille', the system of writing and printing in relief used by the blind. Blind from childhood, he spent nearly all his life in the Institution for the Blind at Coupvray-sur-Marne, becoming a teacher there and an accomplished organist.

Brantôme, PIERRE DE BOURDEILLES, SEIGNEUR and ABBÉ DE (*c.* 1540–1614), b. in Périgord, spent his youth at the court of Marguerite de Navarre, accompanied Mary Stuart to Scotland (1561), soldiered in Italy, Spain, Portugal, etc., and in the civil wars on the side of the Guises (*v. Ligue, La*). Crippled for life (*c.* 1584) by a fall from a horse, he passed the time by composing his memoirs (pub. 1665–6), comprising the *Vies des hommes illustres et grands capitaines français et étrangers* (6 vols.) and the *Vies des dames illustres* (3 vols.; part of this, later known as the *Dames galantes*, related scandalous anecdotes of the court). Writing in a lively style, with uncritical frivolity and absence of morality (but also, when he has personal knowledge of the subject, with obvious sincerity), he throws a vivid light on the externals of military and court life and provides a document for the historian of manners.

Braque, GEORGES (1882–1963), painter, one of the *Fauves* (*v. Impressionism*); the founder, with Picasso, of *Cubism. His fame rests on his still-lifes. He also executed theatre *décors* (e.g. for Diaghilev's company; *v. Cocteau*), a ceiling at the *Musée du* *Louvre* (1953), etc. He recorded his views on life and art in the *Carnet de Georges Braque.*

Braudel, FERNAND (1902–), economic and social historian; professor at the *Collège de France* (1949–72) and the *École pratique des Hautes Études.* His works include *La Méditerranée et le monde méditerranéen à l'époque de Philippe II* (1949; rev. and augm. ed. 1966) and *Civilisation matérielle et capitalisme* (*XVᵉ–XVIIIᵉ siècle*) (vol. I, 1967), in the series *Destins du monde. v.* also *History*, 4 (last §).

Bréal, MICHEL-JULES-ALFRED (1832–1915), an eminent Indo-European philologist, best known as the originator of the study of semantics (and inventor of the term). Besides his famous *Essai de sémantique* (1897), his works include *Mélanges de mythologie et de linguistique* (1877).

Brébeuf, GEORGES DE (1618–61), poet, wrote an epic (1654–5) adapted from Lucan's *Pharsalia*, famous in its day, but condemned by Boileau. His best work was his *Entretiens solitaires, ou Prières et méditations pieuses* (1660).

Brécourt, GUILLAUME MARCOUREAU, SIEUR DE (*c.* 1637–85), a comedian of *Molière's company.

Bremond, HENRI, ABBÉ (1865–1933), historian and critic, spent some years in religious houses in Britain before withdrawing (1904) from the *Jesuit Order to engage in writing and research. His works include, notably, *Histoire littéraire du sentiment religieux en France* (1916–33; 11 of a projected 14 vols., covering, roughly, the 17th c.), a study of the religious element (esp. mysticism) in French literature; also *L'Inquiétude religieuse* (1901 and 1909), essays; *Newman* (1905) and *Fénelon* (1910), studies in religious psychology; *Pour le romantisme* (1923), a plea for romanticism as the element of inspiration in literature; *Prière et poésie* (1925); *La Poésie pure* (1927).

Brendan, St. (484–577), an Irish saint, the subject of the medieval legend of the *Navigation of St. Brendan*. An early 12th-c. *Anglo-Norman version, a poem by a monk named Benedict, describes Brendan's odyssey in search of the earthly Paradise among magic islands in the Western ocean.

Breton, ANDRÉ (1896–1966), poet. After such works as *Mont de piété* (1919) and *Les Champs magnétiques* (1920; with Soupault), showing the influence on him of Apollinaire and his circle, and of an active *Dadaist phase, he emerged in 1924 as the leader and theorist of *Surrealism. He remained until his death a stern guardian of the integrity of Surrealist inspiration and a dedicated exponent of the automatic methods heralded by *Les Champs magnétiques.* His theories may be studied in his three manifestos (1924, 1930, 1942; all in *Les Manifestes du surréalisme*, 1946), in *Qu'est-ce que le surréalisme?* (1934), and in his essays (collected in *Les Pas perdus*, 1924; *Point du jour*, 1934; *La Clé des champs*, 1953; *Perspective cavalière*, 1971). His creative writings, which explore his own feelings and experiences, include the novel *Nadja* (1928), a journal revolving around his encounters with a mysterious woman in Paris; *L'Immaculée Conception* (1930; with Éluard); *L'Union libre* (1931); *Le Revolver à cheveux blancs* (1932); *Les Vases communicants* (1932); *L'Amour fou* (1937); *Arcane 17* (1945), which reflects his increasing interest in occultism; *Ode à Charles Fourier* (1947); the collection *Poèmes* (1948), poems of 1919–48. Apart from its Surrealist qualities, his work is notable for his exaltation of love as mad and revolutionizing.

Breton lays, v. *Romans bretons.*

Bretons, Geste des, v. *Wace.*

Brichemer, the stag in the **Roman de Renart.*

Brid'oison, in Beaumarchais's *Le *Mariage de Figaro.*

Bridoye, in Rabelais's **Pantagruel.*

Brieux, EUGÈNE (1858–1932), dramatist. His works include, notably, *Blanchette* (1892; a study of a country girl educated above her station) and *La Robe rouge* (1900; a study of legal circles); also *L'Engrenage* (1894), *Les Bienfaiteurs* (1897), *Les Trois Filles de M. Dupont* (1899), *Les Avariés* (1901), *La Femme seule* (1913). The dramatic balance of his work was often upset by his preoccupation with moral and social reform. His first play was produced at the **Théâtre Libre.*

Brifaut, CHARLES (1781–1857), author of the tragedy *Ninus* (1813), which underwent a last-minute change of setting from Spain to Assyria to suit Napoleon's dramatic censors, the French army having just crossed the Pyrenees.

Brillat-Savarin, ANTHELME (1755–1826), author of the *Physiologie du goût, ou Méditations sur la gastronomie transcendante* (1825), a sophisticated, amusing, very readable and quotable collection of anecdotes, *pensées*, and aphorisms, inspired by an academic interest in food rather than over-addiction to the pleasures of the table. Born in Bresse, a province renowned for good food, he was a barrister by profession (a deputy of the **Tiers État* in the **Assemblée constituante* of 1789, and later attached to the **Cour de cassation*), a man of wit and culture, welcomed in literary **salons*, and very different from his contemporary Grimod de la Reynière.

Brinvilliers, MARIE-MADELEINE D'AUBRAY, MARQUISE DE (1630–76), a famous murderess, poisoned several members of her family, largely from motives of cupidity. When her lover—and instructor in the art of poisoning—died while experimenting, evidence incriminating her was found among his effects. She fled to England, but was later trapped and arrested in Liège. Mme de Sévigné recounts her execution (17 July 1676).

Brioché, JEAN (fl. c. 1650), a famous mountebank, said to have invented marionettes. He performed at the fairs of Paris.

Brissot or **Brissot de Warville,** JEAN-PIERRE (1754–93), journalist, a member of the **Convention*, and leader of the faction known as the *Brissotins*, then of the **Girondins* (his paper *Le *Patriote français* was their organ). He died on the scaffold.

Britannicus, a tragedy by Racine, based on Tacitus; produced 1669.

The scene is Rome in the early years of Nero's reign. Néron, who has begun to resist the restraining influence of Burrhus and the authority of his mother Agrippine, objects to the proposed marriage of his half-brother Britannicus (son of Messalina) to Junie (a lady of the imperial house), seeing him as a possible rival for the throne. He causes Junie to be brought to the palace, falls in love with her himself, but fails to shake her devotion to Britannicus, whom he now arrests. Unmoved by Agrippine's reproaches (though feigning contrition), then yielding to Burrhus's expostulations, Néron is finally swayed by Narcisse, Britannicus's treacherous tutor, and poisons his half-brother under pretence of a reconciliation. The fierce invective the crime draws from Agrippine is prophetic of his evil future. Junie escapes from the palace to become a vestal; Narcisse, who tries to arrest her, is killed by the mob.

Brizeux, AUGUSTE (1803–58), poet, of Irish descent. His verse, mainly about his native Brittany, includes *Marie* (1836), lyrics of childhood; *Les Ternaires* (1841; *v. Ternaire*); *Les Bretons* (1845); *Primel et Nola* (1852); *Histoires poétiques* (1855).

Brocéliande, a vast forest in Brittany, now the forest of Paimpont, often figures in medieval romances, e.g. as the haunt of *Merlin.

Brodeau, VICTOR (*c.* 1502–40), poet, a favourite pupil of Marot, was in the service of Marguerite de Navarre. He wrote *Louanges de Jésus-Christ notre Sauveur* (1540), a religious poem notable for passages of a vigorous simplicity; and, as a court poet, *rondeaux and epigrams on trivial subjects.

Broglie, a family of Italian origin, distinguished in French history since the 17th c. The duchy of Broglie, in Normandy, was created in 1742. When the Revolution broke out the then duc de Broglie was minister of war. He fled France and fought in the **Armée des émigrés*. His son at first supported the Revolution, but was finally guillotined. The latter's son, Victor, duc de Broglie (1785–1870), a *doctrinaire, leader of the political opposition, and later a minister under Louis-Philippe, married (1814) Albertine, daughter of Mme de *Staël. His *Souvenirs* (1886, 4 vols.) provide a picture of Napoleonic and Restoration France, with many pen-portraits of his contemporaries (e.g. B. Constant, Mme Récamier, Talleyrand). His son, Jacques-Victor-Albert, duc de Broglie (1821–1901), a leading monarchist politician (prime minister 1873–4 and 1877) and an historian, was the grandfather of the physicists Maurice, duc de Broglie (1875–1960) and his brother Louis, prince, then duc, de Broglie (1892–   ; *Prix Nobel* for Physics, 1929).

Brossard, SÉBASTIEN DE, *v. Dictionaries,* 1703.

Brosses, CHARLES DE (1709–77), 'le Président de Brosses', a magistrate of the Burgundy *parlement, remembered for his pleasant *Lettres familières écrites d'Italie en*

1739 et 1740; also for his quarrel with Voltaire over the latter's purchase of a life-interest in the Château de Tournay (near Ferney), which he owned. He also edited Sallust (1777), and was a pioneer in the study of primitive man (*Histoire des navigations aux Terres Australes*, 1756; *Le Culte des dieux fétiches*, 1760).

Brou, Église de, *v. Marguerite d'Autriche.*

Broussel, PIERRE, *v. Fronde.*

Brueys, DAVID-AUGUSTIN, ABBÉ DE (1640–1723), a dramatist chiefly remembered for his collaboration with *Palaprat. He also wrote some comedies of his own and *Gabinie*, a Christian tragedy.

Bruges-la-morte, *v. Rodenbach.*

Brulard, Henri, *v. Stendhal.*

Bruller, JEAN, *v. Resistance.*

Brumaire, *v. Republican Calendar; Revolutions,* 1 (for the *coup d'état du 18 brumaire*).

Brun, 'Bruin' the bear in the **Roman de Renart.*

Brun de la Montagne, a 14th-c. **roman d'aventure*, set in the forest of *Brocéliande.

Brune, GUILLAUME-MARIE-ANNE, *v. Maréchal.*

Bruneau, CHARLES, *v. Brunot.*

Bruneau, MATHURIN, *v. Orphelin du Temple.*

Brunet, JACQUES-CHARLES (1780–1867), bibliographer. His *Manuel du libraire et de l'amateur de livres* (1810, 5th ed. 1860–5) and supplementary *Nouvelles Recherches bibliographiques* (1834) remain authoritative.

Brunet, JEAN, *v. Félibrige.*

Brunet, Pierre-Gustave (1807–96), man of letters and bibliographer. His works include a *Dictionnaire de bibliographie catholique* (1859); also, as 'Philomneste Junior', *Les Fous littéraires* (1880) and *Livres perdus* (1882).

Brunetière, Ferdinand (1849–1906), literary historian and critic, professor at the *École normale supérieure* from 1886 and editor-in-chief of the *Revue des Deux Mondes* from 1893. An admirer of the 17th c., he opposed 19th-c. theories of *l'*art pour l'art* (for art should have a moral purpose); he also held that evolution operated in literature as in science. These views, intensified by his reactionary religious and political beliefs, at times lent an element of *parti pris* to his writing; but this can be discounted. His works include *Études critiques* (1880–1925), *Le Roman naturaliste* (1883), *Histoire et littérature* (1884–6), *L'Évolution des genres dans l'histoire de la littérature* (1890), *L'Évolution de la poésie lyrique au dix-neuvième siècle* (1894), *Manuel de l'histoire de la littérature française* (1897), *L'Art et la morale* (1898).

Brunetto Latini, *v. Trésor, Livre du*.

Brunot, Ferdinand (1860–1938), philologist. The first 10 volumes of his monumental *Histoire de la langue française des origines à 1900* (1905–43; in part with the collaboration of other scholars) carried the history of the language down to 1815; the work has since been continued under the title *Histoire de la langue française des origines à nos jours*, notably by Charles Bruneau (d. 1969), his successor at the University of Paris. The evolution of the language is traced throughout in its relations to political, social, and literary movements of every kind.

Brunschvicg, Léon (1869–1944), philosopher. His chief works, expounding his highly intellectualist philosophy, are *Les Étapes de la philosophie mathématique* (1913) and *Le Progrès de la conscience dans la philosophie occidentale* (1927), which stress the importance of intellectual judgement, and the close connection between scientific and mathematical progress and the evolution of philosophical speculation. His other works, on similar lines, include *L'Expérience humaine et la causalité physique* (1922), *De la connaissance de soi* (1931), *La Raison et la religion* (1939). He also wrote on Descartes and Pascal, and was a noted editor of the latter.

Bruscambille, *nickname of* Des Lauriers, a 17th-c. actor, famous for the prologues he delivered at the *Hôtel de Bourgogne* to amuse the audience while the house was filling, as was then customary. These burlesque satires—imitated from the Italian, and about anything from gout to cabbage—were later printed.

Brut, *v. Wace*.

Brutus, a tragedy by Voltaire, about the Lucius Junius Brutus who freed Rome from the Tarquins; produced 1730. It was dedicated to Lord Bolingbroke, with a preface comparing English and French tragedy.

Porsenna is attacking Rome in order to restore Tarquin. Rome, where Brutus is consul, is holding out, thanks to the brilliant leadership of Brutus's son Titus. But conspirators, aware of Titus's great love for Tarquin's daughter Tullia, who has been a captive in Rome, use her to induce him to betray Rome and himself rule as king, with her as queen. In a moment of weakness he yields to her entreaties. The plot is foiled, and the conspirators perish; but Brutus learns that Tullia's last words have incriminated Titus. The Senate leaves Brutus to decide his son's fate. Confronted by his father, Titus admits his momentary lapse, and elects to die as an example to Rome. Father and son take leave of one another. Brutus sends Titus to his death, then turns to defend Rome.

Bubu de Montparnasse, *v. Philippe, C.-L.*

Buchanan, George (1506–82), a Scot

who became a professor at the *Collège de Guyenne*, Bordeaux, where he taught Montaigne. His Latin translations of Euripides' *Medea* and *Alcestis* (*c.* 1539) and his tragedies *Baptistes sive calumnia* (perf. 1540) and *Jephthes sive votum* (perf. *c.* 1542; a well-ordered dramatization of the story of Jephthah's daughter, more than once trans. into French)—all written for his pupils—have a place in the history of French *tragedy. He later returned to Scotland, and was tutor (1570–8) to James VI and I. His many other works include a *Rerum Scoticarum Historia* (1582).

Buchez, PHILIPPE-JOSEPH-BENJAMIN (1796–1866), publicist and social reformer, parted company (1829) with the *Saint-Simoniens* to expound his own form of Christian socialism in his journal *L'Atelier* (1840–50; it also circulated in England) and in lectures in his own home.

Budé, GUILLAUME, in Latin BUDAEUS (*c.* 1468–1540), one of the first French humanists (*v. Renaissance*), a man of great learning who did much to revive the study of the classics (esp. of Greek, which he was taught by Lascaris). He enjoyed the favour of Louis XII, who sent him as ambassador to the pope, and of François Ier, who appointed him secretary and later royal librarian (*v. Bibliothèque nationale*), and, at his suggestion, instituted the *lecteurs royaux* (*v. Collège de France*). His chief works were Latin translations from Plutarch; commentaries on the Pandects (1508); a dialogue with the king *De philologia*; *De asse* (1514), a treatise on ancient coins; *Commentarii Linguae Graecae* (1529); *Le Livre de l'institution du prince* (1547). He encouraged Rabelais in his humanistic studies.

Bueil, JEAN DE, *v. Jouvencel, Le.*

Buffon, GEORGES-LOUIS LECLERC, COMTE DE (1707–88), naturalist. The son of a magistrate, he studied law and medicine, then produced treatises on scientific subjects and, following his admission to the *Académie des Sciences* (1734), translated (1735) Stephen Hales's *Vegetable Staticks* and (1740) Newton's *Method of Fluxions*. Apart from annual visits to Paris, connected with his curatorship (1739–88) of the *Jardin du Roi* (*v. Jardin des Plantes*), he spent most of his life at his birthplace, the Château de Montbard in Burgundy, improving his estate and composing his great *Histoire naturelle* (1749–1804, 44 vols.). The first 3 vols. (*Théorie de la Terre* and general views on generation and man) appeared in 1749; there followed 12 on quadrupeds (1755–67), 9 on birds (1770–83), 5 on minerals (1783–88), 7 (one the famous *Époques de la Nature*, 1779) on the geological periods of the earth (1774–89). The last 8 vols. (reptiles, fishes, etc.) were completed and published after his death by Lacépède. Other collaborators included Daubenton for anatomical descriptions, and Philibert Guéneau de Montbéliard (1720–85) and the abbé Aimé Bexon (1748–84) for birds. *v. Imprimerie nationale.*

He was the first modern writer to translate the facts of nature into a history. His method, at least in intention, was scientific: he collected information from correspondents all over the world and conducted experiments. His theories and hypotheses were fertile (e.g. his development of geographical zoology and the idea of geological periods), and he trod in paths later followed by Lamarck and Darwin. But at the outset he knew little of botany and entomology; and, in his impatience with the slow methods of science, he advanced theories and systems which were criticized—often rightly—as being based on insufficient evidence. Though he was not hostile to religion, his theory of the history of the earth offended the theologians, and the *Sorbonne condemned (1751) 14 propositions from the *Histoire naturelle*. To avoid controversy he signed a declaration abandoning anything in his work that might contravene the narrative of Moses. He contributed one article (on Nature) to the *Encyclopédie*, but remained aloof from the polemics of its supporters, though they shared his spirit of inquiry into nature. He was a humane man, who denounced slavery and deplored the plight of the peasants.

He aimed at a clear, harmonious, majestic style, suited to the dignity of his subject. (His *Discours sur le style* on his admission to the *Académie française in 1753 contained the well-known dictum, 'Le style est l'homme même'.) He is at his best, not in his animal descriptions (though some are strikingly vivid), but in his great surveys of nature, e.g. in the *Théorie de la Terre* and the *Époques de la Nature*.

Bugeaud de la Piconnerie, THOMAS-ROBERT, DUC D'ISLY (1784–1849), *maréchal de France, remembered as a military and organizing genius (notably during the conquest of Algeria, 1836–40) and as commander of the troops who tried in vain to defend Paris and the monarchy in 1848. He once turned out in response to a night-alarm and, finding he was still wearing his night-cap, cried 'Ma casquette!' (i.e. *képi*)—thus inspiring the well-known soldier's song, long a bugle-call:

> As-tu vu
> La casquette, la casquette,
> As-tu vu
> La casquette au Père Bugeaud?

Bug-Jargal (1826; written 1818), an early novel by Hugo about the negro revolution in San Domingo (*v. Toussaint Louverture*). It is full of horrific and fantastic episodes, but contains descriptive passages which foreshadow the vivid pictorial writing of his later novels.

Bullant, JEAN (1510–78), architect, as controller of royal buildings to Henri II built part of the *Tuileries (*cf. Delorme*, *P.*), but is best known for his books, e.g. his *Règle générale d'architecture* (1568).

Bulletin des lois, an official record of laws enacted by the French government from 1793 to 1931.

Bulliard, PIERRE, *v. Dictionaries*, 1783.

Bullier, *v. Bals populaires*.

Buloz, FRANÇOIS, *v. Revue des Deux Mondes*.

Buonarotti, MICHEL, *v. Babeuf*.

Bureau d'adresse, *v. Renaudot*.

Burgraves, Les (1843), an epic drama by Hugo. Its complete failure ended his career as a dramatist.

Through four generations of burgraves (lawless medieval princes who inhabited the fortified castles of the Rhine) evil and corruption are seen driving out the rough ideas of honour which had hitherto prevailed. The great-grandfather, Job, has suffered lifelong remorse for a youthful crime; his son is brave, but a lawless tyrant; his grandson is corrupt and dissipated; his great-grandson already betrays criminal instincts. A victim of Job's crime, now an old woman, plans to use the young lovers Regina and Otbert, the only creatures he loves, as innocent instruments of her revenge. Providence, in the shape of Barbarossa, intervenes at the last moment to prevent yet another crime, and an old mystery of death and untimely disappearance is solved.

Buridan, JEAN (d. after 1358), Nominalist philosopher, studied under Occam and became rector of the *University of Paris (1327). He is credited with the sophism of the ass ('l'Âne de Buridan'), equally pressed by hunger and thirst, which is placed between hay and water, but must die, having no determining motive of selection. Villon (*Ballade des dames du temps jadis*) refers to a legend that Jeanne de Bourgogne, wife of Philippe V, had him tied in a sack and drowned in the Seine.

Burnouf, EUGÈNE (1801–52), Orientalist and philologist, renowned for his work on the history of Buddhism and (following Anquetil-Duperron) on the *Zend-Avesta*.

Burrhus, in Racine's *Britannicus.

Bussy d'Amboise, LOUIS DE CLERMONT DE (2nd half of 16th c.), a favourite of the duc d'Alençon (brother of Henri III), a noted duellist and marauder, and prominent in the Massacre of St. *Bartholomew. His assassination by Montsoreau, whose wife he had seduced, is the theme of *Dumas *père*'s *La Dame de Monsoreau* and of a tragedy by Chapman.

Bussy-Rabutin, ROGER DE RABUTIN, COMTE DE BUSSY, *known as* (1618–93), a gallant soldier, not without wit and literary taste (he was a member of the *Académie*), but caustic and conceited, and an unscrupulous libertine. His *Histoire amoureuse des Gaules* (1665), portraying, with scandalous anecdotes, various ladies of the court and including an ill-natured sketch of his cousin, Mme de Sévigné, earned him a spell in the *Bastille* and relegation to his estates. His exile lasted 17 years and, though ultimately recalled, he was never restored to favour. Mme de Sévigné forgave him, however, and there are many of his letters in her collected correspondence. Though written in a style of perfect urbanity, they reveal him soured by disappointed ambition. But his book had a wide vogue: we find Pepys reading it, 1 May 1666.

Butor, MICHEL (1926–   ), novelist and essayist, studied philosophy, then taught abroad—in Egypt, England (at Manchester University), Greece, etc. After the novels *Passage de Milan* (1954) and *L'Emploi du temps* (1956; set in a grim English industrial town), he made his name as an exponent of the *nouveau roman* with *La Modification* (1957) and confirmed it with *Degrés* (1960), *Mobile* (1962), *Réseau aérien* (1962), *Description de San Marco* (1963), *Intervalle* (1973), etc. Coming to adulthood in the wake of Proust, James Joyce, the *Surrealists, and Sartre, he has experimented with a rehandling of space, time, and the traditional 'reality' of the novel, progressively abandoning ordered narration. His essays, which show him as an acute and imaginative critic, include *Histoire extraordinaire* (1961; on Baudelaire), *Les Œuvres d'art imaginaires chez Proust* (1964), *Portrait de l'artiste en jeune singe* (1967), and the collection *Répertoire* (1960–74, 4 vols. to date; inc. essays on the novel). He has also published poetry and *Illustrations* (1964–73, 3 vols.), 'une sorte de journal intime.'

Byron, *v. Foreign Influences,* 3.

C

Cabale (Cabbala), esoteric—and traditional as opposed to written—doctrines concerning the mysteries of creation and the nature of God; largely the basis of occult and illuminist philosophies (*v. Illuminisme*).

This mystical interpretation of the Bible, allegedly revealed to elect saints by the Holy Spirit and then preserved in hidden books to be delivered only to a privileged few ('such as be wise'), was bound up with Jewish chronology and messianology, and based on the belief that the 22 letters of the Hebrew alphabet could be so decomposed and rearranged as to reveal hidden truths about the infinite and the finite, and the abstractions or emanations by which the primal substances were gradually condensed into visible matter. These substances were inhabited by creatures purer than man (salamanders in fire, sylphs in air, nymphs in water, gnomes in the earth), over whom the initiate could acquire power. Cabbalists and salamanders ornament A. France's *La *Rôtisserie de la Reine Pédauque*, and before him were taken more seriously by, for example, Nerval and Rimbaud.

Cabale des dévots, *v. Compagnie du Saint-Sacrement.*

Cabanis, GEORGES (1757–1808), physician and materialist philosopher, one of the *idéologues*. His *Traité du physique et du moral de l'homme* (1798–9; republ. as *Rapports du...*, 1802) reduces the spiritual side of man to a function or faculty of his physical nature.

Cabaret, JEAN, v. *History*, 1.

Cabarrus, v. *Tallien*.

Cabet, ÉTIENNE (1785–1856), social reformer, as a political refugee in England (from 1834) came under the influence of Robert Owen. His socialistic romance *Voyage en Icarie* (1842), published after his return to France, depicted a Utopia where fraternity was the only religion and the economic system was based on equality of conditions and community of goods. He made three unsuccessful attempts to establish his 'Icarie' in America. His disciples deserted him, and he finally died of despair.

Cabinet des antiques, Le, v. *Comédie humaine, La* (*Scènes de la vie de province*).

Cabinet du roi, Le, a famous collection of commemorative prints (court festivals, royal triumphs, etc.) formed by Louis XIV, originally for presentation to distinguished visitors. v. *Imprimerie nationale*.

Cabinet noir, a secret bureau at the *Hôtel des Postes* where letters were opened, established by Louis XIV. It was abolished by the *Assemblée constituante* and again, finally, in 1830.

Cabinets de lecture, little libraries or bookshops where, for a small sum, one could read papers, periodicals, new novels, etc.; a feature of 18th- and 19th-c. Parisian life, mentioned in L.-S. *Mercier's Tableau de Paris*, Balzac's *Illusions perdues*, etc.

Cabrion, in *Sue's Les Mystères de Paris*.

Cacambo, in Voltaire's *Candide*.

Cacouacs, Nouveau Mémoire pour servir à l'histoire des (1757), an allegorical pamphlet caricaturing the *Encyclopédistes*, published anonymously by Nicolas Moreau, later librarian to Marie-Antoinette. A *Premier Mémoire sur les Cacouacs* had appeared in the *Mercure de France* earlier in 1757.

Cadet Buteux, hero of Désaugiers's happy parodies (usually sung at *cafés-concerts*) of plays and operas in vogue during the First Empire. Cadet Buteux would roam the streets, pick up the gossip, go to a play or opera, and return late at night to describe it scene by scene, with comments, to his wife. He came to typify the racy wit of the people.

Cadet Roussel, v. *Aude, J.*

Cadignan, Princesse de, heroine of Balzac's *Les *Secrets de la princesse de Cadignan*; also in *Illusions perdues*, Le *Cabinet des antiques*, and Le *Député d'Arcis*.

Cadmus et Hermione, v. *Quinault*.

Cadoudal, GEORGES (1771–1804), under the name 'Georges' led Royalist risings in the *Vendée* (and v. *Quiberon*) and was executed for conspiring with Pichegru and others to depose Napoleon and restore the monarchy. He figures in Sainte-Beuve's *Volupté*.

Café. Coffee is said to have been introduced in Marseilles in 1654, and in 1669 the Turkish ambassador brought Louis XIV a gift of some. Soon afterwards the first *café*, or coffee-house, was opened in the Foire Saint-Germain by an Armenian. The café speedily became a national institution, a place where one could sit and drink (coffee and other beverages), read the papers, write letters, talk literature or politics, or play games. There were 300 in Paris by 1715, and some 900 by 1789. (Early references to them occur in Montesquieu's *Lettres persanes*, 1721.) Some, notably those in the *Palais-Royal* during the Revolution, were hotbeds of political intrigue, e.g. the CAFÉ DE FOY (*v.* below), the CAFÉ DE CHARTRES (Royalists), the CAFÉ CHRÉTIEN (*Jacobins*); others are linked with the literary life of Paris as places where great works received a first hearing, where movements were launched, reviews founded, etc.; and the practice of associating particular cafés with particular movements still persists. In the heyday of *Symbolism, when little reviews pullulated and funds seldom ran to offices, much editorial work was done in cafés.

The CAFÉ ANGLAIS (Boulevard des Italiens) was frequented by the English tourists who flocked to Paris after the Peace of Amiens (1802). When the Peace was broken and the English left, it fell on bad days, but flourished again under the Second Empire as the great centre of luxury and extravagance—the resort of rich dandies, actresses, royalty, etc., who would dine in its private room, 'le Grand Seize'. The CAFÉ DE FOY (est. 2nd half of 18th c., closed 1863; Palais-Royal) was patronized well before the Revolution by politicians (e.g. Desmoulins, on 12 July 1789) and *nouvellistes*, and later by writers and artists. The CAFÉ DE LA RÉGENCE (est. early 18th c.) was a famous resort of chess-players (inc. Robespierre) and also frequented by writers, e.g. Chamfort, Diderot (who mentions it in *Le *Neveu de Rameau*), Grimm, Marmontel, J.-J. Rousseau, Voltaire. The CAFÉ HARDY (Boulevard des Italiens) was fashionable in the early 19th c. ('Au sortir de chez La Rive, we go at Hardy Coffee', Stendhal's *Journal*, 1804) and was also, like many cafés, a restaurant—hence the *mot* 'Il faut être bien riche pour dîner au Café Hardy, et bien hardi pour dîner au Café Riche'. Later, as the MAISON DORÉE, it was patronized by the gilded youth of the Second Empire. The CAFÉ MOMUS (near the *Louvre) figures in *Murger's *Scènes de la vie de Bohème*. The CAFÉ PROCOPE (est. well before 1700; opposite the then home of the *Comédie-Française*—a favourable position) soon became the most famous literary and political café of the day, frequented by Voltaire (whose table there was long preserved), Diderot,

d'Alembert, Buffon, Marmontel, J.-J. Rousseau, etc. It changed hands before the Revolution, became the CAFÉ ZOPPI, and was frequented by such Revolutionaries as Danton, Fabre d'Églantine, Hébert, Marat, and Robespierre; the *bonnet rouge* is said to have appeared there for the first time. Later *habitués* included Balzac, Gautier, Gambetta, Verlaine, Huysmans, and Oscar Wilde. The CAFÉ TORTONI (Boulevard des Italiens) was the most fashionable Paris café during the Empire and Restoration, patronized by politicians, men of letters, and rich foreign visitors. It was a supper resort of the 'dandys' *c.* 1830; and in the afternoons elegant ladies sat outside in their carriages eating ices. The CAFÉ VACHETTE (so called from 1827, earlier the CAFÉ DES GRANDS HOMMES), always popular with students, became a resort of writers in the late 19th c., e.g. Moréas, Louÿs, and Barrès. *Cf. Bals populaires.*

The many literary and artistic cafés of the 20th c. include the COUPOLE, the ROTONDE, and the DÔME, all in *Montparnasse; the DEUX MAGOTS, the BRASSERIE LIPP, and the FLORE, all on the Boulevard Saint-Germain.

Cagliostro, GIUSEPPE BALSAMO, *known as* COMTE (1743–95), a clever Italian charlatan who acquired a great reputation in France as a wonder-worker. One of his chief dupes was Cardinal de Rohan (*v. Collier, L'Affaire du*). His death sentence for heresy (Rome, 1789) was commuted to life imprisonment. He figures in *Dumas *père's* Mémoires d'un médecin: Joseph Balsamo.*

Cahier d'un retour au pays natal, *v.* Césaire.

Cahiers d'André Walter, Les, *v.* Gide.

Cahiers de la quinzaine, Les (1900–14; 238 nos., publ. at irregular intervals), a highly individual periodical f. by Péguy (and issued from his bookshop), each number being devoted to one work or author. It published essays, criticism, poetry, and novels by writers who later became famous (e.g. Benda, Rolland), as well as Péguy's own output. It is in many ways a guide to the ideals and opinions of a whole generation. *v. Halévy* (3).

Cahiers du sud, Les (1915–67; publ. at Marseilles), a notable literary and philosophical review.

Caillavet, GASTON ARMAN DE (1869–1915), son of Mme Arman de Caillavet (*v. France, A.*; *Salon*, 1), author with Flers of sophisticated, sometimes sharply satirical comedies, e.g. *Le Cœur a ses raisons* (1904), *L'Âne de Buridan* (1909), *Monsieur Bretonneau* (1914), *Le Roi* (1908), *Le Bois sacré* (1911; parliamentary life), *L'Habit vert* (1913; *Académie* circles).

Caillé or **Caillié**, RENÉ (1799–1838), explorer. Inspired by *Robinson Crusoe*, he penetrated to Central Africa (1824) and finally reached Timbuctoo (1828), disguised as a Moslem. He was the first European to return alive from these parts.

Caillois, ROGER (1913–78), philosopher and sociologist, an essayist and critic whose work is marked by boldness of thought, classical purity of form, and an anti-romantic spirit; a member of the *Académie* (1971). His essays and studies, on a wide range of subjects, include *Le Mythe et l'homme* (1938), *L'Homme et le sacré* (1939), *Le Rocher de Sisyphe* (1942), *Poétique de Saint-John Perse* (1954), *Méduse et Cie* (1960), *Esthétique généralisée* (1962), *Images, images... Essais sur le rôle et les pouvoirs de l'imagination* (1966), *Cases d'un échiquier* (1970).

Ça ira, a famous Revolutionary song, first sung (to the tune of *Le Carillon national*, a country dance) while Paris was preparing for the *Fête de la *Fédération* of 1790. Like *La *Carmagnole*, it was prohibited by Bonaparte when he became First Consul. The original refrain ran:

Ah! ça ira, ça ira, ça ira!
Le peuple, en ce jour, sans cesse répète:
Ah! ça ira, ça ira, ça ira!
Malgré les mutins, tout réussira.

During the *Terror they sang, as a last line:

Les aristocrates *à la lanterne!

Calas, JEAN (1698–1762), a *Huguenot merchant of Toulouse, tried with the utmost brutality and fanaticism by the Toulouse *parlement*, and then horribly executed, on the false charge of having murdered his son because the latter wanted to become a Catholic. The son had, in fact, committed suicide. After the execution the family moved to Geneva, where Voltaire took up their case with such vigour that the verdict was quashed and Calas's innocence established by the *Conseil d'état* (1765). The case excited widespread sympathy. A subscription list opened in England for the family was headed by the king and the archbishop of Canterbury.

Calendar, *v. Republican Calendar; Year.*

Calepino, AMBROGIO, *v. Dictionaries,* 1502.

Caliban, *v. Drames philosophiques.*

Callias, MME NINA DE, *v. Salon*, 1.

Calligrammes, *v. Apollinaire.*

Callot, JACQUES (1592–1635), a bold, fanciful artist, whose engravings vividly illustrate the France of his day.

Calmet, DOM AUGUSTIN, *v. Dictionaries,* 1720–1.

Calonne, CHARLES-ALEXANDRE DE (1734–1802), controller-general of finances 1783–7. His prodigalities and dishonesty completed the ruin of the monarchy. He was disgraced, fled to England, and was soon rendering dubious service to the royal *émigrés*.

Calonne, ERNEST DE (1822–87), contrived in 1845 to pass off his own comedy, *Le Docteur amoureux*, as a recently discovered work by Molière. It was duly produced at the *Odéon*, with the alleged manuscript on exhibition in the foyer. For a time he fooled everyone except Gautier, who had been suspicious from the outset.

Calotte, a leaden cap with bells, the badge of an 18th-c. company of satirical wits, the *Régiment de la Calotte*. There was a comedy of that name (prod. 1721) by Fuzelier, Lesage, and d'Orneval (d. 1766).

Calvin, JEAN (1509–64), Reformer, b. at Noyon in Picardy. His father, a well-to-do diocesan official, intended him for the Church, and he was educated in Paris at the *Collège de La Marche* and the *Collège de Montaigu*. He then studied canon and civil law but, when his father died (1530), abandoned these studies for Greek and Hebrew. His first work (1532) was a commentary on Seneca's *De clementia*. Meanwhile he had become interested in the doctrines of the Reformers. In 1533 his friend Nicolas Cop, trimestrial rector of the University of Paris, delivered an oration, written by Calvin, showing Lutheran tendencies, and Calvin had to leave Paris for a time. He left again (1535) after the *Affaire des *placards*. In 1536, which saw the first (Latin) edition of his famous *Institution de la religion chrétienne*, he went (as preacher and professor of theology) to help Farel organize the Reformation at Geneva. When expelled from the city (with Farel, 1538), he went to Strasbourg. There he made contact with other Reformers (Luther, Melanchthon, Bucer, etc.), and also married. In 1541 he returned to Geneva, where his party had prevailed, and for the next 14 years devoted himself to establishing a theocratic *régime*. He brooked no opposition: he sent Servetus to the stake (1553), and defended his action in a *Déclaration où il est montré qu'il est licite de punir les hérétiques* (1554). From 1555 he was the unopposed dictator of Geneva. Always delicate, he died exhausted by his labours, remaining poor to the end. *v.* *Huguenots*.

The bulk of his work is in Latin. His writings in French (besides his translation of the *Institution*) include controversial treatises, pamphlets, sermons, and many letters of advice and admonition to Protestant princes and churches. His style, though not elegant, is clear, concise, and forthright, sometimes marked by anger, irony, or contempt. He was one of the first theologians to write treatises in French, and helped to adapt the construction of the French sentence to argument as distinct from narrative.

Camargo, MARIE-ANNE DE CUPIS DE (1710–70), 'La Camargo', a famous Belgian dancer; a great success at the *Opéra*.

Cambacérès, JEAN-JACQUES RÉGIS DE (1753–1824), a magistrate whose prudence and legal training served him well as a member of the *Convention*, then as Second Consul (*v. Consulat*), and later in high official posts under the Empire. Napoleon had great confidence in him. He left memoirs. *v. Code civil.*

Cambrai, L'Archevêque de, *v. Fénelon.*

Cambronne, Le Mot de. At *Waterloo when the *Garde impériale*, under Cambronne, was surrounded and summoned by the English to surrender, he is said to have replied not (as stated on his monument at Nantes) 'La garde meurt et ne se rend pas', but 'Merde!'—a coarse expletive expressing his defiant disgust.

Camelots du roi, *v. Action française.*

Camisards, *Huguenot extremists of the mountain region of the Cévennes who rose in rebellion (1702–5); so called because they wore a white canvas shirt (Prov. *camisa*) over their clothes. Their leader, Jean Cavalier (1680–1740), came to terms with the forces sent to quell the rising, then, mistrustful of his followers, fled to England. He ended his days as governor of Jersey.

Campagnes hallucinées, Les, *v. Verhaeren.*

Campan,   JEANNE-LOUISE-HENRIETTE

GENEST, MME (1752–1822), a gifted and exceptionally well-educated woman, was reader to Louis XV's daughters, then a devoted lady-in-waiting to Marie-Antoinette (1770–92; she left *Mémoires sur la vie privée de Marie-Antoinette*, 1823). Destitute after the *Terror, she opened a girls' boarding-school, where Hortense de Beauharnais was a pupil. Napoleon later made her head of a *pensionnat* for sisters and daughters of members of the *Légion d'honneur*. Her curriculum included domestic economy, which suited his views on the education of women ('Il faut que les femmes tricotent').

Camp du drap d'or, Le (The Field of the Cloth of Gold, near Calais), the scene of an unfruitful meeting (1520) between François Ier and Henry VIII; so called from the magnificence both displayed. *v. Fleurange.*

Campistron, JEAN-GALBERT DE (1656–1723), soldier and dramatist. A professed imitator of Racine, he wrote several rather lifeless tragedies, marked by gentle melancholy, e.g. *Virginie* (1683), *Arminius* (1684), *Andronic* (1685), *Tiridate* (1691; a successful play—possibly his best—about a noble character carried away by a fatal passion); also *Le Jaloux désabusé* (1709), a successful comedy.

Campo Formio, Treaty of, *v. Coalitions* (1).

Camus, ALBERT (1913–60), novelist, dramatist, essayist, and journalist; winner of the *Prix Nobel* (1957). He was born in Algeria, the son of a farm labourer (killed in the 1914-18 war), and his early life (evoked in the essays of *L'Envers et l'endroit*, 1937) was one of extreme poverty. He won his way to the University of Algiers, but ill-health forced him to abandon his studies for the *agrégation*. For some years from 1935, he worked in Algiers as actor and producer with a left-wing theatre company he had helped to found. During the 1939-45 war, he made his name both as a creative writer and as a journalist active in the *Resistance,

emerging at the Liberation as editor (1944-7) of the left-wing daily *Combat*. By the time of his death at the age of 46 in a car accident he had won an international reputation. His meteoric rise to fame may be attributed to the fact that he exactly caught and expressed the mood and the preoccupations of his contemporaries.

He made his name in 1942 with the novel *L'Étranger* and *Le Mythe de Sisyphe*, a philosophical essay, works that are complementary in that they illustrate and define the philosophy of the 'absurd' that underlies all his writing. *L'Étranger* depicts a man who is condemned to death less for a murder he has done his utmost to avoid committing than because he is alienated in a hypocritical *bourgeois* society and refuses to conform to its false values. Though his *homo absurdus* is obviously a close relation of *Existentialist man, Camus refused to be classed as an Existentialist and broke openly with Sartre in 1952. Broadly speaking, he regarded the 'absurd' primarily as a point of departure, and his works are at once a revelation of the human predicament and a quest for means of surmounting it. He brought to the task an innate humanism and a Mediterranean love of life (seen in the sensual pantheism of *Noces*, 1938, essays), and he swiftly emerged as a compelling moralist. His *Lettres à un ami allemand* (1945) and *L'Homme révolté* (1951; essays) reflect the evolution of a moral and metaphysical concept of rebellion against the human condition in sharp contrast to the politico-historical concept of revolution. In another highly successful novel, *La Peste* (1947), where the plague in Oran has reference also to the German Occupation and to human life in general, rebellion takes the form of heroic stoicism (one character aspiring to be 'un saint sans Dieu') and men regain human dignity and give meaning to their existence through social co-operation. *La Chute* (1956) is much less optimistic in its view of man. The masterly *nouvelles* of *L'Exil et le royaume* (1957) illustrate the quality of his prose. His work for the theatre includes *Le Malentendu* (1944), *Caligula* (1945;

written 1938), *L'État de siège* (1948; based on *La Peste*), *Les Justes* (1949), and a series of adaptations. Many of his journalistic articles are collected in *Actuelles* (1950–8, 3 vols.). Two volumes of his notebooks have appeared, *Carnets* (1962–4), covering the years 1935–51.

Camus, JEAN-PIERRE (1584–1652), bishop of Belley, disciple and friend of St. François de Sales. Besides theological works, he wrote religious romances modelled on *L'**Astrée, e.g. *Palombe, ou la Femme honorable.*

Canada, *v. Acadie*; *Cartier*; *Champlain*; *Huron*; *Lahontan*; *Lévis*; *Montcalm*; *Nouvelle France*; *Relations des Jésuites*. For full coverage of Canadian history and of French-Canadian literature *v. The Oxford Companion to Canadian History and Literature* and *The Oxford Companion to the Theatre.*

Canalis, a poet (said to be a caricature of Lamartine) in several novels of Balzac's *Comédie humaine, e.g. *Modeste Mignon, **Illusions perdues.*

Candide (1759), by Voltaire, a philosophical tale demonstrating the calamities that befall man, a satire—provoked by the Lisbon earthquake of 1755—on the optimism of Leibniz and J.-J. Rousseau.
   Candide is a gentle, sensible young man, brought up in the household of a Westphalian baron, Thunder-ten-Tronckh, and taught by the philosopher Pangloss, an invincible optimist who holds that all is for the best in the best of all possible worlds. He is seen making love to Cunégonde, the baron's daughter, and summarily ejected from the house. After being forcibly enlisted in the Bulgarian army and brutally beaten, he meets Pangloss (now in dire distress, but still an optimist) and hears that the baron and his family have been massacred. After a shipwreck, they reach Lisbon, where Candide nearly dies in the earthquake. In an *auto-da-fé* held to avert further tremors, Pangloss is hanged for his optimism and Candide beaten for listening to him. He is now reunited with Cunégonde (who had not been completely massacred, but sold into slavery), kills her lovers, and escapes with her to S. America. Here he has the misfortune to kill her brother; he also, with his servant Cacambo, visits Eldorado. But he pines for Cunégonde, from whom he has been separated, and returns to Europe with Martin, a Manichaean philosopher who holds that God has handed over the world to a maleficent spirit. He falls foul of swindlers in France, then lands at Portsmouth, where Admiral Byng is being executed, because, he is told, 'il est bon de tuer de temps en temps un amiral pour encourager les autres'. In Venice, where he is to meet Cunégonde, he finds six exiled kings, including the Young Pretender. Learning that Cunégonde has been captured by pirates and is washing dishes by the Sea of Marmora, he goes to Constantinople, ransoms her (she has grown very ugly), and finds among the galley-slaves her brother (not completely killed) and Pangloss (not completely hanged). They buy a farm and set to work, Pangloss expounding that all has been for the best. 'Cela est bien dit,' replies Candide, 'mais il faut cultiver notre jardin.'

Candide, *v. Press*, 9.

Canrobert, CERTAIN (1809–95), **maréchal de France*, a famous soldier, served in Algeria, the Crimea, the **Franco-Prussian war. He left memoirs.

Canson, *v. Chanson.*

Cantatrice chauve, La, *v. Ionesco.*

Cantilènes, *v. Chansons de geste*; *Moréas.*

Capetians, 3rd dynasty of kings of France, succeeded the **Carolingians. The dynasty extended from **Hugues Capet (987) in direct line to Charles IV (d. 1328). The throne then passed first to its **Valois, then to its **Bourbon branches. *v.* also *Orléans.*

Capitaine Fracasse, Le (1863), a picaresque novel by Gautier. In the days of Louis XIII, the impoverished baron de Sigognac joins the band of travelling comedians to which his love Isabelle belongs, and plays the part of Capitaine Fracasse (a boisterous soldier of Italian comedy). He squires her through many adventures, both thrilling and comic, and—when she proves to be the daughter of a prince—is rewarded with her hand and a governorship. The opening account of his dilapidated Château de la Misère and its half-starved inmates is one of Gautier's finest descriptive passages.

Caporal, Le Petit, a name given by his soldiers to the young Napoléon Bonaparte. Dumas *père* alleges that when he took command in Italy (1796) he was so young that the troops assumed he must have jumped some promotions and, each time he won a battle, promoted him to a rank he had missed: 'Le Petit Caporal' arose in this way, and became a nickname.

Caprice, v. Un Caprice.

Caprices de Marianne, Les (1833, in the **Revue des Deux Mondes*; 1834, in **Un Spectacle dans un fauteuil*), a 2-act, prose comedy by Musset; produced 1851.
    Octave, a gay libertine in Renaissance Naples, courts Marianne, Claudio's young wife, on behalf of the timid Célio. She is not interested in Célio, but is momentarily attracted to Octave, and gives him a rendezvous. He sends Célio, who falls into a trap set by Claudio, and is killed. Octave, appalled and conscience-stricken, takes a bitter leave of Marianne, who would quite like him to stay.

Captivité de Saint Malc, La (1673), a religious poem by La Fontaine, written at the request of the **Port-Royal* solitaries; based on a story told by St. Jerome.
    Malc is captured by Arab brigands. A virtuous lady, torn from her husband by the brigands, shares his captivity. They escape, and are miraculously delivered from their pursuers by a lioness.

Capus, ALFRED (1858–1922), journalist,

novelist, and playwright, wrote amusing studies of Parisian life, e.g. *Les Honnêtes Gens* (1878), short stories; *Années d'aventure* (1895), a novel; *La Bourse ou la vie* (1900), *La Veine* (1901), *Les Deux Écoles* (1902), *Les Maris de Léontine* (1903), and *La Petite Fonctionnaire* (1904), all comedies.

Carabas, Marquis de. In **Perrault's tale *Le Chat botté* ('Puss in Boots') the cat passes off his master as the wealthy marquis de Carabas. Béranger's *chanson* of this title satirized the arrogance of the nobles after the Restoration.

Carabosse, the wicked fairy in fairy-tales. She is sure to turn up at christenings.

Caractères de Théophraste, Les, v. La Bruyère.

Caran d'Ache (from the Russ. for 'pencil'), *pseudonym of* EMMANUEL POIRÉ (1858–1909), a Russian-born cartoonist whose work was published in *La *Vie parisienne*, *Caricature*, etc. He was noted for his **silhouette drawings, and his shadow-play *L'Épopée* (on Napoleon's victories) drew crowds to the **Chat-Noir*.

Carbonari ('charcoal-burners'; Fr. *charbonniers*), Italian secret societies (meeting at first in charcoal-burners' huts) formed to combat Napoleonic despotism. Later (esp. *c.* 1821) they sprang up in France, where they became anti-monarchical and anti-Catholic. Members of the *Charbonnerie*—Bonapartists, republicans, constitutionalists—were organized in lodges (*ventes*) with fantastic initiation ceremonies. *v. Sergents de La Rochelle.*

Carco, Francis, *pseudonym of* FRANÇOIS CARCOPINO (1886–1958), poet and novelist, b. in New Caledonia. He lived mainly in Paris from 1910 and is remembered for works vividly depicting, with a mixture of irony and sentimentality, the seamy side of Bohemian artist life in **Montmartre. His verse includes *La Bohème et mon cœur* (1912), short **fantaisiste* poems showing his affinities with Laforgue and Verlaine, and *Mortefontaine* (1946). His prose works include the novels *Jésus-la-Caille* (1914), *L'Équipe* (1919), *L'Homme traqué* (1922), *Rien qu'une femme* (1924), *Brumes* (1935), and several volumes of reminiscences, notably *De Montmartre au Quartier latin* (1934).

Carcopino, JÉRÔME (1881–1970), brother of the above, political and literary historian of Roman antiquity. His many works include *César* (1937), *La Vie quotidienne à Rome à l'apogée de l'Empire* (1939), *Les Secrets de la correspondance de Cicéron* (1948).

Carel de Sainte-Garde, JACQUES, *v. Epic Poetry.*

Carême (Lent). Famous Lenten sermons were preached by Bourdaloue (1672–82, 35 in all) and, above all, Massillon (in collections known as the *Grand Carême*, 40 preached 1699-1704; and the *Petit Carême*, 10 preached 1718 before the young Louis XV).

Carême, MARIE-ANTOINE or ANTONIN (1784–1833), a famous cook, trained in Napoleon's kitchens, who served Tsar Alexander I, the Prince Regent (who failed to appreciate cooking as a fine art), Baron Rothschild, Talleyrand (whose kitchen he deemed 'le sanctuaire de la cuisine française'), etc. He wrote *Le Pâtissier pittoresque* (1815), *Le Maître d'hôtel français* (1822), *Le Cuisinier français, ou l'Art de la cuisine au XIXᵉ siècle* (1833), and memoirs (in *Les Classiques de la table*, 1843).

Carillon, *v. Montcalm.*

Carité, *v. Charité.*

Carloman (751–71), king of the Franks (*Carolingian dynasty), son and successor of Pépin le Bref, r. jointly with his brother Charlemagne 768–71.

Carloman (865–84), king of France

(*Carolingian dynasty), 2nd son and successor of Louis II, r. jointly with his brother Louis III 879–82, then alone till 884.

Carmagnole, La, the Revolutionary costume worn by the *fédérés in 1792 (*v. Revolutions*, 1) and adopted by the *Jacobins. Its final form was a short-skirted coat with rows of metal buttons, black trousers, scarlet or *tricolore waist-coat, and red cap. It gave its name to one of the most popular Revolutionary songs (composed 1792, when Louis XVI was imprisoned), sung by troops on the march and at executions. Bonaparte pro-hibited it when he became First Consul (*cf. Ça ira*). It had 11 or 12 verses, subject to constant revision and addition. The original first verse was:

> Monsieur *Véto avait promis
> D'être fidèle à son pays.
> Mais il y a manqué,
> Ne faisons plus quartié.
> Dansons la Carmagnole;
> Vive le son, vive le son,
> Dansons la Carmagnole,
> Vive le son du canon.

Carmen (1847; 1852, in *Nouvelles*), a tale of Spanish gipsy life and love by Mérimée; basis of the libretto by Meilhac and L. Halévy for Bizet's opera *Carmen* (1875).

Carmontelle, LOUIS CARROGIS, *known as* (1717–1806), painter and author of *proverbes dramatiques.*

Carmosine (1850, a *feuilleton in *Le *Constitutionnel*; 1853, in *Comédies et Proverbes), a *proverbe (3 acts, prose) by Musset, produced 1865; based on a tale in the *Decameron*. The king, hearing that Carmosine is nearly dying of love for him, visits her; and he and his queen show her such understanding that she sees a happy future dawning, near him, but married to a man of his choice.

Carnavalet, *v. Musée Carnavalet.*

Carolingians, 2nd dynasty of kings of

France, succeeded the *Merovingians.
The dynasty extended from the accession
of Pépin le Bref (*v. Maire du Palais*) in 751
to the death of Louis V in 987. The death
of Pépin's son Charlemagne was followed
by a period of internal strife (aggravated
by Danish, Hungarian, and Saracen
invasions) under his successors, during
which the kingdom disintegrated. For the
Carolingian Renaissance *v. Alcuin*;
Académie palatine.

Carolus-Duran, CHARLES DURAND,
known as (1837–1917), portrait-painter,
especially of women and children. His
portrait of his wife, *La Dame au gant*
(1869), is well known.

Caron, PIERRE (1875–1952), archivist
(director of the *Archives nationales*, 1937–
41) and bibliographer. His many
compilations include the indispensable
*Manuel pratique pour l'étude de la
Révolution française* (first publ. 1912).

Carrel, ARMAND (1800–36), journalist,
founder (1830, with Thiers and Mignet) of
the daily paper *Le *National*. He was killed
in a duel with É. de Girardin, following a
violent political dispute.

Carrière, EUGÈNE (1849–1906), painter
and lithographer, known for his scenes of
family life and portraits of writers and
artists, e.g. Verlaine, Daudet, Rodin.

Carrosse du Saint-Sacrement, Le, *v.
Théâtre de Clara Gazul.*

Carte de Tendre, La, an allegorical map
of the region of the tender sentiments,
devised by Mlle de Scudéry, assisted by
members of her *salon, and introduced by
her in *Clélie*. Its main features are three
cities of 'Tendre', on three rivers,
'Tendre-sur-Estime', 'Tendre-sur-Re-
connaissance', 'Tendre-sur-Inclination'.
Three roads, each starting from 'Nouvelle
Amitié', lead to the cities, passing through
stages appropriate to their respective
goals, such as 'Sincérité', 'Probité', 'Petits
Soins', 'Empressement'. Wrong turnings
lead to the 'Lac d'Indifférence' or the 'Mer
d'Inimitié'.

Cartesianism, *v. Descartes.*

Cartier, JACQUES (1491–1557), navigator
and explorer. He was sent by François Ier
in 1534 and later years on voyages of
discovery to N. America. On the second
of these he sailed up the St. Lawrence to
the Indian village of Hochelaga, where
Montreal now stands, and took possession
of 'la Nouvelle France' (*cf. Acadie*). His
Voyages have been published more than
once, notably in the Ottawa edition of
1924.

Cartouche, LOUIS-DOMINIQUE BOUR-
GUIGNON, *known as* (1693–1721), the son of
a Paris wine-merchant, allegedly stolen by
gipsies, who became leader of a famous
band of robbers, and was finally broken on
the wheel. He figures in several plays of the
period, e.g. *Arlequin-Cartouche* (*v.
Arlequin*) and *Cartouche, ou les Voleurs.*

Casanova de Seingalt, GIACOMO (1725–
98), an Italian whose memoirs, in
imperfect but lively French, about his
rogueries, adventures, and disreputable
amours all over Europe provide a highly
entertaining account of 18th-c. society.

Casaubon, ISAAC (1559–1614), a famous
Hellenist, son of *Huguenot refugees in
Geneva, son-in-law of H. Estienne. He
was professor at Montpellier, then went to
Paris on the invitation of Henri IV, and
later to England on that of James I.

Cassandre, *v. La Calprenède.*

Cassou, JEAN, *v. Resistance.*

Castel, JEAN (d. 1476), grandson of
Christine de Pisan, a Benedictine of the
Cluniac Order (latterly an abbot),
historiographer and poet (e.g. *Le Spécule
des pécheurs*, a moralizing poem).

Castellio, Castellion, or **Châteillon**,
SÉBASTIEN (1515–63), Protestant theologian, author of a Latin translation of
the Bible (1551; dedicated to Edward VI),
the *Traité des hérétiques* (1554), con-

demning the execution of Servetus (*cf.*
Calvin), etc.

Castelnau, Michel de (1520–92),
diplomat, left important political
memoirs.

Castoiement d'un père à son fils, the title
of two verse translations (late 12th and
13th c. respectively) of the *Disciplina
clericalis* (early 12th c.; written in Spain),
short tales told by a father for the
edification of his son. They set the example
for other *castoiements* or cautionary poems.

**Catalauniques, Les Champs (The
Catalaunian Fields**, near Châlons-sur-
Marne). Here the Romans under Aëtius
defeated Attila (451), a decisive event in
European history.

Cateau-Cambrésis, Treaty of (1559),
between Henri II and Philip II of Spain,
ended France's long conflict with the
emperor Charles V and his son Philip II.
She renounced her claim to Naples and
Milan, and in effect abandoned Savoy and
Piedmont. Her frontier with the
Netherlands was also settled.

Cathédrale, La, *v. Huysmans.*

Catherine II (1729–96), empress of
Russia from 1762, corresponded with
Voltaire, Grimm, and Diderot, and was
the liberal benefactress of Diderot and
Sénac de Meilhan. She left curious
Mémoires in French.

Catherine de Médicis (1519–89),
daughter of Lorenzo de' Medici, duke of
Urbino; wife of Henri II; mother of
François II, Charles IX (she was regent
during his minority), and Henri III. *v.
Bartholomew, Massacre of St.*

Cathos, in Molière's *Les *Précieuses
ridicules.*

Catinat, Nicolas de (1637–1712),
**maréchal de France*, one of Louis XIV's
ablest captains, abandoned the law for the
army and rose solely through merit. He

took Nice and Savoy (1690–1). He left
memoirs.

Caton, Distiques de, *v. Distiques.*

Caturce, Jean de (d. 1532), an early
Protestant, burnt at the stake at Toulouse.
v. Évangélisme.

Caulaincourt,   Armand-Augustin-
Louis, marquis de (1773–1827), served in
the Republican armies and became A.D.C.
to Bonaparte (1802); promoted general
and created duc de Vicence (1804). A man
of upright character, not afraid to speak his
mind, he was one of Napoleon's most
trusted advisers, charged with many
diplomatic missions. He was at his side
during and after the Russian campaign
(1812), and it was he who was sent with
the offer of abdication to the Allied Powers
(1814). His memoirs (1933, 3 vols.) are
illuminating and reliable.

Causeries du lundi, Les, the famous
critical and biographical essays by Sainte-
Beuve which appeared every Monday
(hence the name) in the *Constitutionnel*
(Oct. 1849–Nov. 1852; Sept. 1861–Jan.
1867), the *Moniteur universel* (Dec. 1852–
Aug. 1861; Sept. 1867–Nov. 1868), and
the *Temps* (1869). They were collected in
Causeries du lundi (1851–62, 15 vols.;
articles of 1849–61) and *Nouveaux Lundis*
(1863–70, 13 vols.; articles of 1861–9).
Some of his earlier articles in the *Globe*,
the *Revue de Paris*, the *Revue des Deux
Mondes*, etc.—*cf. Critiques et Portraits
littéraires*—were collected in *Premiers
Lundis* (1874–5, 3 vols.).

Causes grasses, *v. Basoche*; *Coquillart.*

Cavalier, Jean, *v. Camisards.*

Cavalier   Misérey,   Le (1887), by
Hermant, a *Naturalist novel of army life
in peacetime; a severe indictment of
current army conditions which provoked
much indignation and comment. It is the
story of a recruit, a raw, slow-witted, but
good-natured country lad, who goes to
pieces in a brutalizing environment. Much

of it can still be read with interest, e.g. the descriptions of days out on manœuvres.

Caveau, Le, a literary and social club f. 1729 by Piron, the elder Crébillon, and others. It functioned, with various lapses and changes of name (e.g. *Les Dîners du Vaudeville,* 1796–1802; *Le Caveau moderne,* from 1805), till the middle of the 19th c. From 1759 it was frequented by Suard, Marmontel, etc., and *c.* 1805 by Béranger (his *Le Roi d' Yvetot* was first sung there), Désaugiers, Méhul, and Brillat-Savarin.

Caves du Vatican, Les, v. Gide.

Caylus, (1) MARIE-MARGUERITE DE VILLETTE-MURÇAY, MARQUISE DE (1673–1729), a cousin of Mme de Maintenon, noted for her beauty, grace, and wit, acted the name-part in *Esther at the Institut de *Saint-Cyr. Her *Souvenirs* of the court of Louis XIV (dictated to her son and publ. 1770 by Voltaire with preface and notes) contain vivid portraits of court personages. Her letters (chiefly to Mme de Maintenon) have also been published; (2) her son CLAUDE-PHILIPPE DE TUBIÈRES, COMTE DE (1692–1765), a distinguished archaeologist ('antiquaire acariâtre et brusque'— Diderot) and traveller, author of *Tableaux d'Homère et de Virgile* (1757), etc.

Cayrol, JEAN (1911–   ), poet, novelist, and essayist. He began as a *Surrealist poet (*Le Hollandais volant,* 1936), but all his subsequent work, from the poems of *Les Phénomènes célestes* (1939), is broadly religious in inspiration (though with a marked element of oneiric fantasy and, at times, of satire) and reflects the influence on him of Mounier and, above all, of his imprisonment (1943–5) in Mauthausen concentration camp after his arrest in 1942 for *Resistance activities. One theme, in varying forms, pervades his work—'la solitude de l'homme, ses efforts vers la communion, sa méfiance envers une rédemption venue du dehors' (P. de Boisdeffre). *Miroir de la Rédemption* (1944) and *Poèmes de la nuit et du brouillard* (1945), poems inspired by his wartime

experiences, were followed by many other collections of verse and by novels ranging from the notable trilogy *Je vivrai l'amour des autres* (1947–50), evoking the world of the concentration camp, to *Histoire d'une prairie* (1970). His essays include *Lazare parmi nous* (1950), where he writes of the novel and shows his affinity (evident in the novels *L'Espace d'une nuit,* 1954, and *Le Déménagement,* 1956) with the *nouveau roman; Les Pleins et les déliés* (1960); *De l'espace humain* (1969). He collaborated with Alain Resnais in the films *Nuit et brouillard* and *Muriel.*

Cazalis, HENRI, *v. Lahor.*

Cazamian, LOUIS (1877–1965), literary historian and English scholar; author, with Legouis, of a standard *History of English Literature* (1924). His other works include a contribution (on Richardson) to the *Cambridge History of English Literature* (vol. X), a *History of French Literature* (1955) intended primarily for English readers, and *Retour d'un anglicisant à la poésie française* (his Zaharoff Lecture, delivered at Oxford in 1938).

Cazotte, JACQUES (1719–92), a writer with a taste for the occult, remembered only for *Le Diable amoureux* (1772), an original and well-written tale in which a Spaniard evokes the Devil, who assumes the form of a woman, contrives to win his love, and then reveals himself.

Céard, HENRY (1851–1924), *Naturalist novelist, a member of the original *Académie Goncourt, contributed a tale to *Les *Soirées de Médan* and wrote the novels *Une Belle Journée* (1881) and *Terrains à vendre au bord de la mer* (1906).

Cécile, v. Constant, B.

Ceci n'est pas un conte, v. Diderot.

Céladon, in d'Urfé's *L'*Astrée.* His name became proverbial for a constant, timid lover.

Celestina or *Calisto y Melibea* (c. 1500;

trans. into French 1527, 1578, 1633), an early Spanish picaresque romance in dialogue form, attributed to Fernando de Rojas; an influential work in the literary history of Spain and France on account of its vivid realism. Calisto, a young gentleman, falls violently in love with Melibea, a young lady of noble birth; but she is modest and sharply repulses him. On the advice of one of his rascally servants, Parmeno and Sempronio, he enlists the services of Celestina, a crafty old bawd. Her intervention deflects Melibea from the path of virtue and provokes a general catastrophe: the servants murder Celestina for a share of her reward and are put to death, Calisto is killed at one of his secret meetings with Melibea, and she commits suicide in despair.

Célibataires, Les, (1) v. *Comédie humaine, La* (*Scènes de la vie de province*); (2) v. *Montherlant*.

Célimène, in Molière's Le **Misanthrope*.

Céline, Louis-Ferdinand, *pseudonym of* LOUIS-FERDINAND DESTOUCHES (1894–1961), a novelist of humble origin who, having qualified and practised as a doctor, won literary fame with his first novel, *Voyage au bout de la nuit* (1932), which he himself claimed, not unjustifiably, to be important for all that has followed in French literature (*v. Novel*, 3). His account of the life of Bardamu, like himself a doctor in a poverty-stricken suburb of Paris, is expressed in a style which was to be characteristic of his subsequent work. His indignation in the face of human degradation and suffering takes the form of what could often be seen as hatred of his fellow-men, giving rise to violence, obscenity, and lyricism. In due course, the violence of his response, provoked as much by what he sees as human failings as by the conditions of which men are victims, led him to an overt anti-Semitism and an involvement with the Vichy *régime* which he never succeeded in living down (even if he had wished to). His other works include *Mort à crédit* (1936), *Bagatelles*

pour un massacre (1938), *Les Beaux Draps* (1941), *Féerie pour une autre fois* (1952, 2 vols.), *D'un château l'autre* (1957), *Entretiens avec le professeur Y* (1959), *Nord* (1960), *Rigodon* (1969).

Cellini, BENVENUTO (1500–71), Florentine goldsmith and sculptor, worked in France (1540–4, as vividly recorded in his autobiography) at the invitation of François Ier. At his workshop in the Petit-*Nesle he produced his famous sculpture the *Nymph of Fontainebleau*, now in the *Musée du *Louvre*.

Cénacles, groups which formed round the early leaders of *Romanticism. The first was *Nodier's *salon* at the **Bibliothèque de l'Arsenal*. The second, and most famous, met at Hugo's home. The 'petit cénacle' was the group of extreme Romantics led by Petrus Borel (*v. Bousingo*), while the 'cénacle de Joseph Delorme' centred on Sainte-Beuve.

Cendrars, Blaise, *pseudonym of* FRÉDÉRIC SAUSER (1887–1961), novelist and poet of Swiss birth. A visit in youth to Russia (1904–7) and a spell at the University of Berne were the prelude to a life of constant travel in a wide variety of callings (salesman, film-director, journalist, etc.). Before and after the 1914–18 war (when he lost an arm fighting with the *Légion étrangère), he moved in *avant-garde* literary circles in Paris and was closely associated with *Cubism, publishing poetry including *Le Panama, ou les Aventures de mes sept oncles* (1918) and other collections united in *Du monde entier* (1919). His prose writings include swiftly moving novels of travel and epic adventure (e.g. *L'Or*, 1925; *Moravagine*, 1926; *Les Confessions de Dan Yack*, 1929; *Rhum*, 1930) and works directly inspired by his own experiences (e.g. *L'Homme foudroyé*, 1945; *La Main coupée*, 1946; *Bourlinguer*, 1948).

Cendrillon, *v. Perrault*.

Censorship, Dramatic. Censorship, in

the sense of a system designed to prevent, by the requirement of previous licensing, the performance of plays deemed politically or morally obnoxious, was not effectively organized till 1706. Before this, control was mainly repressive: productions considered undesirable were suppressed and those concerned punished. In the 15th c. both the *parlement and the *University of Paris (concerned to restrain the satirical vein of its students) were active in this connection. An attempt in 1442 to exercise a preventive censorship of plays performed by the *Basoche apparently failed, for in 1476 its performances were entirely prohibited. Louis XII restored liberty to the stage, partly to serve his own political ends (v. Gringore). François Ier re-established preventive censorship by the parlement, but disagreed with that body about the performance of *mystères. He repeatedly authorized their production, but the parlement, which disliked them for reasons of public order, later succeeded in prohibiting them in Paris (1548).

Conflicts of authority again arose under the pleasure-loving Henri III, who favoured the loose comedies of the *Italiens. Under Henri IV the growing licence of the players led to the appointment (1609) of a magistrate, the procureur du roi, as dramatic censor; no play was to be produced without his authority. But under Louis XIII there was a large measure of liberty, the main deterrent being fear of incurring the displeasure of the king, the parlement, or Richelieu (who in 1641 required actors, on pain of severe penalties, to refrain from indecency on the stage). Under Louis XIV Molière's *Tartuffe was suppressed, and the Italiens expelled (1697). Finally, in 1706, the king ordered all plays to be submitted to censorship before pro- duction, and gave the lieutenant général de *police absolute control over the theatres. This officer based his verdict on the report of the dramatic censor, usually one of the censors charged with the examination of books (v. Librairie). But sometimes he disregarded the report, or yielded to pressure from the court, the

Church (e.g. from C. de Beaumont), the parlement, etc., which led to lack of consistency in the working of the censorship.

The emergence of the *philosophes led to instances of severer control. Many plays were prohibited, or subjected to varying degrees of modification: Voltaire's Samson was prohibited, his L'*Enfant prodigue altered, his *Mahomet withdrawn at the instance of the parlement. There was a good deal of intrigue, and the position of dramatic censor was not an easy one. Both the elder Crébillon (who faced the first onset of the new philosophical ideas) and, later, Suard (the last defender, in that capacity, of the ancien régime) served with distinction.

There was some relaxation under Louis XVI (e.g. Collé's La *Partie de chasse de Henri IV was now performed), and a curious situation arose when *Palissot's Les Courtisanes was refused by the *Comédie-Française as contrary to public morals, though authorized by the censor and approved by the archbishop. But from about 1783 political unrest led to rigorous measures to exclude from the stage anything capable of being construed as an allusion to current events. Permission to produce Beaumarchais's Le *Mariage de Figaro, at first flatly refused by the king, was obtained only after a hard struggle and with the help of the king's brother, the comte d'Artois.

For the first 18 months of the Revolution the office of dramatic censor in Paris was attached to the municipality. But the spirit of the time made strict control impossible—when Bailly, as mayor, refused to license M.-J. Chénier's *Charles IX he was overruled by the *Assemblée nationale—and in January 1791 dramatic censorship was abolished by law. New theatres, for which prior sanction was no longer required, were to be inspected by municipal officers empowered to prohibit or suspend performances. The extent of their power was debatable, and their suspensions were often revoked by the *Convention. But in 1793 the Convention itself forbade the production of plays of a subversive (i.e.

Royalist) tendency, or with titled characters, and in 1794 it reimposed strict dramatic censorship, both preventive and repressive. In Paris, this was exercised by the *Commission de l'Instruction publique*; in the provinces, by the police or municipal officers. Under the *Consulat and the Empire control became increasingly rigorous. New plays had to be authorized by the *Ministre de l'Intérieur*, and after 1804 by the *Ministre de la Police* (*v. Fouché*). Authorization depended on moral and political suitability, reported on by five dramatic censors attached to the *Ministère de l'Instruction publique*. Imperial sanction was required for new theatres; the repertories of the *Opéra, *Comédie-Française*, and *Opéra-Comique were decided ministerially; and censorship in the provinces was brought under the central authority.

The situation remained much the same until the 1830 *Revolution, when censorship was abolished. But it was not clear whether this included dramatic censorship. Hugo's Le *Roi s'amuse was suppressed (1832) as disrespectful to royalty. He went to law, but lost his case, the judgement being that only censorship of printed matter had been abolished. By an Act of 1835 the government was empowered to require preliminary authorization, and to suspend performances and close theatres. The 1848 *Revolution brought a brief respite, but the Second Empire reimposed even tighter control (*v. Anastasie*). Authorization could be withdrawn at any time, and was not even confirmed till after the dress rehearsal, which was attended by inspectors. Censorship was operated, through examining and inspecting committees, by the minister attached to the imperial household. The laws covered nearly every form of stage spectacle, but after 1864 the requirement of prior sanction for new theatres was dropped. A spell of liberty after the fall of the Second Empire was again followed by censorship (1874), now exercised by the *Ministre de l'Instruction publique*, who delegated the task to the *Division des Beaux-Arts*.

The spirit in which the censorship was exercised varied under successive governments. During and just after the Revolution plays new and old were suppressed or altered in the interests of Republicanism: 'Monsieur' and 'Madame' became 'Citoyen' and 'Citoyenne'; M.-J. Chénier's *Timoléon* was withdrawn because it offended Robespierre; Voltaire's *Zaïre was banned for suspected clericalism; Racine and Molière were edited (*Phèdre's bosom was covered by a *tricolore rosette as she declared her love for Hippolyte). Under Napoleon even such plays as were authorized were mutilated and bowdlerized, often with comic results; and any censor who allowed crowned heads to be discredited or the *philosophes glorified, or who failed to excise even the remotest allusion to religion or politics, incurred the imperial wrath. A similar policy prevailed between 1815 and 1830. The word 'liberté', now suspect, was altered to 'indépendance'; kings, ministers, the Catholic faith, and the *ancienne noblesse* had all to be indulgently represented. Under Louis-Philippe, even after the Act of 1835, censorship was more liberal, though political allusions were still disliked (the *légende napoléonienne caused uneasiness). Under the Second Empire, allusions to high finance were unwelcome (*Mercadet was prohibited), ministers were even more sensitive, religion was too dangerous a subject (even history was frowned on), and the remotest allusions to home or external politics were excised. Morals and manners were less of a stumbling-block: La *Dame aux camélias and *Offenbach's La Belle Hélène were passed without difficulty.

Following the revival of censorship in 1874, more liberal views increasingly prevailed (esp. after the act of 1881 regulating the *Press). Dramatic censorship ended in 1906 with the withdrawal of funds for the remuneration of censors. It remained—and still remains—possible for the government to invoke the security regulations to stop production of a play deemed likely to contravene them (e.g. to provoke crime, to endanger diplomatic relations), and the *maires* (or, in Paris, the *préfet de *police*) have the power to intervene in the interests of public morals or public safety. (The censorship of films began in 1919.)

Censorship, Literary, v. *Librairie*; *Press.*

Centaure, Le, (1) v. *Guérin, M. de*; (2) a literary and artistic quarterly, f. 1896 by Louÿs, H. de Régnier, Gide, and others associated with *Symbolism, which published work by these and other writers, e.g. Valéry.

Cent Ballades, Les, a pleasing collection of late 14th-c. *ballades* on the theme of whether fidelity or inconstancy in love is to be approved; written by 14 nobles and princes of Charles VI's court for a kind of poetical competition, organized by four nobles, including Bouciquaut, who had been in prison together in Cairo (1388–9) during a crusade.

Cent Jours, Les, the Hundred Days—20 March to 6 July 1815—of Napoleon's temporary return to power after his escape from Elba.

Cent Nouvelles Nouvelles, a collection of prose tales (v. *Nouvelle*), presented (*c.* 1460) to Philippe, duc de Bourgogne, by its unknown author (probably a member of the Burgundian court; v. *La Sale*). Most of the tales derive from oral tradition (earlier a source of the *fabliaux*), others from Poggio and Boccaccio; many are licentious. Like those of the *Decameron*, they purport to be related by members of the court, including the duke himself.

Centre national de la Recherche scientifique, a State institution (under the *Ministère de l'Éducation nationale*) which promotes, directs, and finances research work in all fields of knowledge.

Cercle, Le, (1) v. *Palissot*; (2) v. *Poinsinet*.

Césaire, AIMÉ (1913–), West Indian writer and left-wing politician (sometime *député* for his native Martinique); a leading exponent of the literature of *négritude* who has sought to free himself from the traditional forms of Western culture through the medium of *Surrealism. His works, which reflect his hatred of the oppression and abuses of colonialism, include poetry, notably his *Cahier d'un retour au pays natal* (1943; written 1939), rejoicing at the discovery of his African roots and heritage, also *Les Armes miraculeuses* (1946), *Ferrements* (1960), and *Cadastre* (1961); plays, e.g. *Et les chiens se taisaient* (1956), *La Tragédie du roi Christophe* (1963), *Une Saison au Congo* (1966); and essays, e.g. *Discours sur le colonialisme* (1951), *Toussaint Louverture* (1960).

César Birotteau, v. *Histoire de la grandeur et de la décadence de César Birotteau.*

Cézanne, PAUL (1839–1906), one of the first *Impressionists, famous for his landscapes (mostly of his native Provence), still-lifes, and portraits. His long and close friendship with Zola, whom he followed to Paris when allowed to abandon law for art (1861), was broken by Zola's novel *L'*Œuvre.

Chabaneix, PHILIPPE (1898–1982), a poet who has an affinity with the *fantaisistes*; sometime poetry critic on the *Mercure de France. His many collections include *Les Tendres Amies* (1922), *Aux sources de la nuit* (1955).

Chabrier, EMMANUEL (1841–94), a composer of light music whose opera *Le Roi malgré lui* and orchestral rhapsody *España* are still performed. He moved in *Symbolist and *Impressionist circles, and was an early admirer of Wagner.

Chactas, in Chateaubriand's *Atala.*

Chagall, MARC (1887-1985), an artist of Russian birth, closely associated with *Cubist artists and writers. His works (paintings, theatre *décors*, stained glass, ceramics) are often inspired by Jewish history and legend, or by memories of his native land. He executed a ceiling at the *Opéra* (1964).

Cham, *pseudonym of* AMÉDÉE DE NOË, son of the marquis de Noë—hence 'Cham fils de Noë'—(1819–79), a cartoonist in his heyday during the July Monarchy and Second Empire. He excelled at depicting street life. *v. Charivari.*

Chambord, HENRI, COMTE DE, DUC DE BORDEAUX (1820–83), son of the duc de Berry (*v. Bourbon* (3)), **Légitimiste* pretender after the death of his grandfather, Charles X, and known to his supporters as 'Henri V'. He lived in exile (1830–83; mainly in Austria) and died without issue. In 1873 *Légitimistes* and **Orléanistes* sank their differences in a plot to restore him, but it failed at the last moment because he refused to abandon the white Bourbon flag for the **tricolore,* which Louis-Philippe and the *Orléanistes* had accepted.

Chambre ardente, a special court of the **parlement* of Paris, draped in black and lit with torches even by day, set up in the 16th c. to try persons accused of exceptional crimes. In 1679 Louis XIV ordered a *Chambre ardente* (also known as the *Chambre de l'Arsenal*) to investigate mounting evidence (in part disclosed by the trial of the marquise de Brinvilliers) that a fortune-teller known as 'la Voisin' and her accomplices were purveying poisons, known as 'poudres de succession', to speed the demise of unwanted relations, and also engaging in abortion, child-stealing, and the worst excesses of black magic. Over 200 persons were arrested, 104 tried, and 34 executed. The affair caused a sensation, for the confessions of the accused implicated a wide circle of their often innocent clients, including even Mme de Montespan (said to have purchased love philtres) and others prominent at court. The king terminated the proceedings in 1682. A later *Chambre ardente* was that set up in 1716 to force the **fermiers généraux* to disgorge their illicit gains.

Chambre des comptes, under the monarchy, an administrative court of 10 *présidents* and 62 *maîtres de comptes*

which revised the public accounts of the realm, exercising jurisdiction over the accountants and even some control over the king. Napoleon restored it in an improved form as the *Cour des comptes.*

Chambre des Députés, *v. Député.*

Chambre des Pairs, *v. Pairs; Sénat.*

Chamfort, NICOLAS-SÉBASTIEN ROCH, *known as* DE (1741–94), of illegitimate birth, author of indifferent plays (e.g. *La Jeune Indienne,* a sentimental comedy, 1764; *Mustapha et Zéangir,* a tragedy, 1776—both successful) and two good critical works, *Éloge de Molière* (1766) and *Éloge de La Fontaine* (1774). These—and his wit—won him social success, a pension, and election to the **Académie.* His penetrating *Maximes, caractères, et anecdotes* (publ. posth.) reveal his gift for succinct irony and also his disillusionment with the high society on which he felt dependent. Though an ardent supporter of the Revolution and a close friend and inspirer of Mirabeau, he became suspect during the **Terror,* attempted suicide, and died soon afterwards. It was he who coined the Revolutionary slogan, 'Guerre aux châteaux, paix aux chaumières', and interpreted 'Fraternité' as 'Sois mon frère, ou je te tue'.

Chamisso, ADELBERT VON (1781–1838), German poet, novelist, and botanist, a friend of Mme de Staël, was born in France (his family left during the Revolution) and became known to the later generation of **Romantics* when his romances and ballads (melancholy and ironical, usually on traditional themes) and novel *Peter Schlemihl* (about a man who sold his shadow to the Devil) were translated. *v. Foreign Influences,* 3.

Champagne or **Champaigne,** PHILIPPE DE (1602–74), painter, a native of Brussels who spent his life in France and is noted for his portraits, e.g. of leading members of **Port-Royal.*

Champavert, contes immoraux, v. Borel, Petrus.

Champ de mai, (1) the political consultative assemblies held under the *Carolingians, invariably in May; (2) the general representative assembly convoked by Napoleon for 26 May 1815—but held, in fact, on 1 June on the *Champ-de-Mars—at which he signed the *Acte additionnel*, swore to defend the independence of the French people, and conferred many honours.

Champ-de-Mars, Le, a large open space on the left bank of the Seine in Paris, originally the parade-ground of the *École militaire*. It was the scene of the first *Fête de la *Fédération* (1790); *Bailly's execution (1793); the *Fête de l'*Être Suprême* (1794); Napoleon's first investiture of the *Légion d'honneur* (1804), and his proclamation of the *Acte additionnel* (1815; *v.* also *Champ de mai*). After the Restoration it was used for horse-racing (in Flaubert's *L'*Éducation sentimentale* Frédéric takes Rosannette to the races there). It was later the site of successive World Fairs (beginning with the *Exposition universelle*, 1867; *v. Tour Eiffel*), until it became a public open space in 1908.

Champ d'oliviers, Le, one of Maupassant's finest short stories.

Champfleury, *v. Tory*.

Champfleury, *pseudonym of* JULES HUSSON or FLEURY (1821–89), novelist (a leader of *Realism), art historian, and latterly director of the *Sèvres porcelain factory. His novels include *Chien-Caillou* (1847), about an engraver; *Les Aventures de Mademoiselle Mariette* (1853), scenes from a much less sentimentalized *vie de Bohème* than that of Murger; *Les Bourgeois de Molinchart* (1855), a study of provincial life which begins with a spirited description of a hunted deer wrecking a toy-shop. He is now perhaps best known for his *Histoire de la caricature* (1865–90), and for such interesting studies of books and personalities of *Romanticism as *Les Excentriques* (1852) and *Les Vignettes romantiques* (1883).

Champier, SYMPHORIEN (1472–1539), man of letters and poet of the Lyons school (*v.* under *Scève*), wrote *La Nef des dames vertueuses* (1503; prose and verse), etc. He also practised, and wrote about, medicine, and founded a medical school at Lyons.

Champion des dames, Le, v. Le Franc, M.

Champlain, SAMUEL (1567–1635), navigator and explorer, founded Quebec (1608), discovered and explored Lakes Champlain and Ontario, and was sent by Louis XIII to govern Canada (1620). He was besieged in Quebec by the British (1628–9) and had to capitulate, but returned as governor when it was restored to the French (1632), and died there.

Champmeslé, (1) CHARLES CHEVILLET, *known as* (1645–1701), actor and dramatist (*v. La Fontaine*); (2) his more famous wife MARIE DESMARES (1642–98), the actress 'La Champmeslé', mistress of the young Racine and celebrated for her performance as *Bérénice, *Roxane, *Phèdre, etc.

Champollion, JEAN-FRANÇOIS (1790–1832), now recognized as the founder of Egyptology, though his claim to be the first to decipher hieroglyphics was for a time disputed. The chair of Egyptian antiquities at the *Collège de France* was created for him.

Champs-Élysées, Les, a district on the right bank of the Seine in Paris which from the 17th c. was progressively laid out and architecturally embellished, reaching heights of splendour and elegance under Napoleon and again during the Second Empire. Its gardens and traffic ways form a prolongation of the *Tuileries from the *Place de la Concorde to the Rond-Point des Champs-Élysées, whence the broad, glittering Avenue des Champs-Élysées— still magnificent, despite commercial-ization—sweeps up to the *Arc de Triomphe. Foreigners make their way here, some welcomed or tolerated as tourists, others sullenly endured—the Cossacks in 1814, the Prussians in 1871, the Nazis in 1940. Here, too, processions begin or end on great national occasions.

Champs-Élysées, Comédie des, *v.* *Jouvet.*

Champs magnétiques, Les, v. Breton, A.

Chamson, ANDRÉ (1900–83), novelist (a member of the *Académie, 1956), a pupil of the *École nationale des Chartes and holder of high administrative posts. Born at Nîmes of Protestant stock, he made his name with novels of life in the Cévennes, with its austerities and *Huguenot traditions, e.g. *Roux le bandit* (1925), *Les Hommes de la route* (1927), *Le Crime des justes* (1928). His later novels reflect his emergence as an *intellectuel engagé* (he was strongly anti-Fascist in the 1930s and fought in the *Resistance) and his preoccupation with the human problems posed by modern civilization, e.g. *La Galère* (1939), *Le Puits des miracles* (1945), *La Neige et la fleur* (1951), *Comme une pierre qui tombe* (1964), *La Superbe* (1967).

Chandelier, Le (1835, in the *Revue des Deux Mondes; 1840, in *Comédies et Proverbes), a 3-act prose comedy by Musset; produced 1848. To distract attention from her intrigue with Clavaroche, an officer of dragoons, Jacqueline, the young wife of Maître André, encourages the adoration of the young clerk Fortunio. He is so loving, so selflessly devoted even when he finds he has been used, that he wins her from the discomfited Clavaroche.

Chanson (Prov. *canson* or *canso*). The medieval *chanson* was originally any poem composed to be sung, from the *chansons à danser, à personnages, and de toile to the *chansons de geste. In the 12th and 13th cs. the term was also used in the specific sense of a Provençal-type love lyric (*v.* Troubadours) of 5, 6, or 7 stanzas in three groups (2+2+1, 2+2+2, or 2+2+3). Each group was usually marked by the repetition of the same rhymes, but there was an infinite variety of detailed arrangements (the art of the courtly poets

required that the form of each song should be different). Gace Brulé's *chansons*, for example, have 5 or 6 stanzas of 7, 8, 9, or 10 lines. The number of syllables in a line may be 7 (rarely less), 8, or 10. There is often an *envoi. The following is a typical example of the scheme of rhymes and syllables in a 10-line stanza:

rhyme   a b a b a b a b c c
syllables   7 6 7 6 7 6 7 6 4 5

Since the time of Marot and Ronsard the term has been applied to light, amorous, bacchic, political, or satirical poems in a wide variety of metres and barely distinguishable from the lighter type of *ode.

Chanson d'Antioche, v. Antioche.

Chanson de Roland, La, the earliest extant and most famous *chanson de geste (*Charlemagne cycle), probably composed, in the form in which we have it, very early in the 12th c. The oldest manuscript (4,002 decasyllables; now in the Bodleian Library, Oxford; v. Michel, F.-X.) was written in England about the middle of the 12th c. The Turoldus mentioned in its last line may be the author of the poem, or of its source, or (less probably) a scribe. It was perhaps an earlier version of this poem which, as recorded by Wace (drawing on William of Malmesbury) in the *Roman de Rou*, the *jongleur Taillefer sang before Duke William at the battle of Hastings:

De Karlemainne et de Rollant,
Et d'Ollivier et des vassals
Qui morurent en Raincesvals.

Charlemagne has conquered all Spain except Saragossa, which is held by Marsile, the Saracen king. Marsile makes perfidious overtures, designed to induce Charlemagne to leave Spain. The members of Charlemagne's council are divided: *Roland is for rejecting the proposals, his stepfather Ganelon for accepting them. When Ganelon prevails, Roland, angered by his taunts, secures his selection as envoy to Marsile—a dangerous mission, for previous envoys have been executed. Ganelon accepts gifts from Marsile, and plans to betray Roland and the rearguard of the army as it withdraws from Spain. On his advice, Roland is put in command of the rearguard of 20,000 men. The army crosses the Pyrenees, and the rearguard is surrounded by 400,000 Saracens in the pass of Roncevaux. Roland is urged by *Olivier to sound his horn and recall the main force, but proudly refuses. Despite the heroism of the *Douze *Pairs*, the French are gradually annihilated. Finally, when only 60 remain alive, Roland sounds his horn; but it is too late. Before Charlemagne can reach them, they are reduced to four, all mortally wounded. Roland and Olivier say farewell, *Turpin gives his last blessing, and Roland delivers his spirit to St. Gabriel. Charlemagne arrives, routs the Saracens, and enters Saragossa; *Aude falls dead when told of Roland's fate; Ganelon is quartered, following a trial by battle.

The narrative is simple and vivid, the characters live and convincing. The poet's sense of dramatic effect and epic breadth is evident in the grandeur and restrained pathos of the closing scenes.

The historical facts are that, at the invitation of two Moslem emirs hostile to the emir of Cordova, Charlemagne took an army to Spain (778), captured Pampeluna and possibly Saragossa, but was then recalled by a revolt in Saxony. On the way home his rearguard was surprised by Basques in the pass of Roncevaux and annihilated.

Chanson des gueux, La, v. *Richepin*.

Chanson des Saxons (or *des Saisnes*), v. *Bodel*.

Chansons à danser, medieval songs, in a variety of metres, originally composed to accompany dances; the oldest extant examples are of the early and mid-13th c. The *carole*, a kind of round dance in which one dancer led the song and the rest replied in a refrain, gave rise to the *rondet* or *rondet de carole*, roughly equivalent to the modern *triolet*. The *ballette* (the ancestor

of the *ballade*), another dance song, had three stanzas with a refrain repeated at the end of each (rhyming, for example, a b a b b c C C—the capitals indicate the refrain). The *virelai* is also sometimes classed as a *chanson à danser*.

Chansons à personnages, or *chansons dramatiques*, terms applied by some modern critics to various types of medieval song in dialogue form, such as the *chanson de mal mariée* (the unfaithful wife and her lover), the *aube* or Prov. *alba* (lovers warned at dawn by the watchman), the *reverdie* (a spring song in which the birds take part); sometimes considered to include the *pastourelle*. Cf. *Romance*.

Chansons de Bilitis, v. *Louÿs*.

Chansons de geste (from L. *gesta*, 'deeds', in the sense of an historical narrative), poems of heroic and often legendary exploits situated, loosely, in the age of Charlemagne and his immediate predecessors and successors; the earliest form of the French *epic*. Some 80–100 survive, in manuscript versions of the 12th-15th cs. which in some cases are regarded by medievalists as rehandlings of much earlier originals. The dates of actual composition assigned to the poems range from the 11th to the 12th–13th cs. (the heyday of the *genre*) and into the early 14th c. Since the revival of interest in the Middle Ages in the early 19th c. (v. *History*, 4; *Romanticism*) nearly all the extant *chansons* have been edited by scholars, and many have been printed in a modernized form for the benefit of the general reader (*cf.* the modernized versions of Chaucer). They may be anything from under 1,000 to over 20,000 lines long; the majority average 8,000–10,000 lines. They are written in monorhyme stanzas (*laisses*) of varying length, with lines usually of 10 (sometimes 8, latterly 12) syllables, joined by *assonance and later by *consonance.

Their origin has been much debated. The 19th-c. view, held by G. *Paris, was that they had been preceded by epic chants (*cantilènes*), roughly contemporary with the events described, and themselves influenced by Germanic traditions and folklore. The *chansons* thus represented popular or family traditions, some with an historical nucleus, developed by poets to satisfy the public demand for the heroic and the marvellous. Early in the 20th c. *Bédier advanced a different view. It rejects the possibility of Germanic origin and holds that the poems are little more than the inventions of *trouvères* and *jongleurs* working on stories told by monks (who drew them from Latin chronicles, lives of saints, or maybe their own imagination) to pilgrims who visited the shrines (many of which lay on pilgrimage routes) connected with the memory of heroes, e.g. Roland, Ogier, Guillaume d'Orange. Bédier's view still holds the field, though his reduction of the historical and traditional element to a minimum has been questioned.

They were composed by *trouvères* to be chanted to music on the *vielle* (a primitive instrument of the viol family), and were sung by *jongleurs* (or by *trouvères*) in the halls of lords or in public places (shrines, churches) as they wandered about France. Variant versions thus arose; or whole new tales or episodes sprang from the parent stock—some connecting existing tales, others carrying the most popular tales back to the heroes' *enfances* or early deeds, or forward to the exploits of their descendants. This led to the poems being grouped (by 13th-c. *trouvères*; *v.* Bertrand de Bar-sur-Aube) in three main cycles or *gestes*: the *Geste du roi* or *Charlemagne cycle, containing the famous *Chanson de Roland*; the *Geste de *Garin de Monglane*, also known as the *Geste de Guillaume* or *des Aimerides*; the *Geste de *Doon de Mayence*. There was also a subordinate cycle, the *Geste des Lorrains* (*v.* Garin le Loherain).

The *trouvères* rarely invented new characters, and a handful of types recur with monotonous uniformity—the valiant hero, the traitor (brave or cowardly), the Saracen giant, etc. Variety was obtained in other ways, especially as time went on and the original themes were rehandled. Into the simple presentation of a heroic past (as in the *Chanson de Roland*) the poet would

introduce fabulous or extravagant features, e.g. the fairy Oberon in *Huon de Bordeaux*, the marvellous horse Bayard in *Renaud de Montauban*. The taste of popular audiences was studied (a comic element is already prominent in the *Pèlerinage de Charlemagne*), and the heroic element tended to give way to the grotesque; even the great figure of Charlemagne was debased and ridiculed, while yeomen and peasants were exalted. The role assigned to women is often ignoble, but there are remarkable exceptions, e.g. Guibourc, in the *Chanson de *Guillaume*.

During the 14th c. the themes of the great, early *chansons* continued to be rehandled. There was also some revival of epic poetry, inspired by contemporary events such as the Hundred Years War (e.g. Cuvelier's *Chanson de Bertrand du Guesclin*, *c.* 1384); but it produced little of merit, and with the early 15th-c. *Geste des Bourguignons* poems in monorhyme stanzas came to an end. Prose adaptations of several *chansons*, e.g. *Fierabras* and *Huon de Bordeaux*, were issued in the early days of printing (late 15th and early 16th cs.).

Though of no historical value as regards the events they relate, the *chansons* shed light on the customs, sentiments, dress, and arms of their period. Their influence on the literature of other countries is seen in the translations and imitations they inspired in English (many of these are noted under the headings of the several poems), German, and especially Italian (in the works of Pulci, Boiardo, Ariosto). For the principal *chansons*, *v.* Aimeri de Narbonne; Anseïs de Carthage; Aspremont; Berthe aux grands pieds; Bodel (for the Chanson des Saxons); Chanson de Roland; Doon de Mayence; Fierabras; Garin de Monglane; Garin le Loherain; Girart de Roussillon; Girart de Viane; Guillaume, Chanson de; Huon de Bordeaux; Ogier le Danois; Pèlerinage de Charlemagne; Raoul de Cambrai; Renaud de Montauban.

Certain poems unconnected with the legendary history of France and its families also took the form (monorhyme stanzas) of the *chanson de geste*, e.g. the Crusade cycle (*v.* Crusades); *v.* also

Alexandre le Grand (1); *Amis et Amile*; *Beuve de Haumtone*; *Horn*.

Chansons des rues et des bois, Les, v. Hugo.

Chansons de toile, short medieval 'sewing-songs' (poems in monorhyme stanzas, with a refrain) relating a love episode, some obviously very old—the latest probably not later than 1200; so named from early times because they often present women sewing or spinning, or because they were sung at the spinning-wheel. They are remarkably vivid and graceful. *Cf. Romance.*

Chant du départ, Le, a famous Revolutionary song (words by M.-J. Chénier, music by Méhul). Probably first sung at the *Fête de la* *Fédération* of 14 July 1794, it was heard again at the *Fête des* *Victoires* (21 Oct. 1794), and subsequently became the official song at national festivals, rendered by choirs of old men, mothers, children, etc. The refrain runs:

La République nous appelle,
Sachons vaincre ou sachons périr:
Un Français doit vivre pour elle,
Pour elle un Français doit mourir.

Chantecler, the cock in the *Roman de Renart*.

Chantecler (1910), a 4-act verse drama by E. Rostand; a satirical allegory. Ordinary creatures of farmyard and forest are represented as animated by human feelings of jealousy, pride, etc.; they are sometimes tender, often fickle or ruthless. Chantecler imagines that his fine song makes the sun rise. His pride has a fall, but he masters his disillusionment and reverts with a good heart to the humbler role of wakening his farmyard.

Chantefable, *v. Aucassin et Nicolette*.

Chantilly (Oise), a town long famous for its *château* and adjacent forest, and now also as a centre for the training and racing

of horses (*v. Jockey Club*). The medieval *château* was rebuilt in pure Renaissance style in the 16th c. and later progressively embellished, notably by the Condé family. It was badly damaged during the Revolution, but was restored by the duc d'Aumale (1822–97; 4th son of Louis-Philippe, and heir of the last Condé), himself a distinguished historian and a member of the *Académie*, who left it and its fine library and art collections—now the *Musée Condé*—to the *Institut de France*.

Chant royal, a poem usually consisting of 5 stanzas of 10 or 11 decasyllables and an *envoi* of 5 to 7 lines; a common rhyme-scheme is a b a b c c d d e d e, with *envoi* d d e d e. The last line of the first stanza forms a refrain, repeated as the last line of every stanza and of the *envoi*. According to the strict rule, the whole poem should be a single allegory, which is fully explained only in the *envoi*. Marot was a master of this verse-form.

Chants du crépuscule, Les, v. Hugo.

Chants du soldat, v. Déroulède.

Chapelain, JEAN (1595–1674), a man of letters and critic highly esteemed by Richelieu, a member of the original *Académie française* (he proposed the preparation of its dictionary and drafted its attack on *Le* *Cid*; *v. Corneille*), an *habitué* of the Hôtel de *Rambouillet*, and an influential champion of the *Classical* form in literature (esp. of the unities; *v. Tragedy*). His writings—less appreciated than his conversation—included a preface to Marino's *Adone* (*v. Marinisme*); *Odes*; and *La Pucelle*, an unsuccessful epic about Joan of Arc (12 cantos, the fruit of 20 years' labour, appeared in 1656, the remaining 12 cantos were not publ. till 1882).

Chapelle, CLAUDE-EMMANUEL LUILLIER, *known as* (1626–86), poet, friend of Boileau, Molière, Racine, and La Fontaine, and disciple of Gassendi; a jovial bohemian. He was author with F. de Bachaumont of the *Voyage en Provence et*

Languedoc (1656; verse and prose), a medley of burlesque descriptions of scenery and meals, and literary satire.

Char, RENÉ (1907–   ), an influential poet. His early work (in *Arsenal*, 1929; *Le Marteau sans maître*, 1934) was *Surrealist, but he soon went his own way and during and after the 1939–45 war (when he fought in the *maquis* of Provence) won fame with the poems, prose poems, and aphorisms of *Seuls demeurent* (1945) and *Feuillets d'Hypnos* (1946), among the finest poems of the *Resistance (united with other work, inc. *Le Poème pulvérisé* of 1946, in *Fureur et Mystère*, 1948). Much of his poetry and prose is gathered in *La Parole en archipel* (1962), *Commune Présence* (1964; a selection), *Recherche de la base et du sommet* (latest ed. 1965), and *Le Nu perdu* (1971). *Trois Coups sous les arbres* (1967) is a collection of plays. His work is often difficult, at times elliptical or oracular. It reveals his love of nature and of his native Provence (always his home), and the strong influence of Hellenism (esp. of Heraclitus), seen in his deep concern for the human condition and his generous humanism. *v. Lyric Poetry*, 4.

Charasson, HENRIETTE (1884–1972), wife of the critic René Johannet, a poetess of religious inspiration who had something in common with Marie Noël and Cécile Sauvage. She wrote of unhappy love (*Attente*, 1919), then celebrated the familiar joys of family life (e.g. *Les Heures du foyer*, 1926; *Deux Petits Hommes et leur mère*, 1928; collections showing her command of the *verset) and of the Christian faith (e.g. *Mon Seigneur et mon Dieu*, 1934; *Sur la plus haute branche*, 1938). She also wrote plays, essays, tales, and literary criticism, and contributed to the *Mercure de France* (from 1909), the *Revue des Deux Mondes*, etc.

Charbonnerie, *v. Carbonari*.

Chardin, JEAN (1643–1713), author of *Voyage en Perse et aux Indes Orientales* (Amsterdam 1711, 3 vols.), a valuable record of his travels. *v. Tavernier*.

Chardin, JEAN-BAPTISTE-SIMÉON (1699–1779), painter of still life and of genre pictures of *bourgeois* life.

Chardri, *v. Barlaam et Josaphat*.

Charenton, a well-known mental hospital near Paris. Anyone guilty of a rash or senseless act may be called a 'pensionnaire de Charenton' or 'digne d'aller à Charenton'.

Charité and *Miserere*, two early 13th-c. religious poems (elaborate exhortations to a godly life) in octosyllabic stanzas, by an author self-styled 'le Reclus de Molliens'; so named from the first word of each.

Charivari, *Le*, the prototype of *Punch*, f. 1832 by Philipon as a daily satirical pamphlet and soon famous for cartoons (by Cham, Daumier, Gavarni, Grandville, etc.) ridiculing the July Monarchy, Louis-Philippe himself, and the *bourgeoisie*. It flourished again under the Second Empire, when it also covered literature and the drama, and survived into the 20th c.

Charlemagne (Charles Ier) (742–814), one of the greatest figures of the Middle Ages, king of the Franks (*Carolingian dynasty), son and successor of Pépin le Bref, r. jointly with his brother Carloman 768–71, then alone till 814; crowned emperor of the West (800) by Pope Leo III (and *v. Iron Crown*). His empire—established by continuous wars, chiefly against the Saxons—extended from the North Sea to the Pyrenees and the Ebro, and in Italy to the Garigliano, and from the Elbe to the Atlantic. He strove both to bring order and justice to this vast realm (*v. Duc, comte, marquis*) and to encourage learning (*v. Académie palatine; Alcuin*). His mother Berthe (daughter of Caribert, comte de Laon), a woman of fine character, helped to guide his policy till her death in 783.

Many almost entirely apocryphal legends about him, chiefly in the role of the divine defender of Christendom against the Saracens, are embodied in the *Geste du roi* or Charlemagne cycle of the *chansons de *geste* (some 20 poems in all; *v. Anseïs de Carthage*; *Aspremont*; *Berthe aux grands pieds*; *Bodel* (for the *Chanson des Saxons*); *Chanson de Roland*; *Fierabras*; *Pèlerinage de Charlemagne*), also in the *Doon de Mayence and *Garin de Monglane cycles (e.g. *Girart de Viane*). His consort is *Blanchefleur or Sébile; his famous sword is called Joyeuse. For his Twelve Peers *v. Pairs*.

Charles II LE CHAUVE (823–77), king of the Franks (*Carolingian dynasty), 4th son and successor of Louis Ier, r. 840–77. *v. Serments de Strasbourg*; *Verdun*.

Charles III LE SIMPLE (879–929), king of France (*Carolingian dynasty), son of Louis II, r. in opposition to Eudes 893–8, then alone till deposed (922) in favour of Robert Ier. He killed Robert in battle, but was soon again deposed (923) in favour of Raoul and died in captivity.

In 911 he gave his daughter and part of his territory to the Norman pirate Rollo, who thus became the first duke of Normandy. *v. Wace*.

Charles IV LE BEL (1294–1328), king of France (*Capetian dynasty; last of the direct line), son of Philippe IV, succeeded his brother Philippe V, r. 1322–8.

Charles V LE SAGE (1337–80), king of France (*Capetian dynasty, *Valois branch), son and successor of Jean II, r. 1364–80.

Charles VI LE BIEN-AIMÉ (1368–1422), king of France (*Capetian dynasty, *Valois branch), son and successor of Charles V, r. 1380–1422. He was mad for the last 20 years of his reign and France was torn by strife between *Armagnacs and Burgundians.

Charles VII LE VICTORIEUX (1403–61), king of France (*Capetian dynasty, *Valois branch), son and successor of Charles VI and regent during his madness, r. 1422–61. His reign saw the episode of *Jeanne d'Arc, also the end of the Hundred Years War.

Charles VIII L'AFFABLE (1470–98), king of France (*Capetian dynasty, *Valois branch), son and successor of Louis XI, r. 1483–98. He invaded Italy to lay claim to the kingdom of Naples. *v. Commines*; *Régence*.

Charles IX (1550–74), king of France (*Capetian dynasty, *Valois-*Orléans line), 2nd son of Henri II and Catherine de Médicis, succeeded his brother François II, r. 1560–74; a patron of letters and friend of Ronsard. His mother was regent during his minority (till 1564) and remained powerful thereafter; *v. Bartholomew, Massacre of St.*

Charles IX (1789), a verse tragedy by M.-J. Chénier. The scene is Paris. Catherine de Médicis and the *Guises have planned the Massacre of St. *Bartholomew, staging a feigned reconciliation with the *Huguenots to disarm suspicion. The final order must be given by the young Charles IX, who is portrayed as cowardly and vacillating. His mother finally rushes him into a decision and the massacre begins. Chénier's allusions to the intrigues and feebleness of royalty delighted Revolutionary audiences. *v. Censorship, Dramatic.*

Charles X (1757–1836), king of France (*Capetian dynasty, *Bourbon branch), previously comte d'Artois, younger brother of Louis XVI and Louis XVIII, successor of Louis XVIII, r. 1824–30. An *émigré* in 1789, he conspired against the Revolution, and spent some years in England. He returned at the Restoration and led the *Ultras*. His anti-liberal, pro-Catholic policy as king led to the 1830 *Revolution and his abdication. Thereafter he lived in exile, at Holyrood and in Prague. *v. Chambord*; *Congrégation* (2).

Charles XII, Histoire de, *v. Histoire de Charles XII.*

Charles Blanchard, *v. Philippe, C.-L.*

Charles Demailly, *v. Goncourt.*

Charles d'Orléans (1391–1465), poet, son of Louis d'*Orléans and Valentine Visconti, daughter of the duke of Milan. He was captured at *Agincourt and spent 25 years in captivity in England. Later, he lived at Blois, where his court was a literary centre (v. Villon). His first poems, graceful and tender *ballades forming what is known as the Livre de la Prison, were written in England. His later ballades and *rondeaux show great technical skill, but lack depth of feeling.

Charles le Gros (839–88), succeeded his father Louis le Germanique as king of Germany (876; emperor from 882), and on Carloman's death (884) also became king of France (*Carolingian dynasty). He was deposed (887) in favour of Eudes.

Charles le Téméraire (Charles the Bold) (1433–77), one of the last powerful feudal vassals of the kings of France, succeeded to the dukedom of Burgundy in 1467, then married (1468) Margaret of York, sister of Edward IV, thus allying himself with England. He was rashly courageous, cruel, arrogant, and highly ambitious, a constant threat to the crown and the growing national unity of France. He hankered after Alsace-Lorraine, to make his territory continuous (besides his duchy he also held a great part of the Low Countries) and so create a new realm, a Middle Kingdom, with Nancy as capital. He was killed in battle while besieging Nancy. He figures in d'*Arlincourt's Le Solitaire, and Scott's Quentin Durward and Anne of Geierstein. v. Commines.

Charles Martel, v. Maire du Palais.

Charlus, Palamède de Guermantes, baron de, in *A la recherche du temps perdu, is the chief vehicle for Proust's serious and compassionate treatment of the theme of inversion. Marcel first realizes Charlus's true nature when he sees him with the tailor Jupien (at the beginning of Sodome et Gomorrhe), and thereafter he dominates the novel. He is highly cultured, at once charming (at times even sweet-natured) and overpoweringly

insolent. With age, and the end of his affair with the violinist Morel (v. Verdurin), he yields increasingly to his instincts and touches the lowest depths of vice. His personality disintegrates, and he falls from arrogance to an abject, palsied affability. v. Montesquiou.

Charmes, v. Valéry.

Charmettes, Les, v. Rousseau, J.-J.

Charpentier, FRANÇOIS (1620–1702), scholar, perpetual secretary of the *Académie, author of L'Excellence de la langue française (1683).

Charpentier, GUSTAVE (1860–1956), composer, notably of the opera Louise (prod. 1900), for which he also wrote the libretto. The heroine, a seamstress (there is a scene in her employer's workroom), leaves home to live with her artist lover in a little house in a garden in Montmartre.

Charrette, Chevalier à la, v. Chevalier à la charrette.

Charrière, ISABELLA VAN TUYLL VAN SEROOSKERKEN, MME DE, self-styled ZÉLIDE (in an early self-portrait), also known as BELLE DE ZUYLEN (1740–1805), a well-born, intelligent, and beautiful Dutch-woman. Her many suitors included James Boswell, and after her marriage to the dull but worthy M. de Charrière (a Swiss tutor) her life was brightened by an ardent intellectual friendship with B. Constant, until she was ousted by Mme de Staël. Her novels (in French) include Lettres neuchâteloises (1784), Mistress Henley (1784), Lettres écrites de Lausanne (1785) and a sequel Caliste (1787), Trois Femmes (1797). Some are largely auto-biographical and reveal the disappoint-ments of her marriage.

Charroi de Nîmes, Le, a *chanson de geste (*Garin de Monglane cycle).

Charron, PIERRE (1541–1603), religious and philosophical writer, a lawyer who became a priest and a successful preacher, a friend of Montaigne. He wrote *Les Trois Vérités* (1593), asserting the truth of God's existence, of Christianity, and of the Catholic faith—against atheists, infidels, and Protestants respectively; *Discours chrétiens* (1600); *De la sagesse* (1601), a work of stoic philosophy after the manner of Montaigne, designed to bring philosophy to the support of religion, but containing chapters which exposed him to the charge of scepticism, as implying that the study of man can produce a moral code independent of religious dogma. He set about revising it, but died before he could appease the theologians.

Charte, La, the constitutional charter granted 4 June 1814 by the restored Louis XVIII at the bidding of the Allied Powers. It upheld the social and administrative order resulting from the Revolutionary and Napoleonic eras; provided for government by a constitutional monarchy, with a largely hereditary *Chambre des *Pairs* (and *v. Sénat*) nominated by the king and an elected *Chambre des *Députés* (the franchise did not extend below a certain income); guaranteed liberty of the *Press (though this could be—and soon was—restricted by law); and recognized Roman Catholicism as the State religion. Ministerial responsibility was not clearly defined, a fact which enabled Charles X to abuse power and so led to the 1830 *Revolution.

Chartier, ALAIN (*c.* 1390–*c.* 1440), poet and prose writer, was in the service of Charles VI and Charles VII and went on missions to Germany, Venice, and Scotland. He was very ugly, but Marguerite d'Écosse is said to have kissed his lips as he slept as a tribute to the beauty that issued from them. He was made a canon of Paris. His works include the *Livre des quatre dames*, a poem written just after *Agincourt (1415), in which four ladies lament the loss of their lovers, expressing the bitter sorrow that followed the defeat of French chivalry; *La Belle Dame sans merci* (1424), a remarkably successful short poem on a lover who dies of despair in consequence of his lady's cruelty; the

Quadrilogue invectif (1422), his best-known prose work, a vigorous appeal for national unity (written at the time of the strife between *Armagnacs and Burgundians and the incursions of Henry V) in the form of a dialogue between France, the nobility, the people, and the clergy, each exposing the others' failings; a *Traité de l'espérance*; a *Bréviaire des nobles*; the *Débat du Réveille-matin*; *De vita curiali* (trans. as *Le Curial*), a satire on court life. His prose style, modelled on the Latin orators, is attributable to an early revival of humanist letters.

Chartier, ÉMILE-AUGUSTE (1868–1951), philosopher, famous as a teacher and essayist (under the pen-name 'Alain', after Alain Chartier above). He studied at the *École normale supérieure*, then embarked on a career as a teacher of philosophy which lasted till 1933, with a break during the 1914–18 war when, at 47, he joined up and served in the ranks. He taught in provincial *lycées (notably Rouen; *v. Maurois*) till 1900, then in Paris at the *Lycée Condorcet* and (from 1909) at the *Lycée Henri IV*; he also lectured at the *Collège Sévigné*, a girls' school of high repute. He was thus a formative influence on French thought, second only, it has been said, to Bergson, for some 40 years. And in 1906, as 'Alain', he had begun a series of daily *Propos d'un Normand* (short essays on divers subjects—happiness, Christianity, aesthetics, education, politics, etc.) in the *Dépêche de Rouen*; they continued over many years, and soon made him known to a far wider public.

He invented no new system of philosophy. His strength lay in his study and understanding of the best of the old systems; in his independent and clear-sighted application of his findings to the problems of life, religion, art, literature, and politics; and in his great gifts as a teacher—he encouraged his pupils to strip inherited values and beliefs of the mass of associations and commonplaces which distort judgement, and to re-think and re-define for themselves. The evolution of his thought can be studied in the absorbing *Histoire de mes pensées* (1936), in *Les Dieux*

(1934), in *Souvenirs de guerre* (1937), and in the volumes of his collected *Propos*. His *Propos de littérature* (1933) are particularly interesting as criticism. They are complemented by the studies *Stendhal* (1935), *Avec Balzac* (1937), *En lisant Dickens* (1945), and by *Commentaires* (1936) on the poetry of Valéry (poetry, to which he came relatively late in life, provoked some of his most stimulating writing). Other works include his *Système des Beaux-Arts* (1920), a guide to the appreciation of the arts, amplified (esp. as regards poetry) in *Vingt Leçons sur les Beaux-Arts* (1931); *Les Idées et les âges* (1927) and *Entretiens au bord de la mer* (1931), philosophical essays; *Visite au musicien* (1927), on Beethoven.

Chartreuse de Parme, La (1839), by Stendhal, a novel of life and intrigues at the court of Parma between 1815 and 1830; inspired by the chronicles of the Farnese family, 16th-c. sovereigns of Parma.

The 16-year-old Fabrice del Dongo joins Napoleon's armies. After many adventures, he returns to Italy after *Waterloo, somewhat suspect because of his French escapades. His aunt, the duchess of Sanseverina ('La Sanseverina', a beautiful young woman of infinite resource who dominates the book), is mistress of Count Mosca, chief minister at the court of Parma. Through her influence he is launched on a promising ecclesiastical career. Mosca's enemies, aware that the duchess loves Fabrice, plot the young man's removal from the capital, reasoning that the duchess would follow Fabrice and Mosca the duchess. The plot succeeds, thanks to Fabrice's imprudent *amours* with an actress. He is imprisoned, but escapes, helped by the duchess, Mosca, and the prison governor's daughter, Clélia Conti. Meanwhile the duchess has contrived to have the reigning prince of Parma poisoned. Through her influence, again, the new prince pardons Fabrice, who becomes a prominent cleric and preacher, and renews his liaison with Clélia, now a married woman. They have a son, Sandrino, whom Fabrice, wanting to have

his child to himself, later kidnaps. The boy dies, and Clélia does not long survive him. Fabrice retires to a Carthusian monastery ('la Chartreuse de Parme'). He dies a year later, and the duchess soon after him.

Chasles, PHILARÈTE (1798–1873), man of letters and critic, did much to familiarize readers of his day with foreign literatures. In early life he worked in England for a firm of publishers, later he was a professor at the *Collège de France* and on the editorial staff of the *Journal des Débats*. His works include *Le XVIII*ᵉ *Siècle en Angleterre* (1846), *Études sur l'antiquité* (1847), *Études sur l'Espagne et sur les influences de la littérature espagnole en France et en Italie* (1847), *Études sur la littérature et les mœurs de l'Angleterre au XIX*ᵉ *siècle* (1850), *Voyages d'un critique à travers la vie et les livres* (1865–8). His *Mémoires* (1876–7, 2 vols.) contain many portraits of his contemporaries.

Chasse au chastre, La (1853; first publ. 1837 in the *Revue de Paris* as *La Chasse d'un artiste*), a tale by Méry. A Provençal musician, out for a day's shooting, puts up a *chastre* (a rare bird), misses it several times, but stalks it so ardently that weeks later he finds himself in Rome. He is arrested as a suspicious character, with a gun and no papers, and speaking an unknown language (Provençal). Dumas *père*'s tale *La Chasse au chastre* (1841; dramatized 1850) relates the same story, which was told him by Méry.

Chasse spirituelle, La. A long prose poem of this title was published in 1949 by the *Mercure de France* as a lost work by Rimbaud, mentioned by Verlaine, but never traced. The real authors, Mme Akakia Viala and Nicolas Bataille, members of an experimental theatre company, came forward at once. They explained that they had concocted this pastiche to prove, in the face of adverse criticism of some of their productions, that they did, in fact, understand Rimbaud. They had handed the typescript, unsigned, to a bookseller, and it had found its way, as an apparently genuine work, to the publishers. At first many critics disbelieved them, and they were unintentionally responsible for one of the most famous literary hoaxes of modern times.

Chasseur vert, Le, v. *Lucien Leuwen.*

Chassignet, Jean-Baptiste (*c.* 1570–1635), a metaphysical poet (*cf. Sponde*; *La Ceppède*), author in youth of *Le Mépris de la vie et consolation contre la mort* (1594; 1967, ed. H.-J. Lope), a sequence of 434 sonnets (interspersed with other poems), a fine example of the baroque; also of verse paraphrases of the Minor Prophets (1600) and 150 Psalms (1613).

Chastelard, Pierre de Boscosel de (1540–64), gentleman of Dauphiné, grandson of Bayard, became infatuated with Mary Stuart, and followed her to Scotland after the death of François II (her first husband); he was discovered in her room, and executed. His story inspired Swinburne's tragedy *Chastelard.*

Chastellain or **Chastelain,** Georges (*c.* 1405–75), a Fleming, became councillor and historiographer to the dukes of Burgundy (Charles the Bold dubbed him a knight of the Golden Fleece with his own hand—a signal honour). His *Chronique* of the years 1419–75, preserved in fragmentary form, is in a style based on Latin models, and judges princes of the day with a high independence; it was continued by Molinet. He was also a *rhétoriqueur* poet and wrote various moral and political pieces, e.g. *Les Princes,* a poem presenting 24 types of bad ruler.

Chastiement des dames, v. *Robert de Blois.*

Chat botté, Le, v. *Perrault.*

Chateaubriand, François-René, vicomte de (1768–1848), b. at Saint-Malo, 10th child of an old Breton family, the outstanding literary genius of the early 19th c. His schooling was intermittent, his childhood being spent mainly at the Château de Combourg (the family home at Combourg, a country town near Saint-Malo). In his *Mémoires d'outre-tombe* he recalls days of wandering in the deserted forests and marshes, alone or with his beloved sister Lucile (1764–1804), and long, silent evenings in the gloomy drawing-room. In 1788 he went to Paris with an army commission, was presented at court, and made literary friends (notably Fontanes). The Revolution interrupted his career and he left (1791) for America, where his travels were fruitful, though not extensive. Learning by chance that the monarchy had fallen, he returned home (1792), fought with the *Armée des émigrés,* was wounded at the siege of Thionville, and escaped to England (1793). Living mainly in London (with a spell at Bungay in Suffolk), he supported himself by translating, wrote *Les *Natchez* (1826) and an *Essai historique, politique, et moral sur les révolutions anciennes et modernes dans leurs rapports avec la révolution française* (London 1797), and began work on *Le Génie du christianisme.*

He returned to France in 1800, won a sudden reputation with *Atala* (1801), and then resounding fame with *Le *Génie du christianisme* (1802). Now high in Napoleon's favour, he was appointed to a post at the embassy in Rome, but resigned in disgust at the duc d'Enghien's execution (1804). He travelled (1806–7) in Greece, the Near East, and Spain, then returned to La Vallée-aux-Loups (a small property near Paris) to devote himself to literature and journalism (he wrote regularly for the *Mercure de France,* 1800–14; also for the *Journal des Débats*). He became increasingly hostile to the Empire and more than once fell foul of Napoleon. On his election to the *Académie* (1811) his *discours de réception* was so provocative that he was not allowed to read it. His political career—as a minister at Ghent (v. *Journal universel*), then French ambassador in London—began with the restoration of Louis XVIII. Under Louis-Philippe he lived in retirement in Paris, editing his *Mémoires d'outre-tombe,* increasingly a grand old man of literature and the central figure of Mme Récamier's *salon*. At his own request he was buried in an island tomb off Saint-Malo (the Rocher du Grand-Bé, memorably described in *Flaubert's *Par les champs et par les grèves*).

He was, by all accounts, a sublime *poseur*, egotist, and day-dreamer. When his grandiose visions were not realized he could persuade himself that he had not desired the reality actively enough, and substitute others. Hence the imaginative melancholy, the continually frustrated yearning for the infinite, the 'volupté mélancolique des horizons', that infused his creative writings (e.g. *René). By his emotional appeal, as by his rhythmic, flowing, and wonderfully evocative style, he was one of the great precursors of *Romanticism, and a lasting influence on French literature.

His other works include Les *Aventures du dernier Abencérage* (1826); *La Vie de Rancé* (1844), a highly subjective biography (v. *Trappe*); Les *Martyrs* (1809); the travel sketches of *Itinéraire de Paris à Jérusalem* (1811), *Voyage en Amérique* (1827), *Voyage en Italie* (1826), and *Voyage au Mont Blanc* (1806), on journeys made in 1806–7, 1791, 1803–4, and 1805 respectively; and various critical writings and political pamphlets, e.g. *De Buonaparte et des Bourbons* (1814), a piece of invective said by Louis XVIII to have been worth an army in propaganda value. v. also *Joubert*.

Chateaubriand et son groupe littéraire sous l'Empire, v. *Sainte-Beuve*.

Châteaubriant, ALPHONSE DE (1877–1951), regional novelist. His works include *Monsieur des Lourdines* (1911; his first novel, awarded the *Prix Goncourt*), about a country squire of Poitou, deeply attached to the soil and in conflict with his prodigal son; and *La Brière* (1923), notable for its picture of the lonely marshes in the region of Saint-Nazaire. He was strongly pro-German, and after France fell in 1940 he founded and edited the collaborationist weekly *La Gerbe*. He died in exile in Austria, having been condemned to death (1945) in his absence.

Châtel, FERDINAND-FRANÇOIS (1795–1857), a tailor's apprentice who became a priest, served as an army chaplain, but was later forbidden to preach because of his unorthodox views. After the 1830 *Revolution he founded the *Église catholique française*, with services in French, no confessional, a married priesthood, and himself as primate. It was suppressed by the police in 1842. During the 1848 Revolution 'l'abbé Châtel' reappeared as an advocate of women's rights and easy divorce. He was convicted of offences against morality and religion (1850), and is said to have ended up as a grocer. His *Code de l'humanité* (1838) preached a return to 'the true God and real socialism'.

Châtelain de Coucy, *v. Coucy*.

Châtelaine de Vergi, La, a verse romance of the second half of the 13th c. The story, told with charm and delicacy, may have some historical basis. It is also the theme of a tale in the *Heptaméron*.

A knight loves the châtelaine de Vergi, niece of the duke of Burgundy; her little dog has been trained to summon him to meet her. She has warned him that he will lose her if he reveals their secret. The duchess of Burgundy falls in love with him, but, faithful to his lady, he repulses her. The mortified duchess denounces him to the duke as having made improper advances. The duke, who esteems the knight, gives him a chance to clear himself, so, in strict confidence, the knight reveals the secret. But the duchess worms it out of the duke, and takes her revenge by publicly alluding to the châtelaine's lover and the dog. The châtelaine, convinced of her lover's infidelity, dies of a broken heart; the knight, finding her dead, kills himself; and the outraged duke slays his wife with the sword drawn from the knight's body.

Châtelet or **Grand Châtelet** (demolished 1802), originally a fortress erected on the right bank of the Seine in Paris to defend the *Pont-au-Change, later a tribunal and prison where the *prévôt*, assisted by a *lieutenant criminel* and a *lieutenant civil*, exercised the royal jurisdiction over the city (*v. Marot*; *Delisle de Sales*). The *Petit Châtelet* (demolished 1782), on the left bank, defending the Petit Pont, was the *prévôt*'s official residence; part of it also served as a prison.

Châtelet, *v. Du Châtelet*.

Châtiments, Les (1853), poems written by Hugo during his first year of exile and expressing his deep sense of outrage at Napoleon III's *coup d'état* of 2 December 1851 (*v. Republics*, 2); some of the finest satirical and invective verse in the language. The work opens with a sinister picture of the night before the *coup d'état*; 100 poems follow, divided into seven books with such ironical titles as *La Société est sauvée* (because the defenders of liberty have been deported) and *L'Ordre est rétabli* (because the innocent have been massacred in the streets). Book V (*L'Autorité est sacrée*) includes the poem *L'Expiation*, describing the retreat from *Moscow, and *Waterloo (*cf. Les *Misérables*). Having denounced 'Napoléon le petit' as a traitor to France, Hugo looks forward (in *Lux*, the last poem) to the restoration of liberty and the establishment of a universal republic.

Chat-Noir, Le, a café and cabaret in *Montmartre, at first a resort of local poets and painters who devised entertainments for their own amusement, became famous *c.* 1880 when its shows attracted a wider audience eager for a glimpse of Bohemian life. Many authors who wrote for the cabaret later had their works produced at the *Théâtre Libre*. Its sign was a black cat (Art) with a terrified goose (the *bourgeoisie*) under its paw.

Chatrian, ALEXANDRE, *v. Erckmann-Chatrian*.

Chats-fourrés, in Rabelais's *Panta-gruel*.

Chatterton (1835), a prose drama by Vigny about an imaginary episode in the life of the English poet Thomas Chatterton (1752–70).

Chatterton hopes, if he can be free to write, to make enough money to pay his debts. He lodges under an assumed name with John Bell, a materialistic business man. A bond of sympathy, which both hesitate to acknowledge, grows between him and Bell's young wife, the tender, compassionate Kitty. He writes to the Lord Mayor of London, an old friend of his father, to ask for employment. While he awaits a reply former friends appear by chance and reveal his identity. The Lord Mayor answers his letter in person, jeeringly offers him a valet's post, and hands him a newspaper in which he finds himself accused of plagiarism. In utter despair, the poet goes to his room, burns his manuscripts, and takes poison. Kitty follows him, intending to declare her love and her faith in him; but she arrives too late and dies of grief.

Chaudon, DOM LOUIS-MAYEUL, *v. Dictionaries*, 1766.

Chaulieu, GUILLAUME AMFRYE, ABBÉ DE (1639–1720), 'l'Anacréon du Temple', poet, an easy-going genius who managed the affairs of the duc de Vendôme and his brother Philippe (being rewarded with benefices) and frequented the epicurean society of the *Temple; a close friend of La Fare and, latterly, of Mlle de Launay. His best poems are possibly his *Fontenay* and *La Retraite*, his lines on death, and some pleasant verses addressed to La Fare.

Chaumeix, ABRAHAM-JOSEPH DE (*c.* 1730–90), an opponent of the *philosophes*, author of *Préjugés légitimes contre l'Encyclopédie* (1758–9). Voltaire called him 'barbouilleur de papier'.

Chaumière indienne, La, *v. Bernardin de Saint-Pierre*.

Chaunu, PIERRE (1923–), social and economic historian, professor at *Paris IV* since 1970. His works include *Séville et l'Atlantique, 1504–1650* (from 1955, 12 vols.; with Huguette Chaunu),

L'Amérique et les Amériques (1964), *La Civilisation de l'Europe classique* (1966) and *La Civilisation de l'Europe des Lumières* (1971), *Conquête et exploitation des nouveaux mondes, XVIᵉ siècle* (1969), *L'Expansion européenne du XIIIᵉ au XVᵉ siècle* (1969), *L'Espagne de Charles Quint* (1973).

Chauvin, NICOLAS, a soldier whose devotion to Napoleon and heroism in the Revolutionary and Napoleonic wars (he was wounded 17 times) gave rise to the word *Chauvinisme*, denoting the sentimental, almost fanatical, patriotism of the soldiers of that period.

Chef-d'œuvre inconnu, Le, v. *Comédie humaine, La* (*Études philosophiques*).

Chemin de paradis, Le, v. *Maurras.*

Chemin de velours, Le, v. *Gourmont.*

Chemins de la liberté, Les, v. *Sartre.*

Chêne de Vincennes, the oak under which Louis IX is said to have administered justice to his subjects; sometimes referred to as a symbol of the king's ancient status as head of the judicature.

Chênedollé, CHARLES-JULIEN DE (1769–1833), a writer chiefly remembered as the friend and admirer of his more famous contemporaries, e.g. Chateaubriand, Mme de Staël (he frequented *Coppet), Rivarol, Joubert. As an *émigré* in *Hamburg he played a devoted, at times critical, Boswell to Rivarol, and later published *L'Esprit de Rivarol* (1808). He returned to France in 1799, and from 1810 held an educational post at Rouen and Caen, living happily among his flowers and orchards. His poetry includes *Le Génie de l'homme* (1807), a didactic poem; and *Études poétiques* (1820), odes marked by a love of nature which brought him into sympathy with the young *Romantics (he occasionally contributed to their reviews, e.g. *La *Muse française*). He is thus of some importance as a link between two contrasting generations of writers.

Chénier, ANDRÉ (1762–94), generally deemed the greatest French poet of the 18th c., b. at Constantinople (where his father was French consul; his mother was Greek), lived in Paris from the age of five. After a year in the army he travelled in Switzerland and Italy, then spent three years—which he did not enjoy—at the French embassy in London (1787–90). He was active in the early Revolutionary movement, but protested against its later excesses. After being imprisoned for four months, he was executed two days before *le 9 thermidor* (v. *Revolutions, 1*).

Only two of his poems were published in his lifetime (the *Serment du Jeu de Paume* and *Hymne sur l'entrée triomphale des Suisses révoltés du régiment de Châteauvieux*). Chateaubriand included extracts from his work in *Le *Génie du christianisme*, and editions of his poems appeared in 1819 (by Latouche), 1874, and 1908–19 (3 vols.; a definitive ed.). His most characteristic work, which won him the name 'the French Theocritus', is in his shorter eclogues, idylls, odes, and elegies (*La Jeune Tarentine, La Jeune Captive, Clytie*, etc.) and a few longer poems such as *L'Aveugle* (a famous poem on Homer) and *Le Mendiant*. They show his intense devotion to classical literature, especially to the Greek elegiac poets. His poems recapture their grace and melody, giving expression in the old pagan spirit to his love of nature, youth, and beauty. His *Iambes*, lyrical satires written in prison (and smuggled out), reveal his despair at the atrocities of the *Terror.

He has been called the last of the Classics and the first of the Romantics because, while purely *Classical in spirit, he prepared the way for *Romanticism by his metrical innovations (e.g. his free use of *enjambement* which restored harmony and suppleness to French verse). His literary doctrine is set forth in the poem *L'Invention*.

Chénier, MARIE-JOSEPH (1764–1811), brother of the above, wrote tragedies (often on themes from French history, e.g. *Charles IX*, 1789); odes; satires and epistles in a sober, vigorous style; also many patriotic songs, often composed to order and first heard at the *Fêtes de la *Fédération, e.g. the *Chant du départ, an Hymne à l'*Être Suprême. His *Épître sur la calomnie* (1797) was an eloquent reply to accusations of complicity in the death of his brother André.

Chennevière, GEORGES (1884–1929), *unanimiste* poet, author of *Le Printemps* (1910), *Appel au monde* (1919), *Le Chant du verger* (1923), *Pamir* (1926), *La Légende du roi d'un jour* (1927), etc.; collected *Œuvres poétiques* (1929). He and Romains produced a *Petit Traité de versification* (1923; v. *Unanimisme*).

Cherbuliez, VICTOR (1829–99), of Swiss origin, wrote successful novels of manners, often with an historical or archaeological setting, e.g. *Le Comte Kostia* (1863), *Un Cheval de Phidias* (1864), *Le Prince Vitale* (1864), *Le Roman d'une honnête femme* (1866).

Chéri and *La Fin de Chéri*, v. Colette.

Chérie, v. Goncourt, E. de.

Chérubin, in Beaumarchais's *Le *Mariage de Figaro.

Cherubini, SALVATORE (1760–1842), an Italian composer, lived in Paris from 1788 and took French citizenship. He wrote much of the official music of the Revolution and was director of the Paris *Conservatoire de musique* from 1821. v. *Méhul*.

Chevalerie Ogier, La, v. Ogier le Danois.

Chevalier, LOUIS (1911–), historian, a leading topographer and demographer; professor at the *Collège de France from 1952. His works include *Démographie générale* (1951), *Classes laborieuses et classes dangereuses à Paris pendant la première moitié du XIXe siècle* (1958), *Les Parisiens* (1968).

Chevalier à la charrette, Le, or *Lancelot*, a *roman breton* by Chrétien de

Troyes, probably written in the 1170s, but left unfinished and completed by Godefroi de Lagny. The subject—*Lancelot's love for *Guinevere—was proposed by Marie de Champagne. *Amour courtois* is here seen in its extreme form, and Guinevere, whose commands override those of every other form of duty, is very different in character from Chrétien's earlier heroines.

Meleagant, son of the king of Gorre, a land 'dont nus estranges ne retorne', has carried off Guinevere. Lancelot and *Gauvain set out in pursuit. They meet a cart driven by a dwarf, and Lancelot asks if he has seen the queen. The dwarf replies that if he will get into the cart he will learn what has become of her. Lancelot hesitates momentarily before consenting to what, for a knight, is utter degradation, then mounts the cart. Braving danger and temptation, he reaches Gorre, defeats Meleagant, and rescues the queen, who receives him with cold contempt because he hesitated before mounting the cart. However, after he has been treacherously seized by Meleagant's men and reported dead, she relents, greets him kindly, and finally admits him to her chamber at night. This occasions a second successful combat with Meleagant and a second treacherous imprisonment, and it is Gauvain who conducts the queen back to Arthur's court. Here, at a tourney, Lancelot is further tested by his lady, for on the first two days, fighting incognito, he is ordered to play the coward, and is not allowed to show his prowess till the third day.

Chevalier à la mode, Le, a prose comedy of manners by Dancourt; produced 1687.

The Chevalier, an adventurer seeking a rich marriage (but also fond of a pretty face), is undecided whether to marry Mme Patin, the foolish widow of a tax-farmer and a typical *parvenue*, or the baronne, another wealthy widow; he has also, by posing as a marquis, won the heart of Mme Patin's pretty niece. Trouble arises when the three ladies find that he has sent each an identical set of verses, but he cleverly extricates himself. An injudicious attempt simultaneously to marry Mme Patin and carry off her niece finally leads to his undoing; but he remains imperturbably impudent.

Chevalier à l'épée, Le, a short, 13th-c. *roman breton*. *Gauvain escapes the attack of a magical sword in the castle of a treacherous knight, and wins his daughter; but she later deserts him for a rival.

Chevalier au barisel, Le, a medieval verse tale of an impious knight who defiantly confesses his sins to a hermit, and is ordered as sole penance to fill a little barrel from a stream. He lightheartedly obeys, only to find that the water invariably runs away. For a year he strives unsuccessfully, then returns to the hermit, who prays for him. Moved by the prayer, the knight lets drop a single tear of humility, which at once fills the barrel. Then, in a state of perfect repentance, he dies.

Chevalier au cygne, Le, with the **Roman de Godefroi de Bouillon** and *Elioxe* (or *La Naissance du Chevalier au cygne*), forms a group of 13th-c. poems in monorhyme stanzas embodying legends about the house of *Godefroi de Bouillon and therefore attached to the Crusade cycle (*v.* Crusades). According to the first poem, Elias, the ancestor of the house, was called 'le Chevalier au cygne' because he came forward in a skiff drawn by a swan as champion of the comtesse de Bouillon. He married her daughter, and Godefroi was their grandson. (*Cf.* the 14th-c. English *Chevalere Assigne*.) In *Elioxe*, a poem of somewhat later date, Elias is one of six brothers changed into swans, of whom he alone recovers human form.

Chevalier au lion, Le, *v. Yvain*.

Chevalier aux deux épées, Le, an early 13th-c. *roman breton* (12,000 ll.) about the adventures of Meriadeuc, called 'the knight of the two swords' because he alone contrives to remove a certain sword from its fastening and girds it beside his own. Many adventures of *Gauvain are woven into the story.

Chevalier de Maison-Rouge, Le, *v. Dumas père*.

Chevalier des Touches, Le (1864), by Barbey d'Aurevilly, a stirring tale of the adventures of a leader of the *Chouannerie. It has a notable opening picture of decayed aristocrats reminiscing.

Chevaliers de la Table Ronde, *v. Romans bretons; Cocteau*.

Chevaux de Diomède, Les, *v. Gourmont*.

Chèvrefeuille, *v. Marie de France*.

Chevreuse, MARIE DE ROHAN, DUCHESSE DE (1600–79), a woman of beauty and restless energy, famous for her part in plots and intrigues against Richelieu, and later Mazarin, down to the time of the *Fronde. After suffering repeated exile (in England for some years from 1648), she finally accepted defeat, and was reconciled with Mazarin.

Chevrillon, ANDRÉ (1864–1957), man of letters and critic, nephew of Taine. His *Études anglaises* and *Nouvelles Études anglaises* (1901 and 1910), *Kipling* (1903), etc., did much to improve French understanding of English writers such as Galsworthy, Kipling, Meredith, Wells. He also wrote *Taine, formation de sa pensée* (1932), a critical study; several volumes of pleasing travel sketches, e.g. *Sanctuaires et paysages d'Asie* (1905), *Un Crépuscule d'Islam: Maroc* (1907), *Marrakech dans les palmes* (1920); and *La Bretagne d'hier* (1925).

Chicanneau, in Racine's *Les *Plaideurs*.

Chicheface, Dit de, a medieval satire (*v. Dit*). Chicheface ('Thin-face'), a monster who feeds only on patient wives, is painfully thin, while Bigorne, who feeds on patient husbands, grows fat. *Cf.* Chichevache in Chaucer's *Clerk's Tale*, ll. 1132 ff.

Chicot, the king's gentleman jester in *Dumas père's *La Dame de Monsoreau*, etc., was drawn from a Gascon nobleman, Antoine d'Anglerays (d. 1592), who became the friend and unofficial adviser of Henri III.

Chien-Caillou, v. Champfleury.

Chien de Montargis. Aubry de Montdidier, a member of Charles V's court, was assassinated (1371) near Montargis by one Richard de Macaire. The victim's dog aroused suspicion against Macaire, and the king ordered a combat between man and dog. The dog overcame Macaire, who confessed, and was executed. *v. Macaire.*

Children's Reading. For long after the invention of printing children had no special reading-matter of their own: they read sacred books, their catechisms and grammars, abridged versions of works read by their elders, and later the stories in the *Bibliothèque bleue* and La Fontaine's *Fables*. As Fénelon—who himself wrote fables and *Télémaque*—suggested in his *Traité de l'éducation des filles* (1687), something more was required. This was supplied by *Perrault's famous Contes de ma mère l'Oye* (1697) and Mme d'*Aulnoy's Contes des fées* (1698).

18th-c. children were steered firmly out of fairyland by Mme Leprince de Beaumont and Mme de Genlis, both of whom had been royal governesses. The former did include the tale of Beauty and the Beast in her *Le Magasin des enfants, contes moraux* (1757), but the latter never deviated from her policy (expounded in *Adèle et Théodore, ou Lettres sur l'éducation*, 1782) of no make-believe, and no marvels save those capable of rational explanation. Her *Les Veillées du château* (1784) is a book of priggish moral tales, designed to be read in the evenings to three children of about 10 as a reward for good behaviour. In 1782 came the first volume of A. *Berquin's immensely popular L'Ami des enfants*, dialogues, tales, and sketches about children who spent their lives helping the (always servile) poor; who were transformed by wise guardians from insufferable bullies into considerate playmates; and who, if seldom convinced, were certainly crushed by their parents' common-sense replies to their questions.

The early 19th c. saw the equally popular *Contes à ma fille* (1809) and *Contes aux enfants de France* (1824–5) by Jean-Nicolas Bouilly (1763–1842). (A. France, who read both Berquin and Bouilly as a child, pays tribute to them in *Le Petit Pierre*.) Some of Bouilly's tales appeared in *Le Dimanche des enfants*, and soon children had a choice of such periodicals, e.g. *Le Journal des enfants* (f. 1833); *La Semaine des enfants* (f. 1857); *La Poupée modèle* (f. 1863), for the very young; *Le Magasin d'éducation et de récréation* (f. 1864), which serialized many of J. Verne's tales and also had pictures and stories for younger readers. The 'comic', with stories told chiefly by pictures, began *c.* 1890, e.g. *Le Petit Français illustré* (1890–6). From *c.* 1850 there were also special children's sets of *Images d'Épinal*.

Children's books were now produced in increasing numbers. The pattern was still very much that set by Berquin and Bouilly: a naturally lively, impetuous child learns by painful experience—under the sadistically stoic eye of its parents—that things are not what they seem. But for all their moralizing the tales were written for children, about children; and they had the detailed fidelity to daily life which children demand even in a fairy-tale. Bound in the bright red of Hachette's *Bibliothèque rose*, a series guaranteed safe reading for the young, they sold in their thousands. By far the most popular were Mme de *Ségur's tales of Sophie (cf. Maria Edgeworth's Rosamund), who cut off her eyebrows to make them grow thick. There were also stories by writers usually associated with an adult public, e.g. *Nodier's La Fée aux miettes* and other tales, *Dumas père's Histoire d'un casse-noisette* and *La Bouillie de la comtesse Berthe*, G. Sand's *Contes d'une grand'mère*, P. de *Musset's Monsieur le Vent et Madame la Pluie*; animal stories, e.g. Mme de Ségur's *Mémoires d'un âne*; the many adventure stories by J. Verne; Erckmann-Chatrian's historical tales; and *v. Malot*. The very young seem to have had no nursery rhymes, but they had songs (*Sur le pont d'Avignon*; *Au clair de la lune*), adaptations of La Fontaine's *Fables*, and the fairy-tales of Grimm and Hans Andersen (trans. *c.* 1840) to add to their own Perrault. It was, in fact, on translations that the older children were chiefly brought up. They enjoyed *Wyss, Fenimore Cooper, and Mayne Reid, and also, as the young elsewhere have done, many books not specially intended for children: *Robinson Crusoe* (recommended by J.-J. Rousseau in *Émile*; there were many *Nouveaux Robinson*); *Gulliver's Travels*; *Don Quixote*; *Baron von Münchhausen*; the *Arabian Nights*; and, above all, Dickens. A later favourite was Kipling, whose *Just So Stories* and *Jungle Books* became minor classics in French.

The 20th c. has seen a vast increase in the volume of children's books, with works ranging from Jacob's *Histoire du Roi Kaboul Ier et du Marmiton Gauwain* and *Le Géant du soleil* (both 1904), *Vildrac's *L'Île rose* and *Les Lunettes du lion*, *Aymé's *Contes du chat perché*, *Saint-Exupéry's *Le Petit Prince*, and tales by Supervielle to the many volumes depicting the adventures of the elephant Babar, Tintin, or Astérix. Moralizing tales have given way to informative stories and handbooks designed to satisfy, or to arouse, the child's curiosity about every activity and aspect of the world around him, to say nothing of space travel. But Perrault's *Contes* are still read, with the Sophie stories a good second.

Chimène, in Corneille's *Le *Cid*.

Chimères, Les (1854, appended to *Les Filles du feu*), 12 sonnets by Nerval. Their beauty and magic of language triumph over an obscurity due to mythological and occult allusions and—a surprisingly modern note—the elliptical quality of the writing. The best known are *El Desdichado* ('Je suis le ténébreux, le veuf, l'inconsolé'; the title is said to be taken from the word *Desdichado*, 'ill-fated', on the shield of the disguised champion in *Ivanhoe*); *Artémis*; and a sequence of five entitled *Le Christ*

aux oliviers, earlier included in *Petits Châteaux de Bohème* (1853).

Choderlos de Laclos, *v. Laclos.*

Choisy, FRANÇOIS-TIMOLÉON, ABBÉ DE (1644–1724), an eccentric, effeminate character (he masqueraded as a woman) who, after years of frivolity and dissipation, became a missionary and made a voyage to Siam (1685; recorded in an agreeable *Journal*). He left *Mémoires pour servir à l'histoire de Louis XIV* (1727), written in a familiar, attractive style, with some striking portraits, e.g. of Colbert.

Choix des élues, *v. Giraudoux.*

Cholières, NICOLAS, SIEUR DE (2nd half of 16th c.), advocate of Grenoble, wrote *Neuf Matinées* (1585) and *Après-Dînées* (1587), conversations between friends giving occasion for tales; similar, but inferior in interest, to *Du Fail's *Propos rustiques* and G. *Bouchet's *Serées*.

Chopin, FRÉDÉRIC-FRANÇOIS (1810–49), the composer, was half French by birth and lived mainly in Paris from 1831 (there are many references to him in *Delacroix's *Journal*). He is of interest in a literary connection for his liaison with G. *Sand.

Chouannerie, La, the Royalist insurrections in Brittany and Normandy during the Revolution (*cf.* Quiberon; Vendée). The insurgents were called *chouans*, a dialect word for 'owls', because they signalled with an owl-like cry at night. Novels on the subject include Balzac's *Les *Chouans*, Hugo's *Quatre-vingt-treize*, Barbey d'Aurevilly's *Le *Chevalier des Touches*, *Bourges's *Sous la hache*.

Chouans, Les (1829; later in *La *Comédie humaine*, *Scènes de la vie militaire*), a novel of the *Chouannerie* by Balzac. Mlle de Verneuil, a beautiful dancer, and the illegitimate child of a noble, is sent to Brittany by the government to seek out the Royalist leader, win his heart, and induce him to betray his forces. She falls in love with him, and dies in a vain bid to save his life.

Chourineur, Le, in *Sue's *Les Mystères de Paris*.

Chrestien, FLORENT, *v. Satire Ménippée*.

Chrétien de Troyes (2nd half of 12th c.), author of the earliest extant *romans bretons*. He frequented the court of Marie de Champagne (daughter of Eleanor of Aquitaine; *v. Troubadours*) and may have visited England. His earliest works (inc. a poem on *Tristan) are lost, with the possible exception of *Philomena* (*v. Romans d'antiquité*). Between *c.* 1165 and *c.* 1190 he wrote *Erec*, *Cligès*, *Le *Chevalier à la charrette* or *Lancelot*, *Yvain* or *Le Chevalier au lion*, and *Perceval* or *Le Conte du Graal*.

He was a great literary figure of the day, and his works were widely imitated and translated. His fame and influence rested on his skill as a narrator (he excelled at interweaving love and adventure), his imagination, his analysis of the moral and psychological problems of love, and his use of the supernatural. He is also remarkable for his subtle delineation of character, elegant style, and easy, varied handling of the octosyllabic couplet. He wrote for a cultivated, aristocratic society, largely dominated by women, where the ideal of *amour courtois* was fostered, and it is this which is chiefly analysed in his poems.

Christ aux oliviers, Le, *v. Nerval*.

Christine de Pisan (*c.* 1364–*c.* 1430), daughter of an Italian physician in the service of Charles V, was brought up in Paris. She was widowed at 25 and, afflicted by private and public misfortunes, ended her life in a convent. She was an intelligent, educated woman (some would say a 'blue-stocking'), and wrote in both prose and verse. Her prose works include *La Cité des dames*, largely a translation of Boccaccio's *De claris mulieribus*; *Le Livre des trois vertus*, a treatise on women's education; *Le livre des faicts et bonnes meurs du roi Charles* (i.e. Charles V). Her poetry includes the *Épître au dieu d'amour* (1399) and *Dit de la Rose* (1400), in which she ardently defended her sex against the strictures of Jean de Meung; *ballades*; longer poems on love themes; and a *Ditié en l'honneur de Jeanne d'Arc*, showing her devotion to the country of her adoption. Caxton printed a translation of this and her other patriotic tales, *The Fayttes of Arms* (1489). Another translation, *The City of Ladies*, was probably first printed by Wynkyn de Worde.

Chronicles, *v. Crusades*; *Froissart*; *Grandes Chroniques*; *History*, 1.

Chronique des Pasquier (1933–45), the covering title of 10 novels by Duhamel (*Le Notaire du Havre*, *Le Jardin des bêtes sauvages*, *Vue de la terre promise*, *La Nuit de la Saint-Jean*, *Le Désert de Bièvres*, *Les Maîtres*, *Cécile parmi nous*, *Combat contre les ombres*, *Suzanne et les jeunes hommes*, *La Passion de Joseph Pasquier*). They are about a family (rather like the author's) who grow up in the late 19th and early 20th cs. The early volumes are dominated by the vigorously drawn character of the father, Raymond Pasquier, who is always embarking on new ventures. He trails his family after him, magnificently unrepentant about their haphazard growth and the embarrassments they suffer. The worlds of music, science, and literature (*v. Abbaye, L'*) are portrayed.

Chronique du règne de Charles IX (1829), an historical novel by Mérimée, the main episode of which is the Massacre of St. *Bartholomew. It lacks the dramatic and poetic quality of its famous contemporaries *Notre-Dame de Paris and *Cinq-Mars*, but is sometimes preferred to either for its fidelity to history and effective sobriety. *v. Foreign Influences*, 3.

Georges de Mergy has renounced his Protestant faith and joined the king's bodyguard. His brother Bernard joins the *Huguenot troops raised by Coligny. In Paris Bernard falls in love with a Catholic, and during the massacre his life is saved by the mere chance that he has been spending the night with her. He escapes to La Rochelle disguised as a monk. In the siege of the town he strikes down a besieger, and finds he has killed Georges.

Chronique scandaleuse, v. History, 1.

Chrysale, in Molière's *Les *Femmes savantes.*

Chute des feuilles, La, v. Millevoye.

Chute d'un ange, La (1838), a narrative poem by Lamartine, the opening fragment of an uncompleted epic intended to depict the gradual purification of the human soul (*v. Jocelyn*). The work was coldly received: its plan and themes required stronger powers of dramatic narration than Lamartine possessed.

The angel Cédar defies divine wrath and assumes human form to win Daidha, a daughter of Eve. Their disastrous adventures (e.g. in the city of the tyrant Nemphed, on the Euphrates) are the occasion for long, strained descriptions of vice, profligacy, and horror. Finally their children die of thirst in the desert, and Daidha succumbs to her miseries. Cédar burns the bodies, then throws himself on to the pyre. A spirit scatters the ashes, prophesying that Cédar will expiate his sin in nine incarnations. The poem ends with the first rains of the Deluge.

Cid, Le, by Corneille, a famous tragedy (at first described as a *tragicomedy); produced 1637 (for the acute controversy it aroused *v. Corneille*). It is based on Guillén de Castro's *Las Mocedades del Cid* (1621), a play about the Spanish hero Rodrigo (Ruy) Díaz de Bivar, *el Cid Campeador* (*el Cid,* 'the lord'; *Campeador,* 'champion'). An English version by Joseph Rutter was produced in England *c.* 1638.

The scene is Seville. Rodrigue, a Castilian noble, loves the high-born Chimène, and their marriage is contemplated. But his father, Don Diègue, quarrels with her father, the count, and receives the unforgivable affront of a slap in the face. Being no match for his younger adversary, Don Diègue calls on Rodrigue to avenge him. After a brief conflict between love and honour, Rodrigue calls out the count and kills him. Chimène rushes to the king, demanding Rodrigue's death. The king temporizes. Rodrigue presents himself to Chimène, proffers his sword, and begs for death at her hand rather than that of the executioner. A fine scene follows, in which Chimène is torn between love and filial duty; and the two, each recognizing the other's noble motives, lament their fate. She refuses to kill him, but will pursue her demand for vengeance, hoping that it may not be granted. A Moorish fleet now threatens Seville, and Rodrigue leads a band of his father's retainers to meet it. By prodigies of valour he destroys the Moors and captures their two kings, who hail him as 'le Cid'. This feat wins him the king's pardon, but Chimène again demands vengeance. The king consents to a duel between Rodrigue and a champion of Chimène; the victor is to win her hand. Rodrigue again visits Chimène: he will not defend himself in the duel, and accepts death. Unable to contemplate this, she urges him to fight and win, if only to save her from an unwelcome marriage. He duly wins, but spares his opponent's life. Chimène, seeing the latter return alive, infers that her lover is dead, and her reaction convinces the king that she still loves Rodrigue. This she admits, but even now cannot reconcile her sense of duty with marriage to her father's slayer. The king sends Rodrigue to command his armies against the Moors, trusting that time and his prowess will solve the conflict. The issue is left uncertain.

Ci-devant, during the Revolution, an aristocrat or a person attached by title or office to the *ancien régime.*

Cigogne, Contes de la, a name for traditional fairy-tales (also called *Contes de ma mère l'Oye; cf. Perrault*), or any fanciful tales.

Cimetière marin, Le (1920, in the **Nouvelle Revue française;* 1922, in *Charmes*), a famous poem by Valéry, a soliloquy on the theme of death. The noonday sun blazes from a clear, changeless sky on to the cliff-top cemetery at Sète (his birthplace); the sea, momentarily still, glitters below. The dead are at peace, now one with the void; it is the living, inactive in contemplation, who may be a prey to the devouring worm. Then, stimulated by the breeze which is now whipping the spray over the rocks, the poet turns back to life—'il faut tenter de vivre!'

Cinna, a tragedy by Corneille; produced late in 1640 (after *Horace). The theme is from Seneca's *De clementia*, with the addition of the character Émilie, invented by Corneille.

Cinna, Pompée's grandson, enjoys the favour of the emperor Auguste, but is leader of a plot to assassinate him and restore the liberty of Rome. The emperor's magnanimity shakes his resolve; but he loves Émilie, who, though she has been nourished in the emperor's house, spurs him on, stipulating that to win her he must avenge her father, a victim of the proscriptions. Maxime, another conspirator (though also in the emperor's confidence), causes the plot to be revealed to Auguste, feigning remorse, but hoping, after Cinna's arrest, to flee with Émilie, whom he secretly loves. Auguste, horrified by Cinna's treachery, but weary of bloodshed, is uncertain how to act. In a final sequence of scenes, Cinna and Émilie (who has spurned Maxime) admit their ingratitude and beg to die together; and Maxime confesses his true motive for revealing the plot. Overwhelmed by this avowal, Auguste decides to master his wrath, pardons all three, and restores them to favour, thus securing their repentance and future allegiance.

Cinq auteurs, Les, five authors—Corneille, Boisrobert, Colletet, C. de L'Estoile, Rotrou—employed by Richelieu, who had literary ambitions, to write plays under his direction. They collaborated in *La Comédie des Tuileries* (perf. 1635 before the king; *v. Corneille*), *La Grande Pastorale*, *L'Aveugle de Smyrne*, etc.

Cinq Grandes Odes, *v. Claudel*.

Cinq-Mars, ou Une Conjuration sous Louis XIII (1826), an historical novel by Vigny; based on the abortive plot against Richelieu led by the king's favourite, the marquis de Cinq-Mars (1620–42), and F.-A. de Thou, both of whom were executed. The book is slow-moving, but poetical in conception and interesting for its historical background—painted in lavish, though not entirely accurate, detail. Notable incidents are the trial of Urbain Grandier (priest of Loudun, burnt at the stake 1634), whom Richelieu wishes to remove; the evening in Marion *Delorme's *salon* when the conspiracy comes to a head, with the young Descartes and Milton among the unwitting guests; the stately progress of Richelieu's barge up the Rhône, towing a barge bearing the captive conspirators.

Cistercians; Cîteaux. In 1098 Robert, abbot of Molesme, founded the Cistercian Order, an offshoot of the Benedictines, at Cîteaux (L. *Cistercium*), near Dijon. *v. Bernard, St.*

Cité, Île de la, the island in the Seine in Paris, the site of the cathedral of Notre-Dame; in Roman times the centre of the city (Lutetia) and a holy place. Two bridges, later known as the Petit Pont and the Grand Pont, connected it with the left and right banks respectively.

Cité antique, La, *v. Fustel de Coulanges*.

Cîteaux, *v. Cistercians*.

Cité des dames, La, *v. Christine de Pisan*.

Cité des eaux, La, *v. Régnier, H. de*.

Cladel, LÉON (1835–92), wrote realistic tales and novels of peasant or vagrant life in the Quercy (the region of Cahors), e.g. *Le Bouscassié* (1869), *Les Va-nu-pieds* (1873), *N'a-qu'un-œil* (1882).

Claire Lenoir, *v. Villiers de l'Isle-Adam*.

Clairières dans le ciel, *v. Jammes*.

Clairon, Mlle, *stage-name of* CLAIRE

LEGRIS DE LATUDE (1723–1803), a fine tragic actress, notably in Voltaire's tragedies. She published *Mémoires* (1799).

Claque, a band of people engaged, in fulfilment of a contract ('entreprise de succès dramatique') between a theatre manager and a *chef de claque*, to applaud at theatres. The latter receives a certain number of tickets nightly in return for a small sum and an undertaking to produce applause for specified passages. Antoine, in his *Souvenirs sur le Théâtre Libre*, recalls theatre-going in youth as one of a *claque*.

Clara d'Ellébeuse (1899; 1903, in *Le Roman du lièvre*), a tale by Jammes. Clara, brought up by adoring, indulgent parents and nuns, amid all the taboos which were the birthright of a gently born young miss of the 1840s, was still, at 17, so romantically ignorant of the facts of life as to imagine that a shy kiss given to a schoolfellow's brother had engendered the 'sad fruit of a lover's embraces'. Tortured by shame and terror, she wasted away before her parents' eyes, till one day she remembered the laudanum in her mother's medicine-chest, and drank it. The story is so poetically written, and so delicately handled, that bathos—which would be easy—is avoided.

Claretie, ARSÈNE-ARNAUD, *known as* JULES (1840–1913), a prolific, versatile, but rather superficial journalist, critic, and chronicler. He published *La Vie à Paris* (20 vols. covering the years 1881–1911); *Portraits contemporains* (1873–5), popular biography; *Profils de théâtre* (1904), collected dramatic criticism.

Clari or **Clary,** ROBERT DE, *v. Crusades.*

Clarke, MARY (1793–1883), a highly gifted Englishwoman who after 1814 lived mainly in Paris with her widowed mother, moved in intellectual circles, and had many distinguished friends, e.g. Ampère, Cousin, Thierry, and especially Fauriel, whom she had hoped to marry. While she and her mother were living at the Abbaye-aux-Bois (1831–8) she often dispensed tea at Mme *Récamier's *salon*. Before, and especially after, her marriage (1847) to Mohl her own *salon* attracted writers, politicians, and *savants*; her English visitors included Thackeray and Mrs. Gaskell.

Classicism, Classical, the terms applied from the 19th c., in a limited sense, to the predominant intellectual attitude (*l'esprit classique*) in France from *c.* 1590 to *c.* 1715, and especially to the conventions (*les doctrines classiques*) which governed literature (mainly poetry and verse drama) at the height of this period (*c.* 1660–*c.* 1690), as opposed to early 19th-c. *Romanticism, which was largely a revolt against the excessive and exclusive observance of these conventions at the end of the 18th c. (e.g. by La Harpe and Delille). The term 'Classical' is also often loosely applied to all writers of the age of Louis XIV and to the many 18th-c. writers who remained firmly attached to the literary ideals of Classicism.

The Classical era may be divided into three periods. First, a formative period (*c.* 1590–*c.* 1660) of reaction against the literary and grammatical precepts of the *Pléiade* and the extravagance and *préciosité* encouraged by Italian influence. The language was now being purified, i.e. freed from archaisms, neologisms, latinisms, dialect words, etc., and transformed into a more lucid—but less lyrically rich—literary vehicle; the technique of versification was being elaborated; *tragedy as a dramatic form was evolving; and the potentialities of a prose literature were being realized. Various influences were also combining to provoke discussion and formulation of the aesthetic and philosophical bases of literature (e.g. the increasing availability of translations of Greek and Latin works, both creative and critical); and the fact that social and political stability, and a revival of Roman Catholicism, had now succeeded years of upheaval encouraged the desire for similar stability and discipline in the arts. *v. Aubignac*; *Balzac, Guez de*; *Chapelain*; *Corneille*; *François de Sales, St.*; *Malherbe*; *Marinisme*; *Pascal*;

Rambouillet, Hôtel de; *Scudéry*; *Vaugelas*; *Critics and Criticism*, 1. Secondly, a 'peak' period, *l'âge de raison* (*c.* 1660–*c.* 1690), when technical, aesthetic, and philosophical principles still largely in accord with the doctrines of revealed religion were further, and it then seemed finally, evolved. This period saw great creative works by Racine, Molière, and La Fontaine, and the critical writings of Boileau. Thirdly, a period of transition (*c.* 1690 to the death of Louis XIV in 1715) to the age of Voltaire and the *philosophes, to ideas of progress (reflected in the **Querelle des anciens et des modernes*), and—with the spread of Cartesian philosophy (*v. Descartes*)—to religious scepticism; these were ultimately to undermine aesthetic dogmatism.

The conventions finally elaborated in period (2) were based on the conviction that the absolute of beauty in literature had already been achieved by *les anciens*, the great writers of classical antiquity. These were the compulsory models, and the principles of the literary craft could be deduced from their creative works and gleaned from the critical writings of Aristotle and Horace. The object of literature was not only to please, but to preserve fidelity to nature. Genius and imagination were obviously indispensable, but must be disciplined by, perhaps almost subordinated to, reason and concern for artistic perfection.

Reason (in the sense of the guiding principle of the mind in the process of thinking) implied intelligence, judgement, and the search for truth (hence examination of character and motives; the exercise of common sense; a check on spontaneity, and distaste for any personal element). It also implied care for probability (*vraisemblance*), because a rational being is interested in, and so pleased by, what is generally rather than exceptionally true: 'Le vrai peut quelquefois n'être pas vraisemblable'; 'L'esprit n'est point ému de ce qu'il ne croit pas' (Boileau, *Art poétique; and *v. Tragedy* for the dramatic unities). Finally, it implied a complete grasp of one's subject: 'Avant donc que d'écrire

apprenez à penser' (Boileau). Artistic perfection was to be achieved by observing *les règles des bienséances et des genres*. The former regulated choice and treatment of subject, exacting from the writer a sense of fitness (grandeur of subject; avoidance of incongruity, coarseness, and triviality) and a sense of proportion (the parts harmonizing with the whole; avoidance of detail and excess); the latter concerned the different literary *genres*, and the language, style, and prosodic forms appropriate to each. *La raison, les bienséances, les genres* were frequently expounded, notably by Boileau.

Taste (*le goût*), increasingly important in period (2), became all-important in period (3). It was the innate discernment and technical artistry which enabled an author both to observe conventions derived from *les anciens* and to please his own public, mainly the leisured, aristocratic, and critical circles of the court. (*Cf.* the idea of the *relativité du goût*—that standards of beauty and artistic perfection must change with the changing spirit of an age—which was espoused by the *Romantics and provided matter for controversy long after their battles had been won; *v. Critics and Criticism*, 2.)

Classiques français du Moyen Âge (1910–), a series of medieval French and Provençal texts.

Claude (1499–1524), daughter of Louis XII and wife of François Ier. The *Reine Claude* greengage is called after her.

Claude, JEAN (1619–87), a learned *Huguenot pastor and theologian, remembered for his controversies with Bossuet. He won such respect that when he was banished after the revocation of the Edict of Nantes Louis XIV provided him with an escort to the Dutch frontier.

Claude de Pontoux, a 16th-c. poet whose sonnet-sequence *L'Idée* was a source of Drayton's *Idea's Mirror*.

Claude Gueux (1834, in the *Revue de Paris; 1845), a tale by Hugo; an indictment of the social system which contains the germ of Les *Misérables. An unemployed, uneducated, but intelligent worker steals a loaf for his starving family, and is sent to prison for five years. He is persecuted by a malicious warder, but his conduct is exemplary till the warder deliberately separates him from a fellow prisoner who has made his life bearable. In cold despair, he murders his persecutor, then tries to kill himself. He is slowly nursed back to health, and executed.

Claudel, PAUL-LOUIS-CHARLES-MARIE (1868–1955), diplomat, poet, and dramatist. Educated mainly in Paris, he frequented *Symbolist circles and *Mallarmé's 'Tuesdays' (c. 1890), but had already entered the foreign ministry and after 1893 spent some 40 years in the consular and diplomatic service (in the U.S.A., S. America, the Far East, and Europe).

He wrote with lyric fervour, bold imagery, and a sensuously religious emotion (he became a Roman Catholic after a mystical experience in 1886). His poetic development was also, by his own testimony, influenced by Aeschylus, whom he often translated, and by *Rimbaud's Illuminations. He nearly always used the verset claudélien, a form of his own invention, inspired by the Bible, half-way between verse and prose, with neither rhyme nor metre.

His early dramas were Symbolist in tendency, and literary rather than dramatic, e.g. Tête d'or (1890) and La Ville (1893), both included—in revised form— in L'Arbre (1901), which also contains La Jeune Fille Violaine. His play Partage de midi (1906, in a limited ed.) only became known when it was produced by Barrault in 1948. The works which firmly established his reputation were L'*Otage (1911) and L'*Annonce faite à Marie (1912; a later version of La Jeune Fille Violaine). Next came Le Pain dur (1918) and Le Père humilié (1920), completing the trilogy begun by L'Otage, and then the very long drama Le Soulier de satin (1925–8; produced by Barrault in a shortened version, with music by Honegger, 1943),

set in Spain, Bohemia, and at sea off the Balearics in the late 16th c., a passionate treatment of his recurrent theme—man, clinging to his earthly, carnal desires and defying God's love, finally experiences the exquisite joy of surrender. v. also Jeanne d'Arc; Milhaud.

His poetry includes, notably, Cinq Grandes Odes suivies d'un Processional pour saluer le siècle nouveau (1910) and Corona benignitatis anni Dei (1914); also Le Chemin de la Croix (1911), Deux Poèmes d'été (1914), Poèmes de guerre 1914–1916 (1922), Feuilles de saints (1925). His prose works include Connaissance de l'Est (1900; essays and prose poems); Art poétique (1907), essays on poetry and his own poetic form; collections of essays on various subjects, including Biblical commentary, e.g. Figures et Paraboles (1936), Un Poète regarde la Croix (1938).

Claude le Lorrain, CLAUDE GELÉE or GELLÉE, known as (1600–82), b. in the Vosges, a famous landscape painter who spent his life in Italy.

Claudine, in Claudine à l'école, etc., v. Colette.

Claveret, JEAN (1590–1666), dramatist, wrote L'Esprit fort (1630), the first French *comedy of manners, presenting the type of man who affects strength of character and independence of public opinion; La Place Royale (1633; the title was borrowed by Corneille), etc.; also a Traité du poème dramatique, in which he attacked the unity of time. He opposed Corneille in the dispute over Le *Cid.

Clélie (1654–60, 10 vols.), a romance by Mlle de Scudéry; based on the Roman legend of Cloelia who, having been given as a hostage to the Etruscan king Porsenna, escaped, swam the Tiber, and returned to Rome. As in Le *Grand Cyrus, the thread of the story is interrupted by numerous digressions and by discussions of points of gallantry (introducing the famous *Carte de Tendre); and various contemporaries, e.g. Louis XIV, Fouquet, Ninon de Lenclos, are depicted under ancient names.

Clemenceau, GEORGES (1841–1929), 'le Tigre', left-wing politician and journalist (founder of *La Justice*, *Le Bloc*, *L'Homme libre*—v. *Press*, 9; political editor of *L'Aurore*—v. *Dreyfus*). He studied medicine, qualifying in 1869, but soon embarked on a political career, becoming leader of the radical opposition (intermittently a **député*), then prime minister (1906–9). Recalled to power as prime minister at a critical phase of the 1914–18 war (Nov. 1917), he applied himself to the defeat of Germany with fearless ardour and characteristic pugnacity, restored morale, and did much to ensure final victory. He retired in 1920, having negotiated the Treaty of Versailles (1919). Collections of his articles and speeches have been published. He also wrote a successful novel, *Les Plus Forts* (1898).

Cléomadès or *Le Cheval de fust*, a late 13th-c. verse romance by Adenet le Roi, in which a flying wooden horse carries its riders to various adventures. The work is of special interest as depicting the mode of life of a **ménestrel*.

Cléopâtre captive, by Jodelle, the first French **tragedy*; performed 1552/3 before the king. It is based on Plutarch, constructed on classical models, and written (apart from the choruses) in **alexandrines* and decasyllables.

In Act I Antoine's shade announces that it has urged Cléopâtre to kill herself to avoid figuring in Octave's triumph; Cléopâtre appears, blames herself for Antoine's death, and elects to die; the chorus moralizes. In Act II Octave debates with his council: he wishes to preserve Cléopâtre to grace his triumph. In Act III Octave and Cléopâtre are confronted; she tries to obtain liberty by surrendering her treasure; her steward denounces her for concealing part of it. Act IV is concerned with her preparations for death. Act V announces her death, which has taken place in the interval, and the chorus laments.

Clermont, v. *Collège de Clermont*.

Clermont, ÉMILE (1880–1916), novelist, died in action in the 1914–18 war, having published two promising novels: *Amour promis* (1910), *Laure* (1913).

Cleveland, v. *Prévost, A.-F.*

Cligès, a verse romance by Chrétien de Troyes, probably written in the 1170s. It contains episodes based on Oriental tradition, but may be broadly classified as a **roman breton*. The poem illustrates Chrétien's acute analysis of love and of moral problems.

In an introductory section Alexandre, son of the emperor of Constantinople, proves his prowess at King Arthur's court, and marries Arthur's niece, Soredamors. Cligès is their son. The main theme of the second part of the story is the devotion of Fénice, daughter of the emperor of Germany, to her lover Cligès. His uncle, now emperor of Constantinople, marries Fénice against her will. Expressly rejecting the example of Iseut (*v. Tristan*), she preserves her virginity by giving her husband a magic potion, but repulses Cligès because she is nominally a married woman. Then, by a simulated death and after a terrible ordeal, she escapes from the palace and also, as she sees it, from her duty as empress, and is reunited with her lover.

Clio and *Nouvelle Clio*, v. *History*, 4.

Clitandre, in Molière's *Les *Femmes savantes*.

Clitandre, v. *Corneille*.

Cloots, JEAN-BAPTISTE DU VAL DE GRÂCE, BARON DE (1755–94), self-styled 'Anacharsis Cloots' and 'l'Orateur du genre humain', a politician of Prussian origin, joined the **Encyclopédistes* in France and adopted Revolutionary principles, advocating a 'universal family of nations' and a cult of reason. The **Assemblée législative* gave him French citizenship (1792), and he was a member of the *Club des *Jacobins* (till expelled by Robespierre) and the **Convention*. He was executed with the *Hébertistes. He wrote *Adresse d'un Prussien à un Anglais* (1790), the 'Anglais' being Edmund Burke; *L'Orateur du genre humain, ou Dépêches du Prussien Cloots au Prussien Hertzberg* (1791); *La République universelle* (1792), etc.

Clotilde de Surville, v. *Surville.*

Clovis Ier or **Chlodovech** (c. 466–511; *Clovis* is an early form of *Louis*), first king of the Franks, founder of the *Merovingian dynasty, succeeded his father in 481 as chief of the Salian Franks. Bold yet prudent, an unscrupulous bandit and assassin, he defeated first the Roman governor Syagrius (486), then the Alamanni, Burgundians, and Visigoths, thus gaining control over most of Gaul. Anastasius, Roman emperor of the East, recognized him as his lieutenant. He married Clotilda, a Christian princess, and was himself baptized at Rheims, probably in 496, allegedly by St. Remigius. It was Clovis who chose Paris as capital.

Clovis, v. *Desmarets de Saint-Sorlin.*

Club Breton, v. *Jacobins.*

Club de l'Entresol, a club which met (1724–31) to discuss public affairs, especially economic reforms, at the home of its founder, the abbé Alary, in the *entresol* of Hénault's house in the Place Vendôme, Paris. Members included Montesquieu, the abbé de Saint-Pierre, and the marquis d'Argenson. It offended Fleury and had to dissolve.

Cluny, Abbaye de, a famous Benedictine abbey, f. 910 at Cluny (Saône-et-Loire); the centre of the Cluniac Order, which separated from the Benedictines in the 11th c. Only a part of the abbey church, among the largest churches in Europe, now survives.

Cluny, Musée de, a museum of national antiquities and industrial art, mainly of the 14th, 15th, and 16th cs.; housed in the former Hôtel de Cluny in Paris, built c.

1490 (on a site beside Roman remains known as 'les Thermes') as a town residence for the abbots of Cluny.

Clytemnestre, in Racine's *Iphigénie.*

Coalitions, military alliances formed against France by other European powers, first in the reign of Louis XIV, then in the Revolutionary and Napoleonic eras. There were seven of the latter, (1) 1791: Austria and Prussia, joined later by Britain, Spain, Sardinia, Sicily, etc., dissolved, some months after the Austrian defeat at *Rivoli, by the Treaty of Campo Formio (Oct. 1797; between France and Austria); (2) 1799: Austria, Britain, Russia, Turkey, and Sicily, broken by Austrian defeats at *Marengo and *Hohenlinden, followed by the Treaties of Lunéville (Feb. 1801; between France and Austria) and *Amiens (March 1802; between France and Britain); (3) 1805: Austria, Britain, Russia and, later, Prussia, broken by the Austro-Russian defeat at *Austerlitz, followed by the Treaty of Pressburg (Dec. 1805; between France and Austria); (4) 1806: Britain, Prussia, Russia, and Sweden, broken by the Prussian defeat at *Auerstadt and *Jena and the Russian defeat at *Friedland, followed by the Treaty of Tilsit (July 1807; between France, Russia, and Prussia); (5) 1809: Britain and Austria, broken by the Austrian defeat at *Wagram, followed by the Treaty of Vienna (Oct. 1809; between France and Austria); (6) 1813: Austria, Britain, Prussia, Russia, Spain, Sweden, and most other European powers, victorious at *Leipzig, ended with the capitulation of Paris (30 March 1814) and Napoleon's first abdication (6 April 1814), followed by the Treaty of Paris (May 1814; France reverted to the territorial limits of Jan. 1792 and lost her colonial gains); (7) 1815: the same powers, ended with Napoleon's defeat at *Waterloo and final abdication (22 June 1815), followed by the Treaty of Paris (Nov. 1815), which was framed in accordance with the resolutions of the Congress of Vienna (1814–15) and stiffened the terms of the 1814 treaty.

Coblenz. During the Revolution this town was the home of one of the largest colonies of *émigrés* ('les gens de Coblentz') and a rallying-point for the *Armée des émigrés*. *Cf.* *Hamburg*.

Cocagne, Dit de, a facetious medieval poem (*v. Dit*) about a fabulous land of luxury and idleness. Roast pigs roam the streets ready to be carved, the gutters run with wine, and 'qui plus y dort, plus y gagne'. *Cf.* the land of Cockayne in early English literature.

Cocagne, Le Roi de, *v. Legrand.*

Coconas, ANNIBAL, COMTE DE (d. 1574), an Italian adventurer conspicuous for his cruelty in the Massacre of St. *Bartholomew. Catherine de Médicis had him executed (with La Mole) for plotting to place the duc d'Alençon on the throne in preference to his brother Henri III. He figures in *Dumas *père*'s *La Dame de Monsoreau.*

Cocteau, JEAN (1889–1963), a versatile writer whose acute intelligence and sensitivity made him the spearhead (and at times the *accoucheur*) of literary and artistic movements between the 1914–18 and 1939–45 wars. His many publications include (1) collected poetry, e.g. *Poésies 1916–23* (1924; inc. *Le Cap de Bonne Espérance*, 1919, and *Vocabulaire*, 1922, poems of a *fantaisiste* or *Cubist tendency; and *Plain-Chant*, 1923, poems modelled on 16th-c. authors), *Opéra 1925–7* (1927; inc. the well-known *Ange Heurtebise*, 1925), *Poésies* (1947), *Poèmes 1916–55* (1956), *Le Requiem* (1962); (2) plays, e.g. *Orphée* (1927), a 'tragédie en un acte et un intervalle', a modern treatment of the story of Orpheus; *Antigone* (1928), after Sophocles, modernized; *La Voix humaine* (1930, one act; *v. Poulenc*), in which a woman talks on the telephone to the lover who has abandoned her; *La Machine infernale* (1934), a tragedy on the Oedipus theme; *Les Chevaliers de la Table Ronde* (1937), Arthurian legend treated flippantly; *Les Parents terribles* (1938), a modern psychological drama; *L'Aigle à*

deux têtes (1946), a romantic drama in the Ruritanian tradition; *Bacchus* (1951); also ballets, sketches, and monologues, often written for Diaghilev's ballet, with music by Satie, *Les *Six*, etc., and *décor* by Picasso, Braque, Dufy, etc., e.g. *Parade* (1919), *Le Bœuf sur le toit* (a farcical ballet, set in '*Le Bœuf sur le toit* or the Nothing Doing Bar'; prod. 1920, with music by Milhaud and *décor* by Dufy), *Les Mariés de la Tour Eiffel* (1924), *Les Biches* (1924); (3) novels, e.g. *Le Potomak* (1913), *Thomas l'Imposteur* (1923), *Le Grand Écart* (1923), *Les Enfants terribles* (1929; a study of four young people who live and for a time flourish, innocent yet sinister plants, in an unreal hot-house world of their own, which inevitably collapses); (4) essays and criticism (largely collected in *Poésie critique*, 1959–60, 2 vols.), e.g. *Le Rappel à l'ordre* (1926; inc., notably, *Le Secret professionnel*); *Opium* (1930), a form of journal written during treatment for drug-addiction. His work for the cinema should also be noted (*Le Sang d'un poète*, 1931; *La Belle et la Bête*, 1945, etc.); and his brilliant *discours de réception* on his election (1955) to the *Académie. The *Cahiers Jean Cocteau, I* appeared in 1969, his correspondence with Gide in 1970.

Code civil. Codification of the law was promised in the *constitution of 1791, but drafts presented by Cambacérès—to the *Convention and again under the *Directoire—were rejected. Under the *Consulat and Empire, thanks to Napoleon's energy, five codes (covering civil law, civil procedure, commercial, criminal, and penal law) were formulated and approved (1804–10). The first, the *Code civil* (voted 1804), was also called the *Code Napoléon*, because Napoleon presided over the drafting commission and engaged vigorously in the discussions. Though since modified, it is still largely operative. Its three books contain over 2,000 articles: book I covers the law in regard to individuals; books II and III deal with the law of property. Stendhal, who greatly admired its style (solely directed to the avoidance of ambiguity, with no frills and, equally, no fear of repetition in the interests of clarity), told Balzac that while writing La *Chartreuse de Parme he read two pages of it each morning.

Code de la Nature, Le, v. Morelly.

Coëffeteau, NICOLAS (1574–1623), a Dominican friar, preacher to Henri IV, whose funeral oration he delivered; latterly bishop of Marseilles. His writings, constantly cited by Vaugelas as models of French prose, included an Histoire romaine (1621).

Coffret de santal, Le, v. Cros.

Coignard, Abbé Jérôme, in A. France's La *Rôtisserie de la Reine Pédauque.

Colardeau, CHARLES-PIERRE (1732–76), poet, wrote Héroïdes (after the manner of Ovid, inc. a famous Lettre d'Héloïse à Abélard), Caliste (1760; a tragedy), an Épître à M. Duhamel, etc.

Colas, v. Vache à Colas.

Colbert, JEAN-BAPTISTE (1619–83), Louis XIV's great finance minister, first made his mark as assistant to Mazarin, who enriched him and commended him to the king in his will. He helped to overthrow N. Fouquet, and replaced him as intendant des finances (1661) and contrôleur général (1665). He made great reforms in the financial system; though sometimes high-handed (e.g. in his arbitrary reduction of the charge for the national debt), too inclined to protect and regulate industry— and constantly thwarted by the king's costly wars (v. Louvois) and the extravagance of the court—he sought to reduce taxation (v. Fiscal System), to remedy abuses, and to make France great through the prosperity of her people. One of his most useful economic ventures was the Canal du Languedoc (or du Midi; inaugurated 1681) linking the Mediterranean to the Atlantic. As minister of marine, he also created a powerful navy. He was the enlightened founder of the

*Académie des Inscriptions et Belles-Lettres, the *Académie des Sciences, and the *École de Rome, a protector of men of learning (e.g. Mabillon; and v. Journal des savants), and a great art collector (v. Louvre, Musée du). He also reorganized the royal library (v. Bibliothèque nationale), and formed a great library of his own.

Colet, LOUISE REVOIL, MME (1808–76), wife of a professor at the Paris Conservatoire de musique, won some renown for her poetry (Fleurs du midi, 1836; Poésies, 1844; Ce qui est dans le cœur des femmes, 1852, etc.) and much notoriety for her violent behaviour and her liaisons with famous men (inc. *Flaubert and Musset)—described in detail in her autobiographical novel Lui, roman contemporain (1851).

Colette, SIDONIE-GABRIELLE (1873–1954), an outstanding woman writer, in early life also a music-hall actress (1906–14) whose miming and dancing, often semi-nude, and amorous entanglements with both sexes shocked many contemporaries; later a revered literary figure, president of the *Académie Goncourt, and the first woman to be accorded a State funeral. Her talent was discovered by her first husband, the novelist and music critic Henri Gauthier-Villars, who brought her to Paris from her native Burgundy, launched her in the demi-monde, and collaborated with her in a series of novels of schoolgirl life, published under his pen-name 'Willy' (Claudine à l'école, 1900; Claudine à Paris, 1901; Claudine en ménage, 1902; Claudine s'en va, 1903). Their engaging freshness and flippantly perverse sensuality aroused interest and some scandal. The collaboration ended in 1904, the marriage in 1906 (she later married the journalist Henri de Jouvenel, and finally the writer Maurice Goudeket). Her subsequent works (as 'Colette Willy' till 1916, thereafter as 'Colette') include Dialogues de bêtes (1904), introducing the dog Toby-chien and the cat Kiki-la-doucette, and continued in La Paix chez les bêtes (1916); La Retraite sentimentale (1907) and Les

Vrilles de la vigne (1908), lyrical impressions of country life; *L'Envers du music-hall* (1913), on music-hall life; the novels *L'Ingénue libertine* (1909), *La Vagabonde* (1910) and its sequel *L'Entrave* (1913; both about music-hall life), *Chéri* (1920), *Le Blé en herbe* (1923), *La Fin de Chéri* (1926), and *La Chatte* (1933; a subtle study of jealousy, involving a wife, her husband, and his cat); also reminiscences of her childhood, her mother, and her literary beginnings (*La Maison de Claudine*, 1923; *La Naissance du jour*, 1928; *Sido*, 1929; *Mes apprentissages*, 1936). Her supple, musical prose admirably conveys her sensuous feeling for Nature and intuitive sympathy with the unexplored or perverse sides of human nature.

Colette Baudoche, *v. Barrès*.

Coligny, GASPARD DE, AMIRAL (1519–72), leader of the *Huguenots under Charles IX, a man of high character and merit. He was a victim of the Massacre of St. *Bartholomew.

Colin Muset, a 13th-c. lyric poet of Lorraine; a *jongleur* who wrote in praise of good cheer, and of love—sometimes parodying the courtly poets. *v. Lyric Poetry*, 1.

Collé, CHARLES (1709–83), dramatist; reader and secretary to the duc d'*Orléans, who appreciated his gaiety, subtlety, and originality. At first he wrote highly popular, topical *chansons*, then turned to the stage with *La Vérité dans le vin*, a comedy of contemporary manners depicting shameless wives and credulous husbands with the coarse realism of the *fabliaux*. Its public performance was prohibited at the instance of the archbishop of Paris. Then came his two successful comedies: *Dupuis et Desronais* (prod. 1763; in *vers libres*), the gay and touching story of the conflict between two lovers, Desronais and Marianne, and her father, Dupuis, who loves them both, but obstinately opposes their marriage for fear of losing their affection; and *La *Partie de*

chasse de Henri IV, also prohibited and not produced till 1774. *v.* also *Proverbe*.

Collège, *v. Lycées and Collèges; Universities*.

Collège de Boncourt, f. 1353, a college of the medieval *University of Paris, later (1638) incorporated in the *Collège de Navarre*.

Collège de Clermont, f. 1562, the first teaching establishment opened by the *Jesuits in Paris. Molière was a pupil. From 1682 it was called the *Collège Louis-le-Grand*; *v. Prytanée*.

Collège de Coqueret, f. 1463, a college of the medieval *University of Paris. When J. Dorat was principal his pupils included Ronsard, J.-A. de Baïf, Belleau, Du Bellay, and Jodelle.

Collège de France, a famous institution in Paris, independent of the University, for the disinterested pursuit of higher studies. Its nucleus dates from 1530 when François Ier, on Budé's advice, instituted royal readers (*lecteurs royaux*) in Greek, Latin, Hebrew, and mathematics to supplement the conservative teaching of the *Sorbonne*. In time they became a corporate body (the *Collegium Regium Galliarum*) with its own institution; new chairs were also created. Unlike most educational foundations, the college survived the Revolution, and its scope was further extended in the 19th c. Though State-maintained, it enjoys—by a decree of 1873—a high degree of autonomy in regard to administration, appointment, and curriculum. Students are not prepared for examinations, and the lecture courses are public and free. Within the past century, its professors have included Bergson, Michelet, G. Paris, Renan, and Valéry.

Collège de Montaigu, f. 1314 by Gilles Aycelin de Montaigu, a college of the medieval *University of Paris; rebuilt and revived under the rectorship (from 1483) of John Standouck of Malines, and often mentioned in 16th-c. literature. Its some 200 poor students (inc. Erasmus, Calvin, Ignatius Loyola) were brought up in extreme asceticism. Both Erasmus (*Colloquies*) and Rabelais (**Gargantua*, ch. 37) refer to its verminous condition. It was suppressed at the Revolution. *v. Hôtel des Haricots*.

Collège de Navarre, f. 1304 by Jeanne de Navarre, wife of Philippe IV, for poor students of the *University of Paris (20 students in grammar, 30 in arts, and 20 in theology were to receive a weekly allowance of 4, 6, and 8 *solidi*—*v. Money*—respectively). Each group was presided over by a master, the master of the theologians being rector of the college. Later, fee-paying students were admitted. Its revenues were confiscated at the Revolution and it closed in 1792. The **École polytechnique* was built on its site on the Montagne Sainte-Geneviève, behind the *Sorbonne. *v. Villon*.

Collège des Quatre-Nations or **Collège Mazarin**, f. 1661 (opened 1688) under the will of Mazarin for 60 young men, preferably of noble birth, from the four provinces ('quatre nations') France acquired by the Treaty of the *Pyrenees. It occupied the site of the Tour de *Nesle. It was suppressed at the Revolution, and since 1806 has been the home of the **Institut de France*. *v. Bibliothèque Mazarine*.

Collège Lemoine, f. *c.* 1302 by Cardinal Jean Lemoine (*c.* 1250–1313), a college of the medieval *University of Paris.

Collège Sainte-Barbe, a Roman Catholic boys' school in Paris (*v. Écoles libres*), had its origin in a college f. 1460 by Geoffroi Lenormant, a teacher of the *University of Paris, as both a hostel and a school for paying pupils. After a chequered career it was finally suppressed at the Revolution, but promptly replaced by a new foundation of the same name. It is now run by an association of former pupils. J.-É.-J. *Quicherat wrote a history of its origins, and D. Halévy's *Notre cher*

Péguy describes the 'Sainte-Barbe' of modern times.

Collège Stanislas, a Roman Catholic boys' school in Paris (*v. Écoles libres*), f. 1804; received its name (after Stanislas *Leczinski) and full status as a teaching establishment from Louis XVIII in 1822. A. France was a pupil.

Collerye, ROGER DE (*c.* 1470–*c.* 1538), one of the last *rhétoriqueurs, secretary to the bishop of Auxerre. Though always poor and unhappy, he wrote amusing monologues and dialogues for the **Enfants sans souci*, and *rondeaux lamenting his poverty and lost youth with a quality of genuine feeling which recalls Villon.

Colletet, (1) GUILLAUME (1598–1659), one of the *cinq auteurs and a member of the original *Académie, wrote indifferent plays, rather better verse—*Divertissements* (1631–3), *Banquet des poètes* (1646), *Épigrammes* (1653)—and left in manuscript *Vies des poètes français*, a work often used by Sainte-Beuve (it was lost in a fire in 1871, but much of it had previously been published or copied out); (2) his son FRANÇOIS (1628–*c.* 1680), a mediocre poet.

Collier, L'Affaire du, the plot (1783–4) by which Jeanne de Valois, comtesse de La Motte (1756–91), a clever adventuress, contrived to steal a diamond necklace from a jeweller, on the pretence that Marie-Antoinette had agreed to buy it. The comtesse, knowing that Cardinal de Rohan, her dupe, was anxious to be restored to favour at court, first convinced him that she was close to the queen (even contriving an interview between him and a woman impersonating the queen), and then led him to believe that the queen wished him to act as her intermediary in the purchase of the necklace. By this means, and with a forged document signifying the queen's acceptance of the terms of purchase, she acquired the necklace, which was broken up and sold. Both parties were arrested: the cardinal was acquitted; the comtesse branded and imprisoned. She escaped to England and wrote her memoirs. The queen's innocence is now established, but much suspicion and discredit attached to her at the time. The episode is the theme of *Dumas *père*'s *Le Collier de la Reine*.

Collin d'Harleville, JEAN-FRANÇOIS (1755–1806), wrote successful verse comedies, notably *Le Vieux Célibataire* (1792; a rich old bachelor is being inveigled into marriage by his housekeeper, but a nephew and his wife turn up in disguise, outwit her, and win the old man's favour), also *L'Inconstant* (1786), *L'Optimiste* (1788), *Les Châteaux en Espagne* (1789), *Malice pour malice* (1803). M. de Crac in his one-act farce *M. de Crac dans son petit castel* (1791) has remained the type of the boastful country gentleman—from Gascony—hero of countless imaginary adventures. His *Théâtre et poésies fugitives* were first collected and published (1805) by his friend Andrieux.

Colline inspirée, La (1913), a novel by Barrès; possibly his best work. It has some factual basis.

Vaudémont and Sion, two ruined pilgrim sites in Lorraine, were pervaded, like many such ancient places, by a mysterious religious emotion that seemed to derive from pagan rites. In the 19th c. the priest Léopold Baillard restored them to their former glory and affluence, but later fell into heresy, became a disciple of *Vintras, and allowed the shrines, and the convent which had been established, to be profaned by sacrilegious orgies. Then persecution followed, and the wrath of the Church, and a return to desolation.

Collot d'Herbois, JEAN-MARIE (*c.* 1750–96), an actor and theatre manager who became a leading Revolutionary (a *Jacobin and a member of the *Comité de salut public) and was president of the *Convention on the day of Robespierre's fall (*v.* Revolutions, I, 1794). He was deported to Cayenne (1795), and died there. His *Almanach du père Gérard* (1791)

was a fine piece of Revolutionary propaganda.

Colomba (1840, in the *Revue des Deux Mondes*; 1841), a long short story by Mérimée; possibly his best work.

Orso returns to Corsica completely Europeanized by years of army service. During his absence his father has been murdered in a vendetta. His sister Colomba, a remarkable girl of great beauty and innocent savagery, expects him to avenge the family honour. At first he refuses, but gradually his native instincts return. He is on his way to meet his English fiancée and her father when the sons of his father's assassin ambush him. He kills them, then takes to the *maquis*. Colonel Nevill and his daughter, who had heard the shooting, save him from being outlawed by testifying that he fired in self-defence.

Colombe, MICHEL (1430–1512), sculptor, a leading artist of the *Renaissance. Among the few surviving examples of his work is the tomb of François II of Brittany at Nantes.

Colombine (Columbine), a stock character of the *commedia dell'arte* (*v.* Italiens); originally a serving-maid and ward of Pantalon, later *Arlequin's ladylove.

Colon, JENNY, *v. Nerval*.

Colonel Chabert, Le (1832; later in *La *Comédie humaine, Scènes de la vie privée*), a novel by Balzac. Hyacinthe Chabert, a highly distinguished officer of the *Garde impériale*, supposed to have died gloriously at Eylau (1807), had in fact managed to escape after being buried alive on the battlefield. After years of terrible hardship he returns to Paris and confronts his 'widow', who has remarried and prospered (on his fortune). She plays on his feelings and tricks him so successfully that he sacrifices himself and disappears again. Years later he is still alive in a pauper institution, as No. 124, Ward 7, whose days are spent in senile preoccupation with tobacco and liquor.

Colonne (originally **Juda**), Jules-Édouard (1838–1910), musician, founded (1873) his own orchestra and the *Concerts Colonne*, Sunday concerts of classical music. *Cf. Lamoureux*; *Pasdeloup*.

Combat (1941–74), a left-wing daily newspaper, born of the *Resistance, which emerged from clandestinity to be sold openly on the streets of Paris while the city was in process of liberation. It was widely read by intellectuals in the post-war decade (esp. under the editorship of Camus, 1944–7) and carried articles by Sartre, Malraux, Aron, Mounier, Bernanos, etc. It was subsequently conducted by Henry Smadja and ceased publication after his death in 1974.

Combat avec l'ange, *v. Giraudoux*.

Combat des Trente, *v. Trente*.

Combourg, Château de, *v. Chateaubriand*.

Combray, in Proust's *A la recherche du temps perdu*, a country town where Marcel spent childhood holidays at his grandparents' home (*cf.* Proust's holidays at Illiers, near Chartres). His daily walks followed one of two directions—*le côté de chez Swann* or *le côté de Guermantes*. For him the first would always symbolize his own cultured, middle-class world; the second an aristocratic world, which scorned (but was finally engulfed by) the *bourgeoisie*.

Comédie-ballet, a dramatic form devised by *Molière, who introduced *ballet* between the acts of a comedy, giving it a satirical or farcical character connected with the theme of the comedy.

Comédie de la mort, La, *v. Gautier*.

Comédie-Française, La, the first State theatre, officially entitled *Le Théâtre-Français*, also known as *La Maison de Molière*; f. 1680, with a subvention from Louis XIV (for its origin and early history *v. Theatres and Theatre Companies*). Its

repertory has always been mainly classical. From 1689 till 1770 the company played in a theatre on the left bank of the Seine, in what is now the Rue de l'Ancienne Comédie, then in temporary quarters in the *Tuileries, and from 1782 in a new theatre built specially for them near the Palais du *Luxembourg, the *Théâtre du Luxembourg* (*v. Odéon*). During the Revolution the company split into Revolutionary and Royalist factions. The first group became the *Théâtre de la République*, but failed by 1799. The second was imprisoned (1793) and though released after the *Terror failed to re-establish itself on a permanent footing. In the end the government reconstituted the original company and installed it in its present home in the Rue de Richelieu, in the theatre known from 1799 as the *Théâtre-Français*. From 1945 till 1959 the company had a second home at the *Odéon*, its two theatres being officially entitled *Le Théâtre-Français, Salle Richelieu* and *Salle Luxembourg*.

When the company was re-formed after the Revolution its constitution (originally regulated by royal command) was redrafted by Napoleon himself, in minute detail and on a basis that has remained fundamentally the same. Its members are known as *pensionnaires* while still on probation, and thereafter as *sociétaires* (i.e. full members, entitled to a pension on retirement).

Comédie humaine, La (1842–8, 17 vols.), Balzac's collected edition of his own novels and tales. For its theme and characteristics *v. Balzac*.

Some grouping had already been achieved in earlier collections—*Scènes de la vie privée* (1830, 2 vols.; 1832, 4 vols.), *Études de mœurs au XIXe siècle* (1834–7, 12 vols.; inc. *Scènes de la vie de province* and *Scènes de la vie parisienne* as well as the *Scènes de la vie privée*), *Études philosophiques* (1835–40, 20 vols. in 4 ser.). These, with new tales inserted and the addition of the *Études analytiques*, formed the basis of the *Comédie humaine*. In 1845 Balzac drew up a catalogue for a second edition, allowing for some regrouping and further insertions; but he did not live to achieve it. This catalogue, as modified by him in later notes, forms the basis of modern editions and of the list given below. The dates are those of first publication, very often as *romans-feuilletons* and sometimes under a different title. † denotes works not included in the first (1842–8) edition.

ÉTUDES DE MŒURS

SCÈNES DE LA VIE PRIVÉE: *La Maison du chat qui pelote* (1830); *Le Bal de Sceaux* (1830); *Mémoires de deux jeunes mariées* (1841–2); *La Bourse* (1832); *Modeste Mignon* (1844); *Un Début dans la vie* (1842); *Albert Savarus* (1842); *La Vendetta* (1830); *Une Double Famille* (1830); *La Paix du ménage* (1830); *Madame Firmiani* (1832); *Étude de femme* (1830); *La Fausse Maîtresse* (1841); *Une Fille d'Eve* (1838–9); *Le Message* (1832); *La Grenadière* (1832); *La Femme abandonnée* (1832); *Honorine* (1843); *Béatrix* (1839); *Gobseck* (1830); *La Femme de trente ans* (1830–4); *Le *Père Goriot* (1834–5); *Le *Colonel Chabert* (1832); *La Messe de l'athée* (1836); *L'Interdiction* (1836); *Le Contrat de mariage* (1835); *Autre étude de femme* (1842).

SCÈNES DE LA VIE DE PROVINCE: *Ursule Mirouët* (1841); *Eugénie Grandet* (1833); *Les Célibataires*—(i) *Pierrette*, (ii) *Le *Curé de Tours*, (iii) *La *Rabouilleuse* (1840, 1832, 1841–2); *Les Parisiens en province*—(i) *L'*Illustre Gaudissart*, (ii) *La Muse du département* (1833, 1843); *Les Rivalités*—(i) *La Vieille Fille*, (ii) *Le Cabinet des antiques* (1836, 1836–8); *Illusions perdues*—(i) *Les Deux Poètes*, (ii) *Un Grand Homme de province à Paris*, (iii) *Les Souffrances de l'inventeur* (1837, 1839, 1843).

SCÈNES DE LA VIE PARISIENNE: *Histoire des Treize*—(i) *Ferragus*, (ii) *La *Duchesse de Langeais*, (iii) *La Fille aux yeux d'or* (1833, 1833–4, 1834–5); *Histoire de la grandeur et de la décadence de César Birotteau* (1837); *La Maison *Nucingen* (1838); *Splendeurs et misères des courtisanes*—(i) *Comment aiment les filles*, (ii) *A combien l'amour revient aux vieillards*, (iii) *Où mènent les mauvais chemins*, (iv) *La Dernière Incarnation de *Vautrin†* (1838–

47); *Les Secrets de la princesse de Cadignan* (1839); *Facino Cane* (1836); *Sarrasine* (1830); *Pierre Grassou* (1840); *Les Parents pauvres*—(i) *La *Cousine Bette*, (ii) *Le *Cousin Pons* (1846, 1847); *Un Homme d'affaires* (1845); *Un Prince de la Bohème* (1840); *Gaudissart II* (1844); *Les Employés* (1837); *Les Comédiens sans le savoir* (1846); *Les Petits Bourgeois†* (1854); *L'Envers de l'histoire contemporaine*—(i) *Madame de la Chanterie*, (ii) *L'Initié†* (1842–4, 1848).

SCÈNES DE LA VIE POLITIQUE: *Un Épisode sous la Terreur* (1830); *Une Ténébreuse Affaire* (1841); *Le Député d'Arcis* (1847; completed 1853 by Charles Rabou (1803–71)); *Z. Marcas* (1840).

SCÈNES DE LA VIE MILITAIRE: *Les *Chouans* (1829); *Une Passion dans le désert* (1830).

SCÈNES DE LA VIE DE CAMPAGNE: *Les Paysans†* (1844–55); *Le *Médecin de campagne* (1833); *Le *Curé de village* (1839); *Le *Lys dans la vallée* (1835).

ÉTUDES PHILOSOPHIQUES

*La *Peau de chagrin* (1830–1); *Jésus-Christ en Flandre* (1831); *Melmoth réconcilié* (1835); *Massimilla Doni* (1839); *Le Chef-d'œuvre inconnu* (1831); *Gambara* (1837); *La *Recherche de l'absolu* (1834); *L'Enfant maudit* (1831–6); *Adieu* (1830); *Les Marana* (1832–3); *Le Réquisitionnaire* (1831); *El Verdugo* (1830); *Un Drame au bord de la mer* (1835); *Maître Cornélius* (1831); *L'Auberge rouge* (1831); *Sur Catherine de Médicis* (1830–46); *L'Élixir de longue vie* (1830); *Les Proscrits* (1831); *Louis Lambert* (1832); *Séraphita* (1834–5).

ÉTUDES ANALYTIQUES

Physiologie du mariage (1829); *Petites Misères de la vie conjugale†* (39 sketches, 1830–45/6).

Comédie larmoyante, *v.* La Chaussée; Drame.

Comédiens sans le savoir, Les, *v.* Comédie humaine, La (Scènes de la vie parisienne).

Comédies et Proverbes (1840; new rev.

ed. 1853), by Musset. The 1840 edition contained the works already published in *Un Spectacle dans un fauteuil* (2nd ser., 1834) plus *La Quenouille de Barberine* (v. *Barberine*), *Le *Chandelier*, *Il ne faut jurer de rien*, *Un Caprice*. The 1853 edition contained five further works: *Il faut qu'une porte soit ouverte ou fermée*, *Louison*, *On ne saurait penser à tout*, *Carmosine*, *Bettine*.

Comedy. Though the origins of French comedy remain to some extent obscure, it appears to derive, at least in part, from the comic element introduced at an early date in the liturgical drama (v. *Fête des Fous*), especially in the explanatory passages in the vernacular with which the Latin text was 'farci' for the benefit of an ignorant audience. There may also have been a connection between the medieval *jongleurs* and the *joculatores*, *mimi*, and *histriones* of the late Roman period. The comic element passed from the liturgical into the vernacular drama, religious or profane—monologues and dialogues, *mystères* and *miracles*. Examples of this are *Bodel's *Jeu de Saint Nicolas*; *Courtois d'Arras*, a 13th-c. adaptation of the story of the Prodigal Son; *Le Garçon et l' Aveugle* (c. 1270), a short dialogue in which a lad tricks and robs a blind man whom he leads about. Early types of a more developed comic drama are Adam de la Halle's remarkable *Jeu de la Feuillée* and *Jeu de Robin et Marion*.

The evolution of comic drama in the 14th and 15th cs. is somewhat obscure, for surviving texts are rare, and comic performances—*moralités*, *soties*, and *farces*, acted by fraternities (e.g. the *Basochiens*, the *Enfants sans souci*), professional actors, or students—though doubtless numerous, were not deemed sufficiently important to be recorded. *Pathelin* and Le *Franc-Archer de Bagnolet* are masterpieces of 15th-c. farce and farcical monologue respectively.

The literary *Renaissance of the 16th c. brought with it true comedy, at first seeking models in classical drama or Italian adaptations thereof. Meschinot, O. de Saint-Gelais, J.-A. de Baïf, C. Estienne,

and others translated or adapted comedies of Plautus and Terence, and Ronsard translated Aristophanes' *Plutus*. The earliest original comedy is Jodelle's *Eugène* (1552/3), soon followed by Grévin's Les *Ébahis* (1561). In all these the pseudo-classical element is artificial and foreign; such life as they have derives from an element of native farce with its realism and *esprit gaulois*. Then come Larivey's comedies from the Italian (1579, the beginning of a phase of Italian influence) and O. de *Turnèbe's fine comedy *Les Contents*. Before Molière's day comedies were usually in verse (octo-syllables), though La Taille, Larivey, and Turnèbe wrote prose comedies.

In the early 17th c. comedy is rare (owing to the vogue of *pastoral drama), but in 1629 we have Corneille's *Mélite* (followed by his other plays of love intrigue) and c. 1630 the beginning of the comedy of manners, e.g. *Claveret's *L'Esprit fort*, Du Ryer's Les *Vendanges de Suresnes*, *Desmarets de Saint-Sorlin's *Les Visionnaires*. Authors now began to use Spanish models (e.g. Corneille's Le *Menteur*—also a fine example of the comedy of character), and soon Scarron introduced the element of burlesque (v. *Jodelet*; *Don Japhet*). Then came Molière, whose best work, broadening the whole domain of comedy, spanned the years 1659-73. Authors of comedies contemporary with him included Cyrano de Bergerac, Racine (Les *Plaideurs*), Quinault (La *Mère coquette*), and Montfleury (L'*École des jaloux*).

Various successors revived certain aspects of Molière's genius, notably Dancourt and Lesage (his realism), and Regnard (his farcical fancy). Lesser authors—such as Dufresny, d'Allainval, and Poinsinet—also wrote comedies of manners and character. But as the 18th c. advanced this comic vein showed signs of exhaustion. Marivaux, a disciple of Racine rather than of Molière, made love the essential, instead of an episodic, element in his plays. Destouches was the first of a group of authors who show a tendency to moralize, e.g. his Le *Glorieux*, Piron's *La *Métromanie*, Gresset's Le *Méchant*.

Then came the sentimental comedy (*comédie larmoyante*) of La Chaussée, a form exemplified in Voltaire's *L'*Enfant prodigue* and *Nanine*, and later developed by *Diderot in his *drame*, by Sedaine (*Le *Philosophe sans le savoir*), and by L.-S. Mercier. Meanwhile, at the *Théâtre de la Foire*, Lesage and his successors had moved in the direction of *opéra-comique*, e.g. *Favart's *Les Trois Sultanes*. Other forms of 18th-c. comedy are the satirical (Voltaire's *L'*Écossaise*; *Palissot's *Les Philosophes*), the historical (Collé's *La *Partie de chasse de Henri IV*), and finally the brilliant plays of Beaumarchais, which envelop bold social and political satire in gaiety and wit.

Comedy did not thrive on a Revolutionary stage invaded by political propaganda, but revived again under the *Directoire*. The leading authors—*Fabre d'Églantine (*Le Philinte de Molière*), *Collin d'Harleville (*Le Vieux Célibataire*), and *Andrieux (*Le Vieux Fat*)—still copied Molière. During the Empire and Restoration, when dramatic *censorship tended to afflict comedy less than tragedy, *Étienne (*Les Deux Gendres*), *Picard (*Les Marionnettes*), and A. Duval (*Le Tyran domestique*) developed the comedy of manners, with lively, often satirical, sketches of daily and provincial life; and *Delavigne wrote the highly successful *L'École des vieillards* (1823). *Lemercier's *Pinto* (1800) introduced a *genre* of historical comedy, or drama, in which historical events were shown arising from petty causes. This was imitated at intervals throughout the 19th c., e.g. by Scribe, Dumas *père*, Ponsard, Sardou. The outstanding innovator of the first half of the century was Scribe, in whose comedies and *vaudevilles* character was rigorously subordinated to plot. His fame was short-lived, but his technique proved highly influential. For the later 19th and 20th cs. *v. Theatre of the 19th and 20th cs.*

Comité de salut public, an emergency body set up in April 1793 by the *Convention* to frame and administer internal and external political and defence measures. Members (originally 9, later 12)

included Danton (briefly), Robespierre, Saint-Just, Collot d'Herbois, Couthon. It was largely responsible for the *Terror, but also for organizing the Revolutionary armies. It was suppressed in 1795.

Comité de sûreté générale, a body set up in October 1792 by the *Convention*. It controlled the police and the prisons and was responsible for arrests.

Commedia dell'arte, *v. Italiens.*

Commines or Commynes, PHILIPPE DE (*c.* 1446–*c.* 1511), b. in Flanders, served Charles the Bold (as squire, then councillor and chamberlain) 1464–72, then entered the service of Louis XI, becoming one of his most influential advisers, and also, thanks to royal favours (and his own initiative), a very rich man. By his marriage he acquired the domain of Argenton in Poitou, and is often referred to in contemporary documents as 'M. d'Argenton'. In the troubles that followed Charles VIII's accession (1483) he was imprisoned at Loches (in an iron cage) and in Paris, then sent into retirement and relieved of much of his wealth. He was restored to favour *c.* 1491 and accompanied Charles VIII on his Italian expedition (1494–5). After the king's death he left the court, but returned in 1505 and took part in the Genoa campaign of 1507.

His *Mémoires*, written for the instruction of princes and statesmen, are marked by a vigorous intelligence rarely equalled in medieval literature. Bks. I–VI (the division into 8 books is by his editors), probably written 1489–90, deal with the political, diplomatic, and military transactions of Louis XI's reign, tracing events to their causes, estimating characters, etc.; bks. VII and VIII, written 1497–8, deal with Charles VIII's Italian expedition, and contain a vivid account of the battle of Fornovo (1495). Commines emerges as a statesman of almost modern quality. He has little use for feudal chivalry, and regards war as a great evil (he deplored the Italian campaign). He wants just and orderly government, no taxation without the consent of the taxpayers, and a king whose power derives from the affection of his subjects (England is the best-administered state, because violence is not done to the people). He judges princes of the day, including Louis XI and Charles the Bold, with impartiality and penetration. But much as he admires foresight and sagacity in the conduct of affairs, he is a religious man of grave and rather melancholy outlook: he frequently refers to divine intervention in the course of events, attributes war and other political evils to the decline of religion (bk. V, chs. 18–20), and discourses on the miserable life of men in general and the great in particular (bk. VI, ch. 12). This serious tone and a total lack of picturesque quality make his memoirs very different from those of Joinville and Froissart; he is closer to Villehardouin. His style—rather flat, with long, involved sentences—is hardly equal to his theme. The work was translated into many languages (Eng., 1596, by T. Danett), and inspired Scott's *Quentin Durward*, in which Commines himself figures.

Committed Writing, *v. Littérature engagée.*

Commune, (1) the *Commune de Paris* and *Commune insurrectionnelle* (1789–94); (2) the *Commune* of 1871; (3) *v. Département.*

1. An improvised assembly which assumed responsibility for the government of Paris (July 1789; *v. Revolutions*, 1). It promptly appointed a mayor (Bailly) and created the **Garde nationale*. It worked at first through a permanent committee, but was more than once reorganized in a vain bid to combat the extremists in its ranks. On 10 August 1792 the extremists formed a *Commune insurrectionnelle*, which expelled the earlier body and forced the **Assemblée législative* to deprive the king of his powers. Thereafter it exerted pressure on the **Convention* and was behind the worst excesses of the **Terror*. It collapsed when Robespierre fell. *v. Maire de Paris.*

2. On 18 March 1871, when German troops were about to enter Paris (starved

into surrender in Jan. 1871; *v. Franco-Prussian War*), Republican insurgents, bitterly resentful of a peace which permitted the German occupation (also of the new monarchist **Assemblée nationale* sitting at Versailles) and still armed from having served in the **Garde nationale*, removed the cannon from the **Champs-Élysées* (destined as German quarters) to the poorer districts, won popular support, and were soon in control of the city. They set up a *Conseil communal* or *Commune* (26 March), intended to govern the whole country. But France did not follow their lead, and the government formed an army of regulars under MacMahon to combat the army of *communards*. The ensuing civil war amounted to a second siege of Paris. The worst period, *la semaine sanglante* (21–8 May, after government forces entered the city), was marked by violent street fighting and massacres. The *Commune* was suppressed by the end of May. The consequent reprisals and punitive measures went on until 1875.

Communistes, Les, *v. Aragon.*

Compagnie de Jésus, *v. Jesuits.*

Compagnie des Quinze, an experimental theatre company (1930–6), largely recruited from Copeau's theatre school in Burgundy, and founded and directed by his nephew and pupil M. Saint-Denis. *v. Obey.*

Compagnie du Saint-Sacrement (or **du Très-Saint-Sacrement de l'Autel), La,** a powerful secret society or **congrégation* for faith and good works which existed from 1627 to *c.* 1665 and whose members included important Counter-Reformationary figures. It had headquarters in Paris, branches all over the country, and a network of agents and informers planted in all walks of life. It never acted as a body, but always through members as individuals, and these religious enthusiasts—or busybodies—shrank from no means, however dubious, that might further their ends. These included laudable good works, but also the hounding of *Huguenots, blasphemers, prostitutes, adulterers, etc., and attempts to suppress plays deemed unsuitable. It was the influence at court of this 'cabale des dévots' that led the king to prohibit (1664) the performance of Molière's *Tartuffe*, which contained veiled attacks on them. But by this time the *Compagnie*'s existence had become known, Mazarin had opposed it, and it was soon to disperse.

Compagnon du Tour de France, Le (1840), by G. Sand, a novel set in a village some years after the Restoration (1815), when liberalism and discontent with the monarchy were rife and secret societies (*cf. Carbonari*) flourished. Two young carpenters fall in love with the grand-daughter and niece respectively of the comte de Villepreux, who has engaged them to restore carvings, and who pays lip-service to social equality until it affects him personally. The young men, who take their ideals more seriously, have been *compagnons du Tour de France*, i.e., having served their apprenticeship, they have travelled France, perfecting their craft and becoming affiliated to one of the trade guilds then still in existence. The slender plot is filled out with information about these *compagnonnages*.

Complaintes, Les, v. Laforgue.

Comput, in medieval literature, a chronological treatise or ecclesiastical calendar, giving scope for moralization. Such didactic works were popular in the 12th and 13th cs. *v. Philippe de Thaon.*

Comte, *v. Duc, comte, marquis.*

Comte, AUGUSTE (1798–1857), one of the great influences on 19th-c. philosophy; the founder of Positivism, a system which recognizes only positive facts and observable phenomena. After passing out of the *École polytechnique*, he taught mathematics, and was briefly attracted to *Saint-Simonisme*. He first outlined his philosophy in lectures delivered in his own rooms and attended by many eminent contemporaries, and also in the journal *Le Producteur* (1825–6). After suffering a mental breakdown, he resumed lecturing in 1828, was appointed external entrance examiner for the *École polytechnique*, and began to publish his *Cours de philosophie positive* (1830–42). In 1842, which marked the end of his most brilliant period, he lost his post as examiner—largely because of his arrogant behaviour. English admirers, headed by J. S. Mill, helped him financially, but their generosity was damped by his assumption that this was no more than their duty. Then Littré raised a fund that enabled him to continue writing and lecturing till his death.

His *Cours de philosophie positive* applied to society the laws, based on observation and deduction, used in what he classified as the six abstract sciences—mathematics, astronomy, physics, chemistry, biology, and sociology itself (a science of which he was, in effect, the founder). He confined himself to the recognition of facts and their objective relations, waiving any attempt to explain ultimate causes because, he contended, such questions belonged to earlier, theological or metaphysical, stages in the history of thought. The two most brilliant sections of the work are his classification of the sciences and his history of social evolution. After 1842 he attempted to transform his philosophy into a religion, in which worship of Humanity replaced that of a deity. This religion (described by T. H. Huxley as 'Catholicism without God') was soon complicated by the introduction of a mystical element, a result of his romantic passion for Mme Clotilde de Vaux (1815–46), daughter of an army officer and the victim of an unfortunate marriage from which the law then afforded no escape (she wrote novels reflecting her dilemma). She contrived to sublimate Comte's love into an idealistic friendship, and he made her the patron saint of Humanity. His other works include the *Catéchisme positiviste* (1852), where, as 'Grand-Prêtre de l'Humanité', he defines the tenets of his religion; his *Système de politique positive* (1851–4, 4 vols.); and a *Calendrier positiviste* (1849) in which great men replace saints.

Comte de Comminges, Le, v. *Arnaud, Baculard d'*; cf. *Tencin*.

Comte de Monte-Cristo, Le (1844–5), by Dumas *père*, one of the best thrillers ever written.

At the time of Napoleon's exile on Elba, Edmond Dantès, a young sea-captain and an alleged Bonapartist conspirator, is imprisoned in the Château d'If, near Marseilles. He is the innocent victim of Villefort, a magistrate, Fernand, a fisherman, and Danglars, a shipbroker's agent—three villains who would profit by his removal. The abbé Faria, a fellow-prisoner from whose vast learning he benefits, tells him of a fabulous treasure hidden on the Island of Monte-Cristo. When the abbé dies, he substitutes himself for the corpse, is flung into the sea from the prison battlements, and miraculously escapes. He finds the island and the treasure and, as the comte de Monte-Cristo, comes to Paris, where his riches give him entry into the highest circles. Then, without disclosing his identity, he proceeds to take his revenge on his three enemies, all now wealthy, titled, and influential. He adopts many personalities, rakes up lurid pasts, and by deploying his millions contrives assassination, poisoning, and suicide. His wrongs finally avenged, he revisits the Château d'If and then, with his beautiful Greek slave Haydée, sets sail for unknown waters.

Comte de Paris, v. *Henri, comte de Paris*.

Comtesse de Charny, La, v. *Dumas père*.

Comtesse de Rudolstadt, La, v. *Sand*.

Comtesse d'Escarbagnas, La, a one-act prose comedy by Molière, ridiculing the affectations of provincial society; produced 1671.

The scene is Angoulême. The comtesse, an old coquette, apes the elegances of Paris (where she has spent two months) and lords it over her admirers, local bigwigs. A country gentleman, while pretending to court her, uses her house to meet his lady-love.

Conciergerie, La, a famous Paris prison, said to be the oldest in Europe, forms part of the *Palais de Justice*; so called because it was originally occupied by the *concierge* (later the *bailli*) *du palais*. Famous inmates have included Ravaillac, the marquise de Brinvilliers, Damiens, Marie-Antoinette (after Louis XVI's execution), C. Corday, Danton, Robespierre. It is memorably described in Balzac's *Splendeurs et misères des courtisanes*.

Concile féerique, Le, v. *Laforgue*.

Concini or **Concino**, an Italian adventurer brought to France by Marie de Médicis, who was dominated by him and his wife Leonora. He was a minister under Louis XIII, being known as the maréchal d'Ancre. His greed and insolence led the king to order his assassination (1617).

Concordat, an agreement between the Roman See and a secular government on matters that concern both. Famous *concordats* were those of (1) 1516, between Leo X and François Ier, which empowered the king to appoint bishops and abbots, and restored to Rome annates it had lost by a pragmatic sanction of Charles VII; (2) 1801, between Pius VII and Bonaparte, which re-established Catholicism and its free practice as the religion of the majority of Frenchmen, defined relations between France and the Holy See, and demarcated the Church's temporal and spiritual powers (e.g. as regards the nomination, institution, and payment of clergy, and claims to Church property)—a settlement which lasted till the Church was disestablished (1905; v. *Republics*, 3).

Concorde, v. *Place de la Concorde*.

Condamnation de Banquet, La, v. *Moralité*.

Condé, L'Armée de, v. *Armée des émigrés*.

Condé, Le Grand, i.e. Louis II, prince de Condé (1621–86), a member of a branch of the *Bourbon family, a great captain in the wars of Louis XIV, the youthful victor of *Rocroi, Nordlingen, and Lens. During the *Fronde he joined the rebels, even allying himself with Spain against Mazarin and the court, but was later pardoned (1659, after the Treaty of the *Pyrenees) and restored to high command. In 1674 he fought the Prince of Orange at Seneffe. He became a patron of literature, and his letters are the work of a skilled writer. Bossuet delivered his funeral oration.

Condillac, ÉTIENNE DE (1715–80), brother of Mably; philosopher, a close friend of leading *philosophes, e.g. Diderot and Helvétius, though he took little part in their controversies. He went beyond his master Locke in tracing the development of the human faculties to their origin in sensations, and held that it was possible to apply logical reasoning in metaphysics and morals as precisely as in geometry, and to proceed by this method from accurate ideas of the external world to social and political science, and even to theology. His works include an *Essai sur l'origine des connaissances humaines* (1746), *Traité des systèmes* (1749), *Traité des sensations* (1754), *Traité des animaux* (1754; mainly polemical, directed against Buffon), *Cours d'études du prince de Parme* (1769–73), a French grammar (1775; on language as the instrument of reasoning), and articles in the *Encyclopédie. v. Idéologues.*

Condition humaine, La (1933), a novel by Malraux, awarded the *Prix Goncourt.* On one level, it is a powerful novel of action about Communist revolutionaries in Shanghai in 1927 and their brutal suppression by Chiang Kai Shek. On a deeper level, through the conversations of the characters, it is a study of the psychology of the revolutionaries, their motives and ideals (or lack of them), their fundamental loneliness as individuals, yet their recognition of a fraternity that unites men in the face of betrayal and failure— as when the Russian Katow, condemned to be burnt alive, gives the cyanide pills he always carries to two young comrades, similarly condemned and in great fear, and goes to his death feeling that this was the great act of his life.

Condom, L'Évêque de, *v. Bossuet.*

Condorcet, ANTOINE-NICOLAS DE (1743–94), mathematician and *philosophe (and v. Idéologues)* of noble birth, later a Revolutionary politician (a member of the *Assemblée législative* and the *Convention).* He was perpetual secretary of the *Académie des Sciences,* a member of the *Académie française,* and a friend of d'Alembert, Turgot, and Voltaire (sharing Turgot's urge to improve the human lot and Voltaire's antipathy to the Church). His fame rests on his *Tableau historique des progrès de l'esprit humain* (1795). He also edited *Pascal's *Pensées* (1776), with notes dissenting from Pascal's estimate of man's vileness, and wrote lives of Turgot and Voltaire (1786 and 1787) and various political dissertations. He was proscribed as a *Girondin, and is said to have been denounced to the authorities by the wife of an innkeeper because he ordered an omelet with a dozen eggs in it—betraying an aristocratic ignorance. He took poison to avoid the guillotine.

Confession de Claude, La, v. Zola.

Confession de minuit, v. Salavin.

Confession d'un enfant du siècle, La (1836), a remarkable early novel of psychological analysis by Musset; partly autobiographical, in that it was inspired by his unhappy liaison with G. Sand and also contains his (frequently quoted) testimony to the disillusionment of the young in the early 19th c. The hero, deceived by a mistress, takes to debauchery, then falls in love with an honest woman, a widow. He is jealous, even of her past, and there are quarrels and reconciliations. His love is killed by possession and revivified by jealousy. He watches her asleep, and soliloquizes. Finally, he effaces himself so that she can be happy with the man she really loves.

Confessions, Les (1781, bks. I–VI; 1788, bks. VII–XII), by J.-J. Rousseau, an autobiography (written 1764–70) covering his life down to 1766. Claiming to present a man 'in all the truth of nature', he describes in vivid and minute detail, and with complete candour (disclosing even his meanest actions and his sexual abnormalities), the incidents of an agitated life, his reactions to them, and his spiritual development. Though written under the influence of persecutions, both real and imaginary, and so to some extent an apologia with some distortions of fact (v. also *Warens*), this seems to be in general a work of sincere self-revelation. Rousseau emerges as the victim not so much of the hostility of his enemies as of his own revolt against current moral and social conventions and his own morbid sensibility. There are exquisite descriptions of scenery and homely life.

Confidences, Les (1849) and **Nouvelles Confidences** (1851), Lamartine's nostalgic and poetical reminiscences of his early years at Milly and Mâcon, of first travel and first love. His *Graziella* and *Raphaël* are largely drawn from the 1849 volume.

Confrérie de la Passion, La, the most famous of the *confréries sérieuses*, societies of players formed by the tradesmen and other citizens of Paris and some provincial towns (the earliest known is that of Nantes, 1371) to perform the *mystères* when the representation of these passed from clerics to laymen. It was licensed at Paris in 1402, and acted *mystères*, especially the *Mystère de la Passion*, at its headquarters in the hospital adjacent to the Église de la Trinité (outside the Porte Saint-Denis), on the church steps, and—on the occasion of royal entries, etc.—in processions through the city. Sometimes it joined forces with the *Enfants sans souci* or the *Basochiens* for performances consisting of a *mystère* followed by a *farce* or a *sotie* (known from the 16th c. as *pois pilés*, i.e. a *purée* or mixture). In 1539 it moved to the Hôtel de Flandre, but its prestige soon began to decline: the authorities alleged that its processions caused public disorder; also the *mystères* were falling into disfavour with all but the illiterate. Forced to leave the Hôtel de Flandre, it built a new theatre on the site of the former *Hôtel de

Bourgogne, but was forbidden (1548) to perform sacred dramas there—though it retained its monopoly (granted 1518) of theatrical performances in Paris. For over a century it struggled to retain its rights. From 1578 it sometimes let its theatre to professional companies, and its own performances there appear to have ceased in 1588. It was dissolved by an edict of 1676.

Congé, a form of medieval lyric of which Bodel provides the first known example. When obliged to retire to a lazar-house *c.* 1202 he took leave of his friends in a poem of 42 stanzas, addressing a stanza to each. This was imitated first by Baude Fastoul, another poet who became a leper, then by Adam de la Halle, in a poem which amounted to a satire on his fellow-citizens, when he left *Arras c.* 1269 following political troubles.

Congrégation, (1), in the Roman Catholic Church, an Order or community such as the *Congrégation de l'*Oratoire*, the *Congrégation de Saint-Maur* (*v. Maurists*), the *Congrégation de la Mission* (*v. Vincent de Paul*). The term was also applied to the lay, or lay and clerical, associations for faith and good works which arose in the 16th c. among pupils of *Jesuit colleges; *v. Compagnie du Saint-Sacrement*. The latter were suppressed during the Revolution, but revived more or less clandestinely under the Empire, and more openly after the Restoration, with a lay and clerical membership drawn from the upper classes; (2) *La Congrégation* (f. 1801 as a Congregation of the Virgin), an influential secret body led for a time by the comte d'Artois (later Charles X) and suspected of involvement in plots to restore religious and monarchical ascendancy. Various partly literary, partly charitable societies f. after 1815 by young men of Catholic and Royalist sympathies (the *Société des bonnes lettres, Société des bonnes œuvres, Société des bonnes études*) maintained contact with *La Congrégation* and shared its unpopularity in some quarters.

Congrégation de Saint-Maur, *v. Maurists.*

Connaissance de l'Est, *v. Claudel.*

Connards, *v. Sociétés joyeuses.*

Connétable, the Constable of France. In 1191, when the office of *grand sénéchal* was suppressed, the *connétable* (originally superintendent of the royal stables) became the chief dignitary of the kingdom and commander-in-chief of the army. Famous *connétables* included Du Guesclin and several members of the de Montmorency family, notably Anne Ier (1493–1567), who fought at *Marignan, defended Provence against Charles V, allied himself with the *Ligue*, and died fighting the *Huguenots. The office was suppressed in 1627. In 1804, Napoleon created his brother Louis *grand connétable* and Berthier *vice-connétable* (*v. Maréchal*). *v. Barbey d'Aurevilly.*

Conon (or Quesnes) de Béthune (d. 1224), poet of Picardy, an imitator of the *troubadours (and *v. Lyric Poetry*, 1), took part in the Crusades (he is commended by Villehardouin), and was regent of the Empire (1219). When mocked at for his provincialisms (*v. French Language*), he retorted:

Encor ne soit ma parole françoise,
Si la puet on bien entendre en françois;
Ne cil ne sont bien apris ne cortois
S'il m'ont repris, se j'ai dit mos d'Artois,
Car je ne fui pas norris a Pontoise [in the *Ile-de-France].

Conque, La (1891, 11 nos.), an exclusive literary review, f. by Louÿs, published work by young poets, e.g. Valéry (most of his early poems), Gide, H. de Régnier. The frontispiece was always a work by an established poet, e.g. Leconte de Lisle, Mallarmé, Swinburne.

Conquérants, Les, *v. Malraux.*

Conquête de Jérusalem, La, *v. Antioche.*

Conquête de Plassans, La (1874), one of Zola's *Rougon-Macquart novels. The ambitious, domineering abbé Faujas arrives in Plassans and, despite his uncouth exterior and dubious past, manœuvres himself by ecclesiastical and political intrigues into a position of supreme importance. He lodges, and spreads himself, with various objectionable relations, in the home of M. and Mme Mouret (a Macquart and a Rougon), and so disrupts their tranquil household that their latent mental instability comes to the surface. The simple, home-loving Marthe develops religious mania; her husband becomes a homicidal maniac, and sets his house, with its undesirable occupants, on fire. There are excellent descriptions of the abbé's intrigues, and also of provincial society— as when the local worthies settle in armchairs, at a safe distance, to gossip and watch the blaze, at once horrified at the manner of his death and glad to be rid of him.

Conrart, VALENTIN (1603–75), man of letters, a *Huguenot, an authority on grammar and style (a close friend of Guez de Balzac), a founder-member and perpetual secretary of the *Académie. He wrote little, and Boileau ridiculed him in the line 'J'imite de Conrart le silence prudent'. His fragmentary *Mémoires* (1824) contain a good account of the *Fronde* (1652).

Conseil de la République, under the Fourth *Republic, replaced the *Sénat as the upper house of the legislature. Its members, still known as *sénateurs*, were indirectly elected.

Conseil des Anciens and **Conseil des Cinq-Cents,** *v. Directoire.*

Conseil d'état.

1. UNDER THE ANCIEN RÉGIME the royal council took definite shape in the reign of Louis XIV, when the term covered four councils, each presided over by the king: (a) the *Conseil d'état* proper (or the *Conseil d'en haut*), which dealt with high matters

of State (foreign affairs; important litigious questions), and was composed of the chancellor and a few selected ministers, e.g. Louvois, Colbert; (b) the *Conseil privé* (or *des parties*), the supreme judicial body, composed of the chancellor (who, in practice, presided), *ex-officio* members (the ministers and secretaries of State; certain financial officials; the *ducs et* *pairs*, who rarely attended), and a number (limited to 30 after 1673) of specially appointed members, mostly lawyers; (c) the *Conseil des dépêches*, which dealt with internal administration, and was composed of the chancellor, the members of (a), and such secretaries of State as were not members of (a). The royal family attended its meetings; (d) the *Conseil des finances*, which—following its reorganization by Colbert (1661)—dealt with taxes (*v. Fiscal System*), the royal domains, the currency, the State accounts, and litigious financial questions. It consisted of the chancellor, a *chef du conseil*, and three *conseillers* (inc. Colbert). It survived in much the same form until the Revolution.

2. THE MODERN CONSEIL D'ÉTAT, which has its origin in the *Conseil d'état* set up under the *Consulat*, is a supreme judicial body, both an advisory council and a tribunal. It deals with the interpretation and execution of laws and decrees, or cases arising out of them, in so far as they affect government departments, or private citizens in their dealings with departments.

Conservateur, Le (1818–20), an ultra-Royalist journal or miscellany (*v. Press*, 5), f. in opposition to *La *Minerve française*. Contributors included Chateaubriand and Lamennais.

Conservateur littéraire, Le (1819-21), a literary review f. by Hugo (aged 17) and his brother Abel (aged 21). At first orthodox and unprogressive, it became a leading *Romantic organ.

Considérant, VICTOR, *v. Fouriérisme.*

Considérations sur les causes de la *grandeur des Romains et de leur décadence* (1734; rev. and augm. 1748), by Montesquieu, a work of history and political philosophy. Denying that chance dominates the destiny of nations, he deduces from a summary history of Rome the causes of its rise and decline. He ignores economic factors and Roman religion, and is quite uncritical with regard to his sources and inclined to hasty generalizations. But the work is interesting for its studies of the Roman spirit and the Republican Senate, and also as an early example of scientific history, in which events are traced to their natural causes, without reference to a guiding Providence.

Consolation de Philosophie, La, the influential *De consolatione philosophiae* of the Roman philosopher Boethius (*c.* 480–524), a work widely translated and commented in the Middle Ages, e.g. by Jean de Meung (*c.* 1285, for Philippe IV).

Consolations, Les, *v. Sainte-Beuve.*

Consonance, agreement in the terminal sounds of two or more metrical lines, such that the last stressed vowel and any sounds following it are the same. This is modern rhyme, as distinct from *assonance.

Consonne d'appui, *v. Rimes riches.*

Constant, *v. Wairy.*

Constant, ALPHONSE-LOUIS, ABBÉ (1810–75), a friend of Esquiros, author of works reflecting his interest in *Fouriérisme and other, more fantastic, forms of semi-mystical socialism, e.g. *La Bible de la liberté* (1840), *Doctrines religieuses et sociales* (1841), *La Mère de Dieu* (1844). Later he took up occultism, and his *Histoire de la magie* (1860; under the pseudonym 'Éliphas Lévi') is a well-known work in this field.

Constant, Benjamin, *pseudonym of* HENRI-BENJAMIN CONSTANT DE REBECQUE (1767–1830), b. at Lausanne, of Protestant stock, a leading politician and polemicist, famous as author of the novel *Adolphe.

He studied at the Universities of Erlangen and Edinburgh. The first half of his career was marked by liaisons with women older than himself, including Mme de Charrière and Mme de Staël. For 17 years (1794–1811) the latter maintained a hold over him which not even the disclosure of his secret marriage to Charlotte de Hardenberg (1808) sufficed to break. He was at her beck and call in Paris, at *Coppet, or on her travels, and when his politics displeased Napoleon (1803) he shared her exile. After they parted he went to live in Germany, where he published De l'esprit de conquête et de l'usurpation (1813), a famous pamphlet attacking Napoleon. In spite of this, he took office under him in Paris during the Hundred Days (v. Acte additionnel). After the second Restoration he went to Brussels, and then to London, where he published Adolphe (1816). In 1818 he returned to France, and embarked on a brilliant political career as a leader of the Liberal opposition in the Chambre des *Députés and a journalist.

His other works include De la religion considérée dans sa source, ses formes, et ses développements (1824–31); Mélanges de littérature et de politique (1829); two posthumous publications of great literary interest, his Journal intime (1895, fragments; 1952, a much more complete ed.) and Cahier rouge (1907; reminiscences of childhood and youth), so called because it was written in a red notebook—the exact title is Ma vie, 1767–1787; also Cécile (publ. 1951 from a recently discovered, fragmentary ms.), again autobiographical, but, like Adolphe, in the form of a tale.

Constantinople, La Conquête de, v. Villehardouin.

Constituante, La; Constituants, the *Assemblée constituante and its members.

Constitution civile du clergé, La (1790), a law by which the *Concordat of 1516 was repudiated. The Church was freed from papal control, reorganized, and subordinated to the government, which soon required every practising cleric to swear acceptance of this measure. Those who complied were known as prêtres assermentés or jureurs. The many who refused, the insermentés or réfractaires, were deemed to have resigned, and were often ruthlessly persecuted (as in Lamartine's *Jocelyn).

Constitutionnel, Le (originally L'Indépendant), f. 1815 (during the Hundred Days) by former Revolutionaries as a liberal, anti-clerical paper, survived suppression for its Bonapartist sympathies to become a highly popular Opposition journal, noted for its literary *feuilleton and its disapproval of *Romanticism. During the July Monarchy, when its circulation flagged, it was bought (1844) and revived by Véron, a recovery largely due to the *romans-feuilletons of G. Sand, Sue, and Dumas père. Under the Second Empire (for which it helped to prepare public opinion) it flourished on the literary side (v. Causeries du lundi).

Constitutions. France's first written constitution was that of 1791, voted by the *Assemblée constituante. It sought to apply the principles of the *Déclaration des droits de l'homme, especially those regarding the sovereignty of the people and the separation of legislative, executive, and judicial powers. These two principles have remained fundamental (though at times weakened) in subsequent constitutions. The notable dates are 1791, 1793, 1795, 1799, 1802 (v. Revolutions, 1; Directoire; Consulat); 1804 (v. Napoleon; cf. Acte additionnel; Charte; Revolutions, 2); 1848, 1852, 1870 (v. Republics, 2; Revolutions, 4); 1875 (v. Republics, 3); 1946, 1958 (v. Republics, 4 and 5).

Consuelo (1842–3), by G. Sand, a long, formless novel of 18th-c. musical life and adventure, set mainly in Austria and Bohemia. Consuelo is a young singer of gipsy extraction. Her genius and innocent sincerity melt the most villainous hearts, bringing her unscathed through adventures (e.g. wandering, in peasant-lad disguise, with the young Joseph Haydn, when the two sing and play their way to Vienna) which culminate in her marriage to the mysterious Count Albert de Rudolstadt a few moments before he dies. *La Comtesse de Rudolstadt* (1843–5) is a sequel.

Consulat, Le, the form of government by three Consuls introduced by the constitution of 13 December 1799 (*v. Revolutions*, 1). It lasted till the proclamation of the First Empire (18 May 1804). Bonaparte was First Consul and virtual dictator. The functions of the Second and Third Consuls (who included Sieyès, and later Cambacérès), as of the various State bodies (**Conseil d'état*, **Sénat*, **Corps législatif*, *Tribunat*), were almost nominal—especially after Bonaparte secured (by the *sénatus-consulte* of 4 Aug. 1802) a change in the constitution making him Consul for life.

Conte, a term sometimes applied in a special sense to a type of short fictitious narrative—distinct from the *roman* (*v. Novel*) and at first also from the **nouvelle*—which does not purport to represent real life, but interests by its wit or charm, by its allegory, or by its moral, e.g. *La Fontaine's *Amours de Psyché et de Cupidon*, *Perrault's *Contes de ma mère l'Oye*, Voltaire's **Candide* and other philosophical tales. The many other 18th-c. writers of *contes* (often licentious) include Hamilton (*Fleur d'épine*, etc.), Crébillon *fils* (*Le Sopha*), Duclos (*Acajou et Zirphile*), Voisenon. For the 19th c. *v. Nouvelle*.

Contemplations, Les (1856, 2 vols.), a famous collection of lyrics by Hugo. Most were written in Jersey, but he dated them according to the events to which they refer and himself called them the *Mémoires d'une âme*. Vol. I, *Autrefois*, contains reminiscences of childhood, love, and the **Romantic* battles. Vol. II, *Aujourd'hui*, is more profound, reflecting Hugo's personal and patriotic afflictions and consequent preoccupation with God, life, death, and the infinite. It includes moving elegies, e.g. *A Villequier* (it was at Villequier, on the Seine, that Hugo's daughter Léopoldine and her husband were drowned in 1843

when out boating), and such semi-philosophical poems as *Ce que dit la bouche d'ombre*.

Contemporains, Les, *v. Lemaître, J.*

Contents, Les, *v. Turnèbe, O. de.*

Contes à Ninon, *v. Zola.*

Contes cruels, *v. Villiers de l'Isle-Adam.*

Contes de la bécasse, *v. Maupassant.*

Contes des fées (Fairy-tales), *v. Aulnoy; Leprince de Beaumont; Perrault; Children's Reading.*

Contes d'Espagne et d'Italie, *v. Musset.*

Contes drolatiques (1832; 1833; 1837), by Balzac, three sets of tales written for recreation, imitating the licentious tales of Rabelais and his contemporaries.

Contes du jour et de la nuit, *v. Maupassant.*

Contes du lundi, Les, *v. Daudet, A.*

Contes et Nouvelles en vers (1664; 1665; 1666; 1671; 1674), by La Fontaine, collections of light verse tales drawn from Ariosto, Boccaccio, Machiavelli, etc. Many are licentious (*v. Joconde*), and have been censured for their immorality; others are not open to such censure (*v. Belphégor*; *Faucon, Le*). After his conversion (1692) La Fontaine publicly disavowed them—though they did not offend such contemporaries as Boileau and Mme de Sévigné.

Conti, a younger branch of the house of Condé (*v. Bourbon*). Armand, prince de Conti (1629–68), brother of 'le Grand Condé' (and *v. Mazarin's Nieces*), figured in the **Fronde*. He befriended Molière, but later turned against the theatre and wrote a *Traité de la comédie et des spectacles* (1666) of some interest. He and his son appear in Mme de Sévigné's letters. For Louis-François, prince de Conti, *v. Temple.*

Conti, Clélia, in Stendhal's *La *Chartreuse de Parme*.

Contrat de mariage, Le, v. *Comédie humaine, La* (*Scènes de la vie privée*).

Contrat social, v. *Du contrat social*.

Contrerimes, Les, v. *Toulet*.

Contr'un, Le, v. *La Boétie*.

Convention or **Convention nationale, La,** the most memorable of the Revolutionary Assemblies, succeeded the *Assemblée législative* (Sept. 1792) and gave way to the *Directoire* (Oct. 1795); v. *Revolutions*, 1; *Marais, Le* (2); *Plaine*. Thomas Paine was elected a member.

Coolus, Romain, *pseudonym of* RENÉ WEILL (1868–1952), author of light, sentimental comedies, e.g. *Les Amants de Suzy* (1901), *Petite Peste* (1905), *L'Enfant chérie* (1906), *Les Vacances de Pâques* (1928).

Copains, Les, v. *Romains*.

Copeau, JACQUES (1879–1949), actor and producer, a founder of the *Nouvelle Revue française*, made his name (with its backing) as director (1913–24) of the experimental *Théâtre du *Vieux-Colombier*. In 1924, he retired to Burgundy and opened a theatre school for the training of young actors, some of whom became members of the *Compagnie des Quinze*. He was later a producer (1936–41) at the *Comédie-Française*. His writings include *Souvenirs du Vieux-Colombier* (1931), an annotated edition of Molière, and translations of Shakespeare.

Coppée, FRANÇOIS (1842–1908), poet (in youth a *Parnassien*) and dramatist, called 'le poète des humbles' because he wrote about the pitiful romances or tragedies of the lowly. His works, which have been accused of banality but had great popular appeal, include *Intimités* (1868), *Les Humbles* (1872), *Le Cahier rouge* (1874), *Promenades et Intérieurs* (1875), and *Les*

Récits et les Élégies (1878), collections of poetry; *Le Passant* (1869) and *Le Luthier de Crémone* (1876), successful short comedies; *Severo Torelli* (1883), *Les Jacobites* (1885), and *Pour la couronne* (1895), etc., romantic verse dramas; *La Bonne Souffrance* (1898), a novel of religious experience—the fruit of his conversion, in later life, to Roman Catholicism. During the *Dreyfus affair he was prominent in the *Ligue de la patrie française*.

Coppet, a *château* on Lake Geneva, acquired in 1784 by the *Necker family. After Mme de Staël's exile from France it became her headquarters (replacing her Paris *salon*) and a centre of European culture. Frequent guests included B. Constant, Schlegel, Sismondi, Mme Récamier. Life there (often described in Sismondi's letters) was passed in conversation, varied by country excursions and private theatricals. v. also *Oton de Granson*.

Coq-à-l'âne, a term applied to a type of nonsense verse in which incoherence was a veil for satire. The fashion was set by Marot. His *Coq-à-l'âne*, written in Ferrara and addressed to Lyon Jamet, contains satirical sallies at the papacy and the magistrature, and also some slight personal notes. v. *Fatrasie*.

Coq gaulois, Le. A cock first appeared as the national emblem on flags, etc., during the Revolution. Its origin is uncertain, for Gaulish standards did not bear this emblem. Confusion may have arisen because Latin *gallus* means both *coq* and *Gaulois*.

Coquelin, CONSTANT-BENOÎT (1841–1909), Coquelin *aîné*, and his brother ERNEST-ALEXANDRE-HONORÉ (1848–1909), Coquelin *cadet*, actors long associated with the *Comédie-Française*. Coquelin *aîné*, the more famous, created the name-part in *Cyrano de Bergerac*, played with Bernhardt in *L'*Aiglon*, and was also well known in London.

Coquillards (from *coquille*, 'shell', the pilgrim's emblem), a band of discharged soldiers, rogues, and vagabonds, who in the mid-15th. c. (after the end of the Hundred Years War) infested the roads, especially in Burgundy. They had a 'king', statutes, and their own cant or *jargon* (*v. Villon*). They are not to be confused with the *Suppôts du Seigneur de la Coquille* (*v. Sociétés joyeuses*).

Coquillart, GUILLAUME (*c.* 1450–1510), poet, later a jurist and canon of Rheims, wrote (1477–80) two *causes grasses* for the *Basoche of Paris, the *Plaidoyer d'entre la simple et la rusée* and the *Enquête d'entre la simple et la rusée*, caricatures of the legal proceedings that arise when two women compete for a man; also *Les Droits nouveaux*, at once a caricature of legal treatises and a political and social satire; a *Blason des armes et des dames*, listing the rival merits of each; *La Botte de foin* (a lover hides in a hay-loft to escape a husband), an amusing monologue.

Coran, CHARLES (1814–83), a minor *Romantic poet, author of *Onyx* (1840), *Rimes galantes* (1847), *Dernières Élégances* (1868), etc.

Corbeaux, Les (1882), by Becque, one of the first *Naturalist dramas. When the wealthy M. Vigneron dies, leaving his affairs unsettled, his widow and three daughters are a prey for the 'vultures'—lawyers, tradesmen, etc.—who fight for the rich pickings. The most unscrupulous is old Teissier, Vigneron's former partner. He takes a fancy to Marie, one of the daughters, who finally marries him as the only way of rescuing her family from their plight.

Corbière, ÉDOUARD-JOACHIM, *self-styled* TRISTAN (1845–75), a poet little known till Verlaine took him up in his *Poètes maudits*, since when his reputation has grown. His poems about seafaring life in his native Brittany, *Gens de mer* (in *Les Amours jaunes*, 1873), are elliptic, at times slangily expressed, but remarkable for their irony and realism; the last of these,

La Fin, is often contrasted with Hugo's *Oceano nox. v. Symbolism.*

Corday d'Armont, CHARLOTTE (1768–93), descended from a sister of Corneille, went to Paris in the summer of 1793 bent on avenging the *Girondins. On 13 July she entered Marat's apartment and stabbed him to death in his bath. She was guillotined on 17 July. *v. Histoire des Girondins.*

Cordeliers, Club des, or **Société des amis des droits de l'homme et du citoyen,** an extremist Revolutionary club f. 1790 by Danton, Marat, and Desmoulins; so called because it met in the former Franciscan convent. Its organ was Marat's *Ami du peuple*, and its power was greatest during the struggle with the *Girondins. Later, as the headquarters of the *Hébertistes, it disowned both Danton and Desmoulins. After Hébert's fall it gradually dissolved.

Cordière, La Belle, *v. Labé.*

Cordon bleu, originally signified the broad blue sash of the *Ordre du *Saint-Esprit*, then came to mean a mark, or a person, of special eminence in a given profession, and later, facetiously, of special eminence in cooking.

Corinne (1807), a long novel by Mme de Staël. Lord Oswald Nelvil, a melancholy, reserved Englishman, visits Italy (the occasion for descriptions of Italian landscape, literature, and art), and in Rome meets Corinne, a beautiful poetess. They fall in love, but he shrinks from marrying this mysterious genius, with her unrestrained, artistic temperament. Also, his father's dying wish has half bound him to Lucile Edgermond, an English girl. Corinne reveals that she is Lucile's half-sister, Lord Edgermond's daughter by his first wife (an Italian), and that she once lived with him and his second wife, enduring the boredom of English country life (an entertaining part of the book). Oswald's father, a family friend, had actually considered her as a possible wife for his son, but had mistrusted her vivacity. She had quarrelled with her stepmother when her father died, and had left England. Oswald returns home resolved to marry Corinne, but yields to convention and family pressure and marries Lucile. Corinne dies of grief.

Corisande, La Belle, a name often given to Diane d'Ando[u]ins, comtesse de Guiche, a mistress of Henri IV. She was grandmother of the comte de Gramont, and a friend of Montaigne, who dedicated an essay to her.

Cormenin, LOUIS-MARIE DE LA HAYE, VICOMTE DE (1788–1868), in youth a poet, later a jurist and politician who, as 'Timon le misanthrope', consistently attacked the July Monarchy in pamphlets (*Très humbles remontrances de Timon...*, 1838; *Questions scandaleuses d'un jacobin...*, 1840); in *Études sur les orateurs parlementaires* (1836), witty, often cruel portraits of contemporary politicians; and in *Entretiens de village* (1846). He was widely read, but not in the same class as Courier.

Corneille, PIERRE (1606–84), a great dramatist of the *Classical era, b. at Rouen of a family of magistrates; brother of the following and uncle of Fontenelle. He was educated at a *Jesuit school, studied law, and purchased two minor offices in the Rouen magistrature, which he held till 1650. He was simple, candid, and devout; yet also proud and sensitive, intellectually timid and self-tormenting, for ever scrutinizing and correcting his work. He was always needy, despite the pension (paid irregularly) he received in 1663, for his plays brought him more fame than money. A love affair of his own, dramatized in the comedy *Mélite* (prod. 1629 or 1630; v. *Theatres and Theatre Companies*), revealed his poetical gifts. Then came the tragicomedy *Clitandre* (prob. prod. 1630 or 1631; the complicated story of Rosidor's love for Caliste, crossed by Caliste's unfounded jealousy and the machinations of Pymante, who vainly loves Caliste's sister Dorise, who loves Rosidor) and a series of comedies (prob.

prod. 1632–3) of only secondary interest (*La Veuve*; *La Galerie du Palais*, set in the *Palais-Royal; *La Suivante*; *La Place Royale*, set in the *Place Royale*). Soon after this, as one of Richelieu's *cinq auteurs*, he probably wrote the third act of *La Comédie des Tuileries*. His first tragedy, *Médée* (prod. winter of 1634–5), was followed by L'*Illusion comique* (prob. 1635), then by Le *Cid* (1637). This great play, which (with *Mairet's *Sophonisbe*) marks the beginning of true Classical *tragedy, introduced the new theme (to which he often returned) of the conflict in a human soul between love and duty. It aroused acute controversy, being highly approved by the public, but attacked by rivals such as Scudéry, who, supported by Richelieu, procured a judgement on it by the *Académie (*Sentiments de l'Académie sur le Cid*, 1638; drafted by Chapelain), criticizing Corneille on points of style and grammar. Discouraged by this, he produced nothing more till 1640, when his great tragedies *Horace and *Cinna were performed. Then came *Polyeucte (prob. winter of 1641–2) and La *Mort de Pompée (winter of 1642–3), tragedies; Le *Menteur (1643) and *La Suite du Menteur* (winter of 1644–5), comedies; the tragedies *Rodogune (winter of 1644–5), *Théodore (1645), and *Héraclius (winter of 1646–7); *Don Sanche d'Aragon (1649), a tragicomedy; *Andromède* (1650), a spectacle-play which owed much of its success to Giacomo Torelli, the Italian master of theatre machinery brought to France by Louis XIV; *Nicomède (winter of 1650–1), his last great tragedy. After the failure of his tragedy *Pertharite (1651), he retired to his home at Rouen and wrote no more plays for seven years. During this period he produced a notable verse rendering of the *Imitation of Christ and other devotional pieces. He returned to Paris in 1662. The works of his decline— *Œdipe (1659), *La Toison d'or* (1660; lyrical tragedy, a spectacle-play to celebrate the king's marriage), *Sertorius (1662), *Sophonisbe (1663), *Othon (1664), *Agésilas (1666; in *vers libres*), *Attila (1667), *Suréna (1674), all tragedies; *Tite et Bérénice (1670) and *Pulchérie* (1672), *comédies héroïques*—are mostly on historical and political themes from which passion is eliminated. They are unequal and of less interest than his earlier works; even so, they contain vivid characters (statesmen, and women involved in state affairs) and much fine verse. He also wrote part of *Psyché* (1671). Many of his plays were produced at the *Théâtre du Marais*, later also at the *Hôtel de Bourgogne* and by Molière's company.

His best plays are remarkable for their great tragic characters, high ethical quality, and majestic style. Instead of lamenting man's impotence in the face of destiny (the Greek tragic notion), Corneille exalts his power to shape his own destiny, or to rise superior to it. His tragic heroes and heroines are depicted, it has been said, as more than life size, possessed of almost superhuman strength of will, pride, and reason; and they are placed in situations where these qualities are brought into conflict with sentiment, instinct, or outward circumstance, and sometimes lead them to sublime self-sacrifice. His tragedies present some definite problem for solution; external incident is admitted only where it contributes to the psychological action. In general—at any rate after *Le Cid*—he observed the unities, not meticulously, but reasonably, in the interests of realism and concentration. His style is distinguished by the force and clarity, the dialectical brilliance, rising at times to passionate ardour, with which his characters argue out their destiny, rather than by warmth or colour. His own *Discours* (prefixed to the 1660 ed. of his plays) and *Examens* (criticisms attached to each play) shed much light on his dramatic theories. Voltaire wrote a *Commentaire sur Corneille* (1764). For a comparison of Corneille and Racine *v. Racine*.

The best 17th-c. English translations of Corneille were those of Mrs. Katherine Philips, the 'Matchless Orinda'. Some were performed.

Corneille, THOMAS (1625–1709), dramatist, the much younger, less talented brother of the above; also a lexicographer (*v. Dictionaries*, 1694 and 1708) and an editor of *Le *Mercure galant*. He was a prolific and skilful playwright (an imitator—at times of his brother—rather than an innovator) who, with Quinault, filled the interval between his brother's zenith and the rise of Racine. His plays include, notably, *Timocrate* (1656; based on an episode in *La Calprenède's *Cléopâtre*), in which he reintroduced into tragedy the element of romantic intrigue, and *Ariane* (1672), on the theme of Ariadne's betrayal and desertion by Theseus—again suggesting the rising influence of Racine; also *Stilicon* (1660), *Camma* (1661), *Maximien* (1662), *Laodice* (1668), and *Le Comte d'Essex* (1678; *v. La Calprenède*), all tragedies; *Le Festin de pierre* (1677), a verse adaptation of Molière's *Dom Juan*; *Le Geôlier de soi-même* (1655), his best comedy.

Corneille des boulevards, Le, *v. Pixérécourt*.

Cornuel, ANNE-MARIE BIGOT, MME (1605–94), a *bourgeoise* famous for her mordant wit. Her *salon* was much frequented by men of letters in the second half of the 17th c.

Corot, JEAN-BAPTISTE-CAMILLE (1796–1875), famous landscape painter (*v. Barbizon*); a forerunner, by his poetical treatment of light, of *Impressionism.

Corps législatif, Le, a term originally applied to the Revolutionary *Assemblée législative*. It was divided under the *Directoire* into the *Conseil des Cinq-Cents* and the *Conseil des Anciens*. Under the *Consulat* it merely adopted or rejected without debate (hence 'Assemblée des muets') measures prepared by the *Conseil d'état* and discussed by the *Tribunat*. Under Napoleon III the *Corps législatif* was the lower house of the legislature, with little effective power in the 1850s.

Correspondances (1857, in *Les Fleurs du mal* (*Spleen et Idéal*)), by Baudelaire, the famous sonnet in which he describes the symbolic relations of scent, sound, and colour ('Les parfums, les couleurs, et les sons se répondent'). *v. Symbolism.*

Correspondence, *v. Letters.*

Corsaire or *Corsaire-Satan, Le* (f. 1823, ceased publication during the Second Empire), a little review which often printed new writing, notably poems by Baudelaire.

Corydon, v. Gide.

Cosette, in Hugo's *Les *Misérables.*

Cosi-Sancta (1784, Kehl ed.; probably written *c.* 1747), a philosophical tale by Voltaire, on the theme (suggested by a passage in St. Augustine) that it is permissible to do a small wrong if a greater good results. Cosi-Sancta by her virtue causes the death of her lover and endangers her husband; but by three infidelities to the latter saves his life and those of her brother and son, and is canonized in consequence.

Cosroès, v. Rotrou.

Costar, PIERRE (1603–60), an *habitué* of the Hôtel de *Rambouillet, and the somewhat pedantic author of *Défense des ouvrages de M. Voiture* (1653), *Entretiens de M. Voiture et de M. Costar* (1654), *Suite de la Défense des œuvres de M. Voiture* (1655), *Apologie de M. Costar,* and letters (1658).

Cotart, JEHAN, *v. Villon.*

Côté de Guermantes, Le, v. A la recherche du temps perdu; Combray.

Cotgrave, RANDLE, *v. Dictionaries,* 1611.

Cotin, CHARLES, ABBÉ (1604–82), a learned preacher and writer of some repute in his day; an *habitué* of the Hôtel de *Rambouillet. He was ridiculed in Molière's *Les *Femmes savantes* (as Trissotin) and Boileau's *Satires.

Cottin, MARIE RISTAUD, MME 'SOPHIE' (1770–1807), the young widow of a rich banker who settled in the country near Paris and produced five novels, popular in their day, which combine morality, sensation, and sentimentality: *Claire d'Albe* (1799); *Malvina* (1801); *Amélie Mansfield* (1803); *Mathilde* (1805), a tale of the Crusades, so successful that it influenced women's fashions; *Élisabeth, ou les Exilés de Sibérie* (1806), the story (later more soberly retold in X. de Maistre's *La Jeune Sibérienne*) of a young girl who makes the difficult journey from Siberia to St. Petersburg, bent on obtaining the Tsar's pardon for her exiled father. Mme Cottin is said to have committed suicide—a sad end to a life that at times reflected the romantic passions of her novels.

Couard, the hare in the *Roman de Renart.

Coucy, GUI, CHÂTELAIN DE, a late 12th-c. lyric poet (*v. Lyric Poetry,* 1). Under the name of his successor Renaut, he was made the hero of a legend (the theme of *Le Châtelain de Coucy,* a verse **roman d'aventure* by a late 13th-c. poet named Jakemon) telling how his heart, sent from the Holy Land to the lady he loved (the Dame de Faiel), was intercepted by her jealous husband, who served it to her in a dish.

Coulanges, (1) CHRISTOPHE DE, ABBÉ DE LIVRY (*c.* 1607–87), uncle and guardian of Mme de Sévigné, 'le bien bon' of her letters; (2) PHILIPPE-EMMANUEL, MARQUIS DE (1633–1716), cousin and correspondent of Mme de Sévigné, author of light poetry and memoirs; his wife, MARIE-ANGÉLIQUE (1641–1723), was also a close friend of Mme de Sévigné.

Coup d'état. For the *coup d'état du 18 fructidor* (4 Sept. 1797) *v. Fructidor;* for Bonaparte's *coup d'état du 18 brumaire* (9 Nov. 1799) *v. Revolutions,* 1; for Louis-Napoléon's *coup d'état* (2 Dec. 1851) *v. Republics,* 2.

Coupée, Dame, a hen in the *Roman de Renart.

Coupe et les lèvres, La, v. Un Spectacle dans un fauteuil.

Couperin, FRANÇOIS (1668–1733), 'Couperin le Grand', composer of harpsichord music and a celebrated organist. There were five generations of musicians in this family.

Courbet, GUSTAVE (1819–77), a landscape painter whose doctrines of *l'art réaliste* were transposed into literature (*v. Realism*). Like many of his literary friends, including Baudelaire (whose portrait he was painting in Feb. 1848) and Champfleury, he was fired by the ideals of the 1848 *Revolution. He was also an active revolutionary during the *Commune of 1871 and died in exile in Switzerland. His famous *Atelier du peintre*, where Baudelaire can be seen bent over a book, was first exhibited in 1855.

Cour de cassation (created 1790, as the *Tribunal de cassation*), the supreme body in the French legal system. Its sole concern is to determine whether the civil or criminal law has been correctly interpreted and legal procedure correctly observed. It has power to nullify a judgement, thereby necessitating a new trial, before a new court.

Cour des aides, under the monarchy, a court of law which tried suits arising out of the collection, farming, etc., of taxes. It also had executive functions in connection with public works, payment and rationing of troops, etc.

Cour des comptes, *v. Chambre des comptes.*

Cour des miracles, a quarter of medieval Paris, on the right bank of the Seine, inhabited by beggars and vagabonds, the cripples and blind of the daytime streets, whose infirmities miraculously vanished once they got home at night. It figures in Hugo's *Notre-Dame de Paris.*

Cour des monnaies, under the monarchy, a court of law which tried suits in connection with the coinage and precious metals.

Courier, PAUL-LOUIS (1772–1825), pamphleteer and scholar, son of a landowner in Touraine, joined the army (1792), served in Italy, and, finding that he could indulge his passion for classical studies in the great Italian libraries, left the army (1809) and studied in Italy till 1812. He came into prominence with his *Lettre à M. Renouard sur une tache faite à un manuscrit de Florence* (1810). Renouard was a scholar, the manuscript an unknown fragment of Longus which Courier and Renouard had discovered. Courier spilt ink on it, either accidentally or to conceal his misreadings; the *Lettre*, ridiculing the affair, was his reply to the consequent scandal. His translation of Longus's *Daphnis and Chloe* appeared in 1810.

After returning (1812) to manage his property in Touraine, he became a champion of the oppressed peasantry, attacking the clergy and local officials in a series of pamphlets (signed 'Paul-Louis, Vigneron') and letters to newspapers. He was killed by a farm labourer he had dismissed. His *Œuvres complètes*, including his *Lettres écrites de France et d'Italie*, appeared in 1829–30. His best pamphlets—e.g. his *Pétition aux deux Chambres* (1816), *Pétition pour des villageois qu'on empêche de danser* (1820), *Le Simple Discours de Paul-Louis, Vigneron de la Chavonnière* (1821)—rank, after *Pascal's Provinciales*, as masterpieces of polemical writing.

Cournot, ANTOINE-AUGUSTIN (1801–77), mathematician, economist, and the philosopher of *Probabilisme*. His doctrine that in matters of knowledge it is not possible to arrive at absolute truth, only to distinguish between degrees of probability, was expounded in his *Exposition de la théorie des chances et des probabilités* (1843), etc.

Couronnement de Renart, Le, v. Roman de Renart.

Courrier de Provence, Le (1789–91;

thrice weekly), a journal f. and ed. by Mirabeau (replacing his *Lettres du comte de Mirabeau à ses commettants* and his earlier *Journal des États généraux*), mainly devoted to lively reports of proceedings in the *Assemblée constituante*; it also published letters.

Courrier des départements, Le, *v.* *Courrier de Versailles à Paris.*

Courrier de Versailles à Paris et de Paris à Versailles, Le (1789–93; known after 1792 as *Le Courrier des départements*), a leading organ of the *Girondins* which violently opposed Marat's *Ami du peuple*. Its founder, Antoine-Joseph Gorsas, a Versailles schoolmaster who became a member of the *Convention*, was guillotined.

Courteline, Georges, *pseudonym of* GEORGES MOINEAUX (1861–1929), probably the greatest comic writer of the modern period, son of a Paris journalist. He tried various careers, all distasteful. When ministerial influence provided him with a post as a civil servant, he arranged for his work to be done by a colleague, who drew his salary, retaining half for his pains. After two years the colleague asked for a holiday, so Courteline resigned. He took to regular humorous journalism in 1883, and in 1890 began his long association with the daily paper *L'Écho de Paris*, in which most of his work first appeared. His prolific output—tales, sketches, comedies, reminiscences—was based on experience and caustic observation of the minor episodes in daily life, and ranged from farce to profound satire. He wrote, notably, *Boubouroche* (1893), a comedy on the eternal theme of the gullible cuckold; *Les Gaîtés de l'escadron* (1886), *Le Train de 8h. 47* (1888), and *Lidoire et la biscotte* (1892), farcical, sometimes grim, sketches of military life; *Messieurs les ronds-de-cuir* (1893), satirical sketches of bureaucrats at work; also *Le Droit aux étrennes* (1896), *Un Client sérieux* (1897), *Les Boulingrin* (1898), *La Paix chez soi* (1903), *Les Linottes* (1912; a novel), *La Conversion d'Alceste* (1905; an attempt at a sequel to

Molière's *Le *Misanthrope*), etc. He ceased writing in 1912.

Courtilz de Sandras, GATIEN DE (1644–1712), soldier and literary adventurer, author of libellous pamphlets, indifferent historical works, and fabricated memoirs—notably his *Mémoires de M. d'Artagnan* (1700), the source of Dumas père's Les *Trois Mousquetaires.*

Courtois d'Arras, *v.* Comedy.

Cousin, VICTOR (1792–1867), a philosopher who, as a professor at the *Sorbonne* (from 1815; his courses were suspended, 1820–7, because of his *doctrinaire* sympathies), director of the *École normale supérieure,* and finally minister of education, greatly influenced philosophic thought, was responsible (with Guizot and Villemain) for the academic fame of the *Sorbonne c.* 1830, and did much (between 1830 and the *coup d'état* of 1851) to organize education in France. He is said to have founded the school of *eclectic* philosophy, because he produced no new system, but applied psychological method to the history of philosophy, making a synthesis of what he deemed the essential parts of earlier systems (sensationalism, idealism, scepticism, mysticism).

The most famous of his brilliant lecture-courses were those of 1818 (publ. 1836 as *Cours de philosophie,* republ. 1853 as *Du vrai, du beau, et du bien*; v. Art pour l'art, L') and of 1828–30 (largely on Hegel, then unknown in France). Besides many philosophical works, he produced writings of a more literary and historical nature (e.g. *La Jeunesse de Mme de Longueville,* 1853; *La Société française au XVIIᵉ siècle,* 1856), also the first and for long the major edition of Descartes's complete works (1824–6).

Cousine Bette, La (1846; later in *La *Comédie humaine, Scènes de la vie parisienne; cf. Cousin Pons, Le*), a novel by Balzac. Lisbeth ('Bette') Fischer is a peasant from the Vosges, greedy, and jealous of her cousin Adeline for being beautiful, saintly, and married to a respected government official, Baron Hulot. When the book opens (in the reign of Louis-Philippe), Hulot has become the depraved victim of his sexual passions, while Bette is sheltering a young Polish artist, Count Wenceslas Steinbock, on whom she lavishes a bullying tenderness. When Bette learns that the young Hortense Hulot and Steinbock have fallen in love and are to marry, she conceals her feelings, but resolves to ruin her relations. To this end, she allies herself with Hulot's latest mistress, Mme Marneffe. This grasping, heartless siren, already in process of ruining Hulot financially and also involved in affairs with the wealthy Crevel (father-in-law of Hulot's son) and a rich Brazilian, contrives, with Bette's assistance, to seduce Steinbock from Hortense. Bette herself, having convinced her relations that she is feigning friendship with Mme Marneffe to guard their interests, nearly succeeds in marrying Hulot's brother, Maréchal Hulot, but he dies of shock on learning that Hulot has embezzled government funds. Hulot, forced to resign, yields shamelessly to his vices and disappears; Bette sends him money to hasten his degradation. Meanwhile, Mme Marneffe, now widowed, has married Crevel; but her Brazilian lover, discovering her treachery, has the pair of them poisoned. Crevel's daughter and her husband, young Hulot, inherit his fortune. The frustrated Bette, seeing wealth restored to her relations, takes a chill and dies. Then Adeline dies of shock on hearing Hulot, who has returned home an apparently reformed character, anticipating her death and proposing to the kitchenmaid. The decrepit Hulot's marriage to the maid ends this powerful study of the havoc wrought by jealousy and libertinism.

Cousin Pons, Le (1847; later in *La* *Comédie humaine*, *Scènes de la vie parisienne*; with *La *Cousine Bette*, it forms *Les Parents pauvres*), a novel by Balzac; a study of a poor relation. Sylvain Pons, a seedy musician, has two passions—

collecting and good food. Having spent his patrimony on the first, he gratifies the second by visits to various rich relations, enduring insults in return for fine fare. He lives with his devoted German friend Wilhelm Schmucke, also a music master. When Pons fails to engineer a marriage between his cousin and the rich Frédéric Brunner, his relations accuse him of plotting to humiliate them, with the result that he falls gravely ill. Mme Cibot, the *concierge*, then discovers that his collection is worth a fortune; and the dying Pons and his naïve friend become the victims of human cupidity. Mme Cibot, the doctor, a dealer, a shady solicitor, the relations— all scheme over the death-bed. Pons manages to will his property to Schmucke. But Schmucke, broken-hearted and no match for the intriguers, signs away his inheritance for a pittance, and soon dies. The triumphant relations now refer to their '*dear* Cousin Pons'.

Couthon, GEORGES (1755–94), a fanatical Revolutionary politician, a member of the *Assemblée législative*, the *Convention*, and the *Comité de salut public*. He, Robespierre, and Saint-Just ('le Triumvirat de la Terreur') were guillotined on the same day.

Coutumes du Beauvaisis, Les, *v. Beaumanoir*.

Crac, Monsieur de, *v. Collin d'Harleville*.

Crainquebille, the title piece in a volume of tales (1904) by A. France. Crainquebille, a costermonger, is imprisoned on a false charge of having said 'Mort aux vaches' ('Down with coppers') to a policeman. Unable to make a living after his release, he decides he would be better off in prison. So he accosts a policeman and shouts 'Mort aux vaches'—only to be tolerantly moved on.

Cramer, PHILIBERT and GABRIEL (18th c.), Genevan publishers, printed most of Voltaire's works from 1755.

Crébillon, (1) PROSPER JOLYOT, SIEUR DE (1674–1762), a dramatist highly esteemed in his day, a member of the *Académie, and dramatic censor (v. Censorship, Dramatic). His best plays—Idoménée (1705), Atrée et Thyeste (1707), Électre (1708), *Rhadamiste et Zénobie (1711), Xerxès (1714), Sémiramis (1717), Catilina (1748)—are less tragedies than highly tragic melodramas, showing a partiality for violent episodes and romantic complications, rather than character study and truth to life; he sought, as he says, to evoke pity by terror; (2) his son CLAUDE-PROSPER JOLYOT DE (1707–77), Crébillon fils, also dramatic censor, wrote tales and dialogues (e.g. Les Égarements du cœur et de l'esprit, 1736; Le Sopha, 1745, a licentious Oriental *conte) reflecting the depravity of the day and containing elements of social satire and literary criticism. One of these led to his imprisonment (1734). His wife was English.

Crécy, Odette de, v. Odette.

Crenne, HÉLISENNE DE (16th c.), authoress, probably of Picardy, whose Les Angoisses douloureuses qui procèdent d'amours (1538) may be classed as the first French sentimental romance. Written under Italian influence (it resembles Boccaccio's Fiammetta; v. Novel, 1), it is the confession of a girl who, having married very young and lived happily for some years with her husband, falls deeply in love with a young stranger. The ensuing mental anguish and domestic troubles are detailed with skill; the subsequent events and unhappy issue are related (in pts. II and III) by her lover Guénélic.

Créqui, RENÉE-CAROLINE DE FROULLAY, MARQUISE DE (1714–1803), friend of d'Alembert, J.-J. Rousseau, and, in old age, of Sénac de Meilhan. Some of her letters have been published; but the grossly inaccurate, though entertaining, memoirs attributed to her were fabricated by one Courchamps.

Crétin, GUILLAUME (d. 1525), a *rhétoriqueur poet, wrote patriotic, allegorical poems on current events and an unfinished epic, La Chronique française (continued by a monk, René Macé), an uncritical versification of old chronicles. Despite his insipidity, he was praised by Marot as 'souverain poète', and quoted by Rabelais.

Crève-cœur, Le, v. Aragon.

Crime de Sylvestre Bonnard, Le (1881), by A. France, a highly successful novel (in diary form). An elderly scholar abducts the daughter (in later eds. grand-daughter) of the woman he had hoped to marry from the boarding-school where she is ill-treated. He sells his precious library to provide a dowry for her.

Cripure, v. Guilloux.

Crispin rival de son maître, a one-act prose comedy by Lesage; produced 1707.

Valère loves Angélique, daughter of Oronte, and she him. But she has been promised to Damis, son of Orgon, a provincial friend of Oronte. Meanwhile, Damis has secretly married another, and Orgon sends his valet to inform Oronte and break off the proposed match. Orgon's valet falls in with Crispin, valet of Valère. The two devise a plot: they will suppress the news of Damis's marriage, and Crispin will pose as Damis (whom no one involved has ever seen), marry Angélique, and make off with her dowry. After a promising start, the plot is finally foiled, and all ends happily—even for the rascally valets, who manage to talk themselves back into favour.

Critics and Criticism. Medieval literature includes many treatises on rhetoric (which covered both oratory and poetics), but down to the 14th c. they treated of, and were written in, Latin. French treatises of the later Middle Ages (e.g. those of Eustache Deschamps and Molinet) are mainly concerned with the techniques of versification. The foundations of literary criticism in the sense of appraisal—and eventually (late 19th c.) of aesthetic interpretation—were laid in the *Renaissance. For literary and critical reviews of all periods v. *Periodicals*; *Press*, 1–9. For literary histories v. *Histories of French Literature*.

1. RENAISSANCE TO 19TH CENTURY. The introduction of printing (1470 in France) made the great body of Greek, Latin, and Italian literature, and of classical criticism, widely available to a public thirsting for knowledge and grown weary of the *rhétoriqueurs*. Then came the Reformation, which intensified the growing cleavage between purely theological and philological studies on the one hand, and a conception of language as an instrument of literature on the other. This conception, with which French criticism may be said to begin, was largely developed by the *Pléiade* poets, notably in Du Bellay's *Défense et illustration de la langue française* (1549); and at first the criticism was verbal, concerned with language and form (mainly that of poetry). Du Bellay's treatise led to an enhanced respect for French as a literary language, and to the acceptance of new themes and forms, based on classical and Italian models (v. *Pléiade*). There were naturally abuses; and by the late 16th c. the language was fast becoming clogged by the neologisms and borrowings advocated by the *Pléiade*. This danger was largely averted by Malherbe, who also prescribed rules of versification which endured for some 200 years.

By the 17th and 18th cs., writers, theorists, and *savants* had moved on to discuss and develop conceptions of literature as one of the arts. Oral discussion proceeded in the *salons* (e.g. the Hôtel de *Rambouillet) and the *Académie*. In 1638 Richelieu invited the *Académie* to judge the merits of Corneille's *Le *Cid*—in fact, to *criticize* it. The *Académie* was also the scene of the opening rounds of the famous *Querelle des anciens et des modernes*. In print, discussion took the form of essays, prefaces, letters, and *arts poétiques*. Among the many whose theories contributed to the evolution of criticism at this time were Chapelain, Corneille, Guez de Balzac, Descartes, Vaugelas, Boileau, Molière,

Racine, Saint-Évremond, Houdar de la Motte, Dubos, Bayle, Voltaire, Diderot.

The general aim of discussion was to determine what made for good or bad literature; what models should be followed; whether pleasure, a necessary factor, could be produced by conforming to *les règles* (i.e. to general principles and rules of composition and diction; v. *Classicism*), or to rules (e.g. the unities; v. *Tragedy*) more precisely adapted to the evolving literary *genres*; how best to represent nature and truth; how to avoid confusing art with nature; the importance of logic and reason (v. *Classicism*) *vis-à-vis* inspiration; the welcome to be extended to ideas of progress (which raised doubts about the adoption of exclusively classical models). (The place of the individual in literature—a question arising largely out of the works of J.-J. Rousseau—received more attention in the 19th c.)

Thus, by the late 18th c., various literary dogmas had been formulated, and were serving as a basis for the development of criticism in the sense of appraisal. In such literary reviews as existed space was now devoted to criticism; and the critic as a type of independent professional journalist now appeared. With rare exceptions, the criticism was dogmatic, a matter of assessing the merits of a work by its conformity to rules, e.g. the critical writings of La Harpe and Suard, reviews by Feletz, Geoffroy, and F.-B. Hoffmann in the *Journal des Débats*.

2. 19TH CENTURY. The spread of education, with the rapid growth of the *Press and a reading public in need of guidance and information, swelled the ranks of the new professional critics. They were of two kinds: those who made literature and literary journalism their career and whose numbers and importance increased as the century wore on; and the academic critics, university teachers whose official standing long lent added weight to their judgements.

From the early 19th c., the basic principles of criticism itself were changing, largely under the influence of Mme de Staël and Chateaubriand. Ideas were gaining ground that literature was the reflection of social history, and that standards of beauty and taste must vary according to the formative influences of race, religion, and culture. Together with the revolutionary distinction between 'classical' and 'romantic' literature they led to the victory of *Romanticism and the undermining of the Classical conventions. This brought into criticism a new sense of relativity, and the conception that a work of art should be judged on its own merits, independently of standards of subject and treatment. Important writings in this connection are Mme de Staël's *De la littérature and *De l' Allemagne; Chateaubriand's Le *Génie du christianisme; Stendhal's *Racine et Shakspeare; Hugo's prefaces to *Cromwell and Les *Orientales, and later, his *William Shakespeare.

Leading critics of the first half of the century include Villemain, among the first (in his Tableau de la littérature française, 1828) to consider new writing in its relation to general and literary history, to see in literature the reflection of an era, and to introduce biographical and historical notes; Saint-Marc Girardin; Nisard; Magnin; also Fauriel and Marmier, who by their studies of foreign literature were forerunners of comparative criticism (Renan later added considerations of anthropology, philology, and archaeology to the comparative field). During the middle years of the century, the scientific spirit of the age and the new trends in criticism were all clearly evident in one man, the great literary journalist Sainte-Beuve. They are seen in his objective approach to literature and belief in documentation, and in the insight and imaginative sympathy of his studies of literary figures, which amount to psychological reconstructions of the writer and his epoch. He died (1869) leaving literary criticism firmly established as a genre in itself, ranking, at its best, second only to the highest creative writing. His contemporaries Schérer and Montégut were widely read in their own and foreign literatures and solidly informative and explicative in their criticism. His successor Taine made the application of scientific methods to criticism almost the raison

d'être of the critic's function, with results ranging from the brilliant to the frankly astonishing. The late 19th c. saw the work of Brunetière and the rise of Lanson; both were literary historians—a growing class from now on (v. Histories of French Literature). Lanson, an eminent critic -whose work was rooted in historicism and positivism, was the father of 20th-c. academic—or 'Lansoniste'—criticism (notably exemplified by Hazard).

'Impressionistic' criticism developed considerably in the late 19th c. Here the critic is not concerned with the general pattern into which a writer can be fitted, but either with the personality or the ideas revealed by the works (e.g. Barbey d'Aurevilly, Faguet), or with his own personal reaction to a particular writer or work (e.g. J. Lemaître, A. *France's Vie littéraire).

3. 20TH CENTURY. The early 20th c. saw the emergence, alongside academic criticism, of a conception of criticism which was anti-intellectual, less concerned with the assessment of merit than with intuitive understanding (i.e. Bergson's intuitionism translated into terms of critical theory), imaginative re-experience, and interpretation. The conception of criticism as interpretation—and so, at times, of the creative artist as the most, if not the only, satisfactory critic—is already present in Baudelaire, whose critical writings long remained unappreciated. Among the first and most important of the anti-intellectualist critics was R. de Gourmont, who was largely responsible for introducing the psychology of linguistics and the 'dissociation des idées' into criticism. He did much to set the tone for the critics associated with the early *Nouvelle Revue française, for 'Alain', and, above all, for Valéry—an outstanding exponent (in his Variété) of a type of modern criticism which attempts to get behind the language itself and to fathom the mysteries of the creative process. v. also Benda; Du Bos; Gide; Jaloux; Lasserre; Proust; Rivière; Suarès; Thibaudet; Visan.

The 1950s saw the gradual emergence of a wide variety of critical approaches of ideological inspiration, stemming variously from *Existentialism, Marxism,

*Structuralism, and psychoanalysis, which have come to be known as the *nouvelle critique*. Though the *nouveaux critiques* have never formed a single school or movement, they share a desire to ground the study of literature on some coherent theoretical basis and a strong antipathy to the broadly subjective approach widely current in modern literary journalism (e.g. the criticism of Kemp, Massis, and Arland) and, above all, to traditional academic criticism. The chief characteristic of the *nouvelle critique* is an attempt to understand the nature of literature itself by a process of critical *interpretation*, and to replace the traditional view of a literary work as the conscious expression of the writer's feelings, which had led to a process of *elucidation* and undue emphasis on biographical studies. A trend in this direction is already apparent in the critical work of Proust, Valéry, Du Bos, Rivière, Thibaudet, and other 'creative' critics of the *Nouvelle Revue française*. The transition to the *nouvelle critique* was effected by critics like Paulhan (whose discussion of criticism in *Les Fleurs de Tarbes* has been very influential), Bachelard, Blanchot, and Bataille.

The largest group of *nouveaux critiques* are those linked by a broad similarity of approach sometimes called thematic criticism, notably Poulet; Starobinski; Jean-Pierre Richard (1922–   ), author of *Littérature et sensation* (1954) and *Poésie et profondeur* (1955); and Jean Rousset (1910–   ), author of *Forme et signification* (1962). Bachelard is in many ways the father of this approach, but all these critics acknowledge a debt to the Swiss critics Raymond and Béguin. In their different ways, they seek to reveal the consciousness of a given writer as expressed in his works. Both psychoanalysis and phenomenology have been of some significance for this approach, but in practice the methods used by all its exponents are based on the maximum identification with the writer by the critic. Existentialist criticism is largely represented by the work of Sartre. Psychoanalysis has had an effect on almost every branch of criticism, but it is best represented by *psychocritique*, originated by Mauron, which uses the psychoanalytical method. The study of a writer's subconscious in his works, *psychocritique* proceeds by looking for hidden associations from which every writer's 'personal myth' can be established. Marxist criticism is best exemplified by the work of Goldmann. The *Tel Quel* group (critics associated with the review of that name, f. 1961 by Philippe Sollers) are attempting to combine a Marxist approach with a formalist one. The chief figures in Structuralist or formalist criticism are Barthes; Gérard Genette (1930–   ), author of *Figures* (1966–72, 3 vols.); and Tzvetan Todorov (1940–   ), associated, as is Genette, with the review *Poétique* (f. 1969) and author of *Poétique de la prose* (1971). It traces its intellectual ancestry back both to Saussure and to the Russian formalists of the 1920s. In an effort to analyse the operations of literary discourse, these critics often resort to linguistic models. One of their major concerns is to elaborate a poetics which could be used as a theoretical basis for individual studies. At the same time, they stress that criticism cannot provide an exhaustive interpretation of its subject, and that its proper function is to reveal the mechanisms whereby the almost infinite possibilities of meaning in a text are created. In this, all aspects of the *nouvelle critique* have their part to play: any angle of approach to literature is regarded as valid, provided it is coherent and states its premisses.

The *nouvelle critique* was the subject of a heated literary dispute in the mid-60s, when the academic critic Raymond Picard (1917–   ), an authority on Racine, launched an attack on it (provoked by Barthes's *Sur Racine*) in the pamphlet *Nouvelle Critique, ou Nouvelle Imposture* (1965). Barthes replied in *Critique et vérité* and was supported by Serge Doubrovsky (1928–   ) in his *Pourquoi la Nouvelle Critique?* (1966). This 'querelle' served to identify even more precisely the differences between the various approaches.

Critique (1946–   ; monthly), a literary review f. by G. Bataille. It covers both French and foreign publications.

Critique de la raison dialectique, v. *Sartre*.

Critique de l'École des femmes, La, a one-act prose comedy, produced 1663, in which Molière ridiculed the critics of his *L'*École des femmes* by staging a conversation in which it is attacked (by the envious dramatist Lysidas, the prudish *précieuse* Climène, etc.) and defended. The main defence is that it has given pleasure; if it infringes the rules, then the rules must be bad. v. *Impromptu de Versailles, L'*.

Critique philosophique, La, v. *Renouvier*.

Critiques et Portraits littéraires (1832, 1 vol.; 1836–9, 5 vols.), by Sainte-Beuve, collections of critical and biographical studies written during the first part of his career as a professional critic (i.e. before the *Causeries du lundi*), and mostly first published in Le *Globe*, La *Revue de Paris*, La *Revue des Deux Mondes*, Le *National*, Le *Journal des Débats*. He revised and augmented them more than once and (from 1844) divided them into the three well-known groups of *Portraits littéraires*, *Portraits de femmes*, and *Portraits contemporains*.

Criton, v. *Maurras*.

Croche, Monsieur, v. *Debussy*.

Croisset, v. *Flaubert*.

Croisset, Francis de, *pseudonym of* FRANTZ WIENER (1877–1937), of Belgian origin, author of successful comedies, e.g. *Le Bonheur, Mesdames* (1906), *Les Vignes du Seigneur* and *Les Nouveaux Messieurs* (1923 and 1926; in collaboration with Flers); and travel sketches, e.g. *La Féerie cinghalaise* (1926), *Nous avons fait un beau voyage* (1930).

Croix-de-Feu, Les, an organization of ex-soldiers holding the *croix de guerre*, f. 1927 and led by Colonel de La Rocque (1886–1946), which soon opened its ranks to civilians (inc. women and young people), began to agitate for social reform, and became increasingly nationalistic, anti-parliamentarian, and militarized. It was often involved in street riots (e.g. in Feb. 1934; v. *Stavisky*) and by 1935 had a membership of 260,000. It was dissolved as a political body in 1936 by the government of the *Front populaire*.

Cromedeyre-le-vieil, v. *Romains*.

Cromwell (1827), a long verse drama by Hugo, based on the life of the Protector. It was not produced in Hugo's lifetime, but his preface, a plea for 'la liberté de l'art contre le despotisme des systèmes, des codes, et des règles', became the prime manifesto of *Romanticism*. He there maintains that the aesthetic conventions governing choice and treatment of subject have hitherto prevented the drama from being a true representation of life and should be discarded. Beauty can exist only if there is ugliness to throw it into relief; the sublime entails the grotesque, and true art must be free to take account of life's contrasts, to choose not necessarily the beautiful, but the characteristic. Language should be freed from the shackles of poetic diction. The unities of time and place should be abolished. Action should take place on the stage instead of being narrated, and, to emphasize the importance of this innovation, historical truth should be respected. He ends with a plea for more objectivity in criticism.

Croque-mitaine, a legendary monster or ogre invoked to frighten children.

Cros, CHARLES (1842–88), was known in youthful *Symbolist circles as leader of the *Zutistes* and for his monologues (a form he is said to have created), e.g. *Le Hareng saur, Le Bilboquet*. His lyrics, prose poems, and *rondes* (in *Le Coffret de santal*, 1873; *Le Fleuve*, 1875) are still mentioned. He was also a pioneer of colour photography and the phonograph.

Crouzet, FRANÇOIS (1922–   ), historian, an authority on British economic history; professor at *Paris IV* from 1969. His works include *L'Économie du Common-wealth* (1950), *L'Économie britannique et le Blocus continental* (1958), an intro-duction to *Capital Formation in the Indus-trial Revolution* (1972).

Crusades. The Crusades inspired a number of medieval works, in both verse and prose, ranging from historical records of varying degrees of accuracy to pure fantasy. These include: *1st Crusade* (1096–9)—the group of poems forming what is known as the Crusade cycle (*v. Antioche*; *Chevalier au cygne*; *Baudouin de Sebourg*); *3rd Crusade* (1188–92)—*v. Ambroise*; *4th Crusade* (1202–4)—*Villehardouin's Conquête de Constantinople*; a prose account of the expedition, at times vivid and interesting, by Robert de Clari, a Picard who had taken part in it; the *Chronique d'Ernoul*, a history of the kingdom of Jerusalem down to 1229 (brief for the early period, fuller from 1183, when the author records events he has witnessed), written from the standpoint of the Christians settled in Syria, who viewed the successive Crusades with a critical eye; *7th Crusade* (1248–54)—*Joinville's Histoire de Saint Louis*; a letter on the beginning of the expedition by one Jean Sarrazin, with an anonymous continuation giving a clearer account of events than Joinville's work. *v.* also *Terre Sainte*, *Livre de la*; *Gesta Dei per Francos*; *Henri de Valenciennes*; *Morée*; *Philippe de Novare*.
  For the Albigensian Crusade *v.* *Albigeois*.

Cry, a solemn proclamation, at crossroads and in public places, of the forthcoming performance of a *mystère*, e.g. a *cry* of December 1540 for a performance of the *Actes des Apôtres* by the *Confrérie de la Passion*.

Cubism, Cubist, a 20th-c. movement seeking to apply to literature the aims of Cubism in art (*cf. Picasso*), i.e. to present several aspects of an object simultaneously, as well as every image associated with it at the moment of writing, and to seize the disordered, often distorted, cinematographic effect of

perceptions imprinting themselves on the brain. Surprise, an essential element, is emphasized by making the word-associations those of sound and suggestion, rather than sense. Some extreme Cubist poems combine the use of words as intellectual symbols with pictorial, emblematic typography, e.g. *Apollinaire's *Il pleut* and Jacob's *Poème en forme de demi-lune* (in *Le Cornet à dés*). The poets most representative of Cubism in its heyday were Apollinaire, Cendrars, Fargue, Jacob, Reverdy, Salmon.

Cujas, JACQUES (1522–90), a famous juristconsult, wrote commentaries on Justinian. There was a long quarrel between him and Bodin.

Culture des idées, La, *v. Gourmont*.

Cunégonde, in Voltaire's *Candide*.

Curé de Tours, Le (1832; later in *La *Comédie humaine*, *Scènes de la vie de province*), by Balzac; a study of clerical life, set in Tours in 1826. The genial but tactless abbé Birotteau offends his landlady, and is so malevolently per-secuted by her and a jealous fellow-lodger, the abbé Troubert, that his health and career are wrecked.

Curé de village, Le (1839; later in *La *Comédie humaine*, *Scènes de la vie de campagne*), a novel by Balzac. The period is the July Monarchy. The abbé Bonnet (the 'curé') has reformed his poverty-stricken and formerly lawless flock at Montégnac, near Limoges. The plot, which is almost like that of a detective story, turns on two murders and a theft committed at Limoges by Jean Tascheron, a Montégnac artisan of good character. He is caught and executed, but his motive remains a mystery. The riddle is solved by the death-bed confession of the owner and revered benefactress of Montégnac, Mme Graslin, rich widow of a Limoges banker, who, encouraged by the abbé, has provided a modern system of irrigation and brought prosperity to her village. This novel is a fine example of Balzac's grasp of technical and financial detail, and of his gift for making it interesting.

Curée, La, v. *Barbier, Auguste*.

Curée, La (1872), a key novel in Zola's *Rougon-Macquart* cycle. Aristide Rougon (brother of Eugène in *Son Excellence Eugène Rougon*), known as Aristide Saccard, makes a fortune in Paris as a shady building speculator. His wife dies, and his young children (Maxime and Clotilde) are sent to relatives at Plassans. He remarries for money and position, and the plot now becomes complicated, with heavy descriptions of vice, seductions, and the frenzied luxury of Second Empire society. The bored, dissipated young wife Renée flirts with, and finally seduces, the vicious, precocious Maxime (who has returned home). Maxime makes a marriage arranged by Aristide, who, mindful of his social position and precarious finances, chooses to ignore what is going on. The distraught Renée finally dies.

Curel, FRANÇOIS DE (1854–1928), dramatist, made his name with *L'Envers d'une sainte* (an embittered woman imperils the happiness of others and finally takes refuge from herself in a convent) and *Les Fossiles* (a family of decayed nobility are so proud that they cover up a scandal rather than let their name die out), both produced in 1892 at the *Théâtre Libre*. His other plays include *L'Invitée* (1893), *Le Repas du lion* (1897), *La Nouvelle Idole* (1899), *La Fille sauvage* (1902), *La Danse devant le miroir* (1914), *L'Âme en folie* (1920). v. *Theatre of the 19th and 20th cs*.

Curie, PIERRE (1859–1906), and his wife MARIE SKLODOWSKA (1867–1934; of Polish origin), physicists famous for their discovery of radium. Marie succeeded her husband as professor of physics at the *Sorbonne*—the first woman to hold such a high academic post.

Curieux impertinent, Le, v. *Destouches*.

Curiosités esthétiques, v. *Baudelaire*.

Curtis, JEAN-LOUIS (1917–), novelist and essayist, originally a teacher of English. His works, marked by humour and irony and little influenced by current literary trends, include the novels *Les Forêts de la nuit* (1947), a dispassionate chronicle of the *Resistance in the Basque country; *Chers Corbeaux* (1951), depicting the literary and student world of Saint-Germain-des-Prés, in Paris, where the young are easily exploited; *La Parade* (1960); *Un Jeune Couple* (1967), etc.; *Le Thé sous les cyprès* (1969), tales; critical studies and *pastiches*, e.g. *Haute École* (1950), *A la recherche du temps posthume* (1957), *La Chine m'inquiète* (1971; amusing *pastiches* of writers from Proust and Claudel to S. de Beauvoir and N. Sarraute, the theme being the rising of May 1968); *La Quarantaine* (1966), a personal stock-taking. He also writes for radio and television.

Custine, ASTOLPHE, MARQUIS DE (1790–1857), remembered as the author of *La Russie en 1839* (1843, 4 vols.), a lively and informative picture of Tsarist Russia (inc. scandalous anecdotes about the morals of the court and high society at St. Petersburg). He also published *Mémoires et voyages, ou Lettres écrites à diverses époques pendant des courses en Suisse, en Calabre, en Angleterre, et en Écosse* (1830, 2 vols.). His homosexual tendencies occasioned much scandal.

Cuvier, GEORGES (1769–1832), a pioneer in the fields of zoology and palaeontology, famous for his *Leçons d'anatomie comparée* (1800–5; collected lectures delivered at the *Jardin des Plantes*) and *Discours sur les révolutions du globe* (the preface to his *Recherches sur les ossements fossiles*, 1821–4). His *Le Règne animal distribué d'après son organisation* (1816) was an important work of zoological classification. He opposed Lamarck and *Geoffroy Saint-Hilaire. v. *Salon*, 1.

Cuvier, La Farce du, v. *Farce*.

Cycle, a group of narrative poems relating the exploits of a central heroic figure, and/or stories of his boyhood (*enfances*), ancestors, descendants, companions. Such are the three main cycles of **chansons de geste* devoted to **Charlemagne, *Garin de Monglane*, and **Doon de Mayence*, and the subordinate cycle of **Garin le Loherain*; also the Crusade cycle (*v. Antioche*; *Chevalier au cygne*; *Baudouin de Sebourg*). The term is also loosely applied to groups of poems on more diverse subjects, but akin in background and tradition; *v. Romans bretons*; *Romans d'antiquité. v.* also *Roman-cycle*.

Cymbalum mundi, *v. Des Périers*.

Cyrano de Bergerac, SAVINIEN (1619–55), author, **libertin*, soldier, and duellist; a studious, imaginative man of grotesque appearance, famous for his long nose. He was a Parisian, Bergerac being the name of a family estate near Paris. He wrote *Le Pédant joué* (1654), a comedy (*v. Fourberies de Scapin, Les*); *La Mort d'Agrippine* (1653), a tragedy reflecting the free-thinking tendencies of the day; the *Histoire comique des états et empires de la Lune* and *Histoire comique des états et empires du Soleil* (1656 and 1661), fantastic romances in which the author visits the moon and the sun and describes their inhabitants and institutions—the occasion for social and political satire.

Cyrano de Bergerac (1897), by E. Rostand, a highly successful cloak-and-dagger drama (in verse).

When Cyrano (based on the historic Cyrano de Bergerac, but here depicted as a Gascon knight) learns that Roxane, whom he loves, is in love with Christian de Neuvillette, he reveals the noble heart beneath his comic exterior by heroically aiding his rival. He writes Christian's love-letters, is even at hand beneath the balcony to prompt him as he woos the lady. Then Christian is killed in battle, and for 15 years Cyrano helps Roxane to keep his memory green, revealing his own love and selfless role only when on the point of death. The whole provides vivid pictures of life in 17th-c. Paris, e.g. a noisy, bustling evening at the theatre (*v. Montfleury*).

D

Dabit, EUGÈNE (1898–1936), a locksmith turned novelist whose most successful work—*Hôtel du Nord* (1930; later a film, starring Jouvet), about life in a small hotel in a poor district of Paris—was hailed as a fine *roman populiste* (*v. Novel*, 3). He left a *Journal intime* (*1928–36*).

Dacier, ANDRÉ (1651–1722) and his wife ANNE LEFEBVRE (*c.* 1654–1720), learned editors and translators of the classics, both involved on the side of the ancients in the **Querelle des anciens et des modernes*. Dacier's work on Horace is mentioned in Congreve's *The Double Dealer*. Mme Dacier's chief works were translations of the *Iliad* (1711) and the *Odyssey* (1716). Houdar de la Motte based his travestied *Iliad* on her version, provoking her to defend the classical text, and so reviving the *Querelle*.

Dacquin, JEANNE-FRANÇOISE ('JENNY') (1811–95), daughter of a Boulogne *notaire*, the 'inconnue' to whom Mérimée wrote almost daily from 1831 till his death in 1870 (*Lettres à une inconnue*, 1873). The correspondence began when she wrote to him in English (she was long a companion in an English family, but later inherited money and lived in Paris) to ask for an autograph, calling herself 'Lady Algernon Seymour'. He afterwards learnt her true identity, but they rarely met.

Dadaism, Dadaist, a short-lived movement—largely, but not wholly, French—in literature and art. It preceded **Surrealism, stressed the importance of instinctive expression, independent of control by the intelligence, and was characterized by incoherence and a destructive spirit ('Dada détruit et se borne à cela'). Words could have a purely fortuitous significance: the name *Dada* (properly 'hobby-horse') is said to have been chosen at random and, for Dadaists, meant nothing at all. The movement began during the 1914–18 war (*c.* 1916) among refugee writers and artists who had drifted to Zürich (notably Tzara, the Alsatian artist and poet Hans Arp, and the German poet and pacifist Hugo Ball) and were joined by a similar group from New York, led by Marcel Duchamp and Francis Picabia. Dadaist reviews and anthologies of the years 1916–19 included *Le Cabaret Voltaire* and *Dada*. In 1920, following the arrival there of Tzara, Paris became the headquarters of Dadaism and the review *Littérature* (1st ser., 1919–21; *cf. Surrealism*) its organ. Dadaists now included Breton, Aragon, Soupault, Éluard, and Péret. A few *matinées* and festivals were held, usually ending in disorder. The movement was more or less spent by the middle of 1922, and Breton and his group moved away from Tzara.

Dadié, BERNARD, *v. Négritude*.

Dagobert, *v. Merovingians*.

Daguerre, LOUIS-JACQUES-MANDÉ (1787–1851), gave his name to the *daguerréotype*, one of the earliest photographic processes (images were fixed on silver-plated copper by use of light), on which he had worked with Joseph-Nicéphore Niepce (1765–1833)—the actual inventor of photography—from 1829 till Niepce's death in 1833. Daguerre had earlier invented the *diorama*, which produced effects of nature by a combination of lighting, scenic painting, and transparent screens.

Daguesseau, HENRI-FRANÇOIS (1668–1751), orator, moralist, an erudite magistrate of moderate views, famous for his *mercuriales* (discourses on the administration of justice, delivered at judicial assemblies on Wednesdays by the presiding magistrate). He became chancellor (1717), but failed as a politician and was twice relegated to his estates. Though unsympathetic to the *philosophes*, he granted, in his official capacity, the *privilège* for the publication of the *Encyclopédie*. He wrote *Méditations sur les vraies ou les fausses idées de justice*, a fine work reflecting his belief in a natural idea of justice, based neither on interest nor on utility; *Instructions* for the education of his son; an impressive life of his father, etc.

D'Alembert, *v. Alembert*.

Damas, LÉON-GONTRAN, *v. Négritude*.

Dame aux camélias, La (1848), a novel by Dumas *fils*, who dramatized it (1852) with great success. It is the basis of Verdi's opera *La Traviata* (1853).

Marguerite Gautier (*v. Duplessis*), a courtesan, called 'la dame aux camélias' from her passion for this flower, falls deeply in love with Armand Duval, and the two live in quiet happiness in the country. Armand's father visits her. He refuses to believe that her love is sincere and, when bribery fails, begs her to leave Armand. She yields and returns to Paris, letting Armand believe she has left him for a rich nobleman. But the sacrifice is too great, and her already consumptive condition grows rapidly worse. Armand learns the truth and hastens to Paris, where she dies in his arms.

Dame de Monsoreau, La, *v. Dumas père*.

Damiens, ROBERT-FRANÇOIS (1714–57), a fanatic executed for attempting the life of Louis XV.

Dancourt, FLORENT CARTON, SIEUR D'ANCOURT, *known as* (1661–1725), came of a good family of magistrates and financiers, studied law, but then married an actress and turned actor and playwright. His witty prose comedies realistically depict contemporary society—a *bourgeoisie* corrupted by wealth, decayed aristocrats, seedy adventurers. His style is loose and careless, but he had a strong sense of a comic situation and a gift for exploiting current topics or events (a fraudulent Paris lottery in *La Loterie*, 1697; the popularity of a restaurant in *Le Moulin de Javelle*, 1696; the refusal of the courts to acquit a woman of murdering her husband though he is still alive in *Le Mari retrouvé*, 1698). His best-known comedy is *Le *Chevalier à la mode* (1687). Others are *Le Notaire obligeant* (1685); *Les Bourgeoises à la mode* (1692; the model for Vanbrugh's *The Confederacy*) and *Les Bourgeoises de qualité* (1700), both on the theme of *bourgeoises* aping ladies of quality; *Les Agioteurs* (1710). He retired from the stage in 1718 and devoted himself to good works.

Dandin, George, in Molière's **George Dandin*.

Dandin, Perrin, the judge in Racine's *Les *Plaideurs* and La Fontaine's fable *L'Huître et les Plaideurs*. The name comes from Rabelais's Perrin Dendin (*Le Tiers Livre... du noble *Pantagruel*, ch. 41).

Dangeau, PHILIPPE, MARQUIS DE (1638–1720), an assiduous courtier whose *Journal* (for the years 1684–1714), though of no literary merit, is of chronological value as an exact, detailed record of incidents at the court of Louis XIV, literary events in so far as they interested the court, and political events as seen from its standpoint. *v. Saint-Simon, duc de.*

Danican, FRANÇOIS-ANDRÉ (1727–95), 'Philidor', composer of many operas (mainly **opéras-comiques*); also a famous chess-player.

Daniel-Rops, *pseudonym of* HENRY PETIOT (1901–65), Roman Catholic man of letters (a member of the **Académie*, 1955), author of essays (e.g. *Le Monde sans âme*, 1931) and novels (e.g. *L'Âme obscure*, 1928; *Mort, où est ta victoire?*, 1934) of religious inspiration; studies of Rimbaud, William Blake, Estaunié, Pascal, Péguy, etc. (e.g. *Où passent des anges*, 1947); and works of religious history, notably his *Histoire de l'Église du Christ* (1948–67, 10 vols.).

Danse macabre (or macabré). The idea of the ubiquity of Death the leveller, vividly expressed in the many 15th- and 16th-c. representations of the Dance of Death, is already present in such works as the *Vers de la mort* (*c.* 1195; *v. Religious Writings*, 1) and the *Dit des *trois morts et des trois vifs* (before 1280). In the 14th c., possibly as a result of the plague and the preaching of the mendicant friars, the idea took more precise form, apparently at first as a mimed sermon or liturgical drama, in which characters representing all classes of society from pope to peasant came forward in turn and were seized by the hand and hurried away by a figure representing a corpse. The first known European painting of this *danse macabre* was the fresco (1425) in the cemetery of the Innocents in Paris which inspired Villon. It was destroyed in the 17th c., but can be broadly reconstructed from such sources as the fine wood-engravings (accompanied by verse dialogues between the dead and the living) in the *Danse macabre* issued in 1485 by Guyot Marchant. These represent 30 couples, each consisting of a member of a different order of society and his corpse. The corpse (which is not, as it later became, a personification of Death in the abstract) seizes and hales off its living counterpart. Marchant's publication was so successful that he issued a second edition (1486), also a volume containing a *Danse macabre des femmes* (of less merit, and attributed to Martial d'Auvergne). Paintings of the *danse* were executed in many French churches and cloisters, and the idea underwent further development in literature and art; the German artists (e.g. Holbein) who depicted the *danse* appear to have drawn on French sources.

Danton, GEORGES-JACQUES (1759–94), Revolutionary politician and orator, president of the *Club des *Cordeliers*, headed the government formed after the fall of the monarchy (1792), and was later a member of the **Convention* (*v. Montagnards*). His views proved too moderate for the extremists of the **Terror*, and the **Tribunal révolutionnaire*, which he himself had initiated, sent him to the guillotine with Desmoulins and Fabre d'Églantine. Though he almost certainly made money out of the Revolution, he was an ardent patriot, a man of violent energy, active in organizing resistance to foreign attack. His rousing speech in the *Assemblée législative urging attack on the Prussians besieging *Verdun (Sept. 1792) contained the famous words: 'Pour les vaincre il nous faut de l'audace, encore de l'audace, toujours de l'audace, et la France est sauvée.'

Darien, Georges, pseudonym of GEORGES-HIPPOLYTE ADRIEN (1862–1921), author of novels and plays inspired by passionate libertarianism and anarchist sympathies, notably the novel Biribi (1890), an outraged and anguished account of his terrible experiences as an insubordinate young soldier condemned to serve in the brutalizing penal corps in Tunisia.

Darmesteter, (1) ARSÈNE, v. Diction-aries, 1890–1900; (2) his brother JAMES (1849–94), Orientalist and philologist, author of many studies of Persian language and literature, also of Les Prophètes d'Israël (1892).

Daru, PIERRE-ANTOINE-NOËL BRUNO, COMTE (1767–1829), a cousin of Stendhal (whose autobiographical writings often refer to him and his family) and author of many works, e.g. an Histoire de la République de Venise (1819). He was officially responsible for supplying Napoleon's armies in the field, notably in Russia.

Dash, Comtesse, pseudonym of the VICOMTESSE DE POILLOÜE DE SAINT-MARS (1804–72), an indefatigable writer (from c. 1840) of sentimental novels, popular guides to life in high society. She left gossipy Mémoires des autres (1896–7).

Dates, v. Year, Beginning of the.

Daubenton, LOUIS-JEAN-MARIE (1716–99), naturalist and anatomist, supplied numerous anatomical descriptions for *Buffon's Histoire naturelle, and also helped him to replan the Jardin du Roi (v. Jardin des Plantes). Pastilles de Daubenton,

to which he gave his name, are ipeca-cuanha lozenges.

Daudet, ALPHONSE (1840–97), novelist, b. at Nîmes, the son of a silk-merchant. After a youth very like that of Daniel in his Le *Petit Chose (games round the family warehouse; school at Lyons; an un-happy period—1855–6—as a pupil-teacher, bullied by both masters and boys), he joined his brother Ernest in Paris (1857) to try his luck as a writer. By 1861 he had published Les Amoureuses (1858; verse), had written tales and theatrical sketches, was contributing to Le *Figaro, and was private secretary to an influential minister, the duc de Morny, Napoleon III's half-brother. He had the money and leisure to write, and proceeded to make his name as a novelist.

He is now chiefly remembered for the Lettres de mon moulin (1866, in Le *Figaro; 1868, as a book), delicately sentimental, humorous sketches of Provençal life (the mill, near Arles, is now a Daudet museum); Le *Petit Chose (1868); and the unforgettable tales about *Tartarin de Tarascon. The novels which made his name have been somewhat unjustly for-gotten. For a time a leading *Naturalist (though never to the exclusion of the warm, fantasy-loving side of his charac-ter), he depicted the business, political, or social world in Fromont jeune et Risler aîné (1874), Jack (1876), Le *Nabab (1877), Les Rois en exil (1879), *Numa Roumestan (1881). His other works include the novels L'Évangéliste (1883; a painful study of re-ligious mania), *Sapho (1884), and L'Im-mortel (1888; v. Vrain-Lucas); the plays L'Arlésienne (1872; with music by Bizet) and La Dernière Idole (1889); Les Contes du lundi (1873) and Contes et récits (1873), short patriotic tales, possibly inspired by his service in the *Garde nationale during the *Franco-Prussian war; Souvenirs d'un homme de lettres (1888); Trente Ans de Paris (1888); Notes sur la vie (1899). He also wrote much of Le Parnassiculet con-temporain (1867; v. Pastiche).

Daudet, LÉON (1868–1942), son of the above, journalist, publicist, and novelist, gave up medicine (1894) for right-wing political journalism, and from 1908 was associated with *L'**Action française*, which he helped to found. His articles were amusing, often brilliant, but violent and biased. He also wrote novels; *Le Stupide XIXe Siècle* (1922), critical essays—a French equivalent of the anti-Victorian reaction in England; *Souvenirs des milieux littéraires, politiques, artistiques, et médicaux de 1890 à 1905* (1914–21).

Daumier, HONORÉ (1808–79), a famous lithographer and caricaturist, flourished during the July Monarchy and Second Empire. His caustic satires of political and legal circles, his scenes from low life, above all his cartoons of Robert *Macaire, helped to make the reputation of *Le* *Charivari, *Caricature*, and *Le* *Figaro. An early cartoon (in *Caricature*, 1832) of a king ('Gargantua') swallowing enormous budgets cost him six months in prison. His eyesight failed after 1875, and he was awarded a State pension.

Daunou, PIERRE-CLAUDE-FRANÇOIS(1761–1840), priest, historian, and *savant* (keeper of the *Archives nationales from 1804; editor-in-chief of *Le* *Journal des savants, 1816–38). He adhered to the *Constitution civile du clergé, and was prominent in Revolutionary politics. He was arrested when the *Girondins fell, but returned to public life after the *Terror, and long took a leading part in organizing important legislative, scholarly, and scientific reforms and innovations. His *Cours d'études historiques* (1842–6, 20 vols.; lectures delivered at the *Collège de France, 1819–30) stressed the importance—not then generally recognized—of method and documentation.

Dauphin, the title borne by the eldest son of the king of France from 1349 to 1830. It was originally borne by the seigneurs of the Viennois, whence the *province subject to them was called the Dauphiné. When the last seigneur of the Dauphiné ceded the province to Philippe VI (1349), he made it a condition that the title should be perpetuated as that of the king's eldest son.

The edition of the classics *ad usum Delphini* was prepared for Louis XIV's son, 'le *Grand Dauphin'.

Daurat, *v. Dorat*.

Dauzat, ALBERT, *v. Dictionaries*, 1938.

David, JACQUES-LOUIS (1748–1825), a painter famous for works depicting contemporary events and personages (e.g. *Le Serment du Jeu de Paume*; *Marat assassiné*; *Marie-Antoinette allant à l'échafaud*; *Le Sacre de l'Empereur Napoléon Ier*; *La Distribution des aigles*; the well-known *Mme Récamier*) and classical subjects (e.g. *Le Serment des Horaces*; *L'Enlèvement des Sabines*). He was court painter to Louis XVI, but soon became an ardent Revolutionary, voted for the king's death, and was a member—and briefly president—of the *Convention. He organized several of the Revolutionary *fêtes*, notably the *Fête de l'**Être Suprême. Both then and under Napoleon he exercised a quasi-dictatorship over art, demanding a return to the formal severity of classical standards. Later, however, his work was tinged with the *Romantic spirit soon to pervade French art, and Delacroix called him 'le père de la peinture moderne'.

David d'Angers, PIERRE-JEAN (1783–1856), a sculptor noted for his statues and medallions of famous contemporaries. He was in sympathy with the *Romantics.

Davout, LOUIS-NICOLAS, *v. Maréchal*.

De arte honeste amandi, *v. Amour courtois*.

Débâcle, **La** (1892), one of Zola's *Rougon-Macquart novels, chiefly interesting as a detailed, realistic study of the *Franco-Prussian war, especially the disaster of Sedan. Later the scene shifts to Paris during the *Commune. The characters are merely figures in a vast historical fresco.

Débat, *v. Dit*.

Débat du corps et de l'âme, Le, v. *Religious Writings,* 1.

Debu-Bridel, Jacques, v. *Resistance.*

Deburau, Jean (1796–1846), b. in Bohemia, a famous clown who after 1830 drew crowds to the *Théâtre des* *Funambules.* He created the modern conception of *Pierrot as at once lovelorn, ludicrous, and pathetic. His death followed a fall on the stage—a fate which may have suggested the end of E. de *Goncourt's *Les Frères Zemganno.*

Debussy, Claude (1862–1918), a composer closely associated with *Symbolism. His *Prélude à l'après-midi d'un faune* was inspired by *Mallarmé's poem; Maeterlinck's *Pelléas et Mélisande* provided the libretto for his one opera; and he set to music poems by Verlaine, H. de Régnier, Louÿs, etc.; v. also *Ys.* 'Monsieur Croche, anti-dilettante' was his mouthpiece for entertaining music criticism (collected under this title, 1921).

Décadent, Le (1886–9; weekly, later fortnightly), a literary review f. by Anatole Baju (1861–1903). Contributors included Lorrain, Renard, Tailhade, Verlaine. When short of material, the editors supplied *décadent* manifestos (v. *Esprit décadent*), abusive criticism, or verse purporting to be written by Rimbaud.

Décade philosophique, littéraire, et politique, La (1794–1807), a notable periodical, especially on the religious and literary (v. *Ginguené*) sides.

Décades, v. *Pontigny.*

Déclaration des droits de l'homme et du citoyen, La, a manifesto of the guiding principles of the *Revolution, modelled on the American Declaration of Independence, and voted (27 Aug. 1789) by the *Assemblée constituante.* It consisted of a preamble and 17 articles, from which the following extracts are drawn: '(1) Les hommes naissent et demeurent libres et égaux en droits; les distinctions sociales ne

peuvent être fondées que sur l'utilité commune...; (2) [Les] droits [naturels et imprescriptibles de l'homme] sont la liberté, la propriété, la sûreté, et la résistance à l'oppression...; (3) Le principe de toute souveraineté réside essentiellement dans la nation...; (4) La liberté consiste à pouvoir faire tout ce qui ne nuit pas à autrui...; (6) La loi est l'expression de la volonté générale...; (11) La libre communication des pensées et des opinions est un des droits les plus précieux de l'homme...' v. *La Fayette, marquis de.*

Decour, Jacques, v. *Resistance.*

Défense et illustration de la langue française, La (1549), by Du Bellay, a prose manifesto of the doctrines of the *Pléiade.*

It maintains that all languages are basically equal and that the noblest themes can be treated in the French language, if its poetry is perfected by the study and assimilation of classical models (mere translation from the classics is not enough). It advocates the invention, within discreet limits, of new words, the recovery of old words, the adoption of terms used by craftsmen, etc. It approves the alternation of *masculine and feminine rhymes, but not as rigorously binding. Above all, it asserts that the natural facility of the poet must be supplemented by labour and art.

Défenseur de la Constitution, Le (1792–3; soon renamed *Lettres de Maximilien Robespierre... à ses commettants*), a journal, or news-letter, f. by Robespierre to expound and defend his theories of the Revolution.

Deffand, v. *Du Deffand.*

Deffoux, Léon, v. *Pastiche.*

Degas, Edgar (1834–1917), painter, associated for a time with the *Impressionists. His most famous works include studies of horses and horse-racing, and pastels of ballet-dancers, all characterized by his genius for capturing movement.

Deimier, PIERRE DE (1570–1618), a mediocre poet at the court of Marguerite de Valois. His treatise *L'Académie de l'art poétique* (1610) contains theories of poetry and poetic diction very like those of his contemporary Malherbe.

Delacroix, EUGÈNE (1798–1863), founder of the *Romantic school of French painting. His *Dante et Virgile*, exhibited at the *Salon of 1822, had a dash and roughness of technique in sharp contrast to the smooth finish then conventional (*cf. Ingres*). It—and his subsequent works—aroused protest and discussion, though he eventually won ample recognition. His *Journal* (1893–5, 3 vols.) and his *Correspondance* (1936–8, 5 vols.) are of great interest, not only as a revealing picture of the artist and the circles he frequented, but also from the standpoint of painting (aesthetics and technique), literature, and music.

De la littérature considérée dans ses rapports avec les institutions sociales (1800), by Mme de Staël, a work of literary criticism which profoundly influenced her contemporaries (*cf. De l'Allemagne*).

The author reviews the literature of previous ages and other countries (Greece, Rome, Italy, Spain, the countries of N. Europe) from the standpoint (then new) that all literature reflects the society and thought of its day, and through its masterpieces influences human progress. She then turns to the France of her own day, and finds its literature torn between formal traditions derived from pagan antiquity, and the philosophical, more imaginative spirit that dates from the rise of Christianity and the influence of the Northern races. (Her comparison of her own age with the decadent Roman Empire gravely offended Napoleon.) Finally, she attempts to forecast the literature that will spring from the current ideals of liberty and equality, and ends with an enthusiastic profession of faith in the perfectibility of man.

De l'Allemagne (1810), an important work of literary criticism by Mme de Staël, first published 1813, in England, the 1810

edition having been seized on the eve of publication (because of her emphasis on the contrast between France and Germany, and her plea that the French should no longer surround themselves with a spiritual Great Wall of China). All but four copies were destroyed, the type was broken up, and the author ordered to leave France within 24 hours.

The work is in four parts: (1) *De l'Allemagne et des mœurs des Allemands*; (2) *De la littérature et des arts*; (3) *La philosophie et la morale*; (4) *La religion et l'enthousiasme*. (1) and a famous chapter in (2)—*De la poésie classique et de la poésie romantique*—return to the theme of *De la littérature*, deriving European literature from two main sources, Paganism and Christianity: pagan antiquity is responsible for the 'classical' literature of the Southern—Latin—races, with its insistence on clarity and form; Christianity and medieval chivalry for the 'romantic' literature of the Northern—Germanic—races. Form is less important than feeling, and it is into the 'romantic' literature of the North that enthusiasm, Nature, and the soul have found their way; it will thrive, because rooted in the soil. The author's studies of German poets and philosophers (e.g. Goethe, Schiller; Kant, Fichte) did much to make them known in France.

De l'amour (1822), by Stendhal, a study of 'les diverses phases de la maladie de l'âme nommée *amour*' (preface).

Love may be *l'amour-passion* (e.g. Héloïse and Abélard), *l'amour-goût* (a drawing-room amusement, played according to rules), *l'amour de vanité* (it is as important to run a love affair as to go to a good tailor), or *l'amour physique* (rough-and-tumble pleasure). In a famous passage, he compares the initial process, much the same in each case, to the process of crystallization in the salt mines of Salzburg. If a bare branch is thrown into the mine it is soon completely encrusted with tiny particles of salt: 'Ce que j'appelle cristallisation, c'est l'opération de l'esprit, qui tire de tout ce qui se présente la découverte que l'objet aimé a de nouvelles perfections.' He outlines views, advanced for his day, on marriage and the position of women, retails anecdotes of Italian society, and also comments upon morals, politics, and literature.

Delandine, ANTOINE-JOSEPH, v. *Dictionaries*, 1766.

Delaroche, HIPPOLYTE, *known* as PAUL (1797–1856), a painter noted for works depicting subjects from English and French history, e.g. *Les Enfants d'Édouard* (the Princes in the Tower), *La Mort de Jane Gray*, *Richelieu remontant le Rhône*, also incidents from the Passion. He used the smooth, solid technique from which Delacroix was the first to depart.

Delarue-Mardrus, LUCIE DELARUE, MME (1880–1945), wife of J.-C.-V. Mardrus, poetess and novelist. Her best poems (in *Par vents et marées*, 1911; *Souffles de tempête*, 1918) are inspired by her native Normandy; many of her earlier poems (in *Occidents*, 1901; *Ferveur*, 1902; *Horizons*, 1904; *La Figure de proue*, 1908) are inspired by Eastern themes or scenes. Her novels of rural life, childhood, and adolescence include *Marie fille-mère* (1908), *Le Roman des six petites filles* (1909), *Comme tout le monde* (1910), *Un Cancre* (1914).

'**De l'audace...**', v. *Danton*.

De Launay, v. *Launay*.

Delavigne, CASIMIR (1793–1843), a dramatist and poet highly popular with the public and with literary critics of the *Classical school. He is now chiefly known for his comedies, notably *L'École des vieillards* (1823), where he departed from the conventional treatment of the elderly infatuated husband as ridiculous and made him a sympathetic character. His tragedies—e.g. *Le Paria* (1819), *Les *Vêpres siciliennes* (1821), *Marino Faliero* (1829), *Louis XI* (1832), *Les Enfants d'Édouard* (i.e. the Princes in the Tower, 1833)—are interesting as transition pieces which relaxed some Classical conventions

without wholly embracing the liberty claimed by *Romantic dramatists. He wrote successful, conventional verse, of no marked poetic quality, e.g. *Les Messéniennes* (1818).

De l'esprit (1758; amplified in *De l'homme*, 1772), an ethical treatise by Helvétius; a work passed by the censorship, but then condemned by the *parlement*, and burnt.

Holding that religion has failed as the basis of morality, and that the true basis of morality and of legislation is the public interest, the interest of the greatest number (in fact, the doctrine of Utilitarianism—and Bentham acknowledged his debt to this work), Helvétius proceeds to the opinion that the interest of the individual is solely his pleasure and pain and that he is actuated only by egoistic impulses. The human mind, at birth, varies little in different individuals: progress and general happiness thus depend entirely on education, institutions, and laws. He was one of the first to conceive the idea of a moral science, for, like Condillac, he held that the effect of moral forces may be calculated in the same way as that of physical forces.

Delibes, LÉO (1836–91), composer of operas (e.g. *Lakmé*), operettas, and ballets (e.g. *Coppélia*, 1870). Many well-known writers provided him with libretti, e.g. Labiche, L. Halévy, Méry.

Délices, Les, v. *Voltaire*, 1.

Délie, objet de plus haute vertu (1544), by Scève, a long poem (449 *dizains*) on sublimated love, often obscurely symbolical, occultistic, or metaphysical, but of a beauty that anticipates the 'pure' poetry of Mallarmé and Valéry. 'Délie', an anagram of *l'idée*, may refer to Pernette du Guillet, whom Scève had long loved.

Delille, JACQUES, ABBÉ (1738–1813), a mediocre poet and a lively talker, popular in his day, wrote descriptive and didactic poems (*Les Jardins*, 1782; *L'Imagination*,

1788; *L'Homme des champs*, 1800; *Les Trois Règnes*, 1809), and translated Virgil's *Georgics* and *Aeneid* (1770 and 1804) and Milton's *Paradise Lost* (1805). He was ridiculed in *Rivarol's *Le Chou et le Navet*. The king, who suspected him of being an *Encyclopédiste*, deferred his admission to the *Académie* from 1772, when he was elected, until 1774.

De l'intelligence, v. Taine.

Déliquescences d'Adoré Floupette, Les (1885), by Beauclair and Vicaire, an amusing collection of 'poèmes décadents' parodying the *Symbolists. Some critics took it seriously at first, and it had the effect of drawing attention to the poems of Verlaine and Mallarmé.

Delisle, Léopold-Victor (1826–1910), medievalist, long head of the *Bibliothèque nationale* and compiler of *Le Cabinet des manuscrits de la Bibliothèque nationale* (1868–81, 3 vols.), an inventory and history of its manuscripts.

Delisle de Sales, Jean-Claude Izouard, *known as* (1741–1816), a *philosophe* of mediocre talent. His *Philosophie de la nature* (1770; an indifferent reproduction of current philosophical commonplaces) was condemned by the *Châtelet*, which imprisoned him and, after lengthy proceedings, sentenced him to perpetual banishment on absurdly inadequate grounds; the sentence was quashed by the *parlement*.

Delorme, Joseph, v. *Vie, poésies et pensées de Joseph Delorme*; *Cénacles*.

Delorme, Marion (c. 1611–50), a famous courtesan of the time of Louis XIII. She was the mistress of Cinq-Mars, and her admirers ranged from Richelieu, Saint-Évremond, the comte de Gramont, etc., to Des Barreaux. She figures in Hugo's *Marion de Lorme*, Vigny's *Cinq-Mars*, and Bulwer Lytton's *Richelieu*.

Delorme, Philibert (c. 1510–70), a

famous architect. He built the Château de Saint-Maur (for Jean du Bellay) and the Château d'Anet (for Diane de Poitiers), and was enriched by Henri II. His plans for the *Tuileries, prepared for Catherine de Médicis, were only in small part executed. He wrote technical works, e.g. a *Traité d'architecture*.

Delphin Classics, v. *Grand Dauphin*.

Delphine (1802), a novel in letter form by Mme de Staël.

Many mishaps and misunderstandings prevent the love between Delphine d'Abbémar, a young widow, and Léonce de Mondoville from running smoothly. The main obstacle is Delphine herself, perhaps the first 'modern woman' in French fiction, whose ideas of how women behave are not those of the conventional Léonce. He marries another, and she takes the veil. Later, when his wife dies and the Revolution releases her from her vows, they are again free to marry, but again the spiritual barriers between them prove too strong. He becomes an *émigré* and is shot. She takes poison.

Demaison, André (1893–1956), author of animal stories (e.g. the series *La Comédie animale*, beginning with *Le Livre des bêtes qu'on appelle sauvages*, 1929) and novels inspired by travel in Africa. He was in some ways a French Kipling.

Demi-Monde, Le, v. *Dumas fils*.

Démocratie en Amérique, La, v. *Tocqueville*.

Démocrite, v. *Regnard*.

Demolder, Eugène (1862–1919), one of the many Belgian authors associated actively or by sympathy with *Symbolism. He wrote novels (*La Route d'émeraude*, 1899; *Le Jardinier de la Pompadour*, 1904; *Les Patins de la reine de Hollande*, 1901) and criticism.

Denis, Mme Louise, v. *Voltaire*, 1.

Denis, St., according to Gregory of Tours, a bishop who was sent *c.* 250 to convert the Parisians, and suffered martyrdom. According to tradition, he and two companions were beheaded on *Montmartre, and there is a legend that he then carried his head to his grave at *Saint-Denis.

Département. By a decree of 1790 the *Assemblée constituante* divided France into 83 *départements* for administrative purposes (civil, religious, military, electoral). They were named after their geographical features (Hautes-Pyrénées, Seine-et-Marne, etc.), and their size was determined by the desire to make the *chef-lieu* ('county town') accessible from any part within a day. In general, care was taken to respect the boundaries of the former *provinces.* Following the loss of Algeria (1962) and the creation (1964) of seven new *départements* (replacing Seine and Seine-et-Oise), Metropolitan France (inc. Corsica) now comprises 95 *départements*; *v.* Map. There are four *départements d'outre-mer* (Guadeloupe, Martinique, Guyane, Réunion).

Each *département* has its *préfet* (assisted by an elected *conseil général*) and is divided into *arrondissements*, *cantons*, and *communes*. *Arrondissements* and *cantons* are, broadly speaking, administrative and electoral subdivisions. The basic territorial unit for local government purposes is the *commune*, which may be large or small, rural or urban, and has a *maire*, elected by, and (with some reservations) responsible to, a *conseil municipal*. Paris is an exception; *v. Maire de Paris.*

D'Épinay, *v. Épinay.*

Dépit amoureux, Le, a 5-act verse comedy by Molière; produced 1656.
Éraste loves Lucile, and shows his rival, Valère, an encouraging letter she has sent him. Valère laughs, believing that he has himself been secretly married to her the previous night. In fact, he has been tricked into marrying her sister Ascagne, who from childhood has been disguised and passed off as a boy, in order to retain an inheritance which would otherwise pass to Valère's family. The marriage, to which Valère is readily reconciled, solves this problem. But meanwhile the misunderstanding has estranged Lucile and Éraste, and there is a charming scene where they renounce their vows and return gifts, only to find they are still in love. There are also amusing scenes involving the young men's valets, Lucile's maid, and a pedant, Métaphraste. (The play consists of two distinct elements. Only the scenes relating to the quarrel and reconciliation of the lovers, which are of Molière's own invention, are normally staged. The rest is a rather laboured imbroglio imitated from the Italian.)

Dépôt légal, *v. Bibliothèque nationale.*

Député, from 1789 an elected member of various national assemblies (the *Assemblée nationale*, *Assemblée constituante*, *Assemblée législative*, and *Convention*; and *v. Directoire*; *Consulat*); from 1814 (*v. Charte*) a member, directly elected (by universal male and female suffrage since 1946), of the lower house of the legislature, variously called the *Chambre des Députés* (1814–48; 1875–1940), the *Corps législatif* (1852–70), or the *Assemblée nationale* (since 1946). *v. Republics*; *Palais-Bourbon*; *cf. Sénat*; *Conseil de la République.*

Député d'Arcis, Le, *v. Comédie humaine, La* (*Scènes de la vie politique*).

Déracinés, Les (1897), by Barrès, pt. I of *Le Roman de l'énergie nationale.*
Seven young Lorrainers, deeply influenced during their last school-year at Nancy by their professor, M. Bouteiller, who expounds Kant's philosophy of pure reason, go to Paris, the only place to make a career. They soon find themselves adrift, for they lack the necessary cultural and spiritual roots. Disillusionment follows, and they react in divers ways. The book is ideological at the expense of plot and character, and calls for knowledge of the

politics of the Third *Republic; but it is a revealing study of the intellectual climate of this generation. Notable passages include the imaginary conversation between Roemerspacher, one of the seven, and Taine; the reunion of the seven at Napoleon's tomb; the description of Hugo's funeral. v. Senghor.

Derème, Tristan, *pseudonym of* PHILIPPE HUC (1889–1942), **fantaisiste* poet, author of *La Flûte fleurie* (1913), *La Verdure dorée* (1922), *L'Enlèvement sans clair de lune* (1924), *Poèmes des colombes* (1929), etc. He experimented freely with rhyme and metre.

Dernière Bande, La, v. Beckett.

Dernier Jour d'un condamné, Le (1829), a tale by Hugo, an indictment of capital punishment and the publicity with which the death sentence was then carried out. It describes the experiences and reflections of a man under sentence of death. After some weeks in the condemned cell at the notorious **Bicêtre*, he is taken across Paris in an open cart to execution.

Déroulède, PAUL (1846–1914), author and politician, founded (1882) the **Ligue des patriotes* and was later exiled for subversive activities. His patriotic verse was very popular, e.g. *Chants du soldat* (1872), *L'Hetman* (1877; a verse drama), *Le Livre de la Ligue des patriotes* (1887), *Refrains militaires* (1889).

Désaugiers, MARC-ANTOINE (1772–1827), wrote popular comedies and **vaudevilles* (*Le Mari intrigué*, 1806; *Le Valet d'emprunt*, 1807; *Les Petites Danaïdes*, 1817); also songs and light verses of the type—but not the quality—of those of Béranger, e.g. *Chansons et poésies diverses* (1808–16, 3 vols.). v. *Cadet Buteux*.

Des Autels, GUILLAUME (1529–81), a poet on the fringes of the **Pléiade* (*Le Repos de plus grand travail*, 1550; *La Suite du Repos*, 1551; *L'Amoureux Repos*, 1553); later a

champion of Catholicism, man of law, and author of court and official poems.

Des Barreaux, JACQUES VALLÉE, SIEUR (1599–1673), poet, a **libertin* and a disciple of Théophile de Viau. Much of his poetry reflects his materialism and licentiousness (some of his amatory pieces celebrate Marion Delorme). He wrote a fine sonnet of repentance, *Recours du pécheur à la bonté de Dieu.*

Desbordes-Valmore, MARCELINE (1786–1859), an actress who began to write poetry during an illness, and continued to do so, though she returned to the stage, long toured France with her actor husband, and after 1839 struggled to support their family by doing hack work for Paris publishers. She wrote some prose, but mainly gentle, unsophisticated, lyrical poems of love and childhood —*Élégies, Marie* [a prose tale], *et romances* (1819); *Élégies et poésies nouvelles* (1825); *Les Pleurs* (1833); *Pauvres Fleurs* (1839); *Bouquets et prières* (1843). Sainte-Beuve edited a collection of her poems (1842), prefacing it with a friendly, appreciative essay; and Verlaine included her in his **Poètes maudits.* v. *Lyric Poetry,* 4.

Descartes, RENÉ (1596–1650), philosopher and mathematician, b. in Touraine; his father was a magistrate, his ancestors gentry of Poitou. Educated by the Jesuits (at **La Flèche*), he served briefly in the army, travelled widely, then went into studious retreat (v. *Songe*), first in Paris, then (1629) in Holland, where he spent 20 years. But his views exposed him to persecution by the theologians, and Queen Christina invited him to Sweden (1649), where he died. His chief works were the *Discours de la méthode* (1637); the *Traité des passions de l'âme* (1649); the *Meditationes de prima philosophia,* including the *Objectiones* of various philosophers, and replies by Hobbes and Descartes (1641); the *Principia philosophiae* (1644). (The Latin works were later translated into French.) The *Discours,* written for a wide public, outlines not only his proposed *method* of philosophical inquiry, but also his general philosophical system (metaphysical, physical, physiological, and moral). Both are more fully developed in the later works, which are, moreover, supplemented by his published letters.

By his method, to which he attached supreme importance, all the sciences, being interconnected, must be studied together, and by a single process designed to distinguish what is certain from what is probable. He rejects the syllogistic method as sterile (the conclusion can contain no more than the premisses) and substitutes a progression by deduction from the most simple and absolute truths, known by intuition, to the more remote. Intuition ('a firm conception arising in a healthy mind attending only to the light of reason') may be of a simple notion or of a relation. His starting-point is the famous *Cogito, ergo sum*, 'I think, therefore I am'. From this, and the notion the mind possesses of infinity and so of perfection, he deduces that God exists, and—since He must be trusted in the interpretation (corrected by reason) of the evidence of the senses—that the material world exists. Intuition and deduction are supplemented by an analysis of the complex into the simple, by a contrary process of ascent from the simple to the complex, and by a general review to ensure that no difficulty has been overlooked. His *Discours* may thus be contrasted with Bacon's *Novum organum* (1620).

The basis of his physics is his conclusion that the essence and sole primary quality of material objects is their extension. Extension or space being capable of quantitative mathematical expression, he arrived at a purely mathematical conception of the universe. He explained its mechanical arrangement by his famous theory of *tourbillons* or vortices, innumerable whirlpools of material particles, varying in size and rotating at different speeds, and affording, in his view, the only possible basis for motion in a closely packed universe. The animal body he regards as no more than a piece of mechanism; but the human body is in relation with a spiritual soul, capable of thought and will (though he advanced no satisfactory explanation of this relationship). The doctrine of free will, which he upheld, coupled with the intuitive knowledge of God and of the immortality of the soul, forms the basis of his remarkable *Traité des passions*, where he shows how the passions, evil only in their excess, can be disciplined and their effects regulated by reason. He advanced mathematics by his development of analytical geometry, and optics by his discovery of the law of refraction; but his theory of vortices was superseded by the discoveries of Newton. His main contemporary critic was Gassendi.

Cartesianism, as his doctrine is called, was widely applauded in his own day for the rational process it inculcated. He was careful to distinguish between the realms of science and faith. Moreover, his method led him to certain conclusions consonant with Christianity (see above); and he had supporters at *Port-Royal* (A. Arnauld, Nicole) and the *Oratoire* (which produced his disciple Malebranche). For a time, therefore, the fundamental lack of harmony between his system and the Catholic faith escaped general notice. But Pascal and Bossuet perceived it. Descartes had, in fact, erected reason into a universal instrument. Applied to politics, it inspired the *Esprit des lois*; applied to religion, the *Encyclopédie*. In the literary sphere, it exalted scientific truth and encouraged order and logic, thus harmonizing with the spirit of *Classicism* (in the *Querelle des anciens et des modernes* it favoured the *modernes*). Descartes exerted a powerful general influence on European philosophy, seen in England, for example, in the works of the Cambridge Platonists and Locke, even when they differ from his conclusions. His style has been variously judged; though not free from defects, it is vigorous and precise, and he was a pioneer in the formation of scientific and philosophic language.

Descaves, LUCIEN (1861–1949), novelist, dramatist, critic; one of five authors who broke away from Zola and issued a manifesto (1887) against *Naturalism. His best novels have a background of social history, e.g. *Les Emmurés* (1894), *La Colonne* (1901), *Philémon, vieux de la vieille* (1913), depicting suburban life in Paris during the *Commune* of 1871; *L'Imagier d'Épinal* (1919; v. *Images d'Épinal*), about small tradespeople, Bonapartists, still harking back to the *légende napoléonienne*. *Sous-offs* (1889) was a controversial study of the horrors of army life in peacetime.

Deschamps (de Saint-Amand), ÉMILE (1791–1871) and his brother ANTOINE-FRANÇOIS-MARIE, *known as* ANTONY or ANTONI (1800–69), minor *Romantic poets. Émile, a founder of *La *Muse française*, was a good friend to younger writers (Hugo, Vigny). His works—translations (of *Romeo and Juliet*, 1839; *Macbeth*, 1844, etc.) and *Études françaises et étrangères* (1828; poems, with a preface on Romantic doctrines)—stimulated interest in German, Spanish, and English literature. Antony, a more feverishly Romantic character, translated Dante (1829). His mind gave way in 1834.

Deschamps, EUSTACHE MOREL, *known as* (*c.* 1346–*c.* 1406), b. in Champagne, and educated by Guillaume de Machaut (possibly his uncle). He held various offices at Charles V's court and in the provinces. He wrote many *ballades and *rondeaux*, not of the conventional type, but on a wide variety of themes (patriotic, moral, satirical), including a *ballade* in praise of Chaucer, 'grant translateur'; a long unfinished poem, the *Miroir de mariage*, a satire on women; an *Art de dictier et de faire ballades et chants royaux*, a prose treatise on versification; the *Farce de Maître Trubert et d'Antroignart*, a *farce in which a crafty lawyer finds his match in the client he intends to dupe; the *Dit des quatre offices de l'Ostel du Roy*, a *moralité* on the subject of gastronomy. His verse is often vigorous, but lacks poetic inspiration.

Desdichado, El, v. *Chimères, Les*.

Désert de l'amour, Le, v. *Mauriac*.

Désespéré, Le, v. *Bloy*.

Des Essarts, NICOLAS HERBERAY, v. *Amadis de Gaule*.

Des Esseintes, in Huysmans's *A rebours*.

Desfontaines, PIERRE-FRANÇOIS GUYOT, ABBÉ (1685–1745), left the *Jesuit Order and lived by his pen. He wrote in the *Journal des savants* (1724–7), translated *Gulliver's Travels* (1727), and conducted various literary periodicals. His *Dictionnaire néologique à l'usage des beaux esprits du siècle* (1726) made fun of the language and works of some of his contemporaries. He is now chiefly remembered for his controversies with Voltaire. v. *Argenson* (2).

Des Grieux, Chevalier, v. *Manon Lescaut*.

Deshoulières, ANTOINETTE LIGIER DE LA GARDE, MME (1638–94), a poetess whose *salon (she continued Mlle de Scudéry's 'samedis') was frequented by Corneille, Ménage, Conrart, Benserade, Fléchier, Quinault, etc., and who was the centre of the clique that attacked Racine's *Phèdre*. When her husband, an adherent of Condé, became involved in the political troubles of the day, she joined him in the Netherlands. She was ultimately ruined, and long suffered from cancer. She is known for some rather insipid pastoral idylls and eclogues preserved in anthologies, but her best verse was inspired by her misfortunes and approaching death.

Desjardins, PAUL, v. *Pontigny*.

Des Lauriers, v. *Bruscambille*.

Desmarets de Saint-Sorlin, JEAN (1596–1676), poet, a member of the original *Académie française*, an adversary of Boileau and of *Port-Royal, a familiar of *Richelieu and holder of high administrative office. He wrote the epics *Clovis, ou la France chrétienne* (1657) and

Esther (1673), and in various writings (e.g. the *Délices de l'esprit humain*, 1658, which provoked *Nicole's *Les Visionnaires*) defended national and Christian themes as fit subjects for the epic—a doctrine condemned in Boileau's *Art poétique*. His romance *Ariane* (1632) is set in Rome under Nero; and the best of his comedies, *Les Visionnaires* (1637), ridicules extravagant types in polished society, with possible allusions to Mme de *Rambouillet and her circle—Molière drew on it in *Les *Femmes savantes*.

Desmasures, Loys (*c.* 1515–74), learned secretary to the cardinal de Lorraine, was secretly converted to Protestantism (*c.* 1550), and in 1562 fled the country to escape arrest for heresy. He wrote a trilogy of religious dramas on the history of David (*Tragédies saintes*, printed 1566), an attempt to reconcile the classical model of *tragedy with the medieval *mystère*; *Bergerie spirituelle*, a *moralité*; and verse translations of the *Aeneid* and of many Psalms.

Desmoulins, CAMILLE (1760–94), a leading Revolutionary; a lawyer, who became a journalist and—following his appeal (12 July 1789) to the Parisians to rise and defy the king's armies—a popular hero; later secretary to Danton and a *Montagnard*. He founded and edited (1789–91) *Les *Révolutions de France et de Brabant* and (1793–4) *Le *Vieux Cordelier*. His *Histoire des Brissotins, ou Brissot dévoilé* (1793) helped to bring down the *Girondins*, but his protest (in *Le Vieux Cordelier*) against the excesses of the *Terror cost him his life. He was executed with Danton and Fabre d'Églantine. His *Discours de la lanterne aux Parisiens* (*v. A la lanterne*), sometimes quoted as a typical inflammatory pamphlet of the day, begins provocatively enough, but continues as an appeal for moderation.

Desnos, ROBERT (1900–45), a poet of Jewish birth who was active in the *Resistance and died in a concentration camp. In the 1920s, he was an enthusiastic *Surrealist, a leading exponent of automatic writing, and author of verse of an oneiric character. His works of this period include *Deuil pour deuil* (1924); *La Liberté, ou l'Amour* (1927), an erotic novel; *Corps et biens* (1930), poems of 1919–30, perhaps his most lasting work. He broke with Breton in 1930 and continued to perfect his poetic technique which, despite his Surrealist associations, was to a considerable degree classical in inspiration. *Choix de poèmes* (1946) contained some of his fine poems of the Resistance (first publ. under pseudonyms). Most of his poetry was later collected in *Domaine public* (1953).

Desorgues, JOSEPH-THÉODORE (1763–1808), wrote Revolutionary songs and hymns, notably an *Hymne à l'*Être Suprême* (with music by Gossec; *cf. Chénier, M.-J.*).

Des Périers, BONAVENTURE (d. by his own hand *c.* 1544), a Burgundian learned in the classics, a friend of Marot, served at the court of Marguerite de Navarre. He collaborated in the preparation of Olivetan's *Bible (1535) and *Dolet's *Commentaires de la langue latine*. His *Cymbalum mundi* (1538), a prose work directed against the Christian faith, liturgy, and discipline, consists of four satirical dialogues in the style of those of Lucian (e.g. Mercury comes to earth to have the Book of Destiny rebound, and it is stolen by rogues, who use it for their own purposes). It was suppressed by the *parlement and only one copy survived. The *Nouvelles Récréations et joyeux devis*, a work attributed to Des Périers (who probably wrote most of it, though it was enlarged by his editor, 1558, after his death), is a collection of short facetious tales (some of Italian origin), admirably told, with occasional vivid pictures of contemporary manners. He also wrote some graceful verse, and translated works of Plato, Terence, and Horace.

Desportes, PHILIPPE (1546–1606), poet, uncle of M. Régnier, enjoyed the favour of Charles IX and more especially of Henri III, who gave him rich benefices (inc. the abbacy of Tiron: he is often called 'l'abbé de Tiron'). He made generous use of his wealth and influence, which therefore aroused no enmity (except in d'Aubigné and Malherbe). Henri IV confiscated his benefices, but later restored them, and he ended his days in peaceful luxury. Though roundly condemned by Malherbe, he was a lucid yet subtle poet, a disciple of the *Pléiade (but also influenced by the contemporary Italian school), whose melodious, polished love poems, celebrating his own loves and those of his royal patrons, were marked by a new delicacy. He wrote sonnets, quatrains and sixains in *alexandrines, and some charming *chansons (e.g. the famous *Ô nuit! Jalouse nuit!*). His *Premières Œuvres* (1573) were added to in subsequent editions. His *Psaumes* (1592 and 1595), versions of the Psalms in a wide variety of metres, show more gravity and nobility of diction than those of Marot. With Ronsard, he exerted considerable influence on contemporary English poets, e.g. Spenser, Daniel, Lodge.

Despréaux, v. *Boileau*.

Desqueyroux, Thérèse, in Mauriac's *Thérèse Desqueyroux*, *La Fin de la nuit*, etc.

Des Roches, MADELEINE and her daughter CATHERINE (16th c.), poetesses and patronesses of literature whose house at Poitiers, then a literary centre, was open to all men of letters. 'La puce de Mme Des Roches'—a flea seen on Catherine's breast at an evening party in 1579—inspired a famous collection of verses in French, Latin, and other languages by such writers as Passerat, S. de Sainte-Marthe, J.-J. Scaliger, O. de Turnèbe.

Destinées, Les, v. *Vigny*.

Destouches, PHILIPPE NÉRICAULT, *known as* (1680–1754), dramatist, in youth an actor, a man with religious convictions who sought to make comedy moral, edifying, and so worthy of esteem. He served as the Regent's diplomatic agent in England (1717–23), and was admitted to the *Académie* on his return. His verse comedies—sometimes lively, but rather lacking in both comic and pathetic qualities—include *Le Curieux impertinent* (1709; Léandre, doubting his devoted Julie's constancy, induces the reluctant Damon to pay court to her, and, when Damon's feigned advances become real and successful, learns to his cost that true love implies confidence), *L'Ingrat* (1712), *L'Irrésolu* (1713), *Le Médisant* (1715), *Le Philosophe marié* (1727; a dramatization of an incident in his own life, a secret marriage contracted in England and disclosed by his indiscreet young sister-in-law), *Le *Glorieux* (1732), *Le Dissipateur* (1753; parts of this recall Shakespeare's *Timon of Athens*), *Le Tambour nocturne* (1733; adapted from Addison's *The Drummer*), *La Fausse Agnès* (1759; a posth. comedy with some amusing scenes). It was he who wrote, in *L'Obstacle imprévu*, 'Les absents ont toujours tort'.

Destutt de Tracy, ANTOINE-LOUIS-CLAUDE, v. *Idéologues*.

Des Ursins, v. *Juvénal des Ursins*.

Des Ursins, MARIE-ANNE DE LA TRÉMOILLE, PRINCESSE (c. 1642–1722), widow of the Italian Prince Orsini (whence her name), a woman of strong political sense and ambition sent by Louis XIV (1701) as companion to the young consort of his grandson Philip V of Spain. She acquired a strong influence over the royal couple, and was prominent in Spanish politics and court intrigues for nearly 13 years. Her correspondence with Mme de Maintenon at this time sheds light on both women, as well as on events of the day.

Deux décembre, Le, v. *Republics*, 2.

Deux Héritages, Les, v. *Mérimée*.

Devéria, ACHILLE (1800–57) and his brother EUGÈNE (1805–65), artists who frequented the Romantic *cénacles*. Achille, an engraver and lithographer, illustrated books by Romantic authors. Eugène, a painter (e.g. *La Naissance de Henri IV*) and lithographer, was a friend of Hugo.

Devin du village, Le, *v. Rousseau, J.-J.*

Dezobry, CHARLES-LOUIS, and **Bachelet**, THÉODORE, *v. Dictionaries*, 1857, 1862.

Diable, Île du (Devil's Island; north of Cayenne, French Guiana), used since *c.* 1854 as a convict settlement (*cf. Galères*). A law hurried through in 1895 permitted its use for political prisoners: Dreyfus was then sent there.

Diable amoureux, Le, *v. Cazotte.*

Diable au corps, Le, *v. Radiguet.*

Diable boiteux, Le (1707), a novel by Lesage; based on Guevara's *Diablo cojuelo* (1641).

Asmodée, 'le diable boiteux', is released by Don Cléophas Zambullo from a bottle in which an astrologer has imprisoned him. To divert his benefactor, he lifts the roofs off the houses of Madrid and shows him what is going on inside—the occasion for a satirical picture of contemporary Parisian society in all its perversity. There is a slender thread of romance: Asmodée contrives Don Cléophas's marriage to the beautiful Seraphina.

Diable et le bon Dieu, Le, *v. Sartre.*

Diaboliques, Les (1874), by Barbey d'Aurevilly, tales (e.g. *Le Dessous des cartes d'une partie de whist*, *Le Bonheur dans le crime*, *Le Rideau cramoisi*, *Un Dîner d'athées*) recalling the 'Satanism' of the last *Romantics; interesting as period (*c.* 1820) pieces.

Diafoirus, in Molière's *Le *Malade imaginaire*.

Dialogue des héros de romans (1713; written *c.* 1665), a Lucianesque dialogue by Boileau; a lively, telling satire of the precious, pseudo-historical, pseudo-

heroic novels (by La Calprenède, Mlle de Scudéry, etc.) in vogue in the early 17th c.

Pluto complains to Minos that the dead are not what they were: they have no common sense, and speak an affected jargon called *galanterie*, despising as *bourgeois* those who object. He cannot believe this to be true of great heroes like Cyrus and Alexander, and to see for himself has summoned a number of the illustrious dead to appear before him. They come, to his increasing wrath and the ironical amusement of Minos, a succession of precious shepherds and shepherdesses, now concerned only with *tendresse*, *galanterie*, *amitié*, and *amour*. But all ends well when Mercury arrives to explain that it was all a joke: these were 'fantômes chimériques, qui... ont eu pourtant l'audace de prendre le nom des plus grands héros de l'antiquité'.

Dialogue de Sylla et d'Eucrate, *v. Montesquieu.*

Dialogues des morts, *v. Fontenelle.*

Dialogues des morts, composés pour l'éducation d'un prince, *v. Fénelon.*

Diane de Poitiers, DUCHESSE DE VALENTINOIS (1499–1566), mistress of Henri II. *v. Delorme, P.*

Diaries, *v. Memoirs.*

Diatribe du docteur Akakia, médecin du pape (Potsdam 1752; the first two eds. were destroyed by order of Frederick the Great), a prose satire by Voltaire, ridiculing Maupertuis (then director of the Academy of Science in Berlin) in connection with the latter's dispute with the German mathematician Koenig.

There were two 16th-c. physicians, father and son, named Akakia; the father, who had changed his name, Sans-Malice, to its Greek equivalent, attended Marot.

Dictionaries and Encyclopedias. Dictionary-making in France, as elsewhere, has its origins in the glosses, glossaries, and word-lists (Latin into

French) found in medieval Latin manuscripts. The first dictionaries were, broadly speaking, of two kinds: (1) the bilingual (Latin–French) dictionary, which in time became polyglot and was then, because it aimed at being universal, often called a *catholicon* (*cf.* Calepino's *Dictionarium* under date 1502 below); (2) the exclusively French dictionary, with derivations, definitions, and equivalents of French words (i.e. the beginnings of the study of etymology and synonyms), and, in due course, examples of literary and proverbial usage and changes of meaning (the beginnings of a philosophy of grammar). At first, type (1) naturally predominated. But once French was firmly established, not only as the literary language, but also as the official language (*v. Villers-Cotterêts*), dictionaries of type (2) rapidly increased.

It is, indeed, with the 17th c. that dictionaries acquire their fascination from the standpoint of literature and become treasure-houses for the writer striving to express himself. The 17th-c. Jesuit Binet, whose lexicographical *Essay des merveilles de la nature* was intended for all who 'font profession d'éloquence' and 'faute de sçauoir le propre mot de quelquechose... vont tournoyant tout autour du pot', has an undeniable spiritual kinship with Zola, labouring over the vocabulary of *L'*Assommoir*, or with Proust. In the 17th c., too, the word *dictionnaire* takes on its wider modern meaning, and we have also what appears to be the first use of the word *encyclopédie* in a title (*v.* under 1657). By the end of the 17th c., the lines of future dictionary-making are already clear: encyclopedic on the one hand, with the field continually expanding from words to persons and things, to biography, the sciences, the arts, and all the various branches of knowledge; specialized on the other, concerned with words *qua* words, their origins, forms, and uses. With the 18th c., 'la fièvre encyclopédique', as Bremond calls it, reaches its height, notably reflected in the famous **Encyclopédie*. In the 19th c., when methods and methodology are improved and elaborated, lexicography becomes a science, encyclopedia-making almost an industry.

The following list is intended neither as a bibliographical guide, nor as a guide to the best French dictionaries: it is at most an attempt to give a bird's-eye view of the evolution of such works in France. It is almost entirely confined to works by Frenchmen and, in the case of dictionaries, to those concerned solely, or partly, with French. Titles (of 1st eds. unless otherwise stated) are nearly all given in full, the better to convey the content and purpose of the work.

1502 *Dictionarium ex optimis quibusquam authoribus studiose collectum...* (Reggio; continually rev., augm., repr.; first printed in Paris in 1514), the life-work of Ambrosius Calepinus (Ambrogio Calepino, 1435–1511), an Italian Augustinian, one of the first great European lexicographers. This was the dictionary most often used in the 16th c. Originally a Latin dictionary, it became a polyglot dictionary of 11 languages. From this work French derives the word *calepin*, 'note-book'.

1539 *Dictionaire françois-latin, autrement dict les mots françois, avec les manières d'user d'iceulx, tournez en latin* (many rev. and augm. eds.), by R. Estienne. This first dictionary of French, or of French and another language, to be printed was a reversal of his *Dictionarium latinogallicum* (1538), in that the French words were now listed alphabetically, with French and Latin definitions. His *Dictionariolum puerorum* (1542) was much the same work.

c. **1550** *Les Mots propres de marine, venerie, et faulconnerie*, by Aimar de Ranconnet (1498–1559); printed in Nicot's *Thrésor...* (*v.* 1666).

1553 *Dictionarium historicum ac poeticum, omnia gentium, hominum, locorum, fluminum ac montium antiqua recentioraque, ad sacras ac prophanas historias poetarumque fabulas intelligendas necessaria, vocabula ... complectens*, by C. Estienne. Though said to have been mediocre, this work was continually read and augmented, and was the basis of later biographical, historical, and geographical dictionaries.

1572 *Dictionnaire des rymes françoises de feu M. Jehan Le Fèvre*, by Jean Lefèvre, canon of Langres; a work better known in the 1587 edition below.

1587 (also **1588**) *Dictionnaire des rymes françoises premièrement composé par J. Le Fèvre..., depuis augmenté, corrigé, et mis en bon ordre par le seigneur des Accords* [i.e. Tabourot, nephew of Lefèvre].

1596 *Le Dictionnaire des rimes françoises selon l'ordre des lettres de l'alphabeth, auquel deux traités sont ajoutez: l'un, des conjugaisons françoises, l'autre, de l'orthographe françoise, plus un amas d'épithètes recueilli des œuvres de Guillaume de Salluste, seigneur Du Bartas*, by Odet de La Noue.

1606 *Thrésor de la langue françoyse tant ancienne que moderne; auquel entre autres choses, sont les mots propres de marine, vénerie, et faulconnerie, cy devant ramassez par Aimar de Ranconnet, suivi d'une grammaire françoise et latine... et d'un Recueil des vieux proverbes de la France*, by Jean Nicot (1530–1600), scholar and diplomat. This work, described by a modern scholar as 'véritablement le premier dictionnaire français', long remained a main source of subsequent dictionaries. Nicot has another title to fame: he gave his name to tobacco (*Nicotiana*).

1611 *A Dictionarie of the French and English Tongues* (London), by Randle Cotgrave (d. 1634?), a scholar of St. John's College, Cambridge. This was by far the best French–English dictionary to date. It gave genders, grammatical rules, illustrative phrases, and explanations of the origins of expressions. It remains valuable as a guide to contemporary usage.

1635 *Invantaire des deus langues françoise et latine assorti des plus utiles curiositez de l'un et de l'autre idiome*, by Philibert Monet (1566–1643), a Jesuit scholar. Here the words were *defined* in French, sometimes at length, before the Latin equivalents were given.

1640 *Curiositez françoises pour servir de supplément aux dictionnaires, ou Recueil de plusieurs belles propriétez, avec une infinité de proverbes et quolibets, pour l'explication de toutes sortes de livres*, by Antoine Oudin (d. 1653); probably the earliest slang dictionary. Oudin, a court interpreter and Italian master to Louis XIV, also compiled grammars and a Spanish–French dictionary.

1643 *Dictionnaire théologique, historique, poétique, cosmographique, et chronologique*, by Juigné Broissinière, sieur de Mollières. Like C. Estienne (*v.* 1553), on whom he drew freely, he was a very popular step on the way to Moreri (*v.* 1674).

1650 *Les Origines de la langue françoise* (called *Dictionnaire étymologique, ou les Origines...* from the 2nd ed., 1694), by Ménage. This notable work, the first properly etymological dictionary (and, despite many errors, a basis for future compilations), may be said to have inaugurated the study of comparative philology. *v.* 1655.

1655 *Trésor des recherches et antiquitez gauloises et françoises* (included, as the *Dictionnaire des termes du vieux françois, ou Trésor...*, in the rev. and augm. 1750 ed. of Ménage, *v.* 1650), by Pierre Borel (*c.* 1620–89), a physician and antiquarian who made a study of *patois*; a dictionary of obsolete Old French words, with illustrative quotations, and a preface on the development of French.

1657 *L'Encyclopédie des beaux esprits, contenant les moyens de parvenir à la connaissance des belles sciences*, by 'le sieur Saunier'; apparently the first use of the word *encyclopédie* in a title.

1660 *Le Grand Dictionnaire des Prétieuses, ou la Clef de la langue des ruelles*, by Somaize. This lists 700 *précieuses*, giving their principal maxims and examples of their writings and locutions. Doubt has been cast on its accuracy.

1674 *Le Grand Dictionnaire historique, ou le Mélange curieux de l'histoire sainte et profane*, the life-work of Louis Moreri (1643–80), cleric and lexicographer; the most notable of the early encyclopedic dictionaries (*cf.* C. Estienne, 1553; Broissinière, 1643). It was extensively corrected (*v. Bayle*) and augmented (1 vol. in 1674; 10 vols. in 1759, 20th ed.) by later editors, and remains of value.

1677 *A New Dictionary French and English, with Another English and French, According to the present Use of the French* (London), by Guy Miege (1644–*c.* 1718), diplomat and grammarian. This includes a 'Collection of Barbarous French', a list of words in Cotgrave (*v.* 1611) which had since become obsolete.

1678 *Glossarium ad scriptores mediae et infimae latinitatis* (3 vols.; constantly re-ed. and augm.: the 6-vol. 1733 ed. and its 4-vol. supplement of 1766, both publ. by the Benedictines, remained the basis for later eds.; an Old French glossary was added to the 1840–50 ed.), by Du Cange. This 'monument gigantesque' (Brunot) remains the great dictionary of medieval Latin, invaluable to the student of Old French.

1680 *Dictionnaire françois, contenant les mots et les choses, plusieurs nouvelles remarques sur la langue françoise; ses expressions propres, figurées, et burlesques; la prononciation des mots les plus difficiles; le genre des noms; le régime des verbes; avec les termes les plus connus des arts et des sciences; le tout tiré de l'usage et des bons auteurs de la langue françoise* (Geneva; repr., re-ed., and variously augm. or abridged well into the 19th c.), by César-Pierre Richelet (1631–98), a barrister turned grammarian and lexicographer, and a friend of d'Ablancourt, who introduced him into literary circles. This is one of the great 17th-c. French dictionaries and is said to be the first compiled on philosophical principles. It is also one of the most entertaining to read, for Richelet, like Johnson, did not fear to be subjective: under *bain* he remarks, 'Quand les médecins ne savent plus où ils en sont ils ordonnent le bain à leurs malades'.

1685 *Dictionnaire général et curieux, contenant les principaux mots et les plus usitez en la langue françoise, leurs définitions, divisions, et étymologies, enrichies d'éloquens discours, soutenus de quelques histoires, des passages des Pères de l'Église, des autheurs et des poètes, les plus anciens et modernes, avec des démonstrations catholiques sur tous les points qui sont contestez entre ceux de l'Église romaine et les gens de la religion prétendue réformée,* by César de Rochefort (d. *c.* 1690), jurist and lexicographer.

1690 *Dictionnaire universel, contenant généralement tous les mots françois, tant vieux que modernes, et les termes de toutes les sciences et des arts...* (Rotterdam, 3 vols.; with preface by Bayle), by Furetière. This was the best dictionary to date, much more complete than that of the *Académie (*v.* 1694). The 2nd edition (The Hague, 1701, 3 vols.; rev. and augm. by H. Basnage de Beauval) was almost entirely the basis of the *Dictionnaire de Trévoux* (*v.* 1704). It was because Furetière was compiling a dictionary of his own, and presumably profiting by material amassed for the *Académie's* dictionary, that he was turned out of the *Académie*. He sued the *Académie*, but died (1688) while the case was proceeding.

1694 *Dictionnaire de l'Académie françoise* (2 vols; for its inception *v. Académie française*). This was intended as, and remains, a dictionary recording the usage of polite society (technical terms being excluded), not a philological dictionary: its chief concern is to give words acceptable from a literary standpoint, and as such it is periodically revised. There have been 8 editions to date: 1694 (grouping words by families); 1718 (from now on the order was alphabetical); 1740; 1762; 1798; 1835 (with a preface by Villemain); 1878; 1932–5 (carefully rev.); and work is proceeding on a 9th edition. The 5th edition was nearly ready for press when the Revolution broke out and the *Académie* was suppressed. The copy was preserved (*v. Morellet*) and, following a decree of the *Convention (1795), finally published—with a preface upholding the principles of the Revolution—by the *Comité de l'Instruction publique* (for the 'Moutardier edition' publ. at this time *v.* 1802). The *Complément du Dictionnaire...* (1842) contained over 100,000 special and technical terms not admitted by the *Académie*. Its *Dictionnaire historique de la langue française, comprenant l'origine, les formes diverses, les acceptions successives des mots...* (1858) did not get beyond the letter 'A'.

1694 *Dictionnaire des arts et des sciences* (2 vols.; the 1731 ed. was rev. by Fontenelle), by T. Corneille; a work sponsored by the *Académie* as a form of supplement to its own dictionary (*v.* above), which—unlike Furetière's (*v.* 1690)—did not cover this field. *v.* 1708.

1697 *Dictionnaire historique et critique, v. Bayle.*

1697 *Bibliothèque orientale, ou Dictionnaire universel, contenant généralement tout ce qui regarde la connaissance des peuples de l'Orient* (much augm. in later eds., notably that of 1777–9), by Barthélemy d'Herbelot (1625–95), Orientalist; an erudite, discursive, and vastly entertaining work.

1703 *Dictionnaire de musique, contenant une explication des termes grecs, latins, italiens, et françois les plus usitez dans la musique* (Eng. trans. 1740), by Sébastien de Brossard (1660–1730); the first French dictionary of music, much used by J.-J. Rousseau (*v.* 1768).

1704 *Dictionnaire de Trévoux,* properly the *Dictionnaire universel françois et latin contenant la signification et la définition tant des mots de l'une et de l'autre langue... que des termes propres de chaque état et de chaque profession... l'explication de tout ce que renferment les sciences et les arts* (*Trévoux, 3 vols.), compiled by the *Jesuits. The 1st edition appears to have been little more than a reprint of Furetière (*v.* 1690), but it later became an entirely independent work; the editions of 1752 (adding many new words) and 1771 (dropping many old ones) were notable. The Jesuits accused the *Encyclopédistes of using it without acknowledgement.

1708 *Dictionnaire universel géographique et historique* (3 vols.), by T. Corneille. *v.* 1694.

1709 *Dictionnaire œconomique, contenant divers moïens d'augmenter son bien et de conserver sa santé,* by the abbé Noël Chomel (*c.* 1623–1712), a rural economist.

1718 *Dictionnaire comique, satyrique, critique, burlesque, libre, et proverbial, avec une explication très fidelle de toutes les manières de parler burlesques... qui peuvent se rencontrer dans les meilleurs auteurs...* (Amsterdam), by Philibert-Joseph Le Roux (d. at Amsterdam; little else is known about him). This included the *Dictionnaire des proverbes françois avec leur explication et leur origine* (1710) of the Belgian printer and bookseller George de Backer.

1720–1 *Dictionnaire historique, critique, chronologique, géographique, et littéral de la Bible* (4 vols.), by Dom Augustin Calmet (1672–1757), a learned Benedictine. *v.* 1845–63.

1726 *Dictionnaire néologique..., v. Desfontaines.*

1726–39 *Le Grand Dictionnaire géographique et critique et historique* (The Hague, 10 vols.; often re-ed. during the next 100 years), by Antoine-Auguste Bruzen de la Martinière (1683–1749), geographer and antiquarian.

1736 *Synonymes françois, leurs significations, et le choix qu'il en faut faire pour parler avec justesse,* by the abbé Gabriel Girard (*c.* 1677–1748), grammarian and linguist; a work highly praised by Voltaire, several times re-edited and augmented (notably by *Encyclopédistes, e.g. Diderot), and incorporated in the dictionaries of Morin (*v.* 1802) and Guizot (*v.* 1809).

1748 *Dictionnaire des proverbes françois et des façons de parler comiques, burlesques, et familières,* by A.-J. Panckoucke.

1750 *Dictionnaire de l'art de vérifier les dates..., v. Art de vérifier les dates...*

1750 *Manuel lexique, ou Dictionnaire portatif des mots françois dont la signification n'est pas familière à tout le monde* (2 vols.), by the abbé Prévost.

1751–80 *L'Encyclopédie..., v. Encyclopédie.*

1752 *Dictionnaire portatif des beaux-arts, ou Abrégé de ce qui concerne* *l'architecture, la sculpture, la peinture, la gravure, la poésie, et la musique, avec... l'explication des termes et des choses qui leur appartiennent*, by Jacques Lacombe (1724–1801), advocate and bookseller. This work was a true ancestor of the modern 'Companions'. *v.* 1781–1832.

1752 *Dictionnaire historique portatif, contenant l'histoire des patriarches, des princes hébreux, des empereurs, des rois et des grands capitaines, des dieux,... des Papes, des SS. Pères, des évêques,... des historiens, poètes,... et mathématiciens, etc., avec leurs principaux ouvrages...; des femmes savantes,... et... de toutes les personnes illustres de toutes les nations du monde* (2 vols.), by the abbé Jean-Baptiste Ladvocat (1709–65), a Hebrew scholar at the *Sorbonne. This work (in turn rev., augm., and again abridged during the next 70 years) was a highly popular abridgement of Moreri (*v.* 1674), though said to be full of errors.

1754 *Dictionnaire portatif historique et littéraire des théâtres...*, by Antoine de Léris (1723–95), man of letters.

1756 *Projet d'un glossaire de l'ancienne langue françoise*, by Jean-Baptiste de la Curne de Sainte-Palaye (1697–1781), a diplomat turned scholar. He compiled a dictionary of French antiquities with a complete glossary of the variations of the language. Only the above 30-page specimen was printed in his lifetime. The rest (61 vols. of ms.) was deposited in the *Bibliothèque nationale*, proving a valuable source for later lexicographers, e.g. Littré. The whole was printed at Niort in 1875–82: *Dictionnaire historique de l'ancien langage françois, ou Glossaire de la langue françoise depuis son origine jusqu'au siècle de Louis XIV* (10 vols.). *v.* 1829.

1759–65 *Dictionnaire universel dogmatique, canonique, historique, géographique, et chronologique des sciences ecclésiastiques* (5 vols.; there were rev. and much augm. eds., notably that of 1822–7, 29 vols.), by the Dominican Charles-Louis Richard (1711–94) and others.

1762–70 *Dictionnaire géographique, historique, et politique des Gaules et de la France* (6 vols.), by the abbé Jean-Joseph d'Expilly (1719–93), traveller and geographer. This, his most popular work, stops at 'S'. He also wrote a *Description historique et géographique des Isles Britanniques...* (1759).

1764 *Dictionnaire philosophique portatif* (London), by Voltaire; a collection of short articles in alphabetical order (e.g. *Âme, Athée, Christianisme, Dieu*), consisting mainly of attacks on religious dogma and reflecting his hatred of falsehood, obscurity, and oppression. It was at once ordered to be burnt in Geneva and later (1765) condemned by the *parlement* and by Rome. Voltaire was obliged to disavow it, though he prepared further, augmented editions (latterly entitled *La Raison par alphabet*). The *Dictionnaire philosophique* in the Kehl edition includes much additional material originally unconnected with it, e.g. the *Lettres philosophiques*.

1764 *Dictionnaire raisonné universel d'histoire naturelle* (5 vols.; many later eds.), by Jacques-Christophe Valmont de Bomare (1731–1807), a naturalist who went on many scientific expeditions, later a distinguished lecturer and teacher.

1766 *Dictionnaire historique portatif, ou Histoire abrégée de tous les hommes qui se sont fait un nom* (Amsterdam; several eds., notably the 8th, 1804, with many biographies of Revolutionary figures). The 1st edition, 'par une société de gens de lettres', was largely the work of Dom Louis-Mayeul Chaudon (1737–1817), a Benedictine of Cluny (he also compiled a *Dictionnaire anti-philosophique*, 1767–9). Later editions bear the name of Antoine-Joseph Delandine (1756–1820).

1766 *Dictionnaire du vieux langage françois* (entitled *Dictionnaire de la langue romane* in a 1768 ed.), by François Lacombe (1733–95); the first complete Old French dictionary to be printed separately (but *cf.* 1650, 1655, 1756). Lacombe was also author of *Ob-*

servations sur Londres et ses environs (1780) and translations from English.

1766 *Dictionnaire portatif des arts et métiers, contenant en abrégé l'histoire, la description, et la police des arts et métiers, des fabriques, et des manufactures de France et des pays étrangers* (2 vols.), attributed to Philippe Macquer (1720–70), minor man of letters. *v.* 1773.

1766–1815 *Dictionnaire pour l'intelligence des auteurs classiques grecs et latins, tant sacrés que profanes* (37 vols.), by François Sabbathier (1732–1807). Lemprière drew freely on this work.

1767 *Dictionnaire historique des mœurs, usages, et coutumes des François* (3 vols.), by François-Alexandre Aubert de La Chesnaye des Bois (1699–1784). He also compiled dictionaries of agriculture and gardening, genealogy and heraldry, the nobility, a *Dictionnaire domestique portatif*, etc.

1768 *Dictionnaire typographique, historique, et critique des livres rares, singuliers, estimés, et recherchés* (2 vols.), by Jean-Baptiste-Louis Osmont (*c.* 1700–73), bibliographer; the first bibliographical manual to list works in alphabetical order.

1768 *Dictionnaire de musique*, by J.-J. Rousseau; an elaboration of some of his musical articles in the **Encyclopédie. v.* 1703.

1773 *Dictionnaire raisonné universel des arts et métiers...* (4 vols.; a 5-vol. 1793–1801 ed. included a technical vocabulary), by the abbé Pierre Jaubert (*c.* 1715–*c.* 1780); an elaboration of Macquer (*v.* 1766), with a similar title.

1777–83 *Dictionnaire universel des sciences morale, économique, politique, et diplomatique, ou Bibliothèque de l'homme d'état et du citoyen* (London, 30 vols.), by Jean-Baptiste-René Robinet (1735–1820), a Jesuit turned **philosophe*. He also compiled an English–French dictionary.

1781–1832 *Encyclopédie méthodique, ou par ordre de matières, par une société de gens de lettres, de savans et artistes...* (201 vols.), a rearrangement of the **Encyclopédie* by subject (i.e. vols. on *Agriculture*, *Architecture*, etc., with the

articles in alphabetical order within each). C.-J. Panckoucke, who conceived the idea, was its first editor. Lacombe (*v.* 1752) was responsible for some of the volumes.

1783 *Dictionnaire élémentaire de botanique* (rev. and improved by later editors), by the botanist Pierre Bulliard (*c.* 1742–93).

1787–8 *Dictionnaire critique de la langue française* (3 vols.), a work still of value, by the abbé Jean-François Féraud (or Ferraud; 1725–1807), who turned from the Church to philology. He also compiled a *Nouveau Dictionnaire des sciences et des arts* (1753), sometimes considered a supplement to the *Dictionnaire de l'Académie* (*v.* both entries under 1694), and a *Dictionnaire général de la langue française* (1761; several eds.).

1788–1825 *Dictionnaire d'architecture* (3 vols.), by Antoine-Chrysostome Quatremère de Quincy (1755–1849), antiquarian. This 1st edition formed the *Architecture* section of the *Encyclopédie méthodique* (*v.* 1781–1832).

1789 *Dictionnaire de grammaire et de littérature* (Liège, 6 vols.), by Marmontel and Nicolas Beauzée (1717–89), grammarian; articles from the **Encyclopédie*, including those reworked in **Marmontel's Éléments de littérature.

1792 *Dictionnaire des arts de peinture, sculpture, et gravure* (5 vols.), by Claude-Henri Watelet (1718–86), completed and published by Lévêque. Watelet, man of letters and book-illustrator, wrote on gardens in the **Encyclopédie* (he created one of the first *jardins anglais* in France).

1800 *Dictionnaire universel de la langue française* (often rev. and augm., e.g. by Nodier in 1834), by Pierre-Claude-Victoire Boiste (1765–1824). This had a treatise on grammar and spelling and a manual of Old French.

1801 *Néologie, ou Vocabulaire des mots nouveaux, à renouveler, ou pris dans des acceptions nouvelles* (2 vols.), by L.-S. Mercier.

1802 *Dictionnaire de l'Académie française. Nouvelle édition, augmentée de plus de vingt mille articles* (2 vols.), an 'unofficial' edition, issued by the Paris publisher Moutardier (who engaged Laveaux, *v.* 1818, as editor) while the **Académie* was suppressed (*v.* 1694). It occasioned disputes and legal proceedings, and was condemned.

1802 *Dictionnaire universel des synonymes de la langue française* (3 vols.), attributed to Benoît Morin (1746–1817), Paris publisher and bookseller; apparently a collation of similar earlier works (*v.* 1736). It was used by Lévizac and superseded by Guizot (*v.* 1807; 1809).

1806–9 *Dictionnaire des ouvrages anonymes et pseudonymes composés, traduits, ou publiés en français, avec les noms des auteurs, traducteurs, et éditeurs* (4 vols.). This work, still constantly used, was by the learned bibliographer Antoine-Alexandre Barbier, official librarian to Napoleon.

1807 *Dictionnaire universel des synonymes de la langue française* (London), by the abbé Jean-Pont-Victor Lacoutz de Lévizac (d. 1813, in London), a grammarian and an *émigré* who taught, edited French classics, etc., in England. This work was compiled from previous similar dictionaries (*v.* 1802).

1808 *Dictionnaire du bas-langage ou des manières de parler usitées parmi le peuple* (2 vols.), by d'Hautel, a Paris publisher and bookseller of whom little is known.

1808 *Dictionnaire raisonné des onomatopées françaises*, an early work by Nodier, who sought to show that speech had originated with imitation of the sounds of nature. He also produced an *Examen critique des dictionnaires de la langue française, ou Recherches grammaticales et littéraires sur l'orthographe... et l'étymologie des mots* (1828); and *v.* 1800.

1809 *Nouveau Dictionnaire universel des synonymes de la langue française* (2 vols.), by Guizot; a hack compilation of his early years in Paris, but the most comprehensive work of its kind to date and one which long held the field. *v.* 1736.

1818 *Dictionnaire raisonné des difficultés grammaticales et littéraires de la langue française* and

1820 *Nouveau Dictionnaire de la langue française, où l'on trouve tous les mots de la langue usuelle, les étymologies, l'explication détaillée des synonymes...* (2 vols.). These, and a dictionary of synonyms (1826), were by the lexicographer Jean-Charles Thibault de Laveaux (1749–1827), who had earlier edited the 'Moutardier edition' of the *Dictionnaire de l'Académie* (*v.* 1802).

1819 *Trésor des origines et dictionnaire grammatical raisonné de la langue française*, by Marie-Charles-Joseph de Pougens (1755–1833; said to be a natural son of the prince de Conti). This was only a specimen of a projected work. Pougens, who went blind at 24 and when ruined by the Revolution turned printer and bookseller, left voluminous notes (227 vols., 150 in the library of the **Institut de France*). These were much used by Littré; an *Archéologie française, ou Vocabulaire de mots anciens tombés en désuétude* (1821–25, 2 vols.) was also compiled from them.

1819–22 *Dictionnaire françois de la langue oratoire et poétique, suivi d'un vocabulaire de tous les mots qui appartiennent au langage vulgaire* (2 vols.; with illustrative quotations), by Joseph Planche (1762–1853), a Greek scholar, sometime librarian at the **Sorbonne*.

1821 *Dictionnaire des proverbes français*, by Pierre de La Mésangère (1761–1831); the most complete work of its kind till that of **Le Roux de Lincy*. In the course of a varied career, La Mésangère wrote books on women's clothing, and owned and edited an *Almanach des modes*.

1829 *Dictionnaire étymologique de la langue française* (2 vols.; with a dissertation on etymology by another author), by Jean-Baptiste-Bonaventure de Roquefort (1777–1834), also compiler of a *Glossaire de la langue romane* (1808; largely based on Sainte-Palaye, *v.* 1756).

1834 *Dictionnaire général et grammatical des dictionnaires français* (2 vols.), by Napoléon Landais (1803–52), grammarian and novelist. Though superseded by Larousse (v. 1866–76), this work remains useful (esp. the rev. 1853 ed. with a complementary section covering biographical and rhyming dictionaries, and dictionaries of homonyms, paronyms, and antonyms).

1838–44 *Lexique roman, ou Dictionnaire de la langue des troubadours, comparée avec les autres langues de l'Europe latine...* (6 vols.), by Raynouard. This work also contains historical and philological articles, a summary of *grammaire romane*, and an anthology of Provençal poetry. As a dictionary it was completed by Emil Levy's *Provenzalisches Supplementwörterbuch* (Leipzig 1894–1924, 8 vols.).

1838–49 *Encyclopédie catholique* (18 vols.; suppl. 3 vols. 1859). This work—covering science, literature, the arts and trades, with biographies of famous men—was an early example of the big 19th-c. encyclopedia.

1841–9 *Dictionnaire universel d'histoire naturelle* (13 vols., with 3 vols. of plates), by a team headed by Charles Dessalines d'Orbigny (1806–76), one of a noted family of naturalists.

1843–6 *Dictionnaire national, ou Grand Dictionnaire critique de la langue française, contenant pour la première fois, outre tous les mots mis en circulation par la presse et qui sont devenus une des propriétés de la parole, les noms de tous les peuples anciens et modernes...* (2 vols.; many later eds.), by Louis-Nicolas Bescherelle (1802–83), assisted by his brother Albert (Bescherelle *jeune*)—both indefatigable compilers of popular dictionaries, grammars, correspondence manuals, etc.

1845–63 *Encyclopédie théologique, ou Série de dictionnaires sur toutes les parties de la science religieuse* (50 vols.; 2nd series, 1851–9, 53 vols.; *Troisième et Dernière Encyclopédie théologique*, 1855–66, 66 vols.). Migne was general editor, and such earlier works as Dom Calmet's dictionary (v. 1720–1) and *L'*Art de vérifier les dates* were among the volumes.

1857 *Dictionnaire général de biographie et d'histoire, de mythologie, de géographie ancienne et moderne...* (2 vols.; often re-ed. in the 19th c., also suppl.), ed. by Charles-Louis Dezobry (1798–1871) and Théodore Bachelet (1820–79); a full, well-compiled biographical and historical dictionary, typical of the period, and still useful. Dezobry was a man of letters, historian, and bookseller; Bachelet was a teacher.

1857 *Dictionnaire des synonymes de la langue française* (later eds., suppl. 1865), by Pierre-Benjamin Lafaye (1809–67), professor of philosophy at Aix-en-Provence. This had an essay on the theory of synonyms.

1862 *Dictionnaire général des lettres, des beaux-arts, et des sciences morales et politiques* (2 vols.), ed. by Dezobry and Bachelet (v. 1857); a much less popular work than that of 1857.

1863–72 *Dictionnaire de la langue française*, (4 vols.; suppl. 1877; repr. 1950), by Littré; the great French dictionary of the 19th c., still an invaluable guide. It has illustrative quotations, very numerous for the post-16th-c. period.

1864 *Dictionnaire critique de biographie et d'histoire*, by Auguste Jal (1795–1873), journalist, art critic, naval historian. His *Glossaire nautique*,... (1848) also remains useful.

1866–76 *Grand Dictionnaire universel du XIXe siècle, français, historique, géographique, mythologique, bibliographique, littéraire, scientifique,...* (15 vols.; suppl. 1877–90, 2 vols.), edited and partly compiled by Pierre Larousse (1817–75), founder of the publishing firm of Larousse; the first of the famous Larousse series of dictionaries, encyclopedias, compendia, etc. These include the *Nouveau Larousse illustré* (1897–1904, 7 vols., suppl. 1907), ed. by Claude Augé (1854–1924); the *Larousse du XXe siècle* (1928–33, 6 vols.; suppl. 1953), ed. by Paul Augé; the *Grand Larousse encyclopédique* (1960–4, 10 vols.; suppl. 1968); the *Grande Encyclopédie Larousse* (1972–81, to comprise 20 vols. and suppl.; and v. 1971–8. The popular one-volume *Nouveau Petit Larousse illustré* first appeared in 1924.

1866 *Dictionnaire de la langue verte. Argots parisiens comparés*, by Alfred Delvau (1825–67), a journalist who wrote on Parisian life.

1881–1902 *Dictionnaire de l'ancienne langue française et de tous ses dialectes du IXe au XVe siècle* (10 vols., inc. 3 vols. of *complément*), by Frédéric-Eugène Godefroy (1826–97); still the standard dictionary of Old French in the wider sense (i.e. the language down to 1600), though for the earlier period (i.e. down to *c.* 1400) it will be largely superseded by the *Altfranzösisches Wörterbuch* (Berlin, then Wiesbaden, 1925– , 9 vols. to date) of Adolf Tobler and Erhard Lommatzsch.

1885–1903 *La Grande Encyclopédie. Inventaire raisonné des sciences, des lettres, et des arts* (31 vols.), ed. by a body of leading *savants* (inc. Berthelot) and men of letters; a valuable work on the lines of the *Encyclopaedia Britannica*.

1887 *Nouveau Dictionnaire classique illustré*, by Louis-Augustin-Léon Gazier (1844–1922), sometime professor of French language and literature at the *Sorbonne (and *v. Port-Royal*); said to have been the first illustrated dictionary.

1890–1900 *Dictionnaire général de la langue française du commencement du XVIIe siècle jusqu'à nos jours* (2 vols.), by Adolphe Hatzfeld (1824–1900) and Arsène Darmesteter (1846–88), succeeded by André-Antoine Thomas (1857–1935)—all eminent philologists and etymologists; a standard work.

1894 *La Langue verte. Dictionnaire d'argot et des principales locutions populaires, précédé d'une histoire de l'argot par Clément Casciani*, by Jean La Rue.

1897–1904 *Nouveau Larousse illustré*, v. 1866–76.

1922– *Französisches etymologisches Wörterbuch* (some 25 vols. to date), life-work of the Swiss scholar Walther von Wartburg (1888–1971), whose other works include *Évolution et structure de la langue française* (1934); and *v.* 1932.

1925–67 *Dictionnaire de la langue française du XVIe siècle* (7 vols.), by Edmond Huguet (1863–1947).

1928–33 *Larousse du XXe siècle, v.* 1866–76.

1932 *Dictionnaire étymologique de la langue française* (5th ed. 1968), by Oscar Bloch (1877–1937), revised and augmented by Wartburg (*v.* 1922–).

1935–62 *Encyclopédie française* (21 vols.), a work intended to present a conspectus of human knowledge in the 20th c. The first general editor was Febvre. The approach is methodic, in the Baconian sense (*cf.* the *Encyclopédie méthodique*, 1781–1832), not alphabetical.

1936–8 *Recueil général des lexiques français du moyen âge (XIIe–XVe siècle), I. Lexiques alphabétiques* (2 vols.), by Mario Roques; the first of a projected series of reprints of medieval word-lists and glossaries.

1938 *Dictionnaire étymologique de la langue française*, by Albert Dauzat (1877–1955), revised by Dauzat, J. Dubois, and H. Mitterand (1964).

1946 *Dictionnaire des synonymes de la langue française*, by René Bailly.

1950–64 *Dictionnaire alphabétique et analogique de la langue française* (6 vols.), by Paul Robert; a work combining two types of dictionary—the alphabetical, providing derivations and definitions of words, and the analogical, dealing with the association of ideas. It has been called a 'nouveau Littré'.

1951–72 *Dictionnaire des Lettres françaises* (5 vols.: II. *XVIe Siècle*, 1951; III. *XVIIe Siècle*, 1954; IV. *XVIIIe Siècle*, 1960, 2 pts.; I. *Le Moyen Âge*, 1964; V. *XIXe Siècle*, 1971–2, 2 pts.), directed by Cardinal Georges Grente, Albert Pauphilet, Mgr. Louis Pichard, and Robert Barroux.

1960–4 *Grand Larousse encyclopédique, v.* 1866–76.

1971–8 *Grand Larousse de la langue française* (7 vols.); under the direction of Louis Guilbert, René Lagane, and Georges Niobey.

1971– *Trésor de la langue française: Dictionnaire de la langue du XIXe et du XXe siècle, 1789–1960* 8 vols. publ. to date; vol. VIII, 1980, reached FUYARD, under the direction of Paul Imbs.

1972–81 *La Grande Encyclopédie Larousse*, *v.* 1866–76.

Dictionnaire des girouettes (1815), by the comte César de Proisy d'Eppes (1788–1836; man of letters), a satirical guide to contemporaries who had trimmed their convictions to the political winds. Against each name stood as many symbols of weathercocks as the times its bearer had changed his politics.

Dictionnaire des idées reçues, a collection of 'bromides', or trite remarks, compiled with relish by Flaubert over the years, and often mentioned in his letters. He had planned to include them in **Bouvard et Pécuchet*, and after his death some were printed as an appendix to it. They have also been published separately (e.g. *Dictionnaire des idées reçues*, 1951), and translated.

Dictionnaire de Trévoux, *v.* Dictionaries, 1704.

Dictionnaire philosophique portatif, by Voltaire, *v.* Dictionaries, 1764.

Diderot, DENIS (1713–84), son of a cutler of Langres, philosopher, **Encyclopédiste*, novelist, dramatist, art critic; a man of striking personality, affable, generous, loyal, bubbling over with ideas, enthusiasm, and coarse gaiety, but also violent and unbalanced.

After being educated by the **Jesuits*, he decided to embark on a literary career, supporting himself at first by teaching and other modest expedients. He also became deeply interested in natural science, which was to be the basis of his philosophy. One of his first works was a free translation (1745) of Shaftesbury's *Enquiry concerning Virtue*. In 1745, he undertook the direction of the **Encyclopédie*, a heavy burden, of which, with great courage and perseverance, he bore the main share. He now began to visit the **salons* (e.g. those of

Mmes Geoffrin and d'Épinay) and to frequent the house of d'Holbach. His philosophical writings include, notably, the *Pensées philosophiques* (1746; condemned by the **parlement*), designed as an answer to **Pascal's* *Pensées* and showing an attitude of scepticism towards religion, but not yet his later atheism; the **Lettre sur les aveugles* (1749), used as a pretext for temporarily imprisoning him (*v. Vincennes*); the *Suite de l'Apologie de l'abbé de Prades* (1752; *v. Prades*); the *Lettre sur les sourds et muets* (1759), on the development of language and questions of aesthetics; the *Pensées sur l'interprétation de la nature* (1754); the *Entretien d'un philosophe avec la maréchale de **** (1776); the *Essai sur la vie de Sénèque le philosophe* (1779); also various minor works, published posthumously, notably the *Rêve de d'Alembert* (a dialogue on materialistic philosophy, dealing unsparingly with details of human physiology, and not intended for publication) and the *Supplément au Voyage de Bougainville* (a dialogue on monogamy, based on the customs of the Tahitians; *v. Bougainville*). His other writings, apart from art criticism and plays, include *Les Bijoux indiscrets* (1748), a licentious romance, containing some serious criticism, notably of the French drama; *Les Deux Amis de Bourbonne* (1773), a simple moral tale; *La *Religieuse*, **Jacques le fataliste*, *Le *Neveu de Rameau*, and various shorter tales (e.g. *Ceci n'est pas un conte*), all published after his death; an *Éloge de Richardson* (1761), praising the novelist's insight, compassion, and sound moral teaching (the influence of which he acknowledged). The most remarkable of his letters (publ. posth.) are those to Mlle Sophie Volland, an intelligent, cultured woman, whom he loved ardently. He won the favour of Catherine II of Russia, who bought his library, left it in his hands, and paid him to act as her librarian; he visited Russia in 1773–4.

His *Salons*—the accounts of nine exhibitions of contemporary art (1759–81; *v. Salon*, 2), contributed to his close friend **Grimm's* *Correspondance littéraire*— inaugurated the *genre* of art criticism in France. They are good examples of the literary criticism of art, marked by freshness and sincerity, and written in a lively, conversational style combining descriptions of pictures, anecdotes, and digressions with vigorous judgements—though his basic principles are often fallacious and many of the works of little merit.

He wrote two prose *drames, Le Fils naturel (1757; prod. 1771) and Le Père de famille (1758; prod. 1761), mediocre sentimental dramas, written in an unnatural, inflated style, moral, edifying, and totally humourless. They were illustrations of his dramatic theory (expounded in Entretiens appended to Le Fils naturel; Dissertation sur le poème dramatique, 1758; Réflexions sur Térence; and Paradoxe sur le comédien, mainly on actors and acting) that between tragedy and comedy there is an interval to be filled by plays that are neither tragic nor comic, but serious discussions of the domestic problems of bourgeois life. His other drames, which were not acted, include Est-il bon? Est-il méchant? and an adaptation of Edward Moore's The Gamester.

As a philosopher, he was a determinist and an experimental materialist (i.e. he advocated a materialism based on the ascertained facts of natural science), anticipating in some respects later evolutionary ideas. Though opposed to traditional morality, he was an ardent moralist, holding that man is naturally inclined to virtue (which he reduced to beneficence)—is, indeed, incited to it by self-interest—but that his innocent nature has been perverted by society. The basis of morality is thus to be found in conscience, experience, and interest, which are thwarted by bad example, bad education, and bad laws. In politics he was a moderate, practical reformer, no violent revolutionary.

He is important for the wide span of his constructive conceptions, for his scientific approach to philosophical problems (here he was superior to Voltaire and J.-J. Rousseau), and for the ardour and success with which he disseminated and popularized scientific knowledge and philosophic doctrines, chiefly through the Encyclopédie. He wrote as fluently, often as coarsely, as he talked, setting down ideas as they poured from his teeming brain, without order or composition. He lacked the temperament to produce a single great work. v. Naigeon.

Didier, in Hugo's *Marion de Lorme.

Diên Biên Phu (N. Vietnam). Here, from December 1953 till May 1954, a beleaguered French garrison held out against greatly superior Vietminh forces. The fall of this stronghold in May 1954 effectively ended French involvement in Indo-China.

Dierx, LÉON (1838–1912), *Parnassien poet, b. on the *Île Bourbon (like Leconte de Lisle, by whom—as also by Baudelaire—he was strongly influenced, esp. in his often very pessimistic verse). The best of his collections (united in Œuvres complètes, 1872, augm. ed. 1888) was Les Lèvres closes (1867), containing the fine poem Lazare and other evocations of Biblical scenes. In 1898, following an inquiry conducted by La *Plume and Le *Temps, he was chosen to succeed Mallarmé as 'Prince des poètes'.

Dieu, v. Légende des siècles, La.

Dieux ont soif, Les, v. Vieux Cordelier, Le; France, A.

Dilecta, La, Balzac's name for his Egeria, Mme de Berny, said to have inspired Mme de Mortsauf in Le *Lys dans la vallée. Some 20 years his senior, she died, to his great grief, in 1836.

Dimanche, Monsieur, in Molière's *Dom Juan.

Dimanches d'un bourgeois de Paris, Les, v. Maupassant.

Dîme de pénitence, La, a late 13th-c. moral poem, of the same type as Le *Besant de Dieu, by Jean de Journi, a Picard knight who had settled in Cyprus.

Dîme royale, La, v. *Vauban.*

Dindenault, in Rabelais's **Pantagruel.*

Dîners Magny, fortnightly dinners (1862–c. 1875) at the *Restaurant Magny* (in the **Quartier latin), initiated, in an attempt to distract Gavarni, by François-Auguste Veyne (1813–75), physician and friend of many 19th-c. writers and artists. Regular *convives* included Flaubert, Gautier, Renan, Sainte-Beuve, Taine, the Russian novelist Turgenev, and the Goncourt brothers (their **Journal* has many descriptions of the company and conversation).

Diop, ALIOUNE, v. *Négritude.*

Dipsodes, in Rabelais's **Pantagruel.*

Directoire, Le, the form of government which, in accordance with the constitution of 22 August 1795, succeeded the **Convention* on 27 October 1795 and obtained until 9 November 1799 (v. *Revolutions,* 1). Two chambers, the *Conseil des Cinq-Cents* and the *Conseil des Anciens,* shared the legislative power; the executive power was exercised by a *Directoire exécutif de la République française* of five members (elected by the *Anciens* from 10 candidates proposed by the *Cinq-Cents*). The first five elected, all former *conventionnels,* included Barras. v. *Babeuf; Fructidor.*

Disciple, Le (1889), a long, heavy novel by Bourget; an indictment of positivism.

Adrien Sixte, a positivist philosopher (said to be drawn from Taine), leads a life of monastic regularity, but believes that human sensibility is of animal origin and that actions which are the inevitable outcome of natural laws cannot be classed as morally good or bad. His 'disciple', Robert Greslou, formerly tutor in the family of the marquis de Jussat and now in prison awaiting trial for the murder of the marquis's daughter Charlotte, sends Sixte a memorandum proving his innocence, but prohibits its use. He had taken a dislike to André, Charlotte's brother, a quite ordinary army officer in whom he yet sensed a certain nobility lacking in himself. To compensate for his sense of inferiority, he determined to seduce Charlotte. When he threatened suicide, she yielded on condition that after a night together they should kill themselves. When the time came Greslou recanted, but Charlotte committed suicide after warning him that she had sent a confession to André. Greslou, arrested on circumstantial evidence of murder, now refuses to clear himself, wishing to prove that he, too, can act like a 'gentilhomme'. His memorandum shows that Sixte's philosophy had provided him with authority at every stage, but, being now overwhelmed with remorse, he begs for intellectual comfort and support from his master. Sixte, appalled at being held ultimately responsible, attends the trial. At the last moment André reveals Greslou's innocence, procures his discharge, and then shoots him. Sixte, watching Greslou's mother pray over his body, wonders whether those in trouble would pray instinctively to 'Our Father...' if no heavenly Father existed.

Disciplina clericalis, v. *Castoiement d'un père à son fils.*

Discours, by J.-J. Rousseau, on two themes proposed by the *Académie de Dijon* (v. *Vincennes): Si le rétablissement des sciences et des arts a contribué à épurer les mœurs* and *L'Origine et les fondements de l'inégalité parmi les hommes.*

His *Discours sur les sciences et les arts* (1750) maintains that man, originally simple and natural, has been corrupted by the advance of art and science, which has bred suspicion, treachery, conquest, inequality, and luxury (bringing in its train cowardice and other vices).

The *Discours sur l'inégalité* (1754) is largely occupied with a description of primitive man as Rousseau pictured him. At first he lived in isolation in the forests, self-sufficient, and equal to, because independent of, his fellows. Then he gradually formed primitive societies, based on the family and its sense of mutual obligation. Thus far, he was happy and free. But with the advent of the idea of property (arising from the cultivation and enclosure of land), the natural differences between men in point of strength and intelligence led to the enrichment of some, the poverty of others, violent disorders, and the precarious tyranny of the strong, with a stifling of the primitive instinct of pity. The final stage in the evolution is that, to remedy these disorders, a constitution is set up which, on the pretence of establishing peace and justice, perpetuates the inequalities between men. Rousseau asserts that all government is founded on a contract between the people and their rulers (*cf.* his *Du contrat social*). His account of the evolution of society is quite unscientific; the importance of the work lay in its forcible denunciation of contemporary social conditions.

Discours de la lanterne, *v. Desmoulins.*

Discours de la méthode, *v. Descartes.*

Discours sur les révolutions du globe, *v. Cuvier.*

Discours sur l'histoire universelle, *v. Bossuet.*

Discours sur l'universalité de la langue française, *v. Rivarol.*

Dispute, *v. Dit.*

Distiques de Caton. The *Disticha Catonis*, a collection of gnomic Latin verses containing advice on conduct (a very popular work, used as a school-book in the Middle Ages), was translated into *Anglo-Norman in the 12th c., and into French, by Adam de Suel and others, in the 13th c.

Dit, in medieval literature, a rather vague term for a verse composition, sometimes purely descriptive (e.g. on an object and its qualities; a profession; the streets or cries of Paris), sometimes of a more didactic or moralizing nature, sometimes used as the equivalent of *fabliau. v.*

Cocagne, Dit de; *Chicheface, Dit de*; *Trois morts et des trois vifs, Dit des.*

The *débat* or *dispute* is a variety in dialogue form of the didactic *dit*, the dialogue being usually between personifications (e.g. the *Débat de l'hiver et de l'été*); some have religious themes (e.g. the *Débat du corps et de l'âme*; *v. Religious Writings*, 1). *v. Rutebeuf*; *Villon.*

Ditié d'Urbain, Le, *v. Urbain le courtois.*

Divagations, *v. Mallarmé.*

Dive Bouteille, L'Oracle de la, *v. Pantagruel.*

Divoire, FERNAND (1883–1951), *simultanéiste* poet of Belgian birth. His collections include *La Malédiction des enfants* (1910), *Orphée* (1922), *L'Homme du monde* (1926).

Dix, Les, the ten members of the *Académie Goncourt.*

Dix-huit brumaire, Le (9 Nov. 1799), *v. Napoleon*; *Revolutions*, 1.

XIXᵉ Siècle, Le (f. 1871), one of the most popular conservative dailies during the early years of the Third Republic; ed. from 1872 by About. He and his staff were all ex-pupils of the *École normale supérieure* and anti-clerical in their opinions.

Dizain, in French prosody, a stanza of 10 lines, most commonly in decasyllables, rhyming ababbccdcd.

Djinns, Les, *v. Orientales, Les.*

Docteur amoureux, Le, *v. Calonne, E. de.*

Docteur Pascal, Le, *v. Rougon-Macquart, Les.*

Doctrinaires, Les, a small but powerful party of moderate, constitutional Royalists, led by Royer-Collard and Guizot. Their policy, the translation into action of a clearly reasoned and expressed political philosophy, was to steer a middle course ('le juste milieu') between rabid monarchism and the sovereignty of the people. They wanted a constitutional monarch, and for them the people, whose voice should influence the government, signified the *bourgeoisie*. Their influence was strongest under Louis XVIII, waned under the ultra-Royalist Charles X, and had disappeared by 1848. Their chief organs were *Les *Archives philosophiques* and *La *Revue française*.

Doctrinal, *v. Rhétoriqueurs*.

Dolet, ÉTIENNE (1509–46), b. at Orleans, humanist and ardent Ciceronian; a printer of learned works, suspected of materialism if not atheism (he was probably indifferent to religious dogma); a friend of Marot and Rabelais. His chief works were his *Dialogus de imitatione Ciceroniana* (1535), defending the Ciceronian cult against Erasmus; *Commentarii linguae Latinae* (1536–8; *v. Des Périers*), discussions of Latin words, classed according to the ideas they express, a valuable contribution to scholarship; various translations from Cicero, Plato, etc. He set up as a printer at Lyons in 1538, and over the next five years issued works by Marot, Rabelais, and others. But, though devoted to literature, he was vain, quarrelsome, and given to intemperate language in controversy—failings which brought him many enemies and repeated imprisonment, and contributed to his death. In 1536 he killed a man, apparently in self-defence, and obtained the royal pardon (an occasion celebrated by a famous banquet, attended by leading figures of the *Renaissance—Budé, Marot, Rabelais). In 1542 the master printers of Lyons, whom he had antagonized, had him tried (before Mathieu Ory, Rabelais's 'notre maître Doribus') for publishing heretical books (e.g. translations of the Scriptures). He was sentenced to death, but once more pardoned by the king. Later, he was again arrested, convicted of blasphemy and other offences, and executed in the Place Maubert, Paris, where a statue commemorates him.

Dolopathos, a French verse translation, made *c.* 1222–5 by one Herbert from a Latin text, of a collection of tales, three of which are identical with tales in the *Roman des *Sept Sages*, though there are marked differences between the two works. Lucinien, son of Dolopathos, king of Sicily, is condemned to death on the accusation of his stepmother; but his execution is adjourned by the successive arrival of seven sages, who relate tales. Finally Virgil appears, denounces the queen, and effects his liberation.

Domaine public, public property preserved, administered, or exploited by, or on behalf of, the State or a local authority in the common interest, e.g. roads, rivers, museums, etc. A book is spoken of as 'tombé dans le domaine public' when the copyright expires (i.e., in the case of books published during the author's lifetime, 50 years from the year after that of his death).

Domat, JEAN (1625–96), jurist, a friend of Pascal, wrote *Les Lois civiles dans leur ordre naturel* (1694).

Dom Garcie de Navarre, ou le Prince jaloux, an unsuccessful comedy by Molière; produced 1661. (Until the 18th c. French often uses *Dom* for Spanish *Don*.)

Don Garcie loves Elvire, princess of Léon, and she him; but his incurable jealousy arouses her resentment. He finds half a torn letter in her writing, evidently to a lover; the lover proves to be himself. He sees her embracing a man, who proves to be her friend Doña Ignès in disguise. He finds her in the arms of a supposed rival, who proves to be her brother. There is a good situation in Act IV, when she offers to justify herself, but adds that, if he accepts, she will never be his. Jealousy defeats love, and he accepts. But all ends, rather weakly, in reconciliation and marriage. Molière used many of the lines in later plays, e.g. *Le *Misanthrope*.

Dominique (1863), by Fromentin, one of the few French novels of psychological analysis before *c.* 1890. It is a study, partly autobiographical and presented with a sobriety bordering on flatness, of a man (Dominique de Bray, the narrator) who has missed supreme happiness in love and in work, but has learnt to content himself with the second best.

Dom Juan, ou le Festin de pierre, a 5-act prose comedy by Molière; produced 1665. Though highly successful, it provoked violent disapproval and was suppressed within a month. *v. Corneille, T.*

Don Juan Tenorio, an insolent, unscrupulous libertine (like certain noblemen of the day), having carried off Elvire from a convent and married her, has deserted her to pursue other amorous intrigues. He is unmoved by his wife's pleas, and mocks at the protests to which his conduct moves even his valet, Sganarelle. Arriving by chance at the tomb of the Commander, a gentleman he has killed, he brazenly tells Sganarelle to invite the dead man's statue to supper: the statue bows its head in assent. Don Juan, though shaken, is soon his arrogant self again. As he sits at supper, the statue arrives, and he receives it with bold effrontery. It invites him to supper the next night. Don Juan now becomes hypocritically devout, and even more odious. The statue arrives to lead him to supper. As it takes his hand, he cries out in agony; a burning chasm opens and swallows him up.

This grim drama is relieved by a few pleasant scenes, e.g. Don Juan's interview with his creditor, M. Dimanche, whom he so overwhelms with civilities that the poor man dare not mention the debt.

Doña Sol, in Hugo's *Hernani*.

Donat, a name, especially in the Middle Ages, for the *Ars grammatica* of the 4th-c. grammarian Aelius Donatus, long a standard Latin grammar. The young *Gargantua received instruction in it.

Don Bernard de Cabrère, a good *tragicomedy by Rotrou; produced 1647. The main theme is the perverse, positively comical ill-luck that dogs Don Lope, a gallant soldier. Whenever his brave deeds

are related to the king, the latter is either preoccupied, crossed in love, or half asleep. And he is equally unfortunate in love. With him is contrasted the king's favourite, Don Bernard, for whose hand noble ladies contend. In the end, however, Don Lope's luck begins to turn.

Don César de Bazan, in Hugo's *Ruy Blas*.

Dondey, THÉOPHILE, *v. O'Neddy*.

Dongo, Fabrice del, in Stendhal's La *Chartreuse de Parme*.

Don Japhet d'Arménie, a comedy by Scarron; produced 1652, with great success.

Don Japhet, a crazy countryman whose follies have briefly diverted the emperor Charles V, has acquired an exaggerated idea of his own dignity. His self-importance and grandiloquent language, and the grotesque humiliations he suffers, provide an element of buffoonery. There is a slender thread of romance in the adventure of Don Alphonse, a young cavalier, who takes service with Don Japhet to pursue a courtship.

Donnay, MAURICE (1859–1945), playwright, began by writing comic sketches for the *Chat-Noir*. His *Lysistrata* (1893; Aristophanes modernized) was well received, but he made his name with elegant, never very profound comedies of Parisian life, notably *Amants* (1895), which turns on a *demi-mondaine*'s struggle between affection for her protector (father of her child) and love for another; also *La Douloureuse* (1897), *L'Affranchie* (1898), *L'Autre Danger* (1902), *Les Éclaireuses* (1913).

Donneau de Visé, JEAN, *v. Mercure galant*.

Don Ruy Gomez de Silva, in Hugo's *Hernani*.

Don Sanche d'Aragon, a fine, but unsuccessful, *tragicomedy by Corneille (who called it a 'comédie héroïque'); produced 1649.

Fearing that his infant son, Don Sanche, will fall into the hands of the rebels who are soon to usurp his throne, Fernand, king of Aragon, has sent him away in the care of Don Raymond, his confidant. The child has been left with the wife of a poor fisherman, together with a casket which, when he grows up, is to reveal his identity. The boy, known as Carlos, runs away at 16, joins the army of Castile, and by his great valour wins the high esteem of the king of Castile and his sister, Isabelle. This king dies, and the unmarried Isabelle becomes queen. In default of a royal suitor, she is to choose as husband one of three Castilian grandees proposed to her. About this time, the Aragonese usurpers are overthrown. Don Raymond, released from long imprisonment, at once seeks out Don Sanche. The gallant Carlos is identified and, by general consent, marries Isabelle.

Doon de Mayence, a *chanson de geste* (*c.* 11,500 *alexandrines; *v.* below for its cycle), probably, in its extant form, of the 13th c. The first half, perhaps originally a separate poem, deals with Doon's youth. His father, the comte Gui, having become a hermit, the wicked seneschal Herchembaut seeks to destroy Gui's wife and family. Doon escapes the fate designed for him, rescues his mother, and hangs the traitor. In the second half, Doon, having been slighted by Charlemagne, beards him and exacts the city of Vauclere in Saxony, then held by the Saracen king Aubigant, who is being besieged by Danes. The city is won thanks to prodigies of valour by the French, and Doon marries Aubigant's daughter Flandrine.

Doon de Mayence, Geste de, one of the cycles of *chansons de geste*. Grouped in this cycle are tales of the exploits of various rebels against royal authority, who are, as a rule, finally brought to repentance, e.g. *Doon de Mayence, *Girart de Roussillon, *Gormond et Isembard, La Chevalerie *Ogier, *Raoul de Cambrai, *Renaud de Montauban.

Dorante, a common name for characters in 17th-c. comedy, e.g. in Corneille's *Le *Menteur; Molière's *Le *Bourgeois Gentilhomme, Les *Fâcheux, La *Critique de l'École des femmes.

Dorat, CLAUDE-JOSEPH, CHEVALIER (1734–80), poet (regarded as head of a school of light poets of the day—though he repeatedly failed to gain election to the *Académie), dramatist, sometime mousquetaire, wrote lively, graceful miscellaneous verse (Epistles, inc. *Avis aux sages du siècle* which annoyed Voltaire, *Héroïdes* after the manner of Ovid, *Les Baisers, Le Mois de mai*, fables, etc.) and *La Déclamation*, a descriptive poem. The best of his indifferent plays is *Le Célibataire* (1775; comedy); *Les Prôneurs* (1777; comedy) ridiculed the intellectual *salons or bureaux d'esprit.

Dorat or **Daurat,** JEAN (1508–88), principal of the *Collège de Coqueret* and a *lecteur royal (*v. Collège de France*); sometimes classed as a member of the *Pléiade, less for his remarkable Latin verse than as the humanist who inspired Ronsard, Du Bellay, etc., with a love of the classics.

Doré, GUSTAVE (1832–83), caricaturist and book-illustrator, came to Paris (1847) as a youth, his talent having been discovered by Philipon, who gave him work on *Le *Charivari, etc. His best work as a book-illustrator (produced 1860–70) included illustrations for Rabelais, Dante, *Perrault's *Contes*, Balzac's *Contes drolatiques*, Don Quixote*, and the Bible. He was famous in England for his drawings and paintings of London life and characters. For many years works of his were on permanent exhibition at the Doré Gallery in London, opened in 1867.

Dorgelès, Roland, *pseudonym of* ROLAND LECAVELÉ (1886–1973), author of *Les Croix de bois* (1919), a successful novel of the 1914–18 war; *Le Cabaret de la Belle Femme* (1919), short stories; *Saint Magloire* (1921), a novel; travel literature; and reminiscences of Bohemian life in Paris. He was long president of the *Académie Goncourt.

Dorine, in Molière's Le *Tartuffe*.

Dorval, MARIE (1798–1849), actress, played successfully in *mélodrame* and in Dumas *père*'s *Antony*, but her greatest triumph was as Kitty Bell in *Chatterton* at the *Comédie-Française* (v. *Vigny*).

Dorvigny, v. *Janot*; *Jocrisse*.

Double Ballade, v. *Ballade*.

Double Inconstance, La, a comedy by Marivaux; produced 1723.

Silvia and Arlequin are simple country folk and faithful lovers. But the prince, in the character of a gentleman of the court, has fallen in love with Silvia (whom he has seen while hunting) and has had her brought to the palace. She is pining for Arlequin and, on the advice of Flaminia, a lady of the court, he too is brought to the palace; both are kindly treated, and their minds are set at rest. Gradually they grow fond of their new friends, till they unconsciously forget each other and fall in love with the partners designed for them, Arlequin with Flaminia, Silvia with the prince (who reveals his identity only when certain of her love).

Double Méprise, La, v. *Mérimée*.

Double Veuvage, Le, a prose and verse comedy by Dufresny; produced 1702.

The hypocritical pretence of a husband and wife that they love each other is exposed when each is induced to believe the other dead. The 'widow', in pious memory of her late husband, promptly proposes to marry his nephew; the 'widower', with equal piety, proposes to marry his late wife's niece. 'Widow' and 'widower' are confronted, ostensibly to their joy. Each, to annoy the other, now advocates the marriage of the nephew and the niece.

Doubrovsky, SERGE, v. *Critics and Criticism*, 3.

Doudan, XIMÉNÈS (1800–72), critic and *pensée*-writer, b. at Douai, studied in Paris,

then (1825) entered the *Broglie family as tutor to Alphonse Rocca (v. *Staël*), became their cherished friend and adviser, and spent the rest of his life with them at Broglie, *Coppet, and in Paris. Despite real or imaginary ill-health, he lived a tranquil, happy life, reading widely, delighting friends with his letters and conversation, and writing for reviews, notably the *Journal des Débats*. His *Mélanges et lettres* (1876–7) and *Lettres* (1879), among the most enjoyable 19th-c. letters (combining lively discussion of books, people, and events with pictures of country life—herb-collecting, walks, etc.), inspire real affection for their gentle, witty writer and shed light on the period in question (1823–72). His *Pensées et fragments, suivis des Révolutions du goût* (1881) contains an essay on the continually changing standards of beauty, a theme earlier treated by Stendhal.

Dragonnade, the billeting of dragoons or other soldiers on individuals or communities (esp. the *Huguenots, 1680–5) as a punitive measure.

Drama. For the medieval period v. *Mystère*; *Moralité*; *Miracle*; *Sotie*; *Farce*; *Comedy*; *Basoche*; *Confrérie de la Passion*; *Sociétés joyeuses*; *Puy*. For the period from the 16th c. v. *Tragedy*; *Comedy*; *Tragi-comedy*; *Pastoral*; *Opéra-Comique*; *Drame*; *Mélodrame*; *Proverbe*; *Vaudeville*; *Theatre of the 19th and 20th cs.*; *Theatres and Theatre Companies*; *Censorship, Dramatic*.

Drame, in a specialized sense, a type of play intermediate between tragedy and comedy, developed, in theory and practice, by *Diderot (who held that it should deal seriously with the domestic problems of *bourgeois* life), though earlier examples exist in Voltaire's L'*Enfant prodigue* and *Nanine* and *La Chaussée's *comédies larmoyantes*. Other authors of *drames* include Sedaine and L.-S. Mercier, distant precursors of Augier and Dumas *fils*. v. also *Theatre of the 19th and 20th cs.*; *Kotzebue*.

Drames philosophiques (1878–86), by Renan, four short philosophical dramas reflecting his later, indulgently sceptical view of the universe. In *Caliban* (1878), Shakespeare's Prospero, once more duke of Milan, is ousted by Caliban, who represents the ignorant masses, unresponsive to science and thought. Caliban discovers that it pays him to protect Prospero and exploit his brains. Prospero now has more time for research and in a sequel, *L'Eau de Jouvence* (1881), discovers the elixir of life. In *Le Prêtre de Némi* (1885), the priest Antistius seeks to replace traditional rites and blood sacrifice by a religion of love and good works. He meets with opposition inspired by ignorance, convention, and political motives, and falls a victim to mass hatred. *L'Abbesse de Jouarre* (1886), set in the Revolutionary era (it opens in the notorious *Prison du Plessis*, used for prisoners on the way to the *Tribunal révolutionnaire* or the guillotine), is based on the idea that if the end of the world were known to be at hand no moral or social considerations would check the passion of love.

Dreyfus, L'Affaire. In the summer of 1894 the French Ministry of War came into possession of an unsigned letter from the files of the German Embassy, with an appended memorandum (the *bordereau*) giving details of French military secrets to be sent to the German military attaché, Schwartzkoppen. The handwriting resembled that of Captain Alfred Dreyfus, a Jewish officer of blameless record employed at the War Office. He protested his innocence, but was court-martialled (Dec. 1894), convicted, degraded, cashiered, and sent to solitary confinement for life on the Île du *Diable*. It was soon rumoured that he had been convicted on the strength of secret, doubtfully authentic documents produced by the war minister, but not communicated to the defence.

In March 1896, Colonel Picquart, newly appointed head of the Information Branch of the Secret Service, discovered convincing evidence that a Major Esterhazy, an officer of dubious character, was in German pay, and that his handwriting was that of the *bordereau*: this was suppressed by the War Office.

Picquart's deputy, Colonel Henry, then produced a letter—allegedly from the Italian military attaché, Panizzardi—naming Dreyfus and making his guilt clear. In March 1897, his brother Matthieu Dreyfus also discovered evidence incriminating Esterhazy, and accused him. The resulting outcry led to a court martial at which Esterhazy was acquitted. *L'Aurore*, a pro-Dreyfus (*Dreyfusard*) newspaper (f. 1897; Clemenceau was political editor), then published (13 Jan. 1898) Zola's famous *J'accuse*, an open letter to the president of the Republic denouncing the War Office (in a series of paragraphs beginning 'J'accuse...') for suppressing material evidence and concealing a grave miscarriage of justice. Zola's trial and conviction for libel won Dreyfus many supporters. By now the strong feelings aroused by the affair had split France into two camps; families were divided, friendships broken. Against Dreyfus were ranged the whole military caste, the traditional forces of law and order, and the anti-Semites (*v. Ligue de la patrie française*; *Drumont*); for him was an enthusiastic band of *revisionnistes* (at first largely recruited from the intelligentsia), who held that if an injustice had been done it must be set right, regardless of prestige (*v. Ligue des droits de l'homme*). The latter organized a public petition for a retrial, and eventually became so strong that in July 1898 Cavaignac, the war minister, read the Panizzardi letter—the main proof of Dreyfus's guilt—aloud in the Chamber. A month later, Henry admitted that he had forged it. He was arrested, and committed suicide in prison. The government now decided to press for a reversal of the sentence. But at a new trial by court martial (Sept. 1899) the verdict, contrary to all expectation, was still 'Guilty' (with extenuating circumstances, reducing the sentence to 10 years). The government promptly pardoned Dreyfus. In 1906, when the *Cour de cassation* finally reversed the 1894 sentence, he was reinstated in the army with the rank of major. He later fought in the 1914–18 war, winning promotion and the *Légion d'honneur*. Esterhazy's guilt was again confirmed by published extracts (1930) from Schwartzkoppen's papers.

The impact of this spiritual and political crisis is strongly reflected in French literature, e.g. in *Zola's *Vérité*; A. France's M. *Bergeret à Paris* and *L'*Île des pingouins*; Proust's *A la recherche du temps perdu* (in the early vols. old friendships are broken by the affair) and *Jean Santeuil* (inc. a description of the trial); *Martin du Gard's *Jean Barois*; *Blum's *Souvenirs sur l'Affaire*, *Péguy's *Notre jeunesse*, and *Jaurès's *Preuves*, showing the reactions of the younger generation; works by Gyp, Donnay, and Lavedan, reflecting the anti-Semitic point of view.

Drieu la Rochelle, PIERRE-EUGÈNE (1893–1945), a gifted writer who, having served with distinction in the 1914–18 war, made his name with novels (e.g. *L'Homme couvert de femmes*, 1925; *Le Feu follet*, 1931; *Gilles*, 1939), short stories (e.g. *La Comédie de Charleroi*, 1934), and political essays (e.g. *Mesure de la France*, 1922) vigorously depicting the political disarray and moral malaise of the inter-war years and reflecting the influence on him of Barrès and Nietzsche. His Fascist sympathies came to the fore during the German occupation, when he became editor of the *Nouvelle Revue française* (1940–3) and a notorious collaborator. He committed suicide after the Liberation.

Droits de l'homme, Déclaration des, v. *Déclaration*.

Drouet, JULIETTE (1806–83), actress, met Hugo when she played in his *Lucrèce Borgia*. The meeting led to a liaison which lasted, with the utmost devotion on her side, for the rest of their lives. During his years of exile, she acted as his amanuensis, recopying all his manuscripts. *Tristesse d'Olympio* is one of many poems he wrote for her.

Droz, ANTOINE-GUSTAVE (1832–95), journalist and novelist, helped to ensure the success of *La *Vie parisienne* with his light, sentimental sketches of family life (at times leaving little to the imagination)—*Monsieur, Madame et Bébé* (publ. in book form 1866) and *Entre nous* (1867). His novels (*Autour d'une source*, 1869; *Un Paquet de lettres*, 1870) were more ambitious.

Druidisme, v. *Literary Isms*.

Drumont, ÉDOUARD (1844–1917), a violently anti-Semitic journalist; founder-editor (1892) of *La Libre Parole*, a paper soon to be strongly anti-*Dreyfus. His *La France juive* (1886, 2 vols.) attacked Jews and Jewish financiers. v. *Bernanos*.

Du Barry, JEANNE BÉCU, COMTESSE (1743–93), mistress of Louis XV after the death of Mme de Pompadour; executed under the *Terror.

Du Bartas, GUILLAUME DE SALLUSTE, SIEUR (1544–90), a Gascon gentleman and an important *Huguenot poet. After a studious youth, he took up arms (1566) in the service of Henri de Navarre. He was sent on embassies, being received with distinction at the court of James VI of Scotland (1587). He wrote, notably, *La Semaine, ou la Création du monde* (1578), an epic (in *alexandrines) assembling all the scientific knowledge of the day in the guise of an account of the seven days of the Creation, and *La Seconde Semaine* (1584–1603; only four 'days' were completed), which was to have been an encyclopedic history of mankind; also earlier epics (e.g. *Judit*; *Uranie*; *Le Triomphe de la Foi*) and some lyrics. The execution of his two main works was not equal to their grand design. Despite fine passages (e.g. the opening of canto 7 of the *Semaine*—much admired by Goethe), they are marred by bathos, pedantry, and over-indulgence in neologism (v. *Pléiade*). But his *Semaine*, in particular, was highly successful for a time. His work was praised by English poets (e.g. Daniel, Drayton, Lodge, and Marston—though Dryden thought some of it 'abominable fustian'), and in English translation (*Divine Weekes and Workes*,

1605, by J. Sylvester) appears to have influenced Milton. v. *Gamon*.

Du Bellay, (1) JOACHIM (1522–60), poet, next to Ronsard the most famous member of the *Pléiade*, came of a noble family of Anjou and was a cousin of the brothers (2) GUILLAUME (1491–1543), seigneur de Langey, a distinguished soldier, latterly governor of Piedmont (v. *Rabelais*); (3) JEAN (1492–1560), bishop, cardinal (1535), diplomatic agent of François Ier (notably in England and Italy; v. *Rabelais*), and patron of men of letters; and (4) MARTIN (c. 1495–1559), soldier, administrator, and author of *Mémoires* (1569) supplementing those left by his brother Guillaume (they were publ. together in 1908–19 and cover the years 1513–47).

Joachim du Bellay studied law at Poitiers and literature in Paris. It is related that, as a young man, he met Ronsard at an inn, and that the discovery of their common passion for poetry led him to join Ronsard and his 'Brigade' in Paris, there to embark, under *Dorat's guidance, on the task of reform. His first collections of sonnets and other lyrics (inc. *L'Olive*, 115 sonnets inspired by his cousin, Olive de Sévigné) and his famous *Défense et illustration de la langue française* appeared in 1549–50. In 1553, he accompanied his cousin Jean on a mission to Rome, spending four years there in his service. The impact of Rome and his regret for the 'douceur angevine' inspired the *Antiquités de Rome* and the *Regrets* (1558), which contain some of his finest poetry— dignified, moving, and free from the influence of Petrarch under which he had earlier written. His Latin poems and *Divers Jeux rustiques* also appeared in 1558. Du Bellay was less pagan in spirit than Ronsard, and—unlike Ronsard—a Latinist (familiar with Horace, Ovid, Virgil; translator of the *Aeneid*, bks. IV and VI) rather than a Hellenist. He was a master of the *sonnet, whether he was using it to satirize the life of Rome, to evoke the melancholy of its ruins, or to lament his own exile. He also wrote pleasant *chansons (some, e.g. the *Vanneur*

de blé aux vents, imitated from the Latin of the Italian Navagero) and handled the *alexandrine with ease in his satirical *Poète courtisan*, epistles, etc. Spenser translated some of the sonnets as *Visions of Bellay* and the *Antiquités de Rome* as *Ruins of Rome*.

Dubois, PAUL-FRANÇOIS, v. *Globe, Le*.

Du Boisgobey, FORTUNÉ, v. *Lecoq*.

Du Bos, CHARLES (1882–1939), man of letters and critic of partly American descent, exceptionally well qualified by birth, education (at Oxford), travel, and sympathies to interpret foreign literature and thought to his countrymen; also a remarkable conversationalist who strongly influenced his many literary friends, and a Roman Catholic convert (1927). His writings (limited by chronic ill-health) include *Byron et le besoin de la fatalité* (1929); *Du spirituel dans l'ordre littéraire* (articles in *Vigile*, 1930); *François Mauriac et le problème du romancier catholique* (1933); *Approximations* (1922– 37, 7 vols.), collected essays on religion and the arts; *Qu'est-ce que la littérature?* (1940), lectures delivered in English at an American university (1938); his *Journal* (1921–62, 9 vols.), of particular interest for his remarks on English literature and authors. v. *Critics and Criticism*, 3.

Dubos or **Du Bos**, JEAN-BAPTISTE, ABBÉ (1670–1742), man of letters and historian, wrote an *Histoire critique de la monarchie française* (1734); *Réflexions critiques sur la poésie et la peinture* (1719, completed 1733), a work interesting for his doctrine that poetry cannot be judged by rules, but only by the emotion it produces—though in the *Querelle des anciens et des modernes* he favoured the *anciens*, holding with Boileau that tradition is valuable as indicating the coincidence of many opinions on the merit of certain authors. v. *Critics and Criticism*, 1.

Du Bouchet, ANDRÉ, v. *Lyric Poetry*, 4; *Foreign Influences*, 6.

Duby, GEORGES (1919–   ), medieval

historian, professor at the *Collège de France* from 1970. His works include *La Société aux XIe et XIIe siècles* (1954), *Histoire de la civilisation française* (1958, 2 vols.; with Mandrou), *L'Économie rurale et la vie des campagnes dans l'Occident médiéval* (1962), *Le Dimanche de Bouvines, 27 Juillet 1214* (1973), *Guerriers et paysans, VIIe–XIIe siècle. Premier essor de l'économie européenne* (1973), *Hommes et structures du Moyen Âge* (1973; collected papers), and such large illustrated volumes as *L'Europe des cathédrales* (1966). He was general editor of the Larousse *Histoire de la France* (1970–2, 3 vols.).

Du Camp, MAXIME (1822–94), journalist and novelist, chiefly remembered for his friendship with *Flaubert and for his *Souvenirs littéraires* (1882–3). He also edited the *Revue des Deux Mondes* and wrote *Souvenirs et paysages d'Orient* (1848; travel); *Les Convulsions de Paris* (1878–9; on the *Commune* of 1871); *Les Six Aventures* (1857) and *Les Buveurs de cendres* (1866), novels; art criticism, etc.

Du Cange, CHARLES DU FRESNE, SIEUR (1610–88), a man of great learning, compiler of a famous dictionary (*v. Dictionaries*, 1678) and editor of Joinville and Villehardouin.

Ducasse, ISIDORE, *v. Lautréamont.*

Duc, comte, marquis. Charlemagne's empire was divided for administrative purposes into *comtés* or counties, the *comté* being the territory (which might vary at the emperor's pleasure) assigned to a *comte* (L. *comes*, a 'companion' of the emperor) for him to govern. His main duty was to administer justice, in which he was assisted by a council of notables of the *comté*. He had also to raise the military contingent required of his *comté*, and to report in person annually to the emperor. He had no regular salary, but was entitled to a third of the proceeds of the fines he imposed, and sometimes to other revenues. A *marquis* was a *comte* whose territory lay on the *marches* or frontiers of

the empire; his duties were thus of a more military nature. A *duc* (L. *dux*, 'leader'), who had authority over several *comtés*, was appointed according to the needs of the moment. All these offices were temporary, not hereditary, their holders being officials selected, on grounds of fitness for the post, from members of the emperor's court. But in the late 9th c., with the weakening of the monarchy, these officials tended to become irremovable, and their offices hereditary. Charles II, in an edict of 877, recognized the heredity of such offices. *v. Noblesse; Napoleonic Aristocracy; Provinces.*

Du Cerceau, a family of several generations of architects attached to the court in the 16th and 17th cs., notably JACQUES ANDROUET (*c.* 1510–85) and his sons BAPTISTE (*c.* 1540–90) and JACQUES (d. 1614).

Duchâtel, PIERRE (1480–1552), a learned humanist, librarian to François Ier at *Fontainebleau, taught Greek to Marguerite d'Angoulême.

Du Châtelet, GABRIELLE-ÉMILIE DE BRETEUIL, MARQUISE (1706–49), known for her long liaison with Voltaire, whom she received and protected at her *château* at Cirey-sur-Blaise (near the frontier of Lorraine). She was learned and intelligent, devoted to mathematics, science, and philosophy (she translated Newton's *Principia*), and versed in Latin, Italian, and English; also an honest, devoted friend. She was unpopular in the worldly society of the day and bitterly satirized by Mme du Deffand.

Duchesne, MONSEIGNEUR LOUIS (1843–1922), an eminent religious historian and archaeologist, for a time a leading Modernist (*v. Blondel, M.*); professor at the *Institut catholique de Paris* from 1877, director of the *École française d'Archéologie* in Rome (1895–1922). His works include an edition (1886–92) of the *Liber pontificalis; Les Origines du culte chrétien* (1889); *L'Histoire ancienne de l'Église chrétienne* (1906–10).

Duchesse de Langeais, La (1833–4; later in *La *Comédie humaine, Scènes de la vie parisienne*, part of the trilogy *Histoire des Treize*), by Balzac. The beautiful, witty duchesse, a leader of Parisian society during the Restoration, plays fast and loose with the marquis de Montriveau. When he seems to tire of her, she is brokenhearted, compromises herself trying to win him back, then disappears from Paris. After years of searching, he finds her in a convent on a Mediterranean island, speaks to her in the presence of the Mother Superior, and later plots (with his friends, 'les Treize') to kidnap her. But the kidnappers find her dead in her cell. They take her body and bury it at sea.

Ducis, Jean-François (1733–1816), dramatist, author of mediocre tragedies and of verse adaptations of Shakespeare's plays which, though feeble, helped to introduce Shakespeare to the French stage (*Hamlet*, 1769; *Roméo et Juliette*, 1772; *Le Roi Léar*, 1783; *Macbeth*, 1784; *Othello*, 1792). Knowing no English, he used the versions of P.-A. de Laplace and Letourneur and, to suit French taste, introduced confidants and preserved the life of Desdemona: Sainte-Beuve called him a 'profanateur innocent'.

Duclos, Charles Pinot or Pineau (1704–72), historian, moralist, and novelist; historiographer from 1750, perpetual secretary of the *Académie from 1754; a friend of Voltaire and J.-J. Rousseau and in sympathy with the *philosophes and the *Encyclopédie. He wrote, notably, an *Histoire de Louis XI* (1745), full, but colourless; *Considérations sur les mœurs de ce siècle* (1750), penetrating and judicious, but discreet in its censures; and (drawing freely on the duc de *Saint-Simon's ms.) *Mémoires secrets sur les règnes de Louis XIV et de Louis XV* (1790), dealing less with events than with the characters and intrigues of those involved in them (e.g. Law); also romances, e.g. *Histoire de Mme de Luz* (1741) and *Confessions du comte de **** (1742), which illustrates the loose morals of the day (contemporaries enjoyed

its portraits of real persons). His fragmentary memoirs of his dissipated youth are also of some literary interest. His style is concise, rather dry and abrupt, at times caustic and epigrammatic (he was a brilliant conversationalist). He shows sincerity, but little heart; energy and common sense rather than high talent.

Du contrat social (1762), a treatise on political philosophy by J.-J. Rousseau. *Cf. Discours.*

Its central doctrine is that since man is born free, and force cannot be the source of right, his subjection to the authority of government must be based on a compact. Primitive man, to overcome threats to his safety in a state of nature, sought a form of association with his fellows such that each, uniting with all the rest, yet obeyed only himself and remained free. He thereby created a moral collective personality called the *sovereign* when active, the *State* when passive. Each person is at once a member of the sovereign (and as such a *citizen*) and a subject of the State. From this association arises moral duty, justice now replaces instinct, and man gains civil liberty and right of property (subject to limitations). Sovereignty is inalienable and indivisible; it cannot be transferred to representatives (the English wrongly deem themselves a free people: they are so only at the time of an election). Law is the definition of rights and duties, and the main objects of legislation are liberty and equality (to the extent that the exercise of power shall be in conformity with the law, and the enjoyment of wealth shall preclude the servitude of the poor). *Government* is an intermediate body (prince or magistrates) between the sovereign people and the individual citizens, an agent of the sovereign, charged with the execution of the law and the maintenance of liberty. It may be democratic, aristocratic, monarchic, or mixed, according to the size of the governing body. Its establishment is a legislative and executive act of the sovereign, not a compact. Citizens should be required to profess a civil religious faith. Its articles, determined by the sovereign, must be few and simple: belief in an intelligent, beneficent God, a future life, and retribution; acceptance of the sanctity of the social compact and the law.

The work is written with an air of simplicity and dry precision which tends to conceal its disregard for historical fact and for the complexity of human affairs. It cites such questionable sources as the laws of Minos and the constitution of Lycurgus, and turns for historical illustrations to the small states of ancient Greece—though it is only fair to add that Rousseau's doctrines envisage a small community like Geneva or Corsica. Its influence was at first slight, for it was prohibited in France and copies were hard to come by. But, especially after 1789, its proclamation of the sovereignty of the people, not of a single order or ruler, contributed to the growth of new ideas, and its famous opening words— 'L'homme est né libre, et partout il est dans les fers'—echoed far beyond France.

Du côté de chez Swann, v. *A la recherche du temps perdu*; *Combray*.

Ducray-Duminil, FRANÇOIS-GUILLAUME (1761–1819), wrote highly popular sensational novels with a moral strain, e.g. *Alexis, ou la Maisonnette dans les bois* (1788), *Victor, ou l'Enfant de la forêt* (1796), *Cœlina, ou l'Enfant du mystère* (1798), *Les Petits Orphelins du hameau* (1800). Many were dramatized; v. *Pixérécourt*.

Du Deffand, MARIE DE VICHY-CHAMROND, MARQUISE (1697–1780), one of the most famous Frenchwomen of the 18th c. Her *salon* was frequented, not only by the cream of society, but also by Turgot, Hénault, d'Alembert, and other *philosophes* (though she was hostile to the *Encyclopédistes* as a sect). When she became blind in later life she employed Mlle de Lespinasse as reader, with the result that many *habitués* of her *salon* defected to that of her charming companion. The two quarrelled and parted, causing no little stir in the literary world. She was deeply attached to Horace

Walpole, whom she met at the age of 68 (v. his letter to Gray of 25 Jan. 1766), and to whom she left all her papers. Her correspondence with Walpole, her intimate friend Hénault, and others, written in admirable prose, reveals her sound, independent judgement and also the social and intellectual characteristics of the period.

Du Fail, NOËL (1520–91), a Breton gentleman who held high judicial office in his province. His chief work, written as a young man under the anagrammatic pseudonym 'Léon Ladulfi', was *Propos rustiques* (1547), conversations of old villagers under an oak (they compare old customs with new, describe a broil between villages, etc.), partly didactic in intention, but remarkable for its vivid, sympathetic portrayal of village life and rural types; his main theme is the happiness of the simple rural life. He also wrote *Baliverneries d'Eutrapel* (1548), more mixed in subject-matter; the *Contes et discours d'Eutrapel* (1585), anecdotes and conversations, rather more didactic and satirical, and in part autobiographical—the three interlocutors being Eutrapel (Du Fail himself), his brother Polygame, and the shifty lawyer Lupolde.

Du Faur de Pibrac, v. *Pibrac*.

Dufay, PIERRE, v. *Pastiche*.

Dufrénoy, ADÉLAÏDE-GILBERTE BILLET, MME (1765–1825), a minor poetess (*Élégies*, 1807; *Poésies diverses*, 1821). She also produced instructional works, *vaudevilles*, and translations of English novels. v. *Minerve littéraire, La*.

Dufresnoy, CHARLES-ALPHONSE (1611–55), painter and poet. His poem *De arte graphica liber* (1668) appeared in English translation (by Wm. Mason, 1783) with annotations by Joshua Reynolds.

Dufresny, CHARLES RIVIÈRE (1648–1724), dramatist and novelist, briefly editor (1710) of Le *Mercure galant*; an original, versatile man, but desultory and a spendthrift. His works include *Le Chevalier joueur* (1697), a prose counterpart of Regnard's *Le *Joueur*, but depicting the vice of gambling with more force and depth; *L'*Esprit de contradiction* (1700) and *Le *Double Veuvage* (1702), very successful domestic comedies; *Amusements sérieux et comiques d'un Siamois* (1699), the impressions of a Siamese visitor to Paris, a prototype of the **Lettres persanes. v. Italiens.*

Dufy, RAOUL (1877–1953), painter, one of the *Fauves* (v. *Impressionism*), later closely associated with *Cubist artists and writers, and with the experimental theatre (v. *Cocteau*). His works included *La Fée Électricité*, a vast decorative piece executed for the *Exposition internationale* of 1937.

Duguay-Trouin, RENÉ (1673–1736), a privateer who ended a glorious career as *lieutenant général des armées navales*. His exploits included the capture of an English convoy (1707) and of Rio de Janeiro (1711). He left *Mémoires* (1740).

Du Guesclin, BERTRAND (*c.* 1320–80), a great captain of the Hundred Years War, **connétable de France* from 1370; ugly, thickset, and illiterate, but lion-hearted and wise. At 17, he held Rennes against the duke of Lancaster, and was soon named captain of *Mont-Saint-Michel*. He cleared France of the *grandes compagnies* (brigand bands) by leading them into Spain to fight Pedro the Cruel and his English allies. He was captured by the English at the battle of Navarette (1367) and ransomed at a high price—fixed by himself as representing his true worth. He defeated Pedro at Montiel (1369) and successfully pursued the war against the English.

Du Guillet, PERNETTE (*c.* 1520–45), b. at Lyons, a poetess of the school of *Scève (and v. *Délie*), who died young, leaving short poems of some merit.

Du Haillan, BERNARD PIRARD, SEIGNEUR (1535–1610), author of a very popular *Histoire générale des rois de France* (1576),

in the main a reproduction of the **Grandes Chroniques*, amplified with imaginary speeches and debates; a pioneer work in the transition from chronicles to history.

Duhamel, GEORGES (1884–1966), poet, novelist, dramatist, and essayist; a member of the **Abbaye* community and for some time an **unanimiste*. He had little settled education, wandered about Europe on foot for some years, then, with considerable hardship, studied medicine. By the time he qualified (1909), he was already writing. His early works include poetry (*Des légendes, des batailles*, 1907, printed at the *Abbaye*; *L'Homme en tête*, 1909, verse and prose; *Selon ma loi*, 1910; *Compagnons*, 1912) and plays (*La Lumière*, 1911; *Le Combat*, 1913). His experiences as an army surgeon in the 1914–18 war evoked *Vie des martyrs* (1917) and *Civilisation 1914–17* (1918; awarded the *Prix Goncourt*), sketches in which, with characteristic compassion, he unsparingly describes the hideous scenes in the hospitals, and the heroism and amazing good fellowship of the wounded. After 1920 his career was mainly literary. His large output includes two cycles of novels (v. *Salavin*; *Chronique des Pasquier*); literary criticism (*Propos critiques*, 1912; *Paul Claudel*, 1913; *Essai sur le roman*, 1925); essays on aspects of modern civilization (*La Possession du monde* and *Entretiens dans le tumulte*, 1919; *Entretien sur l'esprit européen*, 1928; *Scènes de la vie future*, 1930; *Au chevet de la civilisation*, 1938); reminiscences (*Lumières sur ma vie*, 1944–53, 4 vols.); delightful nature studies (*Fables de mon jardin*, 1936); poetry (*Elégies*, 1920; *Voix du vieux monde*, 1925); plays (*L'Œuvre des athlètes*, 1920; *La Journée des aveux*, 1924; *Quand vous voudrez*, 1924).

Du Hausset, MME, v. *Pompadour*.

Dujardin, ÉDOUARD (1861–1949), a **Symbolist (v. *Revue indépendante*; *Revue wagnérienne*), also a writer and lecturer on the history of religious belief. He published verse, e.g. *Poésies* (1913), *Mari Magno* (1922); plays (*Théâtre*, 1920–4, 2 vols.), some of which had earlier been landmarks of Symbolist drama; the novel *Les Lauriers sont coupés* (1888), an early example of the use of the *monologue intérieur* ('stream of consciousness') and said to have inspired the form of Joyce's *Ulysses*.

Dukas, PAUL-ABRAHAM (1865–1935), composed the music for *Maeterlinck's *Ariane et Barbe-bleue* (prod. 1907); the symphonic poem *L'Apprenti Sorcier*, etc.

Dullin, CHARLES, *v. Atelier, Théâtre de l'*; *Theatres and Theatre Companies*.

Du Maine, *v. Maine*.

Dumarsais, CÉSAR CHESNEAU (1676–1756), a grammarian in the *grammaire générale* tradition of *Port-Royal, wrote a *Traité des tropes* (1730) and articles for the *Encyclopédie.

Dumas, ALEXANDRE (1802–70), Dumas *père*, a novelist and dramatist whose output (his *Œuvres complètes* fill 103 vols. in the Calmann-Lévy ed.), popularity, exuberance, earnings, and extravagance were all equally prodigious. His father (son of the marquis Antoine-Alexandre Davy de la Pailleterie and Marie Dumas, a negress) took the name Dumas, rose to be a general in the Revolutionary armies, but died poor. After a scanty education, the young Alexandre—thanks to his fine handwriting—found a post in Paris (1822) in the household of the future Louis-Philippe. He read voraciously, discovered Shakespeare, Scott, and Schiller, found his way into the *cénacles, and began to write. The production of his *Henri III et sa cour (1829) was at once a personal triumph and a notable *Romantic victory. Not only was it written in prose and with a total disregard of the dramatic conventions and unities, it was also, from the box-office standpoint, a good, exciting play. He soon surpassed it with *Antony (1831) and *La *Tour de Nesle* (1832), and maintained his popularity over the next 20 years, notably with *Charles VII chez ses grands vassaux* (1831; tragedy); *Don Juan*

de Marana and *Kean* (1836; dramas, if not melodramas; *Kean* has been adapted by Sartre); *Mademoiselle de Belle-Isle* (1839), *Un Mariage sous Louis XV* (1841), and *Les Demoiselles de Saint-Cyr* (1843), comedies.

About 1839 he began to write novels (mainly historical), with even greater success. He often used collaborators (*v. Maquet*), but—for all the digs at the 'Fabrique de romans A. Dumas et Cie'—they contributed nothing beyond skeletal plots or historical background. He had great gifts of narrative and dialogue, a powerful imagination, little critical sense or concern for historical accuracy, but a genius for seizing the situations and characters that would best render historical atmosphere. He wrote with unflagging gusto and an instinctive conviction, uncomplicated by hankerings after psychology or analysis, that 'l'action et l'amour' were the essential things in life, hence in fiction. His novels usually appeared first as *romans-feuilletons, and for years he kept his public on tenterhooks from one day to the next with love affairs, intrigues, hairbreadth escapes, imprisonments, and duels galore. His most famous novels are the non-historical *Le *Comte de Monte-Cristo* (1844–5) and three series of historical tales: (1) *Les *Trois Mousquetaires* (1844) and its sequels *Vingt Ans après* (1845; period 1648–9, the time of the *Fronde and the execution of Charles I) and *Le Vicomte de Bragelonne* (1848–50; period 1660–73, a picture of the court of Louis XIV); (2) *La Reine Margot* (1845; period 1572–5, with a fine description of the Massacre of St. *Bartholomew—*cf. Chronique du règne de Charles IX*), *La Dame de Monsoreau* (1846; period 1578–9—*v. Bussy d'Amboise*; *Coconas*; *La Mole*; *Chicot*; its English title is *Chicot the Jester*) and its sequel *Les Quarante-cinq* (1848; period 1584–5, dealing with the Guise intrigues); (3) *Mémoires d'un médecin: Joseph Balsamo* (1846–8; a picture of court life and intrigues under Louis XV; *v. Cagliostro*), *Le Collier de la Reine* (1849–50; for its theme *v. Collier, L'Affaire du*), *Ange Pitou* (1853; period 1789, the weeks before and after the fall of the *Bastille), *La Comtesse* *de Charny* (1852–5; period 1789–94, another novel of the Revolution). Also worthy of special mention are *Le Chevalier de Maison-Rouge* (1845; relating the Chevalier de Rougeville's plot to rescue Marie-Antoinette from the *Temple; *v. Maison rouge*) and three tales of country life: *Conscience l'innocent* (1852), *Catherine Blum* (1854), *Le Meneur de loups* (1857). *v.* also *Chasse au chastre, La.*

His many other works include *Impressions de voyage*, travel reminiscences, beginning (1847–8) with his trip to Cadiz in 1846; *Mes mémoires* (1852–5, 22 vols.), the story of his life, told with verve and wit, perhaps a little embroidered (the vols. covering his early years, Romanticism, and the 1830 *Revolution are of special interest); *Histoire de mes bêtes* (1868), about his monkeys, parrots, cats, almost legendary dogs, etc.; many children's stories, e.g. *Histoire d'un casse-noisette*, *La Bouillie de la comtesse Berthe* (both 1845); a study of Napoleon; and—for he was also an inspired cook—a *Grand Dictionnaire de cuisine* (1873). His best work remains thoroughly readable.

Dumas, ALEXANDRE (1824–95), Dumas *fils*, natural son of the above, novelist and dramatist. He took to writing to pay his debts, quickly won fame with his novel *La *Dame aux camélias* (1848), dramatized it (1852) with striking success, and became a leading playwright of the Second Empire. His plays (collected in *Théâtre complet*, 1868–92, 7 vols., with interesting prefaces) include *Le Demi-Monde* (1855), a word he coined to describe the world of the women of easy virtue depicted in this play; *La Question d'argent* (1857); *Le Fils naturel* (1858); *L'Ami des femmes* (1864); *Les Idées de Mme Aubray* (1867); *La Femme de Claude* (1873); *La Princesse de Bagdad* (1881); *Denise* (1885); *Francillon* (1887). They are well constructed, contain some fine dialogue, but are marred by his increasing tendency to preach reform of the evils they freely depict. His *L'Affaire Clemenceau* (1886) is a semi-autobiographical novel. *v. Theatre of the 19th and 20th cs.*

Duméril, ÉDÉLESTAND PONTUS (1801–71), literary historian, philologist, and palaeographer, known for his studies and editions of medieval poetry.

Dumouriez, CHARLES-FRANÇOIS (1739–1823), commander-in-chief of the Revolutionary armies, the victor of *Valmy and *Jemmapes. He went over to the enemy (1793) and died in obscurity in England.

Dunois, JEAN (1402–68), 'le Bâtard d'Orléans', natural son of Louis d'*Orléans (brother of Charles VI), famous for his valour in the Hundred Years War, in which he fought at the side of Joan of Arc.

Dupanloup, MONSEIGNEUR FÉLIX-ANTOINE-PHILIBERT (1802–78), theologian and educationalist, a noted preacher and polemicist, later canon of Notre-Dame and bishop of Orleans. His works, chiefly educational treatises of a reactionary character, include *De l'éducation* (1851) and *De la haute éducation intellectuelle* (1866). His *Lettres sur l'éducation des filles* (1867–8) did, however, advocate greater freedom of education for girls. *v. Littré.*

Dupérier, FRANÇOIS, *v. Malherbe.*

Du Perron, JACQUES DAVY (1556–1618), archbishop of Sens, cardinal (1604), a formidable religious controversialist (victor at the *Conférence de Fontainebleau* (1600), a disputation organized by Henri IV; Duplessis-Mornay was his opponent); also author of light poetry (a disciple of Ronsard) and official heroic poems. He introduced Malherbe to Henri IV.

Dupin, AURORE, *v. Sand.*

Dupin, JEAN-HENRI (1791–1887), wrote over 200 *vaudevilles and comedies, many in collaboration with Scribe (to whom he claimed to have taught his craft) or Dumersan (1780–1849).

Dupin, LOUIS-ELLIES (1657–1719),

religious historian of *Jansenist sympathies. His *Nouvelle Bibliothèque des auteurs ecclésiastiques* (58 vols.) was suppressed by the *parlement (1696) as too critical of papal authority. Later, he lost his chair at the *Collège de France.

Dupleix, JOSEPH-FRANÇOIS (1697–1763), an able governor of French India and a gallant soldier. The rivalry of La Bourdonnais defeated his efforts to extend French rule; he was recalled and his merits went unrecognized.

Duplessis, Marie (1824–47), a well-known Paris courtesan of the 1840s, the prototype of Marguerite Gautier in Dumas *fils*'s *La *Dame aux camélias*. She had started life as Alphonsine Plessis, a poor Norman peasant-girl.

Duplessis-Mornay, PHILIPPE DE MORNAY, SEIGNEUR DU PLESSIS, *known as* (1549–1623), political philosopher, theologian, and *Huguenot leader, wrote, notably, *Vindiciae contra tyrannos* (1578), carrying the theory of popular sovereignty to its ultimate consequence—the right of rebellion; also a broad-minded *Traité de la vérité de la religion chrétienne* (1581), urging religious appeasement, a *Traité de l'Eucharistie* (1598), etc. v. Du Perron.

Du Plessys, MAURICE (1864–1924), poet (v. *École romane*), published *Dédicace à Apollodore* (1891), *Études lyriques* (1896), *Odes olympiques* (1912), etc.

Dupont, PIERRE (1821–70), a popular author of patriotic *chansons, notably about peasant life, e.g. *Les Bœufs* (1846; 'J'ai deux grands bœufs dans mon étable'), *Le Chant des ouvriers* (1848), *Le Chant des paysans* (1849), *Le Chant du pain* (1849). At his best, he was in the same class as Béranger. Baudelaire wrote a laudatory preface to his *Chants et chansons* (1851–4 ed.; with music by Ernest Reyer).

Dupont de Nemours, PIERRE-SAMUEL (1739–1817), *économiste and politician, friend and supporter of Turgot; later a deputy to the *États généraux* (1789) and

(after a period of proscription) a member of the *Conseil des Anciens* (1795). He became hostile to the *Directoire* and went to America.

Dupuis et Cotonet, Les Lettres de, v. Musset.

Dupuis et Desronais, v. Collé.

Durant, GILLES, v. Satire Ménippée.

Duranty, LOUIS-ÉMILE-EDMOND (1833–80), novelist, a leader of the *Realists, later a *Naturalist. His best and most typical novel is *Le *Malheur d'Henriette Gérard* (1860).

Duras, CLAIRE LECHAT DE KERSAINT, MME DE (1778–1828), wife of the duc de Duras, a returned *émigré* who enjoyed the favour of Louis XVIII. Her literary *salon was among the most brilliant of the Restoration period. She wrote two remarkably successful short novels, *Ourika* (1824) and *Édouard* (1825), portraying characters consumed by passions that cannot be satisfied for reasons of social inequality.

Duras, MARGUERITE (1914–   ), novelist and playwright, published her first novel, *Les Impudents*, in 1942. *Le Square* (1955), her sixth novel and a new departure in her use of this form, made her name as a leading writer and led to comparisons with the *nouveau roman. It is a short work, consisting largely of dialogue, which hauntingly conveys the inability of the characters to give adequate expression to their deeper feelings. This situation often recurs in her subsequent novels, which include *Moderato cantabile* (1958), *L'Après-midi de M. Andesmas* (1962), *Le Ravissement de Lol V. Stein* (1964), *L'Amante anglaise* (1967), *Détruire dit-elle* (1969), *L'Amour* (1971). Many of her plays are dramatizations of her novels. She has also written for the cinema, notably the script for the film *Hiroshima mon amour* (1960).

Durendal, *Roland's sword.

Durkheim, ÉMILE (1858–1917), a pioneer of modern sociology (cf. *Tarde*; *Lévy-Bruhl*), founder (1898) of *L'Année sociologique*, the first sociological review. He wrote, notably, *Les Règles de la méthode sociologique* (1895); also *De la division du travail social* (1893), *Le Suicide* (1897), *Les Formes élémentaires de la vie religieuse: le système totémique en Australie* (1912; a study of moral systems as products of social evolution).

Durtain, Luc, *pseudonym of* ANDRÉ NEPVEU (1881–1959), a doctor by profession. He was associated with the *Abbaye and *unanimiste groups. His works include poetry (*L'Étape nécessaire*, 1907; *Pégase*, 1908; *Kong Harald*, 1914, on a sea-trip around Norway; *Le Retour des hommes*, 1920, an army doctor's poems on trench warfare; *Perspectives*, 1924; *Quatre Continents*, 1935); essays (*Face à face, ou le Poète et toi*, 1921); plays (*Le Donneur de sang*, 1929; *Le Mari singulier*, 1937); novels with a generic title, *Les Conquêtes du monde*, signifying a common theme—man's discovery of his true self, hidden by layers of convention and conformism (*Douze cent mille*, 1922; *La Source rouge*, 1924; *Le Globe sous le bras*, 1936; *La Femme en sandales*, 1937, etc.); also *Mémoires de notre vie* (1947–50, 4 vols.).

Durtal, in *Huysmans's *Là-bas*, etc.

Duruy, VICTOR (1811–94), an ancient historian (*Histoire des Romains*, 1843–5, later augm.; *Histoire des Grecs*, 1887–9, etc.) who held office for a time in the *Ministère de l'Instruction publique* and did much to improve the teaching of history in universities.

Du Ryer, PIERRE (*c.* 1600–58), dramatist, a contemporary of Corneille and Rotrou, served in the royal household, then as secretary to the duc de Vendôme, and after 1640 appears to have lived by his pen. His early romantic or heroic *tragicomedies (1630–4)—*Argénis et Poliarque, Lisandre et Caliste, Cléomédon, Alcimédon*—are crowded with incident and devoid of study of character or manners. His *Clarigène*

(1639), on a conflict of generosity between two friends, shows an advance, and his pastoral comedy *Les* *Vendanges de Suresnes (1635) is of some interest. His later tragicomedies include *Bérénice* (1645; prose), *Nitocris* (1650), *Anaxandre* (1655). He is at his best and most impressive in his tragedies, notably *Lucrèce* (1638; on the story of Tarquin and Lucretia) and *Scévole (1647), also *Alcionée* (1640; a successful romantic tragedy, probably prod. *c.* 1637), *Saül* (1642), and *Esther* (1644).

Dussault, FRANÇOIS-JOSEPH (1769–1824), man of letters and critic on the *Journal des Débats. His articles in this paper were collected in *Annales littéraires* (1824).

Dutourd, JEAN (1920–), novelist and essayist, a militant anti-conformist who attacks contemporary evils with sparkling wit and classical elegance of style. His works include the novels *Au bon beurre* (1952; a savage, highly comic study of black marketeers and collaborators in Occupied France), *Les Horreurs de l'amour* (1963), *Pluche, ou l'Amour de l'art* (1967; satirizing snobbery and corruption in artistic circles); and essays on moral and literary themes (he is a gifted critic), e.g. *Le Complexe de César* (1946; on ambition), *Les Taxis de la Marne* (1956), *L'Âme sensible* (1959; in praise of Stendhal), *Le Fond et la forme* (1958–65, 3 vols.; 'une espèce de dictionnaire philosophique').

Du Vair, GUILLAUME (1556–1621), a member of a noble family of Auvergne; statesman and moral philosopher, latterly chancellor of France and bishop of Lisieux. At the *États généraux of the *Ligue (1593) he eloquently supported Henri IV's claim to the throne. He was sent to England (1596) on a mission to Queen Elizabeth. He was important both as a creator of French prose in his political discourses, e.g. the *Exhortation à la paix*, and as a Christian moralist, notably in his paraphrases of some of the Psalms (*c.* 1580), his treatises *De la sainte philosophie* (*c.* 1580) and *De la philosophie morale des*

Stoïques, and his translation of Epictetus's *Manual* (*c*. 1585). In the latter works he called ancient philosophy to the support of the Christian faith. His other works include the *Traité de la constance et consolation ès calamités publiques* (written during the civil war), a remarkable Ciceronian dialogue in which three of his learned friends discourse on constancy in misfortune, the role of Providence, and faith in a future life; and a *Traité de l'éloquence française*, condemning the excessive display of erudition. Malherbe received guidance from him.

Duval, ALEXANDRE (1767–1842), wrote many dramas and comedies, e.g. *Édouard en Écosse, ou la Nuit d'un proscrit* (1802), an historical drama prohibited by Bonaparte's police as likely to arouse monarchist sympathies. He ended a varied career—sailor, soldier, architect, painter, actor—as librarian of the *Bibliothèque de l'Arsenal* and a member of the *Académie*.

Duval, JEANNE, *v. Baudelaire*.

Duval, PAUL, *v. Lorrain, J.*

Du Verdier, ANTOINE (1544–1600), early bibliographer, compiled *La Bibliothèque d'Antoine Duverdier contenant le catalogue de tous les auteurs qui ont écrit ou traduit en français* (1580; *v. La Croix du Maine*).

Du Vergier de Hauranne, JEAN, ABBÉ DE SAINT-CYRAN (1581–1643), theologian and mystic of austere, ardent, and contagious piety, director from 1635 of *Port-Royal*, where he introduced the doctrines of his friend Jansenius (*v. Jansenism*), with whom he had studied the Fathers (from *c*. 1611) at his native Bayonne. Richelieu imprisoned him (1638–43) for reasons which remain obscure—doubtless partly from suspicion of his spiritual power. He wrote religious and controversial works, his *Petrus Aurelius* (1632–3), a collection of Latin pamphlets defending the rights of the bishops against the *Jesuits and monks, being a notable success. His correspondence with Jansenius and others has also been published.

There were three 19th-c. liberal politicians of this name and family.

Duvernois, HENRI (1875–1937), wrote many tales depicting ordinary people and their foibles with mingled irony and indulgence (*Crapotte*, 1908; *Edgar*, 1919). Some were dramatized.

Dynamisme, *v. Literary Isms*.

E

Eau de Jouvence, L', *v. Drames philosophiques.*

Eaux et Forêts, a government service which deals with the conservation of national waterways and forests. It had its origin well back in the *ancien régime*. *v. La Fontaine.*

Ébahis, Les, a comedy by Grévin; produced 1561.

Josse, a greybeard widower, wishes to marry Madelon, daughter of his friend Gerard. But Madelon returns the love of a young advocate. The advocate visits her disguised in some of Josse's clothes (procured by his valet). Gerard sees him and takes him for Josse, which leads to a quarrel between Gerard and Josse. Finally, Josse's wife, a shrew whom he had believed dead, reappears, and he is left discomfited. Another character is Panthaleoné, a caricature of the braggart Italian adventurer, who is tricked and beaten.

École alsacienne, a Protestant boys' school in Paris, f. 1873. Gide was a pupil.

École de Rome or **Académie de France**

à **Rome** (housed in the Villa Medici, Rome), f. 1666 as an offshoot of the *Académie royale de Peinture et de Sculpture* to enable artists to study works of art in Rome; now under the *Académie des Beaux-Arts*. Winners of the *Grand Prix de Rome* are entitled to three years' residence here.

École des bourgeois, L', a comedy of manners by d'Allainval; produced 1728.

The marquis de Moncade plans to restore his fortunes by marrying Benjamine, daughter of a rich *bourgeois* widow, Mme Abraham. He sinks his pride and flatters her family; but a letter to a noble friend, inviting him to the wedding and revealing his contempt for them, falls into the wrong hands and proves his undoing.

École des femmes, L', a 5-act verse comedy by Molière, notable for its psychological element; produced 1662. It was attacked on both literary and moral grounds (certain passages were deemed indecent or irreverent); Molière replied in *La *Critique de l'École des femmes* and *L'*Impromptu de Versailles*.

Arnolphe has always scoffed at cuckolds. He has therefore caused Agnès, supposed to be a peasant's daughter, to be brought up in a state of unsophisticated innocence, and plans to marry her. In his absence, the young Horace meets her, falls in love, and—thanks to her very artlessness—is able to woo and win her. The situation becomes even more comic when Horace, in all innocence, makes Arnolphe his confidant in the affair. Agnès runs away with Horace, who unsuspectingly entrusts her to Arnolphe. Arnolphe is about to hurry her off to a convent when it is discovered that she is the daughter of the wealthy Enrique, who has arranged for her to marry Horace.

École des jaloux, L', a comedy by Montfleury; produced 1664.

Santillane so worries his wife Léonor with his jealous suspicion that, to cure him of his mania, his brother-in-law, the governor of Cadiz, contrives to have the pair carried off by bogus Turkish corsairs. The Grand Turk, it appears, proposes to make Léonor his favourite. She resists, wishing to remain faithful to Santillane. To overcome this obstacle, the Turk proposes to hang Santillane—who now begs her to set aside her scruples in order to save his life.

École des maris, L', a 3-act verse comedy by Molière; produced 1661. It borrows from Terence's *Adelphi* the contrast of two upbringings, one harsh, the other indulgent.

Her guardian Sganarelle has brought up Isabelle with the utmost severity and plans to marry her. His brother Ariste has brought up her sister Léonor with the utmost indulgence. Isabelle hates Sganarelle and, when he says they are to marry in a week, fools him into assenting to her marriage to her lover Valère in the belief that the bride-to-be is not herself but Léonor (so laxly brought up by Ariste) who has taken refuge in Valère's house.

École française d'Archéologie d'Athènes (f. 1846), **de Rome** (f. 1874), State institutions for post-graduate study of classical languages, history, and archaeology. (*Cf.* the similar British Schools.)

École libre des Sciences politiques, *v. Écoles spéciales.*

École militaire, in Paris (adjoining the *Champ-de-Mars, originally its parade ground), the first military college in France, f. 1751 by Louis XV for 500 'fils de gentilshommes nés sans biens ou morts à la guerre'. The college opened in 1760, the chapel (where the *cadet gentilhomme* Bonaparte was confirmed) in 1769. In 1792 the building became a barracks. Bonaparte founded a new college at Fontainebleau (1803; *v. Saint-Cyr*).

École nationale d'Administration. *v. Écoles spéciales.*

École nationale des Chartes, in Paris, f. 1821, the *école spéciale* where archivists and librarians are trained in palaeography, the handling of archives (*chartes*), documentary and bibliographical research, etc.

École nationale des Langues orientales vivantes, *v. Écoles spéciales.*

École normale; École normale supérieure. An *école normale* (*primaire*) is one of the many State training colleges for primary school teachers. The *École normale supérieure* (often referred to as 'the *École normale*') is a famous **école spéciale* for men in Paris. Founded in 1794 (on the initiative of Lakanal) as part of the **Convention*'s vast scheme for State secondary education, it was re-established (1808) as an autonomous body by Napoleon, to ensure a supply of teachers for his **Université impériale*. It was occasionally closed in the following decades, but since 1843 has functioned continuously in its own premises in the Rue d'Ulm near the **Sorbonne*, to which it was affiliated in 1903. *Normaliens*—in general the carefully sifted pick of the nation's **lycées* and *collèges*—follow the recognized university degree courses in arts or science and receive complementary instruction at the *École*. Graduates normally proceed to the **agrégation*; but by no means all become teachers—some of France's greatest writers and statesmen have been *normaliens*. Students form a close corporation, with its own customs and jargon (used, for example, by Jerphanion and Jallez in *Les *Hommes de bonne volonté*), and are often alleged to be imbued for life with the *esprit normalien* (intellectual arrogance, a sceptical outlook, a cynical wit, a taste for paradox, etc.).

There is a similar institution for women (f. 1881 at Sèvres and transferred to Paris in 1940) and, following the reorganization of secondary education in 1945, two further institutions, at Saint-Cloud (men) and Fontenay-aux-Roses (women), acquired the title and functions of *Écoles normales supérieures*.

École palatine (or du Palais), the 'Palace School' (*cf. Académie palatine*) f. *c.*

782 by Charlemagne, who placed **Alcuin* at its head. Its pupils (drawn mainly from the royal palace and the aristocracy, but also including promising children of humble origin) received instruction in the seven liberal arts. *v. Eginhard.*

École polytechnique, in Paris, a famous **école spéciale* of military status, colloquially known as 'l'X'; f. 1794 (*v. Collège de Navarre*) by the **Convention* as a civilian establishment for day pupils, then transformed by Napoleon into a military college for boarders. After two years' intensive scientific and technical training, pupils are commissioned in the artillery or the engineers, take up posts in the field of civil engineering, etc. *Polytechniciens* are noted for their college jargon and their cocked hats (*bicornes*). Recent developments include the admission of women (1972) and a projected change of site.

École pratique des Hautes Études, an **école spéciale* in Paris, a famous graduate school (f. 1868) for advanced study and research in a wide range of subjects. Students prepare a thesis for the award of the school's diploma.

École romane, L', the name adopted *c.* 1891 by the poets Moréas, Maurras, Raynaud, Du Plessys, and La Tailhède, who, in reaction against the **Symbolists* (and also the **Parnassiens* and the **Romantics*), sought to return to the vigour and purity of the classical tradition, to the classical themes, dignity, and restraint of the 16th and 17th cs.

Écoles libres, private schools, generally denominational and mostly Roman Catholic, e.g. the **Collège Sainte-Barbe* and the **Collège Stanislas* (Catholic), the **École alsacienne* (Protestant). *v. Lycées and Collèges.*

Écoles spéciales, the many State institutions of higher education (some affiliated to universities) designed to train students for specialized careers, e.g. the **Écoles normales supérieures, *École* pratique des Hautes Études, *École nationale des Chartes, École spéciale militaire (v. Saint-Cyr), *École polytechnique, Écoles nationales supérieures des Mines (in Paris and at Saint-Étienne), École nationale des Langues orientales vivantes (f. 1795, in Paris), École nationale supérieure des Beaux-Arts (v. Académie royale de Peinture et de Sculpture), Conservatoire national supérieur de Musique (f. 1795, in Paris), Institut d'Études politiques (in Paris; so called since 1945, formerly the École libre des Sciences politiques), École nationale d'Administration (f. 1945, in Paris; a training school for careers in all branches of the higher civil service). Entry is normally by competitive examination, the concours général.

Écolier limousin, L', in Rabelais's *Pantagruel*.

Économie politique, Traité de l', v. Montchrétien.

Économies royales, v. Sully.

Économistes, a name given in the later 18th c. to the physiocrats, pioneers of the science of political economy in France. They included François Quesnay (1694–1774), founder of the school and a protégé of Mme de Pompadour; Vincent de Gournay (1712–59), intendant du commerce in the government service; Dupont de Nemours; Mercier de La Rivière (1720–93). The doctrines of the school, of which Turgot was the most famous disciple, are expounded in Dupont de Nemours's Origine et progrès d'une science nouvelle (1768), Abrégé des principes (1773), etc., and Quesnay's Le Tableau économique (1758), Le Droit naturel (1765), etc. They held that land was the only source of wealth, and increase of the products of the soil the only means to prosperity. Property in land was the basis of the social order. Hence the idea of a single tax, to be levied on the land; the limitation of authority by laws protecting agriculture; the maxim—attributed to Gournay—of 'Laisser faire, laisser passer' (i.e. unrestricted com-

petition between individuals working on an equal footing; the free movement of goods, nationally and internationally). They had some principles in common with the *philosophes*—Quesnay wrote articles on Fermiers and Grains for the *Encyclopédie*.

Écossaise, L', (1) v. Montchrétien; (2) a sentimental comedy (prod. 1760; one act, prose) by Voltaire, interesting only as an episode in the conflict between the *philosophes* and their critics (v. Fréron).

Écriture artiste, v. Goncourt.

Écriture automatique, v. Surrealism.

Édit de Nantes (Edict of Nantes), v. Huguenots.

Édition, in a bibliographical sense, means—as in English—the total number of copies of a book, pamphlet, etc., printed from one setting-up of type. In referring to first editions, French uses the terms édition princeps (usually confined to the first printed edition—issued in the early days of printing—of a work originally circulated in manuscript form), première édition, and édition originale (both used of modern works, édition originale being the term usually employed in the case of modern and contemporary works likely to interest the collector, e.g. modern novels, éditions de luxe). If the work is illustrated the word used may be tirage rather than édition; and the copies are usually numbered serially, for the quality of the illustrations may be better in the earlier copies. If more copies are required, the first run, or printing (tirage, impression), may be followed by reprints from the original type (nouveaux tirages, nouvelles impressions, réimpressions), which still form part of the one edition. But if revisions of the work, loss or dispersal of the type, etc., involve partial or complete resetting of type, the copies then printed belong to a deuxième, or nouvelle, édition.

Éducation des filles, L', v. Traité de l'éducation des filles.

Éducation sentimentale, L' (1869; first drafted 1843–5), a novel by Flaubert, preferred by some critics to his **Madame Bovary*. It belongs to the type of realistic fiction which depicts uneventful lives in detail on a consistently low note—in this case with consummate artistry. The political and social background is painted with such fidelity that the work is also a valuable record of the ideals and enthusiasms of a whole era.

In the reign of Louis-Philippe, Frédéric Moreau, the hero, is in Paris to study law. He has various dreams and ambitions, no driving enthusiasm. He inherits money, and is able to lead a life of pleasure. He is in love with Mme Arnoux, wife of an amiable sensualist and waster, whom he first met by chance as a young student (*cf.* Flaubert and Mme Schlésinger). But his devotion remains idealistic, partly owing to circumstances, but more because it is essentially a prolonged, timid calf-love. He does have a few half-hearted, less platonic affairs (one is at its height in the spring of 1848), and is nearly drawn into marriage. Arnoux and his family disappear from Paris after a financial crash. Frédéric travels aimlessly, then returns to Paris. Once, after nearly 20 years of monotonous, unthinking existence, he is surprised by a visit from Mme Arnoux. They talk of the past and what might have been, for she had guessed his love and returned it. She leaves him a lock of her hair, now white. 'Et ce fut tout.' Sometimes, in the evenings, Frédéric and his friend Deslauriers sit by the fire recalling their youthful companions, ambitions, and escapades.

Effarés, Les, one of 22 poems written by Rimbaud in 1870, when he was 16. Five urchins crouch in the cold against the grid of a bakehouse, lost to everything but the sight of the baker at work and the fine, hot smell of new bread.

Effrénéisme, *v. Literary Isms.*

Eginhard or **Einhard** (*c.* 770–840), a Frankish historian, noted for his Latin life of Charlemagne (possibly a source of the **Chanson de Roland*). A pupil of the **École palatine*, he enjoyed the favour of Charlemagne and Louis Ier, and helped to promote the contemporary revival of letters (*cf. Alcuin*).

Eichendorff, JOSEPH FREIHERR VON (1788–1857), German Romantic, primarily a lyric poet, but also author of short tales (e.g. *Aus dem Leben eines Taugenichts*, 1826) and dramas; a precursor of French *Romanticism (*v. Foreign Influences*, 3).

Eiffel Tower, *v. Tour Eiffel.*

Élan vital, *v. Bergson.*

Elba, *v. Napoleon.*

El Desdichado, *v. Chimères, Les.*

Eleanor of Aquitaine, *v. Troubadours*; *Wace.*

Élections, *v. Fiscal System.*

Éliacin, in Racine's **Athalie.*

Éliante, in Molière's Le **Misanthrope.*

Elioxe, *v. Chevalier au cygne.*

Élisabeth, ou les Exilés de Sibérie, *v. Cottin.*

Élision, in French prosody, the suppression, in pronunciation, of the final 'mute' *e* when followed in the same line by a word beginning with a vowel or a mute *h*; e.g. in the line,

Assise auprès du feu, dévidant et filant,

the *e* of *assise* is elided. *Cf. Hiatus.*

Élixir de longue vie, L', *v. Comédie humaine, La* (*Études philosophiques*).

Elle et lui, *v. Sand.*

Ellénore, in B. Constant's **Adolphe.*

Elmire, in Molière's Le **Tartuffe.*

Éloa, v. Poèmes antiques et modernes.

Éloge de Richardson, v. Diderot.

Elstir, in Proust's **A la recherche du temps perdu*, a famous painter—at one time an *habitué* of the *Verdurin *salon*—whose life touches Marcel's at many points. Marcel gets to know him, and through him Albertine (*v. Albertine disparue*), on his first holiday at *Balbec. He quickens Marcel's interest in the *Impressionist painters.

Éluard, Paul, *pseudonym of* EUGÈNE GRINDEL (1895–1952), a fine lyric poet. He was a *Dadaist, then long a leading *Surrealist. His Surrealist works, which made his name as a love poet, included such notable collections as *Mourir de ne pas mourir* (1924), *Capitale de la douleur* (1926), *L'Amour la poésie* (1929), *La Vie immédiate* (1932), and *La Rose publique* (1934); also *152 Proverbes mis au goût du jour* (1925; with Péret) and *L'Immaculée Conception* (1930; with A. Breton). He broke with Breton in 1938, moved to a wider human concern by political events (the impact of the Spanish Civil War is evident in *Cours naturel*, 1938), and became a 'poète engagé' (and from 1942 a sincere and active Communist). He was a leader of the intellectual *Resistance to the Germans (notably in *Poésie et vérité*, 1942; *Les Sept Poèmes d'amour en guerre*, 1943; *Au rendez-vous allemand*, 1944), often, like Aragon, resisting through the medium of poignant love poetry. His later works include *Poésie ininterrompue* (1946), *Corps mémorable* (1947), *Poèmes politiques* (1948), *Le Phénix* (1951). He had many friends among artists (e.g. Max Ernst, Picasso, Chirico, Man Ray, Arp, Dali) and they often illustrated his works; *v.* also *Poulenc*.

Élus, *v. Fiscal System.*

El Verdugo, v. Comédie humaine, La (Études philosophiques).

Elvire, (1) in Molière's *Dom Juan; (2) *v. Lamartine.*

Élysée, Palais de l', in Paris, built 1718 for the comte d'Évreux, became State property during the Revolution, was later used as a royal residence or for royal guests (e.g. Queen Victoria during the Second Empire), and since 1873 has been the official residence of the *President of the Republic.

Émaux et Camées (1852; later augm. eds.), by Gautier, a famous collection of short poems (many in octosyllabic quatrains) which perpetuate moments, seasons, and landscapes. Their serene beauty and concern for perfection of form mark Gautier as a precursor of the *Parnassiens. They include the graceful *Premier Sourire du printemps*; the *Symphonie en blanc majeur*; *L'Art* (inc. first in the 1858 ed.), which contains the *Parnassien* doctrines in essence, urging the poet to emulate the sculptor and immortalize his inspiration in the *bloc résistant* of form.

Émigré, L', v. Sénac de Meilhan.

Émigrés, *v. Armée des émigrés; Coblenz; Hamburg.*

Émile (1762), by J.-J. Rousseau, a treatise on education (5 bks., Émile and Sophie being the ideal pupils), based on his doctrine of the return to nature and advancing religious views which led to his prolonged persecution. Despite obvious errors and deficiencies, it threw a flood of light on a subject hitherto governed by prejudice and obscurantism, provoking thought and exerting a beneficial influence far beyond France (it was quickly translated into English).

The child should be born and reared in the country, suckled by his mother, and not smothered in swaddling clothes. His early education should be directed to the development of the heart and intelligence by sympathy and example (avoiding verbal lessons, reasoning, books, and authority), and to the development of a healthy body by exercise, cold baths, etc. As he grows older, instruction is to come from the observation of natural phenomena and of the interdependence of the members of a society. He should now learn a handicraft: he will thus acquire an assured place in the social scheme and learn to respect the humbler members of society. His moral education (which rests ultimately on self-love and self-respect) is later further developed by a study of ancient history (esp. the biographies of great men) and by travel. Religion and philosophy enter very late into the scheme, for Émile does not even hear mention of God until his reason is mature. The religious teaching he is to receive is set forth in a famous section entitled *Profession de foi du vicaire savoyard*. Here Rousseau rejects revealed religion (though he refers to it with reverence) and expounds his belief, by a process of deduction from elementary consciousness, in a benevolent Deity, an immortal soul, and an innate principle of justice and virtue (the conscience).

Book V deals with the education of women, who—in surprising contrast to what precedes—should be trained to help and comfort men, while remaining docile, mentally inferior, and submissive. Émile's courtship of the well-trained Sophie forms a charming, but unconvincing, idyll. In a curious sequel, *Émile et Sophie*, she proves unfaithful and their happy marriage breaks down.

Éminence grise, L', *nickname of* JOSEPH LE CLERC DU TREMBLAY (1577–1638), 'le Père Joseph', a Capuchin friar, the trusted adviser and diplomatic agent of Richelieu; used proverbially of an unobtrusive influential adviser.

Emmanuel, Pierre, *pseudonym of* NOËL MATHIEU (1916–84), poet and essayist of religious inspiration, influenced by Jouve; a member of the *Académie (1968). After *Élégies* (1940), he made his name as a poet of the *Resistance and a Christian revolutionary (with Communist leanings till 1947), ardently voicing, in verse steeped in Christian symbols and pagan myth, the profound disquiet of many of his generation. His poetical works include *Tombeau d'Orphée* (1941); *Jour de colère* (1942), *Combats avec tes défenseurs* (1942),

and *La Liberté guide nos pas* (1945), Resistance poems; *Cantos* (1944); *Chansons du dé à coudre* (1947); *Babel* (1951), a notable modern *epic on the theme of the creation, rise, and fall of man (the narrative, attributed to 'le Récitant', is in poetic prose); *Versant de l'âge* (1958); *Évangéliaire* (1961); *Sophia* (1973). His prose works include *Poésie, raison ardente* (1947); *Qui est cet homme?* (1947) and *L'Ouvrier de la onzième heure* (1953), which are autobiographical; *Le Goût de l'Un* (1963); *Baudelaire devant Dieu* (1967).

Empire, First, *v. Napoleon*.

Empire, Second (1852–70: for details of its rise and fall *v. Republics*, 2; *Revolutions*, 4; *Napoleon III*). For the first half of this period political freedom, whether of action or comment, was suppressed (*v. Press*, 8; *Censorship, Dramatic*), and many persons hostile to the *régime* were in compulsory or self-imposed exile. A slightly more liberal attitude obtained after 1860, but no fundamental reforms were introduced till *c.* 1868. Materially, however, the Second Empire was a period of financial and industrial expansion. Banks were founded, means of communication improved (telegraphs, railways, the Suez Canal), and Paris and other cities undertook schemes of urban development (*v. Haussmann*). There was also some improvement in industrial conditions, but socialistic ideas and a new Republican movement were making silent headway. The positivist and materialistic spirit of the time was reflected in the pursuit of money and pleasure and in brilliant social life (Napoleon III's court was the most resplendent in Europe); the Exhibitions of 1855 and 1867 attracted millions of visitors to Paris. France was several times involved in war. She fought in the Crimea (1854–6) and in China (1857–60); helped Italy in her war of independence against Austria (1859); conquered Cochin-China (1859–62); intervened, with unhappy results, in Mexico (1862); and was disastrously defeated in the *Franco-Prussian war.

Life under the Second Empire is

memorably described in the novels of A. Daudet and Zola.

En attendant Godot, v. *Beckett.*

Encyclopedias, v. *Dictionaries.*

Encyclopédie, ou Dictionnaire raisonné des sciences, des arts, et des métiers, par une société de gens de lettres, L' (*privilège* 1746; Diderot's prospectus 1750; 17 vols. of text, inc. d'Alembert's *Discours préliminaire*, and 11 vols. of plates, 1751–72; 4 additional vols. of text, 1 vol. of plates, and a 2-vol. index, 1776–80), one of the great literary monuments of the 18th c., an encyclopedic dictionary of the knowledge of the day. It was suggested by Ephraim Chambers's *Cyclopaedia* (1728), which two publishers, Le Breton and Briasson, proposed to have translated. They approached Diderot, who persuaded them to give the work an ampler scope, the systematic classification of knowledge on Baconian lines.

Diderot was the principal director of the enterprise (though he had no hand in the 7 final vols.), with d'Alembert, in charge of 'la partie mathématique', as his chief assistant (until 1758), and with Jaucourt, Marmontel, and Voltaire in varying degrees as lieutenants. Famous contributors included Voltaire (articles on *Éloquence*, on the literary aspects of *Esprit* and *Grâce*, etc.), Montesquieu (on *Goût*), Turgot (on *Étymologie, Existence, Foires, Fondations*), J.-J. Rousseau (on *Économie politique* and music), Marmontel (numerous literary articles), Diderot (technical descriptions of the mechanical arts). Others who wrote for, or influenced, the *Encyclopédie* included Buffon (whose article *Nature* appears not to have been printed), Condillac, Duclos, Helvétius, d'Holbach (at whose home the *Encyclopédistes* met), Morellet, G. Raynal. But many of these eminent persons gave little beyond their name and support to the venture; the bulk of the work was done by a host of hack-writers supervised by Jaucourt. There were considerable faults of execution (contradictions, errors, etc.; some articles were disproportionately long, a few were absurd) and much unacknowledged copying from earlier dictionaries (e.g. those of Bayle and Moreri). Commercially, the venture was a great success: the outlay is said to have been about 1,000,000 francs, the profit nearly 300 per cent.

The *Encyclopédie* was a great engine of intellectual revolution in which all the energies of the **philosophes*, however divergent their individual views, were embodied and deployed. D'Alembert's *Discours préliminaire* sets forth the objects of the enterprise (to expound the order and connection of human knowledge, the general principles and essential details of the arts and sciences), traces the arts and sciences back to their origin in sensation and classifies them according to the faculties on which they depend (memory, reason, imagination), and outlines the growth of science from the Renaissance, by way of Bacon, Descartes, Newton, and Locke, down to Buffon, Montesquieu, and Voltaire. It has something of the dignity of Bacon's philosophical writings: it sees the universe as one great single fact, and all the sciences that explain it as branches of a single truth. The *Encyclopédie* propagated the scientific spirit and thereby combated superstition and (with Bacon) assigned to science its practical purpose. The system it taught was purely rationalistic: there was no room in it for anything that reason could not explain. Its doctrines were founded on the three main principles of nature, reason, and humanity: under the first, it attacked the supernatural and fabulous in history; under the second, authority as the source of irrational religious doctrines (e.g. eternal damnation) and political institutions; under the third, intolerance and persecution. The articles on religious subjects are outwardly orthodox, even pious: religious dogmas are asserted, then undermined by insinuations of incredibility, thus encouraging scepticism. The political articles are more straightforward: with increasing boldness as the work progresses they censure the unequal distribution of wealth, fiscal privileges, and other abuses, especially in the administration of justice. The monarchical system is not attacked, but the king must be good and just, and there must be civil equality before the law. War, regarded as a last resort, should be made more humane. Reforms in education are also advocated.

The work's sceptical tendency in regard to religion aroused the hostility of the clergy and the official classes (with the notable exceptions of the comte d'Argenson; Mme de Pompadour; and Malesherbes, then in charge of the censorship and therefore a valuable ally). Its chief opponents included Fréron, Nonnotte, Palissot, Barruel-Bauvert, Chaumeix, Pompignan and his brother (bishop of Le Puy), and the *Jesuits (v. Journal de Trévoux; Dictionaries, 1704; also Cacouacs). Publication was twice prohibited, in 1752 through Jesuit influence (and v. Prades), in 1759 after the appearance of d'*Alembert's article Genève and Helvétius's treatise *De l'esprit. It continued nevertheless, the government being only half-heartedly opposed to it and Malesherbes sympathetic (v. Librairie). Volumes VIII–XVII (issued together) were, however, mutilated by the printer Le Breton, who, unknown to the editors, erased everything likely to offend the authorities.

Encyclopédistes, a term loosely applied to the *philosophes and others who, in greater or less degree, promoted or supported the *Encyclopédie, and who, despite some feuds and differences of doctrine, did form a kind of brotherhood. They included Diderot, d'Alembert, Voltaire, Condillac, Helvétius, d'Holbach, Jaucourt, Morellet, G. Raynal, Duclos, Marmontel, Turgot.

Eneas, v. Romans d'antiquité.

Enfances Ogier, v. Ogier le Danois.

Enfantin, BARTHÉLEMY-PROSPER, v. Saint-Simonisme.

Enfant prodigue, L', a sentimental comedy (in decasyllables) by Voltaire,

interesting as an early example of the *drame, otherwise of little merit; produced 1736. The prodigal son returns just in time to save his former fiancée from being married against her will to his pompous, avaricious brother.

Enfants sans souci, Les, the best known of the medieval confréries or *sociétés joyeuses. It existed in Paris, and its members, like those of other sociétés joyeuses, called themselves sots or compagnons du Prince des Sots, their chief officers being the Prince des Sots and Mère Sotte. They always acted in fool's costume with cap and bells, and mainly performed *soties (v. Confrérie de la Passion). They did not, like members of the *Basoches, belong to a specific profession, but their ranks probably included Basochiens (v. Marot). Like the Basoches, the Enfants sans souci flourished under Louis XII, when Gringore and Jean de l'Espine were famous members. They had ceased to exist by the early 17th c.

Enfants terribles, Les, v. Cocteau.

Enfer de la Bibliothèque nationale, L', the section of the *Bibliothèque nationale reserved for books that for reasons of obscenity, etc., are enfermés and shelf-marked 'enfer.' Apollinaire and two friends compiled a work entitled L'Enfer de la Bibliothèque nationale (1913).

Engagement, engagé, v. Littérature engagée.

Enghien, DUC D', the title borne by the eldest son of the prince de Condé (v. Bourbon). LOUIS-ANTOINE-HENRI DE BOURBON (1772–1804), the last Condé to bear this title, fought with his family in the *Armée des émigrés, then settled in Germany (1801). In March 1804 he was kidnapped, taken to *Vincennes, and, after a perfunctory court martial on the charge of plotting to overthrow Napoleon, shot and buried at night in a grave already dug to receive him. There was little doubt that Napoleon, bent on removing possible Royalist rivals, was directly responsible. The incident aroused fierce indignation.

English Literature, French Influence on. (For English influence on French literature v. *Foreign Influences*.)

1. 13TH–15TH CENTURIES. French literature was introduced into England largely by the Norman Conquest (1066) and the establishment of a French-speaking aristocracy; v. *Anglo-Norman*. Its influence can be seen in the 14th- and 15th-c. English verse romances (esp. those inspired by the **romans bretons*), in stories and adventures borrowed from the **chansons de geste* (e.g. *Sir Ferumbras*), from *Marie de France's *lais* (e.g. *Sir Launfal*), and from Benoît de Sainte-Maure's **Roman de Troie*. Chaucer was influenced by such courtly writers as Guillaume de Lorris (*Romaunt of the Rose*) and by writers of **rondeaux* and **ballades*, e.g. Guillaume de Machaut and Eustache Deschamps.

2. 16TH CENTURY. There was now a fresh wave of French influence: Wyatt and Surrey studied the verse-forms of Marot and M. de Saint-Gelais; Daniel was inspired by Desportes; Spenser translated poems by Du Bellay and admired Marot; and v. *Du Bartas*. Translations of French prose works—often themselves translations—included North's version of Plutarch's *Lives* (1579; from Amyot), a work familiar to the Elizabethan dramatists (*cf. Bandello*); Danett's Commines (1596); Florio's Montaigne (1603). Bacon and Shakespeare were both familiar with Montaigne. Rabelais, too, was certainly read at this time, though not translated till much later (from 1653, by Urquhart).

3. 17TH AND 18TH CENTURIES. The exile in France in the mid-17th c. of the English court and many English men of letters favoured French influence, noticeable especially after the Restoration, on the English stage. Even before then, English heroic tragedy was being influenced by the romances of La Calprenède and Mlle de Scudéry, translated, imitated, and long widely read. The main French influence on Restoration comedy was Molière, from whom Etherege, Sedley, d'Avenant, Dryden, Wycherley, Vanbrugh, and others borrowed plots and characters.

Corneille and Racine were translated (v. *Cid, Le*), imitated (e.g. Addison's *Cato*), and adapted (e.g. Ambrose Philips's *The Distrest Mother*, 1712, from **Andromaque*); and there was much discussion of the rules, and comparative merits, of French *Classical drama, e.g. in Dryden's *Essay of Dramatic Poesy*.

The influence of French literary criticism at this time was ultimately even stronger. Dryden recognized Boileau (whose **Lutrin* and **Art poétique* were translated in 1682 and 1683 respectively) as a leading authority of the day. The critical works of R. Rapin, Dacier, and Le Bossu were also studied and are referred to in Congreve's *The Double Dealer*. Bouhours is often mentioned. A revived interest in Montaigne, seen in the essays of Cowley and Temple, led to a new translation (1685) by Cotton. Other translations included *Guez de Balzac's *Lettres* (1638); *Voiture's *Lettres*, works by Scarron, *Pascal's *Lettres provinciales*, and *Descartes's *Traité des passions*, all *c.* 1650; *Pascal's *Pensées* (1688); *La Rochefoucauld's *Maximes* (1694; Lord Chesterfield's favourite reading); *La Bruyère's *Caractères* (1699). Influence was also exerted by Frenchmen in England as residents, exiles, or visitors (e.g. Saint-Évremond—regarded as a literary oracle; the many *Huguenot men of letters then in London; Voltaire and Montesquieu, who both made long stays and many literary contacts between 1726 and 1731, though their full impact came later, after publication of their chief works).

Though writers of the Augustan age still adhered to the French Classical principles, this dominance gradually weakened as the intellectual horizon extended beyond a polished circle of wits. For from *c.* 1730 the English country gentleman was beginning to visit the Continent, and the middle class was beginning to read 'what it really likes, without bothering about Aristotle or M. Bossu'. But French influence on the developing *genre* of the novel was considerable (e.g. Smollett's debt to **Gil Blas*); and by the mid-18th c. the writings of Voltaire and

Montesquieu were profoundly influencing English political and economic thought and the general philosophic and synthetic conception of history (*cf.* Hume, Gibbon, and Robertson). The ideals of J.-J. Rousseau and the early principles of the Revolution were reflected in such works as Godwin's *Political Justice*, and in the passionate belief in progress, liberty, equality, and humanity which inspired his disciple Shelley, the early Coleridge, Wordsworth and Southey, or Burns.

4. 1800–*c.* 1850. The English attitude to France, hostile during the later Revolution and the Napoleonic era, was in general unreceptive for some 50 years after the Restoration. New developments in French literature did not, however, go unnoticed. Hugo's poetic genius and imagination were recognized, and his *Hernani* was praised for its Shakespearian quality. Balzac and G. Sand were acknowledged to be the leading contemporary French novelists (with Kock and Sue surprisingly close behind); but they were seldom recommended or imitated. Perhaps the chief sign that French literature exerted any influence between 1830 and 1850 is that the critics, voicing public opinion, frequently deplored its cynicism and immorality.

5. AFTER 1850. Appreciation of both the traditional and the newer aspects of the French genius was revived and stimulated after 1850, notably by G. H. Lewes, Matthew Arnold (whose admiration of Sainte-Beuve is seen in his demand for 'curiosity' in criticism), and Meredith (*cf.* his *Odes in Contribution to the Song of French History*). Comte's Positivist philosophy—a more real influence on George Eliot than her early reading of G. Sand, and a basis for the philosophy of Herbert Spencer—became known through the works of J. S. Mill and G. H. Lewes and the translations of Harriet Martineau. Medieval and Renaissance writers were increasingly studied and translated.

Stimulating contacts now also developed between the younger artistic and literary groups and their French fellows. The Swinburne of *Poems and Ballads* was a disciple of Hugo, Gautier, and Baudelaire. Through him, Gautier's defiant creed of *l'*art pour l'art*—later developed by Baudelaire, Flaubert, and the **Parnassiens*—influenced the Pre-Raphaelite revolt and, even more strongly (1870–1900), the aesthetic movement associated with Pater. *L'art pour l'art* was later mocked by Gilbert and Sullivan (*Patience*) and over-exploited by Wilde, but it had helped to bring a more objective spirit into both the creative and the critical function.

In the novel, the interest aroused by *Realism and *Naturalism, and the influence of Flaubert, the Goncourts, Maupassant, Zola, Huysmans, etc., is apparent in George Moore (*The Mummer's Wife*; *Esther Waters*; *Confessions of a Young Man*), Gissing (novels of drab London life), Bennett, Conrad, Somerset Maugham, the early work of James Joyce (*Dubliners*), etc. (*Cf.* also the interpretative criticism of Henry James, Edmund Gosse.)

In poetry, *Impressionism and *Symbolism strongly influenced Yeats, Synge, and their group. Visits to Paris and talk with those they regarded as masters (e.g. at Mallarmé's 'Tuesdays') reinforced the influence. T. S. Eliot (attracted to Symbolism by A. Symons's *Symbolist Movement in Literature*) acknowledged the strong influence of Laforgue on his early work. Eliot also translated (1930) *Saint-John Perse's *Anabase*.

During the past 50 years, the interplay of ideas has obviously become more immediate than ever before, the volume of translations has steadily increased, and the work of Beckett, which belongs to both literatures, has created a link between them. (The growing interest of English readers in modern French authors other than Proust, Maurois, and Simenon, who have long been widely read, is indicated by the increasing availability of the works of e.g. Sartre, Camus, S. Weil, Z. Oldenbourg, Robbe-Grillet, and Ionesco in public libraries, often both in translation and in the original.) Clear influences include, notably, that of Proust on the novel, evident in works ranging from Virginia Woolf's *The Waves* to Anthony Powell's *A Dance to the Music of Time*; also those of *Surrealism on such poets as George Barker and David Gascoyne (who also owes much to Jouve), of Sartrean *Existentialism and the works of Sartre and Camus (both freely cited in Colin Wilson's *The Outsider*)—and also those of S. Weil and Teilhard de Chardin—on the post-war intellectual climate in England, and of the Theatre of the Absurd, in particular Beckett and Ionesco, on Harold Pinter (e.g. *The Caretaker*), N. F. Simpson, and James Saunders. *v.* also *Artaud*; *Saint-Denis, M.*

Enjambement, in French prosody (esp. in the *alexandrine), the carrying on of a phrase or sentence beyond the end of one line into the first words of the next. Boileau, however, decreed in his *Art poétique* that breaks in the sense should coincide with metrical divisions. His dictum (based on no good authority and sometimes ignored by great contemporaries like Corneille, Racine, Molière, and La Fontaine) exerted a strong restrictive influence on later poets; but it was deliberately disregarded by the *Romantics (*v. Chénier, A.*; *Hugo*).

Enlèvement de la redoute, L' (1833, in *Mosaïque*), by Mérimée, a short tale of military glory, said to have been based on the swift storming of the redoubt of Schwardino during Napoleon's Russian campaign of 1812.

Ennemi du genre humain, L'. William Pitt, the younger, was so proclaimed by the *Convention, 7 August 1793.

Ennery, ADOLPHE-PHILIPPE D' (1811–99), wrote popular *mélodrames, e.g. *Cartouche* (1859), *Les Mystères du vieux Paris* (1865), *Les Deux Orphelines* (1875); and *v. Mercadet*.

Enquête sur la monarchie, L', *v. Maurras*.

Enragés, Les, an extremist popular movement in Paris during the Revolution,

without representation in the *Convention*. The *Hébertistes, who contributed to their fall (Sept. 1793), adopted many of their slogans. Their leader, the abbé Jacques Roux, committed suicide.

En route, *v. Huysmans*.

Ensorcelée, L' (1854), by Barbey d'Aurevilly, a novel set in Normandy, with fine descriptions of its wild country and old customs.

After a dissolute youth in the monastery of Blanchelande, the abbé de la Croix-Jurgan was involved in the *Chouannerie and crowned his acts of sacrilege by attempting suicide when the rebels were defeated. When the story opens, he is parish priest in a village not far from his former monastery, now a ruin. Everything about him is monstrous—his hideous, scarred face (he was tortured by Republican troops), his stature, his pride. One of his flock, a rich farmer's wife, bewitched by vengeful nomad shepherds, falls passionately in love with him and kills herself. The abbé, who can be convicted of no sin except inordinate pride, is allowed to resume his functions after a period of penance. During High Mass on Easter Sunday, his first Office, he is shot at the altar by the dead woman's husband. In after years, travellers crossing the deserted heath of Lessay can hear the bell of the ruined abbey of Blanchelande. Its windows are strangely lit, and within a phantom priest celebrates a Mass which he can never complete.

Entretiens d'Ariste et d'Eugène, *v. Bouhours*.

Entretiens sur la pluralité des mondes, *v. Fontenelle*.

Envers de l'histoire contemporaine, L', *v. Comédie humaine, La (Scènes de la vie parisienne).*

Envoi, 'sending on the way', the final stanza in certain types of lyric poem, e.g. *ballades, *jeux partis. It often begins with such words as 'Prince', 'Sire', etc.

Éon de Beaumont, CHARLES D', *known as* LE CHEVALIER D'ÉON (1728–1810), political adventurer, employed as a secret agent by Louis XV at the Russian court (where he posed as a woman) and in London, where he died.

Épervier, Lai de l', a typical *fabliau*. A knight loves a lady. One day, when her husband is away, he sends his squire to ask if he may see her. The squire makes love to her. The knight arrives and she hides the squire. As she is talking to the knight, she sees her husband returning. The knight, on her instructions, feigns anger, and goes off uttering threats as the husband enters. She explains to her husband that the knight was chasing his squire, who, having lost his master's hawk, had taken refuge in her house to escape his wrath; then she brings the squire out from his hiding-place.

Epic Poetry, one of the earliest forms of literary activity in France. The medieval epic is principally exemplified in the *chansons de geste*. There is also an epic element in the poems of the Crusade cycle (e.g. the *Chanson d'*Antioche*) and in the *romans d'antiquité* (e.g. the **Roman de Thèbes*). In time, the romantic or comic element prevailed over the heroic, and the medieval epic declined.

There was no real revival until the 16th c., with **Ronsard's Franciade*, in decasyllables, like the earlier *chansons de geste*; d'Aubigné's *Les *Tragiques* and **Du Bartas's La Semaine*, both in **alexandrines*, the form which now prevailed. In the mid-17th c. there was a spate of epics, now largely forgotten, e.g. **Chapelain's La Pucelle*; **Saint-Amant's Moïse sauvé*; **Godeau's Saint Paul*, which contains passages of Christian eloquence; Louis Le Laboureur's *Charlemagne* (1664); Carel de Sainte-Garde's *Childebrand* (1666); **Desmarets de Saint-Sorlin's Clovis*. In the 18th c. Voltaire produced *La *Henriade*, and A. Chénier planned, but did not live to complete, two great epics on human perfectibility.

In 1822 Vigny published *Héléna*, an epic

of Greek antiquity which he removed from later editions of his works. (His **Éloa* and *Le Déluge*, like Lamartine's *La *Chute d'un ange* and **Jocelyn*, are less epics than long narrative poems.) Other epics of the early and mid-19th c. include the historical and patriotic epic, e.g. **Quinet's Napoléon*, **Viennet's Franciade*; the religious, mythological, or mystical epic (sometimes reflecting the romantic humanitarianism of the years before the 1848 **Revolution*), e.g. **Soumet's Divine Épopée*, **Leconte de Lisle's Qaïn* (written 1845; first publ. 1871 in *Le *Parnasse contemporain*) and *La Passion* (1858), **Ménard's Prométhée délivré* and *Euphorion* (1855); the semi-scientific or philosophical epic, e.g. Lemercier's *Atlantide, ou la Théogonie newtonienne* (1812), Bouilhet's *Les Fossiles* (1854), **Sully-Prudhomme's Le Bonheur*; and an epic of rural life, **Laprade's Pernette*. Possibly the most genuinely epic works of this period are Chateaubriand's *Les *Martyrs* and **Quinet's Ahasuérus*, though both are in prose.

In 1859, Hugo emerged as the supreme epic poet of the century with the first series of his **Légende des siècles*. He introduced a new form of short epic, the *petite épopée* (foreshadowed by Vigny's *Le Cor*, in **Poèmes antiques et modernes*, 1826), in which some legend or fable, briefly told, evokes the whole history and spirit of an age, while a series of such poems, linked together, presents successive phases of a ruling theme. In forsaking the older conventions of the epic, Hugo may have been influenced by Leconte de Lisle, whose aim (*c.* 1850–60) in many poems on Biblical, Greek, Nordic, and Celtic themes was the reconstitution of past epochs rather than straightforward narration.

The move away from such narration was itself a sign that the epic was a dying *genre*. 20th-c. attempts to revive or transform it (*v.* *Emmanuel*; *Saint-John Perse*) have done little to discount Baudelaire's comments of 1862: 'Excepté à l'aurore de la vie des nations, où la poésie est à la fois l'expression de leur âme et le répertoire de leurs connaissances, l'histoire mise en vers est une dérogation aux lois qui gouvernent les deux genres, l'histoire et la poésie; c'est un outrage aux deux Muses. Dans les périodes extrêmement cultivées... celui qui tente de créer le poème épique tel que le comprenaient les nations plus jeunes, risque de diminuer l'effet magique de la poésie... et en même temps d'enlever à l'histoire une partie de la sagesse et de la sévérité qu'exigent d'elle les nations âgées.'

Épinay, LOUISE-FLORENCE D'ESCLA-VELLES, MME D' (1726–83), wife of a *fermier général*, was a leading member of the intellectual society of the day, long on intimate terms with Grimm, a protectress of J.-J. Rousseau, a friend of Diderot; and v. *Galiani*. She left letters; *Conversations d'Émilie* on educational topics; and an autobiographical novel (publ. as *Mémoires*, 1818) vividly depicting her circle (some passages blacken Rousseau's character and appear from changes in the ms. to have been worded with the help of Grimm and Diderot).

Épîtres, (1) v. *Marot*; (2) by Boileau, 12 verse dissertations on various subjects (publ. at intervals from 1674 onwards), modelled on Horace's *Epistles*, and addressed to the king and other notabilities. The most interesting are those on literary matters, notably VII (to Racine), IX, and X. No. XII (*Sur l'Amour de Dieu*) brought him into conflict with the *Jesuits.

Époques de la Nature, v. *Buffon*.

Eracle, a verse romance, written *c.* 1165 by Gautier d'Arras.

Eracle, son of a noble Roman, has a miraculous gift of discerning the merits of gems, horses, and women. When his mother is widowed, she sells him and all her goods for the benefit of the poor. He is bought by the emperor's seneschal, in whose employ he shows his gifts as a diviner (an episode related with much charm and humour). Later, he is elected emperor of Constantinople and restores the Cross (removed from Jerusalem by the king of Persia) to the Holy Sepulchre.

Eracles, Livre d', v. *Terre Sainte, Livre de la*.

Erasmus, DESIDERIUS (1466–1536). After leaving the cloister, this great Dutch humanist settled in Paris for a period of study. He supported himself by teaching, learnt Greek, and (aged 30 and already a scholar of repute) was a boarder at the *Collège de Montaigu*. His famous *Adagia*, from which 'toute la lumière de l'antiquité se répand à flots sur le monde', was first published in Paris in 1500 and did much to engender the classical translations, dictionaries, and grammars which were at once the inspiration and the *apparatus criticus* of early *Renaissance literature and scholarship. v. *Tragedy*.

Erckmann-Chatrian, i.e. ÉMILE ERCKMANN (1822–99) and ALEXANDRE CHATRIAN (1826–90), two Alsatians who long collaborated in writing numerous novels of the Revolution and the Napoleonic wars ('romans nationaux et populaires', popular as school prizes), e.g. *L'Illustre Docteur Mathéus* (1859); *Mme Thérèse, ou les Volontaires de 1792* (1863); *L'Ami Fritz* (1864), a genial, sentimental tale of Alsace and of a confirmed bachelor who finally falls in love, successfully dramatized 1877; *Histoire d'un conscrit de 1813* (1864); *Waterloo* (1865); *Histoire d'un paysan* (1868–74, 4 vols.), a homely, day-to-day picture (with no pretensions to be anything but simplified history) of events before, during, and just after the Revolution as they affected an Alsatian village community and, in particular, the aged narrator, once a fervent Revolutionary and a soldier in the Revolutionary armies.

Erec, a *roman breton* by Chrétien de Troyes; written *c.* 1165.

Erec, a knight of Arthur's court, wins his wife Enid by his prowess, and is then mortified to find that she thinks love has made him neglect his knightly duties. So he sets out with her in search of chivalrous adventure, enjoining her to remain absolutely silent, an order she cannot help disobeying every time she sees him in danger, until, in a dramatic scene, her fidelity brings reconciliation.

Ermenonville, *v. Rousseau, J.-J.; Girardin, marquis de.*

Ermitage, L', *v. Rousseau, J.-J.*

Ermitage, L' (1890–5; 1897–1906), one of the most active *Symbolist reviews, with articles on literature, history, philosophy, music, art, the theatre. Contributors included Louÿs, H. de Régnier, Vielé-Griffin, Claudel, Copeau, Gide, R. de Gourmont, Jammes.

Ernoul, Chronique d', *v. Crusades.*

Escoufle, L', a verse *roman d'aventure* of c. 1200, almost certainly by Jean Renart. It is agreeably told and throws interesting light on medieval manners.

Guillaume, son of a gallant Norman Crusader who has won the affection of the emperor of Rome, is betrothed to the emperor's daughter Aelis. But, when his father dies, the match is cancelled through the influence of the emperor's evil counsellors. The lovers elope to Normandy; but they lose one another on the way, when Guillaume chases a kite (*escoufle*) that has carried off Aelis's purse. For years they search for each other, meeting with many adventures. They are finally reunited by another incident involving a kite. They marry, and Guillaume ends as emperor of Rome.

Esménard, JOSEPH-ÉTIENNE (1769–1811), author and publicist, came to Paris as a delegate to the *Fête de la *Fédération* of 1790, left France when the monarchy fell (1792) and travelled on land and sea (an experience utilized in his didactic poem *La Navigation*, 1805). Under the Empire, he was dramatic censor, director of the *Imprimerie*, and special censor of the *Journal de l'Empire* (*v. Journal des Débats*). He incurred Napoleon's displeasure, was exiled, and died in Italy.

Esméralda, in Hugo's *Notre-Dame de Paris*.

Ésotérisme, *v. Literary Isms.*

Esparbès, THOMAS-AUGUSTE, *known as* GEORGES D'* (1864–1944), wrote patriotic and historical novels, usually of the Revolutionary and Napoleonic eras, e.g. *La Légende de l'Aigle* (1893).

Espion des grands seigneurs..., L', *v. Marana.*

Esplandian, in *Amadis de Gaule.*

Esprit, *v. Mounier.*

Esprit, JACQUES (1611–78), man of letters and gifted conversationalist, frequented the *salons of Mme de Rambouillet and Mme de Sablé. His *Fausseté des vertus humaines* was on the same theme as *La Rochefoucauld's *Maximes*.

Esprit décadent, L', the term applied—possibly first by Laforgue—to the state of mind prevalent between 1880 and 1890 in the small literary societies (e.g. the *Hydropathes*) which were to some extent the cradle of *Symbolism. The term may have come from the sonnet *Je suis l'Empire à la fin de la décadence* by Verlaine, who said of the word *décadence*: 'Ce mot suppose... des pensées raffinées d'extrême civilisation, une haute culture littéraire, une âme capable d'intensives voluptés... Il est fait d'un mélange d'esprit charnel et de chair triste et de toutes les splendeurs violentes du Bas-Empire...'

The spirit was one of extreme *langueur*, futility, distaste for moral or religious restraint, horror of banality, and the quest for novel sensations, however unnatural. It was reflected in verse, criticism, and manifestos published in little reviews, e.g. *La *Nouvelle Rive gauche, La *Revue indépendante, La *Revue wagnérienne, Le *Décadent, La *Vogue*. Many *décadents*, finding the resources of the language inadequate to express their complex sensations, coined new words or ingeniously disintegrated old ones. *v. Adam, P.; Arène; Déliquescences d'Adoré Floupette, Les.*

Esprit de contradiction, L', a one-act prose comedy by Dufresny; produced 1700.

Oronte's wife is a termagant with a spirit of contradiction. To obtain her support for his plan to marry their daughter to a rich suitor, he pretends to support the latter's rival, favoured by the daughter. But the daughter warns her mother, who, from the same spirit of contradiction, unexpectedly falls in with her husband's pretended view.

Esprit des lois, De l' (1748; some 20 further eds. were issued within 18 months), by Montesquieu, a treatise (31 bks.) on the general principles and historical origins of law.

He defines laws as necessary relations resulting from the nature of things. Law (*le droit*) being human reason applied to the government of men, the various laws (*les lois*) are applications of this reason to particular circumstances, such as the type of government (despotism, constitutional monarchy, or republic), or the physical and moral conditions of the people (climate, occupation, degree of liberty, wealth, religion). It is this relation between law and circumstances—*l'esprit des lois*—which he now proceeds to examine in the light of innumerable instances drawn from ancient and contemporary constitutions and from the commentaries of political writers (classical, French, English, Italian).

He recognizes the republic, with its underlying principles of virtue (respect for the law, patriotism) and frugality, as the ideal form of government. But it lacks stability, and he favours constitutional monarchy, in which equilibrium is maintained by certain intermediate bodies between prince and people. He praises the English constitution (XI, 6), where the independence of the executive, legislative, and judicial bodies secures a high degree of liberty. He abhors despotism, which is based on fear. His enlightened, humane attitude is shown in his disapproval of slavery and aggressive war, in his censure of religious intolerance (e.g. in the remonstrance addressed by a Jew to the Inquisition—XXV, 13) and the cruelties

of the penal code, and in his scepticism in regard to accusations of witchcraft. The last five books, different in character from the rest, form a technical treatise on the origins, Roman and Germanic, of French law.

The work has been criticized for its lack of a coherent plan, its over-brilliant, epigrammatic style (Mme du Deffand called it 'de l'esprit sur les lois'), and its tendency to generalize from insufficient premisses. Even so, it was the first work to apply the comparative method to the study of social institutions, a great manifesto of reason and humanity, a grave indictment of the abuses of the French monarchy and the defects of contemporary civilization. Its doctrine, which 'changed the thought of the world', was notably reflected in the political experiments of the Revolution and the parliamentary *constitutions that followed 1815, also in the American constitution, with its idea of federation and extreme application of the principle of separation of powers.

Esprit du boulevard, L', a form of wit prevalent in Paris during the Second Empire in the cafés, restaurants, and theatres in the region of the present Place de l'Opéra. It was a wit of *bons mots* and *à-peu-près* (e.g. 'Mme Réclamier' for a lady given to self-advertisement), a blend of gaiety, irony, malice, gossip, and veiled comment on events at a time when the *Press was muzzled. *v.* Scholl.

Esprit gaulois, L', the talent for giving an amusing and good-humoured turn to indecency that is characteristic of certain branches of French literature, e.g. the *fabliaux*. 'Le besoin de rire', comments Taine, 'est le trait national.'

Esprit pur, L' (1864, in *Les Destinées*; written 1863), one of Vigny's last poems. The poet meditates on his noble ancestors, all men of action. Their name will survive, not because of their exploits, but because he, last of the race, has inscribed it 'sur le pur tableau des livres de L'ESPRIT'.

Esprits, Les (1579), a prose comedy by

Larivey; adapted from Lorenzino dei Medici's *Aridosio*, itself a combination of Plautus's *Aulularia* and *Mostellaria* with Terence's *Adelphi*. Cf. Molière's *L'*Avare*; *L'*École des maris*.

Like the *Adelphi*, it presents two brothers, the one brought up harshly (by the father), the other leniently (by an uncle). It is the former who profits by his father's absence to entertain his mistress in the house. The consequences of the father's unexpected return are averted, as in the *Mostellaria*, by the pretence that the house is haunted by ghosts. And, as in the *Aulularia*, a purse which the avaricious father had buried is removed and returned to him only when he agrees to the lovers' marriage.

Esquiros, HENRI-ALPHONSE (1814–76), began as an extreme *Romantic (*cf. Borel, Petrus*), interested in occultism, and a friend of the abbé Constant. He wrote *Les Hirondelles* (1834; verse); *Le Magicien* (1837) and *Charlotte Corday* (1840), novels; and works of idealistic social republicanism, e.g. *L'Évangile du peuple* (1840). He took part in the 1848 *Revolution, was in exile in England during the Second Empire, but later returned to active political life in France.

Esquisse d'un tableau historique des progrès de l'esprit humain, v. *Tableau...*

Essai sur le goût, v. *Montesquieu*.

Essai sur les données immédiates de la conscience, v. *Bergson*.

Essai sur les Fables de La Fontaine, v. *Taine*.

Essai sur les mœurs et l'esprit des nations (1769), by Voltaire. In 1740, he began work on an abstract of general history, from the time of Charlemagne to that of Louis XIV. Fragments appeared in the *Mercure (1745–6, 1750–1). He repudiated an *Abrégé de l'Histoire universelle* (1753) published at The Hague, and in 1756 a complete text was published at Geneva. This was modified in various ways in the final 1769 edition. The work—a compilation, but mainly drawn from good sources—was very successful (some 16 reprints 1753–84).

He sets out to relate the history, not only of kings and wars, but of the human mind, and the development of civilization, commerce, manners, and the arts; and to extend the narrative, not only to Europe, but to the whole world. He tries to establish how people lived at various epochs (citing the prices of bread and meat, the dates of inventions, etc.), shows the progress of humanity under the pressure of its needs and circumstances, and indicates how man has impeded his own progress, notably by war and religious fanaticism—not omitting to blame the writers, whether early chroniclers or later historians, whose adulation of force and fraud has helped to maintain man in his errors.

Essai sur l'indifférence en matière de religion, v. *Lamennais*.

Essais de critique et d'histoire, v. *Taine*.

Essais de morale, v. *Nicole*.

Estang, Luc, *pseudonym of* LUCIEN BASTARD (1911–   ), poet, novelist, and critic; sometime literary editor of *La Croix*. Though he made his name as a poet in the spirit of Péguy and Claudel (e.g. *Les Béatitudes*, 1945) and continued to publish verse (e.g. *Les Quatre Éléments*, 1955), he became better known for novels depicting the moral anguish of human beings overwhelmed by sin, remorse, or doubt, and clearly influenced by his friendship with Bernanos, e.g. *Charges d'âmes* (1949–54, 3 vols.), *L'Interrogatoire* (1957), *L'Horloger du Cherche-Midi* (1959), *Le Bonheur et le salut* (1961), *Que ces mots répondent* (1964). His other works include studies of Bernanos (1947) and Saint-Exupéry (1956), *Invitation à la poésie* (1944; an essay), and *Le Jour de Caïn* (1967; a play).

Estaunié, ÉDOUARD (1862–1942), novelist. Subdued melancholy and a

Roman Catholic bias characterize his studies of superficially placid lives which conceal emotional or spiritual stress, even crime, e.g. *Les Choses voient* (1913), *L'Ascension de M. Baslèvre* (1921), *L'Appel de la route* (1921), *L'Infirme aux mains de lumière* (1924; short stories), *Le Silence dans la campagne* (1925).

Esther, a 3-act tragedy by Racine; based on the Biblical story of Ahasuerus (Assuérus), Esther, Mordecai (Mardochée), and Haman (Aman), and interspersed with songs by a chorus of Israelite girls. It was written for the pupils of the *Institut de *Saint-Cyr*, and produced there in 1689. *v. Caylus.*

Esthétique de la langue française, L', v. Gourmont.

Estienne, in Latin STEPHANUS, a famous family of printers and scholars, including (1) HENRI (d. 1520), who came to Paris from Provence in 1502 and founded a printing-house; (2) ROBERT (1503–59), son of (1), printer to François Ier and, after being exiled as a Protestant, to Calvin in Geneva, compiler of the best Latin dictionary of the day (*Thesaurus linguae latinae*, 1532; and *v. Dictionaries*, 1539); (3) CHARLES (1504–64), son of (1), physician and scholar, tutor to J.-A. de Baif, translator of Terence's *Andria* (1540; prose) and author of miscellaneous works (*v. Dictionaries*, 1553), who took over the family printing business, but failed and died in prison for debt; (4) HENRI (*c.* 1531–98), son of (2), father-in-law of Casaubon, who spent most of his life in Geneva, where he printed for the Republic, but visited France, Italy, Flanders, and England. He was an ardent Hellenist (compiler of a fine *Thesaurus graecae linguae*, 1572). His works in French include the *Apologie pour Hérodote*, a satire on his age (esp. the Catholics), where he humorously justifies Herodotus's credulity by comparing his tales with the Biblical and other marvellous stories believed in the 16th c.; his *Deux Dialogues du nouveau langage français italianisé* (1578), between two courtiers, satirizing

the corruption of the French language by italianisms; the *Précellence du langage français* (1579), a more profound work on a similar theme, the aptness of the language for all purposes of expression. It was he who wrote, 'Si jeunesse savait; si vieillesse pouvait.'

Est-il bon? Est-il méchant?, v. Diderot.

Estoire d'outre-mer, v. Terre Sainte, Livre de la.

Estrées, GABRIELLE D' (1573–99), mistress of Henri IV from *c.* 1591. The ducs de Vendôme were her descendants; *v. Mazarin's Nieces* (1).

Étape, L' (1902), a novel by Bourget, demonstrating the theories that no stability can be found outside the Church of Rome and that no one can rise in one move from the peasant to the professional (in this case professorial) class.

États généraux, under the monarchy, the assembly of representatives of the three Estates of the realm—the higher clergy, the *noblesse, and the *Tiers État (in practice the burghers of the towns)— summoned solely at the king's discretion (its first recorded meeting being that convened by Philippe IV in 1302), without powers of initiative or free discussion, to support or ratify his proposals. It was summoned fairly regularly, though on the whole at lengthening intervals, until 1614 (a turbulent session in Paris on the occasion of Louis XIII's majority). The opening session of its next meeting (5 May 1789) marked the outbreak of the *Revolution. On this occasion, representatives of the clergy and nobility (the *Privilégiés) were directly elected, while those of the Tiers État were elected by *ad hoc* electoral assemblies nominated by the middle- and lower-class voters; also (by a regulation of Jan. 1789) there were two representatives of the *Tiers État* to one of each of the other two Estates.

États généraux, Les, v. Courrier de Provence.

Étienne, CHARLES-GUILLAUME (1777–1845), journalist and dramatist, editor-in-chief of the *Journal de l'Empire* (v. *Journal des Débats*), a founder of *La *Minerve française*, and later editor of the **Constitutionnel*. He wrote successful comedies, e.g. *Brueys et Palaprat* (1807); *Les Deux Gendres* (1810), a comic treatment of the theme of *King Lear*, in which he was accused of plagiarizing *Conaxa* (1710), a play by a Jesuit.

Étienne de Fougères, v. *Livre des manières*.

Étienne Mayran (1910; written *c*. 1860), an unfinished novel by Taine. It opens in a small provincial town during the July Monarchy. At 14, Étienne, the child of a cultured home, finds himself an almost penniless orphan. There is talk of apprenticing him to a trade, but he sees a chance of remaining in the world to which he feels he belongs, and with a cold logic astonishing for his age drives a bargain with the head of a Paris boys' school: in return for board and tuition, he will prove himself a profitable advertisement for the school by his academic prowess (he will win open prizes, pass first into the **École normale*, etc.); should he fail the headmaster will be entitled to his tiny patrimony. Taine depicts his schoolmates and tutors, his dogged application, the sacrifices he makes to fulfil his side of the bargain, and finally, after a period of doubt and depression, his sudden awakening to the world of ideas which lies beyond mechanical study.

Étourdi, L', Molière's first comedy, imitated from the *Inavvertito* of Nicolò Barbieri (or 'Baltrame'); produced 1655 at Lyons. It was adapted by Dryden as *Sir Martin Mar-All*: Pepys, who saw this acted in 1667, 'never laughed so' in his life.

The scene is Messina. Lélie, the *étourdi*, a hare-brained fellow, loves Célie, a slave-girl, but has no money to buy her. Moreover, his father has a bride in view for him, and there are rival suitors for Célie. Lélie's servant Mascarille, an ingenious knave, contrives a series of simple ruses for getting possession of Célie, and the comedy lies in the perversity with which Lélie, a perfect bungler, manages to ruin them by his interference. But all ends well.

Étranger, L', v. *Camus, A*.

Être et le néant, L', v. *Sartre*.

Être Suprême, L'. The cult of the Supreme Being, which Robespierre hoped would replace both Christianity and the orgies more recently celebrated in the name of Reason (v. *Raison, Fêtes de la*), was instituted by a decree (7 May 1794) of the **Convention* (beginning, 'Le peuple français reconnaît l'Être Suprême et l'immortalité de l'âme'...). A *fête*, hurriedly organized by David, took place on 8 June in the Jardin des Tuileries. Robespierre set fire to an effigy of Atheism, while the people sang the *Hymne à l'Être Suprême* (by Desorgues and Gossec). The crowd then marched to the **Champ-de-Mars* to plant an **arbre de liberté*. There was only one *fête*, for the cult perished with Robespierre.

Études analytiques, v. *Comédie humaine, La*.

Études de la Nature, v. *Bernardin de Saint-Pierre*.

Études de mœurs; *Études philosophiques,* v. *Comédie humaine, La*.

Étudiant noir, L', v. *Négritude*.

Étui de nacre, L', v. *France, A*.

Eudes (Odo) (858–98), son of Robert le Fort, became king of France after Charles le Gros was deposed; r. 888–98, from 893 in opposition to Charles III (the two were at war till 897, then made peace).

Eudore, in Chateaubriand's *Les *Martyrs*.

Eugène, by Jodelle, the first original French **comedy*, in octosyllables;

performed 1552/3 before the king. Like many of the old *farces, it is largely a satire on the higher clergy.

The plot turns on the rivalry of Eugène, a rich, licentious abbot, and Florimond, a soldier and the rejected suitor of Eugène's sister, for the favours of Alix, whom Eugène has married for his own purposes to an imbecile, Guillaume. Florimond, an old lover of Alix, returns from the wars to discover her relations with Eugène and Guillaume. He is furious, and terrifies Eugène, who is further harassed by the arrival of a creditor. Eugène solves his difficulties by handing over his sister to Florimond and a benefice to the creditor.

Eugénie, v. Beaumarchais.

Eugénie, Empress, MARIA EUGENIA DE GUZMAN, COMTESSE DE TEBA (1826–1920), daughter of the comte de Montijo, a Spanish grandee, consort of Napoleon III, whom she married in 1853. She was a woman of great beauty, animated and pleasure-loving, under whose influence the court of the Second Empire became the most splendid in Europe; but she did harm when she tried to meddle in politics. After 1870, she lived mainly in retirement in England, at Chislehurst, a widow from 1873, and further bereaved in 1879 by the death of her only son, the *Prince Impérial. *v. Mérimée; Montijo.*

Eugénie Grandet (1833; later in *La *Comédie humaine, Scènes de la vie de province*), a novel by Balzac.

In 1819, in the small town of Saumur, M. Grandet, a rich miser, lives in penurious simplicity with his wife, their daughter Eugénie, and a devoted servant, Nanon. His nephew Charles, a spendthrift young dandy, arrives unexpectedly from Paris, followed immediately by news that the Paris house of Grandet has failed and that Charles's father has killed himself. Charles, now penniless, leaves for India to seek his fortune, taking with him Eugénie's heart and her 'treasure' of gold pieces given her on successive birthdays by her father. M. Grandet's fury on learning of this so upsets his wife that she falls ill

and dies. Eugénie remains alone with her father, now besotted with avarice and a helpless invalid. When he dies, she inherits his fortune and waits faithfully for Charles to return and marry her. But Charles, once more rich and in Paris, writes to tell her of his forthcoming marriage to Mlle d'Aubrion. She also learns indirectly that he has refused to settle honourably with his father's creditors, and that the marquis d'Aubrion will not let his child marry a bankrupt's son. She pays the creditors in full, then writes to wish Charles happiness and encloses the receipts for all his debts. She lives on very simply in Saumur, cared for by Nanon and devoting herself to charity.

Eulalie, Séquence de Sainte, a religious song (14 couplets in praise of the saint) of *c.* 880, one of the earliest extant writings in French.

Eupalinos, ou l' Architecte, v. Valéry.

Eutrapel, Contes et discours d', v. Du Fail.

Évadisme, v. Mapah.

Évangélisme, the term applied to that early phase of the Reformation in France, largely Lutheran in inspiration, which sought religious truth by direct recourse to the text of the Scriptures. It was stimulated by the new interest in ancient languages and by François Ier's appointment of *lecteurs royaux* in Hebrew, Latin, and Greek. A leading figure in the movement was Lefèvre d'Étaples (and *v. Marguerite de Navarre; Berquin; Caturce*). It was bitterly opposed by the theologians of the *Sorbonne, notably Béda; *v. Placards.* Before long, however, it gave way to Calvinism (*v. Huguenots*), which was opposed to free inquiry in pursuit of truth and alienated such humanists as Rabelais.

Évangéliste, L', v. Daudet, A.

Évangile des femmes, L', a 12th-c. satire in quatrains, the effect of three lines in praise of women being demolished in the fourth line of each.

Événement, *L'* (1848–51), a daily paper f. by Hugo, with his son Charles-Victor as co-editor. It stood for a poetical and socialist approach to political controversies. Balzac, Champfleury, Gautier, Karr, and the publicist Alexandre Erdan (1826–78) all wrote for it.

Éviradnus, *v. Légende des siècles, La.*

Évolution créatrice, L', *v. Bergson.*

Exemple (Exemplum), a short edifying tale or parable, introduced by medieval preachers into their Latin sermons. Many survive, both in sermons and in collections made for the use of preachers. *v. Jacques de Vitry.*

Existentialism, Existentialist, the term applied to a number of loosely associated philosophical doctrines, deriving ultimately (as does the term) from the writings of the Danish philosopher Søren Kierkegaard (1813–55), which share a concern with the individual existing person, with human existence in an active sense (rather than the abstract nature of existence or of the universe). In the atheist and Christian forms in which it came into prominence in France during the 1939–45 war, Existentialism is often regarded as a reflection of the spiritual and moral disarray caused by two world wars (and esp. by the fall of France in 1940). The more widely known atheist Existentialism, of which Sartre is the chief exponent, owes much to the German phenomenologist Edmund Husserl (1859–1938) and to his disciple Martin Heidegger (1889–1976), who recast phenomenology in an Existentialist form. Christian Existentialism was developed by the German philosopher Karl Jaspers (1883–1969) and G. Marcel (said to have been the first to use the French term *existentialisme*, in 1925). As a literary and cultural phenomenon, Existentialism was at its most influential from *c.* 1945 until the late 1950s. It was condemned by Rome in 1950, a serious discouragement to its Catholic apologists. Although widely associated with the literary and philosophical works of Sartre, it never formed a single coherent doctrine or a school, and it is best regarded as the dominant characteristic of French thought and literature in the post-war decade (*v. Novel* 3; *Theatre of the 19th and 20th cs.*). Those often associated with Sartre include, besides S. de Beauvoir, Camus and Merleau-Ponty, but it should be noted that there were serious divergences between Sartre and both Camus and Merleau-Ponty.

A feature of Western philosophical systems from the time of Greek antiquity has been the assumption that since the individual forms a part of the general purpose, or essential nature, of the universe, this purpose, or 'essence', common to all men, must precede the actual fact of individual 'existence'. The basic postulate of Sartrean Existentialism is that there is no *a priori* definition of man in either religious or natural terms, i.e. that 'existence' precedes 'essence'. Every individual therefore has absolute freedom: he is 'condamné à être libre' (Sartre). Primarily an ethic of action, Sartrean Existentialism adopts various important concepts of phenomenology, which stresses the dialectical relation between consciousness and its environment. The complex of circumstances into which each individual is born, his particular *situation*, is a void or *néant* within which he is totally responsible for the choices he makes. He cannot be defined otherwise than by the sum of his actions, and he creates himself by his choices. The individual's consciousness of his freedom, in a state of *engagement* in a particular situation in the world and society, is a condition of his 'authentic' existence, and any attempt to escape responsibility for his choices by invoking any form of determinism, or to justify them in terms of external standards (imposed by a philosophy, a religious faith, *bourgeois* morality, etc.), constitutes *mauvaise foi* and 'inauthenticity'. Overawed by the full implications of his freedom, Existentialist man experiences moral anguish, a sense of absurdity, alienation, and despair. In the case of Sartre, in particular, Existentialism soon also acquired a socio-political dimension, involving a close dialogue with Marxist thought and an active connotation for the term *engagement*. In reply to the charge that his philosophy is demoralizing, he has asserted that 'l'angoisse ne se distingue pas du sens des responsabilités' and that 'le désespoir ne fait qu'un avec la volonté', and he has sought to lay emphasis on its humanistic aspects

(*L'Existentialisme est un humanisme*, 1946), on effort, generosity, social co-operation, etc. *v. Littérature engagée*; *Temps modernes, Les.*

Expiation, L', *v. Châtiments, Les.*

Expilly, JEAN-JOSEPH D', *v. Dictionaries*, 1762–70.

Exposition du système du monde, *v. Laplace, marquis de.*

F

Faber Stapulensis, *v. Lefèvre d'Étaples.*

Fables, *v. La Fontaine* and next article; *Florian*; *Houdar de la Motte*; *Marie de France.*

Fables choisies, mises en vers (bks. I–VI, 1668; bks. VII–XI, 1678–9; bk. XII, 1694), by La Fontaine.

The fables are drawn from many sources, both ancient (Aesop, Phaedrus, Horace, Bidpai) and modern, but the originals are only the skeleton which La Fontaine has filled out and vivified with details drawn from his own observation of nature and society. They are cameos of life, universal in their quality, in which, often in the guise of animals and by means of lively dialogues and sudden vicissitudes, men of all classes of society are depicted and their failings gently ridiculed. Writing in a familiar, persuasive style (its fluency is deceptive, for it was the fruit of much labour) and with an inimitable *naïveté* and a semi-pagan feeling for nature, La Fontaine enters into the lives and affairs of his characters, talking and arguing as they would. (It may be noted that he opposed the Cartesian doctrine that animals are *bêtes-machines* or mere automata.) The quaint expressions (e.g. 'la gent trotte-menu' for mice) and somewhat archaic language, the ingenious use of *vers libres*, the mingling of human and animal traits (e.g. the rat dragged under water by the

frog 'contre le droit des gens, contre la foi jurée') all contribute to the charm of the stories. The moral, usually a rather utilitarian and unheroic counsel of prudence and moderation, is indicated at the end or the beginning, or left to be inferred; but in this traditional form the moral is perhaps not of prime importance. In any case, La Fontaine was no moralist, and his fables—which have been criticized from a strict ethical standpoint—reflect his kindly, easy-going epicureanism. Owing to their variety, they cannot be rigidly classified; but those of the second collection are, on the whole, more serious and philosophical, longer, and of a less Aesopic simplicity than those of the first, while the final book (XII) shows some decline. Many lines or phrases have become proverbial, e.g. 'promettre monts et merveilles', 'contenter tout le monde et son père', 'un Tiens vaut mieux que deux Tu l'auras'.

The work was much read in England (though not translated till the 18th c.), and La Fontaine was invited to London, where his admirers 'engaged to find him an honourable sustenance'.

Fabliau, a verse tale, nearly always in octosyllabic couplets, composed between the end of the 12th and the beginning of the 14th c. Some of the themes are of Oriental origin, others can have been invented only in France, but the great majority are not peculiar to any region or period. They are short narratives, often of c. 300–400 lines, episodic and frequently burlesque in character. They are without literary pretension, marked by simplicity, realism, and conciseness, composed in a mocking spirit, and designed solely to amuse. They range from light, ironical presentations of everyday life to the extreme of coarseness (v. *Esprit gaulois*). Many show an acute contempt for women, as incorrigibly perverse (in marked contrast to the doctrines of *amour courtois*, then also prevailing); others a hatred of priests. Their authors included amateur poets like Beaumanoir and Henri d'Andeli; the *jongleur* Rutebeuf; wandering clerks, and minstrels attached to the courts of the nobility. About 150 *fabliaux* survive (a 6-vol. ed. by Montaiglon and Raynaud appeared in 1872–90): v. *Auberée*; *Aveugles de Compiègne*; *Épervier*; *Fole Largece*; *Housse partie*; *Lai d'Aristote*; *Richeut*; *Saint Pierre et le Jongleur*; *Vilain Mire*; *Vilain qui conquit paradis par plaid*. Stories found in the *fabliaux* reappear in Chaucer's *Reeve's Tale* and *Summoner's Tale*; these and others of the *Canterbury Tales* are in some ways the English equivalent of *fabliaux*, written by a great poet.

Fabre, ÉMILE (1869–1955), author of well-constructed dramas of domestic and public life, e.g. *La Vie politique* (1901; the intrigues and upheavals caused by an election in a provincial town), *Les Ventres dorés* (1905; a satire of financial circles), *La Maison d'argile* (1907; the problem of divorce).

Fabre, FERDINAND (1827–98), took to literature after being educated for the priesthood. His novels of life in the Cévennes, notable for their portraits of country clerics, include *L'Abbé Tigrane* (1873), his best work, describing the quarrels and intrigues among the clergy of a country diocese over the appointment of a new bishop; *Les Courbezon* (1862); *Mon Oncle Célestin* (1881); *L'Abbé Roitelet* (1890). He has been compared to both Anthony Trollope and Thomas Hardy.

Fabre, JEAN-HENRI (1823–1915), entomologist, was long a school-teacher in or near Avignon. His *Souvenirs entomologiques* (1919–24, 10 vols.) are of both scientific and literary value. His laboratory at Sérignan, near Orange, was bought by the State and became a museum.

Fabre d'Églantine, PHILIPPE (1755–94), took the name 'Églantine' after winning the *Prix de l'Églantine* at the *Jeux floraux de Toulouse*. He was a dramatist and poet, remembered for a very popular *chanson* (1780), beginning 'Il pleut, il pleut, bergère', and his comedy *Le Philinte de Molière, ou la Suite du Misanthrope* (1790); also a leading Revolutionary journalist, a member of the *Club des *Cordeliers* and the *Convention*. He was guillotined with his friends Desmoulins and Danton. v. *Republican Calendar*.

Fabrice del Dongo, in Stendhal's *La *Chartreuse de Parme*.

Fâcheux, Les, a 3-act verse *comédie-ballet* by Molière; produced 1661 at *Vaux-le-Vicomte. The theme is drawn from Horace (*Satires*, I, ix) and M. Régnier (*Satires*, VIII). A variety of bores, by their untimely importunity, interrupt the course of the hero's courtship: one stops him with a long account of a stag-hunt; another must tell him about a wonderful hand at piquet, etc.

Facino Cane, v. *Comédie humaine, La* (*Scènes de la vie parisienne*).

Fæneste, Les Aventures du baron de (pts. 1–3, 1617–20; pt. 4, 1630), a satirical pamphlet by d'Aubigné. Within the framework of a series of dialogues—the chief interlocutors being Fæneste, a young papist, and Enay, a virtuous old *Huguenot—the papacy and all the enemies of the Reformation are attacked with bitter irony and invective in theological discussions, scandalous tales of monks, etc.

Faguet, ÉMILE (1847–1916), literary historian and critic, for 20 years dramatic critic on the *Journal des Débats*; an indefatigable writer of wide range, seldom profound and inclined to generalize, but stimulating by reason of his lively interest in men and ideas (v. Critics and Criticism, 2). His works include *Le XVIIe Siècle* (1885), *Le XIXe Siècle* (1887), *Le XVIIIe Siècle* (1890), *Le XVIe Siècle* (1894), *Les Grands Maîtres du XVIIe Siècle* (1885), *Politiques et moralistes du XIXe siècle* (1891–1900), *Politique comparée de Montesquieu, de Rousseau, et de Voltaire* (1902); also *Notes sur le théâtre contemporain* (1889–91), *Questions de théâtre* (1890–8), and *Propos de théâtre* (1903–7), collections of his articles in the *Journal des Débats*.

Fagus, *pseudonym of* GEORGES FAILLET (1872–1933), a poet whose affinity with Villon and Verlaine can be seen in, for instance, *Fière tranquille* (1918), *La Danse macabre* (1920), *La Guirlande à l'épousée* (1921), or the shorter poems, often *chansons*, of *Pas perdus* (1926) and *Le Clavecin* (1926).

Faiel, Seigneur and **Dame de,** *v. Coucy.*

Faillet, GEORGES, *v. Fagus.*

Faiseur, Le, v. Mercadet.

Falloux, La Loi, a law of 1850 regulating primary and secondary education; named after it chief sponsor, a Catholic *député*.

Famine, ou les Gabaonites, La, v. Saül le furieux.

Fanfan la tulipe, a 19th-c. nickname for the French soldier, proverbially fond of wine, women, and glory. It came from a very popular song (1819) of this name by Émile Debraux (1796–1831; a *chanson*-writer after the style of Béranger, but less talented), which inspired various *vaudevilles* and comedies, notably *Fanfan la tulipe* (1858) by Paul Meurice (1820–1905), a romantic comedy about a rough but chivalrous soldier in Mme de Pompadour's bodyguard.

Fanny, (1) *v. Feydeau, E.*; (2) *v. Pagnol.*

Fantaisiste, Le Groupe, the name adopted *c.* 1911 by a group of young poets including Derème, Carco, Klingsor, J.-M. Bernard, and Pellerin. They sought to introduce a lighter, more sceptical note into poetry, and their avowed masters were Laforgue, with his discreet sensibility and gift for playful irony, and Toulet (whose *Contrerimes* were already known), with his distrust of romanticism and cynical, amused outlook on life. They were not without influence on Apollinaire and his circle.

Fantasio (1834, in the *Revue des Deux Mondes* and *Un Spectacle dans un fauteuil*), a 2-act prose comedy by Musset; produced 1866.

Fantasio, a young gentleman of Munich, disguises himself as the king of Bavaria's jester to dodge his creditors and obtain free lodging at court. One of his tricks so upsets the dignity of the prince of Mantua, a visitor at the court, that plans for a marriage between the prince and the king's daughter, Elsbeth, come to grief. Though Mantua and Bavaria may now go to war, at least the gentle young princess will not be married off to a pompous fool.

Fantine, in Hugo's Les *Misérables*.

Fantin-Latour, IGNACE-HENRI-JEAN-THÉODORE (1836–1904), painter and lithographer. His many portrait-groups of contemporary writers and artists include *Hommage à Delacroix* (1865) and *Coin de table* (1872; a group of writers from which the seated figures of Rimbaud and Verlaine, soon to leave Paris together, are often reproduced).

Fantômas, the character, probably as well known in the 20th c. as Rocambole and Rouletabille in the 19th, who gives his name to a long series of popular thrillers by Marcel Allain (1885–1969), writing alone or in collaboration. Another familiar character in the series is the mute, stubborn Detective-Inspector Juve.

Farce, a form of drama popular in the later Middle Ages, said to date back to the expulsion from the churches of the *Fête des Fous*. Its average length was *c.* 500 lines, usually octosyllabic couplets (often interspersed with *triolets*). Its object was good-natured fun (*cf. Sotie*): by choice and treatment of incidents (very like those of the earlier *fabliau*) it burlesqued and caricatured the foibles and vices of everyday domestic, and sometimes political or clerical, life. Some 150 medieval *farces* survive out of what must have been a much greater number. They include the famous *Pathelin*; *La Farce du Pâté et de la Tarte*, in which two famished rascals plan to steal an eel-pie and a tart from a pastry-cook's wife, but are caught in the act and belaboured by the pastry-cook; *Le Chaudronnier*, in which a husband loses a wager with his wife as to which will remain motionless the longer when he springs into action to assault a waggish tinsmith for kissing her; *Le Poulier*, in which a miller takes appropriate revenge on two gentlemen who are courting his wife; *Le Cuvier*, in which a henpecked husband is made to compile a list (*rollet*) of the tasks he must perform for his wife, but when she falls into the wash-tub, he finds, on consulting his *rollet*, that pulling her out is not among them. The *farce* later developed into the one-act comedy or farce, and was the ancestor of French *comedy* in its most successful and characteristic form.

Farel, GUILLAUME (1489–1565), a Reformer of extreme, at times almost excessive, zeal. He was converted to Protestantism largely under the influence of Lefèvre d'Étaples, and was later associated with Calvin.

Faret, NICOLAS (*c.* 1600–46), an early member of the *Académie*. His *Honnête Homme, ou l'Art de plaire à la cour* (1633) was modelled on Castiglione's *Il Cortegiano*.

Fargue, LÉON-PAUL (1876–1947), a poet who traversed various literary movements and influenced younger writers. About 1894 he was one of the *Symbolist circle of the *Mercure de France* and wrote *Tancrède* (1895, in the review *Pan*; 1911), a sequence of short poems, and *Poèmes* (1912; 1918, with the addition of *Pour la musique*). Later collections, e.g. *Espaces* and *Sous la lampe* (both 1929), contain sophisticated, ironical verse of his *Cubist phase. His memoirs of life and literary circles in Paris (*Le Piéton de Paris*, 1939) are of interest.

Farrère, Claude, *pseudonym of* FRÉDÉRIC BARGONE (1876–1957), a naval officer who, following in the wake of Loti, wrote novels with exotic settings (much more vigorous than those of Loti, often merely melodramatic), achieving three big popular successes with *Les Civilisés* (1905; Saigon), *L'Homme qui assassina* (1907; Constantinople), *La Bataille* (1911; Japan).

Fatrasie, in medieval literature, rhymed nonsense, comic, and sometimes satirical, in intention; a precursor of the *coq-à-l'âne*.

Faublas, *v. Amours du Chevalier de Faublas, Les.*

Faubourg Saint-Germain, 'le noble faubourg', a quarter of Paris, on the left bank of the Seine; a centre of aristocratic society in the 17th and 18th cs., and again in the 19th c. when the *émigrés* returned (it is well described in Balzac's *La *Duchesse de Langeais*). 'Faubourg Saint-Germain' survives as a figurative expression (e.g. in Proust) for aristocratic society without specific reference to locality.

Fauchet, CLAUDE (1529–1601), author of *Antiquités gauloises et françaises* (1579–99) and *Recueil de l'origine de la langue et poésie française, rime et romans* (1581), a compilation of value for the purposes of literary history.

Faucon, Le, perhaps the pleasantest of La Fontaine's *Contes et Nouvelles*; drawn from Boccaccio.

Fédéric, a once rich Florentine, has wasted all his substance in trying to win a married woman from her husband, and now lives in poverty. He has one falcon and enjoys hawking. The lady's husband dies, and her sick child is likely to die too unless his craving for Fédéric's falcon is satisfied. She decides to humiliate herself by visiting him and asking for it. Fédéric, overwhelmed by the favour of her visit, searches out the scanty materials for a meal. After the meal she humbly asks for the falcon, and he has to confess that, having nothing better to offer, he has killed it and served it to her. The child dies; but the lady, touched by this supreme mark of devotion, marries Fédéric.

Faujas de Saint-Fond, BARTHÉLEMY (1741–1819), geologist. His lively and amusing *Voyage* [in 1784] *en Angleterre, en Écosse, et aux Iles Hébrides* (1797; Eng. trans., anon., 1799, republ. 1907, ed. by Sir A. Geikie) 'makes a third with Johnson's *Journey to the Western Isles* and Boswell's *Tour in the Hebrides*' (W. P. Ker).

Faulkner, WILLIAM, *v. Foreign Influences,* 6.

Fauquembergue, *Journal de Clément de, v. History,* 1.

Faure, ÉLIE (1873–1937), art historian (*Histoire de l'art,* 1909–21, his chief work; *L'Esprit des formes,* 1927, etc.), excelled at appreciating a work of art, not only for its intrinsic beauty, but as the reflection of a whole civilization. Malraux owes much to him.

Fauré, GABRIEL-URBAIN (1845–1924), composer, notably of songs and chamber music. He was associated with the *Symbolists.

Fauriel, CLAUDE (1772–1844), critic, historian, and translator (the *Parthénéide* of the Danish poet Baggesen, 1810; the tragedies of his friend Manzoni, 1823). He also wrote histories of Provençal and Italian literature. *v. Clarke; Foreign Influences,* 3.

Fausses Confidences, Les, v. Marivaux.

Faustin, La, v. Goncourt, E. de.

Faute de l'abbé Mouret, La, v. Rougon-Macquart, Les.

Fauteuils académiques. In the early days of the *Académie française* only the *directeur* sat in an armchair. The story goes that when Louis XIV heard that another member, the ailing Cardinal d'Estrées, had asked leave to bring his own chair, he realized that this might lead to invidious distinctions and tactfully provided 40 armchairs from the royal store.

Fauves, Les, *v. Impressionism.*

Faux Démétrius, Les, v. Mérimée.

Faux-Monnayeurs, Les (1926), a novel by Gide. *v. Novel,* 3.

The many characters fall into groups of various ages: small, vividly unpleasant schoolboys, who attend the Pension Azaïs and whose attempts to circulate counterfeit coins provide the title; undergraduates; the boys' parents; and the boys' grandparents, whose unpleasant characteristics have become more pronounced in old age. The book deals with vitiated people and unpleasant situations from beginning to end, but the characters—especially the nasty little boys and their older brothers—come to life. Its lack of construction and its apparently spasmodic and disconnected happenings are intentional, Gide claiming that a preliminary framework would have deprived his characters of all the uncertainty of real life.

A focal point is provided by Édouard, a novelist, who is himself writing a novel to be called *Les Faux-Monnayeurs* and whose journal recording its progress (which has its counterpart in Gide's own *Journal des Faux-Monnayeurs,* 1926) forms a large part of the book. Édouard is the uncle of Olivier, a student at the *École normale supérieure,* and has a secretary Bernard, Olivier's friend, who has left home to 'live dangerously'. He catches Georges, a ringleader of the schoolboy criminals, stealing in a bookshop, and discovers that he is Olivier's brother and his own nephew. He goes to Switzerland with Laura, a daughter of the Pension Azaïs, who had once been in love with him, but had married Professor Douviers and then taken a lover, who deserted her. He returns from Switzerland with Boris, the young grandson of a music master at the Pension Azaïs.

In the end, Olivier has been corrupted, first by Passavant, a novelist of Satanic character, then by Édouard himself; Laura has returned to live unhappily with her husband, who agrees to accept her child; Boris, dared by his schoolfellows (including Georges), has committed suicide in class; and Bernard has returned to his father.

Favart, CHARLES-SIMON (1710–92), dramatist, director of the *Opéra-Comique*. His many comic operas—witty and gay, in an easy flowing style, and showing the transition from *comédie en vaudevilles* to *comédie à ariettes*—include *La Chercheuse d'esprit* (1741); *Les Amours de Bastien et Bastienne* (1752), a parody of J.-J. *Rousseau's *Le Devin du village*; *Les Trois Sultanes* (1761), in which the lively, self-asserting Roxelane defeats her rivals for the Sultan's favour and brings the prospect of liberal reforms to his court.

Favier, JEAN-LOUIS (c. 1720–84), publicist and wit, a spendthrift who turned his political acumen to account and was employed on State and secret missions. He was often in danger: at one time he fled to Holland, then to England; at another he was imprisoned in the *Bastille*. He left political writings and memoirs, and a translation (*Mémoires secrets de Bolingbroke*, 1754).

February Revolution, v. *Revolutions*, 3.

Febvre, LUCIEN (1878–1956), historian, an authority on the social and economic climate of 16th-c. Europe; leader, with M. Bloch, of an important school of

historiography (v. *History*, 4). His works include *Philippe II et la Franche-Comté* (1911), *La Terre et l'évolution humaine* (1922; 1949), *Civilisation, le mot et la chose* (1930), *Le Problème de l'incroyance au XVIe siècle. La Religion de Rabelais* (1942). v. *Dictionaries*, 1935–62.

Fédération, fédérés. The early months of the *Revolution saw the widespread formation of *fédérations*, or unions of patriots. Delegates (*fédérés*)—often from local detachments of the new *Garde nationale*—met to proclaim themselves citizens of one empire, bound to uphold the decrees of the *Assemblée constituante*. National festivals instituted to celebrate important anniversaries were called *Fêtes de la Fédération*. The first (14 July 1790, the anniversary of the fall of the *Bastille*) was attended by 60,000 delegates from the 83 newly created *départements*. Talleyrand, as bishop of Autun, celebrated Mass in the middle of the *Champ-de-Mars. The king and the delegates then swore allegiance to the new constitution and sang a hymn written for the occasion by M.-J. Chénier. v. also *Victoires, Fête des*.

Feletz, CHARLES-DORIMOND DE (1767–1850), a critic noted for his sound—strongly classical—literary taste and his conversation. He was educated for the priesthood, but refused to accept the *Constitution civile du clergé*. In 1794 he narrowly escaped deportation, being saved by the fall of Robespierre. He turned journalist and in 1801 joined the *Journal des Débats*, becoming one of its leading critics (cf. *Dussault*; *Geoffroy*; *Hoffmann, F.-B.*). Some of his articles are collected in *Mélanges de philosophie, d'histoire, et de littérature* (1828) and *Jugements historiques et littéraires* (1840).

Féli, Monsieur, v. *Lamennais*.

Félibien, a 17th-c. family of architects and historians, notably ANDRÉ (1619–95) and his son JEAN-FRANÇOIS (c. 1658–1733), architects, the father also an historian of art and architecture; JACQUES (1636–

1716), brother of André, theologian and religious historian; MICHEL (1666–1719), son of André, religious historian, later a Benedictine monk.

Félibrige, félibres. The *Félibrige*, a movement to revive interest in Provençal culture and to promote a standard form of Provençal as a literary language, was launched (1854) by seven Provençal poets: Mistral, Roumanille, Aubanel, Jean Brunet (1823–94), Paul Giéra (1816–61), Remy Marcellin (1832–1908), and Anselme Mathieu (1828–1925), who were soon joined by Alphonse Tavan (1833–1905). They took the name *félibres* from an old Provençal tale in which the infant Jesus is found disputing in the temple among 'li sét felibre de la léi' (which Mistral interpreted as 'the seven Doctors of the Law'). They founded (1855) an annual which still exists, *L'Armana prouvençau*, a repertory of Provençal literature and information. The *Félibrige* inspired similar movements (notably one in Catalonia) and stimulated the development of 'regional' literature. *v. Wyse* (2).

Feminine Lines and Rhymes, *v. Masculine.*

Femme abandonnée, La, *v. Comédie humaine, La (Scènes de la vie privée).*

Femme de trente ans, La, *v. Comédie humaine, La (Scènes de la vie privée).*

Femme et le pantin, La, *v. Louÿs.*

Femme juge et partie, La, a comedy by Montfleury; produced 1669.

Bernadille, unjustly suspicious of his wife, abandons her on a small island and, believing her dead, contemplates remarriage. But she returns disguised as a man, becomes provost of the town, summons him before her tribunal, extorts a confession, sentences him to death, enjoys his terror for a while, and then reveals herself.

Femmes savantes, Les, a 5-act verse comedy by Molière; produced 1672.

Fashion had changed in the 13 years since *Les* **Précieuses ridicules*, and Molière is now ridiculing the extravagances of the cult of grammar (as prescribed by Vaugelas), philosophy (after Descartes), and astronomy. The timid, henpecked *bourgeois* Chrysale has a wife Philaminte, a daughter Armande, and a sister Bélise, who are all devotees of the new cult and admirers of the ridiculous Trissotin, a sorry wit and poetaster (in whom Molière depicted the abbé Cotin), and of the pedant Vadius (said to have been modelled on Ménage). In contrast to them, there is the charming Henriette, Armande's younger sister, and her lover Clitandre, an agreeable courtier. Chrysale favours Clitandre's suit, but Philaminte is determined that Henriette shall marry Trissotin. Shamed by the reproofs of his sensible brother Ariste, Chrysale summons up the courage to insist that she shall marry Clitandre. The notary is sent for and receives contradictory instructions from husband and wife. Even now Chrysale wavers; but, on a false report that the family fortune is lost, Trissotin reveals his true motives by withdrawing his suit, and Clitandre triumphs.

Fénelon, FRANÇOIS DE SALIGNAC [or SALAGNAC] DE LA MOTHE- (1651–1715), theologian, of an old Gascon family. As a priest and a disciple of Bossuet, he was appointed Superior of certain Paris convents (1678) and was employed in the conversion of *Huguenots in the west of France after the revocation (1685) of the Edict of Nantes. He became spiritual leader of a devout group at court, including the duc de Beauvilliers (tutor of the duc de Bourgogne, Louis XIV's grandson), and enjoyed the favour of Mme de Maintenon. About this time, he wrote his Platonic *Dialogues sur l'éloquence* (1718) and **Traité de l'éducation des filles* (1687). In 1689, he was charged with the education of the duc de Bourgogne, a refractory pupil whom he successfully transformed. This important post brought him other honours: he was admitted to the *Académie (1693) and named archbishop of Cambrai (1695). But, under the influence of Mme Guyon, he had been captivated by *Quietism. This brought him into conflict with Bossuet, Mme de Maintenon, and the king—especially when he appealed to Rome on the point of doctrine. His *Explication des maximes des saints* (1697), defending Mme Guyon, was condemned by the pope (1699). The surreptitious publication of *Télémaque* (1699) completed his disgrace. He lost his preceptorate and was relegated to his diocese. He remained in touch with his devout followers at court; but his hope of a return to favour, revived when his former pupil became direct heir to the throne, was blighted by the young man's death, and he died unpardoned. His many other works include the *Dialogues des morts* (1712–30), presenting ancient and modern heroes and statesmen for the edification of his royal pupil; the *Traité de l'existence de Dieu* (1713; second part posth.), seeking proof of God's existence in the wonders of nature and in the structure of the human body and mind; the *Lettre à M. Dacier sur les occupations de l'Académie française* (1716), suggesting that, to follow its dictionary, the *Académie should prepare a grammar, treatises on rhetoric, etc., and imaginatively discussing many literary questions; the *Lettre à Louis XIV* or *Lettre secrète* (written *c.* 1694), which is critical of the prevailing political system, but may have been no more than a rhetorical exercise; the *Tables de Chaulnes* (prepared 1711 with the duc de Beauvilliers), a scheme of political reforms for submission to a future king (royal power was to be restricted by a popular element in the constitution); the *Lettres spirituelles* (1718), letters of religious instruction to various persons, showing him as a priest.

He was a man of great charm, affectionate, humane, aristocratic in tastes and ideas, but also obstinate and ambitious with an ironical affectation of humility; a mystic, lacking the male vigour of Bossuet; a blend of politician and priest. (His complex character and chequered career are well described by the duc de Saint-Simon.) He wrote in a simple, harmonious style (*Télémaque* has been described as the first prose poem in French), showing a fertile imagination.

Fénéon, FÉLIX (1861–1944), critic, one of the first to appreciate the importance of the *Symbolist and *Impressionist movements in literature and art, edited the *Revue indépendante* and was responsible (1905–6) for a news column (*Nouvelles en trois lignes*, offering masterly and amusing examples of the art of compression) in the daily paper *Le Matin*. He wrote mostly in reviews. *Œuvres* (1950, ed. Paulhan) contains selections from his writings.

Féraud or **Ferraud**, JEAN-FRANÇOIS, *v. Dictionaries*, 1787–8.

Fermat, PIERRE DE (*c.* 1595–1665), a counsellor to the *parlement* of Toulouse and a mathematician of standing; friend and correspondent of Pascal (who called him 'le premier homme du monde'). He had some lively disputes with Descartes.

Fermiers généraux. Under the monarchy (from the 13th c.) the office of collecting certain indirect taxes (*v. Fiscal System*), which also implied the right to exploit them, was farmed out to private persons (often auctioned to the highest bidder). The way in which these *fermiers généraux* abused the system, regularly amassing vast fortunes, powerfully contributed to the economic discontent of the pre-Revolutionary era.

Ferney, *v. Voltaire*, 1.

Ferragus, in the *Entrée d'Espagne*, a *chanson de geste* of the *Charlemagne cycle, a Saracen giant who defeats 11 of the *Douze *Pairs* in single combat, but is slain by Roland.

Ferragus, *v. Comédie humaine, La* (*Scènes de la vie parisienne*).

Ferronnière, La Belle, a *bourgeoise* of Paris, a favourite of François Ier. She was not the original of Leonardo da Vinci's portrait of the same name.

Fersen, HANS AXEL, COMTE DE (1755–1810), Swedish statesman, sometime French army officer, and a favourite at court. He idolized Marie-Antoinette and it was he, disguised as a coachman, who drove the royal fugitives part of the way to Varennes (1791). His later activities belong to Swedish history.

Festin de pierre, Le, v. *Dom Juan; Corneille, T.*

Fête des Fous, the medieval Feast of Fools, the farcical element introduced by the lesser clergy into the liturgy of cathedrals during the special celebrations between Christmas and the Octave of Epiphany (13 Jan.), e.g. a *sermon joyeux* (a mock sermon), a drinking-bout, the bringing of an ass into the church, the ending of certain liturgical pieces with a bray—the object being to parody the ecclesiastical hierarchy. These revels had mostly been abolished by the mid-15th c.; they were succeeded in the history of the drama by the profane **farces, *moralités, *soties,* etc., performed by the lay **sociétés joyeuses.*

Fêtes galantes, v. *Verlaine.*

Feu, Le, v. *Barbusse.*

Feuillantisme; Feuillants, Club des. The club—so called from its meeting-place in Paris, a former home of the Cistercian Feuillants—was f. 1791 by constitutional Royalists and moderate democrats who seceded from the **Jacobins.* Their opponents, regarding them as no better than aristocrats, dubbed their doctrines *Feuillantisme.*

Feuilles d'automne, Les (1831), lyrics by Hugo, on more intimate and peaceful themes than those of *Les *Orientales,* e.g. family affection, his own childhood (*Ce siècle avait deux ans*), regret for the passing of time.

Feuillet, OCTAVE (1821–90), a novelist and dramatist highly popular in his day, best known for *Le Roman d'un jeune homme pauvre* (1858), the sentimental tale of a chivalrous, impecunious young man who refuses to marry the rich heroine, destroys

the proof that he is the rightful owner of her fortune, but by a miraculous coincidence inherits even greater wealth and is able to marry her after all. His other works include *Monsieur de Camors* (1867) and *Julia de Trécœur* (1872), novels; *Le Pour et le Contre* (1853), *La Belle au bois dormant* (1867), and *La Partie de dames* (1883), plays; and v. *Proverbe.*

Feuilleton, a supplement issued with a newspaper. The most famous early *feuilleton* (c. 1800), printed across the lower part of the page and detachable, was that created by Geoffroy, dramatic critic of the **Journal des Débats.* Other journals soon had literary and dramatic *feuilletons* and, later, **romans-feuilletons.*

Féval, PAUL (1817–87), prolific author of sensational novels (some were early **romans-feuilletons*), e.g. *Les Mystères de Londres* (1844), *Les Amours de Paris* (1845), *Le Fils du Diable* (1846), *Le Bossu* (1858).

Feydeau, (1) ERNEST (1821–73), novelist and archaeologist, a friend of Flaubert (a distant relative) and Gautier, remembered as the author of *Fanny* (1858), a novel on the theme of adultery and jealousy which ranked as a triumph of **Realism and enjoyed a *succès de scandale*; (2) his son GEORGES (1862–1921), the highly successful author of witty, ingeniously constructed, and uproarious **vaudevilles* and farces, e.g. *Tailleur pour dames* (1888), *La Dame de chez Maxim's* (1899), *Occupe-toi d'Amélie* (1908)—all in his *Théâtre complet* (1948–50).

Fiammetta, v. *Novel,* 1.

Fichet, GUILLAUME (later 15th c.), humanist, rector of the **University of Paris, and a pioneer of the literary **Renaissance, was responsible for the installation (1469) in the **Sorbonne of the first printing-press to operate in Paris.

Fierabras, a late 12th- or early 13th-c. **chanson de geste* (**Charlemagne cycle). Fierabras is a giant, son of the Saracen king

Balant; he has taken Rome and removed the holy relics. He defies Charlemagne and his knights, but is defeated by *Olivier, and baptized. His sister Floripas falls in love with the knight Gui de Bourgogne, and when Gui, Olivier, *Roland, and other knights fall into Balant's hands she brings them together, so that they can resist their gaolers. Charlemagne comes to their rescue; Balant is captured, refuses baptism, and is executed; Floripas is baptized and marries Gui; the relics are recovered.

The English verse romance *Sir Ferumbras* and part of the *Sowdone of Babylon* are based on this story or other versions of it.

Fieschi, JOSEPH, *v. Machine infernale*.

Fiévée, JOSEPH (1767–1839), publicist and journalist, sometime editor of the *Gazette de France* and the *Journal de l'Empire* (*v. Journal des Débats*), also officially responsible for supplying Napoleon with confidential surveys of public opinion. His letters—*Correspondance politique et administrative* (1814–19) and *Correspondance et relations avec Bonaparte* (1837)—give a good picture of events and the movement of ideas in the early 19th c. His short novel *La Dot de Suzette* (1798) was praised by Sainte-Beuve.

Figaro, in Beaumarchais's *Le *Barbier de Séville*, *Le *Mariage de Figaro*, and *L'Autre Tartufe, ou la Mère coupable*.

Figaro, Le, a leading daily paper. Originally a minor weekly (f. 1826), it was acquired (1854) and transformed by Hippolyte de Villemessant (1812–79). He drew around him the wittiest journalists of the day (e.g. About, Banville, Monselet, Scholl, Barbey d'Aurevilly) and published his paper twice weekly till 1866, then daily. It typified the spirit of the Second Empire and, at a time when politics were banned, featured successful dramatic and literary columns, satirical (often scandalous) society chronicles, and cartoons by Daumier. The *Figaro* has always maintained a high standard of literary and dramatic criticism, and from 1946 till 1971 issued a weekly *Figaro littéraire. v. Press*, 9.

Fille aux yeux d'or, La, *v. Comédie humaine, La (Scènes de la vie parisienne)*.

Fille de Mme Angot, La, *v. Angot*.

Fille de Roland, La, *v. Bornier*.

Fille Élisa, La (1877), by E. de Goncourt, a typical *Naturalist novel about a girl who becomes a prostitute (in the provinces, then in a poor quarter of Paris), falls in love with a soldier, and murders him in an hysterical rage. She receives a life-sentence, whereupon the book becomes a protest against prison conditions, depicting her vain rebellion and her final lapse into complete imbecility.

Filles de la Charité, *v. Vincent de Paul, St.*

Filles du feu, Les, *v. Nerval*.

Filleul, NICOLAS, *v. Pastoral*.

Filocopo, *v. Floire et Blancheflor; Novel*, 1.

Fils de Giboyer, Le, *v. Augier*.

Fils naturel, Le, (1) *v. Diderot*; (2) *v. Dumas fils*.

Fin, La, *v. Corbière*.

Fin de partie, *v. Beckett*.

Fin de Satan, La, *v. Légende des siècles, La*.

Fiscal System under the Monarchy. France was divided for fiscal purposes into 21 *généralités*, and the *généralités* into *élections*; under the *élections* were the parishes: *c.* 1600 there were 149 *élections* and 23,159 parishes. In each *généralité* a *bureau général*, a board of about 10 *trésoriers de France*, drew up annual estimates of receipts and expenditure. On the basis of these, the royal council (*v. Conseil d'état*, 1) annually decided the amount of taxes payable by each *généralité*. The *bureau général* apportioned this amount among the *élections*, in each of which a *bureau* of about 10 *élus* (at first elected by the taxpayers, later appointed by the king) then apportioned it among the parishes. Each parish elected *collecteurs*, who assessed the individual taxpayers according to their presumed income and were held responsible for collecting the sum due. In five *généralités*, however, known as the *pays d'états* in contrast to the *pays d'élections*, the provincial *états* or assemblies discussed with the king the amount to be paid by the *généralité*, and then apportioned the sum among the parishes on the basis of a cadastre of real property.

The tax thus levied was the *taille*, a direct tax on either real or personal property and the main source of revenue. There were also various indirect taxes, e.g. the **gabelle*, customs (at both provincial and national frontiers), excise, tolls, etc., which were farmed out. The inequitable incidence of the *taille* (the nobility, clergy, and various judicial, fiscal, and municipal officials were exempt) and the rapacity of the **fermiers généraux* helped to bring about the Revolution. *v. Vauban*.

Colbert reduced the annual yield of the *taille* from well over 53 to 35 million *livres* (*v. Money*) and that of the *gabelle* from 24 to 19 million *livres*; even so, the total revenue from taxation increased from 84 to 116 million *livres* during his period of office. The national budget rose to some 200 million *livres* before the Revolution. *v. Chambre des comptes; Cour des aides*.

Fixed Forms, the more elaborate of the poetic forms involving recurrent elements such as a fixed pattern of rhymes, refrains, etc. *v. Ballade; Chansons à danser; Chant royal; Rondeau; Sonnet; Triolet; Villanelle; Virelai*.

Flamberge, *v. Renaud de Montauban*.

Flaubert, GUSTAVE (1821–80), novelist, b. and educated at Rouen (where his father was a surgeon), studied law in Paris (1840–3), but failed his examinations and (partly because he was then subject to something very like epileptic fits) was allowed to return home and devote himself to literature. After his father died (1846), he remained with his mother (d. 1872) and niece Caroline (later Mme Commanville), over whose education he took great pains, in their country house at Croisset, on the Seine near Rouen. He led a hermit-like existence, subordinating everything to his writing; and so high were his self-imposed standards that his first published novel, **Madame Bovary*, did not appear in book form till 1857. He paid occasional brief visits to Paris to see his friends (Gautier, the Goncourts, G. Sand, Renan, Taine, Turgenev, etc.) or his publishers, and twice travelled in the Near East and Tunisia (1849–51, with his friend Du Camp; 1857, to collect material for **Salammbô*).

The man and his life can best be studied in his letters (*Correspondance*, 1887–93; the definitive ed. is that of Conard, 1925–8, suppl. 1954), among the most interesting in French literature. They show him as a schoolboy and student, already writing tales and plays, and with a robust sense of fun he will never lose; as an extravagant **Romantic*, detesting—as he will always detest—everything that is *bourgeois*, platitudinous, or smug; as the lover of Louise Colet (there are many letters to her), at first ardent, then impatient, finally throwing off a yoke that threatens his work (1846–55; but his lasting, though platonic, devotion was to Mme **Schlésinger*, whom he first met as a youth and never forgot); as a devoted son and uncle (in 1875 he sacrificed his modest fortune to help Caroline's husband, with the result that his last years were clouded by money worries); as a generous friend and critic, sparing no pains to help and encourage other writers (his letters, esp. those to G. Sand, abound in valuable literary criticism; and *v. Maupassant*); as an enthusiastic traveller, revelling in all that is gorgeous, luxurious, and unrestrained in the East; and, during the **Franco-Prussian* war, as an intellectual forced to remember the outside world. His letters also reveal the tortures his writing entailed. He aimed at a strictly objective and impersonal work of art, presented in the most perfect form. To this end, he severely restrained the romantic, exuberant side of his nature; and he often worked for days on end over one page, writing, reading aloud, re-writing, attuning his style to his ideal of balanced, harmonious perfection. Because of his meticulously accurate documentation (*Salammbô*, in particular, involved years of research) he was hailed as a *Realist, and later as a *Naturalist. But he disliked such labels, and though painstaking documentation was, indeed, essential for the absolute verity of his backgrounds, it was never for him an end in itself.

Besides those already mentioned, his works include *L'*Éducation sentimentale* (1869); *La *Tentation de Saint Antoine* (1874); *Trois Contes* (1877); *Bouvard et Pécuchet* (1881); *Par les champs et par les grèves* (1885), the record of a walking-tour in Brittany with Du Camp in 1847, written by both, chapter about; early writings— notably *Mémoires d'un fou* and the tale *Novembre*—collected in *Premières Œuvres* (1914-20). *v.* also *Dictionnaire des idées reçues*.

Fléchier, ESPRIT (1632–1710), bishop of Nîmes, a famous preacher (funeral orations on Turenne, Julie d'Angennes, etc.); also an *habitué* of the Hôtel de *Rambouillet and a member of the *Académie. His *Mémoires sur les Grands-Jours d'Auvergne* (*Grands-Jours* at Clermont in 1665; publ. 1844), written to entertain the Rambouillet circle, is an account of his journey to these assizes with one of the magistrates involved and of the proceedings, with descriptions of provincial society, anecdotes, and digressions. He also wrote light verse, letters, etc.

Flers, ROBERT DE (1872–1927), dramatist, collaborated with *Caillavet and, later, with *Croisset.

Fleurange, ROBERT DE LA MARCK,

SEIGNEUR DE (d. 1537), *maréchal de France*. His memoirs of the period 1499–1521 describe the Field of the Cloth of Gold and *Marignan.

Fleurs du mal, Les, v. Baudelaire.

Fleurus, *v. Sambre-et-Meuse, L'Armée de.*

Fleury, ANDRÉ-HERCULE, CARDINAL DE (1653–1743), chief minister of Louis XV, a good administrator who, in conjunction with Walpole, long pursued a policy of peace; even so, he allowed France to be drawn into the wars of the Polish and Austrian Successions.

Fleury, CLAUDE (1640–1723), noted for his *Histoire ecclésiastique* (1691–1720).

Fleury, JULES, *v. Champfleury.*

Fliche, AUGUSTIN (1884–1951), religious historian. He and Mgr Victor Martin were the founders and first editors of the monumental *Histoire de l'Église depuis les origines jusqu'à nos jours* (1934– ; now nearing completion).

Flicoteau, in the early 19th c., a cheap restaurant (named after its proprietor) in the *Quartier latin, frequented by students and seedy journalists. Balzac describes it in *Illusions perdues* (*Un Grand Homme de province à Paris*).

Floire et Blancheflor, an early 13th-c. verse *roman d'aventure. There are two French versions; *cf.* the English *Flores and Blancheflour* (*c.* 1250) and Boccaccio's *Filocopo* on the same theme.

Floire and Blancheflor are brought up together and fall in love. Blancheflor is carried off to Babylon, but Floire, by hiding in a basket of roses, contrives to join her in the emir's seraglio. They are saved from execution by their beauty and mutual devotion. The poem contains a charming picture of the visionary wonders of the East.

Floovent, a 12th-c. *chanson de geste*, the story of the *Merovingian Floovent, son of Clovis.

Floréal, *v. Republican Calendar.*

Florian, JEAN-PIERRE CLARIS DE (1755–94), novelist, dramatist, and fabulist, a favourite of Voltaire (whose niece married Florian's uncle), and a member of the *Académie*, was in the service of the duc de Penthièvre (a grandson of Louis XIV). His works include a series of mild comedies of *bourgeois* life, depicting *Arlequin as a sentimental character (*Le Bon Ménage, Le Bon Père*, etc.); insipid romances (*Galatée*, 1783, adapted from Cervantes; *Numa Pompilius*, 1786, a moralizing imitation of *Télémaque* and *Bélisaire*; *Estelle et Némorin*, 1787, a pastoral; *Gonzalve de Cordoue*, 1791, the capture of Granada in 1492 with romantic episodes); *Fables* (1792), pleasing, but inferior to those of La Fontaine; *Mémoires d'un jeune Espagnol*, recounting his early life.

Foch, FERDINAND (1851–1929), *maréchal de France*, a famous soldier, commander of the Allied armies during the last year of the 1914–18 war.

Focillon, HENRI (1881–1943), author of works on art, notably *Vie des formes* (1934).

Fogg, Phileas, in *Verne's *Le Tour du monde en quatre-vingts jours*.

Foire, Théâtre de la, *v. Theatres and Theatre Companies*; *Opéra-Comique*.

Foire sur la place, La, *v. Jean-Christophe*.

Folantin, Monsieur, in Huysmans's *À vau l'eau*.

Fole Largece, La, a *fabliau* by Beau-manoir. A salt-merchant has to go four leagues to the sea to fetch his salt. He instructs his wife to sell, during his absence, the salt that remains in stock; but she foolishly gives it away to her gossips. To cure her of her folly, he takes her with him on his next trip and makes her carry part of the salt; by the time they get home she is cured.

Folengo, TEOFILO (1496–1544), an Italian Benedictine who left the cloister for a spell in middle life and, as 'Merlin Cocai', wrote a long macaronic poem which influenced Rabelais by its mixture of parody and realism, *Baldus* (Fr. trans. *Histoire mac-caronique de Merlin Coccaie, prototype de Rabelais*, 1606).

Folies amoureuses, Les, a verse comedy by Regnard, a charming trifle on a well-worn theme; produced 1704.

The aged Albert wishes to marry his young ward Agathe and tries by bolts and bars to prevent the access of younger suitors. But love finds a way. She feigns madness—attributed to Albert's harsh restraint. Her lover's valet, disguised as a physician, undertakes to cure her. The distracted Albert eagerly agrees, and the young couple take advantage of the 'cure' to elope.

Folie Tristan, La, *v. Tristan (Tristram).*

Follain, JEAN (1903–71), a poet and essayist whose work has a constant point of reference in memories of peasant and provincial life in the Normandy of his childhood. His collections include *Chants terrestres* (1937), *L'Épicerie d'enfance* (1938), *Exister* (1947), *Chef-lieu* (1950), *Territoires* (1953), *Des heures* (1960), *D'après tout* (1967).

Folle de Chaillot, La, *v. Giraudoux.*

Folle Journée, La, *v. Mariage de Figaro, Le.*

Fontainas, ANDRÉ (1865–1948), Belgian poet and critic, lived mostly in Paris and was closely associated with *Symbolism (a disciple of Mallarmé and a contributor to the *Mercure de France* and other Symbolist reviews). His works include *Les Vergers illusoires* (1892); *Les Estuaires d'ombre* (1896); *Le Jardin des îles claires* (1901); *La Nef désemparée* (1908); *Récifs au soleil* (1922), influenced by Valéry; translations of Keats and Meredith; also *Mes souvenirs du symbolisme* (1929).

Fontaine, CHARLES (1513–87), poet (he called his poems *Ruisseaux de la Fontaine*), defended Marot against Sagon and later against the innovations of the *Pléiade*.

Fontaine, NICOLAS (1625–1709), a humble member of the society of *Port-Royal*, which is vividly described in his memoirs. *v. Le Maître de Saci.*

Fontainebleau, Palais de, a fortress before the 12th c., then a favourite palace of the kings of France (esp. François Ier and Henri IV), who rebuilt and embellished it. Its library (f. 1363 by Charles V) formed the nucleus of the *Bibliothèque nationale*. During the *Terror the deserted palace was used as a prison. Napoleon, who restored it at great cost, used it to confine Pope Pius VII in semi-captivity (1812–13; *cf. Servitude et grandeur militaires*) and later signed his first abdication there. It is now an historical monument.

Fontaine de jouvence, La, in medieval legend, a fountain with the power of restoring youth; first met with in French literature in Alexandre de Bernay's romance (*v. Alexandre le Grand* (1)), where it is a stream in which Alexander and his army bathe and are restored to the prime of youth.

Fontanes, LOUIS DE (1757–1821), statesman and man of letters (*v. Université impériale*), remembered for his encouragement of the young Chateaubriand. His works—strongly influenced by the didactic poets of the 18th c.—include *Fragment d'un poème sur la nature et sur l'homme* (1777), *Essai sur l'astronomie* (1788; poem), and a translation of Pope's *Essay on Man*.

Fontaney, ANTOINE-ÉTIENNE (1803–37), minor poet, frequented the Romantic *cénacles* and was also at one time attached to the French embassy in Spain. He wrote *Ballades, mélodies, et poésies diverses* (1829) and *Scènes de la vie castillane et andalouse* (1835).

Fontanges, MARIE-ANGÉLIQUE, DUCHESSE DE (1661–81), succeeded Mme de Montespan as mistress of Louis XIV. She gave her name to the *fontange*, a tall head-dress of ribbons.

Fontenay-Mareuil, FRANÇOIS DU VAL, MARQUIS DE (c. 1594–1665), soldier and diplomat under Richelieu and Mazarin, ambassador in England 1630–3. His memoirs, chiefly of the period 1609–24, include a faithful picture of Henri IV.

Fontenelle, BERNARD LE BOVIER, SIEUR DE (1657–1757), a writer of wide curiosity, learning, and cool intelligence, began—under the guidance of his uncle, T. Corneille—by producing plays and verse of no literary importance. His chief works include the *Dialogues des morts* (1683), on the Lucianic model; his famous *Entretiens sur la pluralité des mondes* (1686), emphasizing the insignificance of man and of this planet in relation to the universe as a whole, a work which, by its lucidity and graceful presentation (dialogues between himself and a lady of his acquaintance), awakened general interest both in astronomy and in the scientific system of inquiry; the *Histoire des oracles* (1687), disproving their supernatural origin and analysing the causes of human credulity; the *Digression sur les anciens et les modernes* (1688), supporting the *modernes* in the *Querelle des anciens et des modernes*; the *Réflexions sur la poétique* (1742; written c. 1695), classifying tragic interest according to the misfortune that is its source (placing last the Greek notion of fate as a source of misfortune), and observing that, since the object of dramatic rules is the pleasure of the spectator, an irregular drama which pleases must conform to rules not yet discovered.

In general, he was a precursor of the attack science was soon to make on religion, quietly encouraging freedom of thought by substituting the play of mechanical forces for Providence in explanations of natural phenomena. (Voltaire, who satirized him in *Micromégas*, was nevertheless indebted to him.) He was a member of the *Académie française*, the *Académie des Inscriptions*, the *Académie des Sciences* (as perpetual secretary he wrote its history and remarkable *éloges* of members), and the Royal Society of London.

Fontenoy (near Tournai, Belgium). Here, after a stout defence, the English and Dutch under the duke of Cumberland were defeated (1745) by the French under Maurice de Saxe.

Forain, JEAN-LOUIS (1852–1931), artist, book-illustrator, and caustic caricaturist.

Forbin, CLAUDE, COMTE DE (1656–1733), naval officer. His somewhat vainglorious and unreliable memoirs (1729) involved him in a dispute with Duguay-Trouin, whom he disparaged. He describes the Old Pretender's abortive attempt to land in Scotland in 1708.

Force, La, *v. Salpêtrière.*

Forces tumultueuses, Les, v. Verhaeren.

Foreign Influences on French Literature.

1. 1100–1700. Oriental and Byzantine influence, largely the result of the Crusades, can be seen in the fantasy and lavish colouring of the medieval romances. Arabic influence left traces (via Provençal) on courtly poetry and is found in scientific and didactic literature. But the main foreign influences during this period, other than those of classical antiquity (*v. Classicism; Comedy; Critics and Criticism; Renaissance; Tragedy*), were Italian, Spanish, English, and German.

English and German influence was, on the whole, slight, but the connection between France and *Anglo-Norman* England left some traces, and in the 16th c. the works of Luther (some trans. by L. de Berquin) had a powerful effect (the principle of religious liberty and freedom of thought, so prominent in the 17th c. from Bayle onwards, owes more to him than to Calvin).

Italian influence, notably that of Petrarch, on poetry first becomes marked in the early 16th c., especially at Lyons (*v.*

Scève). It is seen in Marot, who spent some time at Ferrara, and in M. de Saint-Gelais. Castiglione's *Cortegiano* (trans. 1537) introduced the Platonic conception of love and the ideal of the court lady, which inspired *Héroët's Parfaite Amie*. Du Bellay mentions Italian poetry among the inspirations of the *Pléiade*, and he, Ronsard, Tyard, and Louise Labé freely used the Italian *sonnet-form*. (Dante, first trans. 1596–7, was little appreciated before the 19th c.)

From the mid-16th c. translations and imitations of Italian plays were common (*v. Larivey*). 17th-c. dramatists often borrowed plots from Italian and Spanish sources (e.g. Corneille's *Le *Cid*; several of Molière's comedies); and there were Italian troupes (*v. Italiens*) in Paris throughout the 17th c. Though Italian and Spanish influence was strongest on comedy, Italian and Spanish pastorals inspired a vogue reflected in the plays of Hardy and others (*v. Pastoral*) and Italian influence helped to develop *tragicomedy as a genre*. Imitations of Spanish burlesque were common in the 17th c.

In prose fiction, Boccaccio was an early influence. His *Decameron* (trans. 1485 and, a better version, 1545; both several times reprinted) was a model as early as 1462 for the *Cent Nouvelles Nouvelles*; two particularly popular tales—those of *Griseldis* and of Guiscard and Gismonde—were published separately. His *Filocopo* was partly translated in 1531, his *Fiammetta* in 1532. The Latin romance of Eurialus and Lucretia by Aeneas Sylvius (Pope Pius II) was several times translated, and material for collections of tales was also drawn from Poggio's *Facetiae* (also in Latin) and *Bandello's Novelle*. Various Italian pastoral romances were also translated. Spanish influence is early attested by translations of many romances (*v. Celestina; Amadis de Gaule*), later by translations of Baltazar Gracián, by the popularity of *Don Quixote*, and by d'Urfé's *L'*Astrée* (which owed much to Montemayor's *Diana*). It continues in the 17th c. with Scarron (his *Nouvelles tragicomiques* were largely imitated from the Spanish) and well into the 18th with

Lesage. The picaresque novels of Scarron and Lesage have a recognizable prototype in the mid-16th-c. Spanish romance *Lazarillo de Tormes*. *v. Novel*, 1 and 2.

The preciosity of the 17th-c. **salons* was reinforced by—though not derived from—the artificial writings of the Italians Guarini and Marino (*v. Marinisme*). Spanish *Cultismo* or Gongorism, a kindred movement which carried mannerism to the point of obscurity, made little impact in France.

2. 1700–*c.* 1800. Interest now turned increasingly to English and German literature, especially after 1750, when it reflected the pre-*Romantic movement of ideas. (Passing mention must also be made of 18th-c. 'Orientalism', notably encouraged by Galland's translation of the *Arabian Nights*, 1704–17.)

The German philosopher Leibniz wrote two of his major works in French (the *Essais de Théodicée*, 1710; *Monadologie*, 1720). He was at first more esteemed in France than in Germany, though Voltaire later ridiculed his optimism in **Candide*. Works by his disciple Christian von Wolff were also translated. From England, political and philosophical ideas reached France before 1750, partly through Voltaire's **Lettres philosophiques* and Montesquieu's *De l'*esprit des lois*, and Bacon, Hobbes, Halifax, Shaftesbury, Newton, and Locke were widely appreciated.

English essayists, playwrights, and novelists were also becoming known (e.g. through the abbé *Prévost's *Le Pour et Contre*). Temple, Addison, Steele, Wycherley, Vanbrugh, Defoe, and Swift were translated or imitated. Fielding and Richardson were translated between 1740 and 1763, Goldsmith's *Vicar of Wakefield* in 1767, Sterne in 1760–87. Diderot imitated Sterne in **Jacques le fataliste* and praised Richardson (*Éloge de Richardson*, 1761), whose method of romantic narrative by means of letters was adopted by J.-J. Rousseau (*La *Nouvelle Héloise*) and *Laclos (*Les Liaisons dangereuses*). The novels of Horace Walpole, Mrs. Radcliffe, and 'Monk' Lewis were much admired (tombs, sensibility, and delirious

passion appealed to such authors as Baculard d'Arnaud, L.-S. Mercier, and Léonard), but the real vogue for the Gothic novel came at the turn of the century.

From Germany, *Goethe's *Werther* (15 transss. 1776–97) had an overwhelming influence on the mental outlook of a whole generation (*v.* 3, below).

In poetry, the sombre qualities of *Young's *Night Thoughts* (trans. 1769 by Letourneur), Gray's *Elegy* (trans. 1769), and *Ossian (trans. 1777 by Letourneur) were much admired. Both English and German influences (Thomson's *Seasons*, trans. 1769; Haller's *Die Alpen*, trans. 1750) served to strengthen the descriptive element which becomes marked about this time in French didactic verse (*v. Saint-Lambert*; *Lemierre*; *Roucher*) and is soon evident in J.-J. Rousseau. Huber's *Choix de poésies allemandes* (1766, 4 vols.; with a history of German literature and notes on authors) and *Grimm's letters helped to make German poetry known. The idyllic poems of the German-Swiss *Gessner were particularly influential. Klopstock's *Messiah* (trans. 1769) was also admired. Wieland's poems, though read, were more fully appreciated in the 19th c.

In the drama, Shakespeare (praised, imitated, and later censured by Voltaire) was more argued about than appreciated. His plays were translated or adapted by P.-A. de Laplace, Letourneur, and Ducis. Other English dramatists made known by Laplace were Otway and Lillo (whose domestic tragedy influenced Diderot and was praised by Voltaire). Moore's *The Gamester* was more than once adapted. Interest in German drama developed more slowly. The plays of Lessing, though sometimes imitated, were rather coldly received; but his *Dramaturgie* (trans. 1785) and *Laocoon* (essays on the limitations of poetry and the plastic arts, trans. 1802) were to contribute, with the repercussions of the *Sturm und Drang* movement, to the reaction against the *Classical form of tragedy and also to the evolution of dramatic criticism.

3. *c.* 1800–*c.* 1830. Foreign influences, weakened during the Revolution, gathered

impetus in the early 19th c. This was accentuated by the emergence of the professional critic (v. *Critics and Criticism*, 2) and the return of *émigrés* and travellers informed about foreign cultures.

Several reviews, miscellanies, and anthologies were devoted to translation and criticism of English, German, Italian, and Spanish literature, e.g. the *Archives littéraires de l'Europe* (1804–7), the *Bibliothèque germanique* (1805), the *Mélanges de littérature étrangère* (1808), the *Collection des chefs-d'œuvre des théâtres étrangers* (1821–2), the *Revue britannique*. Chateaubriand's *Le *Génie du christianisme* renewed interest in English literature. Mme de Staël's *De l'Allemagne* inspired a lasting enthusiasm for German literature and philosophy. Italy, dear to the *Romantics because of Dante and its association with medieval art and Christianity, was put more clearly on the map by her *Corinne*, *Stendhal's *Rome, Naples, et Florence en 1817*, and literary histories by Ginguené and Sismondi. The Spanish *romanceros* (poems on themes from national history and legend), translated by Creuzé de Lesser (*Les Romances du Cid*, 1814 and 1823), were a fruitful source for the Romantics (e.g. Mérimée's *Théâtre de Clara Gazul*; Hugo's *Hernani* and *Ruy Blas*; Émile *Deschamps's *Études françaises et étrangères*). *Don Quixote* was translated several times.

Foreign influences on the Romantics' fight for freedom in the drama included, above all, Shakespeare (trans. by Guizot, 1821; Bruguière de Sorsum, 1826; Vigny, 1827, 1829; also perf. in English in Paris in 1822 and 1827), constantly quoted in defence of Romantic doctrines, e.g. in Stendhal's *Racine et Shakspeare*, Hugo's *Préface de *Cromwell*; also, from Germany, Schiller (*Wallenstein* was trans. 1809 by B. Constant, who appended *Réflexions sur ... le théâtre allemand*; his other plays were trans. from 1816), *Schlegel's *Cours de littérature dramatique* (trans. by Mme Necker de Saussure), and Goethe (whose plays were trans. from 1821, and in whose Faust the Romantics found a fitting companion to the Byronic hero; *v.*

Nerval); and, from Italy, Manzoni (whose *Lettre à M. Chauvet sur les deux unités classiques* prefaced *Fauriel's trans. of his tragedies).

On Romantic poetry, the strongest foreign influence (seen in Lamartine, Musset, etc.) was Byron, translated (1822–5) by Pichot. Pichot's own *Voyage historique et littéraire en Angleterre et en Écosse* included studies of Byron, Shelley, and the Lake Poets (the last an influence on Sainte-Beuve). A collection of *Ballades, légendes, et chants populaires de l'Angleterre et de l'Écosse* (1825) was also much read. German poetry, e.g. Goethe's *Erlkönig*, Schiller's *Lied von der Glocke*, Bürger's *Lenore* (trans. 1830 by Nerval), fostered the vogue for the macabre; and Wieland's *Oberon* (trans. 1825 by Loève-Veimars) was now appreciated. The enthusiasm for Greece and Greek antiquity apparent at this time was stimulated by Chateaubriand's *Itinéraire de Paris à Jérusalem*, *Latouche's edition of A. Chénier, Fauriel's *Chants populaires de la Grèce moderne* (1824–5), and the Greek War of Independence.

In the novel, romantic love, introspection, and the personal element (e.g. in Senancour's *Obermann*, Chateaubriand's *René*, Musset's *Confession d'un enfant du siècle*, *Nodier's *Le Peintre de Salzbourg*) owe much to *Goethe's *Werther*. Other German influences included E. T. A. *Hoffmann, *Novalis, *La Motte Fouqué, *Eichendorff, and *Chamisso. Their fantastic and mystical tales were translated or imitated by Nodier, Nerval, Gautier, Petrus Borel, Loève-Veimars, etc. Another strong influence was Sir Walter Scott (trans. 1822): the sense of history and care for atmosphere evident in Vigny's *Cinq-Mars*, Mérimée's *Chronique du règne de Charles IX*, Hugo's *Notre-Dame de Paris*, etc., derive largely from him. English Gothic novels were also much read and imitated.

4. *c.* 1830–*c.* 1880. Foreign influence now shows most clearly in the work of essayists, historians, and critics. The main source was German Idealist philosophy. Fichte, Schelling, Hegel, etc., became known largely through *Cousin's lectures

and were mostly translated by 1850. A debt to Herder is apparent in Quinet and Michelet; but the influence of German philosophy (Hegel, Goethe, Herder, and Kant, leavened by a study of English philosophers) is above all marked in Taine (Introduction to his *Histoire de la littérature anglaise*) and Renan (*Les Origines du christianisme*; *L'Avenir de la science*).

Its influence can also be seen in poetry, in the vague pantheism and the pessimism of the *Parnassiens* (e.g. Leconte de Lisle, Sully-Prudhomme, Dierx). But it was not the sole foreign influence: *Parnassien* verse also reflects the interest aroused by the advances in Oriental and archaeological studies (*v. Leconte de Lisle*). *Heine's mixture of lyricism and irony had an effect on, for example, Gautier, Banville, and Baudelaire. Baudelaire also translated, and was among the first to be influenced by, Edgar Allan Poe.

In the novel, on the other hand, such foreign influence as there was (mainly after 1850) was almost wholly English. English fiction was reviewed by the critics (notably Montégut), and the humour, realism, and humanitarianism of Dickens, Thackeray, and George Eliot were much appreciated. The importance attached by Flaubert, the Goncourts, Zola, Maupassant, etc., to objective description and documentation has some connection with the English philosophical ideas (e.g. those of Darwin; *v. Royer*) that filtered into literature through the Positivism of Comte and through Taine, the theoretician of *Naturalism (and *cf. Realism*).

5. *c.* 1880–1900. German influence survived the *Franco-Prussian war (Barrès, in *Les *Déracinés*, 1897, deplores the importance attached to Kant in French teaching). In poetry, the pessimism of Hartmann (trans. 1877, *La Philosophie de l'inconscient*) and Schopenhauer (trans. 1880–1, *Le Monde considéré comme volonté et représentation*) is reflected in the *Symbolists' retreat from external reality to a more subjective universe. They were also influenced, even more than the Romantics, by Novalis, and, above all, by *Wagner. Other influences were those of

the Belgians and Americans who were writing Symbolist poetry in French, while Symbolist drama, and the French theatre, owe much to the Scandinavian dramatists (e.g. Ibsen, Bjørnson, Strindberg), whose works were performed in Paris *c.* 1890 at the *Théâtre de l'*Œuvre*, the *Théâtre Libre*, etc.

In the novel, an enthusiasm for Russian writers (largely inspired by Vogüé and Mérimée, and fostered by Turgenev, who was moving freely in Parisian literary circles) coincided with a reaction against *Naturalism. Tolstoy and Dostoievsky were now frequently translated: the novel of ideas (social reform, religion, etc., e.g. Rolland's *Jean-Christophe*) has a debt to Tolstoy; the full impact of Dostoievsky came later, with the spiritual insecurity of the 1920s and 1930s.

The late 19th c. also saw an awakening of interest in Japanese literature and art (*v. Goncourt, E. de*).

6. 20TH CENTURY. There are signs in 20th-c. literature of the interest in Nietzsche aroused by H. Lichtenberger's *Philosophie de Nietzsche* (1898) and by subsequent translations, e.g. in the works of Gide (who was also influenced by, and wrote on, Dostoievsky). Other early 20th-c. influences were those of Walt Whitman on *Unanimisme, and of the Italian poet Marinetti, the founder of *Futurism.

In the period since the end of the 1914–18 war, cultural contacts between nations and the interplay of ideas have obviously become more immediate than ever before, and French writers have also become more receptive to influences of all kinds. In France, as elsewhere, psychoanalytical theories largely of Austrian and German origin, and Russian Communism, have been major influences. Since the 1920s, when Freud's theory of the unconscious inspired the *Surrealists to explore 'les champs magnétiques', psychoanalytical theories have pervaded the intellectual climate. Since the 1920s, too, a great many creative writers have had an active Communist phase, or an interest in Communism (e.g. Gide), which is reflected in their works, and some have become committed Marxist writers (*v.

Littérature engagée). Since the 1950s, both these influences have been seen in the *nouvelle critique* (*v. Critics and Criticism*, 3)—as have those of the Russian formalists and the Russian-born linguist Roman Jakobson (via *Structuralism), and of the Italian critic Umberto Eco (via *Semiology).

In the inter-war years, the influence of Dostoievsky is apparent in the novels of Bernanos and Gide, and that of Tolstoy in those of Martin du Gard. *Existentialism, now in process of evolution, was strongly influenced by German philosophers. This period saw the beginning of the progressive invasion of France by American culture: the novels of Ernest Hemingway, John Dos Passos, John Steinbeck, William Faulkner, etc., jazz music, and films. The general ethos and, above all, the stylistic and technical innovations of the American novel were making an impact seen after 1940 in, for example, the style of *Camus's *L'Étranger*, the technique of *Sartre's *Le Sursis*, *Vian's American-style thrillers.

Major influences since 1940 have been those of Franz Kafka, William Faulkner, and James Joyce. Kafka's bleak and disturbing vision of the human condition appeared at once prophetic and highly relevant in the dark days of 1940 and in the climate of *Existentialism, and almost overnight he became a master for the *avant garde* (the subject of studies by Blanchot, Camus, N. Sarraute, and many others). His influence, which was reinforced by the dramatization of his works (e.g. Barrault's memorable production of *Le Procès*, 1947), is very apparent in the *nouveau roman* and the Theatre of the Absurd (*v. Theatre of the 19th and 20th cs.*). Faulkner's tragic vision and sense of sin were peculiarly in tune with French sensibility and his influence has been more profound and widespread than that of his compatriots. His works were regularly translated from the early 1930s and their impact was reflected after the war in the *nouveau roman* (esp. the work of C. Simon), in Camus's stage adaptation of *Requiem pour une nonne* (1956), in the later work of Giono, etc. Joyce's influence, which has, predictably,

been primarily on technique and the use of language, has been strong on such writers as Larbaud (who experimented with the stream-of-consciousness technique in the 1920s and helped to translate *Ulysses*, 1937), Beckett, and Queneau, and also on exponents of the *nouveau roman*. His full impact has probably not yet been felt. Since 1962, when the poet André du Bouchet (1924–) published a rendering of parts of *Finnegans Wake*, younger writers (e.g. the *Tel Quel* group) have become interested in this work.

The above brief summary is confined to major influences upon which critics are broadly agreed. Many other foreign writers whose impact cannot yet be assessed have aroused great interest since 1945, e.g. Bertolt Brecht and Jorge Luis Borges. There has also been a modest Japanese influence (as in the late 19th c.).

Foreign Legion, *v. Légion étrangère.*

Forgeries, *v. Hoaxes and Forgeries.*

For-l'Évêque, in Paris, originally an episcopal court of justice and prison; after 1674 a royal prison for debtors and, especially, delinquent actors—who were usually allowed out in the evening to play their parts. It was demolished in 1780.

Fort, PAUL (1872–1960), poet (*v. Naturisme*), founder of the *Théâtre d'Art* (*v. Œuvre, Théâtre de l'*) and the review *Vers et Prose*. His *Ballades françaises* (*c.* 1895, in reviews or as pamphlets; when collected they filled over 30 vols.) are poems and *chansons*, at times of high quality, on the general theme of France, her towns and countryside, legends, and history. He uses, and experiments with, rhyme and verse-forms, but to emphasize the all-importance of rhythm, cadence, and assonance the poems are printed as prose. In a referendum organized (1912) by *Gil Blas* he was elected 'Prince des poètes'.

Fort comme la mort, *v. Maupassant.*

Fortune des Rougon, La, v. *Rougon-Macquart, Les.*

Foucault, MICHEL., v. *Structuralism.*

Fouché, JOSEPH (1759–1820), politician, a member of the *Convention,* one of the instigators of mass-shootings of anti-*Jacobin* rebels at Lyons (1793), and later, when president of the *Club des *Jacobins,* an opponent of Robespierre. His talent for intrigue showed itself under the *Directoire* when, despite his record, he became *Ministre de la *Police* and organized a powerful system of espionage. He helped Napoleon to power and retained office—first as *Ministre de la Police,* then as *Ministre de l'Intérieur*—till 1810 (with an interval of two years, 1802–4), being largely responsible for the repressive censorship exercised at this time (v. *Censorship, Dramatic*; *Librairie*; *Press,* 3 and 4). Though dismissed in 1810 (in which year he was created duc d'Otranto), he was too useful to Napoleon to be disgraced. After Waterloo, he regained office under Louis XVIII (with whom he had been secretly intriguing for some years), but soon resigned and later left France.

Foucher, ADÈLE (1803–68), married Hugo in 1822, having known him from childhood. She wrote—largely, it is said, at his dictation—*Victor Hugo raconté par un témoin de sa vie* (1863, 2 vols.). v. *Hugo, E.*; *Sainte-Beuve.*

Fouillée, ALFRED (1838–1912), philosopher. His numerous works expound his system of *idées-forces,* an attempt at a compromise between an idealistic philosophy and materialism.

Fouquet or **Foucquet,** JEAN (c. 1416–80), portrait painter and manuscript illuminator. His works, commissioned by such patrons as Charles VII, Louis XI, and Étienne Chevalier (treasurer of France), include the famous *Livre d'Heures d'Étienne Chevalier* (in the *Musée Condé) and a portrait of Charles VII (*Musée du *Louvre*).

Fouquet or **Foucquet,** NICOLAS (1615–80), an able and unscrupulous financier who, as *surintendant des finances* (from 1653) under Mazarin, acquired a fortune, partly by peculation. He spent it generously, protecting men of letters (Corneille, Gombauld, La Fontaine, Molière, Perrault, Scarron) and building the Château de *Vaux-le-Vicomte. But he made an enemy of Colbert and his tactless ostentation offended the young Louis XIV. He was arrested (1661), condemned for malversation (v. *Pellisson*), and spent the rest of his life imprisoned at Pignerol. Mme de Sévigné was his devoted friend.

Fouquier-Tinville, ANTOINE-QUENTIN (1746–95), the public prosecutor (*accusateur public*) attached to the *Tribunal révolutionnaire,* one of the men most feared during the *Terror. He was later himself executed.

Fourberies de Scapin, Les, by Molière, a farcical comedy (3 acts, prose) based on Terence's *Phormio*; produced 1671.

The scene is Naples. Octave, son of Argante, and Léandre, son of Géronte, have got entangled in love affairs in their fathers' absence. Octave, having found a destitute young lady (Hyacinthe) weeping for her dying mother, has married her, but cannot support her. Léandre has fallen in love with Zerbinette, an Egyptian girl, but lacks the money to buy her from her owners. The fathers return unexpectedly. Argante is furious to hear of Octave's marriage, for he had wanted him to marry Géronte's daughter, who is now due to arrive in Naples with her mother. Scapin, a resourceful valet, contrives to trick the two fathers into providing the money their sons need: he persuades Argante that he has arranged to annul Octave's marriage in consideration of a money payment; and he convinces Géronte that Léandre has boarded a Turkish galley and been carried off to sea and held to ransom (Géronte's famous repeated exclamation, 'Que diable allait-il faire dans cette galère?', and the accompanying scene, were inspired by *Cyrano de Bergerac's *Le Pédant joué*). Scapin's knavery is discovered; but all ends well, for Hyacinthe proves to be Géronte's daughter (the girl Octave was meant to marry) and Zerbinette proves to be the lost daughter of Argante.

Fourest, GEORGES, *v. Pastiche.*

Fourier, Fouriérisme. *Fouriérisme* was a doctrine of economic and social reform advanced by CHARLES FOURIER (1772–1837). It is contained in germ in his *Théorie des quatre mouvements* (1808), i.e. the four categories into which the universe is divided—society, animal life, organic life, and the material universe. The book is a mixture of social philosophy, projects for economic and agricultural reform (later elaborated in his *Traité de l'association domestique et agricole*, 1822; *Le Nouveau Monde industriel*, 1829–30), and a riotously imaginative picture of a universe destined to last 80,000 years, progressing from chaos to the apogee of happiness and then relapsing into chaos. During the 8,000 years of complete Harmony the North Pole would be warm, the sea like lemonade; there would be 37 million poets equal to Homer, 37 million geometricians equal to Newton, 37 million dramatists equal to Molière (these were 'estimations approximatives'), and at least four husbands or lovers for every woman.

The first of a series of *phalanstères* was established (1838) at Condé-sur-Vesgre, near Rambouillet. In principle these were co-operative, mainly agricultural, communities (*phalanges*), each of 100 families, who were to live in complete physical and moral harmony in buildings called a *phalanstère* (a term coined by Fourier from *phalange* and *monastère*). Profits were to be shared; and for women the system implied emancipation and free love. The experiment failed.

The chief *Fouriériste* work was the *Destinée sociale* (1834) of Victor Considérant (1809–93), one of Fourier's most active disciples. *Fouriériste* journals included *Le Phalanstère* (f. *c.* 1833), succeeded by *La Phalange* (1836–43; fortnightly) and *La Démocratie pacifique* (1843–51; daily). Fourier's doctrines are reflected in G. Sand's *Le *Compagnon*

du Tour de France and *Le Meunier d'Angibault* and in *Zola's *Les Quatre Évangiles*; *v.* also *Leconte de Lisle.*

Fournier, HENRI-ALBAN, *v. Alain-Fournier.*

Fracasse, *v. Capitaine Fracasse, Le.*

Fragonard, JEAN-HONORÉ (1732–1806), a painter noted for his charming scenes of gallantry in the 18th-c. manner.

Français moderne, Le (1933– ; quarterly), a learned philological journal.

Franc-Archer de Bagnolet, Le, a lively dramatic monologue (octosyllables), written in 1468 by an unknown author. The speaker is a boastful warrior who is terrified by a scarecrow, and the work is a caricature of the unpopular militia created (1448) by Charles VII.

France, Anatole, *pseudonym of* JACQUES-ANATOLE-FRANÇOIS THIBAULT (1844–1924), novelist, critic, and man of letters, the only son of a Paris book-dealer. His childhood, schooldays at the **Collège Stanislas*, and the more profitable education he acquired by voracious reading are described with tenderness, humour, and some admixture of fiction in *Le Livre de mon ami* (1885), *Pierre Nozière* (1899), *Le Petit Pierre* (1918), *La Vie en fleur* (1922). Soon after leaving school he obtained employment with Lemerre, the publisher. Over the next 20 years, besides his work as publisher's reader and the writing of prefaces to editions of the classics (collected in *Le Génie latin*, 1913), he wrote for reviews and published a study of Vigny (1868), also *Poèmes dorés* (1873) and *Les Noces corinthiennes* (1876; a verse drama), both influenced by the *Parnassiens (*v. Lemerre*). From 1876 to 1890 he was a librarian at the *Sénat, with ample free time, and wrote regularly for *Le Globe* and *L'Univers illustré*, published tales (*Jocaste et le Chat maigre*, 1879; two tales), made his name with *Le *Crime de Sylvestre Bonnard* (1881), and became literary editor of *Le *Temps* (1888). This period saw the beginning of his association with Mme Arman de Caillavet (v. *Salon*, 1), who long inspired and encouraged him (his first marriage ended in 1892). By 1897, the year after his election to the *Académie*, he had come to dominate the literary scene. The *Dreyfus case aroused his strong sympathies and in later years he developed Socialist leanings. Latterly, he retired to La Béchellerie, his property in Touraine. He was awarded the *Prix Nobel* in 1921.

La Vie littéraire (1888–92, 4 vols.; 1950, 1 vol.), an incomplete collection of his fortnightly articles in *Le Temps*, shows him as a subjective critic (v. *Critics and Criticism*, 2) and also illustrates his particular charm as a writer—his graceful erudition; his love of beauty, pagan antiquity, and 18th-c. *Classicism; his scepticism; his subtle, biting irony; his dislike of extremes; his clarity of thought; and his elegant, melodious style. These qualities are even more marked after 1890 in (1) his novels, e.g. *Thaïs* (1890), *La *Rôtisserie de la Reine Pédauque* (1893), *Le Lys rouge* (1894; his one novel of contemporary society, a study of love and jealousy, set mainly in Florence), *L'Histoire contemporaine* (1896–1901; v. *Bergeret*), *L'*Île des pingouins* (1908), *Les Dieux ont soif* (1912; one of the best novels of the Revolution), *La Révolte des anges* (1914; a number of angels, weary of Heaven, decide to live as ordinary mortals in Paris—their adventures afford scope for sharp social satire); and (2) his tales, e.g. *L'Étui de nacre* (1892; inc. *Le Jongleur de Notre-Dame* and *Le *Procurateur de Judée*), *Le Jardin d'Épicure* (1894; a miscellany), *Crainquebille* (1901), *Sur la pierre blanche* (1905; inc. *Gallion*, a tale of the proconsul mentioned in Acts 18: 12–17). v. also *Jeanne d'Arc*.

France littéraire, La, v. *Quérard*.

Franc Gontier, Les Contreditz, in *Villon's *Testament*. The simple rural life of Gontier, the type of the honest labourer, and his wife Hélène having been extolled in *Les Ditz Franc Gontier* by Philippe de Vitry (d. 1351), Villon here replies with

praise of the easy, sensual life, in a *ballade* with the refrain 'Il n'est trésor que de vivre à son aise'.

Franciade, La, v. *Ronsard*.

Francien, v. *French Language*.

Francion, La Vraie Histoire comique de, v. *Sorel, C.*

Franck, César-Auguste (1822–90), composer of Belgian birth, received his musical education in Paris and spent the rest of his life there. Fame came to him late in life: he was long a church organist and later taught the organ at the *Conservatoire de musique*.

François Ier (1494–1547), king of France (*Capetian dynasty, *Valois-*Orléans line), son of Charles, comte d'Angoulême, and Louise de Savoie and great-great-grandson of Charles V, succeeded his father-in-law Louis XII (who died without male issue; v. *Claude*), r. 1515–47. A man of wide interests, much influenced by his sister Marguerite de Navarre, an admirer of Erasmus, Leonardo, and Petrarch, a patron of writers (e.g. Marot, Rabelais) and scholars (e.g. Budé, Lefèvre d'Étaples, R. Estienne), he played a notable part in the development of the *Renaissance in France (v. also *Bibliothèque nationale*; *Collège de France*; *Évangélisme*; *Concordat*). He was an eager patron of art and a great builder of châteaux (Chambord, *Fontainebleau). On the debit side, he was imperious and violent, weak and vacillating, and a cruel persecutor of the *Vaudois. v. *Marignan*; *Pavia*; *Cartier*.

François II (1544–60), king of France (*Capetian dynasty, *Valois-*Orléans line), eldest son of Henri II and Catherine de Médicis, m. Mary Stuart (1558), succeeded Henri II, r. 1559–60.

François de Sales, St. (1567–1622), b. in Savoy, bishop of Geneva from 1602, a leader of the Counter-Reformation (as a young man he worked as a Catholic evangelist among the *Huguenots of Savoy), and founder with Jeanne-Françoise de Chantal (canonized 1767) of the Congregation of the Visitation (1610). He became the centre of French religious life through his preaching (in Paris in 1602 and 1619), letters, and immensely successful *Introduction à la vie dévote* (1609, definitive ed. 1619; trans. into 17 languages), an attempt to foster a life of Christian devotion amid worldly distractions. His letters inculcate a rational system of morality, free from excessive austerity—in contrast to the spirit of *Jansenism, which followed. He also wrote a mystical *Traité de l'amour de Dieu* (1616). His style was free and graceful, with an abundance of similes, his manner amiable and benign.

Françoise, the devoted and dictatorial family servant in *A la recherche du temps perdu*; drawn from Mme Céleste Albaret, Proust's 'servante au grand cœur'.

François le champi (1850), a romance of country life by G. Sand. A *champi* (i.e. a child abandoned in the fields) adopted by a miller's wife, herself little more than a girl, grows up to be her protector when she is widowed, ill, and burdened with her late husband's debts. The bond of affection between them ripens into love, which they confess on the spot where she had found the *champi*. *v. A la recherche du temps perdu*, 2.

Franco-Prussian War. Hostilities had been threatening for some years when, in the summer of 1870, a Prussian prince came forward as a candidate for the vacant Spanish throne. This threat to France's southern frontier aroused such an outcry that he withdrew. France, having failed to obtain assurances that Prussia would oppose any such move in the future, declared war on 19 July 1870. After a number of reverses, the French were crushingly defeated at Sedan (1 Sept. 1870). The situation just before the battle was that part of the army, under Mac-Mahon, had fallen back on Châlons and

been rejoined by Napoleon III, who left Bazaine in command of the main army, then besieged in Metz. The best course for Mac-Mahon's army would have been to move back on Paris, but feeling there was running high and, to avoid revolution, the emperor was urged to relieve Metz. After a delay that ruined any hope of success, Mac-Mahon's army set out for Metz. The Prussian command discovered the movement, diverted two armies then marching on Paris, surprised the French on 30 August, and encircled them at Sedan (on the Meuse, near the Belgian frontier) on 1 September. The French were under heavy shell-fire all day, the cavalry's heroic efforts to make a way for the infantry were vain, and at 5 p.m. Napoleon III ordered the white flag to be hoisted. He was required to surrender unconditionally and taken prisoner, together with a large army. The main army at Metz capitulated on 27 October. Meanwhile, the Second Empire had fallen (*v. Revolutions*, 4; *Republics*, 3) and hastily levied, untrained forces were resisting the Prussian invasion. Paris, besieged for over four months, was starved into surrender (28 Jan. 1871). Three days later the army which, largely organized by Gambetta, had been trying to cut Prussian communications from the east narrowly escaped capture by taking refuge in Switzerland. *v. Garibaldi.*

The German Empire (proclaimed at *Versailles 18 Jan. 1871) imposed a harsh peace (ratified 1 March and concluded, by the Treaty of Frankfort, in May 1871; *v. Commune*, 2), including a heavy war indemnity, severe occupation terms (though the last German troops had left by Sept. 1873), and the surrender of Alsace and Lorraine (which remained in German hands till 1918).

The war is vividly described in Zola's *La *Débâcle*, and v. Soirées de Médan, Les.

Frayssinous, DENIS, ABBÉ DE (1765–1841), a noted preacher, chaplain to Louis XVIII. His addresses at Saint-Sulpice on the *Défense du christianisme et des libertés gallicanes* (1803; publ. 1825) initiated the custom of giving series of theological lectures in churches.

Fredegarius, *v. Gregory of Tours.*

Frederick the Great, i.e. Friedrich II of Prussia (1712–86), r. 1740–86, was educated by a French tutor (Jacques Duhan) and developed a great love of French language and literature, later evident in his patronage of French men of letters, notably *Voltaire and d'*Alembert. His history of Prussia, his narratives of the Seven Years War and other events of his reign, and his correspondence are written in excellent French.

Frénaud, ANDRÉ (1907–), poet, a civil servant by profession. He made his name with the *Resistance poems of *Les Rois-Mages* (1943), written while he was a prisoner of war. Many of his subsequent collections were united in *Il n'y a pas de paradis* (1962) and *La Sainte Face* (1968). He has since published *Depuis toujours déjà* (1970) and *La Sorcière de Rome* (1973). He is a poet of revolt, stoically searching for a meaning to life in the modern world; disillusioned, yet also conciliatory in spirit and mindful of man's resourcefulness. *v. Lyric Poetry*, 4.

French Influence on English Literature, *v. English Literature.*

French Language, The. This is basically the product of the conquest of Gaul by the Romans, who brought with them both classical Latin (taught in the schools and used in the literature of Roman Gaul) and the popular Latin of soldiers and merchants. The latter, driving out Celtic (though a few words of Celtic origin subsist, e.g. *chemin*, *lieue*), established itself among the mass of the inhabitants and gradually evolved into the Romance vernacular known as French (*v. Romance Languages*). Apart from the obvious changes in the pronunciation of words, this evolution included some notable features, e.g. the adoption of *habere* 'to have', followed by a passive participle, to express the meaning of the perfect as distinct from the aorist or preterite; the extension of *esse* with the past participle

to the whole of the passive; the disappearance of the system of case-inflexions (except for a partial survival of a two-case system into Old French) and its replacement by the use of prepositions; the development, from *ille* and *unus*, of the definite and indefinite articles; many changes in the Latin vocabulary, including striking changes of meaning, e.g. *testa* 'pot' came to mean 'head' (*tête*). The Frankish invasion did not modify the Gallo-Romance character of the language, though it added a good many words of Germanic origin, e.g. *fauteuil*, *guerre*, *riche*.

But it was not a single language that thus evolved. South of a line roughly from the mouth of the Gironde to the Alps the language was the *langue d'oc*, a group of dialects which found its literary expression in the Provençal of the *troubadours*; north of this line, it was the numerous dialects of the *langue d'oïl*—*oc*, from Latin *hoc*, and *oïl*, a contraction of *hoc ille*, being the words for 'yes' in the two regions. The crusade against the *Albigenses and the subjection of the southern provinces (13th c.) carried the *langue d'oïl* to the Mediterranean; Provençal survived as the spoken language of the South, but Provençal literature perished (for its 19th-c. revival *v. Félibrige*). Within the *langue d'oïl* there were great differences between the spoken dialects of the various *provinces*, Normandy, Picardy, Lorraine, Anjou, etc. From the 12th c., however, a common language, which was in the main that of the *Île-de-France (hence the name *Francien* applied to it by modern scholars) and of Paris and the court (*v. Conon de Béthune*), gradually acquired pre-eminence. In its continued evolution this common language has undergone changes of various kinds; its vocabulary, for example, has been enriched by the adoption of words from Arabic, especially in the Middle Ages; from Italian, notably—during the *Renaissance, after successive invasions of Italy—in the spheres of literature, art, and war; from Spanish, especially in the late 16th and 17th cs.; and from English throughout the modern period.

The use of French as a written language dates from the 9th c.: the first extant document is the *Serments de Strasbourg, and the first literary work the *Séquence de Sainte *Eulalie*. These texts were, of course, written down by clerks learned in Latin; and written French remained throughout the Middle Ages very much under the influence of Latin, from which it borrowed large numbers of words (esp. for the expression of abstract ideas, e.g. *créature, esprit, justice*); v. also *Pléiade*. For many purposes Latin remained in competition with French as a written language until the 16th c. (v. *Villers-Cotterêts*).

The French language has extended far beyond France. It was from the beginning the language of parts of what are now Switzerland and Belgium, where it produced distinct literatures. In the Middle Ages, the Norman Conquest carried it to England, where it had an important influence on the formation of the English language and greatly enriched English literature (v. *Anglo-Norman*); it had also for political reasons a temporary vogue in Naples, Greece, and Cyprus. It has considerably influenced many other foreign vocabularies, e.g. German, Dutch, Italian, Russian. In more modern times, it has established itself in Canada and in parts of the French colonial empire. Political circumstances, together with its inherent qualities, have made it pre-eminently the language of diplomacy, and in some countries (Germany, Russia) at certain periods the polite language of society and the preferred language of writers. In its literary form it has since the 17th c. been much regulated by grammarians (e.g. Malherbe, Vaugelas) and by the *Académie*.

French learned journals at present devoted to the study of the French language include Le *Français moderne and *Langue française; v. also *Romance Languages; Periodicals* (for British journals). Great scholars in this field include Littré, Gilliéron, Brunot, and Wartburg; v. also *Dictionaries*.

French Revolution, v. *Revolutions*, 1.

Frêne, v. *Marie de France*.

Fréquente Communion, La, v. *Arnauld, Arnauld d'Andilly* (1).

Frères ennemis, Les, v. *Thébaïde, La*.

Frères Provençaux, Les, in the 19th c., a restaurant in the *Palais-Royal much patronized by writers, e.g. Stendhal, Mérimée.

Frères Zemganno, Les, v. *Goncourt*.

Fréret, NICOLAS (1688–1749), historian and archaeologist, perpetual secretary of the *Académie des Inscriptions, author of a *Mémoire sur la certitude historique*, a *Mémoire sur l'origine des Français* (v. *History*, 3), etc.

Fréron, ÉLIE (1718–76), an eminent critic (a disciple of Desfontaines), conducted two early periodicals, *Lettres sur quelques écrits de ce temps* (from 1749) and the *Année littéraire, giving space to his attacks on Voltaire, the *philosophes, and the *Encyclopédie, made with moderation and irony. Voltaire ridiculed him in Le *Pauvre Diable, La *Pucelle, and L'*Écossaise (here as 'Frélon', a rascally journalist and political spy involved in a quarrel between two Scottish families). Dr. Johnson visited him in Paris (Boswell, 14 Oct. 1775).

Friedland (E. Prussia). Here Napoleon defeated the Russians (14 June 1807) in his campaign against the 4th *Coalition. He then took Königsberg.

Frimaire, v. *Republican Calendar*.

Froissart, JEAN (c. 1337–c. 1410), historian and poet, b. at Valenciennes in Hainault, of *bourgeois* origin. He came to England (1361), won the favour of his compatriot Queen Philippa, and visited Scotland, collecting material for his future chronicles. He accompanied the Black Prince to Bordeaux (1366) and the duke of Clarence to Milan (1368). When Queen Philippa died (1369), he retired to Valenciennes, won the favour of new protectors (notably the comte de Blois), and received ecclesiastical appointments. He travelled in Flanders and France, and also revisited England (1394–5).

His *Chroniques*, covering the years 1325–1400 (later carried down to 1444 by Enguerrand de Monstrelet, and then to 1461 by Mathieu d'Escouchi), consist of four books. The first version of bk. I was completed after his return home in 1369 (he issued three versions, in the first drawing freely on the chronicle of Jean *le Bel, later largely substituting his own account of events); bks. II, III, and IV were completed in 1387, 1390, and the last years of the century respectively. The work is mainly a record of the chief events of the Hundred Years War, including many references to the affairs of Italy, Spain, Germany, etc., but principally concerned with the battles, sieges, repressions of popular risings, massacres, and pillage, seen as exploits of the feudal chivalry of France and England. He is mainly interested in the externals of history, the pageant of adventures, e.g. he relates the atrocities of the *Jacquerie without discussion of its origin and deals perfunctorily with the causes of Wat Tyler's revolt. He writes with impartiality and candour, unaware that his narrative constitutes a formidable indictment of the feudal chivalry he so admires, often heedless of the sufferings of its innocent victims (Scott commented on this in *Old Mortality*, ch. 35). The result is a work of extraordinary vividness and—despite errors of chronology and topography—of high historical value. Passages of interest as illustrating his method of diligently collecting information from eye-witnesses of events in the course of his continual travels are the accounts of his visit to the comte de Foix (bk. III), and of his second visit to England and introduction to Richard II (bk. IV). His work was admirably translated into English (1523–5) by Lord Berners.

He was also, by contemporary standards, a considerable poet, author of *Méliador*, a long verse romance packed with chivalrous adventures, written for his patron Wenceslas of Brabant (some of whose lyrics are included); also of the *Dit du florin*, the *Débat du cheval et du levrier*, etc., and of *lais and *ballades.

Frollo, Claude, in Hugo's *Notre-Dame de Paris*.

Fromentin, EUGÈNE (1820–76), novelist, artist, and art critic, published *Un Été dans le Sahara* (1857) and *Une Année dans le Sahel* (1859), fragments from a journal of wanderings in N. Africa (1846–53), partly travel literature and partly an artist's reflections on how best to paint what he sees; and the novel *Dominique* (1863), his chief work. Feeling unable to satisfy his high literary standards, he then returned to painting and later published *Les Maîtres d'autrefois* (1876), essays on Dutch and Flemish painters which remain valuable both as art criticism and as literature.

Fromont jeune et Risler aîné, v. Daudet, A.

Fronde, La, the name (from a boys' game in which slings, *frondes*, were used) given to two revolts against the absolutism of the crown, caused by the unpopularity of Mazarin and the fiscal measures adopted to finance the German and Spanish wars. The *frondeurs* had no united programme and the great leaders were divided by rivalries. The first *Fronde* (1648–9), an alliance between the *bourgeoisie* and certain nobles, was led by the *parlement of Paris. When Pierre Broussel (venerable champion of the *parlement*) was arrested (Aug. 1648), the mob of Paris, led by Gondi (*v. Retz*), rose and erected *barricades. The court soon left Paris, which was besieged by royal forces. Peace was restored in 1649. The second *Fronde* began in 1651, after Mazarin had imprisoned Condé, the famous but arrogant victor of *Rocroi. The intrigues of Gondi, the disaffection of Turenne (who had invaded Champagne with a Spanish army, Dec. 1650), and the activities of such great ladies as the duchesse de Longueville led to Condé's release and Mazarin's flight from France. But Condé and the mutinous nobles who supported him soon lost popularity, Gondi was won over by a cardinal's hat, and Mazarin returned to France and confided the command of the army to Turenne, who had rejoined the royalist party and now helped to recover Paris for the king. The movement ended in Paris in October 1652 (when Condé left for Flanders to join the Spaniards), though in Bordeaux and elsewhere it lasted till 1653. Gondi was imprisoned, Condé was condemned to death for contumacy, and Mazarin returned in triumph to Paris (Feb. 1653).

Frontin, often the name of the valet in comedy, notably in Lesage's *Turcaret*.

Front populaire, Le, a left-wing political combination of Socialists, Radicals, and Communists which won the election of 1936, whereupon L. Blum, as premier, formed the first Socialist government in France. Though short-lived, it introduced measures to improve the lot of the worker, e.g. the 40-hour week, holidays with pay, the principle of collective bargaining.

Fructidor, *v. Republican Calendar.* Royalist plots to overthrow the *Directoire* were frustrated by the *coup d'état du 18 fructidor* (4 Sept. 1797). Its success was largely due to an impressive show of force by Augereau, then in command of the Paris troops. *v. Press,* 3.

Fugitive, La, v. Albertine disparue.

Fuller, MARIE-LOUISE, *known as* LOÏE (1862–1928), an American-born dancer, noted for her *danse du feu, danse serpentine,* etc., exploiting the play of coloured lights on her floating draperies. She made her name at the *Folies-Bergère* in the 1890s and later toured widely with her own company.

Funambules, Théâtre des, a well-known theatre (f. 1816, on the Boulevard du Temple; demolished 1862; *v. Boulevard du Crime*) where pantomimes, *vaudevilles,* and *mélodrames* were played. *v. Deburau.*

Funeral Orations, *v. Bossuet; Fléchier; Lacordaire; Mascaron; Massillon.*

Furetière, ANTOINE (1619–88), lexicographer (*v. Dictionaries,* 1690) and novelist, a friend of Racine, Boileau, Molière, and La Fontaine. Besides his dictionary, he was author of *Le *Roman bourgeois* (1666); the *Histoire des derniers troubles arrivés au royaume de l'Éloquence* (1658); satirical *Poésies* (1666); *Le Voyage de Mercure* (1659), satirizing literary and learned humbugs.

Fusionisme, one of the many fantastic gospels, combining religion with social reform, of the mid-19th c.; propounded *c.* 1850 by one Louis de Tourreil, whose *Doctrine fusionienne* (1846, 2 vols.) spoke of a fusion of spirit and matter, of universal emanations and absorptions, and of universal love and fecundity.

Fustel de Coulanges, NUMA-DENIS (1830–89), the outstanding historian of the second half of the 19th c. (*v. History,* 4), professor at the University of Strasbourg and (from 1878) at the *Sorbonne.* His works include, notably, *La Cité antique: Étude sur le culte, le droit, et les institutions de la Grèce et de Rome* (1864); also *Histoire des institutions politiques de l'ancienne France* (1875–89; re-ed. 1900–7 by Jullian from notes left by the author) and the unfinished *Leçons à l'Impératrice* (1930; originally lectures delivered to the empress Eugénie and her ladies), little masterpieces of simplified French history.

Futurism, Futurist, a short-lived movement, in art and literature, launched by Marinetti in his *Manifeste du futurisme* (publ. in *Le *Figaro* of 20 Feb. 1909). It had enthusiastic supporters in advanced French and Italian circles. In literature, sound and fury were its main features: Futurist poets tried to reproduce the confused, tumultuous noises of the machine age and glorified danger, war, and destruction.

Fuzelier, LOUIS (1672–1752), man of letters (editor of the *Mercure de France,* 1744–52) and mediocre comic dramatist. He collaborated with Lesage; *v. Calotte.*

G

Gabaonites, Les, v. La Taille.

Gabelle, the salt tax. In most parts of France, under the *ancien régime*, there was a government monopoly of salt. It was sold at an exorbitant price, each inhabitant being required to buy a minimum quantity (the *sel du devoir*). But the price varied in different provinces; moreover, some provinces had redeemed their liability to the tax and others were exempt, as were certain individuals. Though condemned by reformers from Vauban onwards, it was not abolished till 1790. v. *Fiscal System*; *Fermiers généraux*.

Gaboriau, ÉMILE (1832–73), father of the *roman policier*, or detective novel, in France, with *Le Crime d'Orcival* (1867), *Le Dossier n° 113* (1867), *Les Esclaves de Paris* (1868), *L'Affaire Lerouge* (1868), *Monsieur Lecoq* (1869), *La Corde au cou* (1873), etc. (usually first publ. as *romans-feuilletons*). His famous detective, M. Lecoq, is a precursor of Sherlock Holmes. Another familiar character is Tabaret, an amateur detective.

Gace Brulé (d. *c.* 1220), a knight of Champagne, an early imitator in N. French of the poetry of the *troubadours*. v. *Chanson*; *Lyric Poetry*, 1.

Gaguin, ROBERT (1433–1501), chronicler, humanist (a pioneer of the literary *Renaissance*), diplomatist, and a professor of rhetoric at the *University of Paris. He wrote (1497) a *Compendium super Francorum gestis*, chronicles of French history from Pharamond to 1491; a treatise on Latin versification, urging study of the ancients; and two poems of some merit—the *Débat du laboureur, du prestre, et du gendarme* and *Le Passetemps d'oysiveté*.

Gaimar, GEFFREI, a 12th-c. *Anglo-Norman poet who composed—in octosyllables, probably *c.* 1140—an *Estoire des Bretons* (cf. *Geoffrey of Monmouth*), which has not survived, and an *Estoire des Engleis*, bringing the story of the kings of England down to the death of William Rufus. v. *Haveloc*.

Gai saber, the 'gay science', the poetry of the *troubadours*, a term popularized by 14th-c. poets of the school of Toulouse. v. *Jeux floraux*.

Gaîtés de l'escadron, Les, v. Courteline.

Galaad (Galahad), v. Lancelot; Perceval.

Galère ('Que diable allait-il faire dans cette galère?'), v. Fourberies de Scapin, Les.

Galères, galériens. From the late 14th c., if not earlier, French kings owned fleets of galleys, manned by oarsmen (*galériens*), for use in the Mediterranean. The majority of the *galériens* were convicts condemned (for anything from murder or heresy to vagabondage) to row in the king's galleys, a form of penal servitude legalized from the reign of François Ier. Conditions in these floating prisons were appalling. From 1749—when galleys manned by oarsmen ceased to be used—until changes introduced during the Revolution, the convicts, still called *galériens*, served their time in the large naval dockyards or arsenals and were housed in specially constructed prisons (*bagnes*). These in their turn were gradually suppressed after the establishment of a penal colony on the Île du *Diable. v. Bonnet rouge.

Galiani, FERDINAND, ABBÉ (1728–87), a Neapolitan, of diminutive size, secretary at the embassy in Paris from 1759, an amusing talker, something of a buffoon, but also learned and original; a friend of Diderot and Grimm and very popular in their circle. His *Dialogues sur les blés* (1770), attacking the more extreme *économistes*, are remarkable for their lively wit and force of argument. From 1769, when he left Paris, till 1783 he corresponded with Mme d'Épinay; his letters to her, to Mme Geoffrin, and to Mme Necker have been published.

Galilée, Empire de, *v. Basoche.*

Gall, FRANZ JOSEPH (1758–1828), a physician of German birth, the founder of phrenology. He lectured on his theories in Vienna (till the government stopped him), then in Germany, arousing both interest and indignation. In 1807, he arrived in Paris with his collection of human and animal skulls (later bequeathed to the *Jardin des Plantes) and, despite ridicule in the press and disapproval in august quarters, made many influential converts. He took French nationality in 1819, visited England (1823), exciting little attention, and died in Paris. *Cf. Lavater; Mesmer; v. Balzac.*

Galland, ANTOINE (1646–1715), Orientalist, translator of the *Arabian Nights—Les Mille et Une Nuits* (1704–17). *Cf. Mardrus.*

Gallicanism, the principles and practice of the school of Roman Catholics which maintains the claim of the French Church to be in some respects self-governing and free from papal control—as opposed to Ultramontanism, which asserts absolute papal supremacy. Its doctrines were authoritatively set out by the French clergy in 1682 (when Louis XIV was in conflict with Innocent XI) in the *Déclaration des quatre articles*, drafted by Bossuet.

Gambara, *v. Comédie humaine, La* (*Études philosophiques*).

Gambetta, LÉON (1838–82), whose father was a Genoese, was born at Cahors and educated there and at Montauban. He studied law in Paris and became a barrister (1860) as the first step to a political career. He soon emerged as a brilliant orator and an opponent of the Second Empire, became *député* for Paris (1869) and leader of the opposition party. He was prominent in the 1870 *Revolution (and *v. Franco-*

Prussian War), and proved the most energetic member of the Government of National Defence. When the Prussians surrounded Paris (Oct. 1870), he left in a balloon, carried on this government from Tours and Bordeaux, organized resistance, and restored morale. But when Paris fell and the government there signed an armistice without consulting him, he soon resigned office. He returned to Paris in July 1871 as a *député* to the *Assemblée nationale* and was instrumental, with Thiers, in consolidating the Third Republic. His influence later declined and he retired in 1882. His death, the result of an accident, was mourned by the whole nation. *v. République française, La* (2); *Numa Roumestan.*

Gamon, CHRISTOFLE DE (1575–1621), *Huguenot poet, wrote *La Semaine, ou la Création du monde* (1609), an epic refuting that of *Du Bartas; *Le Verger poétique* (1597), collected poems on Biblical themes.

Ganelon, in the *Chanson de Roland.*

Garamond, CLAUDE (d. 1561), a type-founder particularly noted for his 'Grecs du roi', the Greek type he cut (1541) for François Ier (hence its name), for use by R. Estienne, the king's printer, in his editions of the classics.

Garasse, FRANÇOIS (1585–1631), *Jesuit opponent of the *libertins. His *Doctrine curieuse des beaux esprits du temps* (1623) attacked, in particular, Théophile de Viau; his *Somme théologique* (1625) attacked Charron, whose *De la sagesse* was deemed to support the views of the *libertins.*

Garat, DOMINIQUE-JOSEPH (c. 1750–1832), man of letters and journalist (editor of the *Journal de Paris*), a member of the *États généraux of 1789, minister of justice (1792) under the *Convention, and a member of the *Sénat under Napoleon. His *Mémoires historiques sur la vie de M. Suard* throw light on the *idéologues.*

Garçon, Le, a grotesque personage

invented by Flaubert and his friends, the type of the respectable, complacent *bourgeois*—an ancestor of M. Homais in *Madame Bovary*.

Garçon et l'Aveugle, Le, *v. Comedy*.

Garde nationale, originally a form of citizen militia set up by the *Commune de Paris* in July 1789 to maintain order (*v. La Fayette, marquis de*); at first voluntary, later (between 1790, when provincial battalions were organized, and 1793) transformed into a compulsory armed force (able-bodied men from 16 to 60, mainly recruited from the taxable middle and lower-middle classes—later open to all) under the control of the civil or municipal authorities. It counted for little under Napoleon (1799–1815), was revived at the Restoration, suppressed (1827) by Charles X, then revived and reorganized after the 1830 *Revolution* (with a higher intake from the *haute bourgeoisie*) as a force to defend the constitutional monarchy and to uphold law and order. (It often figures in novels, *vaudevilles*, and cartoons of this period.) Feeling ran high about its conduct during and just after the 1848 *Revolution*, for in February 1848 some companies fought for Louis-Philippe against the insurgents, while in the riots of June 1848 (*v. Republics*, 2) other companies, recruited from the working classes and of strong socialist sympathies, either did not report for duty or fought against the government at the *barricades* (there are references to this in Flaubert's *L'*Éducation sentimentale*). The force was under much stricter official control during the Second Empire. In 1870, it took part for a time in defensive fighting against the Prussians (*v. Commune*, 2). It ceased to exist after 1871.

Garde républicaine, special divisions—mounted and foot—of the *Gendarmerie nationale*, a familiar sight in Paris. They guard official buildings, are a highly decorative presence on State occasions, and have a famous band.

Gargamelle, in Rabelais's *Gargantua*.

Gargantua, La Vie très horrifique du grand (1534). The success of *Pantagruel* led Rabelais to write the story of Pantagruel's father, Gargantua, on similar lines, again drawing on the chap-book mentioned under *Pantagruel* (e.g. for the names of Gargantua and his parents, Grandgousier and Gargamelle; his gigantic mare; the theft of the bells of Notre-Dame). The fantastic element is more restricted than in *Pantagruel* and there are many allusions to places near Rabelais's birthplace and to local incidents. Gargantua's war with his neighbour Picrochole, for instance, is a comic development of a local quarrel with a landed proprietor, Gaucher de Sainte-Marthe (*cf. Sainte-Marthe, C. and S. de*), over water-rights.

After the description of the giant Gargantua's birth and early years, we are told how, having profited little by instruction at home from old-fashioned pedagogues and schoolbooks (e.g. *Donat), he is finally sent to Paris. There he takes the bells of Notre-Dame to hang on his mare's neck; a deputation from the university under Maître Janotus de Bragmardo asks for their return, the occasion for a caricature of the *Sorbonne and its eloquence. The special education which Gargantua now receives, in contrast to the traditional course, is a development of the views expressed in *Pantagruel*. He is then recalled to help defend his father's territory against Picrochole's invasion. The theatre of war (of Lilliputian dimensions) is around La Devinière (*v. Rabelais*). Gargantua directs operations, but the chief exploits are performed by a remarkable monk, the courageous Frère Jean des Entommeures, who drives the enemy from the abbey close while his sluggish brethren take refuge in prayer in the chapel. Gargantua's victory is celebrated by the erection of the Abbaye de Thélème (designed on the lines of the great *châteaux* of the day). In contrast to ordinary monasteries, it has only one rule, *Fay ce que vouldras* ('Do what thou wilt'), for those who are 'free, well born, well instructed, and conversant in honest Companies, have naturally an instinct and spur that prompteth them ever to virtuous actions, and withdraws them from vice, the which is called honour' (Urquhart's trans.).

Garibaldi, GIUSEPPE (1807–82), the great Italian soldier and patriot, emerged from retirement in 1870 to offer his help, with his famous 'red-shirt' legion, to France, then involved in the *Franco-Prussian war. Gambetta accepted his offer, but he was defeated near Dijon. He was elected to the *Assemblée nationale* (1871) in gratitude, but soon retired and returned home.

Garin de Monglane, Geste de, also known as the *Geste de Guillaume* or *des Aimerides*, a cycle of some 20 *chansons de geste* (notably *Aimeri de Narbonne*, *Girart de Viane*, the *Chanson de *Guillaume*) about the exploits, chiefly against the Saracens in S. France, of the descendants of Garin de Monglane, who are sent out to conquer fiefs for themselves.

Garin le Loherain, one of a cycle of *chansons de geste*, the *Geste des Lorrains*, relating the long war between Hervis of Metz (in Lorraine) and Hardré of Bordeaux and their descendants, pursued with battle and pillage, siege and massacre, from generation to generation, till Hardré's line is exterminated.

Garnier, ROBERT (1534–90), the most important of the early authors of *tragedy, also author of the first French *tragicomedy, *Bradamante*; a disciple of the *Pléiade*. His seven tragedies (perf. 1568–82) were *Porcie*, on the Senecan model, about the death of Brutus and suicide of Portia; *Cornélie* (Eng. trans. by Thomas Kyd), about the wife of Pompey; *Hippolyte*, an early French treatment of the *Phèdre* theme; *Marc-Antoine* (Eng. trans. by the countess of Pembroke); *La Troade*; *Antigone*; *Les Juives*, on the cruel treatment of Zedekiah and his children by Nebuchadnezzar (2 Kings 25 : 7). He was a considerable poet, with style, eloquence, imagination, and lyric power (evident in the songs of the chorus in his tragedies);

Les Juives, in particular, shows force and pathos.

Garnier de Pont-Sainte-Maxence, *v. Thomas Becket.*

Garo, hero of La Fontaine's fable *Le Gland et la Citrouille*, a pretentious ignoramus.

Garonne, La, one of the four great rivers of France.

Gascar, Pierre, *pseudonym of* PIERRE FOURNIER (1916–), originally a journalist (*Chine ouverte*, 1955, etc.), made his name in 1953 with *Le Temps des morts*, a novel inspired by his wartime experiences in a concentration camp, and *Les Bêtes*, *nouvelles* in the tradition of Maupassant, depicting, with a mixture of fantasy, social satire, and horrifying realism, a world in which the relationship between animals and men is far removed from that found in Kipling. His other works include *La Graine* (1955), *Les Femmes* (1955), *L'Herbe des rues* (1957), *La Barre de corail* (1958), *Soleils* (1960), *Les Charmes* (1965), novels and short stories; *Les Pas perdus* (1958), a play.

Gaspard de la nuit, *v. Bertrand, L. (Aloÿsius).*

Gassendi, PIERRE (1592–1655), mathematician (professor at the *Collège de France* from 1645) and philosopher, a critic of his contemporary Descartes, attacked the philosophy of Aristotle and sought to revive the atomic theory of Epicurus. His many Latin works included treatises on these subjects and lives of Tycho Brahe, Copernicus, and Regiomontanus. His literary disciples included Chapelle.

Gaster, Messer, (1) in Rabelais's *Pantagruel*; (2) in La Fontaine's fable *Les Membres et l'Estomac.*

Gastrolâtres, in Rabelais's *Pantagruel.*

Gaudissart, *v. Illustre Gaudissart, L'.*

Gauguin, PAUL (1848–1903), painter, a grandson of Flora Tristan, for a time an *Impressionist and closely associated with *Symbolism. After 1891, having given up his career on the Stock Exchange (1883), and his wife and family, for his art, he lived in Tahiti, returning only once to France (1893–5). He shared the life of the natives, finding inspiration in them and in the landscape, so poor that he was often unable to buy paints and canvases. His letters and diaries have been published and translated; also *Noa-Noa*, a record of his experiences written in collaboration with Morice.

Gaulle, CHARLES DE (1890–1970), soldier and statesman, President of the Fifth *Republic; the son of a teacher at a Jesuit college. He passed with distinction through the *École spéciale militaire de *Saint-Cyr, joined (1913) an infantry regiment commanded by Pétain, and fought in the 1914–18 war until 1916, when he was wounded and captured at Verdun. After the war, he resumed his military career (on Pétain's staff, in the Rhineland, in Lebanon, etc.). In the 1930s, he published works (e.g. *Le Fil de l'épée*, 1931; *Vers l'armée de métier*, 1934; *La France et son armée*, 1938) which brought him into conflict with orthodox military opinion by calling for a defence strategy based on a professional mechanized army, and mobility, rather than on conscription and fortifications in depth (e.g. the Maginot Line).

When war broke out in 1939, he was colonel of a tank brigade; during the campaign of May 1940, he became a general in command of an armoured division. In June 1940, he was briefly under-secretary of state for defence (under Paul Reynaud) and visited Churchill in London. When Pétain replaced Reynaud and sought an armistice, he left France for England and on 18 June broadcast from London his famous appeal to his compatriots to fight on under his leadership. As General de Gaulle, he was thereafter at once the commander of the Free French forces (a stalwart—and strong-minded—ally of the Western powers) and the inspiration of the *Resistance movement. He entered Paris in triumph while the city was in process of liberation (Aug. 1944) and became head of a provisional government (*v. M.R.P.*). He resigned in January 1946 and campaigned against the proposed new constitution (voted Oct. 1946), holding that it would not provide strong and stable government. In 1947, he formed a new party, the *Rassemblement du peuple français* (*R.P.F.*). When this foundered and was disbanded (1953), he retired to his home at Colombey-les-Deux-Églises (Haute-Marne) and embarked on his memoirs. He was recalled to power in May 1958 at the height of the Algerian crisis; for his subsequent career *v. Republics*, 5.

His stature as a statesman cannot yet be assessed, but he was by any standards a great patriot who did much to restore national self-confidence, an inspiring orator, an enlightened soldier, and a man of conspicuous moral and physical courage. He drew to his side writers ranging from Mauriac to Malraux (who held office under him), and both his speeches and his *Mémoires de guerre* (1954–9, 3 vols.) and *Mémoires d'espoir* (1970–1, 2 vols.; covering the period from 1958) testify to his command of the French language. The Place de l'Étoile in Paris was renamed Place Charles-de-Gaulle in his honour.

Gaulois, Le (f. 1867), a leading monarchist daily during the Third Republic; the paper read by Proust's *Guermantes world.

Gaultier-Garguille, *v. Gros-Guillaume*.

Gautier, JUDITH (1846–1917), daughter of T. Gautier, at one time married to Mendès, the first woman elected (1910) to the *Académie Goncourt*; author of *Le Livre de jade* (1867, under the pseudonym 'Judith Walter'), poems from the Chinese, also of essays and novels reflecting her interest in Orientalism and music.

Gautier, Marguerite, in Dumas *fils*'s *La *Dame aux camélias*.

Gautier, THÉOPHILE (1811–72), poet, novelist, and journalist, lived in Paris from childhood. On leaving school, he became an art student and, like his friends Nerval and Petrus Borel, an extreme *Romantic, with a taste for vampirism and Hoffmannesque horrors. He idolized Hugo, and it was he—in a red satin doublet which became legendary—who led the pro-Hugo faction on the first night of *Hernani. By then (1830) he had given up painting in order to write. The works of his extreme Romantic period (1830–40) include *Poésies* (1830); *Albertus, ou l'Âme et le Péché* (1832); *Les *Jeunes-France, romans goguenards* (1833); *Les Grotesques* (1835), studies of 15th–17th-c. authors, e.g. Villon, Théophile de Viau, Scarron; *Mademoiselle de Maupin* (1835; its preface is an early manifesto of l'*art pour l'art*); *La Morte amoureuse,* a famous vampire story, and *Fortunio,* an *Arabian Nights*-like tale, set in Paris (1836 and 1837, both first publ. in book form in *Nouvelles,* 1845); *La Comédie de la mort* (1838), another fantastic narrative poem.

From 1835, when Balzac helped him to a post on the *Chronique de Paris,* the exuberant Romantic was gradually transformed into a busy, successful journalist (writing for *La *Presse, Le *Moniteur, La *Revue de Paris,* etc.) and an important, popular literary personality of the Second Empire ('le bon Théo'). For nearly 40 years he wrote weekly literary, dramatic, and art criticism of a very high order, collected in *Rapport sur le progrès des lettres depuis vingt-cinq ans* (1868), *Portraits et Souvenirs littéraires* (1875), *Histoire de l'art dramatique depuis vingt-cinq ans* (1856, 6 vols.), *Les Beaux-Arts en Europe* (1855, 2 vols.), etc. To this period belong some of his best works, e.g. *Émaux et Camées* (1852), on which his poetic fame largely rests; *Le *Capitaine Fracasse* (1863) and *Le Roman de la momie* (1856), novels; *La Peau de tigre* (1852) and *Nouvelles* (1858), tales; *Théâtre* (1872), ballets and dramatic sketches; his unfinished *Histoire du romantisme* (1874); the many series of travel-sketches which contain some of his finest descriptive writing—*Voyage en Espagne* (1845),

Caprices et Zig-Zags (1845; mostly about English life), *Voyage en Italie* (1852), *Constantinople* (1853), *Voyage en Russie* (1866), etc.

His Romantic frenzies cooled, but his early aesthetic convictions—the principle of *l'art pour l'art,* the conception of beauty as 'éclat, solidité, couleur... Jamais ni brouillard ni vapeur, jamais rien d'incertain et de flottant'—grew stronger and were shared by such friends as Flaubert, Baudelaire, and Banville. The love of visual, palpable beauty became the chief feature of his work. It was intensified by his painter's eye and his command of language, so that many passages of both his prose and poetry read like transpositions from canvas to paper, lending a certain lifelessness to his writing. These qualities are particularly evident in *Émaux et Camées,* where serenity and concern for perfect form mark him as a precursor of the *Parnassiens. v. Grisi.

Gautier d'Arras, a gifted 12th-c. poet, author of *Eracle* and *Ille et Galeron* (a *roman breton).

Gautier de Coincy, v. *Religious Writings,* 1.

Gautier de Metz, v. *Image du monde.*

Gautier d'Épinal, v. *Lyric Poetry,* 1.

Gauvain (Gawain), nephew of King Arthur, figures as the perfect knight in many of the *romans bretons and is the hero of *Le *Chevalier à l'épée* and *La *Mule sans frein;* during the quest of the Grail (v. *Perceval)* he meets his death at the hands of *Lancelot.

Gavarni, *pseudonym of* SULPICE-GUILLAUME CHEVALIER (1804–66), lithographer and caricaturist, close friend of the Goncourt brothers (who wrote his life, 1873). He made his name with sketches of Parisian life (students, *grisettes,* carnival costumes, women's clothes) in illustrated journals. From 1837, he contributed two notable series—*Fourberies de femme en matière de sentiment* and *Les *Lorettes*—to *Le *Charivari*. Later, especially after a stay in London where he observed the misery and vices of the poor, his work became more bitter, e.g. the collections *Masques et Visages* (1857), *Les Douze Mois* (1869). He wrote his own pithy captions. *v. Dîners Magny*.

Gavroche, in Hugo's *Les *Misérables*.

Gaxotte, PIERRE (1895-1982), historian and journalist (*v. Press*, 9) of Royalist and Catholic sympathies; a member of the **Académie* (1953). His works are lively and readable, e.g. *La Révolution française* (1928); *Histoire des Français* (1951); *Histoire de l'Allemagne* (1963); *L'Académie française* (1965), a history of that body.

Gay, SOPHIE MICHAULT DE LAVALETTE, MME (1776-1852), mother of Delphine Gay (*v. Girardin, Mme É. de*), wrote many novels depicting contemporary French society, e.g. *Laure d'Estell* (1802), *Un Mariage sous l'Empire* (1832).

Gazette, *v. Gazette, La; Nouvellistes*.

Gazette, later *Gazette de France, La*, the first French newspaper (*v. Press*, 1), f. 1631 by Renaudot, who edited it under Richelieu's, and later Mazarin's, patronage. It began as a weekly (4, later 8, quarto pp., publ. on Saturdays, price 1 *sol parisis*—*v. Money*), reporting foreign and domestic news without comment and with an honest attempt at truth. Its scope was gradually extended to include official and historical documents, and Richelieu used it as an instrument of policy. From 1762, as the *Gazette de France* (twice weekly), it bore the royal arms and became an official publication under the direction of the minister of foreign affairs. It lapsed after the execution of Louis XVI, but was revived and (as a daily, read by the clergy) was one of the few political papers tolerated by Napoleon. It was the leading Royalist paper during the Restoration, when it acquired a literary **feuilleton*. It continued throughout the 19th c., fiercely **Légitimiste* (under the July Monarchy) and Royalist (*v. Maurras*).

Gazette nationale, v. Moniteur universel.

Gazier, LOUIS-AUGUSTIN-LÉON, *v. Dictionaries*, 1887; *Port-Royal*.

Gazul, Clara, *v. Théâtre de Clara Gazul, Le*.

Geffroy, GUSTAVE (1856-1926), journalist, novelist, and art critic. His articles on artists, exhibitions, **Impressionism, etc., are collected in *La Vie artistique* (1892-1903, 8 ser.), *Les Musées d'Europe* (1902-13, 12 vols.).

Gelée or **Gellée**, CLAUDE, *v. Claude le Lorrain*.

Gelée, JACQUEMART, *v. Roman de Renart*.

Gelosi, *v. Italiens*.

Gendarme; Gendarmerie nationale. *Gendarme* is a singular formed on *gens d'armes*, in the Middle Ages mounted men-at-arms. The *Gendarmerie nationale* (f. 1791) replaced the *Maréchaussée*, a form of mounted, military constabulary, originally under the command of the **maréchaux de France*. The *Maréchaussée* had close links with the *Gendarmerie du roi* (f. 1609), which was attached to the royal household and stemmed from the *gens d'armes* of the *compagnies d'ordonnance* created by Charles VII to curb brigandage. The modern *Gendarmerie nationale* is at once a civil and a military police force (*v. Police; Garde républicaine*).

Gendre de Monsieur Poirier, Le (1854), a comedy by Augier and Sandeau, a satire on the conflict between the *bourgeoisie* and the nobility characteristic of the period.

M. Poirier, a retired merchant in search of a title, marries his daughter Antoinette to the ruined, dissolute marquis de Presle. The marquis, now solvent and living in the lap of luxury, persists in his former habits. He discovers his father-in-law's ambitions and makes game of him while pretending to further them. M. Poirier determines to humble the arrogant marquis, cuts off supplies, and insists on a legal separation between him and Antoinette. After much intrigue and a threatened duel, the marquis falls in love with his wife and resolves to reform; and M. Poirier, professedly cured of his ambition, calculates in an aside how soon he can hope to be 'un pair de France'.

Généralités, v. Fiscal System.

Genet, JEAN (1910–), novelist and dramatist. He was born illegitimate and brought up in institutions and by foster parents. From the age of 15, when he was sent to a reformatory, he was in and out of prisons all over Europe for a variety of criminal offences. His first works were written in prison. After the private publication of his autobiographical novels *Notre-Dame des Fleurs* (1942) and *Miracle de la rose* (1946), he was launched as a writer and befriended by Sartre and Cocteau, who campaigned for the free pardon he eventually obtained. His novels (inc. also *Pompes funèbres*, 1947; *Querelle de Brest*, 1947) and his autobiographical *Journal du voleur* (1948) are a highly poetical portrayal of the world of crime, vice, and obscenity, of violence and betrayal, by an unrepentant thief and homosexual. His total rejection of accepted social values is equally evident in his plays (e.g. *Les Bonnes*, 1947; *Haute Surveillance*, 1947; *Le Balcon*, 1956; *Les Nègres*, 1957; *Les Paravents*, 1961), which are of wider scope than his novels and belong to the Theatre of the Absurd (v. *Theatre of the 19th and 20th cs.*). Highly stylized and largely symbolic, they reveal a concern with the themes of illusion and identity, with ritual and destruction, at times coming close to Artaud's conception of a primitive, visceral theatre. His life and works are the subject of a study by Sartre.

Genette, GÉRARD, v. Critics and Criticism, 3.

Geneviève, St., a semi-legendary young woman of Nanterre who, when the Huns under Attila were menacing Paris (451), calmed the citizens, who were about to flee in panic. She came to be regarded as the patron saint of Paris.

Génie du christianisme, ou les Beautés poétiques et morales de la religion chrétienne, Le (1802; inc. **Atala* and **René*), a work of Christian apologetics by Chateaubriand, published at a time highly conducive to its success—the eve of the service in Notre-Dame, attended in state by Bonaparte, to mark the restoration of Roman Catholicism as the official religion of France (v. Concordat (2)).

The work (in 4 pts.: *Le Dogme et la doctrine, Poétique, Beaux-Arts et littérature, Culte*) was an attempt to revive Christianity as a moral force and to stress its appeal as the most poetical and human, also the most favourable to liberty, of all religions. It is superior by reason of its doctrine (pt. 1), its poetic force (pt. 2), and its art, literature, and ceremonies (pts. 3 and 4). The author points to the influence on man's thought and feeling for Nature of such great literary products of the Christian faith as the Bible and the *Divine Comedy*, and dwells on the beauty of Christian art (notably of Gothic church architecture, then imperfectly appreciated). The work survives for its poetical qualities rather than as a reasoned apologia. v. Ballanche.

Genlis, FÉLICITÉ DUCREST DE SAINT-AUBIN, MME DE (1746–1830), an extremely knowledgeable woman with a mania for instructing others, governess to the children of the duchesse de Chartres (inc. Louis-Philippe), whom she taught on novel, practical-cum-theoretical lines, writing and producing plays and **proverbes* for their benefit (*Le Théâtre de l'éducation*, 1779). After the execution of her husband, the comte de Genlis (1793, the first of the **Girondins* to die), she lived by her pen in England and Switzerland, returning to France in 1802. Napoleon paid her to furnish him with letters on literature, politics, etc. She wrote children's tales, *Les Veillées du château* (1784; v. *Children's Reading*); numerous popular romances, combining sentiment and sensation, morals and history, but involved and humourless, e.g. *Mademoiselle de Clermont* (1802), *La Duchesse de la Vallière* (1804),

Mademoiselle de La Fayette (1813); and somewhat scandalous *Mémoires* (1825). *v. Salon*, 1.

Gentil-Bernard, *v. Bernard, P.-J.*

Geoffrey of Monmouth (*c.* 1100–54), probably a Benedictine monk of Monmouth, bishop of St. Asaph from 1152; author *c.* 1135 of the Latin *Historia Regum Britanniae*, purporting to give an account of the kings of Britain from before the Christian era, and especially of King Arthur and his successors, a work which gave wide currency to the Arthurian legends. He drew on Bede and Nennius, on British traditions, possibly on Welsh documents now lost, and probably on his imagination. Among 12th-c. French versions of his work were the lost *Estoire des Bretons* of Gaimar and *Wace's *Brut*; it appears largely to have inspired the *romans bretons*. He also wrote a Latin version of the prophecies of *Merlin; and a life of Merlin, in Latin hexameters, is doubtfully attributed to him. *v. Wauquelin.*

Geoffrin, MARIE-THÉRÈSE RODET, MME (1699–1777), of *bourgeois* origin, famous for her *salon* where, in succession to Mme de Tencin, she received artists (Boucher, La Tour) on Mondays and men of letters (Fontenelle, Marivaux, Marmontel, Helvétius, d'Holbach) on Wednesdays. Though not learned, she was intelligent, generous, and worldly-wise, and ruled her *salon* by a mixture of severity (no politics or religion) and good offices. Horace Walpole, an *habitué* before he became devoted to Mme du Deffand, admired her good sense (in a letter to Gray of 25 Jan. 1766); Catherine of Russia corresponded with her. Only a few of her letters survive, but her maxim 'Il ne faut pas laisser croître l'herbe sur le chemin de l'amitié' is characteristic.

Geoffroy, JULIEN-LOUIS (1743–1814), journalist. His dramatic criticism in the *Journal des Débats* (*v. Feuilleton*) was largely responsible for the success of that paper. His articles were collected in *Cours de littérature dramatique* (1819–20).

Geoffroy de Paris, *v. History,* 1.

Geoffroy Saint-Hilaire, ÉTIENNE (1772–1844), scientist, was largely responsible for the striking advance in the study of natural science in the late 18th and early 19th cs. His theories of evolution (in his *Philosophie anatomique*, 1818–22) led to a famous dispute (1830) with Cuvier over the fundamental laws of zoology. His influence on 19th-c. literature can be seen in the work of Balzac. *v. Jardin des Plantes.*

George, Mademoiselle, *stage-name of* MARGUERITE-JOSÉPHINE WEIMER (1787–1867), whose acting, beauty, and temper were alike famous. She played in tragedy at the *Comédie-Française* and later, at the *Odéon* and the *Théâtre Saint-Martin*, created the leading role in several *Romantic dramas, e.g. Hugo's *Lucrèce Borgia*, Dumas *père*'s *La *Tour de Nesle.*

George Dandin, a 3-act prose comedy by Molière; produced 1668.

Dandin, a rich peasant, wishing from vanity to rise in the social scale, has married Angélique de Sotenville, daughter of a country gentleman. Without consulting the lady, he has approached her parents, who have arranged the match for the money it will bring. His punishment is the contempt of his worthless wife and her arrogant parents. He discovers that his wife has a lover and complains to her parents, but they readily accept the denial of the couple and seize the opportunity to humiliate him. One night, observing his wife leave the house to meet her lover, he shuts her out and summons her parents, bent on convincing them of her misconduct. The wife, alarmed, begs forgiveness, and when Dandin is obdurate, feigns suicide. When he goes out of the house to see what has happened, she slips in and locks the door on him. The parents arrive and he is again confuted and humiliated. He makes the melancholy comment 'Vous l'avez voulu, George Dandin', and concludes that his best course is to drown himself.

Georges, *v. Cadoudal.*

Gérard de Nerval, *v. Nerval*.

Gerbert d'Aurillac (*c.* 940–1003), Pope Sylvester II from 999, earlier archbishop of Rheims, then of Ravenna; a scholar so deeply versed in mathematics and astronomy that he was reputed to be a magician. He taught Robert II.

Géricault, THÉODORE (1791–1824), *Romantic painter (an early influence on Delacroix), noted for his bold, often violent imagination and his dramatic use of light and shade (e.g. in his famous *Le Radeau de la Méduse*, 1819). He visited England (1820–2) and made many sketches of sporting (horse-racing) and daily life.

German Influence, *v. Foreign Influences*.

Germinal, *v. Republican Calendar*.

Germinal (1885), one of Zola's *Rougon-Macquart* novels; very long, and powerfully written, if at times almost painstakingly revolting.

  Étienne *Lantier, a machinist, has been sacked from his job in Lille. He walks the country looking for work, comes to a mining district, and gets a job in the pits, where pay and conditions are appalling. His developing socialist sympathies are fed by the misery around him, ill-digested reading, and his friend Souvarine, an exiled Russian nihilist. He incites the miners to strike, but is helpless when hunger, sabotage, and fighting result. Finally, the men resume work, having gained nothing. Souvarine engineers a disastrous explosion; the pits are flooded and many die, including Lantier's sweetheart, Catherine. He himself is rescued after 12 days, but dismissed on leaving hospital. It is spring, and as he again sets out to look for work he dreams of a *Germinal*, or seed-time, to be followed one day by the right to life and happiness for all men.

Germinie Lacerteux, *v. Goncourt*.

Géronte, the name given to the stock character of the old man in early comedy. He was increasingly portrayed as foolish, credulous, opinionated, and avaricious—as in Molière's *Les *Fourberies de Scapin*, *Le *Médecin malgré lui*.

Gerson, JEAN CHARLIER DE (1363–1429), a learned doctor, eventually chancellor, of the *University of Paris, and its representative at the Council of Constance (1414); an eloquent preacher and author of discourses on questions of the day, addressed to the king or the people and reflecting his devotion to the Church, the university, and France, also his faith, charity, and humanistic tastes. He supported Christine de Pisan in her defence of women against the strictures of Jean de Meung. The *Imitation of Christ* has been doubtfully ascribed to him.

Gessner, SALOMON (1730–88), German-Swiss painter and writer. His rustic and narrative idylls in verse and prose (trans. into French by Turgot, among others, in 1760–1) were much admired in France and contributed to the 'Back-to-Nature' movement. He had imitators in A. Berquin and Léonard and influenced Bernardin de Saint-Pierre, Florian, and even A. Chénier. *v. Foreign Influences*, 2.

Gesta Dei per Francos, a collection (publ. 1611) of Latin chronicles and historical documents on the Crusades, mainly the work of monks.

Gesta Romanorum, a collection of Latin tales (chiefly of Oriental origin), each with a moral, compiled in the 14th c., when they were also translated into French.

Geste, *v. Chansons de geste*; *Charlemagne*; *Doon de Mayence*; *Garin de Monglane*; *Garin le Loherain*.

Gestes des Chiprois, *v. Philippe de Novare*.

Ghéon, Henri, *pseudonym of* HENRI VANGLON (1875–1944), dramatist, critic, and essayist, also a physician. His association with the early *Nouvelle Revue française* occasioned the interesting essays *Nos directions: réalisme et poésie* (1911). He was converted to Roman Catholicism during the 1914–18 war (*v.* his *L'Homme né de la guerre. Témoignage d'un converti,* 1919) and thereafter wrote many religious dramas, e.g. *Jeux et miracles pour le peuple fidèle* (1922, 2 vols.).

Ghil, RENÉ (1862–1925), poet, a theorist of *Symbolism and exponent (in *Le Traité du verbe,* 1886, and *De la poésie scientifique,* 1909) of the doctrine of *Instrumentisme* or *Instrumentation verbale,* i.e. that the musical quality of a poem could be intensified, and the theme, as it were, orchestrated, by the conscious use of certain groups of vowels and consonants as if they were parts of an orchestra. His poetry, obscure and much influenced by Mallarmé, is in *Légendes d'âmes et de sangs* (1885) and *Œuvres* (1887–97 and 1898–1920, 13 vols. of verse and prose). *v. Literary Isms*

Gide, ANDRÉ (1869–1951), essayist, critic, novelist, and dramatist, winner of the *Prix Nobel* (1947); nephew of Charles Gide (1847–1932), political economist. His father was of Cévenol Protestant stock; his mother came from Normandy, where much of his childhood and later life was spent. He was educated, intermittently owing to ill-health, at the *École alsacienne,* where school contacts introduced him to *Symbolist circles. Comfortable family circumstances enabled him to devote himself to literature, music, and travel.

His writings fall into three groups. First come his early works, influenced by Symbolism, e.g. *Les Cahiers d'André Walter* (1891; publ. anon.), a study of adolescent unrest and an early example of the journal form he often used; *Traité du Narcisse* (1891); *Les Poésies d'André Walter* (1892); *La Tentative amoureuse* (1893); *Le Voyage d'Urien* (1893).

A second group includes works written between *c.* 1896, following three years in Algeria, and 1914. This Algerian visit, the first of many, profoundly affected his

character, causing him to react against restraints and inhibitions imposed by a narrowly Protestant upbringing (described in *Si le grain ne meurt, v.* below) and to feel stifled by the atmosphere of literary Paris. He now became interested in Nietzsche and Dostoievsky (his first study of the latter appeared in 1911). Their influence, and that of Montaigne and Goethe, is often evident in his work; he was also steeped in the Bible to an extent less common in French than in English writers. Works of this second group include *Paludes* (1896), a satire of literary conventionalism, and *Les *Nourritures terrestres* (1897)—books which caused little stir at the time, but were widely read 20 years later; *Philoctète* (1897), like the earlier *Narcisse,* a *traité* or symbolical treatment of a moral question; *Le Prométhée mal enchaîné* (1899), which he called a *sotie, because the intention was satirical and the treatment farcical; two plays (publ. together 1904), *Le Roi Candaule* (prod. 1901) and *Saül* (written *c.* 1895, prod. 1922), where—in contrast to the theme of *Les Nourritures terrestres*—Saul is shown as an old man, worn out through having yielded to all his desires; *L'Immoraliste* (1902), a *récit* (*v. La Porte étroite* below) in which the chief character practises the precepts of *Les Nourritures,* following every impulse, regardless of morals or humanity; *Prétextes* (1903) and *Nouveaux Prétextes* (1911), collected lectures and criticism; *Amyntas* (1906, written earlier), Algerian travel impressions reflecting the intoxicating effect of his first contact with the East; *Le Retour de l'enfant prodigue* (1907), in which the prodigal son returns, but helps his younger brother to run away; *La *Porte étroite* (1909), a *récit* his first use of this term to describe a studiedly simple, but intrinsically ironic, tale told by, and from the viewpoint of, one character (he reserved the term *roman* for works of complicated structure; *v. Les Faux-Monnayeurs* below); *Isabelle* (1911), a *récit* about a family secret and its discovery, a masterpiece of restrained style and subdued background; *Les Caves du Vatican* (1914), a *sotie,* a series of complicated adventures in which one of the chief characters, Lafcadio, lives dangerously (*v. Acte gratuit*).

His first bookshop success was *La Porte étroite*; until then, though known to a small circle and an influence on *avant-garde* literature (he was a founder of the *Nouvelle Revue française*), he had made little impact on the general public. Thereafter his reputation steadily grew (all the more, perhaps, because some critics found, and denounced, a subversive tendency in his work) and in the period after the 1914–18 war he emerged as a leading exponent of the modern literature of introspection (with sexual abnormality as a recurrent theme—*cf. Proust*), self-confession, and moral and religious—at times also social and political—uneasiness; he was also a fine critic. Widely read, and even more widely discussed, he influenced the aesthetic and moral values of a whole inter-war generation. The works he published after 1918, which form a third group, include *La Symphonie pastorale* (1919), *L'École des femmes* (1929), *Robert* (1930), *Geneviève* (1937), *Thésée* (1946), all *récits*; *Les* *Faux-Monnayeurs* (1926), his only novel in his own sense of the term, interesting as an innovation in technique; *Œdipe* (1931; prod. 1932), a prose drama on the moral problem that continually exercised him—'la lutte entre l'individualisme et la soumission à l'autorité religieuse'; *Voyage au Congo* (1927) and *Le Retour du Tchad* (1928), studies severely critical of French colonization in Africa; *Pages de journal* (1934) and *Retour de l'U.R.S.S.* (1936), marked by sympathy, then disillusionment, with Communism; *Les Nouvelles Nourritures* (1935), new counsels, addressed (before disillusionment prevailed) to 'Camarade'; *Dostoïevsky, articles et causeries* (1923), *Incidences* (1924), and *Essai sur Montaigne* (1929), criticism; translations, notably of Shakespeare and Conrad; *Corydon* (1924), Socratic discussions on the theme of homosexuality; *Si le grain ne meurt* (1926), a very frank autobiography of his early life; his *Journal, 1885–1939* (1939), *1939–42* (1946), *1942–9* (1950), followed by two fragments, *Et nunc manet in te* and *Ainsi soit-il, ou les Jeux sont faits*

(1951; posth.); *Feuillets d'automne* (1949), reminiscences and essays. The correspondence of Gide and Claudel (publ. 1949) throws light on two very different men.

Giéra, PAUL, *v. Félibrige*.

Gigogne, Mère, a character in marionette drama, the mother of a numerous progeny.

Gigonnet, nickname of Bidault, the moneylender in several novels of Balzac's *Comédie humaine*, notably *Histoire de la grandeur et de la décadence de César Birotteau*.

Gilbert, GABRIEL (*c.* 1620–80), a mediocre dramatist and poet, of interest for the use others made of his themes and ideas, e.g. his *Rodogune* (1644) was a precursor of Corneille's *Rodogune*, his *Hippolyte* (1646) of Racine's *Phèdre*.

Gilbert, NICOLAS-JOSEPH-LAURENT (1751–80), a promising poet who died young and poor, author of *Le Dix-huitième Siècle* (1775), *Mon apologie* (1778), *Adieux à la vie* (his last and best work). His satires attacked the *philosophes* with bitter shafts at times recalling Tacitus and Juvenal.

Gilberte, in Proust's *A la recherche du temps perdu*, the daughter of Charles *Swann and *Odette. Marcel first sees her in childhood at *Combray. Later, in Paris, she is his first love. Time as a transforming agent—one of Proust's main themes—can be seen at work in Gilberte, who, though her grandfather was an Alsatian Jew and her mother an ex-courtesan, becomes a *Guermantes by her marriage to Marcel's friend *Saint-Loup. One day (at the reception in *Le Temps retrouvé*, ii) her young daughter will represent for Marcel the point at which the Swann and Guermantes paths of his life coalesced.

Gil Blas (1880–1914), a political and literary daily, brilliant, witty, and often scurrilous. Contributors included Maupassant, Mendès, and Richepin.

Gil Blas de Santillane (vols. I and II, 1715; III, 1724; IV, 1735), a picaresque romance by Lesage. It satirizes the ups and downs of life with a total absence of bitterness, a quality which led Sainte-Beuve to refer to its remarkable consolatory character and Scott to comment that it leaves the reader pleased with himself and with mankind; but it has been censured for its levity, e.g. by Joubert. It was translated into English (or the trans. was revised) by Smollett.

Gil Blas, son of humble Spanish parents, is an ordinary young man, intelligent, easy-going, and adaptable, in no way heroic, and with little in the way of scruples or morality. At 17 he is sent off on a mule, with a few ducats in his pocket, to the University of Salamanca. On the way he falls in with robbers, who detain him. This is the start of a long series of adventures. He takes service with Dr. Sangrado, a quack physician, and himself becomes a physician, with the archbishop of Granada (who invites criticism of his sermons, and resents it when given), and with various other persons. A happy chance introduces him to the prime minister, the duke of Lerma, whom he serves as secretary and confidant, acquiring great wealth. But prosperity corrupts him and he grows proud and heartless, a disposition which is checked when he falls into disgrace and is imprisoned. He later returns to court, where Olivares is now prime minister, and is again employed. He has now acquired worldly wisdom, even a little benevolence and morality, from his experiences. When the minister dies, he retires to a quiet country life. By the ingenuous avowal of his faults he has retained the reader's affection, if not his esteem.

Gill, André, *pseudonym of* LOUIS-ALEXANDRE GOSSET DE GUINES (1840–85), caricaturist. His series of political caricatures, *Nos députés*, was much appreciated.

Gilles, a character in pantomime, a silly, timid creature; the subject of a remarkable painting by Watteau.

Gilles de Retz or **Rais,** *v. Retz.*

Gillet de la Tessonnerie (*c.* 1620–60), author of *Le Déniaisé* (1647) and *Le Campagnard* (1657), good and original comedies.

Gilliatt, in Hugo's *Les *Travailleurs de la mer.*

Gilliéron, JULES (1854–1926), philologist, Swiss by birth, French by naturalization, long professor at the *École pratique des Hautes Études* and an authority on the dialectal variants of French words and constructions. With Edmond Edmont, he published an *Atlas linguistique de la France* (1902–1910; suppl. 1920), a collection of nearly 2,000 linguistic maps recording the variants of a given word or phrase (e.g. *abeille*). The data had been collected by Edmont, who visited 639 localities, armed with a carefully framed questionnaire.

Gillot, JACQUES, *v. Satire Ménippée.*

Gilson, ÉTIENNE (1884–1978), a leading authority on medieval philosophy (esp. Thomism) and the influence of Christianity on the development of modern civilization; professor at the *Collège de France* from 1932, founder and director of the Institute of Medieval Studies at Toronto. His works include *La Liberté chez Descartes et la théologie* (1913); *La Philosophie au moyen âge* (1922; augm. 1944); *Le Thomisme: Introduction au système de saint Thomas d'Aquin* (1922); *L'Esprit de la philosophie médiévale* (1931–2), Gifford lectures delivered at the University of Aberdeen; *Les Idées et les lettres* (1932), with a good preface on the value to be attached by literary historians to the study of sources.

Ginguené, PIERRE-LOUIS (1748–1816), a critic of the dogmatic school (*cf. La Harpe*), wrote for reviews, notably the *Décade philosophique.* His *Histoire littéraire d'Italie* (1811–19, 9 vols.; completed by another hand) was widely read. *v. Musical Controversies.*

Giono, JEAN (1895–1970), a novelist of humble, partly Italian origin. He made his name with novels and tales of pastoral life in Provence (often set in or near his native Manosque), depicting in rich poetic language and with a vivid imagination a way of life that is not only simple and idyllic, but hard and close to primitive Nature, seen as a living and healing force, e.g. *Colline* (1928); *Un de Baumugnes* (1929); *Regain* (1930); *Jean le Bleu* (1933), based on his own childhood; *Que ma joie demeure* (1935); *La Femme du boulanger* (1935). His pacifism (the outcome of service in the 1914–18 war—a period treated in *Le Grand Troupeau*, 1931) led to his imprisonment for some months early in the 1939–45 war. His later novels, called *chroniques*, are of wider scope and have prompted comparisons with Stendhal, especially the best of them, *Le Hussard sur le toit* (1951), where the theme is the cholera epidemic of 1838 and one of the characters recalls Fabrice del Dongo. His work shows deep distaste for the modern world, especially urban society. *v. Pagnol.*

Girard, GABRIEL, *v. Dictionaries*, 1736.

Girardin, ÉMILE DE (1806–81) and his wife DELPHINE (1804–55), daughter of Sophie Gay. The husband, a journalist and publicist whose career was marked by duels (*v. Carrel*) and skirmishes with the authorities, founded (1836) *La *Presse* (one of the first cheap dailies; *v. Press*, 6) and various low-priced instructive journals. His works include *De la presse périodique au XIXᵉ siècle* (1837); *De la liberté de la presse et du journalisme* (1842); *Questions de mon temps, 1836 à 1856* (1858, 12 vols.), collected articles. His beautiful, spirited wife—in her youth a *Romantic poetess (*Essais poétiques*, 1824; *Nouveaux Essais poétiques*, 1825), a contributor to *La *Muse française*, and adored queen of the *cénacles*—wrote one of the earliest gossip columns (weekly in *La Presse*, 1836–9, as 'Charles de Launay'; collected in *Lettres parisiennes*, 1843); also short novels and some comedies, e.g. *Le Lorgnon* (1831), *La Canne de M. de Balzac* (1836), *C'est la*

faute du mari (1851), *Lady Tartufe* (1853), *La Joie fait peur* (1854).

Girardin, RENÉ-LOUIS, MARQUIS DE (1735–1808), of Italian descent, friend and protector of J.-J. Rousseau, who tutored his son, and who lived for some weeks, and died suddenly, in a pavilion in the grounds of his *château* at Ermenonville, near Paris. He was an authority on landscape-gardening (*De la composition des paysages, ou des moyens d'embellir la nature*, 1777) and laid out the *château* grounds in the English manner; Rousseau was at first buried on an island in a lake there.

Girardin, *v. Saint-Marc Girardin.*

Girardon, FRANÇOIS (1628–1715), a sculptor noted for his monumental and decorative statuary, e.g. Richelieu's tomb.

Girart de Roussillon, a late 12th- or early 13th-c. *chanson de geste (*Doon de Mayence cycle). Girart, robbed by Charles Martel (*v. Maire du Palais*) of the woman he was to marry, takes up arms against him. Chastened by the trials to which God subjects him, he helps to erect the shrine of the Madeleine at Vézelay. *v. Wauquelin.*

Girart de Viane, a *chanson de geste (*Garin de Monglane cycle) by Bertrand de Bar-sur-Aube. It relates the war between Charlemagne and Garin's unruly and formidable sons Renier and Girart, who are besieged in Viane (i.e. Vienne, S. France), and includes the capture of Charlemagne in the forest of Viane. *v. Olivier.*

Giraudoux, JEAN (1882–1944), a diplomat by career, among the most distinguished and original of modern authors, made his name with novels, written in a highly personal, impressionistic style (and often containing charming portraits of young girls, who are at once highly sophisticated and disarmingly innocent), e.g. *Provinciales* (1909); *Simon le pathétique* (1918);

Suzanne et le Pacifique (1921), a parody of the desert island type of novel; **Siegfried et le Limousin* (1922); **Juliette au pays des hommes* (1924); *Bella* (1926), where two young members of rival families play Romeo and Juliet in a satire of contemporary political life; *Églantine* (1926); *Combat avec l'ange* (1927), where tragedy nearly enters into a gay love affair when one partner, a rich, beautiful South American, develops a social conscience; *Les Aventures de Jérôme Bardini* (1930); *Choix des élues* (1939).

He turned playwright (1928; *v. Jouvet*) with even greater success. His irony, amused sympathy, poetical fancy, and constant use of paradox and imagery (fatiguing at times in the novels) lent themselves to the discipline of dramatic form and stylized dialogue. His characters belong to a world of fairy-tale and classical myth, but their inconsistencies and conflicts symbolize those of humanity. His plays include *Siegfried* (1928; after the novel); *Amphitryon 38* (1929), a modern treatment of a myth dramatized, he calculated, 37 times before this (*cf.* Molière's **Amphitryon*)—Alcmena, one of his most endearing female characters, teaches Jupiter that human friendship may triumph over a god's desire; *Judith* (1931), a psychological tragedy, from the story in the Apocrypha; *Intermezzo* (1933); *La *Guerre de Troie n'aura pas lieu* (1935); *Électre* (1937); *L'*Impromptu de Paris* (1937); *Cantique des cantiques* (1938); *Ondine* (1939; *v. La Motte Fouqué*); **Sodome et Gomorrhe* (1943); *La Folle de Chaillot* (1945), a bitter satire of a 20th c. in which money is the god and only madwomen still believe in love and honour; *L'Apollon de Bellac* (1947); *Pour Lucrèce* (1953)—the last three produced posthumously.

He also published occasional collections of essays, both critical and patriotic, e.g. *Lectures pour une ombre* (1917), *Adorable Clio* (1920), *Les Cinq Tentations de La Fontaine* (1938), *Pleins Pouvoirs* (1939), *Littérature* (1941). Others have appeared since his death, as has *La Menteuse* (1969), a novel (written 1936) discovered among his papers.

Girondins, Les, during the Revolution, a party of moderate Republicans (many were **députés* from the **département* of the Gironde) led by Brissot (they were also called *Brissotins*) and including Condorcet, Pétion, Mme Roland (in whose **salon* they met) and her husband, and Vergniaud; the guiding body of the **Assemblée législative*, later the moderate group in the **Convention*. Once the Republic was established, they were unable to restrain the extremists. Their attempts to maintain law and order and their protests against the violent measures adopted by the **Commune insurrectionnelle* only succeeded in antagonizing the people, and in June 1793 they were overthrown by the **Montagnards*. Twenty-one of their leaders were imprisoned and later executed. *v. Revolutions*, 1; *Corday d'Armont*; *Histoire des Girondins*.

Giry, ARTHUR (1848–99), scholar, compiler of a *Manuel de diplomatique* (1894) and *Nouveau Traité de diplomatique*, standard works on the study of historical documents.

Glatigny, ALBERT (1839–73), minor poet, led a hand-to-mouth existence touring the provinces as prompter, at times play-writer, to a company of actors. When in Paris, he moved in **Parnassien* circles. His verse, strongly influenced by Banville and Leconte de Lisle, includes *Les Vignes folles* (1860), *Les Flèches d'or* (1864), *Gilles et Pasquins* (1872). He also wrote a comedy of stage life, *L'Illustre Brizacier* (1873).

Glissant, ÉDOUARD, *v. Négritude*.

Globe, Le (1824–32), a daily f. by P. Leroux and the journalist Paul-François Dubois (1793–1874), the paper in which Sainte-Beuve began his career as a literary critic with sympathetic appreciations of young **Romantics*. It reflected the political ideas of the **doctrinaires*, and Thiers was a leading contributor. In 1831 it came briefly into the limelight as the organ of the **Saint-Simoniens*.

Glorieux, Le, a comedy by Destouches,

generally considered his masterpiece; produced 1732.

The theme is the conflict between the ruined nobility and the newly enriched *bourgeoisie*. The comte de Tufière, insufferably arrogant and proud of his high birth, conceals the fact that his family is poor and hopes to marry Isabelle, daughter of the purse-proud *parvenu* Lisimon. His vainglory is finally humiliated when his poverty-stricken father turns up and Isabelle's maid proves to be his own sister. Reconciliation and marriage follow. (Destouches had intended to show the comte as incorrigible and rejected, but the actors are said to have insisted on a happy ending.)

Gluck, Gluckistes, *v. Musical Controversies.*

Gobelins, Manufacture des, a tapestry factory in Paris; originally a dye-works f. by Jean Gobelin, head of a family of dyers who came to Paris *c.* 1450 and won fame by discovering a scarlet dye. It was bought for Louis XIV in the 17th c. (*v. Vaux-le-Vicomte*; *Le Brun*) and since then (with a short break during the Revolution) has been run by the State for the manufacture of tapestries, furniture, and carpets. *v. Savonnerie.*

Gobineau, JOSEPH-ARTHUR, COMTE DE (1816–82), diplomat, novelist, and historian, as a diplomat served as secretary to Tocqueville, then in the embassy at Teheran (from 1855), whither he later returned as ambassador. His name was long associated chiefly with his *Essai sur l'inégalité des races humaines* (1853–5), from which 20th-c. pan-Germanists extracted the doctrine known as *Gobinisme*—often far removed from his own philosophy of racial aristocracy, which is also expounded in his correspondence with Tocqueville (1908). His more lasting fame—as a *conteur*—rests on his Oriental tales, notably *Akrivie Phrangopoulo*, one of four in *Souvenirs de voyage* (1872), and the six in *Nouvelles asiatiques* (1876); and on such small masterpieces (publ., if at all in his lifetime, only in newspapers or reviews) as

Mademoiselle Irnois (1847), *L'Abbaye de Typhaine* (1867), *Adélaïde* and *Le Prisonnier chanceux* (1913 and 1925). He also wrote *Les Pléiades* (1874), a novel influenced by Stendhal; *Trois Ans en Asie* (1859); *Les Religions et les philosophies dans l'Asie centrale* (1865); *La Renaissance* (1877), dramatic scenes from the lives of Savonarola, Michelangelo, etc.

Gobseck, *v. Comédie humaine, La* (*Scènes de la vie privée*). Gobseck, a miserly Jewish moneylender, also appears in other novels by Balzac.

Goddam, a nickname, from the English oath, applied to the English by the French during the Hundred Years War.

Godeau, ANTOINE (1605–72), an *habitué* of the Hôtel de *Rambouillet (known there as 'le Nain de Julie'—he was very short) and a member of the original *Académie française*. He wrote profane and sacred poetry; a good preface to Malherbe's works; *Épîtres morales*, with interesting literary allusions; an *Histoire de l'Église* (1653–78); *Saint Paul* (1654), an *epic. Richelieu made him bishop of Grasse and Vence.

Godechot, JACQUES (1907–   ), historian, an authority on the Revolution; professor at the University of Toulouse-Le Mirail. His works include *Les Commissaires aux armées sous le Directoire* (1938), *Les Institutions de la France sous la Révolution et l'Empire* (1952), *La Grande Nation* (1956), *La Contre-Révolution* (1961), *Les Révolutions, 1770–1799* (1963), *La Prise de la Bastille* (1965), *L'Europe et l'Amérique à l'époque napoléonienne* (1967), and a contribution to the *Histoire générale de la presse française* (1969–72, 3 vols.), of which he was an editor.

Godefroi de Bouillon (1058–1100), a leader of the 1st Crusade and first king of Jerusalem. *v. Chevalier au cygne.*

Godefroy, FRÉDÉRIC-EUGÈNE, *v. Dictionaries,* 1881–1902.

Goethe, JOHANN WOLFGANG VON (1749–1832), the great German author, was decorated by Napoleon with the *Grand-Aigle* of the *Légion d'honneur* (1808). His novel *Die Leiden des jungen Werthers* (1774), with its melancholy, appealing hero who turns to nature for an echo of his emotional storms and whose will power is destroyed by excessive sensibility and unrequited love, was a major foreign influence on French literature *c.* 1800. *v.* *Foreign Influences*, 2, 3; *Romanticism*.

Goldmann, LUCIEN (1913–70), a critic of Rumanian birth who elaborated a form of Marxist criticism which he called 'structuralisme génétique'. His chief works are *Le Dieu caché* (1956), a study of the influence of *Port-Royal* on Pascal and Racine, and *Pour une sociologie du roman* (1964). Some of his essays have been collected in *Structures mentales et création culturelle* (1970) and *La Création culturelle dans la société moderne* (1971). Inspired by the work of the Hungarian critic Georg Lukács, and borrowing the tools of sociology, he saw the relationship between literature and society manifested not in content (the traditional Marxist view), but in structures. *v.* *Critics and Criticism*, 3.

Golias, a fictitious personage of uncertain origin, the type of the jovial railer (greedy, drunken, licentious, witty, and insubordinate), patron of wandering scholars, and reputed author of scores of satirical Latin (Goliardic) poems. He came into prominence about the time of the conflict between Abélard and St. Bernard and was dignified with the titles *Episcopus* and *Archipoeta*.

Gombauld, Gombault, or **Gombaud,** JEAN OGIER DE (1570–1666), an *habitué* of the Hôtel de *Rambouillet and a member of the original *Académie française*; a *Huguenot who, nevertheless, obtained a place at court. He wrote elegies and sonnets; forgotten tragedies; *Amaranthe* (1631), a *pastoral drama; *Endymion* (1624), a prose romance expressing, under a transparent allegory, his love for Marie de Médicis, the queen-mother.

Gomberville, MARIN LE ROY, SIEUR DE (1600–74), novelist and a member of the original *Académie française*, wrote pseudo-historical romances of heroic adventure and gallantry—*La Caritie* (1621), *Polexandre* (1629; 1637), *La Cythérée* (1640)—set in distant lands he had never seen (Egypt, Mexico, Senegal, the West Indies). After being converted to *Jansenism, he wrote a sequel to *Polexandre* to atone for its demoralizing effect, *La Jeune Alcidiane* (1651), a kind of Christian romance.

Goncourt, EDMOND (1822–96) and JULES (1830–70) DE, 'les Frères Goncourt', novelists and men of letters who wrote in such sensitive collaboration that they are seldom mentioned apart. They lived in Paris, highly artistic, nervous creatures, with two major interests—literature and the collection of *objets d'art*—and ample means to indulge both. At first they wrote monographs on art and history—social history of a type then novel, based on study of contemporary customs, periodicals, and letters (e.g. *Histoire de la société française pendant la Révolution*, 1854; ...*pendant le Directoire*, 1855; *L'Art du dix-huitième siècle*, 1859–75; *La Femme au XVIII*[e] *siècle*, 1862—all still read and quoted). In 1851 they published their first novel, *En 1851...*, and began the famous *Journal des Goncourt*.

Their novels, now little read and often unsuccessful when first published, made literary history as the first *romans documentaires* and are constantly cited as examples of 19th-c. *Realism and *Naturalism. The brothers held that the novelist should produce an absolutely faithful picture of life, based on authentic observation of existing conditions—'Le roman actuel se fait avec des *documents* racontés, ou relevés d'après nature, comme l'histoire se fait avec des documents écrits' (*Journal*, 24 Oct. 1864). Thus their best-known novel, *Germinie Lacerteux* (1864), is the history of a domestic of their own who served them faithfully for years and was, they learnt later, all the time leading a life of vice and debauchery which led to her death in a workhouse. *Madame Gervaisais* (1869), a study of religious mania, was drawn from a relative, and they spent months in Rome, where she had lived, documenting themselves on actual scenes and events. For *Sœur Philomène* (1861) they studied hospital life from the inside, suffering nervous prostration in consequence. *Les Hommes de lettres* (1860; first entitled *Charles Demailly*) describes a world of highly strung men of letters, while **Renée Mauperin* (1864) and **Manette Salomon* (1867) are more in the nature of novels of manners. In all these novels the brothers adopted a form peculiarly their own: short, impressionistic, almost disconnected *tableaux*, written in a mannered, precious style (they called it *l'écriture artiste*), with many words drawn from the language of painting and many coined by themselves.

The pair felt pursued by animosity: *En 1851...* failed because it appeared the morning after the *coup d'état* of 1851; the production (1865) of their play *Henriette Maréchal* occasioned an anti-government demonstration. They took every mishap personally, and when Jules died Edmond called him a martyr to literature.

Edmond returned to novel-writing with *La *Fille Élisa* (1877); *Les Frères Zemganno* (1879), a fine novel of circus life, written with real feeling (the chief characters are two devoted brothers); *La Faustin* (1882), a study of an actress; *Chérie* (1884), said to be a portrait of Marie Bashkirtseff. He also did much to awaken interest in Japanese art (*L'Art japonais au XVIIIᵉ siècle: Outamaro*, 1891; and *Hokusaï*, 1896). Recognition came to him with the years. His **salon* in 'le Grenier des Goncourt' (two rooms at the top of his house, full of books and collector's pieces) was a meeting-place for young, and older, writers (and *v. Dîners Magny*). In his will he left a fund to found the **Académie Goncourt*.

Gondi, PAUL DE, *v. Retz*.

Gondinet, EDMOND (1829–88), wrote many light comedies, e.g. *La Cravate*

blanche (1867), *Le Panache* (1875), *Les Braves Gens* (1881).

Gongorisme, *v. Foreign Influences*, 1.

Gorgibus, (1) in Molière's *Les *Précieuses ridicules*; (2) in his **Sganarelle*.

Gormond et Isembard, an early 12th-c. **chanson de geste* (the oldest in the **Doon de Mayence* cycle; only a fragment survives). The French knight Isembard, resentful of unjust treatment by King Louis, has joined the pagan king Gormond and induced him to invade France. The invaders are defeated in a great battle in which Isembard, who fights his own father, dies reconciled with the Church.

Gossec, FRANÇOIS-JOSEPH (1734–1829), composer of much official music during the Revolution, e.g. for Mirabeau's funeral, for **Desorgues's Hymne à l'Être Suprême*.

Goubert, PIERRE (1915–), historian, professor at **Paris IV* since 1969. His works include *Familles marchandes sous l'Ancien Régime* (1959), *Beauvais et le Beauvaisis de 1600 à 1730* (1960), *Louis XIV et vingt millions de Français* (1966), *L'Ancien Régime* (1969–73, 2 vols.), and a major contribution to the *Histoire économique et sociale de la France* (*v. History*, 4, last §).

Goujon, JEAN (*fl.* 1540–60), a sculptor famous for the grace and delicacy of his work—Tritons, Naiads, nymphs, caryatids, etc. He collaborated in the decoration of many important buildings, notably the **Louvre*.

Gounod, CHARLES (1818–93), composer, famous for his opera *Faust* (prod. 1859).

Gourgaud, GASPARD, BARON (1783–1852), one of Napoleon's generals, spent two years with him on St. Helena. His *Sainte Hélène. Journal inédit de 1815 à 1818* (1889, 2 vols.) is a good record of life there. *v. also Montholon*.

Gourmont, REMY DE (1858–1915), one of the finest *critics associated with the *Symbolist movement, also an essayist and novelist (cf. *Schwob*), studied at the University of Caen (he came of a Norman family), then settled (1883) in Paris. His interests were primarily literary and scholarly: he edited and modernized old texts, worked at the *Bibliothèque nationale* (1884–91), helped to found, and wrote regularly for, the Symbolist *Mercure de France*. After 1891 a skin disease intensified his recluse-like habits.

His works include criticism and essays, marked by eclectic rather than profound scholarship, intellectual (and erotic) curiosity, and irony, e.g. *Le Livre des masques* and *Le Deuxième Livre des masques* (1896 and 1898; impressionistic sketches of Symbolists), *Promenades littéraires* (1904–27; collected criticism), *Le Latin mystique* (1890; studies and translations of medieval Latin religious and mystical verse), *L'Esthétique de la langue française* (1899; essays on linguistics), *La Culture des idées* (1901; inc. a well-known essay on the *Dissociation des idées*, asserting the need to get away from the unquestioning acceptance of commonplace ideas and associations of ideas, and for thought to proceed by imagery rather than by ideas), *Le Problème du style* (1902), *Le Chemin de velours* (1902), *Physique de l'amour: essai sur l'instinct sexuel* (1904), *Promenades philosophiques* (1905–9); novels, showing a tendency to regard human behaviour in terms of biological urge and a lack of any real generosity of feeling, e.g. *Sixtine: roman de la vie cérébrale* (1890), *Les Chevaux de Diomède* (1897), *Une Nuit au Luxembourg* (1906; a philosophical fantasy), *Un Cœur virginal* (1907); 'precious' short stories, collected in *Histoires magiques* (1895), *Le Pèlerin du silence* (1896), *D'un pays lointain* (1898), *Couleurs* (1908), etc.; poetry, collected in *Divertissements* (1912); two dramatic prose poems, *Lilith* (1892) and *Théodat* (1893); *Épilogues* (1903–7; contemporary commentaries); the *Lettres à l'Amazone* (1921), written to an American woman whose friendship brightened his last years.

Gournay, MARIE DE JARS, DEMOISELLE DE (1566–1645), adopted daughter of Montaigne, issued an edition of his *Essais* after his death and (in pamphlets collected in *L'Ombre*, 1626; *Les Avis, ou les Présents*, 1634) stoutly defended both him and Ronsard against the grammatical censures of the school of Malherbe. She was a blue-stocking (v. *Saint-Évremond*), a prolific writer on moral and feminist themes, on the French language, etc.

Gournay, VINCENT DE, v. *Économistes*.

Gourville, JEAN HÉRAULT DE (1625–1703), memoir-writer and something of an adventurer (Sainte-Beuve compares him to Gil Blas), began as *valet de chambre* to La Rochefoucauld, followed him to the wars, and rose by resource, wit, and good humour to an important position as a negotiator acceptable to both sides in the *Fronde. His aptitude as a man of business won him the favour of N. Fouquet—and involvement in his disgrace. After a period of exile, including a visit to England, he won favour again as financial agent to the Condé family. Even Colbert, who long sought to recover funds he had misappropriated, respected his ability. His memoirs, simply and sincerely written, contain interesting references to William III.

Gouvion-Saint-Cyr, LAURENT, v. *Maréchal*.

Gozlan, LÉON (1803–66), wrote a novel, *Le Notaire de Chantilly* (1836), influenced by his friend Balzac; sensational dramas; somewhat heavy comedies, e.g. *Le Gâteau des reines* (1855), *Il faut que jeunesse se paye* (1858); rather better one-act *proverbes*, e.g. *Le Lion empaillé* (1848), *Une Tempête dans un verre d'eau* (1849), *La Pluie et le beau temps* (1861); also *Balzac en pantoufles* (1856), useful reminiscences.

Graal, Le Saint (The Holy Grail), v. *Perceval*.

Grabinoulor, v. *Albert-Birot*.

Gracq, Julien, *pseudonym of* LOUIS POIRIER (1910–), one of the second generation of *Surrealists, a teacher by profession. His works, broadly in the tradition that proceeds from Arthurian legend by way of *Romantic lyricism to Surrealism, include novels (e.g. *Au château d'Argol*, 1938; *Un Beau ténébreux*, 1945; *Le Rivage des Syrtes*, 1951; *Un Balcon en forêt*, 1958) and, more recently, the three tales of *La Presqu'île* (1970); the play *Le Roi pêcheur* (1948), inspired by the legend of the Grail; prose poems (*Liberté grande*, 1947 and 1958); essays (*André Breton*, 1948; *Préférences*, 1961, inc. *La Littérature à l'estomac*, first publ. 1950, an attack on the commercialization of literature, literary juries, etc.; *Lettrines*, 1967).

Graffigny, FRANÇOISE D'ISSEMBOURG D'HAPPONCOURT, MME DE (1695–1758), wrote *Lettres d'une Péruvienne* (1747); also *Cénie* (1750), a sentimental comedy very popular in its day. In 1985 the Voltaire Foundation began publication ·of *c.*2,500 remarkably spontaneous and informative letters to her friend Devaux (hitherto unpubl. save for *c.*30 shedding light on the life of Voltaire and Mme du Châtelet at Cirey, where she stayed to escape ill-treatment by her husband).

Graindor de Douai, *v. Antioche.*

Graindorge, M. Frédéric-Thomas, *v. Notes sur Paris.*

Grammaire de l'Académie française (1932), a guide to grammatical usage (*v. Académie française*), said to be largely the work of Hermant. It provoked hostile criticism (notably Brunot's *Observations sur la Grammaire de l'Académie française*, 1932) and has never been taken seriously.

Gramont or **Grammont,** (1) ANTOINE, DUC DE (1604–78), *maréchal de France* (his *Mémoires* were composed by his second son); (2) his brother PHILIBERT, COMTE DE (1621–1707), a gambler and libertine, was banished from Louis XIV's court for his attentions to a royal favourite, then lived at the court of Charles II of England, where he married Elizabeth Hamilton.

The comte, whose lack of scruple was judged lightly in his day, is the subject of the well-known *Mémoires du comte de Gramont* (1713), written in admirable French, in an easy, slightly ironic style, by his brother-in-law A. *Hamilton. The first part, covering his adventures down to his exile and apparently dictated to Hamilton, is the most entertaining; the rest, probably composed by Hamilton, throws a vivid light on English court scandals—though the work is of questionable accuracy.

Grand-Bé, Rocher du, *v. Chateaubriand.*

Grand Cyrus, Artamène, ou le (1649–53, 10 vols.), a romance by Mlle de Scudéry; a work highly successful in its day (read in Eng. trans. by Dorothy Osborne and Mrs. Pepys, and drawn on by Dryden and Killigrew), portraying, under names drawn from Persian history, distinguished contemporaries of the author (Artamène is Condé, Mandane is Mme de Longueville, Sapho is Mlle de Scudéry herself).

The main theme is the attempt of the mysterious hero Artamène, commander of the army of the Medes, to rescue his beloved Mandane, princess of Media, who has been carried off by the prince of Assyria. He forces his way into the burning city of Sinope, where she is held captive, only to find that she has been borne off on a ship by another rival and apparently, but not really, drowned. Artamène, it now emerges, is in fact Cyrus (grandson of Astyages), the hostility of his uncle Cyaxares, Mandane's father, having forced him to conceal his identity and to try to win her by exploits in Cyaxares's service. He finally does so, but only after volumes of battles, assaults, and incredible feats, in which he is always on the point of recovering her and always frustrated. Into this theme are interwoven the adventures of scores of other characters facing similar obstacles with equal fortitude. The action is delayed and the tedium increased by long biographies and monologues; and the prudery of the female characters is much more marked than in *L'*Astrée.*

Grand Dauphin, Le, i.e. LOUIS DE

FRANCE (1661–1711), only son of Louis XIV and Maria Theresa, so called after his death to distinguish him from his eldest son, Louis, duc de Bourgogne (1682–1712; *v. Fénelon*), who succeeded him as dauphin, but died 10 months later. His second son, the duc d'Anjou (1683–1746), became Philip V of Spain (1700). The edition of the classics *ad usum Delphini* was prepared for the 'Grand Dauphin'. *v. Bossuet*; *Monseigneur*.

Grande Mademoiselle, La, *v. Montpensier*.

Grandes Chroniques de France, a French translation of the Latin chronicles of the early kings of France, made by Primat, a monk of *Saint-Denis, and presented to Philippe III *c.* 1274; the first important historical work written in French. Other translators carried the work down to later reigns (e.g. Guillaume de Nangis, also a monk of Saint-Denis); from the 14th c. it was written in French from the outset (*v. Juvénal des Ursins*). It was the first French book printed in France (1477).

Grandet, Le Père, in Balzac's *Eugénie Grandet*.

Grandgousier, in Rabelais's *Gargantua*.

Grand Meaulnes, Le (1913, in the *Nouvelle Revue française*), a novel by Alain-Fournier, remarkable for its sensitive treatment, in terms of a childlike dream world, of events which all the time have a rational explanation. *v. Novel*, 3.

Augustin Meaulnes, an uncouth, dynamic 17-year-old, comes to board at a small school in the village of Sainte-Agathe (*v. Alain-Fournier*); the schoolmaster's son, François Seurel (narrator of the story), becomes his devoted friend. At Christmas, François's grandparents, due for their annual visit, are to be met at the local station; but Meaulnes sets out with a pony and trap to meet them at a distant junction. They arrive, and are met, at the local station. Next day, the pony and trap are brought back; a few days later, Meaulnes returns,

exhausted and silent. In time he tells his story to François. He had lost his way in the dark, tethered the pony while he sought a night's lodging, and returned to find pony and trap gone. After wandering all the next day, he came at nightfall on an old house in a wood, all lit up. Within, in what seemed an enchanted world, a gay company, many of them children in bygone dress, were celebrating the engagement of Frantz de Galais, the owner's son. Meaulnes, for whom a fine costume with a scarlet waistcoat was conveniently to hand, was taken for one of a troupe of actors hired for the occasion. In the course of these fairy-tale revels, a deep sympathy sprang up between him and Yvonne, daughter of the house. Back in his room, he found a distraught young man, Frantz himself, home in secret to leave word that rejoicing could cease—his fiancée had disappeared. The stricken company seemed to vanish. Meaulnes was led to a crossroads and set on the road to Sainte-Agathe, where he arrived at daybreak, dreaming of Yvonne and a lost world (for he had found it, and left it, in the dark)—his only tangible souvenir being the scarlet waistcoat.

One day, he recognizes Frantz among some gipsies in Sainte-Agathe, talks with him, and pledges himself, at whatever cost, to help him find his lost fiancée. The quest takes him to Paris and a life different from, but uneasily intermingled with, the past. He interrupts it to marry Yvonne—for François has meanwhile discovered the whereabouts of the lost domain. Finally, his pledge fulfilled, he comes home to find that Yvonne has died in childbirth and that their child is being cared for by François, now the schoolmaster.

Grand Prix des meilleurs romans du demi-siècle. In 1950 a special jury decided that the 12 best novels of the first half of the 20th c. were: Barrès's *La *Colline inspirée*, *Bernanos's *Journal d'un curé de campagne*, Duhamel's *Confession de minuit* (*v. Salavin*), A. *France's *Les Dieux ont soif*, Gide's *Les *Faux-Monnayeurs*, J. de *Lacretelle's *Silbermann*, *Larbaud's *Fermina Marquez*, Malraux's *La

Condition humaine, Mauriac's *Thérèse Desqueyroux*, Proust's *Un Amour de Swann* (v. *Swann*), Romains's *La Douceur de la vie* (v. *Hommes de bonne volonté*), and *Sartre's *La Nausée*. *La Vagabonde* by Colette, a member of the jury, was specially added to the list.

Grands Cimetières sous la lune, Les, v. Bernanos.

Grand Siècle, Le, the age of Louis XIV.

Grands-Jours, extraordinary assizes formerly held by delegations of the *parlement* in provinces where crime, including the misdeeds of tyrannical nobles, was especially rife. v. *Fléchier*.

Grand Testament, Le, v. Villon.

Grandville, *pseudonym of* JEAN-IGNACE-ISIDORE GÉRARD (1803–47), caricaturist and illustrator (notably of La Fontaine's *Fables*), made his name in *Le *Charivari*. He usually satirized people as animals, as in his series *Les Métamorphoses du jour* (1828).

Graziella (1852; v. *Confidences, Les*), a tale by Lamartine, based on an episode in his early life. A young Frenchman, travelling in Italy, lives for a time in the home of a Neapolitan fisherman. A friendship with the daughter of the house ripens into love, more genuine on her side than on his. When he is recalled to France, she falls ill and dies.

Greban, ARNOUL and SIMON, v. *Mystère*.

Green, JULIEN (1900–   ), a novelist of American parentage who was born in Paris and has spent his life in France, apart from the years 1919–22 (at the University of Virginia) and 1940–5 (again in the U.S.A.); a member of the *Académie* (1971). Although he is a deeply religious man (converted to Roman Catholicism in 1916 and, after some years of doubt, again in 1939), he rejects the description 'Catholic novelist': in his view, 'novels are made of sin'. Often sombre in atmosphere and involving murder, madness, sadism, etc., his works depict the anguish and despair that result from the conflict between man's spiritual and carnal desires, combining conventional realism with a vivid apprehension of evil and of an underlying spiritual presence. His writings include the novels *Mont-Cinère* (1926), *Adrienne Mesurat* (1927), *Léviathan* (1929), *Épaves* (1932), *Le Visionnaire* (1934), *Minuit* (1936), *Si j'étais vous...* (1947), *Moïra* (1950), *Chaque homme dans sa nuit* (1960), and *L'Autre* (1971); short stories and plays; his *Journal* (1928–72, 9 vols. to date), a moving record of his spiritual and literary development; *Partir avant le jour* (1963), *Mille Chemins ouverts* (1965), and *Terre lointaine* (1966), autobiographical works; and, in English, *Memories of Happy Days* (1942), evoking his early life.

Gregh, FERNAND (1873–1960), man of letters, critic, and poet; founder (1902) of *Humanisme* (cf. *Literary Isms*), a short-lived poetical movement, advocating—in reaction against both the *Symbolists and the *Parnassiens*—a return to the humanistic spirit of antiquity. His works include *La Maison de l'enfance* (1897), *La Beauté de vivre* (1900), *Les Clartés humaines* (1904), *L'Or des minutes* (1905), *La Chaîne éternelle* (1910), and *La Gloire du cœur* (1932), poetry; also *La Fenêtre ouverte* (1901) and *Étude sur Victor Hugo* (1904), critical and biographical studies.

Gregory of Tours (c. 538–94), bishop of Tours from 573. His *Historia Francorum* (covering Frankish history down to 591), and a continuation (to 642) attributed to one Fredegarius, are essential sources for the *Merovingian period.

Grenier des Goncourt, Le, v. Goncourt.

Gresset, JEAN-BAPTISTE-LOUIS (1709–77), poet and dramatist, a teacher in *Jesuit colleges, made his name with the poem *Ver-Vert* (1734; a charming trifle about a pampered convent parrot, highly decorous and learned in religious phrases, who is invited to show his paces at another convent, but picks up some shocking language on the journey there and scandalizes the good nuns). A further poem, *La Chartreuse* (1735), disquieted his superiors and his connection with the Order was severed. He later wrote *Le *Méchant* (1745), a successful comedy. He was elected to the *Académie* (1748), and ended his days in religious devotion.

Grétry, ANDRÉ-ERNEST-MODESTE (1741–1813), a composer of Belgian birth, noted for his *opéras-comiques*, e.g. *Le Huron* (1768) and the highly successful *Zémire et Azor* (1771; on the theme of Beauty and the Beast)—each with a libretto by Marmontel. *v.* also *Sedaine.*

Greuze, JEAN-BAPTISTE (1725–1805), genre and portrait painter. His works are marked by a charming, sentimental *naïveté.*

Grève, Place de. In the Middle Ages, the *grève*, a sandy stretch by the Seine in Paris, became a market-place for goods unloaded at the Port de Grève, a centre of the water trade and so of the municipal life of the city (the *marchands par eau* were the nucleus of the municipality). After 1357, when a house bordering it became the *Hôtel de Ville*, it was a public open space, the scene till *c.* 1830 (when it was renamed Place de l'Hôtel-de-Ville) of most of the notorious executions in French history and in 1789 of the creation of the *Commune de Paris* and the *Garde nationale*. It was long a meeting-place for insurrectionists and dissatisfied or unemployed workers (hence *faire grève*, 'to go on strike'). *v. A la lanterne.*

Grévin, ALFRED, *v. Musée Grévin.*

Grévin, JACQUES (1538–70), chiefly known as a dramatist, also a versatile man of letters, a physician, and a poet of the school of Ronsard. His works include, notably, *La Mort de César* (1561), an early *tragedy on the Senecan model, and *Les *Ébahis* (1561), one of the first original French comedies (*v. Comedy*); also *La Trésorière* (1559; a satirical comedy against women

and financiers), translations of the classics, and good lyrics. He became a *Huguenot and twice took refuge in England.

Grignan, MME DE , *v. Sévigné.*

Grimarest, JEAN-LÉONOR LE GALLOIS, SIEUR DE (1659–*c.* 1715), the first biographer of Molière—*Vie de M. de Molière* (1705).

Grimbert, the badger in the *Roman de Renart.*

Grimm, FRÉDÉRIC-MELCHIOR, BARON DE (1723–1807), a German, entered Parisian literary society partly through friendship with J.-J. Rousseau (later they quarrelled resoundingly) and, helped by Diderot, became a good literary critic, succeeding G. Raynal as Paris correspondent of various German sovereigns on literary and artistic subjects (1753–73; after 1768 Diderot and Mme d'Épinay often replace him; *v.* also *Meister*). His letters, in effect a sort of private newspaper circulated in manuscript to privileged persons (imperfectly publ. as *Correspondance littéraire, philosophique, et critique*, 1812; re-ed. 1877–82 by Tourneux), contain much sound criticism (e.g. his comparison of Shakespeare and the French dramatists) and valuable appreciations of contemporaries (Voltaire, Buffon, J.-J. Rousseau, Helvétius, etc.). He also corresponded (1774–96) with Catherine of Russia. He was honest and able (his various official posts are indicative of the confidence he inspired); sceptical in philosophy and politics; and an intimate friend of Mme d'Épinay. *v. Musical Controversies.*

Grimod de la Reynière, BALTHAZAR (1758–1838), a noted *gourmand* and eccentric, given to lavish entertainment and practical jokes (at one of his twice-weekly *déjeuners philosophiques* each guest sat with a coffin behind him); also, at various times, a barrister (he practised for eight years without fees), travelling salesman (after release from prison, where his father had him confined for two years by *lettre de cachet in an attempt to curb his appetite and hospitable instincts), and literary journalist (dramatic critic for Le Censeur dramatique, 1797–8, and owner of a set of waistcoats embroidered with portraits of members of the *Comédie-Française). After 1815 he lived in a country château fitted with numerous mechanical devices to facilitate banqueting and practical jokes, rescued from loneliness by the company of a pet pig, with its seat of honour at table. He always wore gloves, for he was hideously web-handed—a fact which may partly explain his eccentricity and the streak of cruelty in his nature. His works include the Almanach des gourmands, servant de guide dans les moyens de faire grande chère (1803–12, 8 vols.), which he founded and largely wrote—with such success that he was inundated with presents in kind; a Manuel des Amphitryons (1808), on table etiquette and 'les éléments de la politesse gourmande'.

Gringoire, a character inspired by Gringore (below) in (1) Hugo's *Notre-Dame de Paris, (2) *Banville's Gringoire.

*Gringoire, v. Press, 9.

Gringore, PIERRE (c. 1475–1538), a Norman of varied talents, a famous member of the *Enfants sans souci (at one time Mère Sotte), writer and organizer of *mystères, *moralités, *soties, and *farces, and a *rhétoriqueur poet. His best work was the Jeu du Prince des Sots et Mère Sotte (perf. in Paris on Shrove Tuesday 1512), a complete tetralogy (*cry, sotie, moralité, and farce). In the sotie and moralité he supported Louis XII in his conflict with Pope Julius II by vigorous satire of the pope: the moralité is entitled L'Homme obstiné (i.e. the pope); in the sotie, Mother Church (Mère Sotte wearing clerical garments over her own) plots with her prelates to increase her temporal power, wages war with princes, and is finally exposed for what she is. His other works include a long mystère, La Vie monseigneur Saint Louis, not without interest in its pictures of feudal life; political and moral poems in the allegorical style of the rhétoriqueurs, e.g. La Chasse du cerf des cerfs (i.e. the pope), the Blason des hérétiques (listing and condemning all the enemies of orthodoxy down to Luther), and Les Folles Entreprises (1505), a remarkable work (at times reminiscent of Sebastian Brandt's Narrenschiff) consisting in the main of disquisitions on political, moral, and theological questions of the day.

Grippeminaud, in Rabelais's *Pantagruel.

Griseldis or **Griselidis,** 'patient Griselda' of the last tale in Boccaccio's Decameron. On Petrarch's Latin translation of this tale were based, besides Chaucer's Clerk's Tale, two French prose versions made before 1400. One of these, by Philippe de Mézières, may have been the source of the Estoire de Griseldis (c. 1395; octosyllables), apparently the first serious secular French play.

Grisette, the name, in the first half of the 19th c., for a young sempstress, milliner, laundress, etc., of the *Quartier latin. The popular idea of her as hard-working, underfed, but invariably amorous and gay, is reflected in the tales of Musset (e.g. *Mimi Pinson) and Gautier, in *Murger's Scènes de la vie de Bohème. etc.

Grisi, (1) CARLOTTA (1819–99), an Italian ballerina at the *Opéra—Gautier, who wrote the scenario of the ballet Giselle for her and corresponded with her for over 20 years, had a long liaison with her sister Ernesta, a singer; (2) her cousin GIULIA (1811–69), opera-singer and a fine tragédienne, a triumphant success in Paris for several seasons from 1832 onwards.

Grognards, Les, a nickname for the veterans of Napoleon's Garde impériale. He treated them with easy familiarity and they responded with almost fanatical devotion, but reserved the right to grouse (grogner) about the hardships involved.

Gros, ANTOINE-JEAN, BARON (1771–1835), painter, a pupil of David, and an early

*Romantic in his sense of life and colour; noted for his scenes from French history, especially battles, e.g. his *Pestiférés de Jaffa* and *Champ de bataille d'Eylau*.

Gros-Guillaume, Gaultier-Garguille, and **Turlupin,** *stage-names of*, respectively, ROBERT GUÉRIN (d. 1634), HUGUES GUÉRU (d. 1633), and HENRI LEGRAND (d. 1637), a trio of actors at the *Hôtel de Bourgogne* in the early 17th c. who delighted the public with their coarse farces. They also played in tragedy as La Fleur, Fléchelles, and Belleville. The term *turlupinade* was applied to the type of poor jokes and puns then in vogue and condemned by Molière and Boileau.

Gros-René, Éraste's valet in Molière's *Le *Dépit amoureux*.

Grotesques, Les, v. Gautier.

Guèbres, Les, by Voltaire, a tragedy directed against religious persecution; produced 1769. Its performance was prohibited. The scene is Apamea, in Syria, where a Parsee sect is being cruelly persecuted by the Roman priesthood.

Guénée, ANTOINE, ABBÉ (1717–1803), author of *Lettres de quelques Juifs.. à M. de Voltaire* (1769), exposing Voltaire's distortions of the Scriptures.

Guenièvre (Guinevere), King Arthur's queen, beloved of Lancelot. She figures in many *romans bretons. v. Chevalier à la charrette*; Lancelot.

Guêpes, Les, v. Karr.

Guérin, CHARLES (1873–1907), minor poet of the post-*Symbolist period, wrote musical, reflective, at times rather morbidly religious verse, e.g. *Le Cœur solitaire* (1899), *Le Semeur de cendres, 1899–1900* (1901), *L'Homme intérieur, 1901–1905* (1905).

Guérin, EUGÉNIE DE (1805–48) and her brother MAURICE DE (1810–39). Eugénie was a melancholy, intensely emotional and religious woman whose possessive love for Maurice absorbed her life. After their mother died, she brought him up at the Château du Cayla, the family home near Albi, which she rarely left. She was a natural poet (as good as, if not better than, Maurice, in Sainte-Beuve's view), but conscience made her feel that time spent in writing was mis-spent. Her repressed emotions, creative gifts, and rare feeling for nature found an outlet in a remarkable *journal intime*, written for her brother from 1834 and continued, after his death, till 1842. It was edited by Trébutien (*Journal et Fragments d'Eugénie de Guérin*, 1862), who had earlier published *Reliquiae d'Eugénie de Guérin* (1855) for private circulation. After Maurice's death, she agitated for publication of his works and was in contact with Trébutien and Barbey d'Aurevilly.

Maurice, educated at the *Collège Stanislas (with Barbey d'Aurevilly, later his close friend) and destined for the Church, entered *Lamennais's community at La Chesnaie (1832). When it was dissolved (1833) he returned to a secular life, having realized that his love of nature and poetry was stronger than his religious vocation. He tried in vain to live by his pen in Paris, then took to teaching—a hard life which, added to emotional stress and social distractions, finally undermined his health. Soon after his marriage (1837) to the sister of a pupil, which brought him money but no great happiness, he was taken home to die of tuberculosis, having published nothing. He is chiefly noted for his prose poem *Le Centaure* (written *c.* 1835; publ. 1840 in the *Revue des Deux Mondes*, with a memoir by G. Sand and extracts from his letters), a rare evocation of pagan Nature, marked by a sensuous perfection of form, rhythm, and language. His works were published in 1861 (*Maurice de Guérin. Reliquiae*, 2 vols.; ed. by Trébutien, with preface by Sainte-Beuve) and again, with additions which include another prose poem, *La Bacchante*, in 1862 (*Journal, lettres, et poèmes*). His introspective *Journal* (for the years 1832–5; also called the *Cahier vert*) is full of a feeling for Nature which recalls the *Notebooks* of G. M. Hopkins in its detailed awareness of sights and sounds. Matthew Arnold (*Essays in Criticism*, 1865) early appreciated the writings of Maurice and Eugénie de Guérin.

Guermantes, the aristocratic family in Proust's **A la recherche du temps perdu*: notably, the duc and duchesse de Guermantes ('Basin' and 'Oriane'), the duc's brother *Charlus, the prince and princesse de Guermantes; also Mme de *Villeparisis, *Saint-Loup, etc. For the young Marcel, day-dreaming among the effigies in *Combray church, the name Guermantes symbolized French history and legend, also the remote fastnesses of Parisian society which he, as a *bourgeois*, could never hope to penetrate. When, thanks to Saint-Loup, this world was thrown open to him, he studied it (as we do through his eyes) on many occasions— at dinners and receptions given by the duchesse or the princesse, at Mme de Villeparisis's *salon*, at the theatre—and was in turn flattered to be made free of it, disillusioned by its banality, and intrigued by its mannerisms or by its latent passions and vices. At the reception in the last volume (*Le Temps retrouvé*, ii), the middle-aged Marcel observes the havoc wrought by time in this magic world of his early fancies. His host, the prince, ruined by war, has remarried—and the new princesse is none other than the former Mme *Verdurin. Charlus, now sunk in vice, no longer moves in society, but his former violinist *protégé*, Morel, the valet's son, is a wartime hero, received everywhere. The aged duc is madly in love with the aged *Odette, once Mme *Swann. Time's transformations are above all evident in the person of young Mlle de Saint-Loup—in her features even, for they recall both her Alsatian-Jewish great-grandfather (*v. Gilberte*; *Swann*) and her Guermantes father.

Guernes de Pont-Sainte-Maxence, *v. Thomas Becket*.

Guerre, MARTIN, a 16th-c. Gascon gentleman who disappeared without trace.

One Arnaud du Thil, who closely resembled Guerre, presented himself as the missing man, was recognized by Guerre's wife as her husband, and lived with her until it was revealed that the real Guerre was in Flanders. After a long trial, which excited great interest, and the final reappearance of Guerre himself, Du Thil was executed (1560).

Guerre de Troie n'aura pas lieu, La (1935), a 2-act drama by Giraudoux, a fine example of his gift for tragic irony and use of wit and paradox to emphasize moral conflicts. Hector returns to Troy victorious, but sickened of war, and finds a new war threatening, for Helen, kidnapped by Paris, is in Troy and the Greeks demand her return. A struggle ensues between those who, like Hector, are convinced that war is evil and want to return Helen to Menelaus, and the warmongers, who back their refusal with appeals to patriotism, heroism, etc. Hector prevails: the great gates of Troy, open only in time of war, are closed, and Helen is to return to Greece with Ulysses, Menelaus's envoy. But the situation is reversed by a chance drunken killing, which provokes the inevitable war. As the curtain falls, the gates of war are seen slowly opening—and behind them Helen, infinitely fickle, is embracing Troilus.

Guesde, JULES BAZILE, *known as* (1845–1922), one of the chief French disciples of Karl Marx (his father-in-law), editor of the Socialist weekly *L'Égalité*, and leader of the *Guesdistes* (a party which worked for an international Labour movement). He was long *député for Lille and became a minister during the 1914–18 war.

Gui, châtelain de Coucy, *v. Coucy*.

Guiart, GUILLAUME, *v. History*, 1.

Guibert, COMTE DE, *v. Lespinasse*.

Gui de Bourgogne, a *chanson de geste (*Charlemagne cycle).

Gui de Warewic, an *Anglo-Norman

verse romance, probably of the first half of the 13th c. The earliest extant English version, *Guy of Warwick*, is of the 14th c.

The poem relates the exploits undertaken by Gui, son of the earl of Warwick's steward Siward, to win the hand of Felice, the earl's daughter. After his marriage and many adventures, he fights for King Äthelstan before Winchester against the giant Colbrand, champion of the Danish invaders. He slays the giant and retires to a hermitage. He finally makes his whereabouts known to Felice, but dies as she reaches the hermitage.

Guignol, a marionette (*cf. Polichinelle*), seems originally to have been introduced into the outdoor puppet shows established at Lyons c. 1815 by the puppet-master Laurent Mourquet (1745–1844). Mourquet later opened a café, where he installed a *Théâtre de Guignol*. Guignol—like the Lyons silk-worker or the Dauphiné peasant—was good-natured and easily duped, but cunning, and never finally worsted.

The children's puppet theatres ('Punch and Judy') in Paris parks are called *théâtres de Guignol*. The *Théâtre du Grand Guignol* of modern times, in Paris, specialized in crude plays of horror and violence.

Guilbert de Pixérécourt, *v. Pixérécourt*.

Guillaume, Chanson de, one of the finest *chansons de geste* (*Garin de Monglane cycle), probably of the first half of the 12th c., and later rehandled in *Aliscans* (a *chanson de geste* of the late 12th or early 13th c.). It is also noteworthy for the prominent role played in it by a woman. Guillaume d'Orange or 'Guillaume au court nez' (his nose was damaged by a Saracen sword), Garin's great-grandson, had an 8th-c. historical prototype in Guillaume, comte de Toulouse (a title he received from Charlemagne), who fought repeatedly with the Saracens and ended his days as a monk at Aniane, near Montpellier, having built near by a monastery later known as Saint-Guilhem-le-Désert.

A small Christian force under Guillaume's nephew Vivien is routed by Saracens in the plain of Larchamp or Aliscans (from *Elysii campi*, the Roman cemetery near Arles). Guillaume, summoned to the rescue by a messenger from Vivien, comes in haste, but is defeated. His wife, Guibourc, has raised another army, but this too is annihilated, together with all Guillaume's followers. He arrives, pursued by the enemy and half-dead, at the gates of Orange. Guibourc, in command there in his absence, at first refuses to recognize her husband in the fugitive who seeks admission. At last she has the gates opened and questions him about his various followers. He tells of the disaster, and then, in silent sorrow, the two go to the great hall, where all is prepared for the expected banquet, but which will now be for ever deserted. The next day, encouraged by Guibourc, he sets out again and, with reinforcements from the king, defeats the Saracens.

Guillaume, Geste de, *v. Garin de Monglane*.

Guillaume d'Aquitaine (1071–1127), 7th comte de Poitiers and 9th duc d'Aquitaine, the earliest known *troubadour*. He led a stormy life, fell foul of the Church, and was finally excommunicated. Some of his few surviving *chansons* are diffident, mannered lyrics of courtly love (*v. Amour courtois*), others are licentious in the extreme.

Guillaume de Champeaux, *v. Universities*, 1.

Guillaume de Digulleville or **de Deguileville**, author c. 1320 of the poem *Pèlerinage de la vie humaine*, a kind of *Pilgrim's Progress*, translated into English by John Lydgate as *The Pilgrimage of Man*.

Guillaume de Dole, by Jean Renart, an early 13th-c. verse *roman d'aventure*, interspersed with songs borrowed from famous *trouvères.

On the strength of a report given of her by his minstrel, the German emperor Conrad falls in love with Liénor, the beautiful and virtuous sister of Guillaume de Dole. He summons Guillaume to his court, is delighted with his knightly prowess, and tells him that he wishes to marry Liénor. A wicked seneschal then traduces her, to the despair of Conrad and Guillaume; but she comes to the court and is able to confound him.

Guillaume de Lorris, v. Roman de la Rose.

Guillaume de Machaut (c. 1300–77), a poet renowned in his day as the chief of a school, also a fine composer (his musical settings probably contributed to the fame of his lyrics). He was long in the service of John of Luxembourg, king of Bohemia (killed at Crécy), and later attached to the houses of Charles, king of Navarre, and the princes of France; from 1337 he was a canon of Rheims. He was among the first to write *ballades and *rondeaux, and helped to establish fixed forms for both. His lyrics usually treat artificially of *amour courtois, though in his Voir Dit ('True Tale') he presents himself as loved in old age, for his literary reputation, by a young lady of high rank. He also wrote long narrative and didactic poems, usually in octosyllables, e.g. the Dit dou vergier, probably his earliest work, a feeble imitation of the allegory of the *Roman de la Rose; the Jugement du roy de Behaingne (i.e. Bohemia), written before 1342, a debate between a lady who has lost her lover and a knight who has been betrayed by his mistress as to which is more to be pitied, decided by the king in favour of the knight; the Jugement du roy de Navarre (c. 1349), an analogous debate, reversing the above verdict (which was apparently unpopular), preceded by an account of the terrible events of 1348–9, the year of the Black Death; the Livre de la fontaine amoureuse, an allegorical poem on which Chaucer drew for his Boke of the Duchesse; the Confort d'ami, addressed to his patron

Charles de Navarre in captivity; the Prise d'Alexandrie, on the deeds of Pierre Ier of Lusignan, king of Cyprus. v. Deschamps.

Guillaume de Nangis, v. Grandes Chroniques.

Guillaume de Palerne, an early 13th-c. verse *roman d'aventure. There is a 14th-c. English version, William of Palerne.

Guillaume, prince of Apulia, is carried off and saved from poisoning in childhood by a werewolf (really the heir to the Spanish throne, put under a spell by his stepmother, the queen). Brought up by peasants, and later taken to the court of the emperor of Rome, he falls in love with Melior, the emperor's daughter, and during his flight with her is again protected by the werewolf. He then fights with the king of Spain, captures him, and forces the queen to break her spell. The werewolf, restored to human form, reveals Guillaume's identity.

Guillaume de Saint-Amour (fl. c. 1250), a secular doctor of theology who took a leading part in the struggle of the University of Paris against the mendicant friars (v. Universities, 1; Rutebeuf). The pope finally banished him from France, on pain of excommunication.

Guillaume le Clerc, v. Besant de Dieu.

Guillaume le Maréchal, Histoire de, a poem on the life of William the Marshal, earl of Pembroke, regent of England during Henry III's minority, written soon after his death in 1219 by some continental subject of the king of England. It is interesting and well written, throwing light both on historical figures and on the social life of the day.

Guillaumin, ÉMILE (1873–1951), wrote novels describing life in Central France (the old province of Bourbonnais), e.g. Tableaux champêtres (1901), La Vie d'un simple (1904), Baptiste et sa femme (1911).

Guillemette, in *Pathelin.

Guilleragues, GABRIEL-JOSEPH DE LA VERGNE, VICOMTE DE (d. 1685), an advocate (*premier président* of the *Cour des aides in Bordeaux), held a post at the court of Louis XIV from 1669, and was appointed (1679) ambassador in Constantinople; a friend of Boileau and Racine. It has recently (1962) been finally established that he was the author (and not merely the translator) of the *Lettres portugaises. His *Valentins*, madrigals and epigrams, were also published anonymously (1669).

Guillet, *v. Du Guillet.*

Guillevic, EUGÈNE (1907–   ), a poet of Breton origin and Communist sympathies who evokes the material world, above all, solid objects (esp. rocks and stones), seeking to 'arracher aux choses ce qu'elles savent de l'homme' (G. Picon). His collections include *Terraqué* (1942), *Exécutoire* (1947), *Terre à bonheur* (1952), *Trente et Un Sonnets* (1954), *Carnac* (1961), *Sphère* (1963), *Avec* (1966), *Euclidiennes* (1967), *Ville* (1969), *Paroi* (1971), *Encoches* (1971), *Dialogues* (1972). His poems are precise and elliptical, often short and arresting, at times brutal. His use of imagery is sparing and effective.

Guillotine, La, the machine whereby capital punishment is effected in France, wrongly supposed to have been invented by Joseph-Ignace Guillotin (1738–1814; a Paris professor of anatomy and a member of the *Assemblée constituante), who merely proposed that beheading, hitherto reserved for the nobility, should be the sole method of execution, and that it should be carried out mechanically. The *Assemblée* adopted his proposal and a German mechanic named Schmidt built a machine to the specifications of Dr. Louis, then secretary of the French College of Surgeons. It was first used on 25 April 1792, and for a while referred to as 'Louisette'.

Guillotine sèche, La, deportation instead of execution, a practice common under the *Directoire.

Guilloux, LOUIS (1899–1980), a novelist of humble origin and left-wing sympathies (he visited Russia with Gide in 1936). His works—broadly *romans populistes* (*v. Novel*, 3), compassionate, at times also bitter in the spirit of Vallès—include, notably, *Le Sang noir* (1935; dramatized 1966 as *Cripure*), the story of a day of civil strife in a Breton town and the crucifixion of an intellectual, the teacher Cripure, by *bourgeois* cruelty and stupidity; also *La Maison du peuple* (1927; largely the story of his early struggles), *Le Pain des rêves* (1942), *Le Jeu de patience* (1949), *La Confrontation* (1968; also semi-auto-biographical).

Guinevere, *v. Guenièvre.*

Guinglain or *Le Bel Inconnu*, an early 13th-c. *roman breton by Renaud de Beaujeu, who refers here and there to his own love affairs, seeking by his tale to win the favour of his mistress. There is a 14th-c. English version of the story.

A young knight of unknown name and parentage comes to Arthur's court and is granted the adventure of the 'Fier Baiser'. In his quest he repeatedly displays his prowess and, coming to the Île d'Or, slays the defender of the bridge leading to the castle of the 'Damoiselle aux blanches mains', who declares her intention of marrying him. But he perseveres in his quest and reaches a mysterious castle, where he undergoes the ordeal of the 'Fier Baiser'—the kiss of a monstrous serpent. The serpent disappears, to be replaced by Blonde Esmerée, queen of Wales, thus released from enchantment. The knight learns that he is Guinglain, son of *Gauvain, and (though distracted for a time by the charms of the Damoiselle) finally marries Blonde Esmerée.

Guinon, ALBERT (1861–1923), dramatist, author of the comedy *Les Jobards* (1891; with Maurice Denier), about a man who is the victim of his own honesty; also of *Le Partage* (1896), *Le Joug* (1902), *Décadence* (1904), etc.

Guiot de Provins (12th–13th c.), in early life a *jongleur* and *trouvère*, later a monk and author of the *Bible Guiot* (early 13th c.; *v. Bible*), a verse treatise reviewing and criticizing the various classes of society—knights, clerics, lawyers, doctors, etc. His strictures are of a worldly rather than a moral order, showing a survival of the jester in the monk.

Guiraud, ALEXANDRE (1788–1847), minor poet (his *Le Petit Savoyard* in *Poèmes et chants élégiaques*, 1823–4, was much praised) and author of conventional tragedies (e.g. *Les Macchabées*, 1822); a founder of *La *Muse française*.

Guirlande de Julie, a vellum book, decorated with flowers by the painter Nicolas Robert (1614–85) and inscribed by the calligrapher Nicolas Jarry (*c.* 1630–*c.* 1670) with 91 poems (nearly all madrigals) by 19 *habitués* of the Hôtel de *Rambouillet, including Chapelain, Conrart, Desmarets de Saint-Sorlin, Gombauld, G. de Scudéry, Tallemant des Réaux. It was presented to Julie d'Angennes, Mme de Rambouillet's daughter, on 22 May 1641 (her saint's day) by Montausier, whom she later married.

Guiscard and **Gismonde**, *v. Foreign Influences*, 1.

Guise, a branch of the princely house of Lorraine. René II, duc de Lorraine, having come to France, fought with the French at *Marignan and was created duc de Guise by François Ier (1527). His eldest son, François (known as 'le Balafré', 'Scarface'), who succeeded him in 1550, was an eminent captain and councillor under Henri II. His second son, Charles, became cardinal de Lorraine. His eldest daughter, Marie, married James V of Scotland and was the mother of Mary Stuart, who married the future François II. During the brief reign of the young François II (1559–60), the Guises, as uncles of the queen, gained control of the government and vigorously repressed the *Huguenots (*v. Amboise*). The accession of a minor,

Charles IX, and the regency of Catherine de Médicis, soon put an end to their power. François de Guise was assassinated (1563). For the revival of the family's influence under Henri, 3rd duc de Guise, *v. Ligue, La*.

Guitry, (1) LUCIEN (1860–1925), long a leading actor (at one time he partnered Bernhardt), also theatre-manager and playwright; (2) his son SACHA (1885–1957), actor, producer, and playwright. His many productions include *vaudevilles, e.g. *Le Veilleur de nuit* (1911), *La Prise de Berg-op-Zoom* (1912); slight, dramatized biographies, e.g. *Deburau* (1918), *Pasteur* (1919), *Béranger* (1924), *Jean de La Fontaine* (1934); light comedies (usually with three characters—wife, husband, and lover—and himself playing the lead), e.g. *Faisons un rêve* (1916).

Guizot, FRANÇOIS (1787–1874), historian and statesman, came of a Protestant family and was brought up by his mother in Geneva, his father having died in the *Terror. He went to Paris (1805) and studied history, paying his way by teaching and journalism (*v.* also *Dictionaries*, 1809). From 1812 to 1830 he was professor of modern history at the *Sorbonne and author of works including *Histoire des origines du gouvernement représentatif en Europe* (1821–2); *Essais sur l'histoire de France* (first publ. 1823 as a suppl. to an annotated text of *Mably's *Observations sur l'histoire de France*), on the development of political institutions down to the 10th c.; *Collection des mémoires relatifs à l'histoire de France* (1823–35) and *Mémoires relatifs à la révolution d'Angleterre* (1823–5), two monumental series of source-collections; *Histoire de la révolution d'Angleterre* (in 3 pts., publ. at intervals 1826–56), tracing the development of the constitutional monarchy in England; and two famous examples of his methodical, solidly documented work and lucid narrative, *Histoire générale de la civilisation en Europe* (1828) and *Histoire de la civilisation en France* (1829–32), tracing the evolution of social, political, and religious institutions, the progress of philosophy and literature, and also the gradual emergence of the middle classes (for him the most active and decisive element in French history, holding the balance between monarchical absolutism and democratic ideals of liberty).

His political career began after the Restoration, when he became a leader of the *doctrinaires and when his advocacy of a constitutional monarchy led to the official suspension of his lectures (1822–8). Under Louis-Philippe (1830–48) his career was wholly political: he was minister of education (1832–7), briefly ambassador in London (1840), then foreign minister and prime minister. His downfall came with the 1848 *Revolution, for which his policy was held largely responsible. After a year in England, he returned to live in retirement in Normandy. His writings of these later years include *Discours sur l'histoire de la révolution d'Angleterre* (1850), *Histoire parlementaire de France* (1863), *Histoire de France racontée à mes petits-enfants* (1870–5), *Mémoires pour servir à l'histoire de mon temps* (1858–68, 9 vols.).

Guttinguer, ULRIC (1785–1866), minor *Romantic poet and man of letters, a contributor to *La *Muse française*. His works include *Nadir* (1822; critical essays); *Mélanges poétiques* (1826); *Recueil d'élégies* (1829); *Arthur* (1837; publ. anon. 1834), an autobiographical novel (Saint-Martin is among its characters); *Fables et méditations* (1837); *Deux Âges du poète* (1844).

Guyart des Moulins, *v. Bible, French versions of*.

Guyau, JEAN-MARIE (1854–98), philosopher, a stepson of Fouillée, who influenced him. His belief in an instinctive force which underlies human activity, and in the need for the voluntary subordination of the individual to the general good of society, had a considerable influence on French thought *c*. 1880. His chief work was *L'Irréligion de l'avenir* (1887), a study of what he considered to be the sociological basis of religion and an attack, not on religion itself, but on religious dogmas.

Guyon, MME, *v. Quietism*.

Guys, CONSTANTIN (1805–92), black-and-white artist and draughtsman, made a reputation, which has steadily increased, with his sketches of the Parisian life of pleasure, in all its varieties, under the Second Empire. Before he settled in Paris (*c*. 1865), he was in London as tutor to the grandchildren of the artist Thomas Girtin, and in the Crimea following the war as artist-correspondent for the *Illustrated London News*.

Guzla, La, *v. Mérimée*.

Gwynplaine, in Hugo's *L'*Homme qui rit*.

Gyp, *pseudonym of* MARIE-ANTOINETTE DE RIQUETTI DE MIRABEAU, COMTESSE DE MARTEL DE JANVILLE (1850–1932), who wrote light, entertaining, sometimes wittily satirical, novels and sketches of society life, much read in their day, e.g. *Petit Bob* (1868), *Autour du mariage* (1883), *Mademoiselle Loulou* (1888), *Le Mariage de Chiffon* (1894).

H

Habert, PHILIPPE (*c*. 1605–37) and his brother GERMAIN (*c*. 1615–54), abbé de Cérisy, were both members of the original *Académie française*. Germain, an *habitué* of the Hôtel de *Rambouillet, contributed to the *Guirlande de Julie*. Philippe, a

friend of Conrart and also a soldier, wrote an elegy on the death of the wife of his friend and patron the maréchal de la Meilleraye, *Le Temple de la mort* (1637).

Hachette, LOUIS (1800–64), founder

(1826) of the publishing house of Hachette.

Hagiography, v. Saints, Lives of.

Hahn, REYNALDO (1874–1947), long director of music at the Casino of Monte Carlo; a leading composer of music for plays and operas, and especially of songs (e.g. his Chansons grises, settings of lyrics by Verlaine; Chansons latines and espagnoles). v. Proust.

Hainaut, Chroniques de, v. History, 1.

Halévy, (1) LUDOVIC (1834–1908), author, with Meilhac, of gay, amusing libretti for *Offenbach's operettas, Bizet's *Carmen, etc., and of drawing-room comedies (e.g. Froufrou, 1869; La Petite Marquise, 1874), a divertingly impertinent mixture of farce, irony, and (in Froufrou) real pathos. This literary partnership lasted for some 20 years. Writing alone, often with equal success, he produced, notably, L'Abbé Constantin (1882), a novel of country life, very sentimental, but entertaining, and highly popular with a public beginning to tire of the *Naturalist novel; also Un Mariage d'amour (1881) and La Famille Cardinal (1883; amusing scenes from the life of a low-class Parisian family in the 1870s). His Carnets (1935, 2 vols.; for the years 1862–70), almost daily jottings about people and politics, bring to life the agitated period before the *Franco–Prussian war; (2) ÉLIE (1870–1937), son of (1), historian. His chief work, left unfinished at his death, was the Histoire du peuple anglais au XIXᵉ siècle (1912–32, 5 vols.; a further vol., based on his notes, appeared in 1948), a study of political, economic, and religious evolution (esp. the rise of nonconformity) in England after 1815, and an attempt to account for the spirit of voluntary obedience which, in his view, underlies the English conception of liberty; (3) DANIEL (1872–1962), son of (1), essayist, critic, and social historian. His works include Charles Péguy et les Cahiers de la quinzaine (1919; he was associated with Péguy in the conduct of the *Cahiers); studies of the

Third *Republic (La Fin des notables, La République des comités, La République des ducs, 1930–7); Pays parisien (1929), reminiscences of late 19th-c. Paris.

Halphen, LOUIS (1880–1950), medieval historian, notably of the *Carolingian period. He and Philippe Sagnac (1868–1954) were the founders and long the general editors of Peuples et civilisations. Histoire générale de l'humanité depuis les origines (1926–   ), a valuable series of historical monographs.

Halteclere, *Olivier's sword.

Hamburg. During the Revolution a colony of some 40,000 émigrés (e.g. Beaumarchais, Rivarol, Mme de Genlis) settled in Hamburg. They had their own theatre, newspapers, and reviews, and a café where they met. Cf. Coblenz.

Hamelin, OCTAVE (1856–1907), philosopher, taught at the University of Bordeaux, then at the *Sorbonne. His system (expounded in his doctoral thesis, Essai sur les éléments principaux de la représentation, presented 1907, shortly before he was accidentally drowned) is a form of dialectical idealism in which intuition plays no part and is thus, in its rationalism, basically opposed to the anti-intellectualism of Bergson. He had some influence on the intellectual climate of the late 19th and early 20th cs.

Hamilton, ANTHONY (c. 1646–1720), grandson of the first earl of Abercorn, a Jacobite who lived in France during the first exile of the Stuarts (1649–60), settled there after 1688, and fought at the Boyne (1690). He was the brother-in-law and intimate friend of the comte de Gramont and compiler of the Mémoires du comte de *Gramont (1713). He also wrote verse in French and some witty *contes (e.g. the Histoire de Fleur d'épine).

Hamon, JEAN (1618–87), a physician who became (1650) a solitary of *Port-Royal, where he tended the nuns and the poor. He wrote devotional treatises (Mme de

Sévigné praised his *La Pratique de la prière continuelle*) and some remarkable letters. He was greatly esteemed by Racine.

Hamp, Pierre, *pseudonym of* PIERRE BOURILLON (1876–1962), a pastry-cook's apprentice, then a railwayman, who became known as a writer when some of his work appeared in the **Cahiers de la quinzaine*. His many long novels usually follow the processes of industry from raw material to final product, e.g. *La Peine des hommes: Marée fraîche* (1908; fish), *Vin de Champagne* (1909; wine), *Le Rail: Vieille Histoire* (1912), *Le Cantique des cantiques* (1922). *Mes métiers* (1931) describes his early life.

Han d'Islande (1823), a romance by Hugo. The scene is 17th-c. Norway. Two young lovers are united after the hero has undergone many adventures, taken part in conspiracies, fought the 'killer' Han d'Islande, a demonic bandit, and rescued the heroine and her father from captivity.

Hanotaux, GABRIEL (1853–1944), diplomat and historian, author of an *Histoire du cardinal de Richelieu* (1893–1903), general editor and part author of the *Histoire de la nation française des origines préhistoriques jusqu'à nos jours* (1920–9, 15 vols.), a standard work.

Hanska, ÉVELINE RZEWUSKA, COMTESSE (1801–82), **Balzac's wealthy Polish 'Étrangère'. They corresponded for 18 years and married in 1850.

Haraucourt, EDMOND (1856–1941), whose poetry belongs to the **Parnassien* aftermath, published *L'Âme nue* (1885) and *L'Espoir du monde* (1899), collected verse; and *La Passion* (1890), a **mystère*.

Hardy, ALEXANDRE (*c.* 1570–*c.* 1632), a prolific playwright, purveyor of plays to a company of actors (the future *Comédiens du Roi*), at first in the provinces, then at the *Hôtel de Bourgogne* (*v. Theatres and Theatre Companies*). Between *c.* 1593 and *c.* 1630 he composed or adapted several hundred plays, of which he published

(1623–8) 34—*tragedies (on classical themes, e.g. the death of Dido or of Achilles; *Mariamne*, in which Herod, torn between love and jealousy, puts Mariamne to death and then repents, is possibly his best), *tragicomedies (on themes drawn from Lucian, Cervantes, Montemayor, etc.), *pastoral and mythological plays. He was without genius, taste, or style, but he had dramatic instinct (unlike his predecessors, whose works were lyrical or declamatory), and his rough, popular dramas show progress in their animation and rapidity, and in the life he gave to some of his characters. He was also an innovator: he dropped the chorus, shortened monologues and recitals, confronted his principal characters with one another, introduced scenes of violence on to the stage, and in general got rid of the Senecan influence. In all this, he aided the transition from medieval drama and the cold tragedies of the 16th c. to *Classical drama.

Harlequin, *v. Arlequin.*

Harmonie du soir, *v. Baudelaire.*

Harmonies poétiques et religieuses, Les (1830), by Lamartine, a collection of odes and lyrics, mainly religious (at times vaguely pantheistic) in sentiment. God's omnipresence in the universe is the theme of *Jéhovah, Le Chêne, L'Humanité*, and *L'Idée de Dieu*, a sequence of four *harmonies. Milly, ou la Terre natale* is a nostalgic description of the poet's early home.

Harpagon, in Molière's *L'*Avare.*

Harpignies, HENRI (1819–1916), a landscape painter of the *Barbizon school; *v.* also *Impressionism.*

Hatteras, Capitaine, *v. Verne.*

Hatzfeld, ADOLPHE, *v. Dictionaries,* 1890–1900.

Haussmann, EUGÈNE-GEORGES, BARON (1809–91), *préfet de la Seine* during the

Second Empire, initiated the large-scale urban development of Paris.

Haussonville, GABRIEL-OTHENIN, COMTE D' (1843–1924), nephew of Victor de *Broglie, editor of Doudan's letters, and author of *Le Salon de Mme Necker* (1882) and biographical studies in English and French.

Hauteroche, NOËL LE BRETON, SIEUR DE (1617–1707), actor and dramatist, an imitator of Molière, e.g. in his successful comedy *Crispin médecin* (1674), ridiculing the medical profession.

Hauteville House, v. Hugo.

Hautpoul, ANNE-MARIE DE MONT-GEROULT DE COUTANCES, COMTESSE D' (1760–1837), author of verse, novels and pastoral romances (e.g. *Zilia*, 1796; verse and prose), and instructional tales for the young.

Hauts-Ponts, Les, v. Lacretelle, Jacques de.

Haveloc, Lai d', a 12th-c. *Anglo-Norman romance (1,112 octosyllables). The story also forms an episode in *Gaimar's *Estoire des Engleis*; and there is a 14th-c. English version, *The Lay of Havelok*. It appears to have been inspired by the romantic career, in the 10th c., of Aulaf Cuaran, son of a Viking chief, who married the daughter of Constantine III of Scotland.

Haveloc is the son of Gunter, king of Denmark. A mystic flame issuing from his mouth when he sleeps marks his royal birth. Gunter has been treacherously killed and supplanted by Odulf, but before dying has entrusted Haveloc to one of his men, Grim. Grim takes the boy in a boat to England, landing at the future Grimsby, where he is brought up. Achebrit, king of this region, has entrusted his daughter Argentille to her uncle Edelsi: when she is of age, she is to marry the strongest man in the land. Haveloc, now called Cuaran, takes service as scullion with Edelsi and distinguishes himself by his great strength.

Edelsi, seeking in his own interest to degrade Argentille, chooses his scullion as husband for her. A dream and the mystic flame lead Argentille to discover her husband's royal lineage. Haveloc returns to Denmark, is there recognized, slays Odulf, and recovers his own kingdom and afterwards the English kingdom of Argentille.

Hazard, PAUL (1878–1944), scholar and literary historian (v. *Histories of French Literature*), an authority in the field of comparative literature; professor at the *Sorbonne* and the *Collège de France*. His works include *La Crise de la conscience européenne, 1680–1715* (1935) and *La Pensée européenne au XVIIIᵉ siècle de Montesquieu à Lessing* (1946, 3 vols.), notable contributions to the history of European thought; *Les Livres, les enfants, et les hommes* (1937), a graceful, scholarly study of children's books. v. *Critics and Criticism*, 2.

Heaulmière, Les Regrets de la belle, v. Villon.

Héautontimorouménos, L', v. Baudelaire.

Hébert, Hébertistes. After the *Girondins* fell, the *Montagnards* split into two factions: the *Hébertistes*, led by JACQUES-RENÉ HÉBERT (1755–94; a leader of the *Commune insurrectionnelle* and founder of the notorious *Le *Père Duchesne*) and including Cloots and other violent atheists and Revolutionaries; and the less extreme *Indulgents* (Danton and his party). Robespierre triumphed over both factions (v. *Revolutions*, 1; *Cordeliers*). v. also *Enragés, Les*.

Heine, HEINRICH (1797–1856), the German poet, settled permanently in Paris after his democratic sympathies (strengthened by the 1830 *Revolution) brought him into disfavour in Germany. In receipt of a pension (1836–48) as a 'political refugee', he moved freely in literary circles and considerably influenced French literature (v. *Foreign Influences*, 4). His works (trans. into

French separately; then in a complete ed., 1852-68, 14 vols.) include *État de France* and *Lutèce*, amusing short chronicles of life and letters in Paris; the *Nuits florentines*, showing him as a lover and interpreter of Paris; his *Salon* (of 1833-9), essays on French art and the French stage. The translation of his *Reisebilder* (*Impressions de voyage*) opens with an essay on him by Gautier.

Hélinand, *v. Religious Writings*, 1.

Hellequin, *v. Arlequin*.

Hello, ERNEST (1828-85), author of critical and philosophical essays, Roman Catholic and often strongly mystical in tendency. He was an influence on the Roman Catholic revival of the late 19th c.

Héloïse, *v. Abélard*.

Helvétius, CLAUDE-ADRIEN (1715-71), *philosophe* and *Encyclopédiste*, a rich *fermier général* (an office he gave up in 1751); a man of rather narrow and superficial talent. His chief work was *De l'esprit* (1758). His wife, not an intellectual, but charming and kindly, presided over a *salon* frequented by d'Alembert, d'Holbach, Duclos, Turgot, Condorcet, etc.

Hémon, LOUIS (1880-1913), wrote a novel of sporting life (*Battling Malone*, publ. 1925), spent some time in England, then (*c.* 1910) went to Canada. Life among French-Canadian settlers provided material for his novel *Maria Chapdelaine* (1916), which brought him posthumous fame. It is a simple tale—poetically rather than brutally realistic—of a family in an isolated settlement: life is governed by the rigours of the seasons; love, illness, even death, fall into perspective before the colonists' indomitable pioneering spirit.

Hénault, CHARLES-JEAN FRANÇOIS (1685-1770), 'le Président Hénault', a magistrate of the Paris *parlement*, intimate friend of Mme du Deffand, a man of letters (admitted to the *Académie*, 1723) who frequented the best society. His works include a *Nouvel Abrégé chronologique de l'histoire de France* (1744), showing a bias in favour of absolute monarchy; light verse and forgotten tragedies; *Mémoires*, with interesting historical passages and portraits. *v. Club de l'Entresol*.

Hennique, LÉON (1851-1935), *Naturalist novelist (e.g. *La Dévouée*, 1878; *Élisabeth Couronneau*, 1879; *L'Accident de M. Hébert*, 1883; *Un Caractère*, 1889; *Minnie Brandon*, 1899) and dramatist (e.g. *Jacques Damour*, 1887; *La Mort du duc d'Enghien*, 1888). He contributed a tale to *Les *Soirées de Médan*.

Henri Iᵉʳ (1005-60), king of France (*Capetian dynasty), succeeded his father Robert II, r. 1031-60.

Henri II (1519-59; accidentally killed in a tournament held to celebrate the Treaty of *Cateau-Cambrésis), king of France (*Capetian dynasty, *Valois-*Orléans line), succeeded his father François Iᵉʳ, r. 1547-59. He went to the aid of the Scots against Edward VI, then brought Mary Stuart to France and later married her to the dauphin. *v. Diane de Poitiers*.

Henri III (1551-89; assassinated, *v. Ligue, La*), king of France (*Capetian dynasty, last of the *Valois-*Orléans line), succeeded his brother Charles IX, r. 1574-89. He was Italianate, and dubious, in his manners, given to showering wealth and offices on his favourites (called *mignons* by the people), but also a considerable patron of the arts (*v. Desportes*; *Italiens*).

Henri III et sa cour, an historical drama in prose by Dumas *père*, produced 1829; a notable *Romantic triumph.

The duc de Guise learns that the young courtier Saint-Mégrim is in love with his wife. He forces her, by crushing her wrist in his iron gauntlet, to give Saint-Mégrim a rendezvous at her palace. When her lover arrives, the terrified duchess tells him of the trick. He tries to escape, but is seized in the courtyard by the duke's men. From a window the duke throws them a scarf, to strangle him: 'La mort lui sera plus douce; il est aux armes de la duchesse de Guise.'

Henri IV, HENRI DE BOURBON, ROI DE NAVARRE (1553–1610; assassinated by François Ravaillac), son of Antoine de Bourbon and Jeanne d'Albret, heiress of Navarre; king of France (*Capetian dynasty, first of the *Bourbon branch), r. 1589–1610; m. (1) *Marguerite de Valois (1572), (2) Marie de Médicis (1600). In 1584, as a descendant of Louis IX, this Protestant prince became heir to the childless Henri III. His claim was rejected by the *Ligue, war broke out, and Henri III was assassinated. Henri IV defeated the Ligue and abjured the Protestant faith (1593)—a move which won him general recognition as king. A man of great and supple intelligence, he proved an excellent ruler (v. Sully; Huguenots). His published letters, both official and private (inc. several to Queen Elizabeth, of whom he had a high opinion), contain much of great interest, showing him as a brave soldier, an intelligent ruler, and—less creditably— as a lover (he was nicknamed 'le Vert-Galant'). He writes in a simple, natural style, with occasional vivid, racy expressions. v. Corisande; Estrées; Henriade, La; Vervins.

'Henri V', v. Chambord.

Henri, COMTE DE PARIS, the present Orléaniste pretender; v. Orléans (3).

Henriade, La (1728; an earlier version, La Ligue, ou Henri le Grand, appeared in 1723), by Voltaire, an epic poem (10 cantos) dedicated to Queen Caroline of England) reflecting his hatred of civil discord and religious fanaticism.

The hero is Henri de Navarre, later Henri IV. The poem deals at length with the siege of Paris (held by the *Ligue) by Henri III and Henri de Navarre, recounts the assassination of Henri III, the defeat of the Ligue at Ivry, and the entry of Henri IV into Paris. It opens with an imaginary mission by Henri de Navarre to Queen Elizabeth: he gives her an account of the troubles in France (inc. the Massacre of St. *Bartholomew, perhaps the finest part of the work). The characters of Guise and Duplessis-Mornay are well depicted; but the hero's conversion makes an indifferent end to the whole.

Henri d'Andeli (fl. 13th c.), author of the *Lai d'Aristote, a good *fabliau; also of a Bataille des Sept Arts (where the combatants are Grammar and Dialectic; v. Bataille) and a Bataille des Vins.

Henri de Valenciennes (fl. 13th c.), wrote a vivid and eloquent chronicle (prose in its extant form, possibly originally verse) of the war waged against the Bulgarians by Henri, second Latin emperor of the East (1207–16). He was probably a *ménestrel at the emperor's court.

Henriette, in Molière's Les *Femmes savantes.

Henriette d'Angleterre (1644–70), daughter of Charles I of England and his French queen Henrietta Maria (daughter of Henri IV and Marie de Médicis), wife of the duc d'*Orléans. Her early death was lamented in a famous funeral oration by Bossuet. v. La Fayette, Mme de.

Heptaméron, L', the name given by their editor in 1558 to a collection of 72 tales by Marguerite de Navarre, in a form modelled on Boccaccio's Decameron. They purport to be told on successive days by 10 travellers detained by bad weather at an abbey in the Pyrenees. The travellers (five men and five women) are real persons in Marguerite's circle, under fictitious names. She also claims that the incidents related are true and of recent occurrence, at times specifying date and place. The theme of most of the tales is love, usually depicted as a serious, at times as a tragic, passion (in contrast to the licentious or vulgar gallantry of the *Cent Nouvelles Nouvelles). Each tale is followed by a discussion in which current views on the nature of love, its manifestations, etc., are advanced, then opposed by the more moral and religious views of Marguerite (under the name Parlamente), who censures the laxity which had provided amusement for readers of the earlier tales and *fabliaux*. Despite its coarseness of expression, which was in accordance with the tone of the times, the work was clearly intended to have an elevating and civilizing influence. It throws light on the life and customs of the upper classes.

Heptaplomeres, v. Bodin.

Héraclius, a complicated, but greatly applauded, tragedy by Corneille, on a theme from Baronius's *Annales ecclesiastici*; produced in the winter of 1646–7.

The scene is Constantinople. The plot turns on the fact that the usurper Phocas has not, as he imagines, murdered Maurice, emperor of the East, and both his sons. One son, Héraclius, was saved by his nurse, who substituted him, first for her own son Léonce (sacrificed to this end), then, to make the imposture doubly sure, for her foster-child, Phocas's son Martian. Thus Héraclius grows up as Martian, Martian as Léonce. The web becomes even more tangled when Phocas decides that Maurice's daughter Pulchérie shall marry, as he thinks, his son Martian, in fact her brother Héraclius. There are generous confessions, which are not believed. Phocas, irate and mystified, nearly murders both young men and marries Pulchérie himself; but a timely conspiracy ends his life, and Héraclius ascends the throne.

Herbelot (de Molainville), BARTHÉLEMY D', v. *Dictionaries*, 1697.

Herberay des Essarts, NICOLAS, v. *Amadis de Gaule*.

Heredia, JOSÉ-MARIA DE (1842–1905), b. in Cuba (his father was Spanish), one of the first *Parnassien* poets, was educated in France and lived in Paris from 1861. He studied law, and attended the *École nationale des Chartes*, but soon devoted himself to poetry; from 1901 he was keeper of the *Bibliothèque de l'Arsenal*. His fame rests on the 118 sonnets of *Les Trophées* (publ. in book form in 1893, a year before his election to the *Académie*), among the most beautiful in French literature. They are in five groups: *La Grèce et la Sicile*, *Rome et les Barbares*, *Le Moyen Âge et la Renaissance*, *L'Orient et les Tropiques*, *La Nature et le Rêve*. Inspired by, for example, a line from an ancient text or an ornate Renaissance binding, he captures and fixes a fleeting image of beauty from the past. The effect is one of sculptural perfection, suddenly transcended by the great evocative power of the last lines.

Héritage, L', v. *Miss Harriet*.

Herman de Valenciennes, v. *Bible, French Versions of*.

Hermant, ABEL (1862–1950), novelist, essayist, and critic. His articles on the correct use of French, signed 'Lancelot', were for some years a feature of *Le Temps* (and v. *Grammaire de l'Académie*). After his early *Naturalist* novels, e.g. *M. Rabosson* (1884; satirizing university life) and *Le Cavalier Misérey* (1887), he produced, until c. 1938, an almost constant stream of novels of sentimental analysis, entertaining, satirical, often libertine pictures of rich Parisian life (many grouped in the series *Mémoires pour servir à l'histoire de la Société*).

Hermione, in Racine's *Andromaque*.

Hermite de la Chaussée d'Antin, L', v. *Jouy*.

Hermonyme, GEORGES, v. *Renaissance*.

Hernani, a verse drama by Hugo. Its first two performances (25 and 27 Feb. 1830, at the *Comédie-Française*; v. *Taylor*) count among the great battles of the *Romantics*. News having spread that the play was in every way—subject, treatment, and versification—a break with the dramatic conventions, the theatre was packed with partisans: below, in the expensive seats, were the traditionalists, bent on crushing the play; above were hordes of Hugo's admirers—young writers, artists, and musicians—led by Gautier in a red doublet (he describes the scene in his *Histoire du romantisme*) and Petrus Borel. The latter faction so effectively outclapped and outshouted the former on both nights that the success of *Hernani*—and of the Romantic movement—was thenceforth assured.

Don Ruy Gomez de Silva, a Spanish grandee, proposes to marry his ward Doña Sol, who is preparing to elope with the bandit Hernani. Don Carlos, king of Spain, appears in her room and tries to seduce her, but is interrupted by the arrival of Hernani. Hernani, too chivalrous to kill the defenceless king, helps him to escape. The king rewards him with outlawry. Don Ruy Gomez shelters Hernani (disguised), then discovers that he is Doña Sol's lover. The king arrives suddenly, and, despite their rivalry, Don Ruy Gomez refuses to betray his refugee guest. The king departs in wrath, with Doña Sol as hostage. Hernani obtains permission from Don Ruy Gomez to help in rescuing her on condition that he will kill himself whenever Don Ruy Gomez, by sounding a golden horn that Hernani gives him, so ordains. Don Carlos, now Holy Roman Emperor, frustrates a plot to murder him. He learns that Hernani, one of the conspirators, had acted from motives of vengeance, his father having been murdered by Don Carlos's father. Don Carlos restores Hernani's ancestral titles and gives him Doña Sol in marriage. The two are on their balcony on the wedding night when Hernani hears the distant sound of a horn: it is Don Ruy Gomez, who arrives to hold him to his pledge. Doña Sol snatches the phial of poison meant for Hernani and drinks half of it. Hernani finishes it, and they die in each other's arms. Don Ruy Gomez falls on his sword.

Héroard, JEAN (1551–1628), royal physician. His *Journal* (publ. 1868), a detailed record (1601–28) of the life and health of the young Louis XIII, is of historical interest.

Hérodiade, v. Mallarmé.

Hérodias, v. Trois Contes.

Héroët, ANTOINE (1492–1568), a poet of the circle of Marguerite de Navarre. His poems include the *Parfaite Amie* (1542), a subtle, mystical monologue exalting pure love as the supreme happiness and expounding the Platonic doctrine of love (an early example of the influence of Platonism; v. Foreign Influences, 1; Renaissance), written in reply to the *Amie de cour* in which Marot's friend Bertrand de la Borderie had depicted a cynical court lady who cares only for gallantry; also *Androgyne*, on the myth told by Aristophanes in Plato's *Symposium* to explain the origin of love. He translated Ovid's *Ars amatoria*.

Herr, LUCIEN (1864–1926), a brilliant pupil, then (1888–1926) librarian, of the *École normale supérieure*, an ardent Socialist who influenced Jaurès, Blum, Péguy (for a time), and the many generations of *normaliens* whose reading he guided. He was a founder (1904) of the then Socialist daily *L'Humanité*.

Hervieu, PAUL (1857–1915), dramatist and novelist. His plays turn on family problems, e.g. *Les Tenailles* (1896), *La Loi de l'homme* (1897), *La Course du flambeau* (1900). *Théroigne de Méricourt* (1902), his successful drama of the Revolution, was written for Bernhardt. His best-known novels are *Flirt* (1890); *Peints par eux-mêmes* (1893).

Hiatus, in French prosody, the coming together without *elision of two vowel sounds, of which one ends a word and the other (or the other preceded by a mute *h*) begins the following word, e.g. in Ronsard's line:

Le front si *beau, et* la bouche et les yeux.

Until Ronsard's time, hiatus was permissible; later, it was deemed a fault.

Hippolyte, in Racine's *Phèdre*.

Hirsutes, Les, *v. Symbolism.*

Histoire amoureuse des Gaules, *v. Bussy-Rabutin.*

Histoire contemporaine, L', *v. Bergeret.*

Histoire de Charles XII (1731), by Voltaire, an historical work tracing lightly and with substantial accuracy the adventurous life of Charles XII of Sweden and his struggle with Peter the Great of Russia. Its philosophic conclusion is that the conqueror is inferior to the pacific, beneficent monarch.

Histoire de Jenni, v. Jenni.

Histoire de la grandeur et de la décadence de César Birotteau (1837; later in *La *Comédie humaine, Scènes de la vie parisienne*), a novel by Balzac. César Birotteau, an honest scent-merchant, is unbusinesslike, but flourishes thanks to good luck and his wife's restraining influence. He is decorated for his services as deputy mayor and gets carried away by dreams of wealth and grandeur. He launches a new hair-oil (*Huile céphalique*), speculates, and falls a prey to unscrupulous financiers. To crown all, he gives a great ball, which involves rebuilding his house. His dreams end in bankruptcy. His wife and daughter Césarine slave to help him pay his debts. Aided by a few faithful friends (inc. his former employee Anselme Popinot, who loves Césarine), he pays in full, to the admiration of the business world; then, worn out by his efforts, returns to his old home and dies the same evening.

Histoire de la langue française des origines à 1900, *v. Brunot.*

Histoire de la littérature anglaise, v. Taine.

Histoire des Girondins (1847), by Lamartine, a work of romanticized history, written with extreme revolutionary fervour, which made a profound impression at the time. Well-known passages are the sketches of Robespierre, Charlotte Corday, and Mme Roland; the descriptions of the September Massacres, Louis XVI's trial, and the fall of the *Girondins.

Histoire des Treize, v. Comédie humaine, La (*Scènes de la vie parisienne*).

Histoire d'un crime (1877), one of Hugo's best-known pieces of polemical writing (prose), a savage description of the *coup d'état* of 2 December 1851 (*v. Republics,* 2), written in 1852 immediately after his arrival in Brussels.

Histoire d'une fille de ferme, v. Maison Tellier, La.

Histoire d'un paysan, v. Erckmann-Chatrian.

Histoire littéraire de la France, a vast series of historical and critical studies of the main authors and works of French medieval literature, initiated in the 18th c. by the *Maurists, under the direction of Dom Rivet. Vol. I appeared in 1733; by 1749, when Rivet died, 8 vols. had been published. Publication then lagged; vol. XII (to the mid-12th c.) appeared in 1763. After a complete hiatus due to the Revolution and the dispersal of the Benedictines, the work was resumed (1807) under the aegis of the *Académie des Inscriptions et Belles-Lettres.* With the publication of vol. XXXIX (1962) it had passed the middle of the 14th c. (it will end at the year 1500).

Histoire naturelle, v. Buffon.

Histoire naturelle des animaux sans vertèbres, v. Lamarck.

Histoire philosophique et politique des... deux Indes, v. Raynal, G.

Histoire universelle, v. Aubigné.

Histoire universelle, Discours sur l', *v. Bossuet.*

Histories of French Literature. Literary histories and dictionaries have been produced in increasing numbers since the late 19th c. The following are but a few of the many such works (inc. some in other languages), with the emphasis on recent publications and excluding a host of useful manuals (such as Marcel Girard's *Guide illustré de la littérature française moderne*, 1949 and later eds.), concise dictionaries of authors, and the many short works on periods, movements, etc., in such collections as **Que sais-je?* and *Armand Colin*. The dates are those of first publication; many of the earlier works are available in later editions, in some cases with extended coverage.

General histories and dictionaries: *Histoire de la littérature française* (1894), *v.* Lanson; *Histoire de la langue et de la littérature française des origines à 1900* (1896–9, 8 vols.), ed. Petit de Julleville; *Notre littérature étudiée dans les textes* (1920–1, 2 vols.; origins to 1850) and *La Littérature française contemporaine étudiée dans les textes* (1926; 1850–1925), by Marcel Braunschvig; *Histoire de la littérature française illustrée* (1923–4, 2 vols.), ed. Bédier and Hazard; *Histoire de la littérature française* (1931–64, 10 vols.), ed. Joseph Calvet; *Histoire de la littérature française* (1947, 2 vols.), by René Jasinski; *Dictionnaire des Lettres françaises* (1951–72, 5 vols.), *v. Dictionaries*, 1951–72; *Encyclopédie de la Pléiade, Histoire des littératures*, vol. 3: *Littératures françaises, connexes et marginales* (1958); *Littérature française* (1967–8, 2 vols.; illus.), ed. Antoine Adam and others; *A Literary History of France* (1967–74, 6 vols.), ed. P. E. Charvet; *French Literature and its Background* (1968–70, 6 vols.; 16th–20th cs.), ed. John Cruickshank; *Littérature française* (1968–   ; 11 vols., of a projected 16, publ. to date; illus.), ed. Claude Pichois; *Histoire de la littérature française* (1969–70, 2 vols.), ed. Jacques Roger and J.-C. Payen; *Dizionario critico della Letteratura francese* (Turin 1972, 2 vols.), ed. Franco Simone.

Works on particular periods: *Histoire de la littérature française contemporaine (1870 à nos jours)* (1922), by René Lalou; *A*

History of French Dramatic Literature in the Seventeenth Century (1929–42, 9 vols.), by Henry Carrington Lancaster; *De Baudelaire au surréalisme* (1933), *v.* Raymond; *Histoire de la littérature française de 1789 à nos jours* (1936), *v.* Thibaudet; *Histoire du surréalisme* (1945–8, 2 vols.), by Maurice Nadeau; *Introduction à l'histoire de la littérature française* (1946, 2 vols.), *v. Jaloux*; *Histoire de la littérature française du symbolisme à nos jours* (1947–9, 2 vols.), by Henri Clouard; *Histoire de la littérature française au XVIIe siècle* (1948–56, 5 vols.), by Antoine Adam; *Une Histoire vivante de la littérature d'aujourd'hui* (1958), by Pierre de Boisdeffre; *La Littérature en France depuis 1945* (1970; illus.), by Jacques Bersani and others. *v.* also *Histoire littéraire de la France*.

Historiettes, *v. Tallemant des Réaux.*

History. *v.* also *Memoirs*, 1.

1. MEDIEVAL PERIOD. The earliest records of French history were written in Latin (*v. Gregory of Tours; Eginhard*). The first true historical narratives in French were inspired by the Crusades (for some of these works *v. Crusades*). Early rhymed chronicles on other historical topics, in French or *Anglo-Norman, include those of Gaimar, Wace, Benoît de Sainte-Maure, and Jordan Fantosme.

In the 13th and early 14th cs., various works on French and general history, some of them translations from Latin, were written in prose or verse, notably the **Grandes Chroniques*; the rhymed chronicles of Philippe Mousket, bishop of Tournai (written *c.* 1240–50 and relating historical and legendary events from the siege of Troy down to 1243), Geoffroy de Paris (to 1316), and Guillaume Guiart (to 1304); the anecdotes of the 'Ménestrel de Reims' (or the *Chronique de Rains*), written *c.* 1260–70 and relating events from the time of the 2nd Crusade; the *Chroniques de Hainaut* (or *de Baudouin d'Avesnes*—the noble who commissioned them *c.* 1278). There are also two early 13th-c. prose narratives, probably by the same anonymous author (a native of Artois, known as the 'Anonyme de Béthune'), one dealing with the struggle between John and the English barons, the other a valuable account of the reign of Philippe II, preceded respectively by summary histories of the Norman kings of England and the kings of France. *v.* also *Guillaume le Maréchal*; *Pierre de Langtoft*.

Next for mention are the important works of Jean le Bel and Froissart; the *Livre des faits du bon messire Jean le Maingre, dit Bouciquaut* (*v. Bouciquaut*); the chronicle of Juvénal des Ursins; the *Chronique du bon duc Louis de Bourbon*, on the life of a great 14th-c. feudal lord, written in 1429 by one Jean Cabaret to the order of the comte de Clermont; and the *Chronique de Perceval de Cagny* (interesting on Jeanne d'Arc), also of the first half of the 15th c. The *Journal d'un bourgeois de Paris*, a vivid account of conditions in Paris in the years 1405–49 (the period of English and Burgundian domination) by an anonymous churchman of Paris, and the *Journal de Clément de Fauquembergue* (clerk to the Paris *parlement*, 1417–36) throw light on life in the capital. *Commines's *Mémoires* provide invaluable historical information about the reigns of Louis XI and Charles VIII; the *Journal de Jean de Roye* (or *Chronique scandaleuse*) also covers the reign of Louis XI. *v.* also *Jean d'Auton*; *Chastellain*; *La Marche*; *Sources de l'histoire de France, Les*.

2. RENAISSANCE. The chief historical work of this period was J.-A. de *Thou's *Historia sui temporis*. *Du Haillan's *Histoire générale des rois de France* was the first attempt at a connected history, as distinct from chronicles. É. Pasquier and Fauchet wrote on the early history of France. There are also *Monluc's *Commentaires*, *Brantôme's memoirs, and various minor histories, journals, etc.

3. 17TH AND 18TH CENTURIES. The chief historical work of the 17th c. was *Mézeray's *Histoire de France*. Other notable works were *Péréfixe's life of Henri IV, *Maimbourg's *Histoire de la Ligue*, *Bossuet's *Discours sur l'histoire universelle*, the ecclesiastical histories of Tillemont and C. Fleury and, among historical essays, *Retz's *Conjuration de

Fiesque and the comte de Guiche's spirited *Relation du passage du Rhin* (in 1667). There was a tendency under Louis XIV for history to be hampered by political circumspection and to become official and untrustworthy. (Fréret was imprisoned for views he published on the origins of the French; *v.* also *Dupin, L.-E.*) But the sceptical and critical spirit (exemplified by Bayle) on the one hand, and erudition (exemplified by the *Maurists) on the other, ultimately prevailed. The historical works of chief literary merit in the 18th c. were Montesquieu's *Considérations sur les causes de la grandeur des Romains et de leur décadence*; Voltaire's *Histoire de Charles XII* and *Siècle de Louis XIV*, where style and method combine to produce a readable and substantially accurate historical narrative, and also his *Essai sur les mœurs*, recording the progress of the human mind. For other 17th- and 18th-c. historians *v. Saint-Réal*; *Vertot*; *Félibien*; *Rapin de Thoyras*; *Hénault*; *Duclos*. Among the many historical memoirs of this period (*v. Memoirs*, 1), those of the duc de Saint-Simon call for special mention. *v.* also *Young, A*.

4. 19TH AND 20TH CENTURIES. During the 19th c. history became a subject of live general interest and increasingly specialized study. Till *c.* 1850, historians can be roughly classified as *narrative* or *philosophical*. The former reconstitute and often dramatize the past with a wide sweep of historical imagination. They are notably represented by three historians of early and medieval France: Barante, Thierry, and, above all, Michelet. Such works as *Michelet's *Histoire de France* (vols. I–VI, 1833–43), vividly evoking the Middle Ages, were stimulating reading for generations brought up on Chateaubriand's *Le *Génie du christianisme*, Scott's novels (trans. 1822), and the *Romantic manifestos. *v.* also *Michaud*; *Michel, F.-X.*; *Sismondi*.

The philosophical historians, appreciated by more politically conscious readers, were mainly concerned with political and sociological causes and effects, with the evolution of peoples and institutions, and with the future as well as the past. Notable works of this order are *Guizot's *Histoire générale de la civilisation en Europe* and *...en France*, and *Tocqueville's *La Démocratie en Amérique* and *L'Ancien Régime* (an early example of history based on administrative records). *v.* also *Quinet*; *Mignet*; *Thiers*.

From the early 19th c., opportunities for historical research steadily multiplied. Interest in foreign history and its relation to French history, and in ancient and Oriental civilizations, was stimulated by travel literature, the Greek War of Independence, the rapid progress of archaeological and Oriental studies, etc. It is reflected, for example, in the foundation of the *Société asiatique* (1821), the *École nationale des Chartes* (1821), the *Société française d'Archéologie* (1830), the *Revue archéologique* (1844), the *Société de l'histoire de France* (1833), and the *École française d'Archéologie d'Athènes* (1846); the creation of historical and fine arts commissions (*c.* 1837), also of special chairs of history in many universities, which gave the subject a much higher status; the publication of many series of important historical documents (from *c.* 1830), also of memoirs (e.g. those of the duc de Saint-Simon); the organization of State-sponsored archaeological expeditions.

As the century wore on, historical writing, reflecting the positivist spirit of the age, aspired to become more and more scrupulously objective, the fruit of systematic research and documentation. Fustel de Coulanges, in whose view 'l'histoire n'est pas un art, elle est une science pure', was the originator of modern historical method, the practice of presenting history as a body of documented information with no attempt at romantic colouring. He had eminent contemporaries in Taine and Renan (whose works of religious history helped to inaugurate the study of comparative religion in France). *v.* also *Boissier*; *Duruy*; *Lanfrey*; *Blanc*; *Quicherat*, *J.-É.-J.*

The period from the late 19th c. till well after the 1914–18 war was dominated by historians in the direct line of descent from Fustel de Coulanges and in varying degrees scientific and positivist in their approach, e.g. (in date order of birth) Lavisse, A. Sorel, Duchesne, G. Monod (founder of the *Revue historique*), Alfred Rambaud (1847–1905), Aulard, Hanotaux, Charles Seignobos (1854–1942; remembered for his *Histoire sincère de la nation française*, 1933), Jullian, Langlois (author, with Seignobos, of an *Introduction aux études historiques*, 1898, which was long the positivist historian's breviary), Lot. In France, as elsewhere, the early 20th c. saw major advances in the human sciences: sociology emerged as an independent discipline (*v. Durkheim*); geography acquired an economic and social dimension at the hands of Vidal de La Blache and Albert Demangeon (1872–1940); and such scholars as Simiand, Henri Sée (1864–1936), Paul Mantoux (1877–1956), and Henri Hauser (1866–1946) were working in the fields of economics and economic and social history. But these developments were largely ignored by traditional historians, and the study of history, as established in the universities, remained primarily a meticulous documentation of political and military events in Europe. Despair at the state of historical studies and the limitations of the positivist approach (long under attack from the philosopher Henri Berr, founder in 1900 of the *Revue de synthèse historique*, and from Simiand, Febvre, Petit-Dutaillis, and others) led to the emergence of a new school of historiography, headed by Febvre and M. Bloch. They sought to remove the barrier between history and the other human sciences, to make it a study of every aspect and dimension of a civilization, and of structure and evolution as well as events. The year 1929, when they founded the *Annales* (*v. Annales: Économies, Sociétés, Civilisations*), was a landmark in French historical studies, for though what Berr dubbed 'histoire historisante' was written by many thereafter (e.g. Halphen), and still has its exponents, it no longer held the field.

Historical writing of the past 50 years has been marked by a growing interest in (and emphasis upon) social and economic factors of every kind, in topography, and (esp. since 1945) in demography. The period from 1930 has seen notable works in the field of modern (i.e. 16th–20th c.) social and economic history—*v. Halévy, É.; Lefebvre, G.; Febvre; Labrousse; Braudel; Mousnier; Chevalier; Goubert; Le Roy Ladurie; Mandrou; Crouzet; Chaunu*; in the medieval field—*v. Bloch, M.; Perroy; Wolff, Ph.; Duby*; and in the important field of Revolution studies—*v. Lefebvre, G.; Godechot; Soboul* (others who call for mention include Marcel Reinhard and Daniel Guérin; this period has been treated by 19th- and 20th-c. historians of every type, e.g. J.-C.-D. de Lacretelle, Mignet, Thiers, Michelet, Lamartine, Blanc, Taine, Aulard, Sorel, Jaurès, Mathiez, Henri Sée, Caron, Madelin, Bainville, Gaxotte). Other leading authorities include Renouvin (on international relations), H. Michel (on the 1939–45 war), Carcopino (on ancient Rome), and, among religious historians, Fliche and Martin, Daniel-Rops, and Émile Léonard (author of an *Histoire générale du protestantisme*, 1961–4, 3 vols.).

Large-scale collaborative works and *collections* (a series of studies with a unifying theme or approach, supervised by a general editor or editors) are an important feature of modern publishing, e.g. *Peuples et civilisations* (*v. Halphen*), *Clio* (from 1934), the *Histoire générale des civilisations* (from 1953; ed. Maurice Crouzet), the *Histoire des relations internationales* (*v. Renouvin*), *Destins du monde* (from 1957; f. Febvre and ed. Braudel), *Nouvelle Clio* (from 1963), the *Univers de la France* (*v. Wolff, Ph.*), the *Histoire économique et sociale de la France* (from 1970; ed. Braudel and Labrousse), and the *Nouvelle Histoire de Paris* (from 1970). Many of the works listed in the articles on 20th-c. historians form part of *collections* (inc. the more popular *Que sais-je?* series), and a good number are available in English translation.

Hoaxes and Forgeries, *v. Calonne, E. de*; *Chasse spirituelle, La*; *Courtilz de Sandras*; *Louÿs*; *Mérimée*; *Surville,* *Clotilde de*; *Vrain-Lucas*; and *cf. Libri-Carucci*; *Maugérard*.

Hoche, LOUIS-LAZARE (1768–97), a general of the Revolutionary armies, a man of fine character who began life as a stable-boy and rose by his own efforts to be commander of the Army of the Moselle (1793). After a spell in prison (due to Saint-Just's hatred of him), he commanded (1795–6) the Army of the West which finally pacified the *Vendée (and *v. Quiberon*), then led an abortive expedition intended to seize and hold Ireland against the English. He died suddenly, possibly poisoned, while in command of the Army of Germany.

Hoffmann, ERNST THEODOR AMADEUS (1776–1822), German musician, artist, and writer. The great imaginative force and gruesome or grotesque character of his novels and tales, notably his *Phantasie-stücke in Callots Manier* (1814; trans. into French as *Contes fantastiques*), strongly influenced the later—frenetic—*Romantics. *v. Foreign Influences*, 3; *Loève-Veimars*; *Offenbach*.

Hoffmann, FRANÇOIS-BENOÎT (1760–1828), a leading critic on the *Journal des Débats* (*cf. Dussault*; *Feletz*; *Geoffroy*). He also wrote much for the theatre, notably libretti for opera and light opera. His complete works (10 vols.) appeared in 1828–9.

Hohenlinden (Bavaria). Here the French, under Moreau, routed the Austrians (3 Dec. 1800). *v. Coalitions* (2).

Holbach, PAUL THIRY, BARON D' (1723–89), of German birth, a materialist and atheist *philosophe* and *Encyclopédiste*, a man of wide learning, modest, rich, generous, and cheerful (said to be depicted as Wolmar in *La *Nouvelle Héloïse*). His houses (in Paris and in the country at Grand-Val) were the chief centres of the *Encyclopédistes*; there is much about his circle in Diderot's letters to Mlle Volland. His works include, notably, *Le *Système de la nature* (1770); also *Le Christianisme* *dévoilé* (1761 and 1766), *Politique naturelle* (1773), *Le Système social* (1773). He and Naigeon issued (*c*. 1767–8) numerous anti-religious tracts and pamphlets. *v. Rey.*

Holy Alliance, *v. Alliance, La Sainte.*

Homais, Monsieur, in Flaubert's **Madame Bovary.*

Homme approximatif, L', *v. Tzara.*

Homme au masque de fer, L', *v. Masque.*

Homme aux quarante écus, L' (1768), by Voltaire, a satire on French fiscal legislation, condemned by the **parlement.* Economic and other questions (e.g. the agricultural production and national income of France, the proposed 'single tax' on land, monasticism, the iniquities of judicial procedure) are treated mainly in the form of dialogues between an agriculturist, owner of a piece of land yielding an income of 40 *écus*, and a 'géomètre philosophe'.

Homme obstiné, L', *v. Gringore.*

Homme qui rit, L' (1869), a novel by Hugo. The narrative is often powerful, but obscured by absurdities and digressions. Hugo's picture of late 17th-c. English society is unintentionally funny.

Ursus, a vagabond quack and philosopher, lives in a caravan (the 'Green Box') with Homo, a trained wolf. He succours two children, a boy and a baby girl. The boy, Gwynplaine, struggling through a blizzard after being abandoned on a lonely seashore, had found the girl, Dea, in the snow beside a dead woman: she is blind; his face has been so mutilated that it bears a perpetual, grotesque grin which reduces all beholders to helpless mirth.

In London we meet Lord David Dirry-Moir (destined to succeed the Earl of Clancharlie if no legitimate son turns up), described with ironic gusto as a typical athletic English aristocrat and given to going among the people disguised as 'Tom Jim-Jack', and the Duchess Josiane of Clancharlie, a bastard of the king and a magnificent lump of flesh with pretensions to culture. Both have an enemy in Barkilphedro, Receiver of Jetsam at the Admiralty. Ursus settles in Southwark in his caravan. Gwynplaine and Dea are in love; she imagines him to be beautiful as a god. His fame as 'l'homme qui rit' spreads to the court. Suddenly mysterious officials (including the 'Wapentake') appear and take him away—for among other jetsam Barkilphedro has received a sealed bottle containing proof that he is the long-lost son of the late Lord Clancharlie. (He had been stolen, then abandoned, by *comprachios*, vagrants given to procuring children and deforming or mutilating them for sale as exhibits.) This is Barkilphedro's chance to injure Lord David and Josiane. He has Ursus officially informed that Gwynplaine is dead and that he, Dea, and Homo must leave the country at once. Meanwhile Gwynplaine, now a peer, is introduced to the House of Lords. His appearance so convulses his fellow-peers that he has to leave the chamber. He makes for Southwark and the 'Green Box', but finds the site deserted. Suddenly Homo appears and leads him to the waterside, where Ursus and Dea are on board a boat that is about to sail. Gwynplaine makes himself known, but the shock of joy kills Dea. He thereupon throws himself into the water and is drowned.

Hommes de bonne volonté, Les (1932–47), the collective title of 27 novels by Romains: *Le 6 Octobre, Crime de Quinette, Les Amours enfantines,* and *Éros de Paris* (all 1932); *Les Superbes* and *Les Humbles* (both 1933); *Recherche d'une église* and *Province* (both 1934); *Montée des périls* (1935); *Les Pouvoirs, Recours à l'abîme,* and *Les Créateurs* (all 1936); *Mission à Rome, Le Drapeau noir,* and *Prélude à Verdun* (all 1937); *Verdun* (1938); *Vorge contre Quinette* and *La Douceur de la vie* (both 1939); *Cette grande lueur à l'est* and *Le Monde est ton aventure* (both 1941); *Journées dans la montagne* (1942); *Les Travaux et les joies* (1943); *Naissance de la bande* and *Comparutions* (both 1944); *Le Tapis magique* and *Françoise* (both 1946); *Le 7 Octobre* (1947).

The whole forms a survey of French life and thought, and to some extent of modern civilization, between 1908 and 1933. The work ranges from the worlds of politics (both local and international), diplomacy, the Church, industry, literature (with glimpses of *Académie française* circles and of 'abstract' poets at work), and science, to the very seamy side of life. It includes (vols. XV and XVI) an absorbing and emotional, but restrained, picture of France fighting for her existence in the 1914-18 war (not least against profiteers). It differs from, for example, Balzac's *Comédie humaine*, Zola's *Les *Rougon-Macquart*, or Rolland's *Jean-Christophe*, in having no scientific theory to demonstrate, no central character in whose life-history all the other characters are involved, and no artificial links between the volumes for the sake of plot or unity. Individuals and groups, in high and low life, in Paris and the provinces, are studied for a while and then dropped, perhaps for good, while others come to the fore. Romains's technique, in turn panoramic and detailed, gives the reader a window-seat view of life, with all the sense of the haphazard and the incomplete that this entails. The impression finally intended— and broadly achieved—is of the forces of good will struggling to make headway against the inert and destructive forces of ignorance and greed. Two characters who reappear frequently are Pierre Jallez and Jean Jerphanion, young men of good will, who make friends on entering the *École normale supérieure*. Jallez, a Parisian, already sophisticated, will become a novelist and journalist, an intellectual with a strong streak of sensuality (*La Douceur de la vie* is about an interlude in his life). Jerphanion, a raw, uncouth lad from the Massif central, will become a successful, and honest, politician. Their walks across Paris and conversations about life form the greater part of vols. III and IV; in vol. XX they visit Russia together.

Honorine, *v. Comédie humaine, La* (*Scènes de la vie privée*).

Horace, a tragedy by Corneille, produced 1640; based on Livy's story of the Horatii and the Curiatii, with the addition of the character of Sabine.

Rome and Alba are at war. The issue is to be decided by the combat of three champions on each side: Horace and his brothers for Rome, Curiace and his brothers for Alba. The two families are bound by close ties: Horace is married to Curiace's sister Sabine, Curiace is betrothed to Horace's sister Camille. Horace welcomes this chance to sacrifice all other interests to patriotism; the more sensitive and humane Curiace is appalled, but resolute. In the course of the combat, news is brought that Horace, his brothers having been slain, is fleeing from his three foes. His old father laments his disgrace and vows that Horace shall die for it that very night. A revulsion of feeling comes when it is learnt that Horace's flight was a feint, to enable him to kill his adversaries separately. As he returns victorious, Camille meets him. She laments the death of her betrothed, and her fierce denunciation of Rome so infuriates Horace that he kills her. Brought before the king for this crime, he hardly deigns to defend himself. Sabine, appalled at her fate as the wife of the slayer of her brothers, asks that her life be taken in place of his. His father pleads for him, and the king decides that his glorious deed effaces his crime.

Horla, Le, *v. Maupassant*.

Horn, Roman de, a 12th-c. *Anglo-Norman verse romance (in monorhyme stanzas, the form of the *chansons de geste*). There is an English version, *King Horn*.

The Saracens have occupied the kingdom of Suddene, killed its king, and found his young son Horn hidden in a garden with 15 companions. The children are turned adrift in a boat and carried to Brittany, where they are kindly received by the king, Hunlaf. Horn, educated by the seneschal Herland, comes to excel in knightly qualities, and Rigmel, Hunlaf's daughter, falls in love with him. He valiantly defeats a Saracen invasion, after which he and Rigmel plight their troth.

But Horn's cousin Wikele traduces them to Hunlaf, and Horn is banished, after receiving a magic ring from Rigmel. He goes to Ireland as a poor adventurer named Gudmod. He is well received by the king, Gudereche, and again defeats a Saracen invasion, in which the king's sons are killed. The king offers him his realm and his daughter. Horn, faithful to Rigmel, declines. Hearing that, under pressure from Hunlaf and Wikele, Rigmel is to marry Modin, king of Fenoie, he returns to Brittany with a band of followers, arrives at the marriage feast disguised as a pilgrim, is recognized by Rigmel (thanks to the ring), defeats Modin, and threatens Hunlaf's city. Hunlaf makes peace with Horn and gives him Rigmel. Horn pardons Wikele. He now reconquers Suddene from the Saracens and is reunited with his mother, who had survived there in hiding. He foils a plot by which Wikele attempts to get possession of Rigmel (who has remained in Brittany), slays him, then lives happily with Rigmel in Suddene.

Hôtel Carnavalet, v. Sévigné; Musée Carnavalet.

Hôtel d'Argent, in Paris, near Les Halles, was leased as a theatre in the 16th and 17th cs. to companies from the provinces. v. Theatres and Theatre Companies.

Hôtel de Bourgogne, in Paris, near Les Halles, originally a residence of the dukes of Burgundy. Only the fine Tour (or Donjon) de *Jean sans Peur survives. For its connection with the theatre v. Confrérie de la Passion; Theatres and Theatre Companies.

Hôtel de Rambouillet, v. Rambouillet.

Hôtel des Haricots, a nickname for the former *Collège de Montaigu (its students were said to have been fed mainly on beans), the first place used as a prison for delinquent members of the *Garde nationale. The prison changed quarters several times, but the name stuck. During the July Monarchy—when it was in the Rue de la Gare, behind the *Jardin des

Plantes—certain relatively comfortable cellules des artistes were reserved for artists and writers, who drew and wrote on the walls. These cells were later removed to the *Musée Carnavalet.

Hôtel des Invalides, v. Invalides.

Hôtel des Tournelles, in the *Marais quarter of Paris, a royal residence standing in a wood, used by Louis XI, Charles VIII, Louis XII, and François Ier; Louis XII and Henri II died there. Under Henri IV its site was used to create the *Place Royale.

Hôtel de Ville, the Town Hall or Guildhall in French towns. The Hôtel de Ville in Paris stands on the site of a house in the Place de *Grève bought in 1357 by É. Marcel, prévôt de la Hanse des marchands par eau (the guild which controlled the water trade of the city and out of which the municipality developed), to replace the Parloir aux bourgeois (in the Place du *Châtelet). Soon known as the Ostel de Ville, it was the residence of the prévôt des marchands, enlarged and rebuilt at various dates, and long the centre of the political as well as the municipal life of Paris (e.g. seat of the *Commune de Paris, 1789–94; seat of the provisional government after the 1848 *Revolution). Since the First Empire it has been the seat of the *préfet of the *département in which Paris lies (Seine till 1964, now Ville-de-Paris); v. Maire de Paris. The present building (opened 1880) replaced that occupied and finally burnt down by the *Commune in 1871.

Hôtel-Dieu, L', the oldest hospital in Paris, now a public assistance hospital. It goes back, under various names, to a 7th-c. hospice beside the church of Notre-Dame (where it still stands, though not on the original site). Here, until it was secularized in the 16th c., the aged and sick poor were maintained by the clergy. Louis IX was a notable benefactor (cf. Santé, La).

Hôtel Drouot, the usual name for the

Hôtel des Ventes mobilières, well-known sale-rooms in the Rue Drouot in Paris—the counterpart of Sotheby's or Christie's in London.

Hotman, FRANÇOIS (1524–90), a *Huguenot and a jurist. His works include *Franco-Gallia* (1573; Fr. trans. 1574), professing to show with the aid of history that monarchy should be elective and constitutional (*v. Bodin*); an *Épître envoyée au Tigre de la France*, attacking the cardinal de Lorraine (*v. Guise*); a translation of Plato's *Apology*.

Houdar de la Motte, ANTOINE (1672–1731), a talented poet and critic. He long suffered from paralysis and partial blindness, but frequented the *salons of the day and the court of the duchesse du Maine. His works include *Odes* (in fact, verse dissertations on such themes as 'Bienfaisance', 'Émulation'), accompanied by a discourse on poetry in general (1709); *Fables* (1719); dramas (*Les Originaux*, 1693, comedy; *Les Macchabées*, 1722, a lyrical tragedy; *Inès de Castro*, 1723, a very successful tragedy); and various discourses on tragedy (1730). He supported the *modernes* in the *Querelle des anciens et des modernes* and wrote (1714) a verse adaptation of the *Iliad* designed to suit the manners of a polite age (*v. Dacier*). His literary views were influenced by those of his friend Fontenelle. He advanced the theory that poetry (as distinct from verse) is independent of conventional form (metre and rhyme) and can be expressed in prose. He condemned slavish adherence to the *Classical dramatic conventions (inc. the unities), making the spectator's pleasure the supreme criterion. But he did not often practise these revolutionary precepts in his own plays. *v. La Chaussée*.

Houdetot, ÉLISABETH-SOPHIE DE LA LIVE DE BELLEGARDE, COMTESSE D' (1730–1813), the sprightly, amiable sister-in-law of Mme d'Épinay. J.-J. Rousseau fell passionately in love with her, but she remained faithful to Saint-Lambert. Rousseau's passion influenced the composition of *La *Nouvelle Héloïse*.

Houdon, JEAN-ANTOINE (*c.* 1741–1828), sculptor, noted for his busts and statues of contemporaries, e.g. Voltaire, Buffon, Diderot, J.-J. Rousseau, Washington, Franklin.

Houssaye, ARSÈNE (1815–96), man of letters, sometime director of the *Comédie-Française*, and prominent in literary life. He published informative *Confessions: souvenirs d'un demi-siècle (1830–80)* (1885, 4 vols.; a further 2 vols., 1891, extended the period to 1890), an amusing *Histoire du 41ᵉ fauteuil de l'Académie française* (1855; membership of the *Académie* is limited to 40), and many forgotten novels.

Housse partie, La, a *fabliau. There are many European versions of the story. An ungrateful son, about to drive his aged father from his house, consents to give him a horse-cloth for a cloak, and sends his own son to fetch it. The child cuts it in two and brings only one half to his grandfather. 'Why?' asks the father. 'Because,' replies the child, 'I have kept the other half for you, when you are old in your turn.' The child's father is thus shamed into changing his mind.

Houville, **Gérard d'**, *pseudonym of* MARIE DE RÉGNIER (1875–1963), daughter of Heredia and wife of H. de Régnier. She wrote poems (*Le Diadème de Flores: poèmes en prose*, 1925; *Poésies*, 1930), conventional in form, on themes of love, nature, and death, or, like those of her father, on classical themes; also novels (e.g. *L'Inconstante*, 1903; *L'Esclave*, 1905; *Le Temps d'aimer*, 1915).

Hozier, PIERRE DE LA GARDE D' (1592–1660) and his son RENÉ (1640–1732), genealogists. Their name has been adopted as a generic term for genealogical works.

Hubert, St. (d. 727), bishop of Maestricht and Liège, the patron saint of hunters.

Huc, PHILIPPE, *v. Derème*.

Huet, PIERRE-DANIEL (1630–1721), a

learned scholar, bishop of Soissons and later of Avranches. He began, under Bossuet, the edition of the classics *ad usum Delphini* (i.e. for 'le *Grand Dauphin'). *La Fontaine's *Épître à Huet* is addressed to him, and Ménage corresponded with him. His letters have been published, also various learned works, e.g. *De interpretatione* (1661; a dialogue on translation), *Traité de l'origine des romans* (1670; first publ. as an introduction to his friend Mme de *La Fayette's *Zayde*), *Censura philosophiae Cartesianae* (1689), *Histoire du commerce et de la navigation des anciens* (1716).

Hugo, ABEL (1798–1855), brother of Victor Hugo, with whom he founded *Le *Conservateur littéraire*. His later interests were in Spanish literature and history.

Hugo, CHARLES-VICTOR (1826–71), son of Victor Hugo, co-editor of *L'*Événement* and for a time (1848) Lamartine's secretary at the *Ministère des Affaires étrangères*. He followed his father into exile and on his return to Paris helped to found *Le *Rappel*.

Hugo, EUGÈNE (1800–37), brother of Victor Hugo, had himself begun to write, but in 1822, the day after Victor's marriage to Adèle Foucher, whom he too loved, he suffered a severe mental collapse from which he never recovered.

Hugo, JEAN-FRANÇOIS-VICTOR (1828–73), son of Victor Hugo, followed his father into exile and passed the time studying English. He published translations and studies of Shakespeare's plays (1859–65; with a preface, 1865, by his father) and was the first to translate his *Sonnets* (1857).

Hugo, VICTOR-MARIE (1802–85), the greatest French poet of the 19th c., also novelist and dramatist, and the grand figure of the *Romantic movement. He was born at Besançon, where his father, a general of Napoleon's armies, was stationed. Over the next 10 years the general's military duties took him—and his family—to Corsica, Italy, and Spain.

From 1812, when his parents separated, the young Victor lived in Paris with his mother and his brothers Abel and Eugène (*v. Rayons et les ombres, Les*).

His decision to be a writer (a Chateaubriand or nothing) was taken early. A poem he wrote while still at school was noticed by the *Académie; he also won a prize at the *Jeux floraux de Toulouse. In 1819, he and Abel, aged respectively 17 and 21, founded the *Conservateur littéraire. In 1822—the year of his marriage to Adèle *Foucher—his first collection of poems (*Odes et poésies diverses*) came to the notice of Louis XVIII, who awarded him a small pension. His novel *Han d'Islande (1823) brought him another pension and gained him the friendship of Nodier, leader of the first Romantic *cénacle. The second *cénacle* was led by Hugo himself, and met at his home. This was the period of his close friendship with *Sainte-Beuve: it ended sadly, but had fruitful literary consequences. His third collection of poems, *Odes et ballades (1826), introduced a period of amazing literary productivity—novels, essays, travel literature, five more collections of poems, and most of his plays (*v.* list below). This ended suddenly in 1843. He had been disheartened by the failure of *Les *Burgraves* and prostrated by the death of his eldest daughter, Léopoldine, in a boating accident (*v. Contemplations, Les*): he had also, with success and the years, developed political ambitions.

These now occupied him. After his youthful ultra-Royalism, he had accepted the constitutional monarchy of Louis-Philippe, who duly created him a *pair de France (1845). But, after the 1848 *Revolution, his growing Republican sympathies (already apparent in many poems of *Les Chants du crépuscule*) came to the fore. He was elected to the *Assemblée législative and supported measures for free education, universal male suffrage, etc. Moreover, his articles in *L'*Événement*, a paper he founded in 1848, did much to facilitate the rise to power of Louis-Napoléon (*v. Légende napoléonienne*). Being politically ambitious, he was bitter at not being offered high office in the government formed by Louis-Napoléon as Prince-President. With the *coup d'état* of 2 December 1851, his resentment gave way to full-blooded fury. Preferring exile to the Second Empire, he left Paris, disguised as a workman. After some months in Brussels, he went to Jersey (1853), then settled (1855) in Guernsey, at Hauteville House. His family and a few devoted friends, including his mistress Juliette *Drouet, shared his exile. Friends from the mainland visited him at intervals. At one period he went through a spiritualist phase, and even believed that spirits were dictating poems to him. But his life was essentially solitary; his most real companion was the sea.

When the Second Empire fell (1870; *v. Rappel, Le*), he returned to Paris to find that a *légende Victor Hugo* had arisen in his absence. He was triumphantly elected to the *Assemblée nationale*. But his influence waned: the *Assemblée* was not prepared to accept his gospel of a universal republic; the *Communards* doubted his readiness to translate his Republican sympathies into action. *L'Année terrible* (1872; poems inspired by the events of 1870–1—not his finest verse) restored his prestige and he was elected to the *Sénat. He had no political influence, but was now, by reason of his genius, his age, and his battles for the liberty of the people and the arts alike, a national figure. His health failed after 1878. His funeral has often been described (e.g. in Barrès's *Les *Déracinés*; L. *Daudet's *Souvenirs*). After lying in state under the *Arc de Triomphe, guarded by *cuirassiers* with lighted torches, his body was borne (on a pauper's hearse, as he had wished) across Paris to be buried in the *Panthéon.

His literary career falls into two parts. During the first he was, even if not always the prime innovator, the inspired torch-bearer, champion, and theorist of Romanticism, essaying—and revolutionizing—all *genres*. As a dramatist, he waged war against the old conventions (*v. Cromwell*) and won the day with *Hernani*. His *Notre-Dame de Paris* was a revelation of what an historical novel could be. To

poetry he brought a new sense of the beauty of words and of the lyrical resources of the French language. He also took daring liberties with versification, introducing new rhythms and liberating the *alexandrine with striking *enjambements* and unusual placing of the caesura. These, and his disregard for the periphrases of poetic diction, aroused storms of protest from the critics, though later poets were to adopt them as a matter of course. Generally, as opposed to technically, his great service to French poetry was that he established the *moi*, or continual laying bare of the self, of the Romantics. But as his genius developed the self he had to communicate became increasingly the self in relation to life in general. It was on this wider conception of the poet's function that the first phase of his literary career ended (1843).

The second phase opened with the savage invective of *Napoléon le petit (1852) and Les *Châtiments (1853). A quieter period followed, with the literary and political world of Paris behind him. He now elaborated his theory of the poet (i.e. himself) as a man of ideas, a torch-bearer who should lead the people and interpret the events of history and civilization. To this, as time passed, he joined a vast, phantasmagoric conception of a universe that had come into being through man's imperfection, in which original sin had been transmuted into matter, and where all forms of life, animal, vegetable, or mineral, imprisoned some haunted soul expiating the sins of a previous existence. The philosophy is negligible, though Hugo, whose vanity was as colossal as his genius, insisted on its value. Its importance is that it released a torrent of words, symbols, and images, and some visionary writing of the highest order (e.g. in Les *Contemplations, vol. II; in *La Fin de Satan* and *Dieu*—*v. Légende des siècles*). But such ideas by no means dominated his output in this period. His varied inspiration is sufficiently indicated by the earlier epics of the *Légende des siècles* (and *v. Epic Poetry*), the elegiac verse in *Les Contemplations*, and the lighter, more pastoral lyrics of the *Chansons des* *rues et des bois*; while the novels *Les *Misérables* and *Les *Travailleurs de la mer* reveal his interest in sociological problems and his gift for vivid, pictorial writing.

The following list is merely a selection from his vast output; works already mentioned are included for the sake of chronology. POETRY: *Odes et poésies diverses* (1822), *Nouvelles Odes* (1824), *Odes et ballades* (1826), *Les *Orientales* (1829), *Les *Feuilles d'automne* (1831), *Les Chants du crépuscule* (1835), *Les *Voix intérieures* (1837), *Les *Rayons et les ombres* (1840), *Les *Châtiments* (1853), *Les *Contemplations* (1856), *La *Légende des siècles* (1859–83), *Les Chansons des rues et des bois* (1865), *L'Année terrible* (1872), *L'Art d'être grand-père* (1877; lyrics of family life and love), *Le Pape* (1878), *La Pitié suprême* (1879), *L'Âne* (1880), *Religions et religion* (1880), *Les Quatre Vents de l'esprit* (1881; the last collection publ. in his lifetime, so named because of its division into 4 bks.—satiric, dramatic, epic, and lyric—the forms his inspiration had always taken), *La Fin de Satan* and *Dieu* (1886 and 1891; v. *Légende des siècles*), *Toute la lyre* (1888–93), *Années funestes* (1898), *Dernière Gerbe* (1902). NOVELS: *Han d'Islande* (1823), *Bug-Jargal* (1826), *Le *Dernier Jour d'un condamné* (1829), *Notre-Dame de Paris* (1831), *Claude Gueux* (1834), *Les *Misérables* (1862), *Les *Travailleurs de la mer* (1866), *L'*Homme qui rit* (1869), *Quatre-vingt-treize* (1873). DRAMA: *Cromwell* (1827; verse), *Amy Robsart* (1828; prose), *Hernani* (1830; verse), *Marion de Lorme* (1831; verse), *Le *Roi s'amuse* (1832; verse), *Lucrèce Borgia* (1833; prose), *Marie Tudor* (1833; prose), *Angelo* (1835; prose), *Ruy Blas* (1838; verse), *Les *Burgraves* (1843; verse), *Torquemada* (1882; verse), *Le Théâtre en liberté* (1886; short plays). POLITICAL, CRITICAL, AND OTHER WRITINGS: *Étude sur Mirabeau* (1834), *Littérature et philosophie mêlées* (1834), *Le *Rhin* (1842), *Napoléon le petit* (1852), *Histoire d'un crime* (1877), *William Shakespeare* (1864), *Actes et paroles* (I. *Avant l'exil*, 1841–51; II. *Pendant l'exil*, 1852–70; III, IV. *Depuis*

l'exil, 1870–85), and *Choses vues* (1887–1900), his journal.

Huguenots, a name applied from *c.* 1560 to the Calvinist French Protestants (*v.* Calvin; *Évangélisme*). In 1559, at the Synod of Paris, the French Protestant Church, long ruthlessly persecuted, formally organized itself on a Calvinist basis. The movement was fiercely resisted by the *Guises (who came to power, with the accession of François II, shortly after the Synod; v. *Amboise), but by 1561 there were 2,000 Calvinist churches in France and the Huguenots had become a political faction that appeared to endanger the State. From 1562 to 1594 there was almost continuous civil war between the Huguenots and the Catholic majority, in which both sides had help from abroad (*v. Bartholomew, Massacre of St.*; Ligue, La; Coligny; La Noue; Henri IV*). The famous Edict of Nantes (13 April 1598), whereby Henri IV—having abjured the Protestant faith (a triumph for the Catholic faction) and won recognition as king—sought to pacify his realm, reflected the influence of the *Politiques* (a political party of moderate Catholics who advocated religious toleration and had earlier made an alliance with the Huguenots) and the efforts of such Huguenot leaders as Duplessis-Mornay. By this edict the Protestants were granted liberty of conscience, the right of public worship in the castles of the nobility and certain specified localities, admissibility to all public offices, judicial protection, the right of assembly (every three years their deputies might meet to present their complaints to the government), and, for their better security, the right to garrison over 100 fortified towns (e.g. La Rochelle, Montauban, Saumur, Montpellier, Cognac) at State expense. The Huguenots, now in effect a state within a state, continued to be a disruptive element until their fortress of La Rochelle was reduced in 1628 (*v. Rohan, duc de*). Under Louis XIV, continual attempts were made to nullify the concessions of the edict, and it was finally revoked on 18 October 1685. Many Huguenots were forced by *dragon-*

nades and similar methods to apostatize and some 300,000 sought refuge abroad (in Holland, England, Switzerland, etc.). In 1702–5 Huguenot extremists raised the rebellion of the *Camisards; it failed, and thereafter their influence was negligible. Marriages conducted by Huguenot ministers were not recognized by the State till 1787, and only in 1802 was the legal standing of the Huguenot Church established. For some of the writers, scholars, etc., associated with the Huguenot cause *v. Aubigné; Basnage de Beauval; Claude; Du Bartas; Gamon; Hotman; Jurieu; La Ramée; Montchrétien; Palissy. v.* also *Vache à Colas; Calas; Peyrat.*

Hugues Capet (*c.* 938–996), son of Hugues le Grand (d. 956) and grandson of Robert Ier; king of France (first of the *Capetian dynasty) in succession to Louis V, r. 987–96. He was placed on the throne by the nobles in preference to a *Carolingian claimant.

Huis clos, v. Sartre.

Huitain, in French prosody, a stanza of eight lines (octosyllables or decasyllables) usually rhyming a b a b b c b c. *v. Villon.*

Hulot, Baron, in Balzac's *La *Cousine Bette.*

Humanism, *v. Renaissance.*

Humanisme, *v. Gregh.*

Humilis, *v. Nouveau.*

Hundred Days, The, *v. Cent Jours, Les.*

Huon de Bordeaux, a 13th-c. *chanson de geste (*Charlemagne cycle), typical of the later period in its introduction of marvellous and amusing adventures. An English translation by Lord Berners was printed by Wynkyn de Worde (1534). The story is the theme of Gluck's opera *Oberon* and provided Shakespeare with the fairy king in *A Midsummer Night's Dream.*

Huon, treacherously attacked by Charlot, son of the aged Charlemagne,

kills him, not knowing who he is. Despite Huon's success in an ordeal by battle, Charlemagne condemns him to death, but reprieves him on condition that he will go to the court of Gaudisse, emir of Babylon, bring back his beard and four of his teeth, and kiss his daughter Esclarmonde. Huon, assisted by the fairy king Oberon, performs all these tasks.

Huon de Rotelande, a 12th-c. *Anglo-Norman poet, author of the verse romances *Ipomedon and *Protesilaus.*

Huon le Roi (13th c.), author of *Le *Vair Palefroi.* He, or a different Huon le Roi, also wrote poems on religious themes.

Huret, JULES, *v. Naturalism.*

Huron, Le. The early French settlers in Canada gave the name *Huron* (from *hure,* 'shock of hair') to the Iroquois Indians in the regions round Toronto. In 18th-c. France, 'le Huron' became a term for the uncouth but noble savage who comes to Europe from the wilds and is amazed at the paradoxes of civilization. *v. Lahontan; cf.* Voltaire's *L'*Ingénu.*

Husson, JULES, *v. Champfleury.*

Huysmans, JORIS-KARL (1848–1907), novelist and art critic of Dutch descent, born and educated in Paris. For 30 years, till 1898, he combined his writing with a post in the *Sûreté; from 1899 to 1901 he was an oblate in the Benedictine abbey of Ligugé, near Poitiers. His first publication was *Le Drageoir aux épices* (1874), prose poems and short sketches. For some years thereafter his output—more usually tales than full-length novels—typified *Naturalism at its dingiest, e.g. *Marthe, histoire d'une fille* (1876), *Les Sœurs Vatard* (1879; drawn from two sisters employed in a book-binding business he inherited), *Croquis parisiens* (1880), *En ménage* (1881), **A vau l'eau* (1882), *En rade* (1887), *Sac au dos* (a tale he wrote for *Les *Soirées de Médan,* 1880). His novel *A rebours (1884) is often cited as the supreme expression of the *esprit décadent. A later series of novels, largely autobiographical, follows the spiritual progress of a man named Durtal: he arrives at Roman Catholicism by the perverse route of Satanism (*Là-bas*, 1891); goes into retreat at a Trappist monastery (*En route*, 1895); settles at Chartres (*La Cathédrale*, 1898)—the occasion for an elaborate account of the cathedral, with excursions into ecclesiastical symbolism, French church architecture, and hagiography; and ends, like Huysmans himself, as an oblate (*L'Oblat*, 1903). His art criticism includes *L'Art moderne* (1883) and *Certains* (1889),

some of the earliest appreciations of the *Impressionists; Trois Primitifs* (1904), essays on Matthias Grünewald. All his works are written in an elaborate, mannered style, full of neologisms and syntactical contortions. *v. Mugnier.*

Hydropathes, Les, *v. Symbolism.*

Hylas, in d'Urfé's *L'*Astrée.*

Hymne à l'Être Suprême, (1) *v. Desorgues;* (2) *v. Chénier, M.-J.*

I

Iambes, a name given by A. Chénier and A. Barbier to their satirical verse, in allusion to the Latin satirists who so often wrote in iambics.

Ibrahim, ou l'Illustre Bassa, v. Scudéry, M. and G. de.

Idéologues, a group of thinkers and writers of the Revolutionary and post-Revolutionary period, disciples of Condillac. They included Condorcet, Volney, Cabanis, and Antoine-Louis-Claude Destutt de Tracy (1754–1836), who expounded their philosophy in his *Éléments d'idéologie* (1801–5). They professed to establish a science of psychology (even seeking its basis in physiology) and upheld the doctrine of the perfectibility of man. (Incidentally, they judged literary works by the impression these produced on the reason, sensibility, or imagination, regardless of whether they conformed to the rules.) Under the Restoration, their doctrines were to some extent continued by a group of Republicans, political and philosophical theorists who believed that civil liberty and individual happiness must rest on political liberty.

Idiot de la famille, L', v. Sartre.

Iéna, *v. Jena.*

Igitur, ou la Folie d'Elbehnon, v. Mallarmé.

Île Bourbon, the name of the Île de la Réunion (Reunion Island, Indian Ocean) till the Revolution and again from 1815 to 1848.

Île de France, the setting of Bernardin de Saint-Pierre's *Paul et Virginie,* renamed Mauritius when it became British in 1810.

Île-de-France, one of the oldest *provinces* (and *v.* Map), so named from the 14th c., apparently because in shape it resembled an island formed by the rivers Seine, Marne, Ourcq, Aisne, and Oise. Except for a brief period in the late 10th c., it was always owned by the crown; and Paris was its centre. The name is still constantly used (*cf.* Eng. 'Home Counties'). *v. French Language.*

Île des pingouins, L' (1908), a satirical novel by A. France. Through the agency of an early Christian missionary, a colony of penguins on an Arctic island, metamorphosed into human beings, is transported in a state of primeval innocence to the coast of Brittany. Centuries pass, and the penguin-humans evolve into a modern, progressive people, who accept war and racial and industrial hatred in the name of civilization. There is an ironic description of the *Dreyfus case.

Île sonnante, L', v. Pantagruel.

Il faut qu'une porte soit ouverte ou fermée (1845, in the *Revue des Deux Mondes*; 1853, in *Comédies et Proverbes*), a prose *proverbe* by Musset; produced 1848. This is a witty, fencing dialogue between a comte and a marquise, characteristic of Musset's comedies in that deep emotion is seldom expressed, but is easy to sense. At intervals one or the other speaker opens the door to leave the room in disgust. In the end they admit their love and leave together.

Illuminations, Les, v. Rimbaud.

Illuminés, Les, v. Nerval.

Illuminisme, an occult philosophy based on the *Cabale* and akin to theosophy and the mystical doctrines of *Swedenborg, became known in France in the late 18th c., largely through the writings of Saint-Martin, and influenced such later writers as J. de Maistre, Ballanche, and Balzac. The *illuministes* held that man, an embodiment of God's thought, had been placed by Him in a dark world of symbols. When he had learnt to interpret these by developing his latent faculties, or by occult means, he would become an *illuministe,* one with God's radiance and the universal soul—and so able to understand and to practise the mysteries of divine creation. *v. Rosicrucianism.*

Illusion comique, L', a comedy by Corneille; probably produced 1635.

Clindor's father, filled with remorse at having years before driven him from home by harsh treatment, and anxious to learn his fate, consults a magician. The magician shows him a vision of his son acting as the agent of Matamore (a ridiculous, cowardly braggart) and engaged in an intrigue in which he wins Isabelle from Matamore and another rival, followed by a second vision in which Clindor and Isabelle lose their lives. The father is filled with despair, until it is further revealed to him that the pair are now members of a company of actors, who are seen dividing up the takings after performing the tragedy in which the two earlier appeared to have met their death. The play ends with an eloquent defence of the actor's profession.

Illusions perdues (1837–43; later in *La *Comédie humaine, Scènes de la vie de province*), a novel (in three closely connected tales) by Balzac. Lucien Chardon, an intelligent, handsome young poet, takes his mother's name, de Rubempré, and leaves Angoulême to win fame in Paris. He finds a corrupt literary world, where advancement depends on money and a journalist must be prepared to deride genius, puff filth, and climb to success over the reputation of his best friend. He succumbs to the city's evil influence and ruins his family. On the point of suicide, he meets the abbé Carlos Herrera (*Vautrin in disguise), who promises him wealth and success. His adventures are continued in *Splendeurs et misères des courtisanes. v. Lousteau.*

Illustrations de Gaule, v. Lemaire de Belges.

Illustre Gaudissart, L' (1833; later in *La *Comédie humaine, Scènes de la vie de province*), a novel by Balzac. Gaudissart, the archetypal commercial traveller, vulgar, bouncing, astute, and good-natured, also figures in *Splendeurs et misères des courtisanes, Le *Cousin Pons, *Histoire de la grandeur et de la décadence de César Birotteau, etc.

Illustre Théâtre, L', *v. Molière.*

Il ne faut jurer de rien (1836, in the *Revue des Deux Mondes*; 1840, in *Comédies et Proverbes*), a prose *proverbe* by Musset; produced 1848.

Valentin, the hero, wagers that he can prove that Cécile, whom his uncle wishes him to marry, will be a faithless coquette like the rest of her sex. He fails, for her innocence is incorruptible.

Il pleut, il pleut, bergère, v. *Fabre d'Églantine.*

Image du monde, L', an encyclopedic verse treatise written in 1247 by a cleric of Metz, probably named Gossouin, often called Gautier de Metz.

Images d'Épinal. Épinal, a town in the Vosges, was famous from the mid-18th c. for *images*, sheets of little coloured pictures illustrating legends, Bible stories, historical and contemporary events, life in foreign lands, etc.—a development from the woodcuts in almanacs and the *Bibliothèque bleue*. They were hawked and sold all over France (and are now collectors' rarities). The best were made by the Pellerin family (who figure in *Descaves's L'Imagier d'Épinal*). v. *Children's Reading.*

Imitation de Jésus-Christ. The most famous of many 17th-c. prose translations of Thomas à Kempis's *Imitation of Christ* is that of Le Maître de Saci (1662). There were also verse renderings, notably by Corneille (1651) and Desmarets de Saint-Sorlin (1654).

Imitation de Notre-Dame la Lune, L', v. *Laforgue.*

Immoraliste, L', v. *Gide.*

Immortels, Les, a name often applied to the members of the *Académie française*, possibly because the seal originally used for countersigning its documents bore a laurel wreath and the words 'A l'immortalité'. *Cf.* A. *Daudet's L'Immortel.*

Imposteur, L', v. *Tartuffe.*

Impressionism, Impressionist, a movement in art which had many affinities with *Symbolism in literature.

Manet's *Déjeuner sur l'herbe* had created a sensation at the *Salon des refusés* of 1863 (i.e. works refused for the *Salon proper), and he and a number of like-minded painters soon formed a new school. An exhibition of their works in 1874 (v. *Nadar*) included paintings by Boudin and Harpignies, two older artists; Berthe Morisot (1831–93); Camille Pissarro (1830–1903); Cézanne; Degas; Renoir; and Claude-Oscar Monet (1840–1926), whose picture of the sun rising over water was called *Impression, soleil levant*. Le *Charivari* ridiculed the artists as 'Impressionnistes' and their technique as 'Impressionnisme'.

The Impressionists broke with tradition, not only in technique, but also in their conception of what a painting should represent: 'On ne fait pas un paysage, une marine, une figure: on fait l'impression d'une heure de la journée dans un paysage, dans une marine, sur une figure' (from *Manet raconté par lui-même*, 1945). Just as the Symbolists were followed by various smaller literary groups (v. *Literary Isms*), so the Impressionists were followed by the groups to whom the art critic Roger Fry, in organizing an exhibition of their work in London in 1910, gave the all-embracing name of Post-Impressionists. They included Neo-Impressionists, Expressionists, the *Fauves* (prominent c. 1906, led by Matisse and including Georges Rouault (1871–1958), Maurice de Vlaminck (1876–1958), and Dufy), the *Nabis* (i.e. 'prophets', originally a group of art students, inflamed and exalted by their ideas; their first exhibition was in 1891), Cubists, etc., all of whom expressed some form of reaction against Impressionism. A feature of the increasing sympathy between writers and artists in the 20th c. is that most of these small movements had their counterparts in literature, or vice versa (e.g. *Cubism, *Surrealism). This close creative affinity is very apparent in the reminiscences and letters of 20th-c. writers and artists, e.g. Apollinaire, Breton, Carco, Cocteau, Jacob, Salmon.

Zola's *L'*Œuvre* depicts the first Impressionists and their doctrines. Mallarmé wrote about them and had friends among them (v. *Manet*). Fénéon and Huysmans were among the first critics to appreciate their work.

Impressions de théâtre, v. Lemaître, J.

Imprimerie nationale, L', the State printing office, f. 1640. Besides being responsible for all official government printing (*cf.* H.M. Stationery Office), it has also, from its earliest days, printed editions of French, classical, and Oriental texts which are recognized masterpieces of the art of book production. Sometimes the State undertakes the whole work of editing and production, in the interest of learning or art, sometimes it prints for private publishers. Its types are famous, e.g. *Garamond's 'Grecs du roi'; those designed to the order of Louis XIV, and still used; those specially cut for the printing of Oriental works.

It origins go back beyond its actual foundation. The art of printing (introduced in Paris in 1470) had long enjoyed royal protection. François Ier, when he founded the future *Collège de France* (1530), also encouraged the production of fine types (e.g. by Garamond) for the setting up of classical texts, and later created the office of king's printer. Its holders, men of great learning like the humanist R. Estienne, strove to ensure that royally sponsored printing should reach the highest standards of both beauty and scholarly accuracy. In the 17th c., Louis XIII, largely at Richelieu's instigation, granted privileges and exemptions which brought printing and publishing (*cf. Librairie*) under royal protection; and in 1640 he founded the *Imprimerie royale*, quartered in the *Louvre and entrusted with official printing, private printing for the royal household, and the printing of the great monuments of religion and literature. Time brought changes in both its name and its quarters. The *Imprimerie nationale*—so called during the Revolution and again since 1870—is now in the modern industrial quarter of Javel.

Its notable early productions include *De Imitatione Christi* (the first book it printed), the great collections of Oriental texts now in the *Bibliothèque nationale*, the *Cabinet du roi, *Buffon's *Histoire naturelle*.

Impromptu de Paris, L' (1937), a one-act prose comedy by Giraudoux, modelled on Molière's *L'*Impromptu de Versailles*. The scene is the stage of *Jouvet's *Théâtre de l'Athénée*. The company is about to rehearse when an intruder is spotted. He proves to be a government official seeking worthy outlets for surplus funds. The ensuing lively discussion is a vehicle for Giraudoux's views on the art and aims of the drama.

Impromptu de Versailles, L', a one-act prose comedy by Molière; produced 1663, soon withdrawn, and not published till after his death.

Boursault, believing that he had been ridiculed as Lysidas in Molière's *Critique de l'École des femmes*, had retorted in a play, *Le Portrait du peintre*. The king allowed Molière to defend himself in a comedy to be performed at court. He here presents himself and his company rehearsing a play for performance before the king, in which he ridicules Boursault, mimics the acting of various players of the *Hôtel de Bourgogne* (*v. Montfleury*), and scoffs at pedants, prudes, and the *précieuses* of the Hôtel de *Rambouillet. The mock rehearsal is of great interest as showing his methods behind the scenes. The play provoked various rejoinders, e.g. by Donneau de Visé (*v. Mercure galant*) and by a son of Montfleury.

Impulsionnisme, *v. Literary Isms.*

Incipit des poèmes français antérieurs au XVIe siècle, Les (1917), by Arthur Långfors, a bibliography of French poems down to 1500 (other than *chansons de geste* and lyrics) in the alphabetical order of their opening lines.

Inconstant, L', *v. Napoleon.*

Incorruptible, L', *v. Robespierre.*

Incroyables, young elegants (usually reactionaries) of *Directoire society. Their clothes and hair-styles were exaggerated; and they avoided pronouncing the letter r—'En véité, c'est incoyable!' was a favourite exclamation. *Cf. Merveilleuses*; *Muscadins*.

Indes galantes, Les, v. Rameau.

Indiana (1832), a novel by G. Sand (her first without a collaborator). It is typical of her early period—a farrago of romantic passion punctuated by fainting-fits, but also by fine descriptive passages.

Indiana, a beautiful Creole, escapes from the *Île Bourbon and a sadistic elderly husband to join Raymon de Ramière in France, but finds that this accomplished seducer has no further use for her. She is rescued *in extremis* by 'Sir' Brown, her cold, misunderstood, silently adoring English cousin. On his suggestion, they return to the Île Bourbon to commit suicide in a beauty spot designed by nature for this romantic purpose. They arrive vastly improved in health and spirits by a voyage spent mainly in discussing the virtues of suicide. At the last moment, he unburdens his heart to her, and she realizes that she loves him alone. He takes her in his arms for the death-leap—but plans miscarry. Years later they are found living idyllically, far from inhibiting conventions, in a log cabin.

Indifférence en matière de religion, Essai sur l', v. Lamennais.

Indulgents, v. Hébertistes.

Indy, PAUL-MARIE-THÉODORE-VINCENT D' (1851–1931), composer (symphonies, chamber music, etc.), a disciple of Franck, an admirer of Wagner, and founder of the *Schola Cantorum* (a school of—mainly—religious music). He was associated with *Symbolism.

Inès de Castro, daughter of a Castilian noble at the court of Alphonso IV of Portugal. Prince Pedro married her secretly and they lived in happy seclusion. The marriage was discovered, and the king authorized her murder. On his accession (1357), Pedro avenged her. The story is the theme of a tragedy by *Houdar de la Motte and of *Montherlant's *La Reine morte*, also of works by poets ranging from Camoens to W. S. Landor.

Infâme, L', v. Voltaire, 2.

Ingénu, L' (1767), a philosophical tale by Voltaire. It is a protest against abuses of power (e.g. *lettres de cachet*) and the absurdity of many of our conventions; there are thinly veiled allusions to high officials of the day.

A young French-Canadian, brought up among the *Huron Indians, comes to France and proves to be the lost nephew of an old prior and his sister. His reactions to social conventions and the tenets of Catholicism produce some comic situations. He helps to avert an English invasion of Brittany; and he falls in love with Mlle de Saint-Yves, a young Breton lady. But he is secretly denounced for his sympathy with the *Huguenots (the Edict of Nantes has just been revoked) and put in the *Bastille*. His searching observations on religious sectarianism shake the convictions of his cell-mate, a kindly *Jansenist priest. Mlle de Saint-Yves bravely goes to Versailles to secure her lover's release, but finds that she can only obtain it by giving herself to a powerful minister. Her confessor advises her to comply, which she does, after a cruel mental struggle. Both men are released, but she herself dies of grief and remorse.

Ingres, JEAN-AUGUSTE-DOMINIQUE (1780–1867), a painter (scenes from history, portraits) noted for the classical purity of his work and the firm yet delicate lines of his drawing. There was much rivalry between him and Delacroix. He is said to have fancied himself as a violinist—hence *un violon d'Ingres*, 'a secondary occupation, hobby'.

Institut catholique de Paris, the best known of the Roman Catholic universities established after freedom of education was restored by a law of 1875. Students are prepared for the State examinations.

Institut de France, a learned society. In 1795, the *Convention created an *Institut national* to replace the literary and scientific *Académies suppressed in 1793. This 'création grande et monstrueuse' comprised three *classes*: mathematical and physical sciences; moral and political sciences; literature and the fine arts. In 1803, moral and political sciences were dropped and it was reorganized in four *classes*: physical and mathematical sciences; French language and literature; ancient history and literature; fine arts. In 1806, it moved to its present quarters in the Palais Mazarin (*v. Collège des Quatre-Nations*) and was now called the *Institut de France*. A further reorganization (1816) restored the title *académie* to each *classe*, and priority of rank now followed original priority of creation as royal institutions, i.e. **Académie française* (*2ᵉ classe* of 1803), **Académie des Inscriptions et Belles-Lettres* (*3ᵉ classe* of 1803), **Académie des Sciences* (*1ʳᵉ classe* of 1803), *Académie des Beaux-Arts* (the **Académie royale de Peinture et de Sculpture* amalgamated with other bodies in 1795; *4ᵉ classe* of 1803). In 1832, the **Académie des Sciences morales et politiques* was restored as a fifth academy. All meet regularly as separate bodies and also, in joint session, as the *Institut*.

Institut d'Études politiques, *v. Écoles spéciales*.

Institution de la religion chrétienne (1541; augm. ed. 1560), Calvin's translation of his famous *Christianae religionis institutio* (Basle 1536; Strasbourg 1539, rev. and augm.).

The work was intended as a reply to writings critical of the new religion and as an introduction and guide to the Scriptures. Rejecting the old scholastic methods of theological discussion and writing with passionate earnestness and freedom from pedantry, Calvin bases his defence of morality and the Reformed faith on the character of man as a moral being and on the text of the Scriptures. His dominant doctrine, derived from St. Paul, is that of predestination, by which some are predestined to eternal life, others to eternal damnation. He refutes the contrary opinions of various Fathers, anticipates objections based on human ideas of justice, and criticizes Roman Catholic doctrines.

Instrumentisme; Intégralisme, *v. Literary Isms*.

Intendant, under the monarchy, a direct representative of the king in the provinces, with control over judicial, fiscal, police, and even military administration; an office created 1636 by Richelieu, and soon of growing importance. *v. Provinces*.

Intermédiaire des chercheurs et curieux, L' (1864–1940), a periodical devoted to the interchange of information on points of literary, historical, or antiquarian interest (*cf.* the Eng. *Notes and Queries*, f. 1849).

Intermezzo, *v. Giraudoux*.

Intimé, L', in Racine's *Les* *Plaideurs.

Intimisme, *v. Literary Isms*.

Introduction à la vie dévote, *v. François de Sales, St*.

Inutile Beauté, L', *v. Maupassant*.

Invalides, Hôtel des, in Paris, on the left bank of the Seine, originally a hospice for old and disabled soldiers built (1670–4, for the most part) to the order of Louis XIV; a fine building, designed by Libéral Bruant (d. 1697) and Mansard (dome of the chapel only). At one time it housed some 7,000 *invalides*; today there are barely 200 and it is the seat of the military governor of Paris and the home of the Army Museum. In the crypt under the golden dome of the chapel are Napoleon's tomb and a chamber containing Napoleonic relics (*v. Légende napoléonienne*).

Invitation au voyage, L', *v. Baudelaire*.

Ionesco, EUGÈNE (1912–), dramatist of Rumanian birth (a member of the *Académie, 1970), a leading exponent of the Theatre of the Absurd (*v. Theatre of the 19th and 20th cs.*). He settled permanently in France in 1938 and became a literary critic, writing for the *Cahiers du sud, the **Nouvelle Revue française*, etc. His first play, *La Cantatrice chauve* (1950), subtitled 'anti-play' and parodying every convention and assumption of the naturalistic theatre, already embodied his vision of a world where, owing to the pressures and institutions of organized *bourgeois* society (esp. marriage), man's moral and emotional life has become sterile and essentially absurd, where his individuality is so eroded that identities are interchangeable, and where language has broken down as a means of communication. His subsequent plays (often in one-act form) included *La Leçon* (1951), *Les Chaises* (1952), *Victimes du devoir* (1953), *Amédée, ou Comment s'en débarrasser* (1954), *Jacques, ou la Soumission* (1955), *L'Impromptu de l'Alma* (1956), *Le Nouveau Locataire* (1957), *Tueur sans gages* (1959), *Rhinocéros* (1960), *Le Roi se meurt* (1962), *Le Piéton de l'air* (1963), *La Soif et la faim* (1966), *Au pied du mur* (1966), *Jeux de massacre* (1970). He seeks to create 'a new language of the theatre', dispensing with received ideas of plot and character, of rational coherence and probability, and employing visual imagery, verbal rhythm, gesture, and balletic movement in a bid to penetrate beyond reality. He presents a highly disturbing world where there are no true human relationships, where language can become a lethal physical weapon (*La Leçon*), and where grotesque or horrifying events or objects (e.g. the corpse growing bigger and bigger in *Amédée*) symbolize man's condition. His bizarre juxtaposition of the real and the fantastic, and his free use of puns and dreams, recall the *Surrealists. *La Cantatrice chauve* (*The Bald Prima Donna*), now a classic of the modern repertory, and many of his other plays have been produced in translation in England. He has also published short stories, *La Photo du colonel* (1962); *Notes et contre-notes* (1962), on the theatre; *Journal en miettes* (1967) and *Présent passé passé présent* (1968), autobiographical fragments.

Iphigénie en Aulide, a tragedy by Racine, based, with important changes, on the play of Euripides; produced 1674.

The Greek fleet, ready to sail from Aulis against Troy, is detained by contrary winds. An oracle has demanded, as the price of its release, the sacrifice of Iphigénie. The priest Calchas and Ulysse have insisted that her father Agamemnon shall sacrifice her. Torn between love for his daughter and obedience to the gods, he summons her from Argos on the pretext that Achille, her betrothed, wishes to marry her before he sails, then tries in vain to revoke the summons. Iphigénie and her mother Clytemnestre arrive. She is to be led to the altar in the belief that she is to be married there; but the true intention is revealed. Clytemnestre and Achille are outraged; the gentle Iphigénie, prepared to accept her fate, tries to deter Achille from resisting her father's order. Agamemnon, shaken by Clytemnestre's fierce imprecations, finally tells mother and daughter to depart secretly from the camp. But this plan is disclosed to Calchas by Ériphile (a character invented by Racine), a young captive of Achille, of unknown birth, who loves him and hopes to win him through the death of his betrothed. Iphigénie is led to the altar, and a struggle breaks out between Achille with his supporters and the rest of the army. Calchas now intervenes to declare that the gods have explained their oracle to him: the victim they require is Ériphile, who is a child of Theseus and Helen, named Iphigenia at her birth. Ériphile rushes to the altar and takes her own life.

Ipomedon, a 12th-c. *Anglo-Norman verse *roman d'aventure* by Huon de Rotelande. There are two English versions.

The scene is S. Italy and Sicily. Ipomedon is a young prince in love with a princess who will wed only the best knight in the world. He performs the greatest feats, but always conceals his identity, except from the lady, while ostensibly behaving like a coward and a fool, to her confusion. Finally, his true character is revealed to all, and the lovers are united.

Irène (1778), a 5-act verse tragedy by Voltaire, chiefly memorable as the occasion of his 'apotheosis' (*v. Voltaire*, 1).

The plot turns on the love between Irène, married against her will to the tyrant Nicéphore, emperor of Constantinople, and Prince Alexis Comnenius of Greece, whose throne Nicéphore has usurped. Alexis engineers a revolt in which Nicéphore is killed. Irène, now free to marry him, decides that her very joy means that her love for him was guilty and kills herself.

Iron Crown, The, the gold crown of the Lombard kings in which was set an iron circlet said to have been made from nails of the Cross. Charlemagne was crowned with it after his conquest of the Lombards (774). It is preserved at Monza.

Iron Mask, Man in the, v. *Masque*.

Irrésolu, L', v. *Destouches*.

Isabelle, in Racine's *Les *Plaideurs*.

Isabelle, v. *Gide*.

Isabey, JEAN-BAPTISTE (1767–1855), miniaturist and caricaturist. At first a decorator of snuff-boxes and coat-buttons, he rose to be a painter of royalties and notabilities and a designer of decorations and the settings for ceremonies, e.g. the *Légion d'honneur*, Napoleon's coronation.

Isengrin, v. *Ysengrin*.

Iseut, v. *Tristan* (*Tristram*).

Ismène, in Racine's *Phèdre*.

Isolement, L', v. *Méditations poétiques*.

Isopet, v. *Marie de France*.

Isou, Isidore, v. *Literary Isms*.

Italian Influence, v. *Foreign Influences*.

Italiens, Les, the name given to the various Italian troupes who came to France from the mid-16th c. and were authorized to play Italian *commedia dell'arte* (with such stock characters as *Arlequin, *Colombine, *Polichinelle, *Scaramouche, *Trivelin), notably the *Gelosi*, invited to France in 1576 by Henri III, and the company of Tiberio Fiorillo (a famous Scaramouche), who came to Paris in 1639 and later shared a theatre with Molière's company. With increasing frequency and audacity these gifted and popular players introduced scenes in French into their farces, parodied tragedies, and in general exceeded the limits assigned to their performances. Regnard and Dufresny wrote for them at this time. They were expelled in 1697, ostensibly for indecency, in fact for ridiculing Mme de Maintenon in a piece called *La Fausse Prude*. They returned in 1716 (after Louis XIV's death), and Marivaux and Lesage now wrote for them. In 1762 they were fused with the *Théâtre de la Foire* as the *Comédie-Italienne*. v. *Opéra-Comique*; *Theatres and Theatre Companies*.

Itinéraire de Paris à Jérusalem et de Jérusalem à Paris, L' (1811, 3 vols.), by Chateaubriand, describes his journey of 1806–7 to collect material for the setting of *Les *Martyrs*. Much of it is an historical account of the places visited, with long quotations from the Bible, early histories, voyages, etc.; but the sections on Greece and the Near East contain some of his best descriptive writing.

His servant Julien, who went with him, kept an illiterate record of the journey which was of some use to Chateaubriand when he came to edit his own work. It was published in 1904, *Itinéraire de Paris à Jérusalem par Julien, domestique de Chateaubriand* (ed. É. Champion).

Ivain, v. *Yvain*.

Ivry, Battle of, v. *Ligue, La*.

J

J'accuse, v. *Dreyfus*; *Zola*.

Jacob, Le Bibliophile, v. *Lacroix*.

Jacob, MAX (1876–1944), *Cubist poet of Jewish birth, came to Paris from Brittany and for many years lived penuriously among writers and artists. He was dramatically converted to Roman Catholicism (*c.* 1914) and after 1921 settled (with long absences in Paris or abroad) at Saint-Benoît-sur-Loire near the famous Benedictine abbey, writing and fervently practising his faith. He died in the German concentration camp at Drancy during the 1939–45 war. His works include *Le Cornet à dés* (1917), prose poems, partly autobiographical, written 1904–17; *La Défense de Tartufe: extases, remords, visions, prières, poèmes, et méditations d'un Juif converti* (1919); *Le Laboratoire central* (1921); *L'Homme de chair et l'homme reflet* (1924), a novel; *v.* also *Children's Reading*. His poetry was usually racy, punning, conversational, and ironic, shying away from deep emotion and sometimes mingling the everyday and the macabre in authentic ballad fashion (e.g. *Pour demain soir*, in *Rivage*, 1931).

Jacobins, Club des, the most famous political club of the *Revolution, f. 1789 at Versailles, mainly as a debating club, by a group of radical *députés* and at first called the *Club Breton* (because most of its members came from Brittany). It moved to Paris with the *Assemblée constituante* (Oct. 1789) and met in the former convent of the Dominican (*Jacobin*) friars in the Rue Saint-Honoré. In 1791 it was called the *Société des amis de la constitution*; after the monarchy fell it became the *Société des Jacobins, amis de la liberté et de l'égalité*. From being only mildly democratic, the *Jacobins* became a powerful, highly organized Revolutionary force, eventually dominated by Robespierre. They set up affiliated clubs all over France, and opened their ranks to radical politicians and journalists and their meetings to the public. After Robespierre fell they led a harassed existence and were finally suppressed (Nov. 1794). *v. Feuillants, Club des*.

Jacquemart Gelée, v. *Roman de Renart*.

Jacquemont, VICTOR (1801–32), naturalist, moved in scientific and literary circles in Paris, where his friends included Mérimée and Stendhal. Between 1828 and 1832 he undertook a one-man scientific expedition in British India for the *Jardin des Plantes*, recorded in the *Voyage dans l'Inde* (1841, 3 vols.; 1844, 3 vols. of maps and plates). Armed with many introductions from English scientific circles (he had been in England in 1825, spoke and wrote English, and was well received and popular wherever he went), he spent some months in Pondicherry learning Persian and Hindustani, then proceeded from Calcutta up through Kashmir and the Punjab and along the Tibetan border, travelling with the minimum of servants and equipment and enduring great privations. He died in Bombay, a few months before he was due to return home. His letters to his family and friends (1833, 2 vols.; 1867, a further collection; 1933, letters to Stendhal and the Swiss scientist Jean Charpentier) reveal a gay, affectionate nature, a certain thoughtful remoteness, sound common sense, and stoicism (notably in the sad last letter to his brother). They also give a perceptive, amusing, critical (but never censorious) picture of the British in India.

Jacquerie; Jacques Bonhomme. The peasant rising of 1358 in the *Île-de-France, caused by the suffering consequent upon the English invasion, was called the *Jacquerie*, from 'Jacques Bonhomme', a derogatory term for a peasant.

Jacques de Lalaing, Le Livre des faits de, a prose work of the later 15th c., of unknown authorship (sometimes attributed to Chastellain or La Sale), incorporating passages from contemporary chronicles. Jacques de Lalaing (a real person, who died in the mid-15th c.) is an accomplished knight who goes about Europe performing feats of chivalry at tourneys.

Jacques de Vitry (d. 1240), bishop of Acre. Collections of his Latin *exempla* (*v. Exemple*) have been published.

Jacques le fataliste (1796; 1792, in German—*cf. Le *Neveu de Rameau*), by Diderot, a novel inspired by Sterne's *Tristram Shandy*, which it rivals for incoherence and digressions, but not for quality. Jacques, like the author, is a fatalist and an indefatigable talker. His conversations with his master in the course of their random travels and adventures are vividly recounted. The main thread is the story of his disreputable love affairs, liberally interspersed with many other anecdotes, notably that of the cruel vengeance taken by Mme de la Pommeraye on her lover, the marquis des Arcis, for his infidelity.

Jacques Vingtras, *v. Vallès*.

Jadis et naguère, *v. Verlaine*.

Jal, AUGUSTE, *v. Dictionaries*, 1864.

Jallez, Pierre, in Romains's *Les *Hommes de bonne volonté*.

Jaloux, EDMOND (1878–1949), novelist, and a critic of wide reading and sympathies. His novels, usually nostalgic, sensitive recollections of a happy or unhappy past, include *Le Reste est silence* (1909; an unhappy *ménage* observed by a child), *L'Éventail de crêpe* (1911), *Fumées dans la campagne* (1918), *La Fin d'un beau jour* (1920), *La Balance faussée* (1932). His criticism includes studies of English and German writers. Those of Jane Austen, Meredith, George Moore, Henry James, James Joyce, and Virginia Woolf in the collected essays *Figures étrangères* (1926)

and *Au pays du roman* (1931) are of interest. *L'Esprit des livres* (1923–31) contains the essays and reviews he contributed weekly for many years to *Les *Nouvelles littéraires*. He died before completing his fine *Introduction à l'histoire de la littérature française* (1946, 2 vols.— *Des origines à la fin du moyen âge* and *Le XVIe Siècle*).

Jammes, FRANCIS (1868–1938), poet and novelist, lived mainly in or near Orthez (Basses-Pyrénées), but made many literary friends in Paris when the *Mercure de France* published his poems *De l'angélus de l'aube à l'angélus du soir, 1888–1897* (1898). He wrote with *naïveté* (at times, perhaps, studied) about nature, animals, and the daily round of rustic life, and was associated (*c.* 1895) with *Naturisme (sometimes also called *Jammisme*; *v. Literary Isms*). Beginning with *Clairières dans le ciel, 1902–1906* (1906) his verse became increasingly religious in tone. (He was one of several early 20th-c. writers, e.g. Claudel and Gide, whose conversion, or refusal to be converted, to Roman Catholicism took on the aspect of a literary event. He writes of it in vol. III of his *Mémoires*, 1922–3.) His other collections include *Le Deuil des primevères, 1898–1900* (1901; very personal lyrics of love and piety), *Jean de Noarrieu* (1901; a long pastoral epic), *Les Géorgiques chrétiennes* (1911–12). His prose works include, notably, *Le Roman du lièvre* (1903), collected tales (inc. the tale of the hare who, in Heaven, sighed for the excitements of earthly life); also *Clara d'Ellébeuse* (1899), *Almaïde d'Étremont* (1901), and *Pomme d'Anis* (1904), tales of young girls and their romantic agonies; *M. le curé d'Ozéron* (1918), a novel of clerical life.

Jamyn, AMADIS (1540–93), a prolific poet of the school of Ronsard. He also translated the last 12 books of the *Iliad*, completing the work of Salel.

Janet, PAUL (1823–99), philosopher, a disciple of Cousin (whose life he wrote, 1885) and also influenced by Maine de

Biran; author of *Principes de métaphysique et de psychologie* (1897, 2 vols.), etc.

Janin, JULES-GABRIEL (1804–74), a noted literary and dramatic critic, a personality of mid-19th-c. literary life, solely responsible after 1835 for the weekly dramatic **feuilleton* of the **Journal des Débats*. His criticism was spirited, amusing, and gracefully discursive; the selections published as *Histoire de la littérature dramatique* (1858, 6 vols.) are a guide to some 30 years of French theatrical production. He also wrote novels, notably *L'Âne mort et la Femme guillotinée* (1829), possibly satirizing, or parodying, the more horrific *Romantic fiction; the *Contes fantastiques et contes littéraires* (1832); a witty *Discours de réception à la porte de l'Académie française* (1865, when his first bid for election failed—he was elected in 1870), etc.

Jannequin, CLÉMENT, a famous composer of the first half of the 16th c., one of the first French composers of genius and originality. *v. Ronsard.*

Janot, a character invented by the actor-playwright Dorvigny (pseudonym of Louis-François Archambault, 1742–1812); a grotesque ninny whose way of muddling his words was called *Janotisme*. Cf. *Jocrisse*.

Janotus de Bragmardo, in Rabelais's **Gargantua*.

Jansenism, Jansenist, a religious doctrine derived from the works of St. Augustine by CORNELIUS JANSEN or JANSENIUS (1585–1638), bishop of Ypres in Flanders, and developed in his *Augustinus* (1640). It was introduced at *Port-Royal by Du Vergier de Hauranne. Jansenism approximated to Calvinism, repudiating the efficacy of the human will and asserting predestination and the sole virtue of divine grace as against the Pelagian doctrine of salvation by works. The strength of the Jansenists lay in their moral austerity, which influenced many who did not accept

their doctrines, and their spirited attack on irreligion (they did much to disseminate knowledge of the Scriptures; *v. Le Maître de Saci*). By the late 17th c., their influence, radiating from *Port-Royal*, had permeated the court, society, and literature of France: Brunetière holds that, of the great writers of the day, only Molière and La Fontaine had escaped it. The most famous exponent of the doctrine was Pascal (for others *v. Port-Royal*); it was later defended in the *Nouvelles ecclésiastiques* (1728–1803; periodical pamphlets, at first circulated clandestinely). It was bitterly opposed by the *Jesuits and several times condemned by Rome (*v. Port-Royal*). *v. Pâris, F. de; Pavillon.*

Jardin de Bérénice, Le, v. Barrès.

Jardin d'Épicure, Le, v. France, A.

Jardin des Plantes, the popular name for the *Muséum national d'Histoire naturelle*, in Paris. In 1625, Guy de la Brosse (d. 1641), physician to Louis XIII, founded at royal expense a garden for the cultivation of medicinal herbs, where lectures in botany, natural history, pharmacy, etc., were given—a sign of the growing interest in experimental scientific study. From 1640 this *Jardin royal des Herbes médicinales*, later called the *Jardin du Roi*, was open to the public and became a well-loved haunt of Parisians. In the 18th c., notably under the curatorship (1739–88) of Buffon (assisted by Daubenton), its teaching facilities were extended, and its grounds enlarged and embellished with a mound, a maze, a miniature Swiss valley, and tree-lined avenues. During the Revolution it became State property and was reorganized as the *Muséum d'Histoire naturelle*, thanks largely to the initiative of Lakanal. Under the brief curatorship of Bernardin de Saint-Pierre (from 1792), Geoffroy Saint-Hilaire (then a young member of its staff) created a menagerie for the furtherance of zoological studies. It continued to develop and is now an **école spéciale*, with professorial chairs, specialized museums, laboratories, etc. *v.*

Cuvier; *Jacquemont*; *Jussieu*; *Lacépède*; *Lamarck*.

Jardin des racines grecques, Le, v. Port-Royal.

Jardin du Roi, *v. Jardin des Plantes.*

Jargon, Ballades en, v. Villon.

Jarnac, Coup de, proverbial for an unforeseen and decisive blow, in reference to a duel, fought in 1547 before Henri II and the court, in which Jarnac, a young noble, hamstrung his opponent with an unexpected blow.

Jarry, ALFRED (1873–1907), a writer famous as the creator of 'le Père Ubu' in the satirical farce *Ubu Roi* (1896). Ubu, who makes himself king of Poland, is a grotesque and repulsive puppet-like creature, the embodiment of cowardice, cruelty, and *bourgeois* avarice. *Ubu Roi* had its origin in a puppet-show poking fun at a master at the *lycée* of Rennes and performed there by Jarry and other boys. Later, while trying to make his name as a *Symbolist poet in Paris, he reworked it and it was staged at the *Théâtre de l'*Œuvre*. Its success was one of scandal only, made worse by eccentricities of production; but Ubu became a legendary character—as did his creator who, by the time he died of drink, had affected all Ubu's absurdities (the shrill squeaky voice, fantastic dress, Rabelaisian distortions of words, etc.). His other works—enlivened at times by striking images and a dialectical wit, but often merely blasphemous and scatological—include verse (*Les Minutes de sable mémorial*, 1894; *César-Antéchrist*, 1895), tales (*L'Amour en visites*, 1898; *L'Amour absolu*, 1899; *Le Surmâle*, 1902), other plays and writings about Ubu (collected in *Tout Ubu*, 1962), and *Gestes et opinions du Dr. Faustroll, pataphysicien* (1911; written 1898), expounding his science of pataphysics or imaginary solutions. His professed desire to leave the mind more open to hallucination by emptying it of intelligence and his preoccupation with

absurdity place him among the precursors of *Surrealism and the contemporary Theatre of the Absurd (*v. Theatre of the 19th and 20th cs.*). For the *Théâtre Alfred-Jarry*, v. Artaud.

Jaubert, PIERRE, *v. Dictionaries, 1773.*

Jaucourt, LOUIS, CHEVALIER DE (1704–79), one of Diderot's chief assistants in the preparation of the *Encyclopédie*. He wrote much of it himself and supervised the hack-writers. He was a Protestant, a man of wide knowledge and decent life.

Jaufré Rudel, PRINCE DE BLAYE, a 12th-c. *troubadour*. His famous song celebrating distant love ('amor de lonh') gave rise to the legend that he fell in love with the countess of Tripoli from reports of her brought home by pilgrims, set sail to see her, fell mortally ill on board ship, was carried ashore at Tripoli, and died in her arms. The story inspired E. *Rostand's *La Princesse lointaine* and also figures in Petrarch (*Trionfo d'amore*), Swinburne (*Triumph of Time*), Browning (*Rudel and the Lady of Tripoli*), etc.

Jaurès, JEAN-LÉON (1859–1914), b. at Castres, near Albi (Tarn), studied philosophy at the *École normale supérieure*, passed the *agrégation*, then taught in the provinces, but soon turned to journalism and politics. He was elected *député* (1885) for Albi and thereafter was seldom out of the Chamber. His fervent Socialist principles, fearless honesty (as when he agitated for a revision of the *Dreyfus verdict), charm, and brilliant oratory combined to make him one of the greatest forces for democracy in Europe. He founded (1904) and edited the (then Socialist) daily paper *L'Humanité*. He was general editor of the *Histoire socialiste (1789–1900)* and author of the four volumes on the Revolution (*La Constituante*, 1902; *La Législative*, 1903; *La Convention*, 1903, 2 vols.). He was assassinated in a Paris café a few days before the outbreak of the 1914–18 war. References to his influence and the shock of his death occur in Romains's *Les *Hommes de bonne* *volonté*, Martin du Gard's *Les *Thibault*, **Aragon's *Les Beaux Quartiers*, and the writings of Blum, Péguy, etc.

Javert, in Hugo's *Les *Misérables*.

Jean Ier LE POSTHUME (b. 1316), posthumous son of Louis X, was proclaimed king at birth, but died five days later.

Jean II LE BON (1319–64), king of France (*Capetian dynasty, *Valois branch), succeeded his father Philippe VI, r. 1350–64. He was defeated at Poitiers (1356) by the Black Prince and taken captive to England. He spent most of the rest of his life, and died, in captivity. *v. Marcel, É.*

Jean Barois, *v. Martin du Gard.*

Jean Bodel, *v. Bodel.*

Jean-Christophe (1906–12), by Rolland, a *roman-fleuve* in 10 vols. (*L'Aube, Le Matin, L'Adolescent, La Révolte, La Foire sur la place, Antoinette, Dans la maison, Les Amies, Le Buisson ardent, La Nouvelle Journée*); a work long widely read and translated, and still quoted and discussed as an outstanding novel of its day. It is a study of a musical genius of German birth who makes France his second country (reflecting Rolland's views on the fundamental kinship between the two races). The style is impressionistic, each short volume being little more than a series of sketches strung together.

The period is the later 19th and early 20th cs. Jean-Christophe Krafft grows up in a small Rhineland town (where the local prince still holds court and patronizes the arts), emerges as a musical prodigy, and experiences the usual growing-pains of youth—intensified by his turbulent nature and a family background of poverty and drunkenness. On the threshold of manhood, eager to break away from his clinging widowed mother, already composing furiously and beginning to revolt against accepted conventions and German music, he is involved in a fracas which renders him liable to arrest—and so justifies his

departure: he crosses the frontier and makes for Paris (vols. I–IV). Vols. V–VII and part of VIII, all set in Paris, follow his musical, emotional, and spiritual development. He is disgusted by the speciousness and corruption in musical, literary, and artistic circles (vol. V is often mentioned for its heavy indictment of cultural life in Paris *c.* 1912). Scorning to make his way by flattery or complaisance, he retires into himself and his composition, and nearly starves to death. A new, absorbing interest then enters his life—Olivier Jeannin, a charming, delicate young intellectual, whose sister Antoinette, now dead, he had once met in Germany (vol. VI relates the early life of this pair). Jean-Christophe and Olivier set up house together. Jean-Christophe now learns to know the true France, for Olivier shows him the good and bad sides of French life and thought and also teaches him to understand the struggling, kindly, and uncultured masses. In vol. VIII, the friends are separated by Olivier's marriage, and fame comes at last to Jean-Christophe. In vol. IX, reunited with Olivier (whose marriage has failed), he mixes with revolutionaries and is involved in riots in which he kills a policeman and Olivier is wounded. Friends get him to Switzerland, where he learns that Olivier has died of his wounds. For some months he remains dazed and half mad with grief, and his creative genius seems to have deserted him. A fresh emotional crisis brings him agonizingly back to life, releasing all his passion and misery in music of strange and unparalleled beauty. He realizes, as never before, that the creative fire is like a burning bush: it may burn low, but it is never extinguished. He ends in Paris, successful and well loved. New sorrows befall him, but they are bearable, for he can look back on his long, turbulent life and see the pattern working to its close.

Jean d'Arras, *v. Mélusine.*

Jean d'Auton (*c.* 1465–1528), of Poitou or Saintonge, historiographer to Louis XII, also a poet who displays the worst faults of the *rhétoriqueurs*. His prose *Chroniques* relate clearly what he has seen, or conscientiously inquired into, and give many interesting details.

Jean de Bueil, *v. Jouvencel, Le.*

Jean de Journi, *v. Dîme de pénitence.*

Jean de l'Espine or **de Pontalais,** 'Songecreux', a famous member of the *Enfants sans souci in the early 16th c.; probably also an author (possibly of the satirical *Contredits de Songecreux*). He played before François Ier and was imprisoned (1516) for satirizing the queen mother as *Mère Sotte*. Both Des Périers and Rabelais mention him.

Jean de Meung, i.e. JEAN CHOPINEL or CLOPINEL of Meung on the Loire (d. *c.* 1305), author of the second part of the *Roman de la Rose*, also possibly of the *Testament maistre Jehan de Meun* and the *Codicile maistre Jehan de Meun* (poem. criticizing the various classes of society); translator of Vegetius's *De re militari* (as *L'Art de chevalerie*), Boethius's *De consolatione philosophiae* (v. *Consolation de Philosophie, La*), and the life and letters of *Abélard and Héloïse.

Jean de Paris, v. Jehan de Paris.

Jean de Pontalais, *v. Jean de l'Espine.*

Jean de Roye, *v. History,* 1.

Jean des Entommeures, in Rabelais's *Gargantua*.

Jean de Vignai (14th c.), a Hospitaller of the Order of St. Jacques du Haut Pas. He translated many Latin works, e.g. part of *Vincent de Beauvais's *Speculum majus* (the *Speculum historiale,* as *Miroir historial,* *c.* 1330), Vegetius's *De re militari,* the *Legenda aurea,* itineraries of the Holy Land, chronicles; and *v. Bible, French Versions of.*

Jean le Bel, *v. Le Bel.*

Jean le Maingre, *v. Bouciquaut.*

Jeanne d'Arc (Joan of Arc) (1412–31; canonized 1920), 'la Pucelle d'Orléans', an illiterate peasant girl from Domremy in the Meuse valley. Early in 1429, at the age of 17, she claimed to hear mystic voices summoning her to deliver France from the English. Having convinced those about her of her divine mission, she joined Charles VII and led his army to the relief of Orleans, then besieged by the English. She triumphantly drove the English off, then conducted the king to his coronation at Rheims. Here her mission should have ended; but she remained with the army, showing independence of royal commands. She was captured at Compiègne by the Burgundians (v. *Armagnacs and Burgundians*), handed over to the English, condemned as a heretic by a French court of ecclesiastics, and burnt by the English on 30 May 1431. The many works she has inspired include *Christine de Pisan's *Ditié en l'honneur de Jeanne d'Arc*; Chapelain's and Voltaire's *La *Pucelle*; a famous study in *Michelet's *Histoire de France*; a life by A. France (1908, 2 vols.; romanticized and said to be inaccurate in places); *Péguy's *Le Mystère de la charité de Jeanne d'Arc*; Claudel's *Jeanne au bûcher* (1938; a dramatic poem with music by Honegger); *Anouilh's *L'Alouette*.

Jeannin, PIERRE (1540–1623), magistrate, diplomat, and minister under Henri IV. His *Négociations* record his diplomatic transactions with the Netherlands.

Jeannot et Colin (1764), a tale by Voltaire. Jeannot and Colin, village boys, are devoted friends. Then Jeannot's father moves to Paris and makes money by speculating, and Jeannot comes to despise Colin. Later, when Jeannot's family are ruined and in despair, the faithful Colin, who has made his way by steady industry, comes to their rescue.

Jean sans Peur (1371–1419), a grandson of Jean II, duke of Burgundy (1404–19) at the time of the strife between *Armagnacs and Burgundians. *v. Hôtel de Bourgogne*.

Jean Santeuil, v. *Proust*.

Jean Sbogar, v. *Nodier*.

Jehan, v. also *Jean*.

Jehan de Paris, a late 15th-c. prose romance by an unknown author, possibly inspired by the events attending the marriage of Charles VIII to Anne de Bretagne.

The princess of Spain, though earlier promised to the son of the late king of France, is about to marry the elderly king of England. The young king of France decides to go to Spain incognito to see what she is like before pressing his claim to her. He travels, with imposing pomp, as 'Jehan de Paris', a wealthy *bourgeois*. He falls in with the king of England, on his way to his wedding (and propounds to him riddles derived from *Jehan et Blonde). His magnificent suite, charm, and dignified bearing astonish the Spaniards (their growing admiration and excitement is well described), and when he reveals himself as the king of France he easily ousts his rival, who cuts a rather sorry figure throughout.

Jehan et Blonde, a verse **roman d'aventure* by Beaumanoir, written between 1270 and 1280. There are two English translations, one of *c.* 1440, the other printed *c.* 1510–15 by Wynkyn de Worde.

Jehan, the young son of a French knight, goes to England to seek his fortune, accepts service there with the earl of Oxford, and falls in love with his daughter Blonde. They enjoy two years of innocent happiness together, then Jehan is summoned home, for his father is dying and he must do homage for his fief. Blonde promises to wait one year for him; and when her father gives her hand to the rich earl of Gloucester, she obtains a postponement of four months. As the fatal day approaches, Jehan returns to England, falling in with the earl of Gloucester and his retinue on their way to the wedding. He manages to carry off Blonde and,

though they are pursued to Dover, to get her aboard a boat and escape to France. They marry, and Jehan is made a count by the king of France and reconciled with Blonde's father.

Jemmapes (in Belgium). Here the Revolutionary army under Dumouriez defeated the Austrians (Nov. 1792). *v. Armée des émigrés*; *Coalitions* (1).

Jena (near Weimar, Germany). Here Napoleon routed the Prussians (14 Oct. 1806; *cf. Auerstadt*). *v. Coalitions* (4).

Jenni, ou l'Athée et le Sage, Histoire de, (1775), a philosophical tale by Voltaire, of interest as indicating his later views on religion.

Jenni, a young Englishman, captured by the Spaniards at Montjuich (1705) and in danger of being burnt (because the Inquisitor's mistress has fallen in love with him), is saved by Lord Peterborough's capture of Barcelona. A lively dialogue—in which Jenni's father, Mr. Freind, a wise doctor of theology, convinces a bachelor of the University of Salamanca of the superiority of the Protestant faith—is followed by an account of Jenni's dissipated life in London, flight to America, and rescue from Indians by his father. Then comes the main element in the work, an eloquent defence of the existence of God, in a dialogue between Freind and one of Jenni's atheist companions.

Jérôme Paturot à la recherche d'une position sociale, v. *Reybaud*.

Jerphanion, Jean, in Romains's *Les* **Hommes de bonne volonté*.

Jérusalem, Conquête de, v. *Antioche*.

Je suis partout, v. *Press*, 9.

Jesuits, members of the Society of Jesus (*La Compagnie de Jésus*), f. 1534 by St. Ignatius Loyola to combat the Reformation and convert the heathen, authorized by a papal bull of 1540, and bound by vows of chastity, poverty, obedience, and submission to the Holy See. Their main activities were preaching, teaching (*v. Lycées and Collèges*), and hearing confessions. They became extremely powerful in France and other Catholic countries, but their political and other intrigues provoked bad feeling. In the 17th c., their violent campaign against the *Jansenists brought about the fall of *Port-Royal*. The Jansenists took their revenge when the bankruptcy (*c.* 1755) of La Vallette, Superior of the Jesuits in Martinique (where he carried on a large industrial undertaking), led his creditors to sue the Society. The Jansenist *parlement* condemned Loyola's doctrines, closed the Jesuit schools (1762), and expelled the Society from France (1764). Pope Clement XIV suppressed the Society (1773), and it was not re-established till 1814. *v. Dictionaries*, 1704; *Journal de Trévoux*; *Molinistes*; *Bollandistes*; *Relations des Jésuites*.

Jésus-Christ en Flandre, *v. Comédie humaine, La* (*Études philosophiques*).

Jeu Adam, *v. Jeu de la Feuillée.*

Jeu d'Adam, *v. Religious Writings*, 1.

Jeu de la Feuillée ('leafy bower') or *Jeu Adam*, a dramatic work by Adam de la Halle, first performed *c.* 1262; a curious Aristophanic mixture of satirical comedy and the supernatural. The author tells of his marriage, of his decision to leave his wife and return to Paris, and of his father's avarice. He presents friends and neighbours from *Arras and makes fun of their defects (*cf. Congé*). A physician, a monk with relics, and a lunatic are vehicles for his satire. Then three fairies arrive and bestow gifts; one has been neglected and is vindictive. They display a Wheel of Fortune, with images of Arras notabilities attached to it. The play ends with a tavern scene, and the monk is forced to leave his relics as a pledge for the amount of the bill.

Jeu de l'amour et du hasard, *Le*, a comedy by Marivaux, possibly his best; produced 1730. *v. Legrand*.

Dorante and Silvia are to marry, provided they like each other when they meet. Silvia, the better to judge Dorante, changes places with her maid. But Dorante, with the same object in view, has changed places with his valet. The two, thus disguised, fall in love, which places each in an embarrassing position. Dorante finally confesses his identity to Silvia; but Silvia, to test her lover further, maintains the imposture until, braving social prejudice and his father's wrath, he proposes marriage to her. Meanwhile, a similar situation, similarly resolved, has arisen between the valet and the maid, posing as Dorante and Silvia.

Jeu de mail, *v. Mail.*

Jeu de paume, *v. Paume.*

Jeu de Robin et Marion, by Adam de la Halle, a dramatic pastoral with songs, sometimes described as an early form of *opéra-comique* and intended for a more refined audience than the *Jeu de la Feuillée*; probably performed at Naples *c.* 1283 and later at *Arras. The theme is simple: a knight makes love to Marion, a shepherdess, but she is faithful to her shepherd lover Robin and firmly resists an attempt to carry her off; the approaching marriage of Robin and Marion is celebrated in a rustic feast. The characters are drawn with much spirit and the whole throws light on 13th-c. peasant life.

Jeu de Saint Nicolas, *v. Bodel.*

Jeu du Prince des Sots, *v. Gringore.*

Jeune Belgique, *La*, *v. Waller.*

Jeune Captive, *La*, *v. Chénier, A.*

Jeune Fille Violaine, *La*, *v. Claudel.*

Jeune Parque, *La*, *v. Valéry.*

Jeunes-France, Les, a group of extreme young *Romantics of the second generation (*cf. Bousingo*), led for a time by Gautier, who light-heartedly satirized them in *Les Jeunes-France, romans goguenards* (1833).

Jeune Tarentine, La, v. *Chénier, A.*

Jeu parti (Prov. *joc partit* or *partimen*), a popular form of medieval lyric, invented by the *troubadours and imitated in N. France, in which one poet challenges another to a debate, usually on a theme of *amour courtois, allowing his opponent to choose which side he will support. The *envoi sometimes appeals to an arbitrator to decide the issue.

In the *tenson* or *tenso*, a similar form, rarer in French than in Provençal, two poets or a poet and a fictitious character support opposite views in alternate stanzas.

Jeux floraux de Toulouse, said to have been founded by seven *troubadours, who formed a college of the *gai saber and invited all *troubadours* to meet in 1324 and compete, with a poem on the Virgin, for the prize of a golden violet. Before long, prizes of a silver eglantine and a silver marigold were added, and the festival became a well-known annual event, imitated elsewhere. It later lost some of its importance, but was revived in the 15th c. by Dame Clémence Isaure, who endowed the college with property it still enjoys. Du Bellay attacked the institution in his *Défense et illustration de la langue française. Prizewinners have included Du Bartas, Fabre d'Églantine, Hugo.

Jeux rustiques et divins, v. *Régnier, H. de.*

Je vivrai l'amour des autres, v. *Cayrol.*

Joad, in Racine's *Athalie.

Joan of Arc, v. *Jeanne d'Arc.*

Joas, in Racine's *Athalie.

Joceaume, in *Pathelin.

Jocelyn (1836), a narrative poem by Lamartine, a later episode in the unfinished epic begun in *La* *Chute d'un

ange. It purports to be the diary of a young seminarist, who flees from the Revolution to a hiding-place in the mountains. He shelters the 'boy' Laurence, but trouble brews when Laurence proves to be a girl and the two fall in love. The bishop, his former spiritual director at the seminary, now in prison awaiting execution, wants to ordain Jocelyn so that he may receive the last sacrament from him. Jocelyn pleads his love for Laurence, but is overruled and ordained. In due course, he is sent as priest to the remote village of Valneige (Lamartine's descriptions of the countryside and peasant life there have prompted comparisons with Wordsworth). One day, summoned to a death-bed at the village inn, he finds Laurence, who has tried to forget him by plunging into a brilliant life of dissipation in Paris. He gives her absolution and reveals his identity before she dies. A little later, he dies in an epidemic and his parishioners, knowing his story, bury him beside her.

Jockey Club, Le, f. 1833, on the English model, to improve bloodstock, organize horse races, and regulate matters pertaining to the turf. The *Prix du Jockey Club*, f. 1836 and run yearly at *Chantilly, is the equivalent of the English Derby. But the *Jockey Club* is more than this: it is also a social club, among the most exclusive in France.

Joconde (1664), the first of La Fontaine's *Contes et Nouvelles, based on Ariosto; a gay, licentious tale of a prince of Lombardy and his friend, the two most handsome men on earth, who are mortified to find that their wives are unfaithful, seek consolation elsewhere, and are later reconciled to their lot.

Joconde, La, v. *Louvre, Musée du.*

Joc partit, v. *Jeu parti.*

Jocrisse, the type of the credulous simpleton, originally a stock character in comedy and farce, e.g. in Molière's *Sganarelle and *Le Désespoir de Jocrisse* by

Dorvigny (v. *Janot*). Veuillot dubbed Hugo 'Jocrisse à Patmos'.

Jodelet, JULIEN LESPY, *known as* (c. 1590–1660), a famous comic actor, a member of Mondory's company and later of the company of the *Hôtel de Bourgogne* (v. *Theatres and Theatre Companies*), so called because he played Jodelet, the ancestor of a long line of comic valets, in *Scarron's Jodelet, ou le Maître Valet* and Molière's *Les *Précieuses ridicules*. The name Jodelet came to mean a person who provokes laughter by his absurdities.

Jodelle, ÉTIENNE, SIEUR DE LYMODIN (1532–73), a highly gifted member of the *Pléiade*, noted as a pioneer of the drama. His *Cléopâtre captive* was the first original French *tragedy, his *Eugène* the first original French *comedy. Both were performed before the king in 1552/3 and created a sensation. His other works include *Didon*, a later tragedy (in *alexandrines), based on Virgil's story of Dido; and lyrics, rather serious in tone. He died in extreme poverty.

Joffre, JOSEPH-JACQUES-CÉSAIRE (1852–1931), a famous general of the 1914–18 war. The title *maréchal de France*, in abeyance since 1870, was revived to honour him (1916).

Johannot, ALFRED (1800–37) and his brother TONY (1803–52), painters, etchers, and book-illustrators. Tony, who frequented the *cénacles*, was noted for his delicate illustrations of works by *Romantics.

Joie de vivre, La, v. *Rougon-Macquart, Les*.

Joinville, JEAN, SIRE DE (1224–1317), b. in Champagne, of which province he became *sénéchal* (an office hereditary in his family). He took part in Louis IX's first crusade (i.e. the 7th *Crusade, 1248–54), became an intimate friend of the king, and shared his captivity after the disastrous battle of Mansourah. When they were ransomed, he accompanied the king to Palestine and returned to his home in 1254, after an absence of six years. In 1270, despite the king's entreaty, he refused to take part in his second crusade, arguing that his first duty was to his children and his vassals. He lived to see four successors of Louis IX on the throne. His memoirs, which he called *Histoire de Saint Louis*, are the work of one of the pleasantest of medieval authors, less dry than those of Villehardouin, more moving than those of Froissart. They were composed at the request of Jeanne de Navarre, consort of Philippe IV, completed in 1309 (after her death), and dedicated to her son (the future Louis X). They are mainly the story of Louis IX's first crusade, vivid and detailed (though the account of the military operations is not very clear), and told with engaging simplicity and sincerity. He is modest about his own exploits (he received five wounds, and his horse 15, at Mansourah) and freely admits that he was often terrified. There are many such human touches, and the spirit of the crusaders is well conveyed by the comte de Soissons's remark to the author as the two stood together hard pressed at Mansourah: 'Seneschaus, lessons huer cette chenaille, que, par la Coiffe Dieu,... encore en parlerons nous de cele journee es chambres des dames!' Among the most entertaining features of the work are the conversations between himself and the king, in which the king's devout exaltation contrasts with his own more human piety and good sense. He also has some interesting observations on Egypt and its people, the Nile flood, the Bedouin, the Mamelukes, etc., displaying a curiosity reminiscent of Herodotus.

Joly, GUY (17th c.), a magistrate of the Paris *parlement* who attached himself to Retz, took part in the *Fronde and followed Retz into exile, but later entered the service of the court. His memoirs of the *Fronde* period and Retz's later career (to 1665) are more accurate, if less well written, than those of Retz himself, for whom Joly shows mingled admiration and contempt.

Jongleurs (from L. *joculatores*; *v. Comedy*), the public entertainers of the medieval world, not only reciters of literary works and musicians, but also jugglers, acrobats, even exhibitors of animals. They recited or sang lives of *saints, *chansons de geste, *fabliaux*, romances, etc., to audiences gathered in the halls of nobles and in public places, especially at the shrines and churches on the pilgrim routes; on occasion they accompanied the leader of a military expedition (the *jongleur* Taillefer is said to have sung at the battle of Hastings; *v. Chanson de Roland*). They were sometimes retained in the permanent employ of a prince or noble, when they were usually called *ménestrels*. The *jongleur* was not always distinguished from the *trouvère*: a *trouvère* might sing his own poems, a *jongleur* might have written the verses he sang (e.g. Rutebeuf). They were in their heyday in the 13th c. and much favoured by Louis IX. They declined in the 14th c., and their various functions were distributed among separate classes of artists and performers—poets, musicians, singers, actors, acrobats, etc.—who came to be distinguished according to the quality of their respective talents. Authors and musicians rose in social standing (*v. Ménestrel*), the other categories fell. *v. Puy.*

Jordan Fantosme, a 12th-c. *Anglo-Norman cleric of the diocese of Winchester whose account (in monorhyme stanzas) of Henry II's war (1173–4) against William the Lion, king of the Scots, is of historical value.

Josabet, in Racine's *Athalie.*

Josse, Monsieur, a goldsmith in Molière's *L'*Amour médecin*. He recommends jewellery as a cure for Lucinde's melancholy. Sganarelle's reply—'Vous êtes orfèvre, Monsieur Josse'—has become proverbial.

Joubert, JOSEPH (1754–1824), a doctor's son, educated mainly at Toulouse in a *Jesuit college. He had a small income and after 1778 led an uneventful life, mainly in Paris or the country. He read, meditated, amassed a library, frequented the *salons*, and was surrounded by friends who came to him for advice and inspiration, notably Chateaubriand, Fontanes, Mme Leprince de Beaumont, Mme Récamier. Essentially a perfectionist, he produced no sustained piece of writing; but his reflections on life, literature, philosophy, ethics, education, etc., contain abstract criticism of the highest order, expressed in a concentrated but invariably lucid form. Chateaubriand edited a selection from his notebooks, *Recueil des pensées* (1838; re-ed. and augm. by Pierre de Raynal, *Pensées, maximes, essais, et correspondance*, 1842).

Joueur, Le, a verse comedy by Regnard, treating lightly of the vice of gambling (*cf. Dufresny*); produced 1696.

Valère, an inveterate gambler, borrows money right and left. When he loses and is penniless, he is in love with Angélique; when he wins, he is indifferent to her—hence some amusing changes of situation. Angélique, who loves him against her better judgement, finally revolts when she finds that he has pawned a jewelled portrait she had given him, and gives her hand to his worthy uncle.

Jouffroy, SIMON-THÉODORE (1796–1843), spiritualist philosopher, a noted teacher and lecturer, held appointments at the *École normale supérieure (where he had studied philosophy and been a pupil-teacher) and the *Sorbonne*. He attached great importance to the observation and analysis of human conduct, and held that the inadequacy of man's earthly life is in itself a proof of the immortality of the soul. His chief writings include the preface to his translation of the Scottish philosopher Dugald Stewart (*Esquisses de philosophie morale*, 1826) and his *Mélanges* and *Nouveaux Mélanges philosophiques* (1833 and 1842). He contributed to the *Globe* in its early days.

Joufroi, a *roman d'aventure* of the first half of the 13th c. by an unknown author (who says it was written to please his lady).

It relates, without recourse to fantasy or the supernatural, the knightly and amorous adventures of the comte de Poitiers in England (in the days of Henry I) and France. It has some historical basis.

Jouhandeau, MARCEL (1888-1979), novelist and essayist, a schoolmaster by profession. Many of his numerous novels and tales (*La Jeunesse de Théophile*, 1921; *Les Pincengrain*, 1925; *Les Térébinthes*, 1926; *Monsieur Godeau intime*, 1926; *Monsieur Godeau marié*, 1932; *Chaminadour*, 1934–41, 3 vols.; *Chroniques maritales*, 1938; *L'Imposteur*, 1950, etc.) depict the inhabitants of 'Chaminadour' (a country town near Limoges, drawn from his native Guéret, where his father was a butcher); others form a saga of his relations with Élise, his spirited, eccentric wife, a dancer by profession. 'Théophile', 'Godeau', and 'Juste Binche' (*in Le Parricide imaginaire*, 1930) are projections of the author himself. His essays (*Essai sur moi-même*, 1946; *Éloge de la volupté*, 1952; *Confidences*, 1954, etc.) throw light on what has been called his *mystique de l'enfer*, an approach to the Christian faith which requires a vivid apprehension of evil.

Jourdain, Monsieur, in Molière's *Le *Bourgeois Gentilhomme*.

Jourdain de Blaivies (i.e. Blaye), a late 12th- or early 13th-c. romance in the form of a *chanson de geste*, of some interest because the second part of it is an imitation of the Greek romance *Apollonius of Tyre*—the basis of Shakespeare's *Pericles*.

Jourdan, JEAN-BAPTISTE, *v. Maréchal*.

Journal de la Librairie, *v. Bibliographie de la France*.

Journal de Paris or *Poste du Soir*, *Le* (1777–1840), the first French daily newspaper, modelled on the *London Evening Post*. Besides official edicts and notices, it recorded minor events in Paris and in society, the publication of new books, the proceedings of the law courts and the *Académies*, the weather, and

current prices of commodities; there were also anecdotes, *bons mots*, and verse. In the early days of the Revolution, its politics were guardedly liberal and counter-Revolutionary. It was suppressed (Aug.–Oct. 1792), and reappeared as a moderately Republican paper. Garat was now editor, and contributors included A. Chénier and Condorcet. It was one of the few political papers tolerated by Napoleon. Under the Restoration, it remained a leading journal, constitutional-Royalist in complexion, but its influence gradually waned.

Journal de Perlet, *Le* (1789–97), a political and literary journal f. by Charles Perlet (1765–1828), a bookseller with political interests. It reported proceedings of the *Assemblée nationale* and the *Commune de Paris*, and was moderate in tone and popular with the *bourgeoisie*. It was suppressed by the *Directoire*.

Journal des Débats, *Le*, a famous daily paper; f. 1789, and at first largely devoted to fearlessly ironic reports of discussions in the *Assemblée nationale* and the *Commune de Paris*. In 1799, it was bought for a large sum by the *Bertin brothers, who made it a leading journal, with a circulation of 32,000. Its articles on literature and the drama were celebrated; it was one of the first papers to print a daily *feuilleton*, with reviews of new books and plays, fashion notes, advertisements, etc.; it also had Stock Exchange and correspondence columns. Regular contributors at this time included Bonald, Chateaubriand, Geoffroy, Dussault, Feletz, F.-B. Hoffmann, Nodier, Royer-Collard. Napoleon placed the paper under special censorship, appointed new editors (1807; *v. Esménard*; *Étienne*; *Fiévée*), changed its name to *Journal de l'Empire*, and finally confiscated its property (1811). In 1814, the Bertin brothers regained possession and hastily issued a news-sheet (headed *Journal des Débats*) reporting the entry of the Allied armies into Paris, the Royalist demonstrations in the streets, etc. It was then ultra-Royalist, but soon came to favour a constitutional monarchy and was active in the struggle for freedom of the Press (1830; v. Press, 5). The July Monarchy—when it was read by the bourgeoisie and became less progressive, though always alive to new ideas—was one of its most brilliant periods. Leading historians and critics were on the staff; Janin wrote the dramatic feuilleton and literary criticism, Berlioz was music critic. Under the Second Empire, when it withdrew from active political journalism, it became the most literary newspaper of the day, recruiting such great journalists as S.-U. Silvestre de Sacy, Saint-Marc Girardin, Prévost-Paradol, and Weiss, printing articles by Taine and Renan, also occasional translations of English novels (e.g. by Wilkie Collins, Ouida, Trollope). It was suppressed during the *Commune of 1871, but soon revived and continued at a steady level of excellence till 1939. It was suppressed in 1944 (v. Press, 9). v. also Faguet; Lemaître, J.

Journal des États généraux, v. Courrier de Provence.

Journal des Faux-Monnayeurs, v. Faux-Monnayeurs, Les.

Journal des Goncourt, Le, the famous diary kept by the Goncourt brothers from 1851 and continued by Edmond after Jules's death in 1870. It is a mine of valuable, surprisingly modern, literary criticism, and also of literary and artistic information and gossip, for they regularly transcribed any conversation they had taken part in. Most leading writers of the period 1851–95 figure in it, at times less than kindly treated. The descriptions of life in Paris during the *Franco-Prussian war and the *Commune of 1871 are of great interest, also the many thumb-nail sketches of people and events. Extracts appeared before Edmond's death in 1896, there was an incomplete edition in 1935–6 (9 vols.), and the entire work was published in 1956–9.

Journal des savants, Le, the first literary and scientific periodical in Europe, f. January 1665 by Denis de Sallo, an erudite

magistrate of the Paris *parlement. (The Philosophical Transactions of the Royal Society first appeared in London in March 1665.) It appeared weekly, recording and briefly reviewing new publications in Europe, noting scientific discoveries and literary events. It was favoured by Colbert, and prospered. In 1702, having been bought by the State, it was placed under an editorial committee of scholars; from 1724 it appeared monthly. Publication ceased in 1792 and was not successfully resumed till 1816. It has been sponsored since 1903 by the *Institut de France and associated from 1908 with the *Académie des Inscriptions et Belles-Lettres. It now appears quarterly.

Journal de Trévoux, Le, a literary and critical monthly, f. 1701 (as Mémoires pour servir à l'histoire des sciences et des beaux-arts) by the *Jesuits at *Trévoux (it was transferred to Paris in 1731); well written, well informed, specially directed to the defence of religion against the *philosophes, and hotly attacked by Voltaire and others. Its great days ended with the expulsion (1764) of the Jesuits.

Journal d'un curé de campagne, Le, v. Bernanos.

Journal d'un poète, v. Vigny.

Journalism. For its beginnings v. Press, 1.

Journal officiel, Le, f. 1868 and still in existence, replaced the *Moniteur universel as the official daily medium for the publication of full proceedings in both Chambers, the text of decrees, official appointments, honours, etc. (cf. the London Gazette).

Journal universel, Le, better known as the Moniteur de Gand, f. 1815 (during the Hundred Days) at Ghent by one of the *Bertin brothers, primarily to disseminate information about the government of Louis XVIII. It was edited by four of his ministers, including Chateaubriand. The first number (14 April 1815) published a manifesto signed by official representatives of the *Coalition powers declaring Napoleon an enemy of world peace; the last appeared just after *Waterloo.

Journaux intimes, v. *Memoirs.*

Journée du guichet, La, v. *Arnauld, Arnauld d'Andilly* (2).

Journée du 9 thermidor, La (27 July 1794), the day Robespierre fell; it marked the end of the *Terror. v. *Revolutions*, 1; *Republican Calendar.*

Journées de juin, Les, v. *Republics,* 2.

Journées des barricades, Les, v. *Fronde; Ligue, La.*

Jouve, PIERRE-JEAN (1887–1976), primarily a poet. His early work (often first publ. in the review *Les Bandeaux d'or,* 1906–12, of which he was co-founder, and collected in *Heures,* 1919, and *Tragiques,* 1923, etc.) was influenced in turn by *Symbolism, *Unanimisme,* and the pacifism of Rolland (with whom he campaigned in Switzerland). In 1924, following his divorce and a spiritual crisis leading him to a different, unorthodox conception of Roman Catholicism, he embarked on a 'vita nuova', embraced a new poetic creed, and disowned all his previous work. His subsequent collections, largely the record of an agonizing spiritual quest and showing the influence on him of the Christian mystics, of Baudelaire and Rimbaud, and of Freudian psychology (his second wife was a psychoanalyst), are at once mystical and erotic, and pervaded by a sense of sin and guilt. They include *Les Noces* (1931; inc. *Les Mystérieuses Noces,* 1925; and *Noces,* 1928, which had an epigraph, *Vita nuova 1924–1927,* and a postscript on the beliefs by which he now lived and wrote); *Sueur de sang* (1935; with a preface, *Inconscient, spiritualité, et catastrophe*); *Matière céleste* (1937); *La Vierge de Paris* (1946), poems of the 1939–45 war and the *Resistance, marked by patriotic mysticism of a high order and

unified by his conception of the poet as a witness to the truth at a time of national peril; *Génie* (1948), *Diadème* (1949), *Ode* (1950), and *Langue* (1952), poems notable for his adoption of the *verset-form, his use of Chinese images and symbols, and his approach to the problem of the nature of language; *Moires* (1962); *Ténèbre* (1965). His other works include novels (e.g. *Paulina 1880,* 1925; *Le Monde désert,* 1927), *En miroir: Journal sans date* (1954), and translations of Shakespeare. v. *Lyric Poetry,* 4.

Jouvencel, Le, a military romance written between 1461 and 1468 by Jean de Bueil (d. *c.* 1478), an officer in Charles VII's army. It relates, disguising the names of the participants, some of the main episodes that concluded the Hundred Years War, with interesting details about the conduct of military operations and the pitiful devastation of the country. The hero is no longer a feudal knight, but a professional soldier.

Jouvet, LOUIS (1887–1951), actor and producer, worked with Copeau at the *Vieux-Colombier* (1913–22), then set up on his own as an actor-manager in Paris, first at the *Comédie des Champs-Élysées* and later (1934–51) at the *Théâtre de l'Athénée.* He introduced—and did much to form— Giraudoux as a dramatist. He was particularly successful as an actor and producer of Molière, and of *Romains's comedies (e.g. *Knock*). He also worked in the cinema. v. *Theatres and Theatre Companies.*

Jouy, JOSEPH-ÉTIENNE, *self-styled* DE (1764–1846), author of *vaudevilles; *opéras-comiques;* a tragedy, *Tippo-Saib* (1813), set, with some attempt at local colour, in India, where he had soldiered as a young man; popular satirical sketches of Paris and the provinces in the early 19th c.—*L'Hermite de la Chaussée d'Antin* (1812–14), *L'Hermite en province* (1824).

Joyce, JAMES, v. *Foreign Influences,* 6.

Joyeuse, v. *Charlemagne.*

Judicial System under the Monarchy, v. *Parlement.*

Judith, v. *Giraudoux.*

Juif errant, Le, v. *Sue.*

Juives, Les, v. *Garnier.*

Julie, ou la Nouvelle Héloïse, v. *Nouvelle Héloïse.*

Julien, Chateaubriand's servant; v. *Itinéraire de Paris à Jérusalem.*

Juliette au pays des hommes (1924), a novel by Giraudoux. Juliette, soon to marry, goes to Paris to find the other men she might have loved. At one point, she visits the narrator himself. It is May Day. He has been surveying Paris from the top of the *Tour Eiffel and, like Renan after he saw the Acropolis (v. *Souvenirs d'enfance et de jeunesse*), has come home to write a *Prière (sur la Tour Eiffel)*, which he reads to her. She returns to her native Auvergne rid of phantoms and alive to the beauty of reality in the person of her patient lover.

Jullian, CAMILLE (1859–1933), historian of Gaul (*Histoire de la Gaule*, 1907–27; *De la Gaule à la France*, 1921, etc.). v. *Fustel de Coulanges*; *History*, 4.

Jullien, JEAN (1854–1919), a dramatist associated with the *Théâtre Libre*, wrote *L'Échéance* (1889), *Le Maître* (1890; a realistic study of avaricious peasants), *La Mer* (1891), *La Poigne* (1902).

July Monarchy, the reign of Louis-Philippe (1830–48), so called because it followed the July Revolution.

July Revolution (1830), v. *Revolutions*, 2.

Junie, in Racine's *Britannicus.*

Junot, v. *Abrantès.*

Jurieu, PIERRE (1637–1713), *Huguenot pastor and theologian, an adversary of Bossuet. His *Lettres pastorales adressées aux fidèles de France* (1686–9) were written from Holland after the revocation of the Edict of Nantes.

Jussieu, the brothers ANTOINE (1686–1758), BERNARD (1699–1777), and JOSEPH (1704–79) DE, naturalists. Antoine, also a physician, became professor of botany at the *Jardin des Plantes (then the *Jardin du Roi*). Bernard, the most famous, made several botanical expeditions and did much to enrich and classify the collections at the *Jardin des Plantes*, where he was employed. The great cedar of Lebanon there is said to have sprung from a seedling given him by Sherard, founder of the chair of botany at Oxford. Joseph spent 36 years exploring in S. America and discovered the common heliotrope ('cherry-pie').

Justine, ou les Malheurs de la vertu, v. *Sade.*

Juvénal des Ursins, JEAN (1388–1473), historian and magistrate. His chronicle of the reign of Charles VI was a notable addition to the *Grandes Chroniques. v. *History*, 1.

K

Kafka, FRANZ, v. *Foreign Influences*, 6.

Kahn, GUSTAVE (1859–1936), *Symbolist poet, contributor to reviews (some of which he founded). He wrote much about the *vers libre*, of which he was one of the originators, notably an essay prefacing his collected *Premiers Poèmes* (1897; comprising *Palais nomades*, 1887, *Chansons d'amant*, 1891, *Le Livre d'images*, 1897).

Karr, ALPHONSE (1808–90), novelist and journalist. His novels, a popular blend of wit and sentimentality, include *Sous les* *tilleuls* (1832), *Geneviève* (1838), *Clotilde* (1839). He exercised his biting wit in *Les Guêpes* (1839–47), monthly pamphlets on current events, continued as contributions to *Le *Figaro* and other journals. One of his many epigrams is 'Plus ça change, plus c'est la même chose' (in 1849, apropos of revolutions).

Kellermann, FRANÇOIS-CHRISTOPHE, *v. Maréchal.*

Kemp, ROBERT (1885–1959), a critic of the 'impressionistic' school, highly cultured, conservative and classical in his tastes, and a brilliant stylist. He was dramatic critic on *Le *Monde* from 1944 and literary critic on *Les *Nouvelles littéraires* from 1945; earlier he wrote for *L'*Aurore*, *L'Écho de Paris*, *Le *Temps*, etc. Some of his articles are collected in *La Vie des livres* (1955) and *La Vie du théâtre* (1956).

Kessel, JOSEPH (1898–1979), novelist and journalist of Russian parentage, a member of the **Académie* (1962), author of imaginative novels of action, often inspired by his own experiences as a widely travelled correspondent (his articles have been collected in a series of volumes entitled *Témoin parmi les hommes*). He made his name with novels exalting the heroism of the pilots of the 1914–18 war (of whom he was one), e.g. *L'Équipage* (1923). His later works, peopled by gangsters, anarchists, Russian princes turned taxi-drivers, and seductive *demi-mondaines*, as well as true heroes, include *Nuits de princes* (1928), *Vent de sable* (1929), *Le Coup de grâce* (1931), *Le Tour du malheur* (1950, 4 vols.), *Le Lion* (1958), *Les Cavaliers* (1967).

Kléber, JEAN-BAPTISTE (1753–1800), a famous general of the Revolutionary armies, distinguished himself in the **Vendée*, at **Fleurus*, and with the Army of the Rhine. When Bonaparte left Egypt to return to France (1799), he took command there, and defeated a greatly superior Turkish army at Heliopolis. He was assassinated in Cairo by a Moslem fanatic.

Klingsor, Tristan, *pseudonym of* LÉON LECLÈRE (1874–1966), poet, also a painter, art critic, and musician. He was at first a **Symbolist* (sometime editor of *La *Vogue*), writing in a very musical **vers libre*, and later a light-hearted **fantaisiste*, inspired by the world of fairy-tales and medieval legend. His collections include *Schéhérazade* (1903), sensual love poems later set to music by Ravel; *Le Valet de cœur* (1908); *Humoresques* (1921); *L'Escarbille d'or* (1922).

Knock, ou le Triomphe de la médecine (1923), a robustly satirical farce which made Romains's name as a comic dramatist; first produced by Jouvet, who played Knock.

Dr. Knock arrives at Saint-Maurice, the small centre of a backward mountain district, to take over from Dr. Parpalaid. He finds there are no patients: the locals are too healthy, or too ignorant, to call in a doctor. So he tries a little publicity and an astute system of free consultations, and so successfully exploits the superstitious peasant mentality that the whole countryside is soon in the throes of fevers, colics, or nervous prostration, and eager to pay to be cured.

Kock, CHARLES-PAUL DE (1794–1871), a highly prolific and popular novelist whose comic vigour made up for his total lack of style. His best-known novels—*Georgette* (1820), *Gustave, ou le Mauvais Sujet* (1821), *Mon voisin Raymond* (1822), *L'Amant de la lune* (1847)—rollicking and risky, even frankly coarse, and often sentimental, give a good picture of life and amusements in France *c.* 1820–45. They were widely enjoyed in England (read, for example, by Macaulay and Elizabeth Barrett Browning); *v. English Literature, French Influence on*, 4.

Kostrowitzky, WILHELM APOLLINARIS DE, *v. Apollinaire.*

Kotzebue, AUGUST FRIEDRICH FERDINAND VON (1761–1819), German dramatist, wrote over 200 plays, notably **drames bourgeois*. Several were translated into

French in the *Collection des théâtres étrangers* (1799) and at least two were produced and played often in Paris— *Misanthropie et repentir* (1799), *Les Deux Frères* (1801).

Krüdener, BARBARA JULIANA VON VIETINGHOFF, BARONESS VON (1764–1824), b. in Riga, sometime wife of Baron von Krüdener, Russian ambassador in Berlin. In her youth she was somewhat dissipated and inordinately vain and had literary pretensions. She frequented the Paris *salons* and *Coppet, and her sentimental, semi-autobiographical romance *Valérie* (1803) had some vogue. She became a

religious mystic, welcome, with her great wealth, in various sects, and for a time influenced Alexander I of Russia, whom she accompanied to Paris in 1815. Her claim to have inspired the Holy *Alliance may have had some foundation.

Krysinska, MARIE (d. *c.* 1922), early *Symbolist poetess, claimed (in the introductions to her *Rythmes pittoresques*, 1890, and *Intermèdes*, 1904) to have originated the *vers libre* with poems printed in little reviews—in 1881 in *La Chronique parisienne*, in 1882 in *Le Chat noir* (e.g. *Symphonie en gris*) and *La Vie moderne*.

L

La Balue, JEAN, CARDINAL DE (1421–91), a minister of Louis XI, imprisoned in an iron cage (1469–80) for conspiring with Charles the Bold.

Là-bas, v. Huysmans.

Labé, LOUISE (*c.* 1525–65), 'la Belle Cordière' (her husband was a wealthy rope-maker), poetess of the school of *Scève, wrote lyrics (23 *sonnets and three elegies) expressing the joys and torments of love with the passion and sincerity of Sappho, also a prose *Débat de Folie et d'Amour*. At the age of 16, she is said to have gone to the wars accoutred as a soldier.

La Beaumelle, LAURENT ANGLIVIEL DE (1726–73), man of letters, an adversary of Voltaire.

Laberthonnière, LUCIEN, ABBÉ (1860–1932), Neo-Catholic, Modernist philosopher (*v. Blondel, M.*). His works include *Le Dogmatisme moral* (1898), *Essais de philosophie religieuse* (1903), *Le Réalisme chrétien et l'idéalisme grec* (1904). The last two were placed on the Index.

Labiche, EUGÈNE (1815–88), prolific and highly successful author of non-stop

farcical comedies and burlesques (*Théâtre complet*, 1878–9, 10 vols.), e.g. *Un Chapeau de paille d'Italie* (1851), *Le *Voyage de M. Perrichon* (1860), *Le Misanthrope et l'Auvergnat* (1852), *L'Affaire de la rue Lourcine* (1857), *La Poudre aux yeux* (1862). Some are still played and enjoyed.

La Boderie, *v. Le Fèvre de la Boderie.*

La Boétie, ÉTIENNE DE (1530–63), a magistrate of the *parlement of Bordeaux, greatly loved and respected by his colleague Montaigne. He wrote, notably, *Le Contr'un* or *Discours de la servitude volontaire* (1576), an ardent youthful declamation against the tyranny of princes, supported by passages from Plutarch, Xenophon, and Tacitus; also a *Mémoire sur l'édit de janvier*, showing his loyalty to existing political institutions; a translation of Xenophon's *Oeconomicus*; and some sonnets—preserved by Montaigne (*Essais*, I, 28), who pays tribute to him in his essay *De l'amitié* (I, 27).

La Borderie, BERTRAND DE, *v. Héroët.*

Labrousse, ERNEST (1895–   ), economic historian, a director of studies at the *École *pratique des Hautes Études* from 1930. He was influenced by Simiand and among the first to introduce statistical theories and methods to history. His works include *Esquisse sur le mouvement des prix et des revenus en France au XVIIIe siècle* (1933, 2 vols.) and *La Crise de l'économie française à la fin de l'Ancien Régime et au début de la Révolution* (1944). *v.* also *Mousnier*; *History*, 4 (last §).

Labrunie, GÉRARD, *v. Nerval.*

La Bruyère, JEAN DE (1645–96), was educated for the law, then (on Bossuet's recommendation) entered the service of 'le Grand *Condé' and was tutor to his grandson, the duc de Bourbon. His famous *Caractères de Théophraste, traduits du grec, avec les caractères ou les mœurs de ce siècle* (1688, final augm. ed. 1694; Eng. trans. 1699) consist mainly (apart from the trans. of Theophrastus) of observations on character and conduct (grouped under such headings as *De la cour*; *Des biens de fortune*; *Des ouvrages de l'esprit*—opinions on literary matters and individual authors), interspersed with portraits (often of living people under disguised names) exemplifying the failings he describes. The work reveals him as a pessimist and a master of irony; not a deep or original thinker, but independent, sensitive, and perceptive, soberly scornful of the vanity and frivolity of the world around him, critical of faulty institutions, and alive to the plight of the poor. He writes with great art, in a terse, rapid style, deploying his rich vocabulary to bring his portraits physically, as well as morally, to life. The work indicated his support of the *anciens* in the *Querelle des anciens et des modernes*, and his election to the *Académie (1693) was a triumph for that party. In his retirement he wrote *Dialogues sur le Quiétisme* (*v. Quietism*), supporting Bossuet. His *Caractères* probably influenced early 18th-c. English essayists.

Lac, Le, v. Méditations poétiques.

La Calprenède, GAUTHIER DE COSTES DE (1614–63), wrote competent tragedies and

tragicomedies (e.g. *La Mort de Mithridate*; *Bradamante*; *Jeanne d'Angleterre*; *Le Comte d'Essex*, later rehandled by T. Corneille; *La Mort des enfants d'Hérode*), but is best known for his vast, pseudo-historical romances—not to the modern taste, but much admired, imitated, dramatized, and translated in their day—e.g. *Cassandre* (1644–50, 10 vols.; Cassandre, the heroine, is the daughter of Darius who married Alexander the Great; the chief hero is Orondate), *Cléopâtre* (1647–56, 12 vols.; Cléopâtre, the heroine, is a supposed daughter of Antony and Cleopatra; the hero is *Artaban), *Pharamond* (1661–70, 12 vols., the last 5 by a continuator).

Lacan, JACQUES, *v. Structuralism.*

Lacépède, ÉTIENNE DE (1756–1825), naturalist, completed *Buffon's *Histoire naturelle.* Buffon had got him a post at the *Jardin du Roi* (*v. Jardin des Plantes*) and he later held a chair there. As a young man, he was interested in music and wrote an opera, *Omphale*; late in life, he turned historian and also held high official posts.

La Ceppède, JEAN DE (*c.* 1550–1622), lawyer and metaphysical poet (*cf. Sponde*; *Chassignet*). His *Théorèmes sur les mystères de la Rédemption* and *Seconde Partie des Théorèmes spirituels sur les mystères de la descente de Jésus-Christ aux enfers* (1613–21, 2 vols.) are a mixture of symbolism and crude, vivid realism.

La Chaise, FRANÇOIS DE (1624–1709), *Jesuit priest (a *Moliniste*), confessor of Louis XIV, gave his name to the famous *Cimetière du Père-Lachaise* on a hill in the eastern part of Paris. This was once a Jesuit estate, used as a place of rest by the Order; La Chaise often resided there and interested himself in its development (*c.* 1680). It was bought and converted into a municipal cemetery in 1803–4. *v. Père Goriot, Le.*

La Châtre, EDME, COMTE DE (d. 1645), a courtier prominent in the political intrigues of the last years of Louis XIII

and the beginning of the regency of Anne
d'Autriche. He left memoirs of this period.
v. Lenclos.

La Chaussée, Pierre-Claude Nivelle
de (1692–1754), dramatist. Rich, gay, and
dissipated, he attracted attention at the age
of 40 with a verse *Épître à Clio* (1731),
attacking Houdar de la Motte's conception
of poetry. He was the originator in France
of sentimental comedy, or *comédie
larmoyante* (*v. Drame*; *Comedy*), in which
the pathetic element, drawn from a
realistic presentation of the agonizing
problems of ordinary domestic life,
outweighs or obliterates the comic. He
tended to moralize (*v. Raison raisonnante*),
and Piron dubbed him 'révérend père La
Chaussée'. His chief plays, written in
rather colourless verse, but skilfully
contrived to arouse the interest of his
audience, are *La Fausse Antipathie* (1733)
and *Le Préjugé à la mode* (1735), both pleas
in favour of conjugal love; **Mélanide*
(1741; his masterpiece); *Paméla* (1743;
adapted from Richardson); *L'École des
mères* (1744); *La Gouvernante* (1747). He
was elected to the **Académie* in 1736.

Lachelier, Jules (1832–1918), a
philosopher who continued and clarified
the doctrines of Ravaisson-Mollien,
greatly influencing modern French
philosophy, through his teaching (at the
*École normale supérieure, 1864–75) rather
than his writings.

La Chesnaie, *v. Lamennais.*

Laclos, Pierre Choderlos de (1741–
1803), an army officer of blameless life,
who, aspiring, it is said, to be a moralist,
deployed his gift for psychological analysis
and vivid, dry description by depicting the
professional seducer and his victims in *Les
Liaisons dangereuses* (1782), a novel in
letter form. Valmont is a well-born,
cynical, unscrupulous blackguard who
delights in seducing women. Many of the
letters pass between him and his even more
evil accomplice Mme de Merteuil, relating
the artifices by which he debauches two of
his victims: one is driven to death by

shame and remorse, the other enters a
nunnery. His death in a duel with a rival
brings to light Mme de Merteuil's
machinations. She is publicly ostracized,
and soon so hideously disfigured by
smallpox that she would be better dead.

Lacombe, François, *v. Dictionaries,* 1766.

La Condamine, Charles-Marie de
(1701–74), scientist, one of a mission sent
to Ecuador to measure a degree of the
meridian at the equator (1735; *cf.
Maupertuis*). On his return he descended
the Amazon. He wrote a *Relation abrégée
d'un voyage fait dans l'intérieur de
l'Amérique méridionale* (1745).

Lacordaire, Jean-Baptiste-Henri
(1802–61), Roman Catholic priest, began
as a disciple of **Lamennais*, but remained
in the Church when Lamennais broke with
it, later becoming a Dominican, and a
brilliant orator. Latterly, he was head of
a famous college at Sorèze, near
Carcassonne. His published works include
the funeral orations for which he was
renowned.

Lacretelle, Jacques de (1888–1985),
great-grandson of Lacretelle *jeune* (*v.
below*), novelist (a member of the
*Académie, 1936). After making his name
with *La Vie inquiète de Jean Hermelin*
(1920) and *Silbermann* (1922; a moving
study of a young Jew whose racial pre-
cociousness is at odds with the spirit
of French culture), he published *La
Bonifas* (1925) and two more novels
(originally intended as one) on the
Silbermann theme, *Amour nuptial* (1929)
and *Le Retour de Silbermann* (1930).
Then came *Les Hauts-Ponts* (1932–5,
4 vols.), a successful **roman-cycle* of
provincial life. The chief character, the
lonely, avaricious Lise, half peasant, half
aristocrat, has a tenacious love of property
and only one aim in life, to regain
possession of her birthplace, the Château
des Hauts-Ponts. Her shiftless father had
lost it, and in the end she gets it back, only
to see it sold to pay her son's debts. Her
passion for the land and for nature, and the
many scenes of country life (in the

Vendée), are described with fine poetic sensitivity. Lacretelle's other novels include *Le Pour et le contre* (1946), which contains pictures of literary life in Paris between the wars.

Lacretelle, (1) PIERRE-LOUIS DE (1751–1824), Lacretelle *aîné*; (2) his brother JEAN-CHARLES-DOMINIQUE DE (1766–1855), Lacretelle *jeune*. Lacretelle *aîné*, politician and publicist, was one of a pre-Revolutionary circle that included Condorcet, d'Alembert, and Buffon. He returned to public life under the *Directoire*, and later at one time helped B. Constant to edit *La *Minerve française*. He left writings on politics, also *Mélanges de philosophie et de littérature* (1802–7). Lacretelle *jeune* began (1789) by reporting the proceedings of the *Assemblée nationale* for the *Journal des Débats*, then turned to literature and history, and from 1812 was professor of history at the *Sorbonne*. His *Précis historique de la Révolution française* (1801–6) and *Histoire de la Révolution française* (1821–7) are among the earliest studies of this era. He left memoirs, *Testament politique et littéraire* (1840).

Lacroix, PAUL (1807–84), 'le Bibliophile Jacob', bibliographer, cataloguer, and editor of scholarly and other texts. In his youth, he wrote wildly *Romantic novels, also tales, e.g. *La Dame macabre, histoire fantastique du XVᵉ siècle* (1832), *Contes du bibliophile Jacob à ses petits-enfants* (1831).

La Croix du Maine, FRANÇOIS GRUDÉ, SIEUR DE (1552–92), bibliographer, compiler of *La Bibliothèque française* (1584; the 1776 ed. included *Du Verdier's *Bibliothèque*), etc. He was assassinated at Tours.

La Curne de Sainte-Palaye, JEAN-BAPTISTE DE, *v. Dictionaries*, 1756.

La Devinière, *v. Rabelais*.

Ladvocat, JEAN-BAPTISTE, *v. Dictionaries*, 1752.

La Fare, CHARLES-AUGUSTE, MARQUIS DE (1644–1712), author of light epicurean verse and memoirs. After distinguished military service and a period of fervent admiration for Mme de La Sablière, he left the army (he fell foul of Louvois and was refused promotion) and wasted the last 30 years of his life in idle dissipation, consorting with Chaulieu and the society of the *Temple. His verse and his lyrical tragedy *Penthée* are of little importance; but his well-written *Mémoires* contain interesting portraits, also criticism of the age (notably a stern appraisal of Louis XIV).

La Fayette, MARIE-JOSEPH, MARQUIS DE (1757–1834), soldier and politician. Fired with enthusiasm for the doctrines of the *philosophes*, liberty, and the rights of man, he fought in the American War of Independence and on returning home figured prominently in the Revolution. He was elected to the *États généraux* (1789) and was the prime mover of the *Déclaration des droits de l'homme*; he was also put in command of the newly created *Garde nationale*. But his position as a sort of buffer between the people and the royal family (whom he was powerless to help) undermined his prestige, and in the end he was forced to flee the country. He was again briefly in the limelight during the 1830 *Revolution, when, once more in command of the *Garde nationale*, he helped to put Louis-Philippe on the throne.

La Fayette, MARIE-MADELEINE PIOCHE DE LA VERGNE, COMTESSE DE (1634–93), novelist, settled in Paris in 1659 (having parted from her husband) and became the close friend of *Henriette d'Angleterre (whose life she wrote—*Histoire de Madame Henriette d'Angleterre*, 1720), the intimate friend of La Rochefoucauld in his later years (1665–80), also a friend of Ménage, Huet, Segrais, and Mme de Sévigné. Her chief romances were the short *La Princesse de Montpensier* (1662); the longer *Zaÿde* (1670; *v. Huet*) and *La *Princesse de Clèves* (1678; her masterpiece, possibly influenced by La

Rochefoucauld), both published under the name of Segrais; and *La Comtesse de Tende* (1724), again a short work. *Zaÿde*, loosely connected tales on the model of *Le *Grand Cyrus*, but in a Spanish setting, is mainly a study of love in its less happy aspects (e.g. the happiness of Ximenès and Bélasire is ruined by his morbid jealousy of her dead lover). The other three romances are studies of married life, a field hitherto unexplored by the novelist. The princesse de Montpensier has made a political marriage, the comtesse de Tende a marriage of ambition. Both marriages are loveless and supremely unhappy; both end in tragedy. In *La Princesse de Clèves*, will and duty triumph over passion, as with Corneille; but the moral is melancholy— that to do one's duty does not necessarily bring happiness. With these works Mme de La Fayette may be said to have inaugurated the French novel of character, replacing the grandiloquence, incredible adventures, and tedious length of Mlle de Scudéry's romances by proportion, simplicity, sincerity, and an easy, sober style, without affectation or sentimentality (*v. Novel*, 2). Her *Mémoires de la cour de France* (1731), for the years 1688–9, describe James II's arrival at the French court and his departure for Ireland.

Lafcadio, in *Gide's *Les Caves du Vatican*.

Lafenestre, GEORGES (1837–1919), minor *Parnassien* poet (*Les Espérances*, 1863; *Idylles et chansons*, 1873; *Images fuyantes*, 1902, etc.), also art historian and critic.

Laffitte, PIERRE (1823–1903), philosopher and *savant*, a disciple of Comte. He accepted all his master's doctrines, even his later religious beliefs. His chief work was *Les Grands Types de l'humanité* (1875–6, 2 vols.). The chair of the history of science at the *Collège de France* was created for him (1892).

La Flèche, *v. Prytanée militaire*.

La Fontaine, JEAN DE (1621–95), poet and fabulist, b. at Château-Thierry in

Champagne, where his father held a post in the *Eaux et Forêts*; educated partly at the *Maison de l'*Oratoire* in Paris. He thought of entering the Church, then studied law, but showed a disinclination for steady work and was content to spend the next 10 years in idleness at Château-Thierry and most of the rest of his life as the pensioner of wealthy patrons (N. Fouquet, 1656–61; the duchesse de Bouillon—*v. Mazarin's Nieces* (7); Mme de La Sablière, whose hospitality he enjoyed for some 20 years from *c.* 1672; M. d'Hervart). He married (1647), but later parted from his family; he succeeded to his father's post, but relinquished it. Though a man of weak and inconstant character, absent-minded and 'pesant en conversation' (Saint-Simon), he was affectionate and loyal, highly intelligent, very observant, and impressionable. His ardent literary enthusiasms extended from Plato, Plutarch, and the Latin poets to Boccaccio, Ariosto, Marot, Malherbe, and Voiture, from *Baruch to *L'*Astrée*: in a verse *discours de réception* at the *Académie* (he was elected in 1684, after some opposition from the king) he aptly described himself as a 'papillon de Parnasse'. He began as a disciple of Voiture and the society poets of the day, but his chief work, the famous *Fables* (publ. at intervals from 1668, when he was 47), bears the stamp of his own poetic genius. His other works include the well-known *Contes et Nouvelles* (publ. at intervals from 1664), which he publicly disavowed after his conversion (following a serious illness) in 1692; the famous *Élégie aux nymphes de Vaux* (1661; *v. Vaux-le-Vicomte*), inviting them to implore the king's clemency for his patron Fouquet, for whom he also wrote the poem *Adonis* and *Clymène*, a pleasant comedy; *Le Voyage en Limousin* (written 1663, publ. posth.; prose and verse), six delightful letters to his wife, describing a journey to Limoges; *Les Amours de Psyché et de Cupidon* (1669; *cf. Psyché*), set in the framework of a Platonic conversation in the park of *Versailles; *La *Captivité de Saint Malc* (1673); *Le Quinquina* (1682), a poem in praise of quinine, then a new drug; the poem *Philémon et Baucis* (1685); the *Épître à Huet* (v. *Huet*) and *Discours à Mme de La Sablière* (1687 and 1679), poems of interest for the light they throw on his literary art, his support of the *anciens* in the **Querelle des anciens et des modernes*, and (the latter) his rejection of the Cartesian view of animals. He also appears to have had a hand in the comedies *Ragotin* (1684; from an episode in Scarron's **Roman comique*), *Le Florentin* (1685), and *La Coupe enchantée* (1688); they were produced under the name of the actor Champmeslé.

La Fontaine et ses Fables, v. *Taine*.

Laforgue, JULES (1860–87), *Symbolist poet, b. in Montevideo (where his father taught French), educated at Tarbes (in the Pyrenees), came to Paris (1876) and lived on scanty means. In 1881, influential friends helped him to the post of reader to the empress Augusta of Germany, and for the next five years his life, mainly in Berlin, was comfortable but dull. He then married an English governess, Leah Lee, and returned with her to a life of poverty in Paris. Seven months later he died of tuberculosis. His chief works are the poems collected before his death in *Les Complaintes* (1885) and *L'Imitation de Notre-Dame la Lune* (1886) and posthumously in *Derniers Vers* (1890; inc. *Des fleurs de bonne volonté* and *Le Concile féerique*, a poem in dialogue form, first publ. 1886 and later staged); and, in poetic prose, his *Moralités légendaires* (1887, posth.), six elaborately written, satirical versions of, or embroideries upon, old tales—e.g. *Salomé*, dialogues parodying Flaubert's **Hérodias*. His poetic idiom heralds the **fantaisistes*. He was an inaugurator of the **vers libre*, and conversational, even slangy, in his choice of language. He deflated fantasy with irony, and rose abruptly (and self-consciously) from the mundane to the poetic or philosophical. v. *English Literature, French Influence on*, 5.

La Fosse, ANTOINE DE (c. 1653–1708), wrote *Manlius Capitolinus* (1698), a

tragedy based on Livy's narrative and modelled on Otway's *Venice Preserv'd* (1682).

La Fresnaye, v. *Vauquelin de la Fresnaye*.

Lagneau, JULES (1851–94), a great teacher of philosophy, like his pupil and disciple 'Alain' (É.-A. Chartier). For most of his career he taught at the *Lycée Michelet*, in Paris. *L'Existence de Dieu* (1925) is a version, from notes taken by his pupils, of lectures he gave in 1892–3.

La Grange, CHARLES DE (1639–92), actor, a member of Molière's company from 1659. His register of the plays produced, takings, etc., is an invaluable document for the student of the theatre.

Lagrange, JOSEPH-LOUIS (1736–1813), mathematician and astronomer, director of the Academy of Berlin (from 1766), settled in Paris from 1787, with a pension from Louis XVI. His chief work was *Mécanique analytique* (1788; rev. 1811). He was responsible for important advances in his field of study.

Lagrange-Chancel, FRANÇOIS-JOSEPH DE (1677–1758), wrote *Philippiques*, virulently satirizing the Regent (the duc d'*Orléans); also tragedies, Greek in theme only, e.g. *Oreste et Pylade* (1697), *Méléagre* (1699), *Amasis* (1701), *Alceste* (1703), *Ino et Mélicerte* (1713).

La Halle, ADAM DE, v. *Adam de la Halle*.

La Harpe, JEAN-FRANÇOIS DE (1739–1803), dramatist, journalist, and a typical critic of the late 18th-c. dogmatic school (v. *Critics and Criticism*, 1); a disciple, friend, and critic of Voltaire. His indifferent tragedies include *Warwick* (1763); *Philoctète* (1783); *Mélanie* (1778; never acted), an attack on the cloister, based on the true story of a girl who hanged herself to avoid becoming a nun. A more valuable work is his *Lycée, ou Cours de littérature ancienne et moderne* (1799–1805), lectures he gave as a professor at the **Lycée*. His literary correspondence with the grand duke of Russia (later Paul I) in the years 1774–91 (publ. 1804–7) has many lively comments on literature, people, and events. *v. Musical Controversies.*

Lahontan, LOUIS-ARMAND, BARON DE (1666–*c.* 1715), an early French traveller in Canada. His *Voyages* (1703) influenced both French and English literature (e.g. Chateaubriand's *Les *Natchez*). They contain a *Dialogue curieux entre l'auteur et un sauvage de bon sens qui a voyagé*, the latter being a *Huron.

Lahor, Jean, *pseudonym of* HENRI CAZALIS (1840–1909), minor *Parnassien* poet, a friend of Mallarmé; also a doctor. His verse (*L'Illusion*, 1875 and 1888) reflects his interest in Oriental studies and occultism.

Lai, in medieval literature, a short narrative poem in octosyllables, often on the subject of love and with a supernatural element; sometimes of Breton origin. There are a number of *lais* by Marie de France and others of unknown authorship. The term was also applied to *fabliaux* of a more refined character, e.g. the *Lai d'Aristote*.

In the 14th and 15th cs., the term was applied to lyric poems in a complex fixed form.

Lai d'Aristote, Le, a *fabliau* by Henri d'Andeli. The story is found in collections of Oriental tales.

Alexander the Great, having conquered India, has fallen a victim to the charms of an Indian maiden. Aristotle reproves him and he promises amendment. The maiden, learning why he is melancholy, vows vengeance on the crusty grammarian, bidding Alexander to be watching at dawn on the morrow from a tower overlooking the garden. Next day at dawn Aristotle is distracted from his books by the song of the maiden, who gradually so allures and bewitches him by skilful coquetry that he allows her to ride singing on his back as he crawls on all fours about the orchard, saddled and bridled. Caught in this

ridiculous posture by Alexander, he turns his discomfiture to good account: 'Sire, see how right I was to warn you of the dangers of love. I have added example to precept.'

Lai de l'ombre, Le, an early 13th-c. verse *roman d'aventure* by Jean Renart. A knight seeks to win his lady, is repelled, but contrives, while they dispute, to slip his ring on to her finger. As they sit by a well-head in the castle courtyard she bids him take it back. He says he will give it to the lady he loves next best, leans over the well where her image is reflected, and drops it in. 'See,' he says, 'she has taken it.' His delicate compliment wins the lady's heart.

Lais, Le, v. Villon.

Laisse, an assonanced or (later) rhymed stanza, of indeterminate length and usually of decasyllables or *alexandrines; the metrical form of the *chansons de geste.*

Laissez faire, *v. Économistes.*

Lakanal, JOSEPH (1762–1845), a religious who, when his Order was suppressed at the Revolution, subscribed to the *Constitution civile du clergé*, was elected to the *Convention, and voted for Louis XVI's death. He was passionately interested in education and responsible for many of the educational projects of the Revolutionary era (*v. École normale supérieure; Jardin des Plantes*). His anti-monarchical record led to his exile in 1816. He went to America, was for a time a planter in Alabama, and returned to France in 1832.

Lakistes, Les, the English Lake Poets, met with a deep response in France; *v. Foreign Influences,* 3.

Lalaing, Le Livre des faits de Jacques de, v. Jacques de Lalaing.

Lally, THOMAS-ARTHUR, BARON DE TOLLENDAL, COMTE DE (1702–66), a brilliant soldier of Irish Jacobite descent, was promoted on the field of *Fontenoy (1745) by Louis XV, served at Falkirk

(1746) as aide-de-camp to the Young Pretender, etc. In 1755, he was sent to India in command of an expedition against the English. At first things went well, then difficulties arose, of his own and other people's making; he met with reverses, and in the end surrendered at Pondicherry (1761). While a prisoner of war in London, he heard that he was being accused of treachery in Paris, returned to France on parole, and constituted himself a prisoner in the *Bastille. His trial, after a delay of two years, was a travesty of justice and dragged on till 1766. Louis XV refused to intervene on his behalf, and he was found guilty and executed. His legitimated son, the marquis de Lally-Tollendal, long strove to clear his father's name. He had the support of Voltaire and Louis XVI, but never wholly succeeded.

La Marche, OLIVIER DE (c. 1425–1502), *rhétoriqueur poet and chronicler, entered the service of the dukes of Burgundy and wrote Mémoires of the period 1435–67, chiefly celebrating that house. His poems, mainly courtly, include the Parement et triumphe des dames, a moral allegory in which a lover provides his mistress with a complete outfit of virtues, from slippers of Humility to kerchief of Hopefulness; the Chevalier délibéré, in which the author sets out late in life, accompanied by Thought, to fight Accident and Weakness in the forest of Fate.

Lamarck, JEAN-BAPTISTE DE (1744–1829), naturalist, an originator of the doctrine of biological evolution. His works include Flore française (1778); Philosophie zoologique (1809), outlining his theories of transformism, i.e. the persistence of types, modified by and adapted to environment and always improving; Histoire naturelle des animaux sans vertèbres (1815–22). He was associated with the *Jardin des Plantes.

Lamartine, ALPHONSE-MARIE-LOUIS DE PRAT DE (1790–1869), a great *Romantic poet, also a statesman and a fine orator, came of an old family of Franc-Comtois landowners and soldiers (his father, a Royalist, was imprisoned during the Revolution). He grew up in a tranquil family atmosphere at Milly, a small family property in pleasant country near Mâcon (described in his *Confidences; *Harmonies poétiques et religieuses; and La Vigne et la maison, v. below), went to school at Lyons, ran away after two years, and was then sent to the *Jesuit college at Belley (1803–7). Thereafter, apart from a visit to Italy (where his senses revelled in the colour, light, and warmth) and brief service in the royal bodyguard, he lived quietly at home until 1816.

In 1816, while at Aix-les-Bains for his health, he met and fell deeply in love with Julie Charles, the invalid wife of a Paris physician and the 'Elvire' of many of his poems. He followed her back to Paris. Next spring he was again at Aix, awaiting her arrival; but she was too ill to travel and died that autumn. Inspired by this emotional crisis, he set to work seriously on the *Méditations poétiques (1820), his first published work and an instant success. These melodious, plaintive verses, in which Nature is used to reflect the poet's moods, and the *mal du siècle of *Obermann and *René is expressed in poetic form, restored to French poetry a lyricism that had been lost for centuries. The French, who had recently discovered Byron (v. Foreign Influences, 3), now had a gentler Byron of their own, one whose gloom never turned to revolt and who called from his misery on God and not on Satan.

Meanwhile, Lamartine had married (1820) Anna Eliza Birch, a young Englishwoman of means, and embarked on a diplomatic career, first in Naples, then in Florence (embassy secretary from 1825). His poetic output continued with the Nouvelles Méditations (1823), containing the well-known poems Ischia and Le Crucifix, but inferior to his first collection and coldly received ('Elvire' is now an amalgam of Julie Charles, his wife Anna, and the Italian girl in *Graziella); La Mort de Socrate (1823), a philosophico-religious poem in which (as described by Plato) Socrates talks to his friends before going to his death; Le Dernier Chant du *pèlerinage d'Harold* (1825), a compliment to Byron; *Les *Harmonies poétiques et religieuses* (1830). He abandoned diplomacy after the 1830 *Revolution: his Royalist sympathies had waned, and he began to see himself as a prophet and leader of the people (*cf. Hugo*). He stood for the *Chambre des *Députés*, but was not elected. Postponing his political ambitions, he travelled—*en grand seigneur* with a large retinue—in Greece, Syria (where he visited Lady Hester Stanhope), and Palestine (*cf. Chateaubriand*). The tour is described in *Souvenirs, impressions, pensées, et paysages pendant un voyage en Orient* (1835). Elected to the Chamber in his absence, he took his seat in 1833, allying himself to no particular party. His brilliant speeches (e.g. on the liberty of the press, the abolition of slavery, capital punishment; and *v. Légende napoléonienne*) and lofty, if none too practical, conception of a society free from base self-interest and dedicated to ideals of liberty and justice soon captured the imagination of his countrymen.

**Jocelyn* and *La *Chute d'un ange* (1836 and 1838; fragments of an epic) were followed by *Recueillements poétiques* (1839), a collection containing his last great poem, *La Vigne et la maison*. The highly successful *Histoire des Girondins* (1847) committed him to advanced Republicanism. His courage and rousing speeches during the 1848 *Revolution made him a popular idol, and as head of the provisional government he exercised a power almost amounting to dictatorship. But it was short-lived (*v. Republics, 2*), and he soon retired into private life. Now deeply in dept (he had always been extravagant and generous, and had a passion for speculating in land), he sold Milly and became a literary hack. His wife's death (1863) left him in growing poverty, with failing powers; but after 1867 he enjoyed a government pension.

His other works include *Saül*, a 5-act verse tragedy he wrote in 1818 to take his mind off the death of 'Elvire' (he offered it to Talma, who refused it, but he often read it in the *salons* he frequented); *Raphaël* (1849), a short novel,

romanticizing his love for 'Elvire' (here called Julie); *Le Tailleur de pierres de Saint-Point* (1851); *Les *Confidences* and *Nouvelles Confidences* (1849 and 1851), autobiography; *Œuvres oratoires et écrits politiques* (1864-5), his speeches, etc.; and many volumes of history and biography.

Lambert, ANNE-THÉRÈSE DE MARGUENAT DE COURCELLES, MARQUISE DE (1647-1733), a woman of high principles and refined judgement, famous for her *salon (twice weekly, 1710-33)—frequented by both the aristocracy and the literary world and said to be influential in the selection of members of the *Académie*. She wrote *Avis d'une mère à son fils* (1726) and *Avis à sa fille* (1728), containing much sage counsel; *Réflexions sur les femmes*; and treatises on friendship and old age.

Lamennais or **La Mennais**, FÉLICITÉ-ROBERT DE (1782-1854), 'Monsieur Féli', religious writer and Christian democrat. At 34, with the doubtful equipment of an irregular education, ardent religiosity, and a difficult temperament, he became a priest. He came to the fore with the first volume of an *Essai sur l'indifférence en matière de religion* (1817), seeking to establish the verities of the Catholic faith and urging a return to the active practice of religion. He was hailed as a new Bossuet, and his family home at La Chesnaie, near Dinan, became a centre for his disciples. Three further volumes of the *Essai* (1821-3) and his *De la religion considérée dans ses rapports avec l'ordre politique et civil* (1824) caused uneasiness to Church and State by their—subversively Ultramontane (*v. Gallicanism*)—contention that subordination to religion, and hence to the supreme authority of the pope, was the only salvation for society. He developed this, on less traditional lines, into a conception of a liberal democracy in which the people, discarding outworn monarchical theories, would unite for liberty, taking matters temporal into their own hands, but leaving spiritual authority with the Church. (About this time, his influence was felt by the *Romantics, e.g. Hugo, Lamartine, Sainte-Beuve; *v. also

Guérin, M. de. Later, he would make a deep impact on G. Sand.) He now founded a religious congregation (the *Congrégation de Saint-Pierre*, 1828), an *Agence générale pour la Défense de la Liberté religieuse* (1830), and—assisted by his fervent young disciples Lacordaire and Montalembert—the newspaper *L'Avenir* (1830–2), with the motto 'Dieu et Liberté'. His views incurred censure, and he went to Rome to defend his position—confident that Pope Gregory XVI would place himself at the head of his crusade for freedom; but on the way home he was overtaken by the encyclical *Mirari vos* (Aug. 1832), indicating the Church's deep disapproval. His famous *Paroles d'un croyant* (1834), written at this time of spiritual stress in a sweeping, apostrophic style modelled on the Bible, reaffirmed his belief that democracy has its source in the Gospels, and that men should unite to form a Utopian republic in which religion and mutual love will suffice to guide their conduct; so strong was its emotional appeal that the compositors are said to have wept as they set it up. Book and author were promptly condemned in the encyclical *Singulari nos* (July 1834), whereupon Lamennais broke with the Church and his disciples and went over to the advanced Republicans. He was again more than once in trouble for his writings. Though elected to the *Assemblée constituante* after the 1848 *Revolution, he showed no talent for constructive politics. He retired into private life, embittered by events, after the *coup d'état* of 1851. He died unreconciled with the Church and was buried, as he had wished, in a pauper's grave. His other works include *Le Livre du peuple* (1837), *De l'esclavage moderne* (1840), *Esquisse d'une philosophie* (1841–6, 4 vols.).

Lamentations, *v. Mathieu or Matheolus.*

La Mésangère, PIERRE DE, *v. Dictionaries,* 1821.

La Mesnardière, HIPPOLYTE-JULES PILET DE (1610–63), wrote a *Poétique* (1639; only vol. I was publ.) in which

Aristotle and the Italian classical poets were his guide.

La Mettrie, JULIEN OFFROY DE (1709–51), physician and materialist philosopher. His *Histoire naturelle de l'âme* (1745) and *L'Homme machine* (1748) excited such hostility as being subversive of religious belief that he had to flee in turn from France and from Holland. Frederick II invited him to Berlin, where he wrote *L'Homme plante* (1749) and *Sur l'origine des animaux* (1750).

Lamiel, *v. Stendhal.*

La Mole, BONIFACE DE (d. 1574), executed with Coconas for plotting to place the duc d'Alençon on the throne. He figures in *Dumas père's La Dame de Monsoreau.

La Môle, Mathilde de, in Stendhal's *Le *Rouge et le Noir.

La Monnoye, BERNARD DE (1641–1728), author of *Noëls bourguignons*, a work in the Burgundian *patois* depicting amusing, familiar scenes in the framework of the old *mystères de la Nativité. v. also La Palice.

La Mothe le Vayer, FRANÇOIS DE (1588–1672), a magistrate and a learned *libertin, a member of the *Académie, and tutor to the duc d'*Orléans (brother of Louis XIV). As 'Orasius Tubero' he wrote *Dialogues à l'imitation des anciens* (1630), *Discours chrétiens de l'immortalité de l'âme* (1637), *Considérations sur l'éloquence française* (1638), *Traité de la vertu des païens* (1642), *Hexaméron rustique* (1670), etc.

La Motte, *v. Houdar de la Motte.*

La Motte, COMTESSE DE, *v. Collier, L'Affaire du.*

La Motte Fouqué, FRIEDRICH, BARON DE (1777–1843), German poet and novelist. His choice of medieval rather than classical themes appealed to the *Romantics (*v.* Foreign Influences*, 3). He is noted for his fairy romances *Sintram* and *Undine*. The latter inspired Giraudoux's play *Ondine* (1939), the story of the nymph who married a mortal, realized her ambition to possess a soul, but learnt the meaning of unhappiness.

Lamourette, ADRIEN (1742–94), bishop of Lyons. By a moving speech (7 July 1792) in the **Assemblée législative* he reconciled the various factions—but only for a few hours; whence *un baiser Lamourette*, meaning an ephemeral reconciliation. He was executed in 1794.

Lamoureux, CHARLES (1834–99), orchestral conductor, did much to make Wagner and various Russian composers known in France. He founded (1881) the Sunday *Concerts Lamoureux*, a feature of Parisian musical life. *Cf. Colonne; Pasdeloup.*

Lancelot, one of the heroes of Arthurian legend (*v. Romans bretons*), apparently first mentioned in Chrétien de Troyes's **Erec*, then in his **Cligès* and **Chevalier à la charrette* (where he is the hero and the lover of **Guinevere*). He figures prominently in the vast 13th-c. prose cycle on the quest for the Holy Grail (*v. Perceval*). In *Lancelot du Lac* (the central section of this cycle) he is carried off (after the death of his father, King Ban) and brought up by the Lady of the Lake, then sent to Arthur's court, where he falls in love with Guinevere. In the course of many adventures, he takes the castle of Dolorous Gard (renamed Joyous Gard after he has rid it of enchantments). Here he is visited by Arthur and Guinevere, and the story of his love for her continues (with hostile intervention from Morgain la Fée). He also visits the Grail castle, where, under a spell, he takes the daughter of its king for Guinevere and fathers Galaad (Galahad). His story is resumed in the last branches of the cycle. He is debarred by his sins from the quest for the Grail, and is smitten with remorse. But in the *Mort Artu* he is again the queen's lover, is captured in her chamber, rescues her from death at the stake, and carries her to Joyous Gard. He makes an enemy of **Gauvain* by

unwittingly killing his brother, and slays him in single combat. He finally restores Guinevere to Arthur, and ends his days in a hermitage. Guinevere retires to a nunnery.

In England, apart from the late 14th-c. *Le Morte Arthure* (the story of the Maid of Astolat and of the tragic end of the loves of Lancelot and Guinevere), Lancelot plays no important part in medieval romances until Malory's *Morte Darthur*.

Lancelot, CLAUDE, *v. Port-Royal.*

Lancelot, Monsieur, *v. Hermant.*

Lancret, NICOLAS (1690–1743), a noted painter in the style of Watteau.

Lanfrey, PIERRE (1828–77), historian. His works, anti-clerical and highly critical of Napoleon, include *L'Église et les philosophes au XVIIIᵉ siècle* (1855), *Essai sur la Révolution française* (1858), *Histoire politique des papes* (1860), *Histoire de Napoléon Iᵉʳ* (1867–75; his chief work, unfinished); also *Les Lettres d'Éverard* (1860), a sociological novel in letter form. He was active in politics after the **Franco-Prussian war*.

Långfors, ARTHUR, *v. Incipit.*

Langlois, CHARLES-VICTOR (1863–1929), medieval historian. His works include an *Introduction aux études historiques* (1898; with Charles Seignobos—*v. History*, 4); *La Vie en France au Moyen Âge* (1924–8, 4 vols.).

Langtoft, *v. Pierre de Langtoft.*

Langue d'oc; Langue d'oïl, *v. French Language.*

Languedoc, Canal du, *v. Colbert.*

Langue française (1969– ; quarterly), a learned philological journal.

Languet, HUBERT (1518–81), diplomat, a **Huguenot* who settled in Germany. His *Vindiciae contra tyrannos* (1579), on the relations between ruler and people, is a pioneer work of political science, in which emerges the idea of a contract, and hence the right to rebel.

Lannes, JEAN, v. Maréchal.

La Noue, (1) FRANÇOIS DE (1531–91), 'Bras de Fer', a *Huguenot soldier, fought with Coligny and later with Henri IV at Arques and Ivry. The patriotic and tolerant spirit of his *Discours politiques et militaires* (1587; written in captivity and inc. his memoirs) impressed even his enemies; (2) his son ODET DE (d. 1618), v. *Dictionaries*, 1596.

Lanson, GUSTAVE (1857–1934), literary historian and critic, director of the *École normale supérieure* and professor at the *Sorbonne*. His many works include, notably, his *Histoire de la littérature française* (1894 and many later eds.; one of the most widely used and influential manuals of its kind, illustrating his interest in ideas and their philosophical implications, his gift for analysis, and his rigorously scientific and positivist approach) and *Manuel bibliographique de la littérature française moderne, depuis 1500 jusqu'à nos jours* (1909–12, 4 vols.; v. *Bibliographies*); also *Principes de composition et de style* (1887), studies of Bossuet (1890) and Boileau (1892), *Hommes et livres*, *Études morales et littéraires* (1895), *L'Idéal français dans la littérature de la Renaissance à la Révolution* (1928). v. *Critics and Criticism*, 2.

Lanterne, **La**, v. Rochefort, H. de.

Lantier, **Auguste**, lover of Gervaise Macquart in Zola's *L'*Assommoir*. Their sons Claude, Étienne, and Jacques figure in *L'*Œuvre*, *Germinal*, and *La *Bête humaine* respectively.

Lantier, ÉTIENNE-FRANÇOIS DE (1734–1826), a cavalry officer turned author, dubbed 'l'Anacharsis des boudoirs' following his pseudo-antique romance *Les Voyages d'Anténor en Grèce et en Asie* (1798), a gay, superficial imitation of

*Barthélemy's *Voyage du jeune Anacharsis*, highly popular and widely translated in its day. He also wrote *L'Impatient* (1778), a one-act verse comedy, *Contes en prose et en vers* (1801), etc.

Lanval, v. Marie de France.

La Palice, JACQUES DE CHABANNES, SEIGNEUR DE (c. 1470–1525), *maréchal de France*, served with distinction in the Italian wars and fell at *Pavia. A song about him by La Monnoye, containing such couplets as 'Un quart d'heure avant sa mort Il était encore en vie', has given rise to the expression *vérité de La Palice* or *lapalissade* for a self-evident truth.

La Pérouse, JEAN-FRANÇOIS DE (1741–88), a famous navigator, killed by natives while on a voyage of discovery in Polynesia.

La Péruse, JEAN BASLIER DE (1529–56), poet of the school of Ronsard, died young leaving the tragedy *Médée* (c. 1553; from Seneca) and promising poems.

Lapidaire, a medieval work describing the curative and talismanic properties of precious stones, sometimes with allegorical interpretations, e.g. the Latin lapidary of Marbode, bishop of Rennes (d. 1123), several times translated into French verse in the 12th and 13th cs.; the lapidary of Philippe de Thaon.

Laplace, PIERRE-ANTOINE DE (1707–93), translator. His *Théâtre anglais* (1745–8, 8 vols.) included the first French translations of 10 of Shakespeare's plays (some scenes being merely summarized) and the plots of 26 others, with an appreciative introduction. The work aroused much interest and greatly annoyed Voltaire. v. *Foreign Influences*, 2; *Ducis*; *Letourneur*.

Laplace, PIERRE-SIMON, MARQUIS DE (1749–1827), mathematician and astronomer, son of a Norman peasant and a *protégé* of d'Alembert. His famous treatises include *Exposition du système du monde* (1796), on the planetary system; *La Mécanique céleste* (1799–1825), *Théorie analytique des probabilités* (1812), *Essai philosophique sur les probabilités* (1814). He was prominent in public life after the Revolution—a minister under the *Consulat*, a member of the *Sénat under the Empire (when a report by him led to the dropping of the *Republican Calendar), and later ennobled by Louis XVIII.

La Porte, PIERRE DE (1603–80), was in the service of Anne d'Autriche and later *valet de chambre* to the young Louis XIV. His memoirs for the years 1624–66 are mainly concerned with court intrigues and justification of his own conduct.

Laprade, VICTOR-RICHARD DE (1812–87), poet, professor of French literature at Lyons (1847–61). His large output (*Œuvres poétiques*, 1878–81, 6 vols.)— mainly classical and Biblical in inspiration, with a strong feeling for nature—includes *Psyché* (1841), the narrative poem that made his name; *Odes et poèmes* (1844), containing the well-known elegy *La Mort d'un chêne*; *Poèmes évangéliques* (1852); *Les Symphonies* (1855); *Les Idylles héroïques* (1858); *Pernette* (1868), a rural *epic.

La Ramée, PIERRE DE, in Latin RAMUS (1515–72), philosopher and grammarian, a *lecteur royal* (*v. Collège de France*); famous as an adversary of Aristotle and scholasticism, e.g. in his *Dialectique* (1555), one of the first such works to be written in French. He was a victim of the Massacre of St. *Bartholomew.

Larbaud, VALERY (1881–1957), a wealthy, cultured, and widely travelled novelist and man of letters. His works include novels and tales, e.g. *Fermina Marquez* (1911; a study of the ferment caused in an exclusive boys' boarding-school by the presence in the locality of the Spanish-American sisters of a new pupil), *A. O. Barnabooth: ses œuvres complètes*; *c'est-à-dire un conte, ses poésies, et son journal intime* (1913; introducing a personality of 20th-c. French literature, Archibaldo Olson Barnabooth, a blasé young S. American millionaire with an unsatisfied soul, who wanders about Europe seeking distraction and the Absolute), *Enfantines* (1918; tales of childhood), and *Amants, heureux amants* (1923; tales of love, inc. *Beauté, mon beau souci*, set in England, which Larbaud knew well); many critical studies of French and English literature (collected in *Ce vice impuni, la lecture*, 1925; the title is taken from Logan Pearsall Smith), and translations of Whitman, S. Butler, J. Joyce (he helped to translate *Ulysses*, 1937), A. Bennett, etc.; lyrical prose writings inspired by his travels (*Jaune, bleu, blanc*, 1927; *Aux couleurs de Rome*, 1938); and a notable *Journal* (1955). His career was cut short in 1935, when he was paralysed by a severe stroke.

Largillière, NICOLAS DE (1656–1746), a noted portrait painter under Louis XIV.

Larguier, LÉO (1878–1950), poet, literary journalist, and novelist. His poems are collected in *La Maison du poète* (1903), *Les Isolements* (1906), *Jacques* (1907; a narrative poem), *Orchestres* (1914), *Les Ombres* (1935), *Mes vingt ans et moi* (1944), etc.

Larivey, PIERRE DE (*c.* 1540–1612), dramatist of Italian descent (his name is a pun on that of his father's family, the Giunti, 'les arrivés', famous Florentine printers). He published nine prose comedies (six, inc. *Les *Esprits*, in 1579; three in 1611), lively adaptations from the Italian; translated many other Italian works, and helped to establish Italian literary influence in France. *v. Basoche*; *Comedy*; *Foreign Influences*, 1.

La Rochefoucauld, FRANÇOIS, DUC DE (1613–80), moralist. In youth he was feverishly active in abortive intrigues against Richelieu (with Mme de Chevreuse) and Mazarin (with Mme de Longueville, with whom he was then in love), being severely wounded (1652) in the *Fronde. His susceptibility to female influence and his gentle, meditative, rather irresolute nature (well described in *Retz's *Mémoires*) unfitted him for intrigue and turmoil, and thereafter he lived in retirement, moving in a small, highly intellectual circle (inc. Mme de La Fayette, his devoted friend 1665–80; Mme de Sablé; Mme de Sévigné). His *Mémoires* (1662; an unauthorized, incorrect text—the authentic text was publ. only in recent times) are remarkable for the penetrating portraits of persons he was associated with in his intrigues. His chief work, the famous *Maximes*, properly the *Réflexions, ou Sentences et maximes morales* (The Hague 1664, an anonymous, clandestine ed.; Paris 1665), consists of some 500 gnomic sentences, analysing the motives of human conduct with merciless penetration; the style is highly polished, the phrasing precise and appropriate to a degree (here he profited from the comments of his friends, notably Mme de Sablé). While recognizing the existence, in rare cases, of pure virtue and disinterested sentiments, he finds them tainted, almost universally, with some element of self-love or interested motive. Man, in pretending to virtue, usually deceives himself as well as others, for egoism is his dominating sentiment, and once virtue becomes conscious it loses its purity. In view of the author's character and conduct, and of the fact that he attenuated his doctrine in successive editions, the *Maximes* should perhaps be regarded more as a literary *tour de force*, the maintenance of a paradox, than as the sincerely held convictions of a moralist. Moreover, many of them, and of the *Réflexions diverses* (publ. long after his death), deal less with the motives of conduct than with social relations in general (e.g. the sound remarks on conversation in the latter work). Their bitter, pessimistic philosophy—approved by the *Jansenists as confirming the vileness of fallen man, but later challenged by Vauvenargues—had a wide influence, e.g. on Voltaire (in *Candide*) and Chamfort. Voltaire said that La Rochefoucauld did much to form the taste of the nation: 'Il accoutuma à penser et à

renfermer ses pensées dans un tour vif, précis, et délicat.' There were soon English translations of the *Maximes* (inc. one by Mrs. Aphra Behn).

Laromiguière, PIERRE (1756–1837), philosopher, professor at the *Sorbonne (from 1811). In a famous lecture-course (publ. 1815–18 as *Les Principes de l'intelligence*) he established a form of compromise between sensationalism (*v. Condillac; Idéologues*), in that he recognized the senses as a passive source of knowledge, and spiritualism, because, he held, man's intelligence, moral consciousness, and will depend for their exercise on a more elevated faculty of awareness, or 'sentiment', which once admitted leads to belief in a first cause and in God.

Larousse, PIERRE, *v. Dictionaries*, 1866–76.

La Sablière, MARGUERITE HESSEIN, MME DE (1636–93), a famous literary lady of the day (her *salon was frequented by the *libertins; v. Bernier), remembered as a patroness of La Fontaine and for her love affair with La Fare.

La Sale, ANTOINE DE (1388–*post* 1469), romance writer, served the house of Anjou as squire and soldier, visiting various countries, and was later tutor to the son of René d'Anjou. He wrote, notably, the *Petit Jehan de Saintré (c. 1456); also La Salade (c. 1440), a treatise on government, with lively chapters on his visit to the Lipari islands and the 'Paradis de la Reine Sibylle' (which is connected with the legend of Tannhäuser); La Salle (c. 1451), a treatise on ethics; the Réconfort de Mme de Fresne (1458), on the theme of a mother torn between saving her son (a hostage in enemy hands during the Hundred Years War, who will be executed if her husband does not surrender the place he commands) and sacrificing her son to save her husband's honour. The *Quinze Joyes de mariage and the *Cent Nouvelles Nouvelles have often been attributed to him, almost certainly wrongly.

Lascaris, ANDREAS JOANNES, *v.*
Renaissance.

Las Cases, EMMANUEL-AUGUSTIN-
DIEUDONNÉ-MARTIN-JOSEPH, COMTE DE
(1766–1842), held high office under
Napoleon, followed him to St. Helena
(1815), but was expelled from there in
1816. His much-read *Mémorial de Sainte-
Hélène* (1822–3) was a record of
Napoleon's life in exile, with notes of
conversations in which he expressed his
views on politics, history, etc.

La Serre, JEAN PUGET DE (1600–65), a
mediocre dramatist, author of a successful
prose tragedy, *Thomas Morus, ou le
Triomphe de la foi et de la constance* (1641).

Lassailly, CHARLES (1806–43), a minor
frenetic *Romantic, founded little reviews
and published a fantastic novel, *Les
Roueries de Trialph* (1833), which abounds
in murders and ends in suicide (as did its
author).

Lasserre, PIERRE (1867–1930), literary
critic (for some years on *L'*Action
française*). His works include *Le
Romantisme français* (1907), a highly
provocative defence of *Classicism against
*Romanticism; *Les Chapelles littéraires*
(i.e. literary cliques; 1920), studies of
Claudel, Jammes, and Péguy.

La Suze, HENRIETTE DE COLIGNY,
COMTESSE DE (1618–73), grand-daughter of
Coligny, a *Huguenot who turned Roman
Catholic (after which her marriage to the
drunken, jealous comte de La Suze was
dissolved), a worldly beauty and a
précieuse (she corresponded with Guez
de Balzac and Saint-Évremond, and her
salon is said to have been a kind of annexe
to the Hôtel de *Rambouillet). She was
author, with Pellisson and others, of a
Recueil de pièces galantes (1663), or *Recueil
La Suze-Pellisson*, one of the most popular
17th-c. verse and prose miscellanies.

La Tailhède, RAYMOND DE (1867–1938),
poet, a founder of the *École romane*, lived
in Paris after 1888. His verse is collected

in *De la métamorphose des fontaines, poème
suivi des odes, des sonnets, et des hymnes*
(1895), *Hymne pour la France* (1917), *Le
Deuxième Livre des odes* (1920), *Le Poème
d'Orphée* (1926), etc.

La Taille, JEAN DE (1540–1608), an early
author of tragedies, notably *Saül le
furieux* (1572; with a dedicatory epistle on
the nature of *tragedy, insisting on the
unities of time and place) and *La Famine,
ou les Gabaonites* (1573; a sequel to *Saül*);
also of *Le Courtisan retiré* (1574), a satiric
poem, and *Les Corrivaux* (1574), the first
French *comedy written in prose.

His brother JACQUES (1542–62) left two
mediocre tragedies, *Daire* and *Alexandre*.

Latouche, Henri de, *pseudonym of*
HYACINTHE THABAUD (1785–1851), a well-
known man of letters of the *Romantic
period, editor from 1825 of *Le *Mercure
du XIXᵉ siècle*, the first to edit A. Chénier's
works (1819), translator of Schiller's
Maria Stuart (1820); also author of novels
(*Olivier*, 1826; *Fragoletta*, 1829) and verse
(*La Vallée-aux-Loups*, 1833; *Les Agrestes*,
1845). *v. Foreign Influences*, 3; *Proverbe*.

La Tour, MAURICE QUENTIN DE (1704–
88), noted painter of portraits in pastel,
e.g. of Mme de Pompadour.

La Tour du Pin, HENRIETTE-LUCIE
DILLON, MARQUISE DE (1770–1853), of
partly Irish extraction, married into an old
and distinguished family of the Dauphiné
and was briefly in the service of Marie-
Antoinette. Her memoirs (*Journal d'une
femme de cinquante ans, 1778–1815*, not
publ. till the early 20th c.) vividly describe
crucial events of the Revolution, leading
figures on both sides, and, above all, the
trials and adventures of her own family (on
the run in France, farming in America,
living with relations in England).

La Tour du Pin, PATRICE DE (1911–75),
a member of the same family as the above;
a poet of religious inspiration, consciously
un-modernist in style and approach. He
made his name with *La Quête de
joie* (1933). He gathered this and

subsequent collections of poems and prose poems to form a *summa* reflecting his spiritual progress: *Une Somme de poésie*, I (1946), concerned with the 'jeu de l'homme devant lui-même'; II. *Le Second Jeu* (1959), the 'jeu de l'homme devant le monde'; III. *Carême et Temps Pascal* (*Petit Théâtre crépusculaire*, 1963; *Une Lutte pour la vie*, 1970), the 'jeu de l'homme devant Dieu'.

La Tour Landry, *Livre du Chevalier de*, a book of instructive tales from the Bible and the classics, and examples of conduct from contemporary life, written *c.* 1372 by a member of the provincial nobility for the benefit of his young daughters. It throws light on provincial society of the day. *Cf. Ménagier de Paris.*

La Trappe, *v. Trappe.*

Latude, JEAN-HENRI MASERS DE (1725–1805), an adventurer who tried to advance his fortunes by revealing a plot (concocted by himself) against Mme de Pompadour, but failed and was imprisoned (1749–84). He left memoirs.

Launay, MARGUERITE CORDIER, MLLE DE (1684–1750; her father's name was Cordier, but she took her mother's maiden name, de Launay), a learned, intelligent woman, a friend of Fontenelle, Chaulieu, and Mme du Deffand. She was early left penniless and obliged to accept a humble post in the service of the duchesse du *Maine at Sceaux. She rose to be reader to the duchesse and was to some extent privy to her plot against the Regent. In consequence, she was long imprisoned in the *Bastille. After her release, weary of servitude, she tried to obtain an independent position, but was thwarted by the tyrannical duchesse. She was married (1735) against her will to the baron de Staal, an elderly Swiss, but remained in the duchesse's service. She left letters (those to Mme du Deffand describe a visit by Voltaire and Mme du Châtelet to Sceaux) and *Mémoires*, written with elegant simplicity, of her youth, her unhappy life at Sceaux, and her imprisonment ('le seul temps heureux que j'ai passé en ma vie').

Launay, MARQUIS DE, *v. Bastille.*

Laure persécutée, a *tragicomedy by Rotrou, on a theme from Lope de Vega; produced 1637.

Orantée, son of the king of Hungary, loves Laure, a lady of unknown birth. The irate king, bent on marrying Orantée to an Infanta, arrests him and seeks Laure to put her to death. He tries to convince Orantée of her infidelity by an artifice similar to Borachio's in Shakespeare's *Much Ado*. At first he succeeds, but in the end all is revealed and Laure proves to be a sister of the Infanta.

Lauriers sont coupés, Les, v. Dujardin.

Lautréamont, Comte de, *pseudonym* (said to have been taken from the hero of Sue's *Latréaumont* whose supreme arrogance drives him to revolt and blasphemy) *of* ISIDORE DUCASSE (1846–70). Little is known of his life, except that he was born in Montevideo, the exceptionally gifted son of French parents, came to Paris (1867) to study at the *École polytechnique*, but apparently spent most of his time writing, or declaiming what he wrote, and died there in 1870. In 1868 he published the first of his lyrical fragments in prose, *Les Chants de Maldoror* (republ. 1890, with five more fragments). Maldoror, a demonic figure, expresses his hatred of mankind and of God, and his love of the Ocean (a famous passage), blood, octopuses, toads, etc. There are nightmarish encounters with vampires and with mysterious beings on the seashore. The work is an amazing profusion of apostrophe and imagery, at once delirious, erotic, blasphemous, grandiose, and horrific; but its language and style are also so remarkable that it stands as an example of 'les hallucinations servies par la volonté' (R. de Gourmont). This hallucinatory quality in his work has led the *Surrealists to claim Lautréamont as a precursor (modern eds. of his works include one by Soupault). Before his death he published *Poésies* (1870), with an unfinished preface ironically attacking the type of literature represented by *Maldoror*.

Lauzun, ANTONIN NOMPAR DE CAUMONT, *later* DUC DE (1632–1723), a Gascon gentleman at the court of Louis XIV, a man at once brave, witty, insolent ('le plus insolent petit homme qu'on eût vu depuis un siècle'—La Fare), and servile, condemned by some as a crafty adventurer. He had a chequered career. 'La Grande Mademoiselle' (*v. Montpensier*) fell in love with him and obtained the king's consent to marry him (1670); but the king withdrew it three days later and imprisoned him for 10 years at Pignerol, after which he was restored to favour and the pair were, it is believed, secretly married. But Lauzun, who had been lavishly enriched by her, showed gross ingratitude, and they quarrelled and parted. In 1688, when James II was about to flee from England, Lauzun secretly escorted the queen and the infant prince of Wales to France; and in 1690 he commanded the French troops at the battle of the Boyne.

Lauzun, ARMAND-LOUIS DE GONTAUT-BIRON, DUC DE, *later* DUC DE BIRON (1747–93), a brave soldier and noted Don Juan, brought up in the household of Mme de Pompadour. Ruined by his own extravagance, he turned to soldiering and held high command against the English in W. Africa (1779) and America (1780–3). Having lost favour at court, he joined the duc d'*Orléans, becoming a general in the Revolutionary army. He was executed in the *Terror on a charge of having, by his inactivity, favoured the rising in the *Vendée. His memoirs (1821) of his military and amorous adventures (to 1783, with a not wholly reliable picture of the circle of Marie-Antoinette) gave rise to considerable scandal.

La Vallière, LOUISE DE LA BAUME LE BLANC, DUCHESSE DE (1644–1700), mistress of the young Louis XIV, was supplanted by Mme de Montespan and retired (1674) to a convent. She was modest, tender, and disinterested; Mme de Sévigné calls her a 'petite violette qui se cachait sous l'herbe'. Her daughter, Mlle de Blois, married the prince de *Conti.

Lavater, JOHANN KASPAR (1741–1801), a Swiss pastor with leanings to Roman Catholicism, mysticism, and black magic (he died believing he was the Apostle John), chiefly remembered as a physiognomist. His *Physiognomische Fragmente* (1775–8), advancing theories of little scientific value on the art of divining character, past and future fortunes, etc., from facial conformation, excited great interest when translated into French (1783) and later impressed Balzac (*cf. Gall*; *Mesmer*).

Laveaux, JEAN-CHARLES THIBAULT DE, *v. Dictionaries*, 1818, 1820.

Lavedan, HENRI (1859–1940), dramatist. His comedies of manners, depicting Parisian life in its worldly, frivolous aspect and sometimes introducing social themes or a moral, include, notably, *Le Prince d'Aurec* (1894; a study of impoverished aristocrats) and *Le Marquis de Priola* (1902); also *Le Duel* (1905), *Le Nouveau Jeu* (1907), *Le Vieux Marcheur* (1909).

La Vigne, ANDRÉ or ANDRIEU DE (d. *c.* 1515), poet and dramatist, secretary to the duc de Savoie and later to Anne de Bretagne, accompanied Charles VIII to Italy. His works include *Le Vergier d'honneur*, containing a verse journal of the Italian expedition; the *moralité* of *L'*Aveugle et le Boiteux*, performed 1496 at Seurre (Burgundy) with his *mystère* of St. Martin; *soties*; polemical poems supporting Louis XII against the papacy; *rondeaux* on the death of his patroness Queen Anne.

Lavisse, ERNEST (1842–1922), historian, an authority on the 17th c. and on German history; editor, with Alfred Rambaud, of an *Histoire générale du IVe siècle à nos jours* (1891–1900); general editor and part author of the *Histoire de France depuis les origines jusqu'à la Révolution* (1900–11, 9 vols.) and *Histoire de France contemporaine depuis la Révolution jusqu'à la Paix de 1919* (1920–2, 10 vols.), still standard works. *v. History*, 4; *Vidal de La Blache*.

Lavoisier, ANTOINE-LAURENT (1743–94), a pioneer of modern chemistry, discoverer (simultaneously with Priestley) of oxygen and of the composition of air. Having obtained the office of **fermier général* to finance his experiments, he was condemned during the Revolution and executed. Arthur *Young describes a visit to his laboratory (16 Oct. 1787).

Law, JOHN (1671–1729), son of an Edinburgh goldsmith, escaped from prison while under sentence of death for killing his opponent in a duel, fled to France, and won the favour of the Regent. He persuaded the government to adopt the use of paper money, convertible into coin through the medium of the *Banque générale*, which he founded in 1716 in the Rue Quincampoix, Paris. The bank-notes having proved a great success, he then launched a vast enterprise to exploit colonial commerce, and also took charge of tax-farming (*v. Fermiers généraux*). The *Banque générale* became the *Banque royale* (1718), and early in 1720 he was named controller-general of finance. Though he had introduced some wise fiscal reforms, his operations gave rise to frenzied speculation, which collapsed later in 1720, causing widespread ruin. He had to flee the country, and died in Venice. His 'système' and the Rue Quincampoix are often mentioned in contemporary literature.

Lazarillo de Tormes, *v. Foreign Influences*, 1.

Léautaud, PAUL (1872–1956), essayist and man of letters, long associated with the **Mercure de France*, for a time as dramatic critic (*Théâtre de Maurice Boissard* [his pseudonym] *1907–1923*, 1927); editor, with Adolphe van Bever, of *Poètes d'aujourd'hui* (1929, 3 vols.), a well-known anthology of *Symbolist verse. His *Journal littéraire* (1954–66, 19 vols.; for

the years 1893–1956), though at times cynical and rancorous (he had an unhappy childhood), is of interest as a record of literary life and encounters. His *Le Petit Ami* (1903) is autobiographical.

Le Bel, JEAN (*c.* 1290–*c.* 1370), a rich, well-born canon of Liège. His chronicle of the period 1329–61 is written in a clear, vigorous style with an evident desire for truth and impartiality. Froissart drew freely on it and it provided some of his most admired passages, e.g. the incident of the burghers of Calais.

Leblanc, MAURICE (1864–1925), creator of the character Arsène Lupin, gentleman crook-cum-detective, in the crime novels *Arsène Lupin* (1907), *Arsène Lupin contre Sherlock Holmes* (1908), *Arsène Lupin, gentleman cambrioleur* (1914), etc.

Le Bossu, RENÉ, PÈRE (1631–80), author of a *Traité du poème épique* (1675) and a *Parallèle de la philosophie de Descartes et d'Aristote*. His work was admired by Dryden and quoted by Congreve and Macaulay. *v. English Literature, French Influence on*, 3.

Le Breton, ANDRÉ-FRANÇOIS (1708–79), publisher of the **Encyclopédie*.

Le Brun, CHARLES (1619–90), a noted painter and designer of the reign of Louis XIV, rector of the **Académie royale de Peinture et de Sculpture*, director of the **Gobelins* factory, and for a time the dictator of French art. He helped to embellish the *Louvre and *Versailles.

Lebrun, PONCE-DENIS ÉCOUCHARD (1729–1807), 'Lebrun-Pindare', poet, son of a Paris tradesman, famous in his day for his *Odes* (collected 1811). They are little more than rhetorical exercises, the best being two on the Lisbon earthquake of 1755, one (addressed to Voltaire, 1760) evoking the shade of Corneille in favour of Corneille's destitute niece, and those addressed to Buffon. He ardently supported the Revolution and wrote an ode on *Le Vengeur*, a French man-of-war which allowed itself to be sunk by the British (1794) rather than surrender. He was also a skilful writer of epigrams, which he made the vehicle of literary criticism.

Le Cardonnel, LOUIS (1862–1936), poet, frequented *Symbolist circles in Paris (1881–90), then became a Roman Catholic and was ordained priest (1896), but not charged with parochial duties. His works include *Poèmes* (1904; written 1881–90), *Carmina sacra* (1912; religious poems), *De l'une à l'autre aurore* (1924; inc. war poems).

Leclercq, THÉODORE (1777–1851), author of *Proverbes dramatiques* (1820–30), lively, subtle sketches of ultra-Royalist circles, often performed in the Restoration *salons*. He visited England (*c.* 1802) with his friend Fiévée and was also in *Hamburg, where his *proverbes* entertained the *émigrés*.

Lecocq, ALEXANDRE-CHARLES, v. *Angot*.

Leconte, SÉBASTIEN-CHARLES (1865–1934), a disciple of Leconte de Lisle. His poetry is collected in *La Tentation de l'homme* (1903), *Le Sang de Méduse* (1905), etc.

Leconte de Lisle, CHARLES-MARIE-RENÉ (1818–94), leader of the *Parnassien poets, b. on the *Ile Bourbon (his father, a former surgeon in Napoleon's armies, was a planter there; his mother, a cousin of Parny, belonged to the island). He came to France (1837), studied law at Rennes, and began to write. He returned home in 1843, but lived in Paris from 1846. He was briefly attracted by *Fouriérisme and was on the staff of *Fouriériste* journals. The 1848 *Revolution aroused his enthusiasm, but the consequent abolition of slavery ruined his family and his private allowance ceased. There followed several years of struggle and of disillusionment with political events. Subsisting inadequately on journalism, translations, and private tuition, he now published his most famous works—*Poèmes antiques* (1852), *Poèmes et poésies* (1855), *Poèmes barbares* (1862), the

second being absorbed in augmented editions of the first and third (1872 and 1874 respectively). His disciples, the poets of *Le Parnasse contemporain* of 1866, met in his house. Poverty forced him to accept an imperial pension (1864), and his circumstances were further eased when he was given a sinecure (librarian to the *Sénat*, 1872).

In *Poèmes antiques*, his inspiration is largely Greek, reflecting his friendship with the Hellenist Ménard. He depicts prehistoric, pagan Greece, the beauty of its art and thought, the various stages of its civilization (*La Source*, *Niobé*, *Hélène*, *Khiron*). But he is also inspired by Indian Buddhism (*Bhagavat*, *La Vision de Brahma*; *cf.* the many works publ. by Burnouf and other Orientalists from *c.* 1840). The *Poèmes barbares* (i.e. not Greek or Indian) are inspired by Egyptian or Nordic mythology (*Néférou-Ra*, *Le Voile d'Isis*; *La Vision de Snorr*), Biblical history (*Qaïn*; *v. Epic Poetry*), and nature (exotic scenery and jungle life—*La Fontaine aux lianes*, *Le Jaguar*). Both collections typify the formal perfection and visual rather than emotive beauty of *Parnassien* poetry, and also, to a remarkable degree, its static quality (he evokes both the static archaeological beauty of Greece and the intense stillness of the jungle). His other works include *Les Érinnyes* (1873), a tragedy based on Aeschylus's *Oresteia*; *Poèmes tragiques* (1884); *Derniers Poèmes* (1895). His choice of subject was often dictated by his embittered, pessimistic, and atheistic view of life (*v. Foreign Influences*, 4).

Lecoq, Monsieur, the famous detective created by *Gaboriau. He also figures in novels by the once popular *roman-feuilletoniste* Fortuné du Boisgobey (1821–91), e.g. *La Vieillesse de M. Lecoq* (1878).

Lecouvreur, ADRIENNE (1692–1730), a famous actress (esp. in tragedy), noted for her simple and natural, as opposed to declamatory, style. Her charm, intelligence, modesty, and good sense helped to raise the social status of the French actress. She was the mistress of

Maurice de *Saxe, and when she died in mysterious circumstances soon after he had deserted her for the duchesse de Bouillon there were unfounded rumours that the duchesse had poisoned her. Her friend Voltaire addressed an epistle to her (1723) and wrote an elegy on her death, attacking the Church for refusing her Christian burial. *v. Adrienne Lecouvreur*.

Leczinski or **Leszczynski**, STANISLAS (1677–1766), king of Poland 1704–9. He was obliged to leave Poland (1709) and allowed to settle in France (1718), where his daughter Marie married Louis XV (1725). After an abortive attempt to regain his kingdom (1733), he renounced it in return for the duchies of Lorraine and Bar. He patronized the arts at his court at Lunéville, and left a monument in the fine Place Stanislas at Nancy. *v. Collège Stanislas*.

Le Dain or **Le Daim**, OLIVIER NECKER, *known as* (hanged 1484), of Flemish origin, valet, barber, and counsellor of Louis XI, figures in Scott's *Quentin Durward* and, fleetingly, in Hugo's *Notre-Dame de Paris*.

Ledru-Rollin, ALEXANDRE-AUGUSTE, *v. Revolutions*, 3.

Lefebvre, FRANÇOIS-JOSEPH, *v. Maréchal*.

Lefebvre, GEORGES (1874–1959), historian of the Revolution from the social and economic standpoint, and the first to study its impact on the peasantry. His works include *Les Paysans du Nord pendant la Révolution française* (1924), *La Révolution française* (1930; 1951), *Napoléon* (1935), *Les Thermidoriens* (1935).

Lefèvre or **Lefèvre-Deumier**, JULES-ALEXANDRE (1797–1857), minor poet and novelist, a friend of Soumet, and a contributor to *La *Muse française*, known less for his writings (e.g. *Sir Lionel d'Arguenay*, 1834, a novel; *Œuvres d'un désœuvré*, 1842, verse and prose; *Poésies*,

1844; *Le Livre du promeneur*, 1854, prose poems) than as a figure of the early *Romantic movement. Later, he inherited a fortune and patronized the arts.

Le Fèvre de la Boderie, GUY (1541–98), a friend of Amyot, J.-A. de Baïf, and Ronsard, a fine example of the *Renaissance humanist, at once a scholar (learned in Oriental languages and religions) and a poet. His poetry includes *L'Encyclie des secrets de l'Éternité* (1571), *La Galliade, ou la Révolution des arts* (1578), *Hymnes ecclésiastiques* (1578).

Lefèvre d'Étaples, JACQUES, in Latin FABER STAPULENSIS—whence STAPOUL (1450–1537), b. at Étaples (Picardy), a great humanist (*v. Renaissance*) and a leader of *Évangélisme*. He was among the first to study Greek (stimulated by contact with Pico della Mirandola and Ficino in Italy), and edited Aristotle's *Ethics*, *Politics*, and *Logic*, disregarding the works of the medieval commentators. He applied the same method of rational interpretation of actual texts to the Scriptures, and produced the first complete French translation of the *Bible (1523–8) since the 13th c. François Ier appointed him tutor to his third son; and *v. Marguerite d'Angoulême*.

Lefranc, ABEL-JULES-MAURICE (1863–1952), scholar and critic, author of valuable studies of Rabelais (whom he edited), Marguerite de Navarre, Calvin, etc.; also of *A la découverte de Shakespeare* (1945–50, 3 vols.), maintaining that Shakespeare's plays were written by William Stanley, 6th Earl of Derby.

Le Franc, MARTIN (*c.* 1410–61), secretary to two popes and holder of various preferments, author of *Le Champion des dames* (completed 1442; printed 1485), a poem inspired by the *Roman de la Rose*, attacking its author Jean de Meung and taking up the defence of women with the same medley of allegory and erudition as is found in the earlier work. He sent a fine manuscript copy to the duke of Burgundy, and the fact that the work was neglected at the duke's court provoked his dignified *Complainte du livre du Champion des dames à son auteur.*

Le Franc de Pompignan, *v. Pompignan.*

Légataire universel, Le, a comedy by Regnard; produced 1708.

Géronte, a rich old man on the point of death, has a host of greedy prospective heirs, notably his nephew Éraste, who cannot marry unless he secures the bulk of the inheritance. Géronte's plan to leave large legacies to two relatives is cleverly foiled by Éraste's valet Crispin, who impersonates them and by his outrageous conduct turns Géronte against them. When he faints before making a will and is thought dead, Crispin impersonates him and dictates to the notary a will in Éraste's favour (with handsome legacies to himself and his intended). Géronte recovers, and the conspirators are much embarrassed, but extricate themselves by assuring him that he dictated the will while in a trance and finally induce him to ratify it.

Légende de Saint Julien l'Hospitalier, La, v. *Trois Contes.*

Légende des siècles, La (1859, 1877, and 1883), three series of *epic poems by Hugo.

He sets out to portray man's spiritual and historical development in a succession of scenes from different epochs. He begins with idyllic pictures of the Creation and the early days of Biblical history (*Le Sacre de la femme*; *Booz endormi*, the O.T. story of Ruth), passes fairly rapidly across Oriental, Greek, and Roman antiquity, lingers over the Middle Ages (*Le Mariage de Roland*; *Le Petit Roi de Galice*; *L'Aigle du casque*; *Aymerillot*, inspired by *Aimeri de Narbonne*; *Éviradnus*, set in a Germany resembling that of *Les *Burgraves* in its misty, crenellated savagery and grandeur—the knight-errant Éviradnus symbolizes the gradual triumph of justice in the world, the central theme of the work), passes swiftly down to the 19th c., after the Revolution has brought liberty and made the people conscious of moral

progress (*Jean Chouan*; *Les Pauvres Gens*), and concludes with visions of the future and the Day of Judgement (*Pleine Mer*; *Plein Ciel*; *La Trompette du jugement*).

Hugo had intended to crown the work with two further collections, *La Fin de Satan* (showing the forces of evil destroyed by the angel Liberty, and so giving scope for poems on the Revolution—thus far not covered) and *Dieu* (showing man seeking after light and finally coming to the conception of God as Love). They were published posthumously (1886 and 1891; both incomplete) and contain writing of a remarkable visionary quality.

Légende napoléonienne, La. To the France of 1815, exhausted by war and weary of the despot who had brought her to the verge of ruin, the Allied victors seemed almost like deliverers. But disillusionment soon set in: the peace terms were humiliating, and the hard-won liberties of the Revolution vanished under the Restoration. As a result, there gradually evolved a legend of Napoleon as the incarnation of the Revolutionary ideals of liberty, the hero who had restored France from chaos to order and, but for the hostility of Europe, would have brought peace and liberty to the world; also, more sentimentally, as the lonely father, sorrowing on St. Helena for the son torn from him by Allied persecutors. After his death (1821), the legend grew, fostered, for example, by the memoirs and anecdotes of his companions in exile, brothers-in-arms, and loyal friends (*v. Las Cases*; *Montholon*; *Gourgaud*; *Bertrand, comte de*; *Caulaincourt*; *Marchand*), by *Béranger's *chansons* (e.g. his *Souvenirs du peuple*, in *Chansons inédites*, 1828), by some of Hugo's poems (e.g. *Ode à la Colonne*, publ. 1827 in the *Journal des Débats*; *Lui*, in *Les *Orientales*, 1829; *Napoléon II*, written 1832, in *Les Chants du crépuscule*, 1835; *Ode à l'Arc de Triomphe*, in *Les *Voix intérieures*, 1837), by the *Images d'Épinal*; and *cf.* Balzac's *Le *Médecin de campagne*. In 1833, as a gesture of goodwill, the government restored a statue of Napoleon to the column in the *Place Vendôme, and in 1840 his remains were brought from St. Helena and entombed in the *Invalides*. Hugo called this 'la fête d'un cercueil exilé qui revient en triomphe', but Lamartine (when funds for the 'translation des cendres' were voted) deplored 'cette religion napoléonienne'. In 1848, the newly organized Bonapartist party founded newspapers with such names as *Le Petit Caporal* and *La Redingote grise* (referring to Napoleon's famous grey overcoat), and exploited the *légende* to win the working-class vote for the future Napoleon III.

Barrès, in *Les *Déracinés*, describes the significance of the *légende* for successive generations of Frenchmen.

Léger, ALEXIS, v. *Saint-John Perse.*

Léger, *Vie de Saint*, one of the earliest extant French poems (40 octosyllabic *sixains*), probably of the second half of the 10th c. The author is unknown. v. *Saints, Lives of.*

Légion d'honneur, a non-hereditary Order, created by Bonaparte (1802) as a reward for military and civilian services, and still continuing. The first investiture was held on the *Champ-de-Mars (14 July 1804). There are five classes (in ascending order): *Chevalier, Officier, Commandeur, Grand-Officier, Grand-Croix*. The last was at first called *Grand-Aigle*, after the original medal (v. *Isabey*), one side of which bore the imperial eagle (later replaced by two *tricolores*) and the words 'Honneur et Patrie' (which it still bears).

Napoleon also founded *maisons d'éducation de la Légion d'honneur*, schools for daughters or female blood relations of members of the Order, with both free and fee-paying places (v. *Campan*). Some still exist, notably that at Saint-Denis.

Légion étrangère (Foreign Legion), created 1831, regiments of the French army mainly composed of foreign volunteers (enlisted for limited, renewable periods; often refugees from their own country—if a man's papers are not in order, no questions are asked), though Frenchmen can enlist, *as foreigners* (which

means they must have some special reason for sinking their identity); long based in Algeria (now near Marseilles and in Corsica) and largely officered by French regulars. It to some extent continued the tradition of the foreign mercenaries introduced into their armies by the French kings (in 1789 about a quarter of the army consisted of foreigners). The original force was ceded to Spain in 1835, but another was quickly recruited and expanded, and thereafter fought wherever the French were fighting, e.g. in the Crimea (1854), Italy (1859), Mexico (1863), Indo-China (c. 1875, and again in very recent times), and France itself. The life has always been hard and often adventurous—but never as glamorous as depicted in Ouida's *Under Two Flags* or P. C. Wren's *Beau Geste*.

Législateur du Parnasse, Le, v. *Boileau.*

Législative, La, v. *Assemblée législative.*

Légitimistes, in the 19th c., those monarchists who supported the elder—*Bourbon—branch of the royal family. v. *Revolutions, 2; Chambord; Orléanistes.*

Le Goffic, CHARLES (1863–1932), poet, novelist, and dramatist of Breton life. His poetry, collected in *Poésies complètes* (1933), includes *Amour breton* (1889), *Le Bois dormant* (1889–1900). *Le Crucifié de Kéraliès* (1892) is a typically dramatic novel.

Legouis, ÉMILE (1861–1937), literary historian and critic, long professor of English at the *Sorbonne*, author, with Cazamian, of a standard history of English literature (1924). He also published studies of Wordsworth (1896), Chaucer (1910), and Spenser (1923), and a *Défense de la poésie française à l'usage des lecteurs anglais* (1912).

Legouvé, (1) GABRIEL-MARIE-JEAN-BAPTISTE (1764–1812), author of didactic and descriptive verse, e.g. *Le Mérite des femmes* (1801), and historical tragedies; (2) his son ERNEST-WILFRID (1807–1903), dramatist and man of letters, author, with Scribe, of *Adrienne Lecouvreur*.

Legrand, MARC-ANTOINE (1673–1728), an actor at the *Comédie-Française*, wrote several short comedies played there 1707–27, e.g. *Le Roi de Cocagne* (1718; verse); *Le Galant Coureur, ou l'Ouvrage d'un moment* (prose), said to have inspired Marivaux's *Le *Jeu de l'amour et du hasard*.

Leipzig, Battle of. Here the 6th, or General, *Coalition won a signal victory over Napoleon (16–18 Oct. 1813), paving the way for the invasion of France (Jan. 1814) and fall of Paris (March 1814).

Leiris, MICHEL (1901–), poet, and a notable exponent of so-called *littérature de confession* (*v. Memoirs*, 4); a social anthropologist by profession. He began writing poetry under the aegis of M. Jacob, became a *Surrealist in 1924, and published his first collection, *Simulacre*, in 1925. He broke with Surrealism in 1929, but continued to acknowledge his debt to it, seen in his interest in dreams (e.g. *Nuits sans nuit*, 1945) and in Freudian psychology—sexuality being the explicit key to his first autobiographical work, *L'Âge d'homme* (1939). He has long admired, and is an authority on, the work of R. Roussel, and much of his own writing is a fundamental questioning of language by means of puns and word-play, e.g. *Glossaire: j'y serre mes gloses* (1940). In his autobiographical work *La Règle du jeu*, consisting so far of *Biffures* (1948), *Fourbis* (1955), and *Fibrilles* (1966), he combines this activity with the desire to 'faire un livre qui soit un acte', formulated in *De la littérature considérée comme une tauromachie* (1946). His other works include *Aurora* (1946), a semi-auto-biographical novel, and the poems of *Haut Mal* (1943), *Marrons sculptés pour Miro* (1962), and *Autres Lancers* (1969). *v. Temps modernes, Les*.

Lekain, HENRI-LOUIS CAIN, *known as* (1728–78), actor, played in many of Voltaire's tragedies. He left memoirs.

Le Laboureur, LOUIS, *v. Epic Poetry*.

Lélia, *v. Sand*.

Lélian, Pauvre, *v. Poètes maudits, Les*.

Lemaire de Belges, JEAN (*c.* 1473–*c.* 1525), b. in Hainault (at Bavai, then called Belges—whence his name), one of the last and best of the *rhétoriqueurs*. In the course of his travels as secretary or chronicler to princely houses (notably to *Marguerite d'Autriche and Anne de Bretagne), he paid three visits to Italy and came under the influence of Italian literature (Dante, *v. Terza rima*; Boccaccio; Petrarch). His works reveal his interest in music, sculpture, and painting (he was involved in the erection of the church of Brou); also the influence of such Latin writers as Ovid. They include the *Illustrations de Gaule*, a long compilation of legends about the origins of the French (here traced back to Hector of Troy), interspersed with quotations from the classics, written in harmonious prose, with many picturesque passages; *La Concorde des deux langages* (i.e. those of France and Italy), an allegory proclaiming the spiritual harmony of the two nations and containing some of his best poetry and ideas.

Lemaître, FRÉDÉRICK (1800–76), a famous actor (esp. in the role of Robert *Macaire), played with Deburau at the *Théâtre des *Funambules*, then in *Romantic drama (e.g. *Ruy Blas*).

Lemaître, JULES (1853–1914), long dramatic critic on the *Journal des Débats*, famous for his brilliant, impressionistic, often ironical articles (collected in *Les Contemporains*, 1885–99, 7 vols., 1918, 1 vol.; *Impressions de théâtre*, 1888–98, 10 vols., 1920, 1 vol.). He also wrote plays, over-literary and only moderately successful (e.g. the comedies *Révoltée*, 1889; *Le Député Leveau*, 1891; *Mariage blanc*, 1891; *L'Aînée*, 1898), and short stories (*Sérénus, histoire d'un martyr*, 1886; *Dix Contes*, 1889; *Contes blancs*, 1900).

Le Maître de Saci, LOUIS-ISAAC LE MAÎTRE, *known as* (1613–84), a leading *Jansenist, the learned and prudent director of *Port-Royal* (in succession to Singlin). He collaborated in a translation of the New Testament and—while imprisoned in the *Bastille* (1666–8) in the course of the persecution of the Jansenists—himself translated the Old Testament from the Vulgate; *v. Bible, French Versions of.* For some of his other works *v. Imitation de Jésus-Christ; Port-Royal.* The memoirs of his secretary N. Fontaine, who shared his captivity, record a conversation of great literary interest—*L'Entretien* [de Pascal] *avec M. de Saci sur Épictète et Montaigne.*

Lemercier, NÉPOMUCÈNE (1771–1840), dramatist. His *Pinto, ou la Journée d'une conspiration* (1800; prose) was the first French historical *comedy. Its theme is the revolution of 1640 which drove the Spaniards from Portugal; Pinto, the hero, somewhat resembles Figaro. He also wrote mediocre tragedies, e.g. *Agamemnon* (1797; verse), deemed a masterpiece in its day; and *La Panhypocrisiade, ou le Spectacle infernal du XVIᵉ siècle* (1819), half epic, half verse drama, mainly satirical in intention (Nodier called it 'ce chaos monstrueux de vers étonnés de se rencontrer ensemble'). *v.* also *Epic Poetry.*

Lemerre, ALPHONSE (1838–1912), the publisher associated with the *Parnassiens, who often met in his Paris bookshop. *v.* also *France, A.*

Lemierre, ANTOINE-MARIN (1723–93), wrote descriptive poems—*Les Fastes* (1779) and *La Peinture* (1769)—after the manner of Thomson's *Seasons*; also mediocre tragedies.

Lemoine, JEAN, CARDINAL, *v. Collège Lemoine.*

Lemonnier, CAMILLE (1845–1913), Belgian novelist and art critic. He and others associated with the review *La Jeune Belgique* shared the aims of the French *Symbolists and stimulated a revival of Belgian letters. His works include *Contes flamands et wallons* (1873) and novels ranging from *Naturalistic studies of the dregs and slaves of civilization (e.g. *Happe-chair*, 1886; *Madame Lupar*, 1888; *Un Mâle*, 1892) to lyrical descriptions of country life (e.g. *Au cœur frais de la forêt*, 1899; *Le Vent dans les moulins*, 1900; *Le Petit Homme de Dieu*, 1903).

Le Nain, the brothers LOUIS (1593–1648), ANTOINE (1598–1648), and MATHIEU (1607–77), painters of genre pictures of humble life and rustic scenes.

Le Nain de Tillemont, *v. Tillemont.*

Lenclos, ANNE DE, *known as* NINON DE (1620–1705), a woman noted for her *liaisons* with famous men (e.g. Saint-Évremond) and for the charm, wit, virile intellect, and probity which won her wide respect in later life. Her *salon was then frequented by writers (e.g. Boileau, Racine, Molière, La Fontaine), *libertins, artists, and the aristocracy; Mme de La Fayette and Mme de Maintenon were among her friends; Mlle de Scudéry put her into *Clélie* (as Clarisse); the duc de Saint-Simon wrote of her (*Mémoires*, for 1705). The young Voltaire was presented to her in her old age, and she left him a small legacy to buy books. One of the many anecdotes about her relates how, on leaving for the army, her lover La Châtre obtained from her a written promise (*billet*) that she would be faithful. She promptly broke it, and gaily exclaimed 'Le bon billet qu'a La Châtre!'—an expression since proverbial for an illusory promise. She wrote a short volume of sketches, *La Coquette vengée* (1659); her letters have also been published.

Lenéru, MARIE (1875–1918), spent most of her life in her native Brittany, with occasional visits to Paris. She is noted for her remarkable diary (1922), begun in 1886, when she was a healthy, lively-minded child, at the bidding of her mother. By 1890, she had become completely deaf and was threatened with total blindness. The blindness was averted, and after an interval of three years she resumed her diary (1893). It was now the refuge of a woman isolated by affliction, secretly a prey to bitter depression and resentment, but stoically, almost arrogantly, determined to meet the world smiling and—for she is clearly writing for posterity—to make no secret of the effort involved. She read ferociously, developed her critical faculty and literary style, met and corresponded with many leading writers, and in time won a measure of success as a dramatist, e.g. *Les Affranchis* (1911), *Le Redoutable* (1912).

Lenet, PIERRE (d. 1671), a Dijon lawyer, supported Condé in the *Fronde and left memoirs of that period.

Lenormand, HENRI-RENÉ (1882–1951), dramatist. His interesting, rather gloomy plays exploit Freudian theories of the unconscious. He often uses *tableaux*, series of very short scenes which occupy only one part of the stage, the rest being temporarily blacked out. His best-known play is *Les Ratés* (1918), a study of the spiritual and physical downfall of an unsuccessful author and his mistress, a second-rate actress—in the end he takes to drink, kills her, and commits suicide; others are *Le Temps est un songe* (1919), *Le Simoun* (1920), *Le Mangeur de rêves* (1922), *L'Homme et ses fantômes* (1925), *Le Lâche* (1926).

Le Nôtre, ANDRÉ (1613–1700), designer of the gardens of the *châteaux* of *Versailles, *Vaux-le-Vicomte, *Chantilly, etc.

Léonard, ÉMILE, *v. History*, 4.

Léonard, NICOLAS-GERMAIN (1744–93), poet, an imitator of *Gessner, also of Tibullus and Propertius. His *Idylles et poèmes* (1771–87) at times show sincere melancholy and emotion. His *Thérèse et Faldrui* (1783) is a romance.

Leonardo da Vinci (1452–1519), the great Italian painter, sculptor, and engineer, accepted service under Louis XII (1507) and died in France.

Le Play, PIERRE-GUILLAUME-FRÉDÉRIC (1806–82), social reformer, founded an international society for the practical study of social economics. His works include *Les Ouvriers européens* (1855), a comparative study of family budgets of workers in different industries; *La Réforme sociale* (1864); *L'Organisation de la famille* (1871). His doctrine was basically religious, advocating a parental form of authority in industry as well as in the home.

Lépreux de la cité d'Aoste, Le, *v. Maistre, X. de*.

Leprince de Beaumont, MARIE, MME (1711–80), wrote over 70 books for children, mainly collections of moral, instructive tales, e.g. *Le Nouveau Magasin français, ou Bibliothèque instructive* and *Le Magasin des enfants* (1750–5 and 1757; both publ. in London). She married unhappily (1743) and some two years later went to London, where she lived for 17 years, became a royal governess (her *Éducation complète*, London 1753, was intended 'à l'usage de la famille de la princesse de Galles'), and remarried. From 1764 she lived in Switzerland. *v. Children's Reading*.

Léro, ÉTIENNE, *v. Négritude*.

Leroux, GASTON (1868–1927), author of detective novels, e.g. *Le Mystère de la chambre jaune* (1908), *Le Parfum de la dame en noir* (1909). His amateur detective, Joseph Rouletabille, is a young crime reporter who uses his reasoning powers to solve mysteries while the police are still scratching their heads.

Leroux, PIERRE (1797–1871), philosopher, economist, and idealistic social reformer, abandoned his studies at the *École polytechnique to support his family as a journeyman printer. He was founder, with Dubois, of *Le *Globe (and shared its *Saint-Simonien phase), co-editor (1831–5) of the *Revue encyclopédique, and a founder of the *Revue indépendante. Some of G. Sand's novels were influenced by his vaguely pantheistic religion of humanity, obscurely expounded in *De l'humanité, de son principe et de son avenir* (1840) and *De l'égalité* (1838). He founded a printing business (1843) to put his socialist ideas into practice, but it failed. He proved ineffective as a socialist **député* (1848–9) and after the **coup d'état* of 2 December 1851 retired to Jersey, where he wrote a socialist poem, *La Grève de Samarez* (1863–4).

Le Roux, PHILIBERT-JOSEPH, *v. Dictionaries*, 1718.

Le Roux de Lincy, ADRIEN-JEAN-VICTOR (1806–69), medievalist and bibliographer, sometime librarian at the **Bibliothèque de l'Arsenal*; compiler of *Le Livre des proverbes français* (1842–59, 2 vols.; with an introduction on their history and use in literature), still one of the best collections of proverbs.

Le Roy, ÉDOUARD (1870–1954), Neo-Catholic, Modernist philosopher (*v. Blondel, M.*), professor at the **Collège de France* (1921–41) in succession to Bergson, who strongly influenced him. His works include *L'Exigence idéaliste et le fait de l'évolution* (1927), *Les Origines humaines et l'évolution de l'intelligence* (1928), *La Pensée intuitive* (1930), all collections of lectures delivered at the *Collège de France*; also *Essai sur la notion du miracle* (1906), *Dogme et critique* (1907), and *Le Problème de Dieu* (1929). He was a close friend of Teilhard de Chardin.

Leroy, JEAN, *v. Satire Ménippée*.

Le Roy, LOUIS (1510–77), humanist, translated Aristotle's *Politics* (with commentary), Plato, etc. *v. Renaissance*.

Le Roy Ladurie, EMMANUEL (1929–   ), historian, professor at the **Collège de France* from 1973. His works include *Histoire du Languedoc* (1962), *Les Paysans de Languedoc* (1966, 2 vols.), *Histoire du climat depuis l'an mil* (1967; rev. and augm. in the Eng. trans. of 1972—*Times of Feast,*

Times of Famine), *Le Territoire de l'historien* (1973).

Lesage or **Le Sage**, ALAIN-RENÉ (1668–1747), dramatist and novelist of modest Breton origin, spent a quiet and honourable life supporting himself and his family by unremitting literary work. He began with translations from the Spanish. His first success, both as dramatist and novelist, came in 1707 (when he was nearly 40) with his comedy **Crispin rival de son maître* and his romance *Le *Diable boiteux*. After the production of his comedy **Turcaret* (1709), he fell out with the **Comédie-Française* over its grand style of acting, and subsequently, alone or in collaboration, wrote some 100 farces or comedies of manners, often in an Oriental setting and interspersed with lyrics sung to popular airs (*comédies en vaudevilles*), for the *Théâtre de la Foire* (*v. Opéra-Comique*; *Theatres and Theatre Companies*; *Comedy*). The first volumes of his chief work, the great picaresque romance **Gil Blas de Santillane*, appeared in 1715. His romance *Les Aventures de M. Robert Chevalier, dit de Beauchêne* (a real person), mainly about the wars between England and France in Canada, buccaneers, and Red Indians, appeared in 1732, and other picaresque novels—*Don Guzman d'Alfarache, Estevanille Gonzalès*, and *Le Bachelier de Salamanque*—in 1732, 1734, and 1736 respectively. The theme of the last somewhat resembles that of *Gil Blas*: the hero, Don Chérubin, travels about the world as a tutor and introduces the reader to his pupils and their parents. His minor works include *La Valise trouvée* (1740) and the Lucianic *Une Journée des Parques* (1734).

His charm lies in the good humour with which he depicts human failings and absurdities (except those of the financiers, in *Turcaret*), in his vivid and dramatic presentation, remarkably animated narrative, and fluid, precise style. His work is, however, somewhat lacking in moral elevation, treating rarely of the finer feelings, such as love or filial affection. He was underrated by his contemporaries; Voltaire disliked him. Sainte-Beuve ranks him as a satirist with Fielding and Goldsmith, below Cervantes and Molière; Saintsbury regards him as the immediate precursor of Fielding and Smollett.

Lescot, PIERRE (*c.* 1510–78), a famous architect of the *Renaissance (*cf. Bullant; Delorme, P.*), celebrated by Ronsard. A rich, learned ecclesiastic, with a gift for drawing and architecture, he was invited by François Ier to design the *Louvre, submitted to Henri II the grandiose plan which, in the main, was eventually executed, and spent much of his life supervising the initial construction.

Lescure, JEAN, *v. Resistance.*

Lescure, PIERRE DE, *v. Resistance.*

Lescurel, JEHANNOT DE, a 14th-c. author of *ballades* and *rondeaux*.

Lespinasse, JULIE-JEANNE-ÉLÉONORE DE (1732–76), illegitimate daughter of the comtesse d'Albon, a woman of keen intelligence and passionate nature, devoted friend of d'Alembert (both figure in *Diderot's *Le Rêve de d'Alembert*); companion to Mme *du Deffand from 1754 to 1764, when the two quarrelled and parted company. Her *salon*, to which she attracted many former *habitués* of that of her mistress (e.g. d'Alembert, Turgot, Condorcet), was a meeting-place for the *Encyclopédistes*. Her lovers included the comte de Guibert; her passionate love letters to him have been published.

L'Espine, JEAN DE, *v. Jean de l'Espine.*

Lespy, JULIEN, *v. Jodelet.*

Lesseps, FERDINAND DE (1805–94), diplomat. The construction of the Suez Canal (completed 1869) was due to his initiative. *v.* also *Panama, L'Affaire du.*

L'Estoile, (1) PIERRE TAISAN DE (1546–1611), a lawyer whose *Registre-Journal* (not publ. till the 18th c.), a monthly record of major and minor events of the reigns of Henri III and Henri IV, current

epigrams, topical verse, etc., is both interesting and historically important; (2) his son CLAUDE DE (d. 1652), poet and dramatist, a member of the original *Académie française* and one of Richelieu's *cinq auteurs.*

Le Sueur, EUSTACHE (1616–55), painter, noted for his religious pictures (a series on St. Bruno) and landscapes.

Leszczynski, *v. Leczinski.*

Le Tellier, MICHEL (1603–85), minister of war under Louis XIV, initiated the radical reorganization of the army carried out by his son Louvois. Bossuet delivered his funeral oration.

Letourneur, PIERRE (1736–88), translator, notably of Shakespeare (1776–83, 20 vols.; a prose version), also of Richardson's novels (1758), *Young's *Night Thoughts* (1769), and *Ossian (1777); *v. Foreign Influences*, 2. His version of Shakespeare is conscientiously close (with the occasional mistranslation), but entirely lacks the magic of the original. His appreciative introduction provoked Voltaire (earlier annoyed by P.-A. de Laplace's translation) to write his famous *Lettre à l'Académie* (1776).

Letters. Letters of interest on literary or stylistic grounds, as guides to the intellectual climate of an age, or as human documents, include those left by the following. *17th c.*: Balzac, Guez de; Boileau; Bossuet; Bussy-Rabutin; Chapelain; Condé; Corneille; Descartes; Fénelon; François de Sales, St.; Henri IV; La Bruyère; La Fayette, Mme de; La Fontaine; La Rochefoucauld; Louis XIV; Maintenon, Mme de; Malherbe; Palatine, la Princesse; Pascal; Patin; Racine; Retz; Richelieu; Saint-Évremond; Saint-Simon, duc de; Sévigné, Mme de; Vincent de Paul, St.; Voiture. *18th c.*: Aïssé, Mlle; Desmoulins; Diderot; Du Deffand, Mme; Graffigny, Mme de; Grimm; La Harpe; Launay, Mlle de; Lespinasse, Mlle de; Métra; Mirabeau; Roland, Mme; Rousseau, J.-J.; Voltaire. *19th and 20th* cs.: Ampère, A.-M. and J.-J.; Balzac; Baudelaire; Claudel; Courier; Delacroix; Doudan; Fiévée; Flaubert; Gide; Guérin, E. and M. de; Jacob, M.; Jacquemont; Maistre, J. de; Mallarmé; Martin du Gard; Mérimée; Napoleon I; Proust; Récamier, Mme; Renan; Rivière; Rolland; Sainte-Beuve; Sand, G.; Sismondi; Taine; Tocqueville; Valéry.

Lettre à d'Alembert sur les spectacles (1758), by J.-J. Rousseau, a polemical treatise attacking the theatre.

D'Alembert, at the request of Voltaire, had pleaded the cause of the theatre in his article *Genève* in the *Encyclopédie. (Theatres were prohibited in Geneva, and in France the drama, earlier condemned by Bossuet, was frowned on by the Church and actors were harshly treated by the clergy.) Rousseau argues, with ingenious illustrations, that the drama can never be morally beneficial and may be actively pernicious (since it often presents vice in an attractive form), that it involves a great waste of time and money, and that the Genevan authorities rightly prohibit it. The work contains a notable criticism of Molière's Le *Misanthrope. D'Alembert replied in a *Lettre à J.-J. Rousseau*.

Lettres anglaises, v. *Lettres philosophiques*.

Lettres à une inconnue, v. *Dacquin*.

Lettres champenoises, Les, or *Correspondance politique, morale, et littéraire* (1817–25), a literary review (publ. irregularly, as a miscellany, to evade censorship; v. *Press*, 5). Contributors included Dumas *père*, Hugo, Gautier, and other young *Romantics.

Lettres de cachet, under the *ancien régime*, letters sealed with the king's privy seal, usually directing the imprisonment or exile without trial of the persons named. The practice was much abused in the 17th and 18th cs., especially to confine persons deemed likely to disgrace their families. v. *Mirabeau, comte de; Linguet*.

Lettres de Dupuis et Cotonet, Les, v. *Musset*.

Lettres de Maximilien Robespierre ... à ses commettants, v. *Défenseur de la Constitution*.

Lettres de mon moulin, v. *Daudet, A.*

Lettres du comte de Mirabeau à ses commettants, v. *Courrier de Provence*.

Lettres d'une Péruvienne (1747), by Mme de Graffigny, a series of 41 letters purporting to be written by a young Peruvian lady brought to France when Peru falls to the Spaniards. Her comments on French manners and customs are combined with a mild element of romance. She remains faithful to the Peruvian lover from whom she has been separated, rejecting her amiable, love-stricken French protector, only to find that her lover has transferred his affections to a Spanish lady. The work helped to popularize the epistolary novel.

Lettres d'une religieuse portugaise, v. *Lettres portugaises*.

Lettres d'un voyageur, v. *Sand*.

Lettres écrites de France et d'Italie (1829–30), Courier's letters to his family and friends, written 1787–1812. They include descriptions of French society in Milan and Rome and of his army experiences, also correspondence about his classical studies. Those to his women friends and, latterly, to his wife are good reading, especially the ones to his cousin Mme Pigalle, a lady whose pregnancies followed one another in swift succession. His tone is lively, affectionate, bantering, and at times serious—'Je rêve nuit et jour aux moyens de tuer des gens que je n'ai jamais vus, qui ne m'ont fait ni bien ni mal'.

Lettres écrites de la montagne, v. *Rousseau, J.-J.*

Lettres familières, v. *Patin*.

Lettres françaises, Les (1942–72), a literary and artistic weekly born of the *Resistance. Edited from 1953 by Aragon, it became a leading review (subsidized by the French Communist Party, but far from wedded to the Moscow line), with many distinguished contributors, notably poets.

Lettres juives, v. Argens.

Lettres normandes, Les (1817–20), a witty literary review (publ. irregularly, as a miscellany, to evade censorship; *v. Press*, 5), edited by Léon Thiessé (1793–1854). It was unsympathetic to the *Romantics.

Lettres nouvelles, Les (1953– ; now monthly), a literary review edited by Maurice Nadeau (*cf. Quinzaine littéraire, La*), each issue being either 'un numéro de revue ou un ouvrage'.

Lettres persanes (1721; augm. ed. 1754), by Montesquieu, a series of letters purporting to be written and received by two Persians, Rica and Usbek, who visit Paris in the early 18th c.; a work admirably reflecting the spirit of the age. *Cf. Dufresny; Marana.*

The Persians record what they observe and their reflections form a satirical review of French society, from the monarch (Louis XIV and, later, the Regent) and his methods of government, the clergy and their sectarian quarrels, the magistrates, the academics (a visit to the University library occasions pungent criticism of the various categories of French literature), and the financiers (e.g. *Law's 'système') to the poets, gamblers, and libertines. Some letters of wider scope (on war, international law, the causes of depopulation, etc.) show the author's serious preoccupations and his powerful, original mind. Others vividly depict the passions, intrigues, and tragedies of life in a Persian harem.

Lettres philosophiques (1733, an Eng. version; 1734, 1st French ed.; there had been 10 eds. by 1739), 24 letters by Voltaire, the fruit of his stay in England (1726–9; he often refers to them as *Lettres*

anglaises), most of them probably written 1729–31. (A twenty-fifth letter, unconnected with England, criticizes a great many of *Pascal's *Pensées*, mainly on the ground that their pessimism humiliates and degrades human nature and intelligence.) The *parlement at once ordered Voltaire's arrest and the burning of the work as scandalous and disrespectful.

The letters discuss various aspects of English life, making them the occasion for ironical criticism of French life and institutions. Voltaire begins with religion, writing of the Quakers (whose concern for Christ's moral and spiritual precepts, rather than for dogma and ritual, clearly impressed him), the Anglicans, the Presbyterians, and the anti-Trinitarians. Next come two letters praising the English system of government and tracing its history, then one on trade, and one on vaccination for smallpox. There follow letters on Bacon and Locke, and several on Newton (who is compared with Descartes). He then turns to literature, discussing English tragedy (Shakespeare, Dryden, Addison) and comedy (Wycherley, Vanbrugh, Congreve), the poetry of Rochester and Waller, the satirists (Swift, Butler, and Pope—incidentally showing his own aversion to Rabelais), the respect shown to men of letters in England, and English learned societies. He sometimes attempts French translations of passages from authors under discussion (e.g. Hamlet's soliloquy).

Lettres portugaises, five letters ostensibly written by one Marianna Alcaforado, a Portuguese nun, to her lover, a French officer, Bouton de Chamilly, comte de Saint-Léger (the duc de *Saint-Simon's *Mémoires* for 1703 describe his career). The two had met during the war between Portugal and Spain (1661–8) and he had deserted her. The letters, remarkable for their literary force, express her grief, shame, and resentment. They were published in 1669 in what was said to be a French translation, attributed to Guilleragues, and prompted imitations and replies (an Eng. trans., by Sir Roger l'Estrange, appeared in 1678). It was long suspected that Guilleragues was the real author of the letters, a fact finally established in 1962.

Lettres provinciales, v. Pascal.

Lettres sur les Anglais, v. Lettres philosophiques.

Lettre sur les aveugles à l'usage de ceux qui voient (1749), by Diderot, a philosophical treatise tending to atheism and materialism. He discusses the ideas and methods of reasoning of those born blind, as an illustration of the principle that all knowledge depends on our sensory perceptions. The argument for religion drawn from the marvels of nature is, he holds, of little force for the blind. He bases himself in particular on the case of Nicholas Saunderson (1682–1739), the blind professor of mathematics at Cambridge.

Lettre sur les spectacles, v. Lettre à d'Alembert sur les spectacles.

Lettrisme, v. Literary Isms.

Leurs figures, v. Barrès.

Le Vau, LOUIS, *v. Versailles.*

Le Vavasseur, LOUIS-GUSTAVE (1819–96), minor poet, published *Vers* (1843), poems doubtfully attributed to his friend Baudelaire; *Poésies fugitives* (1846); *Dix Mois de révolution* (1849); *Farces et moralités* (1850), etc.

Le Vayer, *v. La Mothe le Vayer.*

Lévi, Éliphas, *v. Constant, A.-L.*

Lévis, FRANÇOIS-GASTON, CHEVALIER, and from 1784 DUC, DE (1720–87), last commander of the French troops in Canada, took command after the fall of Quebec (1759; *v. Montcalm*). He failed to reconquer any of the territory lost to the British and eventually returned to France.

Lévi-Strauss, CLAUDE (1908–   ), social anthropologist, director of studies at the *École pratique des Hautes Études* from 1950 and professor of social anthropology at the *Collège de France* from 1959; a leading exponent of *Structuralism, to which he was introduced by the Russian-born linguist Roman Jakobson. His works include *Anthropologie structurale* (1958), *Le Totémisme aujourd'hui* (1962), *La Pensée sauvage* (1962), *Le Cru et le cuit* (1964), *Du miel aux cendres* (1967), *L'Homme nu* (1971). His *Tristes Tropiques* (1955), a largely autobiographical work, has prompted comparisons with J.-J. Rousseau. He was elected to the *Académie* in 1973.

Lévizac, JEAN-PONT-VICTOR LACOUTZ DE, *v. Dictionaries, 1807.*

Lévy-Bruhl, LUCIEN (1857–1939), sociologist. His works include, notably, *La Morale et la science des mœurs* (1903); also *Les Fonctions mentales dans les sociétés inférieures* (1910), *Le Surnaturel et la nature dans la mentalité primitive* (1931).

L'Hermite, Tristan, *v. Tristan l'Hermite.*

Lhomond, CHARLES-FRANÇOIS, ABBÉ (1727–94), grammarian, the first to compile a Latin grammar in French, *Éléments de la grammaire latine* (1780), long used in French schools.

L'Hôpital, MICHEL DE (1505–73), humanist, chancellor of France (1560–8), an eloquent orator, famous for his tolerance and his efforts to moderate the passions aroused by the wars of religion (he was one of the *Politiques*; *v. Huguenots*); author of Latin poems and a treatise on justice. Ronsard addressed to him the longest of his Pindaric odes (on the history of poetry).

Liaisons dangereuses, Les, v. Laclos.

Libertins, the free-thinkers, sceptics, or Pyrrhonians of the 17th and early 18th cs., e.g. Saint-Évremond, La Fare, Théophile de Viau, Chaulieu (*v. Temple*), Bernier, and to some extent Bayle and Fontenelle, intellectual descendants of Rabelais and Montaigne and precursors of Voltaire and the **Encyclopédistes*. The more erudite (e.g. Naudé) often wrote in Latin, as being a safer medium for the expression of their particular form of religious epicureanism, irreligion, or blasphemy. They were accused of atheism and dissipated living (*v. Garasse; Mersenne*) and attacked by Bossuet, Bourdaloue, Pascal, etc. The accusations were partially true, and became increasingly so, with the result that *libertin* came to signify a profligate contemptuous of sexual morality (*cf.* Molière's **Dom Juan*; Valmont in **Laclos's Les Liaisons dangereuses*).

Librairie, La. The State concerned itself with the book-trade from the early days of printing. Paris printers and booksellers formed a corporation, restricted in numbers, minutely regulated and supervised, and originally a dependency of the **University of Paris*. An ordinance of François Ier (1521) required all books to be authorized by the University and licensed before printing. An ordinance of 1535 (partly relaxed in 1536) forbade all unlicensed printing under pain of death, and subsequent edicts, down to as late as 1757, continued to prescribe very severe penalties for it. The *privilège*, or licence to print, originally intended to protect author and publisher against piracy, was very soon being withheld in order to repress works deemed subversive or immoral. Its political importance dates from the religious disputes of the 16th c., and the University exercised its censorship chiefly in this connection. In 1653, the function of censorship was transferred to four salaried royal censors, responsible to the chancellor. The only books licensed were those guaranteed by a censor to contain nothing contrary to religion, the State, or morality. The custom of granting general licences to particular authors was abolished (1659), though bishops retained their right to licenses without censorship. The censors increased in number as

literature (inc., from now on, newspapers—*v. Press*, 1) developed (82 by 1750, when Malesherbes became *directeur de la librairie* under the chancellor; 121 by 1763). The office was now unpaid (except after 20 years' service), but carried certain advantages. In addition, special censors selected *ad hoc* for their supposed competence in the field concerned were charged with the scrutiny of particular works (d'Alembert read Rousseau's **Lettre sur les spectacles*, Diderot read Palissot's comedies). Books produced by the royal press (*v. Imprimerie nationale*) were exempt from censorship. *v. Trévoux*.

Sometimes, while a formal *privilège* was refused, a *permission tacite* was granted, or the *lieutenant général de *police* gave a verbal undertaking not to prosecute the printer. The *permission tacite* (officially recorded, but not, as was the *privilège*, printed in the work) afforded protection to printers of works containing opinions unsuitable for publication with express royal authority. Both the *privilège* and the *permission tacite* were revocable. A notable instance of the tacit relaxation of the law was the continued printing of the **Encyclopédie* in Paris after the revocation of its *privilège*, thanks to Malesherbes's sympathy with the enterprise. Large numbers of unauthorized books were printed abroad (Holland, Switzerland); most of these were smuggled into France, a few came in with a *permission tacite*.

In the 18th c., several clandestine presses existed in Paris and often produced works with the imprint of Amsterdam, The Hague, etc. Because authorized booksellers were restricted, for convenience of inspection, to the University quarter, many unauthorized vendors (*colporteurs*) sprang up, carrying books to other quarters of Paris. They even opened shops in places exempt from inspection (e.g. the precincts of the royal palaces), disseminating illicit works. Both the repression of illicit printing and the contraband trade, and the inspection of recognized presses and bookshops, fell to the *lieutenant général de police*, acting under the instructions of the *directeur de la librairie* but himself empowered to authorize certain minor works. Gabriel de Sartine combined both functions (1763–76).

While the granting of *privilèges* rested with the chancellor and his delegate, the *directeur*, three bodies possessed or arrogated to themselves the right to condemn works already published: the *Sorbonne, important during the great religious controversies of the 16th and 17th cs., but ineffectual against the 18th-c. *philosophes; the Church (i.e. the bishops, or the clergy in assembly), active, but without effective power; the *parlement. This last body had real and ostensibly formidable powers: any work might be denounced to it; it could then prosecute the author, imprison or exile him, prohibit the sale of his book, seize it, or order it to be burnt; even the censor who had authorized publication was not immune (as in the case of Helvétius's *De l'esprit). In practice, however, its repressive measures were of little avail in restricting dissemination of a work; they served rather to advertise it.

During the 18th c., this whole system, originally adopted to check the spread of the Reformed doctrines and inconsistently—often unjustly—applied, was finally recognized to be useless and out of date. The liberty of printing was expressly affirmed in 1789 and the *privilège* abolished in 1793.

Under the *Consulat, some measure of control was re-established: from 1800, books were subjected to examination, and possible suppression, by the police before distribution. An imperial decree of 1810 intensified its severity. References inimical to the dignity of the throne or the interests of the State (elastic terms) were forbidden; and a *directeur général de l'imprimerie et de la librairie* was created, with powers to examine, confiscate, and suppress before the printing stage was reached. As the police still retained the powers conferred on them in 1800, books were often passed by the censor for printing, then prohibited by the police before publication (e.g. Mme de Staël's *De l'Allemagne). Napoleon's first abdication ended this state of affairs; and his *Acte additionnel (1815) guaran-

teed full freedom of publication for any matter running to more than 20 pages. The book-trade was thus finally freed from control. But the law still provided, and continues to provide, for prosecution after publication on grounds of offence against public morals (v. *Baudelaire*; *Madame Bovary*). The liberal Act of 1881 regulating the Press (v. *Press*, 9) also covered the book-trade. Cf. *Censorship, Dramatic*.

Libraries, v. *Bibliothèque…*

Libri-Carucci, GUGLIELMUS-BRUTUS-ICILIUS-TIMOLEON, COUNT (1803–69), 'Libri the book-thief', a well-born Florentine mathematician and bibliographer, came to France (1830), settled in Paris, acquired influential friends and high academic distinction, was naturalized French (1833), and later appointed an inspector of libraries and archives. In 1848, persistent rumours that he had for years been systematically pillaging the libraries he visited were confirmed by the discovery of police reports, previously suppressed by his friend Guizot. He had prior warning and made off to London (with a large case of books). His trial, *in absentia*, was notable for the intervention of friends convinced of his innocence, e.g. Mérimée; but he was sentenced by default to 10 years' solitary confinement. He lived in London for some 15 years and amassed a fortune by selling his stolen treasures to unsuspecting collectors (e.g. Lord Ashburnham). Many, however, were traced and repurchased by the French government.

Lichtenberger, ANDRÉ (1870–1940), social historian. Besides works in this field, he wrote fiction, notably *Mon petit Trott* (1898), at once a very popular children's book and a psychological study of the sensitive child in a world of warring adults.

Ligne, CHARLES-JOSEPH, PRINCE DE (1735–1814), Belgian by birth, a general in the Austrian service, a man of culture and wit with a wide circle of acquaintance (Voltaire, Mme de Staël, Frederick the

Great, Catherine II, Marie-Antoinette, etc.). His notable *Mélanges militaires, littéraires, sentimentaires* (1795–1811, 30 vols.; Mme de Staël published a good selection) and his letters contain interesting portraits and narratives, also (in the former) a good treatise on gardens, *Coup d'œil sur Beloeil* (his property in Belgium).

Lignon, Le, v. *Astrée, L'*.

Ligue, La, f. 1576 to defend Roman Catholicism against the *Huguenots and led by Henri, 3rd duc de *Guise (1550–88). Guise, known (like his father) as 'le Balafré', had been prominent in the Massacre of St. *Bartholomew and was in the field as a possible successor to the childless Henri III in preference to the Protestant Henri de Navarre (later Henri IV). The Guises came to an understanding with Philip II of Spain, fighting broke out between the *Ligueurs* and the Huguenots, and 'le Balafré' finally became an overt rebel against Henri III. In 1588, Henri III—driven from Paris by the fighting of 12 May (the *journée des *barricades*)—contrived his assassination, and was in turn himself assassinated by a Dominican friar (1589). The *Ligue*, now led by the duc de Mayenne, brother of 'le Balafré', was defeated by Henri IV at Arques (near Dieppe; 1589) and Ivry (near Évreux; 1590), became unpopular owing to its relations with Spain, and collapsed following Henri IV's conversion to the Roman faith. *Les Seize*, a demagogic committee of the *Ligue* which had assumed a revolutionary authority in Paris from 1587 and in 1591 hanged Brisson, president of the *parlement*, were overthrown when Henri IV entered the city in 1594. v. *Satire Ménippée*.

Ligue de la patrie française, f. 1899 during the *Dreyfus case, typified all that was bigoted, anti-Semitic, and reactionary in public life.

Ligue des droits de l'homme, f. during the *Dreyfus case to safeguard the rights of citizens; the counterpart of the above.

Ligue des patriotes, f. 1882 by Déroulède to avenge France's defeat in the *Franco-Prussian war. It supported *Boulangisme* for a time, and campaigned for revision of the constitution and a plebiscitary republic under a strong leader. v. *Barrès*.

Ligue du bien public, a league formed in 1465 against Louis XI by powerful nobles (the dukes of Brittany and Burgundy, the houses of Alençon, Armagnac, Lorraine, etc.), ostensibly to right wrongs and end oppression—in fact to defend feudal independence. The king allied himself with the *bourgeoisie* (esp. of Paris), arrested the rising by a show of force, and ended it by negotiating separately with the leaders.

Ligueurs, v. *Ligue, La*.

Limbes, Les, a title selected, but later rejected, by Baudelaire for *Les Fleurs du mal*.

Lindor, an 18th-c. name (popularized by *Le Barbier de Séville*) for the type of love-lorn Spaniard who serenades his mistress with a guitar.

Lingendes, JEAN DE (c. 1580–1616), wrote sonnets and light verse (e.g. *Les Changements de la bergère Iris*, 1605) and translated Ovid (*Épîtres*, 1615).

Linguet, SIMON-NICOLAS-HENRI (1736–94), barrister and journalist. Disbarred for the caustic violence of his political writings, he was obliged to leave France for London, where he founded (1777) and edited the *Annales politiques, civiles, et littéraires*. He later returned home, was thrown into the *Bastille (1780–2), but resumed control of the *Annales* in London, then in Paris (1790–2). He was executed in the *Terror. His *Mémoires sur la Bastille* (London 1783) is an eloquent indictment of *lettres de cachet* and conditions in the Bastille.

Lison, La, v. *Bête humaine, La*.

Liszt, FRANZ (1811–86), the Hungarian

pianist and composer, lived in Paris for some years (*c.* 1840) and moved in *Romantic circles there. *v. Agoult.*

Lit 29, Le (1884, in *Gil Blas*), a short story by Maupassant; a grimmer treatment of the *Boule-de-suif* theme.

Literary Academies. These were founded, from the time of Louis XIV, in many provincial towns; some, e.g. those at Arles, Soissons, Nîmes, Marseilles, were affiliated to the *Académie française. v. Montesquieu; Discours* (by J.-J. Rousseau).

Literary Isms. French literary history of the 19th and early 20th cs. abounds in new gospels, propagated by small groups and schools who do not rely on creative effort alone, but found reviews, issue manifestos, and provide themselves with a suitable label. Some, of course, developed into great and influential movements (*Romanticism, *Realism, *Naturalism, *Symbolism, *Surrealism). Some are memorable because they introduced—particularly into poetry (poetry and *isms* seem to be naturally akin)—new aspects of vision, new themes and techniques (*v. Unanimisme; Cubism; Fantaisiste, Le Groupe*). Some are perhaps chiefly remembered for the poets associated with them (e.g. *Gregh's *Humanisme*, the *École romane, *Naturisme, *Simultanéisme*), others because they engendered more lasting movements, or announced their existence with a sound and fury which have not yet quite subsided (e.g. *Dadaism and *Futurism).

There were also ephemeral groups and doctrines, with equally ephemeral labels, which barely survived their first appearance on the literary horizon, but have a certain period interest as the teeming offspring of *Symbolism. The list begins with *Ghil's *Instrumentisme* or *Instrumentation verbale* (*c.* 1887) and his *Scientisme* (*c.* 1888; this had a metaphysical bias and could only be expressed in long poems). Saint-Pol-Roux's *Magnificisme* (a self-explanatory label) and Péladan's *Magisme* (in which Wagner and occultism both had a share)

date from *c.* 1890. The basis of *Anarchisme* (practised *c.* 1891 by Gide and others) was the cult of the individual. The violent, explosive lyricism associated particularly with Verhaeren was sometimes called *Paroxysme. Ésotérisme* coincided (*c.* 1895) with a vogue for spiritualism, theosophy, and the occult. The doctrines of *Naturisme* (also called *Jammisme*, after Jammes) and *Humanisme* were later reflected in the gentle, rather wistful poetry of *Intimisme* (*c.* 1910). *Synthétisme* (*c.* 1901) implied a poetry of synthesis, of small details assembled to form a panoramic whole. *Néo-romantisme* (*c.* 1905) was a mixture of science, religion, and emotion. *Intégralisme* (*c.* 1902), *Néo-Mallarmisme* (*c.* 1904), *Impulsionnisme* (*c.* 1904), *Musicisme* (*c.* 1906; f. by Royère), *Sincérisme* (*c.* 1909), *Intensisme* (*c.* 1910), and *Floralisme* (*c.* 1911) variously stressed the importance of inspiration and spontaneity: some considered rhythm, the natural rhythm of poetic utterance, a prime factor, e.g. *Néo-Mallarmisme, Musicisme*; others wrapped themselves in philosophical arguments, e.g. *Impulsionnisme*, said to have consisted of Florian Parmentier (on whose *Histoire des lettres françaises de 1885 à 1914* the present article is largely based) and one disciple. *Somptuarisme* (*c.* 1903) was concerned to produce a jewelled effect in both verse and prose. *Aristocratisme* appeared *c.* 1906. *Druidisme* (launched by Jacob), *Effrénéisme, Visionnarisme, Primitivisme* (so called to distinguish its essential tranquillity from the destructive spirit of Futurism), *Subjectivisme, Spiritualisme* (anti-fleshly rather than occult), and *Totalisme* all belong to *c.* 1909. The list closes with *Dynamisme* (1913), which was anti-intellectual and stood for spontaneity and free play of the imagination. The era of these minor groups ended with the outbreak of the 1914–18 war.

One movement, Surrealism, dominated the inter-war years. *Populisme*, in the novel (from 1929; *v. Novel*, 3), stood for a realistic portrayal of the life of the people; a *Prix du roman populiste* was founded, and *romans populistes* are still being written. Since *c.* 1940, *Existentialism has had notable repercussions on the novel and the drama. *Lettrisme*, launched soon after the war by the poet Isidore Isou (pseudonym of Isidore Goldstein, b. 1925), regarded the letter, not the word, as the essential element in poetry, which became a matter of sound and typography. It represented a return to the destructive spirit of Dadaism and is expounded in works by Isou and his disciple Maurice Lemaître (e.g. the latter's *Qu'est-ce que le lettrisme?*, 1953). The period since 1950 has been marked by the growing influence of *Structuralism in the field of literary criticism (*v. Critics and Criticism*, 3).

Littérature, *v. Dadaism*; *Surrealism*.

Littérature anglaise, *Histoire de la*, *v. Taine*.

Littérature engagée (Committed Writing). Many creative writers obviously have been, and still are, 'committed' in the sense that they elect to take a stand on political or social questions in some, even many, of their works, Voltaire and, in the 20th c., Péguy, Rolland, and Bernanos being notable examples. But the terms *engagement* and *engagé*, which acquired a socio-political connotation in the early 1930s (*v. Rougemont*) and soon also a metaphysical one from *Existentialism, came to be applied in a special sense to a writer's whole output and view of life. For Sartre, as for many other writers of his generation, literary creation constitutes a social activity, and aesthetic questions cannot receive separate consideration. The writer is inevitably involved in the world, and his 'authenticity' can be measured by the extent to which he acknowledges this through his positive commitment in literature. Sartre, who defined the literary application of Existentialist *engagement* in *Qu'est-ce que la littérature?* (in *Situations*, II), has asserted: 'On ne peut pas tirer son épingle du jeu... L'écrivain est en situation dans son époque... Je tiens Flaubert et Goncourt pour responsables de la répression qui suivit la Commune parce qu'ils n'ont pas écrit une ligne pour

l'empêcher.' In the case of Marxist writers, *engagement* involves presenting an 'official' view of the world. The term *engagé* is also often applied in a more general sense, e.g. to writers of the *Resistance, whose temporary *engagement* was anathema to such *Surrealists as Breton and Péret. The idea of literary commitment ceased to be fashionable in the late 1950s. It is relevant in the work of writers including Sartre, S. de Beauvoir, Aragon, E. Triolet, Camus, and Malraux. *v. Temps modernes, Les*.

Littré, ÉMILE (1801–81), Positivist (a disciple of Comte, though he rejected his later mystical and political doctrines), philologist, and lexicographer. He was obliged to abandon medical studies to earn his living by editing medical journals, translating and editing Hippocrates, etc. After Comte's death, he was widely regarded as the incarnation of atheism and materialism: his election to the *Académie (1873) led Dupanloup to resign from it. His fame rests on his *Dictionnaire de la langue française* (*v. Dictionaries*, 1863–72) 'perhaps the greatest dictionary ever compiled by one man' (*Enc. Brit.*). He himself regarded his Hippocrates, his dictionary, and his *Auguste Comte et la philosophie positive* (1863) as his best works. He also wrote other studies of Comte and Positivism (some in the *Revue de philosophie positive*, which he founded in 1867); an *Histoire de la langue française* (1862); and *Études et glanures* (1880), including reminiscences of the years singlemindedly devoted to his dictionary.

Liturgical Plays, *v. Religious Writings*, 1.

Lives of Saints, *v. Saints, Lives of*.

Livre d'amour, Le, *v. Sainte-Beuve*.

Livre de la Terre Sainte, *v. Terre Sainte*.

Livre de mon ami, Le, *v. France, A*.

Livre d'Eracles, *v. Terre Sainte*.

Livre des douleurs, Le (1840, 5 vols.), last

of the four series of Balzac's *Études philosophiques* (1835–40; *v. Comédie humaine, La*). The title was that of a tale he projected, but never wrote.

Livre des manières, a moral treatise attributed to Étienne de Fougères, bishop of Rennes 1168–78, earlier chaplain to Henry II of England. He admonishes and censures all classes of society, showing unusual compassion for the miserable lot of the villeins.

Livre des masques, Le, *v. Gourmont.*

Livre des métiers, *v. Boileau, É.*

Livre des quatre dames, *v. Chartier, A.*

Livre des trois vertus, *v. Christine de Pisan.*

Livre du conquest, *v. Terre Sainte.*

Livre mystique, Le (1835, 2 vols.), by Balzac, a collection of three tales—*Louis Lambert, Les Proscrits, Séraphita* (set in 18th-c. Norway)—all much influenced by his reading of *Swedenborg and other mystical philosophers. They were later included in the *Comédie humaine* (*Études philosophiques*).

Livry, *v. Coulanges* (1); *Sévigné.*

Lodi (in N. Italy). Here Bonaparte defeated the Austrians (10 May 1796)—his first famous victory. *Cf. Caporal, Le Petit.*

Loève-Veimars, FRANÇOIS-ADOLPHE (1801–54), b. in Paris of German-Jewish parents, literary and dramatic critic (*c.* 1825–40) for the *Revue de Paris*, the *Revue des Deux Mondes*, and Le *Temps*; translator of Wieland, Hoffmann (complete works, 1830), Heine, etc., and author of an *Histoire de la littérature allemande* (1826)—*v. Foreign Influences*, 3. *Népenthès* (1840) is a selection of his tales and articles.

Logique de Port-Royal, La, *v. Port-Royal.*

Loire, La, one of the four great rivers of France. The famous *châteaux de la Loire* lie along its central reaches.

Lois de Minos, Les (1773), by Voltaire, a tragedy celebrating the dismissal of the *parlement* of Paris (1770); its performance was prohibited.

The scene is ancient Crete, where a superstitious, intolerant priestly caste enforces the cruel laws of Minos. These require that Astérie, a captive maiden, be sacrificed to the *manes* of dead heroes. The humane and enlightened King Teucer resolves to save her, discovers that she is his own lost daughter, overthrows the priests, and establishes the rule of justice.

Loisy, ALFRED-FIRMIN, ABBÉ (1857–1940), theologian and exegetist, dismissed (1894) from the staff of the *Institut catholique de Paris* as a Modernist (*v.* under *Blondel, M.*), professor at the *Collège de France* (1909–32). His chief works were *Études bibliques* (1901), *L'Évangile et l'Église* (1902), *Autour d'un petit livre* (1903), *Le Quatrième Évangile* (1903), *Les Évangiles synoptiques* (1907–8), *La Religion* (1917), *La Morale humaine* (1923).

Longepierre, HILAIRE-BERNARD DE (1659–1721), dramatist and Hellenist, author of tragedies (notably *Médée*, 1694) and a *Discours sur les anciens* (1687), against Perrault in the *Querelle des anciens et des modernes.*

Longueville, ANNE-GENEVIÈVE DE BOURBON, DUCHESSE DE (1619–79), sister of 'le Grand 'Condé' (and *v. Nemours*), a woman of great charm and distinction, in early life an *habituée* of the Hôtel de *Rambouillet*. She and La Rochefoucauld were deeply in love for a time, and it was for complicated personal and political reasons, including his restless ambition, that she took a prominent part in the *Fronde*. Remorse for this later led her to seek spiritual guidance at *Port-Royal*, of which she became an ardent supporter.

Longwood, *v. Napoleon.*

Lorenzaccio (1834, in *Un Spectacle dans un fauteuil*), a 5-act prose drama by Musset; first produced 1896 with Bernhardt as Lorenzaccio.

The young Lorenzo de' Medici (Lorenzaccio) plans to rid Florence of its vicious despot, his cousin Alessandro. To succeed he must gain Alessandro's confidence by himself embracing a life of debauchery, and the day comes when he realizes that his vice is no longer feigned, but real. He duly assassinates Alessandro, is even briefly exalted after the deed, because, in his view, this murder is all that remains to him of virtue. But he quickly lapses into despair and, making no attempt at defence, dies at the hands of his cousin's avengers. His horror as he probes into his own evil nature has prompted comparisons with Hamlet.

Loret, JEAN, *v. Press*, 1.

Lorette, a mid-19th-c. term for a 'kept woman'; they were so called from the church of Notre-Dame de Lorette, in Paris, in the neighbourhood of which many of them lived.

L'Orme, de, *v. Delorme*.

Lorrain, Jean, *pseudonym of* PAUL DUVAL (1856–1906), a minor but fervent *Symbolist, also an incisive literary journalist. His output includes *Le Sang des dieux* (1882), *La Forêt bleue* (1883), and *L'Ombre ardente* (1897), poems often inspired by classical or medieval legend; *Brocéliande, Yanthis*, and *Prométhée*, verse dramas typical of productions at the *Théâtre de l'Œuvre c.* 1900; *Monsieur de Phocas* (1899), a morbid Symbolist novel.

Lorrain, Le, *v. Claude le Lorrain*.

Lorrains, Geste des, *v. Garin le Loherain*.

Lorris, GUILLAUME DE, *v. Roman de la Rose*.

Lot, FERDINAND (1866–1952), medieval historian and philologist; professor at the *Sorbonne and the *École pratique des Hautes Études*. His many works include *Études sur le règne de Hugues Capet et la fin du Xe siècle* (1903), *Étude sur le 'Lancelot' en prose* (1918), *La Fin du monde antique et le début du moyen âge* (1927; 1951), *Naissance de la France* (1948).

Loterie nationale. In France, State lotteries are a recognized source of revenue (devoted to pensions for ex-servicemen, compensation for victims of disasters, etc.), and the stalls of ticket-vendors (many of them widows) are a familiar sight at street corners. Lotteries were introduced from Italy in the 16th c. and promoted privately for amusement and to raise money for charity (notably by the *précieuses), or (at the court of Louis XIV) as a means of distributing gifts and largesse on the occasion of royal weddings, visits by foreign royalties, etc. Louis XIV introduced (1700) a system of State-controlled public lotteries, and he and his successors used the proceeds mainly for benevolent purposes, e.g. restoring and building churches (La Madeleine; and *v. Panthéon*). The *Loterie royale*, briefly abandoned during the Revolution, soon reappeared as the *Loterie nationale*, which continued under the Empire and Restoration (providing subjects for such caricaturists as Daumier, Gavarni, Monnier), but was prohibited by a law of 1836. Private lotteries were still promoted, usually for charity, sometimes for other reasons (the impoverished Chateaubriand tried unsuccessfully to get rid of his property La Vallée-aux-Loups by promoting one). The *Loterie nationale* was re-established by a law of 1933.

Lothaire (941–86), king of France (*Carolingian dynasty), son and successor of Louis IV, r. 954–86.

Loti, Pierre, *pseudonym of* JULIEN VIAUD (1850–1923), novelist, b. and brought up at Rochefort. He became a naval officer, and his novels and travel books (some 40 works in about 30 years) were written when his naval duties allowed. His fame now rests on three novels of Breton life— *Mon frère Yves* (1883), *Pêcheur d'Islande*

(1886), *Matelot* (1893)—tales of the sailors who leave home to fish off Iceland, of man's eternal struggle with the sea, and the anxiety and heartbreak of those left behind. But he first made his name with romances of sentimental adventure (variations on the theme of loving and sailing away) in a languorously tropical or Oriental setting, notably *Aziyadé* (publ. anon. 1879; set mainly in Constantinople); also *Le Mariage de Loti*, first called *Rarahu* (1880; Tahiti), *Le Roman d'un Spahi* (1881; Senegal), *Madame Chrysanthème* (1888; Japan), *Fantôme d'Orient* (1892; a sequel to *Aziyadé*), etc. *Ramuntcho* (1897), set in the Basque country, was a novel of the same type. His other works include *Jérusalem* (1895), *Le Désert* (1895), *L'Inde* (*sans les Anglais*) (1903; ridiculing the Cook's tourists he encountered), *Vers Ispahan* (1904), and *Un Pèlerin d'Angkor* (1912), travel books; the semi-autobiographical *Le Roman d'un enfant* (1890), *Prime Jeunesse* (1919), and *Un Jeune Officier pauvre* (1923); the *Journal intime de Pierre Loti* (1928–30, 2 vols.; selections from his voluminous diary, ed. by his son, S.-P. Loti-Viaud). He wrote in a style at once simple, impressionistic, musical, and sensuous, conveying atmosphere (often charged with nostalgia, seldom gay or sunlit) rather than pictorial detail.

Louis Ier LE DÉBONNAIRE, LE FAIBLE, or LE PIEUX (778–840), king of the Franks (*Carolingian dynasty), emperor of the West (814), son and successor of Charlemagne, r. 814–40. He was weak and excessively devout, and was more than once deposed by his sons. For the division of his kingdom between them, and their feuds, *v. Serments de Strasbourg*; *Verdun*.

Louis II LE BÈGUE (846–79), king of France (*Carolingian dynasty), son and successor of Charles II, r. 877–9.

Louis III (860–82), king of France (*Carolingian dynasty), son and successor of Louis II, r. jointly with his brother Carloman 879–82.

Louis IV D'OUTRE-MER (*c.* 921–54), king of France (*Carolingian dynasty), son of Charles III, r. 936–54. He was taken to England by his mother after Charles III's death (hence 'd'Outre-Mer'), brought up at King Athelstane's court, then recalled to France and crowned.

Louis V LE FAINÉANT (966–87), king of France (*Carolingian dynasty), son and successor of Lothaire, r. 986–7.

Louis VI LE GROS or LE BATAILLEUR (1081–1137), king of France (*Capetian dynasty), son and successor of Philippe Ier, r. 1108–37.

Louis VII LE JEUNE (1120–80), king of France (*Capetian dynasty), son and successor of Louis VI, r. 1137–80; first husband of Eleanor of Aquitaine (*v. Lyric Poetry*, 1; *Troubadours*).

Louis VIII LE LION (1187–1226), king of France (*Capetian dynasty), son and successor of Philippe II, r. 1223–6.

Louis IX (ST. LOUIS) (1215–70), king of France (*Capetian dynasty), son and successor of Louis VIII, r. 1226–70 (his mother, Blanche of Castille, was regent during his minority). He died while crusading. *v. Joinville*.

Louis X LE HUTIN (*c.* 1290–1316), king of France (*Capetian dynasty), son and successor of Philippe IV, r. 1314–16.

Louis XI (1423–83), king of France (*Capetian dynasty, *Valois branch), son and successor of Charles VII, r. 1461–83; an astute ruler whose reign was notable for his conflict with *Charles the Bold, his extension of the royal dominions, and his encouragement of the early art of printing. *v. Commines*; *Ligue du bien public*.

Louis XII, LE PÈRE DU PEUPLE (1462–1515), king of France (*Capetian dynasty, first of the *Valois-*Orléans line), son of the poet Charles d'Orléans, succeeded Charles VIII, r. 1498–1515. He invaded Italy to lay claim to the duchy of Milan.

Louis XIII LE JUSTE (1601–43), king of France (*Capetian dynasty, *Bourbon branch), son and successor of Henri IV, r. 1610–43. The real rulers of France in his reign were first Marie de Médicis (his mother, regent during his minority), then Richelieu. *v. Héroard*.

Louis XIV LE GRAND, 'le Roi Soleil' (1638–1715), king of France (*Capetian dynasty, *Bourbon branch), son and successor of Louis XIII, r. 1643–1715. He married the Infanta Maria Theresa of Spain (1660), by whom he had one son (*v. Grand Dauphin*); after her death (1683), he was secretly married to Mme de Maintenon (*v. also La Vallière; Montespan; Fontanges; Mazarin's Nieces* (5)). Until he was legally of age (1651) his mother, Anne d'Autriche, was regent, with Mazarin as chief minister (*v. Fronde*). After Mazarin's death (1661), he governed as an absolute monarch, a masterful and ambitious ruler, served by great ministers (e.g. Colbert, Louvois; *v. also Fouquet, N.*) and soldiers (*v. Luxembourg, duc de; Turenne; Condé; Catinat; Vendôme; Vauban*). His reign was largely a period of wars and conquests, which brought France to the verge of ruin; but it is famous for his encouragement of literature and art. Great men of the day included Corneille, Racine, Molière, La Fontaine, La Rochefoucauld, La Bruyère, Boileau, Pascal, Bossuet, Fénelon, Girardon; and *v. Versailles* and Voltaire's *Siècle de Louis XIV. v. also Huguenots; Régale, Droit de; Chambre ardente*.

His *Mémoires*, compiled from his notes by Pellisson or some other secretary and intended for the education of the dauphin, include an account of his reign during the years 1661–8 and many letters down to the year 1694. They show him judicious and well-intentioned in his earlier years, but later despotic and at odds with public opinion.

Louis XV LE BIEN-AIMÉ (1710–74), king of France (*Capetian dynasty, *Bourbon branch), son of Louis, duc de Bourgogne (*v. Grand Dauphin*), great-grandson and successor of Louis XIV, r. 1715–74 (*v. Régence*). His reign was marked by unsuccessful wars and the degradation of the court, but is famous as the period of Voltaire, J.-J. Rousseau, Montesquieu, the *Encyclopédistes*, etc. *v. Pompadour; Du Barry; Leczinski; Parc aux cerfs; Damiens*.

Louis XVI (1754–93), king of France (*Capetian dynasty, *Bourbon branch), 2nd son of the dauphin Louis (who predeceased his father Louis XV), brother of Louis XVIII and Charles X, m. Marie-Antoinette (1770). He succeeded his grandfather Louis XV (1774), was deposed by the *Assemblée législative* (1792), and executed; *v. Revolutions, 1*. The Revolutionaries called him 'Louis Capet' and 'Monsieur *Véto'*.

'Louis XVII', *v. Orphelin du Temple*.

Louis XVIII (1755–1824), grandson of Louis XV, brother of Louis XVI and Charles X. He fled from Paris (1791; on the same night as the royal family, but by a different route) to Brussels and thence to *Coblenz. He commanded the *Armée des émigrés* and later fomented Royalist conspiracies against Napoleon. After the Treaty of Tilsit (*v. Coalitions* (4)) he fled to England, where he lived, pensioned by the British government, till Napoleon's first abdication (April 1814), when he returned to France. On 3 May, he entered Paris as king (*Capetian dynasty, *Bourbon branch). He fled to Ghent when Napoleon returned from Elba and was again restored to the throne after *Waterloo (1815). *v. Charte, La; Journal universel*.

Louis Capet, *v. Louis XVI*.

Louis de Bourbon, Chronique de, *v. History, 1*.

Louise, *v. Charpentier, G*.

Louis Lambert (1832, and *v. Livre mystique, Le*), a tale by Balzac, said to be semi-autobiographical.

Thanks to a chance encounter with

Mme de *Staël, Louis Lambert, a youthful prodigy of humble birth, is educated at the *Collège des Oratoriens* at Vendôme (as was Balzac). Later, as a distinguished mathematician and philosopher in Paris, he moves in the circles described in *Illusions perdues*. But his mind becomes unhinged and he suffers from delusions, followed by intervals of transcendent, sublime clarity. After fearful torment, he finally goes mad on the eve of his wedding.

Louis le Germanique, *v. Verdun*; *Serments de Strasbourg*; *Charles le Gros*.

Louis-Napoléon, *v. Napoleon III.*

Louison (1849; 1853, in *Comédies et Proverbes*), a 2-act verse comedy by Musset; produced 1849. A young duke falls in love with Louison, a country girl, his mother's god-daughter, brought into his household, decked out, and renamed 'Lisette'. But she is simple and virtuous, prefers her country lover, and contrives to reawaken the duke's love for his own wife.

Louis-Philippe (1773–1850), king of France (*Capetian dynasty, Bourbon-*Orléans line), r. 1830–48 (the July Monarchy). At the Restoration he returned to France from a very modest life in exile, became the hope of the opposition party, and ascended the throne as a constitutional monarch following the 1830 *Revolution. He accepted a revised version of the *Charte, re-established the *tricolore, and affected democratic manners, divesting his court of royal splendour. Industry flourished in his reign, the *bourgeoisie* became the dominant influence in politics, and the prosperous *bourgeois* the butt of the satirists and caricaturists (*v. Prudhomme*; *Daumier*; *Mayeux*). He abdicated following the 1848 *Revolution and thereafter lived in exile in England (at Claremont, Surrey).

Loup (Lupus), St. (d. 479), a famous bishop of Troyes, defended Troyes against Attila the Hun (451).

Lourdes, *v. Zola*.

Loustalot or **Loustallot**, ÉLYSÉE (1761–90), barrister, an ardent Revolutionary orator and journalist (*v. Révolutions de Paris, Les*), a man respected for his noble character and high ideals.

Lousteau, Étienne, the corrupt journalist who strips Lucien de Rubempré of his illusions in Balzac's *Illusions perdues*. He also figures in *La *Muse du département*, *Les *Comédiens sans le savoir*, etc.

Louvet de Couvray, JEAN-BAPTISTE (1760–97), Revolutionary and member of the *Convention, wrote the novel *Les *Amours du Chevalier de Faublas* (1789–90).

Louvois, MICHEL LE TELLIER, MARQUIS DE (1641–91), minister of war under Louis XIV, jointly (1662–c. 1677) with his father (*v. Le Tellier*), then alone; a great administrator, who completely reorganized the army. On the debit side, he encouraged the king's inclination for war (he was largely responsible for the devastation of the Palatinate, 1689) and instigated religious persecutions. His policy constantly conflicted with that of Colbert and there was keen rivalry between the two men.

Louvre, Le, on the right bank of the Seine in Paris, a royal palace (now a museum; *v.* below), said to be on the site of a hunting-lodge of Dagobert Ier (*v. Merovingians*). A fortress built here (1204) by Philippe II was much enlarged and provided with a moat by Charles V, rebuilt under François Ier and Henri II (*v. Lescot*), then enlarged by Catherine de Médicis, Henri IV (architect J. A. du Cerceau), Richelieu, and Louis XIV (*v. Perrault, Claude*). The junction of the Louvre and the *Tuileries was completed in 1857.

Louvre, Musée du, the chief art museum in France, opened 1793 in the above palace (taken over for this purpose by the State earlier in the Revolution). Its most important collections are those of pictures and sculpture. The private collections of the kings of France form the nucleus of the former, which dates from the *Renaissance, notably from François Ier, who imported paintings from Italy (e.g. *La Joconde*—the *Monna Lisa*). Louis XIV added largely to it (Colbert bought many works from the collection of Charles I of England) and it was greatly enriched by the spoils of conquest during the Revolutionary and Napoleonic wars (after 1815, the Allies restored 5,000 works of art to their former owners). Many of the sculptures also come from royal collections; others are the fruit of archaeological missions.

Louÿs, Pierre, *pseudonym of* PIERRE LOUIS (1870–1925), novelist and poet, a disciple (and son-in-law) of Heredia, moved in *Symbolist circles, and was closely involved in the launching of *La *Conque* and *Le *Centaure*. His works include *Chansons de Bilitis* (1894), prose poems 'd'amour antique', said to be translated from the Greek of a poetess contemporary with Sappho—in fact, a highly successful literary hoax, which deceived even scholars; *Aphrodite: mœurs antiques* (1896), a novel of courtesan life in ancient Alexandria, a graceful blend of erudition and licentiousness, much admired in its day; *Les Aventures du roi Pausole* (1900), a less elegant work of the same type; a novel now often deemed his best work—*La Femme et le pantin* (1898), a study of the progressive break-up of a man who becomes the creature of a worthless woman; *Poésies* (1927), including *Astarté* (25 poems 'sur la femme et sur l'eau', said to recall Baudelaire); and his *Journal intime 1882–91* (1929).

Lovenjoul, *v. Spoelberch de Lovenjoul.*

Lowe, SIR HUDSON, *v. Napoleon.*

Loyal Serviteur, Le, *v. Bayard.*

Lucien Leuwen (1894, posth.), an unfinished novel by Stendhal, slower-moving and less tautly written than *Le *Rouge et le Noir* and *La *Chartreuse de Parme*, but absorbing reading for those who enjoy quiet realism. He had considered various titles for it, including *Le Chasseur vert* (used when the first chapters were publ. posth. in a vol. of his *Nouvelles inédites*, 1855) and *Le Rouge et le Blanc* (used for an ed. of 1929).

The period is the July Monarchy. Lucien, son of a rich banker (an ironically tolerant father), is fired with an idealistic Republicanism which leads to his expulsion from the *École polytechnique, after which his attitude to life is indeterminate. He resigns himself to a military career and is posted to Nancy. Here, despite his politics, his wealth and charm give him the *entrée* to the decayed ultra-Royalist *salons. He falls violently in love with a young widow, Mme de Chasteller, and she with him (though she does not declare herself). Before he has had the energy to seduce her or the common sense to override politics and insist on marriage, a far-fetched episode shatters his love and ends his military career. The second part of the novel (to have been called *Le Rouge et le Blanc*) shows him resuming life half-heartedly as a civil servant in Paris and depicts bureaucratic circles, with an excursion to the provinces during an election. A final section (never written) would have followed him on official duties to Italy, and in the end he would have been happily reunited with Mme de Chasteller.

Luçon, L'Évêque de, *v. Richelieu.*

Lucrèce, (1) *v. Du Ryer;* (2) *v. Ponsard.*

Lucrèce Borgia (1833), a prose drama by Hugo. *v. Drouet; George, Mlle.*

Lucrèce, having ordered poisoned wine to be served to five young nobles at a banquet, comes to gloat over their death and finds that their friend Gennaro (an orphan of unknown parentage, oppressed by her inexplicable fondness for him) has also drunk the wine. Distracted, she reveals that he is a Borgia, and implores him to take an antidote. At this point, the dying Maffio calls on Gennaro to avenge him. Gennaro stabs Lucrèce, who dies gasping, 'Gennaro! Je suis ta mère!'

Lugné-Poë, Aurélien-François (1869–1940), actor and producer, acted at the *Théâtre Libre, then at the *Théâtre d'Art*, of which he became director (1893–1929)—changing its name to *Théâtre de l'Œuvre*. His reminiscences (*La Parade*, 1931–3, 3 vols.) are of interest.

Lulli, Jean-Baptiste (1633–87), a Florentine, appointed superintendent of music at court by Louis XIV, wrote the music for many of Benserade's *ballets, several of Molière's *comédies-ballets (La *Princesse d'Élide, L'*Amour médecin, *Monsieur de Pourceaugnac, Le *Bourgeois Gentilhomme), and operatic libretti by *Quinault. He established opera as an art in France; *v. Académie nationale de Musique.*

Lumière, the brothers Auguste (1862–1954) and Louis (1864–1948), pioneers of modern photographic technique (inc. colour photography) and the cinematograph. Their exhibition of moving pictures (1895, in a Paris café; admission one franc) was the first of its kind. Auguste later became an eminent biologist.

Lundis, Les, *v. Causeries du lundi.*

Lunéville, Treaty of, *v. Coalitions* (2).

Lupin, Arsène, in *Leblanc's crime novels.

Lustucru (possibly from *l'eusses-tu cru?*), a credulous simpleton in popular rhymes and songs.

Lutèce (L. *Lutetia*), (1) the ancient name of Paris, first mentioned by Julius Caesar (*v. Cité, Île de la*); (2) *v. Nouvelle Rive gauche, La.*

Lutrin, Le (cantos I–IV, 1674; V–VI, 1683), by Boileau, a mock-heroic poem inspired by a dispute between the treasurer and the precentor of the Sainte-Chapelle in Paris over the position of a lectern (*lutrin*) in the choir.

Developing his theme in epic style, Boileau describes the treasurer's wrath (the precentor has been usurping his functions); the plot to reduce the precentor to obscurity by restoring a huge lectern which used to overshadow his seat; the execution of the plot by night; the fury of the precentor, who appeals to the Chapter and gets the lectern removed; the treasurer's appeal to the Sibyl 'Chicanery'; the meeting of the rival factions in a bookshop, where they bombard each other with works ancient and modern (the occasion for some of Boileau's satirical sallies); the triumph of the treasurer by a stratagem, and the final reconciliation.

Luxembourg, François-Henri, DUC DE (1628–95), *maréchal de France*, a great general under Louis XIV, victor of Fleurus (1690), Steinkerque (1692), Neerwinden (1693).

Luxembourg, Madeleine-Angélique DE Neufville-Villeroi, DUCHESSE DE (1707–87), duchesse de Boufflers by her first marriage. She and her husband—the maréchal de Luxembourg (1702–64), a distinguished soldier—were patrons of J.-J. Rousseau. Her *salon, frequented by the best society, was noted for its refinement and good manners. *v. Boufflers.*

Luxembourg, Palais du, on the left bank of the Seine in Paris, built 1615–20 by Marie de Médicis, who left it to Gaston d'*Orléans, from whom it passed to the duchesse de Montpensier and the duchesse de Guise (his daughters), then to Louis XIV. Under the *Régence* it was the home of the regent's daughter, the duchesse de Berry. During the Revolution it was used as a prison (Danton and Desmoulins were confined there). In 1795 it became the seat of the *Directoire and since 1799 it has been the usual seat of the upper house of the legislature (the *Sénat, Chambre des *Pairs, or *Conseil de la République).

In the 17th c. its precincts were an Alsatia or asylum for thieves and vagabonds, who were removed by order of Colbert. The Jardin du Luxembourg, one of the pleasantest of Paris parks, has many literary and artistic associations.

Luxembourg, Théâtre du, v. Odéon.

Luynes, CHARLES-PHILIPPE D'ALBERT, DUC DE (1695–1758), a descendant of the connétable de Luynes (a favourite of Louis XIII) and grandson of Dangeau; a courtier who frequented the circle of Marie Leczinska, queen of Louis XV. His memoirs (for 1715–57) are a daily record of court life (with minute details of ceremonial), diversified by some interesting anecdotes.

Lycanthrope, Le, v. Borel, Petrus.

Lycée, Le (1786–1848; after 1803, when the term lycée was applied to secondary schools, it was called L'Athénée— L'Athénée royal under the Restoration), f. by the *philosophes, an institution in Paris offering something in the nature of a university extension course. *La Harpe lectured on literature, Marmontel on history, Condorcet on mathematics, others on philosophy, chemistry, physiology, natural history, etc. During its last 20 years lecturers included Comte, B. Constant, Geoffroy Saint-Hilaire.

Lycées and Collèges. A lycée is a State secondary school, headed by a proviseur and staffed by professeurs *agrégés or professeurs licenciés; v. Université de France. A collège is normally also a secondary school, either independent and denominational (usually Roman Catholic; v. Écoles libres), or maintained by a local authority (possibly State-aided). (For the medieval collèges, mainly concerned with higher education, v. Universities.)

From the 16th c. onwards secondary education was greatly developed and many schools were founded by the religious Orders, notably the *Jesuits (e.g. the *Collège de Clermont) and later the Congrégation de l'*Oratoire (e.g. the Collège de Juilly, f. 1638). Most of these (and the medieval collèges) were suppressed during the Revolution, though some were later resuscitated as lycées—the name adopted for the secondary schools under Napoleon's unified system of State secondary and higher education (v. Université impériale). At first, the lycées were run on semi-military lines and established only in the big towns; in the smaller towns it was left to the municipality to provide secondary education by founding and supporting collèges. Famous Paris lycées include the Lycée Condorcet (f. 1804; known at first as Lycée Bonaparte), Lycée Henri IV (f. 1804 as Lycée Napoléon), Lycée Louis-le-Grand (the former Collège de Clermont; v. Prytanée), Lycée Saint-Louis (f. 1820 on the site of the old Collège d'Harcourt).

Lyons, School of, v. Scève.

Lyric Poetry. For poetic forms v. Versification; for reviews v. Press, 1–9.

1. MIDDLE AGES. French lyric poetry of the courtly type appears to have originated among the *troubadours of Provence, reaching its zenith there about the middle of the 12th c. It took the form of short songs (v. Chanson) on themes of courtly love (v. Amour courtois), with elaborate strophic forms and rhyme-schemes. The marriage (1137) of Eleanor of Aquitaine (grand-daughter of a troubadour) to Louis VII helped to spread Provençal literary culture in N. France, as did the courts of her daughters, Marie de Champagne and Aélis de Blois. Poets of the North who imitated the troubadours include Conon de Béthune, the châtelain de Coucy, Blondel de Nesle, Gautier d'Épinal (fl. 1180–1200), Gace Brulé, Thibaud de Champagne. The earliest extant songs in N. French (the langue d'oïl; v. French Language) date from the second half of the 12th c. and closely resemble those of Provence. There were also lyrics of a more popular and bourgeois type in which *jongleurs or other professional poets— notably Bodel, Rutebeuf, Colin Muset, Adam de la Halle (who also cultivated the courtly genre)—sang of love and springtime, of their everyday joys and sorrows, often satirically. Finally, there were the popular songs (usually anonymous, apart from those of Audefroi le Bastart), for which v. Chansons à danser; Chansons à personnages; Chansons de toile.

The period of the Hundred Years War was not a fertile one. Its chief poets are Guillaume de Machaut, Eustache Deschamps, Christine de Pisan, Alain Chartier, and Charles d'Orléans. This period saw the development of fixed forms, notably the *rondeau and *ballade (and v. Lai; Virelai), though in content there was an endeavour to maintain the courtly tradition. The latter part of the 15th c. is made famous by the great name of Villon, a writer of a different order, a poet of death, a satirist, and a realist. Then came the *rhétoriqueurs (notably Lemaire de Belges), the least poetic of all the French schools of poetry.

2. *RENAISSANCE. Marot, though a disciple of the rhétoriqueurs, opened a new era, in which false taste was corrected by the study of the classics, the writers of the Italian Renaissance, and (in the case of himself and some others) the Scriptures (v. Évangélisme). He was perhaps the first to adopt from Italian models the form of the *sonnet (cf. Saint-Gelais, M. de). In the first half of the 16th c. there was the small but remarkable school of Lyons (v. Scève). Then came Ronsard and the *Pléiade, who, despite their pedantic excesses, widened and elevated the sphere of poetry, introducing into it a new sincerity, passion, and enthusiasm, also a wider vocabulary.

3. POST-RENAISSANCE TO PRE-ROMANTIC PERIOD. The reaction against the Pléiade was initiated by Malherbe, who gave a more intellectual cast to poetry, advocating clarity and restraint. Boileau, the great literary critic of the 17th c., roundly condemned affectation (e.g. in Voiture, Théophile de Viau) and the burlesque (e.g. in Scarron), insisting on the pursuit of the natural and true, with the aid of reason, common sense, and the canons of beauty laid down by the ancients (v. Classicism). In general, and not forgetting the mystical and baroque poets of the late 16th and early 17th cs. (e.g. La Ceppède, Sponde, Chassignet) and the lyric quality so often present in La Fontaine, the spirit of the 17th and 18th cs. was inimical to poetry. Versifiers were numerous and the various genres were

carefully maintained, but the prevailing opinion was that anything worth saying would be better said in prose. The elegant verses of such light poets as Chaulieu and Voltaire are typical productions of this period. Many good epigrams were also written.

It is not until late in the 18th c. that the first important poet, A. Chénier, appears. He was purely Classical in spirit, but the depth and sincerity of his emotion (e.g. in his elegies) and his metrical innovations herald the lyric poetry of the *Romantics. He was followed in the pre-Romantic years by two minor poets, Millevoye and Chênedollé, whose work is also marked by unmistakable signs of the new lyric note.

4. *ROMANTIC MOVEMENT TO THE PRESENT DAY. The four major Romantic poets—Hugo, Lamartine, Musset, and Vigny—had in common the great Romantic theme, the self in relation to what is universal, to love, nature, and death. All were essentially lyric poets, writing what French literature had not known for some 200 years, verse dictated by emotional necessity. Such poets needed greater freedom of prosody and diction than the Classical rules allowed, and this was won thanks largely to Hugo's battles over the caesura, *enjambement, etc. He himself, from being the leader of the Romantic poets, ended as a visionary genius whose lyricism was apocalyptic and elemental rather than personal (e.g. in La Fin de Satan and Dieu; v. Légende des siècles). Three other Romantic poets call for mention: Marceline Desbordes-Valmore for her love poems; Nerval, whose sonnet El Desdichado (v. Chimères, Les) is one of the enduring poems of French literature; Sainte-Beuve, because the realistic note already apparent in his *Vie, poésies, et pensées de Joseph Delorme was to become transcendent in quality and at times sinister, or macabre, in Baudelaire's poems of Paris, and to approach the banal with Coppée; also because his freedom of technique influenced Hugo.

The beginnings of a reaction against the intensely subjective emotion of the

Romantics can be seen towards the middle of the century in Gautier's *Émaux et Camées* and in Banville, whose mastery of versification has sometimes obscured his great merit as a poet. Indeed, until about the '80s, it might seem as if lyricism had been stifled by the *Parnassien* conceptions of an impersonal, scientific, or philosophical poetry, by the doctrine of *l'*art pour l'art*, and by an insistence on form entailing suppression of some of the prosodic freedom introduced by the Romantics. But, seen in retrospect, the setback was only temporary. Beneath the surface preoccupation with form, the whole poetic subsoil was changing, so much so that from about the last 20 years of the 19th c. the lyric cannot be considered as a separate *genre*: its subsequent development is neither more nor less than the development of French poetry as a whole, in the light of changing conceptions of the very nature of poetic content and the poetic medium.

The change had been anticipated as early as 1828 by Charles de Rémusat, who wrote in Le *Globe*: 'C'est le moment d'en finir avec tous les genres de convention. . . La poésie en est réduite à sa forme naturelle et primitive, la poésie lyrique.' One poet, Baudelaire, forms the bridge between past and future (he, too, is keenly alive to the artificiality of attempts to confine poetry within *genres*; *v. Epic Poetry*). His *Les Fleurs du mal* has both the serene, unadventurous, formal beauty of the *Parnassiens* and the direct, resentful emotion of the Romantics; but when he dwells on his own lassitude, or probes the uneasy depths of his own soul, he enlarges the whole poetic field. Moreover, by stressing the *correspondances* between nature and the arts, he brought the quality of evocation to poetry. He pointed the way to the *Symbolists'* efforts to communicate by suggestion and analogy rather than description, hence to their preoccupation with the prosodic means (*vers libérés*, the *vers libre*) of making poetry more vague, fluid, musical, and mysterious, hence also to their idealism (which usually took the form of an escape into medieval or mystical legend and may be somewhere behind the

Christian idealism of later poets who had strong affinities with Symbolism, e.g. Claudel, Jammes, Le Cardonnel). At a further remove, it is from his influence on three more immediate precursors of Symbolism—Verlaine, Mallarmé, and Rimbaud—that the main currents of modern French poetry derive. He also largely developed the *prose poem, a form to be widely used by his successors.

The influence of Verlaine, who made the necessary lyricism of poetry, its spontaneity, simplicity, and singing quality, more apparent, is seen in Kahn, Samain, Vielé-Griffin, and the early work of Moréas, H. de Régnier, Jammes, etc.; it may also have some responsibility, through Laforgue and Toulet, for the fantasy, gaiety, and irony of the *Cubists and *fantaisistes* writing *c.* 1911 (e.g. Apollinaire, Jacob, Klingsor, Derème). For Mallarmé, the evocative quality of poetry coincides more closely with its emotive power. His difficult poetry of allusion rather than of analogy or symbols (in which the reader must not so much divine his meaning as strive to participate in his sense of creative inspiration) leads directly to Valéry and 'pure' poetry. With Rimbaud, imagery and association (and dissociation too—the *alchimie du verbe*) are all-important, and the path is set for a poetry that is visionary, at times mystical, yet sensuous and even robust (e.g. Claudel), or so completely visionary and oneiric as to seem hardly more than the fragmentary outcrop of some unconscious deposit (e.g. the extreme *Surrealists, who were also influenced by Lautréamont and, more directly, by Apollinaire and his circle).

Since *c.* 1916 (which saw the emergence of *Dadaism), poetry has strongly reflected the general disruption and moral and political disarray caused by two world wars (and esp. the catastrophe of 1940), and it has been marked by an increasing preoccupation with the plight of man, alienated and helpless in the modern world, with what is known as the 'absurdity' of the human condition; *cf. Novel*, 3; *Existentialism*. The period from *c.* 1930 has seen the emergence of the *poète* *engagé* (at first often a defector from Surrealism—e.g. Aragon, and later Éluard) and the phenomenon of *littérature engagée.*

*Surrealism, which evolved from Dadaism, dominated the inter-war years. Apart from the work of Éluard, the poetry it inspired was often superficial and contrived, and its only important poetic innovation, automatic writing, was often little more than an intellectual game, exciting enough in itself, but rarely producing poetry of profound human significance—certainly little that stands comparison with the work of its greatest precursors, Baudelaire and Rimbaud. Its importance lies in the fact that, as a state of mind and a view of the world, it exerted a powerful fertilizing and liberating influence which few, if any, of the inter-war generation (inc. black poets; *v. Négritude*), even such independent poets as Supervielle and Michaux, entirely escaped, and which has also left its mark on later poets, e.g. Bonnefoy (*v. below*).

The fall of France in 1940 created a poetic climate very rare in the modern period: united with their fellows in intellectual resistance, poets were for a time able to communicate directly with a responsive public, and there was an outpouring of 'accessible' poetry, e.g. the work of Aragon (who returned to familiar traditional forms) and Éluard (for poets and reviews of 1940–5 *v. Resistance*). But this *poésie engagée* did not, as seemed possible at the time, herald a poetic revival; a good deal of it proved ephemeral and is now of historical rather than literary interest. After 1945, poetry again became largely a private experience, and only Prévert has since achieved a wide popular appeal.

The period since 1945 has seen notable works by four major poets—Saint-John Perse, Jouve, Michaux, and Char; but no single poet of dominating stature has emerged, and no important new movements (the impact of the young poets and critics associated with the review *Tel Quel*, f. 1961 by Philippe Sollers, b. 1936, cannot yet be assessed). These and other poets (inc., among those b. since 1900, Prévert; Leiris; Queneau; Frénaud; Guillevic; P. de La Tour du Pin; Emmanuel; Yves Bonnefoy, b. 1923, whose affinities are with Saint-John Perse and Jouve; and André du Bouchet, b. 1924, whose affinities are with Éluard and Char) have been experimenting separately in a wide variety of styles and forms (notably the *prose poem*). The indications are that poets have absorbed, and are now outgrowing, the influence of Baudelaire and the spirit of total revolt emanating from him. In the work of, for example, Saint-John Perse, Jouve, Michaux, Char, Frénaud, Bonnefoy, and Du Bouchet (all poets acutely aware of man's plight in the modern world) there is evidence of a more positive response to experience and, even where revolt is most apparent (Michaux and Frénaud), of a desire for reconciliation.

Between the main lines of development briefly indicated above come many small groups; for some of these *v. Literary Isms.*

Lys dans la vallée, Le (1835; later in *La *Comédie humaine, Scènes de la vie de campagne*), a novel by Balzac. The time is the Restoration, the scene mainly a small *château* in a verdant valley in Touraine. Mme de Mortsauf (*v. Dilecta, La*), wife of a returned *émigré* whose health and character have been undermined by privation, devotes her life to her two delicate children and to hiding her husband's weaknesses from the outside world. Félix de Vandenesse, thwarted as a child, chivalrous, timid, and inexperienced, falls in love with her at a ball. A deep sympathy springs up between them and he becomes an *habitué* of the *château*. She refuses to become his mistress, but with all the white heat of purity keeps his devotion at an unbearable pitch. He leaves for Paris and, partly through her influence, enters court circles. On hearing that he has formed a liaison with Lady Arabella Dudley, she loses all will to live and succumbs to a painful illness. From a letter she leaves Félix learns that, though for the sake of her family she had refused to yield to it, her passion had been as strong as his own.

Lys rouge, Le, v. France, A.

M

Mabillon, JEAN (1632–1707), a *Maurist, author or editor of many Maurist publications. His *De re diplomatica* (1681; suppl. 1704) created the science of Latin palaeography and laid down the principles for the critical study of medieval archives. Colbert offered him a gratuity and pension, but he declined them, saying that he needed nothing.

Mably, GABRIEL BONNOT, ABBÉ DE (1709–85), moralist and historian, half-brother of Condillac; author of *Entretiens de Phocion sur le rapport de la morale avec la politique* (1763), interesting *Observations sur l'histoire de France* (1765), *De la législation, ou Principes des lois* (1776), etc. He developed communistic theories with originality and courage, tracing social evils to the creation of landed property, which led to inequality between citizens.

Macaire, a minor *chanson de geste* (*Charlemagne cycle). *Blanchefleur, traduced by the traitor Macaire, flees to Constantinople under the protection of the peasant Varocher. In the end, her innocence is established. This work contains an early form of the story of the *Chien de Montargis.

Macaire, Robert, a character immortalized *c.* 1830 by the cartoonist Daumier; a sarcastic cad and an exploiter of fools—an inventor with no inventions, a doctor with no patients, a company-promoter with no companies—usually accompanied by his stooge Bertrand (as scraggy as Macaire was well covered). The pair were originally the villains in *L'Auberge des Adrets* (prod. 1823), a *mélodrame by Benjamin Antier (1787–1870) and others. The part of Macaire, who played havoc in a lonely inn and when arrested contrived to blame Bertrand, was created with gusto by F. Lemaître, who saved the play from failure by burlesquing it. He and Antier produced a comic sequel, *Robert Macaire* (1834).

Macdonald, JACQUES-ÉTIENNE-JOSEPH-ALEXANDRE, *v. Maréchal.*

Macette, in M. *Régnier's *Satires.*

Machaut, GUILLAUME DE, *v. Guillaume.*

Machine infernale, an explosive contraption used with criminal intent to destroy life or property. Such devices were used in abortive attempts to assassinate Bonaparte (by Royalists, Dec. 1800; 'la machine infernale de la rue Nicaise'—formerly a street in Paris), Louis-Philippe (by Joseph Fieschi and others, July 1835), and Napoleon III (by Félix Orsini, an Italian, Jan. 1858). Fieschi and Orsini were executed.

Machine infernale, La, *v. Cocteau.*

Mackeat, *v. Maquet.*

Mac-Mahon, EDME-PATRICE-MAURICE, COMTE DE (1808–93), *maréchal de France, soldier and statesman of monarchist sympathies, remembered as a commander in the *Franco-Prussian war (and *v. Commune,* 2) and as a President of the Third *Republic.

Mac Orlan, Pierre, *pseudonym of* PIERRE DUMARCHAIS (1883–1970), an author best known for his novels of fantastic adventure, often with an exotic element, and introducing pirates, *légionnaires,* deserters, crooks, and on occasion the Devil (e.g. *Le Chant de l'équipage,* 1918; *La Cavalière Elsa,* 1921; *La Vénus internationale,* 1923; *Le Quai des brumes,* 1927; *La Bandera,* 1931; *L'Ancre de miséricorde,* 1941). He also wrote humorous tales (e.g. *Le Rire jaune,* 1914), poetry and songs, and reminiscences of life in *Montmartre (*La Clique du Café Brebis*) and of his seafaring youth (*Villes*).

Macquart, *v. Rougon-Macquart, Les.*

Macquer, PHILIPPE, *v. Dictionaries*, 1766.

Madame, used alone, was the courtesy title from the 17th c. of the eldest daughter of the king or the dauphin, or of the wife of 'Monsieur', the king's eldest brother (at Louis XIV's court the duchesse d'*Orléans was 'Madame'). The king's eldest daughter was also called 'Madame Royale'. 'Mesdames' or 'Mesdames de France' were the daughters of the royal house, distinguished by their Christian names (e.g. 'Madame Adélaïde'). *v. Bourbon. Cf. Mademoiselle; Monseigneur.*

Madame Bovary (1856, in the *Revue de Paris*; 1857), a novel by Flaubert. Though first published with editorial cuts, the work scandalized many readers and Flaubert, together with the part-proprietor and editor of the *Revue de Paris*, was prosecuted for offences against public morals, but acquitted after a trial which was a literary sensation of the day.

The scene is mainly 'Yonville', a little town near Rouen in Normandy. Emma Rouault, a farmer's daughter, leaves the convent where she has been brought up with her head stuffed with sentimental religiosity and dreams of a life full of luxury and Byronic lovers. She marries Charles Bovary, a country doctor, and finds life in Yonville with a loutish, if adoring, husband very unlike the glamorous pictures in novels. Her dreams look like being realized when she becomes the mistress of a local squire, but he soon abandons her. Her next lover, a lawyer's clerk, finds her too romantically exacting. Meanwhile, she has fallen deeply into debt, and her creditor threatens to reveal everything to her husband. In despair, she makes use of an infatuated chemist's assistant to obtain arsenic, and poisons herself.

Flaubert's object was to show the unbalanced, romantically minded Emma at odds with her environment, and he paints a flat, devastating picture of a petty provincial town and the local worthies—notably M. Homais, an apothecary, the type of the self-satisfied country busybody, who never opens his mouth without making a speech, is ready to settle the affairs of the world at any moment, and prides himself on being anti-clerical and *Voltairien* (*v. Garçon, Le*).

Madame Chrysanthème, *v. Loti.*

Madame Déficit, *v. Marie-Antoinette.*

Madame de la Chanterie, *v. Comédie humaine, La* (*Scènes de la vie parisienne*).

Madame Firmiani, *v. Comédie humaine, La* (*Scènes de la vie privée*).

Madame Mère, Napoleon's mother; *v. Bonaparte Family.*

Madame Putiphar, *v. Borel, Petrus.*

Madame Sans-Gêne, a comedy of love and intrigue at Napoleon's court, by Sardou and Émile Moreau (1852–1922); produced 1893. The chief character is the maréchale Lefebvre (wife of F.-J. Lefebvre, a *maréchal de l'Empire*), originally a laundress and nicknamed 'Madame Sans-Gêne'.

Madame Thérèse, ou les Volontaires de 1792, *v. Erckmann-Chatrian.*

Madame Véto, *v. Véto.*

Madeleine Férat, *v. Zola.*

Madelin, LOUIS (1871–1956), historian. His *Histoire du Consulat et de l'Empire* (1937–54, 16 vols.) contains vivid descriptive passages as well as solid information. His *Fouché* (1901) was also much praised.

Madelon, in Molière's *Les *Précieuses ridicules.*

Madelon, La, a favourite song of the soldiers in the 1914–18 war.

Mademoiselle, used alone, was the courtesy title of the first princess of the blood royal while unmarried, or of the daughter of 'Monsieur', the king's eldest brother. For 'la Grande Mademoiselle' *v.* *Montpensier. Cf. Madame.*

Mademoiselle de Maupin (1835), a long, diffuse novel by Gautier. D'Albert, a discontented young poet, in love with love, finds the embodiment of his dreams in Théodore; Rosette, his mistress, also loves Théodore; and Théodore, the young squire who comes riding out of the wood, is Mademoiselle de Maupin. There is much confusion, but by the time 'Théodore' sets out on further adventures everyone has been made happy, in pagan fashion. The true theme, physical beauty, is well served by sensuous descriptive writing that scandalized the public of the day.

Mademoiselle Fifi (1882), the name-tale of a collection by Maupassant. During the *Franco-Prussian war a French prostitute shoots a Prussian officer (called 'Mademoiselle Fifi' because of his effeminate appearance) who has insulted the French flag. The local curé hides her in the belfry of his church till the enemy has left the district.

Mademoiselle Irnois, *v. Gobineau.*

Maeterlinck, MAURICE (1862–1949), Belgian poet, dramatist, and essayist, figured in the *Symbolist movement in both Belgium and France and lived mostly in France after 1890. In 1889 and 1896 he published *Serres chaudes* and *Douze Chansons*, collected poems, but he made his name with vague, allegorical, romantic plays (mostly produced at the *Théâtre de l'*Œuvre*) and with semi-scientific, philosophical essays on nature and insect life. His work reflects his preoccupation with death and his interest, in later years, in mysticism and occultism. His plays include, notably, *La Princesse Maleine* (1889); *Pelléas et Mélisande* (1892); *Intérieur* (1894); *La Mort de Tintagiles* (1894); *Monna Vanna* (1902); *L'Oiseau bleu* (1909), a fairy play; and *Le Bourgmestre de Stilmonde* (1919), a drama of the 1914–18 war, written partly as propaganda; also *Les Aveugles* (1890),

Alladine et Palomides (1894), *L'Aglavaine et Sélysette* (1896), *Ariane et Barbe-bleue* (1901; *v. Dukas*), *Joyzelle* (1903). Even his titles were typically Symbolist. His essays include *Le Trésor des humbles* (1896), *La Sagesse et la destinée* (1898), *La Vie des abeilles* (1901), *L'Intelligence des fleurs* (1907), *La Mort* (1913). He was awarded the *Prix Nobel* (1911).

Magasin des enfants, Le, *v. Leprince de Beaumont.*

Magasin pittoresque, Le (1833–73), the first French popular illustrated journal (weekly to begin with, price 10 *centimes*). It had articles on agriculture, architecture, commerce, history, literature, science, travel, etc., and an imposing list of contributors and illustrators.

Magdebourg, Centuries de, an ecclesiastical history (13 vols., one for each century down to 1400) by a number of 16th-c. Protestant divines, self-styled 'Centuriatores Magdeburgici'.

Magisme; Magnificisme, *v. Literary Isms.*

Magnin, CHARLES (1793–1862), man of letters and dramatic critic (on the *Globe* and the *Revue des Deux Mondes*); author of *Les Origines du théâtre en Europe* (1838), *L'Histoire des marionnettes* (1852), etc. He was noted for learning and good taste.

Magny, *v. Dîners Magny.*

Magny, OLIVIER DE (*c.* 1529–*c.* 1561), poet of Cahors, a disciple of Ronsard, was in Rome with Du Bellay (and a member of the same mission). He was a successful author of familiar odes and sonnets, collected in *Amours* (1553), *Gaîtés* (1554), *Soupirs* (1557; modelled on, though publ. before, *Du Bellay's *Regrets*), *Odes* (1559).

Mahomet (entitled *Le Fanatisme, ou Mahomet* in the 1743 ed.), a tragedy by Voltaire; produced 1742.

The scene is Mecca, after Mahomet (here a cruel, unscrupulous impostor) has won control of Medina. Séide and Palmire, captured as children from devotees of the old religion, have been brought up in his camp; but the girl, Palmire, has been recaptured from him and kindly tended by the aged sherif of Mecca, Zopire (in fact their father, though neither he nor they know this). Séide and Palmire are in love. Mahomet, who has fallen in love with Palmire, demands her surrender, comes to Mecca under pretence of negotiations, and contrives that Séide, whom he hates, shall first kill Zopire and then die of poison. Séide, persuaded that Zopire's murder is an act of religious vengeance and the condition of his obtaining Palmire, reluctantly carries it out, thus unwittingly killing his own father. The truth is now revealed. Séide rouses the citizens against Mahomet, but has been poisoned and soon dies. Mahomet, who represents Séide's death as proof of divine support for his own cause, is robbed of the fruit of his crime, for Palmire kills herself.

Maigret, v. Simenon.

Mail, Jeu de, an open-air game in which a boxwood ball was driven with a mallet (*mail*) through a ring suspended above the ground in a long alley, the object being to do this in the fewest strokes. Pepys refers to it (2 April 1661): 'To St James's Park, where I saw the Duke of York playing at Pelemele, the first time that I ever saw the sport.'

Maillet or **Mailliet,** MARC DE (1568–1628), a minor poet in the service of Marguerite de Valois, allegedly an eccentric Bohemian, vain, quarrelsome, and a butt for other writers. He wrote *Poésies à la louange de la reine Marguerite* (1611 and 1612), *Poésies... dédiées à Madame de Jehan* (1616), *Épigrammes* (1620).

Maimbourg, LOUIS (1610–86), *Jesuit ecclesiastical historian. His *Histoire de la Ligue* (1683) was translated into English by Dryden at the request of Charles II

(1684). He also wrote histories of the Crusades (1675) and of Calvinism (1682).

Mainard, v. Maynard.

Maine, (1) LOUIS-AUGUSTE DE BOURBON, DUC DU (1670–1736), elder son of Louis XIV and Mme de Montespan, was legitimated and declared heir to the throne in default of princes of the blood (1714), but under the *Régence lost the commanding position his father had sought to give him after his death (v. Saint-Simon, duc de); (2) his wife LOUISE DE BOURBON, DUCHESSE DU (1676–1753), grand-daughter of 'le Grand Condé', a restless and ambitious woman, temporarily imprisoned for conspiring (1718, with the Spanish ambassador Cellamare) to overthrow the Regent. Her literary and political *salon at Sceaux (1700–50; frequented by the cardinal de Polignac, the président de Mesmes, Voltaire, Chaulieu, Fontenelle, etc.) was the best known, though not the most important, of the day. With some assistance from members of her court, she wrote *Divertissements de Sceaux* (verse). v. Launay, Mlle de.

Maine de Biran, MARIE-FRANÇOIS-PIERRE GONTHIER DE BIRAN, *known as* (1766–1824), philosopher, spent most of his life in his native Périgord, though from 1797 he was involved in politics and frequently visited Paris. Originally a sensationalist (a disciple of Condillac and the *idéologues) and a sceptic in religion, he ended by holding totally different doctrines and subscribing to Roman Catholicism. He is important because his changed views were the outcome, not of the influence of other philosophers, but of independent thinking and of long, deliberate probing and observation of his own personality and the workings of his own mind. It was he who introduced psychology and introspection into French philosophy.

His works include, notably, a treatise on *L'Influence de l'habitude sur la faculté de penser* (1803), *Mémoire sur la décomposition de la pensée* (1805), *Considérations sur les rapports du physique et du moral* (1811); also *Les Perceptions obscures* (1807–10). In the first of these, he distinguished between what he called *passive* habits, i.e. sensations and impressions which become dulled with repetition, and *active*, i.e. conscious and willed, habits. This led him to maintain the importance of man as a reflective being whose soul, or *ego*, resides in the will, who is free to exercise intellectual and moral choice, and can best arrive at an understanding of the truth by studying his own personality. The difficult stages by which he came to accept the necessity of belief in the existence of a divine force external to man, namely God, can be followed in his *Journal intime* (1927, 2 vols.), an outstanding example of introspective literature.

Maine-Giraud, *v. Vigny.*

Mainet, *v. Berthe aux grands pieds.*

Mains sales, Les, *v. Sartre.*

Maintenon, FRANÇOISE D'AUBIGNÉ, MARQUISE DE (1635–1719), grand-daughter of d'Aubigné, born in prison at Niort, where her parents, both *Huguenots, were confined. She grew up in poverty and dependence, renounced Protestantism (1648), and married the crippled Scarron (1652) to avoid the convent. Her sprightly, amiable character won her admission to good society, but Scarron's death (1660) again reduced her to poverty and for some years she received a pension from Anne d'Autriche, the queen mother. In 1669, she was entrusted with the education of the children of Louis XIV and Mme de Montespan. She replaced the latter in the king's affections (though she was probably never his mistress) and after the queen's death was secretly married (*c.* 1684) to him. She was modest, discreet, and intelligent, capable of great self-control, and inclined to piety. Her influence on Louis XIV's policy has been variously estimated, but does not, in fact, appear to have been very great: she seems, for instance, to have done nothing to mitigate the persecution of the Huguenots after the revocation of the Edict of Nantes. She did,

however, induce the king to found the convent school at *Saint-Cyr and to place it under her direction. Her *Lettres*, written with a concise correctness and fitness of style which rank her little below Mme de Sévigné, reveal her good qualities and knowledge of human nature. She writes not only of personal matters, but of affairs of Church and State, and gives detailed instructions for the curriculum at the *Institut de Saint-Cyr*.

Maire de Paris. The office of mayor of Paris existed during the Revolution of 1789 (*v. Commune*, 1), and again in 1848 and 1870. Since administrative reforms of 1800, the system of local government in Paris has been exceptional, in recognition of the fact that those who control the capital are well placed to usurp the powers of the central government (as did the *Commune* in 1789). Each of the city's *arrondissements* has a centrally appointed *maire*, with various minor administrative functions; otherwise, the powers and duties which elsewhere fall to an elected *maire* are shared between the *préfet de département* (seated at the *Hôtel de Ville*) and the *préfet de *police*. The office of mayor of Paris is to be revived in 1977.

Maire du Palais, under the *Merovingians, the head of the royal household (*major palatii* or *major domus regiae*) and eventually of the notables and officials of the kingdom. He nominated the dukes and counts who represented the royal authority in the country, administered the royal domains, and in the king's absence presided over the royal tribunal and commanded the army. In the 7th c., he was no longer chosen by the king, but by the notables, and after the death of Dagobert Ier (638) became the real ruler, the kings being known to historians as *rois fainéants*. The chief holders of the office were Pépin d'Héristal, who ruled France with vigour (687–714); his son Charles Martel (ruled 714–41; called 'Martel' because he 'hammered' his enemies), famous for his campaigns against Saracen invaders from Spain and his great victory over them near Poitiers (732); the latter's son Pépin le Bref, father of Charlemagne (ruled 741–68; called 'le Bref' because he was short), who, with the support of the Church, deposed the last Merovingian, Childéric III, and usurped the throne (751); his long war with Waïfre, duke of Aquitaine, may be reflected in *Garin le Loherain*.

Mairet, JEAN (1604–86), a *protégé* of Richelieu (for a time one of his *cinq auteurs*) and a stern critic of Corneille's *Le *Cid*, wrote tragedies (notably *Sophonisbe*, perf. 1634) and *pastoral tragicomedies (e.g. *Sylvie*, perf. 1626; *Silvanire*, perf. 1630). It was he who really introduced the dramatic unities (v. *Tragedy*), and his *Sophonisbe* is regarded as the first regular *Classical tragedy, by reason of its noble style, refined sentiment, simple theme, respect for the unities, and exclusion of the comic element.

Maison de Molière, La, v. *Comédie-Française*.

Maison dorée, v. *Café Hardy*.

Maison du berger, La (1844, in the *Revue des Deux Mondes*; 1864, in *Les Destinées*), a famous poem by Vigny. The poet, disgusted with the world and an industrial civilization, will turn to Nature, but not alone, for she is cruel and unmoved by human suffering. He will therefore look at Nature and life only through the eyes of his loved one, whom he invites to share his solitude in the *maison du berger* (the movable hut used by shepherds when their flocks are on distant pastures).

Maison du chat qui pelote, La, v. *Comédie humaine, La* (*Scènes de la vie privée*).

Maison Nucingen, La, v. *Comédie humaine, La* (*Scènes de la vie parisienne*); *Nucingen*.

Maison rouge, La, under the monarchy, two companies of royal musketeers, so called because they wore bright red cloaks.

Maisons de la culture. Since 1960, under a scheme initiated by Malraux as Minister for Cultural Affairs, *Maisons de la culture*—State institutions designed to promote, and provide facilities for, the widest possible variety of cultural activities in their locality—have been opened in Paris and many provincial towns.

Maison Tellier, La (1881), the name-tale of a collection by Maupassant, a masterpiece of irony. One evening in a small seaside town in Normandy the local worthies arrive at Mme Tellier's brothel, their regular meeting-place, sanctified by usage, to find it closed: she has taken the ladies on a trip to attend her niece's First Communion. They have a wonderful frolic in the country and are lusciously overcome by memories and emotion at the ceremony. They return next day, refreshed and in riotous spirits, and the brothel reopens to its overjoyed clients.

This collection also includes *Histoire d'une fille de ferme*, a tale of farm life in Normandy, and the macabre *Sur l'eau*.

Maistre, JOSEPH DE (1753–1821), moralist and Christian philosopher (*cf. Ballanche*; *Bonald*; v. *Illuminisme*), brother of the following. Born of French parents in Savoy (then a possession of the kings of Sardinia, but taken by France in 1792), he studied at the University of Turin, entered the magistracy, and lived in Savoy. In 1793, he refused to swear allegiance to Republican France and fled to Switzerland, expressing his feelings (anonymously) in *Lettres d'un royaliste savoisien* (1793) and *Considérations sur la France* (1796; treating the Revolution as a divine purification). Sent as Sardinian envoy to Russia (1803), with little in the way of subsistence or official backing from his king, he won the respect of the Russian court, but had to leave the country (1817) because of his *Jesuit sympathies. He went to Paris, then to Turin, where he died. His works, admirably clear and vivacious in style, embody the Catholic reaction against the *philosophes*, the views of the *Ultras*, and his opposition to the progress of physical science. They include, notably, *Les

Soirées de Saint-Pétersbourg (1821); also *Essai sur le principe générateur des constitutions politiques* (1810), *Du Pape* (1819; asserting papal infallibility), *L'Église gallicane* (1820), and his voluminous correspondence (in *Œuvres complètes*, 1884–7). It was he who wrote 'Toute nation a le gouvernement qu'elle mérite'.

Maistre, XAVIER DE (1763–1852), novelist. An exile after France took Savoy, he followed his brother (*v.* above) to Russia, rose to be a general in the Russian army, and, apart from travels in Savoy, Italy, and France (1826–39), spent most of his life there. His charming *Voyage autour de ma chambre* (1794), written during his early years of service with the Piedmontese army, describes, with a delicate mixture of sentiment, humour, and exact observation, a period of imprisonment in his quarters at Turin; the underlying idea is that confinement cannot rob us of happiness, which we must find in ourselves. He also wrote *Expédition nocturne autour de ma chambre* (1825) and tales—*Le Lépreux de la cité d'Aoste* (1811), *Les Prisonniers du Caucase* (1825), *La Jeune Sibérienne* (1825; *v. Cottin*).

Maître Cornélius, v. Comédie humaine, La (*Études philosophiques*).

Maître de forges, Le (1882; dramatized 1883), a novel by Ohnet; a sentimental best-seller. Jilted by her ducal fiancé, the nobly born heroine marries a rich ironmaster, Philippe Derblay, who has all the virtues—bar an apostrophe in his name. She treats him with shameful arrogance, but is finally worn down by his cold politeness and comes adoringly to heel.

Maîtres d'autrefois, Les, v. Fromentin.

Maîtres des requêtes, under the monarchy, magistrates whose original duty was to receive and report on petitions presented to the king. Later, under Louis XIV, when the minister for war assumed this duty, they were assigned various special judicial functions, e.g. they assisted the *Conseil d'état* in its judicial capacity. The office could be sold or inherited.

Malade imaginaire, Le, a 3-act prose *comédie-ballet* by Molière; produced 1673. In this, his last play, he again returns to mockery of the medical profession, which 'knows everything about disease, except how to cure it'.

Argan, imagining himself to be ill, credulously submits to the endless medicaments prescribed by doctors Purgon and Diafoirus. A slight show of insubordination on his part, encouraged by the arguments of his sensible brother, provokes a ludicrous imprecation from Purgon, full of long, terrifying words. Argan is even set on marrying his daughter to Diafoirus's son, a pedantic medical student, so as to have a doctor in the family. His second wife, who pretends to love him, but is interested only in his property, hopes to drive the daughter into a convent. Induced to feign death in order to prove his wife's love, he discovers instead her self-interest and his daughter's devotion. A final ballet represents, in macaronic Latin, the burlesque admission of a doctor by the Faculty of Paris.

Malbrouk s'en va-t-en guerre, the first line of an old French song (with a tune similar to that of 'We won't go home till morning'); perhaps going back to a Crusaders' *chanson* about a knight Mambrun or Mambro, but since the 18th c. associated with the great duke of Marlborough. It was popularized through being sung by a nurse as a lullaby to one of Marie-Antoinette's children. Beaumarchais introduced the tune into *Le *Mariage de Figaro.

Maldoror, *v. Lautréamont.*

Mal du siècle, Le, the imaginative, introspective melancholy—ranging from gentle lassitude to violent despair—characteristic of early 19th-c. sensibility, especially of *Romanticism.

Mâle, ÉMILE (1862–1954), art historian.

His valuable studies include *L'Art religieux du moyen âge en France* (1922), *L'Art religieux après le concile de Trente* (1932).

Malebranche, NICOLAS (1638–1715), theologian, scientist, and philosopher, entered the *Congrégation de l'*Oratoire* and devoted himself to meditation and the composition of numerous religious and philosophical works, notably *La Recherche de la vérité* (1674–5; Eng. trans. 1694); also *Conversations chrétiennes* (1676), *Traité de la nature et de la grâce* (1680), *Méditations chrétiennes* (1683), *Traité de morale* (1684), *Entretiens sur la métaphysique et la religion* (1688). He was a disciple of Descartes (except in regard to metaphysics) and, equally, of St. Augustine. He did not distinguish between the realms of faith and reason, but held that divine reason surpassed the imperfect reason of man. He advanced an original solution of the Cartesian dualism of spirit and matter: denying the action of matter on spirit and spirit on matter, he found in God the source of our notions of the material world and the sole and universal cause, operating the movements of external objects and of our ideas so as to produce correspondence between the two; at the same time, he maintained, in some degree, the freedom of the will. His doctrine, with its tendency to pantheism, was contested by the *Jansenists (v. Arnauld, A.*) and by Bossuet, and involved him in much controversy; but he attracted many important admirers, e.g. Leibniz. He was one of the best prose writers of the 17th c.

Malesherbes, CHRÉTIEN-GUILLAUME DE LAMOIGNON DE (1721–94), a man of sterling character, an able and enlightened *directeur de la *librairie* (1750–63; under his father, then chancellor) and a minister (with Turgot) under Louis XVI. While striving to be strictly equitable, he did much to soften the rigour of the censorship (notably in regard to the *Encyclopédie; v. Librairie*), being an advocate of the liberty of the *Press (in his *Mémoire sur la liberté de la presse*, 1790) and at heart in sympathy

with the *philosophes*. He defended Louis XVI before the *Convention and was guillotined.

Maleville or **Malleville**, CLAUDE DE (1597–1647), lyric poet, a member of the original *Académie française*. His sonnet on *La Belle Matineuse* was deemed to excel even Voiture's sonnet on that subject.

Malfilâtre, JACQUES-CHARLES-LOUIS DE (1732–67), a promising poet who died young and unrecognized. He wrote satires, odes, and the poem *Narcisse dans l'île de Vénus* (1769).

Malherbe, FRANÇOIS DE (1555–1628), poet, b. at Caen (Normandy), spent many years in Provence, initially in the service of the chevalier d'Angoulême, then went to Paris as official court poet (1605; *v. Du Perron*), a position he retained till his death. He is famous as a literary legislator, especially in regard to grammar and poetic forms: he severely criticized the school of Ronsard (esp. Desportes) for excess of emotion, over-facility, and addiction to mere ornament; he condemned the latinisms, dialectalisms, and irregular constructions of the *Pléiade in favour of what he deemed common Parisian usage; and he laid down rules of versification (outlawing *hiatus and *enjambement*, regulating the caesura and rhyme) which were to prevail for some 200 years. He was thus one of the architects of *Classicism. His teaching was mainly oral: his views were written down only as marginal comments in a copy of Desportes's poetic works (these comments circulated in ms. form, but he never published them) or in his letters (notably to his friend Peiresc). His immediate disciples included Racan (who wrote his life) and Maynard.

He himself wrote comparatively little. His poetry, marked less by poetic inspiration than by careful, vigorous eloquence, includes verses on high political themes (*Prière pour le roi allant en Limousin*, etc.); paraphrases of the Psalms; and a few personal poems, notably the ode addressed to his friend François Dupérier on the death of his daughter (1599; 'Et,

rose, elle a vécu ce que vivent les roses,
L'espace d'un matin'). His prose writings
include translations of Seneca and Livy.
He wrote very slowly: it is said that he took
so long over a poem on the death of the
présidente de Verdun that by the time it
was finished her husband, whom he sought
to console, had remarried and died. There
are many anecdotes about him (mostly
based on Racan) in *Tallemant des
Réaux's *Historiettes*.

Malheur d'Henriette Gérard, Le
(1860), a *Realist novel by Duranty. A
provincial family persecute their daughter
into marrying a rich old man, who
pathetically dotes on her. On her wedding-
day she learns that the young weakling of
a clerk whom she loves has drowned
himself. She turns on her husband so
violently that he has a stroke, nurses him
with cool efficiency till he dies, and then
makes sure that her family get none of his
money. Her courage and insolent defiance
of her parents are well rendered, and there
are good family squabbles.

Malibran, MARIA-FÉLICIA GARCIA, MME
(1808–36), a famous operatic contralto
with a voice of exceptional range, daughter
of a great Spanish tenor, Manuel Garcia.
She sang to enthusiastic audiences all over
Europe. Her death (in Manchester)
inspired *Musset's *Stances à la Malibran*.

Mallarmé, STÉPHANE (1842–98), poet, a
leading *Symbolist. Soon after completing
his schooling at Sens, he spent a year in
London (1862–3) studying English and
there married Marie Gerhard, a young
German governess who had accompanied
him. Having qualified as a teacher of
English (he never obtained a university
degree), he taught till 1871 in schools at
Tournon, Besançon, and Avignon, then in
Paris *lycées (*Condorcet, Janson-de-Sailly,
Rollin*). He several times revisited
England, where he had many friends (e.g.
Swinburne and, later, Whistler), and in
1894 lectured at Oxford and Cambridge
(*La Musique et les Lettres*, 1895; important
as a statement of his poetic doctrine).
From 1894, having given up teaching, he

lived at his cottage at Valvins, near Fontainebleau. In 1896 he was elected 'Prince
des poètes' in succession to Verlaine.

Teaching was merely his means
of livelihood. His life was almost
exclusively devoted to poetic creation (for
him an agonizing struggle), or to thinking,
talking, and occasionally writing, about
the poetic function. His output, latterly
nearly at a standstill (apart from pleasing
light verse, collected in *Vers de
circonstance*, 1920), included shorter
poems and sonnets, prose poems, and
translations of poems by Poe, usually first
printed in reviews (e.g. 11 poems in *Le
Parnasse contemporain of 1866; prose
poems in the *Revue des lettres et des arts*,
1867–8; *v.* also *Tombeau d'Edgar Poë, Le*);
three fragments of a dramatic poem,
Hérodiade (*Ouverture*, publ. posth., a
monologue by Herodias's nurse; *Scène*,
publ. 1871 in *Le Parnasse contemporain*, a
dialogue between the nurse and Herodias;
Cantique de Saint Jean, publ. posth., a
monologue by the saint); the famous
eclogue *L'Après-midi d'un faune* (1876; *v.*
Debussy; Manet*); *Igitur, ou la Folie
d'Elbehnon* (1925), fragments of a prose
tale; a preface to *Vathek* (1876); *Les Mots
anglais* (1877), a curious study exploring
connections between the sound and sense
of English words; a translation of
Whistler's *Ten o'Clock* (1888). Collections
published during his lifetime included his
Poésies (1887; a limited ed. of 40 copies),
Les Poèmes d'Edgar Poë (1888;
translations), *Pages* (1891; prose), *Vers et
Prose* (1893), *Divagations* (1897; essays on
style and aesthetics, and some prose
poems). His correspondence has recently
been published (1959–84, 10 vols.; ed. H.
Mondor and L. J. Austin). A collection of
Documents Stéphane Mallarmé appeared
from 1968, his correspondence with
Whistler in 1964.

His first poems (55 entitled *Entre quatre
murs*, written 1859–60; 40 were first publ.
in 1954) imitated the *Romantics, but he
was soon writing under the influence of
Baudelaire and Poe. Despite his early links
with the *Parnassiens, their *monde visible*
was not for him: he believed that a poem
should suggest rather than describe, and

that words, as the poet uses them, have an evocative content beyond their everyday meaning. An acute spiritual crisis of 1866 bore fruit in his *credo* 'Beauty alone exists, and it has only one perfect expression, Poetry', and in his project for a great work embodying his vision of the evolution of beauty. (This long-awaited 'Livre', which was to include *Hérodiade*, was never written.) His efforts to evoke an ideal beauty (which led him to use an elaborate symbols and metaphors, and to experiment with rhythm and syntax by transposing words, omitting grammatical elements, etc.) and his theories of the 'musicality' of poetry, and of music and poetry as alternative aspects of the pure idea, made him a great poetic force in his own day and—after 1884, when Huysmans praised him in *A rebours* and Verlaine included him in *Les *Poètes maudits*—a notable influence on his successors. This influence was most strongly exercised through his talk at his famous 'Mardis', the Tuesday evening gatherings (*c*. 1880–94) of poets and other writers, both French and foreign, at his Paris flat (89 rue de Rome).

Some of his work is so obscure as to defeat determined study, e.g. his last poem, *Un Coup de dés jamais n'abolira le hasard* (1897, in the review *Cosmopolis*), where the size of the type and the arrangement of the words on a double page are continually varied in the attempt both to produce the effect of a musical score and to render the 'subdivisions prismatiques de l'idée'. But the sonnets, parts of *Hérodiade*, and the *Faune* have a rare, evocative beauty which leaves the reader silent before 'l'éruptif multiple sursautement de la clarté, comme les proches irradiations d'un lever de jour' (preface to *Un Coup de dés*). *v. Lyric Poetry*, 4.

Mallet du Pan, JACQUES (1749–1800), man of letters and journalist, notable for his political insight, good sense, and vigorous, ironic style. An honest and courageous editor of the *Mercure de France* (*v. Mercure galant*) and a champion of constitutional monarchy, he left France early in 1792 to work in the interests of the *émigrés*. (His *Considérations sur la nature de la Révolution de France*, 1793, is of this period.) Driven from Switzerland, he fled to England (1798), and from London (where he died) published the *Mercure britannique*, which was hostile to Republican France. His *Mémoires et correspondance* (1852), including letters of advice to the *Bourbon family, was highly praised by Sainte-Beuve. *v. Annales politiques, civiles, et littéraires.*

Malleville, *v. Maleville.*

Malmaison, on the outskirts of Paris, was originally a lepers' colony dependent on the Abbaye de *Saint-Denis. A 17th-c. house on the site, bought (1799) and enlarged by Bonaparte's wife Joséphine, was his favourite residence under the *Consulat*. After the divorce, Joséphine remained there with her children. It was eventually bought and presented to the nation (1904), and is now a moving and evocative museum of the Napoleonic era.

Malot, HECTOR (1830–1907), noted for his children's stories, especially *Sans famille* (1878), the adventures of a foundling boy; also *Romain Kalbris* (1869), *En famille* (1893).

Malraux, ANDRÉ (1901–76), novelist and essayist; a left-wing intellectual of compelling personality whose view of life and proven courage as a man of action caught the imagination of his countrymen. Between 1923 (when he left France on an archaeological expedition to Laos) and 1927 he was active among Communist revolutionaries in China (his exact role remains obscure). During the 1930s, he emerged as a militant anti-Fascist and fought in the Spanish Civil War. Taken prisoner early in the 1939–45 war, he escaped and later became a hero of the *Resistance, leader of a section of the *maquis*, arrested in 1944, and released by the Allies to command the *Brigade Alsace-Lorraine* which helped to liberate Alsace.

His novels directly reflect his career and

are in large measure autobiographical (in that his characters are often projections of different sides of himself) and documentary, e.g. *Les Conquérants* (1928), set in Canton in 1925, and *La *Condition humaine* (1933), set in Shanghai in 1927, where the background is Communism in China; *La Voie royale* (1930), inspired by his adventures as an archaeologist in Indo-China; *L'Espoir* (1937), about the Spanish Civil War; *Les Noyers de l'Altenburg* (1943). As a result of his career as a left-wing activist moving in Marxist circles, he was long widely regarded as a committed writer (*v. Littérature engagée*)—and as a renegade when, after the war, he moved to the Right, aligned himself with de Gaulle, and attacked Stalinism. He has, in fact, always been primarily a liberal humanist who could never wholly subscribe to Marxist philosophy; and his affinities as a novelist are with Dostoievsky rather than with Aragon. His works—which established in the novel the idea of the 'absurd'—are the fruit of constant reflection on the metaphysical situation of the modern European, whom he sees as alienated in a civilization where faith and reason have failed and death seems the only reality. He affirms his faith in man, whom he depicts discovering that his greatness—and his hope of regaining a sense of human dignity and fraternity—lies in offering an heroic challenge to the human condition. After 1945, he emerged as a philosopher of art, to which he turned for images of the permanence and nobility of man 'assez puissantes pour nier notre néant', notably in his *Psychologie de l'art* (1947–9, 3 vols.—united in *Les Voix du silence*, 1951). He was also prominent in Gaullist politics, serving as Minister for Cultural Affairs (1959–69). His *Antimémoires*, the first instalment of his memoirs, appeared in 1967 (rev. and augm. 1972); a further instalment appeared in 1974.

Mamamouchi, in Molière's *Le *Bourgeois Gentilhomme*.

Mamelles de Tirésias, Les, v. Apollinaire.

Mamelouks de la Garde, Les, a company of the *Garde impériale* formed 1804 from a native mounted corps created by Bonaparte in Egypt *c.* 1798. They always wore Oriental dress, though a few officers and other ranks were French. They were disbanded in 1815 and many were massacred at Marseilles during the **Terreur blanche*.

Mancini, *v. Mazarin's Nieces.*

Mandarins, Les, v. Beauvoir, S. de.

Mandrin, LOUIS (1724–55), a famous brigand. He was broken on the wheel.

Mandrou, ROBERT (1921–   ), historian, professor at **Paris X*. His works include *Magistrats et sorciers en France au XVIIᵉ siècle* (1968), *Les Fugger, propriétaires fonciers en Souabe* (1969), and *v. Duby*.

Manekine, La, a verse **roman d'aventure* by Beaumanoir, written between 1270 and 1280. There are versions in other languages, the earliest known being in a *Vita Offae primi* probably written at St. Albans in the late 12th c.

A king of Hungary has promised his dying wife that he will only marry a woman resembling herself. His barons urge him to remarry, but the only woman who fulfils the condition is Joïe, his own daughter. Revolted by the idea, she cuts off her left hand. The king orders her to be burnt, but the kindly seneschal sends her adrift in a boat. It carries her to Scotland, where the king shelters her, names her Manekine (for she will not say who she is) and, despite his mother's opposition, marries her. When Joïe gives birth to a son, the old queen substitutes for the letter announcing this news to the absent king another letter saying that she has given birth to a monster. The king orders her to be cared for until his return, but the queen substitutes an order that she is to be burnt. A seneschal again saves her and sends her adrift in a boat, which carries her to the mouth of the Tiber. Seven years later the king discovers her in Rome, where her penitent father also appears. Her severed hand miraculously reappears in a fountain and by the pope's prayer is reunited to her arm.

Manet, ÉDOUARD (1832–83), one of the most famous of the *Impressionists (though he never exhibited with them), was very closely associated with contemporary writers, notably Mallarmé (he painted a well-known portrait of him and illustrated the first ed. of *L'Après-midi d'un faune*); also the *Parnassiens (with whom he forgathered at Lemerre's bookshop), Zola (whom he painted), Baudelaire (who encouraged him in his early days).

Manette Salomon (1867), a novel of artist life by the Goncourt brothers. Four young men of contrasting character first meet as art students. Bazoche, a typical Bohemian, has great facility, but no application or true creative gift. He loves animals and ends as a keeper in the zoo. Chassagnol, a theorist and a bore, ends by living on his wife and continuing to theorize. Garnotelle, a conventional success, becomes a fashionable portrait-painter and marries a foreign princess. Coriolis, a true artist, is rich and a modernist, therefore suspect. He marries Manette, a beautiful Jewish model, and watches her ruin his life. Her relations fill the house; she grows increasingly avaricious and will only let him paint what will sell. There are notable descriptions of Paris, seen from the *Jardin des Plantes*, and of the sojourn of Coriolis, Manette, and Bazoche at *Barbizon.

Manières, Livre des, v. *Livre des manières*.

Manifeste des cinq contre 'La Terre' (18 Aug. 1887, in *Le *Figaro*), a public repudiation—which the authors later regretted—of Zola's *Naturalism and a denunciation (provoked especially by his novel *La *Terre*, then being serialized) of his obscenity. It was signed by five of his former disciples: Paul Bonnetain (1858–99), Gustave Guiches (1860–1935), Descaves, P. Margueritte, J.-H. Rosny.

Manifeste du surréalisme, v. *Breton, A.*

Mannequin d'osier, Le, v. *Bergeret*.

Manon Lescaut, Histoire du chevalier des Grieux et de (1731, as vol. VII of *Mémoires d'un homme de qualité*; later publ. separately), by the abbé Prévost, a romance which owed its immense success to the simple and realistic description of a man's overmastering passion for an unworthy woman. Reprinted in 1733, it created a sensation and was seized by the authorities. Changes in an edition of 1753 tended to emphasize the moral aspect of the story.

Des Grieux, at 17, chances to meet Manon Lescaut, a girl who is about to be made a nun against her will, falls desperately in love, and elopes with her. His blind passion, effacing all sense of honour and dignity, even triumphing over her repeated infidelity (for, though gentle and affectionate, she is quite devoid of moral sense), leads him through a series of unhappy adventures and reduces him to the basest expedients to obtain the means to support the pair of them. At last, with the connivance of his respectable father, she is transported to New Orleans. The despairing des Grieux contrives to accompany her. They live there in comparative happiness, posing as man and wife, until it comes to light that they are not married—whereupon Manon is allotted to the governor's nephew, who has fallen in love with her. Des Grieux and Manon flee on foot from the colony, but she dies, exhausted, in the desert. Thereafter, it is indicated, religion and the punishment he has endured recall des Grieux to greater dignity and fortitude. Important secondary characters are his father; Tiberge, his faithful, sensible friend; and Manon's rascally brother.

Mansard or **Mansart**, (1) FRANÇOIS (1598–1666), architect, gave his name to the *mansarde* or mansard roof; (2) his great-nephew JULES HARDOUIN- (1645–1708), the chief architect employed by Louis XIV from 1670 onwards (v.

Versailles; *Invalides*; *Place Vendôme*; *Marly*).

Manuel des péchés, *v. Religious Writings*, 1.

Manzoni, ALESSANDRO (1785–1873), Italian poet and novelist, author of the famous novel *I Promessi Sposi* (1825–7), leader of the Italian Romantics and an influence on *Romanticism in France. *v. Foreign Influences*, 3.

Mapah, Le, *name* (from *mater + pater*) *taken by* GANNAU or GANNEAU (*c.* 1805–51), a sculptor, who *c.* 1835 founded a synthetic religion called *Évadisme* (from Ève + Adam). It exalted woman, and preached the perfect equality and eventual fusion of the sexes, since 'le véritable Dieu' must embody both the male and the female principle. In his filthy Paris lodging he modelled figures, dubiously symbolic of the mysteries of his religion, which he sent to various *députés* and *pairs de France*. He also addressed missives to the pope, one announcing his own advent and requesting the pope to step down in his favour. He was denounced to the Paris magistrates, but when he appeared for questioning, heavily bearded and in sacerdotal garb of working-man's blue blouse, sabots, and a huge grey felt hat, the matter was dropped, rather than create a stir.

Maquet, AUGUSTE (1813–88), in youth a *Romantic (self-styled 'Augustus Mackeat') and an associate of Gautier and Petrus Borel, is remembered as one of the collaborators who provided Dumas *père* with plots and background for his historical novels. His own works included plays (e.g. *La Maison du baigneur*, 1856) and novels.

Maquis, *v. Resistance*.

Marais, Le, (1) an old quarter of Paris, stretching up from the right bank of the Seine, so called because it was originally a marsh, not drained till the late Middle Ages (*v. Place Royale*; *Bastille*; *Theatres*

and Theatre Companies); (2) a name given partly in derision to a large, floating group of the centre party in the *Convention* (*v. Plaine*).

Marais, MATHIEU (1664–1737), a Parisian *bourgeois* whose *Journal* contains interesting anecdotes and comments on literary events. He assisted Bayle with his dictionary.

Marana, GIOVANNI PAOLO (1642–93), a Genoese, latterly resident in Paris and pensioned by Louis XIV. His *L'Espion des grands seigneurs dans les cours des princes chrétiens, ou Mémoires pour servir à l'histoire de ce siècle depuis 1637 jusqu'à 1682* (1684, 6 vols.), letters purporting to be written from Paris by a Turkish spy, was a model for Montesquieu's *Lettres persanes*.

Marana, Les, *v. Comédie humaine, La* (*Études philosophiques*).

Marat, JEAN-PAUL (1743–93), an impassioned and virulent Revolutionary journalist, founder-editor of *L'*Ami du peuple* (his articles probably helped to provoke the massacres of Sept. 1792; *v. Revolutions*, 1) and a leader of the *Montagnards. A doctor by profession (educated partly in Edinburgh) and a man of encyclopedic knowledge, he believed himself to be the apostle of Liberty. He was assassinated in his bath by Charlotte Corday.

Marbode, *v. Lapidaire*.

Marcabru· (*fl. c.* 1130–50), one of the earliest *troubadours after Guillaume d'Aquitaine, author of the first known *pastourelle. A man of humble origin, probably a professional *jongleur, he was an opponent of courtly poetry and courtly love (*v. Amour courtois*), and reputed to be the founder of the *trobar clus*, or 'closed' (i.e. esoteric) style of Provençal poetry.

Marcadé, EUSTACHE, *v. Mystère*.

Marceau, Félicien, *pseudonym of* LOUIS

CARETTE (1913–   ), novelist and dramatist of Belgian birth. His works, which are marked by sharp observation, irony, and a vein of fantasy, often present a decidedly disenchanted view of life and human relations. His fiction includes novels (e.g. *Chasseneuil*, 1948; *Chair et cuir*, 1951; *Capri, petite île*, 1951; *Bergère légère*, 1953; *Les Élans du cœur*, 1955; *Creezy*, 1969, awarded the *Prix Goncourt*) and short stories (*En de secrètes noces*, 1953; *Les Belles Natures*, 1957). His plays include, notably, the wry comedies *L'Œuf* (1956) and *La Bonne Soupe* (1958), both in the form of scenes illustrating a monologue by the central character; also *L'Étouffe-Chrétien* (1960), *La Preuve par quatre* (1964), *Babour* (1969). In addition, he has published critical studies, e.g. *Balzac et son monde* (1955), on a novelist with whom he has some affinity; and *Les Années courtes* (1968), the story of his youth.

Marceau, MARCEL (1923–   ), an actor who has won world fame as an exponent of mime. After a spell with Barrault's company (1945–6), he devoted himself to mime, evolving from *Pierrot the personage Bip, a white-faced clown in a tight-fitting striped coat and sailor trousers, thin as a rake and moving with comically balletic precision. He has toured widely, appearing as Bip and, with players trained by himself, in mimes of his own composition.

Marcel, chief character and narrator of Proust's *À la recherche du temps perdu*.

Marcel, ÉTIENNE (*c.* 1317–58), a wealthy draper of Paris, *prévôt des marchands* (*v. Hôtel de Ville*). In 1357, after the defeat and capture of Jean II at Poitiers, he led the *bourgeoisie* of Paris in a famous rising against the regent, the duke of Normandy. He was murdered when about to deliver the city to the king of Navarre, an ally of England.

Marcel, GABRIEL (1889–1973), Christian *Existentialist philosopher and dramatist. His philosophical works (e.g. *Journal métaphysique*, 1928; *Être et Avoir*, 1935;

Homo viator, 1944; *Le Mystère de l'Être*, 1951) show the influence on him of Kierkegaard and of his conversion (1929) to Roman Catholicism, though he came to dislike 'l'affreux vocable d'existentialisme', preferring 'néo-socratisme' or 'socratisme chrétien', and latterly judged that his Christianity had grown progressively less 'confessionnel'. His plays, which he aptly described as 'le théâtre de l'âme en exil', depicting man's alienation in the world, reflect his preoccupations as a philosopher and, though over-intellectual and often rather contrived, they include powerful dramas of conscience. He published plays from 1911 and, after 1920, some were staged (e.g. *Le Cœur des autres*, 1921; *La Chapelle ardente*, 1925; *Le Dard*, 1937), but his work was little appreciated until 1949, which saw the production of *Un Homme de Dieu* (a drama on the theme of forgiveness for adultery, written 1925), followed in 1953 by *Le Chemin de crête* (written 1936). Some of his later plays have topical themes, e.g. *Rome n'est plus dans Rome* (1951), on problems posed by the Cold War. He was also a dramatic critic on *Les *Nouvelles littéraires*, etc. (*L'Heure théâtrale*, 1959, contains collected reviews) and a music critic.

Marcelin, *v. Vie parisienne, La*.

Marcellin, REMY, *v. Félibrige*.

Marchand, LOUIS-JOSEPH-NARCISSE (1791–1876), succeeded 'Constant' (*v. Wairy*) as Napoleon's head *valet de chambre* (1814) and served him devotedly to the end. Napoleon created him comte and entrusted him with his will, and he was later one of the escort sent to fetch his remains from St. Helena (*v. Légende napoléonienne*). His memoirs (1952–5, 2 vols.) of the period of his service with Napoleon (1811–21) are sincere and unpretentious.

Marchant, GUYOT, *v. Danse macabre*.

Mardoche, *v. Musset*.

Mardrus, Joseph-Charles-Victor (1868–1949), physician and Orientalist, translator of the *Arabian Nights—Mille Nuits et une nuit* (1898–1904, 16 vols.), a much fuller and more colourful version than that of Galland. *v. Delarue-Mardrus.*

Mare au diable, La (1846), by G. Sand, a tale of rustic life. Germain, a widowed young farmer, sets off to pay court tò an eligible widow in the next village. With him go one of his children and Marie, a girl he has agreed to escort to her first post. They get lost in the mist near a lake reputed to be enchanted. When they have to spend the night as best they can under the trees, Marie's cheerful good sense makes Germain think that he might fare worse for a wife. Next day they complete their journey. Marie soon flees from the obnoxious attentions of her new master; Germain meets, and dislikes, the widow. The tale ends with the marriage of Germain and Marie, a good, old-time country wedding.

Maréchal (de France; de l'Empire). In the Middle Ages, the *maréchal* was a high military officer. At first there was a single *maréchal*, subordinate only to the *connétable*, then the number was increased. There were also *maréchaux* in the *provinces* under the feudal princes (*v. Villehardouin*). In 1788, there were 20 *maréchaux de France*. The dignity was suppressed during the Revolution (1793), but revived by Napoleon (*cf. Connétable*).

The law of 18 May 1804, inaugurating the First Empire, provided for the creation of *maréchaux de l'Empire*, to be chosen from the most distinguished generals, or former generals, of the army. A decree of 19 May announced the first 18 promotions, namely (in alphabetical order): Auge-reau, Pierre-François-Charles (1757–1816), created duc de Castiglione (one of his great victories) in 1808 (*v. Fructidor*); Bernadotte, Jean-Baptiste-Jules (1763–1844), created prince de Pontecorvo (1806), elected heir to the throne of Sweden (1810), fought against France at *Leipzig, became Charles XIV of Sweden (1818); Berthier, Louis-Alexandre (1753–1815), created prince de Neuchâtel (1806), prince de *Wagram (1809); Bessières, Jean-Baptiste (1768–1813), created duc d'Istrie (1809), was killed in battle in Saxony; Brune, Guillaume-Marie-Anne (1763–1815), offended Napoleon and was retired (1807), held a command again in 1815, but surrendered Toulon to the Royalists and was brutally murdered at Avignon; Davout, Louis-Nicolas (1770–1823), created duc d'*Auerstadt (1808) and prince d'Eckmühl (1809), minister of war during the Hundred Days, organized the defence of Paris after *Waterloo; Jourdan, Jean-Baptiste (1762–1833), victor of *Fleurus (1794); Kellermann, François-Christophe (1735–1820), created duc de *Valmy (1804), became president of the *Sénat*; Lannes, Jean (1769–1809), created duc de Montebello (1808), one of Napoleon's most devoted generals, killed at Essling; Lefebvre, François-Joseph (1755–1820), created duc de Dantzig (1808) (*v. Madame Sans-Gêne*); Masséna, André (1758–1817), of Italian birth, created duc de *Rivoli (1808), prince d'Essling (1810; the French were in full retreat at Essling, in Germany, when a bridge broke; Masséna averted disaster); Moncey, Bon-Adrien Jeannot de (1754–1842), created duc de Conegliano (1808), took part in the unsuccessful defence of Paris against the Allies (1814); Mortier, Édouard - Adolphe - Casimir - Joseph (1768–1835), created duc de Trévise (1808), took part in the defence of Paris (1814), was later ambassador in Russia, and was killed by Fieschi's *machine infernale*; Murat, Joachim (1771–1815), m. Napoleon's sister Caroline (1800; *v. Bonaparte Family*), created prince (1805), roi de Naples (1808), a brilliant and audacious soldier, promoted general on the field of Aboukir (1799), latterly intrigued unsuccessfully with Austria and England, had to vacate his throne and was caught, and shot, by Royalists; Ney, Michel (1769–1815), 'le brave des braves', the most famous of them all and the most popular with the troops, created duc d'Elchingen (1808), prince de la

Moskova (1813; v. *Borodino*), urged Napoleon to abdicate (1814) and was charged by him (with Marmont and Macdonald) to negotiate with Russia, then swore allegiance to the restored monarchy, but when sent to check Napoleon's advance (1815) joined forces with him instead, fought heroically at *Waterloo, was tried for treason by the *Chambre des *Pairs*, and shot; PÉRIGNON, DOMINIQUE-CATHERINE (1754–1818), created comte (1808), marquis (1817); SÉRURIER, JEAN-MATHIEU-PHILIBERT (1742–1819), created comte (1808); SOULT, NICOLAS-JEAN DE DIEU (1769–1851), created duc de Dalmatie (1808), fought Sir John Moore at Corunna, rallied to Napoleon in 1815 and fought at Waterloo, later held government office and was promoted *maréchal-général de France* (1847).

There were seven later promotions, namely (in order of date): VICTOR, CLAUDE-VICTOR PERRIN, *known as* (1766–1841), promoted after *Friedland, created duc de Bellune (1808); MACDONALD, JACQUES - ÉTIENNE - JOSEPH - ALEXANDRE (1765–1840), promoted on the field of *Wagram, created duc de Tarente (1809), a professional soldier (son of a Scottish Jacobite who had taken service with Louis XV after the '45), the last of the *maréchaux* to rally to the restored monarchy in 1814; MARMONT, AUGUSTE-FRÉDÉRIC-LOUIS VIESSE DE (1774–1852), promoted after *Wagram, created duc de Raguse (1809), a brilliant soldier—though his conduct after the fall of Paris (1814) was disloyal to the point of treachery and made Napoleon's abdication inevitable (he tried to justify himself in his memoirs, 1856–7), held office under the Restoration, accompanied Charles X to England (1830) and never returned to France; OUDINOT, NICOLAS-CHARLES (1767–1847), promoted after *Wagram, created duc de Reggio (1809), a daring, tough foot-soldier who fought his way up the ranks (he was wounded 35 times); SUCHET, LOUIS-GABRIEL (1770–1826), promoted *maréchal* (1811) and created duc d'Albufera (1812) for services in the Peninsula; GOUVION-SAINT-CYR, LAURENT (1764–1830), created comte (1808), promoted *maréchal*

during the Russian campaign (1812), commanded the army sent against Napoleon at Orleans (1815), making his escape when his troops deserted; minister of war under Louis XVIII, who created him marquis; PONIATOWSKI, JOSEPH-ANTOINE, PRINCE (1762–1813), nephew of Stanislas *Leczinski, commander of the Polish corps in the French army, promoted before *Leipzig (he was drowned in the Elster while covering the French retreat).

These men were Napoleon's chosen band, his brothers-in-arms, commanders of army corps at his famous battles, his representatives sent to administer conquered lands. He listened—if he did not defer—to their advice, bullied them, humoured their rivalries. Since they were the nucleus of his imperial aristocracy, he loaded them with honours and favours, insisted on their maintaining a grand way of life (and provided the means for them to do so), even, on occasion, chose their wives. Most of them had been professional soldiers before the Revolution, others had enlisted in the Revolutionary armies and risen rapidly from the ranks; many had served in the *Garde nationale*. They were mainly of good *bourgeois* or *petit-bourgeois* stock; a few were of noble birth, very few—perhaps only Augereau, Lannes, and Ney—were of very humble origin. After, in some cases even before, Napoleon's first abdication (1814), the large majority rallied to the restored monarchy, receiving honours and office from Louis XVIII both then and after 1815—and later from Charles X and Louis-Philippe. Barely a third rallied to Napoleon during the Hundred Days: some of these few were severely punished (Ney was shot); most of the others were gradually restored to favour. Some of them left memoirs, e.g. Gouvion-Saint-Cyr, Marmont.

After 1815, the title again became *maréchal de France*. The number of *maréchaux* was gradually reduced and after 1870 there were no promotions till that of Joffre (1916).

Maréchale d'Ancre, La, *v. Vigny*; *cf. Concini.*

Maréchaussée, v. *Gendarme.*

Marengo (in Piedmont, N. Italy). Here Bonaparte won his crowning victory over the Austrians (14 June 1800). v. *Coalitions* (2).

Marguerite d'Angoulême or **d'Alençon** or **de Navarre** (1492–1549), sister of François Ier, m. (1) the duc d'Alençon, (2) Henri d'Albret, king of Navarre, by which marriage she was ancestress of the *Bourbons. She was intelligent, broad-minded, and compassionate; eager for spiritual liberty, yet devoutly religious. She supported *Évangélisme* and, at her court of Navarre, protected enlightened men whom the theologians were persecuting, e.g. Lefèvre d'Étaples, Marot, Des Périers, Calvin. She learnt Latin, Italian, and Spanish, studied Hebrew, admired Plato and encouraged the translation of his dialogues. Her chief work was the *Heptaméron*. She also wrote poetry (e.g. the *Miroir de l'âme pécheresse*, 1531, and *Chansons spirituelles*, inc. with other work in *Marguerites de la Marguerite des princesses*, 1547) and plays (e.g. *Comédie à dix personnages*, 1542; *Comédie jouée à Mont-de-Marsan en 1547*).

Marguerite d'Anjou (1429–82), daughter of René d'Anjou, married Henry VI of England (1444, at Nancy).

Marguerite d'Autriche (1480–1530), daughter of the emperor Maximilian, m. (1) Prince John of Spain, (2) Philibert II of Savoy, in whose memory she built the beautiful church of Brou at Bourg-en-Bresse (1511–36; v. *Lemaire de Belges*), celebrated in a poem by Matthew Arnold. She was regent of the Netherlands (1507–30) and negotiated the peace of Cambrai (1529).

Marguerite d'Écosse (1424–44), daughter of James I of Scotland, 1st wife of Louis XI. v. *Chartier, A.*

Marguerite de Savoie (1523–74), daughter of François Ier, sister of Henri II, wife of Philibert–Emmanuel of Savoy.

She wrote verses and was a patroness of the school of young poets led by Ronsard.

Marguerite de Valois (1553–1615), daughter of Henri II and Catherine de Médicis, m. (1572) Henri de Navarre (Henri IV), who, after a long separation, divorced her for political reasons (1599). A patroness of Ronsard, she wrote poems (some with help from Maynard), memoirs (addressed to Brantôme, with a view to helping him with his *Vies des dames illustres*; they contain a vivid account of the Massacre of St. *Bartholomew), and letters in the same clear, precise style as her memoirs.

Marguerites, Les trois, i.e. Marguerite d'Angoulême or d'Alençon or de Navarre, Marguerite de Savoie, and Marguerite de Valois.

Margueritte, the brothers PAUL (1860–1918) and VICTOR (1867–1942), novelists. They collaborated in a series of socio-historical novels about the period of the *Franco-Prussian war under the general title *Une Époque* (1898–1904, 4 vols.), and in the popular children's books *Poum* (1897) and *Zette, histoire d'une petite fille* (1903). Paul, having signed the *Manifeste des cinq* repudiating Zola's doctrines, had earlier been inspired by the Russian novelists then coming into fashion, e.g. in his *Pascal Géfosse* (1887), *La Force des choses* (1890). Victor, an advocate of female emancipation, caused an outcry with his novel *La Garçonne* (1922).

Maria Chapdelaine, v. *Hémon.*

Mariage de Figaro, ou la Folle Journée, Le, a prose comedy by Beaumarchais, a sequel to *Le *Barbier de Séville.* This gay, witty, and immensely popular play had an important political side, for its daring and bitter derision of existing institutions and privileges (notably in a famous monologue by Figaro, V, iii) echoed popular feeling of the day. Its production was delayed from 1781 until 1784 by the royal veto (v.

Censorship, Dramatic), but it was widely read and privately performed.

The comte Almaviva, married for three years to Rosine, has tired of her and is now an unfaithful, though jealous, husband. She still loves him, but shows a dangerous romantic inclination. Figaro, now the comte's door-keeper, loves and is about to marry Rosine's maid, the honest, merry Suzanne. The comte approves, but only in the interests of his own designs on Suzanne. The plot turns on the struggle between the two men for the possession of Suzanne; the comte is supported by feudal privilege and the machinery of the law (in the person of Brid'oison, the type of the ignorant, formalist magistrate), Figaro by the wits and loyalty of his fiancée. The page Chérubin, a budding rake in love with Rosine, complicates matters by arousing the comte's jealousy. Everything conspires to thwart the comte and render him ridiculous. His infidelity is finally exposed when Rosine, posing as Suzanne, keeps a twilight assignation Suzanne has given him. Figaro, and the cause of honourable marriage, thus triumph.

Mariage forcé, Le, a one-act prose comedy by Molière, a trifle hastily written. for an entertainment given by the king at the *Louvre (1664).

Sganarelle, a middle-aged *bourgeois*, is well pleased to have won the hand of young Dorimène—till he learns that she has accepted him only to get her liberty and his money. He decides to take advice as to the chances of her remaining faithful. The absurd conversations between him and the philosophers he consults (Pancrace the Aristotelian and Marphurius the Pyrrhonian), imitated from Rabelais, bring him no comfort. After overhearing a conversation between Dorimène and her lover, he decides not to marry her. But her brother then bids him choose between marrying her and fighting him, whereupon, having no stomach for a duel, he opts for marriage.

Mariamne, wife of Herod the Great, executed by him in a fit of jealousy; the subject of tragedies by Hardy, Tristan l'Hermite, and Voltaire.

Mariana, JUAN DE (1532–1624), a Spanish *Jesuit, taught theology in Rome and Paris. His treatise *De rege et regis institutione* (1598), in treating of regicide, approved the assassination of Henri III and was thought by some to have inspired that of Henri IV.

Marianne, a familiar name, after *c.* 1854, for the republican form of government and, by extension, for the French Republic. It was the password of a secret society formed in the West of France (and directed from a headquarters in London) after the *coup d'état* of 1851 with a view to overthrowing Napoleon III and re-establishing the Republic. In the course of an elaborate initiation ceremony, members were asked, 'Connaissez-vous Marianne?' Its origin has been variously explained.

Marianne, La Vie de (1731–41, 11 pts.), an unfinished romance by Marivaux. Mme Riccoboni wrote a conclusion (pt. 12).

Marianne, a girl of unknown but apparently good birth, tells the story of her life. Having been saved when her parents were killed by robbers, and brought up from infancy in the house of a priest, she acquires a protector in M. de Climal, a hypocrite who makes a pretence of piety and tries to seduce her. She meets Valville, a young man of quality, and the two fall in love. Valville proves to be the nephew of M. de Climal who, to punish her for scorning him, withdraws his support. She then finds a protectress, who turns out to be Valville's mother and to have a different wife in view for him. After a long series of incidents and setbacks, including Valville's temporary infidelity, Marianne, whose virtue is pleasantly tinged with coquetry, finally marries her lover and (in pt. 12) is reunited with her distinguished family. Her reactions are minutely analysed with all Marivaux's knowledge of the female heart, and we are given a picture of Parisian and conventual manners.

Marie, ou l'Esclavage aux États-Unis, v. Beaumont de la Bonninière.

Marie-Antoinette (1755–93), daughter of Francis I, emperor of Austria, and Maria Theresa; wife of Louis XVI, whom she encouraged to resist the Revolution. The people dubbed her 'Madame Déficit' (blaming her extravagance for the disastrous state of the national finances) and 'Madame *Véto'. She was tried by the *Tribunal révolutionnaire and executed. v. Collier, L'Affaire du; Trianon.

Marie de France, a late 12th-c. poetess, a cultured woman who, besides French, knew Latin and English. Little else is known of her. She appears to have been born in France and to have done much or all of her literary work in England. It has been conjectured that she was the Marie who was a natural daughter of Geoffrey Plantagenet (and so half-sister of Henry II) and abbess of Shaftesbury (1181–1215). She wrote about a dozen *lais (dedicated to a 'noble king', probably Henry II)— poems of love and adventure, fairies and marvels, which have a mysterious, romantic character attributed by some critics to Celtic originals—e.g. Lanval, the story, in which Arthur figures, of a poor knight who is secretly loved and enriched by a fairy (there is a 14th-c. Eng. version, Sir Launfal); Frêne, the touching story of a patient Griselda, who as a child was exposed in an ash-tree, whence the title (there is a 14th-c. Eng. version, the Lai le Freine); Chèvrefeuille, a slight, episodic story of *Tristan and Iseut—a hazel stick bearing Tristan's name placed in Iseut's path as she passes through the forest brings about a brief meeting between them. She also wrote a collection of Aesopic fables (based on the lost Eng. version of a collection attributed to King Alfred) to which she gave the name Esope; in the later form Ysopet or Isopet this became the usual name for medieval collections of fables. Finally, she made a French version of the legend of the Purgatory of St. Patrick.

Marie de Médicis (1573–1642), niece of the grand duke of Tuscany, 2nd wife of Henri IV (1600), regent (1610–17; v. Louis XIII). v. Concini.

Marie Donadieu, v. Philippe, C.-L.

Marie Stuart (later **Mary Queen of Scots**) (1542–87), daughter of James V of Scotland and Marie de *Guise, brought up from 1548 at the French court and married (1558) to the dauphin, soon to reign briefly as François II. She returned to Scotland after his death (1560). v. Ronsard; Chastelard; Montchrétien.

Marie Tudor (1833), by Hugo, an historical drama (prose; in 3 'journées') with little factual basis. The queen's lover, Fabio Fabiani, has seduced Jane, the adopted daughter, soon to be the wife, of the worthy craftsman Gilbert. Fabiani knows that she is the lost child of Earl Talbot and thinks that in certain eventualities he might save his own fortunes by marrying her. When his intrigues miscarry, he caps them with murder. There is a tense scene in the final 'journée', when a prisoner, who may be either Fabiani or Gilbert, is led to execution watched by Jane and the queen, who has contrived the arrest and is now overcome by events.

Marignan (Melegnano, near Milan), scene of the defeat of (1) the Swiss by François Ier (1515; referred to by Rabelais, the subject of a famous song by Jannequin, and v. Fleurange); (2) the Austrians (1859) by Napoleon III.

Marigny, JACQUES CARPENTIER DE (17th c.), a supporter of Gondi in the *Fronde, noted for his satirical *mazarinades, comic songs, and parodies.

Marigny, Théâtre, v. Barrault.

Marinetti, FILIPPO TOMMASO (1878–1944), Italian poet, novelist, and critic, educated in France; founder of *Futurism. He lived mainly in Milan, but kept in touch with advanced literary circles in Paris and wrote much in French, e.g. La Conquête des étoiles (1902; an epic), Destruction: Poésies lyriques (1904), La Ville charnelle (1908; poems of Africa), La Bataille de Tripoli (1912).

Marinisme, the term applied to the mannered, euphuistic style of the Italian poet Giovanni Battista Marino, who took refuge (1615–22) at the court of Marie de Médicis, where he was known as 'le Cavalier Marin'. It is exemplified in his *Adone*, a long poem in French (publ. in France 1623, with a preface by Chapelain), and was imitated by some of the **précieux*. *v. Foreign Influences*, 1.

Marion de Lorme (1831), a verse drama by Hugo; written 1829 (before **Hernani*), but vetoed by the dramatic **censorship* and not produced till 1831.

Marion **de Lorme, the courtesan, loves, and is loved by, Didier, who is unaware of her identity. He and the marquis de Saverny, another of her admirers, are arrested for duelling in defiance of a royal decree, inspired by Richelieu, making it a capital offence. To save Didier, Marion sacrifices herself to a magistrate, M. de Laffemas. But Didier, having learnt who she is, prefers death to her help. The characters include Louis XIII and Richelieu, who attends Didier's execution and speaks from behind the curtains of his litter.

Maritain, JACQUES (1882–1973), philosopher and man of letters; long a leading Neo-Thomist (*v. Thomas Aquinas*), though before his conversion to Roman Catholicism in 1906 he was a disciple of Bergson. His works include *La Philosophie bergsonienne* (1914), condemning Bergsonism as the root of all modern intellectual heresy; *Art et scolastique* (1920); *Saint Thomas d'Aquin, apôtre des temps modernes* (1923); *Réflexions sur l'intelligence* (1924); *Trois Réformateurs* (1925), denouncing Luther, Descartes, and Rousseau; *Frontières de la poésie* (1926); *Primauté du spirituel* (1927); *Religion et culture* (1930); *Court Traité de l'existence et de l'existant* (1947); *Christianisme et démocratie* (1948); *La Responsabilité de l'artiste* (1962).

Marivaux, PIERRE CARLET DE CHAMBLAIN DE (1688–1763), dramatist and novelist; in his youth an *habitué* of the **salons* of Mme de Tencin and Mme de Lambert, a supporter of the *modernes* in the **Querelle des anciens et des modernes* and author of an *Iliade travestie* (1717). His comedies (in prose, and often written for the **Italiens*) include *Arlequin poli par l'amour* (1720), *La *Surprise de l'amour* (1722), *La *Double Inconstance* (1723), *La Seconde Surprise de l'amour* (1727), *Le *Jeu de l'amour et du hasard* (1730), *Le Legs* (1736), *Les Fausses Confidences* (1737), *Les *Sincères* (1739), *L'Épreuve* (1740). They are usually on the theme of love and concerned with the trifling incidents of courtship (arising from jealousy, pique, misunderstanding, etc.) in a sybaritic society like that painted by Watteau and Boucher. Their charm and light romantic fancy made Marivaux extremely popular for a time, though he outlived the period of their vogue. His two (unfinished) novels, *La Vie de *Marianne* (1731–41) and *Le *Paysan parvenu* (1735–6), are notable for their delicate analysis of sentiment and realistic picture of middle-class society; they may have influenced Fielding's *Joseph Andrews*. He also wrote, in more serious vein, on ethical and literary subjects, e.g. in his *Spectateur français* (1722; modelled on Addison's *Spectator*). He was admitted to the **Académie* in 1742.

Marlotte, a village near Fontainebleau, a famous artists' colony in the 19th c. *Cf. Barbizon.*

Marly, a fine country house midway between Versailles and Saint-Germain, built by Mansard for Louis XIV, as a secluded retreat. A pump, the *machine de Marly*, raised water from the Seine to form a river and cascades in the gardens. It was demolished during the Revolution, since when the marble *chevaux de Marly* have stood at the foot of the Avenue des **Champs-Élysées*.

Marmier, XAVIER (1809–92), a widely travelled man of letters and critic, well read in foreign literature (*v. Critics and Criticism*, 2). His works include *Histoire de la littérature en Danemark et en Suède* (1839), *Chants populaires du Nord, traduits en français* (1842), travel literature, and a few novels. He moved freely in literary, political, and aristocratic circles, and his *Journal* (1968, 2 vols.; for the years 1848–90) contains much information—and disenchanted comment—about events and prominent persons of the day.

Marmont, Auguste-Frédéric-Louis Viesse de, *v. Maréchal.*

Marmontel, Jean-François (1723–99), a man of wide, but second-rate, literary talent; a friend and disciple of Voltaire, chief contributor of the literary articles in the *Encyclopédie*, editor of the *Mercure de France* (from 1758; thanks to his patroness Mme de Pompadour), a member of the *Académie* (1763; perpetual secretary, in succession to d'Alembert, 1783). His best work is his *Mémoires d'un père* (1804, 4 vols.), containing good sketches of the *Encyclopédistes*. His other works include forgotten tragedies (e.g. *Denys le Tyran*, 1748); serious comedies (*La Bergère des Alpes*, 1766; *Sylvain*, 1770); *opéras-comiques* (v. Grétry); *Contes moraux* (first publ. in the *Mercure*, collected 1761 and 1789–92), slight, edifying tales, agreeably told; two historical romances—*Bélisaire* (1766), in which Belisarius discourses with Justinian and his son on political and social systems (the *Sorbonne* condemned it for a chapter advocating religious toleration, thereby making itself ridiculous and merely advertising a dull book), and *Les Incas* (1777), introducing Las Casas, the defender of the Indians; *Éléments de littérature* (1787; *v. Dictionaries*, 1789), a collection of his literary articles in the *Encyclopédie. v. Musical Controversies.*

Marmousets, grotesque sculptured figures on monuments; a nickname for the *bourgeois* councillors of Charles VI. They were exiled by the duc de Bourgogne during the king's insanity, despite the efficiency of their administration.

Marne, Les Taxis de la. In September 1914, when retreating French and British armies made a stand at the river Marne

against the German sweep on Paris, French reinforcements were rushed up to maintain the counter-offensive. Some of these troops were so exhausted when they reached Paris on their way that the military governor, General Galliéni, requisitioned all the Paris taxis and had them driven to the front. The Germans retreated (9 Sept.).

Marneffe, Madame, in Balzac's *La *Cousine Bette.*

Marot, Clément (1496–1544), poet, son of the following, b. at Cahors, came to Paris with his father (*c.* 1506), became a law clerk and a member of the *Basoche* and the *Enfants sans souci* (for whom he wrote one of his early *ballades*), entered the service of Marguerite d'Alençon (later queen of Navarre) as *valet de chambre* (*c.* 1518), was early inspired by *Évangélisme* and confined in the *Châtelet* (1525) for breach of the Lenten fast, succeeded his father in the king's service (1526). After publishing a collection of his early verse, the *Adolescence Clémentine* (1532), he began work on verse translations of the Psalms, probably at the instance of his protectress Marguerite de Navarre. Being already suspect to the theologians for his Protestant sympathies, he took refuge in Italy after the *Affaire des *placards* (1534), first at Ferrara (the duchess of Ferrara was the Lutheran Renée de France), then in Venice. After a time, on making abjuration of his errors, he was allowed to return to France. He published his *Œuvres* in 1538. Despite his abjuration, he continued to work on the Psalms and published his translations in 1539 (30 psalms, dedicated to the king) and 1541. He was consequently again obliged to leave France, this time for Geneva, where he received encouragement from Calvin. A further edition of his Psalms, with 20 additional translations, appeared in 1543. His conduct proved unacceptable at Geneva (he is said to have played backgammon on Sunday), so he withdrew to Savoy, then to Italy. He died at Turin.

He combined a cheerful, affectionate, hare-brained, yet in some degree religious, disposition with intellectual independence. He wrote a great variety of poems. Some are long, e.g. *Le Temple de Cupidon* (an allegory after the style of the *rhétoriqueurs*, whom he regarded as his masters), *L'Enfer* (on his experiences in the *Châtelet*); but the great majority are shorter pieces, including 65 *épîtres* (mostly in decasyllables), notably two addressed to the king and the *Coq-à-l'âne*; eclogues; *rondeaux*, notably one addressed to a creditor; *chansons*; elegies; *ballades*, notably that of 'Frère Lubin'; and some 300 epigrams, notably that on Semblançay. He also wrote a few *sonnets, being among the first French poets to adopt this form, which he met with in Italy. There, too, he increased his knowledge of the Latin classics: as early as 1530, he had translated part of Ovid's *Metamorphoses*; after his exile, he adapted Virgil's fourth eclogue and translated epigrams of Martial. Another side of his literary taste is reflected in his editions of the *Roman de la Rose* (1527) and Villon (1533). In most of his poems he is essentially a court poet, light, subtle, graceful, and amusing, neither sentimental nor passionate—though his wit, when directed at such enemies as the *Sorbonne theologians, the papacy, or the magistrature, could be mordant. His Psalms, much admired in his day, are remarkable for their harmonious solemnity and metrical variety. In his sincerity, refinement, and deliberate art, his interest in the classics and early use of the sonnet form, he was a good—though not great—poet of the transition from the medieval tradition of allegorical didactic verse to the new spirit of the *Renaissance.

He was much revered by contemporary poets: a scurrilous attack on him (1537) by an obscure rhymer, François Sagon, led to a literary controversy from which he emerged triumphant (v. *Fontaine, C.*). His fame was soon eclipsed by that of the *Pléiade*, but under Louis XIII and Louis XIV he again came into favour and was praised by Boileau ('Imitez de Marot l'élégant badinage'). He had some influence on 16th-c. English poets, notably on Spenser's eclogues.

Marot, JEAN (d. 1526), a mediocre *rhétoriqueur* poet, father of the above, a Norman who settled for a time at Cahors, then came to Paris (*c.* 1506) as secretary to Anne de Bretagne and accompanied Louis XII on his two expeditions to Italy. His verse descriptions of these include a lively account of the adventurers who joined the army in hope of plunder.

Marquis, v. *Duc, comte, marquis.*

Marquis de Villemer, Le, v. *Sand.*

Mars, Mlle, *stage-name of* ANNE-FRANÇOISE-HIPPOLYTE BOUTET (1779–1847), a famous actress of the *Comédie-Française*, notably in the comedies of Molière and Marivaux. She was on the stage from *c.* 1800 to 1841 and was admired for her beauty, intelligence, and fresh, youthful voice. Sainte-Beuve praises her 'ingénuité habile'.

Marsay, Henri de, in many novels of Balzac's *Comédie humaine.*

Marseillaise, La, the French national anthem, written 25 April 1792 by Rouget de Lisle. News of the French declaration of war on Austria had reached Strasbourg and the mayor was entertaining officers, including Rouget de Lisle, destined to take part in the campaign. He deplored the lack of a national anthem and called on Rouget de Lisle to compose one. The young officer is said to have written both words and music that same evening, though his authorship of the music has been disputed. Published in Strasbourg as *Le Chant de guerre pour l'armée du Rhin*, it spread to the South, and the *fédérés* from Marseilles sang it as they massed in the Place de la Bastille the following July (v. *Revolutions*, 1, 10 Aug. 1792). Adopted by the Parisians as *La Marseillaise*, it was sung by official order on the field of *Valmy and thereafter became the national anthem. It was suppressed for a time by Napoleon and again after the Restoration. There were originally six verses, the first being the most famous:

Allons, enfants de la patrie,
Le jour de gloire est arrivé!
Contre nous de la tyrannie
L'étendard sanglant est levé! (twice)
Entendez-vous dans les campagnes
Mugir ces féroces soldats?
Ils viennent jusque dans nos bras
Égorger nos fils, nos compagnes.
Aux armes, citoyens, formez vos
    bataillons!
Marchons! Marchons!
Qu'un sang impur abreuve nos sillons!

Martial d'Auvergne (c. 1430–1508),
author of *Vigilles de Charles VII* (written
1461, on the king's death), a long poem,
divided into 'Psalms' and 'Lessons', and
containing pleasant passages; the *Arrêts
d'amour* (c. 1460–5; repr. at least 13 times
between 1525 and 1537), a prose collection
(with verse prologue) of 51 imaginary law-
suits on questions of gallantry, providing
picturesque details of contemporary
manners; a *Danse macabre des femmes* (v.
Danse macabre). v. also *Amant rendu
cordelier, L'*.

Martin, in Voltaire's *Candide*.

Martin, GABRIEL (1679–1761), bookseller
and bibliographer, drew up (1705–61)
auction sale catalogues for 148 libraries
(e.g. that of Baluze, 1719, 2 vols.). He
applied a new system of classification,
dividing books into five main categories.

Martin, St. (d. c. 396), a Pannonian
soldier of the Roman army in Gaul,
became a disciple of St. Hilary (bishop of
Poitiers), an earnest apostle among the
poor, and eventually bishop of Tours. He
was noted for his charity: the story of his
dividing his cloak with a beggar is a
favourite subject in ecclesiastical art.

Martin du Gard, ROGER (1881–1958),
novelist. After qualifying as an archivist at
the *École nationale des Chartes* (a training
not without influence on his writing), he
published his first novel, *Devenir*, in 1909,
the year of the founding of the *Nouvelle
Revue française*, with which he was long

closely associated. Immediately before and
after serving in the 1914–18 war, he
worked with Copeau at the *Vieux-
Colombier* (their correspondence, 1913–49,
appeared in 1972). Thereafter, he led a
very retired life, devoted to his writing.
His fame rests on the *roman-cycle Les
Thibault (1922–40), which won him the
Prix Nobel in 1937. His other novels
include *Jean Barois* (1913), which
introduces the *Dreyfus case and portrays
characters at grips with problems of
morals and religion; *La Confidence
africaine* (1931); *Vieille France* (1933), a
ferociously realistic study of country life.
His sardonic comedy *Le Testament du Père
Leleu* (1914) also depicts country life. He
published very frank *Notes sur André Gide*
(1951) and their correspondence (1913–
51) appeared in 1968. *Souvenirs du colonel
de Maumort* (a long unfinished novel on
which he had worked for many years), his
Journal, and other correspondence remain
unpublished. He acknowledged the
influence on his work of Tolstoy,
Chekhov, Ibsen, and George Eliot.

Martin le Franc, v. *Le Franc*.

Martinozzi, v. *Mazarin's Nieces*.

**Martyrs, ou le Triomphe de la religion
chrétienne, Les** (1809), by Chateaubriand,
a prose epic (24 bks.) designed as a pendant
to *Le *Génie du christianisme*. Though
tedious as a whole, it contains stirring
evocations of the past; Thierry dated his
vocation as an historian from his schoolboy
reading of the account of a battle between
Romans and Franks (bk. 4).

The time is the 3rd c., during
Diocletian's persecution of the Christians.
The central characters are two young
Greek lovers, Eudore, a convert, and
Cymodocée, a pagan maiden. Both, we
learn in bk. 3, are destined by God as
sacrifices so that other Christians may be
saved. Bks. 4–11 follow Eudore's earlier
life and adventures in Germany, Gaul,
Egypt, and Rome. Bk. 12 resumes the
main narrative. Cymodocée, for love of
Eudore, becomes a Christian. They marry,
events separate them, and after many

vicissitudes they are reunited in Rome, only to suffer martyrdom. Triumph crowns their sacrifice, for in the arena where they have died the victorious Constantine proclaims Christianity as the official religion of the Empire.

Marx, KARL HEINRICH (1818–83), b. at Trier in Germany, founder of Marxist Communism and author of *Das Kapital* (vol. I, 1867). His years in Paris (1843–5), to which the present article is mainly confined, were his most important formative period. He came there from Cologne (when the *Rheinische Zeitung*, which he edited, was suppressed for its radicalism) and found work on a German paper. He proceeded to soak himself in history (notably the causes of the failure of the French Revolution), philosophy, political economy, and the theories of such French social reformers as Saint-Simon, Fourier, Cabet, Proudhon (whose *Philosophie de la misère* provoked his *La Misère de la philosophie*, 1847), and the collectivist Constantin Pecqueur (1801–87). He made French and foreign contacts and friends who shared his awareness of the contemporary social ferment. He joined a communist group of factory workers and artisans. It was now that he parted company with Hegelian doctrine (he wrote a critique of Hegel's *Philosophy of Right* in 1844) and formulated the materialistic conception of the historical process, and the belief in revolutionary communism and the importance of the proletariat, which have extended their influence beyond politics to the literature of the 20th c. His *Manifesto of the Communist Party* (publ. in London a few weeks before the outbreak of the 1848 *Revolution, but not known in France till June of that year) was the culminating work of this period. Soon after his arrival in London (1849), he wrote two pamphlets on events in France, *The Class Struggle in France 1848–50* (1850, in the *Neue Rheinische Zeitung*) and *The Eighteenth Brumaire of Louis Bonaparte* (1852, in a New York review); and in 1871, in a pamphlet later entitled *The Civil War in France*, he described the rise and fall of the

Commune and discussed its historical significance in the process of working-class emancipation. It may also be noted that he admired Balzac and Stendhal (he projected, but never wrote, a study of Balzac as analyst of *bourgeois* society), and that the essays and studies of *German Ideology* (written with Friedrich Engels in 1846) include a study of the social significance of *Sue's *Les Mystères de Paris*.

He was expelled from Paris in 1845. He returned briefly in February 1848 (after his expulsion from Belgium) and—as a very unwelcome visitor—in July 1849 (after his expulsion from Cologne). A month later he went to London, where he lived with his wife and family, most of the time in acute poverty, until his death. His two eldest daughters married French Socialists (*v. Guesde*).

Mary Stuart, *v. Marie Stuart.*

Mascarille, in Molière's *L'*Étourdi, Le *Dépit amoureux, Les *Précieuses ridicules*; the type of the clever, impudent valet.

Mascaron, JULES (1634–1703), a member of the *Oratoire*, bishop of Tulle and later of Agen, a noted preacher (though not the equal of his contemporary Bossuet). He delivered funeral orations on Turenne, Anne d'Autriche, and Henriette d'Angleterre.

Masculine and Feminine Lines and Rhymes. In French prosody, a 'feminine' line is one that ends with an '*e*-mute' syllable (*-e*, *-es*, or *-ent*) not counted in the measure of the line; all other endings are 'masculine'. A masculine or feminine rhyme is one coupling two masculine or two feminine lines. *v. Alternance des rimes.*

Masque de fer, L'Homme au, the unknown 'Man in the Iron Mask' (a black velvet mask with iron hinges) who was imprisoned first at Pignerol (1679), then in the *Bastille*, where he died in 1703. He was probably a diplomatic agent named Matthioli, arrested for treason by order of Louis XIV. The story (in the duc de

Richelieu's memoirs) that he was a twin brother of Louis XIV is discredited. So persistent were rumours that Monmouth had escaped execution in 1685 that Voltaire thought it necessary to deny that he was the 'Man in the Iron Mask' (*Dictionnaire philosophique*, under *Anecdote sur l'homme au masque de fer*).

Masséna, ANDRÉ, v. *Maréchal*.

Massenet, JULES-ÉMILE-FRÉDÉRIC (1842–1912), composer, studied, and later taught, at the Paris *Conservatoire de musique*. His works include the operas *Manon* (1884) and *Werther* (1892), and a number of orchestral suites.

Massillon, JEAN-BAPTISTE (1663–1742), a member of the *Oratoire, bishop of Clermont-Ferrand from 1717, a member of the *Académie (1719), came to Paris (1699, when Bourdaloue was ending his career) and achieved immediate success as a preacher (v. *Avent*; *Carême* (*Lent*)). His manner was quiet and gently persuasive, with some rhetorical affectation. He avoided dogma almost entirely, confining himself to ethics and subtle psychological analysis; he was consequently approved by the *philosophes*. His funeral orations were less admired than those of Bossuet, though his opening words were often impressive (after surveying in silence the magnificent pomp of Louis XIV's funeral, he began: 'Dieu seul est grand, mes frères!').

Massimilla Doni (1839; later in *La *Comédie humaine, Études philosophiques*), a novel by Balzac; slight as regards narrative, but often mentioned as an exposition (in the form of a running commentary on Rossini's opera *Mosè in Egitto*) of his views on music and the effect of passion on creative ability.

Massis, HENRI (1886–1970), a right-wing, Roman Catholic critic and journalist (a member of the *Académie, 1960), wrote for *L'*Action française* and was co-founder and editor of the *Revue universelle*. He made his name, with Alfred de Tarde under the joint pseudonym 'Agathon',

with surveys of public opinion (or certain sections of it), notably *Les Jeunes Gens d'aujourd'hui* (1913), finding that young men were now tough, anti-intellectual, ardently patriotic, and devout—and so, critics alleged in retrospect, already in moral trim for the call to arms in 1914. His subsequent political and literary works included *Jugements* (1923–4, 2 vols.), essays on Renan, A. France, Barrès, Gide, Rolland, Duhamel, and Benda, predictably hostile to Gide and Benda; *La Défense de l'Occident* (1928); *Les Idées restent* (1941); *D'André Gide à Marcel Proust* (1948); *Charles Maurras et notre temps* (1951, 2 vols.). He also left memoirs, *Au long d'une vie* (1967).

Masson, LOYS (1915–69), primarily a Christian poet (though his beliefs—indicated in the essay *Pour une Église*, 1945—were far from orthodox) whose work is passionate and symbolical, marked by an instinctive love of nature and a yearning for the brotherhood of man (critics point to his affinities with Péguy and Milosz); also a novelist and dramatist. He came to France from Mauritius (1939) and made his name as a poet of the *Resistance in *Délivrez-nous du mal* (1942–6). His subsequent works included *Icare, ou le Voyage* (1950), *Les Vignes de septembre* (1955), *La Dame de Pavoux* (1965), poetry; novels, notably tales of adventure in the Indian Ocean (recalling Melville and Stevenson), e.g. *Les Mutins* (1951), *Les Tortues* (1956); and the plays *La Résurrection des corps* (1952) and *Cristobal de Lugo* (1960).

Matamore, a character in Spanish comedy who boasts of imaginary exploits against the Moors. He figures in Corneille's *L'*Illusion comique*.

Mateo Falcone, v. *Mérimée*.

Mathieu or **Matheolus**, author of *Lamentationes*, a late 13th-c. Latin work attacking women which long remained popular in Jehan le Fèvre's French translation (1371 or 1372).

Mathieu, ANSELME, v. *Félibrige*.

Mathiez, ALBERT (1874–1932), historian of the Revolution. He is remembered for his rehabilitation of Robespierre, in opposition to his former master Aulard, an ardent 'Dantoniste'.

Mathilde, Princesse (1820–1904), daughter of Jérôme Bonaparte (v. *Bonaparte Family*), separated (1845) from her Russian husband, Count Demidoff. Under the Second Empire her friendship with her cousin Napoleon III gave her a position of some influence. She enjoyed collecting writers and artists in her Paris *salon and her country house at Saint-Gratien. Flaubert, Gautier, E. de Goncourt, and Sainte-Beuve were among her favoured guests. She figures in *Flaubert's *Correspondance*, the *Journal des Goncourt*, etc.

Matière et mémoire, v. Bergson.

Matines brugeoises, Les, a popular rising (18 May 1302) against the patricians of Bruges, who were supported by the French governor, Jacques de Châtillon. Many French knights were murdered in their beds. Cf. *Vêpres siciliennes*.

Matisse, HENRI (1869–1954), painter, sculptor, designer, and engraver, was leader of the *Fauves*. v. *Impressionism*.

Mauclair, Camille, *pseudonym of* SÉVERIN FAUST (1872–1945), author of poems, collected in *Sonatines d'automne* (1895), *Le Sang parle* (1904); novels, e.g. *Le Soleil des morts* (1898), a picture of young literary circles of the day—the character Calixte Armel is drawn from Mallarmé; literary and art criticism, in *Éleusis* (1894), *L'Impressionnisme* (1904), *Princes de l'esprit* (1920; on Delacroix, Flaubert, Mallarmé, Poe, etc.); also memoirs—*Servitude et grandeur littéraires* (1922).

Maucroix, FRANÇOIS (1619–1708), poet, canon of Rheims, and lifelong friend of La Fontaine. He wrote epigrams, madrigals, etc., and translated the classics, notably Plato and Cicero.

Maufrigneuse, v. *Maupassant*.

Maugérard, JEAN-BAPTISTE (1735–1815), a book-thief (*cf. Libri*). A learned Benedictine with a great knowledge of manuscripts and incunabula and their whereabouts, he left the cloister (of Saint-Arnoul, near Metz) at the time of the *Constitution civile du clergé*, was in Paris for a while, then settled as an *émigré* in Germany. He visited monastic libraries in the parts of the Rhineland conquered by France in the Revolutionary wars, posing as a member of a commission charged with the classification and conservation of documents which were now French property; in 1802 he was, in fact, officially authorized to seek out books and manuscripts in the new *départements* formed in this region. He thus acquired a collection of treasures from which he enriched other libraries, notably the *Bibliothèque nationale* (though some items had to be returned after 1815), and also effectively lined his own pockets. He bought land, and after 1808 lived comfortably on a government pension in Metz.

Maupassant, GUY DE (1850–93), a Norman by birth, education, and sympathies; famous for his *contes* (v. *Nouvelle*), also a novelist and literary journalist. After army service in 1870–1 (an experience which was to bear fruit in *Boule-de-suif, *Mademoiselle Fifi*, etc.), he became an office clerk—conscientious, if never zealous—in the *Ministère de la Marine* (1872–8) and the *Ministère de l'Instruction publique* (1878–82). He reserved his main energies for outdoor pursuits—boating, shooting, fishing—and for hard discipline, under Flaubert's guidance, in the writer's craft (v. *Pierre et Jean*). Flaubert, whose feeling for him was one of delight in his talent combined with affection born of an old family friendship, introduced him to literary circles. There he met Zola and the other *Naturalists with whom he collaborated in Les *Soirées de Médan* (1880). *Boule-de-suif*, his own contribution, made him a celebrity almost overnight, and by 1882 he could safely abandon the civil service for literature. During 10 prodigiously successful years (1880–90)—when he made, and squandered, a great deal of money—he published a volume of verse (*Des vers*, 1880), three collections of travel sketches (*Au soleil*, 1884; *Sur l'eau*, 1888; *La Vie errante*, 1890), 16 volumes of short stories, and six novels, besides contributing regularly to periodicals. From 1890 his reason began to fail. Despite his robust appearance, his health had early been undermined by dissolute living and now collapsed under continual overwork and mental strain. He attempted suicide (Dec. 1891), and spent the last 18 months of his life in a mental home in Paris. *v. Tassart*.

His *contes* were often first published in periodicals (*Les Dimanches d'un bourgeois de Paris*, tales of a civil servant's Sunday outings, appeared weekly in *Le *Gaulois*, 1882; *Le *Lit 29* in **Gil Blas*, 1884), sometimes under pseudonyms, e.g. Joseph Prunier (used for his first tale, *La Main d'écorché*, 1875, in the *Almanach de Pont à Mousson*), Maufrigneuse, Guy de Valmont. The majority are about farm, peasant, or small-town life in Normandy, or the life of tradespeople and petty officials in Paris (a few depict the fashionable world in which he later moved). Some are tales of the *Franco-Prussian war; in others, mystery, hallucination, and horror of death predominate (e.g. *Le Horla*; *L'Auberge*; *Sur l'eau*, the tale, in *La *Maison Tellier*, not the travel sketches; *La Morte*; *L'Endormeuse*). Typical collections published in his lifetime were *La *Maison Tellier* (1881), **Mademoiselle Fifi* (1882), *Contes de la bécasse* (1883), *Les Sœurs Rondoli* (1884), **Miss Harriet* (1884), *Contes du jour et de la nuit* (1885; *v. Parure, La*), **Yvette* (1885), *Monsieur Parent* (1886), *Le Rosier de Mme Husson* (1888), *L'Inutile Beauté* (1890). His excellence as a *conteur* is due to his narrative style—simple, direct, realistic, dispassionate to the point of irony—and his gift for presenting the precise minimum of detail necessary to convey character or atmosphere. Most of his characters move in a material, sometimes brutally sensual, world in which the finer feelings have little place.

His novels—less tautly objective than the *contes*—were *Une Vie* (1883; on a woman's lonely life, in Normandy:

deception and disillusionment are her sole experiences), **Bel-Ami* (1885), *Mont-Oriol* (1887), **Pierre et Jean* (1888), *Fort comme la mort* (1889; an ageing man's life is disrupted by his hopeless love for a young girl), *Notre cœur* (1890). He also wrote a one-act verse comedy, *Histoire du vieux temps* (1879).

Maupeou, RENÉ-NICOLAS DE (1714-92), chancellor under Louis XV, remembered for his suppression of the *parlements*.

Maupertuis, the lair and stronghold of Renart the fox in the *Roman de Renart*.

Maupertuis, PIERRE-LOUIS MOREAU DE (1698-1759), scientist, a member of the *Académie des Sciences* and the Royal Society of London (the first Frenchman to be elected), director (from 1740) of the Academy of Science in Berlin. He early defended the principles of Newton and was one of a mission sent to measure a degree of the meridian in Lapland (1736; *cf. La Condamine*) and so verify the shape of the earth as calculated by Newton. His scientific ability was limited, and Voltaire and he fell out in Berlin (*v. Diatribe du docteur Akakia*).

Mauprat (1837), by G. Sand, a romantic novel, high in the class of readable bad books, on the eternally enthralling theme of a brute transformed by love. Tristan de Mauprat, his eight sons, and their cousin Bernard (the narrator) terrorize the countryside from their feudal stronghold of La Roche Mauprat. They kidnap Edmée, daughter of Hubert de Mauprat (representing a younger, civilized branch of the family). Bernard, startled by his own softer impulses, helps her to escape; in return, she promises to marry none but him. When the *Maréchaussée* (mounted constabulary) storm La Roche Mauprat and kill or banish its inmates, Bernard finds refuge with Hubert and Edmée. His passion for Edmée finally drives him to co-operate in their efforts to tame and educate him. One day while the pair are out hunting, Edmée is mysteriously shot and nearly dies (their wild ride through the forest before the shooting is a well-known episode). Bernard, whose former violence tells against him, is tried for attempted murder, but triumphantly cleared by last-minute evidence. Edmée decides that she can now safely marry him.

Mauriac, CLAUDE (1914–), son of the following, novelist, critic, and essayist; private secretary to de Gaulle (1944–49). As a critic, he has written widely on 19th- and 20th-c. authors (Balzac, Proust, Gide, etc.). His novels (e.g. *Toutes les femmes sont fatales*, 1957; *Le Diner en ville*, 1959; *La Marquise sortit à cinq heures*, 1961; *L'Agrandissement*, 1963; *L'Oubli*, 1966) and his criticism reveal a questioning attitude towards traditional forms of literature which has prompted comparisons with exponents of the *nouveau roman*. His approach is summarized in the word he coined for the title of one of his chief critical works— *L'Alittérature contemporaine* (1958).

Mauriac, FRANÇOIS (1885–1970), primarily a novelist (a member of the *Académie*, 1933; winner of the *Prix Nobel*, 1952), also a dramatist and critic. His novels include *Le Baiser au lépreux* (1922), *Genitrix* (1923), *Le Désert de l'amour* (1925), *Thérèse Desqueyroux* (1927) and its sequel *La Fin de la nuit* (1935), *Destins* (1928), *Le Nœud de vipères* (1932), *Le Mystère Frontenac* (1933), *Les Anges noirs* (1936), *Les Chemins de la mer* (1939), *La Pharisienne* (1941), *Le Sagouin* (1950). With few exceptions (e.g. *Le Nœud de vipères*, a longer study of avarice and family discord; *Le Mystère Frontenac*, largely the story of his own family), they are short, swift-moving, psychological studies from the pen of a fervent Roman Catholic. The scene is nearly always his native Bordeaux or its environs—the wine-growing districts, or the hot, sandy, pine-covered Landes along the coast. Beneath their wealthy, well-ordered respectability, his characters are the helpless victims of disordered, uneasy passions, which he pursues into their most murky recesses. Such passions are continually at war with—may indeed, he

suggests, be of the obverse side of—the religion that purifies the human heart; and this conflict between sensuality and religion forms the dramatic interest of the novels.

His other works include the plays *Asmodée* (1938), *Les Mal Aimés* (1945), and *Passage du malin* (1948); critical studies, e.g. *Le Roman* (1928), *Vie de Jean Racine* (1928), *Trois Grands Hommes devant Dieu* (1947; on Molière, J.-J. Rousseau, and Flaubert); a *Vie de Jésus* (1936); *De Gaulle* (1964); *Mémoires* and *Nouveaux Mémoires intérieurs* (1959 and 1965); *Mémoires politiques* (1967); *Journal* (1934–53, 5 vols.) and *Bloc-Notes* (1958–71, 5 vols.), collections of his journalistic writings from 1932 in *Le *Figaro*, *L'Express*, etc. (reminiscences, jottings, literary and music criticism, political and polemical articles, etc.), forming what he calls a 'journal semi-intime'; also *Resistance writings (often publ. clandestinely under the name 'Forez').

Maurice de Sully (d. 1196), bishop of Paris (1160–96, in succession to Pierre le Lombard), author of a collection of sermons (extant in both Latin and French versions) which was long widely used by preachers. He was associated with the school of the Abbaye de *Saint-Victor (v. Universities, 1).

Maurists, Benedictine monks of the *Congrégation de Saint-Maur* (f. 1618, with a view to reforming the Order; v. *Saint-Germain-des-Prés*). Their learning and literary industry became even more famous than their monastic zeal. Under the impulsion of their first superior-general, Dom Grégoire Tarisse, they carried out an immense amount of historical and critical work in connection with patristic and Biblical literature, monastic and ecclesiastical history, palaeography, and other branches of technical erudition; some travelled widely, researching in monastic libraries. v. *Mabillon*; *Montfaucon*; *Art de vérifier les dates...*, *L'*; *Histoire littéraire de la France*.

Mauritius, v. *Île de France*.

Maurois, André, *pseudonym of* ÉMILE HERZOG (1885–1967), man of letters and novelist (a member of the *Académie, 1938), came of a family of industrialists who left Alsace for Normandy after the *Franco-Prussian war. After service as a liaison officer with the British army in the 1914–18 war, he made a reputation as an interpreter of the English spirit with *Les Silences du Colonel Bramble* (1918), an amusing and perceptive study of an English officers' mess, and *Les Discours du Docteur O'Grady* (1922), then confirmed it with essays on English writers (*Quatre Études anglaises*, 1927; *Magiciens et logiciens*, 1935), *Le Côté de Chelsea* (1929; an amusing *pastiche* of Proust), *L'Anglaise* (1933; three tales), *Édouard VII et son temps* (1933), and highly successful romantic biographies of Shelley (*Ariel*, 1923), Disraeli (1927), and Byron (1930). Besides novels (notably *Climats*, 1928) and tales, he published many more biographical and/or literary studies, e.g. of Lyautey (1931), Voltaire (1935), Chateaubriand (1937), Proust (*À la recherche de Marcel Proust*, 1949), É.-A. Chartier (*Alain*, 1950; he was taught by Chartier at Rouen), G. Sand (*Lélia*, 1952), Hugo (*Olympio*, 1954), Mme de La Fayette (1960), Balzac (1965); popular histories of England (inc. a work on the Norman Conquest, 1968), the United States (he taught at Princeton during the 1939–45 war), and France; collections of literary studies (*De Proust à Camus*, 1963; *De La Bruyère à Proust*, 1964, etc.); also *Mémoires* (1948; another vol. appeared in 1970) and *Soixante Ans de ma vie littéraire* (1966).

Mauron, CHARLES (1899–1966), critic, the originator of *psychocritique* (*v. Critics and Criticism*, 3), which he defined in *Des Métaphores obsédantes au mythe personnel* (1963). His other works include *Introduction à la psychanalyse de Mallarmé* (1950), *L'Inconscient dans l'œuvre et la vie de Racine* (1957), *Psychocritique du genre comique* (1964).

Mauron, MARIE ROUMANILLE, MME (1896–1976), divorced from the above, a school-teacher turned novelist whose stories and studies of Provençal life have prompted comparisons with Colette. They include *Le Quartier Mortisson* (1938), *Lisa de Roquemale* (1945), *La Transhumance* (1955), *Hommes et cités de Provence* (1965), *Châteaux de cartes* (1966).

Maurras, CHARLES (1868–1952), poet and essayist, in later life a notoriously reactionary political journalist; a member of the *Académie (1938). He began his literary career in Paris at 17, contributed essays and criticism to reviews, and not only wrote poetry but, with Moréas, Du Plessys, and others, founded the *École romane. In the next 15 years he published *Le Chemin de paradis* (1894), philosophical tales illustrating the pagan conception of life; *Anthinéa: d'Athènes à Florence* (1901), travel sketches, mostly of Greece; *Les Amants de Venise* (1902), a study of some months in the lives of G. Sand and Musset; *L'Avenir de l'intelligence* (1905), collected essays, including a well-known essay on women writers, *Le Romantisme féminin*. These, and his *Barbarie et poésie* (1925; critical studies), showed his love for the restraint and grace of classical culture and profound distaste for the romantic (i.e. emotional) approach to life. But his literary influence—for a time considerable—was to be undermined by his increasing absorption in reactionary politics. He became a monarchist after the *Dreyfus affair, helped to found the *Action française group, and created a great stir with his *Enquête sur la monarchie* (1901, in the *Gazette de France), the results of an inquiry he had conducted (by means of interviews and correspondence with exiled Royalists, leading authors, etc.) to determine whether French opinion would welcome a return to monarchical government. He was thereafter the moving spirit and editor, with L. Daudet, of the extreme monarchist paper *L'Action française* (his articles were often signed 'Criton'). *Au signe de Flore* (1931) contains his political reminiscences of these years. When France fell, he rallied to Pétain under the slogan 'France alone', opposed alike to the Allies, the *Resistance, and the pro-German collaborators. After the Liberation, he was sentenced to life imprisonment, but was released on health grounds in 1952. The fact that he was totally deaf from an early age is sometimes advanced to explain his bitter fanaticism.

Maury, JEAN-SIFFREIN, ABBÉ (1746–1817), ecclesiastical writer (e.g. a good *Essai sur l'éloquence de la chaire*, final ed. 1810) and politician, defended the monarchy and the Church in the *Assemblée constituante* and was rewarded by Pius VI with a cardinal's hat (1794, after he had left France). He returned to France in 1804, was created archbishop of Paris by Napoleon (1810) and, despite the pope's express prohibition, held the office till 1814.

Maximes, (1) *v. La Rochefoucauld*; (2) *v. Vauvenargues.*

Maximes des saints, v. Fénelon.

Mayenne, CHARLES DE LORRAINE, DUC DE (1554–1611), succeeded his brother Henri, 3rd duc de *Guise*, as leader of the *Ligue*.

Mayeux, a personage—originally a character in the farce *Le Fossé des Tuileries* (1831)—memorably depicted by the caricaturist Traviès. He was the type of the *petit-bourgeois* of the July Monarchy; the hunchbacked hero of preposterous adventures, bumptious, conceited, loose-living, and intensely patriotic.

Maynard or **Mainard,** FRANÇOIS (1582–1646), poet, a favourite disciple of Malherbe, a member of the original *Académie française*, and sometime secretary to *Marguerite de Valois*, spent most of his life as a magistrate at Aurillac. He usually sacrificed vigour to a laborious correctness, but wrote some good odes (e.g. *La Belle Vieille*; *Alcippe, reviens dans nos bois*) and epigrams, e.g. the following, directed at an author's lack of perspicuity:

> Si ton esprit veut cacher
> Les belles choses qu'il pense,
> Dis-moi, qui peut t'empêcher
> De te servir du silence?

Mayor of the Palace, *v. Maire du Palais.*

Mazarin, i.e. GIULIO MAZARINI (1602–61), son of a Sicilian employed as an agent by the Colonna family, in early manhood doctor of laws, soldier, and diplomat, came into prominence as papal agent in 1630 by securing a truce between France and Spain. He was sent to Paris (1634) as papal legate, attracted Richelieu's notice, entered the French service, and was made cardinal. He succeeded Richelieu as prime minister and, despite his intense unpopularity (*v. Fronde*; *Mazarinades*), retained office under Louis XIV by favour of the regent Anne d'Autriche (to whom he may have been secretly married). He was a great collector of books (ably assisted by his librarian Naudé), and from 1643 his fine library (*v. Bibliothèque Mazarine*) was open to the public. During the *Fronde* the *parlement* ordered it to be sold, but he later managed to reconstitute it and bequeathed it to the nation as part of a college to be founded in his memory (*v. Collège des Quatre-Nations*). *v. Pyrenees, Treaty of the.*

Mazarinades, the name given to the numerous pamphlets and satires, in prose and verse, issued against Mazarin during the *Fronde*, and sometimes to any satire published in those years. *v. Marigny.*

Mazarin's Nieces. Mazarin had numerous nieces (daughters of his sisters, married to Girolamo Martinozzi and Lorenzo Mancini). He brought several of them to Paris (1648 and 1653) and arranged great marriages for them.

(1) LAURE MANCINI (d. at 19), m. (1651) the duc de Mercœur, grandson of Henri IV and Gabrielle d'Estrées, and was mother of Vendôme. (2) ANNE-MARIE MARTINOZZI, m. (1654) the prince de *Conti*. She became a pious *Jansenist*. (3) LAURE MARTINOZZI, m. (1656) Alphonse d'Este, heir of the duke of Modena. She was later long regent of Modena. Her daughter married the duke of York (James II). (4) OLYMPE MANCINI, after a boy-and-girl affair with Louis XIV, m. (1657) a prince of the house of Savoy, who was

created comte de Soissons. She was mother of Prince Eugene, victor—with Marlborough—of Oudenarde and Malplaquet. (5) MARIE MANCINI. Louis XIV fell deeply in love with her and proposed to Mazarin that he should marry her. Mazarin opposed the match and removed her from court; the king's marriage to the Infanta ended the episode. She married (1661) Prince Colonna, was unhappy, and left him. (6) HORTENSE MANCINI, a woman of great beauty and charm, sought in marriage by the exiled Charles II and other royal persons, m. (1661) the son of the maréchal de la Meilleraye. Mazarin left them the bulk of his vast fortune on condition that they took his name: she is consequently known as the duchesse de Mazarin. She ran away from her husband (a jealous crank) and her adventurous wanderings took her to Italy, Savoy, and finally England, where—with her fellow-exile and admirer Saint-Évremond—she shone at the courts of Charles II and James II, and where she died (1699). The memoirs bearing her name were probably compiled by Saint-Réal. (7) MARIE-ANNE MANCINI, m. (1662) the duc de Bouillon, a gallant soldier, nephew of Turenne. She was a patroness of men of letters, notably La Fontaine, and prominent among those who induced Pradon to write his *Phèdre et Hippolyte* as a rival piece to Racine's **Phèdre*. She visited Hortense in England (1687).

Mazas, a prison in Paris (built 1845–50; demolished 1898) designed solely for prisoners sentenced to solitary confinement.

Meaulnes, *v. Grand Meaulnes, Le.*

Meaux, L'Aigle de, L'Évêque de, *v. Bossuet.*

Méchant, Le, a satirical comedy by Gresset; produced 1745 with great success. Its background is the soulless society of the **salons* of the day, vividly depicted.

Cléon, 'le Méchant', is a cynical,

perfidious mischief-maker who delights in provoking quarrels and making himself feared and hated. He sets about spoiling the projected marriage of Valère and Chloé, by calumny and other devices. But the love of Valère, aided by the counsels of the firm and upright Ariste and the perspicacity of Chloé's maid, foils his schemes and he is exposed—but unabashed.

Médan, *v. Soirées de Médan, Les.*

Médecin de campagne, Le (1833; later in *La *Comédie humaine, Scènes de la vie de campagne*), a novel by Balzac.

After unhappy experiences in love and in the world of Paris, Benassis has set up in medical practice in an isolated mountain village near Grenoble and has transformed its cretinous, half-starved inhabitants into a healthy, self-supporting, progressive community of which he is now mayor. In the course of rural rides with Genestas, an officer from the Grenoble garrison, he describes how this was achieved and expounds his (i.e. Balzac's) views on politics, religion, social reform, etc. He introduces Genestas to various local characters, including two old soldiers, Gondrin, sole survivor of the pontoneers of the Beresina (*v. Moscow*), and Goguelat, formerly of the *Garde impériale*, both still fanatically devoted to 'l'Empereur' (*v. Légende napoléonienne*). Goguelat is the village story-teller, and in one memorable scene, at night, in a candle-lit barn, he keeps his audience enthralled with fantastic tales of Napoleon.

Médecin malgré lui, Le, a 3-act prose comedy by Molière, probably partly inspired by Le **Vilain Mire*; produced 1666.

Géronte's daughter Lucinde, foiled by his opposition to her marriage to the penniless Léandre, feigns sudden dumbness. Her doctors having failed to cure her, Géronte sends out his servants to look for a specialist. They light on Martine, who is bent on paying out her husband Sganarelle, a woodcutter, for beating her. Having been servant to a doctor, he has a smattering of medical terms, and she assures Géronte's servants that he is just the man they want, but that he is a whimsical fellow who will deny his miraculous powers unless they take their sticks to him. Sganarelle, well beaten, agrees to attend Lucinde, easily hoodwinks Géronte with a little medical jargon, and takes kindly to his new role. When he refers to the heart as being on the right side and the liver on the left and Géronte says he thought it was the other way about, he airily extricates himself with the famous line: 'Oui, cela était autrefois ainsi; mais nous avons changé tout cela.' Bribed by Léandre, he introduces him as his apothecary—whereupon Lucinde recovers her speech with such vigour that Géronte begs Sganarelle to make her dumb again. This Sganarelle cannot do, but he offers to make Géronte deaf instead (a touch borrowed from Rabelais). The lovers elope, and Géronte is reconciled to their marriage when he learns that Léandre has come into a fortune.

Médée, Corneille's first tragedy, depicting the vengeance of Medea, deserted by Jason, and modelled on the plays on the same theme by Euripides and Seneca; produced in the winter of 1634–5. Though the best tragedy to date, it lacks the full dignity and simplicity of his later plays. It contains the famous reply of Médée in the passage:

> Votre pays vous hait, votre époux est sans foi:
> Dans un si grand revers que vous reste-t-il?
>   —Moi!
> Moi, dis-je, et c'est assez....

Médicis, v. *Catherine de Médicis*; *Marie de Médicis*.

Méditations poétiques (1820), by Lamartine, a collection of 24 odes and elegies; notably *Le Lac* and *L'Isolement*, also *Le Soir*, *Le Vallon*, *L'Automne*. In *Le Lac*, the poet is alone by the Lac du Bourget, near Aix-les-Bains, where he had

been the previous year with 'Elvire', now dying in Paris. How intense their happiness had been as they listened to the rhythmical beat of the oars on the water! Then, they had called on time to stand still. And now? Time has swept on, but love itself must linger in this place. *L'Isolement* was written a year after the death of 'Elvire'. Alone in a world where 'un seul être vous manque et tout est dépeuplé', the poet dreams of a mystical reunion in another world and calls on the north wind to sweep him, like a withered leaf, towards 'ce bien idéal que toute âme désire'.

Méhul, ÉTIENNE-NICOLAS (1763–1817), composer of operas, *opéras-comiques, and ballets; also of the music for such great Revolutionary songs as the *Chant du départ, Chant des victoires, Hymne du 9 thermidor, etc. He and Cherubini were musical directors for the service held in Notre-Dame, on Easter Sunday 1802 in the presence of Bonaparte, to mark the official return to the Christian religion.

Meilhac, HENRI (1831–97), author, with L. *Halévy, of comedies and of libretti for *Offenbach's operettas, etc.

Meillet, ANTOINE (1866–1936), philologist. His valuable studies include *Introduction à l'étude comparative des langues indo-européennes* (1903), *Linguistique historique et linguistique générale* (1921), *Esquisse d'une histoire de la langue latine* (1928).

Meister, JACQUES-HENRI (1744–1826), Swiss man of letters, a friend of Diderot and d'Holbach, lived in Paris from 1770 to 1789. He contributed to *Grimm's correspondence and continued it from 1773 to 1790.

Mélanges (as in *Mélanges de philologie offerts à Ferdinand Brunot*), a volume of essays by colleagues and former pupils in honour of a distinguished scholar, the French equivalent of a *Festschrift*, a *Miscellany*, or (*Homage*) *Studies*.

Mélanide, a sentimental comedy in verse by La Chaussée; produced 1741.

The comte d'Ormancé, having secretly married Mélanide and had a son by her, has been forcibly separated from her by his family and later led to believe that she and the boy are dead. Eighteen years later, he again falls in love, this time with a girl of humble birth. Her mother welcomes such a fine match, but the girl herself favours young Darviane—who is, in fact, the comte's son, though neither knows this. The play turns on the conflict in the father's mind when he learns the truth, for he has forgotten Mélanide and at first hates and repudiates the son who is his rival. But Mélanide now appears and wins back her husband's heart, and father and son are reconciled.

Mélicerte, a *pastoral comedy by Molière on a theme from Le *Grand Cyrus*. He wrote only two acts, performed in 1666. The plot is trifling—two shepherdesses in love with a shepherd who loves another— but the form is graceful.

Mélisande, in Maeterlinck's *Pelléas et Mélisande*.

Mélite, a comedy by Corneille, his first play; produced 1629 or 1630.

Éraste loves Mélite, but his love is not returned. He introduces her to his friend Tircis (who claims to be superior to any tender passion), and the two fall in love. Éraste devises a cruel revenge: Tircis has a sister, Chloris, who is betrothed to Philandre; Éraste fabricates a letter from Mélite declaring herself in love with Philandre, and sends it to Philandre. Thus, to ruin the prospects of Mélite and Tircis, he also ruins those of Chloris, for Philandre allows himself to be seduced from his allegiance to her, and also shows Tircis the fabricated letter. Tircis is distraught, and a report of his death is brought to Mélite, who faints away. Éraste, informed that Tircis and Mélite have died of grief, is so crazed by remorse that he believes himself dead and in hell. In the end, Tircis and Mélite are reunited,

and Chloris, who repudiates the inconstant Philandre, is awarded to the penitent Éraste.

Melmoth réconcilié (1835; later in *La *Comédie humaine*, Études philosophiques*). Balzac was much influenced in his early years by the Gothic romances of the Irish writer Charles Robert Maturin (trans. into French *c*. 1820 and widely read). Maturin's 'Melmoth the Wanderer' sold his soul—a transferable bargain—to the Devil in return for long life, discovered all the *ennui* and horror of diabolic omnipotence, but could find no one, however desperate, who did not shrink from relieving him of his pact. Balzac's Melmoth finds no such difficulty in the society of the Restoration, which has replaced 'le principe Honneur par le principe Argent'. He exchanges souls with Castanier, a swindling cashier in fear of discovery, then dies an edifying death. Castanier, in his turn, exchanges souls with a bankrupt stockbroker, who is prepared to accept any pact.

Mélodrame, a sensational drama with incidental music (used to indicate character or to emphasize the action), and sometimes ballet, which may have evolved from *pantomime dialoguée*. Interest depended on violent incident and exaggerated sentiment; and virtue nearly always won a last-minute triumph over vice. For some 30 years from *c*. 1798 *mélodrames* filled the *théâtres du boulevard* in Paris (*v. Theatres and Theatre Companies*; *Boulevard du Crime*), and the form quickly spread to other countries (melodrama was played on the London stage from 1802). The earliest and most prolific author of *mélodrames* was Pixérécourt; *v. also Ennery*; *Soulié*.

Mélusine, a fairy of French folklore, the water-sprite of the fountain of Lusignan in Poitou and legendary ancestress and tutelary spirit of the house of Lusignan. She consented to marry Raimondin of Lusignan on condition that he should never see her on a Saturday, when she resumed mermaid form. He broke the compact, and she fled. The legend was adapted in a prose romance by Jean d'Arras (*c.* 1387) and later further developed.

Memnon (1749), a philosophical tale by Voltaire, also the title of the first version of his *Zadig.

Memnon conceives the idea of being perfectly wise: he will abjure the love of women, avoid excesses of food and drink, live within his means and on good terms with his neighbours. Yet within a few hours he is beguiled by a woman, gets drunk, loses an eye in a quarrel, and is ruined by the bankruptcy of a creditor. In a vision a celestial spirit explains to him that perfect wisdom is impossible in this imperfect world, and that (short of recovering his eye) he may yet live with moderate happiness, provided he abandons his foolish project.

Mémoires de deux jeunes mariées, v. Comédie humaine, La (*Scènes de la vie privée*).

Mémoires d'Hadrien, v. Yourcenar.

Mémoires de Trévoux, v. Journal de Trévoux.

Mémoires d'outre-tombe (1849–50; 1948, the first complete text), Chateaubriand's autobiography, one of the masterpieces of French literature; written between 1811 and 1841. In later life, when in financial straits, he sold the manuscript to a syndicate, stipulating that it should not be published till a year after his death (when it appeared in instalments). It is in four sections (subdivided into books), covering (1) his early years, military career, life in exile, and return to France (1768–1800); (2) his literary career (1800–14); (3) his political career (1814–30); (4) his years of retirement (1830–c. 1840). The first books, which contain reminiscences of childhood and a description of the beginnings of the Revolution, are considered incomparably the finest; but the whole work abounds in memorable and often self-revealing passages—portraits of contemporaries

(notably Napoleon), invariably coloured by the writer's own emotions; descriptions of personal sensations; accounts of travel in Germany, Italy, and Central Europe.

Mémoires du diable, Les, v. Soulié.

Mémoires d'un fou (in *Premières Œuvres*, 1914–20), by Flaubert, a fragmentary, semi-autobiographical work, written when he was 17 and interesting as a record of his first meeting with Mme *Schlésinger— here called 'Maria'.

Mémoires d'un homme de qualité, v. Prévost, A.-F.

Mémoires d'un médecin: Joseph Balsamo, v. Dumas père; Cagliostro.

Mémoires pour servir à l'histoire de France sous Napoléon, v. Montholon.

Mémoires secrets…, (1) *v. Duclos;* (2) *v. Bachaumont, L. P. de.*

Mémoires sur la Bastille, v. Linguet.

Memoirs, Autobiographies, *Journaux intimes*. The chief authors of such works are listed below, broadly classified into four groups—though it will be appreciated that division cannot always be clear-cut. The type of autobiography in which the author is, and expects his readers to be, chiefly interested in himself (or himself in relation to the literary or political scene) is very much a 19th-c. phenomenon; so, too, is the *journal intime.*

1. Memoirs mainly of interest as social, political, or military history (*v.* also *History*):
(a) *Periods before c. 1750*: Antin, duc d'; Argenson, marquis d'; d'Aubigné; Bassompierre; Brantôme; Bussy-Rabutin; Castelnau; Catinat; Caylus, marquise de; Choisy; Commines; Conrart; Dangeau; Du Bellay, G. and M.; Duclos; Duguay-Trouin; Du Hausset, Mme; Épinay, Mme d'; Fontaine, N.; Fontenay-Mareuil; Forbin; Gourville; Gramont, duc de;

Gramont, comte de; Hénault; Héroard; Jeannin; Joinville; La Châtre; La Fare; La Fayette, Mme de; La Noue, F. de; La Rochefoucauld; Launay, Mlle de; Lenet; L'Estoile, P. T. de; Louis XIV; Luynes; Marguerite de Valois; Mazarin, duchesse de (v. *Mazarin's Nieces* (6)); Monluc; Montpensier, duchesse de; Motteville, Mme de; Nemours, duchesse de; Pontis; Retz; Richelieu, cardinal de; Richelieu, duc de; Rohan, duc de; Saint-Simon, duc de; Sourches; Sully; Tallemant des Réaux; Tavannes; Turenne; Vieilleville; Villars; Villehardouin.

(b) *Periods after c. 1750*: Abrantès, duchesse d'; Arago; Beaumarchais; Bernis; Besenval; Boigne, comtesse de; Broglie, duc de; Campan, Mme; Canrobert; Carême, M.-A.; Caulaincourt; Clairon, Mlle; Custine; Gaulle, C. de; Genlis, Mme de; Gourgaud; Gouvion-Saint-Cyr; Guizot; Haussonville; Hugo; Las Cases; La Tour du Pin, marquise de; Latude; Lauzun (duc de Biron); Marchand; Marmont; Marmontel; Ménard; Morellet; Napoleon I; Poincaré, R.; Récamier, Mme; Rémusat, Mme de; Rœderer; Roland, Mme; Staël, Mme de; Tocqueville; Vidocq; Viel-Castel; Vigée-Lebrun, Mme; Villemain.

Memoirs of the above persons which have not been published separately will in some cases be found in the *Collection des mémoires relatifs à l'histoire de France* (1819–29) of Petitot and Monmerqué and the *Nouvelle Collection des mémoires pour servir à l'histoire de France* (1836–8) of Michaud and Poujoulat.

2. REMINISCENCES OF LITERARY, ARTISTIC, AND THEATRICAL LIFE: Ancelot, Mme; Antoine; Berlioz; Carco; Chasles; Copeau; Daudet, A.; Du Camp; Dumas *père*; Goncourt, E. and J. de; Halévy, L.; Houssaye; Léautaud; Lugné-Poë; Marmier; Mauclair; Mauriac; Raynaud; Sachs; Véron.

3. WORKS THAT ARE MAINLY AUTOBIOGRAPHICAL: Arago; Beauvoir, S. de; Chateaubriand; Colette; France, A.; Genet; Gide; Green; Lamartine; Malraux; Maurois; Michelet; Musset; Quinet; Renan; Rousseau, J.-J.; Sand, G.; Sartre;

Schlumberger; Stendhal; Vallès; Verlaine.

4. JOURNAUX INTIMES (diaries, confessions, psychological autobiographies): Amiel, H.-F.; Barrès; Bashkirtseff, Marie; Baudelaire; Bloy; Constant, B.; Delacroix; Du Bos, C.; Gide; Green; Guérin, E. and M. de; Leiris; Lenéru, Marie; Loti; Louÿs; Maine de Biran; Mauriac; Michelet; Ramuz; Régnier, Paule; Renard; Vigny.

Mémorial de Pascal, v. Pascal.

Mémorial de Sainte-Hélène, v. Las Cases.

Ménage, GILLES (1613–92), philologist and man of letters, an *habitué* of the Hôtel de *Rambouillet, said to be Vadius in Molière's Les *Femmes savantes*. His works include *Les Origines de la langue française* (v. Dictionaries, 1650); *Miscellanea* (1652), a collection of satires and other pieces in Greek, Latin, and French; observations on Tasso's *Aminta* (1655); a translation, with commentary, of Diogenes Laertius; Italian etymologies; *Menagiana* (1693), a collection of his sayings, anecdotes, and miscellanies, prepared by him and published posthumously. He was quarrelsome and had controversies with Bouhours, Cotin, and others; but Mme de Sévigné owed much to his instruction in her youth. Despite his merit, he was not elected to the *Académie*.

Ménagier de Paris, Le, a prose work written 1392–4 by a rich elderly *bourgeois* of Paris to instruct his young wife in matters moral and domestic, from religious duties to cooking recipes. It sheds light on the life of the rich *bourgeoisie* of the day. *Cf. La Tour Landry.*

Ménalque, (1) in *La Bruyère's *Caractères*; (2) in Gide's Les *Nourritures terrestres* and *L'Immoraliste*.

Ménard, LOUIS (1822–1901), one of the first *Parnassien* poets, author of the epic *Prométhée délivré* (1844) and collected

Poèmes (1855); but more important as a scholar and thinker (*Rêveries d'un païen mystique*, 1876, prose and verse), a Hellenist whose pagan attitude to life influenced such contemporaries as Leconte de Lisle. His *Prologue d'une révolution* (1849) is a moving account of the rising of June 1848 (*v. Republics*, 2) in which he took part.

Mendès, CATULLE (1842–1909), married for a time to Judith Gautier; *Parnassien poet (founder of the *Revue fantaisiste* and a contributor to *Le Parnasse contemporain*), also a novelist, playwright, and man of letters. His writings include the poetry collected in *Poésies* (1892), *Poésies nouvelles* (1893), *Choix de poésies* (1925); plays—his most successful work, written alone or in collaboration—e.g. *La Reine Fiammette* (1889), *Médée* (1898); many novels, e.g. *Les Folies amoureuses* (1877), a title indicative of their character; and his *Légende du Parnasse contemporain* (1884) and *Rapport sur le mouvement poétique français* (1902), valuable studies of 19th-c. poetry.

Mendiant ingrat, *Le*, *v. Bloy*.

Ménechmes, *Les*, by Regnard, a comedy based on Plautus's *Menaechmi*; produced 1705. Two brothers, who look alike, are mistaken for each other. The one, an unsophisticated provincial, comes to Paris to collect an inheritance; the other, an unscrupulous adventurer, sets about securing for himself both his brother's inheritance and his intended bride.

Ménestrel, originally a paid servant in a household, later extended to include *jongleurs in the permanent employ of a prince or noble, then restricted to these. The fact that the *ménestrel* was in permanent employment, and so free to devote himself to literary creation, favoured the transformation of the old type of *jongleur* into an author or man of letters. There was a corporation of *ménestrels* of Paris from 1321.

Ménestrel de Reims, *v. History*, 1.

Ménippée, Satire, *v. Satire Ménippée*.

Menteur, Le, by Corneille, a comedy adapted from Alarcón's *La Verdad sospechosa*; produced 1643.

Dorante, who has left the law school of Poitiers and come to Paris to take up the profession of arms, is a young man of gallant character with an amazing propensity for telling lies. To win favour with a lady he represents himself as just returned from the wars; to avoid betrothal to another he bamboozles his father with a fantastic tale of a previous marriage; and so on. He finally becomes hopelessly entangled by mistaking the name of the lady he is courting, and only extricates himself by transferring his favour to the other lady.

The success of this play led Corneille to produce a sequel, *La Suite du Menteur* (prod. winter of 1644–5), based on a comedy by Lope de Vega. Though the hero and his valet bear the same names as in *Le Menteur*, there is no real relation between the two plays, for Dorante is now a model of generous self-denial. He endures wrongful imprisonment for the sake of a friend, and is even prepared to surrender his lady to him.

Mérat, ALBERT (1840–1909), minor *Parnassien poet (*Les Chimères*, 1866; *Les Villes de marbre*, 1874; *Au fil de l'eau*, 1877; *Poèmes de Paris*, 1880; *Vers le soir*, 1900, etc.). *v. Valade*.

Méraugis de Portlesguez, an early 13th-c. verse *roman breton by Raoul de Houdenc. The young knights Méraugis and Gorvain Cadrut both love Lidoine, the first for her worth, the second for her beauty. A tribunal of ladies, presided over by *Guinevere, awards her to Méraugis, provided that he proves himself worthy of her in a quest for *Gauvain, who has been absent from Arthur's court for a year. Méraugis sets out, with Lidoine, and ultimately succeeds in the quest. The complicated tale of their magical adventures is skilfully and pleasingly told. The poem is also notable for its discussion of abstract love themes.

Mercadet, a 3-act drama, produced 1851, adapted by d'Ennery from Balzac's 5-act prose comedy *Le Faiseur* (written 1838–40, publ. 1851 as *Mercadet*). It is a powerful, realistic study of a speculator (*v. Censorship, Dramatic*).

Mercier, LOUIS (1870–1935), poet, of peasant extraction, spent most of his life near Lyons. His verse is collected in *Voix de la terre et du temps* (1903), *Le Poème de la maison* (1909), *Les Pierres sacrées* (1919). Such inspiration as it shows comes from religion or the humble, familiar objects of daily life.

Mercier, LOUIS-SÉBASTIEN (1740–1814), is chiefly remembered as a linguistic innovator (*v. Dictionaries*, 1801) and for his *Tableau de Paris* (1779–89, 12 vols.), a mine of first-hand information about the contemporary scene, combining topography with descriptions of various classes of citizens, anecdotes, and short essays on anything from politics to mushrooms. His other works include plays, notably prose *drames* (*Jenneval*, 1768, based on Lillo's *George Barnwell*; *Le Déserteur*, 1782, a protest against war and the rigours of military law; *La Brouette du vinaigrier*, 1784, a plea for social equality), sentimental and didactic, but based on new theories anticipating the *Romantic revolt against *Classical conventions and set forth in his *Nouvel Essai sur l'art dramatique* (1773) and *De la littérature et des littérateurs* (1778); also *Le Nouveau Paris* (1789–94, 6 vols.), a day-to-day record of events of the Revolution. *v. Annales patriotiques*.

Mercier de La Rivière, *v. Économistes*.

Mercœur, ÉLISA (1809–35), *Romantic poetess (*Œuvres*, 1843, 3 vols.).

Mercure de France, Le, (1) *v. Mercure galant*; (2) a famous literary and artistic monthly (1890–1965; in its heyday *c.* 1900), f. by Alfred Vallette, his wife '*Rachilde', and other *Symbolists. It was at first particularly associated with Symbolism, but made a feature of printing original work by writers of all schools and nationalities.

Mercure du XIXe siècle, Le (1823–30), a literary review (ed. Latouche) which stood for a moderate *Romanticism. Senancour wrote for it.

Mercure galant, Le (1672–1820), a periodical f. by Jean Donneau de Visé (1638–1710; author of farces and *vaudevilles*, and a critic, at times acrimonious, of Molière). It carried news of court and literary circles, literary criticism, poetry, etc., combining politics and literature in a light, agreeable form suited to a wide public. Published monthly from 1678, it was highly popular and enjoyed the favour of Louis XIV, though it was attacked from certain literary quarters (La Bruyère said it was 'immédiatement au-dessous de rien'; and *v. Boursault*). In 1724, it became the *Mercure de France*, with a greater literary scope and semi-official status (its editor was appointed by the government and profits were devoted to pensions for men of letters). Just before the Revolution the management was in the hands of C.-J. Panckoucke. Its literary features continued during the Revolutionary era (when for a time it was called *Le Mercure français*), and it was little molested. Napoleon suppressed it (1811), but it reappeared after his fall and was popular with the constitutional party just after the Restoration. Contributors included T. Corneille, G. Raynal, Marmontel, and Mallet du Pan (editors), La Harpe, Chamfort, and Voltaire.

Mercuriale, *v. Daguesseau*.

Méré, ANTOINE GOMBAUD, CHEVALIER DE (1610–85), moralist, a friend of Guez de Balzac, a man of acute, if somewhat pedantic, intelligence; self-appointed arbiter of good manners and polite usage. His *Lettres* (1682), which include anecdotes and tales, are remembered for those addressed to his friend Pascal, whom he advised to adopt an *esprit de finesse* in polite society rather than the bludgeoning tactics of logic. His *Conversations* with the maréchal de Clérambault, *Maximes*, and treatises on polite usage (*De la vraie honnêteté, De l'éloquence et de l'entretien*, etc.) appeared in 1669, 1692, and 1701 respectively.

Mère coquette, La, a verse comedy by Quinault; produced 1665.

The elderly Cremante wishes to marry Isabelle, daughter of Ismène, a middle-aged coquette; Ismène, who thinks herself a widow, her husband having been carried off years ago by the Turks, would like to marry Cremante's son Acante; Acante and Isabelle are in love. Laurette, a rascally maid, contrives to estrange the young lovers, in order to further the designs of their elders. But the unexpected return of Ismène's husband, aided by the true love of Acante and Isabelle, defeats the plot.

Mère coupable, La, v. *Beaumarchais*.

Mère l'Oye, Contes de ma, v. *Perrault*.

Mère Sotte, v. *Enfants sans souci*.

Meriadeuc, v. *Chevalier aux deux épées*.

Mérimée, PROSPER (1803–70), novelist, also archaeologist and historian; great-grandson of Mme Leprince de Beaumont and son of Léonor Mérimée, a mediocre but cultivated artist. He studied law, but preferred literature and, like his close friend Stendhal, was for a time attracted, though not carried away, by *Ro-manticism. His active literary career began with a successful hoax, *Le *Théâtre de Clara Gazul* (1825), followed by another hoax, *La Guzla* (1827), alleged translations, by 'Hyacinthe Maglanowich', of Illyrian national songs and poems. *La Jacquerie* (dramatic sketches; v. *Jacquerie*) and *La Famille de Carvajal* (a drama of incestuous love), published anonymously in 1828, were followed, still anonymously, by his *Chronique du règne de Charles IX* (1829), a novel influenced by Scott. Between 1829 and 1850 he published, usually in reviews (and seldom now anonymously), the tales

on which his fame rests. After 1830, his official career took precedence, at least outwardly, over his creative work. From 1834, as inspector-general of historical monuments, he made long, tiring tours of inspection and presented vigorous reports (e.g. *Voyage dans le midi de la France*, 1835, on church architecture; *Voyage dans l'ouest de la France*, 1836; *Voyage en Corse*, 1840; *Rapport sur les monuments historiques*, 1843). Under the Second Empire he was a member of the *Sénat, prominent at court (largely owing to his close friendship with the empress Eugénie—whom he had known from her childhood—and her mother; v. *Montijo*) and in literary circles. After 1854— perhaps because this year saw the unhappy end of his long intimacy with Mme Valentine Delessert (a cultured, artistic woman whose husband was the Paris *préfet de *police under the July Monarchy)—his creative impulse withered.

His tales (*nouvelles*) are masterpieces of economic, objective narrative, with understatement and an ironic sense of humour keeping the passion and cruelty usually inherent in their themes well under control—hence perhaps their appeal for English readers. (Mérimée knew England well, as he did Spain, and had many English friends.) His first volume of collected tales was *Mosaïque* (1833), including *Mateo Falcone* (1829, in the *Revue de Paris*; a tale of Corsican life), *La Vision de Charles XI* [of Sweden] (1829, in the *Revue de Paris*; a tale of hallucination), *L'*Enlèvement de la redoute*, *Tamango, La Partie de trictrac* (1830, in the *Revue de Paris*; a man cheats at the gaming-tables to provide money for his mistress and is ravaged by remorse), and *Le *Vase étrusque*. *Colomba* gave its name to a volume (first French ed. 1841) of three tales, the others being *Les Âmes du Purgatoire* (first publ. 1836; the exploits of Don Juan de Marana) and *La *Vénus d'Ille*. *Nouvelles* (1852) included *Carmen, Arsène Guillot*, and two translations from Pushkin—*La Dame de pique* and *Le Hussard*. *Dernières Nouvelles* (1873) contained *Lokis* (1870, in the *Revue des Deux Mondes*; a fantastic horror tale) and

La Chambre bleue. La Double Méprise (1833), a longer tale not in the above collections, was possibly originally intended as a novel.

His other works include the one-act comedy *Les Deux Héritages* (1850, in the *Revue des Deux Mondes*; 1853, in book form, with two other short pieces); studies of and translations from Russian literature (he was a friend of Turgenev); historical works, e.g. his *Histoire de don Pèdre Ier, roi de Castille* (1848) and *Les Faux Démétrius* (1852), a study of an episode from 16th-c. Russian history. His *Correspondance générale* (1941–64, 17 vols.) covers the years 1822–70 (earlier eds. of his letters include those to Mlle *Dacquin, *Panizzi, the comtesse de *Montijo, and the Delessert family—the last publ. 1931).

Merleau-Ponty, MAURICE (1908–61), philosopher, professor at the *Sorbonne* and the *Collège de France*. He developed his philosophy on the basis of the phenomenology of the German philosopher Edmund Husserl (1859–1938). He rejects traditional Cartesian dualism, and seeks to strike a balance between the excesses of both empiricism and subjectivism in his notion of the 'body subject' and his emphasis on its dialectical relation with the world. He abhorred absolutes and conclusions, regarding his philosophy more as a vision of reality than as a system. For a time, he was closely associated with Sartrean *Existentialism and helped to found *Les *Temps modernes*; but he and Sartre diverged on many points and went their separate ways. He drew widely on literature to illustrate his philosophy, notably on the work of C. Simon. His best-known work is *Phénoménologie de la perception* (1945); others include *La Structure du comportement* (1941), *Humanisme et terreur* (1947), *Sens et non-sens* (1948), *Éloge de la philosophie* (1953), *Les Aventures de la dialectique* (1955), *Signes* (1960), *Cosmologie du vingtième siècle* (1965).

Merlin, a prophet and magician whose name first occurs in *Geoffrey of Monmouth's *Historia Regum Britanniae*, where he is identified with Ambrosius, a boy with a gift of prophecy of whom *Nennius tells a tale in his *Historia Britonum*. His prophecies occupy the seventh book of Geoffrey's *Historia*. In Robert de Boron's trilogy (*v. Perceval*) he forms the link between the early history of the Grail and the days of Arthur, and the 13th-c. prose versions develop his part in the story. It is he who advises the foundation of the Round Table, and his intervention and counsel constantly influence the course of events. *v. Brocéliande*.

Merlin l'enchanteur, *v. Quinet.*

Mérope, by Voltaire, a tragedy based on Hyginus's version of the legend of Mérope; written 1736, produced 1743, with great success.

Mérope is the widow of Cresphonte, king of Messenia, who has been killed, allegedly by brigands, but in fact by Polyphonte. Two of her sons have also been killed; the third, Égisthe, has been saved by old Narbas and brought up in ignorance of his parentage. Mérope knows nothing of his fate. Polyphonte, who aspires to the throne, wants to marry Mérope and to dispose of Égisthe, if he can be found. Mérope indignantly repels his advances. A young man who has killed another youth—he claims in self-defence—is brought in from the frontier. Mérope suspects, from his resemblance to Cresphonte, that he is Égisthe; but his own account of himself belies this, and there is also some evidence that the dead youth was Égisthe. Polyphonte uses the presumed death of Égisthe to press his suit, and Mérope agrees to marry him if she is allowed to kill Égisthe's murderer with her own hand; she intends to kill herself immediately afterwards. The captive is led to the altar, but as she is about to plunge the dagger in his breast, old Narbas identifies him as Égisthe and reveals that Polyphonte killed Cresphonte. Égisthe seizes the sacrificial axe and slays Polyphonte; the people rally to him, and he is acclaimed king.

Merovingians, 1st dynasty of the kings of all the Franks, f. by *Clovis Ier, so named from Mérovée (d. 458), grandfather of Clovis Ier. After Clovis's death, his kingdom was divided, according to Frankish custom, among his three sons into Austrasia, the eastern territories between the Meuse and the Rhine; Neustria, the north-western territories between the Meuse and the Loire; and the southern territories, including Burgundy. After the death of Dagobert Ier (638), real power passed into the hands of the *Maires du Palais*. The last Merovingian, Childéric III, was deposed by Pépin le Bref in 751. These kings were the brutal and barbarous chiefs of pillaging bands, and their history is an appalling record of family feuds, assassinations, etc. The outstanding members of the dynasty, besides Clovis Ier, were Chilpéric Ier (king of Neustria, 561–84), who showed some literary and artistic ambitions, and Dagobert Ier (king of Austrasia from 622, and of all France from 628), who founded the Abbaye de *Saint-Denis. v. Pharamond; Gregory of Tours.*

Merrill, STUART (1863–1915), poet, of partly French descent, b. in the U.S.A., lived in France from childhood and was closely associated with *Symbolism. The poems of *Les Gammes* (1887) and *Les Fastes* (1891) are largely experiments in versification and in the Symbolist 'orchestration' of verse; those of *Les Quatre Saisons* (1900) belong to a Socialist phase of his career; the lyrics of *Une Voix dans la foule* (1909), his last, and best, collection, are on a deeper note. He also published *Petits Poèmes d'automne* (1895); and *Pastels in Prose* (New York 1890), translations from French poets of the later 19th c.

Mersenne, MARIN (1588–1648), theologian, philosopher, and mathematician; a friend of Descartes and correspondent of scientists all over Europe. He denounced the *libertins (L'Impiété des déistes, 1624).

Merteuil, Mme de, in *Laclos's *Les Liaisons dangereuses.*

Merveilleuses, a name *c.* 1797 for fashionable women who adopted the Greek styles of dress seen in prints and caricatures of the day (e.g. by Carle Vernet). *Cf. Incroyables; Muscadins.*

Méry, FRANÇOIS-JOSEPH-PIERRE-AGNÈS (1797–1866), journalist and man of letters, came to Paris from his native Marseilles (1824), wrote for *Le *Nain jaune* and other journals, and, in collaboration with Auguste Barthélemy (1796–1867), published successful satirical pamphlets in verse (e.g. *Les Sidiennes*, 1825) and notably, after the 1830 *Revolution, *La Némésis*, a weekly series of invective verse (one number attacked Lamartine for prostituting his poetical gifts to politics, provoking his *Ode à Némésis*). His many other writings include *Napoléon en Égypte* (1828), an epic poem; plays and *vaudevilles (alone or with others); novels; and lively short stories, notably *La *Chasse au chastre.*

Meschinot, JEAN (*c.* 1420–91), a *rhétoriqueur poet, employed in the military service of the dukes of Brittany. He wrote poems on moral, satirical, and love themes; also political poems attacking Louis XI (*Innocent feint, tout fourré de malice*) and a political allegory, *Les Lunettes des princes. v.* also *Comedy.*

Mesdames, *v. Madame.*

Mesmer, FRIEDRICH ANTON (1733–1815), an Austrian doctor, the originator of the theory of animal magnetism or mesmerism. He experimented in healing by stroking the body with a magnet, then claimed to be able to communicate magnetism himself and to heal by laying on of hands. He came to Paris (1778), lectured, and held healing *séances* in luxurious, mysteriously lit surroundings. He excited such a furore that, despite allegations of charlatanism from the medical faculty, the government offered him a life annuity—which he declined—for his secret. He influenced Balzac (*cf. Gall; Lavater*).

Message, Le, *v. Comédie humaine, La (Scènes de la vie privée).*

Messe de l'athée, La, v. *Comédie humaine, La* (*Scènes de la vie privée*).

Messidor, v. *Republican Calendar.*

Méténier, OSCAR, v. *Alexis, P.*

Métiers, Livre des, v. *Boileau, É.*

Métra, FRANÇOIS or (?) OLIVIER (*c.* 1714–86), anonymous author of a *Correspondance littéraire et secrète*, published in Holland (1774–93) and reprinted with some changes in London from 1787 as *Correspondance secrète politique et littéraire, ou Mémoires pour servir à l'histoire des cours, des sociétés, et de la littérature en France depuis la mort de Louis XV*. It consists of gossipy comments, professing to be inside information, on political and literary events. Little is known about Métra. He is said to have been a banker, sometime correspondent of the king of Prussia, who got into trouble and fled to Holland, where he compiled his *Correspondance* from material sent to him from Paris.

Metric System. In 1790 the *Assemblée constituante*, at the instance of Talleyrand, decided that France should have a single system of weights and measures. Following reports from various scientific commissions, the value of the basic unit, named *mètre*, was legally fixed (1799) at one ten-millionth part of the quadrant of the terrestrial meridian (i.e. 39·37 inches). The new system was introduced in 1801; a law of 1837 made it compulsory, to the exclusion of other systems, from 1 January 1840. The *mètre* is the unit of length. The other units are those of (1) weight—the *gramme* (the weight of a cubic centimetre of distilled water at the maximum density); (2) surface—the *mètre carré*; (3) volume—the *mètre cube*; (4) capacity—the *litre* (one *décimètre cube*), used for liquids and grains, and the *stère* (one *mètre cube*), used for solids, e.g. firewood. v. also *Weights and Measures.*

Métro, Le, short for *Le Chemin-de-fer métropolitain de Paris*, the system of underground electric railways which is the main form of public passenger transport in Paris. The first line opened in July 1900.

Métromanie, La, by Piron, a verse comedy good-humouredly ridiculing poets (inc. the author) and poetasters; produced 1738, with great success.

Lucile is the daughter of Francaleu, a rhymester who inflicts his verses on anyone he can induce to listen. Dorante woos and wins her with poems written by his friend Damis (who has been sent to Paris to study law, but has turned poet instead), confesses the fraud, and retains her heart. Francaleu dislikes Dorante, who will not listen to his verses, and wants Lucile to marry Damis, because he is a brother poet. But Damis rejects her, having pledged himself to an unknown authoress with whom he has been exchanging love verses in the *Mercure de France*. His 'authoress' proves to be Francaleu (a hit at Voltaire, who had been similarly taken in by the verses of a 'Mlle de La Vigne'). Dorante is reconciled to Francaleu and marries Lucile; Damis remains the devotee of the Muses.

Meudon, Le Curé de, v. *Rabelais.*

Meung, JEAN DE, v. *Jean de Meung.*

Meunier d'Angibault, Le, v. *Sand.*

Meyerbeer, JACQUES or GIACOMO (1791–1864), operatic composer, a German Jew, highly popular in his own country, and in Italy and France. His greatest successes— *Robert le Diable* (1831; with libretto by Scribe), *Les Huguenots* (1836), *Le Prophète* (1849)—were composed for the Paris *Opéra* and first performed there.

Meyerson, ÉMILE (1859–1933), philosopher, an anti-empiricist. His works include *Identité et réalité* (1908), a statement of his position, e.g. his view that hypothesis is a necessary preliminary of research; *De l'explication dans les sciences* (1921); *La Déduction relativiste* (1925); *Du cheminement de la pensée* (1931), examining various modern physical and mathematical conceptions of the universe.

Meysenbug, MALWIDA VON, *v. Rolland*; *Monod, G.*

Mézeray, FRANÇOIS-EUDES DE (1610–83), historian, noted for his *Histoire de France* (1643–51; down to 1598, of especial interest in its later portion). He also wrote an *Abrégé chronologique* (1667) and a treatise *De l'origine des Français* (1682). He succeeded Conrart as perpetual secretary of the **Académie*. Mazarin gave him a pension, but he lost it, under Colbert, for criticizing the tax-system.

Michaud, JOSEPH (1767–1839), publicist and historian, came to Paris (1791), took to journalism, and was more than once in trouble for his Royalist sympathies. His *Histoire des Croisades* (1812–22), a much enlarged version of a preface he wrote for Mme **Cottin's Mathilde*, did much to arouse interest in medieval history. An augmented edition (1840–1) was the fruit of a visit to the Near East, as was his interesting *Correspondance d'Orient* (1833–5). *v. Biographie universelle.*

Michaux, HENRI (1899-1984), b. in Belgium, is among the most original of modern poets. He has never belonged to any school or movement (though some critics consider that he has, in his own way, achieved the most ambitious aims of *Surrealism), and both his approach and his technique are unorthodox (as he declared in the postscript to *Mes propriétés*: 'Rien de l'imagination volontaire des professionnels. Ni thèmes, ni développements, ni construction, ni méthode.'). His writing, which vividly evokes his wide travels (S. America, India, the Far East, etc.), is marked by an acute awareness of man's isolation and vulnerability in the modern world, and by an underlying pessimism. He explores the conflict between the individual and society, between the inner and outer worlds, seeking to exorcize the perilous human condition, to fend off 'les puissances environnantes du monde hostile', through the medium of poetry— inseparable, in his case, from painting (for he is a gifted artist and often illustrates his

writings) and experiments with drugs. His works include *Qui je fus* (1927), *Écuador* (1929), *Mes propriétés* (1929), *Un Certain Plume* (1930; 'Plume' exemplifies the defenceless individual, crushed by society), *La Nuit remue* (1931), *Un Barbare en Asie* (1932), *Voyage en Grande Garabagne* (1936), *Plume* (1937), *Au pays de la Magie* (1941), *Épreuves, Exorcismes* (1945), *Ici, Poddema* (1946), *Ailleurs* (1948), *La Vie dans les plis* (1949), *Passages* (1950), *Face aux verrous* (1954), *Misérable Miracle* (1956), *L'Infini turbulent* (1957), *Connaissance par les gouffres* (1961), *L'Espace du dedans* (1966), *Les Grandes Épreuves de l'esprit* (1966), *Vers la complétude* (1967), *Émergences-résurgences* (1972), *Moments: traversées du temps* (1973). His almost invariable form is the prose poem. *v. Lyric Poetry, 4.*

Michel, FRANCISQUE-XAVIER (1809–87), historian, wrote on aspects of medieval life, e.g. *Recherches sur le commerce, la fabrication, et l'usage des étoffes de soie, d'or ...pendant le moyen âge* (1852–4), *Les Écossais en France et les Français en Écosse* (1862). He edited the newly discovered Oxford ms. of the **Chanson de Roland* (1837) and many other important medieval texts, e.g. the **Pèlerinage de Charlemagne* (1836), **Horn* (1845).

Michel, GEORGES-ÉPHRAÏM, *v. Mikhaël.*

Michel, HENRI (1907–   ), historian, an authority on the 1939–45 war; a director of research of the **Centre national de la Recherche scientifique* from 1966. His works include studies of various aspects of the **Resistance, a Bibliographie critique de la Résistance* (1964), and *La Seconde Guerre mondiale* (1968–9, 2 vols.).

Michelet, JULES (1798–1874), historian, knew poverty and toil in childhood as the son of a struggling Paris printer, who sacrificed much to educate him. In 1826 he became professor of ancient history at the **École normale supérieure*, soon devoted himself wholly to the medieval and modern periods, and embarked on his life's work, a history of France. As keeper of the *Archives nationales* (from 1831) he enjoyed easy access to source materials.

His *Histoire de France* (1833–43, 6 vols.—Celtic origins to the Renaissance; 1855–67, 11 vols.—Renaissance to the reign of Louis XVI) is the most famous example of 19th-c. romantic narrative history (*v. History*, 4), a resuscitation of the past, picturesque, subjective, at times declamatory, but of high literary value. His conception of history as the product of the geographical distribution of peoples, with consequent racial distinctions, interactions, and antagonisms, is reflected in the famous *Tableau de France* (vol. II) describing France province by province and seeing in physical and geographical features the influences responsible for variations in human character. The first six, and most famous, volumes contain a brilliant evocation of the Middle Ages (vol. II) and a moving study of Joan of Arc (vol. V).

From 1838 he held the chair of history at the *Collège de France*. His ardent democratic sympathies, increasingly evident in his lectures, led him to lay aside his *Histoire* and write *La Révolution française* (1847–53, 7 vols.), depicting the men, moods, and events of the Revolution with imaginative insight and democratic fervour; also *Du prêtre, de la femme, et de la famille* (1845; a pamphlet) and *Le Peuple* (1846). He saw his dreams of liberty realized in the 1848 *Revolution, then destroyed by the events of 1849–51. His refusal to swear allegiance to the Second Empire lost him his posts at the *Collège de France* and the *Archives*. Thereafter he lived quietly in the country, completed his *Histoire*, wrote *La *Bible de l'humanité*, and developed an interest in natural science which inspired works in a lyrical vein—*L'Oiseau* (1856), *L'Insecte* (1858), *La Mer* (1861), *La Montagne* (1868). His earlier works also include *Précis de l'histoire moderne* (1827); *Histoire romaine* (1831); *Introduction à l'histoire universelle* (1831); *Principes de la philosophie de l'histoire* (1827), a translation of *La scienza nuova* of the Italian philosopher Vico, whose theories, like those of Herder, had influenced him; *Ma jeunesse* (1844), on his

early life. Publication of his complete *Journal* (for the period 1828–74) began in 1959; it sheds new light on both the writer and the man.

Michel Strogoff, *v. Verne.*

Micromégas (1752), a tale by Voltaire, completed in Berlin (possibly begun as early as 1739). The theme—the relativity of all dimensions and man's insignificance in the universe—is derived from *Cyrano de Bergerac's *Histoire comique* and Swift's *Gulliver*.

Micromégas, 120,000 feet tall, visits Earth from the star Sirius, in company with an inhabitant of Saturn, 6,000 feet tall. They meet and talk with a party of philosophers just returning from the Polar regions (*v. Maupertuis*). They are horrified to hear of the massacres in which futile quarrels have engaged the diminutive human race; surprised to find that while the philosophers are accurately informed about the distance of the stars, etc., they can only give vague and conflicting answers when asked what is meant by 'soul' and 'spirit'; and amused to hear the theologians maintain that the universe exists for the benefit of man. In the Saturnian, who draws the wrong conclusions from what he observes, Voltaire satirized Fontenelle.

Midi, Canal du, *v. Colbert.*

Mignard, PIERRE (1610–95), painter of the reign of Louis XIV, noted for his fresco on the cupola of the *Val-de-Grâce (*La Gloire des bienheureux*: it inspired Molière's poem *La Gloire du Val-de-Grâce*) and portraits of Molière, Mme de Sévigné, Mme de Grignan, etc.

Migne, JACQUES-PAUL (1800–75), theologian, editor and publisher of the great *Patrologiae cursus completus* in over 300 vols. (Latin series 1844–55; Greek series 1856–61). *v.* also *Dictionaries*, 1845–63.

Mignet, FRANÇOIS-AUGUSTE (1796–1884), historian, came to Paris with his friend Thiers (1821), became a liberal political journalist, and helped to found *Le *National*. After the 1830 *Revolution he gave up politics for history. His works— clear, sober, and factual—include *Histoire de la Révolution française* (1824; still read); *Négociations relatives à la succession d'Espagne sous Louis XIV* (1835–42; a collection of diplomatic documents, with a notable introduction); *Marie Stuart* (1851); *Mémoires historiques* (1843), papers read before the *Académie des Sciences morales et politiques*, of which he was secretary.

Mikhaël, Éphraïm, *pseudonym of* GEORGES-ÉPHRAÏM MICHEL (1866–90), a young *Symbolist, author of poems (publ. in little reviews and collected in *L'Automne*, 1886) and verse dramas, e.g. *Briséis* (1892; with Mendès).

Milet, JACQUES, *v. Mystère*.

Milhaud, DARIUS (1892–1974), composer, one of *Les *Six*. His many works include symphonies, chamber music, operas (e.g. *Christophe Colomb*, 1928, with his friend Claudel; *Bolivar*, 1950, with Supervielle), ballets (*v. Cocteau*), incidental music for Claudel's translation of Aeschylus, settings for poems by Ronsard, Gide, Cocteau, etc. His *Notes sans musique* (1949) is an engaging autobiography.

Mille et Une Nuits, Les, *v. Galland*; *cf. Mardrus*.

Millet, JEAN-FRANÇOIS (1814–75), a painter famous for his studies of peasant life. *v. Barbizon*.

Millevoye, CHARLES-HUBERT (1782– 1816), a consumptive poet in whose work may be detected early signs of the *Romantic melancholy and response to Nature. He published *Poésies* (1800), then won literary prizes and some celebrity, notably with *Élégies* (1814; inc. two well-known poems—*La Chute des feuilles* and *Le Poète mourant*). His *Œuvres* (1814–16, 5 vols.; republ. and augm. 1865, with a preface by Sainte-Beuve) contained the *Élégies*, also *Charlemagne à Pavie*, an epic

poem; *Ballades et romances*; and translations of Virgil's *Bucolics*.

Milly, *v. Lamartine*.

Milosz, OSCAR VLADISLAS DE LUBICZ (1877–1939), poet, a Lithuanian (naturalized French in 1930) of French education; Lithuanian minister in Paris (1919–28). His works are marked by nostalgia for his native land and a mystical religiosity (his quest for Love and Truth latterly led him to engage in esoteric research and Biblical exegesis). They include poetry (*Le Poème des décadences*, 1899; *Les Sept Solitudes*, 1906; *Les Éléments*, 1911; *La Confession de Lémuel*, 1920; *Poèmes, florilège 1895–1927*, 1929); the novel *L'Amoureuse Initiation* (1910); *Miguel Mañara* (1912) and other 'mystères'; collections of Lithuanian tales and fables.

Mimi, the consumptive heroine of *Murger's *Scènes de la vie de Bohème*.

Mimi Pinson (1843), a tale by Musset. Mimi, a Parisian shop-girl (*v. Grisette*) who leads a gay, hand-to-mouth existence and pawns her one frock to help a starving friend, is a typical figure of the student *vie de Bohème*.

Minerve française, La (1818–20), an influential literary and political miscellany (publ. irregularly to evade the censorship, though it finally succumbed), f. by Béranger, B. Constant, Étienne, and others. It was liberal in spirit, seeking to spread knowledge and break down political and literary prejudices. *v. Conservateur, Le*.

Minerve littéraire, La (1820–2), a literary review hostile to the new *Romantic doctrines, edited by Mme Dufrénoy. Senancour, usually deemed a precursor of Romanticism, contributed criticism 'fort peu romantique'.

Minotaure, *v. Surrealism*.

Miomandre, Francis de, *pseudonym of* FRANCIS DURAND (1880–1959), a novelist who depicts the fantastic and the marvellous. His works include *Écrit sur de l'eau* (1908); *Le Veau d'or et la vache enragée* (1917), one of his many novels of Provence; *Direction Étoile* (1937), a fantasy with the *Métro for setting; *L'Âne de Buridan* (1946); and translations of Cervantes and Góngora.

Mirabeau, HONORÉ-GABRIEL DE RIQUETTI, COMTE DE (1749–91), son of the following, a great Revolutionary statesman and orator. As a young man he was violent and immoral, constantly in debt and in revolt against a harsh father, who more than once had him imprisoned by *lettres de cachet*. While thus confined at the Fort de Joux, near Pontarlier, he met (*c.* 1775), and later escaped to Holland with, Marie-Thérèse ('Sophie') de Ruffey, young wife of the elderly marquis de Monnier. The lovers were arrested (1777); he was sent to the prison of *Vincennes, she to a convent. While in prison, he studied prodigiously and wrote many treatises on politics and finance, notably *Des lettres de cachet et des prisons d'état* (Hamburg 1782), expounding his theories of constitutional monarchy, and *Dénonciation de l'agiotage* (1787). He also wrote almost daily to 'Sophie', letters which were a mixture of passion, literary criticism, plans for his career, tirades against his father, and hints on such matters as ante-natal care and how to grow a good head of hair; with other letters to his father and family friends, they form the *Lettres écrites du donjon de Vincennes* (1792).

In May 1789, he was returned to the *États généraux as *député du *Tiers État for Aix-en-Provence. His notoriety, and a reputation for venality, had preceded him; his manner was *gauche*, his face repulsively swollen and pitted with smallpox—but such was his political genius and power of oratory (he had a fine voice and, when he chose, great charm) that he quickly dominated the *Assemblée nationale. The day after the *États généraux* opened he began publication of his *Journal des États généraux* (*v. Courrier de Provence*). He took his stand on the need for a constitutional monarchy, with the rights of the people

fully recognized. The fact that in 1790, when deeply in debt, he was receiving money from court sources has prompted allegations that his political convictions were not entirely disinterested. His popularity gradually waned, though to the last he could still carry the day by sheer force of oratory. His death caused general consternation, and he was given a public funeral. Opinion later turned against him, and his remains were removed from the *Panthéon.

Mirabeau, VICTOR DE RIQUETTI, MARQUIS DE (1715–89), father of the above and a close friend of Vauvenargues; a member of the minor nobility of Provence. He was a combination of feudal baron and revolutionary theorist; an enemy of the *philosophes and a champion of religion, yet also an enemy of priests and financiers. He was imprisoned, then banished to his estates, for the liberal views expressed in his *Théorie de l'impôt* (1761). His *L'Ami des hommes, ou Traité de la population* (1756) and *La Philosophie rurale* (1763), treatises on political economy, held, with the *économistes, that land is the only source of wealth.

Miracle, a medieval drama or narrative in which the chief incident is the miraculous intervention of the Virgin Mary or a saint in response to the appeal of a penitent. Narrative *miracles* include those of Gautier de Coincy (*v. Religious Writings,* 1); dramatic *miracles* (which seem usually to have been performed by the *puys at solemn festivals in honour of the Virgin) include, notably, the *Miracles de Notre-Dame par personnages,* also *Rutebeuf's Miracle de Théophile* and *Bodel's *Jeu de Saint Nicolas*.

Miracles de Notre-Dame par personnages, a 14th-c. collection of 40 short dramatic *miracles* (1,000–3,000 octosyllables), composed for performance by a *puy (probably in Paris). They are on themes drawn from high, low, and clerical life, or from religious and national legend, usually painful and melodramatic in character and realistic in detail. Despite their devout nature (most include a short sermon, usually in prose), the Church is treated with great freedom and clerics (even the pope), as well as kings, are often shown in an unfavourable light.

Mirame, v. *Richelieu*.

Mirari vos, v. *Lamennais*.

Mirbeau, OCTAVE (1848–1917), author of novels, e.g. *Le Jardin des supplices* (1899), *Le Journal d'une femme de chambre* (1900), *Les Vingt et Un Jours d'un neurasthénique* (1901); a good satirical play about an unscrupulous financier, *Les Affaires sont les affaires* (1903); tales; and dramatic criticism (collected in *Gens de théâtre*, 1924).

Mirèio (1859), by Mistral, an epic of rural life, written in Provençal strophic verse; usually deemed his masterpiece and later the theme of Gounod's opera *Mireille*.

Mirèio loves Vincent, a penniless basket-maker; but her parents, wealthy farmers, strongly disapprove. Hoping for a miracle, she sets off on foot across the lonely Camargue on a pilgrimage to the little church of Les Saintes-Maries-de-la-Mer. Her parents and Vincent follow, and find her dying of exhaustion and sunstroke.

Miroir de mariage, v. *Deschamps*.

Misanthrope, Le, a 5-act verse comedy by Molière; produced 1666. It was not a great success, but was admired by persons of judgement, e.g. Boileau. Wycherley drew on it in *The Plain Dealer*.

The plot is very slight, the play being mainly a fine portrait of Alceste, an honest, cantankerous gentleman who sets himself to attack the perfidies and flatteries, even the minor hypocritical conventions, of polite society. Contrasted with him is his friend Philinte, an intelligent man who admits that society is corrupt, but is prepared to accept its conventions; also the courtier Oronte ('l'homme au sonnet'), whose bad verses draw frank comment from Alceste, and two ridiculous fops. By a stroke of Molière's genius, Alceste loves Célimène, a back-biting coquette; he is

aware of her faults, but cannot break free. The other female characters are Arsinoé, a pretended prude, who has designs on Alceste (she and Célimène have an entertaining passage of arms; III, 5), and the gentle, sincere Éliante. Though Célimène's heartlessness is exposed, Arsinoé fails to win Alceste. Finally, infuriated by unjust defeat in a lawsuit, he decides to abandon society and live in solitude. Even now, he asks Célimène to accompany him; but she cannot renounce the world, and he departs in indignation.

Misérables, Les (1862), a novel by Hugo. The story is complex and punctuated by many long historical, political, and sociological digressions, notably an account of *Waterloo, a study of the years just before 1830 and the figure of Louis-Philippe, a famous description of the Paris sewers, and pictures of Paris and its underworld. v. *Claude Gueux*.

In 1815, Jean Valjean is released after serving 19 years' penal servitude for stealing bread to feed his starving nephews. Once a slow-witted, kindly peasant, he is now an astute criminal. He tries to rob the saintly Monseigneur Myriel, and meets with such kindness that his heart begins to soften. Unfortunately, another theft, no sooner committed than regretted, renders him liable to life imprisonment.

Posing as 'Monsieur Madeleine', he sets up in business in a small town in N. France, prospers, becomes mayor, and is widely revered. He is kind to Fantine, an unfortunate woman of the town, and promises to rescue her illegitimate child Cosette from foster-parents living near Paris, the rascally innkeeper Thénardier and his wife. Then he suddenly learns that a prisoner at the local assizes is being charged in his name. After a struggle of conscience, he attends the trial and confesses his identity. He is placed in the custody of Javert, a police officer in whom devotion to duty has killed all human feeling and who has for some time suspected him. He is again sent to the convict settlement at Toulon, but soon escapes in such a way that his death is

presumed. He now fulfils his promise to
rescue the half-starved, terrorized Cosette.
They live in semi-hiding in Paris; Cosette
grows into a happy, carefree child,
believing Valjean to be her father. One
day, Javert, now in Paris, meets and
recognizes Valjean. After an exciting
chase, Valjean and Cosette escape to a
convent. He works there for some years as
gardener, while she is educated by the
nuns. Then, as 'Monsieur Fauchelevent',
he again ventures into the world. She is
now a beautiful young girl, he an
apparently venerable citizen; they live on
money he had hidden in former days.
Cosette falls in love with Marius, a young
student who has left a wealthy home to
become a democrat. When he is wounded
fighting at the barricades in the riots of 5–
6 June 1832, Valjean comes to the rescue
and drags him, unconscious, through a
manhole into the great sewer of Paris.
After a terrifying progress, he emerges, deposits the unconscious youth at his grandfather's house, and disappears. Marius's
grandfather consents to his marriage with
Cosette, believing her to be the daughter
of the respectable 'Fauchelevent'. After the
wedding, Valjean tells Marius that he is an
ex-convict and not Cosette's father.
Marius, shocked, and knowing neither the
whole story nor that he owes his life to Valjean, acquiesces in the old man's plan to
disappear gradually from their lives. Eventually, his eyes are opened and there is a
happy reconciliation; but in the meantime
Valjean, sorrowing for Cosette, has lost the
will to live, and his death follows. Other
strands in the story are Valjean's later
efforts to elude Javert, the subsequent
career of the Thénardiers and their connection with Marius, the touching episode
of the gay, heroic little guttersnipe Gavroche, the secret society of Marius's
student friends, etc.

Miserere, v. *Charité*.

Miss Harriet (1884; a reworking of *Miss
Hastings*, 1883, in *Le *Gaulois*), name-tale
of a collection by Maupassant.
    An artist on holiday at a Norman inn
finds that the only other guest is an elderly

English spinster, a grotesque creature who
gradually responds to his kindly, semi-
flirtatious teasing. Suddenly aware that
she has taken him seriously, he tells the
innkeeper at dinner that he must leave the
next day. Later, while out for a walk, he
turns from kissing a farm servant to
discern Miss Harriet running distractedly
off into the dusk. Next day her body is
found in the well.
    This collection also includes *L'Héritage*,
a cruel tale of a couple who will inherit
a fortune if they have a child within a given
time.

Mississippi Company, v. *Law*.

Mistral, FRÉDÉRIC (1830–1914),
Provençal poet, leader (with Roumanille)
of the *Félibrige*, was born in Provence of
wealthy farming stock (he owed much of
his great knowledge of Provençal custom
and legend to his mother) and, apart from
a spell in Paris (1858), spent most of his
life there. His works, in Provençal, include
Mirèio (1859); *Calendau* (1867), the
exploits of a Provençal fisherman; *Lis Isclo
d'or* (1875), lyrics; *Nerto* (1884), a
narrative poem based on a medieval
legend; *Lou Pouèmo dóu Rose* [i.e. Rhône]
(1897); *Lis Oulivado* (1912), songs of the
olive harvest. He spent many years
compiling *Le Trésor du Félibrige* (1878–
86), a dictionary of Provençal words,
proverbs, legends, etc. His writings won
him the *Prix Nobel* (1904).

Mithouard, ADRIEN (1864–1919), author
of symbolical and religious poetry (*Le
Récital mystique*, 1893; *Le Pauvre Pêcheur*,
1899; *Les Frères marcheurs*, 1902), and of
essays reflecting his belief in the cultural
importance of Western Europe, with
France as its centre (often first publ. in the
review *L'*Occident*, which he founded,
and collected in *Le Tourment de l'unité*,
1901; *Traité de l'Occident*, 1903; *Les Pas
sur la terre*, 1908; *Les Marches de
l'Occident*, 1910).

Mithridate, by Racine, a tragedy based on
the story of Mithridates VI, the great
enemy of Rome, with considerable

alteration of the historical facts; produced 1673.

The Greek maiden Monime (one of the most appealing of Racine's heroines, tender and modest, yet proud and fearless when her honour is threatened) has come to Nymphaeum in the Tauric Chersonese to marry the aged Mithridate, who has fallen in love with her. But he has been defeated by Pompey and is reported killed. His sons Pharnace and Xipharès both love Monime. Pharnace is pro-Roman in sympathies; Xipharès shares his father's hatred of Rome. On the report of Mithridate's death, Pharnace demands that Monime shall marry him forthwith. Monime, who hates him, appeals to Xipharès for protection. The brothers quarrel, at which point Mithridate appears. He is incensed by Pharnace's conduct, but remains ignorant of Xipharès's love for Monime. To test Pharnace, he expounds to his sons his great project for the invasion of Italy; Pharnace is to marry a Parthian princess and so secure the Parthian alliance. Pharnace tries to dissuade his father, is ordered to leave at once for Parthia, demurs (thus confirming his father's suspicions), is arrested, and promptly reveals that Xipharès also loves Monime. Mithridate, at first incredulous, discovers from Monime herself, by a stratagem, that this is true and that she returns Xipharès's love. She now refuses to marry the king, preferring death. Pharnace provokes a mutiny and leads a Roman force against his father. Having sent Monime poison to take, Mithridate, hard pressed by the Romans, stabs himself. Xipharès repels the Romans and rescues the dying king, who spares Monime and bestows her on Xipharès.

Mockel, ALBERT (1866–1945), a Belgian *Symbolist, founder of the review *La *Wallonie*, lived in Liège till *c.* 1890, then in Paris. His works include *Chantefable un peu naïve* (1891), a 'symphonic' poem in the *vers libre*; and *Propos de littérature* (1894), studies of Symbolist poets.

Modeste Mignon (1844; later in *La*

Comédie humaine, Scènes de la vie privée), a novel by Balzac. The year is 1829. Modeste and her blind mother remain at Le Havre with the faithful M. and Mme Dumay while M. Mignon is overseas trying to restore the family fortunes. The romantic Modeste writes under an assumed name to *Canalis, a famous poet. He is blasé and weary of anonymous admirers, but his secretary, Ernest de la Brière, uses his name on an impulse and replies. Soon love letters are exchanged. Modeste contrives to see 'Canalis', tells him her father is on his way home with a fortune, and advises him to visit M. Mignon in Paris and get his consent to their marriage. The real Canalis, learning what has happened, regrets having let slip a fortune. M. Mignon, having heard the whole story from Ernest, who would gladly marry Modeste without a dowry, invites the real and the sham Canalis to Le Havre so that she may choose for herself; a third suitor is the impoverished duc d'Hérouville, a well-meaning nonentity. Modeste, at first furious with Ernest, is soon impelled to contrast his true worth and charm with the egotism and cynical parade of Canalis. The tale ends with Canalis restored to the clutches of an elderly mistress, the duc retained as a friend, and the young lovers on the verge of wedded bliss.

Mohl, JULES (1800–76), Orientalist of German birth (later naturalized French; and *v. Clarke*), professor of Persian at the *Collège de France*, and editor and translator of Firdusi (*Le Livre des rois*, 1838–78).

Moinaux, GEORGES, *v. Courteline*.

Moïse, *v. Poèmes antiques et modernes*.

Moissy,   ALEXANDRE-GUILLAUME MOUSLIER DE, *v. Proverbe (dramatique)*.

Molé, La Conférence, a debating society in the form of a miniature parliament, f. 1832 by the statesman Louis-Mathieu Molé to train young barristers for political life. It was merged (1877) with the similar

Conférence Tocqueville to form the *Conférence Molé-Tocqueville*.

Molière, JEAN-BAPTISTE POQUELIN, *known as* (1622–73), the great comic dramatist, b. in Paris, the son of an upholsterer attached to the court; educated at the *Collège de Clermont* (where, according to modern scholarship, he was *not* a pupil of Gassendi). In 1643, with Joseph and Madeleine Béjart and others, he founded a dramatic company (the *Illustre Théâtre*) in Paris and became an actor, from 1644 under the stage-name 'Molière'. Having failed to pay its way in Paris, the company toured the provinces (1645–58). Molière wrote for it slight pieces or sketches for improvised comedies in the Italian manner; some of the titles survive and in two cases (*Le Médecin volant*; *La Jalousie du Barbouillé*) the doubtful text. His first plays of any importance were *L'*Étourdi* (1655) and *Le *Dépit amoureux* (1656). In October 1658, his company settled in Paris in the *Théâtre du Petit-Bourbon* (part of the *Louvre), granted to him by the king; in 1661, it moved to a hall in the *Palais-Royal (again by the king's favour), where it played till Molière's death. The year 1659 saw his first great comedy of manners, *Les *Précieuses ridicules*; then came *Sganarelle* (1660), *Dom Garcie de Navarre* (1661, at the Palais-Royal; a failure), *L'*École des maris* (1661), and *Les *Fâcheux* (1661, at *Vaux-le-Vicomte)— the first of his 14 *comédies-ballets* (several with music by Lulli, which were to prove highly popular at court. In 1662, he married Armande Béjart, younger sister (*not* daughter) of Madeleine Béjart; the marriage was not happy. The severe criticism levelled at *L'*École des femmes* (1662) showed that, though he had many friends and supporters (inc. the king and Boileau), his unsparing ridicule had also made him many enemies, especially rival authors; he defended himself in *La *Critique de l'École des femmes* and *L'*Impromptu de Versailles* (both 1663). 1664 saw *Le *Mariage forcé*, *La *Princesse d'Élide*, and the first performance of one of his greatest plays, *Le *Tartuffe*, which

drew a storm of protest from the devout and was prohibited (*v. Tartuffe*). *Dom Juan* (1665), also the object of violent attacks, was removed from the repertory. There followed *L'*Amour médecin* (1665); *Le *Misanthrope* (another masterpiece) and *Le *Médecin malgré lui* (both 1666); *Mélicerte*, *La *Pastorale comique*, and *Le *Sicilien—three slighter pieces (winter of 1666–7); and *Amphitryon* (1668). The company had been experiencing hard times, but this last play was a considerable success. It was followed in the same year by *L'*Avare* and *George Dandin*; *Monsieur de Pourceaugnac* (1669); *Le *Bourgeois Gentilhomme* and *Les *Amants magnifiques* (both 1670); *Psyché* (in collaboration with Corneille and Quinault), *Les *Fourberies de Scapin*, and *La *Comtesse d'Escarbagnas* (all 1671); *Les *Femmes savantes* (1672); and *Le *Malade imaginaire* (1673). While playing Argan in this last comedy, Molière was taken ill and died soon after. The clergy made difficulties about his burial, which took place at night without pomp.

He may be said to have created modern French comedy by giving it a serious basis, where there had previously been little but farces and comedies of intrigue on Italian or Spanish models. His genius lay in his great gift for observing the complexities and foibles of human nature and then presenting them in their amusing aspect— that is, short of the point where they turn to tragedy (though some of his greatest plays reach the borderline). In general, the theme of his more serious comedies is the exposure of hypocrisy and affectation in all their forms. His lighter pieces, on the other hand, shine by their gaiety and absurdity. He was thus a master of both high comedy and farce (though said by his friends to have been of a melancholy disposition). He has left a whole portrait-gallery of 17th-c. types (for, broadly speaking, in contrast to Shakespeare, he depicts types rather than individual characters): noblemen of the court and of the provinces; doctors, lawyers, merchants, and their wives (though, oddly enough, no financiers); servants and peasants. He borrowed plots and episodes from many sources, but these borrowings were no more than raw material, to be converted into a work of art. His plots are slight, his dénouements often clumsy or conventional, for he was less interested in these than in the exposition of character. He has been criticized for defects of style (often due to hasty composition), and Boileau reproached him for descending to buffoonery. English Restoration dramatists—D'Avenant, Dryden, Wycherley, Vanbrugh, etc.—drew freely on his plays. *v. Mignard.*

Molinet, JEAN (1435–1507), chronicler and **rhétoriqueur* poet, entered the service of the dukes of Burgundy and continued **Chastellain's Chronique* down to 1506. He was highly esteemed as a poet and wrote a treatise on poetry, *L'Art et science de rhétorique* (1493).

Molinier, AUGUSTE, *v. Sources de l'histoire de France.*

Molinistes, followers of Luis Molina (1535–1600), a Spanish *Jesuit, who sought to reconcile free will with the doctrines of grace and divine prescience. The *Molinistes,* who included Père de La Chaise, Louis XIV's confessor, were in conflict with the *Jansenists in the 17th c.

Molinosistes, *v. Quietism.*

Monarchie de juillet, La, *v. July Monarchy.*

Moncade, (1) in *Baron's *L'Homme à bonnes fortunes;* (2) in d'Allainval's *L'*École des bourgeois.*

Moncey, BON-ADRIEN JEANNOT DE, *v. Maréchal.*

Moncrif, FRANÇOIS-AUGUSTIN PARADIS DE (1687–1770), a witty writer, popular in his day; a friend of Voltaire and reader to the queen. He wrote comedies, tales, and *chansons; his *Aventures de Zéloïde et d'Amanzarifdine* (1714) was an Indian tale, his *Histoire des chats* (1727) an erudite pleasantry.

Mondain, Le (1736), by Voltaire, a verse satire in praise of the luxury of the age,

directed at the *Jansenists. In his *Défense du Mondain* (1737) he condemned the hypocritical censure of pleasure.

Monde, Le (Dec. 1944–   ), the 'quality' daily newspaper (publ. in the evening) which—under the direction of Hubert Beuve-Méry, followed (Dec. 1969) by Jacques Fauvet and then (July 1982) André Laurens—succeeded *Le *Temps,* inheriting its general character and high standards, and also some of its contributors. *v. Press, 9.*

Monde comme il va, Le, *v. Babouc.*

Monde où l'on s'ennuie, Le, *v. Pailleron.*

Mondory or **Montdory,** GUILLAUME DESGILBERTS, *known as* (17th c.), chief actor of the *Comédiens du Prince d'Orange,* a company associated with the young Corneille (*v. Theatres and Theatre Companies*); noted for the energy and grandeur of his acting, e.g. as Herod in Tristan l'Hermite's *Mariamne.

Monet, CLAUDE-OSCAR, *v. Impressionism.*

Money. From the 10th to the 18th c., the money of account, i.e. the terms in which values and money transactions were recorded, was entirely distinct from the money in actual circulation. The origin of the money of account (and also of the English £. *s. d.*) was the division by Charlemagne of the pound of silver or *libra argenti* (*livre*) into 20 *solidi* (*sols, sous*) and of each *solidus* into 12 *denarii* (*deniers*). From the time of the *Capetian kings, the terms *livre, sol,* and *denier* ceased to signify their original weights of bullion, and the coins actually minted were given a wide variety of names (*v.* below). Their value was, however, defined by the government of the day in terms of *livres, sols,* and *deniers* of the money of account (which retained their primitive relation to each other). This system prevailed until the Revolution.

But, after the break-up of the *Carolingian empire, the money of account was not uniform over France, and the *livre, sol,* and *denier* were variously designated *parisis, tournois, angevin,* *poitevin*, etc. The *livre tournois* (originally current in Tours), in general use in the South, and the *livre parisis*, in general use in the domains of the Capetians, were the most important. After the incorporation of the South in the royal domains, both were retained side by side, the *livre parisis* being valued one-fourth higher than the *tournois*. The *livre parisis* gradually went out of use and was abolished (1667) by Louis XIV.

The *livre* was subjected to a fairly continuous process of depreciation: from a value of perhaps some 7,000 grains of silver under Charlemagne it had fallen by the 18th c. to a value of about 70 grains. This depreciation of the *livre* in terms of precious metal was due largely to deliberate policy, since it facilitated the payment of royal debts expressed in terms of the money of account.

The distinction between currency and money of account was swept away at the Revolution. A law of 1795 introduced a decimal system of currency based on the *franc* (divided into 10 *décimes* or 100 *centimes*), a coin of 5 grammes (77 grains) of silver of a fineness of nine-tenths. Neither weight nor fineness varied much during the 19th c. v. *Cour des monnaies*; *Fiscal System*.

Monetary terms often met with in French literature include: FRANC, a gold coin with the legend 'Francorum Rex' (whence its name, thereafter used for various other coins), struck by Jean II, value a *livre tournois*. Henri III reintroduced it as a silver coin, value 20 *sols* or a *livre*. From then till the Revolution the term *franc* was used as the equivalent of *livre* of the money of account; AGNEL or MOUTON, a gold coin with the *Agnus Dei* on the obverse, first struck by Louis IX, value 10 *sols*; SALUT, a gold coin with the Angelic Salutation on the obverse, first struck by Charles VI, value 25 *sols*; ÉCU, a gold coin showing the king holding a shield, first struck by Philippe VI, value 20 *sols* or a *livre*. It was repeatedly appreciated. The silver *écu*, value 3 *livres*, dates from the 16th c.; TESTON, a silver coin issued under Louis XII (and by succeeding kings to Henri III), bearing for the first time the king's head on the

obverse (whence its name), value 10 *sols*; DENIER, a silver or base metal coin corresponding to the *denier* of the money of account. The name was also used at different times for a variety of other coins; LIARD, a small coin first struck by Charles VI, value 3 *deniers*; LOUIS or LOUIS D'OR, a gold coin with the king's head on the obverse, first struck by Louis XIII, value 20 *livres* or more before, and 20 *francs* after, the Revolution. Later, it bore Napoleon's head and was called a *napoléon*; MAILLE, a small coin worth half a *denier*; MARC, the measure adopted in the 11th c. in place of the *livre* of 12 oz. for stating weights of bullion; it contained 8 oz. (4,608 grains); PISTOLE, originally a Spanish gold coin, value the same as the *louis d'or*.

The expression 'placer l'argent au denier dix' or 'au denier douze', often met with in 17th-c. literature, means to put money out at interest at the rate of one-tenth or one-twelfth of the capital sum.

Mon frère Yves, v. *Loti*.

Monge, GASPARD (1746–1818), geometrician and physicist, a founder of the *École polytechnique and one of the first professors at the *École normale supérieure. He was with Bonaparte in Egypt and received many honours at his hands. He left memoirs.

Monime, in Racine's *Mithridate.

Moniteur de Gand, v. *Journal universel*.

Moniteur universel, La Gazette nationale, ou le, a daily paper of liberal trend, modelled on the English newspapers, f. November 1789 by C.-J. Panckoucke. It printed official documents, reported the proceedings of the *Assemblée constituante, and was noted for its political and literary articles (La Harpe was one of its first editors). Thanks to its skill in tempering its views to those of the government, it survived the Revolution. Under the *Consulat it acquired a semi-official status which it retained till 1868, when it fell into disgrace and was replaced by the *Journal officiel. Napoleon had it read aloud at mealtimes in the *lycées, to indoctrinate the young; he also found it a good medium for sounding public opinion. It published the ordonnances of July 1830 (v. Press, 5), which provoked the 1830 *Revolution. Later, it widened its literary scope, lowered its price, doubled its size, and acquired such famous contributors as Dumas père, Gautier, Mérimée, Musset, and Sainte-Beuve.

Monluc or **Montluc**, BLAISE DE LAS-SERAN-MASSENCÔME, SEIGNEUR DE (1502-77), *maréchal de France (1574), fought in nearly every war of his day, surviving five pitched battles, 17 assaults, and 11 sieges. Finally incapacitated by a wound, he wrote and constantly revised his Commentaires (1592), historical memoirs, partly intended as a manual for young officers, concerned with strategy in the field and giving a vivid picture both of the warfare of the day (notably his defence of Siena against the Imperialists, 1556) and of himself as a cool, brave, ruthless, and mildly vainglorious soldier.

Monnier, HENRI, v. Prudhomme.

Monod, GABRIEL (1844-1915), historian, founder of the *Revue historique; a keen supporter of Dreyfus. His works include, notably, Études critiques sur les sources de l'histoire mérovingienne (1872-85, 2 vols.), also Les Maîtres de l'histoire (1894), with studies of Renan, Taine, and Michelet. He married Olga Herzen, daughter of the Russian anarchist and ward of Malwida von Meysenbug (cf. Rolland). v. History, 4.

Monod, JACQUES (1910-76), biologist (Prix Nobel for medicine, 1965), professor of molecular biology at the *Collège de France from 1967. His less specialized writings include Le Hasard et la Nécessité. Essai sur la philosophie naturelle de la biologie moderne (1970).

Mon oncle Benjamin, v. Tillier.

Monseigneur, used alone, courtesy title of the dauphin from the time of Louis XIV. Cf. Madame.

Monselet, CHARLES (1825-88), a critic on Le *Figaro, a typical literary journalist of the Second Empire—witty, competent, and well read. His collected writings include Statues et statuettes contemporaines (1851), Les Oubliés et les dédaignés. Figures littéraires de la fin du XVIIIe siècle (1857; studies of Linguet, L.-S. Mercier, Grimod de la Reynière, etc.), Les Tréteaux du Sieur Charles Monselet (1859), De Montmartre à Séville (1865); also Les Vignes du Seigneur (1854), poems.

Monsieur, used alone, courtesy title of the king's eldest brother. Cf. Madame.

Monsieur Croche, anti-dilettante, v. Debussy.

Monsieur de Camors, v. Feuillet.

Monsieur de Phocas, v. Lorrain, J.

Monsieur de Pourceaugnac, a 3-act prose *comédie-ballet by Molière; produced 1669. v. Lulli.

Orgon, a Parisian, has arranged to marry his daughter Julie to Pourceaugnac, a provincial lawyer whom neither he nor Julie has met. Her lover Éraste resolves to foil the plan. When Pourceaugnac arrives from Limoges, Éraste lures him into the custody of doctors (here again ridiculed by Molière), who treat him for lunacy. Orgon is led to believe that Pourceaugnac is heavily in debt, Pourceaugnac that Julie is a hussy. Two women claim to be already married to Pourceaugnac and he is threatened with prosecution for bigamy. He is thankful to escape from Paris, and Éraste wins Julie by pretending to have rescued her from an attempt by Pourceaugnac to carry her off.

Monsieur des Lourdines, v. Chateaubriant.

Monsieur Féli, v. Lamennais.

Monsieur Le Trouhadec saisi par la débauche, v. *Romains*.

Monsieur Parent, v. *Maupassant*.

Monsieur Véto, v. *Véto*.

Monsoreau, v. *Montsoreau*.

Monstrelet, ENGUERRAND DE, v. *Froissart*.

Montagnards, Les, the extreme Revolutionary party in the *Convention*, so named because they sat on the highest benches (*cf. Marais, Le* (2); *Plaine*); led at various times by Danton, Marat, and, above all, Robespierre. They held, in opposition to the more federal policy of the *Girondins*, that complete centralization of government was necessary for the survival of the Revolution and victory in the Revolutionary wars. At first a small group, they finally numbered more than a third of the *Convention*. They overthrew the *Girondins*, directed the policy of the *Jacobins*, initiated the *Terror, and finally brought down Robespierre, but were soon victims of the *réaction thermidorienne*. v. *Revolutions*, 1; *Commune*, 1.

Montaigne, MICHEL EYQUEM DE (1533–92), essayist, b. at the Château de Montaigne in Périgord, son of Pierre Eyquem, a merchant and mayor of Bordeaux. He learnt Latin as a child, before French. He was sent to the *Collège de Guyenne*, in Bordeaux, but profited little (his father being opposed to any constraint in his education), though he acted in the Latin plays of Buchanan and other professors. He became a magistrate of the *parlement* of Bordeaux and a close friend of *La Boétie. After his father's death (1568), he retired to his *château* and soon began work (1572) on his *Essais*; the first two books appeared in 1580. He then travelled, partly in search of health (he suffered from stone), in Germany and Italy; his journal of these travels has been published. Elected mayor of Bordeaux (1581–5) at a time of religious strife (v. *Ligue, La*), he proved moderate and wise.

He supported the royal authority and the cause of Henri de Navarre, but without fanaticism, and was sought as an intermediary by both parties. He has been reproached—though not by contemporaries—for refusing, on relinquishing office, to go to plague-stricken Bordeaux to surrender the keys of the city, as custom required. A much enlarged edition of bks. I and II of the *Essais*, together with bk. III, appeared in 1588. Until his death he continued to annotate and amplify a copy of this edition. There have since been over 100 editions of the *Essais* (inc. the early ed. by his adopted daughter Marie de Gournay and an ed. of his annotated 1588 text).

The work began as a kind of commonplace book in which, reading and meditating in his library (described in III, 3), he noted and commented on memorable maxims and examples he found in the classics (esp. Plutarch; v. *Amyot*). It developed into a collection of studies of the human mind, 'vain, divers, et ondoyant', in all its manifestations, as gathered from self-examination and from observation of the opinions and prejudices of his contemporaries and of writers of all nations and ages. Examined in chronological order, his writings reveal a striking evolution in his thought. At first, inspired by Seneca and Cato of Utica, he aims at a stoical indifference to death and misfortune. He then passes through a phase of scepticism. He had translated for his father the *Theologia naturalis* of Raymond of Sebonde (a 15th-c. Spanish professor of theology and medicine at Toulouse), a work claiming that it is possible for the human reason to discover the contents of the Christian revelation in nature alone. Now, in the strange guise of an *Apologie de Raimond Sebond* (II, 12), he demonstrates, by a great mass of instances drawn from all sources, the utter fallibility of the human mind and its inability to know anything with certainty. He concludes that judgement must be suspended, and adopts the motto 'Que sais-je?' (1576). From this Pyrrhonian attitude he finally proceeds to a personal philosophy of an epicurean tendency, based on his own experience of life; virtue now consists in an orderly and harmonious exercise of all the human faculties. In religion he may be described as a tolerant deist, though outwardly a Catholic. He has left a vivid picture of himself: he was, he says, short, inactive, gay, talkative (in a loud voice), and frank, without memory, a dreamer, a vagabond, averse to all obligations, incontinent, unsuited for marriage or paternity.

Though capable of lofty eloquence, he usually writes in an easy, familiar style and in vigorous, racy language, with freshness and gaiety and many apposite, amusing, and memorable illustrations, passing abruptly from idea to idea and often digressing. The content of a chapter has often little connection with its title. An amusing example of his lack of method is *Des coches* (III, 6). His many serious and instructive essays include *De la physionomie* (III, 12), on consolation in public calamities; *De l'institution des enfants* (I, 25), on education; *Du repentir* (III, 2), on repentance; *De l'art de conférer* (III, 8), on conversation; *Que philosopher c'est apprendre à mourir* (I, 19), on the thought of death.

Though regarded with suspicion by the Church and placed on the Index (1676), his work won the admiration of his own and succeeding generations and was the basis of the philosophical expansion of the 17th c. Translated into English by Florio (1603) and Charles Cotton (1685), it was quoted by Shakespeare (in *The Tempest*) and drawn on by Webster, Marston, Burton, and Browne. It inspired the English essay, as developed by Bacon, Cowley, Temple, and Dryden.

Montaigu, Collège de, *v. Collège de Montaigu.*

Montalembert, CHARLES-FORBES-RENÉ, COMTE DE (1810–70), publicist, historian, and orator, b. in London of a Scots mother and an *émigré* father (later ambassador in Sweden); a disciple of Lamennais, and associated with him and Lacordaire in a fight for liberal Catholicism. Like Lacordaire, he remained in the Church when Lamennais left it and he was later a leader of the militant Catholics. His works include a *Vie de sainte Élisabeth de Hongrie* (1836) and an *Histoire des moines d'Occident depuis saint Benoît jusqu'à saint Bernard* (1860–77, 7 vols.).

Montalte, Louis de, *v. Pascal.*

Montargis, Chien de, *v. Chien de Montargis.*

Montausier, CHARLES DE SAINTE-MAURE, DUC DE (1610–90), a man of upright character who, having served king (Louis XIV) and country, was chosen to supervise the upbringing of the dauphin. After 14 years' courtship, he married Julie d'Angennes (*v. Guirlande de Julie*). He may have inspired Alceste in Molière's Le *Misanthrope.*

Montbéliard, PHILIBERT GUÉNEAU DE, *v. Buffon.*

Montcalm de Saint-Véran, LOUIS-JOSEPH, MARQUIS DE (1712–59), general, a great figure in French colonial history. Sent to defend French Canada against the British (1756), he had some initial success, notably his victory (8 July 1758) over a much larger British force under Abercrombie at Fort Carillon (a point of great strategic importance; later Fort Ticonderoga, New York State)—an event often mentioned in early 19th-c. French-Canadian patriotic literature. Soon, however, the British strengthened their forces and launched the series of attacks which led to the conquest of Canada. In 1759, Montcalm was besieged in Quebec by General Wolfe. In the battle of the Heights of Abraham (12 Sept.), which ended the siege, Wolfe was killed outright, Montcalm mortally wounded. Quebec surrendered a few days later.

Montchrétien, ANTOINE DE (c. 1575–1621), dramatist and economist, a man of active intelligence and turbulent spirit. In the course of a singular career, he was left for dead in a youthful brawl and obtained a large indemnity, was obliged to leave France as the result of a duel, visited England and Holland and studied their industries and commerce, founded steelworks in France, and was killed fighting in the *Huguenot rising of 1621. In his earlier years, he published six tragedies (retaining the chorus, which gave scope for his marked lyrical gifts): *Sophonisbe (1596); La Reine d'Écosse (or L'Écossaise; on the death of Mary Stuart), Les Lacènes (on the fortitude of the Spartan king Cleomenes, prisoner of Ptolemy), David (the story of David and Bathsheba), and Aman (the story of Haman, Esther, and Ahasuerus)—all published 1601, with the long poem Susane, ou la Chasteté (the story of Susanna and the elders); Hector (1604); also a prose and verse Bergerie (1601), an early *pastoral play. These he later followed with a remarkable Traité de l'économie politique (1615; he is said to have coined the term économie politique), which inspired Richelieu and Colbert. Drawing some of his ideas from earlier writers, notably Bodin, he proceeds from a detailed study of industries and trades (e.g. the manufacture of hats; the cod and herring fisheries) to general rules of policy, showing himself a retaliatory protectionist in the situation in which France then found herself, but with aspirations to free trade.

Mont des oliviers, Le (1864, in Les Destinées), by Vigny, a poem on the Agony in the Garden; written 1843, except for the conclusion, added in 1863 by Vigny at his most bitterly stoical.

Montdory, v. Mondory.

Monte-Cristo, v. Comte de Monte-Cristo, Le.

Montégut, ÉMILE (1825–95), a critic on the *Revue des Deux Mondes (from 1847) and other reviews, noted for his solid, well-informed articles on English, American, and, later, contemporary French writers. His works include Libres Opinions morales

et historiques (1858), Essais sur la littérature anglaise (1883), Nos morts contemporains (1884), Écrivains modernes de l'Angleterre (1885–92), Mélanges critiques (1887); also translations of Emerson, Macaulay, and Shakespeare. v. Foreign Influences, 4.

Montespan, FRANÇOISE-ATHÉNAÏS DE ROCHECHOUART, MARQUISE DE (1640–1707), mistress of Louis XIV after La Vallière; a woman of taste, who encouraged Quinault, Racine, and Boileau. Her sons by the king were the duc du *Maine and the comte de Toulouse; v. also Antin.

Montesquieu, CHARLES DE SECONDAT, BARON DE (1689–1755), political philosopher, b. at the Château de la Brède, near Bordeaux, of a good Guyenne family; a kindly man of simple habits, devoted to his family, a good citizen not only of France but of the world. He entered the magistrature, inherited a fortune (1716), and in the same year was admitted to the Académie de Bordeaux, where he gave various dissertations on political and scientific subjects. His first important work was the *Lettres persanes (publ. anon. 1721). In the following years, he published some political treatises and slight political tales, e.g. the Dialogue de Sylla et d'Eucrate (1722; Sulla, after his surrender of the dictatorship, defends his past tyranny and proscriptions), and prose poems, e.g. Le Temple de Gnide (1725; purporting to be translated from a Greek work—the narrator describes the temple of Aphrodite at Cnidos and its frequenters, a terrifying visit to the cave of Jealousy, and the restoring effect of the temple of Bacchus). In 1727, he was admitted to the *Académie; he was also a member of the *Club de l'Entresol. He travelled about Europe, part of the time with Lord Chesterfield, spent the years 1729–31 in England, then settled at La Brède, and in 1734 published his *Considérations sur les causes de la grandeur des Romains et de leur décadence. De l'*esprit des lois, his greatest work, appeared, at first anonymously, in 1748; the subject had, he tells us, interested him since he first studied law and he had devoted 20 years to the book. His defence of it, *Défense de l'Esprit des lois* (1750), contains (in its third part) some of his best writing. Failing eyesight then restricted his output. An unfinished *Essai sur le goût dans les choses de la nature et de l'art* appeared as the article *Goût* in the *Encyclopédie*. His works reflect his great learning; his usual style is sober and grave, with occasional affectation.

Montesquiou (Montesquiou-Fezen-sac), ROBERT, COMTE DE (1855–1921), a member of an old aristocratic family, poet and aesthete, now chiefly of interest for his association and correspondence with Proust and because his luxurious habits and grotesque mannerisms—the subject of many anecdotes—are said to have inspired Proust's *Charlus and Huysmans's Des Esseintes (v. A rebours)*. He wrote precious and elaborately symbolical poetry (*Les Chauves-Souris*, 1892; *Le Chef des odeurs suaves*, 1893; *Les Hortensias bleus*, 1896; *Les Perles rouges*, 1899), essays (*Roseaux pensants*, 1897; *Autels privilégiés*, 1898), memoirs (*Les Pas effacés*, 1923, 3 vols.), etc.

Montfaucon, in the Middle Ages, a place of execution outside the walls of Paris.

Montfaucon, BERNARD DE (1655–1741), scholar, soldiered under Turenne in Germany, then became a *Maurist, devoting himself to the study of manuscripts in monastic libraries in France and Italy. His chief work, *Palaeographia graeca* (1708), did for the science of Greek palaeography what *Mabillon's *De re diplomatica* had done for Latin palaeography.

Montfleury, (1) ZACHARIE JACOB, *known as* (1600–67), an actor of the company of the *Hôtel de Bourgogne*, ridiculed in Molière's *L'*Impromptu de Versailles* and ordered off the stage by Cyrano in Rostand's *Cyrano de Bergerac* (an incident which may have occurred in real life); (2) his son ANTOINE JACOB, *known as* (1640–85), actor and dramatist, rival and

enemy of Molière. His comedies include, notably, *L'*École des jaloux* (1664) and *La *Femme juge et partie* (1669); also *La Fille capitaine* (1672), *La Dame médecin* (1678).

Montgolfier, JOSEPH (1740–1810) and his brother ÉTIENNE (1745–99), inventors of the hot-air balloon, first successfully used to carry a passenger in 1783.

Montherlant, HENRY DE (1896–1972), novelist, essayist, and dramatist (a member of the *Académie, 1961); a controversial figure—admired as a passionate moralist with a gift for irony and a fine prose style, attacked for his arrogant egotism, attitudinizing, and Fascist leanings. His earlier works exalt war and manly sports (e.g. bull-fighting) and advocate a haughty nobility of spirit (he always felt a spiritual affinity with Renaissance Spain), e.g. *Le Songe* (1922) and *Les Bestiaires* (1926), novels; *Aux fontaines du désir* (1927), *Mors et vita* (1932), *Service inutile* (1935), essays. His later novels include *Les Célibataires* (1934), a realistic study of three unpleasing bachelor brothers; the sensational series (1936–9) *Les Jeunes Filles*, *Pitié pour les femmes*, *Le Démon du bien*, *Les Lépreuses*, depicting a famous and sensual novelist (a projection of the author) beset by obstinately adoring women; *Le Chaos et la nuit* (1963); *Les Garçons* (1969); *Un Assassin est mon maître* (1971). In later life, he enhanced his reputation with powerful dramas on historical and/or religious themes, e.g. *La Reine morte* (1942; *v. Inès de Castro*), *Malatesta* (1946), *Le Maître de Santiago* (1947), *La Ville dont le Prince est un enfant* (1951), *Port-Royal* (1954; *v. Arnauld, Arnauld d'Andilly* (5)), *Brocéliande* (1956), *Don Juan* (1958), *Le Cardinal d'Espagne* (1960), *La Guerre civile* (1965). He died by his own hand.

Montholon, CHARLES-TRISTAN, COMTE DE (1783–1853), one of Napoleon's generals, at his side during the Hundred Days and for the whole period of his exile on St. Helena. He published *Mémoires pour servir à l'histoire de France sous Napoléon* (1823; in collaboration with

Gourgaud), based on notes dictated by Napoleon; also *Récits de la captivité de Napoléon à Sainte-Hélène* (1847, 2 vols.).

Montijo, MARIA KIRKPATRICK Y GREVIGNÉ, COMTESSE DE (1794–1879), mother of the empress Eugénie. She was long a friend of Mérimée; their correspondence (1930, 2 vols.) throws light on the Spanish and French social and political scene in the years 1839–70.

Montjoie or **Montjoie-Saint-Denis,** the medieval battle-cry of the French, already used in the *Chanson de Roland ('Munjoie escriet, c'est l'enseigne Carlun').

Montluc, v. Monluc.

Montmartre (possibly from *Mons martyrum*; v. Denis, St.), a district in the north of Paris, a centre of Bohemian artist life (evoked by Carco, Dorgelès, Mac Orlan, etc.) and of artistic and literary cafés and cabarets.

Montmorency, ANNE DE, v. Connétable.

Mont-Oriol, v. Maupassant.

Montparnasse, a district in Paris on the left (south) bank of the Seine, a centre for artists and cabaret life (*cf.* *Montmartre, in the north). In the 17th c., it was a *butte*, or small hill, outside the walls, where the students used to declaim their verses, and which they named *Butte du Mont Parnasse*.

Montpensier, LOUISE D'ORLÉANS, DUCHESSE DE (1627–93), 'la Grande Mademoiselle', daughter of Gaston d'*Orléans. She actively supported Condé in the second *Fronde, showing bravery and decision. She had aspired to marry a reigning prince (e.g. Charles II or the Emperor), but finally, at 42, fell in love with a Gascon adventurer (v. Lauzun, A. N. de Caumont, duc de). She left interesting and vivacious *Mémoires* and published two mediocre romances (*La Relation de l'île imaginaire*; *La Princesse de Paphlagonie*) under the name of *Segrais.

Montre, v. Basoche.

Montreux, v. Nicolas de Montreux.

Mont-Saint-Michel, a rocky island crowned by a monastery, now connected by a mole to the north coast of France, near Avranches. It held out for 70 years against English attacks in the Hundred Years War (v. Du Guesclin). Here Louis XI instituted the Order of Knights of Saint-Michel.

Montsoreau, CHARLES DE CHAMBES, COMTE DE (1549–1619), the assassin of Bussy d'Amboise, who had seduced his wife. The story is the theme of *Dumas *père*'s La Dame de Monsoreau.

Montyon, JEAN-BAPTISTE-ANTOINE, BARON DE (1733–1820), philanthropist, founded prizes for edifying works and for acts of virtue (1782). v. Prix littéraires.

Moralité, in the later Middle Ages, a form of drama in which personified abstractions were used to inculcate a moral teaching; not always distinguishable from the *farce, because of the frequent introduction of comic elements and burlesque scenes from everyday life. A typical edifying *moralité* is *Bien-avisé et Mal-avisé*. Bien-avisé and Mal-avisé set out together, but soon separate. Bien-avisé follows Reason, who leads him to Faith, whence he passes on to meet Contrition, Confession, Prayer, Chastity, etc., and finally, in the care of Good-End, reaches Heaven. Mal-avisé's path is dogged by Laziness, Debauchery, Despair, etc., and Evil-End leads him to Hell. Others of this type include the very long *L'Homme juste et l'homme mondain*; *L'Homme pécheur* (a young man yields to all the vices, then repents and dies in a state of grace); *La Condamnation de Banquet* (Gout, Dropsy, etc., fall on the feasters); *Charité*; *Les Blasphémateurs*. Sometimes the theme is a simple parable, e.g. the Prodigal Son. For satirical *moralités* v. Coquillart; Baude; Gringore; La Vigne.

Moralités légendaires, Les, v. Laforgue.

Morand, PAUL (1888–1976), novelist and

career diplomat, a member of the *Académie* (1968), made his name with impressionistic studies of night life in Europe in the 1920s. His works include *Tendres Stocks* (1921; with a preface by Proust), *Ouvert la nuit* (1922), *Fermé la nuit* (1923), *La Folle amoureuse* (1956), *Fin de siècle* (1957), tales; *Lewis et Irène* (1924), *Le Flagellant de Séville* (1951), novels; *Journal d'un attaché d'ambassade* (1947), *Bains de mer, bains de rêve* (1960), reminiscences; *Londres* (1933) and *Le Nouveau Londres* (1963), portraits by an amused observer of the British way of life.

Moréas, Jean, *pseudonym of* IANNIS PAPADIAMANTOPOULOS (1856–1910), poet, of Greek birth, but wholly French by culture and tastes and resident in Paris after 1880. At first an ardent *Symbolist, he wrote for little reviews and was known in such groups as the *Hydropathes* and *Zutistes*. The sonnets and lyrics of *Les Syrtes* (1884), showing the influence of Verlaine, and *Les Cantilènes* (1886), showing the Symbolist love of medieval and archaic terms, belong to this phase; *v.* also *Thé chez Miranda, Le.* After a third collection, *Le Pèlerin passionné* (1891), he moved away from Symbolism and, with Maurras and Raynaud as disciples, launched the *École romane*. His *Poèmes et sylves, 1886–1896* (1907), including the well-known *Énone au clair visage* and *Ériphyle*, reflect this phase and show him abandoning the *vers libre*, which he had earlier used with great skill. His finest poems, notably the lyrics of *Les Stances* (1899, bks. I–II; 1901, bks. III–VI; 1920, bk. VII), belong to his final phase, when he became on the whole soberly classical in theme, form, and style.

Moreau, Frédéric, in Flaubert's *L'*Éducation sentimentale*.

Moreau, GUSTAVE (1826–98), a painter much admired by *Symbolists. His works, 'désespérées et érudites', moved Des Esseintes (in Huysmans's *A rebours*) to 'longs transports... jusqu'au fond des entrailles'. They can be seen at the *Musée Gustave Moreau*, once his house in Paris.

Moreau, HÉGÉSIPPE (1810–38), minor *Romantic poet. His best poems (in *Le Myosotis*, 1838) are of country life; the bitter *Ode à la faim* is a reminder that his dissipated life ended in the workhouse. He also wrote *Contes à ma sœur* (1851; prose).

Moreau, JEAN-VICTOR (1763–1813), a famous general in the Revolutionary armies, victor of *Hohenlinden. Later exiled for his part in Royalist plots (1804) against Napoleon, he went to America, returned (1813) to fight for Russia against France, and was killed in action.

Morée, *Livre de la conqueste de la princée de la*, a chronicle, by a Frenchman living in the Morea, of the French principality set up there as a result of the 4th Crusade. It covers the years 1204–1305 and sheds light on the life of the French knights established in Greece.

Morellet, ANDRÉ, ABBÉ (1727–1819), man of letters and *philosophe*, wrote articles (mainly on theology and metaphysics) for the *Encyclopédie*, visited Italy in early life and later England (1772, as the guest of Lord Shelburne). A member of the *Académie* from 1785, he worked steadily on its dictionary (*v. Dictionaries*, 1694) and, when the *Académie* was suppressed during the Revolution, contrived to preserve the copy of a new edition, then ready for the printer. He was ruined by the Revolution and had to subsist on literary hack work, e.g. translating English novels. His works include the witty, polemical *Petit Écrit sur une matière intéressante: La Tolérance* (1756); *Manuel des inquisiteurs* (1762), a digest of the *Directorium inquisitorum* of Nicolas Eymeric (14th-c. inquisitor-general of Aragon), a book that had deeply shocked him when he came on it in an Italian library; *Traité sur les délits et les peines* (1765; a trans. of Cesare Beccaria's *Trattato dei delitti e delle pene*, on penal reform, 1764), a work much read by the *Encyclopédistes* and approved by Voltaire; *Mélanges de littérature et de philosophie au XVIIIᵉ siècle* (1818, 4 vols.), his own selection of his best writings. His *Mémoires* (1822, 2 vols.), of interest as a study of France before and during the Revolution, reveal a dry yet often engagingly light-hearted philosopher, who finds compensation for his many misfortunes in 'le bonheur inestimable... d'avoir été toute ma vie un particulier obscur... le maître de mes travaux, de mes loisirs'.

Morelly, an 18th-c. political theorist of whose life nothing is known. In two audacious works—*Naufrage des îles flottantes, ou la Basiliade du célèbre Pilpai* (1753) and *Le Code de la Nature* (1755)— he anticipates J.-J. Rousseau, and to some extent Babeuf and Fourier, by contending that man is naturally good and that private property and the errors of legislators are the root of all evil. In the first work (a prose epic, purporting to be a translation of a poem by Bidpai), the 'îles flottantes' are the prejudices that prevent man's happiness, and the 'Basiliade' is the reign of the philosopher-king who restores the laws of nature in his realm. In the second work Morelly sets out his own code of laws for a model society.

Moreri, LOUIS, *v. Dictionaries*, 1674.

Morice, CHARLES (1861–1919), an early *Symbolist poet and a theorist of Symbolism, a friend of Verlaine and Mallarmé. His *La Littérature de tout à l'heure* (1889) stressed the need for vagueness in poetry. *v. Gauguin.*

Morin, BENOÎT, *v. Dictionaries*, 1802.

Morin, SIMON (*c.* 1622–63), a mystic with a large following who believed that he was Christ reincarnated and called himself 'le Fils de l'Homme'. He was twice confined in the *Bastille*, failed to abide by his recantations, and was finally arrested (a matter in which Desmarets de Saint-Sorlin had some part) and burnt.

Mornay, *v. Duplessis-Mornay.*

Morny, CHARLES - AUGUSTE - LOUIS- JOSEPH, DUC DE (1811–65), natural son of Queen Hortense (mother of Napoleon III;

v. Bonaparte Family (5)) and the comte de Flahaut (son of Mme de Souza), led the world of fashion (*c.* 1840), helped to engineer his half-brother's *coup d'état* of 1851, and became a brilliant political figure of the Second Empire (ambassador in Russia, 1856–7), still a dandy and also, less reputably, a speculator. He figures prominently in A. Daudet's *Le *Nabab.*

Mort Artu, *v. Perceval*; *Lancelot.*

Mort de César, La, (1) *v. Grévin, J.*; (2) *v. Voltaire*, 1.

Mort de Pompée, La, a tragedy by Corneille; produced in the winter of 1642– 3. The theme, drawn in part from Lucan's *Pharsalia*, is the assassination of Pompey (following his defeat by Caesar at Pharsalia) by order of Ptolemy of Egypt.

Mort de quelqu'un, *v. Romains.*

Mort de Socrate, La, *v. Lamartine.*

Mort du loup, La (1843, in the *Revue des Deux Mondes*; 1864, in *Les Destinées*), a poem by Vigny; written 1838. Man should learn from the wolf which, when cornered by the huntsmen, licks its wounds and dies silently: 'Seul le silence est grand; tout le reste est faiblesse.'

Mort d'un chêne, La, *v. Laprade.*

Mortier, ÉDOUARD-ADOLPHE-CASIMIR- JOSEPH, *v. Maréchal.*

Mortsauf, Mme de, in Balzac's *Le *Lys dans la vallée.*

Morts sans sépulture, *v. Sartre.*

Mosaïque, *v. Mérimée.*

Mosca, Count, in Stendhal's *La *Chartreuse de Parme.*

Moscow, The Retreat from. After *Borodino, Napoleon occupied Moscow (14 Sept. 1812). It was almost deserted, and the next day it was swept by a great fire said to have been started by the Russians before they left. Further disconcerted by their refusal to negotiate, Napoleon hesitated for five weeks, then abandoned his plan to winter in Moscow and ordered a retreat. The army set out (19 Oct.), with a fortnight's provisions, across devastated country; starvation, and the extreme cold, took a fearful toll. Arriving at last at the river Beresina, they found themselves hemmed in by three Russian armies, and unable to cross because a sudden thaw had loosened the ice. After 24 hours' labour, the pontoneers managed to construct two narrow bridges, and men, horses, and vehicles fought their way across in a confused mass under Russian fire, the more fortunate reaching the other bank over the bodies of their comrades (25-9 Nov.). Napoleon started the campaign with some 400,000 men; of these he lost 380,000, 90,000 in the retreat from Moscow alone. It is memorably described in Tolstoy's *War and Peace*. Old Goguelat's account in Balzac's *Le *Médecin de campagne* also deserves mention.

Moskova, Bataille de la, *v. Borodino.*

Motin, PIERRE (1566–1613), poet, a disciple and friend of M. Régnier, noted in his day for his amorous and licentious verse (publ. in *Le *Parnasse satirique*, *Le Cabinet satirique*, etc.). Boileau ridiculed him (*L'*Art poétique*, IV, 3940).

Motteville, FRANÇOISE BERTAUT, MME DE (1621–89), niece of Bertaut, was for 22 years lady-in-waiting and friend of Anne d'Autriche and also well acquainted with Henrietta Maria of England. Her memoirs of the period of Anne's regency and Mazarin's power include a valuable account of the *Fronde*, and passages on the civil war in England and the exiled Stuarts.

Mouches, Les, *v. Sartre.*

Mounet-Sully, JEAN-SULLY MOUNET, *known as* (1841–1916), a famous tragic actor at the *Comédie-Française*. His brother PAUL (1847–1922) also acted there.

Mounier, EMMANUEL (1905–50), philosopher, completed his studies at the *Sorbonne (*agrégation* in philosophy, 1928), but in 1932 turned aside from an academic career to launch and thereafter lead a movement based on a moral and social philosophy known as *Personnalisme*, with the political and literary review *Esprit* as its organ. *Personnalisme*, which was Christian (but not denominational), broadly left-wing, and always more a state of mind than a coherent system, is sometimes compared with *Existentialism and Marxism as one of the three modern philosophies of existence. It had its origin in the reaction of many young men of the inter-war generation against the spiritual and political apathy of an age which seemed to them menaced by the total collapse of civilization. They sought to combat this apathy by a new approach to the problems of existence, one less exclusively dependent on moral or economic principles than those propounded by theologians and academics, and more concrete, because based on the individual's *sense of his responsibility* as a being free to choose and to act in a universe which he takes for granted. As Christians of the Left, they were bent on dissociating Christianity (and, in particular, the Roman Catholic Church) from the 'désordre établi' of its liaison with the Right. Mounier himself was much influenced by Péguy, and for his followers he was in many ways the Péguy of their generation. During the 1939–45 war he was imprisoned for a time by the Vichy government and *Esprit*, now a focus of the intellectual *Resistance, was suppressed (1941). After the Liberation, when *Personnalisme* (already widely established in France by 1939) spread to other European countries, Mounier emerged for a time as the 'spiritus rector des chrétiens engagés'. Those closely associated with the movement have included Rougemont, Béguin, P.-H. Simon, Cayrol, and the philosophers Jean Lacroix and Paul Ricœur. Its doctrines may be studied in Mounier's works (e.g. *La Révolution personnaliste et communautaire*, 1935; *Traité du caractère*,

1946; *Le Personnalisme*, 1949), in *Mounier et sa génération. Lettres, carnets, et inédits* (1956), and in the review *Esprit*, where the debate continues.

Mousket, PHILIPPE, *v. History*, 1.

Mousnier, ROLAND (1907–   ), historian, professor at the *Sorbonne from 1955. His works include *La Vénalité des offices sous Henri IV et Louis XIII* (no date; 2nd ed. 1971); vol. IV (1953; 5th ed. 1967) and, with Labrousse, vol. V (1953; 5th ed. 1966), covering together the 16th, 17th, and 18th cs., in the *Histoire générale des civilisations*; *Progrès scientifique et technique au XVIIIᵉ siècle* (1958); *L'Assassinat d'Henri IV* (1964); *Fureurs paysannes. Les Paysans dans les révoltes du XVIIᵉ siècle (France, Russie, Chine)* (1968); *La Plume, la faucille, et le marteau. Institutions et société en France du Moyen Âge à la Révolution* (1970); *Les Institutions de la France sous la monarchie absolue* (vol. I, 1974).

Mouton Blanc, Le, in the 17th c., a tavern in Paris frequented by writers.

Moyen de parvenir, Le, *v. Béroalde.*

M.R.P., the *Mouvement républicain populaire* (f. Nov. 1944 by a group inc. Maurice Schumann and Georges Bidault), the party of the Christian Democrats. Bidault and others took office under de Gaulle in 1944, and Bidault replaced him as premier in 1946.

Mugnier, ARTHUR, ABBÉ (1853–1944), a Benedictine, long priest of Sainte-Clotilde, a church in the fashionable Faubourg Saint-Germain in Paris; the wise and learned friend and spiritual adviser of many late 19th- and early 20th-c. writers, in some cases responsible for their conversion, or return, to the Church. He greatly influenced Huysmans (the abbé Gevresin, spiritual director of Durtal in *En route*, is drawn from Mugnier).

Mule du Pape, La (1866, one of the *Lettres de mon moulin*), the most famous of A. Daudet's tales of Provence. There is, he says, a saying 'Comme la mule du Pape qui garda sept ans son coup de pied', and he has consulted his 'bibliothèque des cigales' for the explanation. A small boy, a born *arriviste*, curried favour with the good Pope Boniface of Avignon by lavishing endearments in public on the pope's beloved mule, though in private he tormented it unmercifully. He was sent to Rome for his education, and the mule bided its time. On his return, he got himself a fine post in the pope's retinue, and turned up confident and bedecked for the ceremony of his installation. As he went to the dais, he stopped before his old 'friend' the mule, who with one mighty kick let fly the stored-up rancour of seven years.

Mule sans frein, La, a 13th-c. *roman breton* (1,136 ll.), an episode in the life of *Gauvain. A damsel arrives at Arthur's court on a mule with a head-stall but no bit. She tells the king she has been robbed of the bit; she will give herself to any knight who recovers it, and will lend her mule as guide. Keu (Kay) sets out, but soon returns terrified by the perils involved. Gauvain takes his place and by his courage and loyalty achieves the quest.

Muller, CHARLES, and **Reboux**, PAUL, *v. Pastiche.*

Multiple Splendeur, La, *v. Verhaeren.*

Murat, AMÉLIE (1888–1940), author of love and nature poems—*D'un cœur fervent* (1909), *Bucoliques d'été* (1920), *Le Sanglot d'Ève* (1923), *Chants de minuit* (1927), etc.

Murat, JOACHIM, *v. Maréchal.*

Muret, MARC-ANTOINE DE, in Latin MURETUS (1526–85), a learned humanist of the *Renaissance, taught the classics in Paris (to Grévin, S. de Sainte-Marthe, and Vauquelin de la Fresnaye), Bordeaux (to Montaigne), and elsewhere; edited Latin authors; and wrote letters, orations, a frigid *tragedy on the classical model (*Julius Caesar tragoedia*, 1544) in elegant Latin, and a commentary on *Ronsard's

Amours (explaining the mythological allusions).

Murger, HENRY (1822–61), b. in Paris, had a scanty education, then—encouraged by a tenant in the building where his father, a German, was *concierge*—tried his hand at painting and literature. He wrote some verse (collected in *Poésies*, 1855), but his talent was for poeticized, sentimental descriptions of humble life or of the rackety, precarious existence of the artists, writers (like himself), and *grisettes* who people his well-known *Scènes de la vie de Bohème* (1848, serialized in *Le *Corsaire*; 1851, in book form; dramatized 1849; the theme of Puccini's opera *La Bohème*, 1896); *v. Mimi*; *Musette*. His other works, usually variations on the same theme, include *Les Buveurs d'eau* (1854); *Scènes de campagne* (1857); *Le Bonhomme Jadis* (1852), a one-act comedy.

Muscadins, a name for the gilded youth (dandies, perfumed with musk) active in anti-*Jacobin* demonstrations during the *réaction thermidorienne* (1794–5; *v. Revolutions*, 1). *Cf. Incroyables*; *Merveilleuses*.

Muse du département, La, *v. Comédie humaine, La* (*Scènes de la vie de province*).

Musée Carnavalet, the *Musée historique de la ville de Paris*, created 1866, when the municipality of Paris bought the fine Renaissance Hôtel Carnavalet (near the former *Place Royale; the home of Mme de Sévigné, 1677–96) to house a most interesting and evocative collection of portraits, prints, porcelain, *bibelots*, costumes, etc., notably of the Revolution and Empire periods.

Musée Condé, *v. Chantilly*.

Musée Grévin, a museum of waxworks in Paris, created 1882 on the model of Mme Tussaud's in London by Alfred Grévin (1827–92), a caricaturist noted for gay sketches of Parisian life.

Muse française, La (1823–4), a short-lived but famous literary review associated with the early *Romantics, f. by Guiraud, Soumet, Émile Deschamps, and younger writers, including Hugo and Vigny. It published many of the Romantic manifestos and made a point of fostering new talent. Nearly all the great Romantics wrote for it.

Muse historique, La, *v. Press*, 1.

Muset, COLIN, *v. Colin Muset*.

Musette, in *Murger's *Scènes de la vie de Bohème*. She sings the *Chanson de Musette*, his best poem.

Muséum national d'Histoire naturelle, *v. Jardin des Plantes*.

Musical Controversies. There was a resounding dispute *c.* 1752 over the comparative merits of French and Italian music, with J.-J. Rousseau (in a *Lettre sur la musique française*, 1753) and Grimm (in a pamphlet *Le Petit Prophète de Boehmischbroda*, 1753) vocal on the Italian side. Later, *c.* 1774–80, the musical world of Paris was divided by a dispute over the respective merits of the German composer Gluck (whose revolt against Italian operatic conventions was largely due to Rameau's influence) and the Italian composer Piccini, both then in Paris. The *Gluckistes* were led by the abbé François Arnaud (1721–84; man of letters and wit) and Suard; the *Piccinistes* by Marmontel, La Harpe, and Ginguené. The affair is satirized in Marmontel's poem *Polymnie* (publ. posth. 1819) and reflected in comedies and memoirs of the day.

Musicisme, *v. Literary Isms*.

Musset, ALFRED DE (1810–57), poet, novelist, and dramatist, born and educated in Paris (his father was a government official), began to write after attempts to study law and medicine. Sainte-Beuve, scenting a new talent, introduced him to Nodier and Hugo, and so to the *Romantic *cénacles*—a new atmosphere for a young dandy used to fashionable *salons*.

His first published work was *L'Anglais mangeur d'opium* (1828), a very free translation of De Quincey's *Opium Eater*. *Contes d'Espagne et d'Italie* (1830), his first collection of poems (plus a short verse play, *Les Marrons du feu*), contained narrative poems (e.g. *Mardoche*) at times reminiscent of Byron, also a *Ballade à la lune* comparing the moon to the dot over an 'i', which drew protests. Then came *Un Spectacle dans un fauteuil* (1833 and 1834), two series of dramatic poems, historical dramas (notably *Lorenzaccio*), comedies, and *proverbes*; and *Rolla* (1833, in the *Revue des Deux Mondes*), another Byronesque poem. In 1833, he fell passionately in love with George Sand. The two went to Italy, where first, in Genoa, she went down with fever and he was bored and unfaithful, then, in Venice, he himself fell dangerously ill. George Sand and a young Italian doctor, Pietro Pagello, devotedly nursed him back to life, but she became Pagello's mistress. Musset returned to Paris (March 1834) broken in spirit and still feeble. George Sand returned with Pagello in the summer of 1834, but he was soon dismissed back to Venice. The liaison between her and Musset was resumed, then broken again, and the two tore at each other for some months till the final break in March 1835. This unhappy affair is described in his *Confession d'un enfant du siècle* (1836) and he made a fantastic satire of it, and of Romanticism, in *Histoire d'un merle blanc* (1842); *v.* also *Nuits, Les*; *Souvenir*.

The years 1834–43 saw some of his finest work—lyrics, most of his comedies and *proverbes*, and the best of his *nouvelles* (e.g. *Emmeline, Frédéric et Bernerette*, *Mimi Pinson*)—usually first published in the *Revue des Deux Mondes* and collected with earlier writings in *Poésies complètes* (1840), *Premières Poésies. Poésies nouvelles* (1852, 2 vols.), *Nouvelles* (1840), *Comédies et Proverbes* (1840 and 1853), etc. The music and genuine passion of his lyrics (e.g. *Les Nuits*; *Souvenir*) put him in the front rank of French poets, while his comedies hold their own in French literature by their wit, grace, lyricism, psychological insight, and dramatic

quality. Other works of this period include the well-known poem *Stances à la Malibran* (*v. Malibran*); *Une Soirée perdue* (1840), verses in praise of Molière; *Le Rhin allemand* (1841); *Les Lettres de Dupuis et Cotonet* (1836–8, in the *Revue des Deux Mondes*), a satire of Romanticism in the form of letters purporting to be written by two provincial worthies who are puzzled by the new literary terms (the first, and best-known, letter wittily describes the plain man's efforts to distinguish between Classicism and Romanticism; he finally decides with relief that Romanticism is merely a matter of adjectives run wild). After 1843 Musset's output declined (his manner of life was disastrous to both health and character), and by 1852, when he was elected to the *Académie*, it had almost ceased.

He is usually classed with Hugo, Lamartine, and Vigny as one of the four great Romantics; and he does, even more directly than they, communicate his innermost self (the *moi* of the Romantics) and his sufferings. On the other hand, after the exaggerated and at times hardly serious Romantic mannerisms of his early work, he took pains to dissociate himself (in *Les Lettres de Dupuis et Cotonet*) from the 'rhyming school' of Hugo and his disciples.

Musset, PAUL DE (1804–80), brother of the above, author of *Lui et elle* (1859), a thinly disguised account of his brother's affair with George Sand and a bitter reply to her *Elle et lui*; a life of his brother (1877); and *Monsieur le Vent et Madame la Pluie* (1860), long a minor classic of children's literature.

Mystère, the name (possibly derived from L. *ministerium* confused with *mysterium*) given from the 14th c., and especially in the second half of the 15th c., to a religious drama representing Scriptural scenes (for early examples, performed in or in front of churches, *v. Religious Writings*, 1). This form of drama developed greatly all over France in the 14th c., through the agency of fraternities somewhat similar to the *puys* (*v. Confrérie de la Passion*). The repertory of one of these appears to be

represented by a manuscript in the
Bibliothèque Sainte-Geneviève, con-
taining a Nativity, a play of the Three
Kings, a Passion, and a Resurrection.

The early 15th c. saw a further evolution
of the *mystère*, increased prominence being
given to the Virgin Mary and to a realistic
presentation of the sufferings of Christ.
Performances now often occupied several
days and became very elaborate, with a
huge cast (ordinary citizens, members of
the *confréries*, or professional actors), a vast
stage including many scenes, and rich
costumes. There was no limit of time
or place to the incidents represented,
which were drawn from the O.T.,
the N.T., the Apocrypha, the *Legenda
aurea*, etc. Buffoonery was included,
and contemporary life was realistically
presented, the nobility and clergy often
being unfavourably depicted. The style of
writing was generally vulgar and prolix,
without literary pretension. The usual
metre was the octosyllable, though many
others were used. An important and
common feature of the prologue was the
Procès de Paradis (inspired by Psalm
85:10) in which Justice, Mercy, Peace,
and Truth plead before God the cause that
is resolved by the Crucifixion. The *mystère*
was intended to edify; it was also an act
of piety, sometimes designed to avert
pestilence, or as a thanksgiving. Performances, announced by a *cry* and
the occasion of a general holiday, were
witnessed by large, enthusiastic crowds.
The cost was often borne in part by
municipalities or private individuals.

The most important 15th-c. *mystères*
were the *Passion d'Arras*, probably by
Eustache Marcadé (d. 1440; a learned

ecclesiastical functionary of Corbie in
Picardy), covering the life of Christ from
the Nativity to the Ascension; and the
Passion (*c.* 1450) of Arnoul Greban
(organist and choirmaster of Notre-Dame,
later canon of Le Mans; a man of learning
and poetic gifts), a work of considerable
power, covering the same events (it was
rehandled by Jean Michel, who had it
sumptuously performed at Angers, 1486,
over a period of four days). Arnoul Greban
and his brother Simon wrote a long *Actes
des Apôtres* (60,000 ll.; one of several
mystères of this title), following the
Apostles all over the world in a
monotonous series of sermons, con-
versions, miracles, and martyrdoms; it
was performed as late as 1540 (*v. Cry*).
Other 15th-c. *mystères* include the *Mystère
du Viel Testament*, and two on profane
themes—the *Mystère du siège d'Orléans*
(the deliverance of Orleans by Joan of
Arc), and the *Mystère de la destruction de
Troye la grant* (1450–2; 30,000 ll.) by
Jacques Milet (*c.* 1428–66), a work much
admired in its day, though it is uncertain
whether it was ever performed.

The performance of *mystères* was
suppressed in Paris in 1548 (*v. Censorship,
Dramatic*), and gradually ceased all over
France. The *mystère* had by then fallen into disfavour except among the illiterate: it
was condemned by the pious as irreverent
(the Protestants regarded it as a
profanation of the Bible), and by the
cultured as out of harmony with the spirit
of the *Renaissance. v. Tragedy.

Mystère Frontenac, Le, *v. Mauriac.*

Mystères de Paris, Les, *v. Sue.*

N

Nabab, Le (1877), a novel by A. Daudet;
a good study of Second Empire society.
The 'nabab', Bernard Jansoulet, the son of
Provençal peasants, returns to France in
his sixties, having made a fortune in Tunis.
He establishes himself with great pomp in

Paris, determined to cut a figure in society
and to enter politics. He is exuberantly
vulgar, yet touchingly loyal to his humble
origins; shrewdly ready to disburse vast
sums in order to further his social
ambitions, yet for all his experience

innocently certain that the world will share his delight at his romantic fortunes. He is soon beset by flatterers and swindlers. An associate of his Tunis days, now a rich Paris banker, plots to entangle him in a shady financial venture, while making it impossible for him to obtain money from Tunis (where he still has millions unrealized). He is elected a *député, but his enemies spread libellous stories about his private life, the election is annulled, and his sycophantic friends desert him. His end is pitiful. In his private box at a theatre which exists on his generosity he finds himself scorned and shunned by his former followers. He tries to defy them, but the blow is too heavy and he dies of a seizure.

Nabis, Les, v. *Impressionism.*

Nadar, *pseudonym of* FÉLIX TOURNACHON (1820–1910), a figure in the Paris of the Second Empire, in turn journalist, caricaturist, photographer (his *Panthéon-Nadar*, a collection of photographs of celebrities, was well known), and aeronaut. The *Impressionists held their first exhibition (1874) in his studio. He experimented hazardously with his huge balloon, 'Le Géant', and in the *Franco-Prussian war was head of a corps which observed enemy movements from captive balloons.

Nadaud, GUSTAVE (1820–93), wrote popular light verse—*Chansons* (1849; 1867; 1875, etc.); *Contes, proverbes, scènes et récits en vers* (1870), etc.

Nadeau, MAURICE, v. *Lettres nouvelles, Les*; *Quinzaine littéraire, La*; *Histories of French Literature.*

Naigeon, JACQUES-ANDRÉ (1738–1810), man of letters (editor of *Montaigne's Essais,* 1802) and *philosophe,* friend of Diderot (he published his works, 1798, and wrote a *Mémoire* of him), and an associate of d'Holbach in his anti-religious writings.

Nain jaune, Le, (1) a newspaper of

Bonapartist sympathies (f. 1814, after the first Restoration), noted for its caricatures and lively, satirical articles; (2) a short-lived paper of similar character, f. 1863 by Scholl.

Naissance du Chevalier au cygne, La, v. Chevalier au cygne.

Namouna, v. *Un Spectacle dans un fauteuil.*

Nana (1880), one of Zola's *Rougon-Macquart* novels. Nana, daughter of Gervaise in L'*Assommoir*, becomes an actress and for a time leads a life of luxurious and highly profitable vice—the occasion for detailed descriptions of this side of Second Empire society.

Nanine, ou le Préjugé vaincu, a sentimental comedy (in decasyllables) by Voltaire; produced 1749. It is mainly of interest as an early example of the *drame. The theme—a nobleman defies social prejudice to marry a beautiful girl of low birth—had already been treated in *La Chaussée's *Paméla.*

Nanteuil, CÉLESTIN (1813–73), a book-illustrator, notably of works by the *Romantics, e.g. Hugo's *Notre-Dame de Paris.*

Nanteuil, ROBERT (1630–78), pastel-portraitist and a noted engraver. His portrait of Mazarin is well known.

Napoleon. NAPOLÉON BONAPARTE, EMPEROR NAPOLEON I (1769–1821; v. *Bonaparte; Bonaparte Family*), b. at Ajaccio, Corsica, was a French citizen of Corsican and Italian descent and patrician origin, educated in France (Autun, the military college of Brienne, and the *École militaire*), then commissioned (1785) in an artillery regiment. He rose rapidly in the Revolutionary armies, and his prompt action saved the situation when the *Convention was attacked by insurgents (Oct. 1795; v. *Revolutions,* 1). By 1796, when he was 27 (v. *Caporal, Le Petit*), he was in command of the campaign against

Austria in N. Italy. He emerged victorious (v. *Rivoli*; *Coalitions* (1)). Now a military hero, he kept himself in the public eye by his conquest of Egypt (1798). His plan to make this the successful preliminary to the destruction of British power in India was largely foiled by Nelson's naval victory at Aboukir Bay (1–2 Aug. 1798), and he took advantage of a political crisis in France to return home (Oct. 1799) with his fame still high. He promptly engineered the *coup d'état du 18 brumaire* (9 Nov. 1799; v. *Revolutions*, 1) and emerged as First Consul (v.*Consulat*), with the powers of a dictator. After an interval during which he increased his stature by defeating the 2nd Coalition, he was elected Consul for life (1802), and by the *sénatus-consulte* of 18 May 1804, confirmed by plebiscite, constituted himself emperor. He crowned himself with his wife Joséphine (v. *Beauharnais*) in Notre-Dame (2 Dec. 1804; Pope Pius VII celebrated Mass). Life at his court—very unlike those of the *ancien régime*—has been well described by Mme de Rémusat (and v. *Napoleonic Aristocracy*). He had no children by Joséphine, and with a view to founding a dynasty he divorced her (1809) and married the archduchess Marie-Louise of Austria (1810), who bore him a son (v. *Napoleon II*).

At home, Napoleon restored order and unity to France, and showed a genius of which the effects still remain in reconstructing her internal economy, e.g. local and central government; financial, judicial, and legal systems; Church government; secondary and university education; v. *Code civil*; *Concordat*; *Lycées and Collèges*; *Université impériale*; *Légion d'honneur*. He also instituted many works of public utility and architectural embellishment. But he ruthlessly crushed conspiracies, real or imaginary (v. *Cadoudal*; *Enghien*), and established drastic systems of espionage and censorship (v. *Censorship, Dramatic*; *Librairie*; *Press*, 4), controlling the Press almost out of existence. His influence on literature was bad and shackling, for he disliked independence of spirit and expected to impose his will on thinkers and

writers as he did on his ministers and generals; he cold-shouldered Chateaubriand and exiled Mme de Staël, the greatest writers of the day.

By 1810, after an almost unbroken series of campaigns (1805–9; v. *Armée, La Grande*), his empire, including confederate or vassal states, covered most of Europe excluding Russia; and he had distributed territories to his kinsfolk and favourites (v. *Maréchal*). But he had not gained command at sea, nor, after *Trafalgar (1805), could he hope to do so; and he unwisely persisted, in the teeth of widespread resistance, with the Spanish campaign and the blockade of Britain (v. *Blocus continental*). Following his ill-fated Russian campaign (1812; v. *Moscow*) and defeat at *Leipzig (1813), the Allies invaded France (Jan. 1814) and Paris capitulated (30 March). On 6 April he abdicated unconditionally; he was allowed to retain the title of emperor and sovereignty of Elba (a small, now Italian, island in the Mediterranean), to which he retired (20 April). Ten months later he escaped in the brig *L'Inconstant* and landed, with 700 soldiers, on the French coast near Antibes (1 March 1815). Amid scenes of wild enthusiasm, he made his way to Paris, where he was borne in triumph to the *Tuileries (20 March)—Louis XVIII having fled to Belgium. But the enthusiasm was not general. The *bourgeoisie* were lukewarm, despite his introduction of liberal government (v. *Acte additionnel*); the Royalists of the West, an old centre of disaffection (v. *Vendée*), rose against him; and the 6th Coalition at once re-formed to destroy him. Decisively defeated at *Waterloo (18 June 1815), he again abdicated (22 June), went to Rochefort with the idea of leaving for America, but finally decided to claim the protection of the British government. He boarded H.M.S. *Bellerophon* (15 July) and—after the hasty passage of a bill 'for the more effectually detaining in custody Napoleon Buonaparté'—was transferred at sea to the flagship *Northumberland* and taken to the British island of St. Helena (in the Atlantic) for internment. There, in failing health, with a handful of devoted followers for company, he lived out his life in the villa of Longwood, composing and dictating his memoirs, and subjected to the closest supervision by Sir Hudson Lowe, the governor. He had reduced France to a state of physical and military collapse, and the Treaty of Paris (Nov. 1815) left her territorially smaller than before the Revolution; yet within a few years of his death the *légende napoléonienne* was already in being.

His correspondence (1858–70, 32 vols.; ed. and publ. by order of Napoleon III) includes three volumes of works dictated at St. Helena, his will, and other papers. His many proclamations, orders of the day, etc., are models of their kind—terse, to the point, at times magnificently inspiring. v. *Vol d'aigle*.

Napoleon II. JOSEPH-FRANÇOIS-CHARLES (1811–32), only son of Napoleon and Marie-Louise of Austria, was proclaimed *Roi de Rome* in infancy and recognized as Emperor Napoleon II by the government at the time of Napoleon's second abdication (1815), but never reigned. He and his mother left Paris in 1814, and spent the rest of his life, as duc de Reichstadt, with his grandfather, the emperor of Austria, at the castle of Schönbrunn in Vienna. He died of phthisis. He is the hero of Rostand's *L'*Aiglon*.

Napoleon III. CHARLES-LOUIS-NAPOLÉON BONAPARTE (1808–73), 3rd son of Louis Bonaparte, king of Holland (v. *Bonaparte Family*), and his queen, the former Hortense de *Beauharnais, and so nephew of Napoleon and grandson of the empress Joséphine. After the fall of the First Empire his mother, now separated from her husband, took him to Switzerland. He served in the Swiss armies and was later involved with the *Carbonari*. On the death of Napoleon's son (v. above), he became Bonapartist pretender to the throne and twice attempted to overthrow Louis-Philippe. The first time (1836) he was deported to the U.S.A., but soon managed to return to Europe and from London published

(1838) *Les Idées napoléoniennes*, in which he spoke of his duty to realize the social reforms dreamed of by Napoleon. The second time he was imprisoned for life in the fortress of Ham (near Péronne, N. France), but escaped to London (1846) disguised as a mason by the name of 'Badinguet' (thereafter his nickname). He returned to France at the outbreak of the 1848 *Revolution and was elected to the *Assemblée constituante*. Within the year he was elected Prince-President of the Republic, and four years later, having increased his power by the *coup d'état* of 2 December 1851, he was proclaimed Emperor Napoleon III (Dec. 1852; for fuller details v. *Republics*, 2; *Empire, Second*). He married (1853) the daughter of the comte de Montijo, a Spanish grandee (v. *Eugénie, Empress*). His health was bad in the later years of his reign, which may have accounted for his vacillating policy at home and abroad. On the outbreak of the *Franco-Prussian war (1870) he took command of his armies in the field. He was disastrously defeated and captured at Sedan, and the Second Empire fell (v. *Revolutions*, 4). After a spell in prison in Germany, he joined his wife and son (v. *Prince Impérial*) in exile at Chislehurst, near London, where he died.

Napoléon, Prince, v. *Bonaparte Family* (8).

Napoleonic Aristocracy. Napoleon provided himself with a court and instituted many titled offices (*grand dignitaire de l'Empire, grand officier*, etc., in descending scale) necessitating elaborate rules of precedence. In 1808, he systematized things by creating the *noblesse impériale*, a peerage, in some cases hereditary, with a hierarchy of *ducs, princes, barons, comtes,* and *chevaliers* (for members of the *Légion d'honneur*) into which the *grands dignitaires*, etc., were all fitted. v. *Noblesse*.

Napoléon le petit (London 1852), by Hugo, a history (4 bks., prose) of the period December 1848 to April 1852, from start to finish a savage, rhetorical indictment of Napoleon III—'Je me lève devant lui comme le remords en attendant que tous se lèvent comme le châtiment.' It was written in Brussels, in 16 days.

Napol le Pyrénéen, v. *Peyrat.*

Narcissus, v. *Romans d'antiquité.*

Natchez, Les (1826), by Chateaubriand, a prose epic (12 bks.) written in England and originally intended to form part of *Le *Génie du christianisme.* It continues the story of René in America and of Chactas after Atala's death (v. *René; Atala*). The Natchez were a tribe of American Indians in the region of New Orleans. They revolted against the French colonists (*c.* 1730) and were nearly exterminated.

Natiònal, Le, a daily paper f. 1830 by Thiers, Mignet, and Carrel just before publication of the *ordonnances* abolishing the liberty of the Press (v. *Press,* 5). A protest drafted by Thiers, signed by editors of other papers, and issued from the *National*'s offices did much to provoke the 1830 *Revolution. After 1830 the paper stood for a constitutional monarchy on the English model. Later, it objected to Louis-Philippe's policy of peace at any price and turned Republican. The *coup d'état* of December 1851 ended its existence.

Nattier, JEAN-MARC (1685-1766), a noted portrait-painter.

Naturalism, Naturalist, a movement in the novel and the drama (*c.* 1865–*c.*1895), developed out of *Realism, with which it had much in common, not least the influence of Taine. After 1865—largely owing to Taine's determinist philosophy of the influence of 'la race, le milieu, et le moment' on the formation of character, and his view that a novel should be a kind of human case-history—the documentary and scientific aspects of the novel were more heavily emphasized and it became more brutal, depicting the lowest side of human nature and characters who were often pathological cases at the mercy of inherited criminal or vicious instincts. It was also held that, to be a faithful study of human life, the novel should dispense with action, most lives being uneventful (a typical Naturalist novel where nothing happens is Céard's *Une Belle Journée*).

The chief difference between Realism and Naturalism lay in the pseudo-scientific character given to the Naturalist movement by its leader, Zola. Drawing a false analogy between the functions of the scientist and the novelist, he sought to apply to fiction the methods of observation and experiment advocated by the physiologist Claude *Bernard (*Introduction à l'étude de la médecine expérimentale,* 1865). He was also influenced by the *Traité philosophique et physiologique de l'hérédité naturelle* (1847–50) of Dr. Prosper Lucas. He elaborated his theories in *Le Roman expérimental* (1880), which stands as the manifesto of Naturalism and is in great part a naïve transposition of Bernard's treatise (substituting the word *romancier* for *médecin*); also in the studies and reviews collected in *Les Romanciers naturalistes* and *Le Naturalisme au théâtre* (both 1881). In his *Rougon-Macquart* novels, written to illustrate his theories, he selects his situation and endows his characters with conflicting temperaments (always shown to be the result of heredity and environment), then proceeds, by the accumulation of details, to a logical demonstration that there can only be one inevitable conclusion.

Zola's doctrines, carried by him to extremes, coloured the work of his five disciples of the 'groupe de Médan' (v. *Soirées de Médan, Les*)—Maupassant, Huysmans, Céard, Alexis, and Hennique—and also of A. Daudet. Flaubert (esp. with *L'*Éducation sentimentale*) and E. de Goncourt are also often called Naturalists (and the Goncourts did, in fact, originate the *roman documentaire*), but they were not involved in the extreme Naturalist campaign. Naturalism influenced the theatre through the dramatization of works by Zola and the Goncourts (v. *Alexis*), and even more effectively through the plays of Becque and the work (1887–96) of the *Théâtre Libre.

Reaction against Naturalism was evident before 1890. Many influences were at work: a growing conviction among public and authors alike that Naturalism and monotony were becoming synonymous, the decline of positivism, new trends in philosophy (e.g. Bergsonism), a revival of interest in religion, the appearance of the psychological novel (*v. Bourget*), and the repercussions of *Symbolism. In 1883, Brunetière had attacked the movement in *Le Roman naturaliste*. In 1887, five of Zola's disciples publicly repudiated his doctrines and his obscenity (*v. Manifeste des cinq*). Zola himself was finding *Les Rougon-Macquart* a depressing task; Maupassant's novels were becoming psychological (and his characters less humble); Daudet, with his irrepressible good humour, was never by temperament a Naturalist; and Huysmans was turning to religion. In 1890, a questionnaire (organized by the journalist Jules Huret) was circulated to 64 leading writers, asking whether they thought Naturalism was dead or dying. Alexis sent a frantic wire 'Naturalisme pas mort. Lettre suit', but the general trend of the replies (publ. 1891, in *L'Écho de Paris*) was that the movement was incurably moribund.

Naturisme, a poetic movement, began *c.* 1895 in reaction against *Symbolist vagueness and lack of contact with real life. The *naturistes*—notably Jammes, Fort, the comtesse de Noailles, Saint-Georges de Bouhélier—sought to return to Nature (not *Naturalism) and wrote of rustic life, everyday joys and sorrows, social justice, and universal brotherhood.

Nau, John-Antoine, *pseudonym of* ANTOINE TORQUET (1860–1918), a widely travelled poet and novelist (for a time he sailed before the mast). His works, which have a marked exotic element, include the novels *Cristobal le poète* (1912; set in Algiers) and *Thérèse Donati* (1921; set in Corsica), and the poems collected in *Au seuil de l'espoir* (1897), *Vers la Fée Viviane* (1908), *En suivant les goélands* (1914).

Naudé, GABRIEL (1600–53), a learned *libertin, friend of Patin, and librarian in

turn to Cardinal de Bagni (in Italy), Richelieu, and Mazarin. His works include, notably, the *Apologie pour les grands personnages faussement soupçonnés de magie* (1625); also an *Advis pour dresser une bibliothèque* (1627; Eng. trans. by John Evelyn, 1661); *Mascurat* (1649), a dialogue in defence of Mazarin; a *Jugement de tout ce qui a été imprimé contre le cardinal de Mazarin*, containing a mass of miscellaneous information; and historical writings.

Naundorff, CHARLES, *v. Orphelin du Temple*.

Nausée, La, *v. Sartre*.

Nautilus, Le, *v. Verne*.

Navarre, *v. Collège de Navarre*; *Henri IV*; *Marguerite d'Angoulême*.

Necker, JACQUES (1732–1804), father of Mme de Staël, a Genevan banker who settled in Paris and directed the finances of France with honesty and wisdom from 1776 (after the fall of Turgot) to 1781, when his famous *Compte rendu* (a financial report) led to his resignation. He was in office again in 1788–9, on the very eve of the Revolution, and in 1789–90. He wrote an *Éloge de Colbert* (1773) and *La Législation et le commerce des graines* (1775).

His wife was Suzanne Curchod (1739–94), the Swiss girl whom the young Gibbon had wished to marry. Her Paris *salon (from 1764) was frequented by men of letters. She lacked the taste and easy grace of the true Parisian, but her conversation and miscellaneous writings reflected her intelligence, rectitude, and kindliness. She was a friend of Buffon and tells us much about him.

Necker de Saussure, ALBERTINE, MME (1766–1841), daughter of the Swiss scientist Horace-Bénédict de Saussure, cousin by marriage and intimate friend of Mme de Staël. Her works include a *Notice sur le caractère et les écrits de Mme de Staël*

(1820); *L'Éducation progressive, étude du cours de la vie* (1828–32, 3 vols.), a treatise on children's education and the position of women, much read in its day; a translation of *Schlegel's lectures on the drama.

Négritude, a phenomenon which was at the origin of nationalism in French-speaking Africa and also of a new literature reflecting the aspirations of black writers of French language. *Négritude* is difficult to define, for it has meant different things to different people, but it is basically a new consciousness of Negro-African cultural values—a black consciousness. It had its origin among young black intellectuals—mainly West Indians and Africans—in Paris in the early 1930s, and it emerged against a background of growing concern over the depredations of the white man in Africa (reflected in *Gide's *Voyage au Congo*, 1927, and *Le Retour du Tchad*, 1928) and of growing interest in negro arts and culture (greatly increased by the Colonial Exhibition in Paris in 1931). *Négritude* was born within a group which included Senghor; Césaire, who is said to have coined the term; the poet Léon-Gontran Damas (1912–   ), author of *Pigments* (1937) and *Black Label* (1956); the *Surrealist poet Étienne Léro (1909–39), author with others of the militant manifesto *Légitime Défense* (1932); and the Nardal sisters, one of whom, Paulette, edited the short-lived, but highly influential, *Revue du Monde noir* (1931–2). Another important review of the 1930s was *L'Étudiant noir*, which sought to break down the clannish barriers between black students from different colonies. Sartre's acclamation and analysis of *négritude* in *Orphée noir* (1948, prefacing *Senghor's *Anthologie*) did much to crystallize it as a militant philosophy and also to arouse public interest in the new black writers. The many others associated with the literature—and often also the politics—of *négritude* include the Malagasy poet and politician Jacques Rabemananjara (1913–   ), the poets Alioune Diop (founder in 1947 of the review *Présence africaine*), Bernard Dadié (1916–   ), and Édouard Glissant (1928–   ).

Némésis, La, *v. Méry.*

Nemo, Capitaine, *v. Verne.*

Nemours, MARIE DE LONGUEVILLE, DUCHESSE DE (1625–1707), stepdaughter of the duchesse de Longueville, author of memoirs of the period of the *Fronde. The duke of York (then in exile, later James II) proposed to marry her, but Anne d'Autriche, then regent, disapproved.

Nennius (*fl. c.* 800), putative author or reviser of the Latin *Historia Britonum*, one of the sources of *Geoffrey of Monmouth's *Historia Regum Britanniae* and of interest for the account it purports to give of the historical Arthur. Nennius lived on the borders of Mercia and was a pupil of Elbod, bishop of Bangor.

Neo-Impressionists, *v. Impressionism.*

Néo-Mallarmisme, *v. Literary Isms.*

Néo-romantisme, *v. Literary Isms.*

Neo-Thomism, *v. Thomas Aquinas.*

Nepveu, ANDRÉ, *v. Durtain.*

Néricault, PHILIPPE, *v. Destouches.*

Néron (Nero), in Racine's *Britannicus.*

Nerval, Gérard de, *pseudonym of* GÉRARD LABRUNIE (1808–55), primarily a poet and author of short stories. While his father, a doctor, fought with Napoleon's armies, he had a country upbringing (*v. Sylvie*) with cousins and the run of his uncle's library of occult books. Later, he attended the Lycée Charlemagne in Paris. He was soon an extreme *Romantic, one of the *Jeunes-France and, like them, a *bousingo, inspired by the German Romantics. At 20, he published a translation of *Faust* (1828), which Goethe himself praised. His writings indicate that in the 1830s his life was profoundly affected by his love for the gay, capricious Marguerite ('Jenny') Colon (1808–42), an actress at the *Opéra-Comique. Now, and later, he travelled in

Germany, Austria, and the Near East (*Voyage en Orient*, 1851; *Loreley: Souvenirs d'Allemagne*, 1852), forming lasting vagabond habits; eventually he was to drift through life with no settled abode, relying on the casual hospitality of friends or the odd sleep in a café. He had his first mental breakdown in 1841. A spell in a private asylum restored his balance for a time, but latterly he was continually on or over the verge of insanity. His body was found hanging from a railing in the Rue de la Vieille Lanterne, one of his favourite haunts in Paris.

His considerable output (usually first publ. in reviews) comprised poetry (inc. translations and political and satirical verse), short stories, essays and portrait sketches, literary and dramatic criticism, and some plays. Works collected and published in book form in his lifetime include *Les Illuminés, ou les Précurseurs du socialisme* (1852), studies of Cazotte, Cagliostro, Restif de la Bretonne, etc.; *Petits Châteaux de Bohème* (1853), prose and poetry, including five sonnets entitled *Le Christ aux oliviers* which later formed part of *Les *Chimères* (12 fine sonnets appended to *Les Filles du feu*; v. below); *Contes et facéties* (1853), including *La Main enchantée* (first publ. 1832, as *La Main de gloire*), a highly Romantic piece of jocose Gothic with an historical background and a hand, newly severed from a corpse, that performs blood-curdling antics; *Les Filles du feu* (1854), tales (with *Les Chimères* appended) which include *Sylvie*, his masterpiece; *La Bohème galante* (1855), prose (inc. criticism) and poetry; *Aurélia, ou le Rêve et la vie* (1855; prose). This last collection contains a remarkable record of his deranged visions and the various phases of his insanity which has earned him a place as a precursor of much of the consciously hallucinatory writing of modern times; the matter is delirious, the language lucid to a degree that led Gautier to describe the work as 'la Raison écrivant les mémoires de la Folie sous sa dictée'.

Nervèze, ANTOINE DE (*c.* 1570–*c.* 1625), a writer in whom the *précieux* style can be

seen at its most exaggerated (*Les Amours de Filandre et de Marizée*, 1603; *Les Aventures guerrières et amoureuses de Léandre*, 1608, etc.).

Nesle, Tour de; Hôtel de. The Tour de Nesle (demolished 1663; v. *Collège des Quatre-Nations*), originally called the Tour Hamelin, was a large fortified tower at thè western extremity of the wall of medieval Paris (where it reached the left bank of the Seine). It took its name from the adjacent Hôtel de Nesle, a spacious residence erected in the 13th c. by a sieur de Nesle, and was associated with the legendary crimes of Marguerite de Bourgogne (the theme of Dumas *père*'s *La *Tour de Nesle*). The Hôtel du Petit-Nesle, where Benvenuto Cellini lived and worked during much of his stay in Paris, was part of the Hôtel de Nesle, but distinct from the main building; it stood on the city wall.

Neustria, v. *Merovingians.*

Neveu de Rameau, Le (1823; 1891, the first printing from the original ms.), Diderot's most characteristic work, a character-sketch in the form of a dialogue, probably written between 1761 and 1774. It first became known through a German translation by Goethe and was then printed (1823) from a copy of Diderot's manuscript.

The subject, the composer Rameau's nephew (a real person, of whom L.-S. Mercier has also left a picture), is an original, a crack-brained parasite who is lazy, sensual (and utterly frank in his depravity), a gifted mimic, and passionately fond of music. The dialogue gives amazing vigour and animation to the portrait and also throws light on the corrupt society of the day.

Newspapers, v. *Press,* 1–9.

New Year, v. *Year.*

Ney, MICHEL, v. *Maréchal.*

Nicaise, CLAUDE, ABBÉ (1623–1701), antiquarian, a native of Dijon, pursued his interests in France and Italy and corresponded with Leibniz, Huet, Bayle, etc.

Nicaise, Rue, v. *Machine infernale.*

Nicolas, Jeu de Saint, v. *Bodel.*

Nicolas de Montreux (*c.* 1561–1608), a gentleman of Maine, a dramatist and novelist who wrote under the pseudonym 'Olenix du Mont-Sacré'. His works include mediocre tragedies and comedies written in early life (*Le Jeune Cyrus, Annibal, Joyeuse,* etc.); *Les Bergeries de Juliette* (1585–93), a long *pastoral romance; other romances of a moral tendency, e.g. *Les Chastes et Délectables Jardins d'Amour* (1594); pastoral plays, notably *Arimène* (perf. at Nantes with great splendour, 1596; a complicated story of thwarted love and threatened suicide, with magic superadded), also *Athlette* (1585), *Diane* (1592); and two further plays (publ. 1601), *Sophonisbe and Joseph le chaste.*

Nicolas de Troyes (16th c.), a saddler, a native of Troyes who lived at Tours. He left in manuscript a collection of short tales, *Le Parangon des nouvelles nouvelles.* The first part is lost and the second was in part printed in 1867. Most of the surviving tales are drawn from Boccaccio, the *Cent Nouvelles Nouvelles,* the *Quinze Joyes de mariage,* etc.

Nicole, PIERRE (1625–95), moralist and theologian, a learned solitary of *Port-Royal,* collaborated with A. Arnauld in the *Logique de Port-Royal,* helped him draft his *La Perpétuité de la foi de l'Église catholique touchant l'Eucharistie,* sought to moderate him in his religious controversies, followed him into exile, but soon made his accommodation and was allowed to return home. His own works include *Essais de morale et instructions théologiques* (from 1671), much admired by Mme de Sévigné; *Les Imaginaires, ou Lettres sur l'hérésie imaginaire* (from 1664), a work after the manner of *Pascal's Lettres provinciales,* designed to show that

the alleged *Jansenist heresy was a matter of little importance; *Les Visionnaires, ou Seconde Partie des Lettres sur l'hérésie imaginaire* (1667), directed against Desmarets de Saint-Sorlin (who had attacked Jansenism). This last work bitterly condemned novelists and dramatists, provoking a sharp reply from Racine, who was now breaking away from *Port-Royal.*

Nicolette, v. *Aucassin et Nicolette.*

Nicomède, one of Corneille's most remarkable tragedies; produced in the winter of 1650–1.

Nicomède returns from his conquest of Cappadocia to the court of his father Prusias, king of Bithynia. He encounters the hostility of his stepmother Arsinoé (who wants to see her own son Attale succeed to the throne), of the king (ruled by Arsinoé), and of Flaminius the Roman ambassador (who rules both king and queen and has procured the death of Hannibal, a refugee at their court). Moreover, Attale is his rival for the hand of Laodice, queen of Armenia. He meets all intrigues with magnanimous prudence and cool irony; and when his enemies make a last effort to ship him off as a prisoner to Rome he even wins the help of Attale to foil them.

Nicot, JEAN, v. *Dictionaries,* 1606.

Niepce, JOSEPH-NICÉPHORE, v. *Daguerre.*

Nimier, Roger, *pseudonym of* ROGER NIMIER DE LA PERRIÈRE (1925–62), a novelist and journalist who, before his early death in a car accident, made his name with novels in the tradition of Laclos and Stendhal, at once provocative, cynical, and romantic (e.g. *Le Hussard bleu,* 1950; *Les Enfants tristes,* 1951; *D'Artagnan amoureux,* 1962), and for his insolent rejection of current literary and political ideologies (e.g. his essay *Amour et néant,* 1951, against Sartre; the journalistic writings collected in *Journées de lecture,* 1965, showing him as a 'disengaged' critic).

Ninon de Lenclos, *v. Lenclos*.

Nisard, DÉSIRÉ (1806–88), literary historian and critic, began as a political journalist on the **Journal des Débats* and the **National*, then held various academic and government appointments (e.g. professor of French eloquence at the **Sorbonne*, in succession to Villemain; director of the **École normale supérieure*, 1857–67). His works—notably *Histoire de la littérature française* (1855–61), also *Mélanges d'histoire et de littérature* (1868) and *Nouveaux Mélanges...* (1886)—were marked by a strong distaste for the **Romantics and the belief that little of merit had been written since the 17th c.

Nivelle de La Chaussée, *v. La Chaussée*.

Nivôse, *v. Republican Calendar*.

Noailles, PRINCESSE ANNA-ÉLISABETH DE BRANCOVAN, COMTESSE MATHIEU DE (1876–1933), b. in Paris of Rumanian and Greek ancestry, a gifted poetess (associated with **Naturisme* and the group known as the 'Nouvelle Pléiade'); also a novelist. Her poetry—classical in form, but strongly romantic, often pagan, in spirit, and intensely subjective in its sense of personal communion with Nature—is at its most characteristic in *Le Cœur innombrable* (1901), which contains beautiful descriptions of landscape (esp. of the **Île-de-France), and in *L'Ombre des jours* (1902) and *Les Éblouissements* (1907), where the themes are love of life and youth, travel, and the East. Her later collections, on a more melancholy note, include, notably, *Les Vivants et les morts* (1913) and *Les Forces éternelles* (1920), also *Poème de l'amour* (1924), *L'Honneur de souffrir* (1927). Her novels, which are diffusely sensuous, include *La Nouvelle Espérance* (1903), *Le Visage émerveillé* (1904), *La Domination* (1904).

Nobel Prize, *v. Prix Nobel*.

Noble, the lion in the **Roman de Renart*.

Noblesse, La. The pre-Revolutionary aristocracy originated in the feudal *noblesse de parage* (i.e. by birth), based on possession of land ('Point de seigneur sans terre') and carrying with it, besides various privileges and exemptions, the right of direct male succession. By the 12th c. the officials of Charlemagne's creation (*v. Duc, comte, marquis*) formed the highest ranks of a growing class of hereditary landowners, warriors (*la chevalerie*) who needed to possess lands in order to meet the heavy expenses of knightly life. The hierarchy extended downwards from the king through *ducs*, *comtes*, and *vicomtes* (the *grands feudataires* who took their titles—e.g. duc de Bourgogne—from their domains or provinces, where they exercised sovereign authority) to *seigneurs* (usually called *sire* or *baron*) and *chevaliers*, and below these (a 13th-c. extension) to *écuyers* (who were called *gentilshommes* and became the country gentry). This hereditary nobility was further extended from the 13th c., when the kings began to issue *lettres de noblesse* ennobling rich commoners or to bestow offices carrying entitlement to noble rank.

By the 16th c. some hereditary rights and privileges had disappeared, but many remained (e.g. exemption from taxes, vested right to certain high offices) and led to abuse (*cf. Privilégiés*). By then, too, the *noblesse d'épée* had come into being, so called because, at first, military service over a specified period counted as entitlement to hereditary noble rank. Here, with the years, the tendency was to confine military promotion solely to the *noblesse d'épée*. The 16th and 17th cs. also saw the evolution of the hereditary *noblesse de robe* (conferred on holders of high judicial or legal office) and more humble *noblesse municipale* or *de cloche* (for magistrates and municipal officials). Again, there was great scope for abuse, for traffic in titles was a means of procuring revenue. Moreover, when the families of the original *ducs* and *comtes*—whose rank had been the badge, so to speak, of their functions—became extinct, the same rank, but without office, was sometimes conferred on lesser nobles who were the king's favourites or a possible source of profit to him. During, and especially after, the reign of Louis XIV, a distinction between *noblesse de cour* and *noblesse de province* led to much abuse. The former lived for most of the year at court and tended to obtain all the high offices, while the latter remained in the country, often, if they belonged to the lesser nobility, in poverty and precluded by the very circumstances of their birth from any but a military career.

All hereditary titles and offices were abolished by decree (Jan. 1790) of the *Assemblée constituante*. Napoleon, in creating his *Napoleonic aristocracy, reintroduced some of the old titles. The pre-Revolutionary aristocracy was revived during the Restoration and Napoleon's *noblesse impériale* maintained. Titles were again abolished in 1848, but revived in 1852. *v. Provinces; cf. Pairs.*

Noces, Les, *v. Jouve.*

Nodier, CHARLES (1780–1844), novelist and man of letters, librarian (from 1824) of the *Bibliothèque de l'Arsenal*, where his *salon (vividly described in *Dumas père's memoirs) was the first *Romantic *cénacle. In early life, as a librarian in his native Besançon, he sometimes visited Paris seeking other employment, and on one such trip was imprisoned (1803) for writing and circulating a rhymed pamphlet (*La Napoléone*, 1802) disrespectful to Napoleon. He was literary assistant (1807–9) to the eccentric Sir Herbert Croft and Lady Mary Hamilton, who lived near Amiens. In 1813, at Laibach (in Illyria, then occupied by France), he combined the duties of municipal librarian, editor of a tetraglot newspaper, and secretary to Fouché. After 1814 he lived in Paris with his wife and his daughter Marie (*v. Arvers*).

He was a prolific writer, at his most typical in novels, e.g. *Le Peintre de Salzbourg, journal des émotions d'un cœur souffrant* (1803; much influenced by *Goethe's *Werther*), *Jean Sbogar* (1818; a mysterious, high-souled bandit defies

cramping laws and conventions from the fastness of his Illyrian castle), *Thérèse Aubert* (1819; a story of unhappy love and the risings in the *Vendée), and in fantastic tales with a strong foretaste of Romantic extravagance, e.g. *Smarra, ou les Démons de la nuit* (1821), *Trilby, ou le Lutin d'Argail* (1822), *L'Histoire du roi de Bohème et de ses sept châteaux* (1830), *Mademoiselle de Marsan* (1832), *La Fée aux miettes* (1832; set, like *Trilby*, in Scotland), *Inès de las sierras* (1837); *v. Foreign Influences,* 3; *Children's Reading.* His other works include poetry (*Essais d'un jeune barde,* 1804), *Le Vampire* (1820; a *mélodrame*), a *Bibliographie entomologique* (1801), *Questions de littérature légale* (1812), *Mélanges de littérature et de critique* (1820), *Mélanges tirés d'une petite bibliothèque* (1829), *Rêveries* (1832; containing essays significant of their period, e.g. *Du fantastique en littérature*), *Souvenirs de la jeunesse* (1832); and *v. Dictionaries,* 1808; *Journal des Débats.*

Noël, a lyrical piece connected with Christmas.

Noël, Marie, *pseudonym of* MARIE-MÉLANIE ROUGET (1883–1967), author of *chansons* (often with music) and lyrics of religious inspiration and popular appeal, e.g. *Les Chansons et les heures* (1920), *Les Chants de la Merci* (1930).

Noëls bourguignons, *v. La Monnoye.*

Nœud de vipères, Le, *v. Mauriac.*

Nohant, Château de, *v. Sand.*

Nonnotte, CLAUDE-FRANÇOIS, ABBÉ (1711–93), *Jesuit author of *Les Erreurs de Voltaire* (1762), pointing out Voltaire's errors of historical fact. He was consequently involved in controversy with Voltaire, who often ridiculed him. He attacked the *Encyclopédie.

Normands, Geste des, *v. Wace.*

Norpois, Marquis de, in Proust's *A la recherche du temps perdu,* a diplomat of the old school; a friend of Marcel's father and lover of Mme de *Villeparisis (and so a link between the *Swann and *Guermantes sides of Marcel's life). His habit of elaborate discourse, without ever committing himself, is well conveyed.

Nostradamus, MICHEL DE NOSTRE-DAME, *known as* (1503–66), astrologer and physician. His *Centuries* (1555; in quatrains), a book of obscure prophecies, had a wide vogue, but was finally condemned by Rome. Catherine de Médicis summoned him to court and he was physician to Charles IX. He is mentioned by Mme de Sévigné (11 March 1676), in Pepys's diary (3 Feb. 1667), in the first scene of Goethe's *Faust*, etc.

Notables, Les, under the monarchy, members of the privileged orders (*v. Privilégiés*). The king could at will convoke an *Assemblée des Notables*. An assembly convoked in February 1787 refused to agree to proposals for taxation which would touch both the *Privilégiés* and the *Tiers État*. The ensuing crisis led to the convening of the *États généraux* of 1789.

Notes sur l'Angleterre, v. Taine.

Notes sur Paris. Vie et opinions de M. Frédéric-Thomas Graindorge (1868), by Taine, studies, at times ironical, of Parisian life under the Second Empire. M. Graindorge, Taine's mouthpiece, left Paris at 12 and returns 35 years later. He has been educated at Eton and Heidelberg, and has made a fortune out of canned pork in America. The chapters *Aux Italiens* and *Tête-à-tête*, reflecting Taine's love of Mozart and Beethoven, are of great interest.

Notre cœur, v. Maupassant.

Notre-Dame de Paris (1831), by Hugo, a novel of 15th-c. Paris. Despite many historical and topographical digressions, it vividly evokes the teeming medieval city clustered around the cathedral of Notre-Dame, which dominates all. The character Pierre Gringoire is a travesty, antedated, of Gringore.

Claude Frollo, archdeacon of Notre-Dame, falls in love with Esméralda, a gipsy dancer popular with the idle Paris crowds. He employs his *protégé* Quasimodo, the grotesque, hunchback bell-ringer of Notre-Dame, to kidnap her. She is rescued by Phébus de Châteaupers, captain of the Royal Archers, falls in love with him (taking him for a hero—he is really a loose-living braggart), and gives him a secret rendezvous. Frollo follows her, stabs Phébus, and leaves her to be arrested and sent to the gallows. Quasimodo, whom she has enslaved by one casual act of kindness, snatches her from the scaffold itself and takes her secretly to sanctuary in Notre-Dame. Frollo so engineers matters that the band of gipsies and vagabonds to which she belongs (*cf. Cour des miracles*) learns her whereabouts and resolves to rescue her. They attack the cathedral at midnight (a highly dramatic scene) and are repulsed by Quasimodo, single-handed. Meanwhile Frollo, in disguise and assisted by Gringoire, has persuaded Esméralda to fly with him. She suddenly recognizes him and chooses to be handed over to the authorities rather than yield to his threats. Frollo, enraged, goes to find the officers of the guard, leaving her in charge of a half-mad old woman. Seeing an amulet Esméralda is wearing, the woman recognizes her as her daughter, kidnapped years ago by gipsies. The archers now appear and with great difficulty wrest Esméralda from her mother, who is left dying on the pavement. From one of the towers of Notre-Dame the distraught Quasimodo sees Esméralda swinging on the gallows, turns to find Frollo gloating over the scene, and with one movement hurls him from the balustrade to the cobblestones far below. One day, in the vault where criminals' bodies are flung, Quasimodo's skeleton is found beside that of Esméralda.

Nourritures terrestres, Les (1897), by Gide, prose and verse fragments of great sensuous and musical appeal, counselling Nathanaël, an imaginary youth, to live fully, in and for the moment, to be ruled by desire and impulse instead of disciplined morality, to be *disponible*, ready to accept *all* experiences and sensations (for to choose is to renounce all that one might have chosen), and so finally to make self-emancipation the way to self-realization. Ménalque, invoked in the course of the work as a mentor, also figures in *L'Immoraliste*.

Nouveau, GERMAIN (1852–1920), poet, self-styled 'Humilis'. After a Bohemian youth (inc. a spell in London with Rimbaud), he was influenced by Verlaine (the Verlaine of *Sagesse*), became a devout Roman Catholic, and wrote *Poèmes d'Humilis* (1911). *Poésies d'Humilis et vers inédits* (1926) is a posthumous collection.

Nouveau roman, a term first used in 1957 to describe a form of novel which had already been recognized as a new phenomenon and had provoked a literary outcry. The chief exponents of the *nouveau roman* are Robbe-Grillet; Butor; N. Sarraute; C. Simon; Claude Ollier (1922–), with *Le Maintien de l'ordre* (1961); Robert Pinget (1919–), with *L'Inquisitoire* (1962); and Jean Ricardou (1932–), with *La Prise de Constantinople* (1965). They are linked, not as a school, but by a shared conviction that the forms of the novel should not be taken for granted (*cf. Anti-roman*), and that they inevitably imply a certain view of reality; early targets were the traditional concepts of character and plot. These novelists are broadly agreed on a literary ancestry which begins with Flaubert and continues with Proust, James Joyce, Kafka, Virginia Woolf, and William Faulkner. The work of R. Roussel has also strongly influenced some of their ideas about the construction of fiction. Several of them have published essays on the theories underlying their work, and a growing interest in the laws of fiction (as opposed to the laws of reality, psychological or social) has been paralleled in the *nouvelle critique* (*v. Critics and Criticism*, 3). Writers whose work has a marked affinity with the *nouveau roman* include M. Duras, Cayrol, and C. Mauriac. *v. Novel*, 3.

Nouveaux Lundis, *v. Causeries du lundi.*

Nouvelle, a rather vague term for a short fictitious narrative (comic or tragic, usually in prose), which critics have distinguished from the *roman* (*v. Novel*; *cf. Conte*) in that it deals with a single situation (usually from everyday life), aspect of a character, or contrast of characters, throwing this into strong relief and leading up to an issue in some degree dramatic or unexpected. Though elements of the *nouvelle* may be seen in the early **lais* (e.g. some of those of Marie de France), the **fabliaux*, the Oriental tales of the *Roman des *Sept Sages*, etc., there seems to be no direct line of evolution from these to the *nouvelle*. A closer approximation to it may perhaps be seen in the realistic and dramatic descriptions of incidents of married life in the 15th-c. **Quinze Joyes de mariage* and in some works of La Sale (the *Réconfort de Mme de Fresne*; the final episode of the **Petit Jehan de Saintré*). The *nouvelle* proper finally emerges (under Italian influence; *v. Foreign Influences*, 1) with the **Cent Nouvelles Nouvelles* (*c.* 1460). Other 15th-c. works with some features of the *nouvelle* are **Martial d'Auvergne's Arrêts d'amour* and the tale **Jehan de Paris*. Later examples of the *genre* range from Marguerite de Navarre's **Heptaméron* (1558), the *Nouvelles Récréations* (*v. Des Périers*), and **Scarron's Nouvelles tragi-comiques* (1655–7) to the masterly tales of Voltaire. The many 19th-c. authors of tales and short stories (now called either *nouvelles* or *contes*, the two terms having become largely interchangeable) include Nodier; Musset; Vigny (**Servitude et grandeur militaires*); Méry (*La *Chasse au chastre*); Nerval; Mérimée, who introduced an objectivity and a forceful economy of construction rivalled by few except Maupassant, whose tales are among the finest examples of purely objective writing in French literature; Gobineau; Flaubert (**Trois Contes*); A. Daudet; Villiers de l'Isle-Adam; Schwob; and A. France, another master of this form. 20th-c. authors who call for mention include Larbaud, Morand, Supervielle, Giono, Aymé (*Le Passe-Muraille*), Camus (*L'Exil et le royaume*), Sartre (*Le Mur*), Arland,

Gascar (*Les Bêtes*), and F. Marceau (*En de secrètes noces*). For children's stories *v. Children's Reading*.

Nouvelle critique, *v. Critics and Criticism*, 3.

Nouvelle France, La, the French-Canadian territory in the St. Lawrence valley. *v. Cartier; cf. Acadie*.

Nouvelle Héloïse, Julie, ou la (1761; 72 eds. by 1800), by J.-J. Rousseau, a highly successful and influential romance in letter form; written 1756–8 (*v. Houdetot*). Its portrayal of conjugal fidelity may be said to have effected something of a moral revolution in the empty, dissipated society of the day, while its ideal picture of a happy, prosperous countryside contrasted with the misery then prevailing among the peasantry. It also contains a notable attack (curiously attributed to the character Lord Edward) on the social privileges of rank when rank is not accompanied by corresponding worth.

The young Saint-Preux is tutor in the house of Julie's father, the baron d'Étanges. He and Julie fall deeply in love, the baron's pride prevents their marriage, and they yield to their passion. Remorse soon follows. Saint-Preux is saved from suicide by the generous intervention of Lord Edward Bomston, an Englishman, who offers the pair asylum on his estate and, when this is refused, puts Saint-Preux aboard the ship in which Admiral Anson is leaving for his voyage round the world. Julie obeys her father and marries the elderly baron Wolmar, a kindly, judicious foreigner (*v. Holbach*). Saint-Preux returns after some years, and Wolmar invites him to stay with them. Julie has confessed to Wolmar her earlier relations with Saint-Preux (in fact, he knew already) and he deems it wiser to regulate their attachment, by trusting them to be loyal to him, than to oppose it. Moreover, he makes Saint-Preux tutor to his children. There follows a picture of orderly, virtuous, contented family life, in which Julie and Saint-Preux bravely struggle against a renewal of their passion. She

encourages him to share her religious devotion, also to marry her cousin. Her untimely death ends the story, and she dies confessing the survival of her love.

Nouvelle Revue, La, *v. Adam, Juliette*.

Nouvelle Revue française, La (1909–43; 1953–), a famous review (monthly) of literature and the other arts. Its founders included Schlumberger, Copeau (the review later backed his *Théâtre du *Vieux-Colombier*), and Gide (the moving spirit). They shared the conviction that the *Symbolist aesthetic was inadequate for what the younger generation had to say, but it was only with time that their own aims emerged at all clearly. They upheld the importance of literary method, sensibility, and what they termed 'esprit'—in fact, of the enduring aesthetic values independent of intellectual and moral prejudices or fashions in writing. They were anxious to encourage new trends and obscure authors, and in 1911 founded a publishing house under the direction of Gaston Gallimard, who was a member of the group. An impressive list could be made of the 'little-known' authors the review printed in the early days—Claudel, Martin du Gard, Romains, Giraudoux, Péguy, Valéry, Gide himself. It failed in literary perceptiveness in refusing (1913) Proust's *A la recherche du temps perdu*, but made good the lapse when it bought the literary rights of the work in 1917. The review lost its intellectual independence during the 1939–45 war (*v. Drieu la Rochelle*) and ceased to appear in 1943. A special number, *Hommage à Gide*, was produced in 1951. Publication was resumed in 1953, with the title *La Nouvelle Nouvelle Revue française* till 1959. Editors have included Rivière, Paulhan, and now Arland.

Nouvelle Rive gauche, La (1882–6; weekly), an early *Symbolist review (better known, from 1883, as *Lutèce*), printed work by P. Adam, Laforgue (*Les Complaintes*), Moréas, H. de Régnier, etc.

Nouvelles à la main, *v. Nouvellistes*.

Nouvelles de la République des Lettres,
v. Bayle; Basnage de Beauval.

Nouvelles ecclésiastiques, v. Jansenism.

Nouvelles littéraires, Les (1922– ;
weekly), a journal f. by André Gillon
(1880–1969) and others as *Les Nouvelles
littéraires, artistiques, et scientifiques.*
Gillon, creator of this type of French
illustrated weekly in newspaper format,
was long its director and moving spirit.
Jaloux, Kemp, and G. Marcel contributed
criticism.

Nouvelles Méditations, v. Lamartine.

Nouvelles Nourritures, Les, v. Gide.

Nouvelles Récréations et joyeux devis, v.
Des Périers.

Nouvelle Table ronde, La, v. Table ronde,
La.

Nouvellistes, persons who, in the 17th c.,
before the development of the *Press,
assembled at various points in Paris to
hear, retail, and discuss the news of the
day. The collection of news for persons of
importance eventually became a paid
profession. Manuscript newsletters,
known as *Nouvelles* [or *Gazettes*] *à la main*
and often satirical and propagandist, were
also clandestinely circulated, even after the
advent of printed gazettes. *v. Loret* (under
Press, 1).

Novalis, *pseudonym of* FRIEDRICH
LEOPOLD FREIHERR VON HARDENBERG
(1772–1801), a German Romantic who
influenced the French *Romantics and
*Symbolists. His fragmentary output—
poetry, tales, an unfinished novel—has a
mystical, semi-philosophical, often
fantastic strain. *v. Foreign Influences,* 3, 5.

Novel, The. The word *roman,* 'novel',
comes from Old French *romanz,* which at
first meant the vernacular (*v. Romance
Languages*), and from the 12th c. a work
actually or ostensibly translated from
Latin into the vernacular. By the 14th c.,

romanz or *roman* was applied more
specifically to the romances of antiquity
or chivalry (*v. Roman courtois*), which
were usually—though not invariably, *cf.*
Lancelot—in verse. By the 16th c., the
advent of printing (1470 in Paris) had
produced a reading public for whom
roman had come to denote any prose
narrative relating the exploits of a hero.
From the 17th c., *roman* was used in the
sense, which it still largely retains, of a
prose work of imagination, usually of some
length, portraying characters and actions
representative of real life. *v. Conte;*
Nouvelle; Foreign Influences.

1. MIDDLE AGES TO LATE 16TH CENTURY.
The verse *romans courtois,* remote
ancestors of the modern novel, are long,
episodic narratives woven round highly
idealized themes of love (a refined,
disciplined emotion; *v. Amour courtois*),
destined to be read aloud (not, like the
chansons de geste, sung), mainly to
audiences of women. Lovers are separated,
encounter perils, monsters, and marvels
(often in foreign lands, where the
*Crusades take them), and in the end are
usually happily reunited. The knight
performs feats of endurance and prowess,
described at prodigious length, to prove
his love for his mistress, who may be a
married woman. She accepts his love, but
tests it (sometimes cruelly), and does not
always reward it.

The *romans courtois,* especially those
termed *romans bretons,* were often
reproduced in 16th-c. prose compilations,
but with the sentimental element
weakened, for tastes had changed. With
the dissolution of feudal society, interest
in fictional entertainment had spread from
courtly to *bourgeois* circles and a more
cynical, earthy type of narrative had
evolved, as seen in the *fabliaux* (verse) or
the prose tales of the *Quinze Joyes de
mariage.* Conduct is now on a lower level:
the clergy are venal; men eat, drink, and
make love coarsely; women are inconstant,
if not frankly lecherous, lovers more often
under their mistresses' beds than engaged
on perilous quests. (*Cf.* also the satire of
the later parts of the *Roman de Renart*;
the cynical derision of women in the

second part of the *Roman de la Rose*, in contrast to the exaltation of *amour courtois* in the first.) This was a notable advance, for such tales convey an illusion of real life (e.g. the lifelike dialogues in the 15th-c. *Cent Nouvelles Nouvelles*). Adventures and episodes are still of prime importance, but are interludes in the daily life of real men and women, even if the characters themselves are rarely convincingly differentiated (the vivid descriptions and character-drawing in the later part of La Sale's *Petit Jehan de Saintré, c.* 1456, are exceptional). In the 16th c., various minor writers—Du Fail, G. Bouchet, Yver—depict rustic scenes, *bourgeois* society, or country-house life, while one genius—Rabelais—combines, in his *Gargantua* and *Pantagruel*, extravagant fantasy and a vivid portrayal of the life of all classes of people. His was the first work of sustained prose fiction, in that its successive books continue the story from father to son; it might also be called the first philosophical novel, for his genius played over life in all its manifestations.

From the late 15th c., the great popularity of translations from foreign literature (*v. Foreign Influences,* 1) undoubtedly helped to make love the central theme of fiction—passionate love rather than *l'amour courtois* or the Platonic love favoured by such writers as Marguerite de Navarre, Héroët, or Scève. The *Thirteen Questions*, or love problems, of bk. V of Boccaccio's *Filocopo* (a prose romance; *cf. Floire et Blancheflor*), translated into French in 1531, are often cited as an influence on the development of the French novel. His *Fiammetta* (trans. 1532; the tale of a married woman who falls in love with a stranger and is deserted by him) appears to have strongly influenced Hélisenne de *Crenne's Les Angoisses douloureuses qui procèdent d'amours* (1538), a work which heralds the novel of sentimental analysis. Translations from the Spanish, notably Herberay des Essarts's *Amadis* (1540–8), gave new life to tales of chivalry and romantic love (hence the *romans courtois* in prose compilations).

2. 17TH AND 18TH CENTURIES. By the

early 17th c. the paths along which the novel will proceed to its great period of expansion in the 19th c. are clearly discernible.

First, there is the sentimental tale which follows the course of true love to a happy ending. It has a plot (for plot, albeit rambling and interrupted by subsidiary plots, now comes definitely into the picture) and a young girl rather than a married woman for heroine. It is not necessarily concerned with verisimili-.tude. D'Urfé's *L'*Astrée* (1607–27) —sentimental, precious, interminably episodic (some 5,000 pp.), and clearly inspired by the Spanish and Italian *pastoral romances—is a first landmark. Its success confirmed the vogue (associated with the little world of the Hôtel de *Rambouillet and such authors as Mlle de Scudéry, Gomberville, and La Calprenède) for long, unreal, insipid, heroic-sentimental works in which courtiers of the day are thinly disguised in pastoral or classical trappings. In *L'Astrée*, however, the shepherds and shepherdesses are individuals, whose shades of feeling are indicated, and whose very number emphasizes the sense of the complicated interplay of passions. The vogue was ridiculed (*v. Sorel, C.*; *Boileau*) and petered out. The love story *qua* story then goes to ground for a time. It re-emerges in J.-J. Rousseau's *Nouvelle Héloïse* (1761), with an element of irregular passion to emphasize a moral purpose (a feature that has come to stay), and much hampered by philosophical and didactic trappings. In Bernardin de Saint-Pierre's *Paul et Virginie* (1787) it is simple, lyrical (as with Rousseau), and pathetic, and brings in nature (as had Rousseau, but here in an exotic setting). Eventually, touched by English and German influence, it reaches Gothic realms and a delicious, swooning sensibility.

Secondly, there is the equally formless narrative which, rejecting sentimental invention, seeks to create an atmosphere of real life by depicting society (usually *bourgeois*, or frankly low), scenes, and manners, e.g. C. *Sorel's Francion* (1623), Furetière's *Roman bourgeois* (1666),

*Restif de la Bretonne's *Le Paysan perverti* (1775), Diderot's *La *Religieuse* (1796). Even when the narrative is picaresque (under Spanish influence, notably of *Lazarillo de Tormes* and *Don Quixote*; and v. *Lesage*) the background remains realistic, as in Scarron's *Roman comique* (1651–7), Lesage's *Gil Blas* (1715–35). Even, again, in the pseudo-Oriental and licentious *contes* or the philosophical romances fashionable in the 18th c. (e.g. those of Crébillon *fils* and Voltaire) the satire is aimed at contemporary manners.

Thirdly, there are a few narratives—e.g. Mme de La Fayette's *La *Princesse de Clèves* (1678), the abbé Prévost's *Manon Lescaut* (1731), *Laclos's *Les Liaisons dangereuses* (1782)—which, in their concern with human problems and the analysis of emotions, are true precursors of modern psychological fiction. To some extent they continue the narrative of sentimental adventure, but the adventures are primarily those of the soul at grips with the cruel, dangerous, and no longer idealistic passion of love.

3. 19TH AND 20TH CENTURIES. The exuberant and self-conscious development of the novel in the 19th c. was encouraged by an avid novel-reading public (created by the spread of education, and the reviews and serialized fiction in the daily and periodical Press; v. *Critics and Criticism*, 2; *Roman-feuilleton*) and took the form of prolonged bursts of creative energy alternating, or at times coinciding, with phases of concentration on technique. The result was a vastly enlarged conception of what constitutes the appropriate form and matter of fiction.

Between c. 1800 and 1850 creative genius was particularly evident. Chateaubriand, Senancour, and B. Constant portray the state of mind of individuals whose emotions, whether love or spiritual loneliness, mean more to them than outward events (v. *René*; *Obermann*; *Adolphe*; *Romanticism*), inspiring a long line of novels of introspection and self-revelation, beginning with Musset's *Confession d'un enfant du siècle* and Sainte-Beuve's *Volupté*. Mme de Staël evokes the loneliness of the woman who dares to be unconventional (*Corinne*; *Delphine*); she also paves the way for the *roman à thèse*. Chateaubriand and, to a lesser extent, Mme de Staël develop the exotic element introduced by Bernardin de Saint-Pierre.

The greatest novelists of this period were Balzac and Stendhal. Balzac's genius has the universal quality which defies classification because succeeding ages find in it new sources of inspiration. His great *Comédie humaine* contains studies of life and character that can be described variously as historical novels (*Les *Chouans*) or as novels of ideas (*La *Cousine Bette*; *Le *Père Goriot*), illustrating the havoc wrought by vice or uncontrolled passions. Crime fiction and the *roman noir* (a novel permeated by the influence of one sinister character) owe much to his master-criminal *Vautrin and to *La *Rabouilleuse*. His method of linking the main divisions of his *Comédie humaine* (and also the tales within them) by reintroducing the same character in roles of varying importance foreshadows the 20th-c. *roman-fleuve* or *roman-cycle*. Stendhal was a writer of less universal genius, but his penetrating, scrupulously objective studies of character and motives (*Le *Rouge et le Noir*; *La *Chartreuse de Parme*) bore fruit c. 1890 in the novel of psychological analysis.

From c. 1830 George Sand was steadily turning out novels combining sentiment, passion, melodrama, and (in her second phase) ideology. The ever popular story of true love also flourished, sometimes well spiced with licentiousness or satire, or serving as a lively portrait of contemporary society (v. *Kock*; *Karr*), sometimes sugary (e.g. Lamartine's *Graziella*). Heroines died pitifully young of broken hearts, but the novel of sensibility, full of tears and fainting-fits, languished after the disappearance early in the century of such writers as Mme de Genlis, Mme de Souza, and Mme de Duras. A passing phase of extravagant *Romanticism, exemplified in novels and tales by Gautier (with exceptions such as his picaresque *Capitaine Fracasse* and lyrical, and unique, *Mademoiselle de Maupin*), is later reflected in Barbey d'Aurevilly (e.g. *Les *Diaboliques*) and Villiers de l'Isle-Adam (*Claire Lenoir*;

Contes cruels). The **romans-feuilletons* of Soulié and Sue (one of the first novelists to depict the underworld) are marked by melodramatic extravagance.

The historical novel, inspired by Scott, also came to the fore between 1800 and 1850, with Vigny's **Cinq-Mars* (1826), soon followed by Balzac's *Les *Chouans*, Mérimée's **Chronique du règne de Charles IX*, and Hugo's **Notre-Dame de Paris*. The vogue continued throughout the century: Dumas *père* exploited French history as the background for countless adventure stories; Barbey d'Aurevilly combined history with fantasy (*L'*Ensorcelée; Le *Chevalier des Touches*); the later Hugo combined it with sociology (*Les *Misérables; *Quatre-vingt-treize*); Flaubert wrote **Salammbô*, Zola *La *Débâcle; v.* also *Erckmann-Chatrian; Esparbès; Margueritte*. The 20th c. has seen works including A. **France's Les Dieux ont soif*, the two 'Verdun' volumes of Romains's *Les *Hommes de bonne volonté*, the novels of Z. Oldenbourg, Troyat, and M. Yourcenar, and **Aragon's La Semaine sainte*.

Between 1850 and *c.* 1890 novelists were preoccupied with questions of form, technique, and function. The positivist spirit of the day manifested itself in the novel in **Realism* and **Naturalism* (*cf.*, in poetry, the **Parnassiens*). The Realists, bent on depicting life as it is actually lived, set themselves to *document* their novels, with results ranging from the minute portrayal of everyday life practised by Champfleury, E. Feydeau, Duranty, and to some extent A. Daudet, to the unrelieved portrayal of vice, squalor, and disease practised by the Goncourts and the Zola of **Thérèse Raquin*. Flaubert, who dominates this period, cannot properly be classed as a Realist. Not only did he object to such literary labels; his meticulous documentation was never an end in itself, but stemmed from his view of the novel as an impersonal work of art. **Madame Bovary* and *L'*Éducation sentimentale* are among the great novels of French literature: they also happen to be great realistic novels. The tendency of Realism to photographic and formless representation of life was exaggerated by the Naturalists, led by

Zola. Naturalism was, moreover, influenced by the determinism of Taine and by contemporary interest in heredity and experimental physiology. Zola alone rigorously practised his own theories (*v. Rougon-Macquart, Les*), but they influenced Maupassant, Huysmans, Céard, Alexis, Hennique, and A. Daudet.

Between *c.* 1890 and 1913 no literary giants appeared to change the course of evolution. The outstanding novelists were Barrès and A. France, whose work is marked by elegance, sophistication, and style rather than great creative energy. But the novel was quietly expanding its province by reflecting and exploiting contemporary interests and ideologies. It took little from **Symbolism*, but absorbed new humanitarian (and later psychological) ideas from the Russian writers. Psychology and idealistic philosophy replaced positivism as its intellectual background.

About 1890, after one strangely isolated precursor in Fromentin's **Dominique* (1863), the novel of psychological analysis developed. Its chief concern was with human character and the gradual, cumulative process by which habits are formed. It had its origins in the 17th c. (*v.* 2, above); more immediately, it derived from Stendhal and the critic Taine. Bourget was long regarded as its chief exponent; another was Maupassant (with **Pierre et Jean*).

Some writers—e.g. Bourges, Huysmans (in his later phase), Estaunié, C.-L. Philippe—made philosophy, psychology, religious experience, or vague, sentimental humanitarianism the staple of their work, and had an appeal which still remains for small circles. Others—e.g. P. Adam, R. Bazin, Feuillet, Mirbeau, M. Prévost—contrived to combine similar themes with just sufficient realism and attention to the contemporary scene to ensure wide popularity if not lasting fame.

We have already noted the birth of the exotic novel, with Bernardin de Saint-Pierre and Chateaubriand. Balzac's *Scènes de la vie de province* (*v. Comédie humaine, La*) were early regional novels. They were followed by G. Sand's idylls of country life (*La *Mare au diable; *François le champi*), then by F. Fabre's novels of life in the Cévennes, and novels and sketches of Provençal life by A. Daudet, Aicard, and Arène. From the late 19th c. until the present day, the exotic novel and the regional novel have flourished and developed in the hands of writers including Loti, Farrère, the Tharaud brothers, Hémon, Larbaud, Morand, R. Bazin, Boylesve, Bordeaux, Guillaumin, Ramuz, Châteaubriant, Pourrat, Giono, Chamson, Bosco, and M. Mauron; *v.* also *Mauriac, F.*; *Lacretelle, J. de*; *Aymé*. The exotic novel is often, as with Farrère, a novel of adventure—another type of novel which has flourished in the 20th c. (*v. Benoit*; *Mac Orlan*; *Kessel*; *Masson*).

The period since *c.* 1920 has been one of change and experiment, leading after 1950 to a radical departure from existing conventions by exponents of the *nouveau roman*. Many factors have played their part, notably the increasing openness of French writers to foreign influences of all kinds (*v. Foreign Influences*, 6), the impact of two world wars, and a growing preoccupation with the plight of man in modern society and the essential 'absurdity' of the human condition. 1913 saw the publication of two works which had a great impact on the form and content of the novel: the first volume of Proust's *A la recherche du temps perdu* and Alain-Fournier's *Le *Grand Meaulnes*. Proust, by far the greater influence, invaded the hitherto unexplored realms of instinct and intuition, the dark, uneasy world of the subconscious (to become darker and uneasier as Freudian theories gained currency); Alain-Fournier largely introduced the novel of fantasy and poetic adventure, situated in the strange, luminous world that hovers between dream and reality (the return of poetry and fantasy to the novel, a reaction against *Naturalism that had been in progress since the late 19th c., is also evident in the pre-war work of Miomandre, Giraudoux, Colette, Larbaud, etc.). Both novels were subversive of objectivity and chronological plot, and led to technical innovations to suit a new, amorphous content. In the novel of fantasy, which was particularly

open to the influence of *Surrealism, content became disjointed and as unselective as dreams themselves, or (as with Giraudoux) reached almost mystifying heights of imagery and paradox. The novel deriving from Proust was long, discursive, and infinitely complicated, and the Proustian structure lent itself to such innovations as the form of Gide's *Les *Faux-Monnayeurs*, where the reader shares in the creative process through the journal of the character Édouard, who is himself writing a novel entitled *Les Faux-Monnayeurs*.

In the post-war decade, poetry and fantasy invaded the novel and there was an outpouring of poetic and imaginative fiction of all kinds, e.g. *Giraudoux's *Suzanne et le Pacifique*, *Aragon's *Le Paysan de Paris*, *Ramuz's *La Beauté sur la terre*, *Breton's *Nadja*, *Cocteau's *Les Enfants terribles*; and *v. Larbaud*; *Morand*. The success at this time of the novel of fantasy reflected the widespread desire to escape from reality, from the memory of war and the problems of peace. The rapid growth from now on of the detective novel (*v. Simenon*) was another aspect of escapism. Meanwhile, in the hands of Gide, Mauriac, J. de Lacretelle, Jouhandeau, Bernanos, Green, and Radiguet, the novel of psychological analysis became a novel of interior conflict, depicting the soul beset by moral, religious, and political uncertainty, by the uneasy preoccupation with sin and sex and the growing sense of 'la part du diable' which marked the period. During the inter-war years, several novelists, following in the wake of Balzac and Zola in the 19th c. and Rolland in the early 20th c., developed the *roman-fleuve* and *roman-cycle*; *v. Duhamel*; *Martin du Gard*; *Lacretelle, J. de*; *Romains*. This period also saw the continuing work of Colette, a writer unique in her subtle exploration of physical sensitivity.

The birth in 1929 of the *roman populiste* at the hands of Léon Lemonnier (1890–1953) and André Thérive (pseudonym of Roger Puthosté, 1891–1967) marked a return to *Naturalism (but in a muted, more lyrical form) and a reaction against introspection and fantasy in the novel. The *roman populiste*, sympathetically depicting the life of the common people, is well exemplified by *Dabit's *Hôtel du Nord*. A similar reaction against the flight from reality was very evident in the novelists who came to the fore in the later '20s and largely dominated the '30s, e.g. Malraux, who asserted that 'le roman moderne est un moyen d'expression privilégié du tragique de l'homme, non une élucidation de l'individu' and whose novels of action treated of the 'absurdity' of the human condition (henceforward a recurrent theme), Aragon, Bernanos, Montherlant, Saint-Exupéry, Giono, Drieu la Rochelle. Different though they were in many respects, these novelists were united by a common ethical concern. In their hands, the novel became a vehicle for questioning the accepted values of the modern world and for professing faith in new ones—heroism with Malraux, social justice with Aragon, etc. Under the pressure of the moral and political crises of the '30s, and in the climate of *Personnalisme* (*v. Mounier*), there emerged the concept of *littérature engagée* which is relevant in the work of many creative writers of the inter-war and post-war years. At the same time, there were signs of a new intellectual climate in such works as *Céline's *Voyage au bout de la nuit* and *Queneau's *Le Chiendent*. They, too, depict an 'absurd' world, but, with Céline in particular, it is a world without values, seen in all its nakedness. Moreover, both writers mount an attack on the literary language, and Céline's use of the spoken language was to have a great impact on the style of the novel. Their world heralds that of the so-called *roman existentialiste*, which emerged in 1938 with *Sartre's *La Nausée* and dominated the scene till the mid-1950s—though the war years also saw the literature of the *Resistance (e.g. Vercors's *Le Silence de la mer*), and experience of the Occupation and of the concentration camps was to provide material for novelists including Vailland, Dutourd, Gascar, and Cayrol. The novels of Sartre and Camus are commonly associated, with some justification, under the label of *Existentialism, though it should be noted that this label is an over-simplification and was, in fact, rejected by Camus. Broadly speaking, Sartre and Camus gave the novel a metaphysical rather than ethical content and a new structure, and their work reflects the impact of the style and techniques of the American novel. In the view of the critic Gaëtan Picon, each of their novels 'was constructed like a theoretical essay, its aim being to analyze fully a proposition. Hence an important stylistic change. There was no longer any question of being carried away by an impulse, of arousing the emotions, or seeking to transmute experience. The aim was to be complete, clear, accessible, simple.' Their writing was as unpoetic as their vision of man's plight: Picon has described the literature they dominated as 'metaphysical naturalism rather than existentialism'. *v. Grand Prix des meilleurs romans du demi-siècle*.

The appearance in 1948 of N. Sarraute's *Portrait d'un inconnu* (*v. Anti-roman*) heralded the *nouveau roman*, which emerged *c.* 1955. Its chief exponents—N. Sarraute, Robbe-Grillet, Butor, and C. Simon (for others *v. Nouveau roman*)—are very different writers, but they share the conviction that the possibilities of the traditional novel that seeks to tell a story and to bring characters to life have been exhausted, and they are united in their rejection of traditional forms and in their search for forms better adapted to modern sensibilities. Their work represents the culmination of a trend in the French novel attributable to the combined influence of such innovators as Proust, Joyce, Kafka, R. Roussel, and the American novelists, and also to the *Surrealists' challenge to literature—a trend evident in the work of writers including Céline, Queneau, G. Bataille, Blanchot, Genet, and Beckett, all of whom in varying degrees reject or undermine the traditional forms of the novel and often also the accepted values of language. The general characteristics of the *nouveau roman* include an absence or near-absence of continuous plot, chronological sequence, and conventional suspense; an attempt to abandon characters—and their psychological analysis—in the accepted sense (i.e. the type of the lover, the unfaithful wife, the miser, the hypocrite, etc., whose feelings and motives are analysed by himself or others), and to start from much lower depths—'the elementary stammerings and visceral shivers of people' (Henri Peyre), e.g. from N. Sarraute's *tropismes*; a preoccupation with objects, continuing a trend away from anthropomorphism in the novel that was already evident in the work of Sartre and Camus. The *nouveau roman* often takes the form of what Sartre has called 'le roman d'un roman qui ne se fait pas' and Butor 'le roman comme recherche' (e.g. C. *Simon's Le Vent*, where the narrator, instead of relating a story, is in search of it), and the reader is often left to create the novel himself from the raw materials provided.

Alongside these developments, there flows the mainstream of the traditional novel, which has remained remarkably vigorous in the hands of writers who, though open to stylistic and technical innovations of all kinds, do not seriously challenge the novel as such. Besides the continuing work of established writers like Aragon, Arland, Gracq, Green, Guilloux, Mauriac, Montherlant, and some of the exponents of the historical novel, the exotic novel, the regional novel, and the novel of adventure listed above (e.g. Bosco, Chamson, Giono, Kessel, Troyat, M. Yourcenar), the post-war period has seen the emergence of many new novelists broadly in the traditional convention, such as H. Bazin, Curtis, Dutourd, Gascar, F.

Marceau, Nimier, Z. Oldenbourg, Peyrefitte, C. Rochefort, F. Sagan, and Vailland.

Novembre, v. Flaubert.

Nucingen, Baron Frédéric de, in Balzac's *Comédie humaine* (notably in *La Maison Nucingen, Le *Père Goriot, *Splendeurs et misères des courtisanes, *Histoire de la grandeur et de la décadence de César Birotteau*), a repulsive Jewish financier from Alsace who laid the foundations of his wealth by speculating on the outcome of *Waterloo.

Nuits, Les (1835–7, in the *Revue des Deux Mondes*), four famous lyrics by Musset, *La Nuit de mai, La Nuit de décembre, La Nuit d'août, La Nuit d'octobre*. In dialogues with his Muse, the poet dwells on the anguish he has suffered through disappointed love, but in the end prefers to relive his agony rather than forget it.

Nuit vénitienne, La, v. Un Spectacle dans un fauteuil.

Numa Roumestan (1881), a novel by A. Daudet, a perceptive study of the contrast between the French of the North and the *gens du Midi*. Numa Roumestan, a typical *méridional* (said to be drawn from Gambetta), studies law in Paris and, thanks to his natural exuberance and powers of oratory, carries all before him, finally rising to be minister of education. But he cannot realize that, in the eyes of the cold, realistic Northerners with whom he comes into contact, promises must be kept; and his expansiveness nearly ruins both his private and his public life.

O

Obermann (1804; 1795, in embryonic form, as *Aldomen*), by Senancour, a famous pre-*Romantic novel (in letter form; there is no real plot). It was to appeal increasingly to generations tortured by the *mal du siècle*, and its influence can be seen in, for example, Balzac's Le *Lys dans la

vallée, Sainte-Beuve's *Volupté, G. *Sand's Lélia.

The hero writes to a friend over a period of many years, describing his state of soul. He is melancholy, frustrated, unhappy in love, and powerless to rouse himself to any kind of active life. He often writes of his surroundings (a remote Alpine valley; the Forest of Fontainebleau), investing them with his own gloom.

Obey, André (1892–1975), dramatist and actor-manager. His works include *Noé* (1931; handling the story of Noah with poetic freshness and wit), *Le Viol de Lucrèce* (1931; the rape of Lucretia, treated as a Greek tragedy; later the basis of an opera by Benjamin Britten), and *La Bataille de la Marne* (1932), all produced by the *Compagnie des Quinze*, with which he was closely associated; *Le Trompeur de Séville* (1937) and *L'Homme de cendres* (1950), both on the Don Juan theme; *Lazare* (1952); *Les Trois Coups de minuit* (1958); and v. *Amiel, D.*

Oblat, L', v. Huysmans.

Occident, L' (1901–10; 1912–14), f. by Mithouard, one of the most representative literary (mainly poetical) reviews of the early 20th c. Others associated with it included Jammes, Morice, Vielé-Griffin, Visan.

Oceano nox, v. *Rayons et les ombres, Les*.

Ode, a lyric poem in a series of metrically similar stanzas, usually composed of lines of varying length and complex rhyme-scheme. The name was first used by Ronsard, who imitated both the Pindaric and Horatian odes. From the 17th c. the *ode* was used for heroic, religious, philosophical, and satirical themes, usually in a more simplified metrical form. A lighter type of *ode*, sometimes called *odelette*, is hardly distinguishable from the *chanson*. v. *Malherbe*; *Rousseau, J.-B.*; *Chénier, A.*; *Lamartine*; *Hugo*; *Banville*.

Odéon, Théâtre de l', f. 1797 in the *Théâtre du Luxembourg* (near the Palais du *Luxembourg*), built 1782 for the *Comédie-Française*. The original intention was to include opera in the repertory (hence the name *Odéon*, in reference to the theatre built by Pericles in Athens for musical competitions). It

was burnt down in 1799, reopened in 1808 as the *Théâtre de l'Impératrice*, damaged by fire again in 1818, and reopened in 1819, completely reorganized, as a second *Théâtre-Français* (v. *Comédie-Française*). It had a chequered career till 1841, but thereafter established itself as the second national theatre, with both a classical and a modern repertory. From 1945 till 1959 its company was merged with that of the *Comédie-Française*, and it became the *Théâtre-Français, Salle Luxembourg*, with a mainly modern repertory. In 1959 it regained its independence as the State-subsidized *Odéon-Théâtre de France*, with Barrault as director.

From 1873 till recent times the 'Galeries de l'Odéon', covered arcades along three sides of the theatre, belonged to a firm of publishers and booksellers and were a favourite haunt of book-lovers: books lined the walls and were enticingly piled on long trestle tables.

Odes et ballades (1826; inc. *Odes et poésies diverses*, 1822, and *Nouvelles Odes*, 1824; augm. 1828), a collection of poems by Hugo, prefaced by one of his first *Romantic manifestos. Some of the *odes* are intimate and domestic, more are political (e.g. *Le Sacre de Charles X*), celebrating events of the restored monarchy. The *ballades* (e.g. *Le Géant*; *La Fiancée du timbalier*) are already picturesquely Romantic.

Odes funambulesques, v. Banville.

Odette (de Crécy), in Proust's *A la recherche du temps perdu* (notably in *Du côté de chez Swann* (*Un Amour de Swann*)), a *demi-mondaine* of the Second Empire (the mysterious 'dame en rose' who visited Marcel's worldly uncle Adolphe; the 'Mlle de Sacripant' painted by *Elstir) and a *protégée* of the *Verdurins, then the mistress of Charles *Swann, who marries her for the sake of their daughter, *Gilberte. Marcel first sees her as Mme Swann, on his walks as a child at *Combray. When his life becomes linked with the Swann *ménage* through his love for Gilberte, his friendship with Swann, etc., he observes her profiting by the *Dreyfus scandal and the admiration of her men friends to create a *salon* and rise in society. After Swann's death she marries M. de Forcheville, a former lover. She ends (at the reception in *Le Temps retrouvé*, ii) as mistress of the duc de *Guermantes.

Œdipe, (1) a tragedy by Corneille, based on Sophocles' *Oedipus tyrannus* (Oedipus, king of Thebes, discovers that not only has he unwittingly killed Laius, the late king, whose widow Jocasta he has married, but that he is, in fact, the son of Laius and Jocasta); produced 1659. Corneille spoils the simple grandeur of the original by adding the invented character Dircé, daughter and heiress of Laius, and her love affair with Thésée, prince of Athens.

(2) Voltaire's first tragedy; successfully produced 1718 (publ. 1719). He, too, added a romantic element, also polemical allusions to religious and political questions.

Œil-de-bœuf, L', an antechamber adjoining the king's bedroom at *Versailles where courtiers awaited the king; so called from an oval window inserted (1701) in one of its walls.

Œnone, in Racine's *Phèdre*.

Œuvre, L' (1886), one of Zola's *Rougon-Macquart* novels, less dedicated to his general thesis than the rest of the series and of interest as a picture of the early *Impressionists. *v. Cézanne; Manet*.

Claude *Lantier (often identified as an amalgam of Manet and Cézanne) inherits money and becomes an artist in Paris, exhibiting his great picture *Plein Air* at the *Salon des refusés* (*cf.* Manet's *Déjeuner sur l'herbe*). His revolutionary technique excites derision, but it also initiates the *École de plein air* and various mediocre artists make their names by discreetly imitating it. He sacrifices his fortune and family to his art, but finally becomes impotent before his own theories and commits suicide. His novelist friend

Sandoz is a mouthpiece for Zola's theories of his own *Rougon-Macquart* novels.

Œuvre, Théâtre de l', f. 1890 in Paris as the *Théâtre d'Art* by the poet Fort (then 18) in reaction against *Naturalism in the theatre (*v. Théâtre Libre*). It staged *Symbolist plays (e.g. by Maeterlinck), adaptations of poems by Laforgue, Mallarmé, Rimbaud, etc. Young artists (Gauguin, Bonnard, Vuillard) painted the scenery and illustrated the programmes. Under the direction (1893–1929) of the actor Lugné-Poë, who renamed it *Théâtre de l'Œuvre*, it became an influential *avant-garde* theatre, staging works by young or unknown French dramatists (Lugné-Poë excelled at discovering new talent) and by foreign dramatists, e.g. Jarry (*Ubu Roi*), Claudel, Salacrou, Achard, Sarment, Ibsen, Bjørnson, Strindberg, Wilde (*Salomé*). *v. Theatres and Theatre Companies*.

Œuvres et les hommes, Les, *v. Barbey d'Aurevilly*.

Offenbach, JACQUES (1819–80), composer, b. at Cologne, the son of a German Jew, lived in Paris from 1833 (when he arrived to study music at the *Conservatoire*), and later took French nationality. He began as a violoncellist in the orchestra at the *Opéra-Comique*, made his name as a virtuoso at private recitals, and became leader of the orchestra at the *Comédie-Française* (1850–5). He then leased a small theatre, the *Bouffes-Parisiens*, to produce his own operettas (a mixture of *vaudeville and *opéra-comique*), with good, amusing libretti by Meilhac and L. Halévy, e.g. *Orphée aux enfers* (1858), *La Belle Hélène* (1864; about Helen of Troy), *La Vie parisienne* (1866), *La Grande-Duchesse de Gérolstein* (1867), *La *Périchole* (1868). Few memoirs and social histories of the Second Empire fail to mention him, for his infectiously gay, melodious works were the rage of Paris and seem to have reflected the pleasure-loving, ironic spirit of the day. He died just before the production of his most lasting work, *Les Contes d'Hoffmann* (1880; based on

*Hoffmann's *Phantasiestücke*), with libretto by Jules Barbier and Michel Carré, minor dramatists. *v. Schneider.*

Ogier, FRANÇOIS, *v. Tyr et Sidon.*

Ogier le Danois, hero of the **chanson de geste* (**Doon de Mayence cycle) *La Chevalerie Ogier,* a rehandling (*c.* 1200) attributed to Raimbert de Paris of a lost earlier poem; also of **Adenet le Roi's *Enfances Ogier.* He also figures in poems of the **Charlemagne cycle, including the **Chanson de Roland.* He is identified with the historical Autcharius, a Frankish warrior who fought Charlemagne and was then reconciled to him. His legend was early associated with the abbey of St. Faro at Meaux.

In the *Chevalerie Ogier* he is at Charlemagne's court, a hostage for his father, and wins favour by his exploits in Italy. But his son is killed by Charlemagne's son in a quarrel, whereupon, seized with rage, he kills the queen's nephew and even attempts to kill the king himself. He is pursued, besieged, and imprisoned, but later released to fight the Saracens.

Oh! les beaux jours, v. Beckett.

Ohnet, GEORGES (1848–1918), a novelist whose snobbishly sentimental best-sellers (also usually dramatized), e.g. *Serge Panine* (1881), *Le *Maître de forges* (1882), *La Comtesse Sarah* (1883), *La Grande Marnière* (1885), aroused the disgusted wit of such critics as A. France and J. Lemaître.

Oiseau bleu, L', v. Maeterlinck.

Oiseaux s'envolent et les fleurs tombent, Les, v. Bourges.

Oldenbourg, ZOÉ (1916–), novelist of Russian birth, author of lively, well-documented historical novels (e.g. *Argile et cendres,* 1946; *La Pierre angulaire,* 1953; *Les Brûlés,* 1960, about the **Albigeois*; *Les Cités charnelles,* 1961; *La Joie des pauvres,* 1970) and studies (*Le Bûcher de Montségur,*

1959, also on the *Albigeois*; *Les Croisades,* 1965).

Olenix du Mont-Sacré, *v. Nicolas de Montreux.*

Olim, Les, registers recording enactments (1254–1318) of the **parlement* of Paris.

Olimpie, a tragedy by Voltaire; produced 1764. Olimpie (daughter of Alexander the Great and his wife Statira) loves and is about to marry Cassandre, king of Macedonia. She knows nothing of her parentage, nor that Cassandre has earlier killed her father and, as he believes, her mother—a deed he has bitterly regretted. Antigone, a rival king, discovers the secret of her birth and he and Cassandre fiercely contend for her hand. Meanwhile, Statira reappears, recognizes Olimpie, and—convinced that Cassandre will prevail over Antigone—takes her own life, commanding Olimpie to marry Antigone. Olimpie, torn between love and duty, throws herself on her mother's pyre.

Olive, L', v. Du Bellay.

Olivet, PIERRE-JOSEPH THOULIER, ABBÉ D' (1682–1768), man of letters, translator, and grammarian; sometime tutor to Voltaire, whom he later 'received' into the **Académie.* He carried **Pellisson's *Histoire de l'Académie française* down to 1700 (1729).

Olivetan, PIERRE ROBERT, *known as* (d. 1538), *v. Bible, French Versions of.*

Olivier, in the **chansons de geste,* one of Charlemagne's *Douze *Pairs*; son of Renier and nephew of Girart, the unruly sons of **Garin de Monglane*; bosom friend of **Roland.* His prudent valour contrasts with Roland's proud impetuosity. His early exploits are related in **Girart de Viane.* He (with his sister Aude) is among the defenders of Viane, Roland among the besiegers. Roland falls in love with Aude and tries to carry her off, but Olivier rescues her. It is decided that

Roland and Olivier shall fight a duel to decide the issue of the war. Their long duel, fought with great chivalry, is finally stopped by divine intervention; they swear eternal friendship, and Aude is betrothed to Roland. Olivier also figures in the *Pèlerinage de Charlemagne, *Fierabras, the fight with *Ferragus, etc. He dies at Roncevaux, fighting heroically with his sword Halteclere (v. Chanson de Roland).

Olivier de la Marche, v. La Marche.

Olivier le Dain, v. Le Dain.

Ollé-Laprune, LÉON (1830–99), a philosopher whose works, e.g. De la certitude morale (1880), Le Prix de la vie (1885), La Philosophie et le temps présent (1895), influenced later Neo-Catholic philosophers (v. Blondel, M.).

Ollier, CLAUDE, v. Nouveau roman.

Olympie, v. Olimpie.

Olympio, v. Tristesse d'Olympio.

Ombre, Lai de l', v. Lai de l'ombre.

O'Meara, BARRY EDWARD (1786–1836), an Irishman, surgeon on H.M.S. Bellerophon, was authorized to go with Napoleon to St. Helena as his physician. He was there for three years, but fell out with Sir Hudson Lowe and was recalled. A French translation of his reminiscences of Napoleon in exile appeared in 1822.

Ondine, v. Giraudoux; La Motte Fouqué.

O'Neddy, Philothée, pseudonym (an anagram) of THÉOPHILE DONDEY (1811–75), a *bousingo whose poems, Feu et flamme (1833), typify the writings of the later, frenetic *Romantics. He also wrote short stories and a romance of chivalry, L'Histoire d'un anneau (1842; prose and verse). Later he was a dramatic critic.

On ne badine pas avec l'amour (1834, first in the *Revue des Deux Mondes, then

in *Un Spectacle dans un fauteuil), a 3-act prose comedy by Musset; produced 1861. It lacks the gay note of his other comedies.

Perdican is eager to comply with his uncle's wishes and marry his cousin Camille, but she rejects him. To punish her, he pretends to fall in love with Rosette, a village girl, and even decides to marry her. This breaks Camille's resistance, and she and Perdican pledge their love in a scene of reconciliation. A sudden cry reveals that Rosette has overheard them from a hiding-place. She dies; and Perdican and Camille part, unable to build their happiness on such a sacrifice.

On ne saurait penser à tout (1849, as a *feuilleton in the paper L'Ordre; 1853, in *Comédies et Proverbes), a one-act prose *proverbe by Musset, based on Carmontelle's proverbe Le Distrait; produced 1849. It is about a marquis who is young, charming, and in love, but so absent-minded that he forgets to propose.

Onuphre, the pious hypocrite in *La Bruyère's Caractères.

Opéra, Théâtre de l', v. Académie nationale de Musique.

Opéra-Comique, a State-subsidized theatre in Paris, the home of light opera, now under the same direction as the *Opéra. The opéra-comique had its origin in comedies or farces interspersed with lyrical passages sung at first to well-known airs (comédie en *vaudevilles) and later to music specially composed (comédie à ariettes). The players of the Théâtre de la Foire (v. Theatres and Theatre Companies) obtained the right to perform these c. 1713; the chief authors who wrote for them were Lesage and Piron, followed by Favart, Sedaine, and J.-J. Vadé. Despite opposition (both the Opéra and the *Italiens objected to their use of music), the players persisted, with public support, and in 1762 combined with the Italiens under the official title of Comédie-Italienne, paying the Opéra an annual tribute for their privilege. The Italian element gradually disappeared, surviving only in the name Boulevard des Italiens. From 1780 the company was known officially as the *Opéra-Comique*, and in 1783 it moved to the *Salle Favart*, on the site it still occupies. The growing popularity of light opera from now on culminated in the great vogue for it in Paris in the mid-19th c. *v. Danican*; *Grétry*; *Méhul*; *Boïeldieu*; *Auber*; *Bizet*; *Offenbach*.

Opinions de Jérôme Coignard, Les, *v. Rôtisserie de la Reine Pédauque, La.*

Oraisons funèbres, *v. Funeral Orations.*

Orasius Tubero, *v. La Mothe le Vayer.*

Orateur du genre humain, L', *v. Cloots.*

Orateur du peuple, L' (1790–95), a newspaper f. by Stanislas Fréron (1754–1802), son of É. Fréron (*v. Année littéraire*) and a member of the *Assemblée nationale*. For a time a disciple of Marat, he at first conducted the paper on violently Revolutionary lines. After Robespierre's fall (1794) he—and his paper—became violently reactionary. He went with Leclerc to San Domingo (*v. Toussaint Louverture*), and died there.

Oratoire, Congrégation de l', a congregation of priests f. 1611 in France by Cardinal Pierre de Bérulle, on the basis of that f. 1564 in Rome by St. Philip Neri. It sought to meet the need for educated, dedicated priests, and was an important factor in the Counter-Reformation. Members included Malebranche, Massillon, and Mascaron. It came to have some 75 establishments in France; also several teaching institutions (*v. Lycées and Collèges*), which played an important part in the education of the laity.

Orbigny, CHARLES DESSALINES D', *v. Dictionaries*, 1841–9.

Ordonnances of 26 July 1830, *v. Revolutions*, 2; *Press*, 5.

Oresme, NICOLAS (d. 1382), professor of theology, bishop of Lisieux, chaplain and councillor of Charles V. His works include important translations (1370–7; from a Latin text) of Aristotle, e.g. the *Ethics* and *Politics*; a famous *Traité des monnaies*, condemning the debasement of coinage (*cf. Money*); treatises on cosmography and astronomy (which he distinguished from astrology).

Oreste, in Racine's **Andromaque.*

Oreste, *v. Voltaire*, 1.

Orgon, in Molière's *Le *Tartuffe.*

Oriane, *v. Guermantes.*

Orientales, Les (1829), a collection of lyrics by Hugo (e.g. *Le Feu du ciel*; *Clair de lune*; *Les Djinns*; *Grenade*; *Sara la baigneuse*; *Mazeppa*); mainly on Oriental themes. With imagery and rhythmical effects new to French verse, he vividly conveys his idea of the heat, languor, and savagery of the East.

Oriflamme, the small red three-pointed banner of the kings of France; originally the banner of the abbots of *Saint-Denis. *Cf. Montjoie.*

Origines de la France contemporaine, Les (1875–94, 6 vols.), by Taine, an historical study of pre-Revolutionary France (vol. I, *L'Ancien Régime*), the Revolution (vols. II–IV, *L'Anarchie*; *La Conquête Jacobine*; *Le Gouvernement révolutionnaire*), and the Napoleonic and post-Napoleonic eras (vols. V–VI, *Le Régime moderne*). Two long surveys of the state of the Church and of education (VI) were to have been followed by other surveys of the social scene, but Taine died before completing them. His fame as an historian rests on this work, the volumes on the Revolution being the most generally read. Later historians have, however, found his documentation incomplete and unmethodical, and have criticized him for allowing his anti-Revolutionary convictions (which had been intensified by his horror at the events of the *Commune of 1871) to lead him into unwarranted generalizations. But as literature, if not as history, the whole work is characteristically brilliant and eloquent, and highly readable.

Origines du christianisme, Les, v. Renan.

Orléanistes, in the 19th c., those monarchists who supported the younger— *Orléans—branch of the royal family, i.e. Louis-Philippe and his descendants. v. Revolutions,* 2 and 3; *Chambord; Légitimistes.*

Orléans, a name borne by younger princes of the blood from 1392, when Charles VI made the duchy of Orléans an apanage of the crown and bestowed it on his brother Louis. There were three branches of the house of Orléans.

(1) The *Valois-Orléans branch, which began with the above Louis, duc d'Orléans (1371–1407). His grandson (by his son *Charles d'Orléans, the poet) became Louis XII. His great-grandson (by his 2nd son, Jean, duc d'Angoulême) became François Ier. This branch ended with the death of Henri III (1589).

(2) The first *Bourbon-Orléans branch, whose only male representative was Gaston, duc d'Orléans (1608–60), 3rd son of Henri IV and Marie de Médicis, brother of Louis XIII, and father of 'la Grande Mademoiselle' (*v. Montpensier*).

(3) The second *Bourbon-Orléans branch, descended from Philippe, duc d'Orléans (1640–1701; 2nd son of Louis XIII and Anne d'Autriche and only brother of Louis XIV; *cf. Palais-Royal*) through his second wife, the Princesse *Palatine (his first wife was *Henriette d'Angleterre). Members of this branch include Philippe, duc d'Orléans (1674–1723), son of the above and regent during Louis XV's minority (*v. Régence*); Louis-Philippe-Joseph (1749–93), great-grandson of the above regent and cousin of Louis XVI, who threw in his lot with the Revolution from the outset, took the name 'Philippe-Égalité' on his election (1792) to the *Convention, voted for the death of Louis XVI, and died on the

scaffold; Louis-Philippe, son of 'Philippe-Égalité', who became king in 1830 and whose great-great-grandson, Henri, comte de Paris (b. 1908), is the present pretender.

Orme du mail, L', v. Bergeret.

Orondate, in *La Calprenède's *Cassandre.*

Oronte, in Molière's *Le *Misanthrope.*

Orphée, v. Cocteau.

Orphée aux enfers, v. Offenbach.

Orphelin de la Chine, L', a tragedy by Voltaire; produced 1755.
  Genghis Khan, having overrun China and slain the emperor and five of his sons, demands the surrender of a surviving son, whom the dying emperor had entrusted to the mandarin Zamti. Zamti substitutes his own son for the infant prince and gives him up, but his wife Idamé, unable to bear the sacrifice of her child, rushes forward and reveals the deception. Now Genghis had once loved, and still loves, Idamé; and he threatens to kill Zamti and his child unless the prince and Idamé are surrendered. But the courage of Zamti and Idamé, who prefer death to dishonour, finally wins the conqueror's admiration and teaches him to conquer himself.

Orphelin du Temple, L'; Orpheline du Temple, L', Louis-Charles de France, the dauphin, and his sister Marie-Thérèse-Charlotte de France, children of Louis XVI and Marie-Antoinette (*v. Bourbon* (1)), imprisoned with their parents in the *Temple in August 1792. After his father's execution (when, for the *émigrés* and the foreign powers, he became Louis XVII) the boy was taken from his mother and put in charge of the guard Simon, a cobbler. He is said to have died in prison in 1795, but the circumstances were mysterious and some believed that his escape had been contrived and a sickly child substituted for him. There were later some 30 pretenders ('faux dauphins'), notably Charles Naundorff (d. 1845), a

Prussian clockmaker, whose claim was taken to the French courts and gained credence in some quarters, and Mathurin Bruneau (d. *c.* 1825), a Norman peasant, the son of a cobbler.

Marie-Thérèse was handed over to the Austrians (1795) in exchange for eight French prisoners. She married (1799) the duc d'Angoulême (*v. Bourbon* (3)) and went into exile with him after the 1830 *Revolution.

Orsini, Félix, *v. Machine infernale.*

Ossian. In 1762–3, James Macpherson, a Scottish man of letters, published long epic poems alleged to be translations from the Gaelic of Ossian, a 3rd-c. warrior-bard. Though later found to be a hoax, they were much admired at the time. Translated into French in 1777 (by Letourneur) and again in 1810 (with a preface by Ginguené), they were a strong influence in the pre-*Romantic era (*v. Foreign Influences*, 2; *cf. Young, E.*) and were more than once imitated. Their wild, romantic quality served to emphasize Mme de Staël's distinction between the literatures of the North and the South.

Otage, L' (1911), a drama by Claudel, produced 1914; the first of a trilogy about the Coufontaine family, completed by *Le Pain dur* and *Le Père humilié.*

The period is 1812–14. Sygne and her cousin Georges are the last members of the old family of Coufontaine, ruined by the Revolution. Georges rescues the pope (confined in France by Napoleon) and takes him to the derelict abbey of Coufontaine. Turelure, a vile, low-born, ex-Revolutionary, now Napoleon's man and local *préfet*, discovers the escape and exacts Sygne's hand in marriage as the price of his silence. She is pledged to Georges, but sacrifices love and honour to save the pope. The last act opens in 1814,

just before Napoleon's first abdication. Turelure, now *préfet de la Seine*, tells Sygne that he will hand over Paris to Louis XVIII if she can induce Georges to make over all his Coufontaine rights to the son born of her marriage. Georges arrives as the king's envoy to treat with Turelure and after a painful interview with Sygne signs the necessary deed. He tries to shoot Turelure, but Sygne intercepts the bullet and dies. Georges is also killed. Turelure receives Louis XVIII and the Allied sovereigns in front of the bier on which their bodies have been laid.

Othon, one of Corneille's less successful tragedies; produced 1664. The theme (from Tacitus) is the struggle for the succession to the Roman emperor Galba.

Oton de Granson (d. 1397), the French poet imitated and translated by Chaucer, who called him 'Graunson flour of hem that make in France'. Froissart mentions him as fighting at the siege of La Rochelle (1372) with the earl of Pembroke. After this he was in England. Later, he played an important part at court in his native Savoy and died in a duel defending himself against a charge of complicity in the murder of the count of Savoy. His father-in-law was lord of *Coppet.

Oudinot, Nicolas-Charles, *v. Maréchal.*

Ozanam, Frédéric (1813–53), critic and literary historian, professor of foreign literature at the *Sorbonne from 1844. He was also a founder of the Society of St. *Vincent de Paul, and his eloquent, poetical lectures at Notre-Dame were a feature of the religious life of Paris. His writings—intended to show religion glorified by history—include *Les Poètes franciscains en Italie au XIIIᵉ siècle* (1852).

P

Pagello, PIETRO, *v. Musset.*

Pagnol, MARCEL (1895–1974), dramatist and film-writer (a member of the *Académie, 1946), made his name with the satirical comedy *Topaze* (1928; a master in a seedy private school is dismissed for being honest about his pupils' progress when a few sycophantic lies would be better policy; he finds work as unwitting stooge to a local big-business crook and, when his eyes are at last opened, becomes so efficient that he outwits his employer) and the trilogy *Marius* (1929), *Fanny* (1931), and *César* (1936; a film—later a play), comedies of life in Marseilles. His other film dialogues (some of them adaptations of works by Giono) include those for *Angèle, Regain, La Femme du boulanger, Carnaval, La Fille du puisatier*. His memories of his childhood in Provence (*La Gloire de mon père*, 1957, etc.) are characteristically gay and moving.

Pailleron, ÉDOUARD (1834–99), dramatist, wrote, notably, *Le Monde où l'on s'ennuie* (1881), a lively satire of a world in which 'culture' is an amusement for society women and political and literary honours depend on skilful wire-pulling; also *Le Monde où l'on s'amuse* (1868), *Les Faux Ménages* (1869), *L'Âge ingrat* (1879), etc. His young girls are drawn with skill and sympathy.

Pain dur, Le, *v. Claudel.*

Pairs, Les Douze; Pairs de France. The *Douze Pairs* ('Twelve Peers') were Charlemagne's paladins, his chief warrior lords. The list differs in the various *chansons de geste. In the *Chanson de Roland they are *Roland, *Olivier, Gérin, Gérier, Bérengier, Otton, Samson, Engelier, Ivon, Ivoire, Anséis, Girard.

In the early 13th c. there were, in fact, 'Twelve Peers of France' forming a Court of Peers (six ecclesiastical, six lay), which in 1202 declared King John of England deprived of Normandy and his other fiefs in France. These peerages were later suppressed. The dignity was afterwards revived and existed, though without its former importance, till the Revolution (*v. Saint-Simon, duc de*). There were again *pairs de France* from the Restoration (1814) till the 1848 *Revolution. These peers, members of the *Chambre des Pairs* (*cf. Sénat*), the upper house of the legislature, were created by the king, the dignity being for life only after 1831.

Païva, La, often mentioned in literary memoirs and correspondence of the later 19th c., was THÉRÈSE LACHMANN (b. 1819), a Russian Jewess of humble birth, who left her husband (a tailor), arrived in Paris *c.* 1840, and became known in artistic circles. She married (1849) the marquis de la Païva, a rich Portuguese. She soon left him (but retained his name) to live, still in Paris, with a rich Prussian, keeping open house for writers, artists, and musicians. Some time in the 1870s she was suspected of political intrigue and had to leave Paris.

Paix du ménage, La, *v. Comédie humaine, La* (*Scènes de la vie privée*).

Paix perpétuelle, Projet de, *v. Saint-Pierre, abbé de; Rousseau, J.-J.*

Paladins, *v. Pairs.*

Palais-Bourbon, on the left bank of the Seine in Paris, on the site of a residence erected *c.* 1728 for the daughter of Louis XIV and Mme de Montespan. It has been in turn the seat of the *Conseil de Cinq-Cents* (under the *Directoire), the *Corps législatif (under the *Consulat and Empire), the *Chambre des* *Députés (after the Restoration and under the Third *Republic), the *Corps législatif* (under Napoleon III), and the *Assemblée nationale (under the Fourth and Fifth Republics).

Palais-Royal, on the right bank of the Seine in Paris (on a quadrilateral site fronting on to the Rue Saint-Honoré and flanked by the *Comédie-Française*), a palace and gardens (surrounded by arcades) with many social, political, and literary associations. It was built c. 1636 for Richelieu and known first as the Palais Cardinal. Its gardens were open to the public and became a place of popular resort. Corneille made it the scene of an early comedy (*La Galerie du Palais*).

Richelieu left it to Louis XIII. Louis XIV lived in it as a child with his widowed mother, Anne d'Autriche. He placed one of its halls at the disposal of *Molière's company (1661; cf. Académie nationale de Musique*) and later (1692) gave it to his brother, the duc d'Orléans. As the residence of the *Orléans family it was a notorious place of revelry during the *Régence* and in the time of Philippe-Égalité, who began the construction of wooden arcades, the *galeries de bois*, on three sides of the garden, with a view to letting them as shops and dwellings. During the Revolution and early 19th c.—when the palace was called the Palais-Égalité (1792-9) and the Palais du Tribunat (from 1799 it was the seat of the *Tribunat—v. Consulat*)—the cafés on the ground-floor of the *galeries de bois* were hotbeds of political intrigue (*v. Café*), while the restaurants, gaming-houses, and private dwellings on the upper storeys were the haunt of gamesters and prostitutes. (There are good descriptions in, for example, A. *France's Les Dieux ont soif*; Balzac's *Illusions perdues*.) Louis-Philippe, who occupied the palace for some years from 1814, demolished the wooden *galeries* and spent much money on restoration. It was badly damaged by fire in the *Commune* of 1871, but again restored. The main buildings are now in government occupation. The gardens are a place of repose and recreation, the shops of the stone arcades (replacing the *galeries de bois*) are a lure for collectors of postage-stamps and *antiquités*, the dwellings above are still inhabited, or coveted, by writers and artists.

Palaprat, JEAN (1650-1721), a dramatist remembered for his collaboration with Brueys in comedies and farces, notably *L'Avocat Pathelin* (1706; an adaptation of *Pathelin*), also *Le Grondeur* (1691).

Palatine, CHARLOTTE-ÉLISABETH DE BAVIÈRE, PRINCESSE (1652-1722), b. at Heidelberg, great-granddaughter of James I and cousin of George I; second wife of the duc d'*Orléans (brother of Louis XIV) and mother of the regent (*v. Régence*). Her letters (translated for the most part from the German) show her a woman of strong character, simple, sensible, humorous, and outspoken. She provides much valuable information about life at court, is very critical of Louis XIV and Mme de Maintenon (whom she detested), and also refers to the exiled Stuarts, William III, the duke of Marlborough, etc.

Palinod, *v. Puy.*

Palissot, CHARLES PALISSOT DE MONTENOY, *known as* (1730-1814), a dramatist highly inimical to the *philosophes* (though in later life he drew nearer to them, and seems to have remained on good terms with Voltaire). His works include *Les Originaux, ou le Cercle* (1755), a light comedy caricaturing various social types, some resembling J.-J. Rousseau, Mme du Châtelet, and Voltaire; *Petites Lettres sur de grands philosophes* (1757); *Les Philosophes* (1760), a comedy modelled on *Les *Femmes savantes*, a rather coarse attack on the *Encyclopédistes*, but a considerable success despite their wrath; *Les Courtisanes* (1782; *v. Censorship, Dramatic*), a comedy violently satirizing the courtesans then prominent in Parisian life. *v. Poinsinet.*

Palissy, BERNARD (c. 1510-89), a famous potter, also author of works on natural science; a *Huguenot who died imprisoned in the *Bastille*. A low-born, self-educated man of scientific and inquiring mind, he devoted many years to experiments in enamels and in the production of high-relief ware, achieving results which won him the protection of Catherine de Médicis and lasting fame.

His *Recette véritable par laquelle tous les hommes de la France pourront apprendre à multiplier... leurs trésors* (1563) and *Discours admirable de la nature des eaux et fontaines...* (1580; inc. a vivid account of his early poverty and setbacks) reflect his strong, elevated character and his love of nature.

Palma-Cayet, PIERRE-VICTOR (1525–1610), chronologer royal under Henri IV, author of records of his reign entitled *Chronologie novénaire* and *Chronologie septénaire*.

Palmes académiques, an Order instituted in 1808 to reward academic merit. There are three classes: *Chevalier*, *Officier*, and *Commandeur* (formerly *Officier d'Académie* and *Officier de l'Instruction publique*).

Paludes, *v. Gide.*

Pamphile et Galatée, a 14th-c. version by Jehan Bras-de-Fer of the 12th-c. Latin poem *Pamphilus*, a dialogue on love (*amour courtois*).

Panama, L'Affaire du, the resounding scandal over the widespread official corruption and abuse of funds revealed by the failure in 1889 of a company promoted in 1881 (largely by de Lesseps, of Suez Canal fame) to finance the construction of a canal across the Isthmus of Panama. It forms the background of *Barrès's Leurs figures*. (The canal was completed in 1914 by American enterprise.)

Panard, CHARLES-FRANÇOIS (1674–1765), prolific author of songs, *vaudevilles*, and *opéras-comiques* of a moral and sentimental cast.

Panckoucke, a distinguished family of publishers in the 18th and 19th cs., originally of Bruges, later of Lille, including (1) ANDRÉ-JOSEPH (1700–53), resident in Lille, who wrote burlesque poems (at times attacking Voltaire) and

compiled manuals, notably a dictionary of proverbs (*v.* Dictionaries, 1748); (2) CHARLES-JOSEPH (1736–98), son of (1), the most famous member of the family and noted for his liberal treatment of authors. He came to Paris in 1760, acquired various periodicals (e.g. the *Mercure de France*; the *Journal des savants*), founded the *Moniteur universel*, and initiated the *Encyclopédie méthodique* (*v.* Dictionaries, 1781–1832). *v.* Suard; (3) CHARLES-LOUIS-FLEURY (1780–1844), son of (2), who edited and published various large-scale works.

Pangloss, Maître, in Voltaire's *Candide*.

Panizzi, ANTONIO, *later* SIR ANTHONY (1797–1879), an Italian political exile who settled in England (1823), obtained a post at the British Museum (1831), and rose to be Keeper of Printed Books (1837–56). He and Mérimée became warm friends after early official contacts and some of Mérimée's most delightful letters were written to him (*Lettres à Panizzi*, 1850–70, 1881).

Pantagruel (1532 or 1533), by Rabelais, the first book of his great work. He followed it with *Gargantua* (1534), which comes first in the chronological order of the story. Then came the *Tiers Livre... du noble Pantagruel* (1546), the *Quart Livre* (1548, the prologue and 11 chs.; 1552, the complete book), and the *Cinquième Livre* (1562, 16 chs., under the title *L'Île sonnante*; 1564, the complete book).

The title *Pantagruel* is taken from the name of a devil in the *Actes des Apôtres* (by the Greban brothers; *v.* Mystère) who puts salt in drunkards' throats, and Pantagruel often appears as a being who induces thirst in others. The work was inspired by the success of a recent chap-book, *Les Grandes et Inestimables Chroniques du... géant Gargantua*, a fantastic romance about a giant created by *Merlin who overcomes the enemies of King Arthur. Rabelais makes Pantagruel Gargantua's son; he has a giant's strength, thirst, and appetite, but these characteristics are sometimes overlooked (they disappear almost entirely in the later books). His extraordinary birth and childhood parody the *chansons de geste*. As a youth he goes a round of the universities of France: at Orleans he meets the *Écolier limousin* (the occasion for ridicule of the latinized mode of speech); at Paris, where he installs himself, he visits the library of the Abbaye de *Saint-Victor (the occasion for a satirical catalogue of some of its books; *v. Béda*). A letter of advice from his father about his studies reveals Rabelais's enlightened views, in the spirit of the early *Renaissance, on the subject of education. On the model of *Folengo's *Baldus*, Pantagruel acquires a number of companions whose names indicate their salient qualities, notably Panurge (cunning roguery), also Epistemon (knowledge), Eusthenes (strength), Carpalim (speed).

Recalled from Paris to defend his country of Utopia (a name taken from Sir Thomas More) against the invading Dipsodes ('Thirsty People'), he sets out with his companions on a voyage round the Cape of Good Hope to the Far East (where Utopia lies). Aided by the stratagems of Panurge, he destroys the invaders and conquers their kingdom. Epistemon has his head cut off in the process, but, recovering, relates his experiences in Hell, where he has seen heroes of antiquity, knights of the Round Table, and popes set to the most incongruous occupations.

The *Tiers Livre* is very different in character from the two earlier books. Pantagruel, now rarely a giant, figures as a serene, sensible, good-humoured prince, while Panurge has become a fluent, pusillanimous buffoon. The scene at first is still Utopia, but soon shifts to Touraine. The prologue reflects the political situation of the day, the efforts then made to secure France against attack by Charles V. After a brilliant apologia for borrowing and lending by Panurge (who has been made lord of Salmigondin and has squandered its revenues), the question arises whether or not he would do well to marry. It is investigated by opening Virgil at random, by consulting a witch, a dumb man (who answers by signs), the old poet

Raminagrobis, the fool *Triboulet, etc.; it proves impossible to obtain the opinion of Bridoye, the judge, for he has been required to defend before the *parlement* his practice of deciding cases by throwing dice. These inquiries having proved inconclusive, it is decided to consult the oracle of the *Dive Bouteille* ('Holy Bottle') and a fleet is equipped for the purpose (the occasion for a disquisition on the virtues of the herb *Pantagruelion*, or hemp).

The *Quart Livre* relates the adventures of Pantagruel and his companions on their voyage to Cathay (via the North-West Passage) to consult the oracle, including the famous meeting with a ship carrying sheep and the bargaining between Panurge and Dindenault the sheep-merchant, also a great storm at sea (vividly described). They visit various islands, and their inhabitants provide material for satire, e.g. the episodes of the *Papefigues* (condemned to misery for having mocked the pope's image) and the *Papimanes* (devotees of the pope and the decretals), which are openly hostile to Rome. Other subjects of satire are the institution of the Lenten fast and the greed and idleness of the monks (*Gastrolâtres*).

The *Cinquième Livre* (of doubtful authenticity; *v. Rabelais*) shows a marked decline in quality and interest. It conducts the travellers to the temple of the *Dive Bouteille*, where the priestess Bacbuc conveys to them the advice of the oracle, which is 'Trinch' ('Drink'). The chief episodes are those of the *Île sonnante*, where bells ring all day and the natives are ecclesiastics of various grades in the form of birds; and of the *Chats-fourrés* ('Furred Law-cats') and their archduke Grippeminaud, a crude satire on the administration of justice.

Pantagruelion, *v. Pantagruel*.

Panthéon, Le, on the left bank of the Seine in Paris (in the Place du Panthéon), the secular burial-place of famous men accorded a State funeral. It is a vast building in the shape of a Greek cross, erected (1757–90; largely with money raised by a *loterie) to replace the almost derelict collegiate church of *Sainte-Geneviève. It was barely finished when the *Assemblée constituante decreed (1791) that it should be used solely for the purpose it has since served. It was named the Panthéon français and the words 'Aux grands hommes la Patrie reconnaissante' were carved over the portal. Mirabeau was the first to be buried there, and soon the remains of Voltaire and J.-J. Rousseau were transferred there. Hugo's funeral (1885) was among the most memorable.

Panurge, in Rabelais's *Pantagruel.

Papadiamantopoulos, IANNIS, v. Moréas.

Papefigues; Papimanes, in Rabelais's *Pantagruel.

Paquebot 'Tenacity', Le, v. Vildrac.

Paraclet, Le, v. Abélard.

Paradoxe sur le comédien, v. Diderot.

Parallèlement, v. Verlaine.

Parallèles des anciens et des modernes, v. Perrault.

Paravents, Les, v. Genet.

Parc aux cerfs, at Versailles, the notorious seraglio of Louis XV, so called, it is said, because the house stood in a district earlier used by Louis XIII as a kind of deer-farm.

Paré, AMBROISE (1517–90), surgeon, devoted his life to the improvement of surgery and was the first to effect the ligature of arteries and veins. He is said to have been devout and modest, always ending reports of cases he had cured with the words 'Je le pansai, Dieu le guérit'. He wrote surgical treatises (in French, which angered the medical faculty), e.g. his Méthode de traiter les plaies faites par harquebutes (1545), and left an auto-biography, Apologie et voyages.

Parents pauvres, Les, v. Comédie humaine, La (Scènes de la vie parisienne).

Parfaict, FRANÇOIS (1698–1753) and his brother CLAUDE (1705–77), joint authors of important records of the French drama.

Parfaite Amie, La, v. Héroët.

Pari de Pascal, Le, v. Pascal.

Paris, v. Zola.

Paris I, II, etc., Université, v. Universities, 1.

Pâris, Les frères, the brothers ANTOINE, CLAUDE, JOSEPH (known as PÂRIS-DUVERNEY; 1684–1770), and JEAN, financiers under the *Régence and Louis XV. Sons of an innkeeper, they showed their financial ability in the commissariat of the French army in Flanders, and after the collapse of *Law's système were entrusted with the national finances. Pâris-Duverney, the best known of them, fell foul of Fleury and was imprisoned (1726–8), but was favoured by Mme de Pompadour. He enriched *Beaumarchais.

Pâris, FRANÇOIS DE (1690–1727), a *Jansenist deacon who repudiated the papal bull Unigenitus and continued his life of rigorous austerity in a poor quarter of Paris, devoting himself to the people. After his death the belief grew among the Jansenists that miraculous cures, attended by violent convulsions indicative of the struggle between life and death for the body of the sick person, were worked at his tomb in the cemetery of the Église Saint-Médard. Crowds flocked there daily, fell into trances and convulsions, prophesied, and indulged in various, often unseemly, forms of religious ecstasy. Such were the activities of these convulsionnaires de Saint-Médard that the cemetery was officially closed (1732); even so, they long continued their practices furtively.

Paris, GASTON (1839–1903), a leading 19th-c. medievalist, succeeded his father Paulin Paris (also a pioneer in medieval scholarship) in the chair of Medieval French at the *Collège de France and held it for nearly 40 years. His works (inc. innumerable articles in learned journals) reflect his wide range of interests. They include *Histoire poétique de Charlemagne* (1865), *La Poésie au moyen âge* (1885 and 1895, 2 ser., in which he discusses the origins of the *chansons de geste*), *La Littérature française au moyen âge* (1888), *Mélanges linguistiques* (1905), and (alone or with others) many critical editions of medieval texts.

Paris, Treaty of, v. Coalitions (6), (7).

Parisienne, La (1885), a play by Becque. Clotilde, the chief character, plays elegant acrobatics with a husband, a lover who is jealous of him, and a second lover brought in to maintain the equilibrium.

Parisiens en province, Les, v. Comédie humaine, La (*Scènes de la vie de province*).

Parlamente, Marguerite de Navarre, in her *Heptaméron.

Parlement, an offspring of the *curia regis* or royal court, gradually developed and specialized from the time of Louis IX as a powerful judicial assembly, subordinate only to the *Conseil d'état.* By 1789 the number of *parlements* had risen to 13: Paris, Toulouse, Grenoble, Bordeaux, Dijon, Rouen, Aix, Rennes, Pau, Metz, Douai, Besançon, Nancy. The word *parlement*, used alone, usually refers to that of Paris, the most ancient. Its jurisdiction extended over half France, and it comprised 200 magistrates. It sat in general assembly only to consider the gravest questions of State (e.g. the verification and registration of the king's edicts required to give these force of law). It was divided into separate benches to deal with ordinary suits and with appeals from lower jurisdictions (v. Bailli); a special bench—the *Tournelle*—dealt with criminal cases. The other *parlements* were organized on similar lines, but had

fewer magistrates. Besides *présidents* and *conseillers*, a *parlement* included magistrates known as the *parquet* (a *procureur général*, *avocats généraux*, and their deputies, whose duty it was to defend the interests of king and State), so called because when the king presided over a session of the *parlement* they knelt in the centre of the hall, on the *parquet*. The *parlements* and subordinate magistratures had control of the *police. Officials of the *parlements* were irremovable; their offices were hereditary and could be purchased.

The *parlement* of Paris played an important part in the first *Fronde. As a privileged body of hereditary lawyers it was naturally opposed to administrative reform and new philosophies, and its influence was never more unfortunate than in the 18th c. Even so, it enjoyed some popularity as the chief seat of opposition to a corrupt court: Maupeou's suppression of all the *parlements* (1771) met with disfavour, and they were reconstituted amid general rejoicing by Louis XVI (1774).

Par les champs et par les grèves, v. Flaubert.

Parloir aux bourgeois, v. Hôtel de Ville.

Parmentier, ANTOINE-AUGUSTIN (1737–1813), agriculturist and chemist, discovered the virtues of the potato during long, hungry spells of captivity in the Seven Years War, and thereafter successfully devoted himself, with royal encouragement, to popularizing this vegetable among a people who had hitherto regarded it as fit only for animals and as a possible cause of leprosy. He wrote treatises on potatoes, grains, bread and bread-making, etc.

Parnasse contemporain, Le, v. Parnassiens.

Parnasse satirique, Le (1622), a collection of licentious verse. v. Théophile de Viau; Motin.

Parnassiculet contemporain, Le, v. Pastiche.

Parnassiens, Les, a group of poets who, from *c.* 1860, represented in poetry the scientific and positivist spirit of the age and its reaction against *Romanticism (*cf.* *Realism and *Naturalism in fiction and the drama). Their chief precursor was the Gautier of *Émaux et Camées*, the apostle of *l'*art pour l'art*; others were Banville and Baudelaire, in their concern for perfection of form. They included, notably, Leconte de Lisle (soon the acknowledged leader, in whose house they met and whose doctrines they accepted), Heredia, and Sully-Prudhomme; also Mendès and Ricard (co-founders of the group), Dierx, Ménard, Mérat, and the young Coppée. At first they were associated with various short-lived reviews: the *Revue fantaisiste* (1861; f. by Mendès); the *Revue du Progrès moral, littéraire, scientifique, et artistique* (1863–4; f. by Ricard), which had political tendencies and favoured scientific poetry; and *L'Art* (1865–6; f. by Ricard), which voiced the doctrines of *l'*art pour l'art*. At intervals during 1866 the publisher Lemerre issued the first series (in 18 fascicules) of *Le Parnasse contemporain. Recueil de vers nouveaux*, poems by members of the group, hence the name *Parnassiens*. The second series, prepared in 1869, was delayed by the *Franco-Prussian war and appeared in 1871; the third appeared in 1876 (3 vols.). Other contributors to this publication included Baudelaire (with *Nouvelles Fleurs du mal*, 16 poems), Banville, and the young A. France, Mallarmé, and Verlaine.

Eschewing the lyrical egotism and technical liberties of the Romantics, the *Parnassiens* strove to be objective, impersonal, restrained, and impeccable in form (rhythm was all-important). They confined themselves to descriptions of nature, remarkable for their static, pictorial quality and often introducing an exotic element; evocations of an historic or archaeological past; or attempts to convey philosophical conceptions, often pessimistic (*v. Foreign Influences*, 4). *Leconte de Lisle's *Poèmes antiques* and *Poèmes barbares* and *Heredia's *Les Trophées* perfectly express the *Parnassien*

ideals of serene imagery and measured rhythm.

Parny, ÉVARISTE-DÉSIRÉ DE FORGES, VICOMTE DE (1753–1814), poet, b. in the *Île Bourbon and a friend of Bertin. His *Poésies érotiques* (1778) are elegies on the vicissitudes of love, simple, elegant, and sincere, revealing at times an exotic descriptive talent that anticipates his kinsman Leconte de Lisle. His later work is inferior. Voltaire addressed him as 'Mon cher Tibulle'.

Paroles d'un croyant, v. Lamennais.

Paroxysme, *v. Literary Isms.*

Partage de midi, v. Claudel.

Partenopeus de Blois, a 12th-c. verse *roman d'aventure*. There are two 15th-c. English versions.

The story resembles that of Cupid and Psyche, with the roles reversed. Partenopeus is borne by enchantment to a fine palace where he enjoys the love of the lady Melior on condition that he does not try to see her. At last one night he turns the light of a lamp upon her, with results disastrous for both of them. But after many trials, he finally gains her hand.

Partie de chasse de Henri IV, La, by Collé, an early historical comedy (prose). The main theme is the frustration of a double intrigue by *Concini to overthrow the minister *Sully and to rob an honest miller lad of his fiancée. An episode showing the king hobnobbing with his humbler subjects (inspired by the story of Henry II and the Miller of Mansfield) was deemed disrespectful to royalty, and the play was prohibited by the *censorship under Louis XV. It was finally produced in 1774.

Partie de trictrac, La, v. Mérimée.

Parure, La (1884, in *Le *Gaulois*; 1885, in *Contes du jour et de la nuit*), a tale by

Maupassant. A young civil servant and his wife are invited to a big reception. She wears a diamond necklace borrowed from a rich friend, but loses it on the way home. The distraught couple find and buy an exact duplicate, which they return, saying nothing. Payment over the years reduces them to a coarse, spiritless poverty. One day the wife meets her friend, tells her the story, and learns that the lost necklace had been paste.

Pascal, BLAISE (1623–62), physicist and philosopher, one of the great French prose writers; b. at Clermont-Ferrand, the son of a magistrate who was an ardent student of the sciences. He showed a precocious genius for mathematics: at 16 he wrote an *Essai sur les coniques* (on conic sections); in the years 1642–52 he developed the first calculating machine. He came under *Jansenist influence (1646), but retained his scientific interests (he made notable experiments confirming Torricelli's theories of atmospheric pressure) and led a somewhat worldly life—though his *Préface d'un traité du vide*, *Prière pour le bon usage des maladies*, and *Lettre sur la mort de M. Pascal père* (all of 1648–51) show his profoundly religious disposition. The *Discours des passions de l'amour*, discovered in the 19th c. and doubtfully attributed to him, is assigned to a slightly later date. In 1654, after a period of discouragement and repeated meditations, he had a mystical experience which effected his conversion to a religious life. He recorded his devotion in an ecstatic prayer—the *Mémorial*—which he always carried with him. In 1655 he took up residence near *Port-Royal* and thereafter published nothing further in his own name. The works for which he is famous—his *Lettres provinciales* and *Pensées*—were written in the remaining years of his short life. His health had always been precarious and he died after sufferings aggravated by self-mortification.

His eighteen *Lettres de Louis de Montalte à un Provincial de ses amis et aux RR. PP. Jésuites sur la morale et la politique de ces Pères* (1656–7), known as the *Lettres provinciales*, were prompted by attacks by the *Jesuits on Jansenism and on A. *Arnauld in particular. Writing with polite irony and the utmost simplicity, lucidity, and objectivity, he defends the Jansenist doctrine of divine grace (his views on this are also expressed in his *Écrits sur la grâce* of uncertain date) and attacks the Jesuits for the laxity of their ethical code and their casuistry, making a vigorous appeal to public opinion by quotations from Jesuit works and by means of dialogues in which Jesuits are made to condemn themselves out of their own mouths. The work was a great success, and, though the Jesuits were soon to bring down *Port-Royal*, it dealt them a blow from which they never fully recovered. It was placed on the Index and the *Conseil d'état* ordered it to be burnt (1660).

His *Pensées* are fragmentary, disjointed notes (ranging from mere headings to developed expositions) for an *Apologie de la religion chrétienne*, a work conceived in his last years but never completed. It was to have been primarily directed at the *libertins* and designed to confound the rational basis of incredulity by showing the impotence of reason in metaphysical matters. For reason, suspended between two infinities which it cannot grasp, and so unable to seize the whole, can, he submits, know nothing but 'some appearances in the midst of things'. Faith, on the other hand, is not contrary to reason, but above it. We must venerate the Christian faith, for the story of the Fall and the Redemption alone explains the contradictions of human nature. Moreover, its truth is attested by the miracles and prophecies (he devotes much attention to these). Finally, faith is desirable because it brings true happiness. Even if man cannot attain to certainty in religious belief, his reason must force him to accept the Christian mode of life, for by so doing he hazards only a few years of chequered pleasure against an infinity of future happiness (an argument known as *le pari de Pascal*). But faith comes only by grace, and to obtain this one must discipline the body. The spirit of the whole may be summed up in the words: 'C'est le cœur qui sent Dieu et non la raison : voici ce que c'est que la foi : Dieu sensible au cœur.' The work is notable for its acute analysis of human nature, its many memorable sayings, its combination of powerful reasoning with passionate devotion, and the perfection of its style— at once that of a persuasive philosopher and of a lyric poet. It was imperfectly published in 1670. The importance attached to it in the 18th c. is indicated by the criticism it drew from Voltaire (*v. Lettres philosophiques*); and *v. Condorcet*; *Diderot*. The first critical edition was that of Prosper Faugère in 1844, since when a series of editors have tackled the difficult task of establishing an authentic text.

Pasdeloup, JULES-ÉTIENNE (1819–87), orchestral conductor, founded (1861) the *Concerts Pasdeloup*, popular Sunday concerts of classical music. *Cf. Colonne*; *Lamoureux*.

Pasquier, *v. Chronique des Pasquier*.

Pasquier, ÉTIENNE (1529–1615), jurist, humanist, and historian, noted for his *Recherches de la France* (1560, bk. I; 1621, the complete work) in which, writing in a pleasant, ingenuous style and without pedantry, he assembles much valuable information about French history (he favours toleration, condemns religious wars, and is highly critical of the Vatican's claim to interfere in French affairs), literature (he refers to the **Pléiade*, Montaigne, etc.), and the University of Paris. He also wrote *Lettres* (1586 and 1619), disquisitions on learned subjects; a *Catéchisme des Jésuites* (1602), an attack on the **Jesuits in dialogue form (in 1565 he had pleaded the case of the University of Paris in its bid to deny the Order the right to teach); and poems in Latin and Greek.

Passepartout, *v. Verne*.

Passerat, JEAN (1534–1602), humanist and poet, a professor at the **Collège de France*, and a collaborator in the **Satire Ménippée*. His pleasant lighter pieces

include *Le Premier Jour de mai*, a **chanson*; and *J'ai perdu ma tourterelle*, a **villanelle*.

Passeur, STÈVE (1899–1966), dramatist. His plays include, notably, *Je vivrai un grand amour* (1935), a psychological drama, set in the 17th c.; also *L'Acheteuse* (1930), *Le Témoin* (1936), *La Traîtresse* (1946).

Passion d'Arras, de Sainte Geneviève, etc., *v. Mystère*.

Passion de Clermont, *v. Religious Writings*, 1.

Pasteur, LOUIS (1822–95), chemist and biologist, famous as the pioneer of bacteriology. The conception and practice of curative and preventive inoculation against virus diseases, and the introduction of antiseptic and aseptic methods into surgery, derive almost entirely from his researches. After his most dramatic discovery, the virus of rabies, he began (1885) to inoculate human beings against hydrophobia. The *Institut Pasteur* in Paris was founded (1888) in his honour. Pasteurization, the heat treatment of liquids to destroy bacteria, is named after him.

Pastiche, a literary exercise which consists in reproducing, not only a writer's style and mannerisms, but also his mode of thought and approach to his subject. According to the degree of irony and caricature involved, and the claims made for it by the author, it can range from parody to forgery (*v. Hoaxes and Forgeries*). It is no new phenomenon (there are examples in *Le Cabinet satirique*, 1618, a collection of licentious verse, and **Marmontel's Éléments de littérature* has an article *Pastiche*), but it has been increasingly practised in the 19th and 20th cs. Examples of this period include Balzac's **Contes drolatiques*, pastiches of Rabelais; *Le Parnassiculet contemporain* (1867), largely the work of Arène and A. Daudet, a very good parody of *Le *Parnasse contemporain* of 1866; *Les *Déliquescences d'Adoré Floupette* (1885), so convincingly *Symbolist and *décadent* that some critics were taken in; *La Négresse blonde* (1909), amusing, irreverent verses by Georges Fourest; the *Anthologie du pastiche* (2nd ed. 1926) by Léon Deffoux and Pierre Dufay; *A la manière de...* (latest ed. 1950) by Paul Reboux and Charles Muller, brilliant *pastiches* of 19th-c. French authors (also of Racine and of English writers, e.g. Kipling and Conan Doyle); *Proust's Pastiches et mélanges* (1919); *Queneau's Exercices de style* (1947); *Curtis's *La Chine m'inquiète* (1971).

Pastoral Romance and Drama. Though passing mention should be made of Adam de la Halle's **Jeu de Robin et Marion* (*c.* 1283) and Amyot's translation of *Daphnis and Chloe* (1559), the pastoral had its true beginning in France in the latter part of the 16th c. and came from Italy and Spain, inspired by translations from 1544 onwards of Sannazaro's *Arcadia*, Tasso's *Aminta*, Guarini's *Il Pastor fido*, Montemayor's *Diana*, etc. (*v. Foreign Influences*, 1). *Belleau's *Bergerie*, though no more than a pastoral frame for a number of complimentary poems, is a sign of their influence on the *Pléiade*. The first true pastoral works are probably the *Ombres* (perf. 1566) of Nicolas Filleul, a poet of Rouen, and Belleforest's *Pastorale amoureuse* (1569), a dramatic eclogue with four characters. Then came *Nicolas de Montreux's *Bergeries de Juliette* (1585–93) and his pastoral plays, followed by a spate of pastoral plays by many other writers, e.g. *Montchrétien's *Bergerie* (1601) and *Les Amantes, ou la Grande Pastourelle* (1613) by Nicolas Chrestien des Croix. These early works deal monotonously with the loves and jealousies of shepherds and shepherdesses, complicated by the intervention of satyrs, magicians, Druids, and such deities as Diana, Pan, and Cupid. They consist largely of long tirades and laments, with little dramatic action, and are in lines of eight, ten, or twelve syllables. Hardy's five pastoral dramas (1623–8; in decasyllables) introduce more liveliness and action; they are, in fact, simple comedies of love and rivalry, with

some addition of the mythical and marvellous. D'Urfé's *L'*Astrée*, a long romance in pastoral form (*v. Novel*, 2), largely inspired by Montemayor's *Diana*, appeared between 1607 and 1627. Pastoral drama reached its zenith about the end of this period with such works as *Racan's *Bergeries*, *Mairet's *Sylvie* and *Silvanire*, and *Gombauld's *Amaranthe*, all in *alexandrines. They still include the old features, but show a transition towards comedy in their omission of the more outrageous and unnatural incidents and their greater delicacy and elegance of style and treatment. After 1631, pastoral drama declines, then fades out, losing itself in *comedy, *tragicomedy, or *opéra-comique*. C. *Sorel's *Le Berger extravagant* (1627), ridiculing *L'Astrée*, had helped to show the absurdity of many pastoral works; and though Molière wrote some pastoral comedies (e.g. *Mélicerte*; *Les *Amants magnifiques*) his more characteristic attitude was that of M. *Jourdain—'Pourquoi   toujours   des   bergers?'

Pastorale comique, La, by Molière, a *comédie-ballet* written for a royal festival late in 1666. Only part of the text survives.

Pastourelle (Prov. *pastorela*), a medieval song in stanzas of relatively complex metrical form, usually with a refrain, relating an encounter between the poet and a peasant girl. *Cf. Chansons à personnages*; *v. Marcabru*.

Pâté et de la Tarte, Farce du, *v. Farce*.

Pathelin, Maistre Pierre, a famous medieval *farce* (in octosyllables), written *c.* 1464 by an unknown author. *v. Palaprat*.

Pathelin, a rascally lawyer, tricks the draper Joceaulme out of a piece of cloth. When Joceaulme comes to Pathelin's house for payment, Pathelin, abetted by his wife Guillemette, feigns illness and gabbles deliriously in various dialects and finally in Latin. Meanwhile, Joceaulme has discovered that he is being robbed of his sheep by his shepherd, Aignelet, whom he hales before the judge. Aignelet enlists

Pathelin's services as advocate. Joceaulme, confused to see the rascal Pathelin in court, mixes up his two grievances, keeps referring to the loss of his cloth, and is called to order by the judge with the words 'Revenons à ces moutons' (the origin of the proverbial 'Revenons à nos moutons'). Aignelet, who obeys Pathelin's orders to reply to every question with a bleat, is discharged as an idiot. But the tables are turned on Pathelin when he demands his fee, for Aignelet's answer is a bleat.

Patin, GUI (1602–72), physician, dean of the Paris faculty of medicine (1650–2), a man of an original and satirical turn of mind. His lively *Lettres* (publ. posth.) contain much curious information about his times and some good literary judgements, besides revealing the intolerant, pedantic attitude of the faculty in his day (*v. Renaudot*) and his aversion to apothecaries and *Jesuits.

Patriote français, Le (1789–93), a journal f. by Brissot. It set out to be 'libre, impartial, et national' and carried good reports of proceedings in the *Assemblée constituante*. It was the organ of the *Girondins*, and its later numbers are of interest as reflecting their conflict with the *Montagnards*.

Patriotes, *v. Ligue des patriotes.*

Patru, OLIVIER (1604–81), an advocate noted for his forensic eloquence and as an authority on literary taste and style; a friend of Vaugelas, Guez de Balzac, d'Ablancourt, Boileau, and La Fontaine. His speech of thanks on his admission to the *Académie* (1640) initiated the custom of the formal *discours de réception*. His *Plaidoyers* were published, and some of his letters are worth reading; otherwise he wrote little.

Paul et Virginie (1787, in *Études de la Nature*), by Bernardin de Saint-Pierre, a romance with didactic digressions. For all its sentimentality, this short work contains many charming passages, especially the descriptions—in which J.-J. Rousseau's influence can be seen—of an idyllic life in exotic surroundings. It had an immense vogue, was translated into many languages, and retains its popular fame.

Paul and Virginie, two fatherless children who have loved each other from infancy, are brought up in poverty and innocence, far from the corrupting influence of society, on the tropical *Ile de France. Virginie, to the despair of both, is recalled to France by a harsh and wealthy aunt. She is unhappy, and after two years returns to the island. But her ship is wrecked as it nears the shore, and she drowns in the sight of Paul. Had she been willing to strip off her clothes and jump into the raging sea with the naked sailor who tried to rescue her, she could have survived; but she repulsed him with dignity, awaiting death with 'une main sur ses habits, l'autre sur son cœur'. Paul dies of a broken heart, the melancholy moral being that man should not depart from nature.

Paulet, *v. Paulette.*

Paulette, La, under the *ancien régime*, an annual tax of one-sixtieth of the price of a judicial or financial office, payment permitting the holder to acquire full right of property in it. It was named after CHARLES PAULET, a financier under Henri IV, the first farmer of the tax. He was father of ANGÉLIQUE PAULET (1592–1651), an *habituée* of the Hôtel de *Rambouillet and known as 'la Lionne' from her character and the colour of her hair. Some of Voiture's most entertaining letters are addressed to her.

Paulhan, JEAN (1884–1968), critic and essayist, a member of the *Académie* (1963). His dedication to clarity of language and thought made him a stimulating and influential editor of the *Nouvelle Revue française* (1925–40, then from 1953 with Arland). His works include *Entretiens sur des faits divers* (1930), *Les Fleurs de Tarbes* (1941; *v. Critics and Criticism*, 3), *Clef de la poésie* (1944), *Petite Préface à toute critique* (1951), *La Preuve* *par l'étymologie* (1953), *De mauvais sujets* (1960). *v. Resistance.*

Pauline, in Corneille's **Polyeucte.*

Paul-Louis, Vigneron, *v. Courier.*

Paume, Jeu de, the game of royal tennis. A distinction was made between *courte paume*, played in an enclosed court (e.g. the *Salle du Jeu de Paume* at Versailles, scene of an historic meeting of the **Assemblée nationale* in 1789; *v. Revolutions*, 1), and *longue paume*, played in an open space.

Pauvre Diable, *Le* (1758), by Voltaire, a verse satire on the Horatian model, directed mainly at the literary profession and ridiculing Fréron, Pompignan, and others.

Pavia (in Lombardy). Here François Ier was defeated by the Imperial army (1525) and taken prisoner. He wrote to his mother: 'De toutes choses il ne m'est demeuré que l'honneur et la vie qui est sauve' (often quoted in the form 'Tout est perdu fors l'honneur').

Pavillon, NICOLAS (1597–1677), bishop of Alet, a leading champion of the *Jansenists during their persecution.

Paysan du Danube, *Le*, a fable by La Fontaine. An untutored peasant under Roman domination protests against corrupt officials with a vigour that reaches Rome itself and produces reforms. The title has become proverbial for a rough but forcible critic.

Paysan parvenu, *Le* (1735–6), an unfinished romance by Marivaux, a counterpart of his *Marianne. Jacob, a sturdy young peasant, comes to Paris from Champagne, makes his way in the world thanks to his good looks, becomes a *fermier général, and marries a countess.

Paysan perverti, *Le*; **Paysanne pervertie**, *La*, *v. Restif de la Bretonne.*

Paysans, *Les* (1844–55; later in *La* *Comédie humaine, *Scènes de la vie de campagne*), a long, rather disconnected novel by Balzac. It turns on the intrigues whereby the crafty, surly peasants of the Morvan (Burgundy) finally drive Général de Montcornet to sell his property. The period is *c.* 1825.

Pays d'élections; Pays d'états, *v. Fiscal System.*

Peau d'Âne, one of **Perrault's fairy-tales, originally in verse.

To avoid a criminal marriage, a fair princess escapes from her father's court under the protection of a fairy, her face disguised with soot and wearing an old ass's skin. She wanders far afield, but with her sluttish looks the only place she can obtain is that of a drudge on a farm. She lives alone in a hovel and sometimes comforts herself by resuming her beauty and gay clothes. One day, a prince who is out hunting looks from curiosity through the keyhole of the hovel and discovers her thus. He asks who she is and is told 'Peau d'Âne'. He falls ill from love of her and insists that nothing will cure him but a cake made by Peau d'Âne. His whim is humoured, and as he eats the cake he finds a ring that has slipped off her finger. Now he will marry only the woman who can fit the tiny ring on her finger. All the women of the realm try it on in vain. Finally Peau d'Âne is brought in, amid the derision of the courtiers. The ring fits her, she again becomes a beautiful princess, and her royal birth is revealed.

Peau de chagrin, *La* (1830–1; later in *La* *Comédie humaine, *Études philosophiques*), a novel by Balzac. A magic piece of shagreen (ass's skin) has the power to grant its owner's wishes, but with every wish granted it shrinks and the owner's life is shortened.

Pêcheur d'Islande, *v. Loti.*

Pécuchet, *v. Bouvard et Pécuchet.*

Pédauque, Reine, *v. Rôtisserie de la Reine Pédauque, La.*

Péguy, CHARLES (1873–1914), essayist and poet, b. at Orleans in humble circumstances. He won his way to the *Collège Sainte-Barbe*, then to the *École normale supérieure*, which he left without taking his degree. In 1900, having run a Socialist bookshop for some years, he founded, and was thenceforth the moving spirit of, the *Cahiers de la quinzaine*. His passion for justice (he was deeply stirred by the *Dreyfus case) and unswerving loyalty to the truth as he understood it won him the love and admiration of many of his generation. At first an ardent, anti-clerical Socialist, he ended as a keen patriot and nationalist, and a fervent, almost mystical—though never practising— Roman Catholic. He died in action at the battle of the *Marne.

Until 1909 his output (nearly all first publ. in the *Cahiers*) consisted mainly of polemical prose, e.g. *Notre patrie* (1905; an ordinary citizen, returning to Paris from the country to find the air heavy with the threat of German invasion, becomes more vividly aware of what France and her culture mean to him); *A nos amis, à nos abonnés* (1909) and *Notre jeunesse* (1910), both about the Dreyfus case and its enduring impact on his generation; *Victor-Marie, comte Hugo* (1911). His poetry is dominated by his intense veneration for Joan of Arc, whose gradual awakening to her vocation forms the theme of his three dramatic poems, *Le Mystère de la Charité de Jeanne d'Arc* (1909; a reworking of his *Jeanne d'Arc*, 1897), *Le Porche du Mystère de la Deuxième Vertu* (1911), and *Le Mystère des Saints Innocents* (1912). The collections called *Tapisseries* (*Tapisserie de Sainte Geneviève*, 1912; *Tapisserie de Notre-Dame*, 1913, inc. the *Présentation de la Beauce* [the great fertile plain beyond Chartres] *à Notre-Dame de Chartres*) also reflect his love of Orleans and the Loire valley. *Ève* (1914), a very long poem, contains the famous *Prière pour nous autres charnels*, with its litany-like repetition and variation of the first line ('Heureux ceux qui sont morts pour la terre charnelle'). Repetition and variation of words and phrases are features of his style, in both prose and poetry.

Peignot, ÉTIENNE-GABRIEL (1767–1849), a bibliographer who combined immense learning with wit and sound judgement. His vast output includes a *Dictionnaire... des principaux livres condamnés au feu, supprimés, ou censurés* (1806, 2 vols.); a *Manuel du bibliophile* (1823, 2 vols.); *Recherches historiques et littéraires sur les danses des morts et sur l'origine des cartes à jouer* (1826), perhaps his best work; and innumerable pamphlets and articles in periodicals.

Peintre de Salzbourg, Le, v. Nodier.

Peiresc, NICOLAS-CLAUDE FABRI DE (1580–1637), magistrate, antiquarian, and naturalist; a friend of Malherbe and a correspondent of learned men all over Europe.

Péladan, JOSÉPHIN (1859–1918), man of letters and playwright, author of essays (*Le Vice suprême*, 1884; *La Décadence esthétique*, 1888–98) and mystical dramas (*Les Fils des étoiles*, 1895; *La Prométhéide*, 1895; *Le Prince de Byzance*, 1896, etc.). He was involved in a revival of *Rosicrucianism (c. 1888) and founded (1890) the *Théâtre de la Rose-Croix* in opposition to the *Naturalism of the *Théâtre Libre. v. Literary Isms.*

Pèlerinage de Charlemagne à Jérusalem, a *chanson de geste (*Charlemagne cycle) in *alexandrines, probably of the mid-12th c. Charlemagne, irritated by his wife's indiscreet praise of Hugo, emperor of Constantinople, sets out to see for himself whether she is right. He goes first to Jerusalem, where he acquires precious relics. His subsequent visit to Hugo is the occasion for some crudely comic incidents and leads to the conclusion that his wife was much mistaken.

Pèlerin passionné, Le, v. Moréas.

Peletier, JACQUES (1517–82), 'Peletier du Mans' (he was born at Le Mans), mathematician and poet, inspired Ronsard and Du Bellay with their first ideas of poetic reform and figures in Ronsard's original list of members of the *Pléiade. His views were expounded in a preface to his translation of Horace's Ars poetica (1545) and in his own L'Art poétique (1555).

Pelléas et Mélisande (1892), by Maeterlinck, one of the best-known *Symbolist dramas, especially after Debussy set it to music (1902). It is about two ill-fated lovers—Mélisande, a frail, mysterious maiden, found weeping in the forest by Golaud, a king's son, who marries her, and Pelléas, Golaud's brother. The lovers talk by a fountain and Mélisande loses her ring, the gift of Golaud, in the water. Golaud's jealousy mounts. He surprises them taking a last farewell of each other and kills Pelléas. He seeks forgiveness, too late, from Mélisande. Mélisande dies.

Pellerin, JEAN (1885–1920), author of *fantaisiste poems of modern life, collected in La Romance du retour (1921), Le Bouquet inutile (1923), etc.

Pellisson, PAUL (1624–93), man of letters and secretary to N. Fouquet, whom he defended in eloquent discourses addressed to Louis XIV. Involved in Fouquet's disgrace, he spent five years in the *Bastille, but was then released by the king, who made him historiographer. His short Histoire de l'Académie française (in the form of a letter to a friend, relating its inception and proceedings down to 1652; v. Olivet) won him a seat in that body; Sainte-Beuve commends it as a most finished and agreeable work. v. La Suze.

Peltier, JEAN-GABRIEL (1765–1825), founder-editor of the famous Royalist journal Les *Actes des Apôtres. When the monarchy fell (1792), he fled to England, where he edited L'Ambigu, a paper at first anti-Revolutionary, then anti-Napoleon.

Pensées de Pascal, v. Pascal.

Pensées philosophiques and **Pensées sur l'interprétation de la nature,** v. Diderot.

Pépin d'Héristal; Pépin le Bref, v. Maire du Palais; Carolingians.

Perceforest (first printed 1528), a vast, very popular, 14th-c. prose romance linking the legends of Alexander and Arthur. Alexander, after conquering India, is driven by a storm on to the coast of Britain. He makes his companion Perceforest (so called because he has slain a magician who lived in a thick forest) king of the land. Perceforest creates an Order of Knights of the Franc Palais. Under his grandson the Grail is brought to England. The many adventures related include that of the 'Belle au bois dormant' (Sleeping Beauty).

Perceval. The basis of the story of Perceval was probably a folk-tale about a boy, brought up by his widowed mother in ignorance of the world, who comes by chance to the king's court, becomes a brave knight, and ultimately avenges his father. In his Perceval or Le Conte du Graal, Chrétien de Troyes introduced into this story the motif of the graal ('grail') or mysterious dish which, together with a bleeding lance, Perceval sees in a strange castle, but of which he fails to inquire the significance; reproached for this negligence, he devotes himself to the quest of the graal, which takes on a mystical import. Chrétien left his poem unfinished, but the story was continued by other poets in whose work the graal assumed a character apparently not contemplated by him—that of the dish in which Joseph of Arimathea received the blood of Christ on the Cross, brought according to legend to the mysterious castle of Corbenic in Britain. Towards the end of the 12th c., Robert de Boron or Borron wrote a trilogy—Joseph d'Arimathie, Merlin, Perceval (only the first poem and the beginning of the second survive)—in which he developed the early history of the Holy Grail and linked it (through the figure of *Merlin) to the Arthurian tradition. Various prose versions followed early in the 13th c.; the most notable, known as the 'Vulgate' version, is an immense cycle consisting of five sections:

the *Estoire du Saint Graal*, *Merlin*, *Lancelot du Lac*, the *Queste du Saint Graal*, and the *Mort Artu*; v. *Lancelot*. Perceval is here replaced as hero of the quest of the Grail by Galaad (Galahad), son of Lancelot.

The story has been widely treated in other languages, notably in the *Parzifal* of Wolfram von Eschenbach (and *cf* Wagner's *Parzival*), in the Welsh Mabinogi *Peredur*, and in English above all by Sir Thomas Malory in his *Morte Darthur*.

Perceval de Cagny, Chronique de, v. *History*, 1.

Perdican, in Musset's **On ne badine pas avec l'amour*.

Père de famille, Le, v. *Diderot*.

Père Duchesne, Le (1790–4; thrice weekly, 355 nos. in all), a Revolutionary journal f. by Hébert and widely read by the masses. Its articles, by no means ill-written, were notorious for their foul-mouthed violence, and Hébert left few personalities or events untouched. 'Le Père Duchesne' (apparently originally a stock character of the *Théâtre de la *Foire*, to whom were gradually attributed opinions or anecdotes that could not be voiced openly) was pictured in a vignette at the head of the paper, at first with a pipe in his mouth and tobacco in his hand, later with pistols in his belt and brandishing an axe over the head of the kneeling abbé **Maury*. The motto beneath read: 'Je suis le véritable Père Duchesne, foutre.' His name was also in use for another, much less violent, pamphlet-series, the *Lettres bougrement patriotiques du Père Duchesne* (1790–2), and was revived for one of the short-lived papers founded in 1848.

Péréfixe, HARDOUIN DE BEAUMONT DE (1605–71), archbishop of Paris (he forbade the performance of Molière's *Le *Tartuffe* in 1667) and historian; author of a life of Henri IV, written for Louis XIV, to whom he was tutor.

Père Goriot, Le (1834–5), a key novel in Balzac's **Comédie humaine* (*Scènes de la vie privée*). Eugène de **Rastignac* is in Paris to study law. He is ambitious, impatient of poverty, and resolved to conquer Parisian society. His fellow-boarders at the dingy Maison Vauquer include the mysterious **Vautrin* and M. Goriot, a retired merchant. Vautrin urges him to use all means of advancement, even crime, and unfolds a plan for a murder leading to marriage with an heiress. He is about to consent when Vautrin is arrested as a notorious criminal. Goriot, obviously poverty-stricken, is the butt of the boarding-house, for no one believes his story that the baronne Delphine de **Nucingen* and the comtesse Anastasie de Restaud are his daughters. But Rastignac meets Anastasie at a ball and learns that the story is true. Goriot has impoverished himself in order to give his daughters large dowries and pay their debts; they are now ashamed of him and only visit him with a view to bleeding him still further. Out of pity, Rastignac befriends the old man and also, as a stepping-stone to a career, becomes Delphine's lover. Goriot falls mortally ill after a last desperate effort to pay Anastasie's debts and avert a scandal. Dying, he calls piteously for his daughters, but only Rastignac and Bianchon, a medical student, are beside him. Rastignac sells his watch to pay for the lonely burial. The book ends with him surveying Paris from the heights of the cemetery of **Père-Lachaise*. She sprawls beneath him like a monster, only to be conquered after the most cynical struggle; and with the words 'A nous deux maintenant!' he turns to begin the fight.

Père humilié, Le, v. *Claudel*.

Père Joseph, Le, v. *Éminence grise*.

Père-Lachaise, Cimetière du, v. *La Chaise*.

Péret, BENJAMIN (1899–1959), poet; a **Dadaist*, and then a **Surrealist* who remained loyal to Breton and never abandoned automatic methods. Some of his many collections (e.g. *Dormir, dormir dans les pierres*, 1927) were united in *Main forte* (1946) and *Feu central* (1947). He held that a poet must be a revolutionary (*Je ne mange pas de ce pain-là*, 1936) and fought in the Spanish Civil War, but in 1941 he left France for Mexico (with Breton) and attacked the use of poetry for patriotic ends (*Le Déshonneur des poètes*, 1945; *v. L'Honneur des poètes* under *Resistance*). *v. Éluard*.

Périchole (Perricholi), La, a peasant girl found singing in the streets of Lima who became famous as an actress and singer, and for her colourful life in 18th-c. Peru. She figures in Mérimée's *Le Carrosse du Saint-Sacrement* (*v. Théâtre de Clara Gazul, Le*), *Offenbach's *La Périchole*, and, more recently, in Thornton Wilder's *The Bridge of San Luis Rey*.

Pérignon, DOMINIQUE-CATHERINE, *v. Maréchal*.

Periodicals and Reviews, *v. Press*, 1–9. Those which are the subject of separate articles will often be found under *Annales..., Année..., Archives..., Cahiers..., Journal..., Lettres..., Nouvelle(s)..., Revue...* For current learned journals *v.* also *French Language; Romance Languages*. Current British learned journals wholly or partly devoted to French language and literature include *French Studies* (1947–   ; f. by Alfred Ewert), *The Modern Language Review* (1906–   ), and *Forum for Modern Language Studies* (1965–   ), all quarterly.

Pernelle, Madame, in Molière's *Le *Tartuffe*, the mother of Orgon.

Péron, FRANÇOIS (1775–1810), naturalist, author of a well-known book of travel and discovery, *Voyage de découverte aux terres australes* (1811–16)—the fruit of his experiences as a zoologist attached to a scientific expedition to the southern hemisphere (1800–4; led by Nicolas Baudin). He brought back a large and valuable collection of animals.

Perrault, CHARLES (1628–1703), poet and critic, the most famous of four distinguished brothers, the others being CLAUDE (1613–88), physician, architect (he designed the colonnade of the *Louvre), and translator of Vitruvius; PIERRE (d. 1680), a receiver-general; NICOLAS (1611–61), theologian and *Jansenist. He was a versatile, amiable man of original mind, employed by Colbert as adviser in matters of art and letters and a member of the *Académie* from 1671. He was a leading champion of the *modernes* (as were his brothers Claude and Pierre) in the *Querelle des anciens et des modernes*, which he revived with his poem *Le Siècle de Louis le Grand* (1687), setting Régnier, Malherbe, Molière, Rotrou, and others above the ancients. There followed his *Parallèles des anciens et des modernes* (1688–97), lively dialogues making fun of the pedants (but betraying his ignorance of classical antiquity), *Apologie des femmes* (1694), in reply to Boileau's *Satire X* (*v. Satires*), and *Les Hommes illustres qui ont paru en France pendant ce siècle* (1696–1701). Most of his famous collection of fairy-tales, no doubt based on French popular tradition and told with simplicity and charm, appeared in 1697 (over the name of his young son) in his *Histoires et contes du temps passé, avec des moralités. Contes de ma mère l'Oye*. This included *La Belle au bois dormant* ('Sleeping Beauty'), *Le Petit Chaperon rouge* ('Little Red Riding Hood'), *La Barbe-bleue* ('Bluebeard'), *Le Maître Chat, ou le Chat botté* ('Puss in Boots'; *v. Carabas*), *Cendrillon, ou la Petite Pantoufle de verre* ('Cinderella'), *Le Petit Poucet* ('Tom Thumb'), *Les Fées* ('The Fairy'), and *Riquet à la houppe* ('Riquet with the Tuft'), all in prose. *Grisélidis*, **Peau d'Âne*, and *Les Souhaits ridicules*, in verse, were added later. His 'Mother Goose's Tales' were translated into English by Robert Samber (1729). *v.* also *Children's Reading*.

Perrette, in La Fontaine's fable *La Laitière et le Pot au lait*, the milkmaid who carries her milk to market on her head, skips as she thinks of the calf she will buy with the proceeds skipping in the field, and upsets the pail.

Perrichon, Monsieur, v. *Voyage de M. Perrichon, Le.*

Perrin, CLAUDE-VICTOR, v. *Maréchal* (Victor).

Perrin Dandin, in Racine's *Les *Plaideurs.*

Perrot d'Ablancourt, v. *Ablancourt.*

Perroy, ÉDOUARD (1901–74), medieval historian, professor at the *Sorbonne* from 1950. His works include *L'Angleterre et le grand schisme de l'Occident* (1933), *La Guerre de cent ans* (1945), *Le Moyen Âge: l'expansion de l'Orient et la naissance de la civilisation occidentale* (1955, 5th ed. 1967; with others), *Le Monde carolingien* (1974), and editions of medieval records (e.g. the diplomatic correspondence of Richard II of England, 1933).

Perse, v. *Saint-John Perse.*

Personnalisme, v. (1) *Renouvier*; (2) *Mounier.*

Pertharite, a tragedy by Corneille; produced 1651. It was a complete failure. Voltaire says that the sentiments expressed are extravagant or feeble, the versification poor, the very names of the characters repellent.

Pertharite, king of the Lombards, has been dethroned by Grimoald, who reports that he is dead. Grimoald, though betrothed to Pertharite's sister Edvige, falls in love with Pertharite's wife Rodelinde. She resists a marriage she regards as criminal, but finally consents to it on the strange condition that Grimoald will kill her son. Pertharite returns and Grimoald declares him an impostor. But when he finds that Pertharite only wants to recover his wife, he is so struck by his magnanimity that he abandons the kingdom to him and returns to Edvige.

Peste, La, v. *Camus, A.*

Pétain, HENRI-PHILIPPE (1856–1951), *maréchal de France* (1918), a great general of the 1914–18 war (v. *Verdun*). After the fall of France in the 1939–45 war it was he who signed the armistice with Germany and then headed the collaborationist Vichy government (v. *Republics*, 3). After France was liberated, he was tried (1945) and condemned to death, but the sentence was commuted to one of life imprisonment. He was confined in a fort on the Île d'Yeu till shortly before his death.

Pétaud, Le Roi, the name (facetiously derived from L. *peto*, 'I beg') formerly given to the chief of the community of French beggars. His authority was slight, and 'la cour du roi Pétaud' was proverbial for an assembly where everyone is vocal and self-assertive (*cf. Le *Tartuffe*, I, i). It was sometimes applied to the court of Louis XV.

Pétion de Villeneuve, JÉRÔME (1756–94), a leading Revolutionary writer and politician, mayor of Paris (1791). He escaped after the fall of his party, the *Girondins*, but committed suicide after months of wandering.

Petit Chaperon rouge, Le, v. *Perrault.*

Petit Chose, Le (1868), by A. Daudet, a semi-autobiographical novel in two parts. The first follows fairly closely the early years of Daudet and his brother Ernest, called Daniel and Jacques Eysette; the second, after the two come to Paris, is almost purely fiction. Both fall in love with Camille, daughter of a porcelain manufacturer. She loves Daniel, who becomes entangled with an actress. Jacques dies; and Daniel, who had meant to write, marries Camille and settles for a solid career in his father-in-law's factory.

Petit de Julleville, LOUIS (1841–1900), medievalist, an authority on the origin and evolution of the drama in France. v. *Histories of French Literature.*

Petit-Dutaillis, CHARLES (1868–1948), medieval historian, an authority on the feudal system (*La Monarchie féodale en France et en Angleterre*, 1933).

Petite Fadette, La, v. Sand.

Petites Affiches, Les (f. 1751), a journal mainly composed of advertisements of all kinds, law notices, etc., now of interest for its information on 18th-c. literary affairs. v. Renaudot.

Petites Écoles de Port-Royal, Les, v. Port-Royal.

Petites Misères de la vie conjugale, v. Comédie humaine, La (*Études analytiques*).

Petit Jean, in Racine's *Les *Plaideurs*.

Petit Jehan de Saintré, Histoire du (c. 1456), a prose romance by La Sale, notable for its sharp delineation of character and the realism of its later scenes. Jehan de Saintré was a 14th-c. knight (Froissart says he was deemed the best French knight of the day); he fought and was captured at the battle of Poitiers.

Saintré, a page at the court of Jean II, wins the favour of the Dame des Belles Cousines. She sets herself to teach him to be a perfect knight, showing him a growing affection, which he returns. The first part of the work is a veritable manual of chivalry, with much about the etiquette of tourneys, blazons, trappings, etc. Saintré becomes a great knight, famous for his exploits against the Saracens. But his lady, piqued by his decision to leave her for a while in order to win fresh laurels, takes another lover in his absence, Damp (i.e. Dom) Abbé, a rich, burly monk, and on his return subjects him to the disgrace of wrestling with the monk in her presence and being defeated. (This supplanting and defeat of a knight by a *bourgeois* may reflect the author's awareness of the decline of feudal chivalry.) The signal revenge he takes on the monk and the humiliation of the lady before the court bring the story to a close.

Petit Philosophe, Le, v. Poinsinet.

Petit Pierre, Le, v. France, A.

Petit Poucet, Le, v. Perrault.

Petits Châteaux de Bohème, v. Nerval.

Petit Traité de poésie française, v. Banville.

Petit Traité de versification, v. Unanimisme.

Petrarch, v. Foreign Influences, 1; Vaucluse.

Peuples et civilisations, v. Halphen.

Peyrat, NAPOLÉON (1809–81), a Protestant pastor, friend of Lamennais and Béranger, remembered for his *Histoire des pasteurs du désert depuis la révocation de l'édit de Nantes jusqu'à la Révolution française, 1685–1789* (1842–3, 2 vols.). The poems of his *L'Arise, romancero religieux, héroïque, et pastoral* (1863) include *Roland*, a fine *Romantic ode written in early life, when he styled himself 'Napol le Pyrénéen'.

Peyrefitte, ROGER (1907–), novelist. He was educated by the Jesuits and served as a career diplomat until 1944. He made his name with his first novel, *Les Amitiés particulières* (1944), a moving and ironical study of adolescent homosexual love in a Jesuit college. After less successful novels and *La Mort d'une mère* (1950), a frank avowal of unfilial conduct, he turned to satire, with provocative, at time vicious, attacks on the diplomatic service (*Les Ambassades*, 1951; *La Fin des ambassades*, 1953) and the Roman Catholic Church (*Les Clés de Saint Pierre*, 1955; *Chevaliers de Malte*, 1957; *La Nature du Prince*, 1963). He also continued to write on homosexual themes, e.g. *Jeunes Proies* (1956), *L'Exilé de Capri* (1959). The documentary element in much of his writing is very marked in such later works as *Les Juifs* (1965) and *Des Français* (1970).

Peyronnet, La Loi, v. Press, 5.

Phalange, La, (1) v. Fourier; (2) an important literary review (1906–14; f. by

Royère) which continued the traditions of *Symbolism, but also sponsored new writers. Contributors included Apollinaire, Jammes, Vielé-Griffin.

Phalanstère, Le, v. Fourier.

Pharamond, legendary ancestor of the *Merovingians; the subject of a romance by La Calprenède. He is supposed to have reigned from 420 to 428, but his name is not found in reliable chronicles.

Phébus, as in parler Phébus, to speak or write with such affectation as to be obscure. There are examples of this in the romances of Mlle de Scudéry, La Calprenède, etc.

Phèdre, a tragedy by Racine; produced 1677. It is based on the Hippolytus of Euripides and in some degree on that of Seneca, with certain changes, notably the addition of the character Aricie. The extreme passion depicted in this great play shocked the audience of the day.

Hippolyte, son of Thésée and Antiope, is at his father's court at Troezen. Thésée has long been absent, and Hippolyte is about to set out to seek him; he dreads his growing love for Aricie, a princess of royal Athenian blood but of a family hostile to Thésée, held captive at the court with her confidant Ismène. Phèdre, wife of Thésée, conceals a guilty passion for Hippolyte. A report of Thésée's death reaches Troezen. Phèdre, on the pretext of taking leave of Hippolyte, reveals her love to him and he repels it with horror. News now comes that Thésée is alive and on his way home. Phèdre greets him with a few words of guilty confusion; Hippolyte, no less perturbed, asks permission to withdraw from the place where Phèdre is living. Thésée, shocked by his reception, seeks the explanation. Phèdre's old nurse and confidant Œnone, who has encouraged her to give rein to her passion, accuses Hippolyte to Thésée of dishonourable advances to her mistress. Thésée, outraged, calls on his protector Neptune to destroy Hippolyte. Hippolyte denies the charge, and, while hinting that the guilt

lies elsewhere, refrains from accusing Phèdre; he declares his own love for Aricie. Phèdre, already distraught by love and remorse and now consumed by jealousy of Aricie, curses Œnone for leading her on. Aricie, who is aware of Hippolyte's love and returns it, boldly asserts his innocence to Thésée and warns him of his error. Thésée, now less sure of his son's guilt, is about to question Œnone further when he learns of her suicide. This news is swiftly followed by the arrival of Hippolyte's tutor and confidant Théramène to describe (in a famous passage known as le récit de Théramène) his death by the intervention of the god invoked by Thésée. Phèdre, who has taken poison, dies confessing Hippolyte's innocence and her own guilt.

Phèdre et Hippolyte, v. Pradon.

Philaminte, in Molière's Les *Femmes savantes.

Philémon et Baucis, v. La Fontaine.

Philidor, v. Danican.

Philinte, in Molière's Le *Misanthrope.

Philipon, CHARLES (1800–62), lithographer, caricaturist, and journalist, founder-editor of Caricature (1830) and Le *Charivari (1832), satirical journals famous, and often prosecuted, for their cartoons ridiculing the bourgeoisie and the July Monarchy, especially Louis-Philippe who, from the shape of his head, was often represented as a pear.

Philippe Ier (1053–1108), king of France (*Capetian dynasty), succeeded his father Henri Ier, r. 1060–1108.

Philippe II, PHILIPPE-AUGUSTE (1165–1223), king of France (*Capetian dynasty), succeeded his father Louis VII, r. 1180–1223. One of the greatest of the early kings, he did much to achieve national unity and to expel the English. His reign was also a landmark in the development of Paris and its university.

Philippe III LE HARDI (1245–85), king of France (*Capetian dynasty), succeeded his father Louis IX, r. 1270–85.

Philippe IV LE BEL (1268–1314), king of France (*Capetian dynasty), succeeded his father Philippe III, r. 1285–1314. He was also, by his marriage to Jeanne de Navarre, king of Navarre. *v. États généraux.*

Philippe V LE LONG (1293–1322), king of France (*Capetian dynasty), 2nd son of Philippe IV and brother of Louis X, whom he succeeded (following the death of Jean Ier); r. 1316–22.

Philippe VI, PHILIPPE DE VALOIS (1293–1350), king of France (*Capetian dynasty, first of the *Valois branch), came to the throne after the death of Charles IV, r. 1328–50.

Philippe, CHARLES-LOUIS (1874–1909), novelist, a cobbler's son, largely self-educated, who came to Paris and, thanks to Barrès, found work which gave him a pittance and the leisure to write. His novels—all primarily studies of poverty, described with realism and a compassion that sometimes borders on sentimentality—include *Bubu de Montparnasse* (1901), his first success, a study of the dregs of humanity in Paris in which the influence of Tolstoy and Dostoievsky has been variously recognized (e.g. in the humble clerk's effort to redeem a prostitute); *Le Père Perdrix* (1903); *Marie Donadieu* (1904); *Croquignole* (1906); *Charles Blanchard* (1913; unfinished), based on his father's early life.

Philippe de Beaumanoir, *v. Beaumanoir.*

Philippe de Champagne, *v. Champagne.*

Philippe de Mézières (c. 1327–1405), soldier and diplomat, chancellor of Cyprus under Pierre Ier of Lusignan, later the friend and trusted adviser of Charles V. Even after the king's death, when he retired to a Paris cloister and devoted himself to writing, his political influence remained considerable. His works, written in French or Latin and reflecting his crusading zeal, include, notably, the *Songe du Vieil Pèlerin*, a long moral and political allegory, intended for the king (various allegorical personages, guided by the author under the name 'Ardant Désir', travel in the East and the West, and finally in France itself, passing judgement on morals, customs, and institutions; the last part of the work is a veritable manual of government); also a version of the story of *Griseldis.

Philippe de Novare (d. c. 1265), a Lombard who spent most of his life in Cyprus. His very varied writings include an *Estoire* (interspersed with satirical topical songs) on the war (1228–43), in which he fought, between the emperor Frederick II and Philippe d'Ibelin for the regency of Cyprus (a continuation of this work down to 1309, by Gérard de Montréal, is known as the *Gestes des Chiprois*); the *Livre en forme de plait*, a treatise on jurisprudence; the *Quatre Âges de l'homme*, an ethical treatise, the fruit of his own experience; poems amatory and pious; memoirs.

Philippe de Thaon or **Thaün** (*fl.* early 12th c.), an *Anglo-Norman cleric, author of the earliest *Bestiaire, also of a *Comput and a *Lapidaire.

Philippe-Égalité, *v. Orléans* (3).

Philomena, *v. Romans d'antiquité.*

Philomneste Junior, *v. Brunet, P.-G.*

Philosophe inconnu, Le, *v. Saint-Martin.*

Philosophes, Les, a general term for those 18th-c. literary men, scientists, and thinkers who, though often widely different in their individual tendencies, were united by their belief in the sovereign efficacy of human reason and in their desire to overthrow the old creeds, institutions, and abuses that obstructed its effective supremacy. Cartesian philosophy, with its exaltation of reason, the worldly scepticism of the *libertins*, Fontenelle's popularization of science, Bayle's direct attack on dogma, and the influence of English Deism all helped to prepare their intellectual path, while the development of their doctrine was favoured by sectarian dissensions within the Church (the rift between *Jesuits and *Jansenists; Bossuet's dispute with Fénelon) and the fact that absolute monarchy had been discredited by the disastrous wars and ruinous and inequitable taxation of the end of Louis XIV's reign.

The movement was moderate and restrained in the first half of the 18th c., a period dominated by Montesquieu and Voltaire (in his earlier phase). Thereafter, with the development of Voltaire's attack, the emergence of Diderot, J.-J. Rousseau, Buffon, Condillac, Turgot, Condorcet, d'Alembert, Morellet, d'Holbach, Marmontel, Helvétius, G. Raynal, and others, and the publication (from 1751) of the *Encyclopédie*, it increasingly gained momentum. The *philosophes* were bitterly attacked by the Church (e.g. in the Jesuit *Journal de Trévoux* and the *Jansenist *Nouvelles ecclésiastiques*) and the *parlement* (which had many of their works burnt), and satirized by Palissot, Laurent Gilbert, and others. Many were imprisoned (Voltaire, Diderot, Marmontel, Morellet). But their opponents were divided, and they won over many influential persons (e.g. Malesherbes). They contributed to the Revolution both by their doctrines, which served to discredit the government, the magistrature, and the Church, and by their own example of rebellion.

Philosophes, Les, v. Palissot; cf. Poinsinet.

Philosophe sans le savoir, Le, by Sedaine, a good *drame bourgeois* (with none of the pathos and moralizing of Diderot and La Chaussée); produced 1765. In its scenic effects and loose handling of the unity of time it anticipates the *Romantic drama.

M. Vanderk is a man of noble birth (which he conceals under an assumed name) whom circumstances have made a merchant and who is proud of this calling. His home is happy and orderly, and he is about to marry his daughter to a magistrate. On the eve of the wedding, his son hears another young man abusing all merchants as scoundrels and challenges him; the duel is fixed for the wedding day. Vanderk tries in vain to prevent it and is left in dread of the issue. The son is at first reported killed; but it later transpires that the adversaries were reconciled after a first encounter, and the day ends happily.

Phlipon, *v. Roland, Mme.*

Phocas le jardinier, v. Vielé-Griffin.

Physiocrates, *v. Économistes.*

Physiologie du goût, v. Brillat-Savarin.

Physiologie du mariage, ou Méditations de philosophie éclectique sur le bonheur et le malheur conjugal (1829; later in *La *Comédie humaine, Études analytiques*), by Balzac (first publ. anon.), collected studies of marriage and passion, some satirical, some coarsely facetious, some with a pseudo-sociological interest. (The term *physiologie* is here used in the contemporary, non-scientific sense of a collection of character-sketches.)

Pibrac, GUY DU FAUR DE (1529–84), magistrate and moralist, a man of classical culture and distinguished career, narrowly escaped death under Henri II for boldly advocating religious toleration, and under Charles IX was one of three envoys sent to defend the Gallican Church at the Council of Trent (1562). He is noted for his *Quatrains moraux*, 126 moralizing quatrains (the first 50 publ. 1574), long regarded as a code of conduct and a necessary part of a liberal education (Gorgibus, in Molière's *Sganarelle*, commends them to his daughter). A. France found him 'le plus ennuyeux mortel qui ait jamais écrit'.

Picard,   LOUIS-BENOÎT   (1769–1828),

actor, theatre-manager, and playwright, left the stage on his election (1807) to the *Académie. He wrote many popular and amusing comedies of manners (often of early 19th-c. provincial life), e.g. *La Petite Ville* (1801), *Les Provinciaux à Paris* (1802), *Les Marionnettes* (1806), *Les Ricochets* (1807), *Les Deux Philibert* (1816); also many *vaudevilles*.

Picard, RAYMOND, v. *Critics and Criticism*, 3.

Picasso, PABLO RUIZ BLASCO, *known as* (1881–1973), painter and sculptor of Spanish birth, one of the most important—and most discussed—artists of modern times. He lived and worked mainly in France from 1904 and moved freely in *avant-garde* literary and theatrical circles. As the founder, with Braque, of Cubism in art, he was closely associated with *Cubist writers (Apollinaire's *Les Peintres cubistes*, 1913, includes a study of his work). Later, he was similarly associated with the *Surrealists, notably Éluard. v. also *Cocteau*.

Piccini, Piccinistes, v. *Musical Controversies*.

Picciola, v. *Saintine*.

Pichat, MICHEL (1790–1828), poet and dramatist. His conventional tragedies *Léonidas* (1825) and *Guillaume Tell* (1830) were praised in their day.

Pichegru, CHARLES (1761–1804), a Revolutionary general, conqueror of Holland, who was condemned to death for conspiring with Cadoudal and others to depose Napoleon. He died in prison, probably by his own hand.

Pichot, AMÉDÉE (1795–1877), man of letters, editor (1835–77) of the *Revue britannique*. His translations of Byron, Shakespeare, Scott, Dickens, etc., and his *Voyage historique et littéraire en Angleterre et en Écosse* (1825) did much to popularize English literature in France. v. *Foreign Influences*, 3.

Picrochole, in Rabelais's *Gargantua*.

Pierre de Langtoft (*fl.* 14th c.), a canon of Bridlington (Yorkshire), who shortly after 1311 wrote, in French *alexandrines, a summary of the history of England to the death of Edward I.

Pierre et Jean (1888), a novel by Maupassant, usually considered his best. In a notable preface, he expounds his ideas on the novel and the novelist's function, and describes how Flaubert taught him to write.

Pierre and Jean Roland are the sons of a retired Paris jeweller, living at Le Havre. Pierre is a doctor, a nervous, unsteady character; Jean, more placid by nature, is a lawyer. Both love Mme Rosémilly, a young widow. When Jean suddenly inherits a fortune from M. Maréchal, an old family friend, Pierre, who gets nothing, is puzzled, jealous, then seized by suspicion of his mother's earlier adultery. She reads his thoughts, and both live in torture. Beside himself with rage to learn that Mme Rosémilly has consented to marry Jean, Pierre blurts out his suspicions to him. Jean, learning from his mother that Pierre is right, resolves to rid the family of a disturbing presence and continue his life as if nothing had happened. He manoeuvres Pierre into a post of doctor on a transatlantic liner, and the story ends as the ship sails with Pierre on board.

Pierre Faifeu, La Légende joyeuse de Maître, a poem relating the exploits of a rascally student of Angers of the type of Villon, written in 1527 by Charles Bourdigné, an Angevin priest.

Pierre Grassou, v. *Comédie humaine, La* (*Scènes de la vie parisienne*).

Pierre le Lombard (Peter Lombard) (*c.* 1100–60), 'Magister sententiarum', b. at Novara, a theologian who taught at the Cathedral School of Paris (v. *Universities*, 1) from *c.* 1139 and finally became bishop of Paris (1159). His *Sententiae* (written 1148–50), a collection of opinions of the

Fathers (notably on the sacraments), became the standard textbook of Catholic theology during the Middle Ages.

Pierre l'Hermite (Peter the Hermit) (d. 1115), a gentleman of Picardy, a soldier turned monk who preached the 1st *Crusade and led a host of his followers into Asia Minor (1096). They nearly all died or were killed at the siege of Nicaea before the regular crusaders arrived. He survived to accompany these crusaders eastwards in 1097 and was present at the siege and counter-siege of Antioch. *v.* *Antioche, Chanson d'*.

Pierre Nozière, *v. France, A.*

Pierrette, *v. Comédie humaine, La (Scènes de la vie de province).*

Pierrot, a character in pantomime, thievish, greedy, artless, and amoral; dressed in loose white garments, with his face whitened. *v. Deburau; Marceau, M.*

Pigal, EDME-JEAN (1794–1872), comic artist and lithographer. His sketches of working-class life were popular in the late 1820s.

Pigalle, JEAN-BAPTISTE (1714–85), sculptor, noted for his statue of Maurice de Saxe, bust of Voltaire, etc.

Pigault-Lebrun, CHARLES-ANTOINE-GUILLAUME PIGAULT DE L'ÉPINOY, *known as* (1753–1835), author of lively, licentious novels, widely read *c.* 1800 (e.g. by Miss Crawley in Thackeray's *Vanity Fair*), including *L'Enfant du carnaval* (1792), *Mon oncle Thomas* (1799), *La Folie espagnole* (1799), *M. de Kinglin* (1801), *Tableaux de la société* (1813).

Pilon, GERMAIN (1539–90), sculptor, noted for his tombs of François Ier and Henri II at *Saint-Denis and for a group of the Three Graces. He enjoyed the favour of Catherine de Médicis.

Pimbesche, Comtesse de, in Racine's *Les *Plaideurs*.

Pinget, ROBERT, *v. Nouveau roman.*

Pinson, Mimi, *v. Mimi Pinson.*

Pinte, Dame, a hen in the *Roman de Renart*.

Pipelet, La Mère, in *Sue's *Les Mystères de Paris*.

Piramus et Tisbé, *v. Romans d'antiquité.*

Piron, ALEXIS (1689–1773), a light, witty poet and dramatist. His works include, notably, the comedy *La *Métromanie* (1738); also *Arlequin-Deucalion* (1722), a farce in which, to comply with the ban on the employment of more than one speaking actor by the *Théâtre de la *Foire*, he takes as theme Deucalion re-creating mankind after the Flood; *Les Fils ingrats* (1728), a comedy; verse tales, satires, etc., not free from coarse buffoonery; and many good epigrams. Louis XV vetoed his election (1753) to the *Académie on account of a licentious *Ode à Priape* he had written in youth. He had a formidable gift of repartee, and he is said to have worsted even his enemy Voltaire.

Pisan, CHRISTINE DE, *v. Christine de Pisan.*

Pisançon, ALBÉRIC DE, *v. Alexandre le Grand* (1).

Pithou, PIERRE, *v. Satire Ménippée.*

Pitoëff, GEORGES (1886–1939), a Russian-born actor and producer, settled in Paris after the 1914–18 war and formed his own company, playing from 1924 at the *Théâtre des Arts* and from 1934 at the *Mathurins*. He staged many foreign plays in translation: e.g. Shakespeare, Shaw, Pirandello, Ibsen; also plays by Claudel, Cocteau, Anouilh, etc. His wife LUDMILLA (1895–1951), a fine actress who ran the company after his death, excelled as Shaw's St. Joan. His son SACHA (1920–   ) is also an actor and producer. *v. Theatres and Theatre Companies.*

Pixérécourt, RENÉ-CHARLES GUILBERT

DE (1773–1844), 'le Corneille des boulevards', a prolific author of comedies, *vaudevilles, *opéras-comiques, and, above all, *mélodrames, a type of play then new which he popularized in the *théâtres du boulevard* (v. *Theatres and Theatre Companies*), where over 100 of his plays (often adapted from novels of the day) were produced in the years 1798–1835. They included *Victor, ou l'Enfant de la forêt* (1798), *Les Mystères d'Udolphe* (1798; from Mrs. Radcliffe's *Mysteries of Udolpho*), *Cœlina, ou l'Enfant du mystère* (1800); v. *Ducray-Duminil*.

Placards, L'Affaire des, a famous incident in the early Reformation (v. *Évangélisme*). On 18 October 1534 Paris was found placarded with denunciations of the Mass. This gave rise to general indignation and many Protestants were arrested and executed. Both Calvin and Marot fled from Paris at this time.

Place de la Concorde, a famous open space in Paris, to the north-west of the *Tuileries, created by Louis XV and at first known as the Place Louis XV. During the Revolution it was called the Place de la Révolution and a statue of Liberty was erected there, also the guillotine on which so many perished. In October 1795, after the Terror, the *Convention* renamed it the Place de la Concorde. It was again the Place Louis XV during the Restoration, then (1830) once more the Place de la Concorde.

Place de l'Hôtel-de-Ville, v. *Grève*.

Place des Vosges, v. *Place Royale*.

Place Royale, now the Place des Vosges, a residential square in the centre of the *Marais quarter of Paris (on the site of the earlier *Hôtel des Tournelles) which still retains much of its 17th-c. architectural unity. Construction began—to designs by J. A. du Cerceau—under Henri IV. In the 17th and 18th cs. it was a centre of fashion and culture, also often the scene of duels. Richelieu lived there, as did the courtesan Marion Delorme; Mme de Sévigné was born there (Hôtel de Coulanges) and later lived near by (Hôtel Carnavalet); Corneille set an early comedy, *La Place Royale*, there. 19th-c. residents included Hugo (1833–48, at no. 6, now the *Musée Victor-Hugo*), Gautier, and A. Daudet.

Place Vendôme, a large square in Paris, in part constructed—to designs by Mansard—under Louis XIV, when it had a statue of the king in the centre and was called the Place Louis-le-Grand. The statue was torn down in the Revolution and replaced (1806) by a column (the *Colonne de la Grande Armée*) inspired by Trajan's Column in Rome, its bronze bas-reliefs being made from captured cannon; a statue of Napoleon stood on top (v. *Légende napoléonienne*). The column was thrown down in the *Commune* of 1871, but re-erected in 1873.

Plaideurs, Les, by Racine, a farcical comedy on a theme derived from the *Wasps* of Aristophanes; produced 1668. It is an amusing satire on legal procedure, with allusions to corrupt judges, false witnesses, pompous advocates, and absurd sentences. Some of Racine's friends, e.g. Boileau and La Fontaine, helped in its composition.

Perrin Dandin is a magistrate whose passion for his profession has driven him crazy, so that his son has to keep him locked up. The *bourgeois* Chicanneau and the comtesse de Pimbesche are equally ardent litigants. Dandin, shut up in his house, tries to hear their case from a garret window, then through the air-hole of his cellar. He is induced to exercise his judicial functions over the members of his household. His dog, caught eating a capon, is formally tried, with absurd speeches for the prosecution and defence by two servants, Petit Jean and L'Intimé. It is sentenced to the galleys, but the appearance of its puppies moves the judge to compassion. His son, by a stratagem of legal procedure, wins the hand of Chicanneau's daughter Isabelle. The saying 'Point d'argent, point de suisses' comes from this play.

Plaine, La, the deputies (numerically the strongest element of the assembly) who occupied the middle benches in the *_Convention_, between the *_Girondins_ and the *_Montagnards_, siding intermittently with both. _Cf. Marais, Le_ (2).

Plaisirs et les jours, Les, v. Proust.

Planche, GUSTAVE (1808–57), literary and art critic on the *_Revue des Deux Mondes_ after 1831; also associated, as editor or contributor, with the *_Journal des Débats_, the _Chronique de Paris_ (bought by Balzac in 1836), etc. His collections of articles—many on English literature—include _Portraits littéraires_ (1836–49, 4 vols.), _Nouveaux Portraits littéraires_ (1854), _Études sur les arts_ (1855–6). He was a hard-hitting critic, especially of the *_Romantics_, and made many enemies.

Planchon, ROGER, _v. Theatres and Theatre Companies._

Plantin, CHRISTOPHE (1514–89), a famous printer of French birth, established at Antwerp.

Plassans, _v. Rougon-Macquart, Les._

Pléiade, La, the name (from the seven stars of the Pleiades) given to the seven leading Greek poets in the time of Ptolemy II and applied in the 16th c. to the poets of Ronsard's 'Brigade' or circle. He listed the seven as himself, Du Bellay, Tyard, J.-A. de Baïf, Jodelle, Belleau, and Peletier (for whom contemporaries substituted J. Dorat, as the humanist who inspired the school).

Fired by a lofty idea of the role of the poet, the _Pléiade_ effected a literary revolution, sweeping away the medieval poetical tradition, with its popular and frivolous themes and finicking, *fixed forms, in favour of a new poetry, based on a profound study of Greek, Latin, and Italian literature (notably Homer, Pindar, Horace, and Petrarch), inspired by classical and Italian models, and treating of noble and aristocratic themes. It further sought to renew the French language, to

enrich it by borrowing from or imitating Greek and Latin (e.g. it introduced the word _patrie_), by using archaic, dialectal, and technical terms, and by coining derivatives of existing words (e.g. new verbs derived from nouns). Du Bellay, whose *_Défense et illustration de la langue française_ (1549) was a manifesto of the _Pléiade_'s doctrines, and Ronsard, its greatest poet, laid down precepts of versification (dealing with caesura, *_enjambement_, *masculine and feminine rhymes, inversion, *hiatus, etc.), the best of which were later adopted by Malherbe (a stern critic of some manifestations of the school). The _Pléiade_ revived and established the *alexandrine and was largely responsible for introducing the *sonnet-form from Italy. Its eclipse was due to its excessive erudition, its too servile imitation of the classics, and the artificiality of much of its poetry. _v. Critics and Criticism_, 1; _Lyric Poetry_, 2; _Foreign Influences_, 1; _Renaissance._

Pléiades, Les, v. Gobineau.

Plessis, FRÉDÉRIC (1851–1941), a poet influenced by the *_Parnassiens_. His work was collected in _La Lampe d'argile_ (1886), _Vesper_ (1887), etc.

Plessys, _v. Du Plessys._

Plon-plon, _v. Bonaparte Family_ (8).

Plowert, Jacques, _v. Adam, P._

Pluche, Dame, in Musset's *_On ne badine pas avec l'amour._

Pluche, NOËL-ANTOINE, ABBÉ (1688–1761), a popularizer of scientific knowledge. His _Spectacle de la Nature_ (1732) was very widely read.

Plume, La (1889–1904; fortnightly), a *Symbolist review, soon extended its scope and became an excellent guide to all new trends in literature and art. It often devoted a whole number to one author or movement. It published work by Mallarmé, Moréas, Verlaine, etc.; Barrès,

A. France, and Morice were among its literary critics.

Plutarch, *v. Amyot.*

Pluviôse, *v. Republican Calendar.*

Poème moral, v. Religious Writings, 1.

Poèmes antiques, v. Leconte de Lisle.

Poèmes antiques et modernes (1826; 1837, with 10 additional poems publ. anon. in 1822), a collection of poems by Vigny. It includes, notably, *Éloa* (first publ. 1824), a narrative poem which he called a *mystère*, and *Moïse. Éloa* is the story of an angel of pity who leaves Paradise to find and save the banished Lucifer. She meets him on the confines of Hell, 'jeune, triste, et charmant', an outcast and exile. Her innocence momentarily fills him with nostalgia for his lost purity, but when he sees her half-sensing danger and about to take wing he again becomes 'l'ennemi séducteur' and swears that only her love and voluntary exile from Paradise can save him. She turns back. In *Moïse*, Moses, alone on a mountain-top overlooking the Promised Land, cries to God for release from the heavy burden of his responsibilities— 'Vous m'avez fait vieillir puissant et solitaire, Laissez-moi m'endormir du sommeil de la terre.'

Poèmes barbares, v. Leconte de Lisle.

Poèmes saturniens, v. Verlaine.

Poèmes tragiques, v. Leconte de Lisle.

Poésie 40, v. Resistance.

Poète mourant, Le, v. Millevoye.

Poètes maudits, Les (1884), by Verlaine, short critical and biographical studies, with plentiful quotations, of six poets whom he considered to be insufficiently appreciated. They were Corbière, Marceline Desbordes-Valmore, Villiers de l'Isle-Adam, Mallarmé, Rimbaud, and 'Pauvre Lélian' (an anagram of his own name).

Poétique, v. Critics and Criticism, 3.

Poil de Carotte, v. Renard.

Poincaré, (1) HENRI (1856–1912), a mathematician and *savant*, some of whose works (e.g. *La Science et l'hypothèse,* 1902; *La Valeur de la science,* 1906; *Science et méthode,* 1908) reached beyond a purely scientific public and were widely translated; (2) his cousin RAYMOND (1860–1934), politician and statesman, President of the *Third Republic (1913–20), who left memoirs (*Au service de la France,* 1929–33, 10 vols.) of much interest for the political history of the period leading up to the 1914–18 war and of the war itself.

Poinsinet, ANTOINE-ALEXANDRE-HENRI (1735–69), dramatist, a man of credulous nature and the victim of many practical jokes. He wrote tragedies, *opéras-comiques*, and comedies, notably *Le Cercle* (1764), a one-act prose comedy in which, imitating *Palissot's *Les Originaux, ou le Cercle* and perhaps also *Saurin's *Les Mœurs du temps*, he ridiculed prominent figures in Parisian society of the day. In an earlier comedy, *Le Petit Philosophe* (1760; in *vers libres*), he had parodied Palissot's *Les Philosophes*.

Poirier, Monsieur, *v. Gendre de M. Poirier, Le.*

Poisons, L'Affaire des, *v. Chambre ardente.*

Pois pilés, *v. Confrérie de la Passion.*

Polexandre (1629; 1637, a longer version in 5 vols.), by Gomberville, a heroic romance much admired in its day. Alcidiane, queen of an 'inaccessible island', is so beautiful that, on seeing her portrait, many kings of distant lands ask her hand in marriage. She sends her knight Polexandre to chastise their presumption, and he has a long series of adventures all over the world.

Police. Under the *ancien régime* responsibility for maintaining law and order was vested by the king or the *parlements* in *baillis*, *sénéchaux*, *prévôts*, *intendants*, and similar officers. They often operated through the *Maréchaussée* (*v. Gendarme*). In Paris, where responsibility lay partly with the *prévôt des marchands* (*v. Hôtel de Ville*), Louis XIV created (1667) the office of *lieutenant général de police*. Its first holders, Gabriel-Nicolas de La Reynie and Marc-René d'Argenson, set up 11 *bureaux* (covering public safety, morals, religion, etc.) and laid down general lines for the maintenance of order.

For a time during the Revolution police responsibilities were divided among committees. A *Ministère de la Police générale* was created in 1796 (*v. Fouché*), but its functions were later returned to the *Ministère de l'Intérieur*. In Paris, the office of *lieutenant général de police*, which had been suppressed, was in effect revived when Bonaparte created (1800) the office of *préfet de police*. Since then, for reasons of history, politics, and administration (*v. Maire de Paris*), police powers in the Paris region have been vested in the *préfet de police* and not, as elsewhere, in the *préfet de* *département*.

France is now policed by two bodies (reorganized 1966–9): the *Police nationale* (under the central control of the *Direction générale de la Sûreté nationale*, known as the *Sûreté*, a department of the *Ministère de l'Intérieur*) and the *Gendarmerie nationale* (under the *Ministre des Armées*), each covering the whole country. The various directorates of the *Sûreté* reflect a broad division into *police administrative* or *générale* (mainly uniformed forces, concerned with crime prevention in general, with the maintenance of State security and of law and order, with frontier control, traffic control, decency, hygiene, etc.) and *police judiciaire* (mainly plain-clothes forces, concerned with criminal investigation and often acting on orders from the judicature; the counterpart of the English C.I.D.). Broadly speaking, the policing of urban areas falls largely to the departmental public security services of

the *Police nationale* (there are also some 40 forces of *police municipale*, which are employed by the *communes* and may be reinforced by officers of the *Police nationale*), while the policing of rural areas falls largely to the departmental *Gendarmerie*. In every *département* (except Ville-de-Paris), responsibility for the *police générale* (except in certain specialized fields) is vested in the *préfet*, who has the co-operation of the departmental *Gendarmerie* commander. In Ville-de-Paris, control of the *police générale* falls to the *préfet de police* (who is directly responsible to the *Ministre de l'Intérieur*); he also controls the *police judiciaire* in the region comprising Ville-de-Paris, Hauts-de-Seine, Seine-Saint-Denis, and Val-de-Marne.

For the benefit of readers of crime fiction, a *gardien*, *brigadier*, *officier-adjoint*, *officier*, and *commissaire* of the *Police nationale* are roughly equivalent to an English constable, sergeant, inspector, chief inspector, and superintendent; an *agent*, or a *sergent de ville*, is a municipal, uniformed policeman; a *garde-champêtre* is a rural policeman; the 'P. J.' or 'Quai des Orfèvres' is the Paris headquarters of the *police judiciaire*; the 'Rue des Saussaies' is the *Sûreté*.

Polichinelle, French form of the Italian *Policinello*, *Pulcinella*, name (of uncertain origin) of a character in Neapolitan farce, introduced by Molière in the first interlude of *Le *Malade imaginaire*; popularized by a puppet show (Eng. *Punchinello*, *Punch and Judy*). *Cf. Guignol.*

Polignac, JULES-AUGUSTE-ARMAND-MARIE, COMTE, later PRINCE, DE (1780–1847), a Royalist and Roman Catholic of the most reactionary type, imprisoned (1804–13) for his part in the *Cadoudal-Pichegru conspiracy. He was ambassador in London (1823–9). As foreign minister, then prime minister (1829–30), he was held largely responsible for Charles X's repressive policy. He was arrested during the 1830 *Revolution, and when his life sentence was commuted to exile (1836) he retired to England for some years. He published *Études historiques, politiques, et morales* and *Réponse à mes adversaires* (both 1845).

Politiques, Les, v. *Huguenots.*

Politique tirée de l'Écriture Sainte, v. *Bossuet.*

Polyeucte, a tragedy by Corneille; probably produced in the winter of 1641–2. It is based on the *Vitae sanctorum* of Surius, a 16th-c. German monk.

The scene is Armenia in the time of the emperor Decius. Polyeucte is married to Pauline, daughter of Félix, the Roman governor. He is the friend of Néarque, a Christian, and is himself on the point of conversion. Pauline is disquieted by a dream: she has seen her former lover Sévère (whom she wrongly believes to be dead) and witnessed the death of Polyeucte, killed by her father. Polyeucte is baptized. Sévère, now the emperor's favourite, arrives in the town to do sacrifice, hoping to claim Pauline as his bride. He sees Pauline, who still loves him, learns that she is married, and honourably renounces her. Polyeucte and Néarque attend the sacrifice and revile the Roman gods. Néarque is executed, Polyeucte imprisoned. He desires martyrdom, and surrenders Pauline, whom he dearly loves, to Sévère. Pauline's admiration of her husband now turns to love, and she refuses Sévère, who nobly resolves to save Polyeucte. But the weak, time-serving Félix, afraid that Sévère will denounce him if he shows leniency, orders Polyeucte's execution. The sight of his martyrdom converts Pauline to Christianity. Sévère upbraids Félix for sacrificing Polyeucte to save himself. Félix announces his own conversion.

Polymnie, v. *Musical Controversies.*

Pomme de Pin, La, a Paris tavern, mentioned by Villon, Rabelais, and M. Régnier.

Pompadour, ANTOINETTE POISSON, MARQUISE DE (1721–64), a woman of the rich *bourgeoisie*, mistress of Louis XV. She was an intelligent patroness of the arts, but her political influence over some 20 years (esp. in regard to war and foreign affairs) was less fortunate. The memoirs (1809) of Mme du Hausset, her *femme de chambre*, throw light on her long period of power. It was she who said to Louis XV, 'Après nous le déluge!'

Pompignan, JEAN-JACQUES LE FRANC, MARQUIS DE (1709–84), a learned magistrate and a poet of some merit. He wrote *Didon* (1734), a tragedy; *Prométhée*, a satirical opera directed against Voltaire; an ode on the death of J.-B. Rousseau, whose disciple he was; *Poésies sacrées*, etc. He was admitted to the *Académie (1760), where he declaimed against the *Encyclopédistes, but was thereafter undeservedly overwhelmed by Voltaire's ridicule. v. *Arnaud, Baculard d'.*

Pomponne, v. *Arnauld, Arnauld d'Andilly* (4).

Ponge, FRANCIS (1899–), poet. He was associated with the **Nouvelle Revue française* in the 1920s and briefly with *Surrealism in 1930. Between 1937 and 1947 he was a militant Communist, active in the intellectual *Resistance from 1942. His work consists largely of detailed descriptions or definitions of objects (a shrimp, a pebble, a glass of water, etc.); in form, it rejects the traditional apparatus of poetry and attempts to subvert accepted uses of language in an effort to 'found a new rhetoric'. His publications include *Douze Petits Écrits* (1926), *Le Parti pris des choses* (1942), *Proêmes* (1948), *Le Peintre à l'étude* (1948), *La Seine* (1950), *La Rage de l'expression* (1952), *Le Grand Recueil* (1961, 3 vols.), *Pour un Malherbe* (1965), *Le Savon* (1967), *La Fabrique du pré* (1971).

Poniatowski, JOSEPH-ANTOINE, PRINCE, v. *Maréchal.*

Pons, Sylvain, in Balzac's *Le* **Cousin Pons.*

Ponsard, FRANÇOIS (1814–67), dramatist, a leader (with Augier) of the *école du bon sens*, a movement in the theatre which marked a reaction against the exaggerations of *Romantic drama, though it profited by some of its innovations. His works, nearly all in verse, include the Classical *tragedy *Lucrèce* (1843; with Rachel as Lucrèce), produced with striking success just after the failure of Hugo's Les *Burgraves; *Agnès de Méranie* (1846) and *Charlotte Corday* (1850), tragedies; *L'Honneur et l'argent* (1853) and *La Bourse* (1856), comedies satirizing the mid-19th-c. worship of money; *Le Lion amoureux* (1866), a lively historical comedy of *Directoire society which long remained popular. *v. Theatre of the 19th and 20th cs.*

Ponson du Terrail, PIERRE-ALEXIS, VICOMTE DE (1829–71), a highly prolific, best-selling novelist and *roman-feuilletoniste*. His hero Rocambole went through countless adventures, told with a serene, often comic, disregard for plot and style, in 22 volumes of *Les Exploits de Rocambole* (1859) and many sequels.

Pont-Allais, *v. Jean de l'Espine.*

Pont-au-Change, originally the Grand Pont (*v. Cité, Île de la*), so called from the money-changers established there by the king in the 12th c.

Pontigny, Les Décades de, the gatherings, a mixture of a retreat and a summer school, instituted *c.* 1905 by the critic and philosopher Paul Desjardins (1859–1940) at his home, the former Cistercian Abbey of Pontigny, in Burgundy. There were several every summer, each lasting ten days, down to 1939. The purpose was study, and free discussion of topics of spiritual, cultural, and academic interest. They were attended by intellectuals from all over the world.

Pontis, LOUIS DE (1583–1670), a soldier who after some 50 years' service ended his days as a solitary at *Port-Royal*. He left memoirs.

Pont-Neuf, the bridge connecting the western end of the Île de la *Cité with the right and left banks of the Seine; begun 1578 by Henri III and completed 1607 by Henry IV. It was the first bridge in Paris which was not lined with shops, and was long a mixture of a fair and a market. There are allusions in 17th-c. literature to the *chansonniers* or *colporteurs* of the Pont-Neuf, and in the 18th c. 'un pont-neuf' was a colloquial term for a popular song or air. *v. Tabarin.*

Pont-Sainte-Maxence, GARNIER DE, *v. Thomas Becket.*

Pontus de Tyard, *v. Tyard.*

Populisme, *v. Novel, 3.*

Poquelin, *v. Molière.*

Porte étroite, La (1909), by Gide, a fine, but painful, example of the type of novel he called a *récit*.

There is no reason why Alissa should not marry her cousin Jérôme, except her initial fear that marriage may profane love. This fear soon turns to a form of exacerbated religious scrupulosity against which he can make no headway. Striving after holiness, she mortifies spirit and flesh, turning her back on love, joy, and human contacts, finally on life itself. Jérôme tells the tale, with the aid of quotations from her diary which suggest that, with less high-souled diffidence on his part, her scruples might have collapsed.

Porthos, in Dumas *père*'s Les *Trois Mousquetaires.*

Porto-Riche, GEORGES DE (1849–1930), dramatist, became known with *La Chance de Françoise* (1889), a one-act comedy produced at the *Théâtre Libre. He was an innovator of the so-called *théâtre d'amour*, i.e. dramas of psychological analysis, studying the relations between men and women in love. His greatest successes were *Amoureuse* (1891), a study of three unhappy people (Étienne Fériaud, a scientist, tells his wife Germaine to take a lover and leave him in peace; she chooses his friend Pascal Delannoy; Étienne suspects this, Pascal is ashamed, and Germaine still loves Étienne); *Le Passé* (1898); *Le Vieil Homme* (1911).

Portraits contemporains; *Portraits de femmes*; *Portraits littéraires*, v. *Critiques et Portraits littéraires*.

Port-Royal, a Cistercian convent (f. 1204) in the Vallée de Chevreuse, south-west of Paris. In the early 17th c., its discipline (much relaxed, as in other convents at this time) was firmly restored by its young abbess Jacqueline Arnauld, 'la Mère Angélique de Sainte-Madeleine'. In 1625, the nuns moved to larger premises in Paris, distinguished as *Port-Royal de Paris* from the older foundation, thereafter called *Port-Royal des Champs*. Du Vergier de Hauranne (abbé de Saint-Cyran), director of the convent from 1635, introduced the *Jansenist doctrines of which *Port-Royal* became the centre and the symbol. *v.* also *Singlin*; *Le Maître de Saci*.

Meanwhile, the deserted *Port-Royal des Champs* had been occupied by a group of Jansenist solitaries. When some of the nuns returned from Paris (1648), the *solitaires* moved to a neighbouring hill. Here and in the vicinity they founded some small schools (the *Petites Écoles de Port-Royal*) and were soon famous for the excellent education they provided (Racine was a pupil). Jansenists of *Port-Royal* such as A. Arnauld, Nicole, and Claude Lancelot (1615–95) prepared educational works of high quality, e.g. the *Logique, ou l'Art de penser* (1661) by Arnauld and Nicole; the *Grammaire générale* (1660) by Arnauld and Lancelot; the *Jardin des racines grecques* (1657), a versified Greek dictionary by Lancelot and Le Maître de Saci; Lancelot's *Nouvelles Méthodes* of learning Greek, Latin, Italian, and Spanish.

The greatest writer associated with *Port-Royal* was Pascal. Arnauld was the most important of its later leaders. Its chief enemies were the *Jesuits, bent on retaining their monopoly of education and spiritual direction. They secured the condemnation (1653) by Pope Innocent X of five propositions from Jansenius's *Augustinus*, the censuring of Arnauld by the *Sorbonne*, the closing of the *Port-Royal* schools, the dispersal of the solitaries, and the prolonged persecution of the nuns. The nuns firmly refused to sign a formulary condemning the doctrines attributed to Jansenius and had many supporters in high places, even among the clergy. Some were removed to other convents (*v.* *Arnauld*, *Arnauld d'Andilly* (5)); then all were reunited at *Port-Royal des Champs*, but kept in a state of sequestration. An accommodation was reached in 1668 when Clement IX became pope, and there was a truce (*la paix de l'Église*) for some 10 years; but the persecution was then resumed owing to the king's annoyance at the revived popularity and influence of the sect. Arnauld was driven into exile, and from 1679 the convent was forbidden to accept novices and was thus doomed to extinction. Before this came about, however, the abolition of *Port-Royal* was decreed by papal bull (1708), the remaining nuns forcibly removed (1709), the buildings razed to the ground (1710), and the bodies in the graveyard dug up and dispersed (1711). In 1713, in the bull *Unigenitus Dei Filius*, Clement XI condemned 101 propositions in the *Réflexions morales sur le Nouveau Testament* (1671; re-ed. 1699) of Pasquier Quesnel (1634–1719), who succeeded Arnauld as leader of the Jansenists.

Works on *Port-Royal* include *Racine's *Abrégé de l'histoire de Port-Royal*, Sainte-Beuve's *Port-Royal*, and Gazier's *Histoire générale du mouvement janséniste* (1922). *v.* also *Montherlant*.

Port-Royal (1840–59), Sainte-Beuve's greatest work of re-creative criticism; the published form of lectures on the theme of *Port-Royal*, delivered 1837–8 in Lausanne. This long, meandering masterpiece is the work of Sainte-Beuve the poet, penetrating 'le mystère de ces âmes pieuses', and of Sainte-Beuve the seeker after truth, who found, as he proceeded, that poetry disappeared, for 'la religion seule s'est montrée..., et le christianisme dans sa nudité'. But the poetry lingered in his approach, which he called a 'procédé de peintre,... plein de retouches et de revisions,... de scrupules et de repentirs, cheminant petit à petit', and in his style.

There are six books. Bk. I, *Origine et renaissance de Port-Royal*, covers the early history of the convent, detailing the reforms effected by Jacqueline Arnauld. The whole Arnauld family is described, the characters of St. François de Sales and the abbé de Saint-Cyran (Du Vergier de Hauranne) are contrasted, and an examination of contemporary doctrines of Grace leads to various literary digressions, e.g. a study of Corneille and his *Polyeucte*. Bk. II, *Le Port-Royal de M. de Saint-Cyran*, is mainly about the solitaires. Their many literary, philosophic, and social connections lead to studies of Guez de Balzac, *Jansenism, Descartes, the duc and duchesse de Luynes (who built a *château* near *Port-Royal des Champs*), etc. Bk. III (in 2 pts.), *Pascal*, is a famous study of the life, death, and works of Pascal, with no less famous digressions on Montaigne and Molière (notably his *Tartuffe*). Bk. IV, *Écoles de Port-Royal*, is about the schools founded by the solitaires and their textbooks. There are pen-portraits of masters and pupils, also of the abbé de Rancé. Bk. V (in 2 pts.), *La Seconde Génération de Port-Royal*, moves to the years 1660-9. It includes studies of Angélique Arnauld d'Andilly and Nicole; also of persons connected with *Port-Royal* in a more literary or worldly way, e.g. La Fontaine (*v. Captivité de Saint Malc, La*), Mme de Sablé, Mme de Longueville. Bk. VI (in 2 pts.), *Le Port-Royal finissant*, covers the final years of persecution and destruction (1679-1711). Arnauld is studied at length, and Boileau as his friend and defender. The second part is almost entirely devoted to Racine, and a long study of *Athalie* crowns 'cette histoire... modestement commencée à la journée du Guichet' (*v. Arnauld, Arnauld d'Andilly* (2)).

Positivism, *v. Comte, A.*; *Littré*; *Laffitte.*

Pot-Bouille, *v. Rougon-Macquart, Les.*

Pougens, MARIE-CHARLES-JOSEPH DE, *v. Dictionaries*, 1819.

Poujadisme, a political movement led by Pierre Poujade (1920–), founder in 1954 of the *Union de défense des commerçants et artisans*. The *Poujadistes*, widely supported by small shopkeepers, etc., in a campaign against taxation, had some success at the elections of 1956, but were soon divided.

Poulenc, FRANCIS (1899–1963), composer, one of *Les *Six*, wrote airs for many poems (by Ronsard, Moréas, Apollinaire, Jacob, Éluard, etc.); lyrical works, notably adaptations of *Apollinaire's *Les Mamelles de Tirésias* (as a light opera, 1947) and *Cocteau's *La Voix humaine* (1958); ballets; religious music, etc.

Poulet, GEORGES (1902–), critic and university teacher, a Belgian who taught French literature at the University of Edinburgh, then in the U.S.A. and Switzerland. His works include *Études sur le temps humain* (1949–68, 4 vols.), *Les Métamorphoses du cercle* (1961), *L'Espace proustien* (1963), *Le Point de départ* (1964), *Mesure de l'instant* (1968), and *La Conscience critique* (1971), which contains essays on critics and criticism. His criticism is based on a total identification with the author in question. He believes that, by seeing how a writer perceives and expresses such phenomena as time, space, and form, the critic is able to reveal the individual consciousness which lies at the heart of the work. *v. Critics and Criticism*, 3.

Pourceaugnac, *v. Monsieur de Pourceaugnac.*

Pour et Contre, Le, *v. Prévost, A.-F.*

Pour et le Contre, Le, (1) a poem (1722) by Voltaire in support of Deism, in the guise of arguments for and against Christianity; (2) v. *Feuillet*.

Pourrat, HENRI (1887–1959), noted for his novels of Auvergne, especially the cycle *Vaillances, farces, et gentillesses de Gaspard des Montagnes* (1922–31).

Poussin, NICOLAS (1594–1665), a great historical and landscape painter. His works include *Le Déluge*, *Moïse sauvé des eaux*, *L'Enlèvement des Sabines*. His *Correspondance* appeared in 1824.

Prades, JEAN, ABBÉ DE (1720–82), an *Encyclopédiste* who successfully sustained (1751) before the *Sorbonne* a thesis later found to throw doubt on the credibility of the Christian miracles. It was condemned by the *parlement*, and he fled to Berlin to escape arrest. He defended his position in an *Apologie*, and Diderot wrote a *Suite de l'Apologie de l'abbé de Prades* (1752); but he later recanted. The affair contributed to the suppression (1752) of the first two volumes of the *Encyclopédie*.

Pradon, JACQUES, *known as* NICOLAS (1644–98), an obscure tragic poet, brought into notoriety by his *Phèdre et Hippolyte* (1677), which he was induced by the cabal hostile to Racine to compose in rivalry with Racine's *Phèdre*. It was staged two days after *Phèdre*. v. *Mazarin's Nieces* (7).

Prairial, v. *Republican Calendar*.

Preachers. The 17th c. was the great age of religious oratory in France (v. *Bossuet*; *Bourdaloue*; *Fléchier*; *Massillon*; *Mascaron*). There was some revival in the 19th c. (v. *Lacordaire*; *Dupanloup*; *Frayssinous*; *Ravignan*).

Pré-aux-Clercs, v. *Saint-Germain-des-Prés*.

Précellence du langage français, v. *Estienne* (4).

Précieuses ridicules, Les, a one-act prose comedy by Molière; produced 1659. Here, for the first time, he derided the absurdities of contemporary society, but took care to distinguish in his preface between the 'véritables *précieuses*' and their imitators.

Madelon and Cathos, daughter and niece of Gorgibus, a *bourgeois* from the provinces, are infatuated with the affected manners and speech of Parisian society. They spurn the suitors who propose marriage to them without the circumlocutions and preparatory adventures described in the Scudéry romances. The suitors arrange for their valets, who are similarly inclined to ape persons of condition, to visit the ladies in the guise of the marquis de *Mascarille* and the vicomte de *Jodelet*. An amusing scene follows, the ladies being enthralled by the extravagant language and dress of their visitors, which they take for the height of fashion, and correspondingly deflated when the trick is revealed.

Précieux,   Précieuses. *Préciosité*, brought into fashion by Mme de Rambouillet and her circle (v. *Rambouillet, Hôtel de*; *Sablé*; *Pure*; *Somaize*), was in origin the pursuit of elegance and delicacy in thought, language, and manners. In language, it led to the coining of metaphorical expressions (some have survived, e.g. *travestir sa pensée*), the avoidance of low or barbarous words, and a general attempt to achieve clarity and precision. But in checking coarseness it also inhibited spontaneity, and in time it was carried to excess, e.g. in the cult of periphrasis for its own sake. The *précieuses*, the ladies who practised it, were ridiculed for their pedantry and affectation, and Boileau, Racine, and Molière reacted against it.

Préfet, the executive head of a *département*, an important civil office created 1800 by Bonaparte. There is also a *sous-préfet* for each *arrondissement*. Both are appointed centrally. The *préfet* has police powers, except in the *département* (Seine till 1964, now Ville-de-Paris) in which Paris is situated (v. *Police*; *Maire de Paris*). The *préfet*, his wife *la préfète*, and the *sous-préfet* figure largely in 19th-c. fiction.

Préfet de police, v. Police.

Premiers Lundis, v. Causeries du lundi, Les.

Prémontrés, Ordre des, the Order of the Premonstratensians, f. 1120 by St. Norbert at Prémontré, near Laon; so called because the site of their first house is said to have been prophetically indicated to St. Norbert.

Présence africaine, v. Négritude.

Présidente, La, the name given (it is said by Flaubert) to Mme Apollonie-Aglaé Sabatier, a well-known mid-19th-c. beauty. At one time an artist's model, she was the friend of many writers and artists, and the Sunday evening gatherings at her flat are often referred to in letters of the period. She inspired some of Baudelaire's finest poems (e.g. *Que diras-tu ce soir*; *Harmonie du soir*; *Hymne*).

Presidents of the Republic, v. Republics, 2, 3, 4, 5; *Élysée, Palais de l'*; *Rambouillet, Château de.*

Press, Development of the.

1. PRE-REVOLUTION. The periodical and daily Press began in the 17th c., with *La *Gazette,* f. 1631 by Renaudot; *La Muse historique* (1650–65), weekly letters or gazettes recording events of the day in burlesque verse, addressed by Jean Loret to his patroness Mme de Longueville; and the sheets circulated by the *nouvellistes.* Initial development was slow. As with the book-trade, a licence to print—the *privilège* granted by the *directeur de la *librairie*—was required, and the few licences granted created a virtual monopoly for journals which enjoyed them. Political journals were subject to censorship, but this was often evaded, e.g. by printing and circulating them clandestinely; by printing them abroad and introducing them to subscribers in France; or by claiming that they dealt with a subject exempt from censorship (e.g. medicine). The liberty of the Press was a burning subject almost from the start and was advocated by the *parlement* in a decree of 1778.

Other publications founded before the Revolution include *Le *Mercure galant, Le *Journal de Paris, Les *Annales politiques, civiles, et littéraires, Le *Journal des savants, L'*Année littéraire, Le *Journal de Trévoux, Le Pour et Contre* (v. Prévost, A.-F.).

2. REVOLUTION. Development was rapid in the months before the Revolution. The convoking of the *États généraux* unleashed a flood of pamphlets (with such titles as *Manière de s'assembler, Considérations sur les intérêts du Tiers État,* etc.) impossible to control by licensing or censorship; v. Sieyès. With the opening of the assembly (May 1789) many new, mainly political journals (termed indiscriminately *gazette, journal, bulletin, chronique, feuille,* etc.) were founded, often by former pamphleteers. They were designed to keep the nation informed of events, to report the proceedings of the *Assemblée nationale* (e.g. the famous *Journal des Débats*), to voice the views of party leaders, etc. Publication was daily, weekly, three or four times weekly, or at irregular intervals. Size varied: a daily might run to four quarto pages, sometimes printed in double columns; the others were usually from two to five pages octavo. Some covered literature and gossip, but many were little more than news-sheets, often ill-written, at times obscene, and vituperative rather than soberly informative. They were circulated to subscribers, or sold by street-vendors (*colporteurs*), who shouted their wares in competition and were potential disturbers of the peace.

Freedom of the Press was assured by the *Déclaration des droits de l'homme* (art. 11) and confirmed by the *constitution of 1791. But editors, printers, or vendors were increasingly denounced and prosecuted for disseminating opinions calculated to undermine law and order. Many journals had to suspend publication while their editors were in prison or in hiding. Those of Royalist or constitutionalist sympathies lost the freedom to publish when the monarchy fell (1792); their type was dispersed and their editors pursued by the *Tribunal révolutionnaire*. From the fall of the *Girondins* (1793) to that of Robespierre (1794) the Press was virtually controlled by the *Jacobins*, some journals being subsidized by the *Comité de salut public*.

Papers founded at this time include *Les Actes des Apôtres, Le *Courrier de Provence, Le *Moniteur universel, L'*Ami du Roi, des Français...*, La *Quotidienne*—all Royalist or liberal, and mainly counter-Revolutionary; *L'*Ami du peuple, Les *Annales patriotiques et littéraires, Le *Courrier de Versailles à Paris...*, Le *Journal de Perlet, L'*Orateur du peuple, Le *Patriote français, Les *Révolutions de Paris, Les *Révolutions de France et de Brabant, Le *Vieux Cordelier, Le *Père Duchesne, Le *Défenseur de la Constitution*—all Revolutionary or Republican. Reviews published at this time include *La *Décade philosophique*.

3. DIRECTOIRE. The principle of freedom of the Press was again broadly affirmed in the constitution of 1795 inaugurating the *Directoire*. But the many new, counter-Revolutionary journals (e.g. *L'*Accusateur public*) born of the *réaction thermidorienne* (1794; *v. Revolutions*, 1) soon abused their liberty, while journals of all parties combined to attack the *Directoire* and hamper its efforts at peaceful government. A law of 1796, the first of its kind in France, made it a penal offence for the Press to agitate for the overthrow of the government or the restoration of the monarchy. It proved ineffective, and after the *coup d'état du 18 *fructidor* ('La Saint-Barthélemy des journalistes') the editors and printers of several journals were imprisoned or deported on charges of conspiring against the internal security of the Republic with intent to restore the monarchy. Their presses were destroyed. A law was then passed subjecting all periodical publications to strict police surveillance (and possible suppression) for a period of 12 months.

4. CONSULAT AND EMPIRE. Napoleon deprived the Press of its little remaining liberty. He suppressed (1800) all but 13 of

73 political papers produced in the Paris region and forbade the creation of any new ones. The survivors were subjected to severe police control, exercised through a Press Bureau. The provincial Press was controlled by the *préfets*. Certain topics, e.g. religion, were prohibited or had to be treated on set lines. Further, specially appointed censors supervised the tone of any journal disliked by Napoleon. Sometimes he even nominated journalists to editorial staffs to write articles specified by him, or dictated the way in which profits were to be used. In 1810, he issued a decree re-establishing censorship of the periodical Press and of books; in 1811, he reduced the number of tolerated political papers from 13 to four—*La *Gazette de France, Le Journal de l'Empire* (i.e. *Le *Journal des Débats), Le *Journal de Paris, Le *Moniteur universel*. Non-political periodicals were tolerated if they published nothing capable of being interpreted as critical of the government. During the Hundred Days, however, Napoleon finally granted liberty of the Press (*v. Acte additionnel*).

5. RESTORATION. The *Charte* granted by Louis XVIII in 1814 guaranteed liberty of the Press, but 'la liberté selon la Charte' was soon being severely restricted by laws hotly debated on their passage through both Chambers. Royal sanction was made necessary for the publication of even remotely political journals of all kinds, and pamphlets of less than 20 pages were subjected to censorship. This regulation was often evaded by publishing in miscellany form at irregular intervals (e.g. *La *Minerve française; Le *Conservateur*).

The restrictions were lifted by three constructive laws of 1819. Full freedom of publication (subject to certain preliminary guarantees, financial and otherwise) was accorded to newspapers and periodicals, the censorship was abolished, the duties of editors and printers were defined. A year later, however, and again under Charles X, censorship was re-established in a more reactionary form than ever. *La loi Peyronnet*—a bill introduced in 1827 by the comte de Peyronnet, one of Charles X's ministers—threatened to destroy any liberty remaining to the Press and the book-trade. It prompted many petitions to the king, including one from the *Académie*, and after a debate notable for a fine attacking speech by Royer-Collard it was eventually withdrawn. Matters finally came to a head with the *ordonnances* of 26 July 1830, which entirely suppressed the liberty of the Press. Feeling ran so high that Le *National and Le *Temps*, with several other journals, issued a signed protest calling on the nation to resist. The ensuing disaffection led to the 1830 *Revolution.

Daily and other papers founded between 1814 and 1830 included Le *Constitutionnel, Le *Figaro (as a small weekly), Le *Globe, Le *Journal universel, Le *Nain jaune, Le *National, Le *Temps. The period was fertile in new conceptions of politics, philosophy, religion, and aesthetics; and informed discussion of these in daily papers and periodicals made the Press a powerful factor in the movement of ideas. There was also a great development of the predominantly literary Press (cf. Critics and Criticism, 2). The many new reviews which now appeared were roughly of three types: those of the old school, edited by liberals or monarchists reared on the pseudo-*Classicism of the 18th c., e.g. Les *Lettres normandes, La *Minerve française, La *Minerve littéraire; those founded and supported by the ultra-*Romantics (in part the younger generation of writers, in part the returned émigrés), e.g. Les *Lettres champenoises, Les *Annales de la littérature et des arts, La *Revue de Paris (to some extent), and, above all, Le *Conservateur littéraire and La *Muse française; those of the *doctrinaires, for whom the literature of every age was one expression of its social and political development and who welcomed the new literary theories in so far as these agreed with their own views, e.g. Les *Archives philosophiques, La *Revue française. The famous *Revue des Deux Mondes (f. 1829) did not at once develop its literary side. v. also Revue encyclopédique, La; Foreign Influences, 3.

6. THE JULY MONARCHY. With the advent of Louis-Philippe in 1830 the Press regained a freedom not effectively impaired by laws of 1834–5 controlling street-vendors of pamphlet literature and dealing with slander, seditious writings, etc. It became less important politically: in 1848, for instance, it was only indirectly responsible for the fall of the monarchy; more was effected by *banquets.

This period saw the development of the idealistic, socialistic, and humanitarian Press, reflecting the ideas of Lamennais, P. Leroux, the *Saint-Simoniens, and the *Fouriéristes; the satirical and cartoonist Press, e.g. Le *Charivari; the feminist Press, e.g. La Gazette des femmes (1836–7 and 1841–3), edited solely or mainly by women, and Le Miroir des dames (f. 1841; fortnightly); and the *roman-feuilleton. At this time, too, the chronicle-writers or columnists made their appearance (e.g. Janin; Mme Émile de Girardin), as did periodicals for children (v. Children's Reading). The outstanding innovation was the cheap daily, relying largely on advertisements for its income, e.g. La *Presse and Le *Siècle (both f. 1836). The older papers, at first strongly opposed to advertisements, soon followed suit, halved their subscription rate, and increased their circulation. In 1835, when the population was c. 35,000,000, there were some 70,000 subscribers to newspapers published in Paris and the provinces; by 1836 there were 200,000 subscribers to daily papers published in the Paris region alone. v. also Magasin pittoresque, Le; Univers, L'.

7. 1848 AND THE SECOND REPUBLIC. After the 1848 *Revolution the provisional government ended the system of laws and penalties regulating the conduct of the Press. Universal male suffrage was now a live issue, and a spate of newspapers appeared to voice the opinions of the many political parties on such questions of the day, e.g. La *République française, L'*Assemblée nationale, L'*Événement, Le Représentant du peuple (f. by Proudhon); most were to be short-lived. There was also a crop of papers devoted to topical satire and caricatures, or to sensational news and gossip. Semi-political journals for women included La Voix des femmes and La Politique des femmes.

Soon after Louis-Napoléon Bonaparte became President he reintroduced the Press laws recently repealed and in 1850 made the signature of political articles obligatory. Quick to recognize the propaganda value of the Press, he then launched what amounted to a Press campaign in 'inspired' journals (e.g. Le *Constitutionnel*) to prepare public opinion for his *coup d'état* of 1851 and swift emergence as emperor (v. *Republics*, 2).

8. THE SECOND EMPIRE. The *coup d'état* had entailed wholesale suppression of newspapers and the compulsory or voluntary exile of their editors. Decrees of 1852 again subjected the Press to police control, reinstituted a rigorous system of taxes, preliminary deposits, and obligatory authorization and supervision of papers of political or economic character, and empowered the government to suspend or suppress any paper which contravened the law. Official censorship was not reimposed, but the effect of the decrees was to make each editor his own censor. Political papers almost ceased to exist (only 11 were allowed to continue) and free comment long remained impossible. Many papers consequently developed their literary, dramatic, musical, and art criticism (e.g. Le *Figaro*; L'*Univers*; Le *Charivari*); new papers appeared solely devoted to these features or to non-political news and cartoons (e.g. Le *Nain jaune*), and illustrated papers increased (v. *Vie parisienne, La*). Le Petit Journal (f. 1863, price one *sou*) brought the daily paper within reach of all classes; it carried miscellaneous information, gossip, and a *roman-feuilleton*, and soon had a record circulation. The 1860s also saw the foundation of Le *Temps* (1861) and Le *Gaulois* (1867), and of literary reviews associated with the *Parnassiens*. From 1868, when the law requiring authorization before publication was repealed, a host of new journals appeared, all critical of the *régime*, e.g. La Lanterne (v. *Rochefort*), Le *Rappel*, Le *Réveil*.

9. 1870 AND AFTER. Though several new, mainly short-lived, papers appeared when the Second Empire fell, the Press was virtually under military control during the *Franco-Prussian war and freedom of comment was not immediately regained. Many leading journals suspended publication while the Prussians occupied Paris; others followed the government and were printed at Tours or Bordeaux. There was an outcry when the military governor of Paris used his emergency powers to suppress some of the violently Republican papers and prohibit new ones, and the *communards* of 1871 called for liberty of the Press. Within weeks, however, the *Commune in its turn suppressed some of the more hostile conservative papers and created new ones, reviving titles used in the Revolution of 1789.

Successive governments thereafter busied themselves with legislation concerning the position and conduct of the Press. A thoroughly liberal bill enacted in 1881, and subsequently little modified, has since then regulated the periodical Press (and the book-trade). It safeguarded the liberty of printers and booksellers, permitted full comment and criticism, but stipulated that nothing must be published that constituted a political misdemeanour or a threat to public safety, also that any official correction of mis-statements must be inserted prominently, free of charge. In exceptional circumstances, such as time of war, freedom of publication could be limited and censorship introduced. (This happened in the 1914–18 war, while before and after the outbreak of the 1939–45 war, and again in May–June 1958 (v. *Republics*, 5), the freedom of the Press was restricted by various special decrees.)

The years 1870–1914 were marked by polemical journalism of unprecedented violence (generated by the fate of the *communards*, monarchist and anarchist plots, *Boulangisme*, the *Panama scandal, the *Dreyfus case, the *Action française*, the growing threat of war, etc.). The many new papers—primarily journals of *opinion*— founded at this time include Le *XIXᵉ Siècle* (1871), La *République française* (1871), Le Cri du peuple (1871; v. Vallès), L'Intransigeant (1880; v. Rochefort), *Gil Blas* (1880), La Croix (1883; a Roman Catholic paper), La Libre Parole (1892; v. Drumont), L'*Aurore

(1897; *v. Dreyfus*) and other papers associated with Clemenceau, *L'*Action française* (1899), *L'Humanité* (1904; *v. Jaurès*). Others engaged in polemical journalism included Veuillot (in *L'*Univers*) and Barrès (in *L'Écho de Paris*).

In France, as elsewhere, the development of the rotary press led to the rapid growth of the popular Press—primarily journals of *information*, reporting 'news' of every kind, in due course with photographs (here *Excelsior*, f. 1910, was a pioneer). By 1914, Paris had five papers with very large circulations: *Le Petit Journal* (*v.* above), *Le Petit Parisien* (f. 1876), *Le Matin* (f. 1882), *L'Écho de Paris* (f. 1884), *Le Journal* (f. 1892). Easier production and transport favoured the development of a highly influential, more solidly political provincial Press (e.g. *La Dépêche*, f. 1870 at Toulouse; *La Gironde*; *Le Phare de la Loire*; *Le Journal de Rouen*). There was also a vast increase in the number of cheap sporting papers, women's magazines, and specialist journals of all kinds.

The polemics ceased abruptly in 1914 (except in Clemenceau's *L'Homme libre*, which was suppressed and re-emerged as *L'Homme enchaîné*). Papers founded during the war included *L'Œuvre* (1915) and *Le Populaire* (1918), left-wing dailies; and *Le Canard enchaîné* (1915), an irreverent satirical weekly which enjoys a continuing success. In 1921, *L'Humanité* became the official organ of the Communist Party and *Le Populaire* (ed. by Blum) that of the Socialist Party. The inter-war years saw the foundation of *Paris-Soir* (1924), an evening paper which had a circulation of 1,500,000 by 1939 (it published the women's weekly *Marie-Claire* and, from 1937, the illustrated weekly magazine *Match*—the model for *Paris-Match*, f. 1949); also of the right-wing political and literary weeklies *Candide* (1924–44; ed. by Gaxotte), *Gringoire* (1928–44), and *Je suis partout* (1930–44; directed till 1937 by Gaxotte; later it was overtly pro-German and ed. by Robert Brasillach—*v. Resistance* and *cf. Châteaubriant*).

The fall of France in 1940 was followed by the appearance of a host of clandestine papers and news-sheets associated with the *Resistance, some of which circulated widely and became highly influential, e.g. *Combat*. Various pre-war papers also appeared clandestinely, e.g. *L'Humanité* and *Ce soir* (both suppressed in 1939); others moved to the Unoccupied Zone, e.g. *Le *Figaro*, *Paris-Soir*, *La Croix*. Shortly after the Liberation in 1944, all papers which had not ceased publication after June 1940 in the North, or after November 1942 in the South (i.e. when the Germans moved in), were suppressed. There were some notable casualties, e.g. *Le *Temps*, *Le *Journal des Débats*, *Paris-Soir*, *Le Petit Parisien*, *Le Petit Journal*, *Le Journal*, *Le Matin*, *L'Œuvre*, *L'*Action française*. Only six Paris dailies survived the war: *Le Figaro*, *La Croix*, *Le Populaire*, *L'Humanité*, *Ce soir*, *L'Aube*. The gap was filled by Resistance papers (sometimes with changed titles), e.g. *Combat*, *Le Parisien libéré*, *France-Soir*, *Le Franc-Tireur*, *Libération*, and by the foundation in 1944–5 of a host of new papers, e.g. *Le *Monde*, *L'Aurore*, *Paris-Presse*. Some of these took over the presses of suppressed papers and were in varying degrees their successors, e.g. *Le Monde* of *Le Temps*, *France-Soir* of *Paris-Soir*, *L'Aurore* of *L'Œuvre*. This recovery was short-lived, for in France, as elsewhere, the post-war period has been marked by closures (e.g. *L'Aube*, 1951; *Ce soir*, 1953; *Libération*, 1964; *Le Populaire*, 1969; *Combat*, 1974) and mergers (e.g. *Paris-Presse* with *France-Soir*, 1970), especially of journals of opinion. Paris dailies, reduced from over 30 in 1946 to about 10 in 1974 (excluding a few professional papers), now include the morning papers *Le Figaro*, *Le Parisien libéré* (with the largest circulation), *L'Aurore*, *L'Humanité*, and smaller papers such as *La Nation* (a Gaullist daily f. 1962) and *Libération* (f. 1973 by Sartre and unconnected with the defunct *Libération*); and the evening papers *Le Monde*, *France-Soir* (with the largest circulation), and *La Croix*. Current political weeklies include *L'Express* and the more left-wing *Nouvel Observateur*.

Though the number of provincial dailies has fallen from 175 to about 80 since 1946, the surviving papers have gained ground at the expense of the national dailies. They include *Dernières Nouvelles d'Alsace* (Strasbourg), *La Dépêche du Midi* (Toulouse), *La Nouvelle République du Centre-Ouest* (Tours), *La Voix du Nord* (Lille), *Le Dauphiné libéré* (Grenoble), *Le Progrès* (Lyons), *Ouest France* (Rennes), *Paris-Normandie* (Rouen), *Sud-Ouest* (Bordeaux).

Literary, or partly literary, reviews and periodicals founded since 1870 include *La Nouvelle Revue* (1879; v. *Adam, J.*); the reviews listed under *Symbolism, notably *Le* **Mercure de France*; *La* **Revue encyclopédique* (1891); *La* *Revue de Paris (1894); *Les* **Cahiers de la quinzaine* (1900); *L'**Occident (1901); *Vers et Prose (1905); *La* *Phalange (1906); *La* **Nouvelle Revue française* (1909); *Les* *Cahiers du sud (1915); the little reviews associated with the *fantaisiste, *Futurist, and *Cubist poets (v. *Bernard, J.-M.*; *Albert-Birot*; *Reverdy*); those listed under *Dadaism and *Surrealism; *La* **Revue universelle* (1920); *Les* **Nouvelles littéraires* (1922); *Candide, Gringoire*, and *Je suis partout* (listed above); *Esprit* (1932; v. *Mounier*); the reviews born of the *Resistance, notably *Poésie 40* and *Les* **Lettres françaises* (1942); *La* *Table ronde (1944); *Les* *Temps modernes (1945); *Critique (1946); *Les* **Lettres nouvelles* (1953); *La* **Quinzaine littéraire* (1966); *Tel Quel* (1961) and *Poétique* (1969)—v. *Critics and Criticism*, 3. For other reviews of various kinds v. *Barrès*; *Durkheim*; *Jouve*; *Négritude*; *Proust*; *Renouvier*; also *Periodicals and Reviews*.

Pressburg, Treaty of, v. *Coalitions* (3).

Presse, La (1836–1928; 1934–5), one of the first cheap daily papers (v. *Press*, 6), f. by É. de Girardin. It was a paper of democratic sympathies and carried both a *roman-feuilleton and a scientific *feuilleton*. Early contributors included Balzac, Dumas *père*, Gautier, Hugo, G. Sand, Sue. It soon had a large circulation—still among the largest of the day in 1900.

Pretenders, v. *Chambord*; *Orléans* (3); *Bonaparte Family* (8).

Prétextes and **Nouveaux Prétextes,** v. *Gide*.

Prêtre de Némi, Le, v. *Drames philosophiques*.

Prévert, JACQUES (1900–77), a poet who owes his wide popular appeal to a skilful blend of satire (broadly anti-establishment), humour, and sentimentality. His *Tentative de description d'un Dîner de Têtes à Paris-France* (1931), a bitterly satirical story-poem (often deemed his best work), showed the influence of an initial *Surrealist phase (1926–9). He thereafter produced a stream of poems, stories, and writings for the cinema (collaborating with Marcel Carné in the films *Quai des brumes*, *Le Jour se lève*, *Les Enfants du paradis*, etc.). The poems at last collected in *Paroles* (1946) were an instant success and were soon being sung to the airs of Joseph Kosma in Paris music-halls, recited in student cafés, etc. (e.g. *Barbara, Inventaire, Les Feuilles mortes*). His later works include *Spectacle* (1951), *La Pluie et le beau temps* (1955), *Fatras* (1966).

Prévost, ANTOINE-FRANÇOIS, ABBÉ (1697–1763), 'Prévost d'Exiles', novelist. Educated by the *Jesuits with a view to an ecclesiastical career, he twice entered and left the army, then became a *Maurist, taking his vows 'with internal reservations'. His taste for a worldly life unfitted him for the austerity of the Maurist cloister, and he fled from it (1728), relying on a papal brief he had obtained permitting his transfer to *Cluny. But the formalities were incomplete, and, finding himself in a dangerous position, he took refuge in Holland and England till 1734. He was again briefly in exile in 1741 for his part in a scandalous publication. His life was spent in arduous literary work, including novels, translations, and such vast compilations as an *Histoire générale des voyages* (v. also *Dictionaries*, 1750). His fame now rests on his *Histoire du chevalier* *des Grieux et de* *Manon Lescaut* (1731, as vol. VII of his first romance—*Mémoires d'un homme de qualité*, 1728–31). His other novels include *Le Philosophe anglais, ou les Mémoires de Cleveland* (1732–9; often shortened to *Cleveland*), the love story and startling adventures of a supposed natural son of Oliver Cromwell who becomes king of a tribe of South American Indians—a work in some respects anticipating the political philosophy of J.-J. Rousseau; *Le Doyen de Killerine* (1735–40), another romance of adventure, the hero being an Irish ecclesiastic; *Histoire d'une Grecque moderne* (1741); *Mémoires d'un honnête homme* (1745). He did much to acquaint his countrymen with English literature and the English character as he saw it, both through some of his own novels and his translations of those of Richardson (*Paméla*, 1742; *Clarisse Harlowe*, 1751; *Grandisson*, 1755–8) and as founder-editor (1733–40) of *Le Pour et Contre*, a literary periodical similar in form to those of Addison, Steele, and Johnson. *v. Foreign Influences*, 2.

Prévost, JEAN, *v. Resistance.*

Prévost, MARCEL (1862–1940), author of many 'society' novels of a type popular at the end of the 19th c., e.g. *L'Automne d'une femme* (1893), *Les Demi-vierges* (1894), and the series *Lettres à Françoise* (1902–28). He specialized in feminine psychology.

Prévost-Paradol,   LUCIEN-ANATOLE (1829–70), a noted Second Empire journalist. A brilliant student of the *École normale supérieure*, he rejected an academic career, joined the staff of the *Journal des Débats*, then founded the weekly *Courrier du dimanche*, which was suppressed for attacking the government. His attitude softened when government policy became more liberal, and he went to Washington as ambassador (1870), his mission being to assure the United States that Europe was at peace. When this was swiftly belied by the outbreak of the *Franco-Prussian war, he committed suicide. His works include *Essais de politique et de littérature* (1859–63), collected articles (notably *De la liberté des

cultes en France) and book reviews exemplifying his firm moral and political convictions and lucid, ironical style.

Prévôt, under the *ancien régime*, a royal agent exercising judicial, political, financial, and military functions over a small area (*châtellenie*). His powers conflicted with those of the feudal lords and were further restricted by the creation (*c.* 1190) of *baillis* and *sénéchaux*, who were set over him. Even so, the *prévôt de Paris* in particular, seated in the *Châtelet*, long wielded great power as chief magistrate of the city. For the *prévôt des marchands*, *v. Hôtel de Ville*.

Prière sur l'Acropole, La, *v. Souvenirs d'enfance et de jeunesse.*

Prière sur la Tour Eiffel, La, *v. Juliette au pays des hommes.*

Primat, *v. Grandes Chroniques.*

Primitivisme, *v. Literary Isms.*

Prince Impérial, Le, title of Napoléon-Eugène-Louis-Jean-Joseph Bonaparte (1856–79), only son of Napoleon III. He shared his parents' exile in England and was sent to the Royal Military Academy at Woolwich. He was killed while taking part in the British expedition against the Zulus.

Princesse de Babylone, La (1768), by Voltaire, an Oriental tale of a princess who, in company with a wise phoenix, roams the world in pursuit of her lover—giving the author the chance to compare and criticize the customs and beliefs she encounters.

Princesse de Clèves, La (1678), a novel by Mme de La Fayette. An English version appeared in 1688.

The scene is the court of Henri II. Mme de Chartres marries her daughter to the prince de Clèves for worldly reasons. The princess, a woman of the highest character, cannot return her husband's love, but is scrupulously loyal to him. When the duc de Nemours, an Admirable Crichton, falls in love with her, and she with him, she strives from a sense of duty to hide her feelings from him. At last, hoping to be fortified in her virtue, she avows the situation to her husband. Their mutual esteem is increased, but his life is embittered by jealousy and he dies of a broken heart. She retires to a convent and does not long survive him.

Princesse d'Élide, La, a **comédie-ballet* by Molière; produced 1664. It was written for a festival at *Versailles, begun in verse, then completed under pressure of time in prose. *v. Lulli*.

The prince of Elis is holding games in the hope that one of the young princes of Greece will win the heart of his daughter, who professes to disdain all men. Euryale, prince of Ithaca, who loves her, adopts a stratagem: unlike the other suitors, he pretends to be indifferent to her. Much piqued, she tells him that she intends to marry the prince of Messenia, whereupon he tells her that he loves her cousin Aglante. She is now jealous, and her resistance crumbles when she finds him apparently asking her father for Aglante's hand.

Princesse lointaine, La, *v. Rostand, E.*

Princesse Maleine, La, *v. Maeterlinck.*

Prisonnière, La, *v. A la recherche du temps perdu.*

Privilège, *v. Librairie*; *Press*, 1.

Privilégiés, Les. At the outbreak of the Revolution there were two parties—the *Privilégiés* (most of the *noblesse and the higher clergy, possessing the greater share of the wealth of the kingdom and innumerable hereditary rights whereby they both levied and avoided taxation; *cf. Notables*) and the *Non-Privilégiés* or **Tiers État*. *v. États généraux.*

Prix Goncourt, *v. Prix littéraires.*

Prix littéraires. The *Guide des prix littéraires* lists the remarkable number of prizes available for award in France and French-speaking countries. They cover a very wide field, from imaginative literature and criticism, history, philosophy, etc., to aviation, gastronomy, rural economy, and sport. Their money value varies greatly and is often less important than their effect on the winner's reputation and sales. The awards which create most stir are those made annually for works of imaginative literature, usually novels, e.g. the *Prix Goncourt* (*v. Académie Goncourt*), *Prix Femina*, *Prix Théophraste-Renaudot*, *Prix Interallié*, *Prix des critiques*. Other important annual prizes are the *Grand Prix du roman* and *Grand Prix de littérature* awarded by the **Académie française* (this body alone has well over 100 prizes in its gift, inc. the various *Prix Broquette-Gonin* and the *Prix *Montyon*), the *Grand Prix national des lettres* (for outstanding men of letters), and the *Grand Prix de la critique littéraire*. The many other awards include those made by the other *Académies* of the **Institut de France* (for works in their separate fields), by such bodies as the **Société des gens de lettres* (for prose fiction, poetry, criticism, etc.), by a host of provincial literary *Académies* (e.g. the *Académie des *Jeux floraux de Toulouse*), and by various municipalities. *v. also Grand Prix des meilleurs romans du demi-siècle*; *Prix Nobel.*

Prix Nobel. The Nobel Prize for Literature (f. 1901) has been awarded to the following French authors: Sully-Prudhomme (1901), Mistral (1904), Rolland (1915), A. France (1921), Bergson (1927), Martin du Gard (1937), Gide (1947), Mauriac (1952), Camus (1957), Saint-John Perse (1960), Sartre (1964; he refused it). In 1911 it was won by the Belgian writer Maeterlinck, in 1969 by the Irishman Beckett.

Procès de Paradis, *v. Mystère.*

Procope, Café, *v. Café.*

Procurateur de Judée, Le (1892, in *L'Étui de nacre*), one of A. France's finest tales. The aged Pontius Pilate is discussing old times, especially his years in Judaea, with a friend. The friend mentions one 'Jesus the Nazarene', who was crucified for some crime or other. Does Pilate remember? He does not.

Profession de foi du vicaire savoyard, v. *Émile*.

Progrès de l'esprit humain, Tableau historique des, v. *Tableau historique*.

Promenades littéraires, v. *Gourmont*.

Prométhée mal enchaîné, Le, v. *Gide*.

Propos d'Alain, v. *Chartier, É.-A.*

Proscrits, Les, v. *Livre mystique, Le*.

Prose Poem, a form which emerged in the mid-19th c. and reflected a reaction against the restrictions of the traditional rules of *versification (later seen in *vers libérés* and the *vers libre*). The *poème en prose*, which obeys no such rules, was largely developed by Baudelaire (who acknowledged his debt to A. *Bertrand's *Gaspard de la nuit*) and adopted in the 19th c. by Mallarmé, Rimbaud, Lautréamont, and others. It is widely used by 20th-c. writers, e.g. Gide, M. Jacob, Fargue, Saint-John Perse, Reverdy, Éluard, Breton, Ponge, Michaux, Char.

Prose (*pour des Esseintes*) (1885, in the *Revue indépendante*; 1887, in *Poésies*), a poem by Mallarmé, of interest for his aesthetic theories. The dedication acknowledged Huysmans's praise of him in *À rebours*.

Protesilaus, v. *Huon de Rotelande*.

Proudhon, PIERRE-JOSEPH (1809–65), publicist and social reformer. Of humble origin and partly self-educated, he worked for a firm of printers in his native Besançon, then won a scholarship to Paris (1839) and took up economics. His first work of note, *Qu'est-ce que la propriété?* (1840), began with the famous paradox 'La propriété, c'est le vol', and went on to

maintain that the theory of property was a denial of the principles of justice, liberty, and equality, since it enabled some men to exploit the labour of others; property was justifiable only when it resulted from work and was shared by all in a society where the rights of the individual were safeguarded.

After managing his own printing firm in Besançon, he worked in business in Lyons, then settled in Paris (1847), hoping to live by his pen. He was now a well-known writer on social questions (e.g. *Avertissement aux propriétaires*, 1842, again on property; *Système des contradictions économiques, ou Philosophie de la misère*, 1846, attacking Utopian reformers—v. *Marx*). After the 1848 *Revolution, when he was elected to the *Assemblée constituante* and founded a newspaper (v. *Press*, 7), his journalistic violence landed him in prison (1849–52). He then retired into private life, but a further work of 1858—*La Justice dans la Révolution et dans l'Église*—attacked Church, State, and other institutions so fiercely that it was confiscated and he had to flee to Brussels to escape arrest. Hardship undermined his health and he died three years after his return (1862) to Paris.

His works—including also *Confessions d'un révolutionnaire* (1849), *La Théorie de l'impôt* (1861), *La Guerre et la paix* (1862; studies of might and right)—were hard-hitting and dialectical, full of diatribe and paradox, with none of the Utopianism or mysticism of the *Saint-Simoniens* and *Fouriéristes*. They considerably influenced later Socialist thinkers.

Proust, MARCEL (1871–1922), novelist, famous as the author of *À la recherche du temps perdu* (1913–27), was born, and died, in Paris. He seldom left it except for holidays (as a child, with relations at Illiers, near Chartres; in later life, on the coast of Normandy; *cf.* *Combray*; *Balbec*) or short literary and artistic pilgrimages. His father, Adrien Proust (d. 1903), was a professor of medicine; his mother (d. 1905), whom he adored, was of Jewish descent.

Educated at the *Lycée Condorcet*, he did his military service at Orleans (1889–90), then studied law and political science (1891–3). Severe asthma, from which he had suffered since childhood, precluded any regular profession. He was also from his early years neurotic—a condition probably aggravated by his efforts to conceal his homosexual tendencies (the subject of perversion was to be treated at great length in his novel). In any case, his ambition was to write. He contributed to literary reviews and was part-founder of the review *Le *Banquet*. *Les Plaisirs et les jours* (1896), a little collection of his short stories, sketches, and poems (with illustrations by the fashionable painter Madeleine Lemaire, musical settings by his intimate friend and correspondent Reynaldo Hahn, and an amiable preface by A. France) was indulgently received; some of the stories are interesting anticipations of his novel. Other early writings (many first publ. in *Le *Figaro*; *cf. Salon*, 1), collected in *Pastiches et mélanges* (1919), show his talent for *pastiche*. For some years, when his health allowed, he seems to have devoted most of his ingenuity to satisfying his ambition to move in aristocratic circles. His charm, wit, and wealth all helped him to secure introductions. This snobbish phase was to yield immense profit, for the social world to which he gained the *entrée* became the setting of his great work. As time went on his health deteriorated and he stayed more at home, entertaining, sometimes writing for periodicals, and translating Ruskin (*La Bible d'Amiens*, 1904; *Sésame et les lys*, 1906), whose artistic ideas influenced his own. (Another influence, noticeable in his approach to the theme of time in his novel, was that of Bergson.) After his mother's death he lapsed into invalidism and led the life of a recluse. He wrote constantly to his friends, but if they were summoned to visit him, or if he ventured out, it was usually at night; very occasionally, when he was well enough, he visited the country or the sea. He spent most of his time in bed; the windows of his room were tightly shut, the air thick with inhalants, the walls cork-lined to exclude noise. He wrote

feverishly, for he now had the idea for his novel and feared that he might not live to finish it.

His writing was something of a mystery to his friends, but from papers found after his death it seems that he first wrote substantial fragments of a novel—*Jean Santeuil* (1952, 3 vols.)—which was the germ, at times even a first draft, of *A la recherche du temps perdu*. (Other fragments, similarly retrieved, and bearing the same relation to the later work, appeared in 1954, together with *Contre Sainte-Beuve*, an enlightening study of the critical practice of Sainte-Beuve and of his own, opposed, theories of intuitive criticism.) From 1910 he was definitely at work on *A la recherche du temps perdu* itself. He finished it in its first form in 1912 (for details of publication *v. A la recherche du temps perdu*). The first volume, *Du côté de chez Swann* (1913), made little stir at the time, but gradually it attracted readers both in France and abroad. The award of the *Prix Goncourt* (1920) for *A l'ombre des jeunes filles en fleurs* enhanced his reputation, and by the time he died it was clear that the writer whom few had at first taken seriously was one of the great novelists of the 20th c. *v. Novel*, 3.

Provençal Literature, *v. Troubadours*; *Lyric Poetry*, 1; *Félibrige*.

Proverbe (dramatique), a short dramatic sketch written to illustrate, or 'point', a proverb. The *genre* originated in the 17th-c. *salons, where private theatricals were very popular, and had been preceded by the *jeu des proverbes*, a kind of parlour-game (fashionable under Louis XIII) which involved conversing in proverbs. The early *proverbes* resembled charades, in that the audience had to guess the proverb; sometimes scenes and dialogues were only roughly indicated, amplification being left to the actors. Later, the proverb was disclosed at once as the title, and repeated as the last line, of what was, in effect, a short, usually one-act, comedy.

A small collection of *proverbes* by a Mme Durand was printed at the end of the 17th c., and about this time Mme de Maintenon was writing *proverbes* (publ. 1829) for performance by the young ladies of *Saint-Cyr*. But the great vogue for this type of entertainment began in the middle of the 18th c. and lasted until the Revolution destroyed the society in which it flourished. Collé wrote *proverbes* for the private theatre of the duc d'Orléans. Carmontelle, in all but date very much the creator of the *genre*, published his amusing *Proverbes dramatiques* (1768–87), also written for the duc d'Orléans. He had several imitators, and his work was later to inspire Musset. Edifying *proverbes* were written for the young, e.g. by Mme de Genlis (whose *Mémoires* contain many references to performances in *salons*) and Alexandre-Guillaume Mouslier de Moissy (1712–77), an inveterate gambler whose *Les Jeux de la petite Thalie* (1769) were designed to 'former les mœurs' of young persons. Just before the Revolution, *proverbes* were occasionally performed in public theatres.

After the Restoration, they were again read or performed in the *salons*. The most popular were *Leclercq's *Proverbes dramatiques* (1820–30). Other authors included Antoine-Marie, baron Rœderer (1782–1865; son of P.-L. Rœderer), with *Comédies, proverbes, et parades* (1824–5); Latouche (e.g. *On fait ce qu'on peut et non pas ce qu'on veut*); and, later, Feuillet (*Scènes et proverbes*, 1851) and Gozlan. By this time, however, Musset, the master of the *genre*, had transformed the *proverbe* from a passing entertainment into a high form of art, the purest, most delicate comedy (*v. Comédies et Proverbes*).

Proverbes au vilain; **Proverbes au comte de Bretagne**, medieval collections of homely proverbs, e.g. 'Ne sont pas tous chevaliers qui en cheval montent'. Some shed light on the life of the period.

Proverbes français, Le Livre des, *v. Le Roux de Lincy*.

Provinces. Though the word *province* did not pass into the language of

administration until about the 14th c. and never seems to have had any very precise or consistent administrative significance, the entities known as the *anciennes provinces* (*v.* Map) are tied up historically and ethnically with the evolution of the French as a nation. For many official purposes the Frenchman is a man of his *département*; but as an individual he is more likely to regard himself as a man of his *province*, with customs, tastes, idiosyncrasies of language and physique, and territorial loyalties that differentiate him from natives of other *provinces*.

The *provinces*, usually much larger areas than the *départements*, were the administrative subdivisions of pre-Revolutionary France. They go back ultimately to the tribal territories of Ancient Gaul, but more directly to the *duchés* and *comtés* of *Merovingian, and especially *Carolingian, times (*v.* Duc, comte, marquis*; *Noblesse*). At the height of the feudal period, many *duchés* and *comtés* were in fact separate domains which, with the offices attached to them, had been appropriated as their hereditary right by the great military and land-owning warriors. They had their own customary laws, their own administrative—and often also monetary—systems, their own dialects or even languages.

Originally, the kingdom of France was merely one such feudal domain. Hugues Capet, the first *Capetian king, ruled his own domain directly (it then roughly corresponded to what was later known as the *Île-de-France), but was accepted by the other great warriors as their suzerain lord. The subsequent progressive consolidation of the monarchy was accompanied by what is known as the *progrès du domaine royal*, a process of conquest and annexation, or acquisition by death, marriage, purchase, or barter, by which the vassal states and some frontier territories were absorbed into the crown property and from which the *provinces* more immediately derive.

The bringing of these territories within the fiscal, judicial, and other systems of the realm often involved haphazard improvisation, resulting in division into purely artificial areas (v. *Fiscal System*; *Parlement*). For military purposes, however, division by the 16th c. was into *gouvernements généraux*, and these were the areas that most nearly preserved the outline of the territories absorbed. Each had its *gouverneur*. At first his duties were purely military, but in time he became the direct representative of the king, the *gouverneur et lieutenant général du Roi* and of the *états de la province*. An early 18th-c. geographical primer used in the *Collège Louis-le-Grand* poses the question 'Comment divisez-vous la France?', requiring the answer 'En trente provinces, qui sont autant de gouvernements'.

By the beginning of the 17th c., when the monarchy was firmly consolidated, there were 12 *grands gouvernements* or *provinces*: Auvergne, Bourgogne, Bretagne, Champagne, Dauphiné (v. *Dauphin*), Guyenne (which had included the *duché* of Gascogne since 1052), Île-de-France, Languedoc, Lyonnais, Normandie, Picardie, Provence. Between then and 1789 new *provinces* were annexed or ceded to the *domaine royal* (e.g. Alsace, Artois, Franche-Comté, Flandre, Lorraine, Corsica), old ones were split up (some into such small units that their names are barely remembered), and the number of *gouvernements* nearly trebled. In the 18th c., with the increase in the number and powers of the *intendants*, the functions of the *gouverneurs* often became largely decorative. By 1789 there were over 30 areas called *intendances*, and these, too, were often termed *provinces*.

The *esprit de province*, however, had resisted partitioning and dismemberment. Indeed, it became all the stronger after 1750 as the monarchy weakened its own authority by a series of capitulations to the growing pretensions of the *parlements* and of the provincial *états* (v. *Fiscal System*), privileged bodies which claimed to represent local custom and law. The Revolutionaries of 1789, convinced that provincial privilege and particularism had helped to ruin France, were suspicious of the *provinces* and the *esprit de province*, identifying both with sectional and vested interests. In their view, the *esprit de province* would, if allowed to persist, militate against national unity and was thus an added reason for radically reorganizing the administrative and territorial bases of government. The first step was taken by a law of 1789 establishing the principle of the creation of *départements*. The drawing of their boundaries occasioned much dispute, but in the end the dividing-lines between the old *provinces* were in general respected.

Provinciales, Lettres, v. *Pascal*.

Prudhomme, M. Joseph, the type of the prosperous *bourgeois* under the July Monarchy, able by his large stomach and loud voice to impose himself and his platitudes on any assembly. He was created by the caricaturist Henri Monnier (1799–1877), who spent 20 years developing him from his first, lightly sketched appearance in *Scènes dessinées à la plume* (1830). When the type was dying out, Monnier made a play of him (*Grandeur et décadence de M. Joseph Prudhomme*, 1852) and recorded his life and sayings (*Mémoires de M. Joseph Prudhomme*, 1857).

Prunier, Joseph, v. *Maupassant*.

Prytanée. Under the *Directoire* and the *Consulat*, the *Collège Louis-le-Grand* (earlier the *Collège de Clermont*, later the *Lycée Louis-le-Grand*) became the *Prytanée* (so called after the Prytaneum of ancient Greece). Lectures were given and it became a form of boarding-school, intended as the nucleus of a reorganized educational system, on lines proposed by Lucien Bonaparte. To some extent it was the germ of the Napoleonic *lycées*.

Prytanée militaire de La Flèche, a State military school (primarily for officers' sons) at La Flèche, near Le Mans; f. 1760 as a preparatory school for the *École militaire*. It replaced a famous college f. 1603 by Henri IV and given by him to the *Jesuits* (Descartes was a pupil, 1604–12).

Psalms, The, v. Religious Writings, 2.

Psalters, v. Bible, French versions of.

Psichari, ERNEST (1883–1914), grandson of Renan, a professional soldier who wrote militaristic, semi-mystical novels (he was a Roman Catholic convert), e.g. L'Appel des armes (1913; two members of a military expedition in the Sahara discover how far the glories of a soldier's life outweigh its trials) and Le Voyage du centurion (1915; the study of a religious conversion—the setting is again military life in Africa). He died on active service.

Psyché, (1) a *comédie-ballet in *vers libres by Molière (who wrote the prologue, Act I, and the first scene of Act II and of Act III, and planned the whole), Corneille (who wrote most of Acts II–V, contributing some very fine verse), and Quinault; produced 1671. The story is an adaptation of the fable of Cupid and Psyche from the Golden Ass of Apuleius— a theme recently treated in *La Fontaine's Les Amours de Psyché et de Cupidon; (2) v. Laprade.

Psychocritique, v. Critics and Criticism, 3; Mauron, C.

Psychologie de l'art, v. Malraux.

Publiciste parisien, Le; Publiciste de la République française, Le, v. Ami du peuple.

Puce de Mme Des Roches, La, v. Des Roches.

Pucelle, La (i.e. Jeanne d'Arc), (1) v. Chapelain; (2) a mock-heroic poem (1755) by Voltaire, an unseemly burlesque, containing a good deal of licentious matter.

Puget, PIERRE (1622–94), sculptor and painter of the period of Louis XIV.

Pulchérie, v. Corneille.

Pure, MICHEL, ABBÉ DE (1634–80), author of works including Ostorius (1659), a tragedy, and La Prétieuse, ou le Mystère des ruelles (1656–8), a novel in which, in the course of conversations on the subject of marriage, the different types of *précieuse are defined. He is remembered for the ridicule he suffered in Boileau's *Satires, on account of a libel Boileau believed he had circulated—though he appears to have been a quiet, harmless man.

Purgon, in Molière's Le *Malade imaginaire.

Putain respectueuse, La, v. Sartre.

Puvis de Chavannes, PIERRE (1824–98), painter, a master of decorative art, responsible for murals in the *Sorbonne, the *Panthéon, and other public buildings in France. His idealistic, poetical work was much admired by the *Symbolists.

Puy or Pui, a medieval fraternity of *jongleurs and ordinary burghers at *Arras and other towns of N. and W. France, which held contests at which lyric poets competed. The name may come from Le Puy-en-Velay, where such contests, at first in honour of the Virgin, are said to have originated, apparently in the 12th c. Most of the poems submitted were of a religious nature. The *Miracles de Notre-Dame par personnages were probably written for a puy in Paris. The puy of Rouen, f. in the latter part of the 15th c. in honour of the Immaculate Conception and devoted to poems on that subject, was known as the Puy des Palinods. There were other such puys at Caen and Dieppe.

Pyat, FÉLIX (1810–99), a revolutionary and an idealistic social reformer (in the wake of the *Fouriéristes), active—and in and out of prison—between 1830 and 1848. His plays championing the rights of the people (e.g. Une Révolution d'autrefois, 1832; Le Chiffonnier de Paris, 1847) were quite successful in their day. He lived in exile in England during the Second Empire.

Pyrenees, Treaty of the (1659), a treaty

between France (whose plenipotentiary was Mazarin) and Spain. France restored many of her conquests to Spain, but acquired Roussillon and Cerdagne on the Spanish border and territory in Artois and

Flanders (*cf. Collège des Quatre-Nations*). The marriage of Louis XIV and the Infanta Maria Theresa was also arranged.

Pyrrhus, in Racine's **Andromaque*.

Q

Qaïn, v. Leconte de Lisle.

Quadrilogue invectif, v. Chartier, A.

Quai des Orfèvres, *v. Police*.

Quai d'Orsay, the *Ministère des Affaires étrangères* or Foreign Office, so called because it is on the part of the Seine embankment (left bank) known as the Quai d'Orsay.

Quarante, Les, *v. Académie française*.

Quarante-cinq, Les, v. Dumas père.

Quartier latin, earlier also called the *Pays latin*, the university quarter of Paris, on the left bank of the Seine. It extends roughly from the Seine up to the Montagne-Sainte-Geneviève and from the Rue du Bac on the west to the Rue Cardinal-Lemoine on the east.

Quasimodo, in Hugo's **Notre-Dame de Paris*.

Quatre Âges de l'homme, v. Philippe de Novare.

Quatre Évangiles, Les, v. Zola.

Quatremère de Quincy, ANTOINE-CHRYSOSTOME, *v. Dictionaries*, 1788–1825.

Quatre offices de l'Ostel du Roy, Dit des, v. Deschamps, Eustache.

Quatre Vents de l'esprit, Les, v. Hugo.

Quatre-vingt-treize (1873), by Hugo, a novel about the Royalist risings in Brittany

(*v. Chouannerie, La*; *Quiberon*) and the **Vendée during the Revolution. The Royalists—*les blancs*, led by the marquis de Lantenac—wage a savage guerrilla war against the Republican forces—*les bleus*—led by Gauvain, the marquis's nephew. On the marquis's orders, his men capture and use as hostages three refugee children adopted by the Republicans. The Royalists are gradually defeated, and the marquis and a few of his men take refuge in his ancestral castle. They escape by a secret passage, leaving the children in an inaccessible wing, to which they have set fire. The *bleus* try in vain to reach the children. Suddenly the marquis, who has the only key to the burning wing, returns, rescues the children, and gives himself up. Gauvain, deeply moved by his uncle's bravery, helps him to escape from the condemned cell and takes his place. When this is discovered, Gauvain is tried by a special court of three men, including one of the chief characters in the book, Cimourdan. The one sign of humanity in this fanatical Revolutionary, an ex-priest, has been his devotion to Gauvain, his former pupil. Now, torn between his principles and his affections, he gives the casting vote that sends Gauvain to the guillotine, then shoots himself.

Notable passages include the descriptions of the forests of Brittany and the Vendée, with their underground tunnels and refuges known only to the natives; also, when the scene shifts to Paris, the conversation between Danton, Robespierre, and Marat, followed by a meeting of the **Convention*.

Queneau, RAYMOND (1903–76), a poet and novelist of wide culture (editor of the

Encyclopédie de la Pléiade) whose work stems from a serious interest in language and style. He began as a *Surrealist (1924–9) and later made his name with works in which he exposed, with ironic, and often malicious, humour, the fatuity of various received ideas about language, literature, and the nature of inspiration, introducing popular speech into poetry, parodying sacrosanct forms, and ignoring the distinctions between *genres*, e.g. the anti-poems of *Les Ziaux* (1943); *Exercices de style* (1947), the same story told in 99 different styles by a master of *pastiche*; *Cent Mille Milliards de poèmes* (1961), 10 sonnets, with interchangeable lines. A similar spirit informs his other verse (e.g. *Chêne et chien*, 1937, an autobiography; *Petite Cosmogonie portative*, 1950, a history of the world in *alexandrines; the collections *Si tu t'imagines*, 1951, *Fendre les flots*, 1969, etc.) and his novels (or anti-novels), e.g. *Le Chiendent* (1933), embodying reflections on Cartesianism; *Les Enfants du limon* (1938); and the more burlesque and fantastic *Saint Glinglin* (1948) and *Zazie dans le Métro* (1959). He has also written for the cinema. *v. Novel*, 3.

Quérard, JOSEPH-MARIE (1797–1865), bibliographer, compiled, notably, *La France littéraire, ou Dictionnaire bibliographique des savants, historiens et gens de lettres de la France, ainsi que des littérateurs étrangers qui ont écrit en français, plus particulièrement pendant les XVIIIe et XIXe siècles* (1827–39, 10 vols.; suppl. 1854–64, 2 vols.), a work continued by *La Littérature française contemporaine* (1827–49, 6 vols.) of Louandre, Bourquelot, and Maury; also *Les Supercheries littéraires dévoilées* (1845–56, 5 vols.), a dictionary of apocryphal and pseudonymous writers.

Querelle des anciens et des modernes, a dispute—at its height in the last decades of the 17th c.—between the advocates of imitation of the literature of classical antiquity (*v. Classicism*) and the champions of progress, new ideas, and self-sufficiency. Desmarets de Saint-Sorlin was one of the first supporters of the *modernes*, defending in a series of writings the choice of a Christian national hero in his epic *Clovis*. His doctrine was roundly condemned by Boileau in the *Art poétique*. Some years later, Charles Perrault and his brothers, supported by Fontenelle, entered the lists on the side of the *modernes*. Stung by Perrault's contention that the age of Louis XIV compared favourably with that of Augustus and that modern writers represented the maturity of the human intellect, Boileau returned to the attack (first in the *Académie, then in print), supported by La Bruyère and La Fontaine (in his *Épître à Huet*). The dispute died down, and in his *Lettre à M. Perrault* (1700) Boileau recognized, within certain limits, the equality in literary merit of the 17th c. to any period of antiquity. Besides the above writers, *v. Dubos; Dacier; Houdar de la Motte; Longepierre; Marivaux.*

Que sais-je? (1941–), a vast encyclopedic series of informative works (a pocket-size volume to a subject) for the general reader. Many leading scholars have contributed to this *collection*.

Quesnay, FRANÇOIS, *v. Économistes.*

Quesnel, PASQUIER, *v. Port-Royal.*

Quesnes de Béthune, *v. Conon de Béthune.*

Quiberon, a small peninsula on the southwest coast of Brittany, the scene in July 1795 of a disastrous Royalist rising. A party of *émigrés*, escorted by a British squadron, landed and was joined by rebels from the *Vendée led by Cadoudal. Republican forces commanded by Hoche (who had orders to take no prisoners) drove them back to the sea. The efforts of the British to cover the re-embarkment were futile, and over 1,200 Royalists perished.

Quicherat, (1) JULES-ÉTIENNE-JOSEPH (1814–82), a leading 19th-c. archaeologist, also an historian; author of *Procès de* *condamnation et de réhabilitation de Jeanne d'Arc* (1841–9); *Histoire de Sainte-Barbe* (1860–4), a history of the *Collège Sainte-Barbe, of interest for its details of life in the medieval colleges; *Mélanges d'archéologie et d'histoire* (1885–6); (2) his brother LOUIS-MARIE (1797–1884), philologist (*Mélanges de philologie*, 1879), compiled Latin-French and French-Latin dictionaries, wrote on Latin and French versification and on music.

Quietism, a form of religious mysticism consisting in passive devotional contemplation, with total extinction of the will and complete abandonment to the Divine Presence, originated by the Spanish priest Miguel de Molinos (*c.* 1640–97). It was promoted in France by Mme Guyon (Jeanne-Marie Bouvier de La Motte-Guyon, 1648–1717), who, in company with her spiritual director Lacombe, a Barnabite friar, began (1681) a five-year journey through the country propagating her beliefs. The two were arrested (1687) on suspicion of heresy and immorality, but Mme Guyon was freed by the efforts of Mme de Maintenon. She now became prominent in the royal circle and often lectured at the *Institut de* *Saint-Cyr. She strongly influenced *Fénelon and was soon to involve him in an acute controversy with *Bossuet, to whom any relaxation of the will and personal energy in the pursuit of virtue was repugnant. Meanwhile, Molinos had been arrested (1685) by the Inquisition. He was imprisoned for life and his doctrines condemned (1687). Mme Guyon, now under increasing attack, demanded a theological commission to clear her. The resulting Conference of Issy (1695) condemned her and she was imprisoned (1695–1702), being released on her submission. *v. La Bruyère.*

Quinault, JEANNE-FRANÇOISE (*c.* 1700–83), a gifted actress, remarkable also for her literary taste and judgement. Her house was a meeting-place for writers and *philosophes (e.g. d'Alembert and Diderot). Voltaire addressed several letters to her.

Quinault, PHILIPPE (1635–88), son of a Paris baker and educated by Tristan l'Hermite; a dramatist who, with T. Corneille, filled the interval between the zenith of P. Corneille and the rise of Racine. His tragedies, in which the element of love predominates, include *Astrate, roi de Tyr (1664), the most successful (it was ridiculed by Boileau); *La Mort de Cyrus* (1656); *Amalasonte* (1657). His comedies, which show greater talent, include the very successful *La* *Mère coquette (1665), also *L'Amant indiscret* (1654; Dryden drew on this in his adaptation of Molière's *L'**Étourdi). After 1670 he devoted himself to opera, and wrote libretti for the composer Lulli. Their principal operas were *Cadmus et Hermione* (1673), *Alceste* (1674), *Thésée* (1675), *Atys* (1676), *Persée* (1682), *Phaéton* (1683), *Amadis de Gaule (1684), *Roland* (1685), *Armide (1686). *v.* also *Psyché.*

Quincampoix, Rue, *v. Law.*

Quinet, EDGAR (1803–75), primarily an historian interested in the philosophy of history. After a period as professor of foreign literature at Lyons, he moved (1842) to a chair at the *Collège de France. Here his views on politics and education (he was active in the cause of educational freedom) led to the suppression of his lectures (*cf.* his friend Michelet, with whom he wrote *Les Jésuites,* an attack on *Ultramontanism). He was elected to the *Assemblée nationale in 1848 and again after 1870 (having spent the years after the *coup d'état* of 1851 in exile in Belgium and Switzerland). He was an idealistic patriot, and fundamentally religious for all his anti-clericalism. His *Histoire de mes idées* (1855) is an interesting account of his early years.

His many works on history, philosophy, and religion include *Idées sur la philosophie de l'histoire de l'humanité* (1827), a translation, with a prefatory essay, of Herder's *Philosophie der Geschichte* (*v. Foreign Influences,* 4); *L'Allemagne et la révolution* (1831), a prophetic study of the Prussian threat to France; *Les Révolutions d'Italie* (1848–52); *Histoire de la*

Révolution (1865); also *Le Génie des religions* (1842), one of a contemplated series of works which would have formed a universal history of religious and social revolutions. He also wrote several poetical works, semi-philosophical, obscurely symbolical and allegorical, and often heavy, but showing a powerful imagination. Some of them may have influenced Rimbaud. They include *Ahasuérus* (1833), a dramatic epic in dialogued prose, in which the Wandering Jew incarnates man's journey through the ages; also *Napoléon* (1836; verse), *Prométhée* (1838; verse), *Les Esclaves* (1853; a verse drama, with Spartacus for hero), *Merlin l'enchanteur* (1860, 2 vols.; a long allegorical work in poetic prose). *v. Epic Poetry.*

Quinquina, Le, v. La Fontaine.

Quinzaine littéraire, La (1966–), a literary review in newspaper format, edited by the literary critic Maurice Nadeau (1911–).

Quinze Joyes de mariage, Les, a prose satire on marriage, formerly attributed to La Sale, but probably the work of an early 15th-c. ecclesiastic. It was translated into English as *The Fifteen Comforts of Matrimony* (1682).

A husband is likened to a fish which, seeing other fishes in a net, is not satisfied till it gets inside, never to escape. The husband here depicted is a poor creature, weak, credulous, and stupid. His tribulations, dealt with under 15 heads, are attributed to the failings of his wife—her frivolity, avarice, infidelity, love of fine clothes, habit of bullying while posing as a martyr, etc. There are notably lively and realistic scenes from everyday life, e.g. the incidents of a pilgrimage, the wife's cajoleries, her scheming with her gossips, and the plot in which they—and even the confessor—join to convince the husband that his eyes misled him when he found his wife with her lover.

Quinze-Vingts, Hospice des, now a national hospital for the blind, was founded *c.* 1260 by Louis IX, allegedly for 300 crusaders released by the Saracens after their eyes had been put out. In the Middle Ages it was a hospice for blind paupers and beggars, who made it a flourishing self-governing community.

Quotidienne, La (1792–7; 1814–47), an outspokenly anti-Revolutionary daily paper, which existed precariously till 1797. Revived in 1814, it was Royalist and **Légitimiste* during the Restoration and July Monarchy, widely read in clerical and ex-*émigré* circles all over France. La Harpe and Fontanes were early contributors.

R

Rabbe, ALPHONSE (1786–1830), a publicist and hack historian who moved in *Romantic circles and left a remarkable *Album d'un pessimiste* (1835), containing essays and meditations (with such titles as *Philosophie du désespoir*; *Horreur*; *L'Enfer d'un maudit*) written under the stress of a painfully disfiguring infection contracted in youth.

Rabelais, FRANÇOIS (*c.* 1494–*c.* 1553), physician, humanist, and satirist, b. near Chinon (Touraine), where his father was a lawyer, probably at La Devinière, a small farm (now State-owned) belonging to the family. By 1520 he was a member of the Franciscan convent of Fontenay-le-Comte (Poitou). He remained there till 1524, and was ordained priest. During these years, fired by the spirit of the early *Renaissance, he studied Greek (encouraged by Budé), won a reputation for learning among his friends (e.g. Tiraqueau), but was persecuted by his monastic superiors. In 1524, thanks to the protection of the enlightened Geoffroy d'Estissac, bishop of Maillezais, he obtained leave to transfer to the Benedictine abbey there. He became the bishop's secretary, travelling with him around his estates in Poitou and meeting men of learning. He left Poitou *c.* 1528 and probably spent the next two years visiting provincial universities and perhaps studying medicine in Paris. He now abandoned the cowl and went to Montpellier, where he obtained the degree of bachelor of medicine (Dec. 1530) and lectured on Hippocrates and Galen (1531). In 1532 he settled at Lyons (then a centre of great literary activity), published editions of medical works (e.g. Hippocrates's *Aphorisms*), and was appointed (Nov. 1532) physician to the municipal hospital. *Pantagruel, the first of the five books of his famous work, written as 'Alcofribas Nasier' (a pseudonym he often used—an anagram of his own name), appeared in 1532 or 1533 (for other dates of publication and summaries of the story *v. Pantagruel; Gargantua*). He wrote it, he tells us, in moments of relaxation for the solace of the sick. He thrice visited Rome (1534; 1535–6, when he obtained absolution from the pope for his breaches of ecclesiastical discipline; 1548–50) as physician to his friend and patron Cardinal Jean du Bellay; in 1540–1 he was in Turin, in the suite of the cardinal's brother, Guillaume du Bellay, governor of Piedmont. He lost his post in Lyons for being absent without leave. In 1550 he obtained the livings of Meudon, near Paris, and Jambet, near Le Mans, but he does not appear to have discharged the duties of either personally. He wrote no other important original work, his *Prognostication Pantagrueline* (1533, as 'Maître Alcofribas') being merely a facetious parody of popular almanacs foretelling events of the coming year. He was much esteemed by contemporaries as a physician, a pioneer of humanism, and author of an entertaining book.

The five books of his great work, written at intervals over 20 years, do not form a single artistic whole, for, though loosely held together by a thread of narrative, they vary greatly in character and quality and abound in digressions. The *Cinquième Livre* (publ. posth.) is of doubtful authenticity. It certainly contains work by other hands and was possibly worked up from fragments or rejected drafts left by Rabelais; towards the end, in particular, it consists largely of translations and imitations. The interest of the whole lies in the vivid picture it provides both of the society of the day and of the Protean author himself. He portrays all conditions of men: rustics and artisans at work and play, merchants, monks, and country gentlemen; above all, doctors, lawyers, and academics (both professors and students) and their professional solemnities, pomposities, diversions, squabbles, and jargon. In so doing, he reveals his own enthusiastic humanism, his love of life in all its forms, his thirst for knowledge of every kind (Pantagruel's voyage through the North-West Passage to Cathay reflects his interest in recent voyages of discovery to North America), his hatred of asceticism, above all his contempt for monkery and scholasticism. His enlightened views on education can be seen in the systems he drew up for Pantagruel and Gargantua. His Abbaye de Thélème (*v. Gargantua*) is inspired by faith in the essential rightness of human instincts. His precise attitude to religion is difficult to determine. Though certainly a supporter of early *Évangélisme, he was repelled by the rigidity of Calvin, and his works suggest that he had little use for religious dogmas. He is above all a realist, continuing and developing Jean de Meung's cult of uncorrupted nature. He is often censured for his lapses into gross indecency and his physiological and medical obscenities. These may be explained partly as the work of an irrepressible jester writing for a coarse, outspoken society, partly as that of a realist—or, indeed, a humanist—presenting life in the round, in the belief that no aspect of it should be despised or concealed.

His style is remarkably vivid and racy, the wealth of his vocabulary amazing. He draws words from the French dialects, Latin, and Greek, and often coins his own terms. His handling of dialogue is particularly successful. He makes lavish use of quotations from the classics, adroitly weaving them into his text.

His work incensed the theologians and was condemned by the *parlement. He issued a revised edition (1542) of the first two books, attenuating his insulting references to the theologians, but it failed to placate the *Sorbonne and both books were again condemned in 1543. The Quart Livre was condemned in 1552, his friend Tiraqueau being among the judges. But Rabelais had had the ear of François Ier (d. 1547) and the enlightened classes, and his open hostility to Rome in the Quart Livre reflected the attitude of the court at that time. He has been variously judged by later ages: Molière drew on him, Voltaire and Balzac imitated him; but many have censured his obscenity. His work was soon known in England (e.g. to Gabriel Harvey, John Donne, Francis Bacon) and influenced various later writers (e.g. Sterne). The first three books were translated by Sir Thomas Urquhart (1653, bks. I and II; 1693, bk. III), the last two by Peter Anthony Motteux (1693–4).

Rabemananjara, JACQUES, v. Négritude.

Rabouilleuse, La (1841–2; later in La *Comédie humaine, Scènes de la vie de province), a novel by Balzac.

The Bridau brothers are contrasting characters. Joseph, a painter of genius, sacrifices himself to care for his mother. Philippe, the elder and his mother's favourite, has become a debauched cad and profligate since his army career was cut short by the fall of Napoleon. Thanks to his excesses and crimes, affairs reach such a pass that Mme Bridau and Joseph go from Paris to the provincial town of Issoudun in the hope of raising money from her rich brother, M. Rouget, whom she has not seen since girlhood. They fail, for the old man is in the toils of his housekeeper and mistress Flore Brazier ('la Rabouilleuse'—a dialect word for the person who, in fresh-water crayfishing, troubles the water, causing the fish to rise

into the nets; Flore had acted as rabouilleuse for her uncle in childhood). She and her lover Max Gilet (who is installed in the house and, like Philippe, is a former army officer turned gangster) plot to get hold of Rouget's fortune, but are beaten at their own game of criminal intrigue by the arrival of Philippe, who provokes a duel, kills Max, and gets Rouget and Flore into his power. Now nothing but a heartless, calculating monster, he persuades Rouget to marry Flore and make over his money to her, then causes Rouget's death by indirect methods and marries Flore himself, thus securing the money. He throws in his lot with the Royalists, regains a high position in the army, and aspires to a title and—if he can get rid of Flore—a rich marriage. His dying mother begs him to help Joseph, whom he had earlier robbed, and his cold, insulting refusal finally opens her eyes to his hateful character. Meanwhile Flore, as he had planned, is dying of drink and vice. But from now on his plans miscarry, his wickedness is recognized or suspected, he speculates and loses heavily during the 1830 *Revolution, has to return to active service, and is killed. Joseph inherits what money he leaves.

Notable passages in this powerful novel are the descriptions of the enforced deterioration in the Bridau way of life, of the parsimonious household of M. and Mme Hochon (Mme Bridau's godmother) at Issoudun, and of the malicious, gossiping inhabitants of that town.

Racan, HONORAT DE BUEIL, SEIGNEUR DE (1589–1670), poet, was page to Henri IV, later served in the army, but chose to retire to his estates in Touraine at the age of 39. He was a disciple of Malherbe (whose life he wrote) and, within rather narrow limits, a true poet, inspired by love of the countryside. He wrote several good lyrics, notably Stances sur la retraite (c. 1618; on the theme of Horace's Beatus ille qui procul negotiis); also Bergeries (1625; previously produced as Arthénice, 1619), a kind of *pastoral comedy, containing graceful and harmonious verse, but weak on the dramatic side. Latterly, he paraphrased the Psalms in a wide variety of metres.

Rachel or **Mademoiselle Rachel**, *stage-name of* ÉLISABETH FÉLIX (1820–58), a famous tragic actress of Jewish descent, b. in Switzerland. Originally a street-singer, she had her first triumph as Camille (1838) in Corneille's **Horace*. She acted in Corneille and Racine, and was also very successful in the name-part of **Adrienne Lecouvreur*. Sainte-Beuve notes the revival of the **Comédie-Française* under her influence. She visited England in 1841.

Rachilde, *pseudonym of* MME ALFRED VALLETTE, *née* MARGUERITE EYMERY (1860–1953), literary critic and author of some 60 novels (most of them daring in a ninetyish manner); co-founder, with her husband and others, of *Le *Mercure de France*. Her memoirs (*Quand j'étais jeune*, 1948) give a good picture of *Symbolist circles.

Racine, JEAN (1639–99), a great dramatist of the *Classical era, b. at La Ferté-Milon near Soissons, the son of a *procureur* in that area. Soon left an orphan in the care of a *Jansenist grandmother, he was educated from 1655 at the schools of **Port-Royal*, where he acquired both the Jansenist doctrines and a very wide knowledge of the classics. In 1658, having already revealed his poetic gifts in some odes on the scenery around *Port-Royal*, he went to the *Collège d'Harcourt* (*v. Universities*, 1). From now on, *Port-Royal* and the profane world contended for him. He frequented the society of actors, wrote an ode on Louis XIV's marriage (*La Nymphe de la Seine*, 1660), was protected by Chapelain, and obtained a small pension. With a view to his entering the Church, his family placed him in the care of a clerical uncle at Uzès, in Languedoc; but he returned to Paris (1662), published more odes, and was on more or less friendly terms with Boileau (who had a considerable influence on him), Molière, and La Fontaine. His first two tragedies, *La *Thébaïde* (1664) and **Alexandre le Grand* (1665), were both produced by Molière, but he soon transferred the second play from Molière's theatre to the **Hôtel de Bourgogne*, which led to a breach between him and Molière. Though not masterpieces, these plays made his name. He now definitely parted company with *Port-Royal*, intervening with acrimony on the side of Desmarets de Saint-Sorlin in the latter's dispute with *Nicole. His **Andromaque* (1667) rivalled Corneille's *Le *Cid* in its success, and in 1669—after his comedy *Les *Plaideurs* (1668)—he challenged the older dramatist on his own ground with the political play **Britannicus*. The contest was repeated in 1670, when his **Bérénice* and Corneille's **Tite et Bérénice* appeared almost simultaneously—and this time the younger poet was deemed the victor. His other great plays followed—**Bajazet* (1672), **Mithridate* (1673), **Iphigénie* (1674), **Phèdre* (1677). He was admitted to the **Académie* in 1673. But from the days of *Alexandre* he had always had critics and enemies. A rival *Iphigénie* was hastily concocted by inferior poets to damp the success of his *Iphigénie*, and an influential cabal (*v. Deshoulières*; *Mazarin's Nieces* (7)) contrived that his *Phèdre* should be opposed by *Pradon's *Phèdre et Hippolyte*. He now resolved to abandon the theatre, repented of his dramatic writing, and was reconciled with *Port-Royal*. The year 1677 saw his marriage and his appointment, with Boileau, as historiographer to Louis XIV. He took his new duties seriously, accompanying the king on journeys and campaigns. In 1689 and 1691, at Mme de Maintenon's request, he wrote the religious dramas **Esther* and **Athalie* for performance by the young ladies of the *Institut de *Saint-Cyr*. His later works include four *Cantiques spirituels*; a memorandum on the sufferings of the people (said by Louis Racine to have offended the king); and a notable *Abrégé de l'histoire de Port-Royal* (1742, in part; 1767, in full)—but nothing more for the theatre. *v. Champmeslé.*

In their main features—concentration on the exposition of character and acute spiritual conflict, observance of the unities, and exclusion of everything irrelevant to the main theme—his tragedies follow those of Corneille. But they differ from them in certain important respects. With Corneille, the will triumphs over instinct and circumstance; with Racine, it is feeble and vacillating (here the influence of Jansenism may be suspected), and the interplay of conflicting motives leads to the final solution. His characters are thus more real and human than those of Corneille: La Bruyère said of Corneille and Racine that 'celui-là peint les hommes comme ils devraient être, celui-ci les peint tels qu'ils sont'. Racine 'inaugurated the literature of the passions of the heart' (Brunetière), and his most striking characters are women (Phèdre, Andromaque, Hermione, Monime, Roxane, Athalie); but in his plays love and women are subversive, anti-social forces, leading not to heroism but to neglect of duty, misery, and crime, and he was widely criticized in his own day for what was regarded as his crude realism (esp. in *Phèdre*). His style is simple and natural, smooth and polished, less oratorical than that of Corneille. His choice of so many Greek themes points to the influence of Hellenism in his education.

His work was at first less appreciated in England than that of Corneille, and it was not till the early 18th c. that adaptations of his plays (Edmund Smith's *Phaedra and Hippolitus*, 1706; Ambrose Philips's *The Distrest Mother*, from *Andromaque*, 1712) met with marked success.

Racine, LOUIS (1692–1763), son of the above, educated by the *Jansenists. He wrote indifferent didactic verse (on *La Grâce*, 1720; *La Religion*, 1742, his chief work); pious, but not wholly reliable, memoirs of his father; essays on poetry and the drama; and a prose translation of Milton's *Paradise Lost*.

Racine et Shakspeare (1823, 1825), by Stendhal, two pamphlets in defence of *Romanticism. Dealing particularly with the drama, he defines Romanticism as the element in literature which satisfies a continually changing criterion of beauty. All great writers were romantic in their day, becoming classic only with the lapse

of time. Racinian and Shakespearian tragedy could both be termed romantic, the first because it depicted the passions, the second because it treated the catastrophic events of history and laid bare the workings of the human heart. Shakespearian tragedy, because unhampered by the unities of time and place, was the more truly romantic: it could emphasize the eternal theme of tragedy, change of heart, and so more easily follow the psychological development of the characters. Romantic tragedy of the future should spread the action over several months and several events; and it should be written in prose, to secure perfect freedom of expression.

Radiguet, RAYMOND (1903–23), died at 20, having written two brilliant novels of psychological analysis, notable also for their clear, confident style: *Le Diable au corps* (1923), a study of adolescence forced to a precocious maturity in time of war; and *Le Bal du comte d'Orgel* (1924), which, from the analogies of situation and treatment, might be called a kind of latter-day *Princesse de Clèves*.

Ragotin, in Scarron's *Roman comique*.

Ragueneau, CYPRIEN or FRANÇOIS (d. 1654), pastry-cook (in Paris, c. 1640–50), actor, and poet. He failed as a cook no less than as a poet, and was a humble member of travelling companies of actors (inc., it is said, that of Molière). He figures in Rostand's *Cyrano de Bergerac*.

Rains, Chronique de, v. History, 1.

Rais, v. Retz or Rais.

Raison, Fêtes de la, celebrations instituted during the Revolution in an attempt to eradicate Christianity. The first was held in Notre-Dame in November 1793. The interior of the cathedral was draped (to hide the trappings of Catholicism) and a small temple was erected with the inscription 'A la Philosophie', flanked by busts of Voltaire and J.-J. Rousseau. An actress played the part of the Goddess of Reason and emerged from the temple to receive the homage of the people. *Cf. Être Suprême.*

Raison par alphabet, La, v. *Dictionaries*, 1764.

Raison raisonnante, La, a term applied by Taine to the dogmatic and pedantic disquisitions, verging on the sermon or the political harangue, common in drama of the later 18th c., notably in La Chaussée and Diderot, and even in Voltaire.

Rambaud, ALFRED, v. *Lavisse*; *History*, 4.

Rambouillet, Château de, some 20 miles south-west of Versailles, originally a seat of the Angennes family (v. next article), passed into the hands of Louis XVI, became State property at the Revolution, and is now the country residence of the President.

Rambouillet, Hôtel de, on part of the site of the present *Palais-Royal, the intellectual centre of the best Parisian society from *c.* 1618 to 1650. It was the town house of Catherine de Vivonne, marquise de Rambouillet (1588–1665), a kindly, intelligent woman, learned without being pedantic, who had been married at 12 to Charles d'Angennes, later marquis de Rambouillet. Mme de Rambouillet (known in her circle as 'Arthénice'—an anagram of her Christian name), assisted by her daughter Julie d'Angennes (v. *Montausier*; *Guirlande de Julie*), received, besides many of the nobility, most of the leading writers and wits of the day, including Malherbe, Racan, Gombauld, Conrart, Vaugelas, Chapelain, Voiture, Saint-Évremond, La Rochefoucauld, the Scudérys, Ménage, Costar, Mme Cornuel, and even Bossuet and, for a time, Corneille. The conversation was on every kind of subject—the news or scandal of the day, the latest literary event (e.g. the dispute about the sonnets of *Benserade and Voiture), points of ethics, the meaning of certain words, the precise nature of certain feelings. This *salon*, though not the first of its kind, set the example for

many others, e.g. those of Mme de Sablé and Mme de Longueville. Its influence on literature, at its height *c.* 1642–8, has been variously estimated, for it brought *préciosité* into fashion (v. *Précieux*, *Précieuses*).

Rameau, JEAN-PHILIPPE (1683–1764), long an organist by profession, won fame in middle life as a composer of operas, ballets (e.g. *Les Indes galantes*, 1735, an opera-ballet), and music for the harpsichord, and as author of important musical treatises (*Traité de l'harmonie*, 1722; *Nouveau Système de musique théorique*, 1726, etc.). Louis XV gave him a pension and he held a post at court. v. *Neveu de Rameau, Le*.

Raminagrobis, in Rabelais's *Pantagruel*.

Ramond de Carbonnières, LOUIS-FRANÇOIS (1755–1827), geologist, a pioneer in the study of mountains. His *Observations faites dans les Pyrénées* (1789) and *Voyages au Mont-Perdu* (1801) contain remarkable descriptions of mountain scenery.

Ramus, v. *La Ramée*.

Ramuz, CHARLES-FERDINAND (1878–1947), a novelist of Swiss birth who lived for some years in Paris before 1914. His many novels of French–Swiss country life include *Aline* (1905), *Vie de Samuel Belet* (1913), *La Grande Peur dans la montagne* (1926), *La Beauté sur la terre* (1927), *Derborence* (1935). His *Journal* (1943) runs from 1896 to 1942.

Rancé, ARMAND DE, v. *Trappe*.

Randon, GABRIEL, v. *Rictus*.

Raoul or **Rodolphe,** duc de Bourgogne and son-in-law of Robert Ier, became king of France when Charles III was deposed for the second time (923) and reigned till 936.

Raoul de Cambrai, a 12th-c. *chanson de

geste (*Doon de Mayence cycle), interesting for the light it throws on feudal sentiment. Raoul, awarded the estate of Herbert of Vermandois by the king, invades it to oust Herbert's sons and sacks the town of Origny, burning its convent and nuns. Bernier, Herbert's grandson, who is also Raoul's squire and faithful to his liege lord, sees his mother burnt to death. Only when Raoul strikes him down for lamenting these calamities does Bernier renounce his allegiance. He later kills Raoul, but is ever after tormented by his broken oath and spends his life seeking to allay his conscience by pilgrimages. Guerri, Raoul's uncle, finally kills him in the place where he himself had killed his lord.

Raoul de Houdenc, a 13th-c. poet, author of the *Songe d'enfer* (v. *Religious Writings*, 1) and the *Roman des ailes* (a description of the chivalrous virtues), didactic allegories; and of **Méraugis de Portlesguez*, a *roman breton.

Raphaël, v. Lamartine.

Rapin, NICOLAS (c. 1535–1608), a gentleman of Poitou and a poet of the school of Ronsard (*Les Plaisirs du gentilhomme champêtre, augmentés de quelques nouveaux poèmes et épigrammes*, 1583, etc.). He fought for Henri IV at Ivry and collaborated in the *Satire Ménippée.

Rapin, RENÉ (1621–87), 'le Père Rapin', a *Jesuit and an able literary critic. His *Réflexions sur la Poétique d'Aristote* (1674), translated into English by Rymer (1674), was highly praised by Dryden (v. *English Literature, French Influence on*, 3). He also wrote a *Traité de la manière d'écrire l'histoire*.

Rapin de Thoyras, PAUL DE (1671–1725), historian, a *Huguenot who found refuge in Holland and went to England with William of Orange. He wrote an *Histoire d'Angleterre* down to 1688 (1724; Eng. trans. by N. Tindal, 1723–31).

Rappel, Le, a newspaper f. 1869 to voice opposition to the Second Empire (v. *Press*, 8; *Hugo, C.-V.*). The first number carried a stirring letter from Victor Hugo, calling for the 'rappel de la liberté par le réveil de la France'. The paper was very popular with the working classes and continued into the 20th c.

Raspail, FRANÇOIS-VINCENT (1794–1878), chemist and politician. He was intended for the Church, but developed strong Republican sympathies after 1815, rejected a clerical career, studied science in Paris, and soon made his name as an organic chemist. After 1830, and again in and after 1848, he was active in advanced revolutionary politics. He served a long term in prison in the early years of the Second Empire, then lived in Belgium. He returned to France in 1869 and was later a *député.

Rastignac, **Eugène de**, a leading character in Balzac's *Comédie humaine. A member of the impoverished provincial nobility, he comes to Paris from near Angoulême in 1819 to study law and lodges at the Maison Vauquer, where he meets Goriot and *Vautrin (v. *Père Goriot, Le*). In **Illusions perdues* and **Splendeurs et misères des courtisanes* his fortunes are to some extent linked with those of Lucien de Rubempré. In *L'Interdiction*, *La *Peau de chagrin*, *Une Fille d'Ève*, *La Maison Nucingen*, *La *Cousine Bette*, etc., he is seen pursuing riches, becoming a successful politician and a *pair de France, and finally marrying the daughter of Mme de Nucingen, his first mistress.

Ratisbonne, LOUIS (1827–1900), a minor *Parnassien poet, also translated Dante and wrote pleasing and popular tales and poems for children, e.g. *La Comédie enfantine* (1860).

Ravachol, FRANÇOIS-CLAUDIUS KŒNIG-STEIN, *known as* (1859–92), anarchist, one of a group responsible for bomb outrages. He was guillotined.

Ravaillac, FRANÇOIS (1578–1610), the assassin of Henri IV.

Ravaisson-Mollien, FÉLIX (1813–1900), philosopher, one of the first to react against the eclecticism of Cousin. Strongly influenced by Maine de Biran, he rejected a purely scientific explanation of the universe as inadequate and insisted on the need for spiritual belief; his philosophy is sometimes called Neo-criticism or Neo-spiritualism. His works include *De l'habitude* (1838), his doctoral thesis; *Essai sur la métaphysique d'Aristote* (1837–46), one of the great philosophical treatises of the 19th c.; a remarkable *Rapport sur la philosophie en France au XIXᵉ siècle* (1867), written for the Great Exhibition of 1867.

Ravel, MAURICE (1875–1937), composer, lived mainly in Paris and, like Debussy, was closely associated with *Symbolist writers and *Impressionist painters. He set many poems—e.g. by Mallarmé, Verlaine, Klingsor—to music, also A. *Bertrand's *Gaspard de la nuit*.

Ravignan, XAVIER DE (1795–1858), a noted *Jesuit preacher, initiated the famous practice of Lenten sermons for men only at Notre-Dame. His own were delivered between 1837 and 1846.

Ravisius Textor, *v. Tixier de Ravisi*.

Raymond, MARCEL (1897–1957), critic, of Swiss birth. His works include *De Baudelaire au surréalisme* (1933), a fine historico-critical study. *v. Critics and Criticism*, 3.

Raynal, GUILLAUME, ABBÉ (1713–96), historian, *Encyclopédiste*, sometime editor of the *Mercure de France*, and originator (1747) of the literary correspondence with German sovereigns continued by *Grimm. His long *Histoire philosophique et politique des établissements et du commerce des Européens dans les deux Indes* (1770) stressed the moral obligations of the Europeans, combining a wealth of entertaining information on a wide variety of subjects with disquisitions against religion, despotism, slavery, etc. (probably supplied in part by Diderot), which

encouraged such revolutionaries as Toussaint Louverture. The work was suppressed (1772) and he was obliged to leave France (1775); but it was widely read (some 30 eds., with numerous additions, had appeared by 1789). In 1791 he reproved the *Assemblée constituante* for its errors and intolerance, with the result that his property was confiscated and he died in extreme poverty. He was a fellow of the Royal Society of London, and his work was praised by William Cowper (in a letter of 7 May 1778) and Horace Walpole—though Walpole found the author himself a tiresome bore and feigned deafness to escape him.

Raynal, PAUL (1885–1971), dramatist, made his name with *Le Maître de son cœur* (1920), a drama of love and jealousy, and *Le Tombeau sous l'Arc de Triomphe* (1924), a controversial play contrasting the misery of the soldiers in the trenches in the 1914–18 war with the comfort and security of civilian life at home. *La Francerie* (1933) and *Le Matériel humain* (1948) were also concerned with such moral problems.

Raynaud, ERNEST (1864–1936), poet, began as an ardent *Symbolist, then helped to found the *École romane. He was also in at the beginnings of the *Mercure de France*. His works include *Le Signe* (1887), *Chairs profanes* (1889), *Les Cornes du faune* (1890), and *La Tour d'ivoire* (1899), collected poetry; also *La Mêlée symboliste* (1918–23, 3 vols.), reminiscences.

Raynouard, FRANÇOIS (1761–1836), medievalist and philologist (*Des troubadours et des cours d'amour*, 1817; and *v. Dictionaries*, 1838–44). His tragedy *Les Templiers* (1805) was one of the most successful of the day, perhaps owing to Talma's acting. He was perpetual secretary of the *Académie from 1817.

Rayons et les ombres, **Les** (1840), a collection of lyrics by Hugo, the last of his first period. It contains some of his most famous poems, e.g. *Ce qui se passait aux*

Feuillantines vers 1813, memories of childhood at his home in Paris; *Tristesse d'Olympio*; *La Statue*; *Oceano nox*, a lament for sailors lost at sea, without even a humble tombstone to keep their memory alive—often contrasted with *Corbière's *La Fin* (a defiant and ironical treatment of the same theme); *Fonction du poète*, indicating his conception, elaborated in later life, of the poet as seer and torch-bearer.

Réaction thermidorienne, La, *v.* *Revolutions*, 1 (1794).

Realism, Realist, a movement in the novel, at its height *c.* 1850–65, reflecting the interest of a progressively positivist and scientific age in material facts and the general distaste for the vague enthusiasms of the *Romantics. The Romantics had called for 'la liberté dans l'art': the new slogan was 'la sincérité dans l'art'.

Realism owed something to Stendhal, who had claimed that the actions of his characters proceeded logically from the many small factors that composed their natures and influenced their motives (though it is to be noted that his factors were moral rather than material). Balzac, who claimed for his novels a sociological value as studies of society, was more truly a precursor. The theory of documentation, so important in both the Realist and the *Naturalist novel, may be said to have derived from the scrupulous exactitude with which he set the stage for his stories, from his detailed observation of the material facts of his characters' lives—their houses, habits, business transactions, etc. These aspects of Balzac and Stendhal were emphasized by *Taine, who was a major influence on Realism and Naturalism. (For the main differences between these two schools, which had much in common and are often confused, *v. Naturalism*.)

The Realists owed a more immediate debt to the painter Courbet, who in 1848 had announced that he would in future paint only the modern and the vulgar. His theories of *l'art réaliste* attracted a number of artists and writers and were transposed into literature by Champfleury, who became leader of the movement. He wrote a number of now more or less unreadable novels and a manifesto of the new doctrines (*Le Réalisme*, 1857).

The intransigent Realists aimed at a scrupulous reproduction of life in all its aspects and at a novel documented with the same careful regard for truth as a work of history (*v. Goncourt*). Every fact, every detail of background, must be recorded without softening, exaggeration, incidental description, or concern for style. Imagination and sensibility, love of form, the effort to convey an idealized, unreal beauty, no longer counted. Involved plots, catastrophic events, or shattering passions, were falsifications of the truth. Subjects should be taken from contemporary, everyday life, preferably lower-class or industrial life, which offered a more naked reality. The extreme Realist novel, when not merely the unselective accumulation of monotonous events, became the laborious depiction of vice, ugliness, and squalor—a trend to be intensified by the Naturalists.

Flaubert's *Madame Bovary* was hailed as a triumph of Realism (and later of Naturalism—though Flaubert himself disliked such labels) because of its close observation of life and because the action stemmed by an inevitable sequence of cause and effect from the psychology of the characters. Its greatness as a work of art was seldom noticed, or noticed only in negative fashion when certain extreme Realists decried it as too carefully written. A more truly Realist novel was the *Goncourts' *Germinie Lacerteux*, though this again by its style—the nervous, impressionistic style peculiar to the Goncourts—differed from the norm. Other Realists were E. *Feydeau with *Fanny* and Duranty with *Le *Malheur d'Henriette Gérard*.

Réaumur, RENÉ-ANTOINE FERCHAULT DE (1683–1757), physicist and naturalist, remembered as the inventor of the Réaumur thermometer. He published *Mémoires pour servir à l'histoire naturelle des insectes* (1736–42).

Rebatet, LUCIEN (1903–72), a journalist (on *L'**Action française, etc.) and novelist whose record as a collaborator during the 1939–45 war (and esp. his anti-Semitic pamphlet *Les Décombres*, 1943) delayed recognition of his undeniable literary talent—particularly evident in the novel *Les Deux Étendards* (1952), an outstanding work, despite its violence and vulgarity.

Rebell, Hugues, *pseudonym of* GEORGES GRASSAL (1867–1905), who wrote poetry (*Chants de la pluie et du soleil*, 1894) and novels, usually with elaborate historical settings and said to resemble those of Louÿs (e.g. *La Nichina*, 1897; *La Femme qui a connu l'Empereur*, 1901; *La Saison à Baïa*, 1901).

Reboux, PAUL, and **Muller,** CHARLES, *v. Pastiche.*

Récamier, JEANNE-FRANÇOISE BERNARD, MME (1777–1849), a woman of great beauty, charm, and tact, the wife from 1793 of a rich, elderly Paris banker and famous for her *salon, frequented by the greatest writers and politicians of the Napoleonic and Restoration periods. She stirred the hearts of many men and had the gift of transforming them into devoted friends; B. Constant worshipped her in vain (*c.* 1815), to his great exasperation. She was Mme de Staël's closest—perhaps only—woman friend. From 1819, after some reverses of fortune, she lived at the Abbaye-aux-Bois, a Paris convent with which was combined a kind of select *pension*. Her *salon* there, and her own life, henceforward revolved around Chateaubriand. It was there that friends and admirers met to hear him reading passages from 'work in progress', his **Mémoires d'outre-tombe*. Her *Souvenirs et correspondance* were edited by her niece Mme Lenormand. There are famous portraits of her by David and Gérard.

Recherche de l'absolu, La (1834; later in *La* **Comédie humaine, Études philosophiques*), a novel by Balzac. Balthazar Claes, respected head of an old family of Flemish weavers and a devoted husband

and father, develops a sudden passion for scientific research. In his zeal to find the 'absolute', the philosopher's stone which will convert all it touches to wealth, he ruins himself. His wife dies. His daughter restores the family fortunes for a time, but in vain. He dies a victim to his mania, leaving the family to face disaster.

Recherche de la vérité, La, v. Malebranche.

Recherches de la France, v. Pasquier, É.

Reclus, ÉLISÉE (1830–1905), geographer and revolutionary. Forced into political exile in 1851, he travelled in Europe and America, observed conditions, wrote about his travels, and became a Communist. He returned home in 1857, but was exiled after the *Commune of 1871. His *Géographie universelle* (1875–94) was written abroad.

Reclus de Molliens, Le, *v. Charité.*

Recueillement, v. Baudelaire.

Recueillements poétiques, v. Lamartine.

Redon, ODILON (1840–1916), painter and lithographer (he illustrated Flaubert), was associated with *Symbolism. He is mentioned in Huysmans's *A rebours.

Réflexions sur Longin (1694), a work in which Boileau uses a series of passages from the Greek treatise known as *Longinus on the Sublime* (which he had earlier translated) as texts of dissertations in defence of the ancients, especially Homer and Pindar, against Charles Perrault.

Réfractaires, *v. Constitution civile du clergé*. In the mid-19th c. the term was applied (e.g. by Veuillot and Vallès) to the journalistic hacks, hangers-on of literary circles, who had expected to succeed without sacrifice and hard work and were ending their days in embittered poverty.

Régale, Droit de, the right, claimed by the kings of France, to collect the revenues of vacant archbishoprics and bishoprics and to nominate to benefices dependent on them. It was the subject of a violent dispute (1677–82) between Louis XIV and the papacy.

Régence, La, a term applied in particular to the regency (1715–23) of Philippe, duc d'*Orléans, during the minority of Louis XV. It was a period of profligate reaction from the moral austerity latterly required by Louis XIV and of liberal reaction from his political absolutism; *v.* also *Law*. Other notable regencies were those of Anne de Beaujeu during the minority of her brother Charles VIII, Marie de Médicis during the minority of Louis XIII, and Anne d'Autriche during the minority of Louis XIV.

Régie, La. An industry or institution is said to be *mise en régie* (or *sous la régie*) when controlled or monopolized by the State. The term is well known as applied to the State tobacco monopoly, which goes back to 1674.

Regnard, JEAN-FRANÇOIS (1655–1709), dramatist, was long regarded as the nearest successor to Molière. His best comedies— written first for the *Italiens* and from 1695 for the *Comédie-Française*—are *Le *Joueur* (1696), *Le Distrait* (1697), *Démocrite* (1700), *Les *Folies amoureuses* (1704), *Les *Ménechmes* (1705), *Le *Légataire universel* (1708). He was no moralist, but depicted a corrupt world with boundless gaiety, in a rich, picturesque style and in excellent verse. His other works include *La Provençale*, a romance treating an incident in his early travels when he was taken by corsairs (1678) and held at Algiers till ransomed; *Voyage en Laponie*, also about his travels; verse epistles and satires.

Régnier, HENRI DE (1864–1936), poet and novelist, b. at Honfleur of a family whose interesting ancestral associations he sometimes used in his novels; husband of Marie de Heredia (*v.* Houville, Gérard d'). His first collections of poems—*Lendemains* (1885), *Apaisement* (1886), *Sites* (1887; sonnets), *Épisodes* (1888)—were faintly

reminiscent of the *Parnassiens*, but he soon became famous as a *Symbolist and for his musical, supple use of the *vers libre*. The lyrics and *odelettes* collected, from the little reviews in which they first appeared, in *Poèmes anciens et romanesques* (1890), *Tel qu'en songe* (1892), and *Jeux rustiques et divins* (1897) are typical of this phase. He then returned to classical forms and to themes chosen mainly from antiquity, e.g. *Les Médailles d'argile* (1900), sonnets dedicated to A. Chénier; *La Sandale ailée* (1906); *Le Miroir des heures* (1911). In *La Cité des eaux* (1902) he wrote of the deserted splendours of *Versailles. Later collections were *1914–1916; poèmes* (1918) and *Vestigia flammae* (1921; inc. the tenderly evocative *Te souviens-tu, ô Roméo?*).

Having already made his name as a poet, he published several successful novels and tales. Some, in 17th- and 18th-c. settings, are written with an elaborate libertinism and in a highly decorative, precious style, e.g. *La Canne de jaspe* (1897; tales); *La Double Maîtresse* (1900), his best-known novel; *Les Rencontres de M. de Bréot* (1904). Others, in a modern setting, are *Le Mariage de minuit* (1903), including a character modelled on Montesquiou, and *Les Vacances d'un jeune homme sage* (1903), an indulgent, amused, and highly sophisticated picture of provincial life and calf love.

Régnier, MATHURIN (1573–1613), satirist, a nephew of Desportes. He visited Italy several times, notably in the suite of Cardinal de Joyeuse, French envoy at the papal court (1593), but his dissolute habits hindered his advancement. The first collection of his *Satires*, poems (in *alexandrines) modelled on the satires of Horace and Juvenal and compared by Sainte-Beuve to Flemish paintings, appeared in 1608. With vigorous and amusing traits, he depicts the physician, the poet, the hypocrite, the Gascon adventurer, etc. Satire IX shows him firmly opposed to the petty reforms of Malherbe and the purists. His general philosophy— reflecting his easy-going good humour— is that of Montaigne: everything varies with the point of view of the individual, who should act as his own reason or situation dictates. His *Satires* raised him high in the public esteem (even in that of Malherbe, and later of Boileau) and prepared the way for Molière (Macette, the hypocritical old woman in Satire XIII, was a prototype of *Tartuffe; and *v. Fâcheux, Les).

Régnier, PAULE (1888–1950), novelist. Badly deformed by an illness in infancy, poor, and sensitive, she had an instinctive love of literature and began to write when she was about 20. About 1912 she formed a deep friendship, which turned to unhappy love on her side, with a poet, who was killed in battle in 1915. She never got over his death. After her mother died (1926) she became more and more of a solitary, a prey to spiritual perplexities which conflicted with her desire for faith and increasingly overwhelmed by the material struggles of existence. She finally committed suicide. Her novels include *L'Abbaye d'Évolayne* (1933), which was moderately successful; also *Octave* (1913), *La Vivante Paix* (1924), *Les Filets dans la mer* (1949). Her *Journal* (1951), a diary kept until the night before her suicide, is more likely to preserve her memory.

Régnier-Desmarais, FRANÇOIS-SÉRA-PHIN (1632–1713), grammarian and poet (*Poésies françaises, italiennes, latines, et espagnoles*, 1707–8), helped to prepare the first edition of the *Dictionnaire de l'Académie française* (*v.* Dictionaries, 1694). His *Traité de la grammaire française* (1705) was both highly praised and hotly attacked.

Regrets, Les, *v. Du Bellay*.

Reichstadt, DUC DE, *v. Napoleon II*.

Reinach, (1) JOSEPH (1856–1921), politician and publicist, a vigorous opponent of *Boulangisme and a champion of Dreyfus; (2) his brother SALOMON (1858–1932), philologist, archaeologist, and art historian, and author of valuable works in all these fields.

Reine Margot, La, *v. Dumas père*.

Réjane, *stage-name of* GABRIELLE-CHARLOTTE RÉJU (1857–1920), a leading actress in light comedy (1880–1915), notably as *Madame Sans-Gêne and as Clotilde in Becque's *La *Parisienne*. She played in London, the U.S.A., etc.

Relations des Jésuites. The early *Jesuit missionaries in Canada had to furnish annual reports of their work to their Superior-General in Quebec, who used them to compile the *Relations de ce qui s'est passé en la Nouvelle France* (publ. in Paris 1632–72 and later eds.). These *Relations* are of great interest for the early history of Canada.

Religieuse, La (1796; written 1760), by Diderot, a romance—based on a true story—about a girl whose parents, having exhausted their means in endowing her elder sisters, condemn her to be a nun. It describes the cruel treatment by which she is forced to take the veil, the sufferings to which she is subjected in the cloister, her transfer to a convent under a dissolute superior, her escape and subsequent misfortunes.

Religious Writings. *v.* also *Bible, French Versions of*.

1. MEDIEVAL PERIOD. Most of the earliest extant writings in French belong to this category: the *Séquence de Sainte *Eulalie* (*c.* 880); two 10th-c. poems, the *Passion de Clermont* (the earliest French text based on the Bible; in octosyllabic quatrains) and the *Vie de Saint *Léger*; the 11th-c. *Vie de Saint *Alexis*. Religious writings in verse and prose were frequent from the 12th c., notably narrations and legends from the early Church about the Virgin Mary and a host of saints and martyrs (*v.* Saints, *Lives of*). Well-known poems about the Virgin are the *Miracles de la Sainte Vierge* (*c.* 1220), instances of her mercy to humble sinners, compiled by Gautier de Coincy (*c.* 1177–1236; a Benedictine); and the *Tombeur de Notre-Dame*, the story of a poor *jongleur who devotes his skill as an acrobat to the service

of the Virgin (it inspired A. *France's *Le Jongleur de Notre-Dame*).

Apart from French versions of sermons (e.g. those of St. Bernard and Maurice de Sully), didactic works of Christian ethics were also numerous, e.g. *La *Dîme de pénitence*; *Le *Besant de Dieu*; *Charité and *Miserere*; the eloquent *Vers de la mort* (*c.* 1195), adjuring the worldly to think of the life hereafter, by Hélinand, a monk of noble birth; the *Poème moral* (13th c.), a sincere exhortation to renounce worldly joys, accompanied by many examples, including the life of St. Thaïs. Some of these works took dialogue form, e.g. the *Débat du corps et de l'âme* (12th c.; in hexasyllables), where the soul reproaches the body for causing its damnation, and the body retorts; the *Dit des *trois morts et des trois vifs*. Others were allegorical, e.g. Raoul de Houdenc's strange *Songe d'enfer*, where Lucifer devours sinners. The *Somme des vices et des vertus* or *Somme le Roi* (1279), a treatise on Christian ethics dedicated by a Dominican named Laurens to Philippe III, sheds light on 13th-c. society. William of Wadington's *Manuel des péchés* (13th c., in *Anglo-Norman; adapted in Eng., as *Handlyng Synne*, by Robert Mannyng) similarly illuminates English customs. 13th-c. literature also includes a number of edifying narrative poems; *v. Barlaam et Josaphat*; *Chevalier au barisel, Le*.

The drama in France, as in England, had in its earliest phase a close connection with the Church. The liturgical plays, originally in Latin, performed by the clergy at Christmas and Easter in churches or their precincts were gradually transformed into plays in the vernacular performed by lay fraternities. These early liturgical plays, of which few survive, dealt with such themes as the Annunciation, the Nativity, the Resurrection, or the raising of Lazarus. The earliest in which the vernacular is used is the *Sponsus* play (in Latin mixed with Provençal), a verse dramatization of the parable of the Wise and Foolish Virgins; it is probably of the 11th c. In the 12th c. we have the important *Jeu d'Adam* (in Anglo-Norman octosyllables and decasyllables, with stage directions in Latin), representing the Fall, the death of Abel, and the prophets of the Redemption. A later dramatic poem, also in Anglo-Norman, is the *Resurrection*, of which the extant fragments (in octosyllables) deal with the Descent and Entombment, and present apocryphal incidents connected with Joseph of Arimathea, Longinus, and Nicodemus. Other religious plays represented incidents in the lives of saints or miracles performed by them: early examples are *Bodel's *Jeu de Saint Nicolas* (partly comic) and *Rutebeuf's *Miracle de Théophile*. For the later development of religious drama *v. Mystère*; *Miracle*; *Confrérie de la Passion. v.* also *Danse macabre*.

2. 16TH AND 17TH CENTURIES. The Reformation added theology to the field of French literature. Calvin's French version (*Institution de la religion chrétienne*, 1541) of his earlier *Christianae religionis institutio* was the first theological work to be written in French and inspired many others; it was also a formative influence on French prose style.

The poets of the *Pléiade*, though primarily pagan in inspiration, turned at times to the Bible—e.g. Du Bellay's *Monomachie de David et de Goliath* (1560), Belleau's paraphrases of Ecclesiastes and the Song of Solomon and *Les Amours de David et de Bethsabée* (in his *Bergerie*)—or, like Ronsard in his *Discours*, defended the Catholic faith against the Protestant reform. The great poet of Protestantism was d'Aubigné, above all in *Les *Tragiques*. Another notable Protestant epic was *Du Bartas's *La Semaine*. Other authors of religious epics included Montchrétien, Saint-Amant, Desmarets de Saint-Sorlin, and Godeau. Many poets, following the example of Marot, wrote paraphrases of the Psalms, and religious canticles, e.g. Bertaut, Desportes, Malherbe, Godeau, and Racan. The poets Sponde, La Ceppède, and Chassignet have appealed to the 20th-c. interest in metaphysical and baroque verse.

The period from *c.* 1640 was notable for the writings of the *Jansenists, above all *Pascal's *Lettres provinciales* and *Pensées* (*v.* also *Arnauld, A.*; *Nicole*; *Le Maître de Saci*). Other leading religious writers of the 16th and 17th cs. include Charron, Du Vair, St. François de Sales, and the great clerics and preachers of the reign of Louis XIV (Bossuet, Bourdaloue, Massillon, Fléchier, Fénelon). *v.* also *Maurists*.

In the field of drama, the Bible provided themes for *Buchanan's *Baptistes sive calumnia*, *Bèze's *Abraham sacrifiant*, La Taille's *Saül le furieux*, *Desmasures's *Tragédies saintes*, *Garnier's *Les Juives*, *Montchrétien's *David* and *Aman*, *Du Ryer's *Saül* and *Esther*, Racine's *Esther* and *Athalie*. Corneille, in *Polyeucte* and *Théodore*, dramatized the conflict between paganism and Christianity.

3. 19TH AND 20TH CENTURIES. Religious writings had been no feature of the 18th c., though the Jesuit *Journal de Trévoux (f. 1701) and *Jansenist *Nouvelles ecclésiastiques* (f. 1728) were among the earliest French periodicals. After the *Concordat* of 1801, giving Roman Catholicism official status as the national faith, religious sentiment revived and could again be openly expressed. Chateaubriand's *Le *Génie du christianisme*, published aptly in 1802 (and to some extent anticipated by a work by Ballanche), did much to awaken the enthusiasm for medieval piety and *le merveilleux chrétien* which marked the early phases of *Romanticism.

Early in the 19th c., in the works of J. de Maistre and Bonald, theories of papal infallibility and of the divine origin of monarchical authority combined to form a political philosophy. This period also saw the publication of *Lamennais's famous *Essai sur l'indifférence en matière de religion*, followed in 1834 by his impassioned *Paroles d'un croyant*. Montalembert and Lacordaire, at one time Lamennais's disciples, were also religious writers of note.

19th-c. developments in philosophy, journalism, and Biblical and literary criticism and history widened the significance of the term 'religious writings'. It came to include, for instance, the work of a long line of 19th- and 20th-c. spiritualist philosophers from Maine de Biran, Ravaisson-Mollien, Lachelier, and Fouillée to the Neo-Catholics (*v.* under *Blondel, M.*), Gilson, Maritain, Teilhard de Chardin, and G. Marcel; also that of Roman Catholic essayists and journalists from Veuillot and Hello to Bernanos and Daniel-Rops. Other 19th- and early 20th-c. writers who call for mention include Renan, if only, in the present connection, for the respect and sympathy for orthodox religion in which he clothed his inability to accept it; Ozanam; Quinet; Migne; and, among literary critics, Sainte-Beuve (for his *Port-Royal*) and Bremond. More recently, there has been a marked religious element in some of the writings of Mounier and his followers, and in those of S. Weil.

In purely creative writing, the religious element is apparent early in the 19th c. in Chateaubriand's *Les *Martyrs* and in Lamartine's poetry. Later, some poems in Hugo's *Légende des siècles* (e.g. *Booz endormi*) have Biblical themes. Religious sentiment and emotion are the very essence of poems by Péguy and Claudel, and are strongly present in the work of such of their contemporaries and successors as Jammes, Le Cardonnel, Nouveau, Fagus, H. Charasson, M. Noël, Cayrol, Estang, Jouve, P. de La Tour du Pin, Masson, and Emmanuel; *v.* also *Milosz*; *Spire*. Claudel calls for mention not only for his poetry and later essays (many of which are commentaries on the Bible), but as one of the few dramatists of religious inspiration in this period, though G. Marcel has also written dramas of conscience and Montherlant has treated religious themes. Claudel was also among a number of later 19th- and early 20th-c. writers who found matter for literature in their conversion, or their return, to the Roman Catholic faith (e.g. the novelists Huysmans, Bourget, and Bloy; the poets Jammes, Le Cardonnel, Verlaine, Nouveau, and Jacob; the critic Du Bos; and *v. Mugnier*). Later novelists whose work contains a strong religious element include, notably, Mauriac, Bernanos, and Green; *v.* also *Cayrol*; *Daniel-Rops*; *Estang*; *Simon, P.-H.* Cf. *Illuminisme*; *Rosicrucianism*.

Remarques sur la langue française, v. Vaugelas.

Rémusat, (1) CLAIRE-ÉLISABETH GRAVIER DE VERGENNES, COMTESSE DE (1780–1821), lady-in-waiting to the empress Joséphine, left *Mémoires* (1879) and *Lettres, 1804–14* (1881) shedding light on life at court, her anecdotes and character-sketches of Napoleon, the Bonaparte relations, and Talleyrand being of particular interest; (2) her son CHARLES, COMTE DE (1797–1875), politician and author of works on philosophy, English politics and history, etc., e.g. *L'Angleterre au XVIIIe siècle* (1856), *Channing* (1857), *John Wesley et le méthodisme* (1870).

Rémusat, JEAN-PIERRE-ABEL (1788–1832), a famous Orientalist, professor of Chinese at the *Collège de France (a chair specially created for him). Besides many philological studies, he left interesting *Mélanges asiatiques* (1825–6) and *Mélanges d'histoire et de littérature orientales* (1843).

Renaissance, The, the great literary and artistic revival that took place in the 16th c. under the influence of Greek and Latin models, to the gradual exclusion of the medieval tradition. By the end of the 15th c., under the pressure of a narrow dogmatic theology and of scholastic philosophy, the inspiration of the Middle Ages had become exhausted: a cynical, materialistic spirit prevailed; poetry tended to be trivial in content and complicated and artificial in form (*v. Rhétoriqueurs*). The reaction is often partly attributed to the successive invasions of Italy (1494–1525) by Charles VIII, Louis XII, and François Ier: these, by bringing the French into contact with Italian culture and Italian humanists, led to a refinement of taste and a better understanding of classical authors—notably Aristotle and Plato. The movement was powerfully supported by men of learning like Lefèvre d'Étaples, Gaguin, and Fichet, and by the arrival of teachers of Greek such as Hermonymus (Georges Hermonyme) and Andreas Lascaris. Boccaccio's *Decameron* had already been translated and was widely read (*v. Foreign Influences,* 1); and the sojourn of Petrarch himself at Avignon and Paris in the 14th c. had not been without some preparatory influence. The new spirit was especially fostered at the courts of François Ier and his sister Marguerite de Navarre, where writers, artists, and scholars enjoyed protection. The study of the humanities, *disciplinae humaniores,* as distinct from the formal logic and barbarous Latin of the scholastics, had to a limited extent been adopted at the *University of Paris before the end of the 15th c.; the printing of Greek books began in Paris in 1507; in 1530 François Ier founded the future *Collège de France. *v.* also *Erasmus.*

Among the many exponents of the new humanism were Budé, R. Estienne, Dolet, Rabelais, and Amyot; *v.* also *Scaliger* (2); *Turnèbe*; *Muret*. Its first literary effects are perceptible in the work of Lemaire de Belges, Marot, Scève, and Héroët; then, in more revolutionary fashion, in that of Ronsard and the *Pléiade. Thanks largely to the *Pléiade,* the century of the Renaissance saw a vast change in the character and capacity of French literature (*v. Tragedy; Comedy; Epic Poetry; Alexandrine; Sonnet*) and a great (though somewhat indiscriminate) enrichment of the language.

At first humanism and Protestantism (*v. Évangélisme*) went hand in hand, but after the *Affaire des* *placards (1534) their paths diverged, for Protestantism became Calvinism, which was opposed to free inquiry in pursuit of truth.

Renan, ERNEST (1823–92), historian, Hebrew scholar, philologist, and critic, was educated for the priesthood, notably (1843–5) at the seminary of *Saint-Sulpice. Here his philological training (before long he was teaching as well as learning Hebrew) and critical study of Biblical texts led him to question first the divine inspiration of the Bible, then the fundamental doctrines of orthodox, revealed religion. Following a period of spiritual crisis, he left (1845) without taking his vows. He became a pupil-teacher, *au pair*, in a private school, living in modest circumstances while preparing for his *agrégation in philosophy (1848). He was already a distinguished Semitic scholar: essays he contributed in the next few years to the **Revue des Deux Mondes* and the **Journal des Débats* are among his collected *Études d'histoire religieuse* (1857) and *Essais de morale et de critique* (1859). In 1849 a visit to Rome to work on his doctoral thesis (*Averroès et l'Averroïsme*, 1852) deepened his interest in classical antiquity and the arts, but it was not till 1865, in Athens, that it was passionately aroused (*v. Souvenirs d'enfance et de jeunesse*). He was appointed (1851) to a post at the **Bibliothèque nationale* (manuscript dept.) and devoted himself mainly to Biblical studies. In 1860–1 he headed a government archaeological expedition in Phoenicia and Palestine, then remained to visit the scenes of the Gospel story. The tour was overshadowed by the death of his beloved sister Henriette, who had gone with him (*Ma sœur Henriette*, written for private circulation at the time and publ. 1895, expresses his grief).

In 1862 he became professor of Hebrew at the **Collège de France*. His inaugural lecture on the part played by the Jews in the history of civilization was heterodox— he denied the divinity of Christ, 'un homme incomparable'—and provoked his suspension by government order. He was dismissed from his chair after the publication of his *Vie de Jésus* (1863), the first volume of a long-projected work, *Les Origines du christianisme* (1863–83; the subsequent vols. were *Les Apôtres*, 1866; *La Vie de Saint Paul*, 1869; *L'Antéchrist*, 1873; *Les Évangiles*, 1877; *L'Église chrétienne*, 1879; *Marc-Aurèle*, 1881; and an Index, 1883). This is a study of the origin of the Christian tradition in the beliefs of a small Jewish sect, the gradual emergence of a monotheistic doctrine, the founding of the Church and its triumph over Greek and Roman opposition. The treatment is critical, from the standpoint (following the example of German scholarship) of Biblical exegesis; but it is also biographical and psychological in so far as the approach is through the figures of the founders of Christianity. The value of the work as a scientific study has been disputed, but the *Vie de Jésus* in particular caused an undeniable sensation—for beneath a lyrical picture of the carpenter's son growing up amid the flowers of Galilee lay a total rejection of the supernatural element in his life. The *Vie de Saint Paul* and *Marc-Aurèle* are notable as indicating the development both of Christianity and of Renan's own philosophy. His later *Histoire du peuple d'Israël* (1887–93, 5 vols.) forms a prelude to the whole.

After the 1870 *Revolution he was reinstated at the *Collège de France*, of which he became head (1883). He was now, by reason of his erudition and literary knowledge, the persuasive force of his reasoning and of his style, and the controversy surrounding his works, a famous literary personality, ranking as a major representative of French thought. His intellectual appeal combined three elements: a romantic (and—from his Breton origin—Celtic) spiritualism, a materialism which believed that the future of the world lay in the progress of science, and a reluctance to deny a place to an ideal towards which the universe is striving. His attitude, already discernible in *L'*Avenir de la science* (written 1848), is clearly seen in his *Dialogues et fragments philosophiques* (1876) and his *Examen de conscience philosophique* (1888). In the **Drames philosophiques* (1878–86) the 'haute impartialité philosophique qui ne s'attache exclusivement à aucun parti' has become, in the view of some critics, a form of intellectual dilettantism. The notes and memoranda of his *Cahiers*, and *Nouveaux Cahiers, de jeunesse* (1906 and 1907) reflect the formation of his views on religion, philology, philosophy, and literature. His correspondence with Henriette, his friend *Berthelot, and many contemporaries covers a wide range of subjects. *v. Foreign Influences*, 4.

Renard, JULES (1864–1910), novelist; a native of the Morvan (a rather isolated district of Burgundy where farming is difficult and the inhabitants tend to be dour) and latterly mayor of his home town there. At first he had a hard struggle to live by his pen and private teaching in Paris, but his position in advanced literary circles was assured when he joined (1890) the original staff of the *Symbolist *Mercure de France*, and he was to be among the first members of the *Académie Goncourt*.

His writings have few of the characteristics usually associated with Symbolism. His ironic humour and acidulously keen gifts of observation and description were often exercised on human nature in its meanest, sourest, and most rebarbative aspects. But sympathy and poetic feeling did sometimes break through, as in *Poil de Carotte* (1894; dramatized 1900, and later filmed), the work which made his name. It is a tale of the sufferings (till he learns the painful art of self-preservation) of a dreamy, sensitive child in the country, bullied by his mother and neglected by his father. His other works include *L'Écornifleur* (1892; dramatized 1903 as *Monsieur Vernet*), a study of a 'literary' scrounger, who shamelessly imposes on the credulous M. and Mme Vernet; *Coquecigrues* (1893); *Le Vigneron dans sa vigne* (1894); *Les Philippe* (1898); *Les Bucoliques* (1898); *Histoires naturelles* (1896) and *Nos frères farouches* (1908), highly unsentimental sketches of life (inc. animal life) in the country; and one-act plays in the *Naturalist tradition (*Le Plaisir de rompre*, 1898; *Le Pain de ménage*, 1899; *Huit Jours à la campagne*, 1906). His *Journal inédit, 1887–1910* (in *Œuvres complètes*, 1925-7, 9 vols.) has many notes on contemporary literary events and personalities and interesting, at times painful, accounts of his family life; it is also a constant revelation of a bitter, dissatisfied man.

Renart, JEAN, an early 13th-c. poet, probably from the *Île-de-France. His verse *romans d'aventure—Le *Lai de l'ombre*, *Guillaume de Dole*, L'*Escoufle*, and possibly *Galeran de Bretagne*—are remarkable for their delicate charm and their vivid sketches of domestic life and little portraits of characters.

Renart, Roman de, v. *Roman de Renart*.

Renart le Bestourné; *Renart le Contrefait*; *Renart le Nouvel*, v. *Roman de Renart*.

Renaud de Beaujeu, v. *Guinglain*.

Renaud de Montauban or *Les Quatre Fils Aymon*, a late 12th- or early 13th-c. *chanson de geste* (*Doon de Mayence cycle). Renaud and his three brothers, sons of Aymon de Dordogne, escape from court after Renaud has killed Charlemagne's nephew in an affray. A long war follows. The brothers resist valiantly (Renaud on Bayard, his wonderful horse, and wielding his sword Flamberge), but are beleaguered and endure great suffering. Charlemagne, under pressure from his paladins, pardons them on condition that Renaud surrenders Bayard and goes to Palestine. Bayard, thrown into the river with a millstone round his neck on Charlemagne's orders, contrives to escape. Renaud, after further exploits, meets his death while helping, as a humble workman, to build the shrine of St. Peter at Cologne. Charlemagne plays an inglorious part (he is dishonourable and vindictive, and fooled by the enchanter Maugis), and the sympathy of the author and his readers is with the defeated rebels.

Renaud figures as Rinaldo in Boiardo's *Orlando Innamorato* and Ariosto's *Orlando Furioso*; and v. *Bibliothèque bleue*. During the German occupation of Belgium (1940-4), *Les Quatre Fils Aymon*, a play on the theme, banned by the Germans as subversive, was performed 'underground' to enthusiastic audiences.

Renaudot, THÉOPHRASTE (1586–1653), a physician and publicist of original and enlightened views. He founded *La *Gazette*, the first French newspaper; the *Bureau d'adresse et de rencontre*, an advertising and information centre which issued sheets of advertisements (the prototype of *Les *Petites Affiches*) of articles wanted or for sale, situations vacant, etc., and where lectures were given; and the first *mont-de-piété* (pawnshop), for the benefit of the poor, which involved him in accusations of usury. He also opened a centre for the distribution of free medicine to the poor, incurring the wrath of the Paris faculty of medicine, led by Patin, who called him *nebulo hebdomadarius*.

René (1802, in *Le *Génie du christianisme*; publ. separately 1805), a tale of great poetic beauty by Chateaubriand, originally intended (like *Atala) as part of *Les *Natchez*. René is a romantic, melancholy youth, brought up, like the author, in the deepest solitudes of nature in close companionship with an adored sister, Amélie. Realizing that her love for him is more than sisterly affection, Amélie takes desperate refuge in a convent. René learns the reason for her flight on the day she takes her vows. Grief and horror drive him to the wilds of America, where he tells his story to Chactas (*v. Atala*) and Père Souël, a missionary.

René incarnates all the vague, unsatisfied yearnings, the *mal du siècle, the passion for nature in its most melancholy and terrifying aspects, that typify early *Romanticism. Sainte-Beuve's reaction, 'René, c'est moi!', was shared by countless other young men.

René d'Anjou, DUC D'ANJOU and COMTE DE PROVENCE (1408–80), 'le bon roi René', titular king of Naples, the two Sicilies, and Jerusalem, a devotee of knight-errantry, tilting, and hunting, and a patron of writers (e.g. La Sale) and musicians. His court at Aix-en-Provence is described in Scott's *Anne of Geierstein*. His own literary works include *Regnault et Jehanneton*, a poem in the form of a pastoral celebrating his love for his second wife, Jeanne de Laval; the *Livre du cueur d'amour espris*, a romantic work in verse and prose. *v. Marguerite d'Anjou*.

Renée Mauperin (1864), a novel by the Goncourt brothers. The petted, attractive young Renée is too impulsive and credulous, a disturbingly incalculable member of her rich, conventional family. Her brother Henri, a calculating, pushing young man, long carries on a liaison with a rich neighbour's wife, then becomes engaged to the daughter. Shocked and disgusted at this, Renée stirs up trouble so successfully that he has to fight a duel and is killed. Stricken by remorse, she then goes into a decline and dies. The bereft parents seek consolation in travel.

Renoir, PIERRE-AUGUSTE (1841–1919), painter, one of the first *Impressionists.

Renouvier, CHARLES (1815–1903), philosopher. His system of Neo-criticism, or *Personnalisme*, gave a place to moral liberty and freedom of choice, making a rigidly scientific conception of the universe untenable. His influence was considerable *c.* 1870–90 when Positivism was losing ground. His works include his *Essais de critique générale* (1854–64; rev. and augm. till 1897, when they filled 13 vols.), one of the most important philosophical works of the 19th c.; *La Science de la morale* (1869); *Les Dilemmes de la métaphysique pure* and its sequel *Histoire et solution des problèmes métaphysiques* (both 1901); *Le Personnalisme* (1903), a final statement of his doctrines. He founded two famous journals, *L'Année philosophique* (1867–9) and *La Critique philosophique* (1872–9). The second carried articles on politics and religion as well as philosophy.

Renouvin, PIERRE (1893–1974), historian, professor at the *Sorbonne (1933–64). His works include *La Crise européenne et la Première Guerre mondiale (1904–1918)* (1948; 5th ed. 1969); vols. V–VIII (covering the period 1815–1945) of the *Histoire des relations internationales* (1953–8, 8 vols.), of which he was general editor; *Introduction à l'histoire des relations internationales* (1964; with J.-B. Duroselle); *L'Armistice de Réthondes* (1968).

Republican Calendar. This was introduced by a decree of 5 October 1793 and backdated to 22 September 1792, the first day of the First *Republic (*An I* thus ran from 22 Sept. 1792 to 21 Sept. 1793). It remained in force till 1 January 1806.

The aim was to break with the Christian traditions and nomenclature of the Gregorian Calendar (*v. Year*). The chronology of the Republican Calendar was the work of Romme. It usually began on 22 or 23 September (depending on the date of the autumnal equinox) and consisted of 12 months of 30 days, each month being divided into three *décades* (periods of ten days) instead of weeks. This left five intercalary days (six in a leap year), called *sans-culottides* and observed as national festivals. The task of renaming the months was entrusted to Fabre d'Églantine, who gave them their seasonal significance, as follows: *Vendémiaire, Brumaire, Frimaire*, the autumn months of vintage, mist, and frost; *Nivôse, Pluviôse, Ventôse*, the winter months of snow, rain, and tempest; *Germinal, Floréal, Prairial*, the spring months of seed-time, flowers, and meadows; *Messidor, Thermidor, Fructidor*, the summer months of harvest, heat, and fruit. The days were renamed *primidi, duodi, tridi, quartidi, quintidi, sextidi, septidi, octidi, nonidi, décadi* (the day of rest). The saints' days gave way to days named after metals, plants, agricultural implements, etc.

Republics

1. FIRST REPUBLIC. This was the outcome of the Revolution of 1789 and was proclaimed on 21 September 1792. It lasted till 18 May 1804, when Napoleon Bonaparte became emperor. It falls into three periods, those of the **Convention, *Directoire*, and **Consulat*. For fuller details *v. Revolutions*, 1.

2. SECOND REPUBLIC. This was proclaimed on 25 February 1848 and lasted till 2 December 1852. It was humanitarian and pacific in its ideals, but its leaders (*v. Revolutions*, 3) had no practical experience of government and were soon divided: some wanted to improve existing conditions, others to establish a new social order. The socialists had the upper hand at first, but at the elections for an **Assemblée constituante* (April 1848) the country showed its dislike of their measures, notably of the **ateliers nationaux*. The abolition of these brought

republican and socialist discontent to a head. Serious riots ensued, with four days of bitter street fighting (23–6 June 1848, *les journées de juin*). The government declared Paris in a state of siege, suppressed the rising with difficulty, and took very severe reprisals. The reactionary spirit triumphed and the class struggle became marked, the *bourgeoisie* and the peasants being ranged against the industrial workers. All three were disappointed with the Republic, with the result that Bonapartism gained ground (*v. Légende napoléonienne*).

The new constitution (voted 4 Nov. 1848) provided for an *Assemblée législative* and a President of the Republic with executive power (for a four-year term), both to be elected by universal manhood suffrage. The Bonapartist party, supported by the *parti de l'ordre* (the largest party in the country, bent on restoring 'moral order' and including **Légitimistes, *Orléanistes*, and Catholics), came forward with Louis-Napoléon Bonaparte (*v. Napoleon III*) as candidate for the presidency. He was elected Prince-President by a large majority (Dec. 1848) and swore fidelity to the Republic. In fact, he spent the next three years preparing for the *coup d'état* of 2 December 1851 (*v. Press*, 7; *Saint-Arnaud*) by which he abolished the *Assemblée législative* (which had been elected in May 1849). He followed this by a plebiscite on a limited franchise (14–21 Dec. 1851), when the electorate by an overwhelming majority empowered him to frame a new constitution (introduced 14 Jan. 1852), thus consolidating him in a position of absolute authority. A second, even more emphatic plebiscite (20 Nov. 1852) ratified a *sénatus-consulte* of 7 November re-establishing 'the imperial dignity in the person of Louis-Napoléon'. He was proclaimed emperor on 2 December 1852. (Flaubert's *L'*Éducation sentimentale*, **Ménard's Prologue d'une révolution*, Hugo's **Histoire d'un crime*, **Tocqueville's Souvenirs*, and G. Sand's *Souvenirs et idées* bring this period to life.)

3. THIRD REPUBLIC. This was proclaimed on 4 September 1870 (*v.*

Revolutions, 4) and lasted till 1940. For the period till May 1871 *v. Franco-Prussian War*; *Commune*, 2; *Gambetta*; *Thiers*. The government which signed the peace treaty with Germany (May 1871) had been elected in February 1871 and functioned as an *Assemblée nationale* until three constitutional laws, generally known as the constitution of 1875, definitely consolidated France as a republic. (There had been an abortive attempt to restore the monarchy in 1873; *v. Chambord*.) There were in all 14 Presidents of the Third Republic (elected for a seven-year term by the *Chambre des *Députés* and *Sénat* voting as one, and vested with executive powers): Thiers, in office 1871–3; Mac-Mahon, 1873–9; Jules Grévy, 1879–87 (re-elected 1885); Marie-François-Sadi Carnot, 1887–94 (assassinated); Jean Casimir-Périer, 1894–5; François-Félix Faure, 1895–9; Émile Loubet, 1899–1906; Armand Fallières, 1906–13; Raymond Poincaré, 1913–20; Paul-Eugène-Louis Deschanel, 1920 (resigned for reasons of health); Étienne-Alexandre Millerand, 1920–4; Gaston Doumergue, 1924–31; Paul Doumer, 1931–2 (assassinated); Albert Lebrun, 1932–40 (re-elected 1939; resigned July 1940).

Internally, the period between *c.* 1880 and the outbreak of the 1914–18 war was marked by *Boulangisme*, the *Panama scandal, and the *Dreyfus case; by a conflict between Church and State (esp. over education—a law of 1882 made primary education free, compulsory, and lay), culminating in the *loi de la séparation* (Dec. 1905) by which the Roman Catholic Church was disestablished and disendowed (*cf. Concordat*); by the rapid growth of Socialism, Trade Unionism, and Syndicalism (the *Confédération générale du Travail* or *C.G.T.*, the French equivalent of the Trades Union Congress, was formed in 1895; *v.* also *Jaurès*); and by heated polemical journalism (*v. Press*, 9). Externally, France's colonial expansion (1880–1900) was notable, also her restoration to the position of a great power. She concluded an alliance with Russia (1892) and the *Entente cordiale* with Britain (1904). The years immediately

before 1914 were clouded by the growing German menace (*v. Agadir*).

The 1914–18 war brought a progressive disruption of the country's ordered economy and great changes in the social fabric. (The war as a factor in accelerating and intensifying social change was studied by Proust in the last volume of *A la recherche du temps perdu*, a work of great interest for the social history of the Third Republic.)

The inter-war years were dominated by the precarious international situation, which bred general discontent, political instability, and spiritual malaise (all increasingly reflected in literature; *v. Novel*, 3). Internal dissension was increased by the fact that attempts by successive governments to introduce long overdue social reforms were hampered by considerations of national defence (esp. after the rise of Hitler). A split in the trade union movement (1922) led to the formation of the *Confédération générale du Travail unitaire* (*C.G.T.U.*) with a strong Communist bias. Many creative writers were attracted to Communism from now on (*v. Surrealism*); at the opposite extreme, the *Action française* had many adherents (and *v. Croix-de-Feu*). The 1930s, which saw the increasing political *engagement* of intellectuals (*v. Littérature engagée*), were marked by the influence of *Personnalisme* (*v. Mounier*), the rise of *négritude*, the *Stavisky scandal, the brief administration of the *Front populaire*, the profound impact of the Spanish Civil War (esp. on intellectuals, e.g. Bernanos, Malraux, S. Weil), and the Munich agreement with Hitler.

On 3 September 1939, France declared war on Germany. In May 1940, the Germans overran Holland and Belgium, broke through, as in 1870, at Sedan, and entered Paris (16 June). Paul Reynaud, then premier, resigned and was succeeded by Pétain (aged 84), who signed an armistice with Germany (22 June). On 9–10 July, a depleted *Assemblée nationale*, sitting at Vichy, voted a revision of the constitution which gave him special powers. These he used to constitute himself executive and legislative head of the State. June 1940 saw the birth of the *Resistance (v. Gaulle, C. de).

Novels depicting the social and political scene between 1870 and 1939 include (besides *A la recherche du temps perdu, mentioned above) works by Zola, Maupassant, and A. Daudet, *Barrès's Le Roman de l'énergie nationale, Rolland's *Jean-Christophe, Martin du Gard's Les *Thibault, Romains's Les *Hommes de bonne volonté, *Sartre's Les Chemins de la liberté. The moral and political climate of the war years is reflected in works ranging from M. *Bloch's L'Étrange Défaite and the *Resistance writings to *Vailland's Drôle de jeu and *Dutourd's Au bon beurre.

4. FOURTH REPUBLIC. This was officially inaugurated in January 1947 and ended in October 1958. It had existed provisionally since June 1944, when the Comité français de Libération nationale (formed in Algeria in 1943) became the Gouvernement provisoire de la République française (v. Gaulle, C. de). Two constituent assemblies were then elected to draft a new constitution, endorsed by a plebiscite of October 1946. This gave women the vote and provided for two elected bodies: an *Assemblée nationale and a *Conseil de la République. The Presidents of the Fourth Republic (elected for a seven-year term by the above bodies, voting as one) were Vincent Auriol, 1947–54; and René Coty, 1954–8. v. Diên Biên Phu; Poujadisme.

5. FIFTH REPUBLIC. This was inaugurated in October 1958. In May 1958, when army leaders in Algeria defied the government in Paris and France was threatened with civil war, de Gaulle was recalled to power, appointed prime minister (June), and vested with executive and legislative powers. He introduced a new constitution (endorsed by a plebiscite of Sept. 1958): executive power was to rest with the President (with wider powers than heretofore) and a prime minister appointed by him; legislative power with an *Assemblée nationale, elected by universal suffrage, and a *Sénat, indirectly elected. De Gaulle was elected President (Dec. 1958, for a seven-year term). The granting of independence to Algeria

(overwhelmingly endorsed by a plebiscite of April 1962, but bitterly opposed to the last by the 'Algérie française' lobby and the militant Organisation armée secrète, or O.A.S.) ended a long and divisive war (1954–62). De Gaulle was re-elected President in 1965 (by universal suffrage, following a revision of the constitution). He resigned in April 1969, midway through his second term, which saw the student rising of May 1968 (v. Universities, 1). He was succeeded (June 1969) by Georges Pompidou (1911–74), who died in office and was succeeded (May 1974) by Valéry Giscard d'Estaing (1926–) in turn succeeded (May 1981) by François Mitterrand (1916–).

République, Six Livres de la, v. Bodin.

République française, La, (1) a daily f. 1848 (v. Press, 7) to air the new doctrines of socialism (e.g. free education, electoral reform, and a better life for the workers)—contributors included G. Sand and Bastiat; (2) the organ (f. 1871) of Gambetta's parliamentary group, sometimes called Le Journal des Débats de la démocratie.

Réquisitionnaire, Le, v. Comédie humaine, La (Études philosophiques).

Resistance, The, the term applied to the underground opposition to the Germans, in both Occupied and Unoccupied France (the latter under Pétain), from the fall of France in May 1940 until the Liberation in June 1944. For historical works on the Resistance v. Michel, H. The present article is no more than a brief survey of the part played by men of letters within France, and it should be remembered that millions of patriots were inspired and sustained from without by the example, indeed the very existence, of the Free French forces led by de Gaulle; by B.B.C. broadcasts in French from London, notably 'Les Français parlent aux Français' (v. Saint-Denis); and by the writings and patriotic activities of those intellectuals who spent all or part of this period in voluntary exile, e.g. Jouve in Switzerland, Bernstein, Green, Maritain, Maurois, Romains, Saint-Exupéry (later to die in action), and Saint-John Perse in the U.S.A., Bernanos (who had left in 1938) and Supervielle in S. America, Aron, Saint-Denis, S. Weil, and others in England. It should also be noted that some writers were in enemy hands, e.g. P. de La Tour du Pin, Cayrol, Gascar, Frénaud.

Within France, the Unoccupied Zone naturally became the resort of 'résistants' of all kinds, though the dangers increased after November 1942, when the Germans moved in. Some writers fought with the nation-wide network of guerrilla groups known as the *maquis* (the name for the Corsican bush, the traditional resort of outlaws), e.g. Chamson, Char, Jean Cassou (*v.* below), Malraux, and the essayist and novelist Jean Prévost (1901–44), who was killed in the Vercors, a wooded plateau in the Alps (Drôme and Isère) which was a centre of the movement. Many more engaged in intellectual resistance through their writings and, whether or not they were active in other ways (as they often were), risked arrest for involvement with clandestine publications. Early in 1942, a group including Paulhan (who had already been arrested—and released at the instigation of Drieu la Rochelle—for issuing clandestine papers), the novelist Pierre de Lescure (1891–1963), 'Jacques Decour' (pseudonym of Daniel Decourdemanche, 1910–42, teacher and author), the writer and politician Jacques Debu-Bridel (1902–), and Vildrac, all members of the newly formed *Comité national des écrivains* (or *C.N.E.*), attempted to launch an organ for 'free' writers, *Les *Lettres françaises*. Decour wrote a manifesto for the first issue, but he was arrested and shot (30 May) and the copy was destroyed. The first mimeographed number appeared in September 1942 and in October 1943 it became a printed review. Contributors, who used pseudonyms, included Aragon, Éluard, the poet Jean Lescure (1912–), the critic and poet Louis Parrot (1906–48), Mauriac, and Sartre. It was also in 1942 that P. de Lescure and Debu-Bridel launched the *Éditions de minuit* with *Le Silence de la mer* by 'Vercors' (pseudonym of the novelist and essayist Jean Bruller,

1902–), a tale which caused a sensation at the time, for it depicted the dilemma of a 'good' German officer. Forty volumes appeared before the Liberation, including works by Aragon (*Le Musée Grévin*), Benda, the art critic and novelist Jean Cassou (1897– ; *33 Sonnets composés au secret*), Gide, Mauriac (*Le Cahier noir*), Paulhan, E. Triolet and also *L'Honneur des poètes* (a notable collection of verse by 22 poets, which was organized by J. Lescure and Éluard). The poets, above all, and, in particular, Aragon, Éluard, Desnos, Jouve, and Emmanuel (one of a host of young poets who emerged at this time), bore inspiring witness to their patriotism, love of liberty, and concern for human dignity. Two reviews call for special mention: *Poésie 40, 41*, etc. (a continuation of *Poètes casqués*, f. 1939; it appeared monthly and survived till 1949), founded, and edited at Villeneuve-lès-Avignon, by the poet and publisher Pierre Seghers (1906–), a friend of Éluard (with whom, in May 1944, he launched the series *Poètes d'aujourd'hui*) and of Desnos; and *Messages*, conducted by J. Lescure and others, which published work by poets including Emmanuel, Follain, Masson, Ponge, and Queneau, and a special number, *Domaine français*, with contributions from a wide range of 'free' writers, including, besides many already mentioned, Camus, Claudel, and Duhamel (who, as perpetual secretary of the *Académie, was instrumental, with Valéry and others, in suspending elections to that body until the Liberation). Many of the other literary reviews associated with the intellectual resistance were published, like *Poésie 40*, in the Unoccupied Zone, or outside France, e.g. *Confluences* (Lyons), *Positions* (Saint-Étienne), *Pyrénées* (Toulouse), the *Cahiers du sud* (Marseilles), *Fontaine* (Algiers), the *Cahiers du Rhône* (a Swiss review, f. by Béguin). Another important centre of resistance in the Unoccupied Zone was Dieulefit (Drôme), where Mounier (and others associated with his review *Esprit*) and creative writers including Emmanuel found refuge. *v. Lyric Poetry*, 4.

The many intellectuals who died in consequence of their Resistance activities, and/or of their Jewish birth, included, besides those already mentioned, M. Bloch, Desnos, M. Jacob, and numerous Communists (e.g. the philosopher Georges Politzer, who was shot with Decour).

With regard to the various writers branded as *collaborateurs*, a distinction is often made between those who rallied to Pétain as 'le plus Français des Français' (Maurras) and who were anti-democratic and/or anti-Semitic rather than pro-German, and the very few who were actively pro-German, e.g. Drieu la Rochelle, Châteaubriant, the critic and novelist Robert Brasillach (tried and executed in 1945), and Rebatet. *v. Press*, 9.

Rességuier, BERNARD-MARIE-JULES, COMTE DE (1789–1862), a minor, very early *Romantic, author of verse and one novel (*Almaria*, 1835); also a *Légitimiste*.

Restif (or Rétif) de la Bretonne, NICOLAS-EDME (1734–1806), novelist, son of a peasant and himself a working printer, wrote some 250 volumes of realistic, didactic romances, of little literary merit, but providing a keenly observed picture of the life of peasants and of women of the humbler classes in the 18th c., e.g. *Le Paysan perverti* (1775; the tragic tale of a young peasant corrupted by the evil influences of Paris), *La Paysanne pervertie* (1776), *La Vie de mon père* (1779), *Les Contemporaines* (1780–5), *Monsieur Nicolas* (1796–7). His work was admired by contemporaries, though some thought it marred by melodrama, obscenities, and a coarse style. *v. Novel*, 2.

Restoration, The. After Napoleon's first abdication (1814) there were two periods of restored *Bourbon monarchy: April 1814 till March 1815 and June 1815 till July 1830. For details *v. Napoleon*; *Louis XVIII*; *Charles X*; *Revolutions*, 2.

Retour de l'enfant prodigue, Le, v. Gide.

Retour des cendres, *v. Légende napoléonienne.*

Retté, ADOLPHE (1863–1930), *Symbolist poet, edited *La *Vogue* and *L'*Ermitage* and wrote much about the theories of Symbolism and the *vers libre* (notably an essay on rhythm in poetry, first publ. in the *Mercure de France* and later included in his reminiscences—*Le Symbolisme*, 1903). His collections of verse include *Une Belle Dame passa* (1893); *L'Archipel en fleurs* (1895); *Campagne première* (1897); and the more exclusively nature poems of *Lumières tranquilles* (1901) and *Dans la forêt* (1903). Later, after his conversion to Roman Catholicism, he wrote sentimental religious prose, also further reminiscences.

Retz or Rais, GILLES DE (*c.* 1396–1440), *maréchal de France*, fought at the side of Joan of Arc against the English. Later, he engaged in necromancy and was executed for kidnapping and murdering children. In the folklore of Brittany, where he had estates, he is identified with Bluebeard—though he had only one wife, who left him.

Retz, PAUL DE GONDI, CARDINAL DE (1613–79), a man who, without the least vocation, became archbishop of Paris (1654–62; in succession to his uncle, to whom he was coadjutor from 1643) and a cardinal (1652). He aspired to become a minister of Louis XIV, but had a weakness for intrigue and was active in the *Fronde*. He was afterwards imprisoned, but escaped and was pardoned (1662) on condition he resigned his see. He was esteemed and defended by Mme de Sévigné and was fond of her daughter (who did not return his affection). His *Conjuration de Fiesque* (1655) is an account, written in youth, of the conspiracy of Fiesco of Genoa against Andrea Doria. His *Mémoires* (1717) are a lucid and vivacious, if unreliable, account of his chequered career and political events in which he was involved. They contain many incisive portraits (Condé, Turenne, etc.) and aphorisms worthy of La Rochefoucauld. *v. Joly.*

Revanche, La, *v. Ligue des patriotes;* Boulanger, G.

Rêve, Le, *v. Rougon-Macquart, Les.*

Rêve de d'Alembert, Le, *v. Diderot.*

Réveil, Le, *v. Press,* 8.

Revenons à nos moutons, *v. Pathelin.*

Reverdie, *v. Chansons à personnages.*

Reverdy, PIERRE (1889–1960), poet. From 1910, he moved in *Cubist circles in Paris, published verse (e.g. *La Lucarne ovale,* 1916), and founded the review *Nord-Sud* (1917–19), which brought together the future *Surrealists. He was a solitary man, haunted by spiritual doubt, and after 1919 he took little active part in literary movements, though he shed light on the aims and methods of the Surrealists (in *Le Gant de crin,* 1927) and they greatly admired his work. From 1926, he led a retired and ascetic life near the Abbey of Solesmes, vainly seeking a solution through religious faith. Having published such collections as *Les Épaves du ciel* (1924) and *Ferraille* (1937), he collected his poems (in the *vers libre) and prose poems in *Plupart du temps* (1945) and *Main-d'œuvre* (1949). Shorn of all ornament, at times poignantly lyrical, and unified by muted anguish and a sense of desolation, they are, in his own words, like 'cristaux déposés après l'effervescent contact de l'esprit avec la réalité'. *Le Gant de crin* (1927), *Le Livre de mon bord* (1948), and *En vrac* (1956) are prose works containing his reflections on life and literature.

Rêveries du promeneur solitaire, Les (1782), by J.-J. Rousseau, 10 meditations on various phases of his life, written in his last years. They contain some of his most pleasing pages, especially the third (on his early years and mental development) and the fifth (describing his stay on the island of Saint-Pierre in the Lake of Bienne).

Reviews, *v. Periodicals and Reviews.*

Révolte des anges, La, *v. France, A.*

Revolutionary Calendar, *v. Republican Calendar.*

Revolutions. There were four major revolutions in France between 1789 and 1870: (1) the great Revolution of 1789 (always called the *Révolution* or the *Révolution française,* with no other distinguishing adjective, and referred to in the present volume as 'the Revolution'), which shattered the absolute monarchy and ended the *ancien régime;* (2) the 1830 or July Revolution (*Révolution du 29 juillet*), which overthrew Charles X; (3) the 1848 or February Revolution (*Révolution du 24 février*), which overthrew Louis-Philippe; (4) the 1870 or September Revolution (*Révolution du 4 septembre*), which overthrew Napoleon III.

1. REVOLUTION OF 1789. The Revolutionary era began in the summer of 1789 and lasted until the establishment of the *Consulat* in December 1799. During this period many thousands of aristocrats and Royalists were executed, fled from France (*v. Coblenz; Hamburg*), or went into hiding; *v. Armée des émigrés.* The following is a summary of the main sequence of events. For members of the royal family in 1789 *v. Bourbon;* for historical studies of the period *v. History,* 4; for periodicals *v. Press,* 2 and 3.

1789. 5 May: The *États généraux,* convoked to decide on reforms of taxation, meet at Versailles and at once disagree. The *Privilégiés* insist that each order should deliberate separately; the *Tiers État* holds that reform is possible only if they deliberate and vote together. 17 June: The *Tiers État,* now self-styled *Assemblée nationale,* constitutes itself the controlling body for purposes of taxation. 20 June: The *Assemblée nationale,* excluded by royal command from the building intended for meetings of the combined orders, retires to the *Salle du Jeu de *Paume* and swears (*Serment du Jeu de Paume*) not to dissolve till it has framed a constitution. 23 June: Louis XVI, addressing a special session of the combined *États généraux,* declares that the recent decisions of the *Assemblée* *nationale* are null, and orders the whole assembly to disperse and to resume sittings the next day to consider his own programme of ineffective reforms. The *Tiers État* (*Assemblée nationale*) refuses to obey, and Mirabeau declares: 'Nous sommes ici par la volonté du peuple et... on ne nous arrachera que par la force des baïonnettes.' 9 July: The *Assemblée nationale*, reinforced by a majority of the clergy and a minority of the nobles, calls itself the *Assemblée constituante* and begins to frame a constitution. This marks the end of the absolute monarchy. 12 July: Desmoulins calls on the people of Paris to rise. 14 July: The people take the *Bastille*. The *Commune de Paris* is set up. The *Assemblée constituante* undertakes the drafting of the *Déclaration des droits de l'homme*. 15 July: The king adopts the *tricolore* and agrees to the new order. 27 Aug.: The *Assemblée constituante* votes the *Déclaration des droits de l'homme*, which the king, holding to his right of *véto*, refuses to sanction till 5 October. 5 Oct.: A mob (mainly women) marches from Paris to Versailles and forces the royal family to return to the *Tuileries. 16 Oct.: The *Assemblée constituante* moves from Versailles to Paris.

1790. 14 July: The first *Fête de la *Fédération*. King and nation swear fidelity to the new order.

1791. 21–4 June: Measures such as the confiscation of the *biens nationaux* and the *Constitution civile du clergé* have increased the king's hostility to the *Assemblée*. The royal family attempt to escape from Paris, but are arrested at Varennes, and brought back. The *Assemblée*'s decree suspending the king from his functions splits the Revolutionary party into Republicans (at first the minority) and constitutional monarchists. 3 Sept.: The *Assemblée* votes the *constitution. Both Royalists and extreme Republicans dislike it. 14 Sept.: The king swears to uphold it and is re-established as a constitutional monarch. 1 Oct.: The *Assemblée législative* succeeds the *Assemblée constituante*, and at first strongly favours a constitutional monarchy.

1792. 20 April: The *Assemblée* declares war on Austria, forestalling the attack of Austro-Prussian forces bent on restoring the king's authority. This marks the beginning of the Revolutionary wars, which will lead on to the Napoleonic wars (*v. Coalitions*). 10 July: The *Assemblée* declares 'la patrie en danger' owing to increasing pressure on the Revolutionary armies by foreign forces and the *Armée des émigrés*. National defence is organized. Discontent now grows, largely over the king's refusal to sanction the *Assemblée*'s decrees. The movement to depose him gathers strength. 10 Aug.: The monarchy falls. The people of Paris, aided by provincial detachments of the *Garde nationale* (esp. by the *fédérés* from Marseilles; *v. Marseillaise*), storm *Tuileries. The *Assemblée* deprives the king of his powers, assumes executive functions, and summons the country to elect a *Convention nationale* to frame a new constitution. The royal family are imprisoned in the *Temple, and a temporary Revolutionary government is formed with Danton at its head (*v. Commune, 1; Bonnet rouge*). 2–5 Sept.: The continuing defeats of the Revolutionary armies are attributed to Royalist treason. The people invade the prisons (e.g. the *Prison de l'*Abbaye*; the *Salpêtrière*) and kill over 1,200 prisoners (*les massacres de septembre*, instigated by the *septembriseurs*—notably Marat). 20 Sept.: Defeat of the Prussians at *Valmy. 21 Sept.: The *Convention nationale* succeeds the *Assemblée législative* and decrees the abolition of the monarchy. 22 Sept.: First day of the *Republic. The struggle between the different factions in the *Convention* now begins (*v. Cordeliers; Girondins; Jacobins; Montagnards*). Oct.: *Comité de sûreté générale* established. 11 Dec.–20 Jan. 1793: Trial of Louis XVI

1793. 21 Jan.: Execution of Louis XVI. From now on the power of the *Montagnards* increases. 11 March: *Tribunal révolutionnaire* established. 6 April: *Comité de salut public* established. 31 May–2 June: An organized insurrection in the *Convention* overthrows the *Girondins*; their leaders are arrested or flee. 13 July: Marat is assassinated. July:

Robespierre comes to full power. 10 Aug.: As Paris celebrates the inauguration of the new constitution (voted 23 June) the *Convention* renders it void by deciding not to dissolve till the wars are over. 17 Sept.: The *Convention* passes the *loi des suspects*, ordering the arrest of everyone suspected of disloyalty to the Revolution, and the *Terror begins. 5 Oct.: *Republican Calendar introduced. 10 Oct.: A Revolutionary government is established by decree of the *Convention*, the supreme authorities being the *Convention*, its commissaries, the *Comité de sûreté générale*, the *Comité de salut public*, and the *Tribunal révolutionnaire*. 16 Oct.: Execution of Marie-Antoinette. 31 Oct.: Execution of *Girondins* (inc. Brissot); more will die in the coming months. During the winter of 1793–4 the Revolutionary armies are victorious, but at home Robespierre's policy is opposed by both the *Hébertistes and Danton and his party (the *Indulgents*).

1794. 13 March–5 April: *Hébertistes* (inc. Hébert himself) and *Indulgents* (inc. Danton, Fabre d'Églantine, and Desmoulins) arrested and executed. 5 May: *Culte de l'*Être Suprême* instituted. Opposition to Robespierre becomes marked. 10 June (*le 22 prairial*): By the *loi du 22 prairial* the trial of suspects becomes purely nominal, and the Terror reaches its height. Opposition to Robespierre mounts. 27 July (*le 9 thermidor*): Robespierre falls. 28 July: He and his followers (inc. Saint-Just and Couthon) are executed.

1794 (Aug.)–1795 (Oct.). The period of *la réaction thermidorienne*, consequent upon the fall of Robespierre. The extreme Revolutionaries are in retreat and many surviving moderates return to Paris. 12 Nov.: *Club des Jacobins* closed. May (1795): There are Royalist risings in the provinces (brutally suppressed; *v. Chouannerie*; *Vendée*; *Terreur blanche*) and in Paris. 22 Aug.: The *Convention* presents a new constitution providing for government by a *Directoire*. The Revolutionary armies remain victorious and France's frontiers are extended. 5–12 Oct.: Resentment at the prolonged

existence of the *Convention* leads to risings against it, notably that of 5 October (*le 13 vendémiaire*), one of the bloodiest of the period, suppressed by the prompt action of the young Napoleon Bonaparte. 26 Oct. (*le 4 brumaire*): The *Convention*, meeting for the last time before giving way to the *Directoire, decrees a general amnesty for anti-Revolutionary acts, except those of deported priests, *émigrés*, and *vendémiaires* (*v.* above); capital punishment is abolished (*v. Place de la Concorde*).

1795 (Oct.)–1799. The *Directoire* is feeble and divided; famine and bankruptcy threaten, and the country is scandalized by the profligacy of a section of the *nouveaux riches* and returned nobility (*v. Incroyables*; *Merveilleuses*; *Muscadins*; *Press*, 3). Republics on the French model are set up in the conquered territories of Holland, Switzerland, and Italy. Other European states grow alarmed. Bonaparte comes to the fore. By November 1799 the *Directoire* has brought France to the brink of disaster. On 9 November (*le 18 brumaire*) Bonaparte seizes the military command of Paris. A provisional government is formed (10 Nov.), and on 13 December (*le 22 frimaire*) a new constitution, the result of a plebiscite of the electorate, establishes the *Consulat.

2. REVOLUTION OF 1830. Discontent with the government of Charles X came to a head in 1829 when he dissolved the *Chambre des *Députés* for attacking his reactionary policy. The electorate returned a new Chamber with a much larger opposition party, whereupon, disregarding the theory of ministerial responsibility, the king issued *ordonnances* (26 July 1830) which again dissolved the Chamber, ended representative government by changing the electoral law, and violated the *Charte of 1814 by abolishing the liberty of the Press. There was immediate resistance from journalists (*v. Press*, 5), politicians, and the people of Paris. Street rioting, which turned to fighting, began on 27 July and lasted for three days (*les trois glorieuses*). Charles X then abdicated in favour of his young grandson (*v. Chambord*). At this stage, the

Orléaniste faction of the opposition, exploiting a victory largely won by the Republicans, engineered the establishment of a constitutional monarchy (7 Aug.), with Louis-Philippe as king.

3. REVOLUTION OF 1848. This had direct causes in general discontent with the government of Louis-Philippe (esp. with its refusal to introduce measures of democratic reform), and in acute food shortages (1845–7), which had already led to risings in the provinces. In a wider sense, it was a manifestation of the socialistic ideas that had for some years been fermenting all over Europe, also a symptom of the growing awareness, among a working class partly created and now menaced by industrialism, of the importance of the individual's right to work and social security. *v. Press*, 6.

Rioting began on 22 February, following the government's prohibition, backed by a display of military force, of a patriotic *banquet*. It took a serious turn on the night of 23 February, and on 24 February Louis-Philippe abdicated in favour of his 10-year-old grandson, the comte de Paris. The insurgents, rejecting the comte, invaded the *Chambre des *Députés* and successfully demanded a provisional government. This was headed by the poet Lamartine and included the *savant* Arago, the politician Alexandre-Auguste Ledru-Rollin (1807–74), and, before long, the socialist Blanc. The Second *Republic was proclaimed on 25 February.

4. REVOLUTION OF 1870. Discontent with the *régime* of Napoleon III came to a head in the first month of the *Franco-Prussian war. After Sedan (1 Sept. 1870) the Second Empire crumbled. On 4 September, a crowd headed by the Republican leaders Gambetta and Jules Favre (1809–80) interrupted a session of the *Corps législatif*, then proceeded to the *Hôtel de Ville* and proclaimed the Third *Republic. There was no bloodshed. Until mid-February 1871 the country was kept going by an improvised *gouvernement de la Défense nationale* (all moderate Republicans). It sat partly in Paris and partly in delegation at Tours, with Louis-

Jules Trochu (1815–96), military governor of Paris, as premier. *v. Press*, 8 and 9.

Révolutions de France et de Brabant, Les (1789–91 and, as *La Semaine politique et littéraire*, 1791–2), a weekly f. by Desmoulins and widely read because of his stirring articles. It had some illustrations, mainly caricatures.

Révolutions de Paris, Les (1789–94), one of the most widely read Revolutionary journals (about 50 pp. octavo, with topical engravings—e.g. small maps of the new *départements*), f. by Louis-Marie Prudhomme (1752–1830), publisher and journalist. Its success was largely due to fervently idealistic articles by Loustalot.

Revue blanche, La (1891–1903), a *Symbolist review, f. by Alexandre Natanson. Contributors included Mallarmé, H. de Régnier, Vielé-Griffin, Blum (literary and dramatic critic), Debussy (music critic). It was one of the first reviews to introduce Ibsen and Tolstoy to French readers.

Revue britannique, La (1825–1902), a review which at first published translations and abstracts of articles from English reviews, then widened its scope to include original work in English and other foreign languages. *v. Pichot.*

Revue critique d'histoire et de littérature, La (1866–1935), a learned journal f. by Paul Meyer and G. Paris.

Revue de linguistique romane (1925– ; twice a year), a learned philological journal.

Revue de littérature comparée (1921– ; quarterly), a learned literary journal.

Revue de métaphysique et de morale 1893– ; quarterly), a leading philosophical journal.

Revue de Paris, La, (1) a mainly literary

review (1829–45; 1851–8); f. by Véron, partly with a view to helping unknown writers. Contributors included B. Constant, Musset, Vigny, Mérimée, Sainte-Beuve. It was the first literary review to serialize novels (v. *Roman-feuilleton*; *Madame Bovary*); (2) a literary review (1894–1970; monthly).

Revue des Deux Mondes, La, f. 1829 as a review largely devoted to home and foreign affairs, was acquired in 1831 by François Buloz (1803–77), sometime editor of the *Revue de Paris and director of the *Comédie-Française. He developed its literary and philosophical sides and made it one of the best periodicals of its kind in Europe (publ. fortnightly from 1832). Early contributors included Balzac, Hugo, Musset, Vigny, G. Sand, Sainte-Beuve, Mérimée. It survives (merged with *Hommes et Mondes* in 1956) as the *Nouvelle Revue des Deux Mondes* (monthly).

Revue des langues romanes (1870– ; twice a year), a learned philological journal.

Revue d'histoire littéraire de la France (1894– ; quarterly), the organ of the *Société d'histoire littéraire.*

Revue du Monde noir, La, v. *Négritude.*

Revue encyclopédique, La, (1) a popular literary and scientific review (1819–35), f. by Jullien de Paris (and v. *Leroux, P.*); (2) an encyclopedic review (1891–1900), became the *Revue universelle* (1901–5), then *Larousse mensuel* (1907–37).

Revue fantaisiste, La, v. *Parnassiens.*

Revue française, La (1823–30), an organ of the *doctrinaires, f. on the English model by Guizot; a leading review of the Restoration period, devoted to philosophy, history, political economy, and criticism.

Revue historique (1876– ; quarterly), a learned historical journal, f. by Monod.

Revue indépendante, La, (1) a literary and socialist review (1841–7; fortnightly), f. by P. Leroux, G. Sand, and Louis Viardot (1800–95); (2) a review (1884–95) devoted to literature, the arts, and (at first) politics. There were four series. During the third (1886–9; ed. by Dujardin and Fénéon) it became a leading *Symbolist review. Contributors included Barrès, Laforgue, Mallarmé (dramatic criticism, also *Prose (pour des Esseintes)), Moréas, Wyzewa (on the Russian novel).

Revue parisienne, La (1840; 3 nos. only), a review of which Balzac was part-founder and sole editor. He contributed tales (inc. *Z. Marcas), a savage attack on Sainte-Beuve's *Port-Royal, and a discerning, appreciative study of Stendhal's *La Chartreuse de Parme.*

Revue philosophique de la France et de l'étranger (1876– ; quarterly), a leading philosophical journal, f. by Ribot.

Revue universelle, La, (1) v. *Revue encyclopédique* (2); (2) a review (1920–44) f. by Bainville (editor 1920–36) and Massis (editor 1936–44) and supported by intellectuals of the *Action française.*

Revue wagnérienne, La (1885–8), a literary and musical review f. by Dujardin and others. It reflected the *Symbolists' cult of Wagner. Mallarmé contributed sonnets and the article *Richard Wagner, rêveries d'un poète français;* and v. *Wyzewa.*

Rey, MARC-MICHEL (18th c.), a publisher at Amsterdam, printed most of the works of J.-J. Rousseau and d'Holbach.

Reybaud, MARIE-ROCH-LOUIS (1799–1879), man of letters and publicist, remembered for his novel *Jérôme Paturot à la recherche d'une position sociale* (1843), a satire on life under the July Monarchy. After unsatisfactory experiences as a *Romantic poet, a *Saint-Simonien, a company-promoter, etc., the hero returns to the prosperous but unexciting family business of selling cotton nightcaps.

Jérôme Paturot à la recherche de la meilleure des républiques (1848), a sequel, was less successful.

Reynaud, JEAN (1806–63), a philosopher whose chief work, *Terre et ciel* (1854), influenced Hugo.

Rhadamiste et Zénobie, a tragedy by the elder Crébillon; produced 1711.

The complicated, melodramatic plot turns on the struggle for the hand of Zénobie (daughter of Mithridate, king of Armenia) between her cousin Rhadamiste, his brother Arsame (whom she loves), and their father Pharasmane (Mithridate's brother). Finally, Pharasmane, horrified at having unwittingly killed Rhadamiste, yields Zénobie to Arsame.

Rhétoriqueurs, Les, a school of poets which flourished, especially in Burgundy, in the later 15th and early 16th cs., occupying the interval between Charles d'Orléans and Clément Marot. The *grands rhétoriqueurs* (some of whom were also chroniclers) included Chastellain, Molinet, Meschinot, La Marche, O. de Saint-Gelais, Crétin, J. Marot, Gringore, J. Bouchet, and—the best of them—Lemaire de Belges. The characteristics of the school (already present in some degree in writers of the preceding period, e.g. Guillaume de Machaut) were a lack of sincere emotion, neglect or contempt of nature, undiscriminating admiration of Latin literature, a tendency to moralize on outworn themes (largely taken from Jean de Meung's *Roman de la Rose), and frequent use of allegory, dreams, and mythology for didactic purposes. The *rhétoriqueurs* were often pretentious and inclined to intellectual arrogance. The types of poems they affected were the *doctrinal* (purely didactic), the *débat* (*v. Dit*), the *complainte* or *déploration* (dirge), the *testament*, the *blason* (a minute description of the qualities of an object). They paid special attention to metrical technique and complication of rhyme, and greatly elaborated the *fixed forms of verse (Molinet lists 19 of these).

Rhin, Le (1842, 2 vols.; rev. and augm. 1845), by Hugo, a work based on descriptive letters written to his wife during his visits to the Rhineland in 1839–40. He padded it with history and legend (notably the medieval *Légende du beau Pécopin et de la belle Bauldour*, which he invented), then added a conclusion of much topical and political interest (*cf. Rhin allemand, Le*)—a study of the balance of power in Europe from the 17th c., with a proposal of his own for a policy of mutual aid and concession between France and Germany, with a view to an alliance and so to peace in Europe.

Rhin allemand, Le (1841), a satirical poem by Musset in reply to a provocative *Hymn of the Rhine* (1840) by the German poet Becker. Each verse of Becker's poem began 'Ils ne l'auront pas, le libre Rhin allemand' (in the French trans.); the first few verses of Musset's reply began 'Nous l'avons eu, votre Rhin allemand'. Lamartine also replied, on more dignified, humanitarian lines (*La Marseillaise de la paix*, in the *Revue des Deux Mondes, 1841). *Cf. Rhin, Le.*

Rhône, Le, one of the four great rivers of France.

Rhumbs (1926), by Valéry, a collection of *pensées*, aphorisms, etc. Explaining his use of the navigational term *rhumb*, Valéry says: 'Comme l'aiguille du compas demeure assez constante tandis que la route varie: aussi peut-on regarder les... applications successives de notre pensée... comme des écarts définis par contraste avec je ne sais quelle constante dans l'intention profonde et essentielle de l'esprit.'

Rhyme, *v. Versification.*

Ribot, THÉODULE (1839–1916), an influential philosopher, founder of the *Revue philosophique de la France et de l'étranger. His work lay mainly in the fields of psychology and (latterly) psychopathology. He established experimental psychology as an independent science in France, holding that it should be studied objectively, like the natural sciences, and had nothing to do with metaphysical enquiry into the nature of the soul. His works include *La Psychologie anglaise contemporaine* (1870), which has a notable introduction and reflects the influence on him of such 18th- and 19th-c. English philosophers as Hartley, J. S. Mill, Herbert Spencer, and Bain; *Essai sur l'imagination créatrice* (1900).

Rica, *v. Lettres persanes.*

Ricard, Louis-Xavier de (1843–1911), founder, with Mendès, of the **Parnassien* group of poets (who first met in the **salon* of his mother, the marquise de Ricard) and of short-lived reviews (*v. Parnassiens*). His collections include *Les Chants de l'aube* (1862).

Ricardou, Jean, *v. Nouveau roman.*

Riccoboni, Marie-Jeanne Laboras de Mézières, Mme (1713–92), wrote sentimental romances (*Ernestine, Le Marquis de Crécy*, etc.) and a conclusion to Marivaux's *La Vie de *Marianne.*

Richard I Cœur de Lion (1157–99), king of England (1189–99), was the author of two extant **serventois*. One of these, written during his imprisonment and lamenting his fate, is of historical interest. *v. Blondel de Nesle.*

Richard, Jean-Pierre, *v. Critics and Criticism*, 3.

Richard Cœur de Lion, *v. Sedaine.*

Richard de Fournival, *v. Bestiaire.*

Richelet, César-Pierre, *v. Dictionaries*, 1680.

Richelieu, Armand du Plessis, cardinal de (1585–1642), the great minister of Louis XIII. The son of a gentleman of Poitou, he came to the fore as bishop of Luçon at the **États généraux*

of 1614, entered the council of Marie de Médicis *c*. 1616, and was chief minister from 1624. He effected the ruin of the **Huguenot cause in France, consolidated the autocratic power of the monarchy, and extended the frontiers of France at the expense of Austria. He left a *Testament politique*, which depicts his character and policy, and *Mémoires* (compiled by others), which reproduce in part his own reports to the king. These, and his letters and State papers, testify to his remarkable political ability, but show no great literary talent. Nevertheless, he interested himself in literature, founded the **Académie française* (and invited it to pass judgement on Le **Cid*; *v. Corneille*), and employed five authors to write plays under his direction (*v. Cinq auteurs*). With some help from Desmarets de Saint-Sorlin, he wrote a mediocre tragicomedy, *Mirame*, and had it produced in a hall of the **Palais-Royal specially built for the purpose (and later used by Molière's company).

Richelieu, Armand, duc de (1696–1788), great-nephew of the above, **maréchal de France*. He fought at **Fontenoy and took Port-Mahon (1756), but was above all noted for his gallantries. Memoirs of his life, depicting the depraved courts of the Regent and Louis XV, were compiled from his notes by Jean-Louis Soulavie (1753–1813), a literary abbé of doubtful reputation.

Richepin, Jean (1849–1926), poet and dramatist, became known with *La Chanson des gueux* (1876), poems about tramps and vagrants, using their cant with much verbal dexterity. *Les Caresses* (1877), *Les Blasphèmes* (1884), and *Interludes* (1922) were poems of much the same type. His real success came from his plays, usually in verse: *La Glu* (1883), *Nana Sahib* (1883), *Le Flibustier* (1888), *Par le glaive* (1892; a heroic drama), *Le Chemineau* (1897; a drama of country life, highly popular in its day).

Richeut, a satirical narrative poem, written *c*. 1170; often described as the earliest **fabliau*.

Richeut, a successful and unscrupulous courtesan, trains her son Samson so well that he becomes as great a scourge to women as she is to men—with the result that she is irked by his reputation and contrives, by humiliating him, to prove the superior cunning of women.

Rictus, Jehan, *pseudonym of* GABRIEL RANDON (1867–1938), who wrote poems and ballads of Parisian low life (*Soliloques du pauvre*, 1897; *Les Doléances*, 1899; *Les Cantilènes du malheur*, 1902; *Le Cœur populaire*, 1914), slangy, elliptic, and often genuinely moving.

Ridadondaine, La, a name for the *Théâtre de la *Foire*.

Rideau cramoisi, Le, *v. Diaboliques, Les*.

Rigaud, HYACINTHE RIGAU Y ROS, *known as* (1659–1743), painter, notably of portraits of Louis XIV, Bossuet, Boileau, La Fontaine, etc.

Rigolboche, *stage-name of* MARGUERITE BADEL, a popular variety actress of mid-19th-c. Paris.

Rimbaud, ARTHUR (1854–91), a poet of precocious genius and violent, unstable character who began to write at 15, abandoned literature for a life of action some five (or possibly ten) years later, and died at 37, unaware that he had become a master for the Symbolists. He is now recognized as one of the strongest influences on modern, and not only French, poetry (*v. Symbolism; Surrealism; Lyric Poetry*, 4).

He was born at Charleville in the Ardennes and brought up, with his brother and sisters, by his mother, a dour woman of peasant stock. His father, an able and highly intelligent army officer, had forsaken the home. He was star pupil at the *Collège de Charleville*, but in August 1870, excited by the outbreak of the *Franco-Prussian war and by revolutionary ideas, and irked by a repressive family environment, he ran

away to Paris. He was arrested for travelling without a ticket and sent home. Ten days later he ran away to Belgium (and wrote some of his first original poems), but again had to return home. A second brief flight to Paris coincided with the German entry into the city (March 1871). After this he was at home again, a defiant, unruly adolescent, reading feverishly in the public library, writing poetry, and already forming his poetic doctrine, the *théorie du voyant*. He decided that the poet, to get beyond good and evil, and express the inexpressible, must develop his creative faculty by experimenting with evil and with self-induced states of delirium. In the late summer of 1871 he sent some verses to Verlaine, who invited him to Paris—whereupon, in a burst of enthusiasm, he wrote *Le *Bateau ivre*, perhaps his finest poem. In Paris (from late Sept.) he met Verlaine, who became passionately attached to him, and other poets, who admired his work, but found him boorish and arrogant. In the summer of 1872 he left Paris with Verlaine and the pair led a dissolute life in Brussels and London. More than once, sick of the life and the relationship, he returned alone to France, and on one such occasion began *Une Saison en enfer*. The end came after a drunken quarrel in Brussels (July 1873), when Verlaine fired at him and injured his arm. Verlaine went to prison, Rimbaud back to Charleville. He now finished *Une Saison en enfer* (publ. Oct. 1873 at his own expense), a work variously interpreted as his submission to, and as his continued denial of, religion. It consists of nine fragments (prose and poetry) of remarkable psychological retrospection and of desperate spiritual confession and self-examination; in the last—*Adieu*—the poet abandons the hells he had deliberately entered in search of experience. It was poorly received and he burnt the manuscript and his papers. In 1874 he again visited England, this time with the poet Nouveau. He was in London and Reading (where he taught French), and possibly wrote some of the prose poems of *Les Illuminations*. By 1875 he may—

though this is not certain—have definitely abandoned literature. For five years he wandered: in Germany and Italy (1875; in Stuttgart he met Verlaine and gave him the manuscript of *Les Illuminations*); with the Dutch army in Batavia (1876; he soon deserted); in Europe again (1877–8; part of the time as interpreter-manager with a circus); in Cyprus (1879). In 1880 he found work in Aden with a firm of coffee exporters and was sent to Harar (not then part of Abyssinia). In time, bent on making money, he set up on his own as trader and explorer, travelling in the interior of Abyssinia and at one time trafficking in arms. He wrote home constantly, but never mentioned literature. In May 1891 he returned to Marseilles, in agony, with a neglected tumour on the knee. His leg was amputated and in late July he managed to get home to Charleville, but soon had to return to hospital and died in November. According to his sister Isabelle, he was converted at the end to active acceptance of the Roman Catholic faith in which he had been nurtured.

Meanwhile, his fame had grown in Paris, thanks largely to Verlaine, who included him (and his *Sonnet des voyelles*) in Les *Poètes maudits* and published *Les Illuminations* (1886, in La *Vogue*). This work (prose poems and two poems in the *vers libre*—the 1886 ed. included other poems, now thought to be extraneous) shows how strongly Rimbaud was influenced by Baudelaire, also by works on illuminist and occult philosophies (*v. Illuminisme*), or the semi-mystical writings of Ballanche.

He went further than any poet before him in the exploration of the subconscious and, technically, in experimenting with rhythm and the use of words as units, without syntactical relationship, purely for their evocative and sensational value. He said of himself: 'J'écrivais des silences, des nuits, je notais l'inexprimable. Je fixais des vertiges.' *v. Effarés, Les; Chasse spirituelle, La.*

Rimes (*v.* also *Alternance des rimes; Masculine and Feminine Lines and*

Rhymes). The principal kinds of rhyme recognized in French prosody are:

Rimes croisées, the alternation of masculine and feminine lines to produce a rhyme-scheme a b a b.

Rimes embrassées, the alternation of masculine and feminine lines to produce a rhyme-scheme a b b a.

Rimes équivoques or *équivoquées*, rhymes in which the last two, three, or more syllables of the lines are identical in sound. They were greatly favoured by the *rhétoriqueurs* and still approved by Sebillet, but condemned by Du Bellay (*Défense et illustration*). In modern times they have been used only for comic effect.

Rimes mêlées, rhymes in haphazard order (except that they observe the rule of *alternance des rimes*), common in 17th-c. light verse. When the lines were also of varying length they were called *vers libres* or *vers irréguliers* (as in La Fontaine's *Fables*). They retained the regular syllabic metres, unlike the *vers libre* of the *Symbolists.

Rimes plates or *suivies*, rhymed couplets (rhyme-scheme a a b b).

Rimes riches, rhymes in which not merely the last accented vowel and any following consonant or vowel are identical (*rimes suffisantes*), but also the preceding consonant or consonants (*consonne d'appui*). They were much used by the *rhétoriqueurs, and in the 19th c. by Hugo and the *Parnassiens*.

Rimes suffisantes, v. Rimes riches.

Riquet, M. *Bergeret's dog.

Riquet à la houppe, (1) *v. Perrault*; (2) *v. Banville.*

Rire, Le, *v. Bergson.*

Rivalités, Les, *v. Comédie humaine, La* (*Scènes de la vie de province*).

Rivarol, ANTOINE DE (1753–1801), man of letters, journalist, and pamphleteer, the son of a Provençal schoolmaster, came to Paris in 1777 and was soon famous for his learning, wit, and brilliant conversation. His dissipated life hindered his literary work, yet he had serious aspirations and was capable of elevated thought. His translation (1783) of Dante's *Inferno* was praised, and his *Discours sur l'universalité de la langue française* (1784; containing the famous saying 'Ce qui n'est pas clair n'est pas français') won him a prize from the Academy of Berlin and a small pension from Louis XVI. His many amusing literary and political satires delighted all but his victims, e.g. *Le Chou et le Navet* (1782; against Delille); *Le Petit Almanach de nos grands hommes, année 1788; Petit Dictionnaire des grands hommes de la Révolution* (1790). The most pungent satires in *Les *Actes des Apôtres*, if not actually from his pen, were reports of his sayings. He left France in 1792, was in Brussels till 1794, then went to England and was respectfully welcomed by Pitt and Burke. But he found English society, and the English climate, uncongenial and soon joined the *émigrés* in *Hamburg, remaining there till 1800. During this time a Hamburg publisher wrung from him the *Discours préliminaire du nouveau dictionnaire de la langue française* (1797; a study of the disruptive social effect of contemporary philosophy, perhaps his best work), the first instalment of a vast treatise and dictionary intended to present the human mind through the evolution of language. Like so many works he projected, the rest of the book existed only in his conversation, but existed so vividly that whole fragments of it are reported in the memoirs of his friends. He died in Berlin. His *Œuvres complètes* (5 vols., in fact very incomplete) appeared in 1808, his *Pensées inédites* in 1836. *v. Chênedollé.*

Rivière, JACQUES (1886–1925), critic, essayist, and novelist, a literary personality of his generation, became secretary (1910), then editor (1919–25) of the **Nouvelle Revue française*. His published works include *Études* (1912) and *Nouvelles Études* (1947), collected criticism (literary, art, and music) and essays (notably on the novel); *Marcel Proust* (1924); *De la sincérité envers soi-même* (1926); the novels *Aimée* (1922) and *Florence* (1935; unfinished). His correspondence with his friend Alain-

Fournier (1905–14; publ. 1926–8, 4 vols.), whose sister he married, is the exchange of ideas and experiences between two young intellectuals; that with Claudel (1902–14; publ. 1926) shows him returning, under Claudel's guidance, to the Roman Catholic Church; that with Proust (1911–22; publ. 1955) reflects Proust's strong influence on him in later life. *v. Critics and Criticism,* 3.

Rivoli (near Mantua, N. Italy). Here Bonaparte won his most brilliant victory over the Austrians (14 Jan. 1797) in his first Italian campaign. *v. Coalitions* (1).

Robbe-Grillet, ALAIN (1922–), novelist, originally an agricultural engineer. His first novel, *Les Gommes*, appeared in 1953. *Le Voyeur* (1955), which won the *Prix des Critiques* and aroused much critical interest and antagonism, established his reputation as a leading figure in what was to become the *nouveau roman. His theoretical writings on the novel were collected in *Pour un nouveau roman* (1963). His other novels include *La Jalousie* (1957), *Dans le labyrinthe* (1959), *La Maison de rendez-vous* (1965), *Projet pour une révolution à New York* (1970). He has also collaborated in a number of films, the scripts of which have been published as *ciné-romans*, e.g. *L'Année dernière à Marienbad* (1961). Initially a response to a new view of man's relation to the world, defined as non-tragic and non-anthropomorphic, his novels have increasingly abandoned any basis of realism in a deliberate attempt to demonstrate the independence of writing and fiction from reality.

Robert Ier (*c.* 865–923), king of France, r. 922–3 (*v. Charles III*). He was the second son of Robert le Fort and was grandfather of Hugues Capet, the first *Capetian king.

Robert II LE PIEUX (*c.* 970–1031), king of France (*Capetian dynasty), son and successor of Hugues Capet, r. 996–1031.

Robert, PAUL, *v. Dictionaries,* 1950–64.

Robert de Blois, a 13th-c. poet, author of *Beaudous*, a *roman breton; *Floris et Lyriopé*, a **roman d'aventure*; and various religious and didactic works, notably the *Chastiement des dames*, a manual of conduct for courtly ladies.

Robert de Boron, *v. Perceval.*

Robert de Clari, *v. Crusades.*

Robert le Diable, the subject of a legend in which a childless woman obtains a son by praying to the Devil; he is strong and wicked and lives a lawless life, but finally repents and is reconciled with the Church. The tale was attached to Robert, duke of Normandy (father of William the Conqueror), who was notoriously violent and cruel. It was the theme of a médieval **roman d'aventure*, of which there were various versions (inc. Eng. versions), also of one of the **Miracles de Notre-Dame. v.* also *Bibliothèque bleue*; *Meyerbeer*.

Robert le Fort (d. 866), comte d'Anjou from 864, father of Eudes and Robert Ier. He valiantly defended his territory against the Normans (hence 'le Fort') and was killed in battle.

Robespierre, FRANÇOIS-MAXIMILIEN-JOSEPH DE (1758–94), one of the great leaders of the Revolution, also one of its great orators (*cf. Danton*; *Mirabeau*), was educated at the *Collège Louis-le-Grand* (*v. Collège de Clermont*), then practised as a barrister in his native Arras until his election as *député du* *Tiers État for Arras to the *États généraux of 1789. After the monarchy fell (1792), he came into full prominence as leader of the *Jacobins. He led the *Montagnards in the *Convention, was a member of the **Comité de salut public*, and virtual dictator during the *Terror. He was overthrown on 27 July 1794 (*le 9 thermidor*) and executed the next day. *v. Revolutions*, 1.

He has aroused more controversy than any other figure of the Revolution. The people trusted him and, impressed by the integrity of his private life and his rigid, logical adherence to his democratic ideals,

called him 'l'Incorruptible'. Carlyle, in *The French Revolution*, constantly refers to him as 'The Seagreen Incorruptible', an epithet possibly inspired by Mme de Staël, who said of him: 'Ses traits étaient ignobles, son teint pâle, ses veines d'une couleur verte' (*Considérations sur... la Révolution française*, 1818).

Robinet, JEAN-BAPTISTE-RENÉ, *v. Dictionaries*, 1777–83.

Robin et Marion, *v. Jeu de Robin et Marion.*

Rocambole, *v. Ponson du Terrail.*

Rochefort, CHRISTIANE (1917–), novelist. Her works—marked by realism, humour (often coarse), and a vigorous style—include *Le Repos du guerrier* (1958), the story of a girl who is sexually spellbound by an alcoholic, told in intimate and often scabrous detail; *Les Petits Enfants du siècle* (1961); *Les Stances à Sophie* (1963); *Une Rose pour Morrison* (1966).

Rochefort (Rochefort-Luçay), HENRI DE (1830–1913), political journalist. He contributed to *Le* *Nain jaune and *Le* *Figaro and wrote *vaudevilles. In 1868 he founded *La Lanterne*, a widely read weekly (small, bright red pamphlets) in which, with a savage wit, he attacked Napoleon III and helped to undermine the *régime*. He was soon prosecuted, but escaped to Belgium, where he continued his paper for a time. In 1869 he was elected *député for Paris. After the 1870 *Revolution he was a member of the Government of National Defence and for a time of the **Assemblée nationale*. He described his varied career, which included further arrests, deportation, and the founding of two other papers (*La Marseillaise*, 1869; *L'Intransigeant*, 1880), in *Les Aventures de ma vie* (1896–8, 5 vols.).

Rocher du Grand-Bé, Le, *v. Chateaubriand.*

Rochers, Les, *v. Sévigné.*

Rocroi (in the Ardennes), the scene of a famous battle (1643) in which Condé, then only 22, defeated the Spanish army.

Rod, ÉDOUARD (1857–1910), novelist and critic of Swiss origin, lived in Paris for some years from 1878 and was a professor in Geneva from 1886. He wrote over 40 novels. Some early ones are *Naturalist (e.g. *Palmyre Veulard*, 1881; *La Femme d'Henri Vanneau*, 1884), others reflect the vogue for the Russian novel (e.g. *La Course à la mort*, 1885, where the narrator observes himself slipping discontentedly into futility), but most are psychological studies of struggles of conscience, ill-fated passionate entanglements, or general moral problems (e.g. *Le Sens de la vie*, 1889; *Les Trois Cœurs*, 1890; *Le Message du Pasteur Nauche*, 1898; *La Vie privée de Michel Teissier*, 1893; *L'Ombre s'étend sur la montagne*, 1907). *Études sur le XIXᵉ siècle* (1888) and *Les Idées morales du temps présent* (1892) are collected criticism.

Rodenbach, GEORGES (1855–98), Belgian poet and novelist, did much to extend *Symbolism to Belgium (cf. *Maeterlinck*; *Verhaeren*). He went to Paris *c.* 1876 to continue his law studies, frequented the early Symbolist groups (e.g. the *Hydropathes*), left after some years to practise at the bar in Brussels, but gave this up for literature and lived in Paris after 1887. His collections of poems include *Les Foyers et les champs* (1877), *Les Tristesses* (1879), *La Jeunesse blanche* (1886), *Le Règne du silence* (1891), *Les Vies encloses* (1896), *Le Miroir du ciel natal* (1898). They contain musical, gently melancholy descriptions of landscapes and life in the villages and old towns of Belgium. His best-known novel is *Bruges-la-morte* (1892; dramatized 1901 as *Le Mirage*).

Rodilard, 'bacon-gnawer', a name used by La Fontaine (following Rabelais) for the cat.

Rodin, FRANÇOIS-AUGUSTE-RENÉ (1840–1917), sculptor. His first masterpiece (*L'Âge d'airain*, 1877) created a scandal, as did others of his huge, architecturally conceived works, but it was eventually bought by the State. By 1900 he was himself very much a national monument. The *Musée Rodin* is housed in his former home in Paris. He profoundly influenced the Austrian poet Rainer-Maria Rilke, who was his secretary for some years.

Rodogune, a tragedy by Corneille, based on a passage in Appian; produced in the winter of 1644–5. Some critics share Corneille's view that this was his greatest play.

The scene is Seleucia. Démétrius Nicanor, king of Syria, has been captured by the Parthians. Cléopâtre, his ruthlessly ambitious queen, believing him dead, has married his brother Antiochus and sent away his twin sons to Egypt. Antiochus has been killed and Nicanor, angered by Cléopâtre's remarriage, has set out for Syria, announcing that he will marry Rodogune, a Parthian princess. Cléopâtre, to avoid losing her throne, has killed Nicanor in an ambush and captured Rodogune. She has recalled her twin sons, Antiochus and Séleucus, from Egypt, intending to declare which is to be king. Both sons fall in love with Rodogune, but each is prepared to renounce her and the crown in favour of the other. Cléopâtre tells them she will cede the crown to whichever will kill her hated rival Rodogune; Rodogune tells them she will marry whichever will kill Cléopâtre—but later confesses her love for Antiochus and withdraws her stipulation. Cléopâtre pretends to accept their marriage and to grant Antiochus the crown; but she kills Séleucus and prepares a poisoned nuptial cup for Antiochus and Rodogune. She drinks from it to reassure Antiochus and falls dead.

Rodolphe, (1) in *Sue's *Les Mystères de Paris*; (2) in *Murger's *Scènes de la vie de Bohème*; (3) in Flaubert's *Madame Bovary*.

Rodrigue, in Corneille's *Le *Cid*.

Rodrigues, OLINDE, *v. Saint-Simonisme*.

Rœderer, PIERRE-LOUIS (1754–1835), politician, economist, historian, and journalist. At 25 he was already a counsellor of the *parlement in his native Metz and known for his liberal principles. He was elected to the *Assemblée constituante and was active in public affairs in Paris, especially under Napoleon, who was quick to appreciate his exceptional financial and administrative ability. After 1815, when his public career ended, he turned to the study of the 17th c., reconstructed in his house a *salon in imitation of the Hôtel de *Rambouillet, and compiled *Mémoires pour servir à l'histoire de la société polie en France* (1835) which did much to arouse interest in 17th-c. society. His *Chronique de cinquante jours, du 20 juin au 10 août 1792* (1832) gives a good picture of a critical period in the Revolution. His *Journal* (1909) is useful for the study of Napoleon. For his son Antoine-Marie *v. Proverbe.*

Roger Bontemps. The allegorical character Bon Temps figures in medieval *moralités and *soties; in the form of Roger Bontemps (perhaps under the influence of Roger de Collerye) he became the embodiment of the hopes, fears, and illusions of the people. The 'gros Roger Bontemps' immortalized by Béranger (in the *chanson called *Roger Bontemps*) is gay, carefree, and content with simple pleasures.

Rohan, ÉDOUARD, PRINCE and CARDINAL DE (1734–1803), *v. Cagliostro; Collier, L'Affaire du.*

Rohan, HENRI, DUC DE (1579–1638), chief military leader of the *Huguenots in the civil wars of the reign of Louis XIII, in which he played a brave, arduous, and unsuccessful part. He was exiled, but later returned to favour and held high command in the war against the Imperialists (1635). He died of wounds. His *Mémoires* of the period 1610–29 are of considerable historical interest.

Roi Candaule, Le, v. Gide.

Roi de Rome, Le, *v. Napoleon II.*

Roi des montagnes, Le, v. About.

Roi d'Yvetot, Le, v. Béranger.

Roi s'amuse, Le (1832), a verse drama by Hugo; *v. Censorship, Dramatic.* (Verdi adapted the plot for his opera *Rigoletto*, 1851.)
The jester *Triboulet has brought up his adored only daughter in secret. François Ier and his court discover her existence and the king seduces her. Triboulet in despair plots to have the king murdered while he is pursuing his amours in disguise in a low quarter of the city. He goes at midnight, as arranged, to collect the sack containing the king's body. Just as he is about to throw it into the Seine the stitches give way and a flash of lightning reveals the face of his daughter. The girl, still in love, had contrived to take her seducer's place as victim.

Rois en exil, Les, v. Daudet, A.

Rois fainéants, *v. Maire du Palais; Merovingians.*

Roi Soleil, Le, Louis XIV.

Roland, in the *chansons de geste (notably the *Chanson de Roland), one of the *Douze *Pairs, son of a sister of Charlemagne (Berte or Gilain) and, according to one version, of Milon d'Angers, a humble seneschal, with whom she elopes. Roland, with his sword Durendal, is the legendary hero of many feats of arms. He is depicted as proud and impetuous, but his character softens at the approach of death. For the story of Roland and Olivier, and of Roland's betrothal to Aude, *v. Olivier.*

Roland was an historical character, warden of the Breton marches under Charlemagne, and accompanied the emperor to Spain in 778 (*v. Chanson de Roland*, last §). He figures as Orlando in the poems of Boiardo and Ariosto. In medieval English literature he appears in *Sir Ferumbras* and *Roland and Vernagu.*

Roland, MARIE-JEANNE PHLIPON, MME (1754–93), wife of Jean-Marie Roland de La Platière (1734–93; an economist and politician who held office during the Revolution). A woman of high intelligence and a generous enthusiasm, a lover of nature and literature, an ardent admirer of J.-J. Rousseau, she was the inspirer of the *Girondins, who met in her *salon. She was guillotined following their overthrow by the *Montagnards. As she mounted the scaffold she uttered the now famous words 'Ô liberté, que de crimes on commet en ton nom!' Her husband killed himself on hearing of her death. She left interesting Mémoires and letters, also a spirited Appel à l'impartiale postérité (1795), written in prison.

Roland de La Platière, v. Roland, Mme.

Rolland, ROMAIN (1866–1944), novelist, playwright, essayist, and historian and critic of music and painting; winner of the *Prix Nobel (1915). After a rather intense childhood in Burgundy, much influenced by his widowed mother and also by music and solitary reading, he was sent to the Lycée Louis-le-Grand in Paris, proceeded to the *École normale supérieure, passed his *agrégation in history (1889), then spent two years at the *École française d'Archéologie in Rome. Tolstoy's doctrine of joy through suffering had already impressed him. In Rome he became a friend of the aged Malwida von Meysenbug, a German socialist of *Huguenot descent who had found refuge there (cf. Monod). Her talk of Wagner and Nietzsche, whom she had known, and of Goethe and Beethoven, awakened his sympathy with the struggles of genius and his lifelong conviction that spiritual freedom must transcend all bonds of race, religion, and prejudice. He returned to Paris (1895) to teach history at the École normale supérieure and the history of music at the *Sorbonne (1900–12). He was now writing on music (Histoire de l'opéra en Europe avant Lulli et Scarlatti, 1895; the essays Musiciens d'autrefois and Musiciens d'aujourd'hui, not publ. till 1908, etc.) and for the theatre (three poetical tragédies de

la foi: Saint Louis, 1897; Aërt, 1898; Le Triomphe de la raison, 1898; and three dramas of the Revolution: Les Loups, 1898; Danton, 1900; Le 14 juillet, 1902). He had a sudden success with a lyrically written life of Beethoven (1903). Similar studies of Michelangelo (1908) and Tolstoy (1911) proved equally successful. He campaigned with Péguy in support of Dreyfus and afterwards collaborated in the *Cahiers de la quinzaine. The friendship later cooled, but before then several issues of the Cahiers had been devoted to publishing his most famous work, *Jean-Christophe (1906–12), a long *roman-fleuve.

When the 1914–18 war broke out he was living in retirement in Switzerland. He remained there, working in the pacifist cause. His pamphlet Au-dessus de la mêlée (1915), appealing to intellectuals on both sides to agitate for peace, aroused resentment in many quarters. For some years after this he was a rallying-point for pacifist intellectuals. He also became interested in Buddhism and Communism. This gradual evolution of his thought is reflected in, for example, the essays collected in Les Précurseurs (1919), Quinze Ans de combat (1919–34) (1934), Par la Révolution, la Paix (1935), Essai sur la mystique et l'action de l'Inde (1929–30, 3 vols.). His other works include Colas Breugnon (1919), sketches of Burgundian peasant life; Clérambault: histoire d'une conscience libre pendant la guerre (1925); Pierre et Luce (1925); and another roman-fleuve, L'Âme enchantée (1922–33, 7 vols.), this time with a woman as central figure. The Cahiers Romain Rolland (1948–   ) contain correspondence of great interest, e.g. with Richard Strauss, Malwida von Meysenbug, Gandhi.

Rollin, CHARLES (1661–1741), historian, rector of the *University of Paris (1694), then principal of the Collège de Beauvais (1699), but obliged to retire in 1712 because of his *Jansenist views. He wrote a valuable Traité des Études (1726–8).

Rollinat, MAURICE (1846–1903), a poet of the transition from the *Parnassiens to the

*Symbolists. The poems collected in *Dans les brandes* (1877) and *Paysages et paysans* (1899) are calm descriptions of nature and country life; those in *Les Névroses* (1883) and *L'Abîme* (1886) are more often morbid or despairing.

Romains, Jules, *pseudonym of* LOUIS FARIGOULE (1885–1972), poet, playwright, essayist, and novelist; a member of the *Académie* (1946). The son of a schoolteacher, he was brought up in Paris, proceeded from the *Lycée Condorcet* to the *École normale supérieure*, and passed the *agrégation* in philosophy in 1909. His literary career began *c.* 1908 when he was associated with the *Abbaye* community, though never a member. They printed *La Vie unanime* (1908), the poems in which he first expressed the convictions that underlie all his writings (*v. Unanimisme*), as well as those of the *unanimiste* group of poets of which he was soon the moving spirit. His subsequent volumes of poetry include *Un Être en marche* (1910), *Odes et prières* (1913), *Europe* (1916), *L'Ode génoise* (1925), *L'Homme blanc* (1937). *Choix de poèmes* (1948) is a good representative collection.

The bulk of his output consists, however, of novels, tales, and plays. Apart from what may be called their philosophical message, these are characterized by brilliance, irony, fine powers of observation and description, a lively, if heavy, sense of the burlesque, a facility and an encyclopedic knowledge that at times border on the superficial, and a remarkable gift for holding the reader's attention through long passages of *reportage*. This gift is particularly evident in his chief work, the 27 novels of *Les *Hommes de bonne volonté* (1932–47). His other novels include *Mort de quelqu'un* (1911), about the unconscious bond created between persons even remotely affected by the death and funeral of an insignificant railway employee; *Les Copains* (1913), *unanimisme* in terms of broad farce; *Psyché* (*Lucienne*, 1921; *Le Dieu des corps*, 1928; *Quand le navire*, 1929), a lavishly amorous novel, with excursions into psycho-physiological phenomena. His plays (collected in *Théâtre*, 1924–35, 7 vols.) include *Knock, ou le Triomphe de la médecine* (1923), *M. Le Trouhadec saisi par la débauche* (1923), and *Le Mariage de M. Le Trouhadec* (1925), three of the most successful farcical comedies of modern times, all produced and played by Jouvet; also *L'Armée dans la ville* (1911) and *Cromedeyre-le-vieil* (1920; an isolated mountain village returns suddenly to primitive customs), both in verse and treating the theme of group emotion seriously, at times lyrically; and, in collaboration with Stefan Zweig, an adaptation (1928) of Jonson's *Volpone*. His best tales are *Le Bourg régénéré, conte de la vie unanime* (1906), where an incidental discovery gives a village a sense of its own entity and new life; *Le Vin blanc de la Villette* (1914), tales of humble life in Paris; *Donogoo-Tonka* (1920; later dramatized), where a political imposture becomes matter for *l'unanimisme*.

Roman, *v. Novel.*

Roman à tiroirs, a novel constructed as a series of episodes with little or no connecting thread, e.g. Lesage's *Gil Blas.*

Roman bourgeois, Le (1666), by Furetière, a novel which differs sharply from the romances of the day (e.g. *L'*Astrée, Le *Grand Cyrus*; *v. Novel,* 2) by presenting a group of Parisian *bourgeois*—magistrates, advocates, merchants, shopkeepers, sacristans, and their families—and describing with simple realism (though without charm or gaiety) their love affairs, quarrels, elopements, lawsuits, marriage contracts, food, clothes, etc. There is no general plot, merely incidents and scenes, notably (bk. I) the courtship of Javotte (daughter of Vollichon, a swindling lawyer) by a young *bourgeois* who apes the man of fashion, and (bk. II) the loves of Charroselles (an unsuccessful writer—a caricature of C. Sorel) and Mlle Collantine (daughter of a police official), who are both so addicted to litigation that they go on suing one another even after marriage.

Romance, a French term applied to a type of medieval song; it usually comprises the *chansons de toile*, sometimes also the *chansons à personnages*.

Romance Languages (Langues romanes), the term applied to the group of languages descended from Latin, notably French, Provençal, Italian, Spanish, Portuguese, and Rumanian. The French word *roman* (like the Eng. word *romance*) comes from Old French *romanz*, the equivalent of the popular Latin adverb *romanice*—*romanice loqui* meaning 'to speak in the manner of the Romans' in the territories conquered by Rome. In Old French, *romanz*, treated as a noun, at first denoted the vernacular, both spoken and written, as opposed to the language of the Germanic invaders, and then (much more commonly) the vernacular as opposed to Latin, whether classical or popular. For the way in which the French language developed out of this vernacular *v. French Language.* French learned journals devoted to the study of the Romance languages include *Romania,* the *Revue des langues romanes,* the *Revue de linguistique romane.*

Romanceros, *v. Foreign Influences,* 3.

Romances sans paroles, v. Verlaine.

Roman comique, Le (1651, pt. I; 1657, pt. II), an unfinished romance by Scarron. It is a lively account, written in a gay, unaffected style, of the love affairs and adventures of a travelling company of actors, with passages of both coarse buffoonery and delicate romance. Some of the characters are well drawn: Le Destin (a young man of good family) and Mlle de l'Estoile (a lady he has rescued from a persecutor); the old players La Rancune and Caverne; the comic little lawyer Ragotin, who writes plays for the troupe (*cf. Molière; Hardy*) and is the general butt and the victim of ludicrous misadventures. Tavern life of the period is vividly depicted and the whole is a good guide to the conditions in which touring companies then lived and worked. In 1663 the publisher Offray issued a conclusion (pt. III) by an anonymous author (called the *Suite d'Offray* to distinguish it from later conclusions publ. in 1679 and 1771).

Roman courtois (Courtly Romance), a general term for the various types of medieval romance, the *roman breton,* *roman d'antiquité,* *roman d'aventure,* etc. They are nearly all in verse (octosyllables). *v. Novel,* 1.

Roman-cycle, in modern fiction, a series of self-contained but interrelated novels concerned with one central character or family, one generation or period, e.g. Duhamel's *Salavin* series and *Chronique des Pasquier,* Martin du Gard's *Les Thibault,* Romains's *Les Hommes de bonne volonté,* *Troyat's Tant que la terre durera,* etc. *v. Roman-fleuve.*

Roman d'Alexandre, v. Alexandre le Grand (1).

Roman d'aventure, a term applied to a type of romance which developed and became highly popular in the 12th–13th cs. The *romans d'aventure* resemble the *romans bretons* in that they deal with love (*amour courtois*) and chivalry, present a refined civilization, and in general exalt the role of women (for whose entertainment, unlike the *chansons de geste,* they were chiefly intended), but differ from them in that their background is not Arthurian and in that their period is often vaguely contemporary (they shed much light on manners of the day). Most are in harmonious verse (usually octosyllables), e.g. *Ipomedon,* *Partenopeus de Blois, Le Lai de l'ombre,* *Guillaume de Dole,* Le Châtelain de *Coucy,* *Guillaume de Palerne,* *Floire et Blancheflor,* *Robert le Diable.* They also include *Aucassin et Nicolette* (prose and verse) and such prose romances as *Le Conte du roi Constant l'empereur* and *Le Roi Flore et la Belle Jeanne. v. Novel,* 1.

Roman de Godefroi de Bouillon, v. Chevalier au cygne.

Roman de la Poire, a medieval allegorical verse romance, in which a lover is besieged by Love in a tower; an imitation of the *Roman de la Rose*.

Roman de la Rose, a poem in octosyllables, of which the first part (some 4,000 ll.) was written probably *c.* 1230–40 by Guillaume de Lorris (nothing certain is known about him; he may have come from Lorris, near Orleans), and the second (some 18,000 ll.) *c.* 1275–80 by Jean de Meung.

The first part is an 'Art of Love' on the model of Ovid, love being the *amour courtois* of the day and the form an elaborate allegory. The poet relates a dream in which Idleness admits him to a garden where, amid trees, flowers, and birds, the company includes such personages as Courtesy, Sweet-Looks, Gladness, Mirth, Richesse, Largesse, and the God of Love himself. He finds a beautiful Rose and wishes to pick it. He falls victim to the God of Love, who instructs him in the code of courtly love and tells him of the torments and compensations of his service. The Lover's efforts to reach the Rose are helped or foiled by allegorical personages representing his lady's impulses or the influences on her mind: Fair-Welcome, Danger, Evil-Tongue, etc. Thwarted in his efforts, he is dissuaded by Reason from persisting. Then Pity and Venus intervene and he is allowed a kiss. But Evil-Tongue raises an outcry, the Rose is more strictly guarded, walls are built round her, and a Duenna set to watch her. Here the poem of Guillaume de Lorris ends.

Jean de Meung continued the work in a very different strain. The first part had been an allegory, not without picturesque quality, designed to amuse an aristocratic audience. This allegory, though continued, now becomes the pretext for long, erudite digressions covering almost the whole field of medieval thought, addressed to a more general public, written from a *bourgeois* standpoint, often with coarse, realistic vigour, and showing a bold, independent spirit. The allegory continues with the siege of the fortress.

False-Seeming (usually found, it is alleged, in the cloister) comes to the aid of love and subdues Evil-Tongue; the Duenna is won over to the Lover's side; Nature intervenes on his behalf; the firebrand of Venus repels Danger, Shame, and Dread; and the Rose is won. Between the successive incidents come the digressions (showing familiarity, by quotation or imitation, with the ancients and with more recent authors, e.g. Boethius, Abélard, Roger Bacon, John of Salisbury): satires on women (a reaction against their glorification by the *troubadours* and the occasion of a heated controversy in the early 15th c.; *v. Christine de Pisan; Gerson; Le Franc*); attacks on the magistrates, the hereditary nobility (expressing the feelings of the humbler people, then being sorely oppressed by their feudal lords), and the mendicant friars; disquisitions on the origin of society and of the royal power, on property, pauperism, marriage, the relation between nature and art, hallucinations and sorcery, and the physical sciences. When the allegory presents Nature preaching obedience to her laws we have the essence of Jean de Meung's doctrine: everything contrary to nature is vicious, and this is the criterion by which social institutions, and also true nobility, wealth, and love, are to be judged. His doctrine of nature as the sovereign guide was later developed by Rabelais.

The popularity of the poem is attested by the large number of surviving manuscripts and by the influence it exerted on poets of the 14th and 15th cs. As many as 40 editions were printed by 1538 (one by Marot); and even Ronsard and J.-A. de Baïf, who had little use for medieval authors, praised Jean de Meung. The English *Romaunt of the Rose*, in which Chaucer had a hand, is a translation, with amplifications, of the first part of the French poem and portions of the second.

Roman de l'énergie nationale, Le, v. Barrès.

Roman d'Eneas, a poem (10,000 octosyllables) written *c.* 1160 by an unknown author; one of the chief *romans d'antiquité*. It is based on Virgil's *Aeneid*, but increases the romantic and marvellous elements and shows the influence of Ovid.

Roman de Renart, a group of verse tales, of which the earliest and best, written *c.* 1175–1205 by different authors (mostly unknown), present feudal society of the day through the adventures of various animals—Renart the fox, Noble the lion, Ysengrin the wolf, Brun the bear, Tibert the cat, Chantecler the cock, Tiécelin the crow, Grimbert the badger, Couard the hare, Belin the ram, Brichemer the stag, Roonel the mastiff, etc., and their wives, each with his peculiar animal characteristics. The stories derive partly from Greco-Roman fables, but to a greater extent from the general popular traditions of Europe and more directly from the Latin *Ysengrimus* (completed 1148 at Ghent). The general theme of the early tales, so far as they have one, is the conflict of wit and cunning with brute force. The best are marked by wit, a gay absurdity, and flashes of mild, genial satire, and show narrative and dramatic skill and delicacy of touch. In the well-known *Jugement de Renart* Dame Pinte the hen demands justice at the court of Noble the lion, accusing Renart of killing her sister Dame Coupée (at whose martyr's tomb miracles are said to take place). After a burlesque trial, in which the animals display their various characters, he is sentenced to death, but obtains a reprieve on condition that he ends his days in the Holy Land expiating his crimes. He duly sets out, but as soon as he reaches a safe distance throws away his pilgrim's staff and heaps insults on the august assembly. Further branches of the work, generally inferior in invention, continued to be produced in the first half of the 13th c. In some, the animals lose their distinctive characteristics and are just names for human beings; in others, Renart does not figure at all. The satire becomes more bitter, and Renart, originally an agreeable rascal, becomes Evil personified.

So popular were these tales that *renard* replaced the older *goupil* as the ordinary

word for a fox. A Flemish version of the group, no longer extant, was translated and printed by Caxton (1481). Goethe wrote a free translation, *Reineke Fuchs*, in 1794. Chaucer's *Nun's Priest's Tale* is derived from an episode in the French work.

Related works are Rutebeuf's *Renart le Bestourné*, a pungent satire in which Renart, no longer a jolly rascal, symbolizes the mendicant friars and gets control of Noble the lion, to the detriment of the realm; *Le Couronnement de Renart* (2nd half of 13th c.), a bitter attack on contemporary society in which Renart, the embodiment of hypocrisy, greed, and other vices, contrives to be proclaimed king in place of Noble; *Renart le Nouvel* (2nd half of 13th c.), by Jacquemart Gelée, a poet of Lille, a long, chaotic satirical allegory, interspersed with songs, and directed mainly at the clergy and religious orders; *Renart le Contrefait* (early 14th c.), by an unfrocked cleric of Troyes, another allegory, again attacking contemporary abuses and including erudite discourses on all manner of subjects.

Roman de Rou, *v. Wace.*

Roman des Sept Sages, *v. Sept Sages.*

Roman de Thèbes, one of the chief *romans d'antiquité* (*c.* 10,000 octosyllables), written in the mid-12th c. by an unknown author. It tells the story of Oedipus, then that of Eteocles and Polynices and the siege of Thebes (here mainly following Statius's *Thebaid*, but adding romantic episodes and all kinds of military incidents). It ends with the intervention of Theseus to secure the burial of the dead besiegers, the destruction of Thebes, and the death of Creon.

Roman de Troie, by Benoît de Sainte-Maure, one of the chief *romans d'antiquité* (*c.* 30,000 octosyllables), probably written *c.* 1160 and dedicated to Eleanor of Aquitaine; an extremely popular work, widely diffused, translated, and imitated. It tells the story of Troy from the

Argonauts to the death of Ulysses after his return home from the siege, making Hector rather than Achilles the main hero, adding romantic episodes (e.g. the story of Troilus and Cressida, here called Briseida, which the author appears to have originated), and in many respects depicting antiquity in the guise of feudal society of the day. But the main interest lies in the elaboration of the lyrical monologue and the analysis of various types of love.

Roman d'un jeune homme pauvre, Le, v. Feuillet.

Roman expérimental, Le, v. Naturalism.

Roman-feuilleton, a novel published in instalments in a daily paper or periodical (*cf. Feuilleton*). The practice began *c.* 1830 in the fortnightly and monthly periodicals and spread to the daily press in 1836, when *Le *Siècle* carried a few chapters of a translation of the Spanish romance *Lazarillo de Tormes*, then Balzac's *La *Vieille Fille*. Other dailies, notably *La *Presse*, quickly followed suit, and the *roman-feuilleton* was the making of many papers. The masters of the art, in its heyday in the years 1836–50, were Sue, Soulié, Balzac, Dumas *père*, and, in a lesser degree, G. Sand. They often wrote from one day to another with no preconceived plan, piling up the intrigue and breaking off at a moment of suspense. Drawings of the period show people in the provinces gathering in one another's houses on the day the papers arrived for a reading of the *roman-feuilleton*.

Roman-fleuve, a term attributable to Rolland, who said that his *Jean-Christophe* (which is typical of the *genre*) 'm'est apparu comme un fleuve;... il est, dans le cours des fleuves, des zones où ils s'étendent, semblent dormir,... ils n'en continuent pas moins de couler et changer...'; since applied to any *roman-cycle* or novel of this type, sometimes also to a tediously meandering novel.

Romania (1872–   ; quarterly), a learned

journal devoted to the *Romance languages and literatures. The first editors were G. Paris and Paul Meyer.

Romans bretons, narrative poems in octosyllables, written *c.* 1150–1250, relating to the 'matière de Bretagne' (*v. Bodel*), i.e. recounting adventures directly or indirectly connected with the court of Arthur, king of Britain, and his Knights of the Round Table. They include Chrétien de Troyes's *Erec*, *Cligès*, Le *Chevalier à la charrette*, *Yvain*, and *Perceval*, also *Tristan*, *Guinglain*, *Méraugis de Portlesguez*, La *Mule sans frein*, etc. Greatly extended prose versions of some of these were produced in the 13th c. (*v. Perceval; Tristan*) and again in the early days of printing (late 15th and early 16th cs.); *v. also Bibliothèque bleue*. The main source of inspiration was apparently *Geoffrey of Monmouth's *Historia Regum Britanniae* (*c.* 1135), adapted in French in *Wace's *Roman de Brut* (1155); but authors of individual romances drew for their plots on tales and legends of various origins (Celtic, classical, etc.) and sometimes on their own imagination. In their portrayal of love the *romans bretons* are inspired by the conception of *amour courtois* and contrast sharply with the *chansons de geste* in the position assigned to women. *v. Novel*, 1.

Romans d'antiquité, a group of medieval verse romances on themes drawn from Latin authors (the 'matière de Rome la grant'; *v. Bodel*), but increasing the romantic and marvellous elements, often showing the influence of Ovid, and depicting antiquity largely in the guise of feudal society of the day. They include, notably, the *Roman d'Alexandre* (*v. Alexandre le Grand* (1)), the *Roman de Troie*, the *Roman de Thèbes*, and the *Roman d'Eneas*; also *Piramus et Tisbé*; *Narcissus*; *Philomena* (Ovid's story of Procne and Philomela), tentatively ascribed to Chrétien de Troyes. *v. Novel*, 1.

Romanticism, Romantic, a great revolutionary movement affecting the whole field of literature, and also music and painting, which began in France, and not in France alone, in the first years of the 19th c.

The outstanding characteristic of 18th-c. French literature had been the great importance it attached to reason, and to clarity and objectivity in both the conception and the expression of ideas. By about 1800 a new spirit was abroad: literature was tending to become a matter of the senses and emotions. There was a growing awareness of Nature, hitherto an almost unremarked background. Men now admired its intrinsic beauty, but, above all, they increasingly found in it a reflection of their own moods (esp. the introspective melancholy known as le *mal du siècle) and perplexities.

Several influences contributed to the birth and development of the Romantic movement: the writings of J.-J. Rousseau; the political upheaval of the Revolution and its intellectual repercussions; the chaotic educational system of the succeeding years and the unsettled world in which the young grew up; the return of the émigrés, with minds broadened by contact with other cultures; the discovery of novel beauties, far removed from the French canons, in foreign literatures (v. Foreign Influences, 2, 3); the revival of interest in the Middle Ages; and, most directly, the works of the two great precursors of Romanticism— Chateaubriand, who as a creative writer expressed the essence of the young Romantic spirit (e.g. in *René and *Atala), and Mme de Staël, who as a critic (in *De la littérature and *De l'Allemagne) familiarized the French reader with foreign authors and originated the distinction between 'classical' and 'romantic' literature. (The word romantisme was not used before 1822, and romantique served both as noun and adjective.)

The first Romantic *cénacle was Nodier's *salon at the *Bibliothèque de l'Arsenal. Writers to be seen there in 1823 included Lamartine (infrequently), Hugo (soon to be leader of the second, more famous cénacle), and Vigny, all of whom had already published poems strongly

impregnated with the new spirit; later they were joined by Musset and Dumas père. Stendhal, meanwhile, was publishing his *Racine et Shakspeare. Through their chief spokesman, Hugo (whose Préface de *Cromwell was the most famous of the many Romantic manifestos), and in literary reviews associated with the movement (for titles v. Press, 5) the Romantics called for 'liberté dans l'art' (cf. Realism), i.e. freedom in their choice and treatment of subject and in their choice of words, asserting that the *Classical doctrines and conventions were shackles impeding the true representation of life, with its mixture of the sublime and the grotesque, and the free play of moods and sensations. The poet's mission was to relate the colours and harmonies of Nature to his own changing moods, to lay bare his innermost self; he could not fulfil this mission unless the Classical restrictions on the vocabulary of poetry were lifted and the rules of versification relaxed.

The first and fiercest Romantic battles were fought in the theatre. Notable dates were the production of Dumas père's *Henri III et sa cour (1829), of Vigny's adaptation of Othello (1829), and, above all, of Hugo's *Hernani (1830). After these striking and unexpected successes the Romantics were no longer upstarts: they were a conquering force. Romantic drama introduced lasting technical innovations (many of which applied equally to poetry), but it was unwieldy and slow-moving and did not wear very well. In other literary fields the influence of Romanticism was more dynamic. Preoccupation with the self produced a note of lyrical expansiveness that dominated the poetry of the period and resounded in many of the novels, e.g. those of G. Sand; in its more uneasy aspects it also produced or reflected such early psychological novels as Senancour's *Obermann, B. Constant's *Adolphe, Sainte-Beuve's *Volupté, and Musset's *Confession d'un enfant du siècle, all in some degree dissections of the authors' own souls. v. Lyric Poetry, 4; Novel, 3.

Like all such revolutions, the Romantic movement had its excesses and its decadent offshoots. The yearning for the infinite, the eternal questioning, led to a morbid preoccupation with death and the horrors of the tomb, while the cult of the individual—usually a sardonic, Byronic creature of superior intelligence, whose very crimes were grander than the virtues of ordinary mortals—encouraged contempt for the *bourgeois* and the desire to shock. Hence the *genre* of frenetic Romanticism that flourished among the wild young **bousingos* and **Jeunes-France* of the 1830s, with their taste for vampirism, lurid crimes, and so-called 'Satanism'. But this extravagance exhausted itself with the years: Gautier, in youth the most truculent of Romantics, later found that his loudly proclaimed theories of *l'*art pour l'art* led him far away from the cult of the individual; some of his wilder companions died young, others took to respectability and journalism; a few later survivors, such as Barbey d'Aurevilly, have a place in literature almost as anachronisms. On the other hand, though Romanticism and Classicism provide seemingly eternal subjects for controversy, the grand Romantic figures—Chateaubriand, Hugo, Lamartine, Vigny, the Musset of *Les *Nuits*—are now classics of French literature.

The Romantic movement in music was dominated by Berlioz, who was as strongly influenced by Goethe and Shakespeare as were his literary contemporaries. Géricault and Delacroix were the outstanding Romantic painters. Mention must also be made of the many painters and engravers (*v. Devéria*; *Johannot*; *Nanteuil, C.*) whose illustrations were such an important feature of books by Romantic authors (an aspect of the movement studied in **Champfleury's Les Vignettes romantiques*).

Rome, *v. Zola*.

Rome, Naples, et Florence en 1817, *v. Stendhal*.

Romme, GILBERT (1750–95), mathematician and a member of the **Convention*,

was responsible for the chronology of the **Republican Calendar*.

Roncevaux, *v. Chanson de Roland*.

Rondeau, formerly also *rondel*, a fixed verse-form derived from the *rondet de carole* (*v. Chansons à danser*) and very popular in the 14th and 15th cs. The lines (usually octosyllables or decasyllables) were all on two rhymes, e.g. ABA abAB abaABA, or ABBA abAB abbaABBA, or (*rondeau double*) AABBA aabAAB aabbaAABBA (capital letters indicate lines repeated by way of refrain). From the 15th c. it became usual to reduce the refrain to its first few syllables, giving schemes such as abba abR abbaR, or (the form most commonly used by modern poets like Musset and Banville) aabba aabR aabbaR (where R consists of the first word or words of the first line and does not rhyme in either a or b).

Rondet, *v. Chansons à danser*.

Ronsard, PIERRE DE (1524–85), the chief poet of the **Renaissance* and leader of the **Pléiade*, came of a good family of the Vendômois (his father, also a man of letters, served with distinction in Italy under Louis XII and François Ier). He became a page at court, visited Scotland (1537–9) in the suite of the two successive French queens of James V (Madeleine de France and Marie de **Guise*), and attended the humanist L. de Baïf at a religious conference at Haguenau. About 1541, owing to incipient deafness, he turned to the study of letters, came under the influence of Peletier and Dorat, and was led to pursue the reform of French poetry through study of the classics. For five years Ronsard, with Du Bellay (for the story of their meeting *v. Du Bellay*) and J.-A. de Baïf, studied at the **Collège de Coqueret* under Dorat. His *Odes* (bks. I–IV) appeared in 1550, the collection of sonnets entitled *Les Amours* (and bk. V of the *Odes*) in 1552, a reprint of the *Amours* (with a commentary by **Muret*) and four more odes (inc. the famous *Mignonne*, *allons voir si la rose*) in 1553, his *Bocage* in 1554, his *Hymnes* celebrating the king and other notables (now mainly of interest as showing his adaptation of the *alexandrine to moral and philosophical themes, narratives, and allegories) in 1555–6. These works, with additions, were collected in *Œuvres* (1560). His *Odes* and *Amours* were received with enthusiasm by the cultured, and, after a time, by the court. The arrogance with which he and Du Bellay announced their new doctrines offended M. de Saint-Gelais, leader of the old school, but a reconciliation was effected. By 1560 he was probably at the height of his fame. He occupied the position of court poet, enjoying the protection of Charles IX and his sister Marguerite de Valois, also the admiration of Mary Stuart, who later sent him a present from her place of imprisonment. Before long he was granted an annual stipend and two priories in the Vendômois and Touraine (Saint-Côme, where he died). In 1561–3 he published his chief political poems: the *Institution pour l'adolescence du Roi très chrétien*, on the reciprocal duties of a king and his subjects; the *Discours des misères de ce temps* (i.e. the wars of religion); and the *Remontrance au peuple de France*, urging the nation to support the king in the struggle with the *Huguenots. Here patriotic ardour overcomes his erudition and produces some of his most natural and eloquent alexandrines. There followed his *Abrégé de l'art poétique français* (1565); his *Élégies, mascarades, et bergeries* (1565), lyrical pieces for court entertainments, dedicated to Queen Elizabeth (and inc. poems addressed to her, to Dudley, and to Cecil); the *Franciade* (1572, 4 bks.), his not very happy attempt at an *epic, relating the legend of Francus, son of Hector of Troy and fabled ancestor of the French kings (the metre, decasyllables instead of alexandrines, was imposed by Charles IX). After the king's death (1574) he abandoned the *Franciade* and gradually withdrew from court to a retired and studious life, largely spent in his priories. His last great collection, the *Sonnets pour Hélène* (first publ. in the 1578 ed. of his

Œuvres), perhaps partly provoked by the rivalry of a new court poet, Desportes, contains some of his finest poems (e.g. the famous *Quand vous serez bien vieille*). Of the women chiefly celebrated in his love poems, 'Cassandre' was Cassandre Salviati, daughter of a Florentine banker settled in France; 'Marie' was an Angevin peasant girl; 'Hélène' was Hélène de Surgères, a maid-of-honour to Catherine de Médicis.

He was the moving spirit of the poetic revolution effected by the *Pléiade*. He made his first public contribution thereto in his *Odes*, introducing great lyrical poetry on the model of Pindar, assuming for the poet a lofty role, celebrating great events and distributing praise or blame to the mighty. They were intended to be sung (hence certain metrical innovations, such as the *alternance des rimes*), and airs written for them by composers of the day (e.g. Jannequin and Certon) still survive. His Pindaric odes were, however, excessively imitative and pedantic, and overloaded with mythology and metaphor. He soon abandoned this phase of his writing and found models in Horace, Catullus, Anacreon, Ovid, and (for a time) Petrarch. His fame rests on his mastery of the light *ode (erotic, bacchic, or rustic) and the *sonnet, and it was above all in these that he introduced a new rhythm into French poetry. The best of his doctrines prevailed, but his reputation as a poet suffered at the hands of Malherbe and his work was thereafter strangely neglected and despised. His popularity did not revive until the 19th c.

Roonel, the mastiff in the *Roman de Renart*.

Roquefort, JEAN-BAPTISTE BONAVENTURE DE, *v. Dictionaries*, 1829.

Roqueplan, NESTOR (1804–70), a typical wit and dandy of the Second Empire. He was a journalist (part-founder of *Le *Figaro*) and sometime theatre-manager.

Roscelin or **Roscellinus** (d. *c.* 1125), scholastic philosopher and theologian of

French birth, a leading exponent (possibly the founder) of Nominalism. His most famous pupil was Abélard.

Rose, Roman de la, v. *Roman de la Rose.*

Rose-Croix, Frères de la, v. *Rosicrucianism.*

Rose-Croix, Théâtre de la, v. *Péladan.*

Rosicrucianism. Many 17th- and 18th-c. illuminists (v. *Illuminisme*), claiming various forms of secret and magical knowledge concerning the transmutation of metals, the prolongation of life, power over the elements, etc., professed to belong to a society or order of Rosicrucians, or *Frères de la Rose-Croix*, which had originated in the 15th c., when one Christian Rosenkreuz brought the secret wisdom of the East back with him to Germany. The semi-occult, semi-religious philosophy of Rosicrucianism became prominent in Germany in the 17th c., aroused interest in France in the 18th c., when it had a supposed connection with freemasonry, and in the 19th c. influenced such widely differing writers as Balzac (e.g. his *Études philosophiques*) and the *Symbolists (v. *Villiers de l'Isle-Adam*; *Péladan*).

Rosier de Madame Husson, Le, v. *Maupassant.*

Rosine, in Beaumarchais's Le *Barbier de Séville*; also, as the comtesse Almaviva, in Le *Mariage de Figaro* and *La Mère coupable.*

Rosny, BARON DE, v. *Sully.*

Rosny, J.-H., *joint pseudonym of* JOSEPH-HENRI BOEX (Rosny aîné, 1856–1940; v. *Manifeste des cinq*) and his brother SÉRAPHIN-JUSTIN (Rosny jeune, 1859–1948), novelists who usually wrote in collaboration. Some of their novels had a contemporary interest, e.g. *Nell Horn de l'armée du Salut* (1886), London life; *Le Bilatéral* (1887), anarchist circles in Paris; *Le Termite* (1890) and *La Fauve* (1899),

Parisian literary and theatrical life. Others had prehistoric or semi-scientific settings, e.g. *Vamireh* (1892), *Eyrimah* (1895), *La Guerre au feu* (1911), *Le Félin géant* (1920; by Rosny aîné alone).

Rossbach (in Saxony). Here the army of Frederick the Great defeated (1757) the French (under Soubise) and the Imperialists.

Rossini, GIOACCHINO ANTONIO (1792–1868), the Italian composer, spent much of his life in Paris. He was briefly director of the *Opéra-Comique* (from 1820), then *premier compositeur* to Charles X, a post specially created for him. His famous operas included *Il Barbiere di Siviglia* (prod. 1816 in Rome), based on Beaumarchais's comedy; and *Guillaume Tell* (prod. 1829 in Paris), to a French libretto. His fame and influence in France extended beyond music to literature, also to the social world, where his wit and occasional buffoonery were much appreciated (his Saturday evening receptions were crowded to suffocation). His many admirers included Balzac, who refers to him in *Massimilla Doni* and *Gambara*, and Stendhal, whose *Vie de Rossini* (1823) contains long analyses of the operas and much interesting, fundamentally *Romantic musical and literary criticism.

Rostand, (1) EDMOND (1868–1918), dramatist, won sudden fame with the heroic comedy *Cyrano de Bergerac* (1897) and followed this with L'*Aiglon* (1900) and *Chantecler* (1910). His earlier dramas were *Les Romanesques* (1894), *La Princesse lointaine* (1895; v. *Jaufré Rudel*), *La Samaritaine* (1897); (2) MAURICE (1891–1968), son of (1), author of plays (e.g. *La Gloire*, 1921, v. *Bernhardt*; *Le Secret du sphinx*, 1924, both in verse), poetry, and novels; (3) JEAN (1894–1977), son of (1), biologist and man of letters (a member of the *Académie*), author of works on the nature and general moral significance of modern biological discoveries.

Rôtisserie de la Reine Pédauque, La

(1893), a famous philosophical romance (*cf. Voltaire*) by A. France.

The time is the 18th c. The learned abbé Jérôme Coignard combines a liberal humanism with a deep, ingenuous piety. He loves women. He sustains himself in misfortune with a bottle of wine and a copy of the *Consolation* of Boethius drawn from his cloak pocket. He steals diamonds, but when they prove false and unsaleable he sees it as a manifestation of God's will to preserve him from sin. Preferment continually passes him by. In return for meals at the *Reine Pédauque*, he becomes tutor to Jacques Ménétrier, known as 'Tournebroche' ('Turnspit'), the proprietor's son (and narrator of the story). The pair undertake to translate Greek papyri for M. d'Astarac, an eccentric occultist who lives in a dilapidated *château* in a world of sylphs and salamanders. In a pavilion in the grounds live Mosaïde, supposedly a centenarian scholar learned in the *Cabale* (in fact, an absconding Portuguese banker), and Jahel, not really a salamander, but his niece, beautiful and free with her charms. Following a brawl in Paris, the abbé, Jacques, and a rakish marquis enamoured of Jahel flee the city, taking her with them. Mosaïde pursues them and stabs the abbé, believing him to be Jahel's abductor. The abbé's death is edifying. The marquis and Jahel continue their journey; Jacques returns to Paris, to become a bookseller.

Les Opinions de Jérôme Coignard (1893), ostensibly a collection made by Jacques of the abbé's reflections on life, is a vehicle for A. France's sharp criticism of the contemporary scene.

Rotrou, JEAN DE (1609–50), dramatist, one of Richelieu's *cinq auteurs*, a friend of Corneille and his only real rival in his day. His first play, *L'Hypocondriaque, ou le Mort amoureux* (1628), appeared before he was 20, his tragedy *Hercule mourant* in 1634. His best plays, which show a marked advance in style and romantic quality on those of Hardy, were the tragedies *Saint Genest* (1646), *Venceslas* (1647), and *Cosroès* (1649; the story of a sanguinary

struggle for power at the court of the aged Persian king Cosroès); the tragicomedies *Laure persécutée* (1637) and *Don Bernard de Cabrère* (1647); the comedies *Les Sosies* (1636; the plot, based on Plautus's *Amphitruo*, is the same as that of the *Amphitryon* of Molière, who drew freely on Rotrou's comedies) and *La Sœur* (1645). He drew his themes from many sources, including the Spanish authors Lope de Vega (*Laure persécutée* and *Saint Genest*) and Francisco de Rojas (*Venceslas*). He died at his native Dreux, where he was *lieutenant civil*, having refused to leave his post during an epidemic.

Roucher, JEAN-ANTOINE (1745–94), poet. His *Les Mois* (1779), a descriptive poem on the model of Thomson's *Seasons* (v. *Foreign Influences*, 2), shows a love of nature and includes some good lines, but soon relapses into the commonplace. He was guillotined on the same day as A. Chénier.

Rouge et le Blanc, Le, v. *Lucien Leuwen*.

Rouge et le Noir, Le (1830), by Stendhal, a novel depicting the social order under the Restoration (1814–30). The title has been variously explained as standing for the careers of arms and the Church, for republicanism and clerical reaction, etc.

Julien Sorel, a carpenter's son, combines a sensitive and noble spirit with boundless and calculating ambition. Under Napoleon he might have won glory in the army, now only the Church offers possibilities of advancement, by means of intrigue and hypocrisy, to a youth without birth or fortune. As a first step, he becomes tutor to the children of M. de Rênal, mayor of Verrières, and dares himself to seduce the virtuous Mme de Rênal. Having succeeded, he falls as much in love with her as she with him—a flash of sensibility. To avoid gossip he departs to the seminary at Besançon. Here, though unpopular, he does brilliantly and is sent to Paris as secretary to the marquis de La Môle. Again triumphing over disadvantages, he wins the marquis's confidence, the respect of the household and its frequenters, and the love of Mathilde, the marquis's arrogant daughter. It suits his ambition to respond, and he seduces her. More in love than ever, she insists on marriage. To avoid scandal her father arranges for Julien to be ennobled and commissioned in the army. Wedding preparations are going forward when the marquis gets a letter from Mme de Rênal denouncing Julien as a monster who uses seduction as a means to advancement. Julien, in a cold fury, decides that only her death can satisfy his honour, returns to Verrières, finds her praying in church, and fires at her. He is arrested and, despite the efforts of both Mathilde and Mme de Rênal (repentant and only slightly injured), condemned to death. He goes to the scaffold undaunted and with no regrets, resigned to having lost his battle with destiny. Mme de Rênal dies broken-hearted. Mathilde, in macabre imitation of a 16th-c. ancestress, procures his head and gives it a magnificent burial— a melodramatic episode thought by some critics to be out of keeping with the rest of the novel.

Rougemont, DENIS DE (1906–   ), a Swiss Protestant whose essays reflect his deep commitment to *Personnalisme* (*v.* Mounier) and later to European federalism; founder and director from 1950 of the *Centre européen de la Culture* in Geneva. His works include *Politique de la personne* (1933), introducing the term *engagement* in its political sense; *Penser avec les mains* (1936); *Journal d'Allemagne* (1938); *L'Amour et l'Occident* (1939); *La Part du diable* (1942); *L'Aventure occidentale de l'homme* (1956); *Journal d'une époque, 1926–1946* (1968); *Lettre ouverte aux Européens* (1970).

Rouget de Lisle, CLAUDE-JOSEPH (1760–1836), a very minor poet and musician, famous as the author of the **Marseillaise*. He retired from the army in 1796 and thereafter eked out a living by copying music. His *Chants français* (1825) were settings of songs by various authors. He was pensioned by Louis-Philippe. On 14

July 1915 his ashes were transported to the **Panthéon*.

Rougon-Macquart, Les (1871–93), the collective title of the cycle of 20 novels written by Zola to illustrate his theories of the **Naturalist novel: La Fortune des Rougon* (1871), *La *Curée* (1872), *Le *Ventre de Paris* (1873), *La *Conquête de Plassans* (1874), *La Faute de l'abbé Mouret* (1875), **Son Excellence Eugène Rougon* (1876), *L'*Assommoir* (1877), *Une Page d'amour* (1878), **Nana* (1880), *Pot-Bouille* (1882), **Au bonheur des dames* (1883), *La Joie de vivre* (1884), **Germinal* (1885), *L'*Œuvre* (1886), *La *Terre* (1887), *Le Rêve* (1888), *La *Bête humaine* (1890), *L'*Argent* (1891), *La *Débâcle* (1892), *Le Docteur Pascal* (1893). Zola described the series as 'l'histoire naturelle et sociale d'une famille sous le Second Empire' and intended it as a study of the recurrence and development of transmitted character-istics (mainly vicious) over five generations of one family, the Rougon-Macquarts.

The first novel, *La Fortune des Rougon*, introduces various generations of the Rougons, the legitimate branch, and the Macquarts, the low-class, illegitimate branch—offspring of an affair between the mentally unbalanced Rougon grand-mother, Adèle, and a drunken smuggler. The plot is concerned with the events of the years 1848–52 and with politics, class-warfare, and intrigues in the small Provençal town of Plassans (actually Aix-en-Provence), where the family lives. During the **coup d'état* of 1851 the greedy, ambitious Pierre and Félicité Rougon intrigue surreptitiously with their dissolute half-brother Antoine Macquart and exploit events to secure power and social position.

In subsequent novels the scene shifts about the country and up and down the social scale, depicting the *bourgeois* world of tradespeople and financiers, the worlds of politics, art, the Church, the army, and medicine, the lives of the victims of industrialism in the slums and brothels of Paris, in the mines, and on the railways, and of the peasants in the countryside. In the last novel, *Le Docteur Pascal*, the plot turns on a love affair between the ageing doctor and his niece Clotilde, but the book is mainly of interest as a summary of preceding history and an exposition of the theme of the series. It is prefaced by a family tree with a brief case-history attached to each name. This is attributed to Pascal, who had renounced a promising career to write a great work on heredity, based on his own family. It is in this novel that the drunken Antoine Macquart goes up in flames by spontaneous combustion and is reduced to a spot of grease and a few ashes!

Rouletabille, Joseph, v. Leroux, G.

Roumanille, JOSEPH (1818–91), Provençal poet, leader (with Mistral) of the *Félibrige*. His works, written in Provençal, include *Li Margarideto* (i.e. *Les Pâquerettes*, 1847), *Li Flour de sauvi* (i.e. *Les Fleurs de sauge*, 1859). He also edited *Li Prouvençalo* (1852), a collection of Provençal poetry.

Roumieux, LOUIS (1829–94), Provençal poet, author of comedies; a mock-heroic poem (*La Jarjaiado*, 1878); and collections of verse, some humorous, including *La Rampelado* (i.e. *Le Rappel*, 1868) and *Li Couquiho d'un roumiéu* (i.e. *Les Coquilles* [misprints] *d'un pèlerin*, 1890–4), a punning allusion to the fact that he long worked as a proof-reader.

Rousseau, HENRI (1844–1910), a self-taught artist known as 'le Douanier Rousseau' because, before becoming a professional painter (*c.* 1885), he had worked in the *octroi* (a form of local customs or toll-collection service) outside Paris. His portrait groups and scenes from exotic nature have a remarkable primitive quality which was derided in his lifetime, but brought him posthumous fame.

Rousseau, JACQUES (1630–93), a court artist under Louis XIV. He went to London (1690) to decorate Montagu House and Hampton Court, and died there.

Rousseau, JEAN-BAPTISTE (1671–1741), regarded as one of the chief poets of his age, a man of arrogant temper and caustic humour. He was banished (1707) for some defamatory verses, probably unjustly attributed to him, and spent 30 years in miserable exile, finally pitied even by his enemy Voltaire. A collection of his odes and other poems (1723), mainly panegyrical or on themes drawn from the Scriptures, shows competence rather than vigour or inspiration; he is perhaps at his best in his satirical epigrams and some of his imitations of the Psalms.

Rousseau, JEAN-JACQUES (1712–78), philosopher, b. at Geneva. His mother died when he was born. His father, a watchmaker, was a man of restless, unstable character; he read romances with his son, developing prematurely his sensibility and imagination, but did little to educate him and deserted the home when the boy was 10. After a short period of schooling, Jean-Jacques was set to work with a notary, then with an engraver. Unhappy with both, he left Geneva (1728), wandered about the country, and found a protectress in Mme de *Warens. She sheltered him on and off for some 12 years, first at Annecy, then at Les Charmettes, her small farmhouse near Chambéry in Savoy. She also arranged for him to be received at Turin into the Roman Catholic Church (he was never at heart a Catholic and reverted to Protestantism in 1754). It was in Turin that his taste for music was first aroused, and he subsequently studied it with ardour. After a spell of wandering, during which he took service as a lackey and gave music lessons, he returned to Mme de Warens. At Les Charmettes (from 1738) he applied himself for the first time to methodical study of history, philosophy, science, and mathematics. After an unsuccessful experiment as a private tutor at Lyons, he finally left Mme de Warens *c.* 1742 and went to Paris, taking with him a new scheme of musical notation from which he hoped to obtain a livelihood. He entered literary society and was briefly secretary to the French ambassador in

Venice, the comte de Montaigu, but fell out with him and returned to France (1744). He now formed a lifelong liaison with Thérèse Levasseur, a coarse, stupid servant-girl, with whom he seems to have lived happily for many years, until her affection turned to aversion. He sent her five children (who may not have been his) to a foundling hospital, later claiming that he did so in their own interests. He first came to the fore with two *Discours (1750 and 1754) on themes proposed by the Académie de Dijon (v. Discours; Vincennes). The consideration of these themes was a turning-point in his life and thought, for he emerged from it with the convictions that underlie his chief works: that man is by nature virtuous, free, and happy; that he has been corrupted by society, the source of property, inequality, and despotism; that in order to restore to him some measure of happiness it is necessary to return to nature so far as is practicable (for he recognized that existing institutions must be retained, because 'la nature humaine ne rétrograde pas').

His Discours were widely read and his pastoral operetta Le Devin du village (first played at court, 1752) was also successful, but his main means of livelihood was copying music. In 1755 he wrote the article Économie politique for the *Encyclopédie (he also wrote some of the articles on music). In 1756 he settled at L'Ermitage, a small house in the Forêt de Montmorency (north of Paris) placed at his disposal by Mme d'*Épinay. Here he wrote his letter to Voltaire protesting against the pessimistic doctrine of his poem on the Lisbon earthquake of 1755. Having quarrelled with Mme d'Épinay (and with his friends Grimm and Diderot), he moved (late 1757) to a cottage at Montmorency, where he received kindly hospitality from the maréchal de *Luxembourg and his wife. Here he wrote or completed the *Lettre à d'Alembert sur les spectacles (1758), Julie, ou la *Nouvelle Héloïse (1761), *Émile (1762), and *Du contrat social (1762). Émile incurred the censure of the *Sorbonne and the *parlement, and Rousseau was in danger of arrest. He took refuge in Switzerland (1762), but persecution by the Genevan and Bernese authorities soon drove him to Motiers (on Prussian soil in the Val-Travers near Neuchâtel). He was here for three years; Frederick the Great's Scottish governor, George Keith, 10th Earl Marischal, treated him with kindness, and he met Boswell (whom he urged to visit Corsica, with consequences that are well known). He now issued his dignified reply (1763) to the charges laid against Émile by the archbishop of Paris, Christophe de Beaumont, and his Lettres écrites de la montagne (1764; condemned by the parlement in 1765), nine letters stoutly defending himself and his religious doctrines against the attacks made by his enemies in Geneva and set forth in J.-R. Tronchin's Lettres écrites de la campagne. The clergy of Neuchâtel having now joined the ranks of his persecutors, he lived for a short time on the island of Saint-Pierre in the Lake of Bienne (v. Rêveries du promeneur solitaire, Les), then went to England (1766), where, thanks to David Hume, he found asylum at Wootton in Derbyshire. The British government granted him a pension of £100. He had always suffered from ill-health (possibly of nervous origin) and morbid sensitiveness, and he was now a victim of persecution mania. He quarrelled with Hume and returned to France in 1767, befriended by the elder Mirabeau and Louis-François, prince de Conti. After a period of wandering, he settled in Paris (1770–8), again partly supporting himself by copying music (he refused to draw his British pension). He died at Ermenonville (v. Girardin, marquis de).

His *Confessions, covering his life down to 1766, are supplemented by three dialogues—Rousseau juge de Jean-Jacques (written 1775–6)—exposing the iniquity of his persecutors with exaggerations savouring of mania, and by the *Rêveries du promeneur solitaire, written in a calmer spirit. All of these appeared posthumously. His other works include his abstract and criticism of the abbé de *Saint-Pierre's Projet de paix perpétuelle (abstract, 1761; the whole work, 1782); and v. Dictionaries, 1768; Musical

Controversies; *Rey*. Publication of a new edition of his correspondence (1965- ; ed. R. A. Leigh) is nearing completion.

Rousseau's chief importance—and the source of his great influence—lies in the fact that, though he was one of the *philosophes* and shared their hatred of the old order of oppression and intolerance, he was also the principal adversary of their philosophy in some of its dominant characteristics. Whereas 18th-c. philosophy was in the main critical, atheistic, materialistic, and based on reason, his philosophy was constructive, deistic, and based on sentiment. Recovering from his early failings and arguing from his own spiritual experience, he was led to condemn society, to preach the return to nature, to maintain the existence of God, conscience, personal virtue (as distinct from social benevolence), and the immortal soul. His writings, marred here and there by provincialisms and faults of taste, reflect his highly developed sensibility and sympathy with nature (some of his finest passages are descriptions of Swiss scenery, simple family life, and the work of the farm). Their lyrical and picturesque qualities mark him as an important precursor of the *Romantics.

Dr. Johnson thought him 'a very bad man'. Even so, he profoundly influenced many English writers, from Thomas Day (author of *Sandford and Merton*) to Wordsworth. Byron writes sympathetically of him in *Childe Harold's Pilgrimage* (canto III).

Rousseau, PIERRE-ÉTIENNE-THÉODORE (1812–67), a landscape painter of the *Barbizon school, known as 'le Grand Refusé' because his works were so often unsuccessful at the *Salons*.

Rousseau juge de Jean-Jacques, *v. Rousseau, J.-J.*

Roussel, ALBERT-CHARLES-PAUL-MARIE (1869–1937), composer of symphonies, ballet-music, etc. (e.g. *Le Festin de l'araignée*, 1913; *Bacchus et Ariane*, 1931).

He had many connections with poets and poetry of the day.

Roussel, RAYMOND (1877–1933), a writer whose originality and importance were greatly underestimated in his lifetime. His first two works, *La Doublure* (1897) and *La Vue* (1904), are long narrative poems characterized by a fastidious precision of descriptive language. It was as a result of their lack of success that he devised the *procédé*, disclosed posthumously in *Comment j'ai écrit certains de mes livres* (1935), which is now regarded as his greatest contribution to literature. He would produce two semantically different sentences from the same phonological material, and these sentences would then provide the first and the last of his text; the intervening story was created by the attempt to link them, e.g. the tale *Parmi les Noirs* (publ. posth. in *Comment j'ai écrit...*, ed. of 1963). He defined this device as 'essentially poetic' and compared it to rhyme as a means of producing 'unexpected creations'. In his longer works—the novels *Impressions d'Afrique* (1910) and *Locus solus* (1914), and the plays *L'Étoile au front* (1924) and *La Poussière de soleils* (1926)—the *procédé* is used to generate whole scenes and episodes. *Nouvelles Impressions d'Afrique* (1932), written in verse, is not based on the *procédé*, but it is none the less organized on linguistic principles. His work was much admired, if not always fully understood, by the *Surrealists (esp. Leiris). It has since had a considerable influence on the *nouveau roman* (esp. on the work of Butor, Robbe-Grillet, and Jean Ricardou) and also on the development of certain theories of the *nouvelle critique* (v. *Critics and Criticism*, 3).

Rousset, JEAN, v. *Critics and Criticism*, 3.

Roussin, ANDRÉ, v. *Theatre of the 19th and 20th cs.*

Roustan (d. 1845), a Mameluke presented to Napoleon in Egypt. Napoleon brought him home as his personal attendant, took him everywhere, and lavished favours on him. He decamped when Napoleon abdicated in 1814.

Roux, PAUL, *v. Saint-Pol-Roux.*

Roxane, in Racine's **Bajazet.*

Royaumont, Abbaye de, a Cistercian abbey near Pontoise (Val d'Oise), f. 1228 by Louis IX. The ruins were restored *c.* 1930 and transformed into the Foyer de Royaumont, a residential hostel providing tranquil working conditions for writers and artists. At intervals since 1945 it has been used, on the lines of the former *décades de *Pontigny,* as a meeting-place for discussion groups, and the summer concerts in the chapel soon became a feature of Parisian musical life.

Royer, CLÉMENCE (1830–1902), philosopher and scientist, the first French translator (1862) of Darwin's *Origin of Species.*

Royer-Collard, PIERRE-PAUL (1763–1845), philosopher and statesman, a noted parliamentary orator (*v. Press,* 5). As professor of the history of philosophy at the **Sorbonne* (from 1811) he brought a rare eloquence and clarity of exposition to his lectures. His political career began after the Restoration, when he became leader, with Guizot, of the **doctrinaires.* His influence declined after the 1830 **Revolution,* but he remained prominent in the educational field.

Royère, JEAN (1871–1956), poet and critic, a disciple of Mallarmé and founder of the review *La *Phalange.* His poetry is collected in *Poésies* (1924; inc. *Exil doré,* 1898; *Eurythmies,* 1904; *La Sœur de Narcisse nue*), *Orchestration* (1936), etc. His collections of essays and his critical studies include *Clartés sur la poésie* (1925), *Frontons* (1932), *Le Point de vue de Sirius* (1935), *Mallarmé* (1927), *Le Musicisme: Boileau, La Fontaine, Baudelaire* (1929). He gave the name *Musicisme* to his poetic doctrines (*cf. Literary Isms*).

Royou, THOMAS, *v. Ami du Roi.*

Rubempré, Lucien de, in Balzac's **Illusions perdues* and **Splendeurs et misères des courtisanes.*

Rudler, GUSTAVE (1872–1957), the first Marshal Foch Professor of French Literature at the University of Oxford (1919–49), an authority on B. Constant. Besides many studies of Constant and a critical edition (1919) of his **Adolphe,* his works include *Les Techniques de la critique et de l'histoire littéraires en littérature française moderne* (1923).

Ruelle, the part of their bedroom where 16th- and 17th-c. ladies of quality received visitors.

Rulhière, CLAUDE DE (*c.* 1735–91), historian and poet. His works include an anecdotal account of the revolution which placed Catherine II on the throne of Russia in 1762 (he was there at the time as secretary to the French minister); an account of the Polish troubles of the period, commissioned 1768 by the French government for the instruction of the dauphin, but left (unfinished) in manuscript until published by Napoleon in 1806 as *Histoire de l'anarchie de Pologne et du démembrement de cette république;* his *Éclaircissements historiques sur les causes de la Révocation de l'Édit de Nantes* (1788), supporting Louis XVI's favourable attitude to the **Huguenots* and also written at the request of the government. He had a considerable gift for epigram and light verse. His verse epistle on *Les Disputes* was inserted by Voltaire in his **Dictionnaire philosophique.* He was admitted to the **Académie* (1787).

Russian Influence, *v. Foreign Influences,* 5–6.

Rute, *v. Wyse* (3).

Rutebeuf, a 13th-c. poet, both **trouvère* and **jongleur,* who lived a wretched life in Paris, always destitute and in debt. He was a poet of remarkable versatility and technical skill, a forceful and eloquent satirist with whom literature not only takes on a more personal and lyrical note, but also begins to direct public opinion and to assume something of a journalistic character (e.g. he vigorously supported *Guillaume de Saint-Amour). His works include *fabliaux, *dits and débats (e.g. the Débat du croisé et du non-croisé, putting the case for and against taking part in the Crusades), satires such as Renart le Bestourné (v. Roman de Renart), and pious works such as the Miracle de Théophile (a short dramatic *miracle about an ambitious priest who sells his soul to the Devil, repents, and is saved by the Virgin Mary) and lives of St. Elizabeth and St. Mary of Egypt. His satire is directed at all classes of society, from Louis IX (for the favour he shows to monks and friars), the pope, and the nobility to merchants, officials, and lazy workmen.

Ruy Blas (1838), a verse drama by Hugo. The scene is 17th-c. Spain. Don César de Bazan, a gay but honourable rascal, has squandered his fortune and disappeared; only his relative Don Salluste, an enemy of the queen, knows that he has joined a troop of bandits. Don Salluste, discovering that his valet Ruy Blas, a man more truly noble at heart than any grandee, worships the queen from afar, schemes to avenge a fancied insult by making her fall in love with a servant. He introduces Ruy Blas at court as the missing Don César, threatening him with dire punishment if he refuses to play his part. 'Don César' soon becomes the chief grandee at court, uses his influence with the king for the good of the people, and wins the queen's love. A false letter (from Don Salluste) begs the queen to come to 'Don César's' house at midnight. The real Don César nearly upsets the plot by arriving unexpectedly (down the chimney), but Don Salluste gets rid of him. The queen arrives, and Ruy Blas tries to effect her escape, but Don Salluste enters by a secret door and insults her by revealing her lover's identity. Ruy Blas kills him, then poisons himself at the queen's feet.

S

Sabatier, MME, v. Présidente, La.

Sabbathier, FRANÇOIS, v. Dictionaries, 1766–1815.

Sablé, MAGDELEINE DE SOUVRÉ, MARQUISE DE (c. 1599–1678), a famous *précieuse, a woman of intelligence and sound judgement. A. Arnauld sent her his Logique for criticism and she and members of her *salon, which was almost as important as the Hôtel de *Rambouillet, helped in the composition of *La Rochefoucauld's Maximes. She later lived at *Port-Royal, in semi-solitude. Her letters have been published, also Maximes et pensées diverses (1678; not all by her hand).

Sac au dos, v. Soirées de Médan, Les.

Sachs, MAURICE (1906–45), a writer who, after a wild, dissipated life, finally disgraced himself during the 1939–45 war and died in mysterious circumstances in Germany. He left chronicles and memoirs (e.g. Au temps du Bœuf sur le toit, Le Sabbat, Chronique d'une jeunesse scandaleuse, La Chasse à courre, La Décade de l'illusion, Tableau des mœurs de ce temps—nearly all publ. posth.) vividly depicting Parisian literary and artistic life during the years 1925–39 (inc. fine portraits of Gide, Cocteau, Maritain, Jacob, etc.) and betraying his own cynicism and despair.

Saci, Le Maître de, v. Le Maître de Saci.

Sacripant, Mlle de, v. Odette.

Sacy, (1) ANTOINE-ISAAC SILVESTRE DE

(1758–1838), one of the great Orientalists of the late 18th and early 19th cs.; (2) his son SAMUEL-USTAZADE SILVESTRE DE (1801–79), a critic and political journalist associated with the *Journal des Débats (his articles were collected in Variétés littéraires, morales et historiques, 1858).

Sade, DONATIEN-ALPHONSE-FRANÇOIS, COMTE (known as MARQUIS) DE (1740–1814), author of licentious and obscene writings. The son of a diplomat, he fought in the Seven Years War, married at 23, and led a life of criminal debauchery until he was condemned to death (1772) by the *parlement, a sentence the king commuted to imprisonment. He passed his captivity (mainly in the *Bastille) in writing (Justine, ou les Malheurs de la vertu; Juliette, ou les Prospérités du vice; La Philosophie dans le boudoir, etc.). Freed by the Revolution, he espoused its cause with some zeal. After 1794 he busied himself with the publication of his works. The personalities in his pamphlet Zoloë et ses acolytes (1801) offended Bonaparte, who had him confined as a lunatic at *Charenton, where he died. As recently as 1957 the French courts upheld a ruling of 1814 banning publication of his works. Some 20th-c. critics, however, stress his importance as a precursor of Nietzsche's Superman and as a psychologist and analyst far ahead of his time; they also contend that his style and his influence on such 19th-c. writers as Lamartine and Baudelaire give him a place in literature.

Sagan, Françoise, pseudonym of FRANÇOISE QUOIREZ (1935–   ), best-selling novelist and playwright. She made her literary début at 18 with Bonjour Tristesse (1954), which won the Prix des Critiques. Many people were shocked to find a pessimistic picture of love, ennui, and cynical amoralism in the work of a young woman. She thereafter maintained her reputation with such novels as Un Certain Sourire (1956); Aimez-vous Brahms? (1959); Les Merveilleux Nuages (1961); La Chamade (1966); Un Peu de soleil dans l'eau froide (1969); Des bleus à l'âme (1972), which alternates a story with

a commentary by the author, who answers the charges of frivolity and decadence made against her by the critics. Her plays include Château en Suède (1960) and Le Cheval évanoui (1966).

Sagesse, v. Verlaine.

Sagesse, De la, v. Charron.

Sagon, FRANÇOIS, v. Marot, C.

Saint-Amant, MARC-ANTOINE DE GÉRARD, SIEUR DE (1594–1661), poet (a member of the original *Académie française) and *libertin, accompanied his close friend the comte d'Harcourt on his campaigns and sea-voyages and on a mission to England (1643), and was later a follower of Marie de Gonzague, queen of Poland. He was a remarkable poet, author of picturesque, at times burlesque, lyrics; vivid and realistic songs of the tavern; and a long, tedious epic, Moïse sauvé (1653). The bizarre and whimsical quality of some of his verse is seen in his well-known sonnet Les Goinfres and in the longer poem La Solitude. He was condemned by Boileau.

Saint-Amour, GUILLAUME DE, v. Guillaume de Saint-Amour.

Saint-Arnaud, JACQUES LEROY DE (1801–54), *maréchal de France, a famous soldier and an able administrator; minister of war at the time of the *coup d'état of 1851 and largely responsible for its success.

Saint-Aubin, Horace de, v. Balzac, H. de.

Saint-Barthélemy, La, v. Bartholomew, Massacre of St.; **Saint-Barthélemy des journalistes, La,** v. Press, 3.

Saint-Cyr, a small town near Versailles, once the home of the Institut de Saint-Cyr (or des filles de Saint Louis) and later of the École spéciale militaire de Saint-Cyr.

The Institut, f. 1686 by Mme de Maintenon and Louis XIV, was a convent school for young ladies of noble birth but

small means. Racine's *Esther* and
Athalie were written for, and first
performed by, its pupils. The school was
closed by the Revolutionary government
in 1793. In 1808 the new military college
founded by Bonaparte (v. *École militaire*)
moved from Fontainebleau to the school
premises at Saint-Cyr. This college—
comparable with Sandhurst in England—
became an *école spéciale*, established at
Saint-Cyr till the 1939–45 war (when its
buildings were severely damaged by
bombing) and since 1946 at Coëtquidan
(Morbihan). Cadets wear a distinctive
hat of shako type, with a cockade of white
plumes (the *panache*) in front. The site at
Saint-Cyr is now occupied by the *Collège
militaire de Saint-Cyr* (opened 1966), a
school on the lines of the *Prytanée
militaire de La Flèche*.

Saint-Cyr, v. *Gouvion-Saint-Cyr*.

Saint-Cyran, ABBÉ DE, v. *Du Vergier de
Hauranne*.

Saint-Denis, Abbaye de, a famous
Benedictine abbey, a few miles north of
Paris, f. 626 by the *Merovingian king
Dagobert; burial-place of the French
kings. v. *Denis, St.*; *Oriflamme*.

Saint-Denis, MICHEL (1897–1971), actor
and director, a nephew of Copeau, with
whom he worked at the *Vieux-Colombier*
and in Burgundy, and founder of the
Compagnie des Quinze. During the 1939–
45 war, as 'Jacques Duchesne', he was
head of the French section of the B.B.C.
in London. He later worked in the theatre
in England (director of the Old Vic
Theatre School, 1946–52; a director of the
Royal Shakespeare Company, etc.),
France, the U.S.A., and Canada.

Sainte-Barbe, v. *Collège Sainte-Barbe*.

Sainte-Beuve, CHARLES-AUGUSTIN
(1804–69), critic, was brought up by his
widowed mother and an aunt, who
strained their slender resources to educate
him. He studied medicine in Paris for over
three years from 1823 (with a year as a

hospital extern), but from 1824 combined
it with literary journalism on the newly
founded *Globe*, writing many articles
appreciative of the young *Romantics.
After 1827 he devoted himself entirely to
literature. Some of his *Globe* articles were
collected in his *Tableau historique et
critique de la poésie française et du théâtre
français au XVIe siècle* (1828), which put
the Romantics on the literary map by
tracing their affinity with Ronsard and the
*Pléiade. A review (early 1827) of Hugo's
Odes et ballades won him the friendship
of Hugo and his wife Adèle, with whom
he soon fell deeply in love. This affair
ended his friendship with Hugo, went far
to cool his sympathy with the Romantic
movement, and left him long a prey to
emotional and spiritual stress. He
traversed phases of *Saint-Simonisme and
of sympathy with Lamennais; and
religious doubt may have been the first
cause of his interest in *Port-Royal. In
1837–8, for the sake of distraction, he
lectured on this subject at the Academy of
Lausanne. His great *Port-Royal* (1840–
59) was the book form of these lectures.
From 1829 he was a regular critic on the
Revue de Paris, and from 1831 (when he
left the *Globe*) also on the *Revue des Deux
Mondes*. His articles in these two reviews
form the basis of his *Critiques et Portraits
littéraires* (1832; 1836–9)—in their turn
the nucleus of his *Portraits littéraires*,
Portraits de femmes, and *Portraits
contemporains*. Soon after the 1848
*Revolution he resigned a congenial post
at the *Bibliothèque Mazarine* (held since
1840) and accepted a temporary chair at
the University of Liège. His lectures there
(1848–9) bore fruit in another notable
work, *Chateaubriand et son groupe littéraire
sous l'Empire* (1861).

    During this half of his career his output
was creative as well as critical. He
published *Vie, poésies et pensées de Joseph
Delorme* (1829) and *Les Consolations*
(1830), collections of intimate, reflective
verse; and the novel *Volupté* (1834),
semi-autobiographical and of interest to
students of introspective fiction. He also
printed for private circulation love poems
addressed to Adèle Hugo (*Le Livre

d'amour, publ. posth.), an action some found in questionable taste.

The second half of his career began when he returned to Paris in 1849 and accepted an invitation from Véron to review, in his own fashion and with almost complete freedom in his choice of books, for the *Constitutionnel*. This was the beginning of his famous *Causeries du lundi*, literary articles published each Monday in either the *Constitutionnel* or the *Moniteur universel* (1849–68), and finally in the *Temps* (1869). The change, shortly before his death, from the *Moniteur* (an official government organ) to the *Temps* (an opposition journal) reflected his final disillusionment with the reactionary policy of the Second Empire, particularly in regard to religion and education. Earlier, his over-complacent support of the *régime* had earned him official rewards and some unpopularity: in 1854 he was appointed professor of Latin poetry at the *Collège de France*, but prevented from lecturing by hostile demonstrations (the lectures were publ. as *Étude sur Virgile*, 1857). He later lectured at the *École normale supérieure* on medieval and 16th-c. French literature (1858–61). In 1865 he was made a member of the *Sénat*, which eased his financial situation in his last years of failing health. Publication of his *Correspondance générale* (ed. J. Bonnerot), which is of great literary interest, began in 1935 (vol. 17, 1975).

He is primarily important as the chief founder of modern literary criticism (v. *Critics and Criticism*, 2). He took the view, novel and stimulating in his day, that criticism should be re-creative rather than dogmatic; that the critic should provide data of the formative influences on an author's character (heredity, environment, education, love and friendships, etc.) and then leave the reader to draw his own conclusions. The carefully documented monographs of the *Lundis* and the *Portraits* are the practical expression of his theories. They also illustrate the astonishing range of his reading and the breadth of view that enabled him to approach widely differing authors, and not French alone. Between them, they cover not only the great figures down to, and in some

cases during, his own day, but also many lesser figures (in his view, important influences on thought, and the most profitable approach to the study of any literary age). They remain an indispensable guide to French literature, particularly of the 17th c. He has been reproached with unfairness to his contemporaries, and there seems to be little doubt that he was at times influenced by his temperamental distastes, even by a nervous jealousy of creative exuberance. But it is also the case that for him literature was 'une religion ardemment embrassée dès l'enfance' and that what mattered above all else was truth. For example, he more than once made it clear that he found the work of contemporary *Realists on the whole lacking in charm, overweighted, and thus neither poetically nor historically true; that he accepted it reluctantly, and only because it was less untrue, and more courageous, than the literature blessed by official opinion.

Sainte-Geneviève, École de, a medieval school belonging to the collegiate church of Sainte-Geneviève on the left bank of the Seine in Paris, outside the jurisdiction of the bishop of Paris. Abélard's teaching there brought it great fame. Early in the 13th c. it briefly assumed a position almost of rivalry to the *University of Paris, the abbot of Sainte-Geneviève conferring degrees on students in its territory.

Sainte-Marthe, (1) CHARLES DE (c. 1512–55), poet, author of *Poésie française* (1540; *rondeaux* and epigrams on Platonic themes); (2) his nephew SCÉVOLE DE (1536–1623), humanist and poet of the school of Ronsard (who hailed him, in a dedication, as 'excellent poète'); he wrote in both French and Latin (v. *Des Roches*). The Sainte-Marthe family was known to Rabelais (v. *Gargantua*).

Sainte-Maure, BENOÎT DE, v. *Benoît de Sainte-Maure*.

Sainte-Palaye, v. *La Curne de Sainte-Palaye*.

Sainte-Pélagie, in Paris, originally a

convent-refuge for women, f. under Louis XIV. From the Revolution it was used as a prison, mainly for debtors and political offenders—especially outspoken writers and journalists. It no longer exists.

Saint-Esprit, Ordre du, a great order of knighthood (comparable to the Garter and the Golden Fleece) f. 1578 by Henri III. It subsisted till the Revolution, was revived under the Restoration, and finally suppressed in 1830. *v. Cordon bleu.*

Saint-Évremond, CHARLES DE SAINT-DENIS, SIEUR DE (1613–1703), man of letters, one of the most distinguished of the *libertins*. Born of a good Norman family, he at first followed a military career, but was obliged to leave France (1661) in consequence of his *Lettre sur le Traité des Pyrénées* (*v. Pyrenees, Treaty of the*) condemning Mazarin's treaty with Spain. He spent most of the rest of his life in England at the courts of Charles II, James II, and William III, on intimate terms with courtiers such as Buckingham and writers such as Hobbes, Waller, and Cowley. He was buried in Westminster Abbey. His works—marked by wit and a sober elegance—include numerous essays on a wide variety of literary, philosophical, and other subjects (inc. one on English comedy); the *Réflexions sur les divers génies du peuple romain* (1663), a pioneer work in treating the study of manners and mentality as part of history, but incomplete and unequal; the *Conversation du maréchal d'Hoquincourt avec le P. Canaye,* a good example of his lighter ironic style; the *Comédie des Académistes* (1643), a comedy satirizing the chief members of the original *Académie française* together with Mlle de Gournay. His literary criticism had considerable influence in England. Some of his essays were translated into English (Dryden wrote a character-sketch of their author for a collection of 1692). His works, with a life by Des Maizeaux, appeared in English in 1714.

Saint-Exupéry, ANTOINE DE (1900–44), aviator and author of works which are a direct transmutation into literature of his physical and spiritual experiences in the air. He qualified as a pilot in 1921 and soon joined the heroic pioneers of the transcontinental air lines, flying in North Africa, across the Atlantic, in South America, etc., and often narrowly escaping death. Later he combined flying with journalism. By 1939 he had won fame with three works which may be broadly classed as novels: *Courrier-Sud* (1928); *Vol de nuit* (1931), which made his name; *Terre des hommes* (1939). He served as a pilot at the beginning of the 1939–45 war, went to North Africa when France fell in 1940, and thence to New York. Here he published *Pilote de guerre* (1942; first publ. in English as *Flight to Arras*), describing his experiences and emotions in 1940; *Lettre à un otage* (1943), propaganda of a very high order; and *Le Petit Prince* (1943), a much more profound work than the children's fairy-tale it professes to be, though among the best of these. In 1943 he returned to North Africa and managed to rejoin his unit (by then attached to the American forces). Though well over flying age and disabled by earlier crashes, he was allowed to undertake a limited number of reconnaissance missions; he failed to return from the last of these. His *La Citadelle* (1948; an unfinished work begun in 1936), meditations in the desert, is for some a modern Bible of humanism.

Saint-Gelais, (1) OCTOVIEN *or* OCTAVIEN DE (1468–1502), courtier, prelate, and a *rhétoriqueur* poet, author of *ballades*, *rondeaux*, etc.; the *Histoire d'Eurialus et Lucrèce,* an erotic poem; the *Séjour d'honneur,* a long allegory drawing instruction from his own life and human life in general; and translations of the classics; (2) his nephew or natural son MELLIN DE (1487–1558), a leading poet of the day (*v. Ronsard*), scholar, and musician. After a long sojourn in Italy, he became a priest, almoner to the king, and keeper of his library at *Fontainebleau. He wrote graceful *rondeaux*, madrigals, etc., on frivolous themes for ladies of the court; lively epigrams; *Sophonisbe* (1559), a tragedy from the Italian of Trissino. He was among the first to introduce the *sonnet, and the general spirit of the Italian Renaissance, from Italy into France.

Saint Genest, Le Véritable, a tragedy by Rotrou; produced 1646. Genest, a favourite actor of the emperor Diocletian, is directed to perform before him a play about the obstinacy and martyrdom of a Christian. Genest is himself a Christian convert and, as he prepares his part, a voice from Heaven encourages him in his resolve. During the performance, he abandons his part, boldly professes his faith, then goes cheerfully to the torture and execution to which Diocletian condemns him.

Saint Genet, comédien et martyr, v. Sartre.

Saint-Georges de Bouhélier, *pseudonym of* STÉPHANE-GEORGES DE BOUHÉLIER-LEPELLETIER (1876–1942), *naturiste* poet and dramatist (*v. Naturisme*). His collections of verse include *Chants de la vie ardente* (1902) and *Romance de l'homme* (1912). The best known of his many plays is probably *Le Carnaval des enfants* (1910; verse), a mixture of religious symbolism and social satire.

Saint-Germain, COMTE DE, a mysterious adventurer, possibly a spy, who appeared at court *c.* 1740 and ingratiated himself with Louis XV and Mme de Pompadour. He appeared to be very wealthy, pretended to have lived in past centuries, and laid claim to occult sources of information on all manner of subjects.

Saint-Germain, Faubourg, v. *Faubourg Saint-Germain*.

Saint-Germain-des-Prés, Abbaye de, a famous abbey in Paris on the left bank of the Seine, f. 558 by Childebert Ier (son of Clovis Ier); burial-place of Childebert and many other *Merovingians. In the Middle Ages, ownership of the Pré-aux-Clercs, a meadow in front of the abbey and a kind of playground of the *University of Paris, was the subject of a dispute between the two institutions which led to violent affrays. The abbey was later the chief house of the *Maurists (Montfaucon and Mabillon worked there). Only its church (rebuilt in the 11th-12th cs.) now remains. *v. Abbaye, Prison de l'*.

St. Helena, v. *Napoleon*.

Saintine, Xavier, *pseudonym of* JOSEPH-XAVIER BONIFACE (1798–1865), novelist and dramatist (the latter usually in collaboration with better-known writers, e.g. Scribe). He had a great success with the graceful, sentimental tale *Picciola* (1836), in which a prisoner's captivity is solaced, and his resentful character softened, by his love for a plant that suddenly appears in the courtyard outside his cell.

Saint-John Perse, *pseudonym of* ALEXIS LÉGER (1887–1975), poet (*Prix Nobel*, 1960), b. in Guadeloupe and educated in France. Before 1940, he was best known as a brilliant career diplomat who, having served in Peking and travelled widely in the Far East, returned to Paris after the 1914–18 war and rose to be secretary-general of the *Ministère des Affaires étrangères* (1933–40). He left France in June 1940, was deprived of French nationality by the Vichy government, and lived till 1958 in the U.S.A., where he worked at the Library of Congress and taught at Harvard. His poetry, which has an epic grandeur and a metaphysical quality (though it is neither heroic nor Christian), celebrates the marvels of the world (esp. of Nature, the sea, the elements, etc.) and expresses faith in the resourcefulness of man. He seeks less to describe than to record and recreate reality, deploying his encyclopedic knowledge of subjects ranging from natural history, ethnology, and Oriental culture to numismatics, using the rhetorical devices of litany and enumeration, and showing a taste for rare words and scintillating, at times obscure, images. His prevailing tone is Biblical and Claudelian (he often uses the *verset* and rhythmical prose). Though the early poems of *Éloges* (1911), inspired by his childhood in the

West Indies, showed *Symbolist influence, he thereafter went largely his own way. *Anabase* (1924), a notable *epic, was conceived during journeys on horseback from Peking up to a temple near the great caravan trails of the Gobi Desert. After a long, self-imposed silence, he published *Exil* (1942), reflecting his despair at the fate of France, then such important collections as *Pluies* (1943), *Neiges* (1944), *Vents* (1946), *Amers* (1957), and *Chronique* (1960). *v.* Lyric Poetry, 4.

Saint-Just, LOUIS DE (1767–94), an able and fanatical lieutenant of Robespierre (*cf. Couthon*) and, like him, a theoretician of the Revolution; a leader of the *Montagnards* (and one of their chief orators) and a member of the *Comité de salut public*. He was executed with Robespierre.

Saint-Lambert, JEAN-FRANÇOIS, MARQUIS DE (1716–1803), poet and *Encyclopédiste*. His poem *Les Saisons* (1769), modelled on Thomson's *Seasons* and describing nature from both a romantic and a philosophic standpoint, met with much success, though sound judges such as Grimm, Diderot, and Mme du Deffand condemned it as flat and tedious. He succeeded Voltaire in the affections of Mme du Châtelet and was the successful rival of J.-J. Rousseau in those of Mme d'Houdetot.

Saint-Lazare, Prison de. This Paris prison, demolished in 1935, was originally a lepers' hospital, built *c.* 1100. In the 17th c. it became the priory and headquarters of the *Congrégation de la Mission* (*v. Vincent de Paul, St.*)—hence their name *Lazaristes*; later, part of it was used as a house of detention for loose-living young men of good family. It was sacked by the people during the Revolution, then used as a prison (A. Chénier was confined there). Later, it became a prison for female delinquents and prostitutes.

Saint-Loup, Marquis de, in Proust's *A la recherche du temps perdu*, nephew of the duc de *Guermantes. Marcel first meets him at *Balbec when he comes to visit his

great-aunt Mme de *Villeparisis, who is at the same hotel as Marcel and his grandmother. The young men become friends and through Saint-Loup Marcel is introduced to the duchesse de Guermantes. He later marries *Gilberte, and in the years before his death in action in the 1914–18 war succeeds his uncle *Charlus in the affections of Morel.

Saint-Marc Girardin, *pseudonym of* MARC GIRARDIN (1801–73), a distinguished critic (anti-*Romantic) and publicist associated for over 40 years with the *Revue des Deux Mondes* and the *Journal des Débats*; also professor of French poetry at the *Sorbonne (1833–63), where his lectures on the treatment of the passions in dramatic literature (collected in *Cours de littérature dramatique*, 1843–68, 5 vols.) drew large audiences. His other works include *Essais de littérature et de morale* (1845), *Souvenirs de voyages et d'études* (1852–3), *Souvenirs et réflexions politiques d'un journaliste* (1859; his articles in the *Journal des Débats*), *La Fontaine et les fabulistes* (1867), *Étude sur Jean-Jacques Rousseau* (1870). Latterly, he was active in politics.

Saint-Martin, LOUIS-CLAUDE DE (1743–1803), 'le Philosophe inconnu', philosopher and mystic, was largely responsible for spreading *Illuminisme* in France. His first work, *Des erreurs et de la vérité* (1775), was influenced by his association with Martines Pasqualis (1715–91), a Portuguese Jew prominent in the history of freemasonry. His later works—very obscure and influenced by the writings (some of which he translated) of the German shoemaker-theosophist Jakob Boehme (1575–1624)—include *L'Homme de désir* (1790), *Le Crocodile, poème épico-magique en CII chants* (1794), *Le Nouvel Homme* (1796), *Le Ministère de l'homme-esprit* (1802).

Saint-Maur, Congrégation de, *v.* Maurists.

Saint-Médard, Convulsionnaires de, *v.* Pâris, F. de.

Saint-Pavin, DENIS SANGUIN DE (1600–

70), a poet of the *libertin* school, author of polished verse (sonnets, epigrams, etc.) showing some boldness of thought and vivacity. He figures in Mme de Sévigné's letters, for his father was seigneur of Livry.

Saint-Pierre, Bernardin de, *v. Bernardin de Saint-Pierre.*

Saint-Pierre, CHARLES-IRÉNÉE CASTEL, ABBÉ DE (1658–1743), economist, a member of the *Club de l'Entresol*; author of many projects of political and economic reform, some absurd, others enlightened, but all inspired by his concern for human welfare and hatred of war and despotism, e.g. a *Projet de paix perpétuelle* (1713), proposing a federation of Europe (*v. Rousseau, J.-J.*). He was a Utilitarian before Bentham, and Montesquieu regarded him as his master; but, in general, he was treated as a dreamer or as a bore. He also wrote *Annales politiques* (memoirs of the reign of Louis XIV) and was expelled from the *Académie* for attacking Louis XIV's administration in his *Discours sur la polysynodie* (1718).

Saint-Pierre, EUSTACHE DE (*c.* 1287–*c.* 1371), a burgher of Calais, famous for his courage and devotion to his fellow citizens on the occasion of the surrender of the town to Edward III (1347).

Saint Pierre et le Jongleur, a *fabliau.* St. Peter wins at dice the souls in Hell entrusted by the Devil during his absence to the custody of a *jongleur.*

Saint-Pol-Roux, *pseudonym of* PAUL ROUX (1861–1940), a minor *Symbolist poet, also known as 'Saint-Pol-le-Magnifique' (*v. Literary Isms*). His works, often obscure, include the three collected volumes of *Les Reposoirs de la Procession* (1893–1907) and *La Dame à la faulx* (1899), a dramatic poem with three speakers—a Man, a Woman, and Death.

Saint-Preux, in J.-J. Rousseau's *La *Nouvelle Héloïse.*

Saintré, Petit Jehan de, v. *Petit Jehan de Saintré, Histoire du.*

Saint-Réal, CÉSAR VICHARD, ABBÉ DE (1639–92), author of historical works, notably the *Histoire de la conjuration des Espagnols contre Venise* [an episode of 1618] (1674; Eng. trans. 1675), the source of Otway's *Venice Preserv'd. v. Mazarin's Nieces* (6).

Saints, Lives of. Throughout the Middle Ages, from as early as the 10th c., lives of saints—founded on or inspired by Latin texts, tales of contemporary martyrs, etc.—occupied an important place among the subjects treated by French and *Anglo-Norman poets; for well-known examples *v. Léger, Vie de Saint*; *Alexis, Vie de Saint*; *Brendan, St.*; *Thomas Becket, Vie de Saint.* They are an older literary form than the *chansons de geste,* and a clear influence on these. Originally, they were no doubt closely associated with church services, and they continued to be principally composed by clerks for the edification of church congregations. In due course, however, lives of saints were also written by lay poets (e.g. Rutebeuf and Wace) and came to be included in the repertory of the *jongleurs.* There are also numerous lives in prose. *Cf. Religious Writings,* 1.

Saint-Saëns, CAMILLE (1835–1921), organist and composer of operas, symphonic poems, and chamber music.

Saint-Simon, CLAUDE-HENRI DE ROUVROY, COMTE DE, *v. Saint-Simonisme.*

Saint-Simon, LOUIS DE ROUVROY, DUC DE (1675–1755), famous for his *Mémoires,* came of an old but inconsiderable family of the Vermandois and was maintained by Louis XIV in his father's functions of *duc et pair* (i.e. member of one of the royal councils; *v. Conseil d'état,* 1). He was a little man of sickly appearance, violent temper, and narrow intelligence, excessively occupied with his importance as *duc et pair*; a pious but not intolerant Catholic, with an antipathy to knaves and hypocrites. He resigned from the army (1702) on the grounds that his promotion had been unduly slow. This, and his pride, alienated the king, whom he detested. Even so, he lived at court, hoping for high office, and won the favour of the duc de Bourgogne (v. *Grand Dauphin*). When the duc became heir to the throne, he was one of the cabal which discussed the future constitution. He advocated a reform in the direction of a constitutional monarchy, with greater power for the nobility. The duc's death was a severe blow to him. He now attached himself to the duc d'*Orléans, and with more capacity might have come to the fore during the *Régence*; as it was, his only success was a mission to Madrid (1722) to fetch the Infanta (betrothed to Louis XV). After the regent's death (1723) he retired from court and turned to the preparation of his *Mémoires*. He had first contemplated writing these at the age of 19, and had then begun recording his observations. Between 1740 and 1750, drawing on his notes, on a copy of *Dangeau's unpublished *Journal* (which he obtained c. 1730), and on his remarkable memory, he composed a voluminous record of the later years of Louis XIV (from the siege of Namur, 1692) and of the *Régence*; also a supplement down to the death of Fleury (1743), which is lost. After his death the manuscript was claimed by his creditors and was sequestrated by the State (1760). The first authentic edition did not appear till 1829–30 and was imperfect; a correct edition was published between 1879 and 1928.

His *Mémoires* are not the work of a critical, accurate historian. He aims at the truth, but mingles gossip with facts and admits that impartiality is beyond him. His failure to achieve high office embittered him and warped his judgement, but it gave added vividness and intensity to his descriptions of people and events. He is famous for his brilliant portraits of contemporaries, from the king and the royal family, Mme de Maintenon, Vendôme, Fénelon, and other great generals and prelates, to a host of minor characters (some English, e.g. Sir Richard Temple and Elizabeth Hamilton, wife of the comte de Gramont), often sketched in a few pungent words. He is equally successful at depicting crowded scenes and dramatic incidents, and at evoking their setting—the galleries and terraces of *Versailles. Notable descriptions are those of the scene of consternation at the death of 'le *Grand Dauphin', of the *lit de justice* of 1718 (when the duc du Maine was degraded to the rank of an ordinary peer), and of the king's visit to the camp at Compiègne (1698). As with the portraits, the effect is enhanced by his eye for minute details. He is also much occupied with marriages and other events in high society, with genealogies, with the minute description of ceremonies, and with points of etiquette (e.g. the *droit du *tabouret*). He shows incidental appreciation of Racine, La Bruyère, La Fontaine, etc., but no great interest in literature. His own style is rich and varied, at times impassioned and incorrect; his vocabulary is copious and expressive.

Saint-Simonisme, a system of social philosophy inaugurated by CLAUDE-HENRI DE ROUVROY, COMTE DE SAINT-SIMON (1760–1825), a member of the same family as the above. At 18 he fought in the American War of Independence. He was home again by the Revolution, but stood aside from it. He speculated successfully in *biens nationaux*, travelled, married, and lived extravagantly. Both his marriage and his fortune foundered, and from c. 1808 he was almost destitute. He had always pursued vague political and scientific studies and gradually became convinced of the need for a reorganization of society which would give the controlling share in government to industrialists and scientists, on the grounds that only they work for the moral and physical welfare of mankind. True Christianity, he held, is a social religion of love and charity, not a matter of doctrine; each man's duty is to strive, in a society framed to that end, for the betterment of his poorer brethren. Here he was the apostle of a new humanitarian lay religion. He expounded his doctrines in *Réorganisation de la société européenne* (1814), *Le Système industriel* (1821), *Le Catéchisme des industriels* (1823–4), *Le Nouveau Christianisme* (1825), etc.; also in two short-lived periodicals,

L'Industrie (1816) and *L'Organisateur* (1819).

Saint-Simon's teaching, which won little following in his lifetime, was continued after his death by his disciples (the *Saint-Simoniens*), notably Armand Bazard (1791–1832; author of *L'Exposition de la doctrine saint-simonienne*, 1828–30), Barthélemy-Prosper Enfantin (1796–1864; 'le Père Enfantin', author of *Économie politique*, 1831; *Morale*, 1832, etc.), and Olinde Rodrigues (1794–1851). They held meetings in Paris and the provinces, used *Le *Globe* as their official organ, and within six years developed Saint-Simon's theories far beyond their confused beginnings, exerting a far-reaching influence on their own and succeeding generations. They held that history had alternated between negative *états critiques* (war and antagonism) and constructive *états organiques* (obedience and association), and that hope for the future lay in the spirit of association. To this end, they advocated the abolition of hereditary rights, the introduction of social equality and the disappearance of the exploited classes, the furtherance of education, and the emergence of a State in which finance and industry would be on a level with science and art, with work as the touchstone of merit. They also, in advance of their time, believed in disarmament and the protection of the rights of small peoples. They professed a religion based on fraternity and love, formed themselves into a 'collège', later called an 'église', and introduced a form of sacerdotalism, with Bazard and Enfantin as 'pères suprêmes'. They lived as a community in a house in central Paris (1829) till dissension arose; Bazard and others then seceded, the rest followed Enfantin to Ménilmontant, then a suburb of Paris (1831). They adopted a symbolical dress: white trousers (love), a red waistcoat (work), and a violet-blue tunic (faith), signifying that their creed was based on love, fortified by work, and enveloped by faith; the tunic also symbolized fraternity and mutual help, for it buttoned up the back. Life ran less smoothly at Ménilmontant: confusion arose between the theories of female emancipation and community of property; also, Enfantin's ideas became increasingly mystical and he sent envoys in search of a female Messiah, who was to be his bride (it has been said that Lady Hester Stanhope declined this honour). Meanwhile, the authorities had become uneasy and the sect was disbanded in the interests of public morals.

It was Enfantin who first suggested the piercing of the Suez Canal (*v. Lesseps*), and many former *Saint-Simoniens* later made practical use of their theories of group association by promoting joint-stock companies, schemes of industrial development, etc.

Saint-Sorlin, *v. Desmarets de Saint-Sorlin.*

Saint-Sulpice, a famous seminary for priests (f. 1635) in Paris, figures in literary works ranging from the duc de *Saint-Simon's *Mémoires* to Renan's *Souvenirs d'enfance et de jeunesse*. It was bitterly hostile to the *Jansenists. Fénelon received priestly orders there.

Saint-Victor, Abbaye de, formerly on the left bank of the Seine in Paris, the abbey (built 1113 by Louis VI) of the canons regular of St. Victor (the Victorines, a house f. by Guillaume de Champeaux when, under attack by Abélard, he retired to the then priory of Saint-Victor). In the 16th c., its library, deemed the richest in France, was thrown open to students; Rabelais was familiar with it (*v. Pantagruel*). The abbey was suppressed in 1790 and many of its manuscripts and books eventually found their way to the *Bibliothèque nationale* and the *Bibliothèque de l'Arsenal*.

Saint-Victor, PAUL, COMTE DE (1825–81), man of letters and dramatic critic (notably on *La *Presse*). His chief work was a study of the origin and development of the drama, *Les Deux Masques* (1880–3, 3 vols.).

Saisnes, Chanson des, *v. Bodel.*

Saison en enfer, Une, v. Rimbaud.

Salacrou, ARMAND (1899–), dramatist, in youth a *Surrealist and a Communist journalist. His plays—ranging from tragedy to comedy and ironical farce, often with a streak of poetry—include *Le Casseur d'assiettes* (1925), *Atlas-Hôtel* (1931), *L'Inconnue d'Arras* (1935), *Un Homme comme les autres* (1936), *La Terre est ronde* (1938; a drama of religious fanaticism in Renaissance Italy), *Histoire de rire* (1939), *Le Soldat et la sorcière* (1945), *Les Nuits de la colère* (1946; a drama of the *Resistance), *L'Archipel Lenoir* (1947; satirizing *bourgeois* society), *Boulevard Durand* (1960). Many were produced by his friend Dullin at the *Atelier*.

Salammbô (1862), by Flaubert, a novel of ancient Carthage in which he gave full rein to the romantic side of his nature, his love of colour and magnificence. The background is evoked with a meticulous care for historical and archaeological exactitude which cost him years of labour and, in the view of some critics, weakened the book.

   The time is after the first Punic war, when Carthage was besieged by rebellious mercenaries. Their leader Mathô, a superb Libyan giant, loves Salammbô, daughter of Hamilcar, the Carthaginian leader, and priestess in the temple of the goddess Tanit. Mathô enters Carthage by stealth and steals from Salammbô's guardianship the sacred veil of Tanit. For a time the fate of Carthage is in the balance and the high priest orders her to retrieve the stolen treasure. She goes to Mathô's tent and gives herself to him in return for the veil. The mercenaries are defeated. Mathô is tortured to death and the grief-stricken Salammbô dies soon after.

Salavin, Louis, the hero of Duhamel's *Vie et aventures de Salavin*, a cycle of five novels (1920–32). Under a shabby, unobtrusive exterior he is full of fears and ambitions, diffident to a degree, yet ever at the mercy of overriding impulses. In *Confession de minuit* (1920) he yields to an impulse to touch his employer's fat red ear with his finger and loses his job as a clerk. In *Deux Hommes* (1924), where he loses the friend he has made because he cannot respond generously to simple devotion, his failure is spiritual. In *Le Journal de Salavin* (1927; in diary form) he is a prey to agonies of self-disgust and resolves to become a saint. An effort to stamp out dishonesty around him, the first step in a pitifully farcical martyrdom, merely loses him his job with a fraudulent dairy company; and he again comes to grief when he flees home to live in chastity and seek grace through organized religion. In *Le Club des Lyonnais* (1929) he seeks grace through politics rather than religion, but his experiences with a group of Communists intensify his sense of spiritual failure. He decides that change of soul will never come in Europe, and *Tel qu'en lui-même* (1932; a title taken from Mallarmé's *Le *Tombeau d'Edgar Poë*) finds him in Tunis, nominally running a gramophone shop. He works daily at the native hospital, doing sickening menial tasks that others shun. He also tries to reform his nauseous Arab servant, who shoots him. His wife, a devoted, inarticulate creature, from the outset in the background, is sent for and gets him back to Paris, where he dies. The reader is left to decide how nearly he achieved spiritual perfection.

Salel, HUGUES (*c.* 1504–53), poet, almoner to François Ier; author of an early verse translation of the *Iliad* (*v. Jamyn*), *blasons*, and other occasional pieces.

Sales, FRANÇOIS DE, *v. François de Sales*.

Saliat, PIERRE, a 16th-c. translator of Herodotus (*Les Neuf Livres des histoires*).

Salic Law, the code of law (in Latin) of the Salian Franks. It stipulates that a woman can have no portion in the inheritance of Salic land. It was supposed, wrongly, to be by virtue of this law that women were deemed incapable of succeeding to the throne of France (*v. Valois*).

Sallo, DENIS DE, *v. Journal des savants*.

Salmasius, *v. Saumaise*.

Salmon, ANDRÉ (1881–1969), poet, novelist, and art critic; one of a *Cubist group which included Apollinaire, Jacob, and the painter Picasso. His works—a mixture of fantasy and realism, simplicity and irony, in the Cubist manner—include *Les Féeries* (1907), *Le Calumet* (1910), *Prikaz* (1919), *Peindre* (1922), *Tendres Canailles* (1913; a novel of the underworld of the *Quartier latin*), *La Négresse du Sacré-Cœur* (1920), *L'Entrepreneur d'illuminations* (1921).

Salomé (1893), by Oscar Wilde, a one-act drama in French, based on the Biblical story of Salome and John the Baptist. Its public performance was banned in England (1893), and it was first produced in Paris in 1896, while Wilde was in Reading Gaol. The composer Richard Strauss later made an opera of it.

Salomon et Marcoul, Dialogues de, a 13th-c. work in which Solomon propounds lofty maxims, each of which Marcoul contradicts with a common proverb. One of the exchanges is quoted by Rabelais (*Gargantua*, ch. 33).

Salon, (1) an assembly held regularly (usually on one or more days of the week) in a private house, presided over by the lady, or sometimes the master, of the house and frequented by a more or less constant company; (2) an exhibition of work by living artists.

1. The intellectual *salon*, from the outset notable for the influence it enabled women to exert, may be said to have taken shape in the assemblies presided over in the 17th c. by Mme de Rambouillet, Mme de Sablé, and others. In its early days it favoured the growth of polite manners, delicacy of sentiment, and purity of language; it also helped society to recover from the divisive effects of the wars of religion. Then, and later, the *salons* sometimes degenerated into coteries, mutual admiration societies,

or centres of intrigue (both literary and political), creating or destroying reputations, promoting admissions to the *Académie*, etc., and fostering a literature that was witty, luminous, and instructive, but impersonal and colourless. The *salon* suffered a decline during the later years of Louis XIV's reign and the *Régence*, when Parisian society was drawn to *Versailles and the courts of the princes. After this, however, a host of new *salons* came into being, each with its special characteristics, largely dependent, as always, on the taste and temperament of the hostess, and often also on her political sympathies. During the second half of the 18th c. the *salons*—now the meeting-places of the *philosophes and the *Encyclopédistes, and eventually of budding Revolutionaries, as well as of less committed writers, artists, and scholars—reached the height of their influence and were a power in the land. The great days of the *salon* as a formative influence on culture and taste ended with the Revolution, which dispersed the society in which it had thrived. For some of the famous *salons* and centres of pre-Revolutionary society v. *Cornuel*; *Delorme*, *Marion*; *Du Deffand*; *Épinay*; *Geoffrin*; *Helvétius*; *Holbach*; *Lambert*; *Lenclos*; *Lespinasse*; *Luxembourg, duchesse de*; *Maine, duchesse du*; *Necker*; *Palais-Royal*; *Rambouillet, Hôtel de*; *Sablé*; *Scudéry, Mlle de*; *Staël*; *Suard*; *Temple*; *Tencin*; and cf. *Dorat, C.-J.*; *Rœderer*.

The few *salons* of the Revolutionary era were less sophisticated and urbane and more political (e.g. that of Mme Roland). There was some revival of the *salon* under the *Consulat* and Empire, with the return of the *émigrés* and the creation of the *Napoleonic aristocracy; moreover, Napoleon encouraged his officers to marry and their wives to open *salons*. Notable *salons* of this period were those of the marquise de Condorcet; Mme de Staël (in Paris, when Napoleon tolerated her presence there, and also at *Coppet); the duchesse d'Abrantès; Mme de Montesson, who organized Napoleon's court at the *Tuileries and whose *salon* revived an aristocratic past; Mme de Genlis, who received in her rooms at the

Hôtel de l'Arsenal and entertained her guests with *proverbes dramatiques*; and the young Mme Récamier, whose brilliant company included many English visitors (e.g. Fox and Lord and Lady Holland), but too many critics of the *régime* for Napoleon's liking.

After the Restoration (1814) until her death in 1817 Mme de Staël's *salon* in Paris was 'un miroir où se peint l'histoire du temps'; her guests included Wellington. During this Restoration period (1814-30) Mme Récamier's *salon* (at the Abbaye-aux-Bois from 1819) was again a centre, with reading, acting, and music by way of entertainment. Other notable *salons* and gatherings of these years were Nodier's *salon* at the *Bibliothèque de l'Arsenal*, the first of the Romantic *cénacles* (within a few years the second *cénacle* was meeting at Hugo's home in Paris); Cuvier's Saturday evenings at his home at the *Jardin des Plantes*, frequented by Stendhal, Mérimée, Delacroix, Jacquemont, etc.; Mme Ancelot's *salon*, which flourished well into the Second Empire (it was called 'une porte d'entrée de l'Académie française') and where poets, social reformers, and historians would soon be enjoying recitations by the young actress Rachel; the baron Gérard's Wednesday evenings at his studio, where Balzac could be seen.

During the July Monarchy two Englishwomen, Mary Clarke (later Mme Mohl; *v.* next §) and her mother, became firmly established among the intellectual hostesses of Paris society. Mme Récamier's *salon*, now in its last phase, was increasingly a shrine for Chateaubriand. Other *salons* of this period included those of Mme Émile de Girardin (frequented by writers, journalists, and politicians); the comtesse de Boigne; the Russian princesse de Lieven (frequented by Guizot and the *doctrinaires*); the Italian princesse Belgiojoso (frequented by Mignet, Thierry, Musset, etc.); the Russian Mme Schwetchine, a Roman Catholic convert, who lived in Paris (1825-57) and was active in religious and educational controversies (frequented by Lacordaire, Montalembert, etc.).

Literary and artistic *salons* of the Second Empire included those of the princesse *Mathilde*; the marquise de Ricard (frequented by the young *Parnassiens*; *v. Ricard*); Mme d'Agoult (frequented, on Sunday afternoons, by writers, historians, philosophers, and most of the political opposition; Thiers would lecture brilliantly on any question put to him); and Mme Mohl (*née* Mary *Clarke*), who is said to have dispensed tea and biscuits to the 'élite des hommes du jour', French and foreign. Artists, writers, and musicians were entertained in more Bohemian fashion by Mme de Païva and Mme Sabatier (*v. Païva, La; Présidente, La*), and by the young Mme Nina de Callias (one-time wife of a journalist), who befriended many young members of her circle, including Verlaine.

Most of the *salons* of the later 19th c. revolved around one particular figure, e.g. Dumas *fils* in the very strictly ruled *salon* of Mme d'Aubernon (herself a brilliant talker), A. France in that of Mme Arman de Caillavet (frequented by the young Proust), J. Lemaître in that of Mme de Loynes, where the temper was strongly anti-*Dreyfus*; *v.* also *Adam, Mme*. Proust described some of the *salons* of the day in articles contributed to *Le *Figaro* (1900-5; collected in *Chroniques*, 1927) and conveyed an even better idea of them in his *À la recherche du temps perdu* (*v. Verdurin; Villeparisis*).

2. The first such exhibition in France was organized by the *Académie royale de Peinture et de Sculpture* at the instigation of Colbert and held in 1667 in one of the large rooms (a *salle* or *salon*) in the *Louvre*. There were exhibitions at irregular intervals until 1795, with periods when they were biennial or annual. They were resumed biennially after the Revolution and became annual after 1849. The right to exhibit was at first limited to the 40 members of the *Académie royale*. Since the mid-19th c. there has been a selection committee, and the *Salons* are now held in the Grand Palais des Champs-Élysées. In time, the word *Salon* was used for other art exhibitions, e.g. the *Salon des indépendants, Salon d'automne, Salon des refusés* (*v. Impressionism*). *Diderot's Salons* in-

augurated the *genre* of art criticism in France and *Baudelaire's *Salons* marked its progress in the 19th c.

Salpêtrière, La, now a famous hospital in Paris (also an institution for the aged and incurable). It was originally a prison (built *c.* 1650 on the site of an arsenal and salt-petre works) for vagrants and prostitutes, later also for lunatics and, during the Revolution, for political offenders (confined in a part of the building called *La Force*—the scene of some of the worst of the September Massacres; *v. Revolutions*, 1 (1792)). It was to this prison, notorious for filth and vice, that *Manon Lescaut was sent.

Samain, ALBERT (1858–1900), a poet, poor and consumptive, who worked as a clerk and devoted his spare time to literature. His verse shows *Symbolist influence and he helped to found the *Mercure de France*, but he belonged to no one school. His poetry is collected in *Au jardin de l'infante* (1893), sonnets and elegiac verse of great beauty which brought him sudden renown; *Aux flancs du vase* (1898), short, less successful poems of Greek antiquity; and *Le Chariot d'or* (1901). He also left tales (*Contes*, 1903) and a verse drama, *Polyphème* (1906; prod. 1904 at the *Théâtre de l'*Œuvre).

Saman, Madame de, *v. Allart de Méritens.*

Sambre-et-Meuse, L'Armée de, the most famous of the Revolutionary armies. Under Jourdan, it won the important victory of Fleurus (in Belgium; June 1794), defeating the united Austrian and Netherlands armies.

Sand, George, *pseudonym of* AURORE DUPIN, BARONNE DUDEVANT (1804–76), novelist. Her father, an army officer and a descendant of Maurice de Saxe, died when she was very young. She was brought up on Rousseauesque lines at his family home (later to be her own), the Château de Nohant in Berry, with a background of quarrels between her paternal grandmother and her mother. After a convent education in Paris, she was again at Nohant, running wild and reading J.-J. Rousseau, Byron, Shakespeare, Chateaubriand ('Il me sembla que René c'était moi'), etc. In 1822 she married the baron Dudevant, a retired army officer, and subsequently bore him two children (Maurice and Solange). By 1831, with his acquiescence, she was leading an independent, trousered life in Paris, trying to live by her pen. She collaborated at first with Jules Sandeau, under the pseudonym 'Jules Sand', publishing articles and a novel, *Rose et Blanche, ou la Comédienne et la religieuse* (1831). Then, writing alone and for the first time as 'George Sand', she published the novel *Indiana* (1832), the first of many successes. Over the next 40 years she produced a stream of novels, tales, biographical and critical essays, and, later, plays. She wrote effortlessly and with complete conviction, and was a born storyteller, with a lyrically descriptive style that could often carry off her most astonishing flights of imagination. Her work usually echoed whatever men or ideas were foremost in her personal life (Renan called her 'la harpe éolienne de notre temps'), and her large output (105 vols. in the Michel Lévy collected ed.) falls roughly into three periods.

The first—*Romantic *par excellence*— was marked at the outset by her liaison with Musset (for details *v.* Musset; she gave her own version of the affair in *Elle et lui*, 1859, and wrote of their ill-fated trip to Italy in her *Lettres d'un voyageur*, 1834–6, which also covers her early years in Paris). To this period belong, besides *Indiana*, the novels *Valentine* (1832), *Lélia* (1833), *Jacques* (1834), *Mauprat* (1837). Her theme is romantic passion, and the right of the individual to follow his, or rather her, heart and defy conventional morals—'l'amour heurtant son front aveugle à tous les obstacles de la civilisation', as she said of *Indiana*. Towards 1840, now legally separated from her husband and about to embark on a liaison (1838–47) with Chopin (her *Un Hiver à Majorque*, 1841, describes their unhappy stay on the island in the early stages of the affair), she entered a phase of uncritical enthusiasm for the various 'isms' of the day and their exponents, e.g. humanitarianism (*v. Leroux, Pierre; Revue indépendante* (1)), Christian socialism (*v. Lamennais*), Republicanism. This was reflected in, for example, *Spiridion* (1838), a mystical hotchpotch; *Les Sept Cordes de la lyre* (1839); *Le *Compagnon du Tour de France* (1840); **Consuelo* (1842–3) and its inferior sequel, *La Comtesse de Rudolstadt* (1843–5); *Le Meunier d'Angibault* (1845). But she also now began to write the simple, idyllic romances of country life on which her fame rests, e.g. *La *Mare au diable* (1846), *La Petite Fadette* (1848), **François le champi* (1850). Political journalism claimed her for a time during the 1848 *Revolution, but thereafter she lived mainly at Nohant and her writing became, as she said, 'plus sobre et mieux digérée'. She kept open house for her friends, amused herself with a miniature theatre, and came to be known as 'la bonne dame de Nohant'. During this last period she wrote plays (seldom successful when produced); many more novels, e.g. *Les Maîtres Sonneurs* (1852), *L'Homme de neige* (1856), *Les Beaux Messieurs de Bois-Doré* (1858), *Le Marquis de Villemer* (1861; dramatized 1864), *Mademoiselle de Quintinie* (1863); and her *Histoire de ma vie* (1854–5, 4 vols.; vol. IV contains interesting appreciations of her contemporaries). Publication of her complete correspondence, which includes letters of great literary interest (e.g. to Flaubert), began in 1964 (ed. G. Lubin).

Sandeau, JULES (1811–83), a writer most often mentioned as a collaborator in his student days with the baronne Dudevant (*v. Sand*), and later with Augier in the comedy *Le *Gendre de M. Poirier* (1854). He had one success to his sole credit, *Mademoiselle de la Seiglière* (1848; dramatized 1851), a novel of the conflict between love and noble birth. The more realistic *Sacs et parchemins* (1851), a study of business life, and *La Roche aux mouettes* (1871), a tale for young people, are also remembered.

Sandras, *v. Courtilz de Sandras.*

Sangrado, Le Docteur, in Lesage's **Gil Blas de Santillane.*

Sans-culottes, a contemptuous name given by the aristocrats to the Revolutionaries of 1789, who had taken to wearing trousers instead of breeches. The Revolutionaries soon applied it to themselves in the sense of 'patriots'.

Sans-culottides, *v. Republican Calendar.*

Sanseverina, La, in Stendhal's *La *Chartreuse de Parme.*

Sans famille, v. Malot.*

Sanson, CHARLES (1740–93) and his son HENRI (1767–1840), the official executioners in Paris during the Revolution. The father beheaded Louis XVI, the son Marie-Antoinette.

Santé, La, f. in the 13th c. by Marguerite de Provence (widow of Louis IX) as an overflow hospital for the **Hôtel-Dieu*, was later used as an annexe of the prison of **Bicêtre* and, like *Bicêtre*, had many lunatics among its inmates. In the mid-19th c. it became a prison mainly for offenders serving short sentences.

Santeuil, Jean, *v. Proust.*

Sapho, *v. Grand Cyrus, Le.*

Sapho (1884), a *Naturalist novel by A. Daudet; a study of the gradual moral and spiritual collapse of a young artist who comes to Paris from Provence and forms a disastrous liaison with the model Sapho. It somewhat resembles the Goncourts' **Manette Salomon.*

Sarasin, JEAN-FRANÇOIS (1603–54), poet, prose-writer, and wit, a friend of Ménage and Mlle de Scudéry. He wrote **ballades* and other light verse; also *La Conspiration de Wallenstein* (*c.* 1645), an historical essay. Mazarin banished him (1647) for some satirical verses.

Sarcey, FRANCISQUE (1827–99), a noted dramatic critic of the second half of the 19th c. For over 30 years he wrote weekly articles—sound and independent, though not profound—in *Le *Temps* (collected in *Quarante Ans de théâtre*, 1900–2).

Sardou, VICTORIEN (1831–1908), author of well-constructed, but rather lifeless, comedies and historical dramas. His success, though not lasting, for a time rivalled that of his predecessor Scribe, on whom his technique was modelled. His plays include *Les Pattes de mouche* (1860), *Nos intimes* (1861), and *La Famille Benoîton* (1865), comedies of manners; *Rabagas* (1872), a political comedy; *Divorçons* (1880), a *vaudeville; *Fédora* (1882), a drama of revenge in a Russian setting; *Tosca* (1887), the melodrama used by Puccini for his opera (1903); *Patrie* (1869) and *Thermidor* (1891), historical dramas; *Madame Sans-Gêne* (1893; with Émile Moreau), an historical comedy. *v. Bernhardt.*

Sarment, Jean, *pseudonym of* JEAN BELLEMÈRE (1897–1976), dramatist, in youth an actor at the *Vieux-Colombier* and the *Théâtre de l'*Œuvre*. His comedies—often evoking the melancholy disenchantment and romantic dreams of characters at odds with real life—include *Le Pêcheur d'ombres* (1921), *Le Mariage d'Hamlet* (1922), *Je suis trop grand pour moi* (1924), *Léopold le bienaimé* (1927), *Peau d'Espagne* (1933), *Le Discours des prix* (1934). At his best, he recalls Musset.

Sarrasine, v. Comédie humaine, La (Scènes de la vie parisienne).

Sarraute, NATHALIE (1902–   ), Russian-born novelist, a leading exponent and theorist of the *nouveau roman*. She practised at the bar until 1939. Her first publication, *Tropismes* (1939), was a collection of short prose pieces. Its title is a key term in her work and refers to minute and elusive sensations on the borders of consciousness which constitute the underlying motivation of all behaviour. She uses the novel as an instrument of research, in

need of constant modification, to capture this new reality. Her first novel, *Portrait d'un inconnu* (1948), was published with a preface by Sartre (*v. Anti-roman*), but it was only with the publication of *Martereau* (1953) that she was noticed and became associated with the *nouveau roman*. Her other novels are *Le Planétarium* (1959), *Les Fruits d'or* (1963), *Entre la vie et la mort* (1968), *Vous les entendez?* (1972). Her most important essays on the novel are in *L'Ère du soupçon* (1956). She has also written radio plays.

Sarrazin, JEAN, *v. Crusades.*

Sartine, GABRIEL DE, *v. Librairie.*

Sartre, JEAN-PAUL (1905–80), philosopher, novelist, dramatist, critic, and political commentator; the chief exponent of atheist *Existentialism. He studied philosophy at the *École normale supérieure* and came first in the *agrégation* of 1929 (Simone de Beauvoir, whom he met in that year and whose name has been associated with his ever since, took the second place). His teaching career was interrupted by a year (1933–4) spent in Berlin, where he became familiar with the phenomenology of Husserl (*v. Existentialism*). He was mobilized in 1939 and taken prisoner in June 1940. On his release in April 1941, he returned to teaching in Paris and became involved in the *Resistance. The Liberation was followed by a great 'existentialist' vogue and by considerable success and fame for Sartre personally; from then on, his life became one of continuous publication, the editorship of *Les *Temps modernes* (f. 1945; and *v. Littérature engagée*), and political activities of varying degrees of effectiveness. His lack of political success may have been the result of what some would see as the ambiguity of his attitudes: though consistently a man of the Left, his own thought as well as his refusal to accept some of the aims and methods of 'official' Communism effectively made it impossible for him to join the Party. In 1948, he helped to create the *R.D.R.* (*Rassemblement démocratique* *révolutionnaire*), but resigned from the group in 1949 as a result of differences with the other organizers. In later years, even when not in particular sympathy with their views, he increasingly tended to give his support to small groups of the extreme Left, on the grounds that his involvement guaranteed them a freedom of expression they might not otherwise enjoy. In 1964, he was awarded the *Prix Nobel: he refused it because, in his view, acceptance might be misconstrued as approval of capitalist and *bourgeois* society at a time when that society was under attack (esp. in the Third World) following the American involvement in Vietnam.

It is clear from his autobiography, *Les Mots* (1964), that literature occupied a big place in his life from his earliest years, and his evolution as a philosopher in due course developed in parallel with his literary preoccupations: after *L'Imagination* (1936) and *Esquisse d'une théorie des émotions* (1939), *L'Imaginaire* of 1940 (a 'phenomenological psychology of the imagination') is a study of the imaginary, among other things, in its relation to the work of art, and is therefore a philosophical working-out of one of the main themes of the novel *La Nausée* (1938). In that work, the nausea experienced by Roquentin, and described in his diary, arises from his awareness of his contingency as a physical existence in a physical world, and of the incompatibility between that contingency and his desire to be able to conceive of his being as something necessary. The solution he in due course envisages is linked to the production of a work of art: if he can write a novel, an imaginary, non-contingent object, owing its being to his imagination (a function of his consciousness), then his consciousness will be as necessary as the work of art it creates. The question raised is to do with our relationship to the world, but also to other people, and is closely bound up with the problem of identity for a being who is born with no ready-made definition. The theme is elaborated in the short stories collected in *Le Mur* (1939) and leads to the major philosophical work of 1943: *L'Être et le*

néant, a 'phenomenological ontology' which attempts to describe the manner of our being. Some critics view this work as in some way a definitive expression of Sartrean Existentialism and regard such later studies as *Questions de méthode* (1957) or *Critique de la raison dialectique* (1960) as a betrayal of true Existentialism. It must be remembered, however, that *L'Être et le néant* was elaborated during Sartre's non-political pre-war period, subsequently he held the view that philosophy cannot be a study divorced from the political reality of the world, and *Critique de la raison dialectique* is an attempt to bring together Marxism (which he regarded as the only philosophy of consequence in our age) and Existentialism (thus relegated to the more modest position of an ideology). The attempt was to be less than a total success, rejected by the Marxists, inaccessible to a wide public, and unfinished—he had to abandon the work because he saw no hope of being able to carry out the necessary research in his lifetime.

This is not the only example of uncompleted work by Sartre: only three of the four projected volumes of his major novel, *Les Chemins de la liberté*, appeared (*L'Age de raison* and *Le Sursis*, both 1945; *La Mort dans l'âme*, 1949); there exist 223 manuscript pages of the fourth volume, entitled 'La Dernière Chance', and some previously unpublished sections have appeared in the recent Pléiade edition of the *Oeuvres romanesques* (1981). The three completed volumes cover the period from Munich to the fall of France in 1940 and, through a large number of characters and events, as well as stylistic experimentation, trace the evolution of a teacher of philosophy, Mathieu Delarue, from a position of radical defence of his freedom towards political commitment and involvement with his fellow-men. The final volume would have dealt with the Occupation and Resistance; in an interview of 1959, Sartre explained that he could not complete it because it did not make sense in the complexities and ambiguities of the post-war world to write about the essentially simple choices facing the French of the Resistance.

In any case, the novel was for him a worked-out *genre*, in that the war also brought the revelation of the theatre as a medium for which he was gifted and through which he could communicate with a wide public. It could not be said that he was a major innovator in the theatre (indeed, some of his plays tend to formlessness and show signs of lack of discipline in the writing); but he had a talent for dramatic writing which brought him several major successes, even though, as might be expected, the subject-matter of his plays echoes his philosophical, political, and ethical concerns. *Les Mouches* (1943) is a reworking of the Orestes story in terms of liberty, identity, and commitment to action in society; *Huis-clos* (1944), set in a hypothetical Hell, gives a negative account of personal relationships in a situation where each character seeks to make use of the other and therefore suffers through the other; *Morts sans sépulture* (1946) develops the theme in a frankly sado-masochistic context, echoing *L'Être et le néant* in its presentation of the conflict of wills between the torturing *milice* and a group of captured Resistance fighters in Occupied France; in *La Putain respectueuse* (1946), the domination is of one social group by another: the Negro and Lizzie the prostitute are incapable of resisting the privileged whites of the American South. In *Les Mains sales* (1948), Sartre treats a subject with more obviously contemporary political references: how can the left-wing intellectual, nourished on political theory, engage in authentic revolutionary action? Hugo, a *bourgeois* idealist, fails to find the answer, largely because his motives are ultimately self-interested; it is only with Goetz who, in *Le Diable et le bon Dieu* (1951), learns to abandon self-interest for the sake of efficacy of action, that Sartre shows the path to follow—and this play was, in fact, written at about the time when he himself, as is revealed in *Les Mots*, realized that effective action is incompatible with attempts to achieve salvation through absolutes or ideals—or the production of works of art. *Kean*

(1954; adapted from *Dumas *père*'s *Kean*) and *Nekrassov* (1956) are further discussions of the question of personal identity, as is his last play, *Les Séquestrés d'Altona* (1959), where the main character, Frantz, faced with the inability to act effectively, retreats into a mythologizing situation. *Les Troyennes* (1965) is an adaptation of Euripides. He also wrote film scenarios, e.g. *Les Jeux sont faits* (1947) and *L'Engrenage* (1948).

Besides essays on various themes (e.g. *Réflexions sur la question juive*, 1947; and v. *Négritude*), throughout his career he produced works of criticism, many of which, together with occasional pieces on other topics, have been collected in *Situations* (1947-76, 10 vols to date). Among his more extensive critical works are his *Baudelaire* (1947; an introduction to the *écrits intimes*), *Saint Genet, comédien et martyr* (1952; a major 'Existentialist psychoanalysis' of Jean Genet), and, above all, the massive study of Flaubert, *L'Idiot de la famille* (1971-2, 3 vols.). This project—which Sartre had intended to complete with a fourth volume but which failing eyesight forced him to abandon—is as much a working-out of his own ambiguous relationship with Flaubert as a study of Flaubert himself; although it suffers from diffuseness lack of discipline, and sheer length, it contains many pages of brilliant analysis (e.g. of some of Flaubert's youthful writing, and of various well-known episodes from the mature works). Posthumous publications include *Les Carnets de la drôle de guerre* (1983) and *Lettres au Castor* (1983, 2 vols).

On any evaluation, Sartre must be seen as a major figure of his time: despite his own disappointment with himself and his achievements, his body of writing has been of considerable importance in the post-war world, and he himself, both through his positive contribution to intellectual life and through his questioning of accepted values, has exerted an undoubted influence on more than one generation. (*K. O. Gore*)

Satie, ALFRED ERIC LESLIE, *known as* ERIK

(1866–1925), whose mother was a Scot, was an original and eccentric composer, a pioneer of polytonality and atonality, latterly admired by Debussy and Ravel, and, above all, by young musicians (e.g. *Les* *Six). His chief work was the oratorio *Socrate* (1918). His music for ballets (e.g. *Cocteau's *Parade*) was simple, realistic, and unconventional.

Satire Ménippée (1594), a satirical pamphlet (prose and verse) parodying the assembly of the *États généraux in 1593 and supporting the cause of Henri IV against the *Ligue and its Spanish allies; so called after the Cynic philosopher Menippus of Gadara (3rd c. B.C.), who wrote satires in this form, its full title being *De la vertu du Catholicon d'Espagne et de la tenue des États de Paris.* It was written by Jean Leroy, a canon of Rouen, in collaboration with Passerat, N. Rapin, Jacques Gillot (b. *c.* 1560), Pierre Pithou (1539–96), and Florent Chrestien (1540–96)—middle-class functionaries, lawyers, ecclesiastics, or scholars. It is in three parts. The first, after an introduction in which two charlatans (cardinals from Spain and Lorraine) extol the panacea Catholicon, contains a burlesque description of the opening procession of the assembly and of the allegorical tapestries with which the hall is hung. The second, after a list of the chief *Ligueurs* (and their failings), contains imaginary speeches by various real personages. Most of these are amusing caricatures of what the several speakers might have said, but that of d'Aubray, representing the *Tiers État, is a solemn and eloquent indictment of the *Ligue* (written by Pithou) and the most important element in the work. The third part consists of various appended satires and epigrams, notably *Le Trépas de l'âne ligueur* by Gilles Durant (1550–1615), jurist and poet. This lively, mocking pamphlet appeared opportunely at the time of the *Ligue*'s defeat and was highly successful.

Satires of Boileau, 12 verse satires (I–VII, 1666, together with a complimentary *Discours au Roi*; VIII and IX, 1668; X, 1694; XI, 1701; XII, 1711); written at various dates from 1660 onwards, and modelled on the satires of Horace, Juvenal, Persius, and M. Régnier. Boileau used to read them to his friends and they were famous before they were published. They are important because they served to mould public taste and helped to found literary criticism in France. Writing with good sense, caustic wit, and the precision and vigour of a skilful artist, Boileau constitutes himself the judge of literary reputations, condemning in particular the affectations of the *précieux and *précieuses* (e.g. Cotin), the extravagant romances of Mlle de Scudéry, the frigid epic of Chapelain, and the mild tragedies of Quinault, and contrasting with them the work of Racine, Molière, and La Fontaine. Some of the satires deal with moral subjects (e.g. V, on what constitutes true nobility; XI, on honour) and are rather heavy and commonplace; but VI (on the dangers of the city of Paris) and X (a diatribe against women; *v. Perrault*) contain passages of powerful realistic writing. In IX, regarded by some critics as the best, Boileau draws his own literary portrait and makes his defence, with incidental hits at contemporaries. XII (*Sur l'Équivoque*—on ambiguity in religion, written from the *Jansenist standpoint) offended the *Jesuits, and the king forbade its publication (it appeared just after Boileau's death).

Saül, (1) *v. Du Ryer*; (2) *v. Voltaire*, 1; (3) *v. Lamartine*; (4) *v. Soumet*; (5) *v. Gide*.

Saül le furieux (1572), a tragedy by La Taille. The general theme is the mystery of divine Providence, under which man seems at times to suffer unjustly. The play traces the progressive humiliation of the proud spirit of Saul, culminating in his despair and death. A sequel, *La Famine, ou les Gabaonites* (1573), shows the curse on Saul extending to his descendants. The famine which is devastating Israel is to be relieved only when his sons and grandsons have been delivered to the Gibeonites, with whom he has broken faith.

Saumaise, CLAUDE DE, in Latin SALMASIUS (1588–1653), a *Huguenot and an eminent scholar. At 19, he discovered in the Palatine Library at Heidelberg, and first copied, the famous 10th-c. manuscript collection of Greek epigrams known as the *Palatine Anthology*. He was later a professor at the University of Leyden, and Charles II, then in exile at The Hague, commissioned him to draw up a defence of Charles I and an indictment of the regicide government. This he did in a *Defensio regia pro Carolo I* (1649); Milton, ordered to reply, wrote his *Pro populo anglicano defensio* (1651).

Saurin, BERNARD-JOSEPH (1706–81), dramatist, a friend of Helvétius (who helped him financially) and Voltaire, and a member of the *Académie. His plays include *Spartacus* (1760), a successful philosophical tragedy, composed largely of declamations on liberty and humanity; **Blanche et Guiscard* (1763), a tragedy; *Béverlei* (1768; in *vers libres), a *tragédie bourgeoise* on the career of a gambler, based on Edward Moore's *The Gamester*; *Les Mœurs du temps* (1760), a successful one-act prose comedy (*v. Poinsinet*).

Saussure, FERDINAND DE (1857–1913), Swiss philologist and linguist. His *Mémoire sur le système primitif des voyelles dans les langues indo-européennes* (1879) made his name as an Indo-European philologist while he was still a student, but his fame rests on his *Cours de linguistique générale* (publ. 1916, from notes of his lectures taken by students), which constitutes one of the foundations of modern descriptive linguistics. He saw a given state of language as essentially a system (or set of systems) of relations between elements (sounds, words, etc.), each of which owes its validity to its relation to the rest. This 'structural' approach has been extended to many other fields of human activity. *v. Structuralism*; *cf. Semiology*.

Sauvage, CÉCILE (1883–1927), mother of the composer Olivier Messiaen, a poetess who spent her life in Provence and was first encouraged to write by Mistral. She is remembered for her poems of maternal love (in *Œuvres de Cécile Sauvage*, 1929).

Savoir (originally **Posznanski**), ALFRED (1883–1934), a dramatist of Polish origin, wrote satirical comedies and farces, e.g. *La Huitième Femme de Barbe-bleue* (1921), *Banco* (1922), *La Grande Duchesse et le garçon d'étage* (1924), *Lui* (1929; a mysterious stranger's impact on a Swiss resort), *La Petite Catherine* (1930; set in 18th-c. Russia and the court of Catherine the Great), *La Voie lactée* (1933; about theatre life).

Savonnerie, La, on the right bank of the Seine near Passy, was originally a soap-works. In the 17th c. it became a State factory for the manufacture of Oriental-style carpets and for a time pauper children were trained there as carpet-weavers. It was merged with the *Gobelins in the 18th c.

Saxe, MAURICE DE (1696–1750), **maréchal de France*, natural son of Augustus II, Elector of Saxony. He was a great and successful general in the French service and the victor of *Fontenoy. *v. Lecouvreur*; *Sand*.

Saxons, Chanson des, *v. Bodel.*

Scaliger, (1) JULIUS CAESAR (1484–1558), an Italian-born scholar who settled in France as physician to the bishop of Agen, came to the fore with polemical writings against Erasmus, and is chiefly remembered for his long Latin treatise on poetics (1561), a dogmatic exposition of the classical rules of literary perfection; (2) his son JOSEPH JUSTUS (1540–1609), the greatest scholar of the *Renaissance, who revolutionized classical chronology by his edition of Manilius, his *De emendatione temporum*, and his reconstruction of the chronicle of Eusebius.

Scapin, the name for a type of resourceful, rascally valet, taken from Molière's *Les *Fourberies de Scapin*.

Scaramouche (derived from Ital. *scaramuccia*, 'skirmish'), a stock character of the *commedia dell'arte* (*v. Italiens*), a caricature of the Spanish don, dressed in Spanish costume (usually black). He is a cowardly, foolish boaster, constantly cudgelled by *Arlequin.

Scarmentado, Histoire des voyages de (1756), a philosophical tale by Voltaire, who later developed its theme in *Candide.

Scarmentado, son of a governor of Candia, relates his travels about the world, including England at the time of the Gunpowder Plot. He witnesses the stupidity, cruelty, and religious intolerance of mankind, often narrowly escaping death and finally enslaved by negro pirates because his nose and hair are different from theirs.

Scarron, PAUL (1610–60), an author who rebelled against the artificiality and preciosity of contemporary literature and whose burlesque writings helped to discredit the grand style (mythological and heroic) in prose and poetry; v. Novel, 2. Severely crippled by rheumatism from the age of 30, he received a pension from Anne d'Autriche and in 1652 married the young Françoise d'Aubigné (later Mme de Maintenon). His works include, notably, Le *Roman comique (1651–7, 2 pts.; unfinished), the prototype of Gautier's Le *Capitaine Fracasse, and the comedies Jodelet, ou le Maître Valet (1645; v. Jodelet) and *Don Japhet d'Arménie (1652); also a Recueil de quelques vers burlesques (1643); Typhon (1644), a burlesque mythological poem; Virgile travesti (1648–52), an unfinished parody of Virgil; Nouvelles tragi-comiques (1655–7), notable early examples of the *nouvelle (inc. Les Hypocrites and La Précaution inutile which inspired Molière and Sedaine). v. Foreign Influences, 1.

Sceaux, v. Maine, duchesse du.

Scènes de la vie de Bohème, v. Murger.

Scènes de la vie privée; ...de la vie de province; ...de la vie parisienne; ...de la vie politique; ...de la vie militaire; ...de la vie de campagne, v. Comédie humaine, La.

Scève, MAURICE (c. 1510–64), leader of a school of lyric poetry at Lyons (v. Du Guil-

let; Labé; Champier), then a centre of great literary activity and much under Italian influence (esp. that of Petrarch and Bembo; v. Foreign Influences, 1). His works include *Délie, objet de plus haute vertu (1544) and La Saussaie (1547), an eclogue on rustic life on the banks of the Saône. He won fame while a student at Avignon by discovering there the alleged tomb of Petrarch's Laura.

Scévole (1647), a tragedy by Du Ryer, regarded as his masterpiece; probably produced 1644. It is based on the legend of the Roman Mucius Scaevola as told by Livy.

Porsenne (Porsenna), the Etruscan king, is besieging Rome in order to restore the Tarquins. He is represented as a wise and generous ruler, in contrast to the overbearing, ungrateful Tarquin. He and his son Arons both love Junie, a Roman captive in their camp; and so does their enemy Scévole, who has saved Arons's life. The action consists mainly in the various influences that act on Porsenne: the bravery of Horatius Coclès in defence of the bridge, Junie's appeal to him to raise the siege and the advice of Arons in the same sense, his growing hostility to Tarquin, and, above all, the heroism of Scévole (after he has entered the Etruscan camp in a vain bid to kill Porsenne). Porsenne finally abandons the siege and pardons Scévole, to whom Arons generously surrenders Junie.

Schelandre, JEAN DE (c. 1585–1635), dramatist, a gentleman of Verdun, who was killed fighting under Turenne. His long tragedy *Tyr et Sidon (1608) was remodelled as a *tragicomedy (1628) under the influence of Hardy. He spent some time in London, where (1611) he dedicated to James I the ridiculous poem Stuartide, tracing the king's genealogy to Astraea and Banquo. He may have known Shakespeare.

Schérer, EDMOND (1815–89), a leading critic, on the staff of Le *Temps from 1861. He was of Swiss descent (a Protestant, till he lost his faith) and had taught and written on philosophy and theology before turning, in middle life, to literature and foreign languages. His articles in *Le Temps* (collected in *Études critiques sur la littérature contemporaine*, 1863–95, 10 vols.) contained valuable criticism and discussions of critical theory by one whose aim was to observe 'le caractère essentiellement relatif de la vérité'. Moral prejudices biased his judgement of such writers as Chateaubriand, Baudelaire, and Gautier.

Schiller, *v. Foreign Influences*, 3.

Schlegel, August Wilhelm von (1767–1845), German scholar, translator (Shakespeare, Calderón, Hindu literature), and critic. He was a friend of Mme de Staël, tutored her children, stayed at *Coppet, and travelled with her in Europe. His views on the distinction between the 'classical' and the 'romantic' in literature no doubt helped to form hers. They were expounded in his Berlin (1801) and Vienna lectures on the drama, translated by Mme Necker de Saussure as *Cours de littérature dramatique* (1809 and 1814). He also published (1817; in French) a comparison of Racine's *Phèdre* and Euripides' *Hippolytus*, not favourable to Racine. These works were widely read and helped to make French critical theory more independent of the older conventions. *v. Foreign Influences*, 3.

Schlésinger, Élisa Foucault, Mme (1810–88), wife of a Paris music publisher, said to have been the one woman Flaubert loved, for all that the affection was platonic. She was the Mme Arnoux of *L'*Éducation sentimentale* (Émilie Renaud in the first draft) and the Maria of *Mémoires d'un fou*.

Schlumberger, Jean (1877–1968), novelist and critic, a founder of the *Nouvelle Revue française*. His works include the novels *Un Homme heureux* (1920), *Le Camarade infidèle* (1922), and *Saint-Saturnin* (1931); also *Éveils* (1950), reminiscences of late 19th-c. family life in Alsace and Normandy, the emotions aroused by the *Dreyfus case, the early days of the *Nouvelle Revue française*, etc.

Schmucke, Wilhelm, in Balzac's *Le *Cousin Pons*.

Schneider, Hortense (1838–1920), a famous comic-opera star of the Second Empire, notably in *Offenbach's *La Belle Hélène*, *La Grande-Duchesse de Gérolstein*, etc.

Scholl, Aurélien (1833–1902), a well-known wit and journalist of the Second Empire. His talk and writings—in *Le *Nain jaune* (which he founded), *Le *Figaro*, *L'*Événement*, etc.—sparkled with the famous *esprit du boulevard*.

Schwetchine, Mme, *v. Salon*, 1.

Schwob, Marcel (1867–1905), came of an old family of Jewish intellectuals and, like his contemporary R. de Gourmont, was at once an essayist and critic of wide-ranging erudition (associated with the *Symbolist movement and the early days of the *Mercure de France*) and a creative writer. He studied in Paris, then turned to research and literary journalism. As a scholar, his interests lay mainly in classical and medieval studies (esp. the language and times of Villon) and in philology. He was also fluent and exceptionally well read in English and German. His career was cut short by a serious operation in 1895. His works include *Étude de l'argot français* (1889) and *Le Jargon des coquillards en 1451* (1890), scholarly studies; *Moll Flanders* (1893), translated from Defoe; *Spicilège* (1896), critical and philosophical essays, including studies of Villon, Meredith (whom he introduced to French readers), R. L. Stevenson, and trends in modern fiction; *Les Vies imaginaires* (1896), reconstructions of the lives of characters encountered in his reading; *Cœur double* (1891), *Le Roi au masque d'or* (1892), *Mimes* (1894), *Le Livre de Monelle* (1894), and *La Croisade des enfants* (1896), tales, sometimes realistic, more often morbid or ornate, influenced by Symbolism, and based on classical, Oriental, or medieval legend (e.g. *La Croisade des enfants*).

Scott, SIR WALTER, v. *Foreign Influences,* 3.

Scribe, EUGÈNE (1791–1861), probably the most successful dramatist of the first half of the 19th c., highly skilled in plot-construction and stagecraft (for him the essential qualities in a playwright). His vast output (over 300 plays, inc. libretti for *opéras-comiques*, many written with collaborators, e.g. Auber, J.-H. Dupin, and E.-W. Legouvé) consists mainly of *vaudevilles* (e.g. *Une Nuit de la Garde nationale*, 1815; *Le Solliciteur*, 1817) and light-hearted comedies of manners, excellent pictures of *bourgeois* life (e.g. *Le Mariage de raison*, 1826; *Le Mariage d'argent*, 1828; *La Camaraderie, ou la Courte Échelle*, 1837; *Une Chaîne*, 1841, his best work; *Bataille de dames*, 1851). He also wrote historical and political comedies (e.g. *Bertrand et Raton*, 1833; *Le Verre d'eau*, 1842). His fame was short-lived, for his plays were lifeless and superficial, his characters seldom more than types subordinated to the artifices of the plot; but his sound craftsmanship contrasted with the over-literary drama of the *Romantics and influenced many later dramatists. v. *Theatre of the 19th and 20th cs.*

Scudéry, GEORGES DE (1601–67), dramatist, a ruffling soldier and a vainglorious writer. His many tragedies, tragicomedies, and comedies—marked by abundant imagination, excessive rhetoric, and extraordinary incidents and situations—include the *Comédie des Comédiens* (1635), in which a company of actors is staged (as later in Corneille's *Illusion comique*); *L'Amour tyrannique* (1638), a tragicomedy which Richelieu supported as a rival to Corneille's *Le *Cid* (Scudéry was among the chief critics of *Le Cid*); *Axiane* (1643), a prose tragicomedy. His long epic *Alaric* (1654), dedicated to Queen Christina of Sweden, was ridiculed by Boileau. He had some hand in his sister Madeleine's romances. He prefaced her *Ibrahim* with interesting reflections on the art of the novel, advocating a main plot with strictly subsidiary episodes, an action

confined within definite temporal limits (beyond which the method of indirect narration should be preferred), sparing use of coincidences and marvels, and the relation of deeds to motives.

Scudéry, MADELEINE DE (1607–1701), novelist, sister of the above; a woman of good education, plain and virtuous, intelligent, and acutely observant. Her house was a meeting-place of literary society on Saturdays, her famous 'samedis'; and she was known in her circle as 'Sapho'. With some help from her brother (under whose name many of her works were published), she wrote a number of long heroic-sentimental romances of the type then in vogue (v. *Novel,* 2), notably *Le *Grand Cyrus* (1649–53) and *Clélie* (1654–60); also *Ibrahim, ou l'Illustre Bassa* (1641; v. *Scudéry, G. de*), the story of a Christian who falls into the hands of the Turks, becomes the Sultan's favourite, takes the name Ibrahim, and after countless adventures is reunited with the noble Italian lady he has loved throughout; and *Almahide, ou l'Esclave reine* (1660–3), a story of the Moors in Spain. *Le Grand Cyrus* and *Clélie* were immensely popular in their day (admired, for example, by Mme de Sévigné), for many of the characters were portraits of well-known contemporaries, while the conversations introduced into the stories (which are the best part of these works and were extracted and publ. separately) contained sound ideas on such subjects as the education of women. But this type of romance—tediously long, insipid, and unreal—was condemned by *Boileau, and is as a whole quite unreadable today.

Scythes, Les, a tragedy by Voltaire; produced 1767.

The Scythians, primitive and poor, but equal and free, are here contrasted with the Persians, highly sophisticated and wealthy, but corrupt and slaves of the great king. Sozame, a Persian general, and his daughter Obéide have sought refuge in Scythia from the persecution of Athamare, heir to the Persian throne, who has tried to carry off Obéide. After long residence in Scythia, Obéïde has agreed to marry Indatire, a young Scythian, though, in fact, she loves Athamare. Athamare, now king of Ecbatana, comes to Scythia in the guise of friendship, hoping to recover Obéïde. He finds her just married, kills Indatire in single combat, and is himself captured. Required by Scythian custom to kill her husband's slayer with her own hand, Obéïde takes her life.

Seagreen Incorruptible, The, *v.* **Robespierre.**

Sebillet or **Sibilet,** THOMAS (*c.* 1512–89), author of an *Art poétique français* (1548) which shows signs of the transition from the poetry of the *rhétoriqueurs to that of the *Pléiade. He regards 'divine inspiration' as the true essence of poetry, rhyme and other artificial adornments being superficial adjuncts.

Sebond, RAIMOND, *v.* **Montaigne.**

Secrets de la princesse de Cadignan, Les, v. *Comédie humaine, La (Scènes de la vie parisienne); Cadignan.*

Sedaine, MICHEL-JEAN (1719–97), dramatist, began life as a poor stonemason and combined wit with a kindly, honest, and independent character. His best plays are *Le *Philosophe sans le savoir* (1765), a *drame bourgeois, and *La Gageure imprévue* (1768), a light one-act comedy of society after the manner of Marivaux. He also wrote the libretti of several comic operas (or dramas interspersed with songs; *v.* *Opéra-Comique*), usually about working folk and peasants, often on themes from La Fontaine, and with a marked element of pathos, e.g. *Rose et Colas* (1764), *Les Sabots* (1768), *Le Déserteur* (1769; a more ambitious attempt to combine tragic and comic elements). His *Richard Cœur de Lion* (1784; with music by Grétry), on that king's imprisonment and liberation through *Blondel, includes the well-known song:

Ô Richard, ô mon roi,
L'univers t'abandonne;
Sur la terre il n'est que moi
Qui s'intéresse à ta personne.

Sedan, *v.* **Franco-Prussian War.**

Sée, EDMOND (1875–1959), playwright and critic. His comedies of manners (*La Brebis*, 1896; *L'Indiscret*, 1903; *Saison d'amour*, 1918; *La Dépositaire*, 1924, etc.) recall 18th-c. classical comedy. His *Théâtre français contemporain* (1928) is a guide to the development of modern drama.

Sée, HENRI, *v.* **History**, 4.

Ségalen, VICTOR (1878–1919), who travelled widely as a ship's doctor, wrote works including *Stèles* (1914), prose poems in the Chinese manner; *Les Immémoriaux* (1907) and *D'après René Leys* (1923), novels of Tahiti and China.

Seghers, PIERRE, *v.* **Resistance.**

Segrais, JEAN REGNAULT DE (1624–1701), man of letters, for 24 years secretary to the duchesse de Montpensier (who published two romances under his name); also a friend of Mme de La Fayette (whose *Zaïde* and *La *Princesse de Clèves* appeared under his name). He translated Virgil's *Aeneid* and *Georgics* into French verse, and wrote the pastoral poem *Athis*, some elegant but uninspired eclogues, and the short tales collected in *Les Divertissements de la princesse Auréliane* (i.e. the duchesse de Montpensier).

Ségur, SOPHIE ROSTOPCHINE, COMTESSE DE (1799–1874), b. at St. Petersburg, wrote many children's books (originally tales she told to her own children, for she was an invalid and could not play with them), e.g. *Nouveaux Contes de fées pour les petits enfants* (1857), *Les Petites Filles modèles* (1858), *Les Vacances* (1859), *Mémoires d'un âne* (1860), *François le bossu* (1864), *Les Malheurs de Sophie* (1864), *Le Général Dourakine* (1864), *Un Bon Petit Diable* (1865). They were highly popular in their day and, though they belong to an era of moral tales, some are still much enjoyed. *v.* *Children's Reading.*

Seignobos, CHARLES, *v.* **History**, 4.

Seillière, ERNEST-ANTOINE-AIMÉ-LÉON, BARON (1866–1955), moralist, sociologist, and critic; exponent of a philosophy that he termed *Impérialisme*. He set forth his theories time and again, notably in the four volumes of *La Philosophie de l'impérialisme*: I. *Le Comte de Gobineau et l'Aryanisme historique* (1903), on racial Imperialism; II. *Apollôn ou Dionysos* (1905), on the individual, as represented by Nietzsche; III. *L'Impérialisme démocratique* (1907); IV. *Le Mal romantique* (1908), on irrational Imperialism (in essence a revolt of sentiment or instinct against reason)—a study of five generations of romantics, beginning with J.-J. Rousseau and going on to Fourier, Stendhal, and 19th-c. thought in general.

Seine, La, one of the four great rivers of France.

Seize, Le Grand, *v. Café* (Café anglais).

Seize, Les, *v. Ligue, La.*

Semaine, La, *v. Du Bartas.*

Semaine politique et littéraire, La, *v. Révolutions de France et de Brabant.*

Semaine sainte, La, *v. Aragon.*

Semaine sanglante, La, *v. Commune, 2.*

Semblançay, JACQUES DE BEAUNE DE (1457–1527), treasurer of François Ier, executed for malversation, though probably innocent. Marot has an epigram on the fortitude with which he met his death.

Semiology or **Semiotics,** the science of signs, first fully elaborated by the American philosopher Charles S. Peirce (1839–1914). His near contemporary Saussure saw linguistics as part of a science of signs. Closely related to *Structuralism, semiology is at present being developed in a number of different directions by critics and philosophers including Barthes (e.g. in his *Éléments de sémiologie*, 1965;

Mythologies; and *Système de la mode*), Algirdas J. Greimas (in *Du sens*, 1970), and Julia Kristeva (in *Semeiotikè*, 1969).

Sénac de Meilhan, GABRIEL (1736–1803), man of letters, son of a physician to Louis XV, held provincial administrative posts till 1789, travelled Europe as an *émigré* from 1791 (usually managing to find some benevolent protector, e.g. Catherine II of Russia), and finally settled in Vienna, where he died. His works include *Considérations sur l'esprit et les mœurs* (1787), depicting worldly society in the last years of Louis XVI; *Du gouvernement, des mœurs, et des conditions en France avant la Révolution* (1795), a political treatise of some merit; *Portraits et caractères des personnages distingués de la fin du XVIIIe siècle* (1813); *L'Émigré* (1797), a short novel in letter form, slight but sensitively written, the story of a nobleman in the *Armée des émigrés* (he is wounded, takes refuge in a castle on the Rhine, and falls in love with the *châtelaine*, who is widowed during his stay; but before they can marry honour compels him to rejoin the army, and he is captured and executed).

Senancour, ÉTIENNE PIVERT DE (1770–1846), remembered for his novel *Obermann* (1804), which, like Chateaubriand's *René*, inspired several novels of romantic introspection and marks him as a precursor of *Romanticism. Sainte-Beuve, in an appreciative preface to the second edition (1833) and in articles in the *Lundis*, was among the first to recognize his influence. Matthew Arnold introduced him to English readers in the poems *Obermann* and *Obermann once more* (1852 and 1867) and the essay *Obermann* (Oct. 1869, in *The Academy*).

Born in Paris in comfortable circumstances, he was intended for the Church, but cut free and went to Switzerland. The Swiss scene intensified a bent for *rêverie* stimulated by early reading of J.-J. Rousseau, Bernardin de Saint-Pierre, *Goethe's *Werther*, etc., and he dreamed of settling in a remote valley alone with Nature and his soul. His marriage (1790) proved unhappy and had almost broken down by the time he returned to Paris in 1794; later, his son and daughter lived with him, and at one time he also had his wife's illegitimate son on his hands. In Paris he drifted along, enfeebled in body, disillusioned, a prey to neurotic melancholy and lethargy. At one time he thought he had found a soul-mate in a Mme de Walckenaer (the 'Mme Del**' of *Obermann*), at another he experimented with drugs and intoxicants. He had some money, soon spent, from his parents (d. 1795). For two years *c*. 1800 he was tutor to Mme d'Houdetot's grandson. Thereafter (until 1833, when he received a pension) his chief means of livelihood was hack writing (articles for an encyclopedia, journalism, some criticism, etc.). Besides *Obermann*, his creative works include *Rêveries sur la nature primitive de l'homme* (1799), on man's need to find the guiding principles of conduct in an understanding of his own nature rather than in religious dogma; *De l'amour considéré dans les lois réelles et dans les formes sociales de l'union des deux sexes* (1805), a semi-philosophical treatise; the *Libres Méditations d'un solitaire inconnu* (1819), a work of Christian philosophy; *Isabella* (1833), another novel in letter form.

Sénat. The *Sénat conservateur* was the most important of the legislative bodies created by the constitution of 1799 (*v. Consulat*). It issued decrees (*sénatus-consultes*), but, like the other bodies, was very much under Napoleon's thumb. The majority of its members (who were life-members) were, or could be, nominated by him. He often bestowed the high and lucrative office of *sénateur* on his generals and drew largely on the *Sénat* for his imperial aristocracy (*v. Napoleonic Aristocracy*). Having, at the invitation of the Allies, declared his reign at an end and voted a provisional government (April 1814), the *Sénat* was abolished by the *Charte* of 1814; but about two-thirds of its members became members of the new upper house, the *Chambre des *Pairs* (the lower house being the *Chambre des

Députés). Under the Second Empire (1852–70) the *Sénat français* was the upper house of the legislature (the lower being the *Corps législatif*). Its functions were determined, and its members nominated, by Napoleon III. Under the Third *Republic (1870–1940) the *Sénat français* was soon again the upper house (the lower being the *Chambre des Députés*). Its functions were determined by the constitution of 1875. After 1884 all its members were (indirectly) elected for fixed periods. For the subsequent period *v. Conseil de la République; Republics*, 4 and 5. *v.* also *Luxembourg, Palais du*.

Sénecé, ANTOINE BAUDERON DE (1643–1737), minor poet, wrote agreeable verse tales, also madrigals, epistles, epigrams, etc.

Sénéchal, *v. Bailli; Sénéchal.*

Senghor, LÉOPOLD SÉDAR (1906–), President of Senegal from 1960; an African intellectual of Roman Catholic faith and French education, at once a poet, a teacher, and a politician, who did much to define and develop the concept of *négritude*. He came to Paris from Senegal in 1928 and became a pupil at the *Lycée Louis-le-Grand*. Georges Pompidou, a fellow-pupil and long a close friend, introduced him to the works of Barrès, which made a great impact on him (he traces his full realization of his own uprooted state to a reading of *Les *Déracinés* in 1929). Others who influenced him included Mounier and, later, Teilhard de Chardin. His most formative years were those spent as a student in Paris in the 1930s, when, in company with other black intellectuals (*v. Négritude*), he rediscovered his African roots and heritage and generated a new black consciousness. Having passed the *agrégation* in 1935, he entered the teaching profession in France and became active in *Front populaire* politics. In 1937, he delivered a notable speech in Dakar on the theme 'Let us assimilate, not be assimilated'. After the 1939–45 war (in which he served and was taken prisoner), he became a leading African *député* in the *Assemblée nationale* and increasingly involved in politics. Most of his life was spent in France, and the tension caused by his longing for Africa found an outlet in his poetry, which is rooted in memories of his African childhood and where he goes far to bridge the gulf between the cultures of Christian Europe and Africa. His collections (united in *Poèmes*, 1964) include *Chants d'ombre* (1945; poems of the 1930s), *Hosties noires* (1948; mainly poems of the war years), *Éthiopiques* (1956), *Nocturnes* (1961; inc. love poems). In 1948, he published an *Anthologie de la nouvelle poésie nègre et malgache de langue française*, with a preface by Sartre. Many of his lectures and articles of the years 1937–64 are collected in *Liberté I: Négritude et Humanisme* (1964).

Sept Cordes de la lyre, Les, v. Sand.

September Revolution, *v. Revolutions,* 4.

Septembriseurs, *v. Revolutions,* 1 (1792).

Sept Sages, Roman des, an anonymous French prose translation (2nd half of 12th c.) of the Latin version of a collection of Oriental tales derived from those of the Indian philosopher known as Syntipas or Sindabar. The seven sages, to defend the king's son against an accusation brought by his jealous stepmother, each relate a tale designed to show the perfidy of women; the queen retorts with seven tales calculated to discredit the sages. *v. Dolopathos.*

Séraphita, v. Livre mystique, Le.

Serées, Les, v. Bouchet, G.

Sergents de La Rochelle, Les Quatre, four young sergeants of the line, members of the *Charbonnerie* (*v. Carbonari*), who were incited by *agents provocateurs* to attempt (1822) a republican uprising at La Rochelle. They were arrested and executed. Their youth, and the cir-

cumstances of the case, excited public sympathy.

Serment du Jeu de Paume, *v. Revolutions,* 1 (1789).

Serments de Strasbourg, an oath of mutual support (*sacramentum firmitatis*), and of alliance against their brother Lothaire, sworn by Louis le Germanique and Charles II (sons of Louis Ier and grandsons of Charlemagne) in the presence of their respective armies assembled at Strasbourg in 842 (the year before the Treaty of *Verdun). It was sworn in French by Louis, so as to be understood by Charles's army, and, similarly, in German by Charles; then, in a modified form (*sacramentum fidelitatis*), it was sworn in German by the followers of Louis and in French by those of Charles. Both texts are given in a Latin history of the strife between the sons of Louis Ier, written by one of the earliest French chroniclers, Nithard (*c.* 790–858), a grandson of Charlemagne. The French text is the earliest extant document in the French language and so of great philological interest (*v. French Language*).

Sermon joyeux, *v. Fête des Fous.*

Serres, OLIVIER DE (1539–1619), a landed proprietor of the Vivarais, a *Huguenot, and a favourite of Henri IV; author of a *Théâtre d'agriculture et ménage des champs* (1600), on the management of rural property. He introduced the culture of the silkworm to France.

Serres chaudes, v. Maeterlinck.

Sertorius, a tragedy by Corneille; produced 1662. The theme is the historical struggle of Sertorius in Spain against the senatorial army under Pompey, the assassination of Sertorius by his lieutenant Perpenna, and Perpenna's execution by Pompey. Corneille has introduced two female characters (Aristie, the divorced wife of Pompey, and Viriate, queen of Lusitania) and a certain love interest; but the play remains essentially political.

Sérurier, Jean-Mathieu-Philibert, v. *Maréchal*.

Serventois, a poetic form originally taking its name from the Provençal *sirventes*, which was a satirical or polemical poem in the form of the **chanson*. The French term was, however, most frequently applied in the 14th and 15th cs. to poems in honour of the Virgin, in a form very like the **chant royal*, but usually without a refrain.

Servitude et grandeur militaires (1835), by Vigny, three fine tales (*v. Nouvelle*) illustrating the selfless devotion to duty of Napoleon's armies—*Laurette, ou le Cachet rouge*; *La Veillée de Vincennes*; *La Vie et la mort du capitaine Renaud, ou la Canne de jonc*. In *La Canne de jonc*, as it is usually called, an old officer of the *Garde impériale* reminisces. He tells of his years as a prisoner on parole in British ships under Collingwood (inc. the *Victory*), also of an interview he witnessed between Napoleon and the pope (then confined at **Fontainebleau*).

Servitude volontaire, Discours de la, v. *La Boétie*.

Sévère, in Corneille's **Polyeucte*.

Séverine, *pseudonym of* CAROLINE RÉMY, MME GUEBHARD by her second marriage (1855–1929), probably the best woman journalist of her day, much read and loved by the people. Introduced to journalism by Vallès, she edited her own paper (*Le Cri du peuple*), then gave it up to become a free-lance. Papers of all complexions employed her and allowed her to express her decidedly left-wing views. She left an autobiography, *Line* (1921), and some volumes of collected articles.

Sévigné, MARIE DE RABUTIN-CHANTAL, MARQUISE DE (1626–96), famous for her letters, grand-daughter of Mme de Chantal (founder, with St. François de Sales, of the Order of the Visitation) and first cousin of Bussy-Rabutin. She was orphaned very young and brought up by her uncle, the abbé de Livry (*v. Coulanges*), to whom she remained deeply attached. She married (1644) the marquis de Sévigné, an agreeable man, but an unfaithful, extravagant husband. He was killed in a duel (1651), leaving her with a son, witty and devoted, but irresponsible, and a daughter, considered a great beauty, but cross-grained and cold-hearted. The daughter married (1669) the comte de Grignan, lieutenant-governor of Provence, and settled in the South. Her passionate devotion to this daughter, from whom she was thus separated for long periods and who, moreover, was not in full sympathy with her mother, was at once the chief joy and the chief torment of her life. She lived mainly in Paris (at the Hôtel Carnavalet; *v. Musée Carnavalet*; *Place Royale*) and at her country house (Les Rochers) near Vitré in Brittany; but she was sometimes with her uncle at the abbey of Livry near Paris, and occasionally with her daughter in Provence. She was a cultured woman, who knew Latin, Spanish, and Italian (her instructors included Chapelain and Ménage); also a woman of great charm, witty, intelligent, and friendly, with a playful imagination that pervades her letters, outwardly cheerful if at times given to melancholy reflection. She was an *habituée* of the Hôtel de **Rambouillet* in the period of its decline and an intimate friend of Mme de La Fayette. Publication of her correspondence (over 1,500 letters in all, the majority to her daughter) began in 1725 with a collection of 31 letters. Writing naturally but not carelessly, in a racy, picturesque style, she gives a revealing and amusing picture of the life of the nobility, at court, in the country, and in their social and domestic relations, describing such events as the trial of N. Fouquet (to whom she was steadfastly loyal), the execution of the marquise de Brinvilliers, the suicide of Vatel, a performance of Racine's **Esther* at **Versailles*, Lauzun escorting James II's queen and infant son in their flight from England. Her letters also show her enjoying the society and diversions of Paris and occasionally of Versailles, delighting in the countryside (looking after her woods and rents at Les Rochers and showing a knowledge of nature unusual in her day), passing judgement on the books she reads, and pouring out her anxious affection for her daughter. The collection also includes a number of letters from her friends (e.g. Mme de La Fayette; and *v. Bussy-Rabutin*).

Sèvres, a suburb of Paris famous for its porcelain factory, which was acquired by the State in the mid-18th c. *v.* also *École normale supérieure.*

Seyssel, CLAUDE DE (1450–1520), humanist and diplomat, archbishop of Turin, author of *La Grande Monarchie de France* (1519; a work of political philosophy, praising the French constitution) and translator of classical Greek authors.

Sganarelle, (1) in Molière's *Sganarelle*; (2) in his *Dom Juan*; (3) in his *Le Médecin malgré lui*.

Sganarelle, ou le Cocu imaginaire, a one-act verse comedy by Molière; produced 1660.

Célie loves Lélie, but her father Gorgibus, a *bourgeois*, requires her to marry a richer suitor. By a chain of accidents and misunderstandings, Sganarelle, another *bourgeois*, is led to believe that his wife loves Lélie; Lélie that Célie has married Sganarelle; Mme Sganarelle that her husband loves Célie; and Célie that Lélie is unfaithful to her. The muddle is cleared up, and Célie's rich suitor proves to be already married.

Shakespeare, *v. Foreign Influences,* 2 and 3.

Short Stories, *v. Conte; Nouvelle.*

Sibilet, *v. Sebillet.*

Sicilian Vespers, *v. Vêpres siciliennes.*

Sicilien, ou l'Amour peintre, Le, a one-act prose *comédie-ballet* by Molière; produced 1667.

Don Pèdre, a Sicilian, wishes to marry Isidore, a Greek slave, whom he keeps jealously shut up. But Adraste, a French gentleman, has seen her and fallen in love with her. Posing as an artist who is to paint her portrait, he gains access to her, and she contrives to escape from her master's house.

Siècle, Le (1836–1927), one of the first cheap daily papers (*v. Press,* 6). It supplied news, ready-made radical and anti-clerical opinions, and a *roman-feuilleton.* It soon had a record circulation (38,000), mainly among small traders and the working classes.

Siècle de Louis le Grand, Le, v. Perrault.

Siècle de Louis XIV, Le (1751; rev. eds. 1756 and 1768; a 1763 ed. contained as a suppl. a *Précis du siècle de Louis XV*), an historical work by Voltaire, begun in 1734. He prepared the ground by methodical inquiries (he knew many survivors of the great age) and wide reading of memoirs. The result was a solid piece of work, as accurate as was possible in the circumstances. Besides dealing clearly with the great political problems of the day and the characters of the king, Colbert, Mme de Maintenon, etc., he also traces the progress of civilization (with an incidental attack on aggressive war), eliminating, in contrast to Bossuet, the action of Providence. But the plan of the work (the reign is treated under separate headings— political and military history, finance, anecdotes of the court, etc.) has been much criticized.

Siècle de Louis XV, Précis du, v. Siècle de Louis XIV, Le.

Siegfried et le Limousin (1922), a novel by Giraudoux, who later dramatized it as *Siegfried*. It is a study, on the whole gently satirical, of the French and German mentalities, the good and bad points of each, and how they might complement one another. During the 1914–18 war, the Germans pick up a naked, unconscious soldier on the battlefield; there is no clue to his identity and he has lost his memory. He is re-educated as a good German and becomes leader of the Weimar Republic. One day a French journalist is struck by a familiar ring in his writings and speeches and eventually discovers that 'Siegfried' is really Jacques Forestier, a native of the Limousin, and in youth his friend. When Giraudoux dramatized the story he tightened it up considerably and altered the ending.

Sieyès, EMMANUEL-JOSEPH, ABBÉ (1748–1836), a Revolutionary politician, published three famous pamphlets in the winter of 1788–9 (just before the meeting of the *États généraux*): *Essai sur les privilèges*; *Délibérations à prendre dans les assemblées de bailliage*; and *Qu'est-ce que le Tiers État?*, a forcible exposition of the views and ambitions of the *bourgeoisie*, and a sketch of the means by which the *Tiers État* could secure its rights. He was associated with Bonaparte in the *coup d'état du 18 brumaire* (1799) and held high office under the *Consulat*.

Signoret, EMMANUEL (1872–1900), a promising poet, who died young. His *Daphné* (1894), *Vers dorés* (1895), and *La Souffrance des eaux* (1898) were collected in *Poésies complètes* (1908; with a preface by Gide).

Sigogne, v. *Sygognes.*

Si le grain ne meurt, v. *Gide.*

Silhouette, a portrait or picture drawn in solid black or cut out of black paper, so called after Étienne de Silhouette (1709–67), controller-general of finances in 1759. Opinions differ as to why his name was applied to it.

Sillonisme, a short-lived Christian democratic movement led by the publicist and social reformer Marc Sangnier (1873–1950). Its organ was *Le Sillon*, f. 1902 by Sangnier.

Silvestre, PAUL-ARMAND (1838–1901), minor *Parnassien* poet (*Rimes neuves et* *vieilles*, 1862; *Gloire des souvenirs*, 1872; *Les Ailes d'or*, 1880, etc.); also a novelist and dramatist.

Simenon, GEORGES (1903–   ), a highly prolific and successful novelist of Belgian birth, has lived in France, the U.S.A., and Switzerland. Between 1920 and 1973 (when he announced his retirement from writing), he produced some 300 works, progressing from popular fiction (with *Au Pont des Arches*, 1920, and other novels publ. under pseudonyms) to crime fiction with a psychological interest, then to more serious psychological novels (inc. some set in America). His popular fame rests on the series of detective novels (publ. from 1931 and now read in translation the world over) featuring Commissaire Maigret of the Paris *police judiciaire*, who sets himself to discover the motives behind the crime, relying on intuition rather than scientific deduction. Simenon deals in the psychology of loneliness, frustration, and hatred. His characters often move in a vitiated, crapulous underworld, seldom described, but evoked with a remarkable feeling for atmosphere, especially sinister atmosphere, that characterizes all his work. His best novels include *L'Homme qui regardait passer les trains* (1938), *Pedigree* (1948), *La Neige était sale* (1948), *Les Anneaux de Bicêtre* (1963), *La Mort d'Auguste* (1966).

Simiand, FRANÇOIS (1873–1935), economist, professor at the *Collège de France* (1932–5). He laid down principles for the scientific analysis of economic and social facts, and is noted for his theory about phases of economic growth and stagnation in the modern period. His chief work was *Le Salaire, l'évolution sociale, et la monnaie* (1932, 3 vols.). v. *History*, 4.

Simon, CLAUDE (1913–   ), novelist. He began writing in 1938, but remained relatively unknown until the appearance of *Le Vent* (1957), when he became associated with the *nouveau roman*. His other novels include *L'Herbe* (1958), *La Route des Flandres* (1960), *Le Palace* (1962), *La Bataille de Pharsale* (1969), *Les Corps conducteurs* (1971), *Triptyque* (1973). His work constitutes an effort to create a new logic in fiction, replacing conventional chronological development of plot and character. His earlier novels are characterized by a near absence of sentence boundaries and by frequent use of the present participle. His more recent works are grammatically quite conventional, and each one is organized as a system of *collages* linked by a number of transitional hinges or generators.

Simon, PIERRE-HENRI (1903–72), man of letters and university teacher; literary critic on *Le *Monde* from 1961 and a member of the *Académie* (1966). His writings—marked by Christian humanism (he was influenced by Mounier and wrote for *Esprit*)—include moral and political essays (e.g. *Contre la torture*, 1957); literary essays (e.g. *L'Homme en procès*, 1949; *Procès du Héros*, 1950; *Témoins de l'homme*, 1957) and an *Histoire de la littérature française contemporaine* (1956, 2 vols.); novels (e.g. *Les Raisins verts*, 1950; *Les Hommes ne veulent pas mourir*, 1953; *Figures à Cordouan*, 1962–7, 4 vols.); and the poems of *Les Regrets et les jours* (1955).

Simon, RICHARD, *v. Bible, French Versions.*

Simon le pathétique, v. Giraudoux.

Simultanéisme, one of the more ephemeral movements in modern poetry (*v. Literary Isms*, led by Barzun (and *v.* also *Divoire*); an exaggerated mixture of *Unanimisme* and *Cubism, the aim being to produce an effect of simultaneity, not only of images, but of sounds intended to represent the voice of man mingled with the voices of Nature and of the great cities.

Sincères, Les, a comedy by Marivaux; produced 1739.

All promises well for the proposed marriage of Ergaste and the marquise, for they share a love of sincerity and always say what they think. But he is so ill-advised as to reply with sincerity when she asks him about the comparative charms of herself and Araminte, and she retorts with a sincere comparison between him and a rival admirer, Dorante. They part in coolness, she to give her hand to Dorante, he to propose to Araminte, finding that less sincerity will promote happiness in marriage.

Sincérisme, *v. Literary Isms.*

Singlin, ANTOINE (*c*. 1607–64), became a priest, entered *Port-Royal* (1637), and came under the influence of Du Vergier de Hauranne, whom he succeeded as director. He helped to convert Pascal. Some of his sermons were published as *Instructions chrétiennes.*

Singulari nos, v. Lamennais.

Sirventes, *v. Serventois.*

Sismondi, LÉONARD SIMONDE DE (1773–1842), historian and political economist, the son of a Genevan pastor, lived with his family in Italy after the Revolution and took to farming. After publishing a *Tableau de l'agriculture toscane* (1801), he returned to Geneva (then French), dividing his time between writing (*L'Histoire des républiques italiennes du Moyen Âge*, 1809–18, 16 vols.; *De la littérature du midi de l'Europe*, 1813, 4 vols., based on lectures he delivered in Geneva in 1811), frequenting Mme de Staël's circle at *Coppet, or travelling with her. Welcomed in literary *salons* in Paris (1813–15), he astonished his friends by rallying to Napoleon during the Hundred Days. His *Nouveaux Principes de l'économie politique* (1819) is said to have influenced the *Saint-Simoniens. In 1819 he married an Englishwoman and returned for good to Geneva, where he wrote his *Histoire des Français* (1821–42, 31 vols.). His correspondence with a wide circle of friends (inc. the countess of Albany, widow of the Young Pretender and mistress of the Italian poet Alfieri) has been published at various dates.

Six, Le Groupe des, the composers Georges Auric, Louis Durey, Arthur Honegger, Darius Milhaud, Francis

Poulenc, and Germaine Tailleferre, who from 1918 wrote for a time in collaboration. They produced the music for *Cocteau's *Les Mariés de la Tour Eiffel* and an *Album des Six*. *Les Six* were admirers and associates of Satie.

Smarh, v. *Tentation de Saint Antoine, La*.

Smarra, ou les Démons de la nuit, v. *Nodier*.

Soboul, ALBERT (1914–82), a leading historian of the Revolution. His works include *Les Sans-culottes parisiens en l'an II* (1958), abridged as *Mouvement populaire et gouvernement révolutionnaire en l'an II* (1973); *Précis d'histoire de la Révolution française* (1962; 2nd ed. 1964, 2 vols.); *Le Procès de Louis XVI* (1966); *La Première République, 1792–1804* (1968); *La Civilisation et la Révolution française* (vol. I, 1970), a very informative illustrated study. He continues the line of left-wing historians of the Revolution, e.g. Jaurès, Mathiez, and G. Lefebvre, who challenged Aulard's positivist interpretation of events (v. *History*, 4).

Société de l'histoire de France, La, a learned society f. 1833 by Guizot and other historians, and still continuing. Its aim was to publish documents concerning the pre-Revolutionary history of France (chronicles, memoirs, registers, etc.) and to maintain a periodical in connection with its work (the *Annuaire* from 1837 to 1863; the *Bulletin* from 1863). In 1927 it absorbed the *Société d'histoire contemporaine* (f. 1890).

Société des anciens textes français, La, f. 1875 (with G. Paris as first president) on the model of the Early English Text Society, publishes critical editions of medieval French and Provençal texts.

Société des gens de lettres, La, f. 1838 by Louis Desnoyers (1802–68; novelist and man of letters) with the support of the leading writers of the day, is primarily an authors' rights society in matters of copyright, publication, etc. It can also help needy writers; and v. *Prix littéraires*.

Société des textes français modernes, La, f. 1905 by Lanson, publishes critical editions of post-medieval texts.

Sociétés joyeuses, associations for purposes of revelry and amusement which existed in Paris and many provincial towns in the later Middle Ages; probably a lay survival of the *Fête des Fous*. Their members—mainly citizens and tradespeople, with the odd young man of good family—wore fool's costume, and their chief officers were usually called the *Prince des Sots* and *Mère Sotte*. They organized processions, or performed *farces*, *moralités*, and *soties* (and recited improvised verses poking fun at local events and personages) on temporary stages set up in public places. They included, notably, the *Enfants sans souci* in Paris; also the *Infanterie dijonnaise*; the *Connards* (probably originally *Cornards*, from the *cornes* on their fool's caps) at Rouen and Évreux; the *Suppôts* ['myrmidons'] *du Seigneur de la Coquille* ['misprint'] at Lyons, recruited from the printing workers of the town; and the *sociétés* of Amiens, Auxerre, Beauvais, and other towns (mainly in the North). Cf. *Basoche*.

Sodome et Gomorrhe, (1) v. *À la recherche du temps perdu*; (2) a 2-act prose drama (prod. 1943; publ. 1946) by Giraudoux; a study, made all the more bitter by the brilliant, paradoxical dialogue, of enmity and incomprehension between the sexes (God will spare Sodom and Gomorrah if even one couple can be found there who are happy in the normal union of man with woman; hopes centre on the couple Lia and Jean, but they are dashed).

Sœur, La, a comedy by Rotrou, adapted from the Italian; produced 1645.

Lélie, sent by his father to Constantinople to recover his lost mother and his sister Aurélie, falls in love on the way with Sophie, a girl of unknown parentage, marries her, returns, and passes her off as Aurélie. When his father proposes to marry 'Aurélie' to an old gentleman, the ingenious valet Ergaste saves the situation. Then Lélie's mother returns from captivity and recognizes 'Aurélie' as her own daughter. But it turns out that the real Aurélie and another child were secretly exchanged in infancy, so all ends well.

Sœur Philomène, v. *Goncourt.*

Sœurs Rondoli, Les, v. *Maupassant.*

Sœurs Vatard, Les, v. *Huysmans.*

Soirées de Médan, Les (1880), a volume of *Naturalist short stories by Zola and five authors who were then his disciples; so called after Zola's country home at Médan, near Paris, where he entertained his friends. Each tale has a military setting, for it was agreed that Zola's contribution— *L'Attaque au moulin*, an episode of the *Franco-Prussian war—should come first and set the scene for the rest. The other stories, in order of printing, were Maupassant's *Boule-de-suif*, Huysmans's *Sac au dos*, Céard's *La Saignée*, Hennique's *L'Affaire du grand 7*, and P. Alexis's *Après la bataille.*

Soirées de Saint-Pétersbourg, ou Entretiens sur le gouvernement temporel de la Providence, Les (1821; written in Russia), the chief work of J. de Maistre, consists of 11 dialogues, brilliant, witty, and often paradoxical, between a count (the author), a devout Russian senator, and a young French *émigré*. They discuss the place of evil in the scheme of Providence; suffering as the divine punishment for sin; the efficacy of prayer; and the eventual certain triumph of the Catholic Church. The first dialogue contains a famous passage defending capital punishment: were it not for the executioner, agent of the divine will, order would give way to chaos.

Sollers, PHILIPPE, v. *Critics and Criticism*, 3; *Lyric Poetry*, 4.

Somaize, ANTOINE BAUDEAU, SIEUR DE (b. 1630), a man of letters who took exception to Molière's mockery of the *précieuses* and constituted himself their champion and historian in a famous dictionary (v. *Dictionaries*, 1660). He also wrote verse, satirical prose, and the comedy *Les Véritables Précieuses*. Very little is known of his life, except that he was secretary to Marie Mancini (v. *Mazarin's Nieces*).

Somme des vices et des vertus or **Somme le Roi**, v. *Religious Writings*, 1.

Somptuarisme, v. *Literary Isms.*

Son Excellence Eugène Rougon (1876), one of Zola's *Rougon-Macquart* novels.

The ambitious Eugène (son of Pierre and Félicité in *La Fortune des Rougon*; brother of Aristide in *La* *Curée*) leaves Plassans for Paris, throws in his lot with supporters of the Second Empire, wins power and social position as a *sénateur*, and retains them by altering his political views. There are detailed, often satirical, not always accurate, pictures of court and political circles.

Songecreux, v. *Jean de l'Espine.*

Songe de Descartes, Le. Descartes is said to have decided to go into philosophical retreat when, while in Germany in 1619, he had three dreams in one night revealing to him 'les fondements d'une science admirable'.

Songe d'enfer, v. *Religious Writings*, 1.

Songe du Vieil Pèlerin, Le, v. *Philippe de Mézières.*

Sonnet, a poem composed of two quatrains and two tercets of any metre. In the regular form—and there are many irregular forms—the rhyme-scheme is:

$$\text{a b b a } \quad \text{a b b a} \quad \text{c c d} \quad \left\{ \begin{array}{l} \text{e d e} \\ \text{e e d} \end{array} \right.$$

Du Bellay and Ronsard were mainly responsible for introducing it into France from Italy, though there are earlier examples of it in Marot, Scève, and M. de Saint-Gelais. v. *Foreign Influences*, 1.

Sonnet des voyelles ('A noir, E blanc, I

rouge, U vert, O bleu: voyelles, Je dirai quelque jour vos naissances latentes'), a sonnet by Rimbaud, written 1871, first printed in Verlaine's Les *Poètes maudits (1884), and later used to illustrate the *Symbolist doctrine of correspondances. It has been variously interpreted as inspired by a coloured alphabet he used as a child, by the alchemical colours (it was written when he was studying magic), and as a deliberate piece of literary mystification.

Sonnets pour Hélène, v. Ronsard.

Sopha, Le, v. Crébillon fils.

Sophie, Lettres à, v. Mirabeau, comte de.

Sophonisbe, the subject of tragedies by M. de Saint-Gelais, Montchrétien, Nicolas de Montreux, Mairet, Corneille, and Voltaire. The historical Sophonisba, a Carthaginian, married Syphax, king of Numidia, and her influence drew him away from his alliance with Rome during the 2nd Punic War. Syphax was captured by Masinissa, an ally of Rome, and she fell into Masinissa's power. He became enamoured of her and determined to marry her. But Scipio Africanus, fearing her influence, claimed her as a captive to be sent to Rome. Masinissa, to save her from captivity, sent her poison, which she calmly drank.

Sorbonne, La, a college of the medieval *University of Paris, f. 1257 by Robert de Sorbon, chaplain to Louis IX, as a hostel for 16 students. It was always closely associated with the study of theology (from the 14th c. certain theses for degrees in theology were sustained there, and known as *Sorboniques*), with the result that the name 'La Sorbonne' came to be applied to the faculty of theology (esp. from 1554, when that faculty began to hold its meetings, often to consider cases of alleged heresy, in the college premises), and (theology being the dominant faculty) even to the whole University.

The faculty of theology of Paris played an important part in French history. Already before the foundation of Robert de Sorbon's college it had resisted the inroads of the mendicant friars. In the 15th c. it showed bitter animosity to Joan of Arc, and, with greater enlightenment, erected the first printing-press in Paris (1469; v. Fichet). In the 16th c. it played a prominent part by its onslaught on *Évangélisme (v. Béda), hostility to the *Jesuits (on their admission to France by Henri II), and support of the *Ligue. In the 17th c. it was closely involved in the quarrel between Jesuits and *Jansenists, and its condemnation of A. Arnauld provoked *Pascal's Lettres provinciales. In the 18th c. it supported the authorities in vigorous—but ineffectual—efforts to repress the *philosophes, the *Encyclopédistes, etc., attacking, for example, Montesquieu, Buffon, J.-J. Rousseau, Marmontel.

The college was suppressed in 1792. Following the creation of the *Université impériale (1808), its buildings in the *Quartier latin (reconstructed in the 17th c. by Richelieu, who was buried in the new chapel, and completely rebuilt, apart from the chapel, in 1885–1901) became the headquarters of the new Académie de Paris, the seat of the faculties of theology (suppressed 1885), arts, and science of the reorganized University of Paris, and of various affiliated institutions. This remained the general situation until 1968; v. Université de France; Universities, 1.

Sorel, AGNÈS (1422–50), mistress of Charles VII, said to have had a good influence on him during her short period of favour (1444–50).

Sorel, ALBERT (1842–1906), historian. He is noted for his studies of the Revolution in relation to external politics, e.g. L'Europe et la Révolution française (1885–1904).

Sorel, CHARLES (1597–1674), author of novels ridiculing the vogue for romances of the type of L'*Astrée, also of bibliographical works (La Bibliothèque française; La Connaissance des bons livres). In La Vraie Histoire comique de Francion (1623), an early picaresque novel (v. Novel,

2), the hero, a man of quality, is first seen disguised as a pilgrim pursuing his love Laurette to her husband's house, where after ludicrous incidents he ends up in a vat with a broken head. The story of his early life, which he relates to a friend, and his subsequent adventures in pursuit of another love, this time in the guise of a charlatan, provide a realistic picture of the lower ranks of society—penniless poets, lawyers, pedants, bullies, schemers of both sexes. The work was highly successful and much of it can still be enjoyed (e.g. the descriptions of life in a Paris college). In his novel *Le Berger extravagant* (1627), the hero, Lysis, who has lost his wits through over-addiction to *pastoral romances, adopts the life and dress of a shepherd and has a series of grotesque adventures, until those who, for their own amusement, have encouraged his illusions take pity on him and restore him to his senses. At one point he prepares to throw himself into the river (like Céladon in *L'Astrée*), but first sends word to three nymphs to be ready to pull him out, 'car je ne sais nager'.

Sorel is depicted as Charroselles in *Le *Roman bourgeois*.

Sorel, GEORGES (1847–1922), social philosopher, an exponent of revolutionary syndicalism. He was an anti-intellectualist, believing, roughly, that progress and social reform are effected by violence and the spirit of collective enthusiasm it engenders (hence the power of mob action and the general strike, and the relative unimportance of the ideologies, whether *bourgeois* or Marxist, which produce them). His chief works are *Réflexions sur la violence* (1908) and *Les Illusions du progrès* (1908). Some of his other works were first published in part in the *Cahiers de la quinzaine*.

Sorel, Julien, in Stendhal's *Le *Rouge et le Noir*.

Sosies, Les, v. Rotrou.

Sotie or **Sottie,** a kind of satirical farce, closely akin to the satirical *moralités* of the same—later medieval—period. *Soties*

were acted by members of the *sociétés joyeuses*, notably the *Enfants sans souci*, who took full advantage of their fool's costume to poke fun at society, manners, and political events. The characters were usually the *Prince des Sots*, *Mère Sotte* (played by a man), and their supporters. One of the best-known *soties* was *Gringore's *Jeu du Prince des Sots et Mère Sotte*. Another typical *sotie*, *Les Trois Pèlerins* (c. 1521), attacked Louise de Savoie, mother of François Ier, whom the people blamed for most of the misfortunes of his reign.

Gide described some of his satirical tales as *soties*.

Sots, v. Enfants sans souci; Sociétés joyeuses; Sotie.

Souday, PAUL (1868–1931), official literary critic of *Le *Temps* (1912–29) and a champion of the classical canons in literature and criticism. He published *La Société des grands esprits* (1929); critical studies of Proust, Gide, Valéry (all 1927), and Bossuet (1929); an edition (1927) of Voltaire's *Mémoires*; *Les Livres du temps* (1913–30), collected articles and reviews.

Soufflot, JACQUES-GERMAIN (1714–80), architect, notably of the *Panthéon.

Souffrances de l'inventeur, Les, v. Comédie humaine, La (Scènes de la vie de province).

Soulary, JOSEPH-MARIE, *self-styled* JOSÉPHIN (1815–91), poet, wrote delicate verse, often in sonnet form. His collections include, notably, *Sonnets humoristiques* (1858); also *A travers champs* (1838), *Les Cinq Cordes du luth* (1838), *Éphémères* (1846).

Soulavie, JEAN-LOUIS, v. Richelieu, duc de.

Soulié, FRÉDÉRIC (1800–47), one of the earliest writers of *romans-feuilletons, produced at least 40 gloomily sensational novels, best-sellers in their day, e.g. *Les Deux Cadavres* (1832), *Les Mémoires du* *diable* (1837–8), *La Lionne* (1846), *La Comtesse de Monrion* (1847). He also collaborated with Dumas *père* in **mélodrames*.

Soulier de satin, Le, v. Claudel.

Soult, NICOLAS-JEAN DE DIEU, *v. Maréchal.*

Soumet, ALEXANDRE (1788–1845), minor poet and dramatist, wrote didactic verse (e.g. *La Découverte de la vaccine*, 1815, which won a prize from the *Académie), but also moved in *Romantic circles and helped to found *La *Muse française*. His life's work, the long *Divine Épopée* (1841) in which all-redeeming love triumphs over evil, delighted his contemporaries; and his elegy *La Pauvre Fille* (1814) is remembered. His tragedies (e.g. *Clytemnestre*, 1822; *Saül*, 1822; *Les Maccabées*, 1827; *Une Fête de Néron*, 1829) at times herald the transition from *Classical to Romantic drama.

Soupault, PHILIPPE (1897–), poet and novelist. He was a *Dadaist, then a leading *Surrealist, publishing works including *Les Champs magnétiques* (1920; with A. Breton); the poems of *Rose des vents* (1920), *Westwego* (1922), and *Georgia* (1926); and the novels *Le Bon Apôtre* (1923) and *Les Frères Durandeau* (1924). He was expelled from the Surrealist group in 1926 and thereafter combined a career in journalism and broadcasting with creative writing, publishing novels (e.g. *Les Dernières Nuits de Paris*, 1928), poetry (much of his verse is in *Poèmes et poésies* (*1917–73*), 1973), studies of Lautréamont (1927; and an edition of his works, 1946), William Blake, Baudelaire, Labiche, etc.

Sources de l'histoire de France, Les, an invaluable repertory of narrative sources for the history of medieval France, also of such indirect sources as letters, poems, etc. The first part, *Des origines aux guerres d'Italie* (1901–6, 6 vols.), was published by Auguste Molinier, and the work was continued by Henri Hauser, Émile Bourgeois, and Louis André.

Sourches, LOUIS-FRANÇOIS DU BOUCHET, MARQUIS DE (1639–1716), was charged from 1664 with the discipline of the royal court as *prévôt de l'hôtel du roi*. His memoirs (not publ. in full till 1882), covering the period 1681–1712, are of historical importance both in their own right and as a valuable check on those of Dangeau and the duc de Saint-Simon, for he is very well informed, dispassionate, and not much addicted to scandalous anecdotes.

Sous le soleil de Satan, v. Bernanos.

Sous-offs, v. Descaves.

Souvenir (1841, in the **Revue des Deux Mondes*), by Musset, a famous lyric written shortly after he had revisited the Forêt de Fontainebleau, where he had passed happy hours with G. Sand. He cherishes the memory of their love, even though happiness was followed by suffering. *Cf.* Lamartine's *Le Lac* (under *Méditations poétiques*) and Hugo's **Tristesse d'Olympio*.

Souvenirs d'égotisme, v. Stendhal.

Souvenirs d'enfance et de jeunesse (1883), Renan's reminiscences of early life. He describes his childhood in Brittany; his early years in Paris and life at the seminary of *Saint-Sulpice; the stages leading to his break with the Church; the beginning of his new life, etc. The style is typical of Renan at his most limpid, supple, persuasive, and (e.g. the account of Talleyrand's death-bed return to the Church) gracefully ironic. The work contains his invocation to Athene, the *Prière que je fis sur l'Acropole quand je fus arrivé à en comprendre la parfaite beauté.* This was not composed on the spot. He first saw the Acropolis in 1865, brought home a few notes, and at intervals over the next 10 years worked them into one of the most famous passages of 19th-c. French prose (first publ. 1876, in the **Revue des Deux Mondes*).

Souvenirs d'un homme de lettres, v. Daudet, A.

Souza, MME DE, i.e. ADÈLE FILLEUL, COMTESSE DE FLAHAUT, then MARQUISE DE SOUZA-BOTELHO (1761–1836), grandmother of the duc de Morny, wrote sentimental romances about the 18th-c. aristocracy of which she was herself a relic (*cf.* Mme de Genlis), notably *Adèle de Sénanges* (1794; partly autobiographical) and *Eugène de Rothelin* (1808). During the Revolution (when her first husband, the comte de Flahaut, was guillotined) she lived by her pen as an *émigrée* in England (at Mickleham, Surrey; *cf.* Staël), then in *Hamburg. She returned to Paris in 1798 and remarried.

Spanish Influence, v. *Foreign Influences.*

Spectateur français, Le, v. *Marivaux.*

Spire, ANDRÉ (1868–1966), poet of Jewish birth and Biblical inspiration, an ardent Zionist and a high civil servant. His many collections include *La Cité présente* (1903), *Poèmes juifs* (1919; definitive ed. 1959), *Poèmes de Loire* (1929). He writes of everyday reality in a spirit of hope akin to that of the early *unanimistes. Most of his work is in the *vers libre.*

Spiridion, v. *Sand.*

Spiritualisme, v. *Literary Isms.*

Spleen de Paris, Le; *Spleen et Idéal*, v. Baudelaire.

Splendeurs et misères des courtisanes (1838–47; later in *La *Comédie humaine*, *Scènes de la vie parisienne*), a group of four closely connected tales by Balzac. It continues the adventures of Lucien de Rubempré (*v. Illusions perdues*). He accompanies the abbé Carlos Herrera to Paris and soon discovers that his companion (who dominates the book) is the ex-convict *Vautrin. Stifling his scruples, he lives in style on the money Vautrin provides. At the theatre he and the courtesan Esther Gobseck fall in love at first sight. Esther, compelled by Vautrin, becomes *Nucingen's mistress so that she may enrich Lucien, but Nucingen is so vile that she commits suicide rather than stay with him. Unknown to herself, she had been heiress to immense wealth, and after her death Lucien is arrested on suspicion of murder. Innocent, but terrified, he confesses his dealings with Vautrin, then hangs himself in his cell.

Spoelberch de Lovenjoul, CHARLES, VICOMTE DE (1836–1907), a wealthy, erudite bibliophile of Belgian birth, amassed famous collections of books, manuscripts, autographs, and ana, notably those of Balzac, Gautier, Musset, Sainte-Beuve, and G. Sand, and bequeathed them to the *Institut de France. He compiled valuable bibliographical manuals, e.g. *Histoire des œuvres de Balzac* (1879 and later eds.) and *Histoire des œuvres de Théophile Gautier* (1887).

Sponde, JEAN DE (1557–95), poet and humanist, a Protestant by birth and education who later became a Roman Catholic and, after a career at court and in the magistracy, turned to the study of theology. His *Sonnets d'amour* and, more especially, such poems of religious experience as his *Sonnets et stances de la mort*, the long poem *Stances du sacré banquet et convive de Jésus-Christ*, and the *Méditations sur les Psaumes avec un essai de quelques poèmes chrétiens* exemplify the metaphysical trend in some late Renaissance poetry (*cf. Chassignet*; *La Ceppède*). His poetry was occasionally included in 16th- and 17th-c. collections, but seldom published separately in his lifetime (when he was best known as a humanist, a jurist, and a translator). His *Poésies* were published in 1949; his *Méditations sur les Psaumes* in 1954 (ed. A. M. Boase).

Staal, MME DE, v. *Launay, Mlle de.*

Staël, ANNE-LOUISE-GERMAINE NECKER, MME DE (1766–1817), a writer who stands with Chateaubriand as one of the chief precursors of *Romanticism and of modern criticism (v. Critics and Criticism, 2). Her father was Jacques *Necker, her mother the former Suzanne Curchod (Gibbon's early love). Her mother's *salon in Paris served as a sort of intellectual forcing-ground where as a child she listened to the conversation of such men as Buffon, Diderot, Grimm, and Talleyrand. After her first marriage (1785) her own salon was among the most famous of the day, both as a centre of intellectual activity and, later, as a meeting-place for those who shared her antipathy to Napoleon and the Empire. Her husband was the baron de Staël-Holstein, Swedish ambassador in Paris, a man older than herself and for whom she had no affection. She was legally separated from him in 1798, having borne him three children (Auguste, who edited her Œuvres complètes, 1821; Albert, killed in a duel in Sweden; Albertine, who married into the *Broglie family). During the Revolution she emigrated, spent four months in England (early in 1793, when she joined the group of émigrés at Juniper Hall, near Mickleham, Surrey, and met Fanny Burney), then retired to *Coppet. In 1795 she spent nine months in Paris, but aroused the suspicions of the *Directoire and had to return to Coppet. She went back to Paris in 1797 and reopened her salon, but she incurred the disfavour of Napoleon, who repeatedly exiled her (1803, 1806, 1810; v. De l'Allemagne). On these occasions she travelled widely in Germany, Italy, Austria, Russia, Sweden, and England, and Coppet became a centre of European culture. Her travelling companions included Schlegel, Sismondi, and B. Constant, with whom she had a long and stormy liaison (1794–1811). The relationship was notable for their intense intellectual sympathy (Sismondi declared: 'On n'a point connu Mme de Staël si on ne l'a pas vue avec Benjamin Constant. Lui seul avait la puissance, par un esprit égal au sien, de mettre en jeu tout son esprit, de la faire grandir par la lutte...'). She returned to Paris after Napoleon's fall in 1814; v. Salon, 1. In 1816 she was secretly married to Albert Rocca, a young Swiss officer to whom she had become secretly

engaged in 1811. Their son Alphonse was brought up in the Broglie household by his half-sister Albertine, with Doudan as tutor.

Her chief works were *De la littérature considérée dans ses rapports avec les institutions sociales (1800) and *De l'Allemagne (1810). Here, as a critic, she made the crucial distinction between 'classical' and 'romantic' literature and also emphasized that judgement should be relative, not absolute, and should be based on a sense of history (a view strongly contrasting with the rigid *Classical conventions then in force). Here, too, she professed her faith in the perfectibility of man. Her other works include the novels *Delphine (1802) and *Corinne (1807), which reflect the conflict in her own life between a thirst for fame and a longing for human affection; Du caractère de M. Necker et de sa vie privée (1804) and Dix Années d'exil (1821; written 1810–13), memoirs; various political, philosophical, and critical treatises, e.g. Lettres sur les ouvrages et le caractère de J.-J. Rousseau (1788), Essai sur les fictions (1795), De l'influence des passions sur le bonheur des individus et des nations (1796), Réflexions sur le suicide (1813; written 1810), Considérations sur les principaux événements de la Révolution française (1818; written 1813 and 1816); also tales written in early life and plays written for the private theatre at Coppet (some publ. in Essais dramatiques, 1821). Many of her letters have been published. The Lettres à Louis de Narbonne (1960, in her Correspondance générale, 1960–   ; ed. B. Jasinski), which cover her period at Juniper Hall, are of special interest to English readers.

Stances à la Malibran, v. Musset.

Stapfer, PAUL (1840–1917), professor and critic, author of Shakespeare et l'antiquité (1879–80), Molière et Shakespeare (1887), Les Réputations littéraires (1893–1901), Récréations grammaticales et littéraires (1909), etc.

Stapoul, v. Lefèvre d'Étaples.

Starobinski, JEAN (1920–   ), a critic of Swiss birth, first studied medicine and is now professor of the history of ideas at the University of Geneva and a member of the British Academy (1974). He is best known for his *Jean-Jacques Rousseau: la transparence et l'obstacle* (1957). His two collections of essays, *L'Œil vivant* (1961) and *La Relation critique* (1970), contain important contributions on individual authors and on criticism in general. His method is to regard the work as a system of relations between the self and the world, then to study this system. *v. Critics and Criticism*, 3.

Stavisky, ALEXANDRE (1886–1934), a fraudulent financier who engineered a large-scale swindle. His exposure (Dec. 1933) and reported suicide (Jan. 1934) provoked riots (6 Feb.) and allegations that he had been murdered to protect his associates in government circles. This scandal helped to bring down the Radical Socialist premier, Camille Chautemps.

Stello, *v. Vigny.*

Stendhal, *pseudonym of* HENRI BEYLE (1783–1842), novelist and critic. Born and educated at Grenoble, he lost his mother when he was seven and detested his father (an advocate) and his early environment, which was Royalist and devout. He was in Paris by 1799, and influence procured him an army commission. It took him to Milan, and he realized that Italy was his spiritual home. He fell in love—unhappily; and he began to study English. In 1802 he resigned his commission, lived mainly in Paris for a time, but could not afford a dilettante life and returned (1806) to the army. For some years he was mainly engaged in victualling Napoleon's armies in Germany, Russia, and Austria—never in the thick of the fighting, but often enduring severe hardship. In 1813 he left the army with his health impaired, largely through his own excesses. In 1814 he scraped some money together and, realizing his great ambition, went back to Milan. He stayed seven years in Italy (until he was suspected of espionage and had to

leave), absorbed by art, music, literature, society, and a shattering, unrequited passion which he never forgot. ('L'amour', he declared, writing his own obituary, 'a fait le bonheur et le malheur de sa vie'.) In these years he published the *Vie de Haydn, de Mozart, et de Métastase* (1814) and *Histoire de la peinture en Italie* (1817), both consisting largely of unacknowledged extracts from other authors, but interspersed with original critical comment; also *Rome, Naples, et Florence en 1817* (1817), writing for the first time as 'Stendhal'. From 1821 to 1830 he was mostly in Paris, living frugally, writing, frequenting literary **salons* (e.g. Mme Ancelot's). He now published the well-known study **De l'amour* (1822); his *Vie de Rossini* (1823; *v. Rossini*); **Racine et Shakspeare* (1823, 1825); *Armance, ou Quelques Scènes d'un salon de Paris en 1827* (1827), his first novel; *Promenades dans Rome* (1829); and *Le *Rouge et le Noir* (1830), the first of his two great novels. In 1831 he got himself appointed consul at Trieste and was soon transferred to Civitavecchia, a dreary, unhealthy little port, but only 45 miles from Rome. He held this office until his death. In these last years he published *Mémoires d'un touriste* (1838), travel impressions with frequent excursions into criticism; the novel *La *Chartreuse de Parme* (1839), which disputes the place as his greatest work with *Le Rouge et le Noir*; *L'Abbesse de Castro* (1839), a short novel; also tales of 16th-c. Italy contributed to reviews. Boredom and ill-health led him to take increasingly lengthy spells of leave, spent travelling or in Paris, where he died. The words on his tomb in the Montmartre cemetery—'Arrigo Beyle, Milanese, Scrisse, Amò, Visse'—were inspired by the epitaph he had composed for himself in 1837. Later, growing interest in his work led to the publication of his *Vie de Napoléon* (1876); *Lamiel* (1889), fragments of the novel on which he was working in his last years; **Lucien Leuwen* (1894), an unfinished novel; also three works of great interest for the study of a writer whose irony and sensuality often concealed a sensitive, wounded spirit—his *Journal* (1888) for the years 1801–18; *La Vie de Henri Brulard* (1890; unfinished), romanticized autobiography ('Confessions,... comme Jean-Jacques Rousseau, avec plus de franchise'); and *Souvenirs d'égotisme* (1892; unfinished), on his life in Paris 1822–30.

His ironical attitude to life was influenced by his study of the 18th-c. sensationalists and *idéologues*. He believed, briefly, that thought is a consequence of sensation; and that man's behaviour is governed by his passions, hence by his desire for happiness. We should, therefore, recognize without illusion that our actions—our virtues or our avoidance of vice—spring from interested motives. He also considered that the most useful faculty a man could acquire was the ability to deduce character from observation and from analysis of motives. His beliefs were allied to what he called *Beylisme*—a worship of magnificent, all-conquering energy in the pursuit of happiness (whether the conquests were of love or of power). It had in it much that was basically *Romantic; and for a time his *Racine et Shakspeare* linked him with the Romantics, as did his views that art and literature should depict passion and that the *beau idéal*—the criterion of beauty—should change with the conditions and ideas of succeeding generations. But, like his friend Mérimée, he was not carried away by Romanticism, and in general neither his attitude nor his writings had any appeal for a generation concerned with the delights, not the causes, of sensibility. He was not a conscious stylist. He set himself to express his thought, however complicated, with the utmost lucidity, if necessary at the expense of harmony and rhythm (*v. Code civil*). He read a great deal of English (he visited England more than once) and was fond of using English words and phrases (*v. Café* (Café Hardy)). As he had predicted, appreciation of his works came towards the end of the century; Balzac (*v. Revue parisienne*) and Gobineau were exceptional in appreciating him earlier. Taine, *c*. 1880, did much to awaken interest in him, and when writers turned to the psychological observation of life for their raw material (*c*. 1890; *v. Novel*, 3) he joined the ranks of the great French novelists.

Stern, Daniel, *v. Agoult.*

Strasbourg, Serments de, *v. Serments.*

Structuralism, which gained prominence in France and elsewhere from the mid-1960s, is primarily an extension of the 'structural' approach to language associated with Saussure and later linguists (e.g. Roman Jakobson), and the general methodology of structural linguistics, to other human sciences, notably social anthropology (*v. Lévi-Strauss*). It seeks to define any human fact in terms of an organized whole of which it is an element and to explain the latter with the help of models. Though not a system of philosophy, it has been hailed by some as the successor to *Existentialism, its exponents being credited with the doctrine that man's thoughts and actions have been determined down the ages by a network of structures, social and psychological, in which free will plays a minimal part. Those who have adopted a structuralist approach include, besides Lévi-Strauss, the philosopher Michel **Foucault (1926–84; professor at the** *Collège de France* from 1970), notably in *Les Mots et les choses* (1966); the **psychoanalyst Jacques Lacan (1901–81),** in whose view (1953) 'l'inconscient est structuré comme un langage' and whose articles are collected in *Écrits* (1966); the Marxist philosopher Louis Althusser (1918–), author of *Pour Marx* (1965), *Lire 'le Capital'* (1965), etc.; and, to a lesser extent, the critic Barthes (*v. Critics and Criticism*, 3). Structuralism has not as yet won the wide appeal once enjoyed by Existentialism, partly because its exponents tend to write in the technical language of their several disciplines. Its literary influence cannot yet be assessed. *v. Semiology.*

Style, Old and New, *v. Year.*

Suard, JEAN-BAPTISTE (1733–1817), journalist, critic (v. Critics and Criticism, 1 (last §)), and *philosophe; dramatic censor from 1777 (v. Censorship, Dramatic) and a member of the *Académie (1774, the court having opposed and delayed his admission). He wrote much in the Journal étranger, *Gazette de France, and Lettres critiques, and his work includes translations from English. His Mélanges de littérature appeared in 1803–5. He married into the *Panckoucke family and his wife's *salon was frequented by the philosophes. v. Musical Controversies.

Suarès, André, pseudonym of ISAAC FÉLIX (1868–1948), an essayist and critic of wide reading and forceful, independent views. His works include Images de la grandeur (1900) and Voici l'homme (1906), essays; Wagner (1899), Tolstoï vivant (1911), Trois Hommes: Pascal, Ibsen, Dostoïevski (1912), Musique et poésie (1928), Goethe le grand Européen (1932), and Trois Grands Vivants: Cervantes, Tolstoï, Baudelaire (1937), music and literary criticism; Le Voyage du Condottiere (Vers Venise, 1910; Fiorenza, 1932; Sienne, la bien aimée, 1932), travel; also a few plays.

Subjectivisme, v. Literary Isms.

Subventionnés, Les, v. Theatres and Theatre Companies.

Suchet, LOUIS-GABRIEL, v. Maréchal.

Sue, MARIE-JOSEPH, self-styled EUGÈNE (1804–75), a highly successful author of *romans-feuilletons, came of a distinguished medical family and began his career as a ship's surgeon, retiring in 1829 to write seafaring novels, e.g. Plik et Plok (1831), La Vigie de Koatven (1833). Then came Arthur (1838), Mathilde (1841), Le Morne au diable (1842), etc., all fairly successful. But he owed his immense popularity to sensational novels of Parisian low life, written with more exuberance than style, showing a fertile, at times grandiose, imagination and strong dramatic sense, and offering a hotch-potch of contemporary ideals of social and democratic reform. The best remembered of them all is probably Les Mystères de Paris (1842–3; v. Marx). Many of the characters have become familiar names, e.g. Rodolphe, the mysterious prince who haunts the Paris underworld in disguise, punishing evil and rewarding virtue; 'la Mère Pipelet' and her husband, the two concierges who suffer a series of amusing mishaps at the hands of the young artist Cabrion; 'le Chourineur', the redeemed convict; 'le Tortillard', the corrupted street-urchin. Other well-known novels in his vast output include Le Juif errant (1844–5), Les Sept Péchés capitaux (1847–9), Les Mystères du peuple (1849–56).

Suite du Menteur, La, v. Menteur, Le.

Sully, MAXIMILIEN DE BÉTHUNE, BARON DE ROSNY, later DUC DE (1559–1641), the great minister of Henri IV, helped the king to pacify his realm, reorganized the national finances by stringent economies and reform of abuses, and encouraged agriculture. He left memoirs (the shortened title is Économies royales) compiled under his supervision by his secretaries (1638), and addressed to himself, recalling his various actions. He credits Henri IV with a famous scheme (discussed by J.-J. Rousseau) to establish perpetual peace through a kind of federation of the States of Europe, rearranged so as greatly to reduce the power of Austria. The scheme had, he asserts, the warm support of Queen Elizabeth.

Sully-Prudhomme, RENÉ-FRANÇOIS-ARMAND (1839–1907), a leading *Parnassien poet, winner of the *Prix Nobel (1901), studied both science and law, then inherited money and turned to literature and philosophy. At first he wrote gentle, sentimental, faintly melancholy lyrics, collected in Stances et poèmes (1865; inc. Le Vase brisé, which has a place in most anthologies), Les Épreuves (1866), Les Solitudes (1869). Afterwards, the lyrical note was subordinated and he carried the Parnassien theories of impersonality to the point of attempting to turn abstract scientific and philosophical systems into epic verse (*La Justice*, 1878; *Le Prisme*, 1884; *Le Bonheur*, 1888). Latterly, he wrote only prose, collected, with his poetry, in *Œuvres* (1883–1908, 8 vols.).

Supervielle, JULES (1884–1960), poet, novelist, and dramatist. Born in Montevideo of French parents (*cf. Lautréamont; Laforgue*), he was educated in Paris, then settled in Uruguay, but frequently visited France and lived there after 1945. His writing, which is coloured by his familiarity with the S. American scene, has exceptional qualities of pure poetic feeling, humour, and fantasy. It is intimate in tone, humanistic and conciliatory in spirit, marked by a 'pansympathie' with Nature (esp. animals), by a gift for, as it were, domesticating the mysteries of the universe, and by a preoccupation with death. His works include *Poèmes* (1919), *Débarcadères* (1922), *Gravitations* (1925), *Le Forçat innocent* (1930), *Les Amis inconnus* (1934), *La Fable du monde* (1938), *Poèmes de la France malheureuse* (1941; inspired by the fall of France), *Oublieuse Mémoire* (1949), and *Le Corps tragique* (1959), poetry; *L'Homme de la Pampa* (1923), *Le Voleur d'enfants* (1926; dramatized 1949), and its sequel *Le Survivant* (1928), novels; *L'Enfant de la haute mer* (1931), *L'Arche de Noé* (1938), *Le Petit Bois* (1947), and *Premiers Pas de l'univers* (1950), short stories, often on Biblical or mythological themes; *La Belle au bois* (1932) and *Bolivar* (1936; rewritten to form the libretto of an opera by Milhaud, 1950), plays; *Boire à la source* (1933; augm. ed. 1952), reminiscences. He was elected 'Prince des Poètes' in 1960.

Supplément au Voyage de Bougainville, *v. Diderot*.

Sur Catherine de Médicis, *v. Comédie humaine, La* (*Études philosophiques*).

Suréna, a tragedy by Corneille, his last play; produced 1674.

Suréna, the Parthian general who has defeated Crassus, and Eurydice, daughter of the king of Armenia, are secretly in love. But the king of Parthia wants Eurydice to marry his son Pacorus, and, distrustful of Suréna's power, to secure his loyalty offers him his own daughter in marriage. Suréna declines, on the pretext that he is unworthy. But his secret love is discovered, he is assassinated, and Eurydice is left dying of grief.

Sûreté, La, *v. Police*.

Sur l'eau, by Maupassant, a macabre tale in *La *Maison Tellier* (1881); also the title of a volume of travel sketches (1888) which he wrote after a cruise in the Mediterranean.

Surprise de l'amour, La, a comedy by Marivaux; produced 1722. Lélio and the comtesse, who have each firmly renounced all dealings with the other sex, are thrown together by circumstances. The play traces with wit and delicacy their progress (assisted by the sprightly Colombine, the comtesse's attendant) from feigned indifference, through friendship, to love.

Surrealism, Surrealist, a literary and artistic movement (entirely unconnected with *Realism) which evolved in Paris in the early 1920s from the defunct *Dadaist movement and soon spread far beyond France. It was strongly influenced by Apollinaire and *Cubists of his circle (e.g. Reverdy, Albert-Birot), and by psychoanalytic theories. Opinions differ as to the individual importance of its earlier literary precursors, who are said to include Nerval, Baudelaire, Rimbaud, Lautréamont, and Jarry. Artists associated with the movement include Picasso, Chirico, Max Ernst, Salvador Dali, and Man Ray.

The leader and chief theorist of Surrealism was the poet Breton, who in 1922 drew round him a group of young writers including Aragon, Desnos, Éluard, Péret, and Soupault; both Breton and Aragon had studied medicine and were interested in psychiatry, and Breton had visited Freud in 1921. For its first exponents, who carried over from

Dadaism an iconoclastic spirit and the urge (soon more than satisfied) to scandalize, Surrealism was far more than a new literary movement: it was a revolutionary means of totally liberating the mind, of changing man and life. Breton, whose manifestos (1924, 1930, 1942) kept pace with his changing literary (and political) convictions, defined it thus in 1924: 'Automatisme psychique pur par lequel on se propose d'exprimer... le fonctionnement réel de la pensée. Dictée de la pensée, en l'absence de tout contrôle exercé par la raison, en dehors de toute préoccupation esthétique ou morale'; and he cited dreams and madness, where the repressive consciousness is no longer in control, as states in which the mind operates with true creative freedom. In order to set in motion this 'psychic automatism', this 'usage immodéré du stupéfiant image' (Aragon), the early Surrealists practised *écriture automatique* or automatic writing (i.e. they sat prepared with pen and paper and wrote down whatever came into their minds; there was no preconceived subject, and no mental censorship was supposed to operate); they recorded their dreams (Desnos, who had mediumistic gifts, would often relate his aloud in a state of hypnosis), gleaning the vivid, freakishly concerted images that crowd the unconscious; they had recourse to chance as a source of the unexpected, and to *humour noir*; and they experimented through collaboration with another member of the group (Surrealism is notable for works written in collaboration). The movement was at its most productive and influential in the '20s and early '30s, and Breton drew many others to his side (e.g. Leiris, Prévert, Char, Queneau). But his insistence on strict conformity to Surrealist principles led to crises and scandals involving the expulsion of some (e.g. Soupault, Artaud, the dramatist Roger Vitrac, 1899–1952) and the defection of others. The years 1929–31 saw a serious split in the movement. Many Surrealists were also Communists, and a group led by Breton, who was totally opposed to any form of committed writing, now moved towards Trotskyism. Aragon and other Stalinists went their own way, and there were further defections as a result of the Spanish Civil War (e.g. Éluard) and after the fall of France in 1940, when Breton and Péret retired to Mexico. Breton returned to preside over a dwindling band of disciples until his death in 1966, exercising some influence on such later writers as Césaire (and other exponents of *négritude*), Gracq, and Yves Bonnefoy (v. *Lyric Poetry*, 4).

Reviews and anthologies associated with the movement include *Littérature* (2nd ser., 1922–4), *La Révolution surréaliste* (1924–9), *Le Surréalisme au service de la Révolution* (1930–3), *Minotaure* (1933–9), the *Petite Anthologie poétique du surréalisme* (1934; ed. G. Hugnet), *Médium* (1952–5), *Le Surréalisme même* (1956–9), *La Brèche* (1961–5), *L'Archibras* (f. 1967). Though the works and theories of its early exponents scandalized many, Surrealism as an attitude of mind gradually won acceptance, and few young writers of the day entirely escaped its influence. It brought to poetry the 'esprit nouveau' called for by Apollinaire, and its persistent awareness of an irreality concomitant with reality has lent a new sharpness to creative perception. v. *Lyric Poetry*, 4.

Surville, Clotilde de, supposedly a French poetess of the time of Alain Chartier and Christine de Pisan. Poems attributed to her were published in 1803, caused a great stir at this time of revival of interest in the Middle Ages, but soon proved to be a hoax. They were said to have been transcribed, from manuscripts at one time in his possession, by her alleged descendant the marquis Joseph-Étienne de Surville, a Royalist officer with literary ambitions who had been executed under the *Directoire*. They were published by the vicomte de Vanderbourg, a friend of the marquis, who added a circumstantial account of the alleged authoress.

Surville, LAURE BALZAC, MME (1800–71), sister of Balzac, author of *Balzac, sa vie et ses œuvres d'après sa correspondance* (1858).

Suzanne et le Pacifique, v. Giraudoux.

Swann, Charles, in Proust's **A la recherche du temps perdu.* His early history and passion for *Odette (whom he eventually marries for the sake of their daughter, *Gilberte) are traced in *Du côté de chez Swann* (*Un Amour de Swann*, the first of the many detailed studies of love and its sufferings contained in the novel). At *Combray, as the friendly owner of a neighbouring property, he visits Marcel's grandparents and often talks stimulatingly to the boy about the arts. The grandparents accept him almost patronizingly as a simple country gentleman of their own class. They knew his father, an Alsatian Jewish financier; they do not know, but gossip about, his wife. In Paris, this same Swann is a wealthy, cultivated amateur of the arts, a member of the *Jockey Club, who hobnobs at Twickenham with the Prince of Wales (in the 1870s) and is welcomed—without his wife—in the exclusive society governed by the duchesse de *Guermantes. The Swann whose Paris home Marcel later frequents is yet another person, affable to anyone who can further his wife's position in society. When Marcel last meets him (at the princesse de Guermantes's evening party in *Sodome et Gomorrhe*, ii) he is a dying man; the *Dreyfus case has stirred his racial sympathies and in some quarters his welcome is less warm than of yore.

Swedenborg, EMMANUEL (1688–1772), the Swedish scientist, philosopher, and mystic. His theosophic teaching proceeded from the belief that there are two worlds, both emanating from God, who is infinite love and infinite wisdom. One, the New Jerusalem, is the spiritual world to which man will one day be restored by a process of purification through divine love. It stands in the relation of cause and effect to the second world, the world of nature that we know, and there is in it a symbolic counterpart for all that is familiar to us in our world. Many French writers and thinkers were directly or indirectly influenced by his teaching, e.g. Ballanche, Balzac (e.g. in *Le*

Livre mystique), the *Symbolists (in their doctrine of *correspondances*). He was also one of a number of visionaries whose influence can be traced in the various forms of romantic, semi-religious, semi-mystical socialism that were a feature of the French scene in the years before 1848. Cf. *Illuminisme*.

Sygognes or **Sigogne, CHARLES DE BEAUXONCLES, SEIGNEUR DE (1560–1611),** satirical poet, an imitator of the Italians (esp. Berni) in his coarse and violent burlesque satires. He had a chequered career in the army, at court, and as governor of Dieppe.

Sylvester II, v. *Gerbert d'Aurillac.*

Sylvie (1854, in *Les Filles du feu*), a tale by Nerval. The narrator hovers between a never very stable reality and a shifting world of reminiscences of his youth in the country near Paris (the region of Chantilly, Senlis, Rousseau's Ermenonville, etc., and the scene of the author's own childhood), where he had known a simple traditional life of dance and song. His passion for an actress fills the present, yet two loves of the past still hold him—Sylvie, who had finally married a dull, but unhesitant suitor, and Adrienne, who died. They had been, he realizes, 'les deux moitiés d'un seul amour', a substance of which his later love was only a half-shadow, adored for what she evoked.

Symbolism, Symbolist, an important movement in poetry, with a continuing influence, began *c.* 1880, when the poems of Mallarmé (*L'Après-midi d'un faune*, 1876) and Verlaine (*Romances sans paroles*, 1874) were becoming known, and at first gained ground in *décadent* circles (*c.* 1885; v. *Esprit décadent*). Three small literary societies, whose members (mostly young writers and artists) met in cafés to read their work and discuss new aims in literature (esp. poetry) and art, are often mentioned in accounts of its early days: the *Hydropathes* (who included Bourget, Laforgue, Kahn, Moréas, Maupassant,

Coppée), the *Zutistes* (led by Cros), and the *Hirsutes*.

The Symbolists were in revolt against the traditional conventions governing both theme and technique in poetry, and against the 'exteriorization' beloved of the *Parnassiens*. They sought to liberate the technique of versification in every way that would make for 'fluidity', a term much used at the time (*v. Vers libérés; Vers libre, Le*). Nothing was to be crystallized; the function of poetry was to evoke, not to describe; its matter was impressions, intuitions, sensations; and the poet's images should be symbols of his state of soul, inspired by latent affinities rather than resemblances. To Baudelaire, who is recognized as its true precursor, the movement owed its theories of poetic music and of the symbolic relations of scent, sound, and colour (the theme of his sonnet *Correspondances; v.* also Rimbaud's *Sonnet des voyelles*); and these combined with the prevailing cult of *Wagner (at its height *c.* 1885) to produce the Symbolist conception of the essential 'musicality' of poetry. This was, briefly, that the theme of a poem could be, as it were, orchestrated and intensified by the choice of words having colour, harmony, and evocative power of their own (*v. Ghil*). *v. Foreign Influences*, 5; *Lyric Poetry*, 4.

The many writers associated with the movement (some as precursors) include Mallarmé, Verlaine, Rimbaud, Laforgue, H. de Régnier, Moréas (who first, in *Le *Figaro* of 18 Sept. 1886, proposed to replace the term *décadent* by *symboliste* and *symbolisme*), Corbière, Villiers de l'Isle-Adam, Kahn, Vielé-Griffin, Merrill; the Belgians Maeterlinck, Rodenbach, and Verhaeren; and the critics R. de Gourmont and Schwob. Many Symbolist reviews were founded, e.g. *Le *Mercure de France* (the longest-lived), *La *Conque*, *Le *Décadent*, *La *Plume*, *La *Revue blanche*, *La *Revue indépendante*, *La *Revue wagnérienne*, *La *Wallonie*, *La *Vogue*, *La *Nouvelle Rive gauche*, *L'*Ermitage*, *Le *Centaure*. Other writings associated with the movement were *Verlaine's *Art poétique* and *Les *Poètes maudits*, Huysmans's *A rebours*, and *Les *Déliquescences d'Adoré Floupette* by Beauclair and Vicaire. Dramatic works by Symbolists were produced at the *Théâtre d'Art* (*v. Œuvre, Théâtre de l'*). The extreme Symbolist movement, centred on Mallarmé, reached its height *c.* 1890, and the first signs of a reaction against it came in the early 1890s with the *École romane* and *Naturisme. v. Literary Isms.*

For musicians associated with Symbolism *v. Chabrier; Debussy; Fauré; Indy; Ravel*; for painters allied to it by sympathy or style *v. Gauguin; Moreau, G.; Redon; Puvis de Chavannes; Van Gogh*; and *cf. Impressionism*.

Symphonie des fromages, La, *v. Ventre de Paris, Le.*

Symphonie fantastique, La, *v. Berlioz.*

Symphonie pastorale, La, *v. Gide.*

Synthétisme, *v. Literary Isms.*

Système de la nature, Le (1770; abridged as *Le Bon Sens, ou Idées naturelles opposées aux idées surnaturelles*, 1772), by d'Holbach (with some assistance from Diderot), a philosophical treatise which, though somewhat declamatory and repetitious, was the culmination, in literary form, of the revolt against existing political and religious institutions. It was condemned by the *parlement*. D'Holbach passes from a self-consistent, at times eloquent, defence of the materialist and determinist standpoint to a vigorous attack on political institutions and on religion, tracing its origin to man's ignorance of the causes of physical phenomena, to his tendency to give an anthropomorphic form to the causes he imagines, and to the advantage taken of his credulity by priests. In general, he deprecates any attempt to go outside nature, of which man is a part, in search of unattainable knowledge.

T

Tabaret, Le Père, *v. Gaboriau.*

Tabarin, *nickname of* ANTOINE GIRARD (d. 1626), a clown who advertised the drugs sold by his brother Philippe, a charlatan known as 'Mondor', on the *Pont-Neuf in the early 17th c. Sometimes the pair performed short dialogues, with Tabarin in the role of servant. These and other *facetiae* were collected (from 1622) and proved highly popular.

Tableau historique des progrès de l'esprit humain, Esquisse d'un (1795), a treatise by Condorcet, written 1793–4 while he was proscribed as a *Girondin.

This sketch for a more detailed work of political philosophy broadly traces the history of mankind from the dawn of the earliest societies down to the conception of the rights of man worked out in the American and French Revolutions of the 18th c. Much attention is paid to the development of the sciences; and Condorcet claims that man is liberated from tyranny and superstition under the banner of 'Reason, Toleration, Humanity'. In conclusion, he expresses the hope that the future will see the growth of equality, both between nations (the freeing of subject peoples, the abolition of the slave trade, etc.) and among subjects of the same nation (equality of the sexes, of wealth, of education, etc.), and the moral, intellectual, and physical improvement of mankind, which he believed capable of indefinite progress through better laws and institutions.

Table ronde, La (1944–69), a literary review f. by a group of writers including Camus, Malraux, and Paulhan. Despite changes in its character and content, it retained a lively interest in young writers. It was briefly revived in 1970 as *La Nouvelle Table ronde.*

Tabouret, Droit du, under the monarchy, the privilege—accorded to ladies of princely or ducal rank—of remaining seated in the presence of the king and queen. Attempts were often made to obtain an extension of this privilege.

Tabourot des Accords, ÉTIENNE (1549–90), 'le Rabelais de la Bourgogne', a lawyer of Dijon, author of *Les Bigarrures* (1582), *Les Touches* (1585), *Les Escraignes dijonnaises* (1614), etc., medleys of amusing anecdotes, tales, epigrams, riddles, and acrostics; and *v. Dictionaries,* 1572, 1587.

Taches d'encre, v. Barrès.

Taglioni, MARIA (1804–84), of Swedish birth, a famous ballerina at the *Opéra* (1827–47).

Tahureau, JACQUES (1527–55), a poet of the school of Ronsard, wrote love lyrics on the Petrarchan model (e.g. the collection *Mignardises amoureuses de l'Admirée*) and satirical dialogues (1562).

Tailhade, LAURENT (1854–1919), poet and man of letters. His works include the sentimental and semi-religious verse of *Le Jardin des rêves* (1880) and *Vitraux* (1891), collected with additions as *Poèmes élégiaques* (1907); and the invective verse of *Au pays du mufle* (1891) and *A travers les groins* (1897), collected as *Poèmes aristophanesques* (1904).

Taille, *v. Fiscal System.*

Taillefer, *v. Chanson de Roland.*

Taine, HIPPOLYTE (1828–93), philosopher, critic, and historian, did brilliantly at the *École normale supérieure*, but failed (1851) his *agrégation* in philosophy, his views being too daring for the examiners of a reactionary era. He taught for a time in provincial schools, then supported himself by private tuition and literary journalism. He also contrived to read voraciously (physiology, psychology, and mathematics) for his own ends, to take his doctor's degree in literature, and to visit the Pyrenees, Italy, and England. In 1864 he succeeded Viollet-le-Duc as professor of aesthetics and the history of art at the *École des *Beaux-Arts*, a post he held, with a break in 1876-7, till 1883. By the time he was 30, with his reputation already firmly established, his publications included *Essai sur les Fables de La Fontaine* (1853; rev. ed. 1860, entitled *La Fontaine et ses Fables*), his doctor's thesis, in effect a study of 17th-c. society and the court of Louis XIV; *Voyage aux eaux des Pyrénées* (1855; later called *Voyage aux Pyrénées*), notes of a trip from Bordeaux through the Landes to Biarritz, thence to Luchon and back to Toulouse ('Je me suis promené beaucoup; j'ai causé un peu; je raconte les plaisirs de mes oreilles et de mes yeux'); *Essai sur Tite-Live* (1856); *Les Philosophes français du XIXe siècle* (1857) and *Essais de critique et d'histoire* (1858), collected articles. The first three were remodelled in later editions, but even in their early form they contain in germ the theory of 'la race, le milieu et le moment' (v. below) with which his name is lastingly associated. The fourth, which became *Les Philosophes classiques du XIXe siècle en France* (rev. ed. 1868), includes studies of Maine de Biran, Jouffroy, and Cousin. The *Essais de critique et d'histoire* were more than once re-edited and augmented, well-known studies of Balzac and Stendhal being among the additions.

Taine and Renan did more than any other writers of the day to mould the thought of the generation reaching maturity *c.* 1870. Taine's importance lay in his theories of the interdependence of the physical and psychological factors which influence human development, and in his application of the principles of scientific investigation to the study of literature, history, and art. His theories, which owed much to Positivism, are expounded in *De l'intelligence* (1870, 2 vols.), a famous work containing the sum of his philosophical thinking. Nature, he asserts—meaning the inherent impulse that determines man's evolution—consists of a succession of events in the parallel development of the psychological (or moral) and the physical elements in man. The psychological element he relates to man's innermost sensations which, with the images they provoke, constitute ideas; the physical element corresponds to the external manifestations of these sensations. It should thus be possible to explain and predict human personality in terms of significant facts, their interrelation, and what effects the combinations can be expected to produce. In the famous Introduction to his *Histoire de la littérature anglaise* (1863, 3 vols.) he had already stressed the importance, for historians and critics, of studying the physical and psychological factors responsible for cultural and social development. For instance, given a certain literature (or a certain historical figure), what were the causes that determined its evolution, what was its dominant characteristic (*faculté maîtresse*), and what forces had been at work to condition it, e.g. forces arising from racial inheritance (*la race*), from physical, social, and political environment (*le milieu*), and from a combination of the momentum—or driving force of development—of the age and the moment of time in which it emerged (*le moment*)? The problem, he said, was simply one of psychological mechanics, to be solved by the same methods of collection and analysis of significant facts as would be used to solve a problem of physical mechanics, except that the conditioning forces could not be exactly measured or reduced to formulae. *v. Foreign Influences*, 4.

Such were some of the views that made Taine the theorist of *Naturalism and gave point to Zola's use of his axiom 'le vice et la vertu sont des produits comme le vitriol et le sucre' (*Litt. anglaise*) as the epigraph for a second edition of *Thérèse Raquin*. They were also largely behind the conscious development of the novel of psychological analysis (from *c.* 1890; *v. Novel*, 3). But they by no means represent the whole extent of his thought. There are, for instance, passages in *De l'intelligence* (vol. I), on the way in which an unforeseen sensation can awaken an image long obliterated, which herald the exploration of the unconscious to be found in some of the great works of modern fiction. (Novels which allude to his contemporary influence include Barrès's Les *Déracinés and Bourget's Le *Disciple.)

He always wrote with unwavering conviction, pursuing his thought with the controlled logic of a man with a passion for abstract reasoning and emphasizing it with metaphors at once forcible and poetic. At times he drove his theories hard, to the detriment of his famous historical work Les *Origines de la France contemporaine (1875–94); or in Notes sur l'Angleterre (1872; on his visit in 1861–2), where he concludes that Englishwomen owe their long teeth to a heavy meat diet and their large feet to a habit of tramping for miles over rain-sodden soil. His other works include Nouveaux and Derniers Essais de critique et d'histoire (1865 and 1894); La Philosophie de l'art (1885), lectures delivered at the École des Beaux-Arts and other essays; *Notes sur Paris. Vie et opinions de M. Frédéric-Thomas Graindorge (1868); Carnets de voyage: Notes sur la province (1863–5) and Voyage en Italie (1866), travel sketches; *Étienne Mayran (1910), an unfinished novel.

Taizé, Communauté de, a community of Protestant brothers, strongly ecumenical in spirit, f. 1945 at Taizé (Saône-et-Loire).

Tallemant des Réaux, GÉDÉON (1619–92), author of Historiettes (completed c. 1659, except for notes added later; but not publ. till 1834), a collection of 376 anecdotal memoirs arranged under the names of notable persons of his time (there are also a few under general headings). He is obviously a scandalmonger, but many of his statements are confirmed by independent evidence and he provides an amusing and valuable picture of society from the time of Henri IV to the mid-17th c., also biographical details of such literary figures as Guez de Balzac, Corneille, Godeau, La Fontaine, Malherbe, Mme de Rambouillet, Mlle de Scudéry, Mlle de Gournay. v. Guirlande de Julie.

Talleyrand-Périgord, CHARLES-MAURICE DE (1754–1838), a famous diplomat, remembered for his political genius, his wit, his urbanity, and his venality. He was lame from infancy and had little choice but to enter the Church. His great financial and administrative ability soon won him preferment, despite his licentious tastes. As bishop of Autun (from 1788) he represented the clergy of his diocese at the *États généraux of 1789, joined the *Tiers État, supported the *Constitution civile du clergé, and left the Church for a secular career. Between 1792 and 1794 he was engaged in dubious diplomatic activities in London, popular neither there nor in France. He then went to America, amassed money, was back in France by 1796, again won power, but lost it by corrupt practices. He was involved in the coup d'état du 18 brumaire (v. Revolutions, 1 (1799)) and became Napoleon's trusted adviser. He negotiated the treaties of *Lunéville and *Amiens, and was created prince of Benevento (1806). He fell from power over foreign policy, received overtures from the Restoration party, and was prominent in the negotiations before and after Napoleon's fall. He represented France at the Congress of Vienna (1814–15). Towards 1830, aware of the growing unpopularity of the government of Charles X, he entered into relations with the *Orléanistes. After the 1830 *Revolution, as French ambassador in London, he did much to shape the future course of events in Europe. He retired in 1834. Renan's *Souvenirs d'enfance et de jeunesse contains a well-known description of his death-bed reconciliation with the Church. He is also the subject of five long articles in Sainte-Beuve's *Nouveaux Lundis.

Tallien, THÉRÈSE CABARRUS, MME (1773–1835), daughter of a Spanish financier, a woman of seductive charm, was married to the marquis de Fontenay (who divorced her), then to the journalist Jean-Lambert Tallien (1767–1820), one of the leaders in the overthrow of Robespierre (inspired, it was said, by his wife, who became known as 'Notre-Dame de Thermidor'). Under the *Directoire*, when she was the mistress of Barras, she was a leader of fashion and introduced the daring Greek mode. In 1805, having divorced Tallien, she married the comte de Caraman, later prince de Chimay.

Talma, FRANÇOIS-JOSEPH (1763–1826), a famous tragic actor, went on the stage in 1787 and joined the *Comédie-Française*. His first great part was in M.-J. Chénier's *Charles IX*. In the first quarter of the 19th c. he created the principal roles in all the famous tragedies of the day, introducing lasting reforms in acting technique (less artificiality, less declamation) and production (period costume and scenery). He was one of Napoleon's intimate circle and performed at Erfurt under his auspices before a 'parterre de rois'. He left *Mémoires* (1826).

Talon, OMER (1595–1652), a magistrate prominent in the *parlement* during the *Fronde*. His memoirs (mainly his speeches and other documents) are of historical interest.

Tamango (1829, in the *Revue de Paris*; 1833, in *Mosaïque*), a tale by Mérimée. The negroes on a French slave ship rebel, massacre the white crew, then find themselves helpless in mid-ocean, unable to sail the boat. An English frigate later finds an apparently abandoned hulk, but on it, barely alive, is Tamango, an African chief who had been captured by a trick and had led the revolt. He is taken to Jamaica, where he ends his days as a regimental cymbalist. He seldom speaks, drinks heavily, and dies of a chest complaint.

Tancrède, a tragedy by Voltaire; produced 1760.

The scene is Syracuse in 1005, when the city had recovered its liberty, but was threatened by the Moors who held the rest of Sicily. Strife among the nobles of Syracuse is to be settled by the marriage of Orbassan, one leader, with Aménaïde, daughter of another. But she is secretly pledged to Tancrède, a Norman knight born at Syracuse, but exiled and despoiled

of his property. To escape the projected marriage, she sends a message to Tancrède, whom she knows to be again in Sicily. This is intercepted in circumstances which suggest that it was meant for the leader of the Moors, and she is condemned to death. Tancrède, coming unrecognized to Syracuse, learns of her impending fate and, though broken-hearted at her apparent infidelity, comes forward as her champion and defeats Orbassan, her accuser. He then valiantly repels a Moorish attack, but is mortally wounded. As he dies he learns that Aménaïde has always been true to him.

Tarde, ALFRED DE, *v. Massis*.

Tarde, GABRIEL (1843–1904), philosopher and sociologist, professor of philosophy at the *Collège de France*. His works, many of which were studies in criminology, include *Les Lois de l'imitation* (1890), *La Logique sociale* (1895), *L'Opposition universelle* (1897), *La Criminalité comparée* (1898), and *Études de psychologie sociale* (1898).

Tartarin de Tarascon, the hero of three tales by A. Daudet, is a genial caricature of the Frenchman of the Midi, proverbially mercurial and exuberant, and so carried away by his own boasts and tall stories that he often believes them. Tarascon, on the Rhône between Arles and Avignon, is a typical very small, hot, Provençal town; a bridge joins it to Beaucaire, across the river.

In *Tartarin de Tarascon* (1872) this local hero finds that his prestige as a crack big-game hunter is crumbling. Action alone can save him, so after elaborate preparations he sets off to shoot lions in N. Africa. He is ferociously armed and costumed—and decidedly uneasy, for he has never been further from home than Beaucaire. But the desert, invaded by modern civilization, has become such a built-up area that all self-respecting lions have long since left. He does shoot an aged, lethargic lion, and has to pay heavy compensation to the two travelling showmen who own it; and he does acquire—in the sense that he cannot get rid of it—a broken-down camel. He himself proves easy game for a bogus Montenegrin prince, who fleeces him. With the camel, and as near crestfallen as he can ever be, he returns destitute to Tarascon. To his amazement, he meets with an ovation from the townspeople, a hero whom absence has rendered even more heroic. His spirits soar, and as he leaves the station he can be heard starting the first of many sagas: 'Figurez-vous, qu'un certain soir, en plein Sahara...'

In *Tartarin sur les Alpes* (1885) he sets off to plant the banner of the Tarascon mountaineering club (which climbs the local hillocks on its Sunday walks) on top of the Jungfrau, and again survives astonishing adventures.

In *Port-Tarascon* (1890) he heads an expedition of the townspeople to found a colony on a South Sea island. But the island proves to be a British possession, and Governor Tartarin, with his now rebellious colonists (but without his island wife), is repatriated in a British warship. Once home, the great man is disowned by Tarascon, so he crosses the river to end his days in Beaucaire.

Tartuffe, Le, a 5-act verse comedy by Molière. When a version in three acts was performed at *Versailles in 1664 there was an outcry from the devout (*v. Compagnie du Saint-Sacrement*) and the king prohibited its public performance. It was produced again as *L'Imposteur* (with some changes, Tartuffe now figuring as Panulphe) in 1667, but again suppressed by the *parlement* (and *v. Péréfixe*). The interdict was lifted in 1669 and thereafter *Le Tartuffe* was performed freely with great success (despite attacks on it by Bourdaloue and Bossuet).

Tartuffe is an odious hypocrite who, feigning extreme piety, insinuates himself into the household of the credulous Orgon. Despite the opposition of his son and of his sensible brother-in-law Cléante, Orgon proposes to marry his daughter against her will to the impostor, and even makes over all his property to him. His eyes are opened only when, by a device of his wife Elmire, he witnesses an attempt by Tartuffe to seduce her. But Tartuffe, now owner of the house, orders the family out of it and contrives the arrest of Orgon. The king, however, intervenes to defeat fraud, and Tartuffe is hauled off to prison. Dorine, the family servant, proverbial for her outspoken, clear-sighted advocacy of her employers' interests, is one of Molière's best characters of this type.

Tassart, FRANÇOIS, Maupassant's valet, described his master's last years of failing health and reason in *Maupassant (1883-93)* (1911).

Tastu, AMABLE VOÏART, MME (1798-1885), wrote sentimental and elevating verse (*Poésies*, 1826; *Poésies nouvelles*, 1834), children's stories and educational books (e.g. *Le Livre des enfants*, 1836-7; *Voyage en France*, 1845), and translated (1835) *Robinson Crusoe*.

Taureau blanc, Le, v. Voltaire, 1.

Tavan, ALPHONSE, *v. Félibrige*.

Tavannes, GASPARD DE SAULX DE (1509-73), *maréchal de France*, took a leading part in bringing about the Massacre of St. *Bartholomew. His life was written by his son JEAN (1555-1629), an ardent *Ligueur who had an adventurous career. Another son, GUILLAUME (1553-1633), wrote his own memoirs.

Tavernier, JEAN-BAPTISTE (1605-89), author of *Les Six Voyages de Jean-Baptiste Tavernier* (1676), recording his travels in Turkey, Persia, and the Indies. His work, and that of Jean Chardin, aroused an interest in the East soon to be reflected in Montesquieu's *Lettres persanes*.

Taylor, ISIDORE-JUSTIN-SÉVERIN, BARON (1789-1879), patron of literature and the arts, archaeologist, and philanthropist. He was director of the *Comédie-Française at the time of the *Romantic movement and used his position to give the Romantic dramatists their chance (he produced *Hernani). He wrote plays and, more memorably, the many volumes, illustrated by contemporary artists, of *Voyages pittoresques et romantiques de l'ancienne France* (1820–63).

Teilhard de Chardin, PIERRE (1881–1955), a priest who won an international reputation as a palaeontologist and posthumous fame as a religious thinker. Born of an old family of Auvergne and educated by the Jesuits, he entered the Order (1899), taught physics in Cairo (1905–8), completed his theological studies in England (at Hastings), and was ordained (1911). After two years at the *Muséum national d'Histoire naturelle* and service as a stretcher-bearer in the 1914–18 war, he joined the staff of the *Institut catholique de Paris* (1920), becoming professor of geology (1922). He was already writing on religion and now advanced views that gravely disquieted the Church. On the orders of his superiors, he left France (1926) for China and thereafter lived mainly in the Far East, prominently involved in many of the great scientific expeditions of the inter-war years. He was then little known as a religious thinker, for the Church refused to sanction publication of his works (though many were circulated privately by his friends) and effectively silenced him (in 1948 he was required to refuse a chair at the *Collège de France*). Electing to remain, as he put it, 'enfant d'obéissance', he withdrew in 1951 to New York, where he died. Full publication of his many works, letters, and *Cahiers* began in 1955 and is still in progress. His chief works—*La Messe sur le monde* (1923), *Le Milieu divin* (1926–7), *Le Phénomène humain* (1938–40), *Le Cœur de la matière* (1950), *Le Christique* (1955)—are the bold attempt of a Christian mystic to integrate into Christianity the discoveries of modern science, especially on the subject of evolution. One of his most striking concepts is that of 'le Christ-Évoluteur' (Christ in the cosmic function of the motive force of evolution). Attention has been drawn to his optimism, his Christocentric humanism, and his poetical style, also to the influence on him of the Modernists M. *Blondel (their correspondence appeared in 1965) and É. Le Roy (his close friend).

Télémaque (1699), by Fénelon, a didactic romance written for the edification of his pupil, the duc de Bourgogne; a precursor of the political and philosophical tales of Marmontel, Voltaire, and others. It reflected, intentionally or not, on the government of Louis XIV, gave offence at court, and contributed to Fénelon's disgrace. *v. Children's Reading.*

Télémaque (Telemachus, son of Ulysses) sets out from Ithaca in search of his father, long due home from Troy. With him goes the goddess Minerva, in the guise of the wise old man Mentor. He meets with adventures that bear no relation to the *Odyssey*—they are more like those of a knight-errant, in a Greek setting charmingly described. With this story are combined precepts of physical and intellectual education, discussion of political utopias, and moral dissertations. He is shipwrecked on the island of Calypso, relates to her his adventures in various Mediterranean lands, and is rescued from her allurements, and those of her nymph Eucharis, by Mentor, who goes to the length of throwing him into the sea. A Phoenician ship carries them to Salente (a city in Calabria, just founded by Idomeneus), around which, with various episodes (inc. a visit to the Elysian Fields), the rest of the story revolves. Mentor, entrusted with the organization of the State, proceeds to create an ideal—if over-regulated—republic. This part of the work amounts to a treatise on government, especially as regards the high standard of political conduct required of a good king: the welfare and happiness of his subjects should be his first concern; Fénelon even asserts that the law is above the king—a bold statement from a subject of Louis XIV. He repeatedly deplores the folly and cruelty of war, and has notable passages on the need for good faith in international relations and on the wise treatment of a conquered nation. He shows himself ahead of his time in his economic views and in his assertion that, however strong the suspicion, a man must be held innocent until proved guilty. The work is written in a harmonious, rather languid style and has been described as the first prose poem in French, but it is marred by the incongruous mixture of pagan fiction and the Christian didactic spirit.

Tel Quel, v. *Critics and Criticism*, 3; *Lyric Poetry*, 4.

Tel qu'en lui-même, v. *Salavin*.

Temple, Le, a fortified lodge, dating from the late 12th c., of the Knights Templar in Paris. Following the suppression of the Order (1312), it came into the hands of the Knights of St. John; parts of it were demolished, but the famous 13th-c. Tour (or Donjon) du Temple survived. Other buildings were added, such as the fine residence (17th c.) of the *grand-prieur de l'Ordre de Malte*. When Philippe de Vendôme (1655–1727) was *grand-prieur* this was the centre of the free-thinking, epicurean society of the day (inc. such writers as Chaulieu, La Fare, Campistron, Palaprat, and the young Voltaire; *v. Libertins*). A later *grand-prieur*, Louis-François, prince de Conti (1717–76), a distinguished soldier and a patron of J.-J. Rousseau, Beaumarchais, and Florian, also had a *salon* (the young Mozart played there before a brilliant company). The Temple became national property in 1790, and when the monarchy fell (1792) Louis XVI and his family were confined in the tower. The buildings disappeared early in the 19th c. and the site was used for municipal gardens (1857), the Square du Temple.

Temple de Gnide, Le, v. *Montesquieu*.

Temple du Goût, Le (1733), by Voltaire, a short work of literary criticism in the form of a prose and verse allegory describing a visit to the temple of the god of Taste. With gay wit and acute judgement, he distributes praise and blame (mostly blame) among the writers of his own day and the preceding century, criticizing even Corneille, Racine, Molière, La Fontaine, Bossuet, and Fénelon.

Temps, Le, (1) a daily paper (1829–42) devoted to progress in politics, literature, science, and industry, was actively involved in the fight for liberty of the Press (*v. Press*, 5); Guizot was one of its first editors; (2) a famous daily paper (1861–1942), the nearest French equivalent to the English *Times*, f. and edited till 1871 by Auguste Nefftzer, then by members of the Hébrard family. It aimed to follow an enlightened, progressive path in politics, without party affiliations. It maintained a consistently high standard of literary, dramatic, and music criticism, and of general writing; *v. France, A.*; *Sarcey*; *Schérer*; *Souday*; *Weiss*. It was suppressed in 1944 (*v. Press*, 9) and has been largely replaced by *Le *Monde*.

Temps modernes, Les (1945– ; monthly), a left-wing literary and political review, f. by Sartre—from the outset its director and moving spirit—and a group including Aron, S. de Beauvoir, Leiris, and Merleau-Ponty; the organ of Sartrean *Existentialism and a vehicle for exponents of *littérature engagée*.

Temps retrouvé, Le, v. *A la recherche du temps perdu*.

Tencin, CLAUDINE-ALEXANDRINE GUÉRIN, MARQUISE DE (1682–1749), an intelligent, cultured woman of unpleasant character ('cupide, rapace, intrigante'—Sainte-Beuve); mother of d'Alembert, whom she cruelly abandoned as an infant. After a discreditable youth, she later presided with distinction over a *salon* much frequented by intellectuals of the day (e.g. Montesquieu, Fontenelle, Marivaux; also Prior and Bolingbroke). She wrote three romances: *Les Mémoires du comte de Comminges* (1735; *cf. Arnaud, Baculard d'*), a work of some merit (after many ordeals, two lovers find one another in a Trappist convent, recognizing each other by the public confession of their sins); *Le Siège de Calais* (1739), a mediocre historical novel; *Les Malheurs de l'amour*

(1747), a tragic love story distantly resembling La *Princesse de Clèves*.

Tendre, Carte de, v. *Carte de Tendre.*

Tenson, v. *Jeu parti.*

Tentation de Saint Antoine, La (1874), by Flaubert. The saint, in the desert, recalls former temptations and is beset by new ones—the lusts of the flesh and the senses, the onslaught of philosophic doubt. The work, a form of dramatic poem in prose, is remarkable for its beauty of style and language, and its imaginative power; Mallarmé called it 'un idéal mêlant époques et races dans une prodigieuse fête, comme l'éclair de l'Orient expiré'. The idea for it took definite shape at Geneva in 1845, when Flaubert saw Breughel's picture of the Temptation of St. Antony. In 1849 he read a first version to his friends Bouilhet and Du Camp, who advised him to burn it. He did put it aside, but resumed work on it some years later (when fragments appeared in the review *L'Artiste*) and finished it in 1872. An early version was entitled *Smarh.*

Ternaire, in French prosody, a form of three-line stanza, on one rhyme. Brizeux claimed to have been the first to use it.

Terre, La (1887), one of Zola's *Rougon-Macquart* novels; an example of extreme *Naturalism, depicting the seamiest side of farming and peasant life. v. *Manifeste des cinq.*

Terre Sainte, Livre de la, a 13th-c. translation of the *Historia rerum transmarinarum* of William, archbishop of Tyre, relating the proceedings of the Christians in the Holy Land down to 1184, to which were added the *Chronique d'Ernoul* (v. *Crusades*) and various continuations to 1275. The work is also known as the *Livre du conquest, Estoire d'outre-mer,* and *Livre d'Eracles* (after the emperor Heraclius, who is mentioned in the first sentence).

Terreur, La, the reign of terror which began with the passage of the *loi des suspects* (17 Sept. 1793) and ended with the fall of Robespierre (27 July 1794); v. *Revolutions,* 1. Suspects were tried, and almost invariably condemned, by the *Tribunal révolutionnaire.* After the passage of the *loi du 22 prairial* (10 June 1794), they were executed *en bloc* without trial, and there were 1,376 executions in Paris alone in 49 days. During the whole period there were nearly 20,000 executions in France.

Terreur blanche, La, a term applied both to the severe anti-Revolutionary measures taken in the provinces during the *réaction thermidorienne* (v. *Revolutions,* 1 (1794–5)) and to the bloody Royalist reprisals in the South after the Restoration of 1815.

Terza rima, the strophic form used by Dante in the *Divina Commedia* (a b a b c b c d c, etc.), adopted in French by Lemaire de Belges, Tyard, Jodelle, Desportes, etc., and later revived by Gautier, Banville, Leconte de Lisle, Richepin, etc. The verse-line used is in the 16th c. usually the decasyllable (corresponding to Dante's hendecasyllable), in the 19th c. the *alexandrine.

Testament, Grand and *Petit,* v. *Villon.*

Teste, Monsieur, the monster of the intellect who 'ne connaît que deux valeurs... le possible et l'impossible', a character created by Valéry in *La Soirée avec Monsieur Teste* (first publ. 1896, in *Le *Centaure*). Thirty years later Valéry added *Lettre d'un ami,* addressed to M. Teste; *Lettre de Madame Émilie Teste,* describing what it is like to be the wife of a 'mystique sans Dieu'; and *Extraits du Log-Book de Monsieur Teste.*

Tête d'or, v. *Claudel.*

Thaïs (1890), by A. France, a novel of 4th-c. Egypt, based on the tale, in the *Golden Legend,* of the courtesan who became a saint.

Thaon or **Thaün,** PHILIPPE DE, v. *Philippe de Thaon.*

Tharaud, Les frères, the brothers JÉRÔME (1874–1953) and JEAN (1877–1952), who wrote in close collaboration. Their novels and tales, marked by a sober, forcible style, usually had a background of topical interest, e.g. British imperialism in the Transvaal (*Dingley, l'illustre écrivain*, 1902; noticeably influenced by Kipling), French colonization in N. Africa (*La Fête arabe*, 1911; *Rabat, ou les Heures marocaines*, 1918), the Jewish problem (*Quand Israël est roi*, 1920; *Un Royaume de Dieu*, 1920). Jérôme, a fellow-student of Péguy, taught French at the University of Budapest; Jean was secretary to Barrès.

Théâtre de Clara Gazul, Le (1825), Mérimée's first published work and a successful literary hoax, purported to be translations of six short plays by a Spanish actress, 'Clara Gazul'. Her portrait (in fact, the young Mérimée wearing a mantilla) formed the frontispiece. The plays owe much to Calderón. *Le Carrosse du Saint-Sacrement* (in a 2nd augm. ed. of 1830), a one-act comedy on a theme similar to that of Maupassant's *La *Maison Tellier* and equally ironical, has won a place in the permanent repertory of the **Comédie-Française.*

Théâtre de la Foire, *v. Theatres and Theatre Companies.*

Théâtre de la Rose-Croix, *v. Péladan.*

Théâtre et son double, Le, v. Artaud.

Théâtre-Français, *v. Comédie-Française.*

Théâtre Libre, a subscription theatre f. 1887 by Antoine. He staged works by young or unknown French and foreign dramatists (e.g. Becque, Brieux, Courteline, Curel, Porto-Riche, Bjørnson, Ibsen, Strindberg), specializing in *comédie rosse*—the new *Naturalist plays of the 'slice-of-life' type, depicting unrewarded virtue, unpunished vice, etc. His settings—scrupulously copied from real life—heightened the naturalistic effect; and acting became much less artificial.

The theatre failed financially and closed in 1896; but Antoine had by then revolutionized French acting and scenic design, and his experiments are a landmark in the evolution of the modern theatre. *v. Theatres and Theatre Companies.*

Théâtre national populaire (T.N.P.), a State-subsidized theatre in Paris (f. 1920 and housed from 1937 in the Palais de Chaillot), had its origins in the efforts of the actor and producer Firmin Gémier (1865–1933), its first director (1920–33), to bring good theatre to the masses at low prices. It became famous under the direction (1951–63) of Jean Vilar (1912–71), on whose initiative the company began to play at halls in the Paris suburbs (attracting large audiences by offering, at a low inclusive price, two plays, a concert, a dance, and meals), to appear at the *Festival d'Avignon*, and to tour widely. *v. Theatres and Theatre Companies.*

Theatre of Cruelty, *v. Artaud.*

Theatre of the Absurd, *v. Theatre of the 19th and 20th cs.*

Theatre of the 19th and 20th cs., The. After *c.* 1830 it becomes impracticable to consider the development of the theatre by *genres*. (For the earlier period *v.* the cross-references under *Drama*.)

The two main influences on the theatre in the first half of the 19th c. were Scribe, with his insistence on sound craftsmanship, on the need to entertain an audience and to hold its attention by a skilfully complicated plot, artifice, and action; and the *Romantics, who flouted the *Classical conventions and the unities, held that tragedy and comedy, the sublime and the grotesque, should be mixed on the stage as they are in real life, and attached great importance to accuracy of historical setting. Scribe's influence was on technique and bore fruit in the 'well-made' play; the Romantic influence was on the aesthetics of the drama. Though the stage success of Romantic drama ended in 1843 with the failure of *Les *Burgraves*, the triumph of Romantic theories dealt a death-blow to regular Classical *tragedy. Moreover, it can be seen in retrospect to have led to the emergence of the modern, intimate play or drama of contemporary life (very like Diderot's *drame bourgeois*), which shows a small group of characters, individuals rather than types, reacting to a given situation or problem. As developed in the second half of the 19th c., this was nearer comedy than tragedy, but comedy in a serious, often moralizing, vein. It depicted and satirized contemporary society with the faithful attention to detail prescribed by the Romantics (*cf*. also *Realism, in the novel) and switched freely from broad comedy to tragedy or near-tragedy. In its later phases it was often solely concerned to study the effect of passion on character, where the less sophisticated Romantic drama had been content to glorify passion (e.g. Dumas *père*'s *Antony*).

Early examples of the move towards the drama in this more restricted sense were the plays of Ponsard (*L'Honneur et l'argent*; *La Bourse*) and Augier (*Les Lionnes pauvres*; *Maître Guérin*). They owed their solid construction to Scribe's example. In tenor they were far from Romantic, for their authors represented the *école du bon sens* (a reaction against the exaggerations of Romantic drama) and extolled the domestic virtues. They often attacked contemporary failings, e.g. the worship of money. With Dumas *fils*, the leading dramatist of the Second Empire, the new drama came into its own. His plays (e.g. *Le Demi-Monde*; *Les Idées de Mme Aubray*) turned on the problems of those condemned by birth or character to an insecure footing in society. They were *pièces à thèse*, pleading for social reform, but he never lost sight of the importance of plot and dialogue. A feature of his construction imitated by later authors was the introduction of a character, usually a family friend or adviser, who at the outset of the play expounds the situation to be treated. At the end of the century Brieux and Hervieu were still writing *pièces à thèse* of a similar type.

Contemporaries of Dumas *fils* included

Pailleron, Gondinet, Feuillet, and Barrière, with plays ranging from light comedy of manners to drama; also Sardou, who followed Scribe in making plot all-important in his comedies, historical dramas, and *vaudevilles*. Burlesque or farcical comedy, in which characters are whirled riotously through a series of ridiculous situations, also flourished, e.g. Labiche's *Un Chapeau de paille d'Italie* and the gay, frothy comedies of Parisian life by Meilhac and L. Halévy—who also wrote libretti for Offenbach. Musset's comedies and *proverbes* (mostly written in the 1830s, but not staged till 1847–51 or later—in some cases much later) were a *genre* in themselves. As with Marivaux, love was their essential element, but their superficial gaiety concealed a passion and pathos unattempted by the earlier dramatist. Musset's drama *Lorenzaccio* (prod. 1896) is probably the nearest French approach to Shakespearian drama.

A new point was reached with the spread of *Naturalism from the novel to the stage (1880–90; *v. Théâtre Libre*). Plot and action were now subordinated to the faithful reproduction of an often uneventful 'slice of life'. About the same time—again reflecting trends in the novel—an increasing element of psychological analysis became apparent and, combined with the influence of Ibsen, gave rise to the *théâtre d'idées*, or problem play, best exemplified by the works of Curel. Here we are presented with a problem of conscience; sometimes, though not always, the characters themselves find a solution; the author imposes no theories of his own. The plays of Porto-Riche were less ideological, analysing passion and the feminine heart; and, from the early 20th c., passion of a violent or uneasy nature was the theme of plays by H. Bataille and Bernstein.

*Symbolism reached the theatre in the 1890s (*v. Œuvre, Théâtre de l'*), with the plays of Maeterlinck, Dujardin, Villiers de l'Isle-Adam, Saint-Pol-Roux, and Péladan, followed in 1912 by *L'*Annonce faite à Marie* of Claudel, whose stature as a dramatist was not fully appreciated until the 1940s. The success in 1897 of E. Rostand's *Cyrano de Bergerac*, and also of *Richepin's Le Chemineau, led to a passing revival of enthusiasm for verse drama. The period from *c.* 1890 to 1914 was also the golden age of light comedy and farce: Flers and Caillavet, Capus, Donnay, and Lavedan were broadly in the line of descent from Meilhac and Halévy; G. Feydeau and T. Bernard maintained the traditions of farce and *vaudeville*; Courteline was a master of satirical farce. *Jarry's Ubu Roi (1896) enjoyed a *succès de scandale* in *avant-garde* circles.

The period from 1913 (when Copeau founded the *Vieux-Colombier*) to 1940 saw a remarkable revival of the theatre which had its origins in the small experimental theatres of Paris (f. from the late 19th c.; *v. Theatres and Theatre Companies*), where such directors as Lugné-Poë, Copeau, Dullin, Jouvet, Baty, and G. Pitoëff made bold innovations in methods of production and acting, in scenic design, lighting effects, etc. Broadly speaking, these directors and the dramatists associated with them were in reaction against the commercialism of the pre-war theatre and the divorce between literature and the stage, against realism, narrative, and the conventions of the 'well-made' play. Many of the dramatists concerned had started as poets or novelists (after 1920 nearly all the leading French authors wrote for the stage; Proust, Malraux, and Breton were among the very few exceptions); and few, if any, escaped the general fertilizing and liberating influence of *Surrealism and Freudian theories of the unconscious. They included the highly versatile Cocteau; Sarment and Anouilh, seen at the time as 'new Romantics'; Romains; Obey; Achard; Lenormand, J.-J. Bernard, D. Amiel, and Vildrac, who were much influenced by Freudian theories; Salacrou, Passeur, and Zimmer, whose work is marked by satire and cynicism; Artaud, notable for his concept of a Theatre of Cruelty and as founder, with Roger Vitrac, of the short-lived *Théâtre Alfred-Jarry*; and, above all, Giraudoux, who turned to the stage in 1928 with

Siegfried and dominated the 1930s. They shared a concern for literary style, and often also a taste for classical or Biblical themes (e.g. Giraudoux, Cocteau, Obey, and, after 1940, Anouilh); they used the *tableau* form (Lenormand), flash-backs (Salacrou), the technique of silence (J.-J. Bernard), accelerated time, etc. In effect, they created an essentially 'literary' play in which both character and structure were more fluid and flexible than ever before.

Alongside these developments, there flowed the main stream of productions in the Boulevard theatres and the national theatres, where successful dramatists (inc. many of the older generation) broadly maintained the conventions and traditions of the pre-war theatre; *v. Bataille*; *Bernard, T.*; *Bernstein*; *Bourdet*; *Coolus*; *Croisset*; *Donnay*; *Guitry, S.*; *Pagnol*; *Raynal, P.*; *Savoir*; *Sée, E.*; *Wolff, Pierre*. But after 1930 the innovations of the experimental theatres—and also many of their directors and dramatists—progressively invaded both the Boulevard and the national theatres.

The chief developments since 1940 have been the advent of an *Existentialist *théâtre d'idées*, followed by the Theatre of the Absurd. Existentialism reached the stage in the early 1940s with the plays of Sartre, Camus, and S. de Beauvoir, who used conventional forms to treat philosophical and ethical problems. The period after 1940 saw the continuing work of many pre-war dramatists, e.g. Salacrou, Cocteau, Obey, Achard (who went over entirely to the Boulevard), Mauriac (who had turned to the theatre in 1938), and Anouilh (who enjoyed a popular success rivalled only by that of Achard and of André Roussin, b. 1911, a prolific author of gay Boulevard comedies, e.g. *La Petite Hutte*, 1947). They were joined in the '40s and '50s by dramatists including Montherlant (whose powerful dramas on religious and historical themes belong to the 'literary' theatre), Aymé, Audiberti, and F. Marceau. After 1940, Claudel came fully into his own as a dramatist, thanks to the productions of Barrault; and G. Marcel, another long-neglected dramatist, also gained recognition, thanks to the Existentialist vogue.

The early 1950s saw the birth of an *antithéâtre* (*cf.*, in the novel, the **anti-roman* and **nouveau roman*) known as the Theatre of the Absurd. In applying this term to the work of Beckett, Adamov (till 1957), Ionesco, and Genet, and finding 'parallels and proselytes' in Jean Tardieu (1903–), Vian, Arrabal, and Robert Pinget (1919– ; *cf. Nouveau roman*), Martin Esslin (in *The Theatre of the Absurd*, 1962) drew a distinction between theme and form. Broadly speaking, the theme of these dramatists is the 'absurdity' of the human condition, which 'is also the theme of much of the work of dramatists like Giraudoux, Anouilh, Salacrou, Sartre, and Camus'; but 'while Sartre or Camus express the new content in the old convention, the Theatre of the Absurd goes a step further in trying to achieve a unity between its basic assumptions and the form in which these are expressed'. All the trappings of conventional dramatic realism are abandoned—the concepts of character and motivation (characters may change sex, age, or personality, and behave irrationally), logical structure, a fixed scene; and language changes its significance, for what happens on the stage may transcend or contradict what is said there. The Theatre of the Absurd is not a movement or school; and, though centred in Paris, it has a broad basis in Western tradition and exponents in many other countries. Its French exponents have their place in an iconoclastic tradition which includes **Jarry's Ubu Roi* and pataphysics, **Apollinaire's Les Mamelles de Tirésias*, the **Dadaists and **Surrealists, the dramatic theories of Artaud, and Roger Vitrac's *Victor, ou les Enfants au pouvoir* (prod. 1924); but they owe quite as much to Kafka and to James Joyce (*v. Foreign Influences*, 6), and also to modern doubts about the efficacy of language as a means of communication. Though the public was at first predictably resistant to their work, these dramatists swiftly imposed themselves, for such plays as **Beckett's En attendant Godot* and **Ionesco's La Cantatrice chauve* had a poignant and compelling psychological reality which was in perfect accord with the spirit of the times and soon found a response far beyond France.

Theatres and Theatre Companies. For dramatic performances in the medieval period *v. Basoche*; *Confrérie de la Passion*; *Fête des Fous*; *Sociétés joyeuses*. In the 16th c. there was only one permanent theatre in Paris, that on the site of the old **Hôtel de Bourgogne*, owned by the **Confrérie de la Passion*, but from 1578 sometimes let to professional companies. There were, however, intermittent theatrical performances in colleges and other premises, and from the end of the century strolling players were in the habit of erecting their booths at the annual fairs of Saint-Germain (winter) and Saint-Laurent (summer). They presented comic dialogues and were known as the *Théâtre de la Foire*.

From *c.* 1606 the company of the *Hôtel de Bourgogne*, led by Valleran Le Conte (d. *c.* 1628; one of the earliest known professional actors), assumed a fairly permanent character and was known as the *Comédiens du Roi*. It left Paris for a time in 1622, but returned to the *Hôtel de Bourgogne* in 1628. Meanwhile (in 1622, 1624, and 1626), the *Comédiens du Prince d'Orange*, a French company directed by Lenoir, with Mondory as chief actor, were at the *Hôtel de Bourgogne*. In 1629, when this company was in Rouen, Mondory received **Mélite* from the young Corneille; the play was later successfully produced in Paris, where the company hired the **Hôtel d'Argent* and finally established itself in the **Marais* quarter (1634; the *Théâtre du Marais*, where all Corneille's earlier plays were probably produced) as a rival to the *Comédiens du Roi*.

In 1658 Molière brought his company to Paris and founded the *Théâtre du Petit-Bourbon* (in part of the **Louvre*). In 1661 it moved to a hall in the **Palais-Royal*. After Molière's death (1673), the king decided that there should be only two companies in Paris, one, the *Comédiens du Roi*, at the *Hôtel de Bourgogne*, the other at the playhouse in the Rue Mazarine, to which Molière's company had now moved. The best players of the *Théâtre du Marais* were combined with Molière's players to form the second company, soon known as the *Compagnie de Guénégaud*. In 1680 the *Comédiens du Roi* were merged with the *Compagnie de Guénégaud* to form the company that survives as the *Comédie-Française*.

The *Comédie-Française* had keen competitors in Fiorillo's company of Italian actors (*v. Italiens*), who now moved to the *Hôtel de Bourgogne*, and in the irrepressible players of the *Théâtre de la Foire*. Following the expulsion of the *Italiens* (1697), the comic dialogues of the *Théâtre de la Foire* gradually developed into dramatic scenes. The *Comédie-Française* opposed this infringement of its monopoly, but to little effect. About 1713, the players of the *Théâtre de la Foire* were authorized to perform comedy interspersed with songs, a form that was gradually to evolve into comic opera. In 1762 they joined forces with the *Italiens* (who had returned in 1716 and were again at the *Hôtel de Bourgogne*) as the *Comédie-Italienne*, known from 1780 as the *Opéra-Comique*. Besides comic opera, they also produced other types of play, alongside the privileged *Comédie-Française*. By the outbreak of the Revolution there were thus two principal theatres in Paris, the *Comédie-Française*, established from 1782 at the *Théâtre du Luxembourg*, and the *Opéra-Comique*, at first at the *Hôtel de Bourgogne* and from 1783 on the *boulevards*. There were also a few minor playhouses.

In the provinces, as late as the 17th c., there were no theatres, and the travelling companies had to use any premises available (as depicted in *Le Roman comique*). These provincial companies were of considerable importance in the history of the French theatre. They included good actors, such as Mondory; and dramatists of the stature of Hardy and Molière wrote plays for them. From the mid-18th c. theatres sprang up in many provincial towns, e.g. Rouen, Lyons, Amiens, Montpellier, Bordeaux, Nantes.

During the Revolution several new theatres opened in Paris. In 1799, after various misadventures, the *Comédie-Française* was officially installed in its present quarters in the Rue de Richelieu. Napoleon kept a firm hold over the theatres (*v. Censorship, Dramatic*), limiting their number and dividing those in Paris into first-class and second-class theatres. The latter, the commercial Boulevard theatres, staged plays of a more popular character—*vaudevilles*, *mélodrames*, and, in time, the new forms of drama (*v. Theatre of the 19th and 20th cs.*). A maximum of two theatres was permitted in the larger provincial towns and one in the smaller. Until 1864 no new theatre could be opened without prior sanction.

Paris theatres of the 20th c. are, broadly speaking, of three types: the national, State-subsidized theatres (*les subventionnés*), including the *Comédie-Française*, the *Odéon-Théâtre de France*, the *Opéra* and *Opéra-Comique*, the *Théâtre national populaire*, whose repertory, long mainly classical, has become both classical and modern; the commercial Boulevard theatres, which aim to entertain a wide public and whose choice of plays is largely governed by the need for box-office appeal and star parts; and the experimental or *avant-garde* theatres, which explore new techniques and stage plays by young or unknown French and foreign dramatists, new versions of French and foreign classics, etc.

The *avant-garde* theatres, often run by actor-producers who have formed their own companies, had their origin in Antoine's *Théâtre Libre* (1887–96) and the *Théâtre de l'Œuvre* (f. 1890 as the *Théâtre d'Art* and directed 1893–1929 by Lugné-Poë). The most influential of them was Copeau's *Vieux-Colombier* (f. 1913): of the four leading *avant-garde* directors of the inter-war years (who in 1927 formed the group known as the *Cartel*)—Dullin of the *Atelier*, Baty of the *Théâtre Montparnasse*, Jouvet of the *Comédie des Champs-Élysées* and the *Athénée*, G. Pitoëff of the *Théâtre des Arts* and the *Mathurins*—all but Baty had worked under Copeau; *v. also Compagnie des*

Quinze. The appointment in 1936 of Copeau, Baty, Dullin, and Jouvet as producers at the *Comédie-Française (v. Bourdet) indicated the impact they had made on the theatre. Their innovations, and the 'literary' theatre they and the dramatists associated with them had created (v. Theatre of the 19th and 20th cs.), invaded both the national and the Boulevard theatres, blurring for a time the initially clear-cut distinction between, in particular, *avant-garde* and Boulevard productions.

The careers of two of the most important post-war actor-producers— Jean Vilar (1912–71), who began as stage-manager at the *Atelier and director of the little *Théâtre de Poche* in Paris, and Roger Planchon (1931–), director of an *avant-garde* company in Lyons—illustrate the considerable changes that have taken place in the theatrical scene since 1945. Determined efforts have been made to decentralize the theatre (and so end the Paris monopoly of theatrical activity) and also to democratize it, to bring it to the people (esp. to the young and to working-class audiences). From 1946, provincial *Centres dramatiques*, subsidized by the State and the local authorities, were established at Saint-Étienne, Strasbourg, Toulouse, Rennes, Lille, Aix-en-Provence, and Bourges; the *Théâtre de la Cité de Villeurbanne* (an industrial suburb of Lyons), f. 1957 by Planchon, was given a State subsidy in 1959; and the foundation from the early 1960s of *Maisons de la culture (e.g. the *Théâtre de l'Est parisien*) further assisted the process of decentralization and democratization. Although the movement has suffered from a shortage of funds and a failure to strike deep enough roots, both Vilar, as first organizer (from 1947) of the annual open-air *Festival d'Avignon* and, above all, as director (1951–63) of the *Théâtre national populaire, and Planchon, at Villeurbanne, have gone far to realize its aims.

Thébaïde, ou les Frères ennemis, La, Racine's first play, a tragedy on the theme of the fratricidal struggle for the throne of Thebes between Eteocles and Polynices,

sons of Jocasta and brothers of Antigone; produced 1664.

Thèbes, Roman de, v. Roman de Thèbes.

Thé chez Miranda, Le (1886), a novel by P. Adam and Moréas, a typical product of the early *Symbolist era. Adam later used the name of one of the characters, Jacques Plowert, as a pseudonym.

Thélème, Abbaye de, v. Gargantua.

Théocrates, a politico-religious, ultra-Royalist party of the Restoration period (i.e. after 1815; cf. Ballanche; Bonald; Maistre, J. de). Their main thesis was that the social hierarchy, with its inequalities, was of divine origin; any attempt to limit the power of the monarch —God's representative—by man-made constitutions was therefore contrary to Nature. Their theory that a Christian and Royalist literature could help to re-educate the people served to stimulate the interest in chivalry and the Middle Ages noticeable at this time—and so contributed to the initially Royalist complexion of the *Romantic movement.

Théodore, a fine, but unsuccessful, tragedy by Corneille; produced 1645.

The scene is Antioch. The contemptible Roman governor, Valens, has married Marcelle, a wicked widow. Disappointed in her hope of marrying her daughter Flavie to her stepson Placide—because Placide loves Théodore, a princess of the old race of Syrian kings and a Christian— Marcelle schemes with Valens to condemn Théodore to prostitution and so ruin her in Placide's esteem. Théodore is rescued from this fate by another lover, Didyme, a Christian, who changes clothes with her and takes her place—thus arousing the jealousy of Placide. Théodore surrenders herself and a conflict of generosity follows between her and Didyme. Marcelle finally kills them both with her own hands, and Placide takes his own life.

Théophilanthropistes, a Deistic sect f. under the *Directoire, which gave it the use of ten Paris churches. The three articles of its creed—belief in God, virtue, and immortality—owed something to Voltaire and J.-J. Rousseau. Its adherents, who met weekly for purposes of moral reading and the singing of specially composed hymns, included scholars, politicians, and writers (e.g. Bernardin de Saint-Pierre; M.-J. Chénier). It petered out after the re-establishment of Roman Catholicism by the *Concordat* of 1801.

Théophile, Miracle de, v. Rutebeuf.

Théophile de Viau (1590–1626), 'Théophile', poet and *libertin*. In 1617 he produced *Pyrame et Thisbé* (printed 1623), a tragedy—with elements of *pastoral and *tragicomedy—which was very successful, despite its preciosity. Banished in 1619 as a *Huguenot and a free-thinker, he was pardoned in 1621, in which year his *Œuvres* (inc. a free trans. of the *Phaedo—Traité de l'immortalité de l'âme, ou la Mort de Socrate*—and his poems) were first published. In 1623, after the republication under his name of *Le *Parnasse satirique*, he was held responsible for its worst obscenities, accused of being the leader of the free-thinkers, and again banished (1625). He opposed the strict doctrine of Malherbe in regard to style: 'J'approuve que chacun écrive à sa façon.' His work was unequal, for he was often negligent and in general wasted his talent. At his best, in such odes as *Le Matin* and *La Solitude*, and despite the preciosity which led Boileau to attack him for affectation and insincerity, he showed a fine sense of beauty and an eye for, and love of, nature. Other poems which call for mention are *Le Corbeau* and the bitter sonnet *Ton orgueil peut durer*.

Théramène, in Racine's *Phèdre*.

Thérèse Aubert, v. Nodier.

Thérèse Desqueyroux (1927), a novel by Mauriac. Thérèse has made a marriage of convenience, arranged by wealthy landowning parents on both sides. But she is young and intelligent, stifled by life with a loutish husband, among unsympathetic relations. When an opportunity suddenly presents itself, she yields to temptation and sets to work to poison her husband slowly with arsenic. She is discovered, but the family conspire to prevent scandal and she is not committed for trial. After this she breaks away from a state of virtual imprisonment in her husband's home, persecuted and separated from her child, and goes to Paris. Her longing for affection and understanding, her subtle attractiveness, her equally mysterious power of wreaking havoc in other people's lives, and her feeble efforts to avoid doing so, are drawn with great sympathy. *La Fin de la nuit* (1935) describes her last spiritual struggles and mental and physical decay. She also figures in *Ce qui était perdu* (1930) and in two of the stories in *Plongées* (1938).

Thérèse Raquin (1867), a powerful psychological novel by Zola. Consumed by an overmastering passion, Thérèse and her lover Laurent murder her husband Camille, a weakling. Both are soon a prey to nervous terrors, haunted by visions of Camille. They hope that all will be well once they are married and together, but in the event their terrors increase, the corpse seems to be with them whenever they are alone, and their love turns to loathing. To make matters worse, their scenes of terror and hate are enacted under the eyes of Camille's paralysed old mother, who thus learns of their crime, but is physically incapable of telling anyone. The pair finally kill themselves; and the old woman sits watching. *v. Taine.*

Thermidor, *v. Republican Calendar*; *Journée du 9 thermidor.*

Théroigne de Méricourt, i.e. ANNE-JOSÈPHE TERWAGNE (1762–1817), 'la Belle Liégeoise', 'l'Amazone de la Liberté', a Revolutionary heroine about whom many stories have collected. She came to Paris from Belgium (1785) with an elderly protector and was soon fired by Revolutionary ardour. She had a political *salon* (c. 1790), tried to raise a women's army, and was particularly fierce and

vindictive at the time of the fall of the
monarchy (1792). From 1793 her
extremism and her popularity waned
rapidly. Later, her reason failed and she
died in the *Salpêtrière. She is the subject
of a play by Hervieu.

Thésée, in Racine's *Phèdre.

Thésée, (1) v. Quinault; (2) v. Gide.

Theuriet, Claude-Adhémar-André
(1833–1907), a minor *Parnassien poet (Le
Chemin des bois, 1867; Le Livre de la payse,
1883, etc.) and a popular novelist,
especially when he wrote of country and
small-town provincial life. His many
novels (some later dramatized) include,
notably, Raymonde (1877) and Sau-
vageonne (1880); also Le Mariage de
Gérard (1875), La Maison des deux
Barbeaux (1879), Toute seule (1880).

Thibaud or Thibaut de Champagne
(1201–53), comte de Champagne and roi
de Navarre (1234–53), poet and a patron
of men of letters, took part in the crusade
against the *Albigenses. He wrote poems
of courtly love, including *jeux partis, in
imitation of the *troubadours (v. Lyric
Poetry, 1). He is said to have loved the
regent Blanche de Castille, who inspired
some of his songs.

Thibaudet, Albert (1874–1936), a
leading critic, latterly professor of French
literature at the University of Geneva. His
works include La Poésie de Stéphane
Mallarmé (1912; rev. and augm. 1926),
which made his name; Flaubert (1922;
1935); Paul Valéry (1923); Intérieurs:
Baudelaire, Fromentin, Amiel (1924);
Triptyque de la poésie moderne: Verlaine,
Rimbaud, Mallarmé (1924); Stendhal
(1931); an unfinished Histoire de la
littérature française de 1789 à nos jours
(1936); Réflexions sur la littérature,... le
roman,... la critique (1938–41), consisting
mainly of articles contributed to the
*Nouvelle Revue française, with which he
was long associated. v. Critics and
Criticism, 3.

Thibault, Jacques-Anatole-François,
v. France, A.

Thibault, Les (1922–40), by Martin du
Gard, an outstanding *roman-cycle in
seven parts—Le Cahier gris (1922), Le
Pénitencier (1922), La Belle Saison (1923),
La Consultation (1928), La Sorellina
(1928), La Mort du père (1929), L'Été 1914
(1936)—with an Épilogue (1940).

The work follows the lives of Antoine
and Jacques Thibault, beginning when
Antoine is a medical student and Jacques
a schoolboy. They are motherless, and
dominated, as is much of the book, by their
father, a zealous Roman Catholic
sociologist and moral reformer, of
pharisaic character. Antoine accepts his
prosperous bourgeois environment and
heritage. He becomes absorbed in his
profession, yielding occasionally to affairs
of the heart, but adhering to a strict,
unquestioning conception of duty which
simplifies the conduct of his life: he faces
responsibility (e.g. for his brother) and
accepts the need for patriotic self-sacrifice.
He is gassed in 1917 and dies in 1918.
Jacques, a misfit from the start, is not
improved by a spell in one of his father's
pet institutions, a penitentiary for better-
class delinquents. He has barely completed his university studies when he
decamps from home. Some years later,
Antoine finds him in Switzerland, leading
a life of his own choosing. He writes and
is involved in international socialist
politics. The latter, and his father's illness,
bring him back to Paris in the summer of
1914. The international situation grows
daily more tense; in his personal life he is
again beset by hates and complexes and
again yields to his love for the sister of a
schoolfellow. When war comes he refuses
to fight and manages to return to
Switzerland. He undertakes to fly over the
battlefields dropping pacifist leaflets. He is
shot down and captured, and his death is
expedited by a cowardly stretcher-bearer.

Other characters, and the contrast
between Catholic and Protestant milieux,
play their part, but on the whole the novel
stands or falls as a strictly objective,
impersonal narrative. It is unsparingly

realistic (in the tradition of 19th-c. *Realism): the descriptions of Paris on the eve of the 1914–18 war, of the assassination of *Jaurès, and, later, of battle scenes, approximate to social history, while the long, merciless description of M. Thibault's lingering death from uraemia reads rather like a medical case-history, as does Antoine's daily record of his own painful decline.

Thierry, AUGUSTIN (1795–1856), historian, came to history by way of scientific studies, *Saint-Simonisme, and journalism (1817–21); v. also Martyrs, Les. He did much to stimulate the early 19th-c. enthusiasm for historical studies and to extend their scope by basing them more thoroughly on contemporary documents, by going further back in time, and by paying more attention to the role of the common people. His chief works, written in a vivid style and enlivened by anecdote and local colour, were L'Histoire de la conquête de l'Angleterre par les Normands (1825), a study of the Anglo-Saxon spirit of liberty surviving invasion to emerge in the system of parliamentary government, and Récits des temps mérovingiens, retelling stories from *Gregory of Tours's history, preceded by Considérations sur l'histoire de France (1840). He was long totally blind.

Thiers, ADOLPHE (1797–1877), statesman and historian, came to Paris (1821; with Mignet) from the South, soon made his name as a political journalist, and then, with his Histoire de la Révolution française (1823–7), as an historian. After the 1830 *Revolution which, as a founder of Le *National, he helped to bring about, he was one of several historians in the government. In 1840 he went into opposition over foreign policy, retired, and wrote his second great work, Histoire du Consulat et de l'Empire (1845–62). He returned to active politics (Republican opposition) in 1863, led the peace negotiations after the *Franco-Prussian war, became first President of the Third *Republic, and did much to assist France's economic and military recovery. His two works, models of clear exposition, remain standard histories.

Thomas, v. Tristan (Tristram).

Thomas, ANDRÉ-ANTOINE, v. Dictionaries, 1890–1900.

Thomas, HENRI (1912–   ), novelist and poet. His poetry—e.g. Travaux d'aveugle (1941), Signe de vie (1944), Le Monde absent (1947), Nul Désordre (1950)—recalls the *Symbolists. His novels, which are relatively devoid of action and present a sombre view of the world, include Le Seau à charbon (1940), Le Précepteur (1942), La Vie ensemble (1945), Les Déserteurs (1951), La Nuit de Londres (1956), La Dernière Année (1960), John Perkins (1960), Le Promontoire (1961), Le Parjure (1964), La Relique (1969). He has also published short stories (La Cible, 1956) and translations of Shakespeare, Melville, Goethe, and Pushkin.

Thomas Aquinas (Thomas d'Aquin), St. (c. 1225–74; canonized 1323; declared 'Doctor of the Church' 1567), the great Italian Dominican philosopher and theologian, spent three periods in Paris: 1245–8 (with his master St. Albertus Magnus), when, though below the prescribed age, he was admitted to teach; 1252–9, when he taught at the Dominican convent of Saint-Jacques and wrote in defence of the mendicant friars (v. Universities, 1); and 1269–72.

In 1879, by the bull Aeterni Patris, the substance of his teaching (Thomism, since then often called Neo-Thomism)—notably expounded in his Summa theologica—was accepted as the official doctrine of the Church of Rome, a doctrine which reconciles philosophical speculation with belief in the divine origin of the universe. v. Gilson; Maritain; cf. Blondel, M.

Thomas Becket, Vie de Saint, a poem in monorhyme stanzas of five *alexandrines, completed 1174, by Garnier or Guernes de Pont-Sainte-Maxence. The author drew his facts mainly from two Latin lives of the saint, but interest in his subject led him to visit Canterbury in order to supplement and reconcile them. The work shows great vigour and literary skill.

Thomas l'Imposteur, v. *Cocteau*.

Thomisme, v. *Thomas Aquinas, St*.

Thou, (1) JACQUES-AUGUSTE DE (1553–1617), historian, magistrate, director of the royal library (v. *Bibliothèque nationale*) from 1593, noted for his *Historia sui temporis* (1604–20, in 5 pts., the fifth completed by other hands; trans. as *Histoire de mon temps*, 1734), a vast work (138 vols.) covering the years 1543–1607 and showing scrupulous fairness and tolerance in its assessment of the Protestant Reformation and the wars of religion—an attitude which brought the author into disfavour with Rome; (2) his son FRANÇOIS-AUGUSTE DE (1607–42), v. *Cinq-Mars*.

Thunder-ten-Tronckh, Baron, in Voltaire's *Candide*.

Tiberge, in Prévost's *Manon Lescaut*.

Tibert; Tiécelin, the cat and the crow in the *Roman de Renart*.

Tiers État, under the monarchy, the Third Estate of the realm, the Commons who, in contrast to the other two Estates (most of the *noblesse* and the higher clergy—the *Privilégiés*), had to sustain the main burden of taxation. v. *États généraux*.

Tillemont, SÉBASTIEN LE NAIN DE (1637–98), a learned historian, a *Jansenist, author of *Mémoires pour servir à l'histoire des six premiers siècles de l'Église* (1693–1712), a work praised by Gibbon for its accuracy, and *Histoire des empereurs et des autres princes qui ont régné pendant les six premiers siècles de l'Église* (1690–1738).

Tillier, CLAUDE (1801–44), journalist, pamphleteer, and novelist, spent much of his life at Nevers, where he edited a daily paper. His vigorous, ironical pamphlets (in *Œuvres*, 1846) are mainly on politics and religion. His novels include the good-humouredly satirical *Mon oncle Benjamin* (1841).

Tilsit, Treaty of, v. *Coalitions* (4).

Timocrate, v. *Corneille, T*.

Timon le misanthrope, v. *Cormenin*.

Tinan, JEAN DE (1875–99), a minor *Symbolist, author of *Document sur l'impuissance d'aimer* (1894), a piece of introspective writing; *Penses-tu réussir* (1897) and *Aimienne* (1898), exaggeratedly Symbolist novels.

Tiraqueau, ANDRÉ (c. 1480–1558), jurist, a man of vast learning and a friend of Rabelais, came to Paris (1541) from Bordeaux and was entrusted with important missions by François Iᵉʳ and Henri II. He wrote on civil law.

Tiron, L'Abbé de, v. *Desportes*.

Tite et Bérénice, a 'comédie héroïque' by Corneille; produced 1670. *Cf.* Racine's *Bérénice* (also prod. 1670) on the same theme.

The scene is Rome. Tite, having just become emperor, is about to marry Domitie (daughter of a Roman general), when the unexpected arrival of Bérénice revives his passionate love for her and places him in great embarrassment. The situation is complicated by the fact that Domitie and Tite's brother Domitian are in love. Finally Bérénice, recognizing that her marriage with Tite would endanger his position, decides to renounce her hopes and leave him, while Tite surrenders Domitie to Domitian.

Tixier de Ravisi, in Latin RAVISIUS TEXTOR (c. 1480–1524), professor at the *Collège de Navarre* (1500–24) and rector of the *University of Paris. He wrote Latin *moralités* and *farces*.

T.N.P., the *Théâtre national populaire*.

Toast funèbre, *v.* under *Tombeau d'Edgar Poë, Le.*

Tocqueville, ALEXIS-HENRI-CHARLES-MAURICE CLÉREL, COMTE DE (1805–59), an historian of enduring reputation. He studied law in Paris and held a post in the judicature at Versailles (1830–5). After 1835 he lived on his private means, was politically active from 1839 (foreign minister for a time), but left France for Italy and Germany after the *coup d'état* of 1851 and devoted himself wholly to writing.

While at Versailles, he was sent for a year (1831) on an official mission to the U.S.A., with Beaumont de la Bonninière, to study and report on the penal system; and the two collaborated in *Du système pénitentiaire aux États-Unis et de son application en France* (1832). Soon after his return he set down his observations on the American political scene in *La Démocratie en Amérique* (1835 and 1840, 2 pts.), the first of two famous works. He had been impressed, while in America, by the success with which the principles of liberty and equality evolved in the Old World had been applied to meet the needs of a new civilization. He concludes that the trend of history is irresistibly towards equality; and that the future of France, indeed of the Western world, is bound up with the acceptance of democratic principles, which are the only effective means of avoiding subjection to tyranny.

He had always held that the Revolution of 1789, far from constituting a complete break with the past, had actually demonstrated the continuity of history. Its original aims had been both equality and liberty (i.e. political freedom), but the second aim had been dropped, leaving the people a prey to a government much stronger than the one they had abolished; and the administrative principles introduced in 1800 were in the event those of the former monarchy. He had hoped to write a work on these lines, with sections on the *ancien régime*, the events of the Revolution, and the career of Napoleon. *L'Ancien Régime* (1856), the only section he completed and his second great work,

is based on long research into official and municipal records. It studies the social and political fabric of pre-Revolutionary France and seeks to explain why the Revolution broke out in France rather than elsewhere in Europe, how it proceeded from the very society it sought to destroy, and why the collapse of the monarchy was so sudden and complete.

His *Souvenirs* (1893) of the period 1848–9 include good descriptions of the 1848 *Revolution and the *journées de juin*. Much of his correspondence (publ. posth. at various dates) is with English friends, e.g. Henry Reeve of *The Times*, J. S. Mill, Mrs. Grote (wife of the historian). *v. Gobineau.*

Todorov, TZVETAN, *v. Critics and Criticism*, 3.

Toepffer, RODOLPHE (1799–1846), a Swiss artist and writer, wrote and illustrated *Voyages en zig-zag* (1844), on his wanderings in Switzerland. He also wrote short stories, collected in *La Bibliothèque de mon oncle* (1832–4) and *Nouvelles genevoises* (1840). His work was praised by Sainte-Beuve.

Toison d'or, Ordre de la, the Order of the Golden Fleece, f. 1429 by Philippe le Bon, duke of Burgundy. It became the chief order of knighthood in Austria and Spain.

Tolérance, *Traité sur la* (1763), by Voltaire, a treatise on religious toleration, written at the time of his campaign to vindicate Calas. He claims that religious intolerance was unknown to the ancient civilizations and was not taught by Jesus Christ, and asserts that it is the Catholics—and especially the *Jesuits—who are the most given to religious fanaticism.

Tombeau d'Edgar Poë, *Le* (Baltimore 1876, in a memorial volume to Poe), a famous sonnet by Mallarmé ('Tel qu'en Lui-même enfin l'éternité le change'). Like Baudelaire before him and Valéry after him, Mallarmé greatly admired Poe and his aesthetic theories.

Other *in memoriam* poems by Mallarmé

may be noted here: *Toast funèbre*, in *Le Tombeau de Théophile Gautier* (1873); the sonnet 'Le temple enseveli divulgue par la bouche', in *Le Tombeau de Charles Baudelaire* (1895); *Tombeau* ('Le noir roc courroucé que la bise le roule'), said to be his last sonnet, published January 1897 for the first anniversary of Verlaine's death.

Tombeur de Notre-Dame, *v. Religious Writings*, 1.

Topaze, *v. Pagnol*.

Torelli, GIACOMO, *v. Corneille*.

Torquet, ANTOINE, *v. Nau*.

Tortillard, Le, in *Sue's Les Mystères de Paris*.

Tory, GEOFFROY (*c.* 1480–*c.* 1533), grammarian, king's printer, and translator of Greek authors. He developed typography and, in his *Champfleury* (1529), encouraged the practice of writing learned works in French and protested against its excessive latinization.

Tosca, *v. Sardou*.

Totalisme, *v. Literary Isms*.

Toulet, PAUL-JEAN (1867–1920), journalist, poet, and novelist, settled in Paris *c.* 1898 and made a name as a conversationalist and with novels and tales (usually first publ. in *La *Vie parisienne*) which, like his talk, were witty, libertine, cynical, and at times savagely ironical, e.g. *Monsieur du Paur, homme public* (1898), *Le Mariage de Don Quichotte* (1901), *Tendres Ménages* (1904), *Mon amie Nane* (1905), *La Jeune Fille verte* (1920), and the *Contes de Béhanzigue* (1920). But the highly polished verse of *Les Contrerimes* (1921, posth.), where emotion has been crystallized in tranquillity and the irony is alternately sharpened or softened by fantasy, won him a more enduring reputation. (The title refers to the unusual stanzaic form, 8a 6b 8b 6a.) *v. Fantaisiste, Le Groupe*.

Toulouse, Floral Games of, *v. Jeux floraux*.

Toulouse-Lautrec, HENRY-MARIE-RAYMOND DE (1864–1901), painter and lithographer, notably of circus and music-hall scenes. There is a fine collection of his work at his native Albi.

Tour de Nesle, La (1832), by Dumas *père*, an historical drama of medieval times (*v. Beauvoir, R. de*). Every night the turret windows of the Tour de *Nesle are lit for revelry; every morning three corpses lie at the foot of the tower, victims of the secret debauches of the queen (Marguerite de Bourgogne, d. 1315) and her two sisters-in-law. One victim is Gaultier d'Aulnay, brother of the queen's favourite. Another, who escapes, is Buridan, a soldier of fortune, who reveals himself to the queen as her former lover and father of the two sons she abandoned at birth. He gets himself made chief minister and plots to have the queen surprised in her tower with her favourite, the elder d'Aulnay. At the last moment he discovers that his sons by the queen, long presumed dead, are none other than the brothers d'Aulnay. He rushes to forestall his own son at the meeting-place and perishes in his stead.

Tour du monde en quatre-vingts jours, Le, *v. Verne*.

Tour Eiffel, La, one of the famous sights of Paris (and now also a powerful radio-transmitting station), a gaunt, lattice-work iron structure, tapering up to a height of 984 ft., erected 1887–9 in the *Champ-de-Mars to the design of the engineer Gustave Eiffel (1832–1923) for the Exhibition of 1889. This intrinsically hideous erection provoked much dismay and ridicule in its early days, but familiarity has bred affection. Visitors who take the lift to the highest of its three platforms are rewarded with a fine view of the city.

Tournachon, FÉLIX, *v. Nadar*.

Tournelle, La, *v. Parlement*.

Tournelles, Hôtel des, *v. Hôtel des Tournelles.*

Tournier, MICHEL (1924–   ), novelist, publisher, and broadcaster. His first novel, *Vendredi, ou les Limbes du Pacifique* (1967), retells the story of Robinson Crusoe. *Le Roi des aulnes* (1970) won the *Prix Goncourt.*

Toussaint Louverture (1743–1803), negro statesman. In 1791 the present Dominican Republic (eastern half of the W. Indian island of which Haiti forms the other half) was a French possession (San Domingo) with a population of whites, mulattoes (free, but without civic rights), and negro slaves. When the negroes were freed by the *constitution of 1791, the mulattoes were given the privileges of French citizens; but trouble between the white and the coloured population led to the decree being revoked. Toussaint Louverture led a revolt of negroes and mulattoes against the whites, and by 1801, after some years of turmoil, his highly intelligent administration had brought order and prosperity to the whole island, now unified. He sought Bonaparte's approval of a form of constitutional government for the island as a French colony, with himself as governor. Far from consenting, Bonaparte sent a military expedition under his brother-in-law Leclerc (*v. Bonaparte Family* (6)) to subdue the island and restore slavery. After months of fierce resistance the negroes came to terms. Toussaint Louverture laid down his arms, but was captured by a trick, deported to France (June 1802), and imprisoned. He soon died of tuberculosis. The negroes renewed the struggle, and in 1803 such remnants of the French force as had survived massacre and disease (Leclerc died of yellow fever) evacuated the island.

Toute la lyre, v. Hugo.

Trafalgar, the famous British naval victory (21 Oct. 1805) over the French and Spanish fleets, gave Britain undisputed command of the sea and foiled Napoleon's plan to invade England from Boulogne (*v. Armée, La Grande*).

Tragedy. Apart from the tragic element in the *mystères*, tragedy was first known in France in the form of translations from the Greek, at first into Latin, then into French (either direct from the Greek or through Seneca's Latin versions). In 1506 Erasmus printed in Paris Latin translations of Euripides' *Hecuba* and *Iphigenia*; and *v. Baif, L. de*; *Buchanan*; *Muret*; *Bochetel*. The first original French tragedy was Jodelle's *Cléopâtre captive*, acted 1552/3 in the presence of the king, together with his *Eugène* (the first original French *comedy). The two plays caused a great sensation. A considerable number of tragedies followed in the next 20 years, notably *La Péruse's *Médée*, M. de *Saint-Gelais's *Sophonisbe*, *Grévin's *La Mort de César*. A rather different class of play appears to have been partly inspired by the *mystère*, which it sought to bring into harmony with the form of classical tragedy, e.g. *Bèze's *Abraham sacrifiant*, *Desmasures's *Tragédies saintes*, La Taille's *Saül le furieux* and its sequel (two tragedies of considerable power).

These early works have certain prevailing characteristics: a subject taken from mythology or Roman or Christian history; presentation of a tragic fact or situation rather than action (the essential scenes of conflict of characters or passions are avoided); little psychology; monologues in which the characters reveal their feelings; a chorus (to draw the moral, lament the victims, and divide the acts); dreams, maxims, much oratory; unity of time. The prevailing metre is the *alexandrine couplet, the choruses being in a variety of shorter metres. The audiences envisaged were lettered and restricted, such as colleges and the court—though performances at court were rare after 1567. The most important of these early tragedians was Garnier, who wrote seven tragedies (perf. 1568–82) and also the first *tragicomedy. Hardy, who wrote many tragedies and tragicomedies for the popular stage (*c.* 1593–*c.* 1630), was a considerable innovator and largely rid tragedy of the Senecan influence. His contemporaries included Montchrétien and Théophile de Viau (noted for the affectation of his *Pyrame et Thisbé*).

There was no marked change in the nature of tragedy until the time of Mairet and Corneille, when there was a revival of tragedy after its temporary eclipse by tragicomedy and the *pastoral play. Mairet may be said to have introduced the unities, the doctrine (narrower and more categorical than that in Aristotle's *Poetics*, on which it claimed to be based) that a play should consist of one main action, represented as occurring within one day, at one place. It had been formulated briefly by Ronsard (*Art poétique*, 1565) and more fully by *La Taille, and had been largely observed by Jodelle and Garnier. It was then forgotten for half a century. In 1631 Mairet—whose *Sophonisbe* (1634) is generally regarded as the first regular *Classical tragedy—advocated the unities of action and time in a preface to his *Silvanire*. Before long, the practice of representing several different localities side by side on the stage (*décor multiple*) gave way to unity of place (Corneille's *Le *Cid*, 1637, involves three scenes; his *Horace*, *Cinna*, and *Polyeucte*, 1640–2, one only). The three unities—notably championed by Chapelain and d'Aubignac and later memorably defined by Boileau (*v. Art poétique*, *L'*)—were henceforth characteristic of Classical tragedy (though some irregular pieces continued to be written, e.g. by Rotrou). They were important as tending to concentrate drama in psychological rather than physical action.

The period *c.* 1637–45—dominated by Corneille—was highly productive of dramatic works. His chief contemporaries were Rotrou, Du Ryer, Tristan l'Hermite, Scudéry, La Calprenède, and Cyrano de Bergerac, writers of very unequal merit; but a host of other poets (Baro, Claveret, Colletet, Boisrobert, etc.) were producing plays now barely remembered. Experiments were made with prose tragedy (e.g. Desmarets de Saint-Sorlin's *Érigone*, 1639), but this form did not become established. It may be noted that

Corneille and others applied the term *tragédie* to plays with a happy ending if the theme was lofty and the treatment serious.

The interval between the zenith of Corneille and the rise of Racine was filled by Corneille's brother Thomas and Quinault. Racine, while adopting the dramatic form of Corneille, modified the treatment under the influence of his Hellenism and *Jansenism; in particular, he represents the human will as weak, swayed above all by the passions of love and hatred.

The great examples of Corneille and Racine hampered the subsequent evolution of tragedy; their successors, instead of studying life afresh, drew from them various fixed formulas of the tragic art. On the other hand, the public was tiring of psychological analysis and showing a taste for sentiment, and also for a moral purpose, in drama. The only tragedians deserving even passing mention between Racine and Voltaire are Campistron, Longepierre, La Fosse, Lagrange-Chancel, and the elder Crébillon. Voltaire attempted to revive the great tragedy of the 17th c., with Racine as his chief model, sometimes seeking novelty in an exotic setting (*Alzire*; *L'*Orphelin de la Chine*), in themes of national history (*Tancrède*; *Zaïre*), or in a philosophic thesis (*Mahomet*). Houdar de la Motte suggested innovations, e.g. much less strict observance of the unities, but seldom practised his own precepts. From the mid-18th c. translators were adapting the tragedies of Shakespeare for the French stage (*v. Foreign Influences*, 2 and 3). M.-J. Chénier, the outstanding tragedian of the Revolutionary era (notably with *Charles IX*), was succeeded by such writers as Baour-Lormian, Brifaut, de Jouy, G. Legouvé, Lemercier, and Raynouard. Despite the initial success of some of their mediocre works (often due to the acting of Talma), and despite attempts at innovation and resuscitation (more apparent in critical than in creative writings), strictly Classical tragedy became increasingly lifeless and lacking in poetic inspiration.

Several factors contributed to its

decline. Creative writing was undoubtedly stultified by severe dramatic *censorship. The *Romantics were fighting a winning battle against the conventions governing Classical tragedy. The post-Revolutionary theatre public was larger and more heterogeneous than before, and no longer an educated *élite*; people came to the theatre looking for incident and action rather than the opportunity to exercise trained critical faculties. The result was that strict tragedy lost its appeal and was gradually ousted by various forms of drama—historical drama, *drame bourgeois*, *mélodrame*, Romantic drama (*v. Theatre of the 19th and 20th cs.*). The transition is noticeable after 1820 in some of the works of Delavigne and Soumet, which preserve the Classical form, but make use of intrigue and incident. The success of *Ponsard's *Lucrèce* (1843), a skilful conventional tragedy (with chorus and dreams), was a dying flicker, due less to intrinsic merit than to a momentary reaction in the public taste.

Tragicomedy, a form of drama introduced from Italy and inaugurated in France by Garnier's *Bradamante* (publ. 1582). It was notably developed by Hardy (and *v.* Schelandre's *Tyr et Sidon*). Tragicomedy, a term variously defined, provided an escape from the restrictions on pure *tragedy (above all, from the unities); its features were usually a romantic subject (though the characters might be of the heroic kind suited to tragedy), startling but not dire adventures, and a happy ending; it did not necessarily contain a comic element. It became very popular and for a time (*c.* 1628), together with *pastoral drama, almost ousted tragedy and comedy. It remained in vogue till *c.* 1650, but from the time of *Le *Cid* (1637) the distinction between tragicomedy and tragedy became blurred. Some 200 such dramas (inc. those of Hardy) were written in this period, the best being perhaps Rotrou's *Don Bernard de Cabrère*, Corneille's *Don Sanche d'Aragon*, and some of those by Scudéry and Du Ryer.

Tragiques, Les (1616; some parts were in circulation by 1593), by d'Aubigné, an epic poem (*c.* 9,000 alexandrines) conceived *c.* 1577 when he was recovering from a wound received in battle. It is a lyrical satire, inspired by fanatical Protestantism, powerful and violent, lacking in proportion and lucidity, but redeemed by the sombre splendour of many passages. There are seven books: I. *Misères*, a poignant exposition of the sufferings of the people and a fierce denunciation of those responsible for them, especially the Jezebel, Catherine de Médicis; II. *Princes*, a diatribe against her sons Charles IX and Henri III; III. *La Chambre dorée*, an over-long attack on the administration of justice; IV. *Les Feux*, a Protestant martyrology; V. *Les Fers*, on the wars of religion; VI. *Vengeances*, enumerating historical instances of divine vengeance on tyrants; VII. *Jugement*, an evocation of the Day of Judgement. This work, together with *Du Bartas's *La Semaine* (another great Protestant epic) and the tragedies of Garnier, finally established the *alexandrine as the metre of serious poetry.

Trahison des clercs, La, *v.* Benda.

Train de 8h. 47, Le, *v.* Courteline.

Traité de la connaissance de Dieu et de soi-même, *v.* Bossuet.

Traité de l'éducation des filles (1687), by Fénelon, a work written for the duchesse de Beauvilliers, who had eight daughters. Girls have reckless imaginations, which should be restrained. Novels and plays are an insufficiently solid diet for their empty heads; philosophy and theology are equally unsuitable. A girl's education should fit her to become a pious, submissive spouse and a good housewife.

Traité des passions de l'âme, *v.* Descartes.

Traité du style, *v.* Aragon.

Traité du verbe, *v.* Ghil.

Trappe, Abbaye de la, a Cistercian abbey (f. 1140) near Mortagne (Orne), was reformed *c.* 1664 by its abbot Armand-Jean Le Bouthillier de Rancé (1626–1700) and soon became a centre of spiritual life (frequented by such men as Bossuet) and noted for the extreme austerity of its rules, enjoining almost perpetual silence and heavy manual labour. Rancé, who abandoned a dissipated life to enter the cloister, is the subject of a biography (1844) by Chateaubriand.

Travail, v. Zola.

Travailleurs de la mer, Les (1866), by Hugo, a novel dedicated to Guernsey, where it is set.

Mess (i.e. Monsieur) Lethierry has two treasures, his adopted daughter Déruchette and his boat *Durande*, the first steamboat in the area. His boat is wrecked off the coast, but the valuable engine is reported to be intact and Déruchette offers to marry the man who can salvage it. Gilliatt, a fisherman who has long loved her from afar, finally accomplishes this seemingly impossible task, but only after superhuman efforts (inc. a fight with a giant octopus which gives full play to Hugo's descriptive powers). He returns to find that Déruchette loves another man. Nobly, he helps her to marry where her heart is. The newly wed couple sail for England. Gilliatt, sitting on a rock to see their ship pass, allows the tide to rise slowly and engulf him.

Traviata, La, v. Dame aux camélias, La.

Traviès de Villers, CHARLES-JOSEPH, *known as* C.-J. TRAVIÈS (1804–59), caricaturist on *Le *Charivari*, *Caricature*, etc., the creator of *Mayeux.

Trébutien,   GUILLAUME-STANISLAS (1800–70), man of letters, remembered as the friend of Barbey d'Aurevilly from their student days at Caen and as editor of the works of E. and M. de Guérin.

Trente, Combat (or *Bataille*) *des,* a poem of 1351, in the form of a *chanson de geste* in *alexandrines, relating a combat between 30 Englishmen and 30 Bretons in the wars of Edward III.

Trésor, Livre du, an encyclopedic treatise written in French *c.* 1265 by the Florentine Brunetto Latini, Dante's teacher.

Trésor de la langue française, (1) *v. Dictionaries,* 1606; (2) *v. Dictionaries,* 1971– .

Trésor de la langue grecque; Trésor de la langue latine, v. Estienne (4) and (2).

Trésor des humbles, Le, v. Maeterlinck.

Trésor du Félibrige, Le, v. Mistral.

Trésoriers de France, *v. Fiscal System.*

Trévoux, a small town near Bourg (Ain), once capital of the little principality of Dombes. A printing-press was established there in 1671 with a *privilège* granted by the duchesse de Montpensier and continued, when Dombes became his, by the duc du Maine. It became one of the famous 18th-c. centres for books printed outside Paris. *v. Librairie; Dictionaries,* 1704 (for the *Dictionnaire de Trévoux*); *Journal de Trévoux.*

Trianon, Le Grand; Le Petit, two pavilions in the park of the Château de *Versailles. The Grand Trianon, an extensive single-storeyed building, was built by Louis XIV in 1687 to the design of Mansard. The Petit Trianon, built by Louis XV in 1751 and supplemented by a small country-house in 1766, was given by Louis XVI to Marie-Antoinette as her private domain. There she discarded etiquette, played the milkmaid, gave parties, acted in musical comedies, etc.

Triboulet, FÉVRIAL or LE FEURIAL, *known as* (d. *c.* 1536), court jester of Louis XII and François Ier. He is celebrated by Rabelais (III, ch. 45) and figures in Hugo's *Le *Roi s'amuse.*

Tribulat Bonhomet, Le Docteur, a

character created by Villiers de l'Isle-Adam, embodies, at times in almost terrifying fashion, the complacent pseudo-scientific materialism of his age (2nd half of 19th c.). His grotesque person, clothes, and mentality are delineated with ironic care in *Le Tueur de cygnes* and *Claire Lenoir*, tales in the collection (1887) that bears his name. He belongs to a company which includes *Prudhomme, *Homais, *Bouvard and Pécuchet, and *Ubu Roi.

Tribunal révolutionnaire, a central court set up in March 1793 by the *Convention* to try persons accused of counter-Revolutionary activities or attempts against the public safety. Judges, jury, and the public prosecutor (Fouquier-Tinville) were nominated by the *Convention. v. Terror.*

Tricolore, Le Drapeau, the French national flag in the colours blue, white, and red, adopted during the Revolution by combining the blue and red of the city of Paris with the white of the *Bourbons (*v. Chambord*). The term *tricolore* is applied to any emblem—flag, cockade, rosette, etc.—in the national colours.

Trilby, ou le Lutin d'Argail, v. Nodier.

Triolet, a stanza of eight lines, the first being repeated after the third and the first and second after the sixth, rhyming A B a A a b A B (the capitals indicate the lines that are repeated).

Triolet, ELSA (1896–1970), a novelist and journalist of Russian birth who lived in France from 1919, writing at first in Russian. She was the lifelong companion of Aragon (whom she met in 1928), the 'Elsa' of his love poetry, and, like him, a committed Marxist writer (*v. Littérature engagée*). Her works include many novels and short stories, notably *Le Premier Accroc coûte deux cents francs* (1944), awarded the *Prix Goncourt*; also studies and translations of Russian authors, e.g. Chekhov, Gogol, Mayakovsky (her brother-in-law).

Trissotin, in Molière's *Les *Femmes savantes.*

Tristan (Tristram), a hero of medieval romance; *v. Romans bretons.* The earliest extant poem about him is the *Tristan* of an *Anglo-Norman named Thomas, written *c.* 1165–70; only parts of it survive. The theme had probably already been treated and in the hands of Thomas loses some of its primitive character. This appears to be better preserved in the *Tristan* of Béroul (probably a native of W. France), much of which is also lost. Two short poems (one of the late 12th, the other of the early 13th c.), entitled *La Folie Tristan*, narrate an episode in which Tristan disguises himself as a fool. Chrétien de Troyes wrote a poem on Tristan, which is lost, while *Marie de France's *Chèvrefeuille* deals with an episode which is not in the Tristan story proper. Finally, the legend was embodied in a long prose version, known as the *Prose Tristan* (*c.* 1230), where it is combined with that of King Arthur and where Tristan and *Lancelot figure as rivals.

The story concerns two lovers, Tristan and Iseut, wife of Tristan's uncle, King Mark of Cornwall. They are conscious of the tie of kinship and loyalty that binds them to Mark, yet dominated by irresistible passion as the result of a love philtre they have drunk unawares. Béroul traces with great penetration the development of this dramatic situation: their escape from burning at the stake; their hardships in the forest; Mark's pursuit of them with intent to kill, and his discovery of them asleep with a naked sword between them; and, when the philtre finally loses its power, their repentance and separation. Other versions end differently.

In English, *Sir Tristrem* is one of the earliest romances in the vernacular; Malory drew on the *Prose Tristan* for his *Morte Darthur*; and more recently the legend has inspired poets such as Matthew Arnold and Swinburne.

Tristan, FLORE TRISTAN-MORCOSO, *known as* **Flora** (1803–44), feminist and revolutionary socialist, said to have been a beauty of romantic and violent character;

maternal grandmother of Gauguin. Her father, a Peruvian who claimed descent from Montezuma, died when she was eight, leaving his family in poverty. At 17, she went to work for a lithographer, with whom she made a disastrous marriage. She left him in 1825, taking the children, but could not get legally free and was persecuted by him till 1839, when he tried to kill her and was imprisoned. Meanwhile, she had been in England in domestic service and in Peru (1833; to seek help from her father's family). She had also begun to educate herself and to agitate for women's rights and divorce-law reform. She made contact with other social reformers, notably Fourier and some of the *Saint-Simoniens, travelled about France increasingly, and came to regard her fight for the oppressed classes as a sort of apostolic mission. In 1843 she founded the *Union ouvrière*. Her works include *Pérégrinations d'une paria (1833–1834)* (1834, 2 vols.), semi-autobiographical, with an account of her year in Peru, and *Promenades dans Londres* (1840), studies of English social conditions.

Tristan l'Hermite, FRANÇOIS L'HERMITE, *known as* (1602–55), dramatist, poet, and novelist, called himself Tristan after the famous 15th-c. Tristan l'Hermite, with whom his family claimed connection. He was poor, delicate, and an inveterate gambler. His works include four notable tragedies: *Mariamne* (1636), which rivalled *Le *Cid* in popularity; *La Mort de Sénèque* (1644), the finest Roman tragedy after those of Corneille and Racine; *La Mort de Crispe* (1645; Fauste, second wife of Constantin, conceals a guilty passion for her stepson Crispe, who loves his cousin Constance and falls a victim to Fauste's jealousy); *Osman* (publ. 1656; on the struggle between the Sultan and his janissaries); also *Les Amours de Tristan* (1638), lyrics including the ode *Le Promenoir des deux amants*; the *Page disgracié* (1642–3), an autobiographical romance describing his chequered youth in the service of the duc d'*Orléans; *Le Parasite* (1654), a comedy. *v. Quinault*.

Tristan l'Hermite, LOUIS (15th c.), in youth a gallant soldier, became *prévôt des maréchaux* under Louis XI and the king's constant companion and adviser ('mon compère'). His sinister role as the ruthless agent of Louis's vengeance inspired many legends. He figures in Scott's *Quentin Durward*.

Tristesse d'Olympio (1840, in *Les *Rayons et les ombres*), one of Hugo's most famous lyrics; *v. Drouet*. The poet (under the name 'Olympio', since often applied to him) revisits the scene of former happiness to find that Nature has pursued her changing course untouched by the emotions she has witnessed. He concludes that, though everything changes, the memory of past happiness survives. *Cf.* Lamartine's *Le Lac* (in *Méditations poétiques*) and Musset's *Souvenir*.

Triumvirat, Le, a tragedy by Voltaire; produced 1767. It is designed to hold up to abhorrence the cruel abuse of arbitrary power, and presents Octavian and Mark Antony, the chief members of the triumvirate, at the moment of the proscriptions by which they sought to remove their principal enemies.

Trivelin, a rascally valet, a stock character of the *commedia dell'arte* (*v. Italiens*).

Troie, Roman de, *v. Roman de Troie*.

Trois Contes (1877), by Flaubert, three finely contrasted examples of his narrative art. The first, *Un Cœur simple*, is a moving tale of the drab, self-sacrificing life of Félicité who, at 16, becomes a servant in a house at Pont-l'Évêque in Normandy. Her existence centres on her widowed mistress, the widow's children, her own sailor nephew, and a parrot. Time passes, and death robs her of them all. She lives on, and finally dies, in the unsold, mouldering house, enfeebled in mind and body, pious as ever, but confusing the stuffed parrot before which she kneels with the Holy Ghost to whom she prays.

La Légende de Saint Julien l'Hospitalier is a medieval tale, jewelled in style like a stained-glass window (and Flaubert may, in fact, have been inspired by a window in Rouen Cathedral). Julien, who seeks to expiate the crimes of his youth by ferrying people across a dangerous river, is summoned one stormy night to transport a filthy and revolting leper. The leper then demands shelter in his hut, a place in his bed, and finally the warmth of his naked body. Julien does all he asks, whereupon sweetness fills the air, the firmament opens, and he finds himself being borne to Heaven in the arms of his Lord.

Hérodias is a sensuously ornate, yet realistic, evocation of a Biblical past. Herod and Herodias are feasting the proconsul Vitellius. The imprecations of the captive John the Baptist are heard from the cistern in the background. Salome dances, and is rewarded with his head. Later it is discarded, *objet lugubre*, among the remains of the banquet. Three of John's disciples retrieve it and set out, carrying it, towards Galilee. 'Comme elle était très lourde', the tale ends, 'ils la portaient alternativement.'

Trois Glorieuses, Les, *v. Revolutions,* 2.

Trois morts et des trois vifs, Dit des, a religious didactic *dit* in dialogue form. The oldest French version, by Baudouin de Condé, dates from before 1280. In this three young noblemen are confronted by three corpses—in life a pope, a cardinal, and a papal notary—who warn them of the vanity of earthly power, honour, and riches. A rather different version, presenting the incident as the vision of a hermit, was printed in the late 15th c., by which time the story was a common theme for church murals. *Cf. Danse macabre.*

Trois Mousquetaires, Les (1844), by Dumas *père*, one of the best of all cloak-and-dagger novels, based largely on *Courtilz de Sandras's Mémoires de M. d'Artagnan.* For its two sequels *v. Dumas père.*

The time is *c.* 1625, the period of Louis XIII and Richelieu. D'Artagnan, a young Gascon—shrewd, brave, and hot-headed, as Gascons proverbially are—comes to Paris to seek his fortune. He has an introduction to the Captain of the King's Musketeers, the picked body who act as Royal Guard and are on terms of continual hostility with Richelieu's Guard. Barely arrived, he is involved in duels in company with three musketeers: Athos, a typical, polished aristocrat; Porthos, a good-hearted, immensely strong braggart; and Aramis, who means to enter the Church and already displays a Jesuitical subtlety. The four companions (d'Artagnan is admitted to the *Corps des Mousquetaires* in due course) have many adventures, the most exciting being when they protect the queen (Anne d'Autriche) against Richelieu's intrigues. In token of affection, she has given the duke of Buckingham some diamonds presented to her by the king. Discovering this, Richelieu persuades the king to give a ball, at which she will have to wear the diamonds. Learning from d'Artagnan's mistress of the queen's predicament, the four set off at once for England. Athos, Porthos, and Aramis fall by the way, but d'Artagnan reaches the duke, obtains the diamonds, and saves the day. The villain of the book is 'Milady', a mysterious and beautiful spy in Richelieu's pay, who becomes d'Artagnan's deadly enemy. Through her, his mistress is poisoned and the duke of Buckingham assassinated. Years ago, she had tricked Athos into marrying her. He thought her dead, but she had remarried, then poisoned her husband for his money. The four finally discover her identity and, when she falls into their power, agree that she deserves no mercy. The story ends with her death.

Trois Villes, Les, *v. Zola.*

Trompe-la-Mort, *v. Vautrin.*

Tronchin, a Genevese family of French origin, chiefly remembered as friends of Voltaire. JEAN-ROBERT (1702–88), banker and jurist, later a *fermier général* in Paris, helped Voltaire buy Les Délices and was soon managing his financial affairs, also performing such tasks as buying his wine, household goods, plants and seeds, etc. *v.* also *Rousseau, J.-J.* THÉODORE (1709–81), cousin of Jean-Robert and Voltaire's physician, was famous for his treatment of the nervous disorders induced by the artificial, dissipated life of Parisian society. He relied largely on fresh air and exercise. FRANÇOIS (1704–98), brother of Jean-Robert, was active in public life in Geneva and a patron of the arts. Voltaire saw the family often and kept up a lively correspondence (esp. 1755–66) with these and other members of it.

Trophées, Les, v. Heredia.

Troubadours (Prov. form of Fr. *trouveurs*), the medieval poets who wrote in the *langue d'oc* of S. France (*v. French Language*). In the later 11th c. they developed a lyric poetry in the Midi, where social and physical conditions (an easy, peaceful life in a genial climate), in contrast to those further north, favoured its growth. It consisted of *chansons*, elaborate in form and concerned almost exclusively with love and the cult of woman (*v. Amour courtois*), *serventois*, *pastourelles, tensons* (*v. Jeu parti*), *aubes* (*v. Chansons à personnages*), etc. The famous *troubadours* Bertrand de Born and Bernard de Ventadour frequented the court of Eleanor of Aquitaine (granddaughter of Guillaume d'Aquitaine, the earliest known *troubadour*; wife of Louis VII of France, then of Henry II of England); her influence and that of her daughters Marie and Aélis (who married the counts of Champagne and Blois) helped to spread this Provençal poetry to N. France, where it found imitators (*v. Lyric Poetry*, 1). The literature of the South declined after the 13th c. (*v. Albigeois*). *v. Marcabru; Jaufré Rudel; Jeux floraux de Toulouse*. For the 19th-c. revival of Provençal literature *v. Félibrige*.

Trouvères or **Trouveurs,** the medieval poets who wrote in the *langue d'oïl* of N. France (*v. French Language*), especially those who composed courtly *lyric poetry* (influenced by, but by no means wholly derived from, that of the *troubadours*). The *trouvère* might also be a *jongleur* and recite his own works, e.g. Rutebeuf; but

he was equally likely to be a person of good birth or high position, e.g. Conon de Béthune, Thibaud de Champagne.

Troyat, Henri, *pseudonym of* LEV TARASSOV (1911–), a widely read novelist of Russian birth, resident in France since childhood and naturalized French; a member of the *Académie* (1959). His many works, which reflect his admiration for Dostoievsky, Tolstoy, Zola, and Balzac, include novels, e.g. *Faux Jour* (1935), *L'Araigne* (1938), *Le Mort saisit le vif* (1942), *La Pierre, la feuille et les ciseaux* (1972); four *romans-cycles*— *Tant que la terre durera* (1947–50, 3 vols.), *Les Semailles et les moissons* (1953–8, 5 vols.), *La Lumière des justes* (1959–63, 5 vols.), and *Les Héritiers de l'avenir* (1968–70, 3 vols.)—forming a vast fresco of family life and political upheavals in Russia from the mid-19th c. to the Revolution of 1917 and thereafter; another *roman-cycle, Les Eygletière* (1965–7, 3 vols.), about a great French family; tales, e.g. *La Fosse commune* (1939), *Le Geste d'Ève* (1964), *Les Ailes du diable* (1966); biographical studies of Russian authors; plays.

Trubert et d'Antroignart, Farce de Maître, v. Deschamps, Eustache.

Tuileries, La Comédie des, v. Cinq auteurs, Les.

Tuileries, Palais des, a royal residence in Paris (adjoining the *Louvre*, on the site of an old tile-factory—whence its name). Its construction was begun by Catherine de Médicis (1564; *v. Delorme, P.; Bullant*). It was the scene of important events during the Revolution, when its seizure by the mob marked the fall of the monarchy; *v. Revolutions*, 1 (5 Oct. 1789; 10 Aug. 1792). Napoleon I lived in it, also Louis XVIII, Charles X, and Napoleon III. It was burnt down during the *Commune* of 1871, and the Place du Carrousel and Jardin des Tuileries were eventually enlarged to cover the site.

Turcaret, a prose comedy by Lesage;

produced 1709 with great success. It is a vigorous satire on contemporary society (esp. the financiers and *fermiers généraux*, who tried to prevent its performance) and reflects Lesage's hatred of the types, and the general dishonesty, here depicted.

Turcaret is a heartless, unscrupulous tax-farmer and usurer, a *parvenu* who has risen from menial service and deserted his wife. But astute as he is over money, he is easily duped by the Baronne, a gay widow he is courting, herself the dupe of the Chevalier, her pretended lover. The designs of the various parties are interrupted by the exposure of Turcaret (following the arrival of his wife and sister) and his arrest. Meanwhile, the Baronne and the Chevalier are themselves cheated by their own servants, rascals of lower degree.

Turenne, HENRI DE LA TOUR D'AUVERGNE, VICOMTE DE (1611–75), *maréchal de France*, grandson of William the Silent, a great captain in the wars of Louis XIV. His campaigns (1645–8) in Germany made possible the Peace of Westphalia. During the *Fronde*, though at first hostile to Mazarin, he later rallied to the court, fought Condé, and helped the king to recover Paris. His victory of the Dunes (1658) over the Spaniards and their ally Condé paved the way for the Treaty of the *Pyrenees*. He also commanded French armies in the wars of 1667 and 1672, and was finally killed in battle. He left military memoirs, and is credited with the saying 'Dieu est toujours pour les gros bataillons'.

Turgot, ANNE-ROBERT-JACQUES (1727–81), a famous economist and administrator, entered the magistrature and served (1761–74) as *intendant* of the *généralité* (*v. Fiscal System*) of Limoges, one of the poorest, most backward areas of France, where he strove to improve the lot of the humbler classes. He was then made controller-general of finance and during his brief tenure of office (till 1776) sought to introduce reforms inspired by the doctrines of the *économistes*: free importation and free circulation at home

of corn; suppression of the *jurandes* and *maîtrises* (the corporations of craftsmen which restricted the liberty of industry); the removal of various fiscal abuses. These proposals, which he pressed uncompromisingly and injudiciously, provoked much hostility and led to his fall. His works include *Réflexions sur la formation et la distribution des richesses* (1766), showing him in close sympathy with the *économistes*; many treatises, pamphlets, and articles (inc. transs. of the idylls of Gessner); and *v. Encyclopédie*. He associated with the *philosophes*—d'Alembert, Condorcet (a faithful friend who wrote his life), Helvétius, Voltaire (who respected him), Mlle de Lespinasse—but rejected with austere probity such of their doctrines as did not commend themselves to his reason. He also knew Adam Smith, and their general economic views were in harmony.

Turlupin, *v. Gros-Guillaume*.

Turnèbe, (1) ADRIEN, in Latin TURNEBUS (1512–65), a learned humanist, reader in Greek at the future *Collège de France* and director of the royal press (where he printed Homer; *v. Imprimerie nationale*); (2) his son ODET DE (1553–81), humanist, dramatist, and advocate, author of one of the best of the early comedies, *Les Contents* (1584; written *c.* 1580; in prose). It is about two rivals for the hand of a girl, one favoured by the girl, the other by her mother. The former—aided by a go-between of the type of the old bawd in *Celestina*—attains his object by disguising himself in a crimson cloak belonging to the latter.

Turoldus, *v. Chanson de Roland*.

Turpin (d. *c.* 800), archbishop of Rheims, was wrongly credited with a Latin chronicle *De vita et gestis Caroli magni* (the *Pseudo-Turpin*), a work of much later date purporting to recount Charlemagne's exploits in Spain. Turpin's legendary death with Roland at Roncevaux is related in the *Chanson de Roland*.

Tyard or **Thyard**, PONTUS DE (1521–1605), poet and philosopher, a member of the *Pléiade*, later bishop of Chalon-sur-Saône. When young he wrote the sonnet-sequence *Erreurs amoureuses* (1549, 1554, and 1555), an early example of the use of the *sonnet-form in France. Later, he wrote prose *Dialogues philosophiques* of a Platonic cast, also astronomical and other serious works.

Tyr et Sidon (1608), a tragedy by Schelandre; probably never acted. It bears some resemblance to Shakespeare's *Romeo and Juliet*, which Schelandre may have read (though he did not visit England till after his play was written).

Tyre and Sidon are at war, and the sons of their kings have each been captured by the enemy. Belcar, son of the king of Sidon, and Meliane, daughter of the king of Tyre, have fallen in love. Eurydice, nurse of Meliane's elder sister Cassandre, favours the affair, but then discovers that Cassandre, too, loves Belcar and resolves to help her instead. The son of the king of Tyre, a captive in Sidon, is now discovered in adultery and killed. His father, in revenge, condemns Belcar to death. Belcar, by the design of Eurydice, escapes on a ship, accompanied, not as he thinks by Meliane, but by Cassandre. On discovering the trick, he quits the ship in a fury, while Cassandre stabs herself and falls into the sea. Her body is washed ashore and found by Meliane, who is seen by her father drawing the dagger from the wound. Suspected of killing Cassandre and believing herself deserted by Belcar, Meliane maintains an obstinate silence and is executed. Eurydice now discloses the truth, and the king, crazed with grief, brings death upon himself.

Schelandre remodelled this work as a *tragicomedy (1628), which ends happily, with the discovery of Meliane's innocence and the return of Belcar. It has a preface by François Ogier, a learned cleric, defending the irregular drama, as preferable to servile imitation of the ancients, and its mixture of tragic and comic elements, as resembling real life.

Tzara, TRISTAN (1896–1963), a poet of Rumanian birth who came to Paris in 1920, is best known as a founder and dedicated exponent of *Dadaism, e.g. *La Première Aventure céleste de M. Antipyrine* (1916), *Vingt-cinq Poèmes* (1918), *Sept Manifestes dada* (1924), and for *L'Homme approximatif* (1931), a work of his *Surrealist phase (1929–34).

U

Ubu Roi, *v. Jarry.*

Ulm, Rue d', the name of the street in Paris where the *École normale supérieure* is situated; often used to designate the institution itself.

Ultramontanism, *v. Gallicanism.*

Ultras, Les, the ultra-Royalist and Catholic party after the Restoration of 1815. *v. Charles X*; *Polignac*; *Bonald*; *Maistre, J. de*; *Congrégation*; *Théocrates.*

Unanimisme, unanimiste, a literary movement, chiefly in poetry, developed *c.* 1908–11 by Romains (with the poems of *La Vie unanime*, 1908) and other young writers, e.g. Arcos, Chennevière, Duhamel, Durtain, Jouve, Vildrac, most of whom had their association with the *Abbaye* group, as well as other interests, in common. It owed much to the Whitmanesque doctrine of universal brotherhood, also to more recent psycho-philosophical theories of group emotion; Romains himself stressed the influence on him of Hugo and a deeply religious upbringing. The *unanimistes* held that collective sentiment cannot be focused in one representative type; the poet's task is rather to emphasize the *dispersive* element of man's soul, to show how the personality of the individual becomes merged in a greater soul, that of the group—the church, factory, city, etc. ('Je cesse d'exister tellement je suis tout'; 'Nous cessons d'être nous pour que la ville dise "Moi"'). They had their own technique of versification, expounded in *Notes sur la technique poétique* (1910) by Duhamel and Vildrac, and in the *Petit Traité de versification* (1923) by Romains and Chennevière. Symbols, allegory, and all unnecessary adornments were avoided, end-rhymes and even assonance were banished, and the rhythm was variable and strongly accented, suitable to the expression of 'la poésie immédiate'.

Un Caprice (1837, in the *Revue des Deux Mondes*; 1840, in *Comédies et Proverbes*), by Musset, a slight, sentimental comedy (one act, prose) about a husband inclined to stray, a timid, adoring wife, and a friend who saves the situation. It was produced at the *Comédie-Française* in 1847 with great success, having earlier been produced in translation in Russia.

Un Chapeau de paille d'Italie (1851), a farcical comedy by Labiche. Fadinard sets out in his pony carriage, across the Bois de Vincennes, to his wedding. He drops his whip and, when he stops to retrieve it, his pony chews a bunch of straw and poppies. This proves to have been a Leghorn hat, a present from her husband to its owner, who has been flirting in a nearby thicket with a soldier. There are lamentations, and Fadinard, anxious to make good the loss, drives hastily back to Paris to buy a similar hat. He finds himself involved in several intrigues which all turn on a Leghorn hat trimmed with poppies, and chases from place to place, followed by an ever-lengthening stream of interested or irate parties, including his own wedding guests. He at last finds an identical hat and all ends well.

Un Cœur simple, v. *Trois Contes*.

Un Coup de dés, v. *Mallarmé*.

Un Début dans la vie, v. *Comédie humaine, La* (*Scènes de la vie privée*).

Un Dîner d'athées, v. *Diaboliques, Les*.

Un Drame au bord de la mer, v. *Comédie humaine, La* (*Études philosophiques*).

Une Belle Journée (1881), a *Naturalist novel by Céard. A very ordinary married woman goes out for the day with her would-be lover, fully expecting to allow him to seduce her. Over lunch he warms into a talkative vulgarity that leads her to change her mind. Meanwhile, a drenching rain has set in, and the pair are marooned in a shabby restaurant, increasingly bored with each other and with nothing to do but read old papers and exchange banal remarks (all of which are recorded for the reader). It is very late before they can find a cabman willing to drive them home through the rain. The woman reflects that the boredom of marriage is preferable to the boredom of adultery.

Une Double Famille; *Une Fille d'Ève*, v. *Comédie humaine, La* (*Scènes de la vie privée*).

Une Histoire sans nom, v. *Barbey d'Aurevilly*.

Une Page d'amour, v. *Rougon-Macquart, Les*.

Une Passion dans le désert, v. *Comédie humaine, La* (*Scènes de la vie militaire*).

Un Épisode sous la Terreur, v. *Comédie humaine, La* (*Scènes de la vie politique*).

Une Saison en enfer, v. *Rimbaud*.

Une Ténébreuse Affaire (1841; later in *La *Comédie humaine, Scènes de la vie politique*), a novel by Balzac. The highly complicated plot turns on Royalist conspiracies engineered by the Simeuse family, whose former *château* is now owned by the upstart Malin, a figure in the Napoleonic Empire. They are aided by the gamekeeper Michu, outwardly a ferocious

Republican, but at heart devotedly loyal to his old masters. The activities of the police agents Corentin and Peyrade (an astute, unlovable pair who appear elsewhere in Balzac, e.g. as the deadly enemies of *Vautrin) provide the chief interest and make the book in many ways a precursor of modern detective fiction.

Une Vie, v. *Maupassant*.

Une Vieille Maîtresse (1851), by Barbey d'Aurevilly, a novel set mainly in an isolated manor on the wild Cotentin coast, partly also in an elegant Paris drawing-room (*c.* 1830). M. de Marigny marries a girl whom, for all his Byronic past, he truly loves. The pair are blissfully happy until his former mistress, Mme Vellini, re-appears and he finds that, struggle as he may, she is in his blood and he is powerless to resist her. D'Aurevilly writes with typical extravagance, but is continually saved from bathos by his descriptive and evocative force.

Un Homme d'affaires, v. *Comédie humaine, La* (*Scènes de la vie parisienne*).

Unigenitus Dei Filius, v. *Port-Royal*.

Unities, The, v. *Tragedy*.

Univers religieux, philosophique, politique, scientifique et littéraire, L' (1833–60; 1867–1914), a Roman Catholic daily paper, ed. from 1843 by Veuillot and noted for his militant articles. It was twice suppressed by imperial decree.

Université de France, the term long applied to the uniform system of State education (primary; secondary—the *lycées; and higher—the *universities, *écoles spéciales*, etc.), the teachers in its employ, and the officials responsible for its administration. The system derives largely from Napoleon's *Université impériale*, with many later modifications (notably laws of 1881–6, making primary education free, compulsory, and lay; a law of 1885 suppressing the faculties of theology; a law of 1896 which went far to reunite the

separate Napoleonic faculties into single, more autonomous universities). For purposes of educational administration France has been divided since the early 19th c. into regions or *académies*. There were long 16 *académies* (17 inc. Algeria), in each of which higher education was provided by a State university. Each had at its head a *recteur*, who was also *recteur* of the university; he was directly responsible to the *Ministre de l'Éducation nationale* (formerly *de l'Instruction publique*). By 1968, following the creation of three new *académies* in 1961, there were 19 *académies* comprising 21 universities. The growing demand for a reform of higher education (reflected in the student rising of May 1968) was met by the *loi d'orientation* of November 1968, which created many new universities and radically reorganized the whole system. There are now 23 *académies*, still headed by *recteurs* (Paris, Aix-en-Provence, Amiens, Besançon, Bordeaux, Caen, Clermont-Ferrand, Dijon, Grenoble, Lille, Limoges, Lyon, Montpellier, Nancy, Nantes, Nice, Orléans, Poitiers, Reims, Rennes, Rouen, Strasbourg, Toulouse), comprising some 65 university institutions. The universities enjoy greater administrative and financial autonomy than ever before, and both teachers and students have a much larger share in government. Moreover, in a bid to achieve the closest possible association of 'les arts et les lettres aux sciences et aux techniques', the old faculties have been abolished and each university is in principle *pluridisciplinaire*, being basically composed of a number of self-governing *unités d'enseignement et de recherche* (*U.E.R.*). v. also *Centre national de la Recherche scientifique*.

Université impériale, the official hierarchy set up in 1808 by Napoleon to administer and apply a State system of secondary and higher education. The first *grand maître de l'Université*, the highest-ranking official, was Fontanes. The *universities, now broken up into the five faculties of arts, science, law, theology, and medicine, lost their autonomy and much of their corporate spirit. *v. Université de France.*

Universities

1. UNIVERSITY OF PARIS. This had its origins in the Cathedral School of Paris and similar schools attached to the abbeys of *Sainte-Geneviève and *Saint-Victor. Such teachers as the Realist philosopher Guillaume de Champeaux (1070–1121; *v. Saint-Victor*), the first important master of the Cathedral School, and his great pupil and adversary Abélard drew many students to Paris. A *studium generale* (a school of general resort for students from all over Europe) gradually developed, and a Society of Masters was formed (probably *c.* 1170). Early in the 13th c. the University had its first written statutes, being accorded the rights and privileges of an ecclesiastical corporation (inc. the exclusive right to confer degrees). It was at first under the jurisdiction of the bishop and his chancellor; but after the organization of the students of the faculty of arts in four 'nations'—French, Normans, Picards, and English (inc. Germans and students from N. and E. Europe)—and the institution of a rector elected by the united 'nations' (mid-13th c.), the rector gradually became head, not only of the faculty of arts, but of the whole University.

From the early 13th c. the University included masters of three faculties—theology, law, and arts; medicine, though taught, was not yet recognized as a separate faculty. From the first pre-eminent as a centre for the study of theology (*v. Pierre le Lombard*), it now (13th c.) became important as a philosophical school. An affray in which students were killed by the royal police led the University to disperse itself (1229) in protest against this infringement of its privileges; the move succeeded and its privileges were confirmed. Masters and scholars returned (1231) and the University was now placed directly under papal jurisdiction (by the bull *Parens scientiarum*). An acute conflict soon arose between the mendicant friars, who claimed the right to teach in the faculty of theology, and the secular clergy, led by Guillaume de Saint-Amour (*v.* also *Thomas Aquinas*). The University expelled the friars (1253), who appealed to the pope. By a papal decision of 1256 the secular cause was technically defeated, but the participation of the friars in University affairs was also rigorously restricted. This struggle consolidated the organization of the University and helped to sow the seeds of *Gallicanism there. Relations between the University and the friars remained strained till the 15th c.

Before the 14th c. the University and its constituent bodies owned no buildings, but used churches, convents, etc.; at one time their only property was the *Pré-aux-Clercs. Teachers, who appear to have hired their own schoolrooms until the 14th c., were supported by benefices, religious orders, or fees from students—though, in principle, instruction was free. The arts schoolrooms were in or near the Rue du Fouarre (so named from the straw on which the students sat). The colleges were in origin endowed hostels, the first founders seeking merely to provide board and lodging for poor scholars (bursars); but the heads of colleges took a gradually increasing part in education. In time all students, and not only bursars, came to live in colleges, of which some 60 were founded before 1500, beginning with the *Collège des Dix-huit* (f. 1180 by a Londoner for the support of 18 students). They included, notably, the *Collège de *Sorbonne, Collège d'Harcourt* (f. 1280 by Raoul d'Harcourt, a member of a great Norman family, cleric, and counsellor of Philippe IV), *Collège de Navarre, *Collège de Montaigu, *Collège de Boncourt, *Collège de Coqueret*; also the *Collège de Beauvais* (for law students), *Collège Lemoine, *Collège Sainte-Barbe, etc.

In the 14th c. the University became increasingly subject to royal authority; it also became an organ of public opinion. It supported the monarchy against the papacy, playing an important part at the Council of Constance (1414; *v. Gerson*). But with the growth of its political influence, its intellectual and spiritual leadership declined; also, as its wealth increased and it acquired buildings and a library, its lay character became more marked. The conservatism of the University, above all of the *Sorbonne*, was out of harmony with the spirit of the *Renaissance*, though some colleges supported humanism (a memorable outcome of this movement was the foundation by François Ier of the future *Collège de France*, at first as part of the University, but soon distinct from it). Despite Henri IV's attempt to reorganize it (1598), the University entered a period of decline in the 17th c. and many colleges disappeared—though Richelieu enriched the *Sorbonne* and Mazarin founded the *Collège des Quatre-Nations*. During the 17th and 18th cs. the faculty of theology, conservative as ever, became increasingly dominant and the University was closely involved in religious and political controversies, and in general implacably opposed to new movements of philosophical thought (hostile alike to Descartes and to Gassendi, to the ideas of Bacon, Newton, and Locke, to the *philosophes* and the *Encyclopédistes*). Its educational force was thus dissipated, and indiscipline and venality were prevalent. Leadership in the academic field shifted elsewhere, e.g. to the *Académie française* and the *Académie des Inscriptions*, to the *Jansenists and the *Maurists, and to the new colleges founded by the *Jesuits and other Orders. The need for a general reform of education was already widely felt on the eve of the Revolution, and when it came the old system was swept away. The colleges lost their revenues and their property was nationalized (some later became *lycées*; v. *Lycées and Collèges*; *Collège Sainte-Barbe*). The University was suppressed in 1793. Following the creation of the *Université impériale* (1808), the buildings of the *Sorbonne* became the headquarters of the new *Académie de Paris* and the seat of the faculties of theology (suppressed 1885), arts, and science of the reorganized University of Paris.

There were few major changes until recent times. Mounting dissatisfaction with the state of higher education, especially with the overcrowded condition

of the University of Paris, was an immediate cause of the serious rising of May–June 1968, when the students of Paris, led by a group from Nanterre, seized and occupied the *Sorbonne* and many other academic or public buildings. Reform came with the *loi d'orientation* of November 1968 (v. *Université de France*). This created 13 separate Universities of Paris, called *Université Paris I, II, III*, etc. The first seven are in the old university quarter of central Paris (the name 'Sorbonne' survives in the titles *Panthéon-Sorbonne, Sorbonne Nouvelle*, and *Paris-Sorbonne* for *Paris I, III*, and *IV* respectively); the rest are on the outskirts, e.g. *Paris VIII* or *Paris-Vincennes, Paris IX* or *Paris-Dauphine, Paris X* or *Paris-Nanterre*. v. *Bibliothèque universitaire*.

2. PROVINCIAL UNIVERSITIES. On the eve of the Revolution of 1789 there were as many as 21 universities in provincial towns: Toulouse (f. 1229; the oldest), Montpellier (f. 1289; famous for its medical school—v. *Rabelais*), Orleans (f. 1305; famous for its law school), Angers, Perpignan, Aix, Avignon, Orange, Valence, Bourges (v. *Amyot*), Poitiers, Bordeaux (v. *Buchanan*), Besançon, Caen, Nantes, Strasbourg, Douai, Pau, Rheims, Dijon, Nancy. For the modern period v. *Université de France*.

University of Paris, v. *Universities*, 1.

Un Jardin sur l'Oronte, v. *Barrès*.

Un Prêtre marié, v. *Barbey d'Aurevilly*.

Un Prince de la Bohème, v. *Comédie humaine, La* (*Scènes de la vie parisienne*).

Un Spectacle dans un fauteuil (1833 and 1834), by Musset, two series of dramatic works, so called because, when his one-act prose comedy *La Nuit vénitienne, ou les Noces de Laurette* failed on production in 1830, he resolved to write only plays that could be read comfortably in an armchair by the fireside. The first series contained *La Coupe et les lèvres* (his first *proverbe*), *A quoi rêvent les jeunes filles*, and the

Oriental poem *Namouna*—all later in *Premières Poésies*. The second series (2 vols.) contained *Lorenzaccio, Les *Caprices de Marianne, André del Sarto (a 3-act historical drama, produced 1848), *Fantasio, *On ne badine pas avec l'amour, and La Nuit vénitienne—all later in *Comédies et Proverbes.

Un Voyage à Cythère, v. Baudelaire.

Uranie, (1) v. *Voiture* and *Benserade*; (2) the name by which Mme du Châtelet is addressed in two verse epistles by Voltaire.

Urbain le courtois or *Le Ditié d'Urbain*, a collection of precepts of good conduct in *Anglo-Norman verse.

Urfé, HONORÉ D' (1567–1625), novelist, came of an old family of the Forez (Lyonnais), the setting of his vast prose romance L'*Astrée (1607–27; concluded, 1628, by Baro). He also wrote *pastoral plays (*Sireine*; *Sylvanire*, 1627, written for Marie de Médicis) and *Épîtres morales*. In youth an ardent supporter of the *Ligue, he retired after its defeat to the territories of his kinsman the duke of Savoy and died in the course of hostilities between Savoy and Genoa.

Ursins, v. *Des Ursins*.

Ursule Mirouët (1841; later in *La *Comédie humaine, Scènes de la vie de province*), a novel by Balzac. Ursule, a beautiful, gifted orphan, has been brought up at Nemours by her adoring uncle, Dr. Minoret, aided by his friends the curé and a local magistrate. Minoret's many, and detested, relations at Nemours, most of them town worthies, suspect her of scheming to displace them in his will. By careful management he has, in fact, amassed enough wealth to leave her a sizable fortune without touching the money legitimately due to his other relations. On his death-bed he tells her of a letter which will guide her to this fortune, but he is overheard by a cousin, who steals the letter. Ursule, almost penniless, lives on in Nemours, worshipped by Minoret's old friends and loved by Savinien, the young comte de Portenduère, whose bigoted old mother has refused to allow him to marry a humble orphan—despite the fact that Minoret once helped to save the Portenduère family from ruin. A happy ending is achieved by recourse to the supernatural. Minoret appears to Ursule in dreams and explains exactly how her cousin stole the letter. Pressure is then brought to bear on the thief, who confesses, restores Ursule's fortune, and mends his ways. Ursule and Savinien marry and live happily in Paris.

Usbek, v. *Lettres persanes*.

Utrillo, MAURICE (1883–1955), an artist famous for his paintings of Paris streets, especially those of *Montmartre. v. *Valadon*.

V

Vacances d'un jeune homme sage, Les, v. Régnier, H. de.

Vache à Colas, La, a nickname for the *Huguenots. A poor man's cow was said to have strayed into a Protestant church during a service. The enraged congregation killed it, then made a collection to compensate the owner. A popular song ridiculing the episode was sung in the streets to annoy the Huguenots until this was declared an offence (1605).

Vacherot, ÉTIENNE (1809–97), professor of modern philosophy at the *Sorbonne and long director of the *École normale supérieure, sought to combine a positivist with a metaphysical conception of the universe and had considerable influence at a time when positivism was giving way to a more idealist philosophy. His chief work was *La Métaphysique et la science* (1858, 3 vols.).

Vacquerie, AUGUSTE (1819–95), author of poetry, comedies, essays, and criticism, was much influenced by Hugo, whose daughter Léopoldine married his brother.

Vadé, Guillaume, Antoine, and **Catherine,** pseudonyms of Voltaire. Antoine and Guillaume are brothers. Catherine, their cousin, supplies an introduction to the *Contes de Guillaume Vadé* (1764), which includes a *Discours aux Welches* (*v. Velche*) attributed to Antoine.

Vadé, JEAN-JOSEPH (1720–57), author of comic poems, parodies, and light comedies (*comédies en* *vaudevilles), in many of which he used the *poissard* dialect of the Paris markets. His *La Fileuse* (1752), a parody of the opera *Omphale* (of the same year), was a great success; his burlesque poem *La Pipe cassée* was also admired. Beaumarchais drew on his *Le Trompeur trompé* for *Le* *Mariage de Figaro.

Vadius, in Molière's *Les* *Femmes savantes.

Vailland, ROGER (1907–65), novelist. He began as a journalist and made his name with his first novel, *Drôle de jeu* (1945), an ironical story of the *Resistance, in which he had been actively involved. Widely known for his experiences with drugs, alcohol, and women, he was always a social non-conformist, attracted both by the aristocratic ideal and by Marxist revolutionary ideology. He was a member of the Communist Party from 1952 until 1956. All his novels are firmly rooted in an historical context and many have a strong autobiographical element. They include *Les Mauvais Coups* (1948), *Un Jeune Homme seul* (1951), *325,000 Francs* (1955), *La Loi* (1957; awarded the *Prix Goncourt*), *La Fête* (1960), *La Truite* (1964). He also wrote plays and essays (e.g. *Laclos par lui-même*, 1953, on a writer with whom he had

some affinity). His *Écrits intimes* appeared in 1968.

Vair Palefroi, Le, a 13th-c. verse tale by Huon le Roi. A young knight, valorous but poor, falls in love with the daughter of a rich lord, who refuses him her hand. On the lady's advice, the knight seeks help from his wealthy uncle, who promises it, then treacherously obtains the lady for himself, to her despair. The knight has a fine grey (*vair*) palfrey, which the father borrows to carry his daughter to the wedding. As they ride through the forest in the early morning, the palfrey turns off along the familiar track to the castle of the knight, who promptly calls a priest and marries the lady.

Valade, LÉON (1841–84), minor *Parnassien poet (e.g. *A mi-côte*, 1874; *L'Affaire Arlequin*, 1882, in *triolet-form). He collaborated with Mérat.

Valadon, MARIA-CLÉMENTINE, *known as* SUZANNE (1867–1938), mother and first teacher (in an effort to counteract his alcoholism) of the painter Utrillo, and herself an artist of standing. She had earlier been a dressmaker, circus acrobat, and artist's model.

Val-de-Grâce, Le, on the left bank of the Seine in Paris, so called after a Benedictine convent moved to the site (1621) by Anne d'Autriche. She added a church (1645–65) in thanksgiving for the birth of her son (Louis XIV). The cupola (*v. Mignard*) is a famous Paris landmark. The convent became a military hospital under Napoleon, and has so remained, with the addition (1916) of an Army Medical Services museum.

Valentine, v. Sand.

Valentinois, DUCHESSE DE, *v. Diane de Poitiers.*

Valère, in Molière's *L'***École des maris.*

Valérien, Mont, a hill to the west of Paris, the highest in the vicinity of the city.

Before the Revolution it was a place of pilgrimage. A fort built on it after 1830, as part of the defences of Paris, has served on occasion as a prison for State offenders.

Valéry, PAUL-AMBROISE (1871–1945), poet, critic, and essayist, b. at Sète (formerly Cette), a small port near Montpellier. His father was French, his mother Italian. He studied law at the University of Montpellier, then went to Paris (1892), where he already knew Gide and Louÿs. In his first years there he was strongly influenced by *Symbolism, notably by Mallarmé (a lasting influence; v. Lyric Poetry, 4). He published poems in the smaller reviews (e.g. La *Conque), but soon turned from poetry to write two short prose works, the Introduction à la méthode de Léonard de Vinci (1895, in La *Nouvelle Revue) and La Soirée avec Monsieur *Teste (1896). He then gave up creative writing and for some 15 years—in the leisure left him by his career at the War Office (1897–1900) and then (till 1922) in the secretariat of the Havas News Agency—engaged in abstract speculation and study. In 1913 he was persuaded to collect some of his early poems for publication (Album de vers anciens, 1890–1900, 1920). Rehandling them led him to write, partly as an exercise, what he intended as a closing poem for the volume. This alone took him four years and was in the end published separately as La Jeune Parque (1917). There followed Charmes (1922), poems written in the years 1913–22 and including the famous *Cimetière marin, the Fragments du Narcisse, and the odes La Pythie and Ébauche d'un serpent. These poems so effectively made his name that after 1923 he was able to live by his pen. He wrote little more poetry. His prose works included two fine dialogues in Socratic form, L'Âme et la danse and Eupalinos, ou l'Architecte (1923; on dancing as the supreme expression of movement and architecture as the supreme expression of repose); Variété (1924–44, 5 vols.), collections of critical essays and prefaces, or of jottings and aphorisms, on literature, philosophy, politics, education, etc.—the work of a gifted critic (v. Critics and Criticism, 3); *Rhumbs (1926); L'Idée fixe (1932); Regards sur le monde actuel (1933); Pièces sur l'art (1934); Mélanges (1941); Tel Quel (1941–3). He also left an unfinished comedy, Mon Faust (1946). For the last 20 years of his life he was a highly revered poet and man of letters, a member of the *Académie from 1925 and professor of poetry (a chair created for him) at the *Collège de France from 1937.

During his years of silence he came to grips with the philosophical and metaphysical problems he had first tackled in his two early prose works—problems of the nature of genius and the creative process (which led to an interest in linguistics); of the conflicting claims, for the creative artist, of emotion and intellect; of the universe, man, and man's activities, in terms of Being and Not-being. (The idea of Being made possible by Not-being permeates his work. Monsieur Teste, the incarnation of the universal brain, existed in a realm of abstract, sterile contemplation of his own potentialities: to condescend to translate any of them into action would have been to mar his perfection.) Such problems were the stuff of his later writings, both his brilliant, graceful, aphoristic prose and his poetry. His poetry is usually obscure; not, like Mallarmé's, because it seems to be trying to express the inexpressible, but because it is quintessential. The matter of abstract speculation has been seized and worked upon at white heat by the poet's sensuous faculties of emotion, imagery, and fantasy, then condensed into the mould of classical form. (His adherence to form was rigid; and within the traditional, often Racinian, form he made a subtle, intensely musical use of inner assonance and alliteration.) His Cahiers (1957–60, 29 vols.), the notebooks in which, from 1894 until his death, he daily recorded reflections on poetry, language, philosophy, memory and the central problem of consciousness, religion, politics, mathematics, physics, etc., contain the raw material of his ideas and reflect the wide range of his intellectual interests.

Valincour, JEAN-HENRI DU TROUSSET, SIEUR DE (1653–1730), man of letters, friend of Boileau and Racine, *Jansenist, historiographer royal, and member of the *Académie.

Valjean, Jean, in Hugo's Les *Misérables.

Vallée-aux-Loups, La, v. Chateaubriand.

Valleran Le Conte, v. Theatres and Theatre Companies.

Vallès, JULES (1833–85), journalist and novelist, son of a provincial schoolmaster of peasant stock, was sent to Paris to try for the *École normale supérieure (1848) and was soon involved in revolutionary activities. After a spell in prison (1853), he tried to earn money by journalism. His sketches of seamy Bohemianism and street life (Les Réfractaires, 1865, v. Réfractaires; La Rue, 1866) first appeared in Le *Figaro, L'*Événement, etc. He was exiled for his part in the *Commune of 1871 and spent several years in England. He returned (1880) to Paris and left-wing journalism (in Le Cri du peuple; v. Press, 9) and finished his remarkable autobiographical trilogy Jacques Vingtras (L'Enfant, 1879; Le Bachelier, 1881; L'Insurgé, 1886, inc. a fine description of the Commune). This work, dedicated 'A tous ceux qui nourris de grec et de latin sont morts de faim', is written with searing resentment and exceptional vividness of sensation and recollection.

Valmont, Guy de, v. Maupassant.

Valmont, Vicomte de, in *Laclos's Les Liaisons dangereuses.

Valmont de Bomare, JACQUES-CHRISTOPHE, v. Dictionaries, 1764.

Valmy, a village in the Argonne where, on 20 September 1792, the French under Dumouriez and Kellermann halted the Prussian advance. This was the first great victory of the Revolutionary armies; according to Goethe, who was present, it opened a new epoch in world history.

Valois, a royal family, a branch of the *Capetians (and v. Orléans). The first Valois king was Philippe VI (son of Charles de Valois, a brother of Philippe IV), who ascended the throne in 1328, when Charles IV died, leaving only a daughter, and an assembly of nobles decided that a woman could not reign (v. Salic Law). The Valois line ended with the death of Henri III (1589) and was followed by the *Bourbon line.

Valvins, v. Mallarmé.

Vandenesse, Félix de, in Le *Lys dans la vallée and other novels of Balzac's *Comédie humaine.

Van Gogh, VINCENT (1853–90), a leading Post-*Impressionist painter. He was Dutch, but lived mainly, and died (by his own hand), in France. His work, notable for its colour and rhythm, includes many landscapes of Provence.

Vanini, LUCILIO (1585–1619), an Italian philosopher and free-thinker, self-styled 'Giulio Cesare', who settled in Toulouse. His De admirandis naturae (1616; trans. into French as Dialogues), an ironical, anti-religious work, influenced the *libertins. He was accused of practising black magic and burnt at the stake.

Van Lerberghe, CHARLES (1861–1907), Belgian *Symbolist (cf. Maeterlinck; Verhaeren), author of Les Flaireurs (1890), a short prose drama; and the poems of Entrevisions (1898) and La Chanson d'Ève (1904).

Varennes, v. Revolutions, 1 (1791).

Variété, v. Valéry.

Varlet, THÉO (1878–1938), poet, novelist, and translator (e.g. of R. L. Stevenson and Kipling). His poetry — the best of it inspired by a love of the Mediterranean region—is collected in Aux libres jardins

(1923), *Le Démon dans l'âme* (1924), *Paralipomena* (1926), *Ad astra et autres poèmes* (1930), etc.

Vase brisé, Le, v. Sully-Prudhomme.

Vase étrusque, Le (1830, in the **Revue de Paris*; 1833, in *Mosaïque*), a tale by Mérimée. A lover suspects his mistress of infidelity and discovers his mistake too late: he is committed to fight a duel and cannot in honour withdraw. He is killed, and his heartbroken mistress does not long survive him.

Vatel, FRANÇOIS (d. 1671), steward to N. Fouquet, then to 'le Grand Condé'. Mme de Sévigné relates how, fearing the fish would not arrive in time for a Friday's repast given at **Chantilly to Louis XIV, he committed suicide.

Vathek (Paris and Lausanne 1787; preceded by an Eng. trans., London 1786), an Oriental tale by William Beckford (1759–1844), written first in French. Mallarmé discovered the French edition in the **Bibliothèque nationale* and had it reprinted (1876), adding an appreciative preface.

Vauban, SÉBASTIEN LE PRESTRE, SEIGNEUR DE (1633–1707), **maréchal de France*, a great military engineer who directed 53 sieges and fortified France's frontiers. His *Projet d'une dîme royale* (1707), advocating a single tax (the *dîme royale*, a form of combined poll-tax and income-tax) as fairer than the existing tax system, greatly annoyed the king and was suppressed.

Vaucluse. The Fontaine de Vaucluse immortalized by Petrarch was a spring about 16 miles from Avignon, the source of the Sorgue, a small tributary of the Rhône. It gave its name to a **département* which in 1793 replaced the former papal enclave made up of the Comtat d'*Avignon and the Comtat Venaissin (capital Carpentras; territory ceded to the papacy in 1229 by the comte de Toulouse).

Vaudeville, a term (from *vaudevire*; v. *Basselin*) applied in the late 17th and 18th cs. to the series of verses, sung to well-known airs, increasingly introduced into the light comedies of the *Théâtre de la Foire*. The *comédie en vaudevilles* gave rise to both the **opéra-comique* and the *vaudeville*, where the emphasis was on spoken dialogue (prose and rhymed couplets) rather than on music. By the end of the 18th c., and as developed with immense success by Scribe, Désaugiers, J.-H. Dupin, Ancelot, and many others from the early 19th c., a *vaudeville* was a gay comedy of manners (usually one act, at most two), at once topical and farcical (e.g. Scribe's *Une Nuit de la Garde nationale*, 1815), and interspersed with songs. Such *vaudevilles* were often played at the *Théâtre du Vaudeville* (f. 1792) or the *Théâtre des Variétés* (f. 1790). This type of *vaudeville* declined after the mid-19th c. and the term came to be applied to the musical comedies of the variety stage. The old spirit survives in works by G. Feydeau, T. Bernard, S. Guitry, etc.

Vaudois (Waldenses), members of a religious sect which originated in S. France c. 1170 through the preaching of Pierre Waldo (Valdus), a merchant of Lyons, who gave all his money to the poor and turned missionary. They rejected the authority of the pope and various Roman rites and doctrines, and were excommunicated and persecuted (with the **Albigeois*). They survived and eventually became a separately organized church, which associated itself with the Protestant Reformation and still exists. Their persecution by the house of Savoy (1655) inspired Milton's sonnet *Avenge, O Lord, thy slaughtered saints*.

Vaugelas, CLAUDE FAVRE, SIEUR DE (1585–1650), grammarian, a member of the original **Académie française* and, until his death, its most influential authority in matters of language. His *Remarques sur la langue française* (1647) is a collection of decisions on particular questions, with a preface explaining that the usage to be followed is that of the most judicious members of the court, in conformity with that of the most judicious writers of the day. His aim was to make the language of literature and of polite conversation both correct and clear.

Vauquelin, v. Wauquelin.

Vauquelin de la Fresnaye, JEAN (1536– c. 1606), poet, a magistrate by profession, author of light verse (e.g. Foresteries, 1555; Idillies, influenced by Desportes; some good sonnets); Satires françaises, mostly translations of Italian satires; and a verse Art poétique (1605), upholding in the main the doctrines of the *Pléiade.

Vauquelin des Yveteaux, NICOLAS (1567–1649), son of the above, poet, tutor to a son of Henri IV and Gabrielle d'Estrées and later to Louis XIII. He introduced Malherbe at court.

Vauquer, La Maison, v. Père Goriot, Le.

Vautrin, one of the many aliases of Jacques Collin, nicknamed 'Trompe-la-Mort', the master-criminal in Balzac's *Comédie humaine. Having originally escaped to Paris from a wrongful imprisonment for forgery, he presides over an association of thieves and (in Le *Père Goriot) boards for a time at the Maison Vauquer with Eugène de *Rastignac, whom he seeks to persuade that 'il n'y a pas de principes, il n'y a que des événements; il n'y a pas de lois, il n'y a que des circonstances; l'homme supérieur épouse les événements et les circonstances pour les conduire'. He is rearrested, but again escapes, and poses as the Spanish abbé Carlos Herrera, whom he has murdered. He supports Lucien de Rubempré with money from the thieves' association (v. Illusions perdues; Splendeurs et misères des courtisanes). After Lucien's suicide, he forsakes a life of crime and, as Saint-Estève, becomes head of the *Sûreté. He ends, in Rabou's conclusion of Le *Député d'Arcis, as a minister responsible for police and public health in a small Italian principality and is assassinated by a forger. v. Vidocq.

Vauvenargues, LUC DE CLAPIERS, MARQUIS DE (1715–47), moralist, a friend of Marmontel and the elder Mirabeau, left the army after Dettingen (1743), despairing of advancement, and sought employment as a diplomat, but an attack of smallpox ruined his health and he spent the rest of his short life in poverty in Paris, devoting himself to literature. He was a man of high and generous character, whose virtue and sincerity won him the affection even of such sceptics as Voltaire. His Introduction à la connaissance de l'esprit humain, suivie de réflexions et maximes (1746) attracted little notice until the 19th c. In three books he deals with the mind (imagination, reflection, memory); the passions; and the vices and virtues. There follow some 600 detached maxims and reflections. In contrast to La Rochefoucauld, who sees man exclusively under the domination of egoism and vanity, and to Pascal, who stresses his intellectual impotence, Vauvenargues discerns both good and evil in him, refuses to denigrate human nature, and rehabilitates virtue (in which La Rochefoucauld sees little but hypocrisy). He holds that 'les grandes pensées viennent du cœur' (by cœur he means spontaneous impulse, in contrast to the reason) and finds in the passions, properly guided, the springs of moral energy.

Vaux, CLOTILDE DE, v. Comte, A.

Vaux-le-Vicomte, Château de (near Melun, about 25 miles south-east of Paris), one of the finest examples of 17th-c. architecture, built 1656–9 (by 18,000 workmen) for N. Fouquet. As later at *Versailles, Le Vau, Le Brun, and Le Nôtre were responsible for the architecture, decoration, and gardens respectively. The tapestries were woven in a factory specially installed near by (it was transferred to Paris after Fouquet's downfall and became the *Gobelins). Fouquet more than once lavishly entertained Louis XIV here. On the last occasion (17 Aug. 1661) Molière's Les *Fâcheux was performed, having been written and rehearsed in a fortnight.

The evening's entertainment—banquet, spectacle, fountains, and fireworks— inflamed the king against a subject who appeared to be trying to outshine him, and Fouquet was arrested a fortnight later. La Fontaine described the evening in a letter (22 Aug. 1661) to Maucroix, and Fouquet's arrest inspired his *Élégie aux nymphes de Vaux*.

Velche or **Welche** (from Ger. *welsch*, 'foreign'—esp. Italian or French, hence 'barbarian'), a word Voltaire often applied to his compatriots of the 18th c., which he considered a period of literary decadence. *v. Vadé, G., A., and C.*

Venaissin, Comtat, *v. Vaucluse.*

Venceslas, a tragedy by Rotrou, imitated from the Spanish of Francisco de Rojas and regarded as his most finished work; produced 1647.

 Ladislas, a prince of ungoverned passions, son of King Venceslas of Poland, detests Féderic, a gallant soldier and the king's favourite, whom he suspects of aspiring to the hand of Cassandre, a noble lady he has himself in vain pursued with dishonourable attentions. In fact, Féderic's attitude to Cassandre is designed to cloak the courtship of the Infante, Ladislas's younger brother. Ladislas, unable to win Cassandre by dishonest means, proposes marriage to her and is indignantly rejected. To spare her further persecution, the Infante and Cassandre decide to wed secretly forthwith. Ladislas, learning of this and believing Féderic to be the intended bridegroom, hides in Cassandre's house on the wedding night and unwittingly murders his own brother. Cassandre demands justice from Venceslas, who subordinates his love as a father to his duty as a king and orders Ladislas's execution. But the intervention of Ladislas's sister and of Féderic, popular clamour, and the consent of a mollified Cassandre combine to avert his death. Venceslas cedes the crown to his repentant son, as the only way of reconciling his duty and his love.

Vendanges de Suresnes, Les, (1) a *pastoral comedy by Du Ryer, produced *c.* 1633 (publ. 1635), interesting for its contemporary setting (the manners depicted are those of the 17th c., with satirical touches) and its scene on the banks of the Seine; (2) a comedy by Dancourt (1694).

Vendée, Guerre de (1793–6). After the execution of Louis XVI, Royalist risings fomented by nobles and priests in the Vendée (W. France) led to a state of intermittent guerrilla war between Republican troops (*les bleus*) and peasant armies (*les blancs*). The *Vendéens* were led by 'M. Henri' (de la Rochejaquelein), 'Georges' (Cadoudal), Cathelineau, Charette, Stofflet, and others, and were finally pacified by Hoche. Victims of the *Guerre de Vendée* far outnumbered those of the *Terror. v. Quiberon; Chouannerie.*

Vendémiaire, *v. Republican Calendar.*

Vendetta, La, *v. Comédie humaine, La (Scènes de la vie privée).*

Vendôme, LOUIS-JOSEPH DE BOURBON, DUC DE (1654–1712), great-grandson of Henri IV and Gabrielle d'Estrées, an eminent general of the reign of Louis XIV, distinguished himself in the Netherlands, Spain, and Italy. He was defeated at Oudenarde (1708) by Marlborough and Prince Eugène. For his brother Philippe *v. Temple.*

Vendôme, Place, *v. Place Vendôme.*

Ventadour, BERNARD DE, *v. Bernard de Ventadour.*

Ventôse, *v. Republican Calendar.*

Ventre de Paris, Le (1873), one of Zola's *Rougon-Macquart novels. Most of the characters have their place in the *Rougon-Macquart* pattern, but the real theme is Les Halles, the great provision market of Paris. Zola's imagination runs riot as he describes the food and its effect on those who handle it. A famous passage describing the various cheeses has been called the 'symphonie des fromages'.

Vénus d'Ille, La (1837, in the *Revue des Deux Mondes*; 1841, in *Colomba*), a story by Mérimée. In a district of the Pyrénées-Orientales, where Phoenician settlers may once have lived, a bridegroom lingers on the way to his wedding to play a game of long tennis. His diamond ring, destined for his bride, disturbs his grip, so he slips it on the finger of a bronze Venus, a statue of rare but sinister beauty still standing under the olives where it has recently been dug up. His match won, he hurries off, forgetting the ring. After the wedding he goes to retrieve it and finds to his horror that the bronze finger has closed and cannot be opened. He confides in one friend, but otherwise says nothing. Next morning he is found dead, his face contorted, his body marked as if crushed by an iron embrace. His bride, half mad with terror, tells of a mysterious visitor in the night. The diamond ring is on the floor.

Vêpres siciliennes, Les, the Sicilian Vespers, a general massacre of the French in Sicily (Easter Monday 1282, while the bells were ringing for vespers), instigated by emissaries of Peter III of Aragon. In 1262 the pope had ceded Sicily as a papal fief to Charles d'Anjou, brother of Louis IX. Delavigne wrote a tragedy on the subject. *Cf. Matines brugeoises.*

Vercingétorix, a Gaulish prince at the time of Julius Caesar's invasion, regarded by the French as one of their early heroes. A man of high and disinterested character (as Caesar recognizes), intelligent and eloquent, and an able military leader, he became (52 B.C.) the centre of resistance to Rome. He defeated Caesar at Gergovia (in his native Auvergne), but was later besieged in Alesia (in Burgundy) and forced to surrender. He was executed after six years' captivity in Rome.

Vercors, *v. Resistance.*

Verdun, a small fortified town on the

Meuse, has been in a position of prime strategical importance from the earliest days of European history. By the Treaty of Verdun (843) the *Carolingian empire was divided between the three surviving sons of Louis Ier. The youngest, Charles II, received territory corresponding to modern France. Louis le Germanique (806–76) received territory corresponding to modern Germany. Lothaire (d. 855), the eldest son, received a narrow middle strip (the 'Middle Kingdom') extending from the North Sea along the Rhine and Rhône down to N. Italy.

During the Revolution Verdun was occupied by the Prussians (1792; *v. Danton*), but evacuated after *Valmy. In the *Franco-Prussian war, after a two months' siege, it was again occupied by the Prussians. In the 1914–18 war it was violently besieged by the Germans (1916) and for ten months was the centre of the epic resistance ('Ils ne passeront pas'), turning later to an offensive, organized by Pétain (a period described in Romains's *Les *Hommes de bonne volonté*, vols. XV and XVI).

Verdurin, Monsieur and **Madame,** in Proust's *A la recherche du temps perdu*, belong to the wealthy, cultivated *bourgeoisie*, in contrast to the aristocracy typified by the *Guermantes. Though they would never admit it, their *salon* (seen in its early days in *Du côté de chez Swann*) is their ladder to social success. In *Sodome et Gomorrhe*, ii, the *salon* and its *habitués* ('le petit clan') are rising in the world on the tides of aesthetic fashion. It is at Mme Verdurin's that Marcel hears the first performance of the *Vinteuil septet and comes much closer to understanding what life holds for him (*La Prisonnière*). On the same occasion, in one of the most dramatic moments in the whole work, the young violinist Morel, encouraged by Mme Verdurin, insults *Charlus, to whom he owes everything. Mme Verdurin ends (in *Le Temps retrouvé*, ii) as the wife of the widowed prince de Guermantes (her third husband). Her *bourgeois* origins are now forgotten and she is a queen of post-war Parisian society.

Vergniaud, PIERRE-VICTURNIEN (1753–93), a *Girondin*, famous for his speeches in the *Convention* opposing the violent measures advocated by the *Montagnards*. He was guillotined.

Verhaeren, ÉMILE (1855–1916), chief of the Belgian poets associated with *Symbolism, studied law at the University of Louvain, was called to the bar in Brussels, but soon devoted himself to literature. From 1892, after some years of serious illness, he was keenly interested in social questions, but his hopes for a world animated by a spirit of universal brotherhood were destroyed by the 1914–18 war and the German invasion of Belgium. (The poems of *Les Ailes rouges*, 1916, are a bitter indictment of war.) He died in a railway accident at Rouen.

His most notable poetry is collected in *Les Flamandes* (1883), early poems describing in realistic manner the peasant life made familiar by the Flemish painters; *Les Moines* (1886), memories of childhood and of visits to a monastery; *Les Soirs* (1887), *Les Débâcles* (1888), and *Les Flambeaux noirs* (1890), a trilogy showing his mastery of the *vers libre*; and two more trilogies—*Les Campagnes hallucinées* (1893), *Les Villages illusoires* (1895), and *Les Villes tentaculaires* (1895); *Les Images de la vie* (1899), *Les Forces tumultueuses* (1902), and *La Multiple Splendeur* (1906)—describing life in the country and the great industrial towns and the gradual destruction of the countryside by the forces of the machine age. Some of these are written with a violence and a sense of warring cosmic forces reminiscent of the later Hugo. *Les Heures claires* (1896), *Les Heures d'après-midi* (1905), and *Les Heures du soir* (1911) are more peaceful collections, mainly of love poems dedicated to his wife. His other works include *Les Aubes* (1898), *Les Visages de la vie* (1899), *Les Rythmes souverains* (1910), *Les Blés mouvants* (1912), *Toute la Flandre* (1904–11), *Les Flammes hautes* (1917). *v. Literary Isms.*

Vérité, *v. Zola.*

Verlaine, PAUL (1844–96), who wrote some of the finest, most musical lyrics in the French language, was associated first with the *Parnassiens*, then with the *décadents* (*v. Esprit décadent*) and the early *Symbolists. The son of an army officer, he was educated at the *Lycée Condorcet* in Paris, but so neglected his studies at the university that his father preferred to find him regular employment (1864), an unexacting clerical post at the *Hôtel de Ville*. This left time for frequenting cafés and other haunts of the young writers and artists from whom sprang the group of *Le Parnasse contemporain*. His early work—*Poèmes saturniens* (1866) and *Fêtes galantes* (1869)—shows a *Parnassien* care for form and objectivity; the latter poems also recall the sophisticated pastorals of such 18th-c. painters as Watteau and Fragonard.

In 1867 he fell deeply in love with Mathilde Mauté, a girl too timid by nature and upbringing for their marriage (1870) to succeed, even without such complications as his drunkenness (this became serious in the winter and spring of 1870–1, when he served for a time, while Paris was besieged, in the *Garde nationale* or hung about, unemployed, after the *Commune*) and, worse still, his complete subjection to the influence of the boy-poet Rimbaud. In 1872, forsaking wife, home, and employment, he left Paris with Rimbaud. Their vagabond life in London and Belgium inspired the poems of *Romances sans paroles* (1874). It was punctuated by drunken quarrels and ended in July 1873, in Brussels, when Verlaine fired at Rimbaud, wounded him, and was sentenced to two years' imprisonment. While in prison at Mons, he returned to active acceptance of the Roman Catholic faith in which he had been born. His conversion—emotional, but wholly sincere at the time—inspired the fine poems of *Sagesse* (1881), which are the broken prayers of a penitent, eager, but too humble, to believe that God's grace is meant for him. On leaving prison, he spent nearly two years teaching French, Latin, and drawing in English schools (at Stickney, Lincs., and in Bournemouth). He then taught in a Roman Catholic school at Rethel (Ardennes). Between 1878 and 1883, in the company of his 'fils adoptif' Lucien Létinois (who was one of his Rethel pupils and inspired many of the elegies of *Amour*, 1888), he tried to farm in the Ardennes, went to England, and back to Paris, where Létinois died of typhoid. Another spell of rustic life (1883–5), when his drunkenness had the upper hand, ended with a prison sentence for attacking his widowed mother, who was keeping house for him. He ended his days living in poverty in Paris, alternating between lapses into debauchery and spells of repentance, and often dependent on public assistance for shelter (described in *Mes hôpitaux*, 1891, prose).

The poems of *Jadis et naguère* (1884; inc. the well-known *Art poétique*, written 1871–3, and *Les Uns et les autres*, a one-act comedy in an 18th-c. setting) form a transition between his earlier, more objective, and later, intensely personal, verse. After *Les *Poètes maudits* (1884) he became a leader for the younger Symbolists (for his general influence *v.* *Lyric Poetry*, 4). He had a considerable influence on prosody. He did not approve of all the Symbolist innovations, such as the *vers libre, and preferred to employ the less revolutionary *vers libérés*. In the poem *Art poétique* he defined his conception of verse as essentially musical, rhythmic, fluid, and evocative, unfettered by rhyme and regularity ('De la musique avant toute chose... Rien de plus cher que la chanson grise Où l'Indécis au Précis se joint').

His other works include the poems collected in *La Bonne Chanson* (1870; lyrics to Mathilde Mauté), *Parallèlement* (1889), *Dédicaces* (1890; poems dedicated to friends), *Bonheur* (1891), *Chansons pour elle* (1891), *Liturgies intimes* (1892), *Élégies* (1893), *Odes en son honneur* (1893); and, in prose, the autobiographical *Mes prisons* (1893) and *Confessions* (1895; on his early years down to his meeting with Rimbaud). *v.* *Hahn*.

Verne, JULES (1828–1905), a highly prolific author of adventure stories who combined a vivid imagination with a gift for popularizing science. His most popular tales—the delight of young people in his own and many other countries and often first published in the *Musée des familles* (a juvenile magazine f. 1850; *v.* also *Children's Reading*)—included *Cinq Semaines en ballon* (1863), his first success; *Voyage au centre de la terre* (1864), geology; *Les Aventures du Capitaine Hatteras* (1866), polar exploration; *Vingt Mille Lieues sous les mers* (1870), introducing the misanthropic Captain Nemo, a refugee Indian prince, and his submarine *Nautilus*; *Le Tour du monde en quatre-vingts jours* (1873), where Phileas Fogg, accompanied by his imperturbable valet Passepartout, wins a wager that he will travel round the world in the then incredibly short space of 80 days; *Michel Strogoff* (1876), about Russians and Tartars. He also wrote a popular history of exploration (*La Découverte de la terre*, 1878–80) and successful plays.

Vernet, (1) CLAUDE-JOSEPH (1714–89), a noted landscape and marine painter; (2) his son ANTOINE-CHARLES-HORACE, *known as* CARLE (1758–1836), a painter noted for his portraits (esp. of Napoleon) and battle-scenes, also a witty caricaturist; (3) the latter's son JEAN-ÉMILE-HORACE (1789–1863), also an historical painter, particularly of battles.

Véron, LOUIS-DÉSIRÉ (1798–1867), a physician who, having made a fortune with a patent medicine, became a patron of the arts and a well-known Paris character (a noted *bon vivant* and the butt of caricaturists). He founded the *Revue de Paris* (1829), was director of the *Opéra* (1831–5), and bought (1844) and revived the *Constitutionnel*. He published *Mémoires d'un bourgeois de Paris* (1853–5, 6 vols.).

Versailles, Château de, originally a hunting-lodge or country house erected 1624 by Louis XIII, was rebuilt and vastly enlarged at enormous expense by Louis XIV, who made it his chief palace. The first enlargement (*c.* 1661–8), with Louis Le Vau (1612–70) as architect, was no sooner finished than a second was begun, again with Le Vau as architect, though he did not live to see it finished. Before long, when Louis XIV decided to make Versailles the seat of his government, work began on a third great extension, finally completed in 1710; the architect was now Mansard. The interior decoration was supervised by Le Brun, who also designed the fountains and groups of statuary which form an important feature of the vast gardens laid out to the plans of Le Nôtre. The changes made under Louis XV and Louis XVI were mainly in the internal disposition of the apartments. *v.* also *Trianon*; *Œil-de-bœuf*; *Marly*.

Vers de la mort, *v. Religious Writings*, 1.

Verset, a 'verse' in the Biblical sense, used as a poetic form by Claudel and later by Saint-John Perse, Jouve, and others.

Vers et Prose (1905–14), a literary review f. by Fort (who was editor for some years); of interest as a guide to early 20th-c. poetry.

Versification. Traditional French verse is based on the number of syllables in the line (counted, until the *Symbolist period and to a considerable extent even today, on the basis of an archaic pronunciation). The commonest lines are the octosyllable, decasyllable, and dodecasyllable or *alexandrine. Traditionally, also, the lines are connected by rhyme. For less strict forms of verse *v. Assonance*; *Vers libérés*; *Vers libre. v.* also *Alternance des rimes*; *Chanson*; *Élision*; *Enjambement*; *Fixed Forms*; *Hiatus*; *Huitain*; *Masculine and Feminine Lines and Rhymes*; *Rimes*; *Ternaire*; *Vers libres. Cf. Prose Poem*; *Verset*.

Vers libérés. About 1880, the *Symbolists, inspired notably by Verlaine, introduced various relaxations of the rules of *versification (zealously maintained, or reimposed, by the *Parnassiens) governing *hiatus, the position of the caesura in the *alexandrine, the value of the 'mute' *e*, etc.; they also used lines of hitherto unusual lengths, such as 9 or 11 syllables. This 'liberated verse', however, was still syllabic and rhymed, unlike the more sweeping innovation of the *vers libre*.

Vers libre, Le. Almost contemporaneously with the introduction by Verlaine of the *vers libéré*, other *Symbolist poets went much further in relaxing the rules of *versification; they abandoned the syllabic principle and regular strophic patterns, and often contented themselves with *assonance in place of rhyme. The form of a poem was to be dictated only by the poet's impulse, varying according to subject and individual. *Cf. Prose Poem*.

Who first employed the *vers libre*, and what influence the poetry of Walt Whitman had on its development, are disputed questions. Two poems by Rimbaud, *Marine* and *Mouvement*, said to have been written as early as 1872 or 1873, are in the *vers libre*. Verlaine printed them as part of *Les Illuminations* in *La *Vogue* in May and June 1886. Other early *vers-libristes* included Kahn, Laforgue, Dujardin, and Moréas, with poems (later in 1886 and in 1887) in *La Vogue*, *La *Revue indépendante*, and *La *Wallonie*; Marie Krysinska, whose claim to have been the first to get into print (1881) was supported by some critics; also Jammes, H. de Régnier, Verhaeren, and Vielé-Griffin.

Vers libres, the term applied to the verseforms often used in the 17th c., e.g. by Corneille (*Agésilas*), by Molière (*Amphitryon*), and, above all, by La Fontaine (*Fables*). The line-lengths and distribution of rhymes vary according to no fixed pattern, but each line obeys the traditional syllabic rules of *versification. The form is thus quite different from the modern *vers libre*.

Vert-Galant, Le, *v. Henri IV*.

Vertot, RENÉ, ABBÉ (1655–1735), historian, author of a history of the Knights of Malta, etc. It is said that, having tardily received for the purpose of his work some notes on the siege of Rhodes, he disregarded them with the remark 'Mon siège est fait', which has become proverbial.

Ver-Vert, v. Gresset.

Vervins (Aisne). Here, in 1598, Henri IV and Philip II of Spain signed the treaty which ended the wars of religion.

Vestris, GAETANO-APOLLINO-BALTHAZAR (1729–1808), a famous Italian-born dancer, made his *début* at the *Opéra* in 1748 and did not retire till 1781. He was notorious for his vanity.

Véto, Le. In the early days of the Revolution opinion was divided on the question of whether Louis XVI should retain his power to refuse assent to legislation. His stubborn exercise of this royal prerogative increased his unpopularity and won him the nickname 'Monsieur Véto', while Marie-Antoinette became 'Madame Véto'. v. *Carmagnole*.

Veuillot, LOUIS-FRANÇOIS (1813–83), probably the most militant and virulent Roman Catholic writer of the 19th c., editor from 1843 of *L'*Univers*. Everyone who, in his view, undermined religion and morals was a *libre-penseur*, from Héloïse to Vigny (author of the 'revoltingly immoral' *Chatterton*) and G. Sand. His chief writings—*Le Pape et la diplomatie* (1861), *Le Fond de Giboyer* (1863; cf. *Augier*), *Le Parfum de Rome* (1862), *Les Odeurs de Paris* (1867)—are in *Mélanges religieux, historiques, et littéraires* (1857–75, 18 vols.) and *Derniers Mélanges 1873–7* (1908–9). His *Correspondance* (1883–1903) is of interest.

Veyne, FRANÇOIS-AUGUSTE, v. *Dîners Magny*.

Vian, BORIS (1920–59), a Jack-of-all-arts—jazz trumpeter, translator, author of novels, plays, poetry, short stories, and *chansons*—whose talent as a writer went largely unrecognized in his lifetime. It was as a result of this lack of success that he wrote a number of best-selling thrillers in the American style under the pseudonym

'Vernon Sullivan', notably *J'irai cracher sur vos tombes* (1946). His serious novels—*Vercoquin et le plancton* (1946), *L'Écume des jours* (1947), *L'Automne à Pékin* (1947), *L'Herbe rouge* (1950), and *L'Arrache-cœur* (1953)—are marked by a *pataphysique* reminiscent of Jarry and Queneau, full of (sometimes cruel) fantasy, lyricism, and linguistic invention (e.g. the 'pianocktail' in *L'Écume des jours*). His plays, written in much the same style, but giving freer rein to his hatred of war, militarism, and *bourgeois* values, include *L'Équarrissage pour tous* (1950), *Les Bâtisseurs d'empire* (1959), *Le Goûter des généraux* (1962). Further works appeared posthumously, e.g. *Les Lurettes fourrées* (1962; short stories) and *Je voudrais pas crever* (1962; poems).

Viau, THÉOPHILE DE, v. *Théophile de Viau*.

Viaud, JULIEN, v. *Loti*.

Vicaire, GABRIEL (1848–1900), wrote satirical light verse and, with Beauclair, *Les *Déliquescences d'Adoré Floupette*.

Vicaire savoyard, La Profession de foi du, v. *Émile*.

Vicomte de Bragelonne, Le, v. *Dumas père*.

Vicomte inversif, Le, v. *Arlincourt*.

Victoires, Fête des (21 Oct. 1794), a national festival held to mark the victories of the Revolutionary armies and the departure of foreign invaders from French soil. The hymn sung was the *Chant du départ*.

Victor, v. *Maréchal*.

Vidal de La Blache, PAUL (1843–1918), one of the first modern, scientific geographers. His less specialized works included an inspiring introduction to the *Lavisse Histoire de France depuis les origines jusqu'à la Révolution—La France: Tableau géographique* (publ. separately 1908), the equivalent for a later generation of *Michelet's *Tableau*. He was responsible for the well-known *Atlas général Vidal de La Blache*.

Vidocq, FRANÇOIS-EUGÈNE (1775–1857), a baker's son whose career illustrated the saying 'Set a thief to catch a thief'. After years of crime and adventure, he offered his services to the government and was made head of a specially created *Brigade de la Sûreté* (*not* the modern *Sûreté*) composed of ex-criminals familiar with the underworld. He retired (1827) with a great reputation and a fortune, lost his money in an attempt to run a factory manned by ex-convicts, was later a private inquiry agent, and died in poverty. The *Mémoires de Vidocq* (1828, 4 vols.; probably not by him) were known to Balzac and Vidocq may have inspired his *Vautrin.

Vie de Jésus, La, v. Renan.

Vie de Marianne, La, v. Marianne.

Vie en fleur, La, v. France, A.

Vieille Fille, La, v. Comédie humaine, La (*Scènes de la vie de province*).

Vieilleville, FRANÇOIS DE (1510–71), *maréchal de France*, the subject of memoirs (possibly written by his secretary Vincent Carloix).

Viel-Castel, HORACE, COMTE DE (1802–64), great-nephew of Mirabeau, a man of letters and historian remembered for his entertaining *Mémoires sur le règne de Napoléon III* (*1851–1864*) (1881–4, 6 vols.).

Vielé-Griffin, FRANCIS (1864–1937), an early *Symbolist poet, b. in Virginia of French descent, was educated and lived permanently in France. His first poems, in *Cueille d'avril* (1886), were influenced by the *esprit décadent*. Later, more robust, collections were inspired by the countryside of Touraine (*Les Cygnes*, 1887; *La Clarté de vie*, 1897; *La Partenza*, 1899; *Le Domaine royal*, 1923) or by the legends of antiquity, the Middle Ages, and

Scandinavia (*Phocas le jardinier*, 1898, a verse drama of early Christian persecution; *La Lumière de Grèce*, 1892; *La Chevauchée d'Yeldis*, 1893; *La Légende ailée de Wieland le forgeron*, 1900; *L'Amour sacré*, 1906; *Voix d'Ionie*, 1914; *Couronne offerte à la Muse romaine*, 1923). He used the *vers libre* with great success (e.g. in *Joies*, 1889).

Vie littéraire, La, v. France, A.

Vienna, Congress of, v. Coalitions (7); Talleyrand.

Vienna, Treaty of, v. Coalitions (5).

Viennet, JEAN-PONS-GUILLAUME (1777–1868), a prolific writer of fables, epistles, satires, epic poetry (*La Franciade*, 1863), and epic dramas, all adhering lifelessly to classical models. His *Épître aux Muses*, attacking the *Romantics, brought him briefly into the limelight. He also had a career in politics, and it was he who, after the 1830 *Revolution, read the proclamation of Louis-Philippe to the people massed before the *Hôtel de Ville*.

Vie parisienne, La, (1) v. Offenbach; (2) one of the first weekly illustrated papers, f. 1863 by Marcelin (pseudonym of Émile-Marcelin-Isidore Planet, 1829–87, writer and book-illustrator). It was a typical product of the Second Empire, with a staff which included brilliant artists and writers, but no professional journalists. It published Taine's *Notes sur Paris* and work by Droz, L. Halévy, Monselet, Toulet, and Marcelin himself. Matter and illustrations were amusing and witty, sometimes risky in tone. It continued, on a lower level, well into the 20th c.

Vie, poésies et pensées de Joseph Delorme (1829), a volume, mostly of poems, supposedly by a deceased friend of Sainte-Beuve—in fact, by Sainte-Beuve himself. In a prefatory memoir containing much autobiography, he depicts Delorme as a melancholy, misunderstood *Romantic who died young in obscure poverty. The poems describe humble scenes and people, small streets in Paris, etc., and reflect his feeling for the English Lake poets. His gentle, intimate, at times almost prosaic tone was unusual at the time and influenced later poets, as did his prosodic innovations (*v. Lyric Poetry*, 4).

Vies des dames illustres; *Vies des dames galantes*; *Vies des hommes illustres et grands capitaines français et étrangers*, *v. Brantôme*.

Vies des hommes illustres, Les, *v. Amyot*.

Vieux Célibataire, Le, *v.* Collin *d'Harleville*.

Vieux-Colombier, Théâtre du, a famous experimental theatre in Paris, directed (1913–24) by Copeau, who trained his own company (inc. Dullin, Jouvet, M. Saint-Denis) and introduced new techniques of acting and production. He staged notable productions of Molière and Shakespeare (esp. of *Twelfth Night—La Nuit des Rois*), and many new plays by young dramatists of the day. *v. Theatres and Theatre Companies*.

Vieux Cordelier, Le (Dec. 1793–Jan. 1794; 7 nos., publ. at five-day intervals), the most eloquent journal of the Revolutionary era, founded, and wholly written, by Desmoulins. Each number bore the motto 'Vivre libre ou mourir' and the whole series was an appeal for moderation. The third number consisted almost entirely of quotations from Tacitus, cleverly strung together to form a severe indictment of the Revolutionary excesses. The fourth, which people queued for at the bookshops, was a protest (which was to cost Desmoulins his life) against the excessive bloodshed of the *Terror and an appeal for a *comité de clémence*. Desmoulins was arrested while correcting the proofs of the seventh number, which ended with the now famous words 'Les Dieux ont soif' (later used by A. France as the title for a novel about the Revolution). He was executed before it appeared.

Vigée-Lebrun, Élisabeth Vigée, Mme (1755–1842), a painter remembered for her portraits, e.g. of Marie-Antoinette. She left *Souvenirs* (1835–7).

Vignettes romantiques, Les, *v. Champfleury*.

Vignon, Marie-Louise (1888–1948), author of nature and love poems, e.g. *Chants de jeunesse* (1911), *Ciels clairs de France* (1922 and 1932).

Vigny, Alfred de (1797–1863), a great *Romantic poet and novelist, grew up in Paris, in a family circle composed largely of returned *émigrés* with ultra-Royalist sympathies. On leaving school, where he was unhappy, he became an officer in the royal bodyguard. His army career was undistinguished, largely because he was by nature unfitted for a life of action. He soon began to write. Some of his most famous poems (e.g. *Moïse* and *Éloa*, in *Poèmes antiques et modernes*, 1826) belong to this period, and he wrote part of his novel *Cinq-Mars* (1826) while stationed in the Pyrenees in 1824. When on leave he frequented Nodier's *cénacle* and became friendly with Hugo. In 1825 he married Lydia Bunbury, daughter of a wealthy Englishman from Demerara. She soon lapsed into invalidism, and her fortune was a myth, but his marriage, and visits to England, brought him many English friends. By 1827, when he left the army and settled in Paris, he had made his name as a poet and novelist and was in the happiest and most fecund period of his creative life. He now moved less in Romantic circles. Their noisy expansiveness was uncongenial to his reserved nature; also Hugo was less friendly, largely because he was jealous of Vigny's success as a dramatist. This had begun with adaptations of Shakespeare (e.g. *Le More de Venise*, from *Othello*, 1829) and continued with *La Maréchale d'Ancre* (1831; *v. Concini*), a long, complicated historical drama; *Quitte pour la peur* (1833), a short, witty piece in which an absentee husband returns to save his young wife's honour and at the same time discovers her charm;

and *Chatterton* (1835), his masterpiece and a striking success, thanks partly to the acting of Marie Dorval. Vigny, who had had a stormy liaison with this actress since 1831, broke with her finally in 1838 and wrote no more for the stage. Other works of this period include *Stello* (1832), three tales (in the framework of a series of *consultations* between the poet Stello and the docteur Noir) illustrating the sufferings of oppressed and unrecognized poetic genius (represented by N. Gilbert, A. Chénier, and Chatterton), and the fine tales of *Servitude et grandeur militaires* (1835).

After 1835 his life was uneventful and increasingly melancholy. His mother, whom he nursed devotedly, died in 1837. His wife's hopeless invalidism drew from him a selfless care which, added to money worries and a distaste for the battles of life, led him to retire for increasingly long periods, sometimes years, to the manor of Maine-Giraud (near Angoulême), a country property he had inherited. Except for rare visits from close friends, his life was one of seclusion. His days were devoted to nursing his wife and managing his small property. At night, in a small turret-room, he wrote and read. His writing was mainly letters, and the *pensées*, day-to-day jottings, and drafts of seldom-finished works that form the *Journal d'un poète* (1867); but in these years he also wrote the 11 poems collected posthumously in *Les Destinées* (1864), the most famous being *La *Bouteille à la mer*, *L'*Esprit pur*, La *Maison du berger*, Le *Mont des oliviers*, La *Mort du loup*, La Colère de Samson*. They are notable for the way in which, starting with a concrete image, he develops a philosophical idea. All reveal stoical, somewhat bitter resignation to the world as a place of suffering, to life as a process of abnegation, and to God, if He exists, as the ruthless divinity of the Old Testament, of whom it is better to make oneself independent.

His sense of spiritual loneliness was deepened by unsuccessful attempts to enter politics. He returned to Paris in 1853, but still lived in an isolated fashion with few outside interests except his membership of the *Académie* and his contacts with young writers in need of encouragement. When his wife died in 1862 he was already mortally ill and outlived her by only a few months. A short work on the lines of *Stello* (*Daphné*, 1912, in the *Revue de Paris*) was found among his papers.

Vilain Mire, Le, 'The Peasant Doctor', a *fabliau*. v. *Médecin malgré lui, Le*.

A peasant is in the habit of beating his wife, hoping to keep her faithful. She seeks a remedy for her plight. Two messengers of the king ask her for hospitality; they are going to England to fetch a doctor for the king's daughter, who has a fish-bone in her throat. She tells them they need not go so far, for her husband is the best doctor in the world, though he will only display his skill if well beaten. The messengers seize him and carry him off to court. A sound beating sharpens his wits and he cures the princess by making her laugh.

Vilain qui conquit paradis par plaid, Le, a *fabliau*. On being refused admission to Paradise, a peasant maintains his claim against St. Peter, St. Thomas, and St. Paul by caustic references to their earthly lives; an example of the element of irreverence so common in medieval devotion.

Vilar, JEAN, v. *Théâtre national populaire*; *Theatres and Theatre Companies*.

Vildrac, Charles, *pseudonym of* CHARLES MESSAGER (1882–1971), poet and dramatist, a founder-member of the *Abbaye* community and an *unanimiste*. His poetry (e.g. *Poèmes*, 1905; *Images et mirages*, 1907; *Chants du désespéré*, 1920; *Prolongements*, 1946) is marked by a belief in friendship and in man's intrinsic goodness. His plays, notably *Le Paquebot 'Tenacity'* (1920), a minor masterpiece of character study which made his name, and *La Brouille* (1930), are simple in the extreme, suggesting rather than depicting the mysteries of the human personality. He also published some good children's stories (e.g. *L'Île rose*, 1924; *Les Lunettes* *du lion*, 1932) and *Pages de journal, 1922–66* (1968), reminiscences. *v. Resistance.*

Villages illusoires, Les, *v. Verhaeren.*

Villa Médicis, *v. École de Rome.*

Villanelle, a fixed verse-form usually consisting of an indefinite number of tercets ending alternately with the first and third lines of the poem: $A^1 b A^2 \ a b A^1 \ a b A^2 \ldots$, and concluding a b $A^1 \ A^2$.

Villars, LOUIS-HECTOR, DUC DE (1653–1734), **maréchal de France*, commander-in-chief at Malplaquet (1709) and the victor of Denain (1712); also a member of the **Académie* (from 1714) and remembered for his friendship with the young Voltaire, who frequented the Château de Villars in the period 1718–24. His *Mémoires* were, at least in part, compiled after his death; the best edition is that of 1884–91.

Ville, La, v. ˚Claudel.

Villedieu, CATHERINE DES JARDINS, MME DE (1640–83), wrote some 30 short novels (e.g. *Mémoires de la vie de Henriette-Sylvie de Molière*), much read in their day.

Villehardouin, GEOFFROI DE (*c.* 1150–*c.* 1212), historian. He was **maréchal de Champagne* and took part as warrior and diplomat in the 4th **Crusade* (1202–4). His *Conquête de Constantinople*, among the earliest examples of French literary prose, is a record of the Crusade and of subsequent events down to 1207. He describes the negotiations (in which he took part) with the doge of Venice for the transport of the Crusaders. He also explains and defends—in the view of some with questionable candour and sincerity—the transformation of the Crusade into a predatory expedition against Constantinople. His precise, rather dry narrative is lit up by occasional vivid passages, e.g. his account of the sailing of the Crusaders from Corfu (ch. 60) and of their first sight of Constantinople (ch. 64).

He was made *maréchal* of the Latin Empire of Constantinople and died in the East.

Ville lumière, La, a name for Paris, said to go back to 1470, when the *Recueil des lettres de Gasparin de Bergame* (the first book printed in France) was dedicated to Paris as a centre from which knowledge radiated like light from the sun.

Villemain, ABEL-FRANÇOIS (1790–1870), literary historian, critic, and politician (twice minister of education under the July Monarchy). He was among the most brilliant young men of the day and, at 26, became a professor at the **Sorbonne* (1816–30), famous for his lectures on 15th–17th-c. French literature. His approach to literary criticism was then novel, being mainly concerned with literature in its relation to history (*cf.* Mme de Staël, *v. Critics and Criticism*, 2) and with parallels between French and European literature. His works include *Discours et mélanges littéraires* (1823; with notable studies of Montaigne, Montesquieu, Fénelon, Pascal), *Nouveaux Mélanges historiques et littéraires* (1827), *Cours de littérature française* (1828), *Études de littérature ancienne et étrangère* (1846), *Choix d'études sur la littérature contemporaine* (1857). His *Souvenirs contemporains* describe events and opinion under Napoleon (esp. the Hundred Days) and during the Restoration period (e.g. lectures and lecturers at the *Sorbonne c.* 1825; literary and political **salons*).

Villeneuve, MME DE, *v. Belle et la Bête, La.*

Villeparisis, Madame de, in Proust's **À la recherche du temps perdu*, aunt of the duchesse de **Guermantes*, and rather *déclassée* by her long liaison with **Norpois*. In her **salon* Marcel studies human nature and social climbers, and—realizing an ambition—meets the duchesse de Guermantes.

Villequier, *v. Contemplations, Les.*

Villeroi, Nicolas de (1598–1685), *maréchal de France*, tutor to Louis XIV.

Villers-Cotterêts (Aisne). It was from his residence in this small town that François Ier issued (10 Aug. 1539) the famous *Ordonnance de Villers-Cotterêts* which, among other civil and juridical reforms, made French the language of legal judgements and records. *v. French Language*.

Villes tentaculaires, Les, v. Verhaeren.

Villiers de l'Isle-Adam, Philippe-Auguste, comte de (1838–89), novelist and dramatist, came of an old, but impoverished, Breton family, steeped in traditions of grandeur and chivalry, and fervently Roman Catholic. After an education of sorts in Brittany, he made literature the sole object of a vagabond life, living mainly in Paris, always in grinding poverty. He is usually classed as a *Symbolist. His writings, of undeniably poetic quality, are often obscure, ornate in language and rhythm, and heavily influenced by philosophical ideas and all the *isms* of the day (e.g. occultism, spiritualism, Wagnerism). But they are also at times extravagantly *Romantic, e.g. his drama *Axël 1890), the earlier dramas *Elen* (1865) and *Morgane* (1866), and the horrific parts of *Claire Lenoir* (a tale in the collection *Tribulat Bonhomet*). Many of his *Contes cruels* (1883) and *Nouveaux Contes cruels* (1888) also belong to the horrific *genre*; others, perhaps the best, are realistic, ironical, and much more tautly written. His other works include the dramas *La Révolte* (1870), on a theme similar to that later used by Ibsen in *A Doll's House*, and *Le Nouveau Monde* (1880), which won a prize for a play marking the centenary of the American Revolution; and *L'Ève future* (1886), a semi-scientific novel.

Villon, François (1431–after 1463), poet, was brought up in Paris by Guillaume de Villon, chaplain of Saint-Benoît-le-Bétourné, whose name he assumed and who remained his kindly foster-father. While a student at the *University of Paris, of which he became licenciate and master of arts, he made disreputable friends and fell into evil ways. In 1455 he killed a cleric, Philippe Sermoise, in a quarrel. On Christmas Eve 1456 he and some friends broke into the *Collège de Navarre and stole 500 gold pieces. He fled from Paris to avoid arrest. The *Lais* ('Legacy') or *Petit Testament*, his earliest poem that can be dated with certainty, was written at this time. Claiming that he is driven to leave Paris by the perfidy of the woman he loved, he facetiously bequeaths to each of his friends and enemies some worthless memento—a stolen duck, the sword and breeches he has pawned, and to his false love his broken heart. He stayed away for six years, probably spent in wandering about France. He was certainly in Blois, where he took part in a poetic contest organized by Charles d'Orléans. There is some evidence that he was in prison at Orleans *c.* 1457 or 1460. 1461 found him imprisoned at Meung-sur-Loire by order of the bishop of Orleans. He was held there for many months and stoutly maintained that he was cruelly and unjustly treated; he was released (Oct. 1461) under a general amnesty when Louis XI visited the town. Some time in 1461, in a fit of despair caused by ill-health, destitution, and remorse, he had written his *Testament* (the *Grand Testament*), a poem of some 2,000 lines, very different from the *Lais* of 1456. He reviews his life, his mistakes, disappointments in love, and sufferings, and expresses his horror of sickness, old age, prison, poverty, and death (*cf. Danse macabre*). Again parodying the legal forms of a will, he makes various bequests, some pathetic, some ironical, some facetious, e.g. to his old mother, his foster-father, his friends and comrades, the women in his life, innkeepers, the executioner, gaolers, police officers, and court officials. Into this framework he inserted a number of his finest shorter pieces (some written at an earlier date), e.g. the *Ballade des dames du temps jadis*, the *Regrets de la belle* *heaulmière*, the *Ballade pour prier Nostre Dame* (a prayer to the Virgin, put into the mouth of his mother), the *Ballade et oroison pour Jehan Cotart* (an ironical prayer for the soul of the hard-drinking Jehan Cotart, an official of the ecclesiastical court of Paris), the *Contreditz *Franc Gontier*, all *ballades except the second. By its mingled bitterness, melancholy, and humour, its sincerity and deep feeling, the *Testament* contrasts strikingly with the insipid lyrics of his predecessors and with the moralizing of the *rhétoriqueurs who followed him.

Late in 1462 and in 1463, being now back in Paris, he was twice more under arrest. On the second occasion he had been present at an affray in which a papal notary was wounded and he was sentenced to be hanged. The sentence was quashed on appeal, but he was exiled from Paris for 10 years 'in view of his evil life'. The death sentence inspired his moving *Ballade des pendus*, perhaps his finest work, in which he sees himself swinging on the gibbet and appeals to God from the justice of men. His last surviving poems are a gay *ballade* on the success of his appeal and another of thanks to the court. The date of his death is unknown. Rabelais has two anecdotes in which he is mentioned, but no credence is placed in them. The same applies to stories about him in the *Repues franches*, a collection of verse at one time wrongly attributed to him and relating various tricks and misdeeds allegedly performed by him and his associates.

His extant work—only some 3,000 lines in all— is almost entirely in the *Lais* and *Testament*, which (apart from the inserted poems) are written in octosyllabic *huitains. Besides those already mentioned, his other pieces include 'Je meurs de soif auprès de la fontaine', a *ballade* written for the Blois contest; the *Débat du cuer [cœur] et du corps de Villon* (v. *Dit*); and the *Ballades en jargon*, written in the cant of the *Coquillards (with some of whom he had relations) and mainly of philological interest. He found early imitators in Coquillart and Baude, and Marot issued an edition (1533) of 'le

meilleur poète parisien qui se trouve'. Thereafter his work was largely neglected until the 19th c. English translators of his poems have included D. G. Rossetti, Swinburne, and W. E. Henley.

Vimeiro, v. *Abrantès*.

Vin blanc de la Villette, Le, v. *Romains*.

Vincennes, Château de; Donjon de. Originally a royal hunting-lodge on the outskirts of Paris, the *château* was rebuilt (1328–73) as a fortified castle and was long a royal residence (a seat of the court till *Versailles took its place). In the 18th c. the dungeons were used to confine persons imprisoned under **lettres de cachet*, e.g. Diderot and Mirabeau (who wrote much there). It was while walking out from Paris to see Diderot, reading the **Mercure de France* to stop himself going too fast in the heat, that J.-J. Rousseau noticed the themes proposed by the *Académie de Dijon* for the next literary contest and was inspired to write his *Discours. The Young Pretender was briefly held there just after he escaped to France from Culloden. The duc d'Enghien was executed in the moat. Vincennes is now a fort and barracks. v. *Chêne de Vincennes*.

Vincent de Beauvais (*c.* 1190–*c.* 1264), a learned Dominican who enjoyed favour at the court of Louis IX. His *Speculum majus* (v. *Jean de Vignai*) was a vast compilation of all the knowledge of the day. Chaucer mentions him (prologue to *The Legend of Good Women*).

Vincent de Lérins, St. (d. *c.* 450), a religious who retired to the monastery of Lérins (on an island off Antibes) and became renowned for his piety, wisdom, and eloquence. His *Commonitorium pro catholicae fidei antiquitate*, later repeatedly printed and translated, contains the famous three-fold test of Catholicity (the Vincentian canon): *Quod ubique, quod semper, quod ab omnibus creditum est*.

Vincent de Paul, St. (1576–1660; canonized 1737), a shepherd-boy who became a priest, famous for his self-sacrificing labours among the aged and the oppressed, also for his simple eloquence. He founded (1625) the *Congrégation de la Mission* (the Lazarists; *v. Saint-Lazare, Prison de*) and (1633) the *Filles de la Charité* (the Sisters of Charity). He was strongly opposed to *Jansenism.

Vinet, ALEXANDRE (1797–1847), a Swiss of French refugee origin, held chairs of both theology and French literature at Lausanne. His literary criticism (e.g. *Études sur Pascal*, 1848; *Études sur la littérature française au XIXᵉ siècle*, 1849–51, 3 vols.) reflects a high sense of moral values and sound judgement; it was much admired by his fellow critics, e.g. Sainte-Beuve and Brunetière.

Vingt Ans après, *v. Dumas père*.

Vingt Mille Lieues sous les mers, *v. Verne*.

Vinteuil, in Proust's **A la recherche du temps perdu*, a composer whose music is a constantly recurring feature of the novel's emotional and aesthetic background.

Vintras, PIERRE-MICHEL (1807–75), a religious reformer of humble origin who proclaimed himself the prophet Elijah reincarnated to reform the Church, lived in an atmosphere of visions and miracles, instituted a new cult, celebrated a sacrilegious Mass, and was condemned by Rome (1850). When the authorities began to investigate his activities (which also included support of Naundorff's claim to the throne), he fled to London, where he continued to preach his doctrines and to work 'miracles'. He returned to France in 1862 and settled at Lyons. The Baillard brothers, who figure in Barrès's *La *Colline inspirée*, were his disciples.

Viol de Lucrèce, Le, *v. Obey*.

Viollet-le-Duc,   EUGÈNE-EMMANUEL (1814–79), architect, is chiefly re-membered—not always kindly—as a restorer of medieval buildings. His many valuable works include a *Dictionnaire raisonné de l'architecture française du XIᵉ au XVIᵉ siècle* (1854; illustrated by himself).

Violon d'Ingres, *v. Ingres*.

Virelai (earlier *vireli*), a fixed verse-form resembling a sequence of two or three modified *rondeaux* with the same refrain. The rhyme-scheme of one of the simpler forms is $A^1 B^1 A^2 B^2$ cdcdabab $A^1 B^1 A^2 B^2$ cdcdabab $A^1 B^1 A^2 B^2$ (A^1 and A^2 indicate two refrain lines on the same rhyme; the length of the line was variable). The *virelai* was cultivated chiefly by Guillaume de Machaut, Froissart, Christine de Pisan, and Eustache Deschamps; it went out *c.* 1500. *v. Chansons à danser*.

Viret, PIERRE (1511–71), Swiss Reformer, a disciple of Farel, was active in Geneva and Lausanne, and latterly in France. He wrote theological works and many satirical pamphlets.

Virginie, *v. Paul et Virginie*.

Visan, Tancrède de, *pseudonym of* VINCENT BIÉTRIX (1878–1945), who wrote poetry (collected in *Paysages introspectifs*, 1904, and *Le Clair Matin sourit*, 1938; both have valuable introductory essays, on *Symbolism and his own 'credo poétique' respectively); two prose works which may be classed as novels, *Lettres à l'élue: confession d'un intellectuel* (1908) and *En regardant passer les vaches* (1924); and numerous critical studies (sometimes first publ. in **Vers et Prose* and *L'*Occident*) which mark him as one of the most interesting critics of his generation, e.g. *Paul Bourget sociologue* (1908), *Colette et Bérénice* (1909), *Les Élégies et les sonnets de Louise Labé* (1910), *Le Guignol lyonnais* (1910), *L'Attitude du lyrisme contemporain* (1911; collected studies of Verlaine, Vielé-Griffin, Maeterlinck, Verhaeren, and others, of added interest for his remarks on poetic vision, the **vers libre*, etc.), *Un Homme de lettres: le comte de Gobineau* (the preface to a 1913 ed. of **Gobineau's*

Nouvelles asiatiques), *De la culture* (1921), *Essais sur la tradition française* (1921 ; this includes some of the above studies), *Sous le signe du lion* (1935), *Le Visage et le masque* (1942).

Visé, JEAN DONNEAU DE, *v. Mercure galant*.

Vision de Babouc, *v. Babouc*.

Vision de Charles XI, La, *v. Mérimée*.

Visionnaires, Les, (1) *v. Desmarets de Saint-Sorlin*; (2) *v. Nicole*.

Visionnarisme, *v. Literary Isms*.

Vitrac, ROGER, *v. Surrealism*; *Artaud*; *Theatre of the 19th and 20th cs*.

Vitry, JACQUES DE, *v. Jacques de Vitry*.

Vitry, PHILIPPE DE, *v. Franc Gontier*.

Vivien, Renée, *pseudonym of* PAULINE TARN (1877–1909), poetess, b. in London of an English father and an American mother, lived mainly in Paris and wrote in French. Her verse (in *Poésies complètes*, 1901–10, 12 vols.; 1934, 2 vols.)—musical, very sensuous, and influenced by Baudelaire—is written with great purity of form and usually on Lesbian themes.

Vivonne, CATHERINE DE, *v. Rambouillet, Hôtel de*.

Vogue, La, a well-known *Symbolist review (weekly, 32 nos. from 1886), published *Rimbaud's *Les Illuminations* and work by Bourget, Dujardin, Fénéon, Laforgue, Villiers de l'Isle-Adam, Mallarmé, etc. It was briefly revived in 1889 by Kahn and Retté and again in 1899 by Klingsor. *v. Vers libre, Le*.

Vogüé, EUGÈNE-MELCHIOR, VICOMTE DE (1848–1910), novelist and man of letters. His studies of Russian novelists (*Le Roman russe*, 1886) aroused interest in their work and indirectly influenced the French novel (*v. Foreign Influences*, 5). Russian influence

is apparent in his own idealistic novels, e.g. *Jean d'Agrève* (1897), *Les Morts qui parlent* (1899), *Le Maître de la mer* (1903).

Voie royale, La, *v. Malraux*.

Voir Dit, Le, *v. Guillaume de Machaut*.

Voisenon, CLAUDE-HENRI, ABBÉ DE (1708–75), a friend of Voltaire, wrote light verse and *contes (e.g. *Le Sultan Misapouf et la princesse Grisemine*) popular in the *salons of the day.

Voisin, La, *v. Chambre ardente*.

Voiture, VINCENT (1598–1648), poet and letter-writer, one of the chief *habitués* of the Hôtel de *Rambouillet, and a member of the original *Académie française*; a man of brilliant social gifts covering more serious qualities of intellect. He served Gaston d'*Orléans for a time, later held a post at court, and went to Italy and Spain on political missions. His works (publ. posth.) consist of occasional verse, written for Mme de Rambouillet's circle, and of letters which, if too subtle and full of conceits, show a pleasant wit and fancy and contributed to the improvement of French prose. Tallemant des Réaux calls him 'le père de l'ingénieuse badinerie', but he could also write well on serious subjects. *v. Benserade* (for the famous dispute over the sonnets of Voiture and Benserade); *Costar*; *Paulette*.

Voix du silence, Les, *v. Malraux*.

Voix intérieures, Les (1837), a collection of lyrics by Hugo. It includes the poems *A Eugène Vicomte Hugo* (*v. Hugo, E.*), *A l'Arc de Triomphe*, *A Virgile*, *A des oiseaux envolés*.

Vol d'aigle, Le, a term used of Napoleon's escape from Elba and swift, triumphant march on Paris (1815). In a proclamation to his troops he declared, '...L'aigle avec les couleurs nationales volera de clocher en clocher jusqu'aux tours de Notre-Dame!'

Volland, SOPHIE, *v. Diderot.*

Volney, CONSTANTIN, COMTE DE (1757–1820), an **idéologue,* famous in his day for his *Voyage en Syrie et en Égypte* (1787) and *Les Ruines, ou Méditations sur les révolutions des empires* (1791), a singular mixture of picturesque description of ancient ruins and philosophical disquisition on the origin and growth of social, political, and religious institutions. He concludes in favour of the equality of all men before the law, the overthrow of despotism, and toleration and agnosticism in religious matters where truth is not verifiable.

Volpone, v. Romains.

Voltaire, FRANÇOIS-MARIE AROUET, *known as* (1694–1778), poet, historian, and philosopher (*v. Philosophes*).

1. LIFE AND CHIEF WORKS. He was born in Paris, of a family from Poitou; his father was a notary and later a minor official of the **Chambre des comptes.* He was educated by the **Jesuits at the *Collège Louis-le-Grand,* but was soon moving in **libertin* circles (*v. Temple;* also *Lenclos*). An attempt to wean him from such frivolity by sending him as page to the French ambassador in the Netherlands (1713) only resulted in an unfortunate love affair and his enforced return. During an 11-month spell in the **Bastille* (as author of a pungent political lampoon), he finished his tragedy **Œdipe* (publ. 1719 under the name 'Voltaire'—a rough anagram of Arouet—by which he was soon known; *v.* also *Vadé, G., A., and C.*) and worked at his epic *La **Henriade.* Both these writings reflected his nascent political revolt. On his release, he again moved in the highest society (*v. Villars*), where his wit made him welcome. He received pensions from the court, speculated successfully, and became rich. His poem *Le **Pour et le Contre* appeared in 1722, his tragedy **Mariamne* in 1725. In 1726, as a result of a quarrel with the chevalier de Rohan, he was obliged (after a further spell in the *Bastille*) to retire to England. He stayed till early in 1729,

learning English, reading Shakespeare, Milton, and the Restoration dramatists, making the acquaintance of Walpole, Congreve, Gay, and Berkeley, and associating with Bolingbroke, Pope, and Swift. The chief literary fruit of his visit was the **Lettres philosophiques.* After his return to France he produced further tragedies (notably **Brutus,* 1730; *La Mort de César,* which shows Shakespearian influence, 1731; **Zaïre,* 1732); the **Histoire de Charles XII* (1731), his first attempt at history; and *Le **Temple du Goût* (1733), which made him enemies among literary men.

The publication of the *Lettres philosophiques* in 1734 exposed him to danger of arrest, and he left Paris to stay at Cirey with Mme **du Châtelet,* whose love and protection he long enjoyed. His sojourn at Cirey lasted for 10 years and was a period of great literary activity: he wrote (*c.* 1734) his *Traité de métaphysique* (publ. posth.); the dramas **Alzire* (1736), **Mahomet* (1742), and **Mérope* (1743); the poem *Le **Mondain* (1736); the *Éléments de la philosophie de Newton* (1736), a popular exposition of Newton's discoveries; and the *Discours sur l'homme,* a philosophic poem; and he worked at his **Siècle de Louis XIV* and **Essai sur les mœurs.* He also engaged in scientific study and experiments; but here his work was defective and amateurish, for he was impatient and inclined to reject facts which did not seem to square with his theories. After 1743 (when Fleury died) he temporarily recovered a measure of favour at court, where he had powerful advocates (e.g. Mme de Pompadour)—though Louis XV disliked and distrusted him. His *Poème de Fontenoy* (1745) constituted him a sort of official poet; he frequented **Versailles and **Fontainebleau,* was made historiographer, and was granted a pension. He was admitted to the **Académie* in 1746. It was now that he wrote the tale **Zadig* (1748) and—in competition with the elder Crébillon—the plays *Sémiramis* (1748), *Catilina* (1750), and *Oreste* (1750); but this period was on the whole one of sterility.

He sincerely mourned the death (1749) of Mme du Châtelet, though their liaison had been interrupted some time before. (She had turned to Saint-Lambert; but it is clear from letters recently discovered that, even before the break, Voltaire was on most intimately affectionate terms with his niece Mme Louise Denis (c. 1710–90).) In 1750 he yielded to the pressing invitation of Frederick the Great (with whom he was corresponding as early as 1736) and took up residence at Potsdam. There he finished Le *Siècle de Louis XIV (1751), continued work on the *Essai sur les mœurs, and wrote, or completed, *Micromégas (1752). But Frederick and he could not get on together; a crisis was reached in 1753 (Voltaire's *Diatribe du docteur Akakia, 1752, directed against his rival Maupertuis, being a contributory factor) and he left Prussia. He now settled for a time in Switzerland, at Lausanne in winter and at a property he bought near Geneva (Les Délices—now the Musée et Institut Voltaire; v. Tronchin) in summer. La *Pucelle appeared in 1755, but he disavowed its authorship. His tragedy L'*Orphelin de la Chine was also produced in 1755. There followed his Poème sur le désastre de Lisbonne (1756), using the terrible Lisbon earthquake of 1755 as a text for an attack on the doctrine of a free and benevolent Providence (v. Rousseau, J.-J.); the Histoire des voyages de *Scarmentado (1756); and Le *Pauvre Diable (1758). He also supported the *Encyclopédie and wrote several articles for it. His relations with the Calvinists of Geneva were not harmonious and late in 1758 he bought a large estate at Ferney (a village to the north-west of Geneva, in French territory, but close to the Swiss frontier; v. Brosses), where from c. 1760 he combined the life of a country magnate with immense literary activity. He was now very rich, thanks to his skilful management of his funds (in 1768, after vigorous economies, his Ferney budget was fixed at 40,000 livres a year, which provided for 60 servants and 12 horses). His niece—the ugly, vulgar, extravagant Mme Denis—kept house for him, and he was extremely hospitable, receiving distinguished guests of every nation. He had, as always, a host of adversaries (e.g. Fréron,

J.-J. Rousseau, Piron, Guénée, Chaumeix, Pompignan, Nonnotte), with whom he delighted to squabble, but he was also greatly kind and generous to many in distress.

Purely literary work—such as his tragedy *Tancrède (1760), Commentaire sur Corneille (1764), and Lettre à l'Académie against Shakespeare (1776)—hereafter occupied comparatively little of his time; his chief concern was with political, philosophical, and religious questions. His Saül (of which he denied the authorship), a mock tragedy in prose ridiculing parts of the Biblical story of Saul, Samuel, and David, appeared in 1763; his Dictionnaire philosophique in 1764 (v. Dictionaries, 1764); his deistic Lettres de Memmius à Cicéron in 1771. Some of his most telling propaganda is in his tales (called romans, but in fact merely the amusing vehicle for his philosophical, religious, and political views), dialogues, facéties, and private letters, of which he produced a constant stream in the last 20 years of his life. He denied writing many of these (other than the letters), but deceived no one. *Candide (1759) was his finest tale; others not previously mentioned include *Babouc, *Cosi-Sancta, *Memnon, Le *Blanc et le Noir, *Jeannot et Colin, L'*Ingénu, L'*Homme aux quarante écus, La *Princesse de Babylone, Le Taureau blanc (1774; an Oriental tale containing much mockery of Old Testament stories), Histoire de *Jenni. The dialogues, such as the conversation of L'Intendant des menus avec l'abbé Grizel on the excommunication of actors, are very vivid and realistic. It was while at Ferney that, fired by the hatred of intolerance and injustice expressed in his Traité sur la *tolérance (1763), he successfully campaigned to clear the name of Jean *Calas, and also fought for the rehabilitation of Sirven (another *Huguenot, condemned on a rather similar charge), La Barre (a youth executed for a trivial religious offence), and *Lally. The production of *Irène, his last tragedy, in 1778 was the occasion of his triumphal return to Paris. He was too ill to go to the *Comédie-Française until the sixth performance, when he was acclaimed with wild enthusiasm and crowned with a laurel wreath. He died within a few weeks at the home of the marquis de Villette on the quay later named after him. The Church refused him burial, and this had to be carried out surreptitiously; but 13 years later his remains were borne in triumph to the *Panthéon.

2. CHARACTER AND OPINIONS. He was a man of strange contrasts: vain, irritable, vindictive, untruthful, at times servile; yet also humane, generous, a good friend, and a passionate champion of the oppressed. Of the various forms of his literary activity, his philosophical propaganda is perhaps that by which he is best known. His views show a development in the course of his life, from the comparative optimism of, for example, *Babouc* and *Zadig* to the pessimism of *Candide*. While affirming the existence of a Deity (e.g. in the *Sermon des cinquante*, 1761), he had little understanding of religion and bitterly attacked the Christian faith (esp. its minor outward manifestations) with every resource of wit and satire. His repeated war-cry was 'Écrasons l'infâme!' (by 'l'infâme' he apparently meant the intolerant religious fanaticism embodied in any dogmatic religion, but, above all, in Catholicism and its priesthood). For him, true religion consisted in the practice of virtue according to the conscience we have received from God, and this virtue he identified substantially with social justice. With this narrowness of spirit he combined an acute perception of the defective political organization and the practical abuses (e.g. *lettres de cachet* and acts of religious intolerance) of his time. The dominant trait of his writings on political and religious subjects is lack of respect for existing institutions and contempt for authority; he was thus a disruptive influence and prepared the way for the Revolution. But he favoured the idea of government by a beneficent despot, a philosopher king; and he aimed, not at a political upheaval, but at the transformation of political thought through rational criticism, which was to bring in the reign of humanity and justice.

3. LITERARY CHARACTERISTICS. His style is in general simple, precise, and appropriate to the matter in hand. His three main historical works (on Charles XII of Sweden and Louis XIV, and the *Essai sur les mœurs*) are well-documented, rapid, luminous recitals of essential facts, tracing cause and effect, the parts played by the various actors, and their characters; but they are deficient in warmth and life and fail to evoke the periods in question. In his tragedies he broadly adhered to the *Classical canons, though here and there we may trace the influence of Shakespeare (whom he at one time claimed, on the whole with justice, to have introduced to the Continent, but whom he later condemned in his *Lettre à l'Académie* of 1776; *v. Letourneur*). But he is essentially a good playwright, aiming at scenic success rather than psychological study and often using his plays as vehicles for propaganda. Besides the tragedies mentioned above (the best of which are perhaps *Zaïre*, *Mérope*, and *Alzire*), there are interesting features in *Olimpie* (1764), *Le *Triumvirat* (1767), Les *Scythes* (1767), Les *Guèbres* (1769), and Les *Lois de Minos* (1773). His comedies—notably L'*Enfant prodigue* (1736) and *Nanine* (1749), also L'*Écossaise* (1760)—are mediocre, for he lacked profundity of observation. His philosophical tales are marked by rapidity and sharp outline; they utilize trivial, comic, but vividly illustrative facts, substituting the striking concrete example for the abstract theory. This—and his gift for expressing better than anyone else what everyone was thinking—explains their appeal to all classes of readers and their great success. He was also a master of light verse, displaying his lively, felicitous wit and his gift for gentle mockery in occasional trifles, epistles, satires, verse tales, etc. The *Épître à Boileau* and *Épître à Horace* are among his best later works. His private letters, of which a vast number have been published, are regarded by some as his most characteristic writings. Natural, lively, graceful, serious at times but soon reverting to gaiety, they reveal the man in all his defects and also in his broad humanity.

His influence may be gauged from the fact that some 50 editions of his collected works (apart from numerous eds. of separate works) were issued in the period 1740–1840, notably that printed 1784–90 at Kehl (in Baden) by the enterprise of Beaumarchais, who bought for the purpose the type of the English printer Baskerville; *v.* also *Cramer.* The Voltaire Foundation is in the process of publishing the *Complete Works of Voltaire* in *c.*150 vols. (1968– ; ed. W. H. Barber and others); publication of his correspondence (21,221 letters; ed. T. Besterman) is now complete (vols. 85–135).

Volupté (1834), a long novel by Sainte-Beuve, much of it autobiographical. The narrator, Amaury, a priest on his way to America, spends the voyage writing, for the spiritual benefit of a friend, the story of his life before he took orders. There is a confused background of Royalist conspiracy under the *Consulat,* in which Cadoudal and Pichegru figure, but the work is chiefly of interest as the inner history of a man who is a prey to melancholy, frustration, and introspection (*cf. Obermann*; *René*; *Adolphe*; *Confession d'un enfant du siècle, La*), and in whom gross sensuality is continually at war with spirituality. Eventually, he finds sublimation in religion and, after almost mystical agonies of temptation, becomes a priest. There is one approach to a dramatic moment at the end, when, soon after being ordained, he is called to administer the last rites to Mme de Couaën, wife of his former friend and patron. He had always loved her, no matter where his baser instincts led him, but she had remained a model of wifely and maternal virtue.

Voyage, Le, v. Baudelaire.

Voyage au bout de la nuit, v. Céline.

Voyage autour de ma chambre, v. Maistre, X. de.

Voyage aux eaux des Pyrénées, later called *Voyage aux Pyrénées, v. Taine.*

Voyage de Monsieur Perrichon, Le, a farcical comedy by Labiche; produced 1860. M. Perrichon, a wealthy retired tradesman, sets off for a holiday in Switzerland with his wife and his daughter Henriette—followed by Daniel and Armand, friendly rivals for her hand. Armand's stock goes up when he rescues M. Perrichon, who falls off a horse; Daniel's soars when he lets M. Perrichon rescue *him* from a well-managed fall into a crevasse. Complications ensue in gay, see-saw fashion, until the clever Daniel overreaches himself and Armand wins Henriette.

Voyage du jeune Anacharsis en Grèce, Le, v. Barthélemy.

Voyage d'Urien, Le, v. Gide.

Voyage en Orient, v. Nerval.

Voyelles, *v. Sonnet des voyelles.*

Vrain-Lucas (b. 1816), a clever literary forger, a self-educated man of humble origin. He came to Paris (1852), found work with a rather dubious genealogist, and discovered that he had a gift for imitating handwriting. Within a few years he had tricked the eminent mathematician Michel Chasles (1793–1880) into buying some 7,000 forged letters (said to be genuine autographs or 16th.-c. transs.), attributed to Cleopatra, Petrarch and Laura, Mme de Maintenon, Pascal (a letter suggesting that Pascal, not Newton, had discovered the law of gravity), etc. Chasles defended their authenticity in heated discussions at the *Académie des Sciences,* but finally had to yield to evidence that he had been duped. (A. Daudet's novel *L'Immortel,* satirizing him, aroused much indignation.) Vrain-Lucas was heavily fined and imprisoned (1870) for two years, but lapsed again on his release.

W

Wace (*c.* 1100–75), an *Anglo-Norman poet, b. in Jersey, was made a canon of Bayeux by Henry II, for whom he wrote two long historical poems: the *Roman de Brut* or *Geste des Bretons* (completed 1155; in octosyllables), dedicated to Eleanor of Aquitaine (wife of Henry II) and based on *Geoffrey of Monmouth's *Historia Regum Britanniae*, with the addition of much picturesque material, including the story of the Round Table (*v. Romans bretons*); the *Roman de Rou* (i.e. Rollo—*v. Charles III*) or *Geste des Normands* (partly in monorhyme stanzas of *alexandrines, partly in octosyllabic couplets), a history of the dukes of Normandy, based on the Latin chronicles, with additions from popular tradition (*v. Chanson de Roland*), down to the battle of Tinchebrai (1106)—at which point, discouraged by the favour shown to his rival Benoît de Sainte-Maure, he abandoned the work. *v.* also *Saints, Lives of.*

Wagner, RICHARD (1813–83). Wagner's operas were performed in Paris as early as 1860, but his music was little appreciated in France till some years later. Baudelaire, meanwhile, had praised him in various articles and remarked on affinities between his own theory of *correspondances* and Wagner's attempt to make his operas, or music-dramas, syntheses of music and poetry. The *Symbolists made these theories of *correspondances* their own and for many of them Wagner became a master. *v. Revue wagnérienne.*

Wagram (near Vienna). Here Napoleon defeated the Austrians (6 July 1809); *v. Coalitions* (5). At one point in the campaign, while trying to cross the Danube at Essling, the French had narrowly escaped defeat; *v. Maréchal* (Masséna).

Wairy, LOUIS-CONSTANT (1778–1845), 'Constant', son of a Belgian *hôtelier*, became Bonaparte's head *valet de chambre* in 1800 and was his close personal attendant, both at home and on campaign, until 1814, when he abandoned his master and was succeeded by Marchand. His memoirs (1830–1, 6 vols.) were compiled, from his own story, by Charles-Maxime de Villemessant, a journalist.

Waldenses, *v. Vaudois.*

Waller, Max, *pseudonym of* MAURICE WARLOMONT (1860–89), a Belgian poet, founder and moving spirit of *La Jeune Belgique* (Brussels 1881–97), a review famous in the history of the 19th-c. literary renaissance in Belgium. It was primarily sympathetic to the *Parnassien ideals, but for a time many Belgian *Symbolists (e.g. Maeterlinck, Rodenbach, Verhaeren) were contributors.

Wallonie, La (1886–92; monthly), a literary and artistic review f. at Liège by the Belgian poet Mockel. It was the organ of Belgian *Symbolism and also published the first works of many French Symbolists.

Walter, André. For *Les Cahiers* and *Les Poésies d'André Walter*, *v. Gide.*

Walter, Judith, *v. Gautier, J.*

Warens, LOUISE-ÉLÉONORE DE LA TOUR DU PIL, BARONNE DE (1700–62), of Swiss birth, a kindly, benevolent woman of easy morals, famous as the protectress of J.-J. Rousseau (*c.* 1729–42). She had then left her husband and was employed by the priests of Savoy in matters relating to the conversion of Protestants from Geneva; she was also, it seems, a political spy. It is open to question how far Rousseau's idyllic account of their relationship (in *Les *Confessions*) is tinged with imagination.

Wartburg, WALTHER VON, *v. Dictionaries*, 1922– .

Watelet, CLAUDE-HENRI, *v. Dictionaries*, 1792.

Waterloo, a village south of Brussels near which, on 18 June 1815, Napoleon (with a hastily recruited army of *c.* 100,000) was finally and decisively defeated by the United Army, which included forces from Britain, the Netherlands, Hanover, and Brunswick, under Wellington, and the Prussian army, under Blücher; *v. Coalitions* (7). Napoleon's aim was to dispose of Wellington's army before the Prussians arrived. There had been a violent storm in the night and he delayed his attack till midday. The British withstood him throughout the afternoon. By 2 p.m. a first contingent of Prussians had arrived, and attacked Napoleon on the right. They were finally repulsed about 7 p.m., by which time nearly all the French infantry reserves had been used up. Napoleon then launched his famous *Garde impériale* in a desperate bid to break Wellington's squares. They were mown down by British fire as they tried to advance. At this point Blücher appeared with the main Prussian forces, taking Napoleon in the flank, and Wellington ordered a general advance. The exhausted French, attacked in front and on the flank, panicked and were routed, with the exception of the *Garde*, who resisted to the end (*v. Cambronne*). The main fighting took place between the farm of La Haie-Sainte, Wellington's advanced post, and the plateau of Mont-Saint-Jean, where his troops were entrenched.

French authors who have described Waterloo include Stendhal (in *La *Chartreuse de Parme*), Hugo (in *Les *Châtiments* and *Les *Misérables*), Erckmann-Chatrian (in *Waterloo*, etc.).

Watteau, ANTOINE (1684–1721), a famous genre painter, especially of *fêtes galantes* in a rustic setting (shepherds and shepherdesses in the fashionable dress of the day), superficially gay, but with an underlying melancholy. His *L'Embarquement pour Cythère* is well known.

Wauquelin or **Vauquelin,** JEAN (d. 1453), a Picard, was a compiler, translator, and copyist in the service of Philippe le Bon, duke of Burgundy. He translated *Geoffrey of Monmouth's *Historia Regum Britanniae* and Jacques de Guise's *Annales de Hainaut*, and made prose adaptations of *Girart de Roussillon* and the *Roman d'Alexandre*.

Weights and Measures. Before the introduction of the *metric system (1801) a great variety of weights and measures was in use in different parts of France, and the same terms had not everywhere precisely the same meaning. Those most commonly found in French literature include (1) long measure: *pouce* $\frac{1}{12}$ of a *pied*, or about an inch; *pied*, a little more than an English foot; *aune*, about $3\frac{1}{4}$ feet (*cf.* the English ell); *toise*, 6 *pieds*; *lieue*, a league, variable, often about $2\frac{1}{2}$ miles; (2) square measure: *arpent*, just over an acre; (3) capacity: *boisseau*, about $\frac{1}{3}$ of a bushel; *muid*, about 400 gallons; (4) weight: *livre*, about 1 lb.

Weil, SIMONE (1909–43), a left-wing intellectual of Jewish birth who died young and has since won fame for her writings on religion, philosophy, and sociology. A brilliant student of the *École normale supérieure*, she passed the *agrégation* in philosophy (1931), then entered the teaching profession. Her career was interrupted by illness, and even more by her sociological interests (as when, eager for experience of working conditions, she spent a year as a factory-hand at the Renault motor works) and her political militancy (as when, in 1936, she joined the International Brigade in Spain). When France fell in 1940 and the teaching profession was closed to Jews, she worked as a farmhand in the Unoccupied Zone. In May 1942, she accompanied her family to New York. A few months later, bent on joining the *Resistance in France, she came to London to work for the Provisional French Government. But she had ruined her health by privations (self-imposed lest her lot should be better than that of her compatriots) and she died of tuberculosis in an English sanatorium.

She published very little in her lifetime, and the writings assembled and published after her death were largely drawn from her *Cahiers* (1951–6, 3 vols.) and from letters and material sent to friends. They include mystical writings in which she explores her attitude to religious belief, revealing her deep insight into spiritual tribulation and her preference for a life guided and enriched by Christian inspiration, but not limited by acceptance of dogma, e.g. *La Pesanteur et la Grâce* (1947), *L'Attente de Dieu* (1950), and *Lettre à un religieux* (1951); translations and studies inspired by her interest in Greek philosophy, e.g. *La Source grecque* (1953); political and sociological studies showing her hatred of injustice, her consequent distrust of any form of organized social authority, and her concern over the dehumanization of the industrial worker, e.g. *L'Enracinement* (1949), *La Condition ouvrière* (1951), *Oppression et liberté* (1955), *Écrits historiques et politiques* (1960). Though at times paradoxical and didactic, her work is notable for its lucidity and intellectual integrity.

Weimars, v. *Loève-Veimars*.

Weiss, JEAN-JACQUES (1827–91), a brilliant political journalist, also a literary critic, with reactionary views. He wrote for the **Journal des Débats* and *Le *Temps*.

Welche, v. *Velche*.

Werthers, Die Leiden des jungen, v. *Goethe*.

Wiener, FRANTZ, v. *Croisset, F. de*.

Wilde, OSCAR (1854–1900), the Anglo-Irish poet and dramatist, had many associations with French literary circles and latterly lived, and died, in Paris. He wrote his **Salomé* in French in the first instance.

William Shakespeare (1864), by Hugo, a biographical and critical study, dedicated to England as a 'glorification de son poète'. The work is apocalyptic in style, but interesting as one of Hugo's emphatic pleas for a relative approach in criticism (v. *Critics and Criticism*, 2). v. *Hugo, J.-F.-V.*

Willy, v. *Colette*.

Wolff, PHILIPPE (1913–), medieval historian, professor at the University of Toulouse from 1945. He has made a special study of the region of Toulouse (*Histoire de Toulouse*, 1958; *Histoire du Languedoc*, 1967, in the series *Univers de la France et des pays francophones, histoire des provinces*, 1967– , of which he is general editor).

Wolff, PIERRE (1865–1930), dramatist. His works—popular successes of the *théâtre du boulevard*—include *Le Secret de Polichinelle* (1903), *L'Âge d'aimer* (1905), *Les Marionnettes* (1910), *Les Ailes brisées* (1920).

Wolmar, Baron and **Julie de,** in J.-J. Rousseau's *La *Nouvelle Héloïse*.

Wyse, (1) SIR THOMAS (1791–1862), Irish politician and at one time British minister in Greece, m. (1821) Lætitia Bonaparte, a daughter of Lucien Bonaparte (v. *Bonaparte Family*) by his second wife; (2) their son WILLIAM CHARLES BONAPARTE-(1826–92), b. at Waterford and educated in England, became associated with the **félibres* (1859), settled at Avignon, and published two collections of poetry in Provençal—*Li Parpaioun blu* (*Les Papillons bleus*, 1868) and *Li Piado de la princesso* (*L'Empreinte des pas de la princesse*, 1882); (3) their daughter MARIE-LÆTITIA-STUDOLMINE (1831–1902; Mme de Rute by her third marriage, earlier Mme de Solms and the comtesse Rattazzi), b. at Waterford, a novelist. She lived in France after her first marriage, but was not recognized as a Bonaparte by Napoleon III and had to leave in 1853 and again in 1865 (after publication of her novel *Les Mariages de la Créole* had been refused; it was publ. in Brussels, 1866). Her other novels include *Bicheville* (1865), set in Florence.

Wyss, JOHANN RUDOLF (1781–1830), a Swiss professor, author, with his father,

Johann David Wyss (1743–1818; a Swiss pastor), of the German original (1812–13) of the story almost at once translated into English as *The Swiss Family Robinson* and into French as *Le Robinson suisse, ou Journal d'un père naufragé avec ses enfants.*

Wyzewa, TEODOR DE (1862–1917), essayist and critic of Polish birth, widely read in foreign literatures and closely associated with the early days of *Symbolism. He published articles in the *Revue wagnérienne* (on Wagner and Symbolism, collected in *Nos maîtres*, 1895), the *Revue indépendante*, etc.; the novel *Valbert* (1893; the hero lives in a world of books and fantasy and is terrified of real life); *Contes chrétiens* (1901), written after his conversion to Roman Catholicism.

Y

Year, Beginning of the. In different parts of France, and at different times, the year was reckoned as beginning on a variety of dates: 25 December, 25 March, Easter (mobile), 1 January. The first system, from 25 December (*style de la Nativité*), was widely used in medieval times, notably in parts of S. France, in regions under English domination, and in the Dauphiné. The second system, from 25 March (*style de l'Annonciation*), was frequently used until 1564 in documents of the southern provinces and elsewhere, penetrating even to N. France. The inconvenient system of reckoning the year from the mobile feast of Easter (which meant that the last 10 days of March and the first 24 days of April, or some of these, might occur twice, or not at all, in a given year) was adopted by the royal chancellery, probably under Louis VI, gradually spread to the provinces, and was in such wide use during the Middle Ages as to be known as the *style de France*. The year beginning on 1 January (*style de la Circoncision*), adopted from Roman usage, was prescribed by an edict of Charles IX of January 1563/4, soon became general, and remained in force till the introduction (1793) of the *Republican Calendar. From 1806, with the return to the Gregorian Calendar, the year again began on 1 January.

Yonville, v. *Madame Bovary.*

Young, ARTHUR (1741–1820), an English agronomist whose fame chiefly rests on his *Travels in France* (1792), a work of lively interest and great historical value describing three tours made between 1787 and 1790, covering nearly the whole country. He thus saw France just before and during the Revolution, and he draws attention to the social and economic defects of the *ancien régime*. The work was translated into French (1794) and 20,000 copies are said to have been printed by order of the *Convention* for free distribution in rural areas. Selections from his agricultural writings were also translated by order of the *Directoire* (*Le Cultivateur anglais*, 1801, 18 vols.).

Young, EDWARD (1683–1765). The long, gloomy, didactic poem by which this English author is chiefly remembered, *The Complaint, or Night Thoughts on Life, Death, and Immortality* (1742–5), was translated into French by Letourneur (*Méditations de la nuit*, 1769—it is often called 'Les Nuits d'Young') and helped to introduce romantic melancholy into French literature. *Cf. Ossian*; v. *Foreign Influences, 2.*

Yourcenar, Marguerite, *pseudonym of* MARGUERITE DE CRAYENCOUR (1903–), b. in Brussels, resident in America since 1939, a versatile writer whose works, set in many different periods and places, reflect her extensive travels and wide cultural interests. They include, notably, *Mémoires d'Hadrien* (1951), fictitious memoirs of the Roman emperor, in effect the philosophical reflections of a humanist; also novels and tales (e.g. *Alexis, ou le Traité du vain combat*, 1929, set in Austria-Hungary just before 1914; *Denier du rêve*, 1934, set in Fascist Italy; *Nouvelles orientales*, 1938; *L'Œuvre au noir*, 1968); essays (*Sous bénéfice d'inventaire*, 1962); translations of Henry James, Virginia Woolf, the Greek and poetry. The first woman to be elected to the *Académie (1980).

Ys, a legendary city under the sea off the coast of Brittany (Finistère). According to the legend, it once stood on the edge of the sea, protected by a dyke with flood-gates to which the king held the only key. One night, after carousing with her lover, the king's daughter stole the key, opened the gates, and engulfed the city. Sometimes, on a clear morning, the cathedral can be seen rising from the sea, and there is a sound of bells and chanting. The story was adapted by the composer Édouard Lalo for his opera *Le Roi d'Ys* (1888) and inspired one of Debussy's best-known pianoforte compositions, *La Cathédrale engloutie*.

Ysengrin, the wolf in the *Roman de Renart.

Ysopet, v. Marie de France.

Yvain or *Le Chevalier au lion*, a *roman breton by Chrétien de Troyes; written *c.* 1180. There is an abbreviated 14th-c. English version, *Ywain and Gawain*.

Yvain, a knight of Arthur's court, goes to the magic fountain in the forest of *Brocéliande, is challenged by the knight who guards it, and slays him. The knight's widow, Laudine, at first heartbroken and bent on revenge, is gradually persuaded by her maid Lunette to look with favour on Yvain, who, for his part, has been deeply moved by Laudine's beauty. A seemingly impossible marriage is thus achieved. Soon after this, Yvain and Laudine are visited by Arthur and his knights, and *Gauvain urges Yvain not to sink into voluptuous sloth, but to resume his knightly life. Laudine agrees to his departure, but appoints a day for his return: if he fails to come, he will lose her love. Yvain, absorbed by knightly pursuits, forgets his promise, and Laudine sends a messenger to tell him that he is never to return to her. Yvain goes mad, but is healed by magic. He now goes about the world seeking adventures, in the course of which he wins the devotion of a lion by saving it from a flame-breathing serpent. Finally, though with difficulty, he obtains Laudine's pardon.

The poem is remarkable for the subtle delineation of the complex character of Laudine, notably the transference of her love from her dead husband to his slayer (recalling the famous story of the Matron of Ephesus) and her display of wounded pride when Yvain forgets his promise. Here, as in the *Chevalier à la charrette, the knight is wholly dominated by his lady.

Yver, JACQUES (1520–72), a gentleman of Poitou, author of *Printemps* (1572; the title is a play on his own name), five tales of varied character, much read in their day. The setting is what would now be called a house-party in a country house in Poitou. The work sheds light on the conversation and mode of life of the wealthy classes of the day, and also provides a taste of the *esprit gaulois.

Yvetot, *v. Béranger.*

Yvette (1885), the name-tale of a collection by Maupassant. A *demi-mondaine*'s daughter grows up in her mother's house unaware of its true nature, mystifying familiars of the household by her innocent provocativeness. She learns the truth, pens a note of outraged virtue to her mother, and tries to end her life by inhaling chloroform. She is found (as is the note) by one of her most perplexed admirers, who revives her. In the exhilaration of returning to life she is glad to have failed—and to fall, leaving her admirer more puzzled than ever.

Z

Zadig (1748; first publ. 1747 as *Memnon, histoire orientale*—to be distinguished from the tale **Memnon*), a philosophical tale by Voltaire, with some sly hits at the clergy and Catholic dogma.

Zadig, a young man well endowed by nature and fortified by a good education, is puzzled by the vagaries of his destiny. He achieves high office, but is unfortunate in love and, despite his wisdom and moderation, narrowly escapes being strangled in Babylon, roasted alive in Basra, and impaled by bonzes in Serendip, and is actually enslaved in Egypt. In a remarkable chapter entitled *L'Hermite*, he is finally relieved of his perplexity by the angel Jesrad, who reveals to him that there is no evil in the world but some good comes of it; and that there is no such thing as chance, but that all is trial or punishment, recompense or precaution. Zadig marries the queen whom he loves, becomes king, and worships Providence.

Zaïre, a tragedy by Voltaire; produced 1732.

Zaïre, a Christian child carried off by the Turks, has been brought up as a Moslem in the seraglio at Jerusalem. The sultan Orosmane has fallen in love with her, and she with him, and they are about to marry. Nérestan, her former companion in captivity, also carried off as a child, arrives just before the wedding. He had been ransomed and taken back to France, then recaptured and released on promising to bring back from France the ransom of 10 knights. This ransom having exhausted his fortune, he again gives himself up. The generous Orosmane refuses the ransom and frees 100 prisoners. But he excepts from these Zaïre and the aged Lusignan, last of the French kings of Jerusalem. Zaïre, aware of Nérestan's disappointment, persuades Orosmane to release Lusignan. He is brought from his cell, aged and infirm, and when his liberators, Nérestan and Zaïre, are presented to him he recognizes them as his own lost children. Horrified to learn that Zaïre is a Moslem, he prevails upon her to become a Christian; the discovered relationship is to be concealed. Lusignan is dying, and Nérestan presses his sister to be secretly baptized. She arouses Orosmane's suspicions by asking for a postponement of the wedding. Orosmane intercepts a letter from Nérestan arranging a meeting with Zaïre in terms which suggest to him that there is a guilty connection between the pair. Mad with jealousy, he goes to the rendezvous and kills Zaïre. He then learns the truth from Nérestan and takes his own life.

Zélide, *v. Charrière*.

Zémire et Azor, *v. Grétry*.

Zimmer, BERNARD (1893–1964), dramatist, author of *Le Veau gras* (1924), *Les Zouaves* (1925), *Bava l'Africain* (1926), *Le Coup du 2 décembre* (1928), *Le Beau Danube rouge* (1932), etc., mainly satires and farces with a grotesque element reminiscent of **Jarry's *Ubu Roi*.

Z. Marcas (1840, in the **Revue parisienne*; later in *La *Comédie humaine, Scènes de la vie politique*). Zéphirin Marcas is young, gifted, and ambitious, but can make no headway against corruption.

Zola, ÉMILE (1840–1902), novelist, of Italian origin on his father's side, was brought up at Aix-en-Provence, went to Paris (1858), worked for the publishing firm of Hachette (1860–5), began to write verse and short stories for periodicals, and published *Contes à Ninon* (1864; a collection inc. some fairy-tales) and *La Confession de Claude* (1865; his first full-length novel). After this he supported himself by literary and art criticism (he was a friend of Cézanne and Manet) and wrote the **Realist novels **Thérèse Raquin* (1867) and *Madeleine Férat* (1868; later produced as a play at the **Théâtre Libre*—he had first written it as a play, but could not get it accepted, so rewrote it as a novel). He then proceeded to make his name as the theorist and leader of *Naturalism, and as the author of a cycle of novels illustrating his theories (for details *v. Naturalism; Rougon-Macquart, Les; v.* also *Soirées de Médan, Les*). He sometimes carried documentation and scientific exposition to extremes, to the detriment of his *Rougon-Macquart* novels as fiction. But when he forgot his theories he could produce powerful—albeit lurid and often revolting—descriptions of vice and misery ('C'est un colosse qui a les pieds mal-propres, mais c'est un colosse'—Flaubert, *Correspondance*, 18 April 1880), and extra-vagantly lyrical descriptions of nature that are primarily *Romantic in inspiration. He excels, for example, at evoking both the teeming, tumultuous life of Paris and its long vistas, skies, and river through the changing seasons.

His later novels had little to do with Naturalism. The trilogy *Les Trois Villes—Lourdes* (1894; *v. Bernadette, St.*), *Rome* (1896), *Paris* (1898)—is concerned with social and religious problems. The series *Les Quatre Évangiles—Fécondité* (1899), *Travail* (1901; this owed much to *Fouriérisme*), *Vérité* (1903), *Justice* (projected, but never written)—is inspired by humanitarian ideals. His other works include *Mes haines* and *Mon salon* (both 1866), collected essays on realism in literature and art; *Édouard Manet* (1867), a study; *Nos auteurs dramatiques* (1881), criticism; and plays (which met with little success; some of his novels were also dramatized), e.g. *Les Héritiers Rabourdin* (1874; comedy) and *Le Bouton de Rose* (1878; farce).

He was a stout champion of Dreyfus, notably in the famous letter *J'accuse* (1898; *v. Dreyfus*)—which earned him a prison sentence (he fled and spent the year in England)—and the pamphlets (1901) *La Vérité en marche* and *L'Affaire Dreyfus*. The case inspired his novel *Vérité*.

Zutistes, Les, *v. Symbolism.*

FRANCE: DEPARTMENTS AND FORMER PROVINCES
(v. Département; Provinces)

1 COMTAT-VENAISSIN, see *Vaucluse*, p. 643.

2 SAVOIE AND COMTÉ DE NICE. The Duché de Savoie (out of which the *départements* of Savoie and Haute-Savoie were formed) and the Comté de Nice were not finally ceded to France until 1860.

3 TERRITOIRE DE BELFORT, the portion of the *département* of Haut-Rhin which remained in French possession in 1871 after the Franco-Prussian War. It retained its separate administrative status when Alsace and Lorraine were restored to France in 1919 by the Treaty of Versailles, and now ranks as a department.

4 The inset shows the new *départements* of the Paris region, replacing Seine and Seine-et-Oise. Each has its *préfet*; there is also a *préfet de la région parisienne* (which includes Seine-et-Marne).

OXFORD

MORE OXFORD PAPERBACKS

Details of a selection of other books follow. A complete list of Oxford Paperbacks, including The World's Classics, Twentieth-Century Classics, OPUS, Past Masters, Oxford Authors, Oxford Shakespeare, and Oxford Paperback Reference, is available in the UK from the General Publicity Department, Oxford University Press, Walton Street, Oxford, OX2 6DP.

In the USA, complete lists are available from the Paperbacks Marketing Manager, Oxford University Press, 200 Madison Avenue, New York, NY 10016.

Dead Man Leading

V. S. Pritchett

Introduction by Paul Theroux

An expedition to rescue a man missing in the Brazilian jungle becomes a journey of self-discovery for his son. Conradian in conception, the treatment in the novel of obsession, verging on madness, is strikingly original.

'a rich, original and satisfying book'—*Spectator*

The Secret Battle

A. P. Herbert

Introduction by John Terraine

First published in 1919, *The Secret Battle* is an account of the wartime experiences of an infantry officer, Harry Penrose, as he is tested and brought to breaking-point, first in Gallipoli, then with his young wife in London, and finally in the trenches of France. Without melodrama or sensationalism, Herbert conveys the full horror of war and its awful impact on the mind and body of an ordinary soldier.

'This book should be read in each generation, so that men and women may rest under no illusion about what war means.'—Winston Churchill

Elizabeth and Essex

Lytton Strachey

Introduction by Michael Holroyd

Lytton Strachey achieved fame with the publication in 1918 of *Eminent Victorians*; but none of his books brought him greater popular success than his last: this dramatic reconstruction of the complex and stormy relationship between Queen Elizabeth I and the dashing, if wayward, Earl of Essex.

'a brilliant and insufficiently appreciated book'—A. L. Rowse

The Fifth Queen

Ford Madox Ford

Introduction by A. S. Byatt

Ford Madox Ford's vision of the court of Henry VIII brilliantly recreates the struggle between Henry's fifth wife, Katharine Howard, and the tough, unscrupulous Thomas Cromwell for the mind and soul of their King.

'The best historical romance of this century.'—*Times Literary Supplement*
'magnificent'—Graham Greene

His Monkey Wife

John Collier

Introduction by Paul Theroux

The work of this British poet and novelist who lived for many years in Hollywood has always attracted a devoted following. This, his first novel, concerns a chimpanzee called Emily who falls in love with her owner—an English schoolmaster—and embarks on a process of self-education which includes the reading of Darwin's *Origin of Species*.

'John Collier welds the strongest force with the strangest subtlety . . . It is a tremendous and terrifying satire, only made possible by the suavity of its wit.'—Osbert Sitwell

'Read as either a parody of thirties' fiction or just crazy comedy, it deserves its place as a 20th-century classic.'—David Holloway, *Sunday Telegraph*

The Village in the Jungle

Leonard Woolf

Introduction by E. F. C. Ludowyck

As a young man Leonard Woolf spent seven years in the Ceylon civil service. The people he met in the Sinhalese jungle villages so fascinated and obsessed him that some years later he wrote a novel about them. It is his knowledge and profound understanding of the Sinhalese people that has made *The Village in the Jungle* a classic for all time.

'The Village in the Jungle is a novel of superbly dispassionate observation, a great novel.'—Quentin Bell

They were Defeated

Rose Macaulay

Introduction by Susan Howatch

In her only historical novel, the author of *The Towers of Trebizond* skilfully interweaves the lives of Robert Herrick and other seventeenth-century writers with those of a small group of fictional characters.

'To the great enrichment of the English language Miss Macaulay has chosen an historical subject. As a result she has achieved her greatest success—which means she has added something permanent to English letters.'—*Observer*

'One of the few authors of whom it may be said she adorns our century'—Elizabeth Bowen

Seven Days in New Crete

Robert Graves

Introduction by Martin Seymour-Smith

A funny, disconcerting, and uncannily prophetic novel about Edward Venn-Thomas, a cynical poet, who finds himself transported to a civilisation in the far future. He discovers that his own world ended long ago, and that the inhabitants of the new civilisation have developed a neo-archaic social system. Magic rather than science forms the basis of their free and stable society; yet, despite its near perfection, Edward finds New Cretan life insipid. He realizes that what is missing is a necessary element of evil, which he feels is his duty to restore.

'Robert Graves' cynical stab at creating a Utopia is a poetic *Brave New World* filled with much more colour and dreaming than the original *Brave New World* of Aldous Huxley.'—Maeve Binchy

The Aerodrome

Rex Warner

Introduction by Anthony Burgess

Published nearly a decade before Orwell's *1984* shocked post-war readers, *The Aerodrome* is a book whose disturbingly prophetic qualities give it equal claim to be regarded as a modern classic. At the centre of the book stand the opposing forces of fascism and democracy, represented on the one hand by the Aerodrome, a ruthlessly efficient totalitarian state, and on the other by the Village, with its sensual muddle and stupidity. A comedy on a serious theme, this novel conveys probably better than any other of its time the glamorous appeal of fascism.

'It is high time that this thrilling story should be widely enjoyed again'—Angus Wilson

'It is a remarkable book; prophetic and powerful. Many books entertain but very few mange to entertain and to challenge at such a deep level.' *Illustrated London News*

The Unbearable Bassington

Saki

Introduction by Joan Aiken
Illustrated by Osbert Lancaster

Set in Edwardian London, Saki's best-known novel has as its hero the 'beautiful, wayward' Comus Bassington, in whom the author invested his own ambiguous feelings for youth and his fierce indignation at the ravages of time.

'There is no greater compliment to be paid to the right kind of friend than to hand him Saki, without comment.'—Christopher Morley